THE VIKING WORLD

———•◆•———

Filling a gap in the literature for an academically oriented volume on the Viking period, this unique book is a one-stop authoritative introduction to all the latest research in the field.

Bringing together today's leading scholars, both established seniors and younger, cutting-edge academics, Stefan Brink, in collaboration with Neil Price, has constructed the first single work to gather innovative research from a spectrum of disciplines (including archaeology, history, philology, comparative religion, numismatics and cultural geography) to create the most comprehensive Viking Age book of its kind ever attempted.

Consisting of longer articles providing overviews of important themes, supported by shorter papers focusing on material or sites of particular interest, this comprehensive volume covers such wide-ranging topics as social institutions, spatial issues, the Viking Age economy, Icelandic sagas and poetry, warfare, beliefs, language, voyages, and links with medieval and Christian Europe.

Including extensive illustrations, maps and references, this book is essential to the collection of any student or specialist in the Viking period or Scandinavian history.

Stefan Brink is Professor of Scandinavian Studies and Director of the Centre for Scandinavian Studies at the University of Aberdeen.

Neil Price is Professor of Archaeology at the University of Aberdeen.

THE ROUTLEDGE WORLDS

THE VIKING WORLD

Edited by

Stefan Brink
in collaboration with
Neil Price

Routledge
Taylor & Francis Group

LONDON AND NEW YORK

First published 2008. First published in paperback 2012 by Routledge
2 Park Square, Milton Park, Abingdon, Oxon OX14 4RN

Simultaneously published in the USA and Canada
by Routledge
711 Third Avenue, New York, NY 10017

Routledge is an imprint of the Taylor & Francis Group, an informa business

Typeset in Garamond Three by
RefineCatch Limited, Bungay, Suffolk

British Library Cataloguing in Publication Data
A catalogue record for this book is available from the British Library

Library of Congress Cataloging in Publication Data
The Viking world / edited by Stefan Brink; in collaboration with Neil Price.
p. cm,
1. Vikings.   2. Northmen.   3. Archaeology, Medieval.
4. Civilization, Viking.   I. Brink, Stefan.   II. Price, Neil.
DL65.V595 2008   948′.022–dc22   2008001095

ISBN: 978–0–415–33315–3 (hbk)
ISBN: 978–0–415–69262–5 (pbk)
ISBN: 978–0–203–41277–0 (ebk)

Printed and bound in Great Britain by
CPI Antony Rowe, Chippenham, Wiltshire

CONTENTS

——— ·◆· ———

PART I: VIKING AGE SCANDINAVIA

People, society and social institutions

Living space

v

Pre-Christian religion and belief

Language, literature and art

PART II: THE VIKING EXPANSION

The British Isles

Continental Europe and the Mediterranean

The Baltic

— Contents —

Russia and the east

The North Atlantic

PART III: SCANDINAVIA ENTERS THE EUROPEAN STAGE

The coming of Christianity

The development of nation states (*ríki*)

— *Contents* —

ILLUSTRATIONS

———·◆·———

CONTRIBUTORS

———•◆•———

Björn Ambrosiani, Fil. Dr (Ups.), Professor of Archaeology, The National Heritage Board/The Birka Project, Stockholm, Sweden.

Fjodor Androshchuk, Dr Phil. (Kiev), Associate Researcher, Dept. of Archaeology and Classical Studies, University of Stockholm, Sweden.

Símun V. Arge, Cand. Mag., Curator, Føroya Fornminnissavn, Tórshavn, The Faroes.

Jette Arneborg, PhD (Køb.), Curator, Senior Researcher, National Museum of Denmark, Copenhagen, Denmark.

Auður G. Magnúsdóttir, Fil. Dr (Goth.), Lecturer, Dept. of History, University of Gothenburg, Sweden.

Michael P. Barnes, MA, Fil. Dr h.c. (Ups.), Professor Emeritus of Scandinavian Studies, Scandinavian Studies, University College London, England.

James H. Barrett, PhD (Glasgow), Deputy Director, McDonald Institute for Archaeological Research, University of Cambridge, England.

Jan Bill, PhD, Professor of Viking Studies and Curator of the Viking Ship Collection at the Museum of Cultural History, University of Oslo, Norway.

Stefan Brink, Fil. Dr (Ups.), Professor of Scandinavian Studies, Centre for Scandinavian Studies, University of Aberdeen, Scotland; Docent in Scandinavian Languages, Dept. of Scandinavian Languages, Uppsala University, Sweden.

Paul Buckland, PhD (Bham), formerly Professor of Environmental Archaeology, England, University of Bournemouth.

Johan Callmer, Fil. Dr (Lund), Professor für Ur- und Frühgeschichte, Institut für Geschichtswissenschaften, Philosophische Fakultät I, Humboldt-Universität zu Berlin, Germany; Docent in Archaeology, Dept. of Archaeology and Ancient History, University of Lund, Sweden.

Dan Carlsson, Fil. Dr (Stockholm), Associate Professor of Cultural Geography, Section for Social Geography and Ethnology, Gotland University College, Visby, Sweden.

Tom Christensen, Mag. art., Curator in Prehistoric Archaeology, Roskilde Museum, Denmark.

Margaret Clunies Ross, MA, BLitt. (Oxon.), Fil. Dr h.c. (Göteborg) McCaughey Professor of English Language and Early English Literature, University of Sydney, Australia.

Clare Downham, PhD (Cantab.), Lecturer in Celtic, School of Language and Literature, University of Aberdeen, Scotland.

David N. Dumville, PhD (Edinburgh), Hon. MA (Pennsylvania), Professor in History, Palaeography & Celtic, Director of the Centre for Anglo-Saxon Studies and the Centre for Celtic Studies, University of Aberdeen, Scotland; Life Fellow, Girton College, Cambridge, England.

Torsten Edgren, Fil. Dr (Hels.), Professor h.c., Former Director of Archaeology at the National Board of Antiquities of Finland and Lecturer in Archaeology at the University of Helsinki, Finland.

Jan-Henrik Fallgren, Fil. Dr (Ups.), Researcher, Dept. of Archaeology and Ancient History, Uppsala University, Sweden.

Anthony Faulkes, MA, BLitt. (Oxon.), Dr phil. (Reykjavík), Emeritus Professor of Old Icelandic, The University of Birmingham, England.

Gillian Fellows-Jensen, Dr Phil. (Cop.), Reader Emerita, Name Research Section, Dept. of Scandinavian Research, University of Copenhagen, Denmark.

Claus Feveile, MA (Aarh.), Curator, Sydvestjyske Museer, Ribe, Denmark.

Gísli Sigurðsson, Dr Phil. (Reykjavík), Research Professor, Stofnun Árna Magnússonar í íslenskum fræðum/The Árni Magnússon Institute for Icelandic Studies, University of Iceland, Reykjavík, Iceland.

Anne-Sofie Gräslund, Fil. Dr (Ups.), Professor in Archaeology, Dept. of Archaeology and Ancient History, Uppsala University, Sweden.

Svein H. Gullbekk, Dr philos., Associate Professor in Numismatics, Museum of Cultural History, University of Oslo, Norway.

Terry Gunnell, PhD (Leeds), Associate Professor in Folkloristics, Dept. of Anthropology and Folkloristics, University of Iceland, Reykjavík, Iceland.

Dawn M. Hadley, PhD (Bham), Reader, Dept. of Archaeology, University of Sheffield, England.

Richard Hall, PhD (Southampton), Director of Archaeology, York Archaeological Trust, England.

Birgitta Hårdh, Fil. Dr (Lund), Professor in Archaeology, Dept. of Archaeology and Ancient History, University of Lund, Sweden.

Lotte Hedeager, Dr Phil. (Aarh.), Professor in Archaeology, Dept. of Archaeology, Conservation and History, University of Oslo, Norway.

Volker Hilberg, Dr Phil., Researcher, Forschungsgruppe Haithabu, Archäologisches Landesmuseum, Schloß Gottorf, Schleswig, Germany.

Anders Hultgård, Teol. Dr (Ups.), Professor Emeritus of History of Religions, especially Indo-European Religions, Faculty of Theology, Uppsala University, Sweden.

Judith Jesch, PhD (London), Professor of Viking Studies, School of English Studies, University of Nottingham, England.

Jón Viðar Sigurðsson, Dr Art. (Bergen), Professor in History, Institute for Archaeology, Conservation and History, University of Oslo, Norway.

Lars Jørgensen, Curator, The National Museum, Copenhagen, Denmark.

Claus Krag, Cand. philol. (Oslo), Professor in History, Dept. of Humanities and Cultural Studies, Telemark University College, Bø in Telemark, Norway.

Linn Lager, Fil. Dr (Ups.), Researcher, Dept. of Archaeology and Ancient History, Uppsala University, Sweden.

Annika Larsson, Fil. Dr (Ups.), Researcher, Dept. of Archaeology, University of Stockholm, Sweden.

Thomas Lindkvist, Fil. Dr (Ups.), Professor in Medieval History, Dept. of History, University of Gothenberg, Sweden.

John Ljungkvist, Fil. Dr (Ups.), Researcher, Dept. of Archaeology and Ancient History, Uppsala University, Sweden.

Lars Lönnroth, Fil. Dr (Stockholm), Professor Emeritus in Literature, Dept. of Literature, University of Gothenberg, Sweden.

Niels Lund, Dr Phil. (Cop.), Professor in History, Saxo Institute, University of Copenhagen, Denmark.

Egil Mikkelsen, Dr Phil. (Oslo), Professor in Scandinavian Archaeology and Museum Director, Museum of Cultural History, University of Oslo, Norway.

Stephen Mitchell, PhD (Minnesota), Professor of Scandinavian and Folklore, Dept. of Germanic Languages and Literatures, Curator of the Milman Parry Collection of Oral Literature, Harvard University, Cambridge, MA, USA.

J.E. Montgomery, PhD (Glasgow), Professor of Classical Arabic, Faculty of Asian and Middle East Studies, University of Cambridge; Fellow of Trinity Hall, Cambridge, England.

Jens N. Nielsen, Curator, Aalborg Historiske Museum, Denmark.

Guðrún Nordal, D. Phil. (Oxon), Professor in Icelandic, Faculty of Humanities, Háskóli Íslands, Reykjavík, Iceland.

Donnchadh Ó Corráin, Dr Litt., Professor of Medieval History, Dept. of History, University College Cork, Ireland.

Anne Pedersen, PhD (Aarh.), Senior Researcher, The National Museum, Copenhagen, Denmark.

Neil Price, Fil. Dr (Ups.), Professor of Archaeology, Dept. of Archaeology, University of Aberdeen, Scotland; Docent in Archaeology, Dept. of Archaeology and Ancient History, Uppsala University, Sweden.

Catharina Raudvere, Fil. Dr (Lund), Professor of History of Religions, Dept. of Cross-Cultural and Regional Studies, University of Copenhagen, Denmark.

Mark Redknap, PhD (London), Curator of Medieval and Later Archaeology, Dept. of Archaeology & Numismatics, Amueddfa Cymru–National Museum, Cardiff, Wales.

Jean Renaud, Dr (Sorbonne), Professor of Scandinavian Languages, Literature and Civilization, Dépt. d'études nordiques, University of Caen, France.

Julian D. Richards, PhD, Professor of Archaeology, Dept. of Archaeology, University of York, England.

Else Roesdahl, Cand. art., Litt. D. h.c. (Dublin), Professor in Medieval Archaeology, Dept. of Medieval and Renaissance Archaeology, University of Aarhus, Denmark.

Jonas Ros, Fil. Dr (Ups.), Field Archaeologist, Societas Archaeologica Upsaliensis, Uppsala, Sweden.

Jens Peter Schjødt, Dr Phil. (Aarh.), Professor of History of Religions, Dept. of the Study of Religion, University of Aarhus, Denmark.

Jonathan Shepard, D. Phil. (Oxon.), D. Litt. h.c. (Sofia), Independent Researcher, Oxford (former Lecturer in History, University of Cambridge), England.

Søren Michael Sindbœk, PhD (Aarh.), Assistant Professor, Dept. of Medieval and Renaissance Archaeology, Chairman of the Centre of Viking and Medieval Studies, University of Aarhus, Denmark.

Dagfinn Skre, Dr Phil. (Oslo), Professor of Archaeology, Institute for Archaeology, Conservation and Historical Studies, Director of the Kaupang Excavation Project, University of Oslo, Norway.

Gro Steinsland, Dr Phil. (Oslo), Professor of History of Religions, Dept. of Linguistics and Scandinavian Studies, University of Oslo, Norway.

Olof Sundqvist, Theol. Dr (Ups.), Lecturer in History of Religions, University College Gävle, Sweden.

Patricia Sutherland, PhD (Alberta), Curator of Eastern Arctic Archaeology, Canadian Museum of Civilization, Gatineau, Canada.

Heiki Valk, PhD (Tartu), Senior Researcher and Head of the Archaeological Kabinet, Tartu University, Estonia.

Birgitta Wallace, Fil. mag (Ups.), Senior Archaeologist Emerita, Parks Canada, Halifax, Nova Scotia, Canada.

Patrick F. Wallace, Dr, Director of The National Museum of Ireland, Dublin, Ireland.

Gareth Williams, PhD (St Andrews), Curator of Early Medieval Coinage, The British Museum, London, England.

Henrik Williams, Fil. Dr (Ups.), Professor of Scandinavian Languages, Dept. of Scandinavian Languages, Uppsala University, Sweden.

Sir David M. Wilson, Litt. D. (Cantab.), Honorary Professor of Archaeology, University College London, Former Director, The British Museum, London, England.

Inger Zachrisson, Fil. Dr (Stockholm), Docent, Curator Emerita of The Museum of National Antiquities, Stockholm, Sweden.

PREFACE

———·◆·———

Stefan Brink and Neil Price

Why do we need a new book on the Vikings? It is true that syntheses of the period appear with some regularity, most often written for a popular audience, together with well-illustrated catalogues resulting from the frequent exhibitions that are held on this theme. However, these books are not usually prepared with an academic audience in mind, and are understandably organised around particular collections of artefacts or the specific theme of an exhibition. At present there is no single work that gathers the latest research from the complete spectrum of disciplines involved, and that brings together all the leading scholars of the field. It has been our ambition to do this in this volume.

Most overviews of the Viking period have also been produced very much from a British perspective, albeit sometimes with Scandinavian involvement. Bearing in mind the geographic origins of the culture concerned, this brings with it certain inevitable problems of access to material and, not least, language. By contrast, this book covers both the homelands of the Vikings, as well as their impact on areas abroad. The authors include both established seniors of the profession and younger, cutting-edge scholars. We have here collected a team of some seventy authors who represents all the disciplines that go to make up the study of the Vikings – archaeology, history, philology, comparative religion, numismatics and cultural geography – drawn from every leading centre of early medieval studies across Europe, North America and even Australia.

This book has taken a very, very long time to prepare. It was originally proposed in outline by Neil Price, following a commission from the publishers. Having brought Stefan Brink on board, the volume was then planned and designed in detail by both editors, who shared communication with the individual authors. As the first papers began to come in, however, a combination of illness, workloads and extended periods of paternity leave forced Neil to adopt a secondary role. During this period we both have also moved between not only universities but also countries several times. The burden of the editing – that is, the primary work on the volume – has therefore been shouldered by Stefan.

Stefan Brink: I would like to, first and foremost, thank my family, for accepting me as a (more than usual) mental absentee for several years, when 'dad was working on the Viking book'. Secondly, all the authors, who have been extremely helpful and kind, despite the very long process of producing this volume, and thirdly the publisher, Routledge, for their understanding position concerning the delays due to severe illnesses, movements between jobs and overseas, child births, and other academic commitments.

Neil Price: My principal thanks go to Stefan, not only for his friendship and academic fraternity but in particular for his patience, tireless effort and good humour as the weight of the editing fell to him, due to the proverbial circumstances beyond my control: we are both the architects of this volume, but he is without doubt also its engineer. I would also like to thank the contributors, who have similarly borne the substantial delays and dislocations with (mostly) good cheer, and I echo Stefan's respect for Routledge's forbearance. My wife and two children – both of whom were born during the gestation of this book – deserve my gratitude more than anyone, and they have it.

ABBREVIATIONS

———•◆•———

AM	Arnamagnæan manuscript collection (see http://arnamagnaeansk.ku.dk/ and www.arnastofnun.is/)
Ar	Arabic
Da	Danish
DR	*Danmarks runeindskrifter*, 3 vols, L. Jacobsen and E. Moltke (eds), Copenhagen (1941–2)
EHR	*The English Historical Review* (Oxford University Press)
Goth	Gothic
Gs	*Gästriklands runinskrifter* (SRI 15), Stockholm: Almqvist & Wiksell International (1981)
Ir	Irish
KL	*Kulturhistoriskt lexikon för nordisk medeltid från vikingatid till reformationstid* 1–21, Malmö: Allhem (1956–78)
KVHAA	Kungliga Vitterhets Historie och Antikvitets Akademien/The Royal Swedish Academy of Letters, History and Antiquities, Stockholm
Lat	Latin
MW	Medieval Welsh
NIyR	*Norges innskrifter med de yngre runer*, M. Olsen *et al.* (eds) (Norsk historisk kjeldeskrift-institutt. Norges indskrifter indtil reformationen 2), 6 vols, Oslo: Jacob Dybwad/A.S. Bokcentralen/Kjeldeskriftfondet (1941 ff.)
Norw	Norwegian
ODa	Old Danish
OE	Old English
Ög	*Östergötlands runinskrifter* (SRI 2), Stockholm: Almqvist & Wiksell International (1911–18)
OHG	Old High German
OIr	Old Irish
Öl	*Ölands runinskrifter* (SRI 1), Stockholm: Almqvist & Wiksell International (1900–6)
ON	Old Norse
OScand	Old Scandinavian

OSw	Old Swedish
Raä	Riksantikvarieämbetet/Central Board of National Antiquities, Stockholm
RGA	*Reallexikon der germanischen Altertumskunde*, 35 vols, 2nd edn, ed. H. Beck *et al.*, Berlin: de Gruyter, 1973–2007.
ROM	Roskilde Museum, Roskilde, Denmark
Sm	*Smålands runinskrifter*, 2 vols (SRI 4), Stockholm: Almqvist & Wiksell International (1935–61)
SRI	*Sveriges runinskrifter* (KVHAA), Stockholm: Almqvist & Wiksell International, 1900 ff.
Sw	Swedish

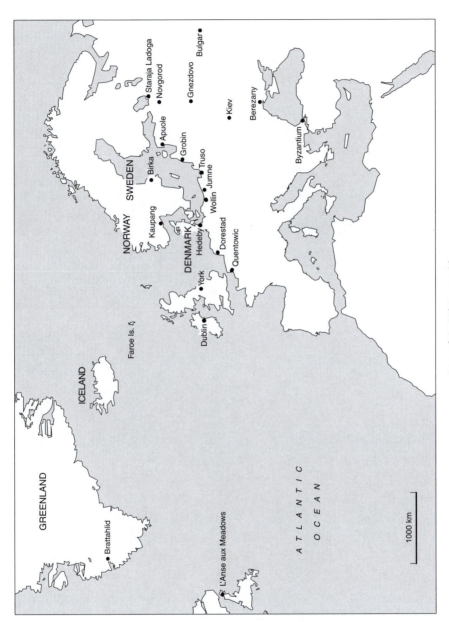

Map of the Viking world.

INTRODUCTION

Stefan Brink

The approach used in this book combines two interactive levels of contributions: longer articles providing overviews of important themes, supported by shorter papers focusing on material or sites of particular interest. The kinds of subjects covered by the latter include spectacular sites or finds, crucial written sources and the results of the latest individual research projects on specialised subjects. In each case we have tried to approach the leading international scholars in the relevant field.

The collection of articles starts with a presentation by *Lotte Hedeager* of the period that preceded the Viking Age, to be able to set the Vikings in a historical context. This is followed by a presentation of people and societies in Scandinavia – the Viking homelands. *Stefan Brink* discusses the polities and the legal customs in Viking Scandinavia, *Inger Zachrisson* the interaction between the Nordic people and the Sámi. Social aspects of society, such as gender roles and women in society, are discussed by *Auður Magnúsdóttir*, while *Stefan Brink* discusses the lowest layer in society, the slaves or the thralls.

The section on landscape and settlement begins with an overview of Scandinavian place names from the period by *Stefan Brink*. The settlement structure of farms and villages is then examined by *Jan-Henrik Fallgren*. An important special case, Tissø, is presented by its excavator, *Lars Jørgensen*. The urbanisation, which in Scandinavia starts in this period, is given an overview by *Dagfinn Skre*. In this section there are also several in-depth articles covering the most important towns and proto-towns of the time, such as Birka by *Björn Ambrosiani*, Hedeby by *Volker Hilberg*, Kaupang by *Dagfinn Skre*, Lejre and Roskilde by *Tom Christensen*, Ribe by *Claus Feveile*, 'Ridanæs' at Fröjel by *Dan Carlsson*, Sebbersund by *Jens N. Nielsen*, Sigtuna by *Jonas Ros*, and Uppåkra and Lund by *Birgitta Hårdh*.

Viking Age economy and the international mercantile endeavours are then highlighted, trade being a major factor for the cultural development of the period discussed by *Søren M. Sindbæk*, and this theme is also covered in an article on coinage by *Svein H. Gullbekk*. Very much tied to this is – for obvious reasons – the study of ships, shipbuilding and maritime voyages, given an overview by *Jan Bill*, followed by presentations by *John Ljungkvist* on handicrafts and *Annika Larsson* on textile technologies. The crucial subject of Viking warfare is covered next, on the mechanics of raiding and

— *Stefan Brink and Neil Price* —

combat, the detail of the weaponry, and fortifications, discussed by *Gareth Williams* and *Anne Pedersen*.

A lot of attention has for a long time been upon the world of beliefs and mentalities, therefore the section on religions in the Nordic area in the period is vital. It starts with an overview by *Anders Hultgård* on the pre-Christian Scandinavian religion. *Jens Peter Schjødt* presents the pagan pantheon, the gods and goddesses of the north, *Olof Sundqvist* discusses the important question of a sacral kingship, while *Gro Steinsland* presents an important aspect hereof, namely a *hieros gamos*, that is, a myth of marriage between a ruler and a giantess. The creation of the mythological and eschatological world of the Vikings is presented by *Margaret Clunies Ross*. The aspects of this supernatural world-view that to a large extent survived into the Christian period are discussed by *Catharina Raudvere*. The material culture of the Old Norse religion and the encounter with Christianity is presented by *Anne-Sofie Gräslund*, together with burial customs presented by *Neil Price*. One of the key elements of the mindset of Viking Age men and women was their interaction with the invisible population of gods and other beings that shared their lives, something which is discussed by *Neil Price* in the chapter 'Sorcery and circumpolar traditions in Old Norse belief'. It is difficult to find an adequate word for this in modern languages, though something like 'sorcery' or 'magic' perhaps comes closest according to Price. In Old Norse we find several different terms for it, the most important being *seiðr*, and in the Old Norse world important agents were the *vǫlur*. Price also discusses links with and the interaction between Scandinavians and Sami on *seiðr* and shamanism.

The Viking world of language, runes, literature and art is covered in the next section. *Michael P. Barnes* discusses the language of the Vikings, which we can reconstruct mainly thanks to the runes, and this importance of the runes for any study of the Viking period is stressed by *Henrik Williams*. One of the main cultural contributions by the Scandinavians has been the sagas and the poetry from the Viking Age and the Middle Ages. *Judith Jesch* presents the Viking poetry (the *Eddas* and skaldic poems), while *Terry Gunnell* explores the way these poems may have been performed. The Icelandic sagas are given an overview by *Lars Lönnroth*, and *Anthony Faulkes* gives a biography of the most famous scholar-politician of them all, Snorri Sturluson. *Guðrún Nordal* discusses the important genre of Icelandic sagas and *Stephen Mitchell* the heroic and legendary sagas, which have seen a lot of attention in recent times. The unique Viking art and artistic tradition are given an extensive presentation by *Sir David M. Wilson*.

We then turn the attention to the exploits that have given the Vikings their international reputation, namely their voyages abroad, their interaction with other cultures, their explorations and colonisation of new land. *Clare Downham* gives an overview for the British Isles, and of the interactions between the Vikings and the Anglo-Saxons, followed by a discussion by *Julian D. Richards* of the form and extent of Scandinavian settlement in England, and special articles on the Danelaw by *Dawn M. Hadley*, the kingdom of York by *Richard Hall* and the Isle of Man by *Sir David M. Wilson*. In a longer article the important primary sources dealing with Vikings – or vikings, as Professor Dumville prefers to label them – in insular sources are discussed by *David N. Dumville*, and *Gillian Fellows-Jensen* gives an overview of the toponymic evidence, in the form of place names. Viking contacts with Wales, Scotland and Ireland are covered by the experts *Mark Redknap*, *James H. Barrett* and *Donnchadh Ó Corráin*, with a special article by *Patrick F. Wallace* on Viking Dublin.

The Viking activities on the Continent are presented by *Johan Callmer*, discussing encounters between the Viking world and the Franks, followed by a survey of colonisation and contact with France, in Normandy by *Jean Renaud* and in Brittany by *Neil Price*, who also discusses Spain and North Africa. The expansion to the east is covered by articles on Viking archaeology in Finland by *Torsten Edgren* and the Baltic by *Heiki Valk*. Viking activities in eastern Europe from an archaeological aspect are discussed by *Fjodor Androshchuk*, and an overview, drawn from the written sources, is presented by *Jonathan Shepard*, who also focuses upon the role played by the Vikings in the emergence of the Russian state. Viking interaction with Byzantium and the Middle East is discussed by *Egil Mikkelsen* regarding Islam, and *J. E. Montgomery* presents an extensive article on Arabic sources on the Vikings.

The Viking expansion into the North Atlantic region is given an overview by *Gísli Sigurðsson*. The discovery and settlement of Iceland is covered in depth by *Jón Viðar Sigurðsson*, looking at its unique laws, power structure and social organisation. *Símun V. Arge* presents the evidence from the Faroes. The colonisation of Greenland is discussed by *Jette Arneborg*, and *Paul Buckland* tells the history of life on a typical farm. The much discussed history of the discovery of America is given an overview by *Birgitta Wallace*, followed by a presentation of the evidence we have of expeditions that set out to North America and the High Arctic by *Patricia Sutherland*.

The volume concludes with the last phase of the Viking period, and Scandinavia's developing links with the medieval, Christian world of Continental Europe. Here *Stefan Brink* explores the process of Christianisation and the organisation of the early Church, while *Anne-Sofie Gräslund* and *Linn Lager* look at the evidence on the runestones. *Anne-Sofie* also presents the material culture and the early Christian burial customs. With Christianisation and the emergence of the medieval kingdoms in Scandinavia, the Viking Age ended. These emerging kingdoms are presented for Norway by *Claus Krag*, for Denmark by *Else Roesdahl* and for Sweden by *Thomas Lindkvist*. An important special case, discussed by *Niels Lund*, is the enigmatic Cnut the Great, king over 'England, Denmark, Norway and parts of Sweden'.

NOTE

In this volume some authors use *viking(s)*, other *Viking(s)*. The background for this different usage is as follows: since the beginning of modern English-language academic discourse, some scholars have written *viking* while others have preferred *Viking*. The implication of the former is that the word is a common noun (what latinate writers would have expressed as *pirata*), of the latter that it is an ethnic term. There is a further complication, 'the Vikings' has become common (especially as a book-title) and it implies our ability to generalise, which some scholars reject by always preferring 'vikings' to 'the Vikings' or 'the Vikings'. In this book, the various authors have been allowed their preferred usage.

WHO WERE THE VIKINGS?

———·◆·———

Stefan Brink

The Viking Age was the period when the Scandinavians made themselves known, or rather notorious. From around 800 to around 1050 Scandinavians stirred up northern Europe in a way they had never done before or since. Norwegians in particular controlled and colonised the whole of the North Atlantic, from Norway, to the Faroes, Iceland, Shetland, the Scottish islands, parts of Ireland, Greenland and all the way to the eastern brim of North America. Especially Danes, but also Norwegians and Swedes, ravaged and had an impact on the political and social development of England and parts of France. Swedes travelled eastward, traded along the Russian rivers, and down to the Byzantine and Islamic world. They established in Kiev, under the name of Rus', a new policy, the embryo of Russia.

Why Scandinavians were able to change the social and political map in such a profound way in northern Europe is still under discussion. Early on one idea was that Scandinavia had been overcrowded with people, or that it was because of years of bad harvests that people had to leave. This cannot be the case. Today we instead stress power struggles within Scandinavia and an escalating incentive to trade. One important factor may be the new kind of sea-going ships that Scandinavians started to build. These ships were long, narrow and shallow; hence they had no need of special harbours: you could make land at any (sandy) beach. The smaller types, used on the rivers in the east, could be dragged or even carried between watercourses.

One side of the Vikings, which has been toned down during the past fifty years, is the ravaging, killing, raping, burning Viking; instead the peaceful, industrious, trading Viking has been on the research agenda. Viking-age Scandinavians, no doubt, spent time on both activities. However, the fear of the Northmen, of which we read in documents and chronicles from Anglo-Saxon England and Ireland, probably had nothing to do with them as traders. Still today, the word *Viking* is in the Anglo-Saxon world associated with pirates and men of violence.

The reason for focusing on Vikings as traders in research during the past decades, is partly because this side of the Northmen was neglected in early, romanticised history writing, but it partly also mirrors society as a whole. Every era uses history for its own purposes; every time shapes its own history. And especially during periods of strong political hegemony and with strong political will in a country, it has been common to present the history which is the most relevant to the political will and struggle, to sanction the politics you pursue. The use of history and the focus on the warrior Viking in Nazi Germany is an obvious example. In post-war Europe, however, battered and tired of war, it was more welcome and natural to focus on the peaceful side of the Vikings, as traders.

THE VIKING AGE

The historical period of the Viking Age is a late construction. The Vikings themselves had, of course, no clue that they were living in the Viking Age. A man-made, constructed historical period must have a beginning and an end. Very often some well-known event has been used as the start and end of a historical period. Regarding the Viking Age two monumental 'events' have framed the period. By tradition the start of the Viking Age has been set at the year 793, which is the year we know that Vikings attacked and plundered the monastery at Lindisfarne, near the coast of Northumberland, mentioned in Anglo-Saxon chronicles. In the same way, by tradition, the end of the Viking Age is usually set in 1066, with the battle at Stamford Bridge, near York, when the English king Harold defeated a large army of Northmen under the command of the Norse king Haraldr Harðráði. In the handbooks it says that after this defeat, no Vikings bothered the British people any more. The Viking era was over.

This is what may be read in a handbook, but it is a qualified truth. In 1070 the Danish king Sven Estridsson came back to England to demand the crown, backed up by the English aristocracy. The new king in England, William, thwarted his plans, and Sven went back to Denmark the same year. In 1075 Knut, son of Sven, came to England with a Danish fleet. And so on. A historically important aspect for the start of Scandinavians beginning to travel outside Scandinavia for trade was obviously the general expansion of trade which took place around 700, which led to the emergence of many towns, or emporia, such as Dorestad, Quentovic, Hamwic, York, Ipswich etc. Here, goods and money were in abundance, and with large quantities of *sceattas* coins, minted by the Frisians, these towns probably were tempting goals for pirates and others. In the light of these circumstances, cases have been made for pulling back the start of the Viking Age to around 700. On the other side, an obvious end to the Viking Age was the introduction of the new Christian religion and the establishment of the Church. And with the Church came a new administration and government based on literacy. This 'Europeanisation' of Scandinavia can – with very good arguments – be said to be the end of the Viking Age. And so we may continue. In my opinion there are no cogent reasons for changing the start and the end of the Viking Age, which anyhow is just an approximation and a late construction to help us understand a complicated past.

THE WORD 'VIKING'

The term which has been synonymous with a raiding or trading Northman during this period is hence *Viking*. This was, however, not the common word used at the time. In Francia these Scandinavians were called 'Northmen' or 'Danes' (in translation), and in England they were called 'Danes' or 'pagans' in contemporary chronicles. In Ireland Scandinavians were at first called 'pagans' ('gentiles'), and then a distinction was made between Norwegians, called *Finngall* 'white foreigners', and Danes, *Dubgall* 'black foreigners'. In the east, Swedes could be called *rus'* or *varjag* (ON *væringi, væringr*). It is in England during the ninth century (outside Scandinavia) that we find the usage of the term *Viking* for ravaging Northmen.

There is no consensus regarding the origin or meaning of the word *Viking*. We find a word *wicing* in the eighth century in Old English, but it is not certain that we are here dealing with the same word. In Old Scandinavian there is masculine *víkingr*, which is normally translated as 'sea warrior', and feminine *víking*, meaning 'military expedition (over sea)'. The words are found in Anglo-Saxon chronicles as well as in runic inscriptions. The latter are especially important for understanding the semantics of the words. *Víkingr* is also used as a Scandinavian man's name, and as a by-name (as in *Toki vikingr* on a runestone).

The masculine word, *víkingr*, seems – according to runic inscriptions – to have been the word used for a man who has gone away on a journey, obviously together with several others – on a 'group journey' we would probably call it today. Most certainly, the majority, perhaps all, of these journeys were raids and military expeditions, conducted by a group of warriors (ON *lið, drótt*) under the leadership of some king or chieftain. One example is found on a runestone from Hablingbo on Gotland, which tells us that Helge had gone westward 'with vikings' (*með vikingum*).

The feminine word, *víking*, has obviously denoted the actual expedition, the journey. This may be exemplified by another runic inscription, from Härlingstorp in Väster-götland, Sweden, where we can read that a man Toli 'was killed in the west in *viking*' (*varþ dauþr a vestrvegum i vikingu*). On another runestone at Gårdstånga in Skåne, Sweden, we are told of several men famous for their expeditions (*Þer drængiaʀ waʀu w{iþa} {un}esiʀ i wikingu*).

But what about the original or etymological meaning of the word *Viking*? It is here that the interpretations start to diverge. A popular hypothesis has been that the name *Viken*, for the large bay up to Oslo, is the origin, hence the word originally meaning 'the people living or coming from Viken'. Another explanation is that the word comes from *vik* 'bay, inlet', referring to 'a person who dwells (or embarks) in bays', or that these Vikings often lie in wait in bays. A third is that it could contain a 'Baltic word' *wic*, a Germanisation of a Latin *vicus* 'harbour, trading place', which we find in names such as *Ipswich, Norwich, 'Hamwich'* (> *Southampton*). This latter idea was much cosseted when the warrior side of the Vikings was toned down, and the Vikings as traders were favoured. A *Viking* would hence have been someone who visited these *vicii* or *wics*, and therefore they were called *wicingas, víkingar* 'persons who visited and traded at these wics'. A fourth, but not so likely hypothesis, has been the idea that *Viking* could be related to a word *vika* 'a distance at sea', hence a *week* (that is, a section or period), with the meaning 'a distance you were able to row between two pauses'. A fifth hypothesis is that it must be related to ON *víkja* 'to move, walk, travel', with an assumed meaning for *Viking* as someone who has digressed from home! All in all, no convincing interpretation has so far been given of the word *Viking*. But from what has been said above, it seems plausible to assume that a *víkingr* (m.) who was out in *víking* (f.) probably had not left Scandinavia for a peaceful trading journey. A warrior-like semantic component seems to be found in the word.

If the word *Viking* was used for a man (or the warrior) or a military expedition to the west of Scandinavia, we have seen that other words have been used for these Scandinavians who went to the south or the east. The ones who travelled on the rivers in

Russia could be called *Rus'* or *Væringar*. The word *Rus'* is most certainly to be connected to the name of the province *Roslagen*, the eastern part of the province of Uppland in Sweden, which we also find in the Finnish name for Sweden, which is *Routsi*. The word goes back to the words *ro* 'row' and *rodd* 'a rowing session'. One idea is that this word *Rus'* for a Swede was succeeded by the word *væringr, væringi*, in Russian *varjag*. The explanation put forward for this latter word is quite interesting. It is supposed that it emanates from the titles for the Scandinavian guard of the Byzantine emperor in Constantinople, as a member of his personal bodyguard. The word probably has the meaning of a person who has given an oath of fidelity (ON **vár* 'oath, promise'), obviously to the emperor. From here the word, so the hypothesis is, was later on transferred to a Swede or a Scandinavian in general.

PART I

VIKING AGE SCANDINAVIA

——·◆·——

CHAPTER ONE

SCANDINAVIA BEFORE
THE VIKING AGE

——— · ✦ · ———

Lotte Hedeager

What is known as the Middle Ages in Scandinavia begins around AD 1000, half a millennium later than the rest of western and central Europe. Only from this date onwards did Scandinavia consist of unified kingdoms and Christianity was established as a serious force in pagan Scandinavia. It is consequently only from this date onwards that Scandinavia has its own written history. This does not, however, mean that the people of Scandinavia were without history, or without any knowledge of ancient events. Quite the opposite, in fact, although their historical tradition was oral, transmitted from generation to generation within the constraints of rulers and traditions of composition and performance.

The archaeological research tradition in the Scandinavian late Iron Age, that is, from the migration period onwards (i.e. from the fifth century), has since the 1990s been juxtaposed with the Old Norse sources from the twelfth to the fourteenth century. This is due to the new approach in archaeology, which focuses on cognitive structures, mentality, cosmology and systems of belief. However, the use of Old Norse sources as an explanatory framework for the late Iron Age causes obvious methodological problems and has been a matter of serious debate in the wake of this new research tradition. Although written down in a Christian context, and although the fact that they may exaggerate and fabricate at some points, these sources contain valuable information on the mentality and cognition of the pre-Christian past. The reason is that structures of collective representations in any society are highly stable and change very slowly. Using the terminology of Fernand Braudel and the Annales school this is 'la longue durée' – and following Pierre Bourdieu we are faced with the concept of 'habitus'. Both of them furnish archaeologists with a general theoretical framework of long-time perspective, enabling them to get beyond the archaeological and textual evidence.

Lacking a modern separation of economic, political and religious institutions, pre-Christian Scandinavia can so far be compared to traditional non-western, pre-industrial communities; in both cases the world-view of a given society tends to fuse these separate domains into a coherent whole. A number of new excavations have contributed to a keener interest in 'central places' and 'cult sites', while major new finds of manorial settlements, gold hoards etc. have encouraged interpretations using terms such as 'kings', 'aristocracy', and the like, providing a concrete counterpart to Old Norse literature, new directions in research into the history of religion, and place-name studies. Among the most important sites in this respect are *Gudme/Lundeborg* on Fyn (Nielsen *et al.* 1994; Hedeager 2001), *Sorte Muld* on Bornholm (Watt 1999), *Uppåkra* in the province of Skåne (Larsson and Hårdh 1998; Hårdh 2003) and *Borg* in Lofoten (Munch *et al.* 2003).

A new, interdisciplinary research movement has developed around these issues where religious, judicial and political conditions are seen as closely interwoven and where an alternative understanding of the connection between political authority, myths and memory, cult activity, skilled craft production and exercise of power in the late Iron Age has emerged (Myhre 2003 and Hedeager 2005 as the latest outlines). The interdisciplinary approach has been developed through the five-year research project *Vägar till Midgård* at the University of Lund (Jennbert *et al.* 2002; Andrén *et al.* 2004; Berggren *et al.* 2004). A similar approach is to be found in some other research projects (Melheim *et al.* 2004, and to a certain degree in Jesch 2002). Earlier studies have been based primarily on the economic character, involving such aspects as agriculture and settlement, economy and society, trade and urbanisation. Combined with burial evidence these topics have usually been the starting point for models of the social and political organisation.

MYTH, MEMORY AND ART

Although without a written history of its own, Scandinavia in the sixth and seventh centuries was nevertheless known to have held quite a special position in the minds of the migration-period Germanic peoples in Europe as the place from which many of them, or at least the royal families, claimed their origin (Hedeager 1997, 2000). This Scandinavian origin myth, repeated by several of the early medieval narrators and maintained by the Germanic peoples of early medieval Europe, was more than just a series of authors copying one another. Myths played a vital role in the creation of a political mentality among the new Germanic warlords and kings in Europe (Hedeager 1997, 1998, 2000; Geary 2003; Hill 2003). Naturally, the factual element within these early European migration myths is much disputed (see Hedeager 2000 and 2005 for references). What is crucial, however, is not to what extent these people once emigrated in small groups from Scandinavia, but that their identity was linked to Scandinavia and that their kings were divine because they descended from *Gautr* or *Óðinn/Wotan*, with this figure's clear association with the Germanic pagan religion and, maybe, the Scandinavian pantheon.

The much later Old English poem *Beowulf* may draw on traditions that have roots in the sixth and seventh centuries. Here there are possible ties between the ruling families of the *Wylfingas*, etymologically identical to the *Wuffingas*, the East Anglian royal family, and the *Wulfings* who were thought to live in what is now south-western Sweden and south-eastern Norway during the late fifth and sixth centuries. Furthermore, there are archaeological indications of kindred relations between the royal families of East Anglia and Scandinavia in the sixth and seventh centuries (Newton 1993: 117), not least the connection revealed between the Sutton Hoo ship burial and the ship burials from Vendel and Valsgärde in the mid-Swedish Mälar area (Bruce-Mitford 1979; Lamm and Nordström 1983).

From the sparse written but rich archaeological material it is evident that close contacts existed between the noble families of southern Scandinavia and those of western Europe during these centuries. The Scandinavian origin myth among the Germanic royal families/peoples, expressed in contemporaneous written sources, is supported by the archaeological evidence, notably weapons, jewellery, and, not least, art and iconography (Hedeager 1998). From about the beginning of the fifth century up until the seventh, the Nordic figurative world was used as a symbolically significant style among the migrating Germanic peoples. It was imitated and elaborated, becoming an impressive elite art style (Salin 1904; Karlsson 1983; Haseloff 1981; Roth 1979; Speake 1980; Näsman 1984: map 10; Hines 1984; Lund Hansen 1992; Høilund Nielsen 1997), until the point when Catholic Christianity put down firm roots during the first half of the eighth century (Roth 1979: 86). In Scandinavia, on the other hand, where a pagan warrior elite persisted during the Viking Age, the Nordic animal style ceased to develop from around AD 1100.

It did not survive the meeting with a new belief system and the political and social implications that this entailed. This can of course be explained through the idea that the people – especially the elite – had acquired different tastes and therefore preferred a new style around 1200 under the influence of the Church. More convincingly, however, it can be argued that the lack of potential for survival and renewal of the animal style in a Christian context had to do with its anchoring in a quite different system of belief (Hedeager 2003). The obvious role of animal style as an inseparable part of the pre-Christian material culture indicates that the animals also may have had an indisputable significant position in the pre-Christian perception of the world (Kristoffersen 1995, 2000b; Hedeager 1997, 1998, 2003, 2004; Jakobsson 2003; Gaimster 1998; Andrén 2000; Glosecki 1989; Magnus 2001; Lindstrøm and Kristoffersen 2001).

The Nordic animal ornamentation does not only incorporate animals, it *is* animals, that is to say, it is entirely a paraphrasing of a many faceted complex of animal motifs which suggests that these styles, structurally speaking, incorporate an overriding abstract principle, reflecting social order and – perhaps subconsciously – also reflecting the physical order of the universe (Roe 1995: 58). As a recurrent theme in the Old Norse texts we find a dualist relationship between man and animal. It is expressed in the words *hugr*, *fylgja* and *hamr*. It consists of protective spirits which attach themselves to individuals, often at birth, and remain with them right through to death, when they transfer their powers to another member of the family. *Fylgja* often appears as an animal and is usually visible only at times of crisis, either in waking or in dreams. It is an externalised 'soul' but also an embodiment of personal luck and destiny, and the concept has much in common with the less attested *hamr* (Orchard 2002; Raudvere 2001: 102 f., 2003: 71).

Acknowledging that contact with the Other World passed through the animals and that the *fylgja* was the embodiment of personal destiny, also helps us understand how animal ornamentation could sustain an organising role in the Scandinavian – and Germanic – society up until the introduction/consolidation of Christianity. It also explains how the animal style was involved in the creation and maintenance of the socio-cosmological order and as such participates in the legitimisation of power (Kristoffersen 1995, 2000a, b; Lindstrøm and Kristoffersen 2001; Hedeager 2003, 2004, 2005).

GOLD AND GIFT-GIVING

The written sources, whether Old Norse or from early medieval Europe, give the impression of gift-giving as the decisive instrument in creating and upholding these political alliances, between lord and warrior-follower and among the warrior elite itself. Items of gold and silver, often lavishly ornamented, played an important role for ritual and ceremonial use in the social reproduction of the late Iron Age. Although the idea of gift-giving was embedded in the cosmological world and as such was highly ritualised all the way through (see Bazelmans 1999, 2000), it is only in the migration period (as in the Viking Age) that the amount of hoards signal an outstanding intense competitive display. During these centuries immense numbers of gold hoards were deposited all over Scandinavia. They consisted of a wide variety of precious objects – bracteates, rings, sword attachments, relief brooches etc. – and they were often highly decorated with animal ornamentation. On this premise, it may be presumed that not only objects but also elements of style – not least the iconographic ones – have been selected with a great deal of care. By means of animal ornamentation these objects were imbedded with special qualities and through time they got their own biography and therefore communicated specific messages.

Broadly speaking, the hoards have been explained in two different ways: as treasures, that is, 'economic' depositions meant to go back into circulation – or as tactical gifts, that is, ritual sacrifices, meant for the supernatural world and a way of creating alliances with the gods. In the past decade the latter explanation has been the dominant approach (for discussion see in particular Geisslinger 1967; Herschend 1979; Fonnesbech-Sandberg 1985; Hines 1989; Hedeager 1991, 1992, 1999; Fabech 1994a; Wiker 1999). Although a great deal of the gold hoards are found in areas which, from a modern and rational economic point of view, are marginal, in an overall perspective they are connected to fertile agricultural areas. This is particularly clear in Sweden where a majority of the gold finds come from the most fertile Swedish provinces of Skåne and Västergötland (approx. 22 kg, i.e. more than half of the gold from mainland Sweden in this period) (Hedeager 1999: 246). The amount of gold in Denmark is about 50 kg, in Norway it is much less (estimated one-third or less) (Hedeager 1999). The hoards have obviously been deposited in deliberately chosen localities in the landscape (see also Johansen 1996: 97). They have been found in central settlement areas, in – or very close to – houses, and they have been found in marginal areas where they are in particular linked to bogs, streams, coasts etc., that means the transitional zone between land and water, and this is where a majority of sacral place names, that is, names with Óðinn, Týr, Freyr and God, are located too (Brink 1996; Andersen 1998: 26; Jakobsson 1997: 91). This transitional zone appears to uphold a special position in the perception of the cultural landscape as places for negotiation with the Other World and the depositions must reflect some kind of past ritual practice. Once deposited, for generations the hoards may have shaped the landscape by creating a sacred topography in people's minds. They may have represented the link between past and present, between this world and the Other World, and as such they gave legitimacy to the land by becoming part of the discursive knowledge of the people who lived in these areas. Although hidden, these hoards remained 'visible' for generations, continuing to play an active role in people's negotiation with the past (Hedeager 1999).

The gold hoards were deposited in a period of great social stress, and gold played a special role as mediator in resource-consuming political alliances and long-distance networks. The hoards may have served as an instrument in organising – or reorganising – the cultural landscape according to the cosmological world in a slightly more hierarchical political structure all over fertile Scandinavia in the migration period.

CENTRAL PLACES FOR ACQUISITION AND TRANSFORMATION

For the Nordic realm before 800, where there is no textual evidence of any specific locations of religious or political power, the archaeological sources and the toponymic evidence provide the only basis for analysing the hierarchical structure in this settlement structure. The concept of 'central places' has been developed in Scandinavian archaeology during the past decades to classify specific rich settlement sites from these centuries, often with great quantities of metal finds indicating extended casting and trade activities (Larsson and Hårdh 1998; Hårdh and Larsson 2002; Hedeager 2001; Jørgensen 2003).

To understand the role of central places in southern Scandinavia it is important to take into consideration the possible symbolic structure underlying the production and acquisition of valuable goods, because the association of the elite with crafts and long-distance trade can not merely be understood as a materialistic and economic phenomenon, but also in terms of qualities and values prevailing within a cosmological frame (Helms 1993; DeMarrais *et al.* 1996; Earle 1990, 2004). It is highly unlikely that any prehistoric society ever saw activities and objects associated with remote distances in a neutral light. The elite was involved in a process by which resources from outside were brought into their society, where they were subsequently transformed, both materially and symbolically, in order to meet local ideological needs. As a result of this, the central places in the late Iron Age were localities where precious metals from the outside were transformed into prestigious objects essential for local ritual purposes. Metal production and craftsmanship are usually regarded as a neutral or even secondary affair, but metallurgy and skilled craftsmanship were in fact closely connected to what these societies conceived of as the quality of power. The role of the metalworkers – especially blacksmiths and jewellers – deserves special attention. Weavers, for example, have been skilled artisans as well, but their activities are more difficult to trace (Holand 2001: 104 ff.). The technicalities of metallurgy and metalwork included a symbolic and ritual element, which gave the practitioners a special status (Herbert 1984, 1993; Hedeager 2001; Jakobsson 2003; Haaland 2004; Gansum 2004).

Given the importance of forging and jewellery associated with any central settlement and big farm from the fifth century until the late Viking Age in Scandinavia, such activities must have served a purpose. This problem may of course be approached from a functional perspective: all big farms needed tools and weapons, and forging must have been an essential part of day-to-day work in all non-urban, pre-industrial societies. Obviously weapons and iron tools were primarily manufactured to meet practical demands, but this is not true of items of gold and silver, which met social requirements. Keeping this in mind it is not surprising that forging and the manufacture of jewellery hold a significant place in the mythological world of pre-Christian Scandinavia (Hedeager 2001; Jakobsson 2003).

Indeed, the Old Norse literature also throws some light on certain essential components of 'powerful' places. For example, the hall assumes great importance in the ideological universe represented in these texts (Herschend 1993, 1997a, 1999: 414; Enright 1996; Brink 1996). Apparently ON *salr* means the kings' and earls' assembly hall, cult hall or moot hall: the place in which the functions of 'theatre, court and church' were united (see the comprehensive account in Herschend 1998). The hall was at the centre of a group of principal farmsteads; it was the heart of the central places from the later part of the Iron Age (a possible ranking of these places can be found in Näsman 1999: 1; Jørgensen 2003), which existed all over Scandinavia, as is now increasingly recognised. Places such as *Gudme/Lundeborg, Sorte Muld, Lejre, Tissø, Toftegård, Boeslunde, Jørlunde, Kalmargård, Nørre Snede, Stentinget, Drengsted* and *Ribe* in Denmark; *Trondheim, Kaupang, Hamar* and *Borg* in Norway; *Slöinge, Helgö, Birka, Uppåkra, Vä, (Gamla) Uppsala, Högom, Vendel* and *Valsgärde* in Sweden (Munch *et al.* 2003; Duczko 1993; Jørgensen 2003; Brink 1996; Callmer 1997; Larsson and Hårdh 1998; Lundqvist *et al.* 1996; Hedeager 2001; Hårdh and Larsson 2002; Skre and Stylegar 2004). Characteristically, many of these sites are located a few kilometres inland, relying on one or more landing places or ports situated on the coast (Fabech 1999). Although this is still a matter of debate, such central places may have served as a basis for some form of political or religious control exercised over a larger area; the radius of their influence went well beyond the site itself. Furthermore, on several of these places a special building seems to have served cultic functions as a pagan *vi*, for example in *Uppåkra* in Skåne (Larsson 2002) and *Tissø* on Zealand, which actually means 'Týr's Lake' (Jørgensen 2003; *Týr* being the war god among the *æsir*).

In addition to their 'official' function as trading and market sites, and as centres where laws were made and cults were established, these central places were also associated with special functions such as the skilled craft of jewellery, weapons, clothing and, furthermore, with special cultic activities performed by religious specialists. These places were also the residence of particularly privileged warriors or housecarls (Brink 1996; Fabech 1998; Hedeager 2001; Jakobsson 2003). Some of the central places go back to the fourth century (e.g. *Gudme/Lundeborg* and *Uppåkra*), but the majority do not come into being until after AD 400. Many of these sites remained centres of power and of economic activity far into the Middle Ages (for an overview of settlements in Scandinavia, see Magnus 2002; Skre 2001).

SCANDINAVIA BEFORE THE VIKINGS

In the aftermath of the West Roman Empire, the Merovingians and subsequently the Carolingians gained supremacy over neighbouring kingdoms by military conquest and networks of long-distance alliances and gift-giving. Their form of political and economic organisation, with centrally localised production sites, markets and emporia, is reflected in the petty kingdoms of Scandinavia. Kings and nobles developed a great need for luxury goods to fulfil the social and ritual obligations necessary to keep them in power. The metal items, primarily weapons, jewellery and drinking equipment, are well known in the archaeological records, while carved wood items, prodigal dress and fur, food, alcoholic drinks, and the like are less well preserved and therefore less recognised. The need for exotic raw material was the background for the increasingly intensive exploitation of resources in northern Scandinavia (Myhre 2003: 91) and a closer contact with the Sámi population, which in turn are manifested through the impact on the Norse religion in the late Iron Age (Price 2002; Solli 2002). The emerging Scandinavian warrior society with its dynamic and changing political configurations based on alliances and military power, demanded extensive agricultural resources for its social institutions as well. The reorganisation of the arable land, intensification in the production process, expansive resource utilisation, a hierarchical settlement structure etc. responded to this need. Manors with high density of buildings and evidence for extensive resource consumption, including highly skilled metalwork and imported luxury goods, developed during these centuries.

Against this background, however, the burial evidence is remarkably sparse. Generally speaking, during the late Iron Age cremation graves dominate and usually the grave goods are therefore so heavily damaged that only small fragments have been preserved. However, they confirm the impression of the rich material culture that existed among the Scandinavian elite. Some impressive grave monuments were constructed during this period, mainly on the Scandinavian peninsula. They are found in the inner part of south-eastern Norway, generally in the best agricultural districts, close to rivers and important land routes, and at strategic places along the coast. A remarkable site is Borre in Vestfold with an impressive burial ground with a number of large mounds; the earliest were built in about AD 600 and the others in the following centuries up to about 900. Borre is mentioned in the skaldic poem *Ynglingatal* as the burial place for the royal dynasty of the *Ynglingar*, whom the poem claims to have reigned in Vestfold during the seventh–ninth centuries (Myhre 1992, 2003). *Ynglingatal* is first mentioned and used by Snorri Sturluson in the 1230s, but ought to be from the ninth century (Myhre 1992: 301). During the same period comparable mounds were erected in Götaland, Svealand and in the province of Medelpad in Sweden. They were also situated in the most fertile areas of the cultural landscape. Close to the old church of (Gamla) Uppsala, three of the largest mounds in Scandinavia are to be found. They were all cremation graves from around AD 500 and the early sixth century and the quality of the fragmented grave goods confirms the status of the deceased. Uppsala, which is known as the religious and political centre of the *Svea* kings in the Viking Age, had probably been so since the migration period. Close to Uppsala two special burial grounds, at Vendel and Valsgärde, are to be found. They contain burial mounds with unburned boat graves and grave goods comparable with those of Sutton Hoo in East Anglia (Lamm and Nordström 1983). The cemeteries are dated from around AD 500 to 800 (Arrhenius 1983: 44).

In Denmark, the rich archaeological material stems from Migration-period hoards and from rich settlements of the sixth, seventh and eighth centuries, while grave finds from this period are sparse. No doubt, cremation burial practice was the norm during these centuries except for Bornholm, where well-equipped humation graves are still in existence (i.e. Jørgensen 1990; Jørgensen and Nørgård Jørgensen 1997). The only impressive burial mound from Denmark is located in *Old Lejre* on Zealand, dated to the sixth century. Old Lejre is mentioned among others in *Beowulf* and in *Gesta Danorum* by Saxo Grammaticus from around 1200 as the royal centre of the *Skjoldungs*, the dynasty of the Danish kings during the migration period. A newly excavated manorial site of extensive size supports Lejre's special position as a royal centre in early Danish history (Christensen 1991; Jørgensen 2003).

Lejre illustrates the kingly organisation of the late Iron Age. The presumed royal seat was established and consolidated during the formative period of the sixth, seventh and eighth centuries, as were the royal centres at Borre and (Gamla) Uppsala. Whether the written evidence contains a core of historical reality or not, the archaeological evidence points to the establishment of a new political structure all over Scandinavia around AD 500. At the same time origin myths, royal genealogies, mythical tales and legends, together with the symbolic language of animal style, ought to be perceived as the ideological articulation of this new warrior elite, and the prerequisite for the emergence of Germanic royalty. In their own way, they played an organisational role in the establishment of these new kingdoms and served to demonstrate common cultural codes all over Scandinavia.

BIBLIOGRAPHY

Andersen, H. (1998) 'Vier og lunde', *Skalk* 1998(1): 15–27.

Andrén, A. (2000) 'Re-reading embodied texts – an interpretation of rune stones', *Current Swedish Archaeology*, 8: 7–32.

Andrén, A., Jennbert, K. and Raudvere, C. (eds) (2004) *Ordning mot kaos. Studier av nordisk förkristen kosmologi* (Vägar till Midgård 4), Lund: Nordic Academic Press.

Arrhenius, B. (1983) 'The chronology of the Vendel graves', in J.P. Lamm and H.-Å. Nordström (eds) *Vendel Period Studies*, Stockholm: Statens Historiska Museum.

Bazelmans, J. (1999) *By Weapons Made Worthy. Lords, Retainers and their Relationship in Beowulf*, Amsterdam: Amsterdam University Press.

—— (2000) 'Beyond power: ceremonial exchanges in *Beowulf*', in F. Theuws and J.L. Nelson (eds) *Rituals of Power. From Late Antiquity to the Early Middle Ages*, Leiden: Brill.

Berggren, Å., Arvidsson, S. and Hållans, A.-M. (eds) (2004) *Minne och myt. Konsten att skapa det förflutna* (Vägar til Midgård 5), Lund: Nordic Academic Press.

Brink, S. (1996) 'Political and social structures in Early Scandinavia', *Tor*, 28: 235–81.

Bruce-Mitford, R. (1979) *The Sutton Hoo Ship Burial*, London: British Museum Publications.

Callmer, J. (1997) 'Aristokratisk präglade residens från yngre järnåldern i forskningshistorien och deras problematik', in J. Callmer and E. Rosengren (eds) *". . . gick Grendel att söka det höga huset . . .": arkeologiska källor till aristokratiska miljöer i Skandinavien under yngre järnålder* (Hallands länsmuseers skriftserie 9), Halmstad: Hallands länsmuseer.

Christensen, T. (1991) *Lejre – syn og sagn*, Roskilde: Roskilde Museum.

DeMarrais, E.L., Castillo, J. and Earle, T. (1996) 'Ideology, materialization, and power strategies', *Current Anthropology*, 37: 15–31.

Duczko, W. (ed.) (1993) *Arkeologi och miljögeografi i Gamla Uppsala. Studier och rapporter* (Opia 7), Uppsala: Dept. of Archaeology, Uppsala University.

Earle, T. (1990) 'Style and iconography as legitimation in complex chiefdoms', in M. Conkey and C. Hastorf (eds) *The Use of Style in Archaeology*, Cambridge: Cambridge University Press.

—— (2004) 'Culture matters in the Neolithic transformation and emergence of hierarchy in Thy, Denmark: Distinguished lecture', *American Anthropologists*, 106: 111–25.

Enright, M.J. (1996) *Lady with a Mead Cup*, Dublin: Four Court Press.

Fabech, C. (1994a) 'Reading society from the cultural landscape: South Scandinavia between sacral and political power', in P.O. Nielsen, K. Randsborg and H. Thrane (eds) *The Archaeology of Gudme and Lundeborg*, Copenhagen: Akademisk Forlag.

—— (1994b) 'Society and landscape: from collective manifestations to ceremonies of a new ruling class', in H. Keller and N. Staubach (eds) *Iconologia Sacra. Festschrift für Karl Hauck*, Berlin and New York: de Gruyter.

—— (1998) 'Kult og samfund i yngre jernalder – Ravlunda som eksempel', in L. Larsson and B. Hårdh (eds) *Centrala Platser – Centrala Frågor. En vänbok till Berta Stjernquist* (Acta Archaeologica Lundensia, Series in 8°, no. 28), Lund: Almqvist & Wiksell International.

—— (1999) 'Centrality on sites and landscapes', in C. Fabech and J. Ringtved (eds) *Settlement and Landscape*, Århus: Jysk Arkæologisk Selskab.

Fonnesbech-Sandberg, E. (1985) 'Hoard finds from the Early Germanic Iron Age', in K. Kristiansen (ed.) *Archaeological Formation Processes*, Copenhagen: The National Museum.

Gaimster, M. (1998) *Vendel Period Bracteates on Gotland. On the Significance of Germanic Art*, Stockholm: Almqvist & Wiksell International.

Gansum, T. (2004) 'Role the bones – from iron to steel', *Norwegian Archaeological Review*, 37: 41–57.

Geary, P.J. (2003) *The Myth of Nations. The Medieval Origins of Europe*, Princeton and Oxford: Princeton University Press.

Geisslinger, H. (1967) *Horte als Geschichtsquelle: dargestellt an den völkerwanderungs- und merowingerzeitlichen Funden des südwestlichen Ostseeraumes* (Offa-Bücher 19), Neumünster: Wachholtz.

Glosecki, S.O. (1989) *Shamanism and Old English Poetry* (Garland reference library of the humanities 905), New York and London: Garland Publishing.

Haaland, R. (2004) 'Technology, transformation and symbolism: ethnographic perspectives on European iron working', *Norwegian Archaeological Review*, 37: 1–19.

Hårdh, B. (ed.) (2003) *Fler fynd i centrum* (Uppåkrastudier 9), Stockholm: Almqvist & Wiksell International.

Hårdh, B. and Larsson, L. (eds) (2002) *Central Places in the Migration and Merovingian Periods. Papers from the 52nd Sachsensymposium Lund, August 2001* (Uppåkrastudier 6), Stockholm: Almqvist & Wiksell International.

Haseloff, G. (1981) *Die germanische Tierornamentik der Volkerwanderungszeit*, 3 vols, Berlin and New York: de Gruyter.

Hedeager, L. (1991) 'Die dänischen Golddepots der Völkerwanderungszeit', *Frühmittelalterliche Studien*, 25: 73–88.

—— (1992) *Iron-Age Societies. From Tribe to State in Northern Europe, 500 BC to AD 700*, Oxford: Blackwell.

—— (1997) *Skygger af en Anden Virkelighed. Oldnordiske myter*, Copenhagen: Samleren.

—— (1998) 'Cosmological endurance: pagan identities in early Christian Europe', *Journal of European Archaeology*, 3: 383–97.

—— (1999) 'Sacred topography: depositions of wealth in the cultural landscape', in A. Gustafsson and H. Karlsson (eds) *Glyfer och arkeologiska rum. In honorem Jarl Nordbladh* (Gotarc Series A:3), Gothenburg: Gothenburg University.

—— (2000) 'Europe in the Migration Period: the formation of a political mentality', in F. Theuws and J.L. Nelson (eds) *Ritual of Power. From Late Antiquity to the Early Middle Ages*, Leiden: Brill.

—— (2001) 'Asgard reconstructed? Gudme – a "central place" in the North', in M. DeJong and F. Theuws (eds) *Topographies of Power in the Early Middle Ages*, Leiden: Brill.

—— (2003) 'Beyond mortality: Scandinavian animal style AD 400–1200', in J. Downes and A. Ritchie (eds) *Sea Change. Orkney and Northern Europe in the Later Iron Age AD 300–800*, Angus: The Pinkfoot Press.

—— (2004) 'Dyr og andre Mennesker – mennesker og andre dyr. Dyreornamentikkens transcendentale realitet', in A. Andrén, K. Jennbert and C. Raudvere (eds) *Ordning mot kaos. Studier av nordisk förkristen kosmologi* (Vägar till Midgård 4), Lund: Nordic Academic Press.

—— (2005) 'Scandinavia (c. 500–700 A.D.)', in P. Fouracer (ed.) *The New Cambridge Medieval History*, vol. 1, Cambridge: Cambridge University Press.

Helms, M.W. (1993) *Craft and the Kingly Ideal. Art, Trade and Power*, Austin: University of Texas Press.

Herbert, E. (1984) *Red Gold of Africa*, Madison: University of Wisconsin Press.

—— (1993) *Iron, Gender and Power*, Bloomington and Indianapolis: Indiana University Press.

Herschend, F. (1979) 'Två studier i ölandska guldfynd. I: Det myntade guldet, II: Det omyntade guldet', *Tor*, 18 (1978–9): 33–294.

—— (1993) 'The origin of the hall in South Scandinavia', *Tor*, 25: 175–99.

—— (1995) 'Hus på Helgö', *Fornvännen*, 90: 222–8.

—— (1997a) *Livet i hallen* (Opia 14), Uppsala: Dept. of Archaeology, Uppsala University.

—— (1997b) 'Striden om Finnsborg', *Tor*, 29: 295–333.

—— (1998) *The Idea of the Good in Late Iron Age Society* (Opia 15), Uppsala: Dept. of Archaeology, Uppsala University.

—— (1999) 'Halle', *Reallexikon der Germanischen Altertumskunde*, 13: 414–25.

Hill, C. (2003) *Origins of the English*, London: Duckworth.

Hines, J. (1984) *The Scandinavian Character of Anglian England in the pre-Viking Period* (BAR: British archaeological reports. British Series 124), Oxford: BAR.

—— (1989) 'Ritual hoarding in Migration-Period Scandinavia: a review of recent interpretations', *Proceedings of the Prehistoric Society*, 55: 193–205.

Høilund Nielsen, K. (1997) 'Retainers of the Scandinavian kings: an alternative interpretation of Salin's Style II (Sixth–Seventh Centuries AD)', *European Journal of Archaeology*, 5: 151–69.

Holand, I. (2001) *Sustaining Life. Vessel Import to Norway in the First Millennium AD* (AmS Skrifter 17), Stavanger: Arkeologisk museum.

Jakobsson, A.H. (2003) *Smältdeglars härskare och Jerusalems tillskyndare* (Stockholm Studies in Archaeology 25), Stockholm: Dept. of Archaeology, University of Stockholm.

Jakobsson, M. (1997) 'Burial layout, society and sacred geography', *Current Swedish Archaeology*, 5: 79–98.

Jennbert, K., Andrén, A. and Raudvere, C. (eds) (2002) *Plats och Praxis. Studier av nordisk förkristen ritual* (Vägar till Midgård 2), Lund: Nordic Academic Press.

Jesch, J. (ed.) (2002) *The Scandinavians from the Vendel Period to the Tenth Century. An Ethnographic Perspective*, Woodbridge: Boydell.

Johansen, B. (1996) 'The transformative dragon: the construction of social identity and the use of metaphors during the Nordic Iron Age', *Current Swedish Archaeology*, 4: 83–102.

Jørgensen, L. (1990) *Bækkegård and Glasergård. Two Cemeteries from the Late Iron Age on Bornholm*, Copenhagen: Akademisk Forlag.

—— (2003) 'Manor and market at lake Tissø in the Sixth to the Eleventh Centuries: the Danish "productive" sites', in T. Pestell and K. Ulmschneider (eds) *Markets in Early Medieval Europe. Trading and 'Productive' Sites, 650–850*, Bollington: Windgather Press.

Jørgensen, L. and Nørgård Jørgensen, A. (1997) *Nørre Sandegård Vest. A Cemetery from the 6th–8th Centuries on Bornholm*, Copenhagen: Det Kongelige Nordiske Oldskriftselskab.

Kaliff, A. (2001) *Gothic Connections* (Opia 26), Uppsala: Dept. of Archaeology and Ancient History, Uppsala University.

Karlsson, L. (1983) *Nordisk Form. Om djurornamentik*, Stockholm: Statens Historiska Museum.

Kristoffersen, S. (1995) 'Transformation in Migration Period animal art', *Norwegian Archaeological Review*, 28: 1–17.

—— (2000a) *Sverd og Spenne. Dyreonamentik og social kontekst*, Kristiansand: Høyskoleforlaget.

—— (2000b) 'Expressive objects', in D. Olausson and H. Vandkilde (eds) *Form, Function and Context*, Stockholm: Almqvist & Wiksell International.

Lamm, J.P. and Nordström, H.A. (eds) (1983) *Vendel Period Studies*, Stockholm: Statens Historiska Museer.

Larsson, L. (2002) 'Uppåkra – research on a central place. Recent excavations and results', in B. Hårdh and L. Larsson (eds) *Central Places in the Migration and Merovingian Periods* (Uppåkrastudier 6), Stockholm: Almqvist & Wiksell International.

Larsson, L. and Hårdh, B. (eds) (1998) *Centrala platser, centrala frågor. Samhällsstrukturen under järnåldern. En vänbok till Berta Stjernquist* (Acta Archaeologica Lundensia, Ser. in 8°, no. 28), Lund: Amqvist & Wiksell International.

Lindstrøm, T.C. and Kristoffersen, S. (2001) 'Figure it out! Psychological perspectives on perception of Migration Period animal art', *Norwegian Archaeological Review*, 34: 65–84.

Lund Hansen, U. (1992) 'Die Rortproblematik im Licht der neuen Diskussion zur Chronologie und zur Deutung der Goldschätze in der Volkerwanderungszeit', in K. Hauck (ed.) *Der historische Horizont der Götterbild-Amulette aus der Übergangsepoche von der Spätantike zum Frühmittelalter* (Abhandlungen der Akademie der Wissenschaften in Göttingen. Philol.-hist. Klasse 3:200), Göttingen: Vandenhoeck und Ruprecht.

Lundqvist, L., Lindeblad, K., Nielsen, A.-L. and Ersgard, L. (1996) *Slöinge och Borg: stormansgårdar i öst och väst* (Raä. Arkeologiska Undersökningar. Skrifter 18), Stockholm: Raä.

Magnus, B. (2001) 'The enigmatic brooches', in B. Magnus (ed.) *Roman Gold and the Development of the Early Germanic Kingdoms*, Stockholm: KVHAA.

—— (2002) 'Dwellings and settlements: structure and characteristics', in J. Jesch (ed.) *The Scandinavians from the Vendel Period to the Tenth Century*, Woodbridge: Boydell.

Melheim, L., Hedeager, L. and Oma, K. (eds) (2004) *Mellom Himmel og Jord* (Oslo Archaeological Series 2), Oslo: Institutt for arkeologi, kunsthistorie og konservering, Universitetet i Oslo.

Munch, G.S., Johansen, O.S. and Roesdahl, E. (eds) (2003) *Borg in Lofoten. A Chieftain's Farm in North Norway* (Arkeologisk Skriftserie 1), Trondheim: Tapir.

Myhre, B. (1992) 'The royal cemetery at Borre, Vestfold: a Norwegian centre in a European periphery', in M. Carver (ed.) *The Age of Sutton Hoo*, Woodbridge: Boydell.

—— (2003) 'The Iron Age', in K. Helle (ed.) *The Cambridge History of Scandinavia*, Cambridge: Cambridge University Press.

Näsman, U. (1984) *Glas och handel i senromersk tid och folkvandringstid* (Aun 5), Uppsala: Dept. of Archaeology, Uppsala University.

—— (1991) 'Sea trade during the Scandinavian Iron Age: its character, commodities, and routes', in O. Crumlin-Pedersen (ed.) *Aspects of Maritime Scandinavia AD 200–1200*, Roskilde: Vikingeskibshallen.

—— (1999) 'The Etnogenesis of the Danes and the making of a Danish kingdom', in T. Dickinson and D. Griffiths (eds) *The Making of Kingdoms* (Anglo-Saxon Studies in Archaeology and History 10), Oxford: Oxford University Committee for Archaeology.

Newton, S. (1993) *The Origins of Beowulf and the Pre-Viking Kingdom of East Anglia*, Woodbridge: D.S. Brewer.

Nielsen, P.O., Randsborg, K. and Thrane, R. (eds) (1994) *The Archaeology of Gudme and Lundeborg*, Copenhagen: Akademisk Forlag.

Orchard, A. (2002) *Cassell's Dictionary of Norse Myth and Legend*, London: Cassell.

Price, N.S. (2002) *The Viking Way. Religion and War in Late Iron Age Scandinavia* (Aun 31), Uppsala: Dept. of Archaeology and Ancient History, Uppsala University.

Raudvere, C. (2001) 'Trolldom in early medieval Scandinavia', in K. Jolly, C. Raudvere and E. Peters, *Witchcraft and Magic in Europe. The Middle Ages*, Philadelphia: University of Pennsylvania Press.

—— (2003) *Kunskap och insikt i norrön tradition: mytologi, ritualer och trolldomsanklagelser* (Vägar till Midgård 3), Lund: Nordic Academic Press.

Roe, P.G. (1995) 'Style, society, myth, and structure', in C. Carr and J.E. Neitzel (eds) *Style, Society, and Person*, New York and London: Plenum Press.

Roth, H. (1979) *Kunst der Völkerwanderungszeit*, Frankfurt am Main: Propyläen Verlag.

Salin, B. (1904) *Die altgermanische Thierornamentik*, Stockholm and Berlin: Asher & Co.

Simek, R. (1996) *Dictionary of Northern Mythology*, Cambridge: D.S. Brewer.

Skre, D. (2001) 'The social context of settlement in Norway in the first millennium AD', *Norwegian Archaeological Review*, 34: 1–12.

Skre, D. and Stylegar, F.-A. (2004) *Kaupangen i Skringssal. Vikingenes by*, Oslo: Universitetets Kulturhistoriske Museum.

Solli, B. (2002) *Seid. Myter, sjamanisme og kjønn i vikingenes tid*, Oslo: Pax.

Speake, G. (1980) *Anglo-Saxon Animal Art and its Germanic Background*, Oxford: Clarendon Press.

Watt, M. (1999) 'Gubber', *RGA* 13: 132–42.

Wiker, G. (1999) 'Gullbrakteatene – i dialog med naturkreftene. Ideologi og endring sett i lys av de skandinaviske brakteatnedleggelsene'. (Unpubl. MA thesis, Dept. of Archaeology, University of Oslo.)

CHAPTER TWO

LAW AND SOCIETY

Polities and legal customs in Viking Scandinavia

———— •◆• ————

Stefan Brink

EARLY POLITIES AND PREHISTORIC PROVINCES

During the Viking Age Scandinavia was finally moving towards the establishment of territorialised and unified kingdoms or states. Although we have no written records for this, we must assume that there were several kingdoms or polities before the establishment of Denmark, Norway and Sweden as major kingdoms. We know of several people (*gens*) in Scandinavia, mentioned by classical authors at the beginning of the first millennium, and by Jordanes in his history of the Goths, *Getica*, from around AD 500. Many of these can be identified and geographically located, for example: *theustes*, which should be the people living in the small province of Tjust; *finnaithi*, the people living in Finnveden; and *ostrogothae*, the Östgötar – all in southern Sweden; *raumariciae*, the people living in Romerike; *grannii*, the people living in Grenland; and *ranii*, the people living in *Ranríki* – all to be found in (medieval) Norway.

The provinces of Scandinavia, today called *landskap*, in prehistoric times called *land*, are certainly prehistoric, no doubt existent in and probably older than the Viking Age. We have for example the name *Jämtland* mentioned on the runestone on Frösön as **eotalont** (J RS1928: 66), and *Hadeland* in Norway mentioned in the inscription on the Dynna runestone (N 68) as **haþalanti**, both runestones dated to the eleventh century.

As is mentioned elsewhere in this book, Denmark and Norway began to emerge as major kingdoms in the tenth century (see Roesdahl, ch. 48, and Krag, ch. 47, below). However, state formation was a process covering several centuries. Many researchers believe today that several smaller polities, *land*, in Denmark were united into a kingdom already in the eighth century (e.g. Olsen 1999: 23–37; Näsman 1999, 2000). For Norway, control of the smaller polities or *land* – especially along the coast – was an obvious struggle in the early tenth century, when the polities along the 'North Way', obviously the coastal route, were united under the control of a king, hence the emergence of the name *Norway*. Sweden, however, remained a very confederate kingdom during all of the Middle Ages, consisting of different provinces (Sw *land* sg., *länder* pl.) (see Lindkvist, ch. 49, below).

The interesting question, extremely difficult to answer due to the lack of written sources, is what was the societal base for these smaller polities or *land*? It is probable that

Scandinavia had a similar situation to the one found for example in early Anglo-Saxon England and early Ireland, with small kingdoms, lordships and short-lived larger kingdoms. However, since we lack written sources in Scandinavia, we have no names for the possible lords, petty kings, kings and 'high kings'. Therefore, the mention by Jordanes of a king Roþulf for the people called *ranii* (hence in *Ranríki*) becomes very important ('ranii, over whom Roduulf was king not many years ago'). It hence seems a possible hypothesis that pre-Viking Age Scandinavia had a similar structure to Anglo-Saxon England, and to the Old Irish *tuath* system, with small kingdoms or at least polities under the control of a king, *dróttinn, jarl* or some other leader.

A toponymic analysis of these small *länder*, together with what we may reconstruct from later written sources, indicates that what seems to have kept these communities together was a common judicial custom. Attempts have been made to reconstruct focal sites in these *länder* (often called *þing, þingbrekka, þinglǫt, þingberg, þingmót, þingvall/vǫllr, þjóðstefna, þjóðarmál, þjóðarlyng, vall/vǫllr/vellir, liung/lyng, lǫt, haugr, fylkishaugr, lǫgberg*), hence mounds, hillocks or plain fields, suitable for assembling, places where people met for legal discussions and settlements (Brink 2003a, b, 2004). It is perfectly clear that these legal communities were not working within an egalitarian peasant society, which was the belief in the nineteenth and early twentieth centuries, but were instead a hierarchical society, with kings, chieftains, free peasants, probably (semi-free) tenants and copy holders, and, at the bottom, slaves. The question is hence, who controlled the *þing* assembly? Was it a king or a chieftain, or was the 'public' important? What was the role of the Lawspeaker and how was he picked out in the community – was he a chieftain that 'took' the position, or was he elected to the office (if so, however, certainly from the upper stratum in society)? Most probably someone 'controlled', maybe even 'owned', the *þing* assembly. But with practically no written sources, we have to make probable models from the few written sources we have, from toponymy and landscape analyses, from retrospective analyses of the Old Icelandic literature and from early medieval documents, and from comparing with the Frankish, Anglo-Saxon and Irish cultures. The important knowledge we gain is that the Viking Age society, or rather societies, were legal societies, for which the borrowing of the word *lǫg* into the English language (*law*, OE *lagu* < Pr.-Nordic **lagu-*) during this period is one obvious piece of evidence.

THE PROVINCIAL LAWS IN SCANDINAVIA

The earliest written laws in Scandinavia emanate from the high and late Middle Ages (roughly eleventh to fourteenth century). They are to be seen as offsprings of the same tradition as the Continental Germanic laws (*leges barbarorum*), such as the laws of the Franks (i.e. *Lex Salica*), the Lombards, the Bavarians, the Anglo-Saxons etc., which, however, started to be written down much earlier than in Scandinavia. The Continental laws were all – in principle – written down in Latin, whereas the laws of the Anglo-Saxon kings and the Scandinavian provinces strangely enough are in the vernacular.

The Scandinavian laws are not contemporary texts from the Viking Age. Therefore a big issue in the discussion of these early provincial laws of Scandinavia has been to decide to what extent they reflect earlier (thus Viking Age) legal customs, or whether they exclusively reflect medieval legal ideology, mainly based on Roman and Canon law. Hence, were these laws orally transmitted legal traditions and customs, which were then written down, or medieval codifications and legislation by political agents in the Middle

Ages, who based their law codes on Continental judicial patterns? In the nineteenth century and more or less up to the middle of the twentieth century, the common stance held, in principle, to the former, whereas today there seems to be solid consensus that the Scandinavian provincial laws mirrored medieval judicial ideology, with a solid foundation in Continental law and jurisprudence. Today researchers are – still – very much occupied with comparing medieval Scandinavian laws with medieval Continental (and Roman and Canon) law, trying to prove Continental influence on Scandinavian laws.

A consequence is that in recent decades a focus has been on the Church laws (ON *Kristinn réttr*, OSw *Kirkiu balker*) within the provincial laws, rules of law which, of course, have a background in Canon and Continental law. In recent times there have been few analyses of other parts of the law, such as the behaviour between neighbours in hamlets (*Viþerboa balker*), the rural system and maintenance of arable fields and meadows (*Iorþar balker*) etc. (one exception is Hoff 1997, 2006). In these cases it would not seem improbable that old, domestic customs are to be found.

With the massive reaction from the 1950s and onwards against earlier sloppy and uncritical views on the medieval Scandinavian laws as codified oral law, mirroring a prehistoric legal society – and more links between Scandinavian provincial laws and Continental law will be found, no doubt – we have today a situation when it is time to turn the whole question around and ask if there are any early intrusions or relics in the laws that have been taken over from a customary, oral legal society.

The historian Elsa Sjöholm (1988) has been the most persistent in declaring that the provincial laws of Scandinavia mirror medieval law, and that it is not possible to trace earlier, prehistoric law. Sjöholm's negative stance for finding early traces in the medieval laws has probably been important for the lack of interest in the provincial laws during the past decades. However, a few have continued to discuss law and legal practice in pre-medieval Scandinavia, first and foremost the Danish legal historian Ole Fenger (1971, 1983, 1987, 1991), but also for example Peter Foote (1987), Bo Ruthström (1988), Martina Stein-Wilkeshuis (1982, 1986, 1991, 1993, 1994, 1998), Anette Hoff (1997, 2006), Birgit Sawyer (1997) and Stefan Brink (1996, 2003a); cf. also Sverre Bagge (1989, 2001), Jan Ragnar Hagland and Jørn Sandnes (1994: ix ff.) and Magnus Rindal (1994). Recently there has been a revival in interest in medieval laws around a research group in Copenhagen (Ditlev Tamm, Michael Gelting, Helle Vogt, Per Andersen; cf. Tamm and Vogt 2005).

TRACES OF PREHISTORIC LEGAL CUSTOMS IN ICELANDIC SAGAS?

In the Icelandic collection of sagas, *Heimskringla*, we have the famous story told by Snorri Sturluson about Thorgny, a lawman among the Svear and at their assembly in Uppsala (*Óláfs saga ins helga* ch. 78), in a sub-province in Uppland. His forefathers had been lawmen for generations, according to Snorri. Thorgny was known as a rich, important and wise man and he had a large military escort (*hirð*). In the same episode Snorri gives us a description of an assembly meeting at the Uppsala *þing* (ch. 80): 'On the first day, when the thing was opened, king Olafr sat in his chair and his *hirð* around him. On the other side of the thing site sat Rǫgnvaldr jarl (from Västergötland) and Thorgny in a chair, and in front of them sat the *hirð* of the jarl and the housecarls of

Thorgny. Behind the chair and around in a circle stood the peasant congregation.' After a persuasive speech by Thorgny that appealed to the congregation, the people made noise with their weapons: 'þá gerði lýðrinn þegar vápnabrak ok gny mikinn' (then the people there clashed their weapons and made a loud noise).

In *Óláfs saga ins helga* there is also the story of the sly lawman Emundr from Skara among the Västgötar, the most influential man in Västergötland after the jarl Rǫgnvaldr. In this episode Emundr has a meeting with the king of the Swedes in Uppsala where he tries to settle a problem, in which the law of the Götar differed from the law of the Svear: 'er lǫg vár greinir ok Upsala-lǫg' (when our law differs from Uppsala law). Thus, at least for Snorri in the thirteenth century, the Västgötar had their law in the early eleventh century, and the Svear theirs.

This is, of course, medieval literature, and we have to take the stories for what they are, literary constructions; but if we can qualify statements and details by Snorri and others with information from sources other than literary sagas, we ought to be able to listen to the authors of the sagas in a more historically observant way.

From what we know, it seems obvious that in early Scandinavia it was the custom to make a noise with weapons at thing assemblies for expressing opinions, thus the divisions of *wapentakes* in the Danelaw inform us, but the custom is also mentioned in the much later Magnus Lagabøter's Law (*landslǫg*) (I:5; NGL 1: 409), where it says that a verdict is not legally valid unless the people on the thing assembly, who stand outside the marked-out and hollowed-out area where the judges sit, *lǫgrétta*, give their consent to the verdict by rattling or raising their weapons in the air (*vápnatak* or *þingtak*).

In a famous episode in the saga of Egill Skallagrimsson the assembly at Gula þing in western Norway is described: 'Where the court was established there was a level field, with hazel poles set down in the field in a ring, and ropes in a circuit all around. These were called the hallowed bands (*vébǫnd*). Inside the ring sat the judges.' How accurate may this account be? Is it to be looked upon as a fictitious literary invention by the author without any historical bearings? Most probably, it is not. In the Gulathing Law itself (ch. 91) it says that the þing site should have a round shape (þinghringr; cf. Robberstad 1937: 198; Schledermann 1974: 374), and in the early Frostathing Law (I:2) the word *vébǫnd* is actually used; it says that the *ármenn* (bailiffs) from all *fylki* shall with *vébǫnd* enclose the place of the men in the *lǫgrétta*. In the so-called *Hundabrævið* from the Faroe Islands *vébǫnd* is mentioned in a context with *lǫgþing*: *Var þetta gort a lǫgþingi innan vebanda* (Barnes 1974: 386), 'This was done at the law þing within the hollow bands.' Finally, the regulation of the use of *vébǫnd* is also found in Magnus Lagabøter's *landslǫg* (3:2) and *bylǫg* (town law) (3:2). The background of the usage of hazel poles to fasten the *vébǫnd* on, mentioned in Egill's saga, may also be based on fact. This custom is for example known from Frankish Law (*Lex Ribuaria* 67:5) in the eighth century.

THE THING SITE

Regarding the legal assemblies in Viking Age Scandinavia, we know for certain of their existence (see Jesch 1998). A famous piece of contemporary evidence is the Bällsta rune monument in the parish of Täby, just north of Stockholm. On two runestones erected here one can read [**ulfkil**] **uk arkil uk kui þir kariþu iar þikstaþ** 'Ulvkel and Arnkel and Gye they made here a þing site (þingstaðr)' (Jansson 1977: 121). Several other þing sites are known from runestones and place names in Sweden (see Brink 2003a, b, 2004). It is also possible to reconstruct *þing* sites through archaeological excavations. One of the most startling ones in recent times is the excavation at Þingnes outside Reykjavík in Iceland. This may be the site of the famous *Kjalarnesþing*, mentioned in the Book of Settlement. Founded by Þorsteinn Ingólfsson, the son of the first settler of Iceland, Ingólfur Arnason, this *þing* may have served as a kind of general assembly until 930, but with no legislative role. A trace of this is that the chieftains of Kjalarnes and the descendants of Þorsteinn Ingólfsson held the honorary title *Allsherjargoði*, the supreme chieftain, whose function was to hallow the National Assembly at Thingvellir every year. Except for the sparse information we get in the Book of Settlement and Ari's words in the Book of the Icelanders, very little is known of the *þing* assembly in Kjalarnes. Therefore it is most interesting that recent archaeological excavations at Elliðavatn by Þingnes have probably revealed this first assembly site (Guðmundur Ólafsson 1987). How old then was the *þing*-institution in Scandinavia? We cannot be certain. However, in a 'Stand der Forschung' article, Per Sveaas Andersen (1974: 347) finds it plausible that it goes back to the early Iron Age (i.e. before AD 600).

RELICTS OF PREHISTORIC LAW IN SCANDINAVIA?

For an analysis of our oldest legal sources in Scandinavia an obvious start would be for example *Baugatal* in the Icelandic law collection, *Grágás*, that is, rules concerning the duty to pay and to accept payment for injuries. Although this law-rule is stuffed with archaic words, it is very dubious, highly controversial and even uncertain if it has ever been in use (see Barlau 1981; Sawyer 1982: 44; 1987; Meulengracht Sørensen 1992: 169 f.; Jesch 1998).

Another possible departure could be the Old Danish 'Vederlov' (*Witherlogh*), the penalty law of the king's *hirð*, found in manuscripts from the late twelfth century, but in two of these stated to be from old Knut's days (understood as being from the time of Canute the Great, thus in the early eleventh century). However, this law is also very problematic regarding origin and age (Kroman 1975; Fenger 1983: 63; cf. Hjärne 1979: 151–208).

The Old Swedish so-called *Hednalagen*, that is, 'Pagan Law', has, as the title of the law fragment indicates, also been assumed to be very old. The codex in which the *Hednalagen* has been written down is from the mid-thirteenth century, but the age of the actual law-rule is not known. The law discusses and regulates *einvígi*, the settling of disputes by fighting, and some phrases have been looked upon as very archaic (see Nelson 1944: 57; Ståhle 1954: 130 f.; Wessén 1968: 51).

In an interesting study, Peter Foote (1987: 63) analyses the Icelandic *Grágás*, especially *Landabrigðisþáttr* and *Rekaþáttr*, and his conclusion is that these parts of the law should be dated to the eleventh century. He even concludes that other parts of *Grágás* must be as old, perhaps even older, that is, from the pre-Christian period (cf. Meulengracht Sørensen 1992: 112 f.).

There are reasons to believe that the provincial laws may have older roots – words, fragments and perhaps even law-rules – in their different provinces (*land*) respectively, which are older than from the twelfth or thirteenth century. The codification, editing and writing down of the provincial laws in books during the twelfth to fourteenth centuries have, of course, seen the use of Continental law, jurisprudence and legal knowledge as the basis for the new product, and the transferring of laws to other regions, as in the case of the Hälsinge Law, which is practically a copy of the Uppland Law. These facts have naturally been revealed. However, for the tracing of older strata and details in the laws, one has to look for things that *differ*. For example, the Hälsinge Law has taken over the administrative structure from the Uppland Law, but used (obviously retained!) a terminology totally unknown in the Uppland Law, which of course must have an explanation.

THE FORSA RUNE RING: THE EARLIEST LAW IN SCANDINAVIA

It is obvious that Viking society was a type of legal society, there is no doubt about this, but it is very difficult to find traces of this and to reconstruct it. We have, however, some – more or less – indisputable evidence of this legal culture in the Viking Age. One is the inscription of the runic iron ring called the Forsa rune ring.

In the parish church of Forsa in the province of Hälsingland, northern Sweden, an iron ring with a runic inscription has been hanging on a door for centuries. The ring was observed and mentioned already in 1599, and the inscription was published and translated around 1700 by the famous Olof Celcius. The ring measures 43 cm in diameter and it contains nearly 250 runes.

Traditionally, and ever since an important and influential analysis of the inscription by the Norwegian Sophus Bugge in 1877, this inscription has been called the oldest legal inscription (law-rule) in Scandinavia. There has been consensus regarding the fact that the inscription contains an ecclesiastical law-rule, regulating tithes, the protection afforded by asylum in a church or the illicit cancellation of divine service. The main argument for this being a church law is the occurrence of two key words, **staf** '(bishops) staff' and **lirþir** 'the learned (clergy)', so read and translated by Bugge. The ring, and the inscription, has therefore been assumed to be from the Christian period, although the runes on the ring are very archaic; the same kind is found on for example the famous Rök runestone in the province of Östergötland (from *c*. AD 800).

In an important analysis of the inscription, made by the Norwegian runologist Aslak Liestøl in the 1970s, he was able to prove that Bugge's reading of **lirþir** was wrong. Instead one should read **liuþir**. This does away with the foundation of the traditional interpretation and dating of the ring. There is nothing that forces us to tie the ring to a clerical context any more.

The inscription reads:

: uksatuiskilanaukauratuastafatfurstalaki :
uksatuaaukaurafiurataþrulaki :
: inatþriþialakiuksafiuraukauratastaf :
aukaltaikuiuarʀifanhafskakiritfuriʀ
: suaþliuþiʀakuatliuþritisuauasintfuraukhalkat :
inþaʀkirþusikþitanunratarstaþum :
: aukufakʀahiurtstaþum :
inuibiurnfaþi :

which may be translated as:

One ox and two **aura** [in fine] [to ?] **staf** [or] **aura staf** [in fine] for the restoration of a cult site (**vi**) in a valid state for the first time; two oxen and four **aura** for the second time; but for the third time four oxen and eight **aura**; and all property in suspension, if he doesn't make right. That, the people are entitled to demand, according to the law of the people that was decreed and ratified before.

But they made [the ring, the statement or?], Anund from Tåsta and Ofeg from Hjortsta. But Vibjörn carved.

Today it seems more obvious to date the Forsa rune ring to the ninth century, which makes its previous title of 'the oldest law-rule in Scandinavia' of course even more accurate (Brink 1996; Källström 2007: 145, 201–2; Williams, ch. 21, below). We here have a legal text, a kind of law-rule, from the early Viking Age. It has been proposed that it regulates the maintenance of a *vi*, a cult and assembly site (Ruthström 1990). For the failure of restoring the *vi* in a legal way, you should pay fines, one ox and two **aura** (*ørar*) for the first time, two oxen and four *ørar* for the second time and four oxen and eight *ørar* the third time, and failing this, all your property was to be suspended. Perhaps the most important part of the inscription is the phrase *svað liuðir æigu at liuðrétti* 'that, which the people are entitled to demand according to the people's right' (hence, the law of the *land*). Thus, we have here evidence of a special kind of law of the people or the *land* (most certainly Hälsingland), a *liuðréttr*, cf. ON *lýðréttr* (see von See 1964: 57 ff.). This statement is unique for Viking Age Scandinavia, to my knowledge, and it actually supports the statement by Snorri Sturluson, that different people had different laws in early Scandinavia. The Forsa rune ring must be looked upon as one of the most important artefacts of the early Viking Age, and for shedding light on early Scandinavian society.

BIBLIOGRAPHY

For runic inscriptions, se *Samnordisk runtextdatabas*: www.nordiska.uu.se/forskning/samnord.htm.

Bagge, S. (1989) [Review of Elsa Sjöholm 1988], (*Norsk*) *historisk tidsskrift*, 69: 500–7.
—— (2001) 'Law and justice in Norway in the Middle Ages: a case study', in L. Bisgaard *et al.* (eds) *Medieval Spirituality in Scandinavia and Europe. A Collection of Essays in Honour of Tore Nyberg*, Odense: Odense University Press.
Barlau, S.B. (1981) 'Old Icelandic kinship terminology: an anomaly', *Ethnology. An international journal of cultural and social anthropology*, 20: 191–202.
Barnes, M. (1974) 'Tingsted', *KL*, 18: 382–7.
Brink, S. (1996) 'Forsaringen. Nordens äldsta lagbud', in E. Roesdahl and P. Meulengracht Sørensen (eds) *Beretning fra femtende tværfaglige vikingesymposium* (Beretning fra Det Tværfaglige Vikingesymposium 15), Højbjerg: Hikuin.
—— (2003a) 'Law and legal customs in Viking Age Scandinavia', in J. Jesch (ed.) *Scandinavians from the Vendel Period to the Tenth Century*, San Marino: CIRSS.
—— (2003b) 'Legal assemblies and judicial structure in early Scandinavia', in P. Barnwell and M. Mostert (eds) *Political Assemblies in the Earlier Middle Ages* (Studies in the Early Middle Ages), Brepols: Turnhout.
—— (2004) 'Legal assembly sites in early Scandinavia', in A. Pantos and S. Semple (eds) *Assembly Places and Practices in Medieval Europe*, Dublin: Four Courts Press.
Bugge, S. (1877) 'Runeskriften paa Ringen i Forsa Kirke i nordre Helsingland', *Festskrift til Det Kgl. Universitet i Upsala . . .* 1, Kristiania: no publ.

Egil's saga, trans. with an intro. by H. Pálsson and P. Edwards, Harmondsworth: Penguin 1976.

Fenger, O. (1971) *Fejde og mandebot. Studier over slægtsansvaret i germansk og gammeldansk ret*, Copenhagen: no publ.

—— (1983) *Gammeldansk ret. Dansk rets historie i oldtid og middelalder* (Ny indsigt), Viby: Centrum.

—— (1987) 'Om kildeværdien af normative tekster', in K. Hastrup and P. Meulengracht Sørensen (eds) *Tradition og historieskrivning. Kilderne til Nordens ældste historie* (Acta Jutlandica 63:2. Hum. Serie 61), Aarhus: Aarhus universitetsforlag.

—— (1991) 'Germansk retsorden med særligt henblik på det 7. århundrede', in P. Mortensen and B. Rasmusen (eds) *Høvdingesamfund og Kongemagt. Fra Stamme til Stat i Danmark*, vol. 2 (Jysk Arkæologisk Selskabs Skrifter 22:2), Højbjerg: Jysk Arkaeologisk Selskab.

Foote, P. (1987) 'Reflections on *Landabrigðisþáttr* and *Rekaþáttr* in *Grágás*', in K. Hastrup and P. Meulengracht Sørensen (eds) *Tradition og historieskrivning. Kilderne til Nordens ældste historie* (Acta Jutlandica 63:2. Hum. Serie 61), Aarhus: Aarhus universitetsforlag.

Frostatingslova, trans. J.R. Hagland and J. Sandnes (Norrøne bokverk), Oslo: Samlaget 1994.

Guðmundur Ólafsson (1987) 'Þingnes by Elliðavatn: the first local assembly in Iceland?', in J. Knirk (ed.) *Proceedings of the Tenth Viking Congress, Larkollen, Norway, 1985* (Universitetets Oldsakssamlings skrifter. Ny rekke 9), Oslo: Universitetets oldsaksamling.

Hagland, J.R. and Sandnes, J. (1994) 'Om lova og lagdømmet', in J.R. Hagland and J. Sandnes, *Frostatingslova* (Norrøne bokverk), Oslo: Samlaget.

Hjärne, E. (1979) *Land och ledung*, vol. 1 (Rättshistoriskt bibliotek 31), Stockholm: Nordiska bokhandeln.

Hoff, A. (1997) *Lov og landskab. Landskabslovenes bidrag til forståelsen af landsbrugs- og landskabsudviklingen i Danmark ca. 900–1250*, Århus: Århus universitetsforlag.

—— (2006) *Recht und Landschaft: der Beitrag der Landschaftsrechte zum Verständnis der Landwirtschafts- und Landschaftsentwicklung in Dänemark ca. 900–1250* (Ergänzungsbände zum Reallexikon der germanischen Altertumskunde 54), Berlin and New York: de Gruyter.

Jansson, S.B.F. (1977) *Runinskrifter i Sverige*, Stockholm: AWE Gebers.

Jesch, J. (1998) 'Murder and treachery in the Viking Age', in T. Haskett (ed.) *Crime and Punishment in the Middle Ages*, Victoria: University of Victoria.

Jordanes' *Getica* = *Getica: om goternas ursprung och bedrifter*, trans. A. Nordin, Stockholm: Atlantis 1997.

Källström, M. (2007) *Mästare och minnesmärken. Studier kring vikingatida runristare och skriftmiljöer i Norden* (Acta Universitatis Stockholmiensis. Stockholm Studies in Scandinavian Philology. NS 43), Stockholm: Almqvist & Wiksell International.

Kroman, E. (1975) 'Vederloven', *KL* 19: 612–14.

Liestøl, A. (1979) 'Runeringen i Forsa. Kva er han, og når vart han smidd?', *Saga och sed*: 12–27.

Meulengracht Sørensen, P. (1992) *Fortælling og ære. Studier i islændingesagaerne*, Aarhus: Aarhus universitetsforlag.

Näsman, U. (1999) 'The ethnogenesis of the Danes and the making of a Danish kingdom', in T. Dickinson and D. Griffiths (eds) *The Making of Kingdoms* (Anglo-Saxon Studies in Archaeology and History 19), Oxford: Oxbow Books.

—— (2000) 'Exchange and politics: the eighth–early ninth century in Denmark', in I.L. Hansen and C. Wickham (eds) *The Long Eighth Century*, Leiden, Boston and Cologne: Brill.

Nelson, A. (1944) 'Envig och ära. En studie över ett fornsvenskt lagfragment', *Saga och sed*: 57–94.

NGL = *Norges gamle Love*, vols 1:1–5, Christiania 1846–95 2:1–2, Oslo 1912–34.

Olsen, O. (1999) *Da Danmark blev til*, Copenhagen: Fremad.

Rindal, M. (1994) 'Innleiing', in B. Eithun, M. Rindal and T. Ulset (eds) *Den eldre Gulatingslova* (Norrøne tekster 6), Oslo: Riksarkivet.

Robberstad, K. (1937) *Gulatingslovi* (Norrøne bokverk 33), Oslo: Det norske samlaget.

Ruthström, B. (1988) 'Oklunda-ristningen i rättslig belysning', *Arkiv för nordisk filologi*, 103: 64–75.

—— (1990) 'Forsa-ristningen – vikingatida vi-rätt?', *Arkiv för nordisk filologi*, 105: 41–56.

Sawyer, B. (1997) 'Viking Age rune-stones as a source for legal history', in A. Dybdahl and J. Sandnes (eds) *Nordiske middelalderlover* (Senter for middelalderstudier. Skrifter 5), Trondheim.

Sawyer, P. (1982) *Kings and Vikings. Scandinavia and Europe AD 700–1100*, London: Routledge.

—— (1987) 'The bloodfeud in fact and fiction', in K. Hastrup and P. Meulengracht Sørensen (eds) *Tradition og historieskrivning. Kilderne til Nordens ældste historie* (Acta Jutlandica 63:2. Hum. Serie 61), Aarhus: Aarhus universitetsforlag.

Schledermann, H. (1974) 'Tingsted', *KL* 18: 373–6.

von See, K. (1964) *Altnordische Rechtswörter. Philologische Studien zur Rechtsauffassung und Rechtsgesinnung der Germanen* (Hermaea. Germanische Forschungen. Neue Folge 16), Tübingen: Niemeyer.

Sjöholm, E. (1988) *Sveriges medeltidslagar. Europeisk rättstradition i politisk omvandling* (Skrifter utgivna av Institutet för rättshistorisk forskning 41), Stockholm: Nordiska bokhandeln.

Snorri Sturluson, *Heimskringla. History of the Kings of Norway*, trans. with introd. and notes by Lee M. Hollander, Austin: University of Texas Press 1964.

Ståhle, C.I. (1954) 'Den första utgåvan av Upplandslagen och dess förlaga', *Arkiv för nordisk filologi*, 69: 91–143.

Stein-Wilkeshuis, M. (1982) 'The right to social welfare in early medieval Iceland', *Journal of Medieval History*, 8: 343–52.

—— (1986) 'Laws in medieval Iceland', *Journal of Medieval History*, 12: 37–54.

—— (1991) 'A Viking-age treaty between Constantinople and northern merchants, with its provision on theft and robbery', *Scando-Slavica*, 37: 35–47.

—— (1993) 'Runestones and the law of inheritance in medieval Scandinavia', *Actes à cause de Mort (Acts of Last Will)*, vol. 4: *Mondes non européens* (Recueils de la Société Jean Bodin 62), Brussels: De Boeck Université.

—— (1994) 'Legal prescriptions on manslaughter and injury in a Viking Age treaty between Constantinople and northern merchants', *Scandinavian Journal of History*, 19: 1–16.

—— (1998) 'Scandinavian law in a tenth-century Rus'–Greek commercial treaty?', in J. Hill and M. Swan (eds) *The Community, the Family and the Saint. Patterns of Power in Early Medieval Europe* (International Medieval Research 4) Turnhout: Brepols.

Sveaas Andersen, P. (1974) 'Ting', *KL* 18: 346–59.

Tamm, D. and Vogt, H. (eds) (2005) *How Nordic are the Nordic Medieval Laws?* (Medieval Legal History 1), Copenhagen: University of Copenhagen Press.

Wessén, E. (1968) *Svenskt lagspråk*, Lund: Gleerup.

CHAPTER THREE

THE SÁMI AND THEIR INTERACTION
WITH THE NORDIC PEOPLES

———•◆•———

Inger Zachrisson

During the Viking Age a large part of the Scandinavian peninsula was inhabited by Sámi (Figure 3.1). Similar populations within the Uralic-speaking zone reveal many common elements of society and culture, cosmology and religion, dwelling types and settlement patterns. Sámi territory was traditionally divided into *sijte* areas, a territorial, economic and social unit. Society was socially and economically stratified; it was changing, dynamic. Some Sámi were probably settled. Regional differences were still existing, but gave way to a more and more 'pan-Sámi' material culture, and an increasing religious and ethnic consolidation.

Central Scandinavia and the north Norwegian coast were important areas for contacts between Sámi and Nordic peoples. The archaeological material shows that there were relatively clear and stable borders between their dwelling areas. Nordic expansion northwards was primarily the result of an inner development, not of immigration. Contacts between agrarian areas and hunting grounds must have been close and the latter not primarily looked upon as 'outlying land' but as 'a homeland', where Sámi relatives still lived (Hansen and Olsen 2004; Schanche 2000; Zachrisson *et al.* 1997).

Most of the written sources emanate from the early Middle Ages, but probably describe the Viking Age as well. They give information about Sámi in *both* northern and central Scandinavia. But everything that is said about them is said by others. The word for Sámi is based on the Old Norse *finnar* (sing. *finn*) – it was through Nordic people that knowledge of the Sámi reached the world. *Finnmark* meant the 'forest' or 'border land' of the Sámi. Their own name, *Saame*, is recorded once, in an Icelandic saga from the thirteenth century, in the word *semsveinar* (ON *sveinn* 'young man').

Skridefinnas ('skiing Sámi') are depicted by king Alfred of Wessex *c.* AD 890 as neighbours to the *svear*. Adam of Bremen writes in the eleventh century about *Skritefini* living between Swedes and Norwegians, in the area of the Swedes, and that some of them were Christianised. *Historia Norwegie* from *c.* 1150–75, probably written in south-east Norway, describes Sámi shamanism, and divides Norway lengthwise into three zones from west to east: the coastal area, the mountains, and the forests of the *finnar*. Snorri Sturluson, in the thirteenth century, and others talk about Sámi in southern Norway, for example Hadeland, Oppland, and possibly Härjedalen (Mundal 1996, 2003; Zachrisson *et al.* 1997).

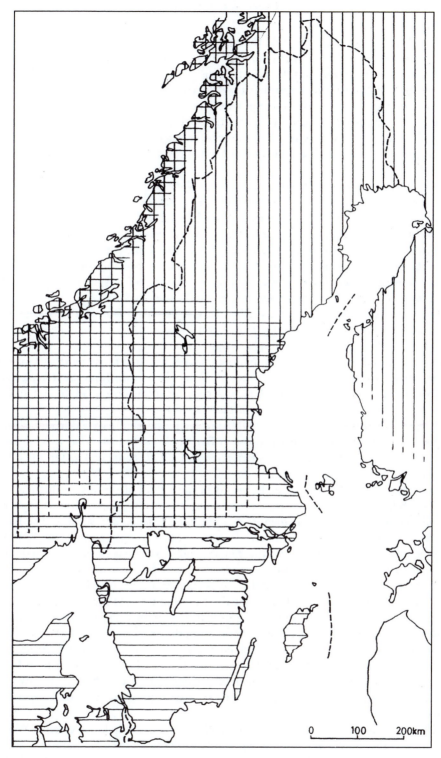

Figure 3.1 A schematic picture of Sámi culture (vertical lines) and Nordic culture (horizontal lines), *c.* AD 1000 (after Zachrisson *et al.* 1997).

The Old Norse sources show that the Sámi were a natural part of Norwegian society; the two peoples lived in a kind of symbiosis. Some Sámi moved to Iceland, according to written sources and grave finds (Einarsson 1994). The borders between the peoples were not sharp. The Norwegians knew that they shared the country with another people – much more than later on. But the Sámi were not looked upon as equals. Local petty kings could have Sámi in their service. Snorri Sturluson tells of a man named Finn, or rather he was a *finn*. He was small and quick, a master on skis and with his bow, the stereotypes of a Sámi. He had long and faithfully been serving king Rörik of Hedmark (Mundal 2003).

Finn was taken up as a Christian name in the Norse culture, and used in some of the most aristocratic families. On the other hand, nearly all the Sámi in the written sources have Norse names. The concept *finnkonge* 'Sámi king' shows Sámi with a special status. Conflicts between Sámi and Norwegians are rarely described – it was considered wrong to mistreat the Sámi. The main criteria of Sámi culture seem to be based on ecological, economical and religious elements. Several people were probably bilingual (Mundal 2003; Zachrisson *et al.* 1997). It was because of contacts, not in spite of such, that the Sámi for so long could maintain their own culture (Odner 1983).

One can distinguish between ten Sámi languages today. During the Viking Age their language area was larger to the south – Sámi was probably the language in central Scandinavia when the Indo-European language arrived (Sammallahti 1996; Strade 1997; Wiik 2002). Influence from Sámi to Nordic may be indicated as far south as Uppland before AD 800 (Kusmenko and Rießler 2000). Many place names from the Iron Age and the Middle Ages in *Finn-* or *Lapp-*, hence identifying ethnic origin, are to be found in southern Norway, especially in the south-east (Olsen 1995).

According to genetic (mitocondric DNA) research, the Sámi have a different genetic disposition compared with other peoples in Europe. It could mean that they emanate from a very old (west) European population (Sajantila *et al.* 1995; cf. Hansen and Olsen 2004).

Differentiated societies are usually rooted in some form of surplus production, and the possibility of using it in a trading position. The many prestige objects from the outside world in Sámi ancient monuments indicate exchange of a surplus. The Norse chiefdoms functioned as redistributive systems (Odner 1983; Hansen 1990). When they became established in the north, they depended on alliances with corresponding societies to the south; one exchanges goods and marriage partners. In the north there were to be found walrus tusks, exquisite furs and gerfalcons, prestige objects sought after by the European elite – things that the Sámi hunters had access to (Hansen and Olsen 2004). Even if tax and plundering expeditions are mentioned, it was probably a more varied reality with co-operation, useful for both parties (Odner 1983). But it does not hinder an asymmetrical relation of power. The saga of *Egill Skallagrímsson* tells about how Þórólfr Kveldulfsson in the tenth century in winter time went from Hålogaland to trade with and tax the Sámi in the mountains. From them he received fur products, afterwards sold in England – 'most went calmly but part of it with fear' (Zachrisson *et al.* 1997).

The north Norwegian chieftain Othere (ON *Óttarr*) reports to king Alfred of Wessex in *c.* AD 890 that the *finnas* live along with and east of the Norwegians, hunting, fishing and catching birds. Othere had 600 unsold tame reindeer, six of which were decoys. The wealth of the Norwegian chieftains was said to be mostly in the tribute of the *finnas*, which was differentiated: 'Each pays according to his rank. The highest in rank has to pay fifteen marten skins, five reindeer skins, one bear skin, ten measures of feathers, a jacket of bearskin or otter skin and two skip-ropes', 60 ells long, one made from walrus-hide and the other from sealskin. The size of the reindeer herd may indicate that it was owned by several Sámi. The chieftains seem to have divided the tribute from the Sámi in exchange for political patronage, goods such as agricultural products, imported textiles or precious metals (Hansen and Olsen 2004). *Historia Norwegie* says about the Sámi: 'There are also by the *finnar* numerous squirrels and hermins, and of the skins of all these animals they every year pay large tributes to the kings of Norway, whose subjects they are.'

When the kings' power in Norway became stronger in the tenth century, the relations between the Sámi and the Norsemen got more strained. During the eleventh century the king got the fur trade as a monopoly. A surplus of fur probably lies behind the many imported metal objects found among the finds of the *c.* ten large Sámi sacrificial sites in the interior of northern Scandinavia. The many Norwegian silver coins in them are from *c.* 1050–1200. The coins were pierced, used as ornaments. But weights here and at a dwelling site, plus non-pierced coins from another site and a grave, indicate that the Sámi by now were part of the 'weight economy' of Scandinavia – perhaps as merchants themselves. Their society was well integrated in the trade and economic system of the surrounding societies (Hedman 2003; Zachrisson 1984; Zachrisson *et al.* 1997).

Some twenty silver hoards from the tenth to the thirteenth century, characterised by necklaces and bracelets, were found in the Sámi areas in the north. The finds have a complementary spread in comparison with the Sámi sacrificial-site finds. The agglomeration in the 'border zone' in Nord-Troms may indicate ritual depositions, perhaps between representatives for both Sámi and Norsemen, a symbolic confirmation of the border between them. Some of the silver ornaments have a very low silver content. Were they especially produced for the Sámi (Zachrisson 1984; Hansen and Olsen 2004)?

Sámi erected 'hunting-ground graves' *c.* 200 BC–AD 1300 in the inland of central Scandinavia, which were as a rule cremation graves under modest stone settings (Zachrisson *et al.* 1997; Zachrisson 2004; Bergstøl 2008; Skjølsvold 1980; Hansen and Olsen 2004). Adopting burial customs from others does not, however, necessarily mean that the underlying ideas were also taken over, but it indicates near contacts. Nordic grave customs spread further and further north among the Sámi in the inland of Sweden. At the same time the agrarian areas at the coast experienced a boom.

Near contacts between Sámi and Norsemen on a high social level are indicated at Vivallen in Härjedalen with twenty rich flat graves with inhumation burials from *c.* 1000 to 1200. They are typical of Sámi graves as regards burial custom (orientation, birch-bark shrouds), combinations of grave goods similar to those of the sacrificial sites (locally made hunting arrowheads and pendants, eastern-type penannular brooches and pendants, western coins and ornaments) and characteristic functional alterations of objects, compared with their areas of production. There were objects of goat skin in three graves. The dwelling site area nearby, from *c.* 800 to 1200, has up to now revealed remains of two Sámi huts with typical stone-filled fire-steads and bones of reindeer and goats/sheep (Zachrisson *et al.* 1997).

In the north so-called *urgraver*, graves of stone, and bear-graves, with ritually buried bears, became characteristic Sámi traits (Schanche 2000; Hansen and Olsen 2004).

The Sámi had a symbolic power in their magic, for which the Norsemen had great respect. Sámi figure as healers, advisers and masters of magic. Sámi and Norse share certain fundamental religious concepts, such as the *seiðr* and the belief in magical weapons and clothes. They fight together against the introduction of Christianity. In the earliest Christian law codes for south-east Norway, written down before *c.* 1120, the Christians are forbidden to go to the land of the *finnar* in order to have their fortune told or to be healed. As far south as in Hedmark a Sámi shaman hammer from about the twelfth century was found at a dwelling site (Bergsland 1970; Zachrisson *et al.* 1997; Zachrisson 2004).

The Nordic peoples interpreted their relationship to the Sámi in the light of myths. The Norse live in Miðgarðr, the Sámi in Útgarðr. The goddess Skaði skis and hunts with bow and arrows, like a Sámi woman, and the Sámi woman Snæfríðr became ancestress to the Norwegian royal dynasty (Mundal 1996, 2003).

The Nordic and Sámi elites exchanged marriage partners. There are women's graves with Nordic types of ornaments in Sámi areas, and women's graves with Sámi types of ornaments – often eastern, of bronze – in Nordic areas (Storli 1991; cf. Schanche 2000; Zachrisson *et al.* 1997). Written sources tell of Sámi women marrying Nordic men of the highest level of society. King Haraldr Hárfagri marries Snæfríðr, daughter of Svási the *finn*-king, who lives in a Sámi hut at the royal mansion at Dovre in southern Norway. They have four sons. In a high-status sphere Sámi were evidently accepted (Mundal 1996).

The 'mats' of birch-bark covering Nordic boat graves in Uppland were originally parts of conical huts, Sámi *gåetie*. Were they trade products or did Sámi live close by? Another question is why typical Sámi items were used at such prestige occasions, whether it was solely for practical reasons, or maybe also symbolical (Zachrisson *et al.* 1997). The Sámi have played a far greater role in both religion and economy than formerly assumed (Price 2002).

The attire of Nordic Viking Age man – and woman – was evidently an ideal for high-ranking Sámi men. Male graves at Vivallen and Långön Island in Ångermanland contained textiles of wool and linen: imported status objects. The richest man's grave at Vivallen shows 'double-gender affiliation' (he was probably a shaman): it consists of an 'oriental' belt belonging to the East Nordic/international male dress, and adornments to high-ranking Nordic women's attire, such as the necklace, knife and linen tunic (Zachrisson *et al.* 1997; Price 2000). Such belts – perhaps signifying a shaman – have been found in other rich Sámi graves in east Scandinavia as well. Swords, on the other hand, in Jämtland and Härjedalen are as a rule found in hunting-ground graves, not in those of the settled areas. Could this be a sign of Norwegian influence on Sámi (Zachrisson *et al.* 1997)?

The Sámi functioned as specialists inside the Nordic economic system. They were hunters and gatherers. *Historia Norwegie* says: 'They are very skilled hunters, . . . nomads who live in tents . . . these they take on their shoulders, fasten smoothed boards under their feet . . . and move with their wives and children faster than the bird . . . whereby the reindeer pull them.'

Sámi women were of old specialists in preparing the pelts of animals, with methods, tools and terminology of their own. The fur trade in the South Sámi area was directed towards Nordic people: the Sámi words for 'marten' and 'to prepare skin' are here borrowed from the Nordic language, while the same words in the North Sámi area are from the Finnish language. The South Sámi word for 'snare' is *giele*, but also *snaarroe*, a word taken over from Nordic. It shows close collaboration (Zachrisson *et al.* 1997).

Historia Norwegie also says about the Sámi: 'There is an enormous amount of wild animals such as bears, wolves, lynxes, foxes, martens, otters, badgers and beavers . . . squirrels and hermins.' The Nordic word for 'fox', ON *refr*, Norw *rev*, Sw *räv*, is probably a loan from Sámi/Fenno-Ugric to all the Nordic languages, which shows it to be an early loan (Bergsland 1970; see Hansen and Olsen 2004). The black (or white) fur of the mountain fox was one of the most valued of all skins from the north.

Trapping pits, usually in systems, for catching big game, elk or reindeer, seem once to have characterised Sámi culture, but later spread also to Nordic culture. In Dovre there were such large systems that the meat, hides and antlers from reindeer caught here must have been for sale at a large market, maybe a result of Sámi–Norse cooperation (Mikkelsen 1994).

Sámi probably made skis for Nordic people. Most of the several hundred prehistoric skis found in Fennoscandia are of Sámi type, several with typical ornamentation. That the Sámi were specialised in skiing is stressed from the ninth to the nineteenth century (Zachrisson *et al.* 1997).

Sámi were of old making exquisitely decorated objects of elk and reindeer antler, often with resin inlay. Reindeer hunters buried in the south Norwegian mountains were also specialised 'comb-makers', working in antler (Christensen 1986).

The much discussed *stalotomter*, a kind of hut foundations, may also indicate specialisation. These Sámi hut foundations, in rows, above the tree-line in Scandinavia, indicate a new use of the mountains. It is debatable whether the dwellings were erected in connection with hunting (Mulk 1994; Hansen 1990), or for reindeer herding. New types of location, with good grazing for reindeer, were now chosen for dwelling sites; this was a new type of Sámi society, based on a semi-nomadic living, which was yet another economic differentiation (Hedman 2003; Storli 1994). Changes in the vegetation indicate reindeer herding at Sösjön in northern Jämtland from at least the thirteenth century and at Vivallen in Härjedalen perhaps earlier (Aronsson 2004; König Königsson in Zachrisson *et al.* 1997). The South Sámi language has words from before AD 800 for driving with and milking reindeer. In all the Sámi languages there are, of old, special words for 'tame reindeer' as well as 'wild reindeer' (Knut Bergsland, see Zachrisson *et al.* 1997: 149).

Iron smithing is also stated during the Viking Age at Sjösjön, and iron arrowheads like those from Vivallen and the sacrificial sites found there (Aronsson 2004). The Sámi seem to have been looked upon as specialists in this field according to written sources, and it is indicated from hunting-ground graves of the Viking Age and before (Zachrisson *et al.* 1997).

Sámi were well-known boat builders. A woman was buried in a sewn boat of Sámi type (Larsson 2007) in a Nordic boat grave in Västmanland, Sweden (Nylén and Schönbäck 1994). The Norwegian king Sigurðr Slembidjákn ordered two sewn Atlantic ships to be built for him by Sámi in Lofoten. The Sámi then made a feast for him – a symbolic act.

On the shores of the border area in northern Norway, in then Sámi areas, there are *hellegroper*, oval/rectangular pits, used to extract train-oil from whale blubber or seal fat. Some pits are so big that the production cannot have been only for local demand (Henriksen 1995; Hansen and Olsen 2004).

Thus, during the Viking Age the interaction between Sámi and Nordic peoples was intensified, especially in central Scandinavia. There was a high degree of reciprocity and social acceptance between them. They had near economic, social and religious contacts. Steadfast forms of collaboration developed, based upon the specialisation of the respective group.

BIBLIOGRAPHY

Aronsson, K.-Å. (2004) 'Tusenårig boplats upptäckt vid Sösjön', *Jämten*, 97: 15–19.

Bergsland, K. (1970) 'Om middelalderens finnmarker', *(Norsk) Historisk Tidsskrift* 1970(4): 365–409.

Bergstøl, J. (2008) *Samer i Østerdalen? En studie av etnicitet i jernalderen og middelalderen i det nordøstre Hedmark* (Acta humaniora 325), Oslo: Unipub.

Christensen, A.E. (1986) 'Reinjeger og kammaker, en forhistorisk yrkeskombinasjon?', *Viking*, 49 (1985–6): 113–33.

Einarsson, B.F. (1994) *The Settlement of Iceland; A Critical Approach. Granastaðir and the Ecological Heritage* (GOTARC. Gothenburg Archaeological Theses B:4), Göteborg: Dept. of Archaeology, University of Gothenburg.

Hansen, L.I. (1990) *Samisk fangstsamfunn og norsk høvdingeøkonomi*, Oslo: Novus forlag.

Hansen, L.I. and Olsen, B. (2004) *Samenes historie fram til 1750*, Oslo: Cappelen Akademisk Forlag.

Hedman, S.-D. (2003) *Boplatser och offerplatser. Ekonomisk strategi och boplatsmönster bland skogssamer 700–1600 AD* (Studia archaeologica universitatis Umensis 17), Umeå: Institutionen för arkeologi och samiska studier, University of Umeå.

Henriksen, J.E. (1995) *Hellegropene. Fornminner fra en funntom periode.* (Unpubl. thesis at the University of Tromsø, Stensilserie B: 42, Tromsø.)

Historia Norwegie, trans. P. Fisher, ed. I. Ekrem and L. Boje Mortensen, Copenhagen: Museum Tusculanum (2003).

Kusmenko, J. and Rießler, M. (2000) 'Traces of Sámi-Scandinavian contact in Scandinavian dialects', in D. Gilbers, J. Nerbonne and J. Schaeken (eds) *Languages in Contact* (Studies in Slavic and general linguistics 28), Amsterdam: Rodopi.

Larsson, G. (2007) *The Ship and the Maritime Society of Central Sweden in Late Iron Age* (Aun 37), Uppsala: Dept. of Archaeology and Ancient History, University of Uppsala.

Mikkelsen, E. (1994) *Fangstprodukter i vikingtidens og middelalderens økonomi. Organiseringen av massefangst av villrein i Dovre* (Universitetets Oldsaksamlings skrifter. Ny rekke 18), Oslo: Universitetets Oldsaksamling.

Mulk, I.-M. (1994) *Sirkas – samiskt fångstsamhälle i förändring. Kr. f.–1600 e. Kr.* (Studia archaeologica universitatis Umensis 6), Umeå: Arkeologiska inst., University of Umeå.

Mundal, E. (1996) 'The perception of the Saamis and their religion in Old Norse sources', in J. Pentikäinen (ed.) *Shamanism and Northern Ecology* (Religion and Society 36), Berlin and New York: Mouton de Gruyter.

——— (2003) 'Vikingane kjende godt til samane', *Daerpies Dierie (Sydsamiskt kyrkoblad)*, 2002(4): 2–3, 2003(1): 8–9, (2): 8–9.

Nylén, E. and Schönbäck, B. (1994) *Tuna i Badelunda. Guld Kvinnor Båtar*, 2 vols (Västerås kulturnämnds skriftserie 27 & 30), Västerås: Kulturnämnden.

Odner, K. (1983) *Finner og terfinner. Etniske prosesser i det nordlige Fenno-Skandinavia* (Oslo occasional papers in social anthropology 9), Oslo: University of Oslo.

Olsen, L. (1995) 'Stadnamn på Finn-. Spor etter samisk aktivitet i Sør-Noreg?', in M. Harsson and B. Helleland (eds) *Stadnamn og kulturlandskapet* (Nasjonale konferensen i namnegransking 7), Oslo: Avdeling for namnegransking, Universitetet i Oslo.

Price, N.S. (2000) 'Drum-time and Viking Age: Sámi-Norse identities in early medieval

Scandinavia', in M. Appelt, J. Berglund and H.Ch. Gulløv (eds) *Identities and Cultural Contacts in the Arctic* (Danish Polar Center. Publications 8), Copenhagen: Danish Polar Center, Danish National Museum.

—— (2002) *The Viking Way. Religion and War in Late Iron Age Scandinavia* (Aun 31), Uppsala: Dept. of Archaeology and Ancient History, Uppsala University.

Sajantila, A. *et al.* (1995) 'Genes and languages in Europe: an analysis of mitochondrial lineages', *Genome Research*, 5: 42–52.

Sammallahti, P. (1996) 'Language and roots', in H. Leskinen (ed.) *Congressus octavus internationalis Fenno-Ugristarum, Jyväskylä 10.–15.8.1995*, vol. 1, Jyväskylä: Moderatores.

Schanche, A. (2000) *Graver i ur og berg: samisk gravskikk og religion fra forhistorisk til nyere tid*, Karasjok: Davvi Girji OS.

Skjølsvold, A. (1980) 'Refleksjoner omkring jernaldersgravene i sydnorske fjellstrøk', *Viking*, 43 (1979): 140–60.

Storli, I. (1991) 'De østlige smykkene fra vikingtid og tidlig middelalder', *Viking*, 54: 89–104.

—— (1994) *'Stallo'-boplassene. Spor etter de første fjellsamer?* (Instituttet for sammenlignende kulturforskning B:19), Oslo: Novus.

Strade, N. (1997) 'Det sydsamiske sprog', in Zachrisson *et al.* (1997).

Wiik, K. (2002) 'On the emergence of the main Indo-European language groups of Europe through adstratal influence', in K. Julku (ed.) *The Roots of Peoples and Languages of Northern Eurasia*, vol. 4, Oulu: Societas Historiae Fenno-Ugricæ.

Zachrisson, I. (1984) *De samiska metalldepåerna år 1000–1350 i ljuset av fyndet från Mörtträsket, Lappland* (Archaeology and Environment 3), Umeå, Inst. för arkeologi, University of Umeå.

—— (2004) 'Idre sameby – sydligast i Sverige', *Idre sameby – med historiska spår i framtiden*, Östersund: Gaaltije.

Zachrisson, I. *et al.* (1997) *Möten i gränsland. Samer och germaner i Mellanskandinavien* (Statens historiska museum. Monographs 4), Stockholm: Statens historiska museum.

CHAPTER FOUR

WOMEN AND SEXUAL POLITICS

———•◆•———

Auður G. Magnúsdóttir

O ne late summer evening in 1238, the prominent politician and writer Snorri
Sturluson was enjoying the company of a few friends in his outdoor bath at
Reykholt. It is said that the men were discussing chieftaincy, which probably included
what characteristics a good chieftain should possess, how he should behave and perhaps
even what material symbols of status were necessary. Doubtless the men consumed
quantities of alcohol and in time started discussing the importance of alliances. Snorri
himself gave an account of his own well-planned ties through marriage, not only his
own, but even those he had planned on behalf of his children. Having been given that
account, the impressed assembly assured him that none within Iceland could match
Snorri's powerful position due to his alliances through marriage (*Sturlunga saga*: 319).[1]
In the struggle for power in contemporary Iceland strong alliances were of utmost
importance. Snorri also believed that he had managed to secure his own position by
joining ties of friendship and marriage with many of the most powerful families in
the country (on Snorri as a politician, see Gunnar Karlsson 1979; see Faulkes, ch. 23,
below). His strategy had been to give his own daughters in marriage to men who were
socially and economically of the same standing as he was. But the social networks Snorri
had struggled for and which had impressed his friends, didn't work out very well. In fact
one of his former sons-in-law was responsible for getting him killed. How could this
have happened?

Modern studies have tended to focus on the important role of marriage in medieval
politics as well as in the political strategies of later times, a view that is well formulated
by Georges Duby (1985: 19): 'Marriage establishes relations of kinship. It underlines
the whole of society and is the keystone of social edifice.' This concentration on marriage
and biological kinship, which in modern society clearly has a different meaning than in
the Middle Ages, has meant that the social functions of other forms of relationship have
been neglected until recently, thus the role of friendship in medieval politics has been an
object of extensive research (i.e. Byock 1988; Althoff 1990; Jón Viðar Sigurðsson 1992;
Hermanson 2000). The treatment of marriage as the 'keystone of the social edifice' has
obscured the fact that monogamous marriage has not always been the norm, that other
forms of cohabitation were socially and politically as important as marriage, and that
kinship is changeable over time. Thus the concept *family* has to be discussed in relation

to the historical context. In the Middle Ages blood ties weren't necessarily the strongest bonds between people. Similarly the phrase 'politics' is in no way unproblematic, not to mention the expression 'sexual politics'. What does it mean? And by whom are sexual politics practised? Before going any further a definition of the phrase is necessary. In Viking Age society – as in later times – women were subordinated to men. This obviously meant that they did not have the formal right to take action in politics; their possibilities of attaining power were thus minimal, as were the opportunities for them to independently control large economic properties. Together with social and personal honour (Pitt Rivers 1966; Henderson Stewart 1994), property is seen as one of the more significant bases for power in medieval society, social honour being the type of honour women could hardly ever achieve (for discussion about wealth and honour as the basis for power in Iceland, see Helgi Þorláksson 1982 and Jón Viðar Sigurðsson 1999; on women, feud and honour, see Auður Magnúsdóttir 2007). It is thus clear that women neither had the formal rights nor the social and economic position to take action in the field of politics. Yet there were women who had influence, some through their husbands, some after they had become widows; in medieval Europe we even have examples of women rising from the status of concubines to queens, which in itself could illustrate the essential meaning of 'sexual politics' (Stafford 1983). On the other hand we have no proof that indicates that these women had *intended* their future position; most of them came to power after the death of their companion, hence they did not exercise sexual politics. In the following the phrase 'sexual politics' will refer to two modes of influence: firstly it signifies the actions of men planning their own and their children's relationships – marriage or concubinage – and secondly it will be used as referring to women's possibilities of exercising influence, through sexuality. This leads us to the two main questions of this chapter: what was the political and social significance of marriage and other sexual relationships in the Viking Age? Secondly, given that the prospects of unmarried women achieving power were minimal, the question of women actually taking part in politics will focus on women having, or having had, sexual relationships with men (similarly, unmarried men were unlikely to achieve essential power).

WHEN DID IT HAPPEN?

The myth of the 'strong' Viking woman, as she is illustrated in the Icelandic sagas, has not been challenged with any intensity, in spite of the critical examination of the sagas in general. The admiration for women like Guðrún Ósvífursdóttir in *Laxdæla saga* and Auður Vésteinsdóttir in the saga of Gísli Súrsson is still visible in recent studies, but the question of this ideal woman's whereabouts in time, space or even as products of the authors' mere fantasy is not raised. However, the historian's possibilities of giving a clear picture of the Viking Age in general are limited, as are the chances of getting a plausible picture of woman's actual situation (Jochens 1995; Jesch 1991). Hence, a study of the political conduct of women during the Viking period is a challenge. The sagas are inevitably at best the product of the thirteenth century, written by educated men of high social standing, many of whom were directly or indirectly involved in the conflicts and social changes that characterised the century. This undoubtedly had an effect on their writing. Furthermore, the Icelandic sagas were composed in the same period as the less known contemporary sagas, most likely by the same men. This in turn makes the striking disparity between the two genres' 'social reality' interesting. Can this disparity be the key to a society going under and a new one evolving?[2]

During the thirteenth century the Church grew strong as an independent institution and accordingly followed the demands of the Church in Rome, among them the demands of celibacy and monogamous sacred marriage. In the contemporary sagas concubinage is common while the Icelandic sagas show a society where monogamous marriage is the rule. In fact the scholar Einar Ólafur Sveinsson (1940: 142) has described the Icelandic sagas as the most monogamous literature in the world. What's more, women in the Icelandic sagas are far more visible than their sisters in the contemporary sagas, and hold a stronger position. This contrast, on the one hand between the depiction of intimate relationships in the two genres, and on the other hand their different images of women, provides one possibility in approaching the use and importance of sexual politics in the Viking Age. Inevitably this means that the point of departure is the thirteenth century, that is, the period of saga-writing, and thus the focus of this chapter will be on the contemporary sagas.

MEN'S POWER – WOMEN'S SEXUALITY?

It is well known that alliances through marriage were meant to create a bond between two families. The obvious goal was to establish a strong horizontal connection between the two groups (Auður Magnúsdóttir 2003: 66). This type of relationship is typical for marriage alliances, in which the families as a rule were of the same or similar social and economic standing. But there were other means of creating effective alliances. Friendship was one, fostering another. However, concubinage can be seen as the most effective way of establishing strong, lasting and loyal alliances. In contrast to the alliances made through marriage, these relationships were concentrated on one person (in most cases of high social standing) and were vertical and hierarchical. In order to show the difference between the two types of alliances it is fruitful to compare Snorri Sturluson's alliances through marriage with Sturla Sighvatsson's relations through concubinage and marriage. Snorri Sturluson and Sturla Sighvatsson were close relatives. Sighvatur, Sturla's father, and Snorri were brothers. Both Snorri, and in due time Sturla, were active in the power struggle in thirteenth-century Iceland and became competitors as Sturla gained age and strong alliances. From 1235 Sturla may be seen as the most powerful chieftain in Iceland, but he was killed in the battle at Örlygsstaðir in 1238.

Before we go any further it is important to emphasise that in Iceland – as in the rest of Scandinavia – the kinship structure was egocentric and bilateral. Each individual had his/her own kindred; in practice this meant that only siblings had the same kindred. This, however, was true only until they married. Marriage created new kinship ties. An individual became a member of a new family and thus acquired new relatives. As a result loyalties changed. The need for effective alliances was great and marriage could strengthen the bonds between families. Within the same family, however, there were several constellations created by marriage or concubinage, and conflicts of loyalty could arise.

MARRIAGE AND SEXUAL POLITICS

When the time had come for Snorri Sturluson to marry, his mother had spent the inheritance he should rightfully have had after his father's death. Thus Snorri, at the age of eighteen, was without property but of high social standing. His brother Þórður and his foster brother Sæmundur Jónsson proposed on his behalf to Herdís Bersadóttir, daughter of Bersi the rich and of Þórður's mistress, Hróðny Þórðardóttir. Snorri had two children with Herdís but the marriage was not a happy one. The couple separated but Snorri continued to control Bersi's property.

Snorri also had a few concubines and with them another three children that we know of. One of Snorri's concubines was Guðrún Hreinsdóttir. She took care of his household at Reykholt. They had several children, but only the daughter, Ingibjörg, survived to adulthood. Guðrún was the daughter of Snælaug Högnadóttir and the stepdaughter of Þórður Böðvarsson, who in fact gave his part of Lundamannagoðorð to Snorri, and in the same year even the important farm Reykholt. Thus the relationship with the concubine brought Snorri even more power and wealth than before (see Auður Magnúsdóttir 2001: 68). Snorri used his children ruthlessly in order to ensure his political and economic situation. His three daughters were married to some of the leading chieftains in the country, and consequently Snorri established important alliances with the Haukdælir, Ásbirningar and Vatnsfirðingar. Through his own relationship to Hallveig Ormsdóttir, the daughter of Ormur Jónsson from Oddi, and by far the richest woman in Iceland, he strengthened his connection with the family of Oddaverjar. It was after having arranged all these marriages that Snorri bragged about his good alliances in the outdoor bath in Reykholt. What Snorri was striving for was to establish strong, horizontal relations between his own social network and the leaders of other social networks, as strong as his own. And, as his friends admitted, his efforts were promising.

However, marriage as a political instrument wasn't always an effective way of creating strong alliances. In contrast to what has been stated about marriage alliances in contemporary Denmark, the relations between fathers and sons-in-law wasn't particularly secure in Iceland. Whereas in Denmark sons-in-law proved to be loyal supporters of their fathers-in-law, and sons not, the circumstances in Iceland were the opposite (Hermanson 2000: 174–5). A possible explanation is that in Iceland one could suppose that sons and fathers had the same or similar ambitions, and strived for the benefit of their own nearest family, the sons-in-law could, as leaders of other alliances, have ambitions which in many cases weren't parallel with those of the father-in-law. A marriage was arranged between two socially and economically equal individuals, and if the new son-in-law had his own political goals and alternative networks, he had the possibility of standing on his own feet, or even opposing his father-in-law. In Snorri's case this meant that he couldn't even be sure of support from two of his most powerful sons-in-law, Gissur Þorvaldsson and Kolbeinn ungi. Thus Kolbeinn as a son-in-law of Snorri, but blood-related to Sturla, chose to support the latter when Sturla and Snorri came into conflict.

Alliances established through marriage were indeed a bond of dependence, but if the interests of the two families came into collision, each of them had the possibility of acting independently. It wasn't even certain that the two families had the same network as a basis of power. This is one of the explanations of the frailty of the system. Strong, horizontal ties could result in difficult conflicts between the leaders of the two networks, as the actors in many cases had the same social standing but an incompatible political position. This, together with the kinship system being bilateral – where you not only had different roles as son, brother, grandson, nephew, uncle, son-in-law and/or brother-in-law, and had obligations to all of your relatives – made marriage an uncertain way of establishing lasting and loyal bonds. This of course created a need for other complementary alliances. Fosterage and concubinage were as a rule vertical connections. Even if the focus here lies on the latter, the character of both relationships makes an interesting comparison to marriage.

CONCUBINAGE AND SEXUAL POLITICS

The insecurity of alliances through blood-relations may be well illustrated in the conflicts between Snorri Sturluson and his nephew Sturla Sighvatsson, in which case affinity was no guarantee of alliance or a peaceful relationship. Furthermore, their conflicts put their common relatives in a difficult position. The question of which of one's relatives one should support appears to be frequent in *Sturlunga saga*, and each time as problematic. (For a short account of the political development during Snorri's and Sturla's 'reign' see Jón Viðar Sigurðsson 1999: 71–83; for the relationship between brothers and nephews during the Icelandic Middle Ages, see Guðrún Nordal 1998 and Torfi H. Tulinius 2000.)

Sturla was an ambitious chieftain, and, like Snorri, he tried to establish strong political alliances in order to secure his own position. As a young and promising chieftain Sturla had a concubine, but in due time married Solveig Sæmundardóttir, daughter of the prominent Sæmundur Jónsson í Oddi. As a political alliance this marriage didn't work out well. Solveig's brothers and sisters were tied to other families through marriage, some of these families being Sturla's prime enemies. As a consequence, Solveig's brothers could never give Sturla any support in his political struggle. Instead, and in contrast to Snorri's networks, Sturla's most important networks were those he established through his relation to the concubine Vigdís Gísl dóttir.

Vigdís' father, Gísl Bergsson, was a significant farmer (*stórbóndi*) in Miðfjörður, a district in which Sturla wished to strengthen his political position. Gísl Bergsson was an influential man in his district, and by choosing his daughter as a concubine, Sturla established a bond between the two families, and even got access to Gísl's own social networks, mainly comprising important farmers in Miðfjörður. As with marriage, the relationship was supposed to bring benefit to both sides. Sturla himself attained the support and loyalty of several farmers, including Gísl's five sons, his nephew, and niece's husband. Their loyalty to Sturla and his father, Sighvatur, continued even after Sturla got married. At least two of Gísl's sons were at Örlygsstaðir, where Sturla and Sighvatur were killed, and they obviously were among Sturla's closest supporters. The association with Sturla was important to Gísl and his sons. Through their relationship they moved upwards in the social hierarchy, which in turn affected their power position. But the relationship was different from similar bonds through marriage. Gísl and his sons were indeed members of Sturla's network, but at the same time they were dependent on him. If they opposed him, or failed in their support, they ran a risk of being excluded from the network and thereby losing the benefits they had gained through the relationship. The ties between Sturla and the family of the concubine were vertical – and hierarchical – and can in many aspects be compared with the patron–client relations in contemporary

Europe. The loyalty caused by the nature of the bond characterises concubinage in twelfth- and thirteenth-century Iceland. As inferiors in social status, the family of the concubine had neither contacts nor position to act independently against the chieftain, which in turn resulted in strong loyalty and explains why these relationships were stronger and more lasting than marriage alliances or even blood-relations. No less important is that even though the chieftain could have several ties of friendship with men of the same social standing as himself, the guardian of the concubine could not establish more than one bond of friendship with a chieftain at a time. He could establish networks with other farmers of the same social standing as himself, and to which the chieftain also had access. In establishing friendship with chieftains, however, he had to make a choice. As the farmer was bound only to one chieftain, problems such as which one of your kinsmen to support never occurred in such relationships. Consequently the relationships created by concubinage can be said to be stronger: loyalty was restricted to one chieftain and could not be broken.

Sturlunga saga throws light on how marriage and other relationships, that is, concubinage and friendship, were used to maintain, extend and strengthen the power position of dignified men. In the Icelandic sagas friendship between men is common, and the circumstances of marriage contracts are frequent objects of narrative. Women do take action in the sagas: they incite to revenge, threaten their husbands and sometimes even take part in fights. Examples of this are to be found in both family and contemporary sagas, not to mention the legendary sagas. A question that remains unanswered is whether the authors were putting forth and thereby preserving stories from the past, or if their narratives contained material from their own lifetime, or if the sagas include a little of both. The form for behaviour, gender roles, social norms and codes must have been familiar to the readers of the sagas, and perhaps the strong woman in many cases is to be seen as a role model for negative behaviour.

Jenny Jochens (1980) has argued for the 'educative' purpose of the sagas, especially regarding marriage and monogamy, while Preben Meulengracht Sørensen (1993) has studied the relationship between author, text and public in several of his works. He underlines that in order to be understood the authors had to adapt their text to the public they addressed. This naturally meant even putting forward certain propaganda and/or opinions. Obviously this is highly relevant when studying women and gender in the texts. Nonetheless the written sources must be seen as reflections of the society they were created in, and perhaps the real position of the Viking woman is to be found in the dissimilarity between the different genres. Let us have a closer look at the position of women in *Sturlunga saga* and the Icelandic sagas.

WOMEN AND SEXUAL POLITICS

In discussing marriage, concubinage as well as other extramarital relations, the concentration is often on the political role of these relationships, which inevitably leads the focus of the analysis to men: men's way of doing politics, men's economic interests and men's struggle for power. But what was the role and status of concubines and was it in any way different from that of the official wife? Under what circumstances could the wife – or concubine – interfere as a recognised actor in the political arena? Through her relationship to a man of a higher social standing, the concubine could advance socially. This fact raises several questions that cannot be answered fully in this chapter. One is if the concubine thereby also advanced politically. Furthermore, it is interesting to discuss the possibilities of women independently establishing relations like friendship and concubinage, in which the man was equal or subordinate.

As stated above, medieval women were subordinate to men, to their fathers, brothers and finally their husbands. However, the sagas show several examples of women who go against their husbands, who take political decisions without consulting them, who divorce their husbands and act independently. These examples in most cases are women who in fact are socially superior to their husbands, and the saga-writers use this difference in social standing as an explanation for the women's behaviour.

Another explanation, which even clarifies the shifting opportunities of women in other societies and periods, is that women can take a man's place in his absence, but have to withdraw when he returns. Nonetheless, none of the famous 'strong' women in Old Norse literature are concubines. The position of the concubine was unavoidably less secure than the official wife's. Besides being subordinate to her 'man' as well as father and brothers, on grounds of gender, the concubine was even subordinate in social standing. This no doubt affected her position and possibilities of interference in politics as well as her possibilities of deciding her own future. Thus Ragnheiður Þórhallsdóttir was nothing but a mere object in the conflict between her lover Jón Loftsson and her brother bishop Þorlákur, and doubtlessly wasn't able to affect the choice of her future husband. When Sturla Sighvatsson got married, his concubine was sent home to her father. And although Gissur Þorvaldsson is said to have loved his concubine dearly, neither she nor her sister, the concubine of Þorgils skarði, are made visible in the saga. An obvious explanation of the lack of 'strong concubines' may be that *Sturlunga saga* focuses on the political struggle of the twelfth and thirteenth centuries where the main actors of course were men. Thus it is difficult to get a clear picture of the concubine's status. However, there was probably a difference in rank between concubines of married and unmarried chieftains. Hence even if Sæmundur Jónsson had several concubines, he also gave them responsibility for his various households, and after his death at least two of his concubines had the same status as widows, which besides being economically independent, meant the possibility of deciding the future marriages of their children (*Sturlunga saga* I: 299). In that way these women, in theory, were able to effect the founding of new political alliances. Even if in *Sturlunga saga* we get a few glimpses of women seemingly independently involved in social networks, only Þórdís Snorradóttir, one of Snorri Sturluson's illegitimate daughters, seems to achieve public acknowledgement as a leader. After the death of Þórdís' husband, Snorri attempted to take control over his daughter and grandson, but failed. Þórdís never married again, but took two lovers and had one child with each of them. She obviously created her own alliances and acted as a politician until her son was old enough to take his inheritance. By that time Þórdís also withdrew from her former role, as she was now the mother of a man who had reached adulthood and was ready and willing to see to his own rights. And, according to tradition, the woman retired.[3]

Sturlunga saga reveals a society familiar to the authors. Sturla Þórðarson, who is the author of the largest part of the compilation, describes events and conflicts he and his close relatives took part in. Þórdís Snorradóttir, mentioned above, was his cousin, and it is not unlikely that he admired her for how she had stood up to her father. Sturla's brother, Ólafur hvítaskáld, has been pointed out as a possible author of *Laxdæla saga*, in which we meet one of the most famous characters in the saga world, Guðrún

Ósvífursdóttir, the image of the strong Viking woman. Furthermore, *Laxdæla saga* can be said to be the only saga in which a woman is the central figure. Indeed the saga contains many exceptional 'strong women'. Here we meet Auður djúpúðga, the slave Melkorka, who turns out to be an Irish princess, Þorgerður, daughter of Egill Skallagrímsson and mother of Kjartan Ólafsson, and Brókar-Auður, the woman who in spite of her two brothers takes revenge into her own hands. On the other hand none of these women can be said to have practised sexual politics, possibly with the exception of Melkorka, who in order to raise money for her son's expedition to Ireland decided to marry a farmer of good fortune (*Laxdæla saga*: 50–1). Clear examples of how women's sexuality can lead to disaster and women using sexuality to accomplish their wishes are on the other hand to be found in Gísli Súrsson's saga. However, none of these examples shows a woman politically active and gaining respect as an actor in the public arena. On the contrary, in most cases the counsels of women in the family sagas lead to disaster, whereas the actions of their sisters in the contemporary sagas do not. The logical question then of course is what conclusions we can reach from this contrast.

NOTES

1 *Sturlunga saga* is a compilation, in which *Íslendinga saga*, by Sturla Þórðarson, constitutes the largest and most important part. It is also in *Íslendinga saga* that we find this tale of the feast in Reykholt. Although we can never be sure of the veracity of the story, it nonetheless gives insight into what qualities and contacts were regarded as important in contemporary Iceland and Scandinavia. For a short but comprehensive account of the *Sturlung Age*, see Helgi Þorláksson (1993).
2 Úlfar Bragason (1991) has argued convincingly for the political significance of *Geirmundar páttur heljarskinns* in the Sturlunga compilation and the political significance of *Sturlunga saga* as a whole. His analysis has relevance for the study of the Icelandic sagas as well.
3 Cf. Laqueur (1990). – Lately Laqueur's theories have been used in order to approach women's social, political and economic situation in medieval and early modern Scandinavia, i.e. Clover (1993); Sjöberg (2001); Auður Magnúsdóttir (2002).

BIBLIOGRAPHY

Althoff, G. (1990) *Verwandte, Freunde und Getreue. Zum politischen Stellenwert der Gruppenbindungen im früheren Mittelalter*, Darmstadt: Wiss. Buchges.
Auður Magnúsdóttir (2001) *Frillor och fruar. Politik och samlevnad på Island 1120–1400* (Avhandlingar från Historiska institutionen i Göteborg 29), Göteborg: Historiska inst., Göteborgs universitet.
—— (2002) '"Var Steinvör þá málóð um hríð". "Sterka konan" og valdamöguleikar íslenskra miðaldakvenna', in Loftur Guttormsson *et al.* (eds) *Íslenskir sagnfræðingar að fornu og nýju. Seinna bindi, Viðhorf og rannsóknir*, Reykjavík: Skrudda.
—— (2003) 'Älskas, giftas, stöttas, slåss. Om svaga och starka länkar som politisk resurs på Island 1180–1270', in Einar Hreinsson and T. Nilson (eds) *Nätverk som social resurs. Historiska exempel*, Lund: Studentlitteratur.
—— (2007) 'Kvinnor i fejd. Ära, kön och konflikt', in E. Opsahl (ed.) *Frid och fejd i middelalderens Norden*, Oslo: Unipub.
Byock, J. (1988) 'Valdatafl og vinfengi', *Skírnir. Tímarit hins Íslenska bókmenntafélags*, 162: 127–37.
Clover, C. (1993) 'Regardless of sex: men, women, and power in early northern Europe', *Speculum: Journal of the Medieval Academy of America*, 68: 363–87 (reprinted in *Representations*, 44 (1993): 1–28).

Duby, G. (1985) *The Knight, the Lady and the Priest. The Making of Modern Marriage in Medieval France*, Harmondsworth: Penguin.

Einar Ólafur Sveinsson (1940) *Sturlungaöld. Drög um íslenska menningu á þrettándu öld*, Reykjavík: no publ.

Guðrún Nordal (1998) *Ethics and Action in Thirteenth Century Iceland* (The Viking Collection 11), Odense: Odense University Press.

Gunnar Karlsson (1979) 'Stjórnmálamaðurinn Snorri', in Gunnar Karlsson (ed.) *Snorri – átta alda minning*, Reykjavík: Sögufélag.

Helgi Þorláksson (1982) 'Sturlung Age', in Ph. Pulsiano (ed.) *Medieval Scandinavia. An Encyclopedia*, New York: Garland.

—— (1993) 'Stéttir, auður og völd á 12. og 13. öld', *Saga*, 20: 63–113.

Henderson Stewart, F. (1994) *Honor*, Chicago: University of Chicago Press.

Hermanson, L. (2000) *Släkt, vänner och makt. En studie av elitens politiska kultur i 1100-talets Danmark* (Avhandlingar från Historiska institutionen i Göteborg 24), Göteborg: Historiska institutionen.

Jesch, J. (1991) *Women in the Viking Age*, Woodbridge: Boydell.

Jochens, J. (1980) 'The Church and sexuality in medieval Iceland', *Journal of Medieval History*, 6: 377–93.

—— (1995) *Women in Old Norse Society*, Ithaca, NY: Cornell University Press.

Jón Viðar Sigurðsson (1992) 'Friendship in the Icelandic Commonwealth', in Gísli Pálsson (ed.) *From Sagas to Society. Comparative Approaches to Early Iceland*, Enfield Lock: Hisarlik Press.

—— (1999) *Chieftains and Power in the Icelandic Commonwealth* (The Viking Collection 12), Odense: Odense University Press.

Laqueur, Th. (1990) *Making Sex: Body and Gender from the Greeks to Freud*, Cambridge, MA: Harvard University Press.

Laxdæla saga, ed. Einar Ólafur Sveinsson (Íslensk fornrit 5), Reykjavík: Hið íslenzka fornritafélag 1934.

Meulengracht Sørensen, P. (1993) *Fortælling og ære. Studier i islændingesagaerne*, Aarhus: Aarhus universitetsforlag.

Pitt Rivers, J. (1966) 'Honour and social status', in J.G. Peristiany (ed.) *Honour and Shame. The Values of Mediterranean Society*, London: Weidenfeld & Nicolson.

Sjöberg, M. (2001) *Kvinnors jord, manlig rätt. Äktenskap, egendom och makt i äldre tid*, Hedemora: Gidlund.

Stafford, P. (1983) *Queens, Concubines and Dowagers. The King's Wife in the Middle Ages*, London: Batsford Academic and Educational.

Sturlunga saga, Jón Jóhannesson, Magnús Finnbogason and Kristján Eldjárn (eds), Reykjavík: Sturlunguútgáfan 1946.

Torfi H. Tulinius (2000) 'Snorri og bræður hans. Framgangur og átök Sturlusona í félagslegu rými þjóðveldisins', *Ný Saga*, 12: 49–60.

Úlfar Bragason (1991) 'Sturlunga: a political statement', in *The Eighth International Saga Conference. The Audience of the Sagas. Preprints*, vol. 2, Göteborg: Göteborgs universitet.

CHAPTER FIVE

SLAVERY IN THE VIKING AGE

——·◆·——

Stefan Brink

Early Scandinavian society was more or less until the 1960s looked upon as an egalitarian peasant society, with free farmers, kings and chieftains (Sw *bygdehövdingar*). In the Icelandic sagas and the earliest provincial laws there were, of course, mentions of slaves, most commonly known as *prælar*. So the existence of a slaving class was known, but not given any particular notice. Kings could have many *prælar*, farmers some. This fact did not alter the view of the prehistoric society; it was still looked upon as fairly homogeneous. When the number of thralls was discussed, some scholars reckoned with large quantities in society, as many as *c.* 25 per cent of the population.

No modern and serious discussion of slavery in prehistoric Scandinavia has, however, seen the light so far. When the topic has been under analysis, the two main sources consulted have been the provincial laws and the Icelandic sagas; the former evidencing the last phase of thralldom in Scandinavia with the manumission of thralls, and for the latter sources – the sagas – we always have the creeping suspicion that they describe more the time of the writing of the sagas (thus mainly the thirteenth century) and what these authors thought of or had heard of thralldom in the Viking Age.

It would hence be hazardous to use sagas and the provincial laws to reconstruct the Viking Age situation of the thralls. In the sagas the thrall is always a stereotype – dark, short and stupid, no doubt used as spice in the narrative to contrast with the blond, tall and wise hero. The descriptions of thralls in these stories are far too stereotypical to use in any serious analysis of Viking slavery (see below). What we can deduce from the stories is the fact that many of the thralls in Iceland seem to have been seized abroad; very often slaves from Ireland are mentioned. Another interesting aspect in the sagas is the stories where a child of a female slave and an Icelander grows up as a free man and makes a reputation for himself.

The provincial laws are the most important sources for us in our study especially of medieval slavery (hence from the twelfth and thirteenth centuries). Here we get a wide range of terms for slave, and we get an insight into the judicial dependence of the slave in society (Nevéus 1974; Iversen 1994); there must have been legal rules in these laws, which were based on old customs, hence older than the Middle Ages. In order to understand prehistoric slavery, and to complement what we can learn from the laws, archaeology, onomastics, and especially the semantic and etymological analysis of slave terminology are vital (Lindkvist and Myrdal 2003; Brink 2002, 2003, 2007, forthcoming).

However, the first question to ask is, what is a slave? This may sound self-evident, but the attempts to define a slave have been complicated, wide-ranging and problematic. One prominent scholar has written on this topic: 'The ambiguities of this word [slave] are indeed so confusing that sociologists might be well advised to eliminate it from their discussion altogether' (Leach 1967: 14). A definition of slave and slavery must contain social, economic as well as judicial aspects. What is characteristic of a slave in all societies is that he or she is the property of another, being looked upon as a tool, a 'thing', not a human being, to be used or abused at the master's will or whim. The slave has no family, hence no social context, and the child of a female slave belongs to the owner. The slave has no legal rights. He or she is a judicial subject insofar as slaves are often mentioned in law-rules, but a slave could not act legally; it was the master of the slave who talked and acted for the slave.

The philosophical justification for slavery, mentioned already by Roman lawmen such as Ulpian and Justinian, was that a man who was defeated and caught in war and not slaughtered had given up his right to live (Watson 1987: 8; Turley 2000: 3). In war all defeated men not killed in battle should be slaughtered afterwards; that was the custom not only in ancient Europe, but also among North American Indians and other people. If their life were spared, they had forfeited their right to be free. They had been given a gift, their life, but had to pay back by giving up their freedom, the right of being looked upon as a human being; instead they became a tool for their master.

When we try to understand early society in Scandinavia it is obvious that it was decisive for an individual to be part of a family and a social group. You were in a way identified by your affiliation to a family, a group and a society. The worst punishment you could thus get was to be cut off from this group and society, to be excommunicated or outlawed, which has been described as a 'social death'. In other words we can see that our forefathers had another concept of freedom than we have. Freedom was not defined as an individual freedom, but a right to belong to a fellowship, to be part of a social group. A stranger was often considered as an enemy. It is from this perspective that we have to understand how our ancestors could accept and even justify slavery.

The natural point of departure for all discussions on slaves in early Scandinavia has been the ancient Edda poem of *Rígsþula*. Here, we find an allegorical description of society, in which named persons represent the social classes, among them the slaves. In the poem, descriptions are also given of each person's (i.e. each social category's) behaviour, name, daily occupation and physical appearance. This poem has therefore been used as a kind of description of the tasks of a Scandinavian slave in the Viking Age ('to make stone fences, to manure the arable land, to herd pigs and goats and to dig peat').

Unfortunately, one has to use the *Rígsþula* with great care and caution, especially if the aim is to use it as a kind of cultural-historical source for life in Viking Age Scandinavia (Dronke 1992: 671 ff.). The poem is a very special one, a mythical allegory, in which the principal character, *Rígr*, as the god *Heimdallr* is called in the poem, bears an Irish name (Ir *rí*, OIr *ríg* 'king'). Also the dating of the poem is problematic. Earlier, the *Rígsþula* was looked upon as an ancient poem, while later research has tended to place it in the thirteenth century (Simek 1993: 294 ff.; Karras 1988: 60). However, there are scholars who even today are prepared, at least tentatively, to place the *Rígsþula* as early as the Viking Age (Meulengracht Sørensen 1993: 164).

The relevant part of the *Rígsþula*, in which we learn about the slaves, starts with Rígr coming to Ái and Edda, and eventually begets a child with Edda:

> Edda bore a child,
> [. . .]
> In rough linen she [wrapped]
> the black-[skinned] boy.
> [Heavy were his eyes] –
> they called him Thrall [*Þræll*].
> [. . .]
> There was on his hands
> wrinkled skin,
> gnarled knuckles,
> [scabbed nails,]
> fingers thick –
> face unlovely,
> bent back,
> long heels.
>
> He began more then
> to test his might
> plaiting bast,
> packing burdens.
> He carried home then
> kindling through the cruel day.
>
> There came to the homestead
> a gadabout girl.
> Soil was on the soles of her feet,
> her arm sunburnt,
> down-curving her nose –
> her name, she said, was Thrallwoman [*Þír*].
>
> Children they bred,
> had a home and were happy.
> I think they were called
> Bawler and Byreboy,
> Clump and Clegg,
> Bedmate, Stinker,
> Stump, Stout,
> Sluggish and Grizzled,
> Stooper and Longleg.
> They fixed fences,
> dunged fields,
> worked at the pigs,

watched over the goats,
dug the peat.

The daughters were
Stumpy and Dumpy,
Bulgingcalves and Eaglenose,
Shouter and Servingmaid [*Ambátt*],
Greatgossip,
Tatteredcoat
and Craneshanks.
From there have come
the generations of thralls [*Þræla ætter*].
(from *Poetic Edda*, vol. 2: *Mythological Poems*,
ed. and trans. U. Dronke (1997)
© Oxford University Press)

It is very clear that the author is following a certain slave topos that is always found whenever slaves are mentioned in Old Norse literature. The thrall was dark, short, stupid, gloomy and ugly; this was in contrast to the tall, blond, handsome and attractive hero. The picture of the thrall is often used in contrast to the free human being (Meulengracht Sørensen 1993: 161 ff.).

It is apparent that we are here dealing with literature. Therefore, one has to approach the text with the utmost care, if one wishes to extract historical facts from it. This literary topos is found again and again in the Old Norse texts. The thralls were not only ugly, but also cowardly and stupid, as in the story of *Þórðr inn huglausi* (*Þórðr* the coward) in the *Gísla Saga Súrssonar*. This *Þórðr* was so cowardly and stupid that he put on another man's clothes, whereby, owing to his stupidity, he was killed in that other man's place.

To sum up, the qualitative aspects of the slaves and their situation during early times are difficult to obtain in the Old Norse literature. The picture drawn here is based on stereotypes and clichés.

THE TERMINOLOGY FOR SLAVES IN EARLY SCANDINAVIA

An excellent point of departure for a discussion on the terms for slaves in Scandinavia is to be found in a paragraph in the Old Law of the Gulathing (198): *Tvær ero hans hinar bezto ambatter. Seta. oc deigia. oc tveir prælar. þionn oc bryti* (i.e. 'Two bondwomen are counted as the best, the housemaid and the housekeeper. Two thralls are counted the best, the foreman and the master's personal servant'; GL trans. by Larson 1935: 144). Here, we see that the early West Scandinavian *ambátt* was obviously some kind of collective term for a female slave, while the male counterpart was *þræll*. The *seta* and *deigja*, and the *þjónn* and *bryti*, were hence slaves with some kinds of special functions.

The most commonly used contemporary term for a slave was ON *þræll*, OSw, ODa *þræl*. This word, which is assumed to go back to a Proto-Scand. **þrahila-*, has an obscure background. Several etymologists connect the word with Goth. *þragjan* and OE *þrægan* 'to run', thus 'the one who runs for someone'. The word *ambátt, ambótt* f. as a name for a female slave is believed to be a loan from Vulgar Lat. *ambactus* 'servant' (cf. Sw *ämbete*). Other names for female slaves were *deigja*, which is derived from the word *deg* 'dough' and which thus had the meaning of 'the one who bakes', and *þý* f. (< **þiujō*), which is closely related to Goth. *þiwi* and OE *þeowu*. There are several other slave words formed on the same stem, such as Goth. *þius* m. 'slave', OE *þéow* m. 'servant' (cf. *þéowian* 'make someone a slave'), ON *þjónn*, OE *þéowen* 'slave, servant', ON *þjá* (< * *þewan*) 'keep in slavery, treat as a slave, torment', Goth. *þiwan* 'keep in slavery' (found in the compounds *anaþiwan* and *gaþiwan*) (Hellquist 1948; de Vries 1962).

In Old Swedish we find the words *fostri* m. and *fostra* f. for male and female slaves. The words have the meaning of 'the one who is brought up in the household/on the homestead', which probably alludes to the fact that these slaves were not prisoners of war, but were born and raised on the farm.

Names for foreigners sometimes have a secondary meaning of 'slave, unfree', which has an obvious background in the fact that prisoners of war and kidnapped or bought foreigners were vital as sources of new slaves. This is obviously the background of the word *slave*, Sw *slav*, which is thus really the ethnic name, and also the word OSw *val*, ON *valir* 'Celt; slave', also in the adjective *valskr*, which goes back to *Wales, Wallonia*, etc. The OE equivalent, *wealh*, pl. *wealas*, with an older meaning 'foreigner, Briton, Welshman', had in Anglo-Saxon a secondary meaning of 'slave', which is believed to have the same background – Britons and Welshmen taken as prisoners in all the battles between the ethnic groups (Bugge 1905: 43; cf. Faull 1975).

The thralls did not make up a homogeneous mass. Some were labourers, working the land and herding the cattle. They were probably – legally and economically – equal to the cattle they herded. However, there were also thralls with some special tasks, such as the *deigja* (above), and some obviously had qualified duties. We are here getting close to a social category of trusted servants and officials. This was the case with the ON *bryti*, originally an unfree servant, according to handbooks, who during the medieval period was transformed into a person of high status. The word *bryti* goes back to a Proto-Scand. **brŭtjan*, a formation from the stem of the verb ON *brjóta* 'break'. Thus, it is believed that the original meaning of *bryti* was 'he who breaks (and distributes the bread)', hence a semantic pendant to the OE *hláfbrytta*. The word *bryti* was also borrowed into Finnish, as *ruttio, ruttia* 'steward, slave'. A *bryti* seems therefore originally to have been some kind of steward on a farm, a supervisor over the rest of the thralls. Later on, we meet the *bryti* as a steward on royal and lordly estates.

However, when we consult contemporary sources, such as runestones, we get a different picture. In for example the inscription on the famous runestone at Hovgården (U 11) on the island of Adelsö, opposite the more famous island of Björkö where Birka is located, we can read: **lit rista toliʀ bry[t]i i roþ kunuki**, *Rett let rista Tolir bryti i Roð kunungi*, which has been translated as 'Tólir the steward of Roþr had them [the runes] rightly carved for the king'. This very important historical runic inscription from probably the middle of the eleventh century is not easy to interpret. Elias Wessén (in U) assumes that the erecting and carving of the inscription was commissioned by the king. Wessén, and many with him, have connected the passage 'bryti i Rodh' with the case in the Östgöta Law (Dråpsb. 14) which deals with *iarls bryti i roþzs bo*, and he thinks that *Tolir bryti* was the king's ombudsman in the district called *Roden* (i.e. the coastal area). Erland Hjärne (1947: 25–55; cf. Rahmqvist 1994: 109) argues – in my opinion quite convincingly – against Wessén's interpretation, and instead proposes that *Tolir bryti* was a bailiff, a manager on the royal farm Hovgården. This runic evidence indicates that a *bryti* in the tenth and eleventh centuries was to be found rather high up the social ladder, in the case of the Hovgården stone a man in close proximity to the king, probably his bailiff, and hence not a slave on the very lowest rung.

It has to be admitted that we have very little knowledge of the status of the thrall and the number of slaves in prehistoric Scandinavia. Probably it is quite wrong to compare the situation of a Scandinavian thrall with that of a slave in the Roman Empire 2,000 years ago or in North America during the eighteenth and nineteenth centuries. According to the etymological evidence of the contemporary terms for 'slave' in early Scandinavia, the diversified meanings found may suggest different kinds of dependence on an authority. The original meaning of several terms is 'servant'. This dependence may not have been an extremely repressive relation between the servant and the master and may instead have been more of a 'client–patron' relationship.

It is not possible to rely on the fact that the meaning 'slave, thrall, unfree', found in lexica and encyclopaedias, was valid and adequate also in prehistoric times. From the etymological list above, it is evident that an often recurring, semantic component was 'servant'. There is nothing that excludes the possibility that a word in an earlier language stage had the meaning '(free) servant', that later on was changed to '(unfree) servant, slave', and vice versa. Hence, it is possible that, for example, in the word ON *þræll* we have a semantic component of 'servant', in the form of a kind of dependence between a superior and an inferior, maybe a warrior, craftsman or a priest, that is, a patron–client relationship.

We know that a free man could give himself as a slave to another, to settle a debt or because of poverty. From this fact it is close to a case where someone is giving up his freedom and accepts a judicial slave status as, for example, a warrior in a hirð. By taking an oath of fidelity a young man could be taken up as a warrior in a king's or a chieftain's personal hirð. By doing this, he accepted to come under the master's personal jurisdiction, literally he laid his life in his hand, but he was probably socially elevated, being close to the king or chieftain, having a seat in his hall. This kind of warrior could be called a *karl*, ON *rekkr*/OSw **rinkr* or *sveinn*. This is to be illustrated with, for example, the ON *væringi*, Sw *väring*, institution (Russian *varjagu*, Greek *varangoi*). A *væring*/*varjag* was the name for a Northman gone east and taken up duty in the hirð of the Byzantine emperor in Constantinople. The word goes back to a Proto-Nordic **wāragangja-*, a compound of *vár*, OE *wær* f., OHG *wāra* 'oath, treaty, fidelity' and the verb *gangjan* 'walk', hence 'someone who takes an oath, enters into a treaty'.

WHAT WERE THE FUNCTION AND THE NUMBERS OF SLAVES?

The numbers of slaves assumed in early research are in my opinion grossly over-estimated. When Northmen were dealing with slaves, in Ireland, Anglo-Saxon England or Francia, large quantities could have been taken. But the custom seems to have been either to take them as hostage and then ask for a large ransom, or to sell them at some slave market. The bringing home of slaves to Scandinavia was certainly a fact, but in my opinion only on a small scale; probably the slave was seen as a precious commodity, to show off. I think slaves were fairly uncommon in society. There might have been working slaves on ordinary farms, but larger quantities were probably only to be found on chieftains' and well-to-do farmers' farms. This could be reflected in some 'double graves', found in Denmark and Sweden, where one of the buried is often beheaded and has his or her hands tied (interpreted as a slave) and the other one is obviously a wealthy man or women with rich grave goods.

Regarding the function of slaves, they were probably of a wide range, from the chattel slave, the *þræll*, working on the fields and herding cattle, sheep and swine, via household slaves, as the *þý, deigja, fostra* and *amma*, to officials and stewards fairly high up on the social ladder, but judicially on a slave rank, as probably were the *bryti*. A warrior in a personal hirð was probably in reality legally unfree, but had a fairly high social status. The slave institution in prehistoric Scandinavia was hence, depending on economic, social and legal aspects, probably rather complex.

BIBLIOGRAPHY

Brink, S. (1997) 'Names and naming of slaves', in J.P. Rodriguez (ed.) *The Historical Encyclopedia of World Slavery*, 2 vols, Santa Barbara, CA: Clio.

—— (1999) 'Social order in the early Scandinavian landscape', in Ch. Fabech and J. Ringtved (eds) *Settlement and Landscape*, Århus: Aarhus University Press.

—— (2002) 'Slavery in Scandinavia, as reflected in names, runes and sagas', in P. Hærnes and T. Iversen (eds) (2002).

—— (2003) '*Ambátt, seta, deigja – þræll, thjónn, bryti*. Termer för trälar belyser träldomens äldre historia', in Th. Lindkvist and J. Myrdal (eds) (2003).

—— (2008) *Lord and Lady – Bryti and Deigja, Some Historical and Etymological Aspects on Family, Patronage and Slavery in Early Scandinavia and Anglo-Saxon England*. (The Dorothea Coke Memorial Lecture in Northern Studies 2004–5), London; Viking Society for Northern Studies, University College London.

—— (forthcoming) *Vikingatidens slaveri*, Stockholm: Atlantis.

Bugge, A. (1905) *Vesterlandenes indflydelse paa nordboernes og særlig nordmændenes ydre kultur, levesæt og samfundsforhold i vikingetiden* (Videnskabsselskapet i Kristiania. Skrifter II, Hist.-filos. Klasse 1904:1), Christiania: no publ.

Dronke, U. (1992) 'Eddic poetry as a source for the history of Germanic religion', in H. Beck, D. Ellmers and K. Schier (eds) *Germanische Religionsgeschichte. Quellen und Quellenprobleme*, Berlin and New York: de Gruyter.

—— (ed. and trans.) (1997) *The Poetic Edda*, vol. 2: *Mythological Poems*, Oxford: Clarendon.

Faull, M. Lindsay (1975) 'The semantic development of Old English *wealh*', *Leeds Studies in English*, 8: 19–44.

Foote, P. (1977) 'Þrælahald á Íslandi. Heimildakönnun og athugasemdir', *Saga. Tímarit Sögufélags*, 15: 41–74.

GL = *The Earliest Norwegian Laws. Being the Gulathing Law and the Frostathing Law*, trans. from the old Norwegian by L.M. Larson (Records of civilization 20), New York: Columbia University Press (1935).

Hærnes, P. and Iversen, T. (eds) (2002) *Slavery across Time and Space. Studies in Slavery in Medieval Europe and Africa* (Trondheim studies in history 38), Trondheim: Tapir.

Harrison, D. (2006), *Slaveri. En världshistoria om ofrihet*, vol. 1: *Forntiden till Renässansen*, Lund: Historiska media.

Hasselberg, G. (1944) 'Den s.k. Skarastadgan och träldomens upphörande i Sverige', *Västergötlands fornminnesförenings tidskrift*, 5(3): 51–90.

Hellquist, E. (1948) *Svensk etymologisk ordbok*, 3rd edn, Lund: Gleerup.

Hemmendorff, O. (1984) 'Människooffer. Ett inslag i järnålderns ritualer, belyst av ett fynd i Bollstanäs, Uppland', *Fornvännen*, 79: 4–12.

Hjärne, E. (1947) 'Rod och runor', *Kungl. Humanistiska Vetenskaps- Samfundets i Uppsala årsbok* (1946): 21–126.

Holm, P. (1986) 'The slave trade of Dublin, ninth to twelfth centuries', *Peritia*, 5: 317–45.

Holmquist-Olausson, L. (1990) ' "Älgmannen" från Birka. Presentation av en nyligen undersökt krigargrav med människooffer', *Fornvännen*, 85: 175–82.

Iversen, T. (1994) *Trelledommen. Norsk slaveri i middelalderen*, Bergen: Dept. of History, University of Bergen.

Jón Hnefill Aðalsteinsson (1986) 'The position of freed slaves in medieval Iceland', *Saga-Book*, 22: 33–49.

Karras, R. Mazo (1988) *Slavery and Society in Medieval Scandinavia*, New Haven: Yale University Press.

Krag, C. (1982) 'Treller og trellehold', [*Norsk*] *Historisk tidsskrift* 61: 209–27.

Leach, E. (1967) 'Caste, class and slavery: the taxonomic problem', in A. de Reuck and J. Knight (eds) *Caste and Race. Comparative Approaches*, London: Ciba Foundation.

Lindkvist, Th. (1979) *Landborna i Norden under äldre medeltid* (Studia Historica Upsaliensis 110), Uppsala: Dept. of History, Uppsala University.

Lindkvist, Th. and Myrdal, J. (eds) (2003) *Trälar. Ofria i agrarsamhället från vikingatid till medeltid* (Skrifter om skogs- och lantbrukshistoria 17), Stockholm: Nordiska museets förlag.

Meulengracht Sørensen, P. (1993) *Fortælling og ære. Studier i islændigesagaerne*, Århus: Århus universitetsforlag.

Nevéus, C. (1974) *Trälarna i landskapslagarnas samhälle. Danmark och Sverige* (Studia historica Upsaliensia 58), Uppsala: Acta Universitatis Upsaliensis, Uppsala University.

Olsson, M. (1999) *Vikingatida träldom. Om slaveriets plats i Skandinaviens ekonomiska historia* (Lund Papers in Economic History 67), Lund: Dept. of Economic History, University of Lund.

Patterson, O. (1982) *Slavery and Social Death. A Comparative Study*, Cambridge, MA: Cambridge University Press.

Rahmqvist, S. (1994) 'Ortnamn påverkade av administration i äldre tid', in G. Ulfsparre (ed.) *Ortnamn värda att vårda*, Stockholm: Raä.

Randsborg, K. (1986) 'The study of slavery in northern Europe: an archaeological approach', *Acta Archaeologica*, 55 (1984): 155–60.

Simek, R. (1993) *Dictionary of Northern Mythology*, trans. A. Hall, Woodbridge: Brewer.

Skyum-Nielsen, N. (1979) 'Nordic slavery in an international setting', *Medieval Scandinavia*, 11 (1978–9): 126–48.

Turley, D. (2000) *Slavery*, Oxford: Blackwell.

U = *Upplands runinskrifter*, 4 vols (SRI 6–9), Stockholm: Almqvist & Wiksell International (1940–58).

de Vries, J. (1962) *Altnordisches etymologisches Wörterbuch*, 2nd edn, Leiden: Brill.

Watson, A. (1987) *Roman Slave Law*, Baltimore: Johns Hopkins University Press.

Wilde-Stockmeyer, M. (1978) *Sklaverei auf Island. Untersuchungen zur rechtlich-sozialen Situation und literarischen Darstellung der Sklaven im skandinavischen Mittelalter* (Skandinavistische arbeiten 5), Heidelberg: Winter.

CHAPTER SIX

NAMING THE LAND

—— ·◆· ——

Stefan Brink

The Viking Age in Scandinavia is – unlike in Francia, Ireland and Anglo-Saxon England – a prehistoric period, hence with practically no written sources. To be able to write the Viking history for Scandinavia we therefore have to rely upon other sources, of which archaeology, of course, is the most important. Another vital source are the place names, especially the names of settlements.

BACKGROUND TO THE TOPONYMIC STUDY IN SCANDINAVIA

The study of place names (toponymy) has a long history in Scandinavia, being more or less the cradle of research in this field. A couple of Scandinavian historians and especially philologists produced some groundbreaking research in this field in the nineteenth century; one to be mentioned is Oluf Rygh, Professor of Archaeology in Oslo, and the founder of the series *Norske Gaardnavne*, which would become a foundation and guideline for future research.

What these early founders of the discipline were attracted by was the possibility of extracting historical information from the old place names after they had been scrutinised and interpreted in a linguistically solid way, according to known language-historical rules. This material also lacks the problems related to letters, hagiographies and chronicles, which are nearly always biased in some respect and difficult to use. On the other hand, although the place names are linguistic entities, we do not get the full historical narratives, only a contextual hint. But since place names are a mass material, their potential as socio- and cultural-historical sources becomes great.

Place names have recently been highlighted again for their potential in landscape studies (Tilley 1994: 18 f.). Since every name carries some historical information, place names can make the landscape 'speak' to us. The names give another dimension to the silent archaeological sources. They become small narratives that can be used in retelling the history of an early landscape, a field of research that I have called *spatial history*, hence whose aim is to write a history where people are not the agents, but the landscape is.

A crucial prerequisite for using place names in this way is to have them dated. This problem has been discussed for nearly two centuries, and we now have a fairly solid chronology for the Scandinavian settlement names (Brink 1983, 1984; Strid 1999: 43 ff.). One important terminus is the transfer of place names, words and elements from Scandinavia to the British Isles, and there especially to the Danelaw. From this evidence we can see that in early Viking Age Denmark the usage of the element *-by* must have been widespread, since so many English place names ending in *-by* of Danish origin are to be found in England, and in the same way elements such as *-þveit* and *-bólstaðr* must have been in use in Norway, since they so often occur in northern England, Scotland and the Isles. On the other hand, ancient Scandinavian elements such as *-vin*, *-heimr*, *-lösa* and *-lev/-löv* are never found in the British Isles, which must indicate that these place-name elements had ceased to be productive in the Viking Age, and hence must be older. (For the Scandinavian place names in Britain, see Fellows-Jensen, ch.28, below.)

The oldest place names we know of in Scandinavia are from the early Iron Age, perhaps some also from the Bronze Age, mainly denoting large features in the landscape, such as lakes: *Vättern* (OSw *Vætur*), *Vänern* (OSw *Vænir* < *VāniaR*), *Siljan* (OSw *Sylghir*), *Mjösa* (ON *Mjǫrs* < *Mersō*), islands: *Ven* (< *Hwaðn?*), *Tjörn* (ON *Þjórn*), *Rådmansö* (< *Ruðma*), bays: *Bleking* (< *Blekungr*), *Fold*, *Sogn*, and large rivers: *Ljusnan* (< *Lŭsn*), *Nidelva* (< *Nið*), *Jostra* (< *Jóstra* or *Jastra*), *Viskan* (OSw *Visk*). From this period some classical authors (e.g. Tacitus, Jordanes) also mention several 'people' in Scandinavia: for example *theustes* 'the people living in Tjust, Småland', *hallin* 'the people living in Halland' (originally obviously the southern part of the later province of Halland), *ranii* 'the people living in Ranríki' (northern Bohuslän), *grannii* 'the people living in Grenland, Norway' and *raumariciae* 'the people living in Romerike, Norway' (Brink forthcoming). The oldest settlement names we today fairly securely date to the Roman period (*c.* 0–400), such as names in *-hem/-heim* (cf. Germ. *-haim* and Eng. *-ham*), *-inge*, *-lev/-löv*, *-lösa*, *-vin* (cf. Goth. *winja* 'meadow').

SETTLEMENT NAMES

The bulk of settlement names for the central areas in Sweden and Norway emanates from the early Middle Ages (corresponding to the late Iron Age in Scandinavia, *c.* AD 500–1100), where very often the parish names (also in Denmark) are from the early Iron Age. The major place-name elements from this period are *-stad* (< OScand. *staðir*), *-by/-bø*, *-land* and *-säter/-set*. The last two most certainly originally denoted some kind of arable land or meadow, whereas the first two probably denoted the actual farm. The *-stad* names normally have a personal name as the qualifier, as in *Gistad* (*Gislastadum* 1375; < OSw *Gisle*) in Östergötland and *Hagnesta* (*Haghnastom* 1384; < OSw *Haghne*) in Helgona, Södermanland, but not always. It is not uncommon with a place name or a topographical word as the first element, for example *Sörviksta* in Hälsingland (< *Viklingsstaðir* where *Viklingr* is a lake name). The Scandinavian *-by* names from this period never contain a personal name. Instead many *-by* names have a first element relating to landscape features, for example *Ekeby* (< *Ekiby* 'the farm by the oak grove'), *Myrby* (< *Myriby* 'the farm by the bog'), *Säby* 'the farm by the lake or sea', which is also the case for the *-land* and the *-säter* names. This trait makes them different from the *-by* names of Scandinavian origin in England, where we often find a personal name as the qualifier. There are great regional differences regarding the distribution of these place names in Scandinavia: *-stad* names and *-by* names are very common in Sweden, *-set* names

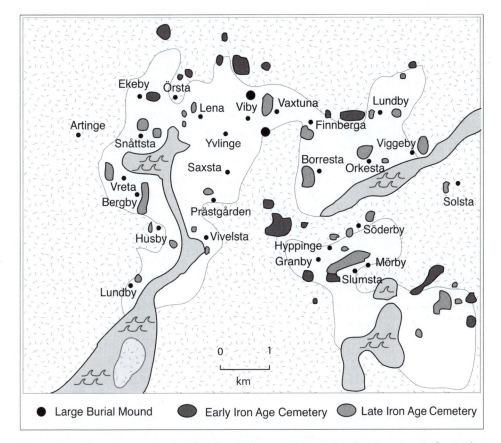

Figure 6.1   The settlement district of Markim-Orkesta in Uppland, Sweden. (Drawing: Stefan Brink.)

are plentiful in Trøndelag in central Norway, while *-land* names are typical in south-western Norway.

For especially eastern central Sweden the place names ending in *-by* and *-stad* make up the large bulk of settlement names within the settlement districts. This is an indication that these districts saw a restructuring or a new colonisation during the middle and second half of the first millennium. It is also an indication that these districts were more or less fully colonised during this period, with no possible expansion with new medieval farms. One example of this kind of 'fossilised' late Iron Age settlement district is the Markim-Orkesta district, north of Stockholm, in the province of Uppland (Figure 6.1). Here we find a couple of place names ending in *-inge* and *-tuna*, which are probably to be placed in an earlier settlement-historical phase than the many *-by* and *-sta(d)* names.

During the high and late Middle Ages (*c.* 1000–1500) new areas were colonised (especially during the twelfth and thirteenth centuries) and many new settlements established. Major place-name elements for these new farms and hamlets are *-torp*, *-rud*, *-ryd*, *-röd/-rød*, *-boda*, *-böle*. Place names ending in *-torp* and *-rød* make up the large part of the Danish settlement names, obviously indicating radical changes in the landscape and settlement structure. It seems likely that several of these *-torp* and *-rød* names are to be dated to as early as the tenth century. Also in southern Sweden place names ending in

-*torp* and -*ryd*, -*röd* are common for medieval settlements, whereas we find names ending in -*boda* and -*böle* in northern Sweden from this period. In Norway the major element from this period of settlement expansion is -*rud*. In these twelfth- and thirteenth-century settlement names normally the first element is a man's name (perhaps the one who first cleared the land).

These 'medieval' place-name elements often denoted a clearance or swidden, as in -*ryd*, -*rud*, -*rød*/-*röd* (< *ruð*-/*rauð*-), -*rönning* (< *rauðning*-), -*sved* (< *swið*-), -*fall* ('chopped-down forest') etc. In other cases the names denoted the new farm or croft, which was often a single farm in the forest, such as -*boda* (-*boþar* 'sheds, barns') and -*böle* (< *bōl-ia*- 'farm'). The element -*torp* (< *þorp*) has probably a special background (cf. Hellberg 1954). It is found all over southern Scandinavia (including southern Norway). It is somewhat problematic, since a few of these names are obviously not from the Middle Ages, but are really ancient, hence should be placed among place-name elements such as -*lev*/-*löv*, -*heim* and -*vin*. The etymology of this ancient *torp* is not clear. The medieval element *torp*, however, must be seen in a context of the huge colonisation in northern Europe during the high Middle Ages, within a new 'feudal' agrarian system with a 'manor' and dependent tenant farms within an estate. In Germany these tenant farms often had the name *dorf* (< *þorp*), and the word for such a dependent farm was spread with the new colonising strategy to Scandinavia. Early on, the element *torp* must have developed into a meaning of secondary farm, a farm detached from a hamlet etc., hence not always denoting a tenant farm within an estate.

DISTRICT NAMES AND THE NAMES OF THE COUNTRIES

The names of the Scandinavian countries are – apart from Iceland and Greenland – much older than the Viking Age. *Denmark* (*Danmark*) contains the word *mark* 'dividing forest' and the name of the people *Danir*. Traditionally the name is understood as a *pars-pro-toto* name, originally denoting the forest that divided the people from the Saxons in southern Schleswig. The meaning of the name of the inhabitants, *Danir*, is obscure and still much debated.

Sweden is a compound of *svear* and *þjóð* 'people', hence originally meaning 'the svea people'. The name of the Swedes (*Svear*) has been interpreted as an autonym, a self-praising name 'we ourselves'. The ethnonym occurs in *Svíaríki* 'the *ríki* of the svear', which can be found in the present-day name of the nation in Scandinavian languages, *Sverige*, and *Svíþjóð* (an old stem composition), which is used as the basis for the name of the Swedish nation in English (*Sweden*), German (*Schweden*) and French (*Suède*). The name of the people, *Svíþjóð*, was commonly transferred to the area where the *Svíar* lived, and there is a consensus today that from early on and into the transitional period between prehistory and history in Scandinavia (around the eleventh century), *Svíþjóð* is to be identified and located to the region around Lake Mälaren in eastern central Sweden, comprising the provinces of *Uppland*, *Södermanland* 'land of the people living to the south' and *Västmanland* 'land of the people living to the west'. Probably *Svíþjóð* was identified with this core area of the *Svíar*, whereas *Svíaríki* and *Svíaveldi* were used for an extended Svía state (*ríki*), later on comprising regions obviously not originally under Svía control, such as the region of the *Götar* (Andersson 2004; Brink forthcoming).

Norway (*Norge, Noreg*) is different from the other two, since it does not contain an inhabitative name. Instead it seems to be a name of the route along the western Norwegian coast, towards Trøndelag and Hålogaland. This is the route (*Norðwegh*) which Othere describes that he travelled from his home down to Kaupang, of which we have a famous description from the 890s (Bately and Anglert 2007). This name became so identified with the land along the route that it gave its name to the country. Hence, *Norway* goes back to a Proto-Nordic *Norð(r)vegr*, originally 'the north way (route)', where the fricative dental must have been lost early, reduced between two other consonants, in the same way as for the adjective ON *norrœnn* 'northerly' (< *norðrœnn*). We may compare it with ON *vestrvegr* 'land to the west', *austrvegr* 'land to the east' and *suðrvegr* 'land to the south' (which could be especially Germany or Italy) (Brink 2007a: 66).

Place names become a very important source for reconstructing a prehistoric and early medieval organisational and administrative structure (Andersson 1965, 1982; Brink 1996, 1997). A basic societal entity in early Scandinavia was the *bygd*, which may be translated as 'settlement district'. A *bygd* was an often naturally demarcated settlement district, comprising several hamlets and single farms with their arable land and meadows, surrounded by forests. We can see that they were looked upon by their neighbours as a unit, and therefore given a name related to some characteristic natural feature in the district (a lake, river, mountain etc.) or a collective name of the people (e.g. a compound with -*ingar*) living in the district. The place names also reveal that the *bygd* was probably a social, judicial and cultic unit, since we are very often able to

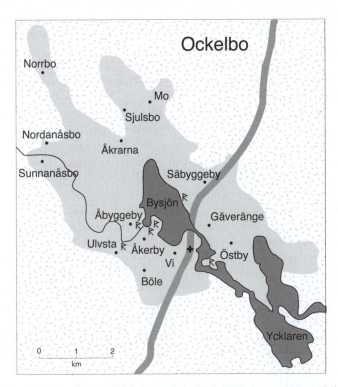

Figure 6.2 The settlement district of Ockelbo in Gästrikland, Sweden, a small, probably Viking Age *bygd* around a lake **Okle* (today Bysjön), with the centrally placed *Vi* 'pagan cult site', where the church was erected. (Drawing: Stefan Brink.)

reconstruct a communal focus, with cultic and judicial indications. One example may be the *bygd* Ockelbo in the province of Gästrikland in Sweden (Figure 6.2). Here we have a small late Iron Age (probably Viking Age) *bygd*, surrounded by deep forests. The name of the *bygd* is a compound of a lake name OSw *Okle* and *bo* 'settlement district'. In the very centre of the *bygd*, where a land route (an esker) and a watercourse (a river) crosses, we find the place name *Vi*, denoting a pagan cult site (cf. German *weihe* 'consecration', *weihen* 'consecrate, make holy', *weihnachten* 'Christmas', i.e. 'The Holy Nights'). In this hamlet a church has also been erected for this parish. It seems more than probable that this place was the communal gathering place, as well as for social and judicial matters, for this district.

Also in eastern central Sweden, but with traces in Denmark and Norway, we find some really interesting place-name milieus, which obviously indicate some political power in the landscape. I have called these milieus 'Central Place Complexes' (Brink 1996: 238), and they seem to be from the Vendel/Merovingian period and the Viking Age, hence the second half of the first millennium. Normally we find as a focus in these districts a place name with *tuna* or *husa*, probably denoting a king's or a chieftain's farm or 'manor'. Close by we nearly always find a place name *Husby* (< *Husaby*), which was the name of a farm belonging to the king's *bona regalia* during the Middle Ages (Brink 2000). The plausible assumption is that the *husaby* has taken over the administrative function from the older 'estate'. Also in the centre of the district we find one or several place names indicating cultic activities: theophoric names, such as *Torsåker* 'the arable land dedicated to the god Þórr', *Ullevi* 'the cult site dedicated to the god Ullr', *Fröslunda* 'the grove dedicated to the god Freyr' etc., names containing a cultic element or obviously associated with cultic activities, *Vi, Hov/Hof, Vang, Åker*, or sometimes the actual focus, the 'estate', has a theophoric qualifier, as in *Ulleråker* 'the arable land dedicated to the god Ullr' and *Torstuna* 'the "estate" dedicated to or in some way linked to the god Þórr'. Moreover, in these milieus we nearly always find place names such as *Kar(le)by* (< *Karlaby*), *Rinkeby/Rickeby* (< *Rinkaby*), *Svenneby* (< *Sveinaby*) or *Tegneby* (< *Tegnaby*), hence with the qualifier in the plural. It has been assumed, with Anglo-Saxon parallels (*ceorl, rinc*), that these words, *karl*, **rinker/rekkr*, *sveinn* and *þegn*, denoted some warriors who were obviously placed in the district. Finally we very often find one place name, *Smedby* (< *Smiþa(r)by*), obviously denoting one or more blacksmith(s), who could forge weapons or jewellery, and one *Gillberga* in these milieus. No one has hitherto been able to explain the background to this last name, but I would tentatively see this in the context of a prehistoric guild (*gille* or *gill) institution, hence a kind of social unit, a communal grouping, of which we know very little, but which could have been similar to the Icelandic *hreppr* institution (see Brink 2008). (For examples of districts of this kind see Hellberg 1979; Brink 1997: 418–31; 1998: 301–22; 1999.)

In the Viking Age we are for the first time faced with administrative districts, in southern Scandinavia called *hærað*, around Lake Mälaren in central Sweden called *hundare*, and in Norway called *fylki*. The *hærað* institution is mentioned in a letter from 1085 and *hundare* is mentioned on one of the Jarlabanki runestones in Täby (U 211), Sweden, dated to *c.* 1050. The word *fylki* is a derivation of the word *folk* 'people', originally probably 'the armed men'; *hærað* is disputed regarding its etymology, but the first element seems to be the word *hær* 'a group of warriors, warband', and one of the interpretations of *hundare* is that it is a compound of *hund* 'hundred' and *hær* 'army, warband'. These administrative districts are thus the Scandinavian equivalents to the

Anglo-Saxon *hundreds* (note, however, that OSw *hundari* is not linguistically identical with OE *hundred*). In other words all these administrative terms are linked to armed men, a force. The traditional explanation for both *hærað* and *hundare* is that they have a background in the naval organisation called the OSw *lepunger*, ODa *lething*, ON *leiðangr* (Andersson 1965, 1982; cf. Lund 1996).

For reconstructing this hundred division the place names become vital. In the same way as for the *bygd*, the hundred names have a background in either a name of the settlement district, the *bygd*, which hence was used as a unit for the hundred, or the assembly place of the district, hence the thing site (Andersson 1965, 1982; the same is the case for the Anglo-Saxon hundreds, see Anderson/Arngart 1934, 1939a, b). For example the name *Møre hærað* in Småland has an older history as a name of a settlement district, a *bygd* or a *land*, mentioned already in the famous journey by Wulfstan in the late ninth century as *Meore* (Brink 2007a: 69), and *Ulleråkers hundare* in Uppland is originally the name of the thing assembly site for this hundred (Vikstrand 2001: 182 ff.).

CULTIC AND THEOPHORIC NAMES

Finally the place names can give an important contribution to our reconstruction of the pagan religion. Since we lack written records from the time of the Viking Age, we have to rely on the Poetic Edda, Snorri's Edda and Saxo Grammaticus, all written down during the Middle Ages. The contribution of the theophoric place names (containing the name of a god or a goddess) are twofold in this respect, they show us: (1) which of the gods and goddesses were actually worshipped, and also (2) where cult was executed, hence giving us a geographical dimension to the analysis. Moreover, we have the cultic place names, hence names containing an element denoting a pagan cult site, such as *vi*, *hov/hof, vang, åker* etc.

Not all of the deities mentioned in the Eddas are found in place names, and thus they probably had no active cult, at least not in the landscape. The deities found in place names are *Óðinn, Þórr, Ullr, Ullinn, Freyr, Týr*, ON *Njǫrðr* and probably also the goddesses *Freyja, Frigg*, OSw *Niærþer* and *Hærn*(?). This is to be compared with the much larger pantheon mentioned by Snorri in his Edda.

When we map all the known theophoric place names in Scandinavia, we find a surprising distribution. For example the gods Ullr and Freyr are, in principle, never found in southern Scandinavia, while the god Týr (Figure 6.3) is only found in Denmark and with a single occurrence in southern (probably Danish-dominated) Norway, and the god Ullinn – never mentioned in the literature, only in place names – is only to be found in south-central and western Norway. This is an indication that the pagan religion in Scandinavia was never homogeneous. It must have had regional variations and cults, where certain gods and goddesses were worshipped (Brink 2007b).

Some place-name elements are certainly, in some cases probably, denoting a pagan cult site (Andersson 1992; Vikstrand 2001). The most 'secure' one is *vi* (see above), Da *væ*, ON *vé*. It is found all over Scandinavia, both as a simplex *Vi/Væ*, and in compounds, such as *Odense* (< ODa *Othæns-væ* 'the cult site dedicated to Óðinn') and *Ullevi* (< OSw *Ullar-vi* 'the cult site dedicated to Ullr'). The element *hov*, ON *hof*, is etymologically not to be placed in a sacral semantic sphere. It originally meant 'hillock'. No doubt in the Icelandic sagas, and also in some place names, the word *hof* denoted a cultic building or site. This is also the case for the compound *hofstaðir*. In the cases where *hof* obviously

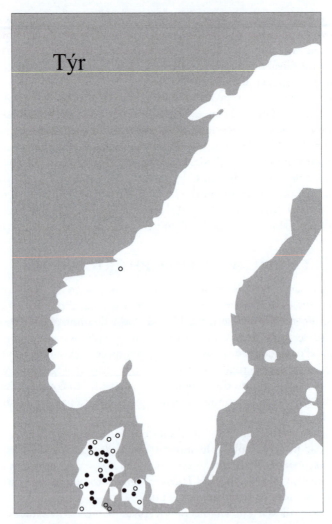

Figure 6.3 The distribution of place names containing the name of the god Týr in Scandinavia (Brink 2007b: 121).

denoted a cultic building or a hall, one cannot disregard the possibility that the Scandinavian word, ON *hof*, has been semantically influenced by the German word *hof* 'mansion, court', whereby a new meaning '(banqueting) hall' has emerged. In the same way as for *vi*, this element occurs both as simplex, *Hov/Hof*, and in compounds: *Frøshov* (Frœyshof 1391) in Trøgstad, Østfold, Norway. A much discussed element and word is **al* (< *alh-*). It was in early scholarship translated as 'temple, sanctuary', but this is inaccurate. This meaning is found for the Gothic equivalent *alhs*, in the Gothic Bible, but a secular usage of the word in the Germanic languages obviously has been 'protected village' etc. If we have examples of this word in Scandinavia (probably *Fröjel, Fryele, Norr-* and *Söderala, Ullerål* and some more), the meaning may have been 'hall, communal building (also for cultic matters)' (Brink 1992).

The word *sal*, ON *salr*, has been much discussed regarding its original meaning. It has been understood as a prehistoric sheiling and also as a barn for hay-fodder. Today there is no doubt that *salr* in place-names must be seen in a much more 'aristocratic' context (Brink 1996: 255–8). It was the Old Scandinavian word for a king's or a chieftain's banqueting hall. The few place names containing this word are prominent places, such as *Uppsala* in Sweden and *Skíringssalr* in Norway. A couple of names contain the god Óðinn's name: *Onsala* in Halland, *Odensala* in Jämtland and the old name of *Huseby* in *Onsøy* (< *Óðins-øy*) in Østfold, Norway. The element *salr* is not primarily to be set in a sacral context, but the denotation 'hall' reveals that cultic matters certainly have been conducted at these places. The word *harg*, ON *hǫrgr* has a similar background. In the Icelandic literature it often has the same meaning as *hof*, hence denoting a cult site or a cult building. The original meaning of the word was 'heap of stones'. The assumption is that from this original meaning a new one, 'stone altar (on the outside)', has emerged, and later on from this 'cult house'. The word is found as simplex *Harg*, and in compounds: OSw *Openshargh*, *Torshälla* (< OSw *Þors-hærghe*), *Skederid* (< OSw *Skæp-hargh*).

Some originally profane words also obviously occur within a cultic and sacral toponymic context, namely *åker* 'arable land', both as simplex *Åker/Aker* and in compounds: *Torsåker* (< OSw *Þors-akir*), *Onsåker* (OSw *Opens-akir*), *Frösåker* (< OSw *Frøs-akir*) (Vikstrand 2002, 2004). Similar is the case of *vang*, ON *vangr*, in Norway, often found as the focal farm in the district, by the church. The word *eke* (< *ek-ia*) 'oak grove' with a sacral toponymic meaning we find in *Onsike* (OSw *Opens-eke*), *Hälke* (< OSw *Hælgha-eke* 'the holy oak grove'), *Alsike* (probably < OSw *Alhs-eke*), and the word *böke* (< *bok-ia*) 'grove of lime trees' has a similar background. The word *lund* 'grove' had, of course, originally a profane meaning, but there is no doubt that the word could eventually appear in a cultic context, not only in compounds (*Torslunda*, *Fröslunda* etc.), but also as a simplex: *Lund*. An interesting case showing this is the name *Oklunda*, found in Östkind's hundred, in Östergötland. Where the farm Oklunda is situated we have a runic inscription carved in the rock, saying that the place (during the Viking Age) was a *vi*, hence a 'cult site', and that cult site must have had the name *Oklunda* 'the (cultic) grove on the yoke' (referring to the topographical situation) (Gustavson 2003; Brink 2003: 93–6). In Denmark there are several cult sites containing the word ODa *hyllæ* (probably) 'shelf', often with the name of the god Óðinn as the qualifier, as in *Vonsild* and *Onsild* (< ODa *Othæns-hyllæ*) on Jutland.

BIBLIOGRAPHY

Anderson (Arngart), O.S. (1934) *The English Hundred-names* (Lunds universitets årsskrift. N.F. Avd. 1, 30:1), Lund: no publ.

—— (1939a) *The English Hundred-names. The South-eastern Counties. With a Survey of Elements Found in Hundred-names and a Chapter on the Origin of the Hundred* (Lunds universitets årsskrift. N.F. Avd. 1, 37:1), Lund: Gleerup.

—— (1939b) *The English Hundred-names. The South-western Counties* (Lunds universitets årsskrift. N.F. Avd. 1, 35:5), Lund: Gleerup.

Andersson, Th. (1965) *Svenska häradsnamn* (Nomina Germanica 14), Uppsala: no publ.

—— (1982) 'Hund, hundare och härad från språklig synpunkt', *Bebyggelsehistorisk tidskrift*, 4: 52–66.

—— (1992) 'Kultplatsbeteckningar i nordiska ortnamn', in G. Fellows-Jensen and B. Holmberg (eds) *Sakrale navne* (Norna-rapporter 48), Uppsala: Norna.

—— (2004) 'Svethiudh. Det svenska rikets kärna', *Namn och bygd*, 92: 5–18.

Bately, J. and Englert, A. (eds) (2007) *Ohthere's Voyages. A Late 9th-century Account of Voyages Along the Coasts* (Maritime Culture of the North 1), Roskilde: Viking Ship Museum.

Brink, S. (1983) 'När bildades våra äldsta bebyggelsenamn?', *Ortnamnssällskapets i Uppsala årsskrift*: 5–17.

—— (1984) 'Absolut datering av bebyggelsenamn', in V. Dalberg *et al.* (eds) *Bebyggelsers og bebyggelsesnavnes alder* (Norna-rapporter 26), Uppsala: Norna.

—— (1992) 'Har vi haft ett kultiskt *al i Norden?', in G. Fellows-Jensen and B. Holmberg (eds) *Sakrale navne* (Norna-rapporter 48), Uppsala: Norna.

—— (1996) 'Political and social structures in early Scandinavia [1]: a settlement-historical pre-study of the central place', *Tor. Journal of Archaeology*, 28: 235–81.

—— (1997) 'Political and social structures in early Scandinavia 2: aspects of space and territoriality – the settlement district', *Tor. Journal of Archaeology*, 29: 389–437.

—— (1998) 'Land, bygd, distrikt och centralort i Sydsverige. Några bebyggelsehistoriska nedslag', in L. Larsson and B. Hårdh (eds) *Centrala platser, centrala frågor. Samhällsstrukturen under järnåldern* (Acta Archaeologica Lundesia, Series in 8°, no. 28), Stockholm: Almqvist & Wiksell International.

—— (1999) 'Social order in the early Scandinavian landscape', in Ch. Fabech and J. Ringtved (eds) *Settlement and Landscape*, Aarhus: Aarhus University Press.

—— (2000) 'Husby', *RGA* 15: 274–8.

—— (2003) 'Law and legal customs in Viking Age Scandinavia', in J. Jesch (ed.) *Scandinavians from the Vendel Period to the Tenth Century* (Studies in Historical Archaeoethnology 5), Woodbridge: Boydell.

—— (2007a) 'Geography, toponymy and political organisation in early Scandinavia', in J. Bately and A. Englert (eds) (2007).

—— (2007b) 'How uniform was the Old Norse religion?', in J. Quinn, K. Heslop and T. Wills (eds) *Learning and Understanding in the Old Norse World. Essays in Honour of Margaret Clunies Ross* (Studies in the Early Middle Ages), Turnhout: Brepols.

—— (2008) *Lord and Lady – Bryti and Deigja. Some Historical and Etymological Aspects of Family, Patronage and Slavery in Early Scandinavia and Anglo-Saxon England* (The Dorothea Coke Memorial Lecture 2004–5), London: Viking Society for Northern Research, University College London.

—— (forthcoming) 'People and *land* in early Scandinavia', in I. Garipzanov, P. Geary and P. Urbanczyk (eds) *Gentes and Gentile Identity in Medieval Europe* (Cursor 5), Turnhout: Brepols.

Gustavson, H. (2003) 'Oklundainskriften sjuttio år efteråt', in W. Heizmann and A. van Nahl (eds) *Runica – Germanica – Medaevalia* (Ergänzungsbände zum Reallexikon der germanischen Altertumskunde 37), Berlin: de Gruyter.

Hellberg, L. (1954) 'Studier i de nordiska *torp*-namnens kronologi', *Namn och bygd*, 42: 106–86.

—— (1979) 'Forn-Kalmar. Ortnamnen och stadens förhistoria', in *Kalmars stads historia*, vol. 1: *Kalmarområdets forntid och stadens äldsta utveckling*, Kalmar: Kulturnämnden.

Lund, N. (1996) *Lið, leding og landeværn. Hær og samfund i Danmark i ældre middelalder*, Roskilde: Vikingeskibshallen.

Rygh, O. *et al.* (1897–1936) *Norske Gaardnavne*, 21 vols, Kristiania (Oslo): Cammermeyer.

Strid, J.P. (1999) *Kulturlandskapets språkliga dimension. Ortnamnen*, 2nd edn, Stockholm: Raä.

Tilley, Ch. (1994) *A Phenomenology of Landscape. Places, Paths, and Monuments*, Oxford: Berg.

Vikstrand, P. (2001) *Gudarnas platser. Förkristna sakrala ortnamn i Mälarlandskapen* (Acta Academiae Regiae Gustavi Adolphi 77), Uppsala: Swedish Science Press.

—— (2002) 'Några tankar om de sakrala åker-namnen och om ortnamnskronologi', *Ortnamnssällskapets i Uppsala årsskrift*: 19–38.

—— (2004) 'Berget, lunden och åker. Om sakrala och kosmologiska landskap ur ortnamnens perspektiv', in A. Andrén, K. Jennbert and C. Raudvere (eds) *Ordning mot kaos. Studier av nordisk förkristen kosmologi* (Vägar från Midgård 4), Lund: Nordic Academic Press.

CHAPTER SEVEN

FARM AND VILLAGE IN THE VIKING AGE

———— · ◆ · ————

Jan-Henrik Fallgren

Despite the fact that the sources concerning the Viking Age settlement in Scandinavia are actually poorer than for the settlement from older periods of the Iron Age, you can nevertheless nowadays state that the general character of the Viking Age settlement in Scandinavia in most aspects was a continuation of how the settlement was formed and organised earlier during the three immediate preceding archaeological periods. The same is also valid in most cases for how the settlement was localised in the landscape. Any larger structural changes of settlement do not occur during the Viking Age. In the main areas of agriculture, medium and large villages dominated. In the woodlands, and in fjord and mountainous areas, there were, on the contrary, mainly smaller units: hamlets and solitary farms (Hvass 1988; Kaldal Mikkelsen 1999; Lillehammer 1999: 13 ff.; Myhre 2002: 132 ff.; Ethelberg 2003; Holst 2004; Fallgren 2006: 80 ff.). In certain regions, however, some important architectonic changes of the old three-aisled longhouses took place during the course of the Viking Age. And in other parts of Scandinavia this old type of house construction came, completely or partly, to be replaced with an entirely new building type, the one-aisled house with roof-supporting walls.

The predominant type of building in Scandinavia had, since the early Bronze Age, been the three-aisled construction of the longhouses, where a number of posts, put in pairs, supported the roof instead of the walls. The tunstall (part of the gable that connects the roof with the walls) was consequently not yet known in Scandinavia. The walls in these houses could be wattle and daub, deal walls anchored in furrows, or made of earth, turf and stone, according to what the local conditions could best provide. In the same way the material for roof-covering shifted – straw, turf or wood – according to the natural environment of each region. The lengths of the houses of the Viking Age varied from 5 to 50 metres. The longest house excavated to date, however, is 80 m long, found at Borg in Lofoten in the northern part of Norway. The houses were as a rule separated into different rooms, which had different functions. The longer the houses, the more rooms and functions inside. These multi-functional houses could contain stable, kitchen, storerooms, rooms for entertaining and for living. The width of the houses was usually between 6 and 7.5 m.

From the end of the ninth century, or at the beginning of the tenth, a new type of three-aisled longhouse started to be built in the south of Scandinavia. These houses were significantly wider: up to 12.5 m in width. They had only two pairs of roof-supporting posts inside the house, which created more spacious rooms. They seem also in general to be considerably taller than the older houses. The height to the roof has been calculated as up to 10 m in the biggest houses. Probably the houses also had an upper floor. This type of house, called the 'Trelleborg house' after the place on Zealand in Denmark where they were first discovered, had substantial, supporting posts heavy at the sides outside long convex walls, which gave the house a resemblance to a boat. These houses could be found, other than in the Danish fortresses from the Viking Age, first and foremost on the largest farms – the farms of the aristocrats – and could have several functions (Figure 7.1). The so-called 'Trelleborg houses' were in use in southern Scandinavia until the beginning of the Middle Ages – the twelfth and the beginning of the thirteenth century. But at that time several of them no longer contained inner roof-bearing posts; instead the houses had developed into one-aisled constructions. Separate smaller one-aisled houses existed even during the Viking Age in the south Scandinavian area, but it was not until later during the thirteenth century that three-aisled houses were completely replaced by one-aisled houses in south and west Scandinavia (Hvass 1988; Skov 1994; Christensen 1999; Rasmussen 1999; Carelli 2001: 48 ff.; Jørgensen 2001, 2002; Ethelberg 2003: 345 ff.; Herschend and Kaldal Mikkelsen 2003: 67 ff.; Söderberg 2005: 111 ff., 192 ff.).

On the other hand this technological building change entered eastern Scandinavia much earlier. On the two large islands in the Baltic Sea, Öland and Gotland, the old three-aisled houses began to be replaced by one-aisled houses with roof-supporting timber-framed walls already at the end of the Merovingian period (Carlsson 1979, 1981, 2005; Thunmark 1979; Fallgren 1994: 120; 1998: 73; 2006: 157 f.), maybe through influences from Slavic and Baltic architecture. During the Viking Age it seems that only one-aisled houses existed on these islands. These new rectangular or square houses were

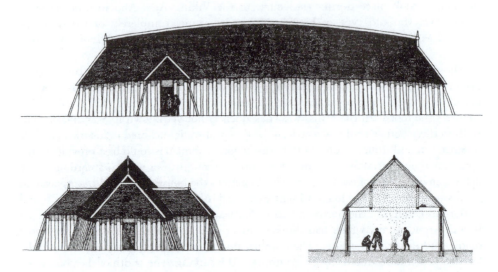

Figure 7.1 Reconstruction of a 'Trelleborg house' from Fyrkat, northern Jutland, Denmark (from Birkebæk & Bau 1982).

in general smaller than the older three-aisled longhouses, and because these houses seldom had several functions the number of buildings per farm became more numerous than before (Figure 7.2). Even on the present Swedish mainland, in the Lake Mälar valley, one-aisled houses appear at the end of the Merovingian period, but became even more common from the tenth century, when they also appear in Götaland and in northern Sweden. But throughout the Viking Age and later during the twelfth century three-aisled houses still remained on certain farms within these regions (Nielsen and Lindeblad 1997; Liedgren 1998; Ramquist 1998; Hållans and Svensson 1999; Borna-Ahlqvist *et al.* 1998; Göthberg 2000: 81 ff.; Åqvist 2006).

In the Viking Age, just as earlier during the Iron Age, one can detect from the widely varying sizes of farms large social differences among the landowning population in Scandinavia. The difference between ordinary smaller farms and the few really big farms was tremendous. The smaller farms could be composed of two or three buildings. These consisted usually of a main building, which housed a dwelling area with or without a stable, and one or two secondary buildings – often a stable or for storage. Sometimes there were also one or two pit-houses – small, partly dug-down buildings, which were used as workshops. The largest farms had between five to seven buildings. The main building was significantly larger than on the smaller farms, and the number of storage buildings, stables and workshops could be considerable. The floor area in the main building on the ordinary farms varied between 150–250 m^2. In the main buildings of the largest farms the floor area was up to 300–650 m^2. The collected floor area for all

Figure 7.2 Reconstruction of a one-aisled house with roof-supporting timber-framed walls excavated at Gotland, Sweden (from Carlsson 1981).

the buildings of the smaller farms amounted to about 200–350 m^2. The collected floor area for the many buildings of the large farms was considerably greater and varied between about 550–1,090 m^2. The largest of these magnate farms seem all to belong to the late Viking Age. To date, the largest Viking Age farms found in Scandinavia are those excavated in Old Lejre and Tissø on Zealand, Denmark, in Järrestad in Scania, Sweden, and at Borg in Lofoten, Norway (Hvass 1988: 86 ff.; Christensen 1999; Jørgensen 2001; Ethelberg 2003: 345 ff.; Herschend and Kaldal Mikkelsen 2003: 67 ff.; Söderberg 2005).

During the late Roman Iron Age, and the Migration and Merovingian periods, there were similar differences between different-sized classes of farms as during the Viking Age. The farms of the aristocrats from these periods could be of the same considerable size as the Viking Age farms. This has up to now most clearly become visible at the excavations in the south Scandinavian area, in south-west Norway and on Öland and Gotland in Sweden (Herschend 1988, 1993, 1997; Hvass 1988; Kaldal Mikkelsen 1999; Myhre 2002; Ethelberg 2003; Fallgren 2006: 26 ff., 143 ff.). On Öland, where a very large number of houses and farms from these archaeological periods are still visible today, one can establish that the floor areas of the existing four different farm sizes varied between 110–834 m^2. The total floor area of the magnate farms varied between 558 and 834 m^2 (Fallgren 1998: 66 ff.; 2006: 26 ff., 143 ff.). In comparison with the great majority of the largest known Viking Age magnate farms, it is actually only the magnate farm at Tissø, with its total floor area of over 1,000 m^2, that is larger than any of the magnate farms on Öland from about AD 300 to 700. The fact that we can find approximately the same classes of farm sizes during the Viking Age as earlier, and that the majority of the largest farms during the Viking Age were of the same size as during the three preceding periods, indicates that the social structure in force and the hierarchy of society was the same during the Viking Age, at least in its main features.

The above-mentioned pit-houses could also be found earlier in the Iron Age on several farms in southern Scandinavia, but became more common in all of the northern territory during the Viking Age. Usually there was only one or at most a few on the farms, but on the largest farms, where particular crafts were practised, as in Lejre and Tissø on Zealand, in Övra Wannborga on Öland and in Järrestad in Scania, they could be found in greater numbers. These farms are also distinguished by archaeological excavation through a considerably greater variety of animal species in the bone waste, with for example more bone from game than on the ordinary farms (Christensen 1993; Fallgren 1994; Jørgensen 2001; Söderberg 2005).

The groupings of the separate farms whether within villages or separate in the landscape could be very different within the different Scandinavian regions during the Viking Age. The same was even true in the way the different buildings within the farms were grouped in relation to each other and to enclosures or other boundaries of the farms. In southern Scandinavia, especially in the south of Jutland, the farmhouses often, but not always, were grouped within very regular-shaped tofts, which were delimited by dug ditches or wooden enclosures. During the Viking Age these tofts become considerably larger than they had been before in this region. The smaller farms in these villages had a plot acreage of about 3,600 m^2, while the plot acreage of the larger farms could amount to 10,000–15,000 m^2. At the end of the Viking Age the tofts in this region became even bigger and acquired the same proportions as the tofts in the later regulated villages during the medieval period. In that period the plot acreage of the villages lay between 9,000–25,000 m^2 and the biggest could have an acreage up to 40,000 m^2 (Hvass 1988: 86 ff.; Jørgensen 2001; Ethelberg 2003: 353 ff.; Holst 2004: 186 ff.). In the rest of Scandinavia these regular toft delimitations of the farms were in general missing throughout the Viking Age. Instead the buildings of the farms in these regions were often irregularly placed and totally or partly adjusted according to the local topography. Often the houses were placed on built-up terraces or plateaus, on smaller ridges or on slopes, or the farms were placed on a limited plane surface in a very hilly landscape. The farms' fences were made of stone and/or wood and were connected to and from the farm in diverse directions, often as cattle paths, which led the cattle from the farm to the pasture on the unfenced outlying land (Liedgren 1998; Olsen 1998; Ramqvist 1998; Lillehammer 1999; Göthberg 2000; Selinge 2001; Myhre 2002; Åqvist 2006).

When it comes to how the villages were structured during the Viking Age, there seem to have been fairly large regional differences within the Nordic area. In the most southern part of Scandinavia there were more regularly shaped villages already at the end of the Viking Age, especially in the south of Jutland, where the farms had developed very regularly formed plot boundaries, and this is most clearly seen in the completely excavated village at Vorbasse (Figure 7.3) (Hvass 1988: 89; Ethelberg 2003: 354; Holst

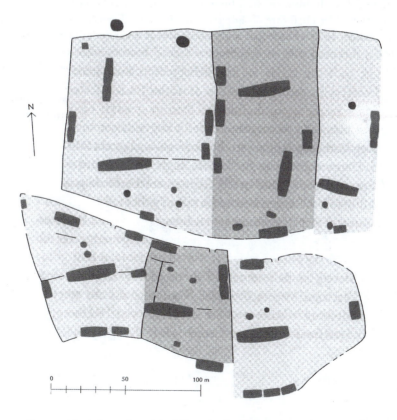

N

0   50   100 m

Figure 7.3 Farms with their yards and buildings in the Viking Age village at Vorbasse, Jutland, Denmark. (Drawing: S. Hendriksen; Museum Sønderjylland. In: *Det sønderjyske landbrugs Historie* 2000: 370 fig. 235.)

2004: 187). Without doubt this structure was strongly influenced by the very regularly formed *Waldhufendörfer*, *Angerdörfer* and *Strassendörfer* within Frankish and German areas, which were the result of the standardised measurements of peasant holdings. But such regulated villages seem only to have existed in an extremely limited quantity during the Viking Age in Scandinavia. Later on in the medieval period, during the twelfth–fourteenth centuries, they became more common, but only in the regions that were totally or partly dominated by the great landowners: the nobility, the Church and the monasteries (Fallgren 2006: 171 ff.).

In the rest of Scandinavia the villages seem in general to have had a totally different and more irregular character, where the farmsteads were placed longer or shorter distances from each other, totally lacking limitations of the plot or with irregular frames of the farmstead yards. The farmsteads in these villages were connected with each other and the common, the grazing area, through cattle paths. The villages with this type of structure lasted long into modern times, particularly in the regions of Scandinavia dominated by self-owning peasants (Figure 7.4). The enclosures that still survive from the Viking Age, or the ones we have found at archaeological excavations, show that the enclosed area of the farmsteads, the arable land and meadows in these villages had been separately enclosed. Every farm had one or several irregularly formed enclosures/infields, which led out directly from the buildings at the farm or the borders that were possibly around the farm. The enclosures of one farmstead adjoined the enclosures of neighbouring farms, which resulted in the farms usually being separated about 50–200 m from each other, and the settlement was spread out over a large area. Some common enclosures or subdivided fields seem not to have been in existence before the Middle Ages in Scandinavia (Fallgren 1993, 2006: 87 ff., 171 ff.). There are no indications of the more regularly formed villages from the Viking Age in southern Jutland having any common fields or enclosures. On the contrary, every farm seems to have had individual infields

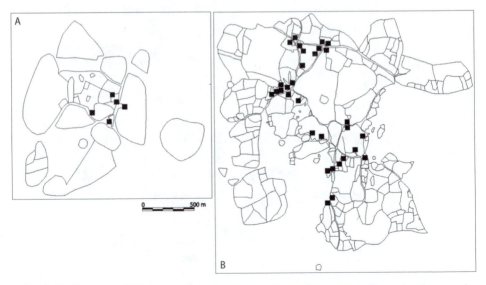

Figure 7.4 Examples of villages with irregular fields and farms (■) with irregular yards. This irregular structure lasted from the Iron Age long into modern times. (A) The village of Enerum 1761, Öland, Sweden, (B) The village of Tällberg 1826, Dalarna, Sweden.

with separate, enclosed long-strips, in exactly the same way as in the regular Frankish, German and Norman villages on the British islands, before a common fallow system and subdivided fields were introduced at the beginning or in the middle of the medieval period (Hoffman 1975: 41; Dodgshon 1980: 75 ff.; Hoff 1984: 102; 1997: 84 ff.; Roberts 1987: 199; Porsmose 1988: 270; Bartlett 1993: 114 ff.; Riddersporre 1995: 172; Holst 2004: 186 ff.). The village sizes in Scandinavia varied widely. Hamlets consisting of two to four farmsteads have primarily been found in woodlands, moraine and mountainous areas, as well as in the Norwegian fjord valleys. Larger villages with fifteen to twenty and up to fifty farmsteads have first of all been found in the central agricultural areas and could include areas of up to 400–500 hectares, settlement and infields included.

Visible remnants of infields, with enclosures and fossil fields, are preserved in southwest Norway, in Östergötland and on Öland and Gotland, and to some extent also in the Lake Mälar area in Sweden. These are mainly composed of demolished stone walls, which are often connected in huge systems. Previously these were mainly considered to belong to earlier periods of the Iron Age, the Roman Iron Age and the migration period, but new excavations and analyses of these have shown that they were also used and constructed during the Viking Age and the medieval period (Fallgren 2006: 31 ff., 159 ff.; Petersson 2006: 187 ff.). These stone walls normally enclosed the meadows and only to a lesser extent the fields. The fields seem to be both few in number and small in area. The farming during the Viking Age, as earlier during the Iron Age, can therefore be characterised as a fairly pastoral economy, where cattle breeding and its products constituted the essential part of agrarian production. This is also something that becomes evident when comparing stables from the Viking Age with stables from the Middle Ages and later: Viking Age stables in general housed more animals, sometimes many more, than stables from the medieval and later periods could accommodate. In the same way the bone material from the excavated farmsteads from the Viking Age shows that cattle breeding was of greater importance than during the medieval period (Myrdal 1999: 39 ff.).

Outside the enclosed fields and meadows, on the border of the outlying land, where the pasture began, the grave-fields of the villages were usually located. However, sometimes they were to be found somewhat further out on the common, and in these cases in connection with more important roads. Often there were several grave-fields around each village, which were normally exposed in order to be visible from the neighbouring villages. The grave-fields seem therefore to have helped define or delimit the enclosed infields of the villages, where the enclosures were the physical manifestations of the land belonging to the different farmsteads in the villages, and where the graves can be interpreted as the symbolic expression of ownership and the rights of inheritance to the land 'enclosed' (Fallgren 2006: 119 f., 136 ff.). There are indications that graves and grave-fields had a function as a declaration of ownership of land and rights of inheritance in the Christian society of Scandinavia (Jørgensen 1988: 50 ff.; Arrhenius 1990: 74; Ringstad 1991: 144 ff.; Gurevich 1992: 194 ff.; Zachrisson 1994; Skre 1998: 199 ff.; Sundqvist 2002: 154 f., 170 ff.).

BIBLIOGRAPHY

Åqvist, C. (2006) *Sanda – en gård i södra Uppland. Bebyggelse från vendeltid till 1600-tal. Uppland, Fresta socken, Sanda 1:1, Raä 147* (UV Mitt. Rapport 2004:15), Stockholm: Raä.

Arrhenius, B. (1990) 'Utgrävningen av den östligaste storhögen på gravfältet Ormknös, Raä111, Björkö, Adelsö sn, Uppland', *Laborativ Arkeologi. Journal of Nordic Archaeological Science*, 4: 65–80.

Bartlett, R. (1993) *The Making of Europe. Conquest, Colonization and Cultural Change 950–1350*, Princeton: Princeton University Press.

Birkebæk, F.A. and Bau, F. (1982) *Sesams Danmarkshistorie. Vikingetiden*, vol. 1: *Rejselystne bønder*, Copenhagen: Sesam.

Borna-Ahlkvist, H., Lindgren-Hertz, L. and Stålbom, U. (1998) *Pryssgården. Från stenålder till medeltid* (Rapport från Raä UV-Linköping 1998:13), Linköping: Raä.

Carelli, P. (2001) *En kapitalistisk anda. Kulturella förändringar i 1100-talets Danmark*, Stockholm: Almqvist & Wiksell International.

Carlsson, D. (1979) *Kulturlandskapets utveckling på Gotland* (Kulturgeografiska institutionen, Stockholms universitet. Meddelanden B 49), Visby: Press.

—— (1981) 'Från stengrund till bulhus – gotländska husformer under yngre järnålder–tidig medeltid. Ett rekonstruktionsförslag utifrån Fjäle i Ala', *Bebyggelsehistorisk tidskrift*, 2: 37–47.

—— (2005) 'Vikingatidens gårdar – en fråga om kontinuitet, *Gotländskt Arkiv*: 90–9.

Christensen, T. (1993) 'Lejre beyond legend: the archaeological evidence', *Journal of Danish Archaeology*, 10 (1991): 163–85.

—— (1999) 'Kongehallen i Lejre', in M. Rasmusen (ed.) (1999).

Dodgshon, R. (1980) *The Origin of British Field Systems. An Interpretation*, London: Academic Press.

Ethelberg, P. (2003) 'Gården og landsbyen i jernalder og vikingetid (500 f Kr–1000 e Kr)', in P. Ethelberg, N. Hardt, B. Poulsen and A.B. Sørensen (eds) *Det Sønderjyske Landbrugs Historie. Jernalder, Vikingetid & Middelalder* (Skrifter udg. af Historisk Samfund for Sønderjylland 82), Haderslev: Haderslev Museum.

Fallgren, J.-H. (1993) 'The concept of the village in Swedish archaeology', *Current Swedish Archaeology*, 1: 59–86.

—— (1994) 'En vendel- och vikingatida grophusbebyggelse i Övra Wannborga på Öland', *Tor*, 26: 107–44.

—— (1998) 'Hus och gård på Öland', *Bebyggelsehistorisk tidskrift*, 33 (1997): 63–76.

—— (2006) *Kontinuitet och förändring. Bebyggelse och samhälle på Öland 200–1300 e. Kr.* (Aun 35), Uppsala: Dept. of Archaeology and Ancient History, Uppsala University.

Göthberg, H. (2000) *Bebyggelse i förändring. Uppland från slutet av yngre bronsålder till tidig medeltid* (Opia 25), Uppsala: Institutionen för arkeologi och antik historia, Uppsala universitet.

Gurevich, A.Ja. (1992) *Historical Anthropology of the Middle Ages*, ed. J. Howlett, Chicago: University of Chicago Press.

Hållans, A.-M. and Svensson, K. (1999) *Arkeologi på väg. Undersökningar för E18. Pollista – bo och bruka under 1 200 år* (UV-Uppsala. Rapport 1998:110) Stockholm: Raä.

Herschend, F. (1988) 'Bebyggelse och folkvandringstid på Öland', in U. Näsman and J. Lund (eds) *Folkevandringstiden i Norden. En krisetid mellem ældre og yngre jernalder*, Århus: Universitetsforlaget.

—— (1991) 'Om öländsk metallekonomi i första hälften av första årtusendet e. Kr.', in Ch. Fabech and J. Ringtved (eds) *Samfundsorganisation og regional variation. Norden i Romersk Jernalder og Folkevandringstid* (Jysk Arkæologisk Selskabs Skrifter 27), Højbjerg: Jysk Arkæologisk Selskab.

—— (1993) 'The origin of the hall in southern Scandinavia', *Tor*, 25: 175–99.

—— (1997) *Livet i hallen. Tre fallstudier i den yngre järnålderns aristokrati* (Opia 14) Uppsala: Inst. för arkeologi och antik histsoria, Uppsala universitet.

Herschend, F. and Kaldal Mikkelsen, D. (2003) 'The main building at Borg', in G. Stamsø Munch, O.S. Johansen and E. Roesdahl (eds) *Borg in Lofoten. A Chieftain's Farm in North Norway* (Arkeologisk skriftserie 1), Trondheim: Tapir.

Hoff, A. (1984) 'Middelalderlige gærder og hegn – ældre og yngre dyrkningssystem i Jydske Lov', *Fortid og nutid*, 31(2): 85–102.

—— (1997) *Lov og landskab. Landskapslovernes bidrag til forståelsen af landbrugs- og landskabsut- viklingen i Danmark ca 900–1250*, Aarhus: Aarhus universitetsforlag.

Hoffman, R.C. (1975) 'Medieval origins of the common fields', in W.N. Parker and E.L. Jones (eds) *European Peasants and their Markets. Essays in Agrarian Economic History*, Princeton: Princeton University Press.

Holst, M.K. (2004) 'The syntax of the Iron Age village: transformations in an orderly com- munity.' (Unpubl. PhD thesis, Dept. of Archaeology, University of Aarhus.)

Hvass, S. (1988) 'Jernalderens bebyggelse', in P. Mortensen and B.M. Rasmussen (eds) *Fra stamme til stat i Danmark*, vol. 1: *Jernalderens stammesamfund* (Jysk Arkæologisk Selskabs Skrifter 22), Højbjerg: Jysk Arkæologisk Selskab.

Jørgensen, L. (1988) 'Family burial practices and inheritance systems: the development of an Iron Age society from 500 BC to AD 1000 on Bornholm, Denmark', *Acta Archaeologica*, 58 (1987): 17–53.

—— (2001) 'From tribute to the estate system 3rd–12th century', in B. Arrhenius (ed.) *Kingdoms and Regionality. Transactions from the 49th Sachsensymposium 1998 in Uppsala* (Theses and Papers in Archaeology B:6), Stockholm: Archaeological Research Laboratory, University of Stockholm.

—— (2002) 'Kongsgård – kultsted – marked. Overvejelser omkring Tissøkompleksets struktur og function', in K. Jennbert, A. Andrén and C. Raudvere (eds) *Plats och praxis. Studier av nordisk förkristen ritual* (Vägar till Midgård 2), Lund: Nordic Academic Press.

Kaldal Mikkelsen, D. (1999) 'Single farm or village? Reflections on the settlement structure of the Iron Age and the Viking period', in Ch. Fabech and J. Ringtved (eds) *Settlement and Landscape*, Højbjerg: Jutland Archaeological Society.

Liedgren, L. (1998) 'Förhistoriska byggnadskonstruktioner i Norrland', *Bebyggelsehistorisk tidskrift*, 33 (1997): 155–68.

Lillehammer, A. (1999) 'Farm and village, the problem of nucleation and dispersal of settlement – seen from a Norwegian perspective', in Ch. Fabech and J. Ringtved (eds) *Settlement and Landscape*, Højbjerg: Jutland Archaeological Society.

Myhre, B. (2002) 'Landbruk, landskap og samfunn 4000 f Kr-800 e Kr.', in B. Myhre and I. Øye (eds) *Norges landsbrukshistorie*, vol. 1: *4000 f. Kr.–1350 e. Kr. Jorda blir levevei*, Oslo: Det norske samlaget.

Myrdal, J. (1999) *Det svenska jordbrukets historia*, vol. 2: *Jordbruket under feodalismen 1000–1700*, Stockholm: Natur och kultur.

Nielsen, K. and Lindeblad, A.-L. (1997) 'Centralplatser i Norrköpingsbygden – förändringar i tid och rum 200–1200 e Kr.', in J. Callmer and E. Rosengren (eds) *'Gick Grendel att söka det höga huset . . .'. Arkeologiska källor till aristokratiska miljöer i Skandinavien under yngre järnålder* (Hallands länsmuseums skriftserie 9), Halmstad: Hallands läsnmuseer.

Olsen, B. (1998) 'Forhistoriske hus i Nord-Norge', *Bebyggelsehistorisk tidskrift*, 33 (1997): 185–94.

Petersson, M. (2006) *Djurhållning och betesdrift. Djur, människor och landskap i västra Östergötland under yngre bronsålder och äldre järnålder*, Stockholm: Raä.

Porsmose, E. (1988) 'Middelalder o. 1000–1536', in C. Bjørn (ed.) *Det danske landbrugs historie*, vol. 1: *Oldtid og middelalder*, Odense: Landbohistorisk selskab.

Ramqvist, P.H. (1998) *Arnäsbacken. En gård från yngre järnålder och medeltid*, Umeå: Prehistorica.

Rasmussen, M. (ed.) (1999) *Hal og højsæde i vikingetid. Et forslag til rekonstruktion af kongehallens arkitektur og inredning* (Historisk–Arkæeologisk Forsøgscenter. Technical Report 5), Lejre: Historisk–Arkæeologisk Forsøgscenter.

Riddersporre, M. (1995) *Bymarker i backspegel. Odlingslandskapet före kartornas tid* (Meddelanden från Lunds universitets geografiska institution. Avhandlingar 124), Trelleborg: Swedala.

Ringstad, B. (1991) 'Graver og ideologi. Implikasjoner fra vestnorsk folkvandringstid', in Ch. Fabech and J. Ringtved (eds) *Samfundsorganisation og regional variation. Norden i romersk jernalder og folkevandringstid* (Jysk Arkæologisk Selskabs Skrifter 27), Aarhus: Jysk Arkæologisk Selskab.

Roberts, B.K. (1987) *The Making of the English Village. A Study in Historical Geography*, London: Longman.

Selinge, K.-G. (2001) 'Orkesta – centralbygd i Attundaland', in M. Elg (ed.) *Plats, landskap, karta. En vänatlas till Ulf Sporrong*, Stockholm: Kulturgeografiska institutionen, Stockholms universitet.

Skov, H. (1994) 'Hustyper i vikingetid og tidlig middelalder. Udviklingen af hustyperne i det gammeldanske område fra ca. 800–1200 e.Kr.', *Hikuin*, 21: 139–62.

Skre, D. (1998) *Herredømmet. Bosetning og besittelse på Romerike 200–B1350 e.Kr.* (Acta Humaniora 32), Oslo: Universitetsforlaget.

Söderberg, B. (2005) *Aristokratiskt rum och gränsöverskridande. Järrestad och sydöstra Skåne mellan region och rike 600–1100* (Raä. Arkeologiska undersökningar. Skrifter 62), Stockholm: Raä.

Sundqvist, O. (2002) *Freyr's Offspring. Rulers and Religion in Ancient Svea Society* (Historia Religionum 21), Uppsala: Acta universitatis Upsaliensis.

Thunmark, L. (1979) 'Burget på Burge – en storgård på gränsen mellan heden och kristen tid', in W. Falck (ed.) *Arkeologi på Gotland* (Gotlandica 14), Visby: Kulturnämnden i Gotlands kommun.

Zachrisson, T. (1994) 'The odal and its manifestation in the landscape', *Current Swedish Archaeology*, 2: 219–38.

MANOR, CULT AND MARKET AT LAKE TISSØ

——— •◆• ———

Lars Jørgensen

One of the Viking magnates' complexes is situated on the west bank of Lake Tissø in west Zealand in Denmark. The settlement is situated at a distance of 7 kilometres from the coast and extends along the west bank for 1.6 km (Figure 7.1.1). The total settlement area is about 50 ha. As early as the nineteenth century weapons and other objects appeared in the lakebed near the settlement when the level of the lake was lower. To date some fifty objects have been found in the lake – swords, axes, lances, brooches and tools – the great majority of which are from the Viking Age. In this connection the name of the lake is interesting – *Tissø*, which actually means *Týr*'s lake. *Týr* was one of the Viking war gods, and probably the lake finds represent offerings. The objects found so far show that this votive tradition goes back at least to around AD 600. The most spectacular find was made in 1977, when a farmer found a tenth-century gold neck-ring weighing 1.8 kg. To this can today be added at least four silver treasures. In 1979 the graves of two executed men emerged at the crossing over the River Halleby Å. The burials can be dated to the mid-eleventh century, which corresponds closely with the end date for the settlement. In the same excavation were found the remains of a 50-metre-long wooden bridge over Halleby Å from the Viking Age.

In the period 1995–2003 extensive excavations took place and *c.* 85,000 m² of the settlement were excavated. Two manors and parts of extensive market and craft areas were investigated. The metal objects show that the settlement began in the mid-sixth century and ended in the first half of the eleventh century. All evidence indicates that the full settlement area was in operation from the beginning of the seventh century and for the next 400 years.

THE FIRST MANOR

The first manor, from the sixth and seventh centuries, comprises an area of *c.* 10,000 m², which is three to four times the size of ordinary Danish farms from the period. The manor consists of a large main building, two largish houses and a few smaller houses. The two largest houses are placed around an inner enclosure. The largest building has a length of 40 m and was unusually well constructed from large timbers and had

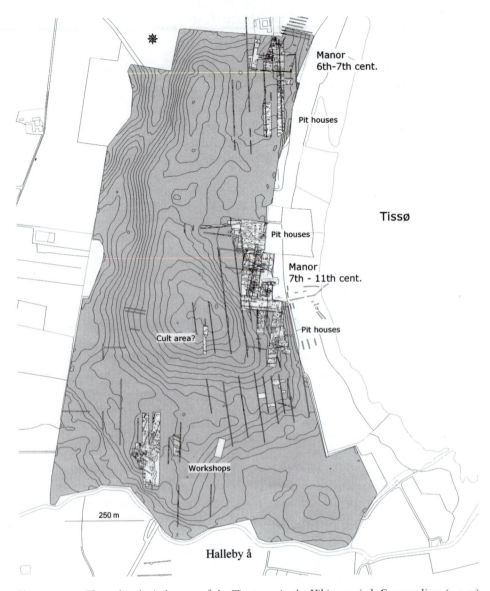

Figure 7.1.1 The archaeological status of the Tissø area in the Viking period. Contour lines (0.5 m) and excavation areas are shown. Just north of the River Halleby Å a workshop area extends along the lake up to the second manor. North of this a pit-house area continues to the north along the lake to the first manor.

white-plastered walls. Probably the whole complex burned down in the middle or second half of the seventh century. On the basis of the metal finds the period of use can be set at *c*. AD 550–650. The finds include brooches, a sword pommel, a spiral bead of gold and a pair of gold pendants with inlaid garnets in cloisonné.

THE SECOND MANOR

The first manor was then superseded by the later manor placed some 600 m further to the south. The ^{14}C datings seem to indicate a beginning around AD 700 and the manor can be followed through four phases. The manor area of Phase 1 is about 10,000 m². At the centre lies the hall building, which is about 36 m × 11 m. A special fenced area was built against the walls of the hall, and in this lay a small building. By the fence at the northern end of the manor was the forge. As a Danish farm complex it is highly atypical, and in the available material there is nothing to suggest agricultural production or permanent livestock at the house complex. It is not only the structure of the house that is odd. The pits dug for the roof-bearing posts in the hall were up to 3 metres deep. The deeply dug posts might indicate high wind pressure on the building – perhaps because it had two floors.

This atypical house structure is repeated in the subsequent Phase 2 from the eighth and ninth centuries. The manor is extended to some 15,000 m². The hall is rebuilt, as well as the separate fenced area. The small building from Phase 1 is replaced by a larger one. As in Phase 1 we can still find the forge at the northern end of the complex.

With Phase 3 from the ninth and tenth centuries there are changes in the structure of the complex (Figure 7.1.2). The area of the manor is extended to about 18,000 m², while its core structure is retained. The hall is just rebuilt, as are the fenced separate area and the related building. The forge is still placed by the north fence of the complex. Along the west fence, though, new buildings are erected at different times. The most striking thing about the development from Phase 1 to Phase 3 is the decided conservatism with respect to the hall and the related separate fenced area with its single building. Over a period of almost 250 years the combination of hall, separate area and smaller building is maintained.

We can interpret the hall as the prestigious main building where the receptions and feast took place, the Old Norse *salr* or *hof*, but the separate area and the small building are clearly something special. Here it is worth noting that there is an unusually high frequency, within the manor, of finds of heathen amulets and jewellery with motifs taken from Norse mythology (Figure 7.1.3). The many heathen amulets and the weapon offerings from the lake might indicate that cult activities were associated with the manor. Perhaps the small building in the special fenced area of the manor could be a cult building, a so-called *hørgr*, often mentioned in the Old Norse sagas.

The concluding Phase 4 embraces the last half of the tenth century and the beginning of the eleventh century. The most spectacular building is a very large hall with 550 m² under the roof. The area is at least 25,000 m². With Phase 4 the structure of the complex changes radically. The hall building is of a new type; the fenced special area disappears, and the other house types are replaced, mainly by houses with diagonal supporting posts.

THE FIND MATERIAL

In general the second manor has a very high percentage of tin-plated and gilded objects of bronze and silver, compared with other productive sites in Denmark. A characteristic element in the inventory of the manor is weaponry: arrowheads, hilts, pommels and other fittings from swords, bridles and spurs. The distribution of the *c.* 100 weapons

Figure 7.1.2   Plan showing the layout of the manor in Phase 3, preliminarily dated to the ninth–tenth centuries.

Figure 7.1.3 Pendants depicting valkyries of the Norse mythology of gilded silver with niello inlays.
(Photo: John Lee, The National Museum of Denmark.)

and weapon parts from the site shows a clear concentration at the manor. Sherds of Carolingian drinking glasses are likewise only found in the manor. Another element is objects from the Carolingian and insular areas. The Carolingian ones include sword-belt fittings, brooches and coins minted under Charlemagne and Louis the Pious. The number of coins totals more than 130 with no fewer than *c.* 110 Arabic coins from the eighth to the tenth century.

MARKET AND WORKSHOP AREA

Both south and north of the large house area there are extensive workshop and market areas. There are thousands of post-holes, in which, however, it is extremely difficult to find any system mainly due to the ploughing-down to which the site has been exposed. One building type in the market areas, however, is the pit-house, of which eighty-five have been excavated. In the southern workshop area iron forging and bronze casting seem to have dominated the activities. Semi-finished material for strike-a-lights, shears, knives and arrowheads are among the finds. Bronze casters worked in the same areas, and among other things casting-moulds for tortoise brooches have been found, patrix dies, models as well as miscast keys, brooches and Thor's hammers. The distribution of molten bronze and lead shows that jewellery was produced over most of the site. Tools in the form of burins, small chisels and hammers for metalwork appear in the southern workshop area.

The distribution of the trading activities is evident from the *c.* 350 weights, many fragments of hack-silver and Arabic coins that have been found all over the area. The distribution of the dateable finds shows that a very large part of the overall market area was functioning at the same time. By contrast there are indications that this was only for a short period at any one time. Compared with the find frequency at emporia such as Ribe, Haithabu, Kaupang and Birka, the quantity of finds is smaller at Tissø. This does not suggest long-lasting occupation in the market and production areas. There seem to have been short, but intense periods of activity.

A ROYAL PALACE?

The find material thus shows that people belonging to the absolute elite were at the Tissø complex throughout its functional period. The distinctive arrangement of the buildings suggests, though, that they did not use it as a permanent residence. The main residence must therefore lie elsewhere, and perhaps we should move up a level as far as the ownership of the complex is concerned. It might have been a royal complex – not a primary residence, but an establishment belonging to the royal estate system of a mobile monarchy (see Jørgensen 2003 for further discussion).

The possible function of the Tissø complex as a royal palace, but not as a main residence, might also be indicated by the fact that no graves have yet been found in connection with the site. If this absence of graves is real, it provides support for the idea that the complex was not the magnate's primary residence as it would be natural to expect rich, dynastic graves in connection with the main residence. As to where such a main residence might have been, we can turn our attention to Old Lejre near Roskilde, where the residential complex has much more of the character of a permanent residence (see Christensen, ch. 8.4, below).

BIBLIOGRAPHY

Jørgensen, L. (2003) 'Manor and market at Lake Tissø in the sixth to eleventh centuries: the Danish "productive" sites', in T. Pestell and K. Ulmschneider (eds) *Markets in Early Medieval Europe. Trading and 'Productive' Sites*, 650–850, Bollington: Windgather Press.

CHAPTER EIGHT

THE DEVELOPMENT OF URBANISM IN SCANDINAVIA

———•◆•———

Dagfinn Skre

The earliest Viking Age is the period when urbanism first gained a foothold in the Scandinavian lands (Figure 8.1). At this time urban communities had for several centuries been abundant further south and west in the Roman Empire, thereafter in the Frankish and the English kingdoms. However, Scandinavia maintained its totally rural

Figure 8.1   Map showing the towns and sites discussed in this chapter.

character almost up to the time when its inhabitants started raiding the coasts of these kingdoms and of Ireland, and penetrating into the Slavonic areas in the Baltic.

This basically rural character was maintained throughout the period and also in the following centuries in spite of urban communities being established in increasing numbers through the Viking Age. At any time during the Middle Ages less than 10 per cent of the Scandinavian population lived in towns. In the late Viking Age the figure was around 1–2 per cent. In the early Viking Age, in the ninth century, a total of only around 3,000–4,000 lived in the four towns of this time: Birka in the land of the Swedes, Ribe, Kaupang and Hedeby in what was then the Danish kingdom. Far the largest of these was Hedeby, which had more inhabitants than the other three counted together. These four towns will be the main focus in the following, but the urban development in the later Viking Age – the eleventh century – will also be touched upon.

The modest size and number of towns should not lead one to underestimate their importance. Towns played an important role in the transformation of the Scandinavian tribal communities of the pre-Viking Age period to the three kingdoms of the late Viking Age. They were also the main arenas for the development of legislation and economic practices in the expanding trade of the period. Craft production underwent major changes in the Viking Age and the establishment of towns was the main condition for this development.

An urban community is composed of people whose main occupation is non-agrarian. Basically they do not produce their own food; they depend on achieving it from the surrounding rural society (Reynolds 1977: ix–x; Clarke and Ambrosiani 1995: 3; Pallister 2000: 5). The typical activities of towns in the Viking Age were craft production and trade. But these were not purely urban activities, in the sense that they took place exclusively in towns. Trade and craft also existed in rural societies before the Viking Age and continued to do so after towns were established (Callmer 1994). It is the dense and permanent settlements inhabited mainly by people who perform these activities that are the hallmark of the Viking Age town. In the late Viking Age, when kings and Church started settling in the towns, bringing with them their courts and clerks, towns also became administrative centres for kingdoms and dioceses, and for the areas immediately surrounding each town.

TWO WAVES OF URBANISATION

The first town to emerge was Birka, the town of the Swedes, established in the mid- or second half of the 700s. Birka was located on a small island, near the middle of Lake Mälaren, the main transport route of that region. Thereafter, three towns were founded in rapid succession within the realm of the Danish king. The first was Ribe, founded in the 790s. The site had been a seasonal marketplace since the first decade of that century, but permanent settlement did not start until the last decade. Like the two other towns of the Danish kingdom it lay in a cultural, political and economic border zone. This southwestern part of the kingdom lay closest to south-eastern England and the north-western Carolingian Empire, where towns and trade flourished at the time. The Frisians in particular were active in the seaborne trade and Ribe was a part of their trade network. Kaupang was established *c.* 800 in the north-western corner of the Danish realm, in Vestfold in present-day Norway, on the border with the Northmen (Skre 2007a). A few years later (808) Hedeby was founded in the south-eastern corner on the border with the Saxons and Slavonic tribes. Today, Hedeby is located close to Schleswig in Germany.

After this half-century of town foundations, two centuries went by without new towns emerging. Then, in the decades around AD 1000, a new wave of urbanisation swept over southern and central Scandinavia. The most important towns established during this period were Sigtuna in Sweden, Århus, Roskilde and Lund in Denmark, and Oslo and Trondheim in Norway (Andrén 1989). All of these towns still exist today, as do most towns from the following centuries. In contrast, all the four towns of the early Viking Age were by the end of the period deserted or had suffered a major downfall. Ribe disappears from the archaeological record around 850. Although it is mentioned as a bishop see in written sources in the following centuries, definite traces of urban activity do not reappear until the twelfth century. Kaupang was abandoned around 930; Birka was deserted around 970, coinciding with the establishment of Sigtuna some miles further north. The same thing happened to Hedeby in the 1060s, around the time when Schleswig was established on the other side of the Schlei fjord.

The reasons for this apparent lack of continuity of the towns from the early to the late Viking Age have been debated among scholars. For Ribe the question of continuity throughout the Viking Age is still open, as the written sources and the continued use of the town's name indicate continuity in the urban community, while the archaeology does not. For the others it has been proposed that the urban function moved elsewhere, which seems to have been the case with Hedeby and Birka. However, this cannot be the case with Kaupang, as there is a gap of about a century between the abandonment of Kaupang and the rise of Oslo and Skien, the next towns to be established in the Oslo fjord area. Only some 30 km north of Kaupang lies Tønsberg, but in spite of extensive archaeological investigations there, no urban traces older than the late eleventh century have been found.

When it is so common in the early Viking Age, both the abandonment and movement of towns need explanations beyond the fate of the individual town. For Hedeby, Birka and Kaupang, poor harbour and sailing conditions have been pointed out as important reasons for abandonment. For Hedeby, the shallow harbour and the increasing size of ships may have been a main cause for building the new town Schleswig across the fjord.

Concerning Birka it has been suggested that the abandonment was caused by the closing of the southern sailing route from the Baltic Sea into Lake Mälaren as a result of land rise. However, the movement of the town to Sigtuna hardly helped in this respect, as it made the approach from the south even longer. In the case of Kaupang, the harbour basin did become somewhat shallower during the town's existence, but the tenth-century depth of 2–5 m was fully sufficient for the ships at that time. For Kaupang and Birka, probably also for Ribe and Hedeby, one must seek other reasons for the abandonment than those caused by nature.

Continuity and discontinuity in urban communities are complex phenomena which need to be explained from a variety of approaches, some connected to the individual town, some to the fundamental social and political structures of society. Of course changes in trade routes and production lead to towns emerging and declining. More importantly, though, the existence and growth of towns always depended on the power structures of society. For trade and craft to flourish, peace and safety must be guaranteed. If not, producers will not settle in town, traders will not bring their goods there and buyers will not bring silver to buy them. Not only did the town need someone to defend it from attacks and plunder, but people also needed to know that disputes would be fairly settled and that someone would see that buying and selling would take place according to the law (Skre 2007b).

In the early Viking Age political power was less institutionalised; it depended more on the personalities of the powerful, their charisma, their skill and luck in war and politics, and their ability to attract important and powerful friends and allies. Therefore control over land and people was rather unstable; a dynasty rarely kept in control for more than a few generations. In the later Viking Age the political structure had changed; the three Scandinavian kingdoms were more or less established. Royal power now depended more on law and institutions and less on the personality of the king. This difference is probably one of the main reasons for the instability of the towns of the early Viking Age and the stability of the towns established in the late Viking Age.

However, there is obviously more to it. There is another type of discontinuity in the late Viking Age: the old rural places of power, commonly called central places (see below), all met their end. In some cases, most pronounced in Lejre–Roskilde and Uppåkra–Lund, a town with central royal and ecclesiastical functions was established in the vicinity around the time when the central place was abandoned. It is the new and strong connection between king and Church which might hold a key to understanding the discontinuity both in towns and in central places around the turn of the millennium. A general conversion to Christianity took place at this time. The Church and the kingdoms entered into a mutually beneficial alliance. The alliance built on the old pagan connection between cultic and secular power now gained a much stronger base as the Church was an international institution with a staff skilled in law, writing and intellectual reasoning (Skre 1998).

To some extent there must have been a sentiment among people, chieftains and kings in the final decades of the Viking Age that a new era had begun. The lack of continuity not only in town and central places might indicate that kings had wanted to put a distance between themselves and the centres of the old society. The vast number of churches and clerical institutions in the major towns of the late Viking Age might indicate that this was the case. To move a town was after all not such a big undertaking; the investment in buildings and infrastructure was very low compared to the masonry churches, monasteries and castles which sprung up in towns in the centuries following the Viking Age. These buildings are the visible sign that towns now filled a wider purpose. While kings and chieftains in earlier times resided on their aristocratic manors, they now moved their household and following into the towns, where they also installed their new ally, the Church. This meant a profound change in the inner life of the new towns compared to the old ones, and in the functions towns had in the overall society. They became more like towns of our own times; they became seats of power.

THE NON-URBAN PLACES OF TRADE AND CRAFT

Before the Viking Age, the typical urban activities of the period – craft production and exchange of goods – took place in a rural context only. From the first millennium AD traces of such activities are found most abundantly in large complexes called central places (e.g. Uppåkra, Tissø, Lejre, Gudme). The full nature of several of these sites is yet unknown, as the task of excavating their deep and complex deposits and analysing their character and development is so overwhelming. ~~Apparently they are first and foremost aristocratic manors with more or less distinct traces of cultic activities, craft, trade, and houses for people attached to the aristocratic household.~~ However, during the long period in which many of them existed, in the case of Uppåkra a whole millennium, there are bound to have been some major changes in their size and functions, about which we as yet know rather little. Many of these central places continued to flourish until the end of the Viking Age.

~~Seasonal marketplaces with archaeological remains of craft and trade were connected to several central places. The archaeological remains of these marketplaces are distinctly different from the four urban sites mentioned. While the objects found are much the same, although with a lower number of items of long-distance trade, there are no remains of permanent buildings. These contrasts to the towns proper speak clearly about the main difference between them – the town formed a separate community organised in a specific way, while the marketplace had only seasonal gatherings of people.~~ Between the gatherings the aristocratic household and its warriors, staff and slaves made up the local community on the manor nearby. Neither in organisation nor in their permanent activities did the central places have an urban character.

Seasonal marketplaces are also found at locations that seem more or less independent of central places. Some are large (Sebbersund, Fröjel), while others, hitherto mostly found in Gotland and Denmark, are very small: only a few pit-houses and scant finds (Carlsson 1991; Ulriksen 1998). The earliest occur in the Roman period (see Thomsen *et al.* 1993; Nielsen *et al.* 1994), but they are more numerous in the Viking Age.

~~Of the four towns only Ribe seems to have developed from a seasonal marketplace.~~ The other three seem to have been founded on virgin land. (The character of the eighth-century Südsiedlung and its relation to Hedeby remains to be fully explored.) Due to only small areas having been excavated, many details of the settling of each town are unknown. Excavations have demonstrated that there has been a period of seasonal activity before people settled permanently there, at Kaupang less than ten years. Nevertheless, the towns were from the start distinctly different from the seasonal markets. The area that developed into a town within a few years was from the earliest period organised in a different way from the marketplaces.

~~Therefore it seems evident that those who organised the towns from the start had a clear idea that they wanted to form a specific type of settlement – a permanent community, not a seasonal marketplace.~~ This demonstrates that from the earliest Viking Age there existed in Scandinavia an idea of what an urban community was and how to organise it. The roots of these ideas are to be found in the Carolingian Empire and England, possibly also in the Slavonic communities along the Baltic coast. But the ideas were from early on adapted to conditions and demands typical of Scandinavia.

THE SCANDINAVIAN VIKING AGE TOWN

~~It is evident that the towns of the Viking Age were *created* and not self-grown communities.~~ Who created them? From the evidence it is clear that kings and petty kings were instrumental in the initial phase. The evidence from Ribe is meagre, although the probable mint in the town from the early eighth century onwards points to a royal connection. On Birka's neighbouring island lies Alsnöhus, the royal manor. *Vita Ansgarii*, which describes the German missionary Ansgar's travels to Birka in 829–30 and 851–2, mentions a royal bailiff in the town. On what was probably the petty king's farm with the name Skiringssal, now Huseby close to Kaupang, the remains of an aristocratic hall have been excavated. The connection between the Danish king and the foundation of Hedeby is testified in the Royal Frankish Annals.

The urban community differed from the rural in many aspects. One of them was their need for separate legislation. The laws for towns and trade in the twelfth century onwards are called *Bjarkøyrett*, literally 'Birka law', in all three Scandinavian countries. There is little doubt that the name refers to the Swedish Viking Age town. The name tells us that the development of legislation for this kind of community started there, probably due to it being the earliest of the four towns. The laws were then transferred, altered and added to in the other towns of the Viking Age and later. The physical borders of the town marked the area within which the law applied. The shallow ditch surrounding Ribe from the early ninth century (Feveile 2006: 43–5) could be an example of this legislative border, possibly connected to the marketplace being converted into a town a few years earlier.

The earliest known version of the *Bjarkøyrett* is no older than the mid-thirteenth century (Hagland and Sandnes 1997) and therefore it is impossible to reconstruct the Viking Age town law in detail. However, by drawing on information in *Vita Ansgarii* some general themes in the early law may be identified. It seems likely that the towns in the first half of the ninth century were under royal administration through the bailiff and that they had their own thing assembly. One of the original tasks of the bailiff may have been to collect the land rent from each household as described in the earliest versions of the law. In the thirteenth-century version the thing assembly gathered to solve conflicts and convict the guilty in certain types of crimes. This may have been the case in the Viking Age as well.

PLOTS, STREETS AND HOUSES

Town plans may be read as a manifestation of the ideas the founders had about what an urban community was and how it should function. The administration of rights to land, the maintenance of communal installations such as jetties and streets, the normal resident's need for space and water, the transport of people and goods within, to and from the town: all of these and many more factors had to be taken into account and realised according to the topographical conditions which each site offered. Some standard solutions to these challenges were developed and a few of them will be described in the following.

From the beginning the town area was divided up into plots, streets, etc. As only a small percentage of each town is excavated, the extent of this original plot division and the number and sizes of later extensions are unknown. However, in at least some of the towns, especially Hedeby, which grew significantly in the tenth century, the town area must have been extended, probably on several occasions.

In Ribe the main focus of activity was the street running through the town, parallel to the river lying at least 40 m further to the south-west. The plots lay on each side of this street, with their shorter end, 6–8 m long, towards it. The finds show that craft and trade were focused on the part of the plot lying along the street, while the back of the plots, extending some 20–30 m off the street, was used for dumping refuse. The town area comprised forty to fifty plots and covered about 1 hectares.

The Ribe plots were established at the beginning of the marketplace period and were basically the same after it was converted into a town. Birka was founded with a somewhat different structure. The main focus here was the harbour. The streets run either parallel to the shoreline or at a right angle to it. The plots have their short end towards the harbour, they have the same width as the Ribe ones; but they are less than half as deep. At its largest Birka covered *c.* 6 hectares and must have had well over 100 plots.

In the two towns established in the early 800s, Kaupang and Hedeby, the structure is much the same as in Birka. Both are focused on the harbour, and the system of streets has the same alignment as Birka's. All the six excavated plots in Kaupang have their short end towards the harbour. In Hedeby the same general rule applies but with some deviations, possibly due to larger surfaces being excavated and therefore more details known. Plots in Kaupang and Hedeby have about the same size as in Birka. Kaupang was in total somewhat smaller than Birka, about 5.4 hectares and 90–100 plots, while Hedeby was the largest town covering *c.* 24 hectares.

The focus on the street rather than the harbour in Ribe is probably an element borrowed from Frisian settlements of the period (Jensen 2004: 243). By the time plots and streets in Birka were laid out the idea of town organisation had changed somewhat. Birka, Kaupang and Hedeby all have their focus on the harbour, probably reflecting the Scandinavian emphasis on seafaring and seaways transport at the time. There is great stability in the width and alignment of plots, as these elements remained nearly unaltered from the laying out of Ribe onwards. The depth of plots was reduced after Ribe, probably as a consequence of more congested space due to several parallel rows of plots being laid out in the other towns. In each town the system of plots and main streets was established from the start and was thereafter rarely altered, although extensions may have taken place.

This rather uniform layout of streets and size of plots differ from what is seen elsewhere in northern Europe during this period. The fact that the same principles were applied when the Scandinavians established their urban communities in York and Dublin later in the ninth century supports the idea that we are faced with a specific Scandinavian way to organise towns.

As mentioned, the settling of each town took some time and initially many plots were uninhabited. In Kaupang one of the six plots excavated in 2000–2 proved never to have had a house; it was probably kept as a pigsty, at least in the first half of the ninth century, which is the period from which the remains of houses etc. were preserved (Pilø 2007). In Birka one of the excavated plots, which used to house a bronzeworker's workshop, was uninhabited for some years, possibly decades, before a new house was built there. But the normal thing in all towns seems to have been that each plot had one building on it, although in Hedeby there was sometimes in addition a shed. Normally, the houses, all of them built of wood, had the same alignment as the elongated plots.

The excavated houses vary somewhat in construction, size and function but are nevertheless, as far as we know them, surprisingly uniform. As only trenches have been excavated in Ribe we know little about houses there. In the three other towns houses are generally about 4–5 m wide and 6–12 m long. In the excavated Hedeby and Birka houses the walls normally carried the roof; in some Kaupang houses it was supported by freestanding posts within the house. Such houses have also been found in the outskirts of Birka. Both construction principles are common in rural settlements of the time, although the rural houses are normally larger.

Also the interior arrangements of houses are common in rural settlements of the time. An open hearth was built on the floor in the central axis of the building, normally in the middle of the main room. A hearth has been found in the corner of a house in Birka. Many houses have permanent benches along the long walls for sitting, working and sleeping. Earthen floors were common although a plank floor has been found at Birka. Many houses seem to be pure dwelling houses and so far few workshops have been securely identified. One exception is the bronze caster's workshop in Birka. In Ribe and Hedeby pit-houses have been found. In Hedeby they seem to be most numerous in the blacksmiths' area of town.

The layout of streets follows the same general pattern in the towns of the late Viking Age, but the plots are normally more spacious. They give room for several houses with a variety of functions probably reflecting the growing diversity in activities and inhabitants in the towns. When the kings' men and wealthy landowners started settling in towns they obviously needed more spacious plots for themselves, their people and their possessions. However, it took time for the new towns to develop this character. It is not until the late eleventh and twelfth centuries that the largest of the new towns reach the size of the towns of the early Viking Age. Most cathedrals, monasteries and royal or clerical residences were built in the twelfth and thirteenth centuries.

CRAFT AND TRADE

Although trade and craft also existed before the Viking Age the urban environment seems to have influenced their character. Craft products became more standardised at the time when the producers moved into newly established towns. Series of identical items, especially bronze brooches and combs, were produced. In earlier times, when these crafts existed in rural communities, they mostly produced unique items, although grouped around certain main types (Callmer 1995).

This probably reflects a change from producing mainly on commission to individuals, to producing identical items for unknown customers in a market-like trade. There can be little doubt what triggered this change. In the towns, sufficiently sized and stable markets were established for this new type of production to be tenable. The higher quantity of buyers is reflected in the fact that many craft products were now much more widely distributed; not only local people came to buy them as was the case in the older seasonal marketplaces. It is also evident that many craft products, such as bronze ornaments and glass beads, were now obtainable for a much wider spectrum of the population than was the case before the Viking Age.

In addition to the crafts already mentioned, remains from ironwork, glass-bead and textile production have been found in all towns. In Hedeby remains from the work of goldsmiths have been identified, and in Ribe the comb-maker, shoe-maker, potter and amber smith have left their traces. The last type of craft was also exercised at Kaupang. One should bear in mind that some crafts, like bead-making and metal casting, leave many and very durable traces, while the remains from others, like carpentry and comb-making, depend on the soil's chemistry and humidity for their survival to the present day. Thus the scope of crafts exercised in each town was certainly broader than archaeologists at present are able to identify. For the same reasons, and because of limited excavations, the volume of the various craft activities is difficult to ascertain.

Several of these crafts demanded highly skilled practitioners and this skill and knowledge was passed on and developed through generations. Although local variations existed, advances in one part of Scandinavia were taken up elsewhere quite swiftly. Sufficiently dense and well-organised networks must have existed within several crafts. To maintain quality and pass on skills in certain crafts, for instance metal casting, well-organised and long-lasting workshops must have existed in several of the towns. The excavation of one such workshop at Birka supports this assumption. Nevertheless, the products demonstrate that skills varied considerably. It is a fact that the quality of glass beads produced in Scandinavia fell rather dramatically from the eighth to the ninth century, never to regain its former level.

Also the character of trade was altered during the early Viking Age and the towns undoubtedly played an important role in this development. To track down these changes it is more illuminating to use the common term *exchange* for the various types of transactions that took place in this period and before (Skre 2001, 2007b). *Trade*, in the sense that one acquires goods with the intention of selling them for a better price, probably also took place, but it hardly dominated the exchange of goods. Trade in this sense was probably mostly performed by people who transported the goods from their areas of origin to markets and towns elsewhere. These goods may have been acquired in different types of exchange, also as gift, tribute, tax or by sheer plunder. In addition, and this may have been the more common type of transaction in towns, craftsmen and other kinds of producers bartered their products to acquire things they needed. Or they may have sold them for silver for which they could buy goods, pay fees, etc.

One given item may have undergone several types of exchange on its way from the producer to its final consumer. The fur trade, in which Birka and possibly other Viking Age towns were heavily engaged, must have involved a variety of exchange types. One would assume that agents for the local aristocracy obtained fur from the hunters, possibly including Sámi, through barter or tribute close to the hunting grounds. The furs were then brought to Birka, probably through channels controlled by the same aristocracy. In Birka the fur was processed, including the cutting off of paws; hence the numerous paw bones from squirrel, marten and fox, even the odd one from bear, found there. Then most of the furs were probably sold in Birka, possibly for silver, and transported further afar for resale or use. This kind of product may also have served as gifts among aristocratic friends and allies.

Although all of these types of exchange existed throughout the period, their relative importance shifted dramatically. By the end of the Viking Age paying with silver made up a much higher proportion of transactions than at the start (Hårdh 1996; Gustin 2004). The towns seem to have been leading this development. In the late tenth century a regular bullion economy existed in south and central Scandinavia. In the eleventh century payment with unminted silver gradually disappeared as coins took over as the dominating means of payment. However, in the tenth century cut-up pieces of Arab silver coins, ingots and ornaments are commonly found in hoards, towns and market-places. At the beginning of the century they are found most frequently in parts of Scandinavia with towns from the same period. Cut-up pieces of silver are much rarer in the ninth century, but excavations in the towns have yielded some, particularly from the second half of the century. At this early stage the majority of the silver fragments weigh less than 2 g, indicating that silver was used in everyday transactions involving items of modest value.

This development is mirrored in changes in weighing equipment. The earliest Viking Age weights were rather imprecise and many local standards seem to have existed. Their shape and material, cylindrical lead weights dominating, made them easy to tamper with, which did not promote trust between trading partners. Around 860/70 a new type and standard of much more reliable bronze weights were introduced in southern and eastern Scandinavia. One would expect that the increased trustworthiness of weights facilitated trade and contributed to the strong growth in exchange where silver was used as a means of payment (Steuer 1997; Gustin 2004).

The need for a trusted means of payment was one of the reasons for the shift to coinage in the final decades of the Viking Age. The trust in the king as a ruler and peacekeeper was extended into the economic sphere and made operational there. One may say that the development in the means of exchange from local weight systems to royal coinage mirrors the fundamental changes that took place in the Scandinavian societies during the Viking Age. The towns were important arenas for the economic, social and political driving forces in this development.

BIBLIOGRAPHY

Andrén, A. (1989) 'State and towns in the Middle Ages: the Scandinavian experience', *Theory and Society*, 18: 585–609.

Callmer, J. (1994) 'Urbanization in Scandinavia and the Baltic region *c.* AD 700–1100: trading places, centres and early urban sites', in B. Ambrosiani and H. Clark (eds) *Development around the Baltic and the North Sea in the Viking Age* (Birka Studies 3), Stockholm: Birka Project, Raä and Statens historiska museum.

—— (1995) 'Hantverksproduktion, samhällsförändringar och bebyggelse. Iakttagelser från östra Sydskandinavien ca. 600–1100 e.Kr', in H. Gjøstein Resi (ed.) *Produksjon og samfunn. Om erverv, spesialisering og bosetning i Norden i 1. årtusen e.Kr.* (Universitetets Oldsaksamling Varia 30), Oslo: Universitetets Oldsaksamling.

Carlsson, D. (1991) 'Harbours and trading places on Gotland AD 600–1000', in O. Crumlin Pedersen (ed.) *Aspects of Maritime Scandinavia AD 200–1200*, Roskilde: Vikingeskibshallen.

Clarke, H. and Ambrosiani, B. (1995) *Towns in the Viking Age*, 2nd rev. edn, London and New York: Leicester University Press.

Feveile, C. (ed.) (2006) *Det ældste Ribe. Udgravninger på nordsiden af Ribe Å 1984–2000* (Ribe Studier 1:1), Højbjerg: Jysk Arkæologisk Selskab.

Gustin, I. (2004) *Mellan gåva och marknad. Handel, tillit och materiell kultur under vikingatid* (Lund Studies in Medieval Archaeology 34), Stockholm: Almqvist & Wiksell.

Hagland, J.R. and Sandnes, J. (1997) *Bjarkøyretten. Nidaros eldste bylov*, Oslo: Det Norske Samlaget.

Hårdh, B. (1996) *Silver in the Viking Age. A Regional-economic Study* (Acta Archaeologica Lundensia 25), Stockholm: Almqvist & Wiksell.

Jensen, J. (2004) *Danmarks Oldtid*, [vol. 4]: *Yngre Jernalder og Vikingetid 400 e.Kr–1050 e.Kr.*, Copenhagen: Gyldendal.

Nielsen, P.O., Randsborg, K. and Thrane, H. (eds) (1994) *The Archaeology of Gudme and Lundeborg. Papers Presented at a Conference at Svendborg, October 1991* (Arkæologiske Studier 10), Copenhagen: Akademisk forlag.

Palliser, D.M. (ed.) (2000) *The Cambridge Urban History of Britain*, vol. 1: *600–1540*. Cambridge: Cambridge University Press.

Pilø, L. (2007) 'The settlement: character, structures and features', in D. Skre (ed.) 2007a.

Reynolds, S. (1977) *An Introduction to the History of English Medieval Towns*, Oxford: Clarendon Press.

Skre, D. (1998) 'Missionary activity in early medieval Norway: strategy, organisation and the course of events', *Scandinavian Journal of History*, 23: 1–19.

—— (2001) 'Kaupang – et handelssted? Om handel og annen vareutveksling i vikingtid', *Collegium Medievale*, 13: 165–76.

—— (ed.) (2007a) *Kaupang in Skiringssal* (Kaupang Excavation Project Publication Series 1), Aarhus: Aarhus University Press.

—— (2007b) 'Towns and markets, kings and central places in south-western Scandinavia *c.* AD 800–950', in D. Skre (ed.) (2007a).

—— (2007c) 'Excavations of the hall at Huseby', in D. Skre (ed.) (2007a).

Steuer, H. (1997) *Waagen und Gewichte aus dem mittelalterlichen Schleswig. Funde des 11. bis 13. Jahrhunderts aus Europa als Quellen zur Handels- und Währungsgeschichte* (Zeitschrift für Archäologie des Mittalters, Beihefte 10), Cologne: Rheinland Vlg & Bonn: Habelt.

Thomsen, P.O., Blæsild, B., Hardt, N. and Kjer Michaelsen, K. (1993) *Lundeborg. En handelsplads fra jernalderen*, (Skrifter fra Svendborg og Omegns museum 32), second edn, Svendborg: Svendborg og Omegns museum.

Ulriksen, J. (1998) *Anløbspladser. Besejling og bebyggelse i Danmark mellem 200 og 1100 e. Kr. En studie af søfartens pladser på baggrund af undersøgelser i Roskilde Fjord*, Roskilde: Vikingeskibshallen.

BIRKA

——·◆·——

Björn Ambrosiani

In the eighth century AD, while Charlemagne still relied on traditions linked to the Roman Empire, western Europe slowly began to distance itself from the ancient world. Increasing economic, political and religious activity led to broader political contacts and emerging trade alliances outside the boundaries of the old empire (McCormick 2001). Two important centres on the routes of travel across the Northern Sea, soon to include the Baltic Sea area, were Quentowic and Dorestad (Clarke and Ambrosiani 1991).

Several places for trade and early towns were established within a broad network as bases for actively collecting raw materials, for example slaves and furs, particularly attractive commodities at the new royal courts and in the towns across the whole of western Europe.

One such place was *Birka*, established on a small island in a bay of the Baltic Sea (Figures 8.1.1 and 8.1.2). Today this island lies in Lake Mälaren *c.* 30 km west of Stockholm in eastern central Sweden. Birka is one of Sweden's most prominent archaeological sites, where archaeological investigations have been carried out at various locations since the 1870s. Birka's finds create the framework for understanding Viking Age chronology in Sweden. Recent excavations have focused on questions concerning the overall structure of the town and contacts between Birka and the greater north European area. The sizeable complex of Birka and the royal manor of Alsnöhus was added to UNESCO's World Heritage List in 1993.

THE TOWN

Eighth-century Birka lay on an island only a few kilometres in size, and in an area still today heavily influenced by land uplift. The political power behind Birka's establishment lay at Alsnöhus on the neighbouring island of Adelsö. Birka's town site, the Black Earth, covers an area of *c.* 5–6 ha and is surrounded by the remains of a complex defence system: a town rampart, an underwater palisade and a hill fort. Extensive cemeteries contain altogether *c.* 2,000 grave mounds and many unmarked inhumation graves which occupy considerable parts of the early island area (Ambrosiani 1992).

Figure 8.1.1   Birka is situated on an island in the Lake Mälaren bay, Björkfjärden, along the route between the Baltic Sea and Uppsala, the centre of the Svear kingdom in prehistoric and medieval times. The royal estate on Adelsö is visible in the foreground. (Photo © Björn Ambrosiani.)

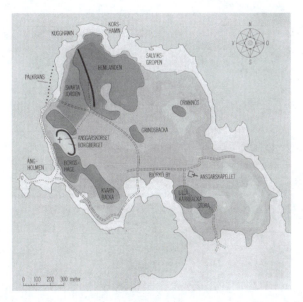

Figure 8.1.2   Map of Birka's town area. The black earth area is protected by a defense construction, the hillfort Borg and the town rampart. By and outside of these lay its cemeteries, of which Hemlanden is the largest with ca. 1600 visible barrows. Coffin- and chamber graves, today lacking visible constructions above the ground, are concentrated to areas closest to the town.
(Map by Bernt Forsblad © The Birka Project.)

Archbishop Rimbert mentions Birka in his ninth-century account, *Vita Ansgarii*, as the place of the first Christian mission to the Svea kingdom (Odelman 1986). Extensive archaeological excavations were initiated by Hjalmar Stolpe in the 1870s, one in the circle of scholars, including Oscar Montelius and Hans Hildebrand, employed by the Museum of National Antiquities (SHM) in Stockholm. Stolpe excavated altogether *c.* 4,500 m² of the Black Earth area (Hyenstrand 1992) and *c.* 1,100 graves (Arbman 1940–3; Arwidsson 1984–9).

The main settlement area was located in a depression adjacent to the water, with several longhouse terraces situated on a slope above the town. Shoreline-bound plots were separated by ditches and later also wooden fences in a fan-shaped pattern following the bay's natural shape. The often rebuilt buildings, primarily of wood with wood or reed roofs, were situated with their gables facing the water (*Birka Studies* forthcoming).

In 1990–5 the Black Earth excavations uncovered part of the mid-eighth-century shoreline, 6 m above present sea level, and the stone foundation of an early jetty from Birka's earliest settlement along with the remains of a bronzeworker's workshop (Figure 8.1.3). This part of the earliest settlement was shore bound until the end of the 700s. Successive changes in land uplift in conjunction with the retreating shoreline exposed new areas for settlement and necessitated the construction of new jetties at lower levels. The workshop ceasing to exist shortly after the mid-800s, its plot was rebuilt after several decades of abandonment. Situated opposite to this and adjacent to the lane leading down to the later jetty, another plot yielded the remains of houses belonging to

Figure 8.1.3   The large stone jetty resting on Birka's original shoreline, allowing for isostatic and eustatistic changes, is situated at ca. 6 m a.s.l., showing that the town must have been established prior to or at about 750 AD. (Photo © Björn Ambrosiani.)

merchants whose contacts reached far to the east: to the Rus', the Khazars, Byzantium and the eastern Caliphate (Ambrosiani 2001).

These Black Earth excavations yielded very rich settlement finds, including workshop products and objects of trade. All of the houses showed evidence of household activities and textile production: spinning, weaving, and the production of fine thread and high-quality fabrics (Andersson 2003). Furs were also produced (Wigh 1998, 2002), as well as combs and glass beads along with cast bronze objects.

DEFENCE

The town Birka was long believed to have been undefended, its earliest recognised built defence being the hill fort Borg. Today an earlier system of ninth-century ramparts is known to have existed, the larger part of which was successively covered by the expanding town. The rampart, still visible today, probably dates to the tenth century at the earliest, and the chronology of Borg has not yet been fully established. Recent excavations have focused on an area outside and adjacent to Borg where evidence of a strong, mainly tenth-century military presence has been uncovered. Terraces with the remains of several generations of longhouses and finds linking to a male, armed presence include sacrifices to the war god *Óðinn* (Holmquist Olausson and Kitzler Åhlfeldt 2002). Comparable finds have not been made in the hill fort itself, where instead graves from *c.* AD 800 lie superficially situated inside its rampart (Arbman 1940–3: 127–31).

GRAVES

Characteristic of Birka are its richly equipped graves (Arbman 1940–3; Gräslund 1980; Arwidsson 1984–9) of which *c.* 1,100 were investigated by H. Stolpe. With altogether *c.* 2,000 mounds, Birka's prehistoric cemeteries are among the largest in Sweden, the majority of the visible barrows covering cremation layers particularly characteristic for the Mälar Basin area in the Viking Age.

Unusual grave traditions for eastern central Sweden at this time are the unmarked wooden coffin and chamber graves, lying in an area inside the later town rampart and the hill fort. Regarding dress and lifestyle, these show links mainly to local traditions. Both men and women were buried fully dressed with jewellery, weapons and tools, but many of these graves also include objects from distant sources. They may have been imported objects available at the local market or as part of the personal belongings brought to Birka by merchants and craftsmen from their own respective home regions.

CHRONOLOGY

The finds from Birka's graves form an important basis for understanding Viking Age chronology, but finds recently uncovered in the bronzeworker's workshop have complicated this picture. Objects dated as deposited in the 900s can be directly linked to the workshop's moulds dating to the early 800s (Ambrosiani and Erikson 1992, 1996). The relationship between production and deposition, of objects in the Black Earth and the grave contexts at Birka, is a central question for future discussion with implications for the chronology of Birka's monuments, but which generally influence Viking Age chronology in various ways.

Several early 'Viking Age motifs' can be shown to have been produced before AD 800, showing that several 'Viking Age' phenomena considerably predate the earliest Viking raids in western Europe in the 790s. This is also seen at Staraya Ladoga and Ribe, implying that the chronological boundary of the Vendel period and the early Viking Age, based on such material expressions, must be reconsidered as they existed already decades earlier (Ambrosiani 1998a). This suggests that as a place for trade Birka existed around the mid-700s at the latest.

In the 970s Birka ceased to exist: artefacts and silver hoards with Arabic coins suggest that Birka still existed *c*. AD 970, but Anglo-Saxon coinage from the 980s and domestic Sigtuna coinage from the 990s are lacking. Birka's disappearance may have been linked to the reorientation of water routes and the use of larger ships. The transition to Sigtuna, where settlement appears to emerge at approximately the same time, has been debated on the one hand as representing a societal change and on the other as purely a relocation of function. If caused by the need for technically better water routes, the latter is more probable.

HINTERLAND

Birka lay at the heart of a considerable hinterland, the area of the Svear: a primarily agrarian area, with good mineral resources and wild game in areas beyond, all of primary importance to the activities at Birka. From this area, produce, fuel and raw materials were delivered to Birka, and, in turn, Birka supplied the hinterland with simple pieces of jewellery, tools and implements. These appear in the many grave finds, until *c*. AD 1000 as traditional cremations covered by a barrow, containing men and women with complete dress equipment (Ambrosiani 1998b).

Birka's products appear in many distant places throughout northern Scandinavia, showing the economic role of furs in the town's trade. This is seen in the thousands of paw bones from squirrels, marten and fox which have been found in Birka's Black Earth, evidence that the skins of wild animals were prepared at Birka for export (Wigh 2002: 120–3).

More difficult to understand is the production of metal, including probably both iron and silver, perhaps copper as well, won from sources within a radius of 200 km from Birka. Also in this respect, Birka could have been an important centre for collecting such regional production (Ambrosiani 1997c).

THE BALTIC SEA REGION AND BEYOND

Birka's contacts with other places for trade/towns near the Baltic Sea were extensive. West Slavonic pottery, amber from East Prussia, soapstone and whalebone from present-day Norway and probably special produce such as honey and salt from the west Slavonic area were important items of trade throughout this interregional network where handicraft production was amazingly similar (Ambrosiani 1997a, b).

Birka's early contacts were directed towards the south-west: to Denmark and the Rhineland. Very few objects have an eastern origin: some Ladoga-type pottery, perhaps the evidence of regional contacts with contemporary Staraya Ladoga (Bäck forthcoming). This situation changes at the end of the 800s: western contacts seem to be replaced by contacts towards the east (Ambrosiani 2001, 2002). This is simultaneous with the appearance of the Rus' and the earliest Scandinavian settlement in western Russia and the Ukraine (Jansson 1997), which were used in establishing direct contact with Byzantium and the eastern Caliphate.

Quantities of silks and silver were thus spread, and Scandinavia created its own weight-based economic system grounded in an Arabian weight standard, apparently though with locally manufactured instruments for weighing (Ambrosiani 2001; Gustin 2004; Sperber 2004). Many phenomena associated with this appear at Birka early in this development, which implies Birka's leading position in Northern Europe.

SUMMARY

Birka can be characterised as a complex early urban society with a diverse mix of local and supra-regional backgrounds: its economy based on trade and handicraft and as part of a contact network spanning the whole of northern Europe first turned towards the south-west and later towards the east. Through this, Birka's society bound together local and outside worlds, which it influenced and was influenced by the changes therein. Today Birka's rich finds are an important key to greater insight into Viking Age chronology and this northern European network of contacts and, therefore, also important to west European archaeology.

BIBLIOGRAPHY

Ambrosiani, B. (1992) 'What is Birka?', in B. Ambrosiani and H. Clarke (eds) (1992).

—— (1997a) 'Birka – stad i nätverk', in *Amico Amici, Festskrift till Gad Rausing den 19 maj 1997*, Lund: Signum.

—— (1997b) 'Birka – part of a network', in G. de Boe and F. Verhaeghe (eds) *Exchange and Trade in Medieval Europe* (Medieval Europe Brugge 1997, vol. 3), Zellik-Asse: Instituut voor het archeologisch patrimonium.

—— (1997c) 'Metallförsörjning i Birka', in A. Åkerlund, S. Bergh, J. Nordbladh and J. Taffinder (eds) *Till Gunborg. Arkeologiska samtal* (Stockholm Archaeological Reports 33), Stockholm: Dept. of Archaeology, University of Stockholm.

—— (1998a) 'Ireland and Scandinavia in the early Viking Age: an archaeological response', in H.B. Clarke, M. Ní Mhaonaigh and R. Ò Floinn (eds) *Ireland and Scandinavia in the Early Viking Age*, Dublin: Four Courts Press.

—— (1998b) 'Birka och omlandet', in P. Bratt (ed.) *Forntid i ny dager*, Stockholm: Raster Förlag and Stockholms Länsmuseum.

—— (2001) 'Eastern connections at Birka', *Viking Heritage Magazine*, 2001(3): 3–7.

—— (2002) 'Osten und Westen im Ostseehandel zur Wikingerzeit', in K. Brandt, M. Müller-Wille and Chr. Radtke (eds) *Haithabu und die frühe Stadtentwicklung im nördlichen Europa* (Schriften des Archäologischen Landesmuseums 8), Neumünster: Wachholtz.

Ambrosiani, B. and Clarke, H. (eds) (1992) *Investigations in the black earth*, vol. 1: *Early investigations and future plans* (Birka Studies 1), Stockholm: Birka Project, Raä and Statens historiska museer.

Ambrosiani, B. and Erikson, B.G. (1991–6) *Birka vikingastaden*, 5 vols, Höganäs and Stockholm: Bra Böcker and Sveriges Radios Förlag.

Andersson, E. (2003) *Tools for Textile Production from Birka and Hedeby* (Birka Studies 8), Stockholm: Birka Project and Raä.

Arbman, H. (1940–3) *Birka*, vol. 1: *Die Gräber*, Stockholm: KVHAA.

Arwidsson, G. (ed.) (1984–9) *Birka*, vol. 2: 1–3, Stockholm: KVHAA.

Bäck, M. (forthcoming) *Eastern Pottery in Birka* (Birka Studies), Stockholm: Birka Project and Raä.

Birka Studies (1992–), 4 vols, ed. B. Ambrosiani and H. Clarke, vols 5– ed. B. Ambrosiani, Stockholm: Birka Project and Raä.

Clarke, H. and Ambrosiani, B. (1991) *Towns in the Viking Age*, Leicester: Leicester University Press.

Gräslund, A.-S. (1980) *The Burial Customs. A Study of the Graves on Björkö* (Birka 4), Stockholm: KVHAA.

Gustin, I. (2004) *Mellan gåva och marknad* (Lund Studies in Medieval Archaeology 34), Stockholm: Almqvist & Wiksell International.

Holmquist Olausson, L. (1990) ' "Älgmannen" från Birka. Presentation av en nyligen undersökt krigargrav med människooffer', *Fornvännen*, 85: 175–82.

Holmquist Olausson, L. and Kitzler Åhfeldt, L. (2002) *Krigarnas hus. Arkeologisk undersökning av ett hallhus i Birkas Garnison* (Borgar och Befästningsverk i Mellansverige 400–1100 e.Kr. Rapport 4), Stockholm: Arkeologiska Forskningslaboratoriet, University of Stockholm.

Hyenstrand, E. (1992) 'Early discoveries in the Black Earth', in B. Ambrosiani and H. Clarke (eds) (1992).

Jansson, I. (1997) 'Warfare, trade or colonisation? Some general remarks on the eastern expansion of the Scandinavians in the Viking period', in P. Hansson (ed.) *The Rural Viking in Russia and Sweden*, Örebro: Örebro kommuns bildningsförvaltning.

McCormick, M. (2001) *Origins of the European Economy. Communications and Commerce, AD 300–900*, Cambridge: Cambridge University Press.

Odelman, E. (trans.) (1986) 'Ansgars liv', in *Boken om Ansgar* (Skrifter utgivna av Samfundet Pro fide et christianismo 10), Stockholm: Proprius.

Sperber, E. (2004) 'Metrology of the weights from the Birka excavations 1990–1995', in B. Ambrosiani (ed.) *Eastern Connections. Excavations in the Black Earth 1990–1995*, vol. 2: *Numismatics and Metrology* (Birka Studies 6), Stockholm: Birka Project and Raä.

Vita Anskarii. Accedit vita Rimberti, recensuit G. Waitz (Monumenta Germaniae historica. Scriptores rerum Germanicarum in usum scholarum separatim editi 55), Hannover: Hahn 1884 (reprint 1988).

Wigh, B. (1998) 'The animal bones from the Viking town of Birka', in E. Cameron (ed.) *Leather and Fur. Aspects of Early Medieval Trade and Technology*, London: Archetype Publications for the Archaeological Leather Group.

—— (2002) *Animal Husbandry in the Viking Age Town of Birka and its Hinterland* (Birka Studies 7), Stockholm: Birka Project and Raä.

CHAPTER EIGHT (2)

HEDEBY: AN OUTLINE OF ITS RESEARCH HISTORY

——·◆·——

Volker Hilberg

The Viking Age emporium of Hedeby is situated at the narrowest part of the Cimbrian peninsula near the Danevirke, which functioned as the Danish border to the south in the Middle Ages. Accessible from both the west and the east, Hedeby possessed a key position in connecting the trading systems of the North Sea to the Baltic Basin. The place is known from written records since 804 and developed in the ninth century to become the leading emporium or proto-town of the Danish kingdom until its final destruction in 1066. Its functions and political role were transferred to Schleswig/Slesvig on the other side of the Schlei/Slie fjord. Hedeby itself is well known for its extensive archaeological research done by German archaeologists since 1900.

EXCAVATIONS AT HEDEBY, 1900–80

In 1897 Sophus Müller, from the National Museum in Copenhagen, had identified an area of *c.* 27 ha inside a huge and well-preserved semicircular rampart at the western side of the Haddebyer Noor, an inlet of the Schlei, with the place mentioned on Viking Age runic inscriptions found nearby as Hedeby (Figure 8.2.1) (Müller 1897: 636–42 figs 395–6). To strengthen his identification small-scale excavation trenches all over this area were started in 1900 (Stark 1988). In the following years, until 1915 and once again in 1921, over 350 small trenches were opened by Wilhelm Splieth and Friedrich Knorr from the Museum für Vaterländische Altertümer in Kiel revealing parts of the emporium. Also *c.* 500–700 inhumation graves from a huge cemetery inside the rampart were excavated between 1902 and 1912; the exact number is very difficult to say because of several superpositions and destructions from younger, overlying settlement structures (Arents 1992 vol. 1: 22–31). Knorr described very briefly the results of all his excavation campaigns in only one article (1924). The documentation of each year's campaign consisted of handwritten reports, drawings true to scale and photos of selected features and also cards with descriptions and drawings of find materials, which survived the decades without any serious losses in the museum's archive. An impressive boat-chamber grave was published in more detail in 1911, and a full analysis was given by M. Müller-Wille in 1976 (Knorr 1911; Müller-Wille 1976; Wamers 1994). But Knorr's excavations also turned the attention from the burials to the thick cultural layers

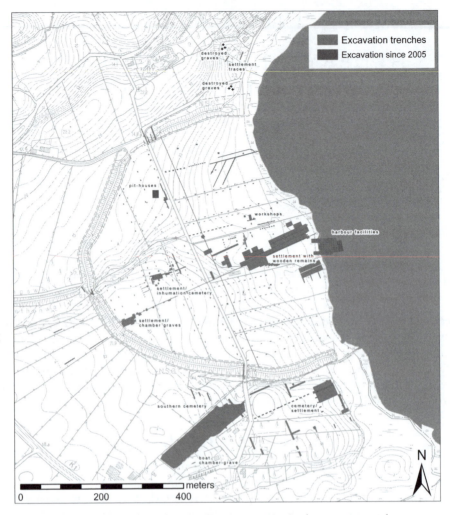

Figure 8.2.1 Map of Hedeby with all excavation trenches between 1900 and 2005.

with conserved wood near the coastline, especially in the depression crossed by a small stream (Knorr 1924: 27).

The resumption of the excavations in 1930 started with a narrow trial trench stretching from west to east and from south to north, which was dug out by the young Herbert Jankuhn. Only in some parts was this trench widened because of special features: in the west, Jankuhn excavated a group of ten chamber burials, which were surrounded by ring ditches, one incineration and two inhumation graves. This part of the cemetery was superseded by a younger settlement of several sunken-featured buildings consisting of different phases with wells and pits. Unfortunately the results of these excavations were never published in detail (Jankuhn 1933, 1986: 93–5 fig. 42; Aner 1952). The Hedeby research of that time is strongly connected with the Nazi regime (Vollertsen 1989; Steuer 2001). From 1935 Jankuhn concentrated his excavations on the low-lying areas near the coastline, which are characterised by well-preserved wooden remains and a stratigraphy up to 2 metres (Jankuhn 1936, 1943). Archaeological research and interest have been focused for decades in this area. The investigations were continued in 1962 by Torsten Capelle and by Kurt Schietzel from 1963 to 1969 (Capelle 1965; Schietzel 1969: 10–59; 1981). The excavated settlement structures form the basis of our knowledge of Hedeby and its layout in the Viking Age (Schietzel 1981, 1984; Jankuhn 1986: 95–100 plan 2; Clarke and Ambrosiani 1991: 138–41). Only *c.* 5 per cent of the area inside the semicircular rampart has been excavated to date, and only a small part has been analysed and published intensively (Schietzel 1981: 21; Radtke 1999: 364). Most of the preserved wooden remains date to the ninth century; for the upper layers no wood preservation could be found. Only a well with a terminus post of AD 1020 possesses the youngest dendrochronological date from Schietzel's settlement excavations (Eckstein 1976; Schietzel 1981: 68 f.).

To the north, lying on the south-eastern slopes of the hill fort, remains of graves destroyed in the nineteenth century and a settlement pit have been found (Jankuhn 1986: 80, 87; Arents 1992 vol. 1: 14–18). In the south rampart remains of inhumation and cremation burials have led to large-scale excavations over several years since 1957. Klaus Raddatz, Heiko Steuer and Konrad Weidemann investigated 890 uncovered burials making up a large part of a huge biritual cemetery. In the eastern area near the coastline Raddatz and Steuer also excavated parts of an older settlement. Only the structures of the settlement were published by Steuer; the cemetery hasn't been published yet in detail (Steuer 1974, 1984: 192–4; Jankuhn 1986: 100–2; Arents 1992 vol. 1: 44–53).

Underwater research from 1953 onwards has found its preliminary culmination in the harbour excavation from 1979 to 1980, when parts of the jetties were excavated, dating from the middle of the ninth century onwards (Kramer 1999; Radtke 1999: 370; Kalmring 2006). In the harbour a lot of different objects and waste were deposited. In front of the jetties also a large warship, measuring about 30 m in length, was recovered. It was dated dendrochronologically to *c.* 982. Besides, we know of three other shipwrecks in front of Hedeby: a huge cargo-vessel of the so-called 'Knorr'-type (t.p. about 1025), a smaller boat of Nordic tradition (t.p. about 965) and a barge dating to the twelfth century (Crumlin-Pedersen 1997).

ARCHAEOLOGICAL AND GEOPHYSICAL INVESTIGATIONS

Another important contribution to the Hedeby research is provided by systematic archaeological prospection. During the 1960s K. Schietzel conducted a systematic field survey inside the semicircular rampart. The materials collected consist mainly of pottery and soapstone sherds, iron slags, and production waste in metal and glass, and this has contributed much to our understanding of the whole settlement complex (Schietzel 1981: 21 f. map 23). Since 2003 systematic metal-detector surveys have been carried out with the assistance of the Bornholmske Amatørarkæologer and a German amateur group of metal-detectorists from Schleswig-Holstein. From five campaigns about 9,700 metal finds were collected and measured precisely with a D-GPS system (Figure 8.2.2) (Hilberg forthcoming). Most of the relevant material dates to Hedeby's younger phases, coming from the disturbed or destroyed upper layers of the emporium. From the area of the southern settlement no materials of pre-Viking Age date could be collected.

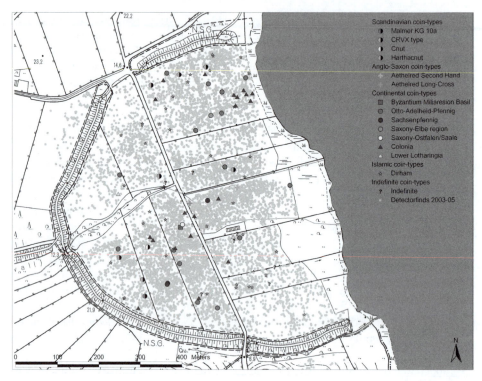

Figure 8.2.2 Map showing finds of early medieval coins dated after *c.* 950 (found by metal-detecting).

With the metal-detected finds our knowledge of the settlement complex enlarged considerably: for many different object types – such as ornaments, coins and weights – larger series are for the first time at our disposal. Besides a typical Scandinavian character in manufacture (Figure 8.2.3), the continental influence on Hedeby is clearly visible from the ninth century onwards.

Also, since 1952 different geophysical methods on sea and land have been used for archaeological purposes (Stümpel and Borth-Hoffmann 1983; Utecht and Stümpel 1983; Kramer 1999). A new project of large-scale geophysical research started in 2002; during fieldwork of three weeks a total of *c.* 29 ha inside and outside the semicircular rampart was analysed by four teams from Kiel, Marburg, Munich and Vienna using Fluxgate- and Caesium-magnetometer and ground-penetrating radar (Figure 8.2.4). The different prospection methods applied in recent years have provided for the first time new data for the whole settlement complex of Hedeby and its development (Hilberg forthcoming).

Inside the rampart the density of anomalies is very high; in the outer surroundings the situation is totally different. The northern part inside the semicircular rampart is characterised in the magnetogram by parallel courses and many rectangular structures with a high magneticism. According to investigations done with ground-penetrating radar some of these structures possess a depth of up to 1.7–1.8 m and could therefore be explained as sunken-featured buildings. Comparable pit-houses were excavated in the surroundings. Schietzel collected from his surface-survey a high amount of iron slags in this north-western part; it was concluded that iron was processed there (Schietzel 1981

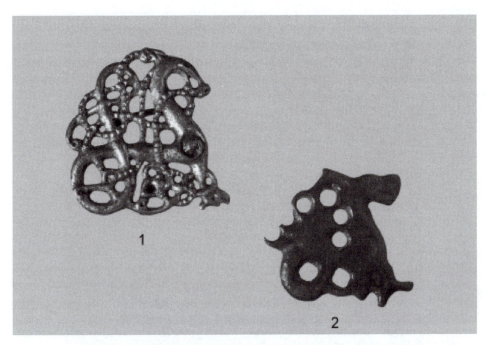

Figure 8.2.3   Metal-detected animal-brooches in the Urnes style from the middle or second half of the eleventh century. (1) Gilded silver, 3.6 × 3.65 cm, (2) bronze, 2.9 × 2.85 cm. (Photo: C. Franz, Stiftung Schleswig-Holsteinische Landesmuseen Schleswig.)

maps 28–9; Westphalen 1989: 28–36 figs 5–7). The magnetic structures in this area of the settlement could be interpreted as workshops (Figure 8.2.5) (Jankuhn 1986: 92); any precise dating is at the moment impossible, but these structures seem to belong to Hedeby's younger phase of the tenth and eleventh centuries. In the north-eastern area inside Hedeby's rampart we also detected a lot of rectangular structures with a high magneticism, sometimes aligned. These could also be interpreted as sunken-featured buildings or workshops. From former excavations we know of workshops for metal casting and glass production, which were lying immediately next to each other and which would be dated to the ninth and tenth centuries. It was this area which Jankuhn designated as the 'quarter of craft activities' in the 1940s and later (Jankuhn 1944, 1977; Hilberg forthcoming fig. 8).

A linear structure runs parallel to the shore and possesses small magnetic structures lying in pairs opposite each other (Figure 8.2.5). It seems to be a street extending along the whole shore with a length of *c.* 530 m, accompanied by houses on both sides. This supposed street crosses the main excavation area of Jankuhn and Schietzel. It is visible there in all layers and was often designated as a main street of the settlement (Jankuhn 1943: 38–40, 49 f. fig. 4; 1986: 98 f. figs 39–40; Schietzel 1969: 19–21; Randsborg 1980: fig. 23). This street also crosses a small stream with a narrow bridge, which is dendrochronologically dated to AD 819 (Eckstein 1976; Schietzel 1969: 21–6 figs 10–14). As a consequence this street must have existed as early as the early ninth century, but without more precise data – for example, provided by new excavations – its extension at that time is still unknown. Streets stretching along the shore seem to be

Figure 8.2.4 Magnetogram of the geophysical research from 2002 (dynamics ca −10/+10 nT).

characteristic of early medieval trading centres, such as Sigtuna or Dublin (Clarke and Ambrosiani 1991: 138–41 figs 5.5 and 4.23). In Hedeby this main street was apparently crossed by several streets running from the harbour to the core areas of the settlement, shown by Jankuhn's and Schietzel's excavations and also detected in the magnetometer survey.

Around AD 900 the settlement still wasn't fortified. Perhaps a ditch existed in the north with a width of *c.* 2.80 m and a depth of *c.* 1.30 m, which we could see in the magnetometer picture for a length of *c.* 210 m (Figure 8.2.5). But at the moment it is very difficult to interpret because it could be proved only in Jankuhn's narrow trial trench.

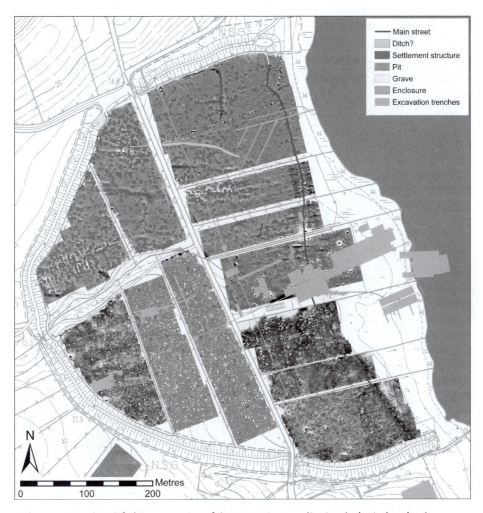

Figure 8.2.5 Simplified interpretation of the magnetic anomalies (on the basis done by the teams from Vienna and Marburg).

To the south-west of the settlement spread a huge cemetery area, with the mid-ninth-century boat grave as a focus. Also, inside the rampart, in the south-west stretching from the rampart to the *c.* 6 m contour, thousands of small anomalies with a lesser degree of magneticism were investigated in 2002 (Figure 8.2.5). They could be interpreted as burials. Ring ditches were also detected in some cases (Steuer 1984: 203–9; Eisenschmidt 1994: 38 f.; 2004: 302). From Knorr's and Jankuhn's excavations a super-positioning of the cemetery with house structures points to the usage of this area for housing and production activities from the tenth century (Jankuhn 1986: 107, 110). Settlement structures in the whole south-western area are proved by the 2002 magnetometer survey; the density of detected houses seems to be less than in the northern parts of Hedeby, but the whole area inside the rampart seems to be settled. Also, the data from the surface-survey and systematic metal-detection point to settlement activities.

Figure 8.2.6   Excavation of a burnt-down pit-house of late tenth-century date. (Photo: D. Stoltenberg, Archäologisches Landesamt Schleswig-Holstein Schleswig.)

But further research is needed to decide if the cemetery area outside and inside the late tenth-century rampart originally formed one burial ground.

The actual state of scientific analysis and publication still remains unfinished in some important respects; for example; no detailed analysis of the settlement structure exists apart from the first summarised reports, but recently a comprehensive study has been finished (Schietzel 1981; Schultze 2006). An analysis of the harbour excavation is also in preparation (by S. Kalmring). All burial finds remain unpublished, but they are studied in Arents (1992), and aspects of burial rite are treated by Steuer (1984). Since 2002 a group of younger researchers has been based in Schleswig using GIS in order to combine all results from field research in Hedeby.

EXCAVATION AND GEOPHYSICAL RESEARCH
SINCE 2005

In 2005 new smaller-scale excavations started to verify the results and interpretations of the geophysical research. The existence of pit-houses in the higher, sandy areas was attested and hundreds of soil samples for further geophysical analyses were collected. Careful excavation and sieving of the spoil revealed a burnt-down pit-house in an excellent state of preservation (Figure 8.2.6) and thousands of small finds dating from the second half of the tenth century to the mid-eleventh century. The high magneticism is due to a younger oven built in the house's debris. The research over the coming years intends to develop new methods in modelling geophysical data and collecting strati-graphically excavated settlement remains. Especially for the late tenth and the eleventh centuries, our knowledge of Hedeby's position and role in the international trading systems has enlarged considerably due to systematic metal-detection (Figures 8.2.2 and 8.2.3) and the new excavations, thus the supposed decline of the emporium around 1000 can now be doubted (Jankuhn 1986: 222 f.; Hill 2001: 107).

BIBLIOGRAPHY

Aner, E. (1952) 'Das Kammergräberfeld von Haithabu', *Offa*, 10: 61–115.

Arents, U. (1992) 'Die wikingerzeitlichen Grabfunde von Haithabu (Kreis Schleswig-Flensburg)', 3 vols, Kiel: Institut für Ur- und Frühgeschichte, Christian-Albrechts-Universität zu Kiel. (Unpubl. PhD thesis.)

Capelle, T. (1965) 'Die Ausgrabungen im Innern des Halbkreiswalles', *Offa*, 21/22 (1964/5): 50–7.

Clarke, H. and Ambrosiani, B. (1991) *Towns in the Viking Age*, Leicester and London: Leicester University Press.

Crumlin-Pedersen, O. (1997) *Viking-Age Ships and Shipbuilding in Hedeby/Haithabu and Schleswig* (Ships and Boats of the North 2), Schleswig: Archäologisches Landesmuseum & Roskilde: The Viking Ship Museum.

Eckstein, D. (1976) 'Absolute Datierung der wikingerzeitlichen Siedlung Haithabu/Schleswig mit Hilfe der Dendrochronologie', *Naturwissenschaftliche Rundschau*, 29(3): 81–4.

Eisenschmidt, S. (1994) *Kammergräber der Wikingerzeit in Altdänemark* (Universitätsforschungen zur prähistorischen Archäologie 25), Bonn: Habelt.

—— (2004) *Grabfunde des 8. bis 11. Jahrhunderts zwischen Kongeå und Eider* (Studien zur Siedlungsgeschichte und Archäologie der Ostseegebiete 5), Neumünster: Wachholtz.

Hilberg, V. (forthcoming) 'Hedeby in Wulfstan's days', in A. Englert (ed.) *Wulfstan's Voyage. New Light on Viking-Age Seafaring within the Ethnic Geography of Mare Balticum*, Roskilde: The Viking Ship Museum.

Hill, D. (2001) 'A short gazeteer of postulated continental wics', in D. Hill and R. Cowie (eds) *Wics. The Early Mediaeval Trading Centres of Northern Europe* (Sheffield Archaeological Monographs 14), Sheffield: Sheffield Academic Press.

Jankuhn, H. (1933) 'Die Ausgrabungen in Haithabu 1930–1933', *Nordelbingen*, 9: 341–69.

—— (1936) 'Die Ausgrabungen in Haithabu 1935/36', *Offa*, 1: 96–140.

—— (1943) *Die Ausgrabungen in Haithabu (1937–1939). Vorläufiger Grabungsbericht*, Berlin: Ahnenerbe-Stiftung Verlag.

—— (1944) 'Die Bedeutung der Gußformen von Haithabu', in H. Jankuhn (ed.) *Bericht über die Kieler Tagung 1939. Jahrestagungen der Forschungs- und Lehrgemeinschaft 'Das Ahnenerbe'*, Neumünster: Wachholtz.

—— (1977) 'Das Bronzegießerhandwerk in Haithabu', in L. Gerevich and Á. Salamon (eds) *La formation et le développement des métiers au Moyen Age (Ve–XIVe siècles). Colloque international organisé par le Comité des recherches sur les origines des villes, tenu à Budapest 25–27 octobre 1973*, Budapest: Akadémiai Kiadó.

—— (1986) *Haithabu. Ein Handelsplatz der Wikingerzeit*, 8th edn, Neumünster: Wachholtz.

Kalmring, S. (2006) 'The harbour of Haiðaby', in L. Blue, A. Englert and F. Hocker (eds) *Connected by the Sea. Proceedings of the Tenth International Symposium on Boat and Ship Archaeology*, Oxford: Oxbow.

Knorr, F. (1911) 'Bootkammergrab südlich der Oldenburg bei Schleswig', *Mitteilungen des Anthropologischen Vereins in Schleswig-Holstein*, 19: 68–77.

—— (1924) 'Schleswig und Haithabu', *Schleswig–Holsteinisches Jahrbuch für 1924* (= *Schleswig Heimatbuch* 1): 24–31.

Kramer, W. (1999) 'Neue Untersuchungen im Hafen von Haithabu', *Archäologische Nachrichten aus Schleswig-Holstein*, 9/10 (1998/9): 90–118.

Müller, S. (1897) *Vor Oldtid. Danmarks forhistoriske Archæologi*, Copenhagen: Det Nordiske Forlag.

Müller-Wille, M. (1976) *Das Bootkammergrab von Haithabu* (Berichte über die Ausgrabungen in Haithabu 8), Neumünster: Wachholtz.

Olsen, O. (1999) 'Da kristendommen kom til Danmark', in O. Olsen, *Da Danmark blev til. Seks radioforedrag*, Copenhagen: Fremad.

Radtke, Chr. (1999) 'Haiðaby', *RGA* 13: 363–81.

Randsborg, K. (1980) *The Viking Age in Denmark*, London: Duckworth.

Schietzel, K. (1969) 'Die archäologischen Befunde der Ausgrabung Haithabu 1963–1964', in K. Schietzel (ed.) *Berichte über die Ausgrabungen in Haithabu*, vol. 1, Neumünster: Wachholtz.

—— (1981) 'Stand der siedlungsarchäologischen Forschung in Haithabu – Ergebnisse und Probleme', in K. Schietzel (ed.) *Berichte über die Ausgrabungen in Haithabu*, vol. 16, Neumünster: Wachholtz.

—— (1984) 'Die Topographie von Haithabu', in H. Jankuhn, K. Schietzel and H. Reichstein (eds) *Archäologische und naturwissenschaftliche Untersuchungen an ländlichen und frühstädtischen Siedlungen im deutschen Küstengebiet vom 5. Jahrhundert v. Chr. bis zum 11. Jahrhundert n. Chr.*, vol. 2: *Handelsplätze des frühen und hohen Mittelalters*, Weinheim: Acta humaniora.

Schlesinger, W. (1972) 'Unkonventionelle Gedanken zur Geschichte von Schleswig/Haithabu', in H. Fuhrmann, H.E. Mayer and K. Wriedt (eds) *Aus Reichsgeschichte und Nordischer Geschichte* (Kieler Historische Studien 16), Stuttgart: Klett.

Schultze, J. (2006) 'Methodische Grundlagen und Auswertungsmöglichkeiten einer archäologisch-dendrochronologischen Strukturierung der Siedlungsgrabung Haithabu', Kiel: Institut für Ur- und Frühgeschichte, Christian-Albrechts-Universität zu Kiel. (Unpubl. PhD thesis.)

Stark, J. (1988) *Haithabu – Schleswig – Danewerk. Aspekte einer Forschungsgeschichte mittelalterlicher Anlagen in Schleswig-Holstein* (BAR International Series 432), Oxford: British Archaeological Reports.

Steuer, H. (1974) *Die Südsiedlung von Haithabu. Studien zur frühmittelalterlichen Keramik im Nordseeküstenbereich und in Schleswig-Holstein* (Ausgrabungen in Haithabu 6), Neumünster: Wachholtz.

—— (1984) 'Zur ethnischen Gliederung der Bevölkerung von Haithabu anhand der Gräberfelder', *Offa*, 41: 189–212.

—— (2001) 'Herbert Jankuhn und seine Darstellungen zur Germanen- und Wikingerzeit', in H. Steuer (ed.) *Eine hervorragend nationale Wissenschaft. Deutsche Prähistoriker zwischen 1900 und 1995* (Ergänzungsbände zum Reallexikon der Germanischen Altertumskunde 29), Berlin and New York: de Gruyter.

Stümpel, H. and Borth-Hoffmann, B. (1983) 'Seismische Untersuchungen im Hafen von

Haithabu', in K. Schietzel (ed.) *Archäometrische Untersuchungen* (Berichte über die Ausgrabungen in Haithabu 18), Neumünster: Wachholtz.

Utecht, T. and Stümpel, H. (1983) 'Magnetische Sondierungen in Haithabu', in K. Schietzel (ed.) *Archäometrische Untersuchungen* (Berichte über die Ausgrabungen in Haithabu 18), Neumünster: Wachholtz.

Vollertsen, N. (1989) 'Herbert Jankuhn, Hedeby-forskningen og det tyske samfund 1934–1976', *Fortid og Nutid*, 36: 235–51.

Wamers, E. (1994) 'König im Grenzland. Neue Analyse des Bootkammergrabes von Haiðaby', *Acta Archaeologica*, 65: 1–56.

Westphalen, P. (1989) *Die Eisenschlacken von Haithabu. Ein Beitrag zur Geschichte des Schmiedehandwerks in Nordeuropa* (Berichte über die Ausgrabungen in Haithabu 26), Neumünster: Wachholtz.

CHAPTER EIGHT (3)

KAUPANG – 'SKÍRINGSSALR'

———·◆·———

Dagfinn Skre

Kaupang is located by the mouth of the Oslo fjord, in the region of Vestfold on the fjord's western side. The region is one of the most fertile in Norway. It is also one of the richest in monuments from the Viking Age. The two Viking ships Oseberg (buried AD 834) and Gokstad (buried AD 900–5) were found in barrows a few kilometres north of Kaupang. The ninth-century town Kaupang lies in a protected bay just by the main sailing route along the coast (Figure 8.3.1). Also important for its location is the mouth of the river Lågen just a few kilometres further west. In this part of Vestfold, Lågen is the main route from the coastal areas inland. In the ninth century inland regions of eastern Norway are known to have produced iron, whetstones and soapstone vessels – all of which were popular trading goods in the Viking Age.

WHERE IS SKÍRINGSSALR?

The history of Kaupang research goes back almost 200 years. One main theme in the early research was to locate a place named *Sciringes heal* in the so-called 'Ohthere's account'. This account was rendered *c.* 890 at the court of Alfred the Great of England by the Norwegian voyager Ohthere, written down by the king's scribes and included in the Old English translation of the history written by the early fifth-century author Orosius. However, the reference here to *Sciringes heal* is brief and raises more questions than it provides answers. There are in fact only two pieces of information in the Old English text. First of all, we learn that Skíringssalr was located about a month's sailing to the south from where Ohthere lived in Hålogaland in northern Norway. Sufficient detail is provided about the route to identify the southern part of present-day Norway, possibly the Oslo fjord area, as the most likely location. Secondly, it is said that Skíringssalr was what in Old English was called a *port*, a word of multiple meanings, covering modern 'port' or 'harbour', 'marketplace' and 'town'.

The first important contribution in the efforts to locate Skíringssalr was made by Jens Kraft (1822), who drew attention to two documents dating from the early fifteenth century. These deal with land transactions in Tjølling parish in southern Vestfold. Some of the farms referred to in the diplomas are said to lie in Skíringssalr, which therefore seems to have been an old and now forgotten name for some part of the parish. Kraft also

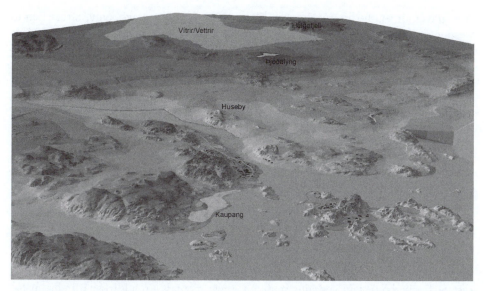

Figure 8.3.1   Digital model of the Kaupang area looking towards the north. The Viking Age sea level, 3.5 m above present, is recreated. The settlement area is surrounded by vast cemeteries. About 1 km north of the settlement, at Huseby, an aristocratic residence was excavated. The hall was built a few decades before the town was established and it was taken down some time at the beginning of the tenth century. A further kilometre north is an ancient assembly site named Þjóðalyng. The assembly site is situated on the shore of a lake called Vítrir or Vettrir, which probably means 'the lake where *vættr* (supernatural beings) dwell'. A cliff on the shore of the lake bears the name Helgefjell, 'the holy mountain'. This complex of assembly place, sacred lake and mountain probably goes back to the Iron Age (second to sixth centuries). (Copyright © Kaupang Excavation Project, University of Oslo.)

notes the farm *Kaupang* in the same parish. The name of this farm, which literally means 'trade-bay', indicates, he writes, that there was once a harbour for trade and seaways transport there (Kraft 1822).

The cartographer and historian Gerhard Munthe, who came to Kaupang in the mid-1830s, was the first to link Kraft's information to Ohthere's account. In his study of geographical details in the sagas of the Norse kings he provides additional information about the excellent harbour and the enormous number of grave mounds on the farm (Munthe 1838). Peter Andreas Munch (1850) drew further on this information, involving a number of written sources, and pointing out the possibility of several *Ynglinga* kings, the mythical lineage of the Norwegian kings, being buried there. He strongly supported Munthe's conclusion that Ohthere's *port* is to be found at Kaupang, and it is fair to say that this contribution exhausted the potential in the written sources for reaching a decision on the matter.

In 1866 the antiquarian Nicolay Nicolaysen began a series of large annual excavations. Solving the Skíringssalr puzzle must have been high on his agenda. In 1867 he began his excavations at Kaupang. In four weeks he excavated 71 of the then 115 remaining mounds north of the settlement and 8 mounds on a small cemetery south of the settlement. Nicolaysen must have hoped to find the royal graves that Munch had suggested should be there. The results were disappointing in both respects. Half the mounds were without finds and the rest contained what may be called 'normal' Viking

Age graves for south-eastern Norway. They were cremation graves only, rather rich in weapons and brooches, but without indications of any 'royal' connection, or of abundant wealth or extensive trade (Nicolaysen 1868; cf. Blindheim *et al.* 1981, 1999).

Nicolaysen's limited results may have been the reason why archaeologists kept away from Kaupang for many decades. Some minor excavations were conducted, but substantial progress was not made until Charlotte Blindheim began excavations in 1950. The low, rocky ridge Bikjholberget had only one small grave mound, but Blindheim discovered that the number of graves there was higher than in Nicolaysen's cemetery. During the following seven years she excavated seventy-four of them, all inhumations in flat graves, the majority of them in boats. The precise number of excavated graves is hard to determine, since every small piece of land was utilised for burial, and the digging of new graves had destroyed some of the older ones.

Flat grave inhumations in boats are rather rare in the region and the number here was extraordinary, indicating, along with the comparable wealth and abundance of imports, that the community that buried their dead at Bikjholberget was of a special kind. The hypothesis that Kaupang was Ohthere's Skíringssalr was substantiated through these finds. Bikjholberget still contains many unexcavated graves and Lamøya, the peninsula east of the harbour, still contains some 94 grave mounds. In addition Blindheim has collected information about several areas with flat graves at Lamøya. She has estimated the original number of graves at Kaupang to be about 1,000.

Only an excavation of the settlement area could give a definite answer as to whether Ohthere's Skíringssalr is to be found at Kaupang. In 1956 Blindheim dug the first trench in the area she believed to be the settlement area – a gentle slope on the opposite side of the shallow bay. Over the following eleven years Blindheim excavated close to 1,500 m^2 of the settlement, which she estimated to have covered some 40,000 m^2. On the basis of 10,000 artefacts she dated the start to the late eighth century and the abandonment to *c.* 900 (Tollnes 1998). The start date coincided with the earliest datings of the cemeteries. But the lack of tenth-century finds from the settlement was something of a puzzle, since both of the excavated cemeteries contained burials right up to the mid-tenth century.

Despite the discrepancies in datings, the evidence for a substantial non-agrarian ninth-century settlement at Kaupang was overwhelming. And when Blindheim published the first summing up of her results in 1969, she concluded that Ohthere's Skíringssalr had been found (see also Blindheim and Tollnes 1972: 91).

WHAT IS SKÍRINGSSALR?

But what kind of place is Skíringssalr and what is the meaning of the Old English word *port*? Munch (1850) was the first to confront this issue, followed by Storm (1901), and it is these two who have produced the main contributions based on the written evidence. Blindheim's excavations created a new basis for discussing these questions. Excavations and surveys in 1998–2003 led by the present author provided even more relevant evidence, which will be considered in the following.

Blindheim's excavations brought for the first time substantial information about the settlement. She found remains that she and her collaborator, architect Roar L. Tollnes (1998), interpreted as those of five houses, none of which had a permanent hearth. It would therefore have been impossible to cook there and also to live in them through the cold Norwegian winters. Blindheim does not state clearly whether she thinks the *kaupang* had its own permanent population or whether it was a seasonal marketplace (see, for instance, Blindheim and Tollnes 1972: 87–8). She used both Munch's term *handelsplass* (trading site) and *markedsplass* (marketplace) (Blindheim 1969; Blindheim and Tollnes 1972; Blindheim *et al.* 1981, 1999; Blindheim and Heyerdahl-Larsen 1995).

As a result of excavations in other Viking towns such as Birka and Hedeby from the 1970s onwards, radical new information was gathered about Scandinavian urban settlements in the Viking Age. Interestingly, Blindheim's results did not fit into this picture. The Kaupang houses indicated a town, but the lack of hearths made their function uncertain and the question of permanent population difficult to assess. The houses were constructed in a completely different manner than in the other towns; their alignment in relation to the shoreline was the opposite of that in the other towns. And although some general regularity could be traced in the placing of the houses, the evidence concerning plot division was at best ambiguous. Besides, there was little or no evidence on the chronology in the development of the settlement through the ninth century.

The difficulty in deciding Kaupang's character and the lack of chronological information were the main reasons why new excavations and surveys were carried out 1998–2003 (Figure 8.3.2; Skre 2007: 197). In the main excavation 2000–2 a site of 1,100 m^2 was opened, and within this site an area of 400 m^2 was dug to the bottom. Additional information was collected through the digging of a water-pipe trench through the whole settlement area, by measurements of the depth of the Viking Age deposits (varying from 0 to 1.1 m) and through metal-detecting and systematic collection of artefacts (*c.* 4,300) in the ploughed field, which covers most of the settlement area.

The analysis of the 100,000 finds and enormous masses of information is ongoing, and many questions are still unanswered. However, the structure of the settlement and the main stages in its development seem fairly clear. From the start in the years around AD 800, in 803 at the latest, the area was divided into plots. In the early stage none of the six excavated plots had a building on them, but all of them had remains of some kind of activity, including crafts, such as blacksmithing and glass-bead production.

In the next stage, probably within a decade of the initial plot division, buildings were erected on five of the six plots, one building on each (Figure 8.3.3). The sixth plot seems to have been an enclosure with a small shed in one corner, possibly a pigsty. In addition to the crafts already mentioned, there are remains of amberworking and textile production, and on one of the plots there are substantial remains of metal casting, seemingly mostly production of jewellery and mounts in lead, bronze, silver and gold (Pilø 2007; Pedersen and Pilø 2007).

Judging from the deposits and the dating of the artefacts, these houses were being utilised for quite a long period, probably several decades. Some of the plots have remains of yet another level of houses on top of these remains, but ploughing during the past hundreds of years has destroyed most of these more recent building remains. The youngest preserved buildings were in use until some time in the mid-ninth century. From the following period only some pits from the mid- or possibly late ninth century were preserved, some of them wells, others with an unknown function.

From the settlement from the late ninth until the mid-tenth century only artefacts from the plough layer are preserved. Therefore very little information exists about the settlement in this period. Interestingly, artefacts recovered from the ploughed soil

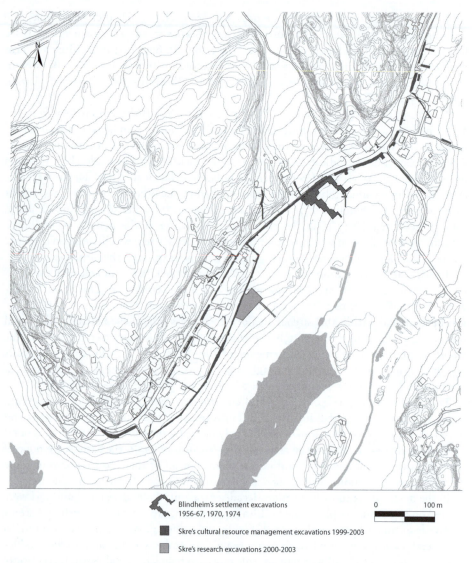

Figure 8.3.2   The extent of Blindheim's (1956–74) and Skre's (1999–2003) excavations in the settlement area at Kaupang. (Copyright © Kaupang Excavation Project, University of Oslo.)

demonstrate that all the activities identified in the ninth century – trade and craft production – continued until the mid-tenth century. But the number of artefacts drops around AD 900–30. There are, for instance, only nine coins from the period 900–60, whereas there are nearly 100 coins deposited in the preceding century. To the extent that the number of deposited coins is a direct result of the intensity in trade, the difference between the two periods is even greater than the number of coins indicates, since the total import of coins to Scandinavia increased many times from the ninth to the tenth century.

Figure 8.3.3 House remains and plot division in the main excavation area 2000–2. Plot division is indicated by ditches and rows of posts. The midden area lies in the *c.* 15 m zone between the houses and the sea. The drainage ditches date from the twentieth century. (Copyright © Kaupang Excavation Project, University of Oslo.)

Nevertheless, this difference in the number of coins must have some other explanation than a drop in economic activity. The reason for this is that the cemeteries give a contrary picture: the number of graves more than doubles from the ninth to the tenth century. The end and start dates of the cemeteries are the same as those of the settlement. Only 204 of the original *c.* 1,000 graves have been excavated or collected, and only 98 of these can be dated more closely. Of these, the number of ninth-century graves is 43 (4.3 per decade) while the number from the tenth century is 55 (11 per decade) (Stylegar 2007). This heavy overweight of nineteenth-century burials strongly indicates that the permanent settlement at Kaupang continued to some time in the mid-tenth century. The reduction in the number of coins and other artefacts from around AD 900 must be due to changes in, for example, waste disposal in the town.

Within the area with plot division there may have been 90–100 plots covering *c.* 2 ha (Figure 8.3.4). Surrounding this area there is a zone with finds from craft and trade but no finds of permanent structure. This zone was probably used for setting up tents or sheds by people who stayed temporarily in the town during market times etc. Based on present knowledge the full extent of the town was *c.* 5.4 ha. Judged on the size of households as well as the total number of graves, Kaupang may have had a population of 400–1,000 people (Stylegar 2007).

No remains of defences have been found at Kaupang neither on land nor in the harbour area. The reason may be that towns in the ninth century generally were without extensive defences. The other towns had their main defences built around the time when Kaupang was abandoned.

In 2000–1 an aristocratic hall was excavated at the farm Huseby *c.* 1 km north of Kaupang (Skre 2007: 223–47). The hall was about 35 m long and 11.7 m wide, narrowing to 7.9 m at the ends. The hall was built in the latter half of the eighth century. There is reason to believe that at Kaupang's time the name of this farm was Skíringssalr, named after the hall. When Ohthere called the town Skíringssalr this is an indication that the town belonged to the chieftain who resided in this hall. The present-day name of the farm, Huseby, indicates that the farm later, maybe in the eleventh century, became one of the royal administrative farms (Skre 2007: 242–3).

Both archaeological and written sources indicate that the land along the Oslo fjord, called Viken, was ruled by the Danish king in most parts of the Viking Age. The initiative to establish a town in this border zone may have come from the Danish king. In that case Kaupang would fit into the same pattern as the two other towns in the realm of the Danish king, Hedeby and Ribe (Skre 2007: 445–69).

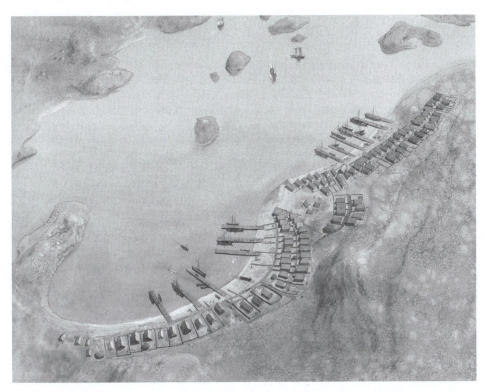

Figure 8.3.4   A tentative reconstruction of the town in the mid-ninth century.
(Copyright © Flemming Bau.)

BIBLIOGRAPHY

Blindheim, Ch. (1969) 'Kaupangundersøkelsen avsluttet. Kort tilbakeblikk på en lang utgravn-ing', *Viking*, 33: 5–39.

Blindheim, Ch. and Heyerdahl-Larsen, B. (1995) *Kaupang-funnene*, vol. 2A: *Gravplassene i Bikjholbergene/Lamøya. Undersøkelsene 1950–1957. Gravskikk* (Norske Oldfunn 16), Oslo: Universitetet i Oslo.

—— (1999) *Kaupang-funnene*, vol. 2B–C: *Gravplassene i Bikjholbergene/Lamøya. Undersøkelsene 1950–1957. Oldsaksformer. Kulturhistorisk tilbakeblikk* [and] *Tekstilene* (Norske Oldfunn 19), Oslo: Universitetet i Oslo.

Blindheim, Ch., Heyerdahl-Larsen, B. and Tollnes, R.L. (1981) *Kaupang-funnene*, vol. 1 (Norske Oldfunn 11), Oslo: Universitetet i Oslo.

Blindheim, Ch. and Tollnes, R.L. (1972) *Kaupang, Vikingenes handelsplass*, Oslo: no publ.

Kraft, J. (1822) *Topographisk-statistisk Beskrivelse over Kongeriget Norge*, vol. 2, Christiania: no publ.

Munch, P.A. (1850) 'Om den gamle vestfoldske Søhandelsplads i Skiringssal og de vestfoldske Konger af Ynglinge-Ætten', *Langes Norsk Tidsskrift* (1950): 101–88. [Reprinted in: Munch, P.A. (1874) *Samlede Afhandlinger. Udgivne efter offentlig Foranstaltning af Gustav Storm*, vol. 2, Christiania: Cammermeyer.]

Munthe, G. (1838) *Geografiske Anmærkninger til Snorre Sturlesons norske kongers Sagaer*, Kristiania: no publ.

Nicolaysen, N. (1868) '[Excavations at Kaupang 1867]', *Foreningen til Norske Fortidsmindemerkers Bevaring. Aarberetning for 1867*: 77–92.

Pedersen, U. and Pilø, L. (2007) 'The settlement: artefacts and site periods', in D. Skre (ed.) *Kaupang in Skiringssal* (Kaupang Excavation Project Publication Series 1), Aarhus: Aarhus University Press.

Pilø, L. (2007) 'The settlement: character, structures and features', in D. Skre (ed.) *Kaupang in Skiringssal* (Kaupang Excavation Project Publication Series 1), Aarhus: Aarhus University Press.

Schmidt, T. (2000) 'Marked, torg og kaupang – språklige vitnemål om handel i middelalderen', *Collegium Medievale*, 13: 79–102.

Skre, D. (ed.) (2007) *Kaupang in Skiringssal* (Kaupang Excavation Project Publication Series 1), Aarhus: Aarhus University Press.

Storm, G. (1901) 'Skiringssal og Sandefjord', *(Norsk) Historisk Tidsskrift*, 4(1): 214–37.

Stylegar, F.-A. (2007) 'The Kaupang cemeteries revisited', in D. Skre (ed.) *Kaupang in Skiringssal* (Kaupang Excavation Project Publication Series 1), Aarhus: Aarhus University Press.

Tollnes, R.L. (1998) *Kaupang-funnene*, vol. 3A: *Undersøkelser i bosetningsområdet 1956–1975. Hus og konstruksjoner* (Norske Oldfunn 18), Oslo: Universitetet i Oslo.

CHAPTER EIGHT (4)

LEJRE AND ROSKILDE

———·◆·———

Tom Christensen

The role played by Lejre and Roskilde in the transition from a pagan tribal society to the Christian state has been greatly debated, primarily on the basis of medieval sagas, chronicles and monastic sources. With variations, these texts relate how the Danes' first royal house, the Skjoldungas, had their seat at Lejre on Sjælland, while the later Viking Age kings established their base at Roskilde, around 10 km east of Lejre at the head of the Roskilde fjord (Skovgaard-Petersen 1977: 23 ff.). Over the past fifty years there have been intermittent excavations at Lejre, which can provide the basis for an evaluation of this site working from material remains. Excavations in Roskilde have also produced new topographical insights.

LEJRE

The Lejre complex covers almost 1 square km and spans a chronological range from the fifth/sixth century until the fourteenth. East of Lejre is an area characterised by three monumental burial mounds and the remains of a ship setting at least 80 m long. Observations made in the eighteenth century indicate that there were once at least five impressive monuments of the latter type. One of the mounds, *Grydehøj*, contained what appears to have been a chieftain's cremation burial from the sixth/seventh century, with extensive animal sacrifices. Parts of a tenth-century cemetery with forty-nine inhumations have also been excavated around the ship setting. The finds here do not differ markedly from those at other contemporary cemeteries (Andersen 1995).

The built area stretches over 500 m along the western bank of the Lejre River, established on some of the small hills characteristic of the landscape in this region. The eldest is a recently discovered settlement at *Fredshøj* (ROM j.nr. 615/84) from the sixth/seventh century, currently (2004) under excavation (Christensen 2004). Two important elements are worth mentioning here: a large hall building, and a heap of burnt stones 16 m in diameter and 0.75 m high. At the periphery of this heap were found pits packed with bones and charcoal. In terms of metal finds, the site is not noticeably different from its contemporaries among large settlements. However, the ceramic material should be noted. The domestic wares are of high quality and unusually richly decorated with

121

similarly remarkable stamps, while the imported pottery is mostly from the Frankish region.

During the seventh century the settlement moved a few hundred metres southwards to *Mysselhøjgård* (ROM j.nr. 641/85). In the 1980s and early 1990s, parts of a settlement complex, dated to the seventh to the tenth centuries, were excavated here. It appears to have had a permanent form, in which the central buildings over at least three phases were raised on the same spot as their predecessors. Two buildings are marked out by their dimensions and construction technique: a structure 42 m long and 7.5 m wide, and most spectacularly the structure 50 m long and 11.5 m wide that from its discovery in 1986 was named the 'Lejre Hall' (Figure 8.4.1; Christensen 1991, 1993, 2001, 2004).

These buildings, set out on a little hill some 7 m high, form the core of the dwelling houses. Downslope is an area characterised by handicraft activities with sunken-featured buildings and a smithy. Most interesting in this context is a pile of burnt stone 35 m in diameter and 1 m high, a parallel to that found on the earlier site at *Fredshøj*.

At some point in the tenth century the great halls were abandoned, and use of the large stone piles ceased. The area was covered by a cultural deposit, with a few

Figure 8.4.1   The hall at Lejre, tenth century. (Photo: Roskilde Museum.
Copyright © Roskilde Museum.)

sunken-featured buildings, from which the finds can be dated to the eleventh century. The residences belonging to this period of occupation may lie on a hill immediately north of the excavation. Test trenches and magnetometer surveys here have revealed the existence of a 150 m × 150 m construction with an impressive palisade, surrounding buildings of similar dimension to the halls on the *Mysselhøjgård* site. It is also possible that this bounded area is at least partly contemporary with the *Myssehøjgård* site itself.

The artefactual material from the excavations represents a broad spectrum ranging from common household equipment to extraordinary metalwork, which forms a striking but not especially common element. In this context we should also note the Lejre hoard, containing among other items a number of silver vessels of Anglo-Irish origin, found a few hundred metres west of the settlement area (Wilson 1960).

Closer to the Lejre River, but still on its west bank and connected with the Iron Age and Viking period settlements, medieval occupation from the twelfth to fourteenth centuries has been found. A stone-built cellar and a twelfth-century windmill are among the finds here. The features here have clear parallels in the period's feudal manor farms (Christensen 1998).

It is thus possible to follow a continual settlement pattern at Lejre from the sixth/seventh century until the fourteenth, and while the site has not been totally investigated it is nonetheless possible to distinguish a number of general trends. The situation of the two or possibly three Iron Age and Viking sites in this hilly landscape leaves no possibility that this is a village of the larger type known from elsewhere at this period. The overall layout seems to consist of at least one central building of impressive dimensions, placed so as to be visible in its surroundings. At *Mysselhøjgård* this is ringed by other buildings, all of which can be followed over several successive construction phases, and the whole site thereby exhibits a marked stability over at least two centuries. If we also recall the hall and large stone pile at the earlier site at *Fredshøj*, then we see two striking elements that appear to have been permanent fixtures in the Lejre settlement for close on half a millennium.

The use of the term *hall* of course makes an assumption about these buildings in their connection to a high-status milieu and pagan cult (Olsen 1966). The occurrence of fire-cracked stone in association with late Iron Age buildings is a recognised phenomenon, and the neutral term *kogesten* ('cooking stones', for boiling water) is the Danish standard. In Norway they are known as *bryggestein* 'brewing stones', referring to their use in historic times for the heating of water as part of beer brewing. The massive number of these stones at Lejre is far in excess of what could be generated by ordinary household activities, and in relation to the great hall buildings must be linked to events involving more people than the residents of the settlement.

In a German source by Bishop Thietmar von Merseburg (*Thietmari Merseburgensis episcopi Chronicon*, written 1012–18) Lejre is mentioned as *caput regni*, where the populace gather regularly every ninth year at the winter solstice (yule), and perform sacrificial rituals on a large scale. It may be these that are reflected in the halls, the stone heaps and the huge quantities of faunal remains at the Lejre settlements. In view of the monumental burial mounds and the ship settings, on archaeological grounds it can be argued that Lejre was the seat of a princely or royal family in the Germanic Iron Age and Viking period, simultaneously functioning as a central cult site. This interpretation is strengthened by the fact that the accumulation of the stone pile ceases, and the hall(s) are abandoned, both together at the end of the tenth century – at the point when the change of religion took place, and when Roskilde makes its appearance on the map.

ROSKILDE

The written descriptions of Harald Bluetooth's burial at Roskilde in 987, which have formed one of the primary arguments for the dating of the town to the tenth century, have been subjected to a critical scrutiny that concludes that these events can hardly have taken place at that site (Lund 1998). Similarly, the archaeological remains cannot support a foundation date prior to the year 1000, as only a couple of objects found within the limits of the medieval town can be dated to the tenth century. The first time the town can be said to appear with certainty in documentary sources is in an English text from *c.* 1022 (Birkebæk 1992: 58). At this time we also find the first archaeological finds in the form of coins minted under Cnut the Great. Results from excavations combined with stray finds and the ecclesiastical topography suggest an extensive settlement, covering a considerable area in the eleventh century.

As is the case with the majority of the early medieval Danish towns, Roskilde was founded on a navigable waterway at the head of a fjord, but the cathedral and – one assumes – its associated royal manor were built on a 40 m high hill some 700 m from the shore. If we add to this the location of the other early churches and an excavated landing site on the fjord from the eleventh century, it seems that the town at this time covered an area of perhaps half a square kilometre (Christensen 2000: 9–21 and Ulriksen 2000: 145–98). The markedly hilly terrain with watercourses and fords has drawn natural boundaries between the churches and their adjacent buildings, giving an impression of a settlement pattern reminiscent of what in northern and western Europe has been called 'the eleventh-century agrarian urban landscape'. This consists of several separate settlements that only in the twelfth century combine to form a cohesive site. When Roskilde gets its town wall in the middle of the twelfth century, and a true settlement develops in the area around the cathedral, at the same time the old 'suburbs' and landing stage by the fjord are cut off.

The background to Roskilde's location does not seem to have been the presence of an existing trading site, nor does trade appear to have played an important role in the first years of the town. Roskilde belongs to a group of bishoprics founded around the turn of the first millennium, which the king and Church needed as administrative centres for a new power structure. First and foremost the desire for good lines of communication between the disparate parts of the realm, and a literally visible placement of church buildings in the landscape, seem together to have determined the location of Roskilde, coupled naturally with its proximity to the old centre at Lejre.

As we have seen, there is an impression of stability about Iron Age and Viking Lejre until the end of the tenth century. At this time comes the disappearance of some of the elements that, it is suggested here, were connected to pre-Christian cult, but the settlement continues during the Middle Ages in the form of a manorial farm. The settlement itself is not abandoned, but to judge from the excavations some of its functions are transferred to the newly founded Roskilde. In this sense it is appropriate to speak of pagan Lejre and Christian Roskilde.

BIBLIOGRAPHY

Andersen, S.W. (1995) 'Lejre – skibssætninger, vikingegrave og Grydehøj', *Aarbøger for Nordisk Oldkyndighed og Historie*, (1993): 7–137.

Birkebæk, F. (1992) 'Fra handelsplads til metropol. 950–1080', in F. Birkebæk *et al. Roskilde bys historie – tiden indtil 1536*, Roskilde: Roskilde Museum Forlag.

Christensen, T. (1991) *Lejre – syn og sagn*, Roskilde: Roskilde Museum Forlag.

—— (1993) 'Lejre beyond legend: the archaeological evidence', *Journal of Danish Archaeology*, 10: 163–85.

—— (1998) 'Middelalder i Gl. Lejre', in *Fra Amt og By. Historiske bidrag i anledning af Ernst Verwohlts 75 års dag 1. oktober 1998* (Historisk årbog fra Roskilde amt), Roskilde: Historisk Samfund for Roskilde amt.

—— (2000) 'Civitas Roscald', in T. Christensen and M. Andersen (eds) *Civitas Roscald – fra byens begyndelsen*, Roskilde: Roskilde Museum Forlag.

—— (2001) 'Lejre', *RGA* 18: 248–54.

—— (2004) 'Fra hedenskab til kristendom i Lejre og Roskilde', in N. Lund (ed.) *Kristendommen i Danmark før 1050*, Roskilde: Roskilde Museum Forlag.

—— (2007) 'A new round of excavations at Lejre (to 2005)', in J. Niles, *Beowulf and Lejre* (Medieval and renaissance texts and studies 323), Tempe, Ariz.: Arizona Centre for Medieval and Renaissance Studies.

Lund, N. (1998) *Harald Blåtands død – og hans begravelse i Roskilde?*, Roskilde: Roskilde Museum Forlag.

Olsen, O. (1966) *Hørg, Hov og Kirke. Historiske og arkæologiske vikingetidsstudier*, Copenhagen: Gad.

Skovgaard-Petersen, I. (1977) 'Oldtid og vikingetid', in A.E. Christensen *et al.* (eds) *Danmarks historie*, vol. 1: *Tiden indtil 1340*, Copenhagen: Gyldendal.

Thietmar von Merseburg, Chronik, W. Trillmich (trans. and ed.) (Ausgewählte Quellen zur deutschen Geschichte des Mittelalters 9), Darmstadt: Wissenschaftlicher Buchgesellschaft 1974.

Ulriksen, J. (2000) 'Vindeboder – Roskildes tidlige havnekvarter', in T. Christensen and M. Andersen (eds) *Civitas Roscald – fra byens begyndelsen*, Roskilde: Roskilde Museum Forlag.

Wilson, D. (1960) 'Irsk-britisk import i Lejre', *Nationalmuseets Arbejdsmark*: 36–7.

CHAPTER EIGHT (5)

RIBE

———·◆·———

Claus Feveile

The written sources about Viking Age Ribe are few (Skovgaard-Petersen 1981). Ribe is mentioned for the first time in the Frankish annals in the 850s when the Danish king Horik the younger gives the missionary Ansgar from the Episcopal residence in Hamburg a piece of land where a church could be erected as well as permission for a priest to take up permanent residence.

Among the participants at the synod in Ingelheim in 948 Bishop Leofdag of Ribe (*Liopdago Ripensis ecclesiae episcopo*) is mentioned. In 965 and 988 Ribe is referred to as an Episcopal residence as well. Finally Ribe occurs in Adam of Bremen's *Gesta* from the 1070s, where the town is described as follows, 'the town is surrounded by a river streaming in from the ocean and through which the ships steer towards Friesland or at any rate to England and our Saxony'.

The first archaeological attempts to locate ancient Ribe were carried out in the 1950s and took place in the area around the present cathedral on the south-west bank of the Ribe River. Here, however, the layers do not date back any further than to the end of the eleventh century. In the 1960s the archaeological search for the town among other things led to excavations outside the town, for example at Dankirke and Okholm (Hansen 1990; Feveile 2001), 6–8 km south-west of Ribe.

The final breakthrough in the archaeological investigation of Ribe came in the 1970s, when Mogens Bencard carried out a long excavation campaign for several years on the north-east bank of the Ribe River. Here remains of the marketplace as well as one inhumation grave dating from the eighth century were found. The excavations in 1970–6 are in course of publication: five volumes have been released and one is in preparation (Bencard 1981, 1984; Bencard *et al.* 1990, 1991, 2004). During 1984–2000 more than twenty excavations were carried out on the north and east banks of the Ribe River. A number of intermediate results and surveys have been released successively (Frandsen and Jensen 1988a and b, 1990; Feveile 1994; Feveile *et al.* 1992, 1999; Feveile and Jensen 2000), while a more comprehensive new series, *Ribe Studier*, dealing with the results from the excavations of 1984–2000 has been initiated (Feveile 2006a).

The oldest part of Ribe is situated on the north and east banks of the Ribe River, whereas from the end of the eleventh century the town centre was situated on the south-west bank of the River. North-east of the river the landscape is dry and sandy, while the south-west side is divided into several small sandy islets, separated by meadow and bogland. The north-east side is mostly flat, *c.* 3–4 m above sea level, but with a few small areas up to 6 m above sea level.

Recent geological research shows a layer of drifting sand in an area of *c.* 6,000 m² dating (by ¹⁴C) from around the birth of Christ, covering a plough-layer with traces of furrow (ardmarks) (Dalsgaard 2006; Aaby 2006). Consequently the marketplace is established on top of a natural sandbank that is several hundred years old and not – as has previously been described – on a man-made layer of sand (Jensen 1991; Feveile 1994). The course of the river in the eighth–twelfth centuries is not known precisely.

In a *c.* 200 m long and 80 m wide area along the river solid culture layers as deep as up to *c.* 2 m have been investigated. The layers consisting of workshop floors, fireplaces, waste layers etc. contain tens of thousands of archaeological objects, documenting an extensive production of crafts (bead-maker, bronze caster, amber polisher, comb manufacturer, shoe-maker, potter) as well as import and trade (raw materials for the craftsmen, ready-made goods such as Frankish ceramics and hollow glass, volcanic basalt, Scandinavian soapstone, whetstones of slate, whalebones and glass beads from the Middle East). The oldest culture layers, which can be dated back to the period 704–10, derive from marketplace activity, the organisation of which is not precisely known. After relatively few years the marketplace was organised in a row of plots *c.* 6–8 m wide and probably up to *c.* 20–30 m long placed at right angles to the river. Probably there have been around forty–fifty plots in all. The individual plots are separated by shallow, narrow ditches, in some places with preserved wattlework along the edges. The basic structure exists unaltered for the next *c.* 150 years, with only small adjustments of the plot boundaries. Until *c.* 770–80 to all appearance the use of the marketplace has been seasonal. Therefore no housing constructions are found on the plots, only a few pit-houses, wells and what appears to have been shelters etc. This, however, changes insofar as at the latest from *c.* 770–80 traces are found indicating actual buildings on the plots throughout the year. Until now the excavations in Ribe have given no answers as to the shape and size of these houses, but it must be presumed that we are dealing with constructions like those known from other contemporary marketplaces in Scandinavia, such as Hedeby, Birka and Kaupang. The growth of the layers stops around the middle or second half of the ninth century for unknown reasons. The next finds made in the marketplace are traces of buildings from the high Middle Ages, twelfth–thirteenth centuries, and later in the form of post-holes, pits etc.

The course of the river in the eighth–ninth centuries is not known precisely and correspondingly no archaeological investigations have been carried out in order to investigate the look of the harbour area.

Behind the area with plots, in many small- and large-scale excavations traces of settlements in the form of pit-houses, post-built houses, wells, fences and road systems have been found. It is essential to note that to no degree worth mentioning are culture layers preserved outside the marketplace area. Consequently we are dealing with so-called flat or areal excavations, where only the features buried in the ground have been preserved. Among the best-documented features are some post-built houses from the second half of the eighth century and the beginning of the ninth. They are of the same shape and size as known from contemporary rural settlements in Jutland. The extent of the excavated area, however, has been so small that there exists no clear evidence of how the settlement was organised: whether it had a farm-like structure or a more dense town-like structure. The material found in the settlement clearly indicates a connection with the marketplace as to a certain degree traces of craft production and trade are also found in the majority of the excavations outside the area with the workshop plots.

It must, however, be emphasised that although no certain permanent settlement dating from the first half of the eighth century has been discovered, this might exist in a number of undated settlement traces. At the same time it is also essential to notice that there are only a very few single finds of objects from the tenth and eleventh centuries, and there are absolutely no real constructions in the form of houses or wells etc. Despite the few written sources about Ribe from the tenth and eleventh centuries it must, from an archaeological point of view, be argued that the town either disappeared or at least diminished considerably during these two centuries (Feveile 2006c: 84 ff.).

About forty-seven graves have been investigated dating to the eighth to eleventh centuries (Figure 8.5.1). They are all situated in a large borderline area to the east and the north of the settlement. The graves have been investigated in five separate excavations, but there is hardly any doubt that originally they formed part of one big or several large graveyards. The majority of the graves – about thirty-three of then – can be dated to the eighth and ninth centuries. Apart from two graves – both inhumation graves with children – they are poorly equipped cremation graves. The majority are without burial gifts, while in some graves there are a few burial gifts in the form of glass beads, iron items etc. One individual cremation grave from the eighth century contained parts of riding equipment, while another grave from the ninth century contained a Frankish sword mount of gilded silver. Fourteen inhumation graves can probably be dated to the tenth–eleventh centuries.

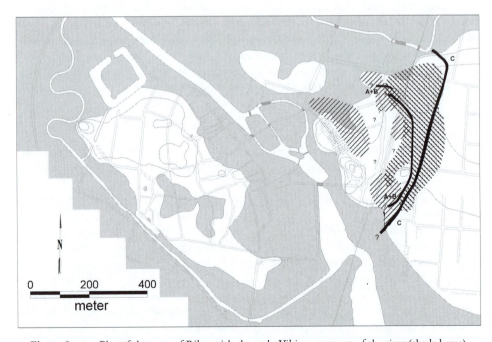

Figure 8.5.1   Plan of the town of Ribe, with the early Viking parts east of the river (shaded area).

At the beginning of the ninth century a ditch was dug around the Ribe, *c.* 2 m wide and 1 m deep (A). In several excavations the ditch was clearly seen to form the border between the developed area on the inside and undeveloped area or graveyard on the outside (Figure 8.5.1). Ditch A is so slight that it cannot be a fortification. Instead the ditch was of a symbolic nature and merely marked the town limits. The ditch that demarcates an area of *c.* 12 ha is well defined towards the east, while its northern and possible western course is not known. Consequently it is not known whether the ditch turns back to the Ribe River forming a semicircle, or whether the ditch stops at the low-lying, wet area to the north of the marketplace. During the second half of the ninth century or probably at the latest at the beginning of the tenth century the town ditch was replaced in more or less the same place by a 6–7 m wide and 1 m deep and flat-bottomed moat (B) with traces of a bank on the inside. During the second half of the eleventh century the town was re-established on both sides of the Ribe River. On the northern side the town now also covered an area in an eastern direction outside moat B. Here a *c.* 10–12 m wide and 2 m deep moat with bank, moat C, was established. This installation probably has to be seen in connection with other fortifications on the southern side of the Ribe River.

Since the first excavations at the marketplace, at regular intervals *sceattas* have been found, so that now 204 are known from Ribe (Bendixen 1981, 1994; Feveile 2006b, 2008). They have been found scattered and single, dropped in connection with trade. The predominant type is 'Wodan/Monster' (85%), followed by 'Porcupine' (11%), 'Continental Runic' (2%) as well as a few other types, all in one single copy. The coins are not only found dropped in layers from the first half of the eighth century, but the dropping – and thereby also the circulation of this type of coin – continues until the beginning of the ninth century. While the British numismatist M. Metcalf thinks the *sceattas* of the 'Wodan/Monster' type were minted in Ribe or south-western Denmark (Metcalf 1993), other researchers think they were minted somewhere in the Frisian area before *c.* 755 (Malmer 2002).

BIBLIOGRAPHY

Aaby, B. (2006) 'Pollenanalyser fra markedspladsen i Ribe, ASR 9 Posthuset og ASR 951 Plejehjemmet Riberhus', in C. Feveile (ed.) (2006a).
Bencard, M. (1978) 'Wikingerzeitliches Handwerk in Ribe. Eine übersicht', *Acta Archaeologica*, 49: 113–38.
—— (ed.) (1981) *Ribe Excavations 1970–76*, vol. 1, Esbjerg: Sydjysk Universitetsforlag.
—— (ed.) (1984) *Ribe Excavations 1970–76*, vol. 2, Esbjerg: Sydjysk Universitetsforlag.
—— (1990) 'The stratigraphy and dating of 8th century Ribe', *Journal of Danish Archaeology*, 7: 225–8.
Bencard, M., Jørgensen, L.B. and Madsen, H.B. (1990) *Ribe Excavations 1970–76*, vol. 4, Esbjerg: Sydjysk Universitetsforlag.
—— (1991) *Ribe Excavations 1970–76*, vol. 3, Esbjerg: Sydjysk Universitetsforlag.
Bencard, M., Rasmussen, A.K. and Madsen, H.B. (2004) *Ribe Excavations 1970–76*, vol. 5, Esbjerg: Jutland Archaeological Society.
Bendixen, K. (1981) 'Sceattas and other coin finds', in M. Bencard (ed.) (1981).
—— (1994) 'The coins from the oldest Ribe (excavations 1985 and 1986, "RibeII")', *Nordisk Numismatisk Årsskrift* (1989–90): 27–43.
Dalsgaard, K. (2006) 'Flygesandsaflejringer ved Ribe', in C. Feveile (ed.) (2006a).

Feveile, C. (1994) 'The latest news from Viking Age Ribe: archaeological excavations 1993', in B. Ambrosiani and H. Clarke (eds) *Developments Around the Baltic and the North Sea in the Viking Age* (The Twelfth Viking Congress; Birka Studies 3), Stockholm: Birka Project.

—— (2001) 'Okholm – en plads med håndværksspor og grubehuse fra 8.–9. århundrede', *By, marsk og geest*, 13: 5–32.

—— (ed.) (2006a) *Ribe Studier. Det ældste Ribe. Udgravninger på nordsiden af Ribe Å 1984–2000*, vols 1:1–1:2, Århus: Jysk Arkæologisk Selskab.

—— (2006b) 'Mønterne fra det ældste Ribe', in C. Feveile (ed.) (2006a), vol. 1:1.

—— (2006c) 'Ribe on the north side of the river, 8th–12th century – overview and interpretation', in C. Feveile (ed.) (2006a), vol. 1:1.

—— (2008) 'Series X and Coin Circulation in Ribe', in T. Abramson (ed.) *Studies in Early Medieval Coinage*, vol. 1: *Two decades of discovery*, Woodbridge: The Boydell Press.

Feveile, C. and Jensen, S. (2000) 'Ribe in the 8th and 9th century: a contribution to the chronology in northwestern Europe', *Acta Archaeologica*, 71: 9–24.

Feveile, C., Jensen, S. and Rasmussen, K.L. (1999) 'Produktion af drejet keramik i sen yngre germansk jernalder. Proviniensbestemmelse ved hjælp af magnetisk susceptibilitet og termoluminiscens', *Kuml*, (1997–8): 143–59.

Feveile, C., Ljungberg, K. and Jensen, S. (1992) 'Endlich gefunden: Ansgars Ribe. Ein bericht über die Ausgrabung 1989 in der Rosenallé in Ribe', *Offa*, 47: 209–33.

Frandsen, L.B. and Jensen, S. (1988a) 'Hvor lå Ribe i vikingetiden', *Kuml* (1986): 21–36.

—— (1988b) 'Pre-Viking and early Viking Age Ribe: excavations at Nicolajgade 8, 1985–86', *Journal of Danish Archaeology*, 6: 175–89.

—— (1990) 'The dating of Ribe's earliest culture layers', *Journal of Danish Archaeology*, 7: 228–31.

Hansen, H.J. (1990) 'Dankirke. Jernalderboplads og rigdomscenter. Oversigt over udgravningerne 1965–70', *Kuml* (1988–9): 201–48.

Jensen, S. (1991) *The Vikings of Ribe*, Ribe: Den Antikvariske samling.

Malmer, B. (2002) 'Münzprägung und frühe Stadtbildung in Nordeuropa', in K. Brandt, M. Müller-Wille and C. Radtke (eds) *Haithabu und die frühe Standtentwicklung im nördlichen Europa*, Neumünster: Wachholtz.

Metcalf, M. (1993) *Thrymsas and Sceattas in the Ashmolean Museum Oxford*, vol. 2 (Royal Numismatic Society. Special publications 27B), London: Royal Numismatic Society and Ashmolean Museum.

Skovgaard-Petersen, I. (1981) 'The written sources', in M. Bencard (ed.) (1981).

CHAPTER EIGHT (6)

'RIDANÆS': A VIKING AGE PORT OF TRADE AT FRÖJEL, GOTLAND

—— •◆• ——

Dan Carlsson

The Viking Age emporium 'Ridanæs' was one of the largest and most important ports on Gotland during that period and was situated between Fröjel church and the present coastline (Figure 8.6.1). We are concerned with an area of some 10 ha, where many traces of early buildings and several cemeteries have been found. Archaeological excavations conducted over several years have revealed a port, and a trading and manufacturing centre in use from the late sixth century to approximately AD 1180.

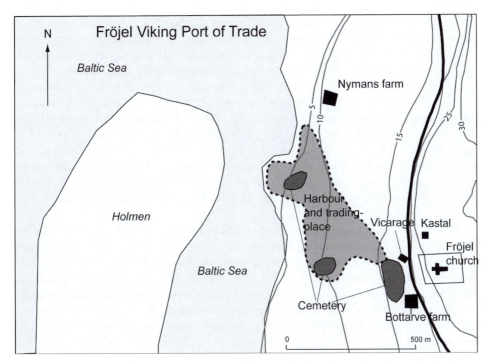

Figure 8.6.1 'Ridanæs', the Viking Age harbour at Fröjel, Gotland.

131

The activities of the port peaked during the eleventh century and the early part of the twelfth century, but continued at a more modest level until the seventeenth century (when it was located on the present coastline). Nowadays, there are no visible signs of the activity that once took place there. Nevertheless, the parish church's position, the presence of a defence tower/storehouse next to it and a large number of Viking Age artefacts in the area are all evidence that we are concerned with an important early medieval commercial centre. The name *Ridanäs* can be found on older maps and indicates the site of the port.

In the late Iron Age/early Middle Ages the harbour site was situated close to a strait, which separated the mainland of Gotland from an outlying island. The former strait, which was well protected from strong winds, the church near to the coast and the existence of a large number of stray finds in the area were reasons to believe that a port might have existed here at an earlier period in the history of the region. A comprehensive phosphate mapping revealed that a large area in direct contact with the eastern shore of the strait had very high phosphate levels, a clear sign of an extensive settlement along the former coastline.

EXCAVATIONS

The archaeological excavations at the site, which are still in progress, have provided clear evidence for human activity in the latter part of the Iron Age and the early Middle Ages (Carlsson 1999). They have revealed traces of settlement, early cemeteries and a large number of artefacts connected with trade and manufacturing. The settlement, which is indicated by rows of post-holes and stone remains, covers the whole area from the former coast up to the school house and the schoolteacher's house. We appear to have an urban community here with obvious parallels at Birka, Hedeby, Wolin and Ribe. The settlement was laid out in a regular pattern, with streets and alleys arranged symmetrically and with rows of houses. We are clearly concerned with early urbanisation here.

A total of some 1,500 m^2 has been archaeologically investigated. Up to the time of writing, the excavations have brought some 35,000 objects to light and in addition large quantities of animal bone, burnt clay, slag, flint and charcoal have been found. The finds are clear evidence for the intensive trade and industrial activity which took place here. We have imports, such as (walrus) ivory from the North Atlantic, semi-precious stones such as carnelian, rock crystal and amethyst from the Arabian peninsula and the area around the Black Sea, imported raw glass material from Italy (for making glass beads) and iron from either the Swedish mainland or from the island of Saaremaa in Estonia.

Many of the objects discovered clearly reflect the trade and contact routes of the Viking Age. Among these objects, there are a resurrection egg from Kiev in the Ukraine, a brooch with arms of equal length from the Swedish mainland, an oval brooch from Finland and more than 150 coins from the Caliphate, Germany, England and Denmark. Most of these coins are German and were struck in the early eleventh century.

The settlement area was fringed by at least three cemeteries. It cannot be ruled out that there are more cemeteries awaiting discovery, since the graves that have been discovered are well below the surface and not visible. Many graves remained untouched by ploughing, since they were up to a metre below the surface.

CEMETERIES

The oldest cemetery is situated at the northern end of the area and was almost entirely covered by later layers of settlement at the harbour. We have both inhumations and cremations, and the cemetery covers the period from the seventh century onwards, remaining in use into the tenth century. Most of the graves were well furnished, especially those of women. They have the typically Gotlandic type of jewellery. The grave goods suggest that most of the persons buried here were natives of Gotland, but new investigation of the DNA of the male population gives a clear indication of the extensive contacts eastwards. About 40 per cent of the male population (or their forefathers) seem to have an origin in eastern Europe, meaning nowadays the Baltic States and Russia.

A second cemetery is situated on the outskirts of the town area in the south and can be dated to the eleventh century. Almost all those buried here are men. Several of them are buried with weapons, such as axes and spearheads. One of the graves can be described as a chamber grave in which the man was put in a timber-framed hole in the ground, this then being sealed by a layer of timber. One of the graves in this cemetery contained several fragments of a bronze bowl, of a type that has been found in large quantities in the graves at the huge cemetery of Barshalder in southern Gotland.

The third cemetery (a Christian churchyard) is situated below the school house and the schoolteacher's house, just east of the harbour site (Carlsson 2000). Excavations were carried out in 1998, and resulted in the discovery of forty-three skeletons, only women and children. The deceased were buried with jewellery, mostly beads, but also an animal-head brooch, decorative brooches, a double-comb and a pendant in the form of an English silver coin struck for King Æthelred the Unready (from around AD 1000). Three of the graves were children's graves. In addition, the skeleton of an infant was discovered together with that of a woman. With one exception, the individuals lay on their backs in an east–west direction with their heads to the west. The exception was a woman lying with her legs pulled up in the same direction as the others but turned around, that is, with the head to the east. The dating of the cemetery is based mainly on the excavation finds. From the shape of the objects and the style of jewellery, it would seem that the graveyard was in use from the early eleventh century onwards, perhaps, more precisely, from around AD 1000. It is not known for how long the cemetery remained in use, but it can be assumed that it continued to be used until the new church was built on the cliff. According to art historians, this took place around 1160.

THE VICARAGE

The remains of the vicarage have also been discovered during the excavations, situated just west of the early churchyard mentioned above. The house was built of stone, had two rooms and 1 m thick walls. The building is not visible on the surface and was discovered by pure chance. A stone stair leads down to a well-built cellar from the floor of the front room of the building. The stone-cut windows opening into the cellar are preserved under a layer of soil. The remains of stained-glass windows are among the most remarkable finds discovered here. Among the fragments, there is one with the name *Pethrus* painted on it.

The building appears to have been in use from the thirteenth century to the early seventeenth century, when it must have been demolished. It is known from written records that Fröjel became a chapel attached to Klinte parish from the sixteenth century onwards, and this could be the reason for the abandonment of the vicarage at Fröjel.

'RIDANÆS' AND ITS SETTING

All things being considered, it can be shown that the harbour and trading site at Fröjel was established in the seventh century, or perhaps even in the late sixth century, and was in continuous use until the high Middle Ages. The extensive area of the settlement, the number of culture layers and the large number of artefacts found here show the importance of the site. There was extensive production of such items as combs, beads, jewellery and other objects of everyday life. The large number of nails and rivets clearly indicates that shipbuilding and ship repair were carried on here. The objects found also reveal contacts with the outside world and show that Fröjel can be added to the early medieval emporia in the Baltic.

The main period of activity was the eleventh century, as is indicated by the coins. From the latter part of the twelfth century, activity at the port declined and around AD 1180 the site was deserted. One of the reasons for this is a drop in sea level, which meant that the strait became too shallow for ships to enter the harbour.

The farm at Bottarve seems to have played a major role in the development of the Viking Age harbour at Fröjel. The farm, which is situated close to the present church and directly above the harbour site, owned most of the land within and adjacent to the harbour in the medieval and early modern periods. Maps show that before 1700 the Bottarve farm was situated further to the north than today.

The physical location of the church, the excavated vicarage and the graveyard at the schoolteacher's house and the school, all indicate that there is a direct connection between the Bottarve farm and the church. In other words, there is much that would indicate that the first church at Fröjel, like the one existing today, was built on land belonging to Bottarve. It is also likely that there was a direct connection between the farm and the harbour that grew up just west of it during the Viking period.

One can detect a strong functional connection between farm, harbour and church, emanating from the farm and its owners. It would seem to be the case that the owner of the farm at Bottarve laid out the graveyard and built the stave church that was probably located on his property. There is every justification for regarding this first church in Fröjel as a kind of mission church. It can be suggested that an individual landowner took the initiative and built one of the first churches in the region. The present church can therefore be seen as its successor serving the whole parish.

BIBLIOGRAPHY

Carlsson, D. (1999) *'Ridanäs': vikingahamnen i Fröjel* (ArkeoDok. Skrifter 2), Visby: ArkeoDok.
—— (2000) *Gård, hamn och kyrka. En vikingatida kyrkogård i Fröjel* (CCC-papers 4), Visby: Centrum för Östersjöstudier, University College Gotland.

CHAPTER EIGHT (7)

SEBBERSUND

———·◆·———

Jens N. Nielsen

The use of metal detectors has led to the discovery of a number of late Iron Age and early medieval settlements of a special character in the eastern part of the Limfjord. One of these settlements is Sebbersund near Nibe.

The Sebbersund site lies on the fjord coast, on a narrow, sandy foreland, part of which is known as 'Skt Nikolaj Bjerg' (St Nicholas' Mountain). The area was ideal for maritime activities, such as anchoring and local and long-distance transportation. Excavations took place here in the 1990s and in 2002 (Birkedahl and Johansen 1993: 3–8; 1995: 160–4; 2000: 25–33; Birkedahl 2000: 140 f.; Christensen and Johansen 1992: 199–229; Nielsen 2002: 6–27).

A TRADING PLACE AND PRODUCTION CENTRE

Approximately 70 pit-houses were excavated north of Skt Nikolaj Bjerg (Figure 8.7.1). Marks in the cornfields show that the total number is considerably larger, perhaps nearly 300. Concentrated and overlapping pit-house remains indicate that when a pit-house fell into disuse, a new one was usually put up almost on the same site. The limited excavations do not allow for a more exact evaluation as to the structure of the pit-house area. Nor do post-holes and other fillings found between the pit-houses allow conclusions to be made as to structures, such as longhouses.

Loom weights and spindle whorls found in half of the pit-houses show the importance of textile production. The rest of the finds come from the filling of the pit-houses. They comprise fragments of earthenware pots and soapstone vessels, glass beads, slate whetstones, numerous combs made from bone and antler, bones from domestic animals, and shells. A rather large amount of teeth from iron eel spears and fish bones indicate that fishing took place in the shallow waters surrounding the foreland.

Post-holes and pits found north-east of Skt Nikolaj Bjerg cannot be identified as remains from houses or other constructions. Several of the pits contained stones and large amounts of flint that had been exposed to fire, as well as charcoal and clinker from forges. The flint was probably used in connection with forge welding. Iron scales and forge remnants show that ironworking was an important activity in this settlement. There are also traces of bronze, silver and gold crafts.

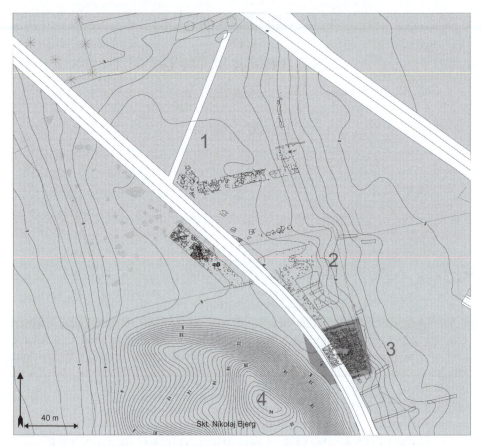

Figure 8.7.1 Plan of the excavated areas and Skt Nikolaj Bjerg. (1) Pit-houses, (2) workshop activity, (3) the wooden church, (4) the stone church.

The investigation results concerning the two areas mentioned indicate the importance of production, probably with textile and iron manufacturing as the chief crafts. Weights indicate that trade also took place here. These activities seem to have begun around AD 700 and continued until the early twelfth century (Christensen and Johansen 1992: 211 f.).

A possible permanent settlement on the foreland would have been of limited size. Sebbersund was probably a seasonal settlement, which attracted the local population as well as people from distant areas, for instance Norway and the British Isles.

THE WOODEN CHURCH

The traces of a wooden church with adjoining churchyard were found south of the workshop area (Figure 8.7.2). The church lies on slightly sloping terrain, which verges on the coast towards the east. The westernmost third of the churchyard has not been investigated. The churchyard measures approximately 40 m × 40 m, and it is bounded by ditches towards the south and north.

Figure 8.7.2   Plan of the wooden church and adjoining churchyard.

A rectangular area without graves in the middle of the churchyard indicates the position of a church. The interpretation of a number of post-holes from a supposed wooden church has caused some problems. However, the most likely hypothesis is the following. The remains are probably from two churches, both of which had a narrow chancel. The first church had wall posts dug into the ground and arranged in pairs. It was succeeded by a church in the same position, but this second church had posts resting on stones dug partly into the earth. The walls of both churches seem to have rested on a sill beam, but the rest of the wall construction is unknown.

THE GRAVES

Approximately 468 graves of different types have been excavated. One of the more remarkable ones is an east–west oriented stone coffin made from split granite boulders, situated south of the church. Its western end consists of a large limestone slab with a round recess for the head. The coffin was sealed with mortar in several places. It contained the well-preserved body of a woman, who had the remains of a 'pillow' under her head (see below). A small hazel stick lay across her pelvis. The woman was around 154 cm tall, a little over sixty years old and of delicate to normal build. She had not had hard, physical work. There was evidence of her having given birth.

In at least twenty burials, wood traces indicate that boats had been used as coffins. In grave no. 267, part of a boat seems to have been placed on top of the buried person. Usually, the stem is pointing towards the east. Men, women and children were buried in boats. A 3.8 m long boat contained the burials of three people, including a child of nine to eleven years. The boat burials are distributed evenly on the excavated part of the churchyard. This and other conditions indicate that the use of boat parts as coffins mainly served a practical purpose, as well as expressing the maritime connection. Several other graves contained iron nails and spikes, probably from boats or boat parts.

A number of graves had traces of wooden coffins. As is the case with the boat graves, the surface of the wood was apparently burnt. Most coffins are rectangular, but trapezium coffins occur. A small group of wooden coffins may be troughs or the like. There are probably graves without any coffin.

THE DEAD

The preservation conditions for the skeletons vary. Several graves contain skeletal parts from more persons, probably due to the overlapping of graves. One person was buried lying on the side, whereas the rest had been placed on the back, always with the head towards the west. In approximately 18 per cent of the graves, boat graves included, the head was supported by a 'pillow'. In most cases, this was probably a turf, but also burnt flint, bones, granite stones or clay were used as 'pillows'. In a few graves, two stones formed a niche around the head.

Anthropological analyses and the height of the skeletons show that women were mainly buried north of the church and men on the southern side. However, this sex-based division was not applied consistently, perhaps due to changes in burial practice over the years. The children's graves clearly tend to be concentrated, for instance near the eastern part of the church and in the north-eastern corner of the churchyard.

Other aspects than sex and age seem to have influenced the choice of burial place. The largest graves tend to lie in groups and have more free space around them. Only in one case, one of these graves was overlapped by another grave (a child's grave). Maybe this tendency reflects the custom of burying leading persons (men especially) or families in specific areas. Perhaps the woman in the stone coffin was buried on the southern side of the church because she was the head of the family.

THE STONE CHURCH

Written sources mention a church situated on Skt Nikolaj Bjerg, and a small-scale excavation in 2002 proved this to be correct. Before the building of the church began, the site was levelled with a sand layer, which was up to 50 cm thick. The church, which was built from granite ashlars, had a length of roughly 20 m. It consisted of a nave and a narrower chancel. Several pieces of mortar with whitewash on one side indicate that the inner walls were whitewashed.

Traces of crafts, such as forging, connected to the building of the church, were noted at several places. A partly intact building layer was found underneath the foundation layer for the floor, which consisted of flint blocks and granite stones, covered by a layer of mortar. Some fashioned lime flags are probably remnants of the floor. In the western end, large flint blocks placed on end created the base of the font. Pieces of fashioned lime blocks found in a nearby layer may have covered the visible part of the font platform. Fragments of yellow bricks of typical medieval shape were found in the eastern part of the chancel. They are probably the remains of a brick altar.

Considerable amounts of iron nails were found inside and outside the church. They are not from coffins, but may be from the church construction, perhaps from a board ceiling. The church is surrounded by graves on all sides, except to the west, where the terrain slopes abruptly. Areas without graves on the southern and northern side of the western part of the nave may indicate doors in the nave walls. The number of graves in the churchyard has been estimated to around 100. The graves seem to have an east–west orientation. Just a few graves were investigated, and they turned out to differ as to construction and other details. A few graves were found inside the church, including four children's graves. Men, women and children are buried in the churchyard.

The present parish church lies 1 km west of Skt Nikolaj Bjerg. This church, Sebber church, which was probably originally part of a Benedictine monastery, was first mentioned in 1268, but is probably older. It may have replaced the stone church on Skt Nikolaj Bjerg.

DATINGS

The trade and crafts settlement came into existence around AD 700 and seems to have existed until the early twelfth century. The settlement appears to have flourished in the eleventh century (Christensen and Johansen 1992: 211 f.). Scientific dating methods indicate that the wooden church was built in the first quarter of the eleventh century and was probably given up during the second half of the twelfth century. It is an obvious conclusion that the building of the wooden church was connected to the activities in the trading settlement. The church was probably built by a local chieftain. The stone church probably existed from the late eleventh century until around 1200. Thus, the two churches may have functioned contemporarily. If this is the case, we are facing some very essential problems concerning the founder and users of the stone church.

BIBLIOGRAPHY

Birkedahl, P.B. (2000) 'Sebbersund', in S. Hvass (ed.) *Vor skjulte kulturarv. Arkæologien under overfladen*, Copenhagen and Højbjerg: Det Kongelige Nordiske Oldskriftsselskab og Jysk Arkæologisk Selskab.

Birkedahl, P. and Johansen, E. (1993) 'Nikolajbjerget', *Skalk*, 1993(1): 3–8.

—— (1995) 'The Sebbersund boat-graves', in O. Crumlin-Petersen and B.M. Thye (eds) *The Ship as Symbol in Prehistoric and Medieval Scandinavia* (Publications from the National Museum. Studies in Archaeology and History 1), Copenhagen: National Museum.

—— (2000) 'The eastern Limfjord in the Germanic Iron Age and the Viking period: internal structures and external relations', in S.S. Hansen and K. Randsborg (eds) *Vikings in the West* (= *Acta Archaeologica*, 71), Oxford: Blackwell.

Christensen, P.B. and Johansen, E. (1992) 'En handelsplads fra yngre jernalder og vikingetid ved Sebbersund', *Aarbøger for Nordisk Oldkyndighed og Historie* (1991): 199–229.

Nielsen, J.N. (2002) *Sebbersund. Handel, håndværk og kristendom ved Limfjorden*, Aalborg: Aalborg Historiske Museum.

—— (2004) 'Sebbersund—tidlige kirker ved Limfjorden', in N. Lund (ed.) *Kristendommen i Danmark før 1050*, Roskilde: Roskilde Museum Forlag.

CHAPTER EIGHT (8)

SIGTUNA

——•◆•——

Jonas Ros

Sigtuna was founded *c.* 980, by the time when the town of Birka ceased to have urban functions, and Sigtuna took over Birka's role of being a port for long-distance trade. Sigtuna also had other functions: it was a centre for craft production, and a market for domestic trade for the town and the hinterland. There was also a mint in the town. King Erik the Victorious probably founded Sigtuna. By founding the town, the king could attach chieftains to him in a new way: he could grant plots in the town to them and he could also grant lordship over hundreds and ship-sokes. Chieftains could then have had jurisdiction over such districts, and could control and man warships. Sigtuna was a centre for the Crown and a meeting-place for the elite.

The oldest mention of the name *Sigtuna* is on coins struck in the town. On the coins, there are short forms of the name, for example *Siht, Stnete* and *Situn* (Malmer 1989: 63 ff.). Sigtuna is also mentioned in the skaldic poetry from the eleventh century. Chieftains who later became kings are said to have visited the town. The name *Sigtuna* is also mentioned in a runic inscription from the town of Sigtuna. The inscription records that: 'Sven . . . carved the stone . . . who transferred her to *Sihtunum*' (i.e. Sigtuna) (U 395). There are different interpretations of the place name *Sigtuna*. According to one, the model for the name is the Celtic word *Segodunon* meaning strong fortification. According to another, it is a compound of the word *sig* 'trickling water' and *tuna*, whose meaning is obscure (Wahlberg 2003: 271 f.). The *Tuna*-places were some kind of central places during the Iron Age.

TOWN PLAN AND EXCAVATIONS

Sigtuna has an S-shaped main street, *Stora gatan*, running east–west parallel to the shore at the south of the urban area. The oldest map of Sigtuna dates from 1636 (Figure 8.8.1). The streets and the blocks have similarities with the present town plan. The main street had its origin from the very beginning of the town. There were plots on each side of the street. Alongside the street there were shops and the street functioned as a market. A model for the town plan has been looked for in England (Schück 1926: 129; Floderus 1941: 65); it has similarities with the contemporary towns Bergen and Trondheim.

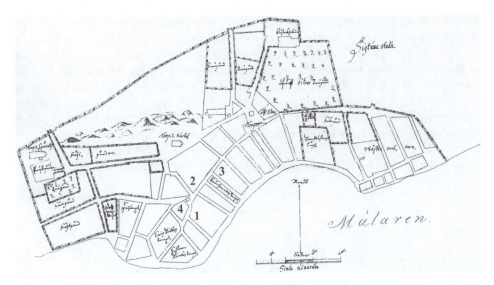

Figure 8.8.1 The oldest map of Sigtuna, dating from 1636. The church of St Per is in the western part of the town. (1) The Urmakaren, (2) the Trädgårdsmästaren, (3) the Professorn blocks, (4) the Sigtuna Museum plot. (Copyright © National Land Survey of Sweden.)

Kings are mentioned in the written sources in connection with the town. One interpretation is that there was a royal residence here, and that this moved to three different places within the settlement area (e.g. Tesch 2003: 8 ff.). However, there is no written or archaeological evidence of royal residences in the town (Ros 2001: 78, 177). Instead, the king had an official, a *geld-exactor*, here, and in 1274 a Sigtuna *Prefect* is mentioned (DS 572, 574). It is probable that there was a *geld-exactor* in Sigtuna from the beginning of the town. A town law was needed to solve conflicts and the *geld-exactor* was probably chairman at the town court. During the Viking Age the kings were itinerant, and they had manors that they visited periodically. To the west of Sigtuna, on the other side of the water Sigtunafjärden/Håtunaviken, there is a royal manor called *Fornsigtuna*, that is, 'Old Sigtuna' – the place name obviously showing a connection to Sigtuna. In the *Ynglingasaga* Snorri Sturluson says that Fornsigtuna was a royal residence during the Iron Age (ch. 5). The king granted Fornsigtuna to the bishop around 1130 (DS 852) and the estate continued to be a royal manor until 1627. Small-scale excavations in Fornsigtuna have given ^{14}C dates to the Iron Age, especially to the Vendel and Viking periods, though some ^{14}C dates are later (Damell 1991: 30, 32 ff., 83 ff.). Extended excavations would certainly show settlement contemporary to the town of Sigtuna. Thus, there was no royal residence in the town of Sigtuna, which was probably at Fornsigtuna. There was a similar situation at Birka, where the royal residence was on the other side of the water, at Adelsö.

The culture layer in Sigtuna covers an area of *c.* 700 m × 100 m and it is at the most 3.5 m thick. There have been many archaeological excavations in the town. To the north of Stora gatan in a block known as Trädgårdsmästaren large-scale excavations have taken place: four and part of a fifth tenement were excavated (Petterson 1995). Excavations to the south of the street in a block known as Professorn show that the plot structure was of the same kind on that side of the street. The most common town plots in Sigtuna were *c.* 8 m wide and sometimes 30–40 m long, with as many as four or five buildings with different functions. At the rear of the plots there was a residential hall with a fireplace on the floor. Another building, with a household function, had a fireplace in one corner. There were also buildings for storage and multiple functions. A great number of tenements probably belonged to manors in the town's hinterland. There was little debris from craft production in the oldest layers; during that period the craftsmen were periodically active in the town. During the eleventh and twelfth centuries, there were shops alongside the street that were rented by craftsmen and traders.

In a block known as Urmakaren, plots of smaller dimensions were excavated (Figure 8.8.2). The buildings along the street had household functions, but there was

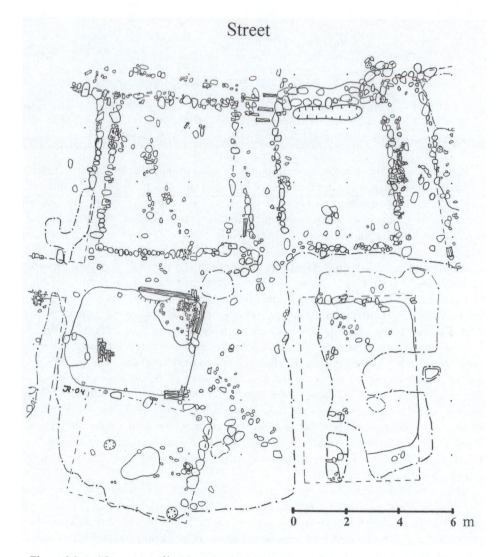

Figure 8.8.2   The remains of buildings on two plots and parts of two other plots in the Urmakaren block in Sigtuna. The buildings date from the mid-eleventh century. (Drawing: J. Ros.)

also debris from craft production in them. There was also debris from craft production in the smaller buildings. The plots were *c.* 6 m wide and there were two or three buildings on them. In the excavated area there were three different kinds of house foundations: sill stone, post-hole and twig holes in lines. The buildings were made by the horizontal-planking technique and wattle and daub, and during the eleventh century the cross-jointing technique was introduced. King Olof Skötkonung's minting-house was found in the excavated area: pieces of lead with the impression of a die were found on the floor (Ros 1991, 2001: 87 ff.). The first Swedish coins were made in Sigtuna: King Olof Skötkonung started coin production *c.* 995 and it continued until his death *c.* 1022. He invited English moneyers to Sigtuna and five moneyers had their names on coins made in the town. Olof might have produced as many as two million coins. Olof's son, Anund Jakob, continued to make coins from *c.* 1022 until 1030/5, then there was a long period without coinage. Production started again in Sigtuna under Knut Eriksson's reign 1167–96 (Malmer 1991: 13, 25).

THE CHURCHES AND THE EPISCOPAL SEE

The foundation of Sigtuna took place during the pagan period. On the outskirt of the town there are late Viking Age inhumation burial grounds (Douglas 1978: 61 f.). There are also some later burial grounds in the town with no visible marking above ground. The graves are Christian, oriented east–west. One of these grave-fields, dating to *c.* 1000, has been excavated in the western part of the town (Hillbom 1987).

Adam of Bremen mentions that Olof Skötkonung had a bishop among his retainers, and later, during the 1060s, there was a missionary bishop named *Osmund* in Sigtuna. Adam calls Sigtuna *civitas magna Sictone* and *Sictonia civitate*. It became a bishopric *c.* 1070, during Stenkil's reign, under Bishop Adalvard the younger, but the bishop abandoned Sigtuna when Stenkil died (*Adam of Bremen* 2: 58, 3: 15, 4: 25, 28 ff.). In a letter from the 1080s the pope expresses his joy that there are preachers among the *Svea* people and the king is asked to send a bishop or priest to Rome (DS 24). It is not known which was the episcopal church in Sigtuna.

In Sigtuna there are churches dedicated to St Per, St Nikolai, St Lars, St Olov, St Gertrud and the Virgin Mary, which belonged to the Dominican monastery. There was also a hospital of St George with a chapel. Archaeological investigations have revealed another two churchyards. Most of the churches are in an east–west sequence north of the settlement area. Only one is located in the settlement area: on the Sigtuna museum plot. One suggestion is that that church was the bishop's church (e.g. Tesch 2003: 9 f.); however, it is more likely that St Per, situated in the western part of the town, was the episcopal church. St Per was built *c.* 1100 (Redelius 1975). Earlier there was probably a wooden church somewhere in the town. St Per might also have been a mother church with a parish comprising the town and the surrounding area (Ros 2001: 147 ff.). This is, however, a hypothetical speculation and the church of St Olov might have been the episcopal church. The episcopal see was moved from Sigtuna to Old Uppsala in the 1130s.

BIBLIOGRAPHY

Adam of Bremen = (1984) *Historien om Hamburgstiftet och dess biskopar. Adam av Bremen*, trans. E. Svenberg (Skrifter utgivna av Samfundet Pro fide et christianismo 6), Stockholm: Proprius, 1984.

Allestav, A. *et al.* (eds) (1991) *Fornsigtuna. En kungsgårds historia*, Upplands-Bro: Stiftelsen Upplands-Bro fornforskning.

Damell, D. (1991) 'Utgrävningens metodik' and 'C14 och termoluminiscensdateringar', in A. Allestav *et al.* (eds) (1991).

Douglas, M. (1978) *Sigtuna* (Medeltidsstaden 6), Stockholm: Raä and Statens historiska museer.

DS = *Diplomatarium suecanum*, vols 1–, Stockholm 1829 ff.

Floderus, E. (1941) *Sigtuna. Sveriges äldsta medeltidsstad*, Stockholm: Geber.

Hillbom, L. (1987) 'Kvarteret Nunnan', in T. Andrae, M. Hasselmo and K. Lamm (eds) *7000 år på 20 år. Arkeologiska undersökningar i Mellansverige*, Stockholm: Raä.

Malmer, B. (1989) *The Sigtuna Coinage c. 995–1005* (Commentationes de nummis saeculorum IX–XI in Suecia repertis. Nova series 4), Stockholm: KVHAA and London: Spink & Son.

—— (ed.) (1991) *Kung Olofs Mynthus i kvarteret Urmakaren, Sigtuna* (Sigtuna museers skriftserie 3), Sigtuna: Sigtuna museum.

Den norsk-islandske skjaldedigtning. Udgiven af kommissionen for det arnamagnaeanske legat, 4 vols, Finnur Jónsson (ed.), Copenhagen: Gyldendalske boghandel, 1912–15.

Pettersson, B. (1995) 'Stratigraphic analysis and settlement stratigraphy in early medieval Sigtuna', *Laborativ Arkeologi. Journal of Nordic Archaeological Science*, 8: 65–77.

Redelius, G. (1975) *Sigtunastudier. Historia och byggnadskonst under äldre medeltid*, Stockholm: University of Stockholm.

Ros, J. (1991) 'Den arkeologiska utgrävningen', in B. Malmer (ed.) (1991).

—— (2001) *Sigtuna. Staden, kyrkorna och den kyrkliga organisationen* (Opia 30), Uppsala: Dept. of Archaeology, Uppsala University.

Schück, A. (1926) *Studier rörande det Svenska stadsväsendets uppkomst och äldsta utveckling*, Stockholm: no publ.

Tesch, S. (2003) *Vyer från medeltidens Sigtuna* (Sigtuna museers skriftserie 10), Sigtuna: Sigtuna museum.

U = *Upplands runinskrifter*, 4 vols (SRI 6–9), Stockholm: Almqvist & Wiksell International.

Wahlberg, M. (ed.) (2003) *Svenskt ortnamnslexikon*, Uppsala: SOFI.

Ynglinga saga, in Snorri Sturluson, *Heimskringla*, 3 vols. (Islenzk fornrit 26–28), Reykjavík: Hið íslenzka fornritafélag 1941–51.

CHAPTER EIGHT (9)

VIKING AGE UPPÅKRA AND LUND

——·◆·——

Birgitta Hårdh

The Iron Age centre Uppåkra is situated on a pronounced height, dominating the plain of Lund. Uppåkra belongs to the group of south Scandinavian central places which have been recorded during the past decades, mainly in Denmark. The central places are defined as multi-functional, regional centres with a long continuity. The finds from Uppåkra show that the site kept the function of a central place during the entire first millennium. With the vast extent of the cultural layer and the distribution of finds, it is, at 40 ha, also the largest Iron Age settlement known from south Scandinavia, and cultural layers measuring up to 2 m thickness have been recorded (Hårdh 2000; Larsson 2001a).

Uppåkra is situated 4 km south of the medieval city of Lund and for a long time there were speculations whether Uppåkra was a predecessor of Lund. Archaeologically it has been stated that the beginning of Lund is about AD 990. The first time that the name of *Uppåkra* appears is in a written document, a donation charter issued by King Cnut the Holy from 1085.

When the new investigations started in Uppåkra in 1996 hardly anything was known of a Viking Age settlement at the site. A number of field names containing the word *toft*, known from cadastral maps from the eighteenth century, were possible indications of a Viking Age settlement. Unfortunately agriculture has destroyed most structures from the Merovingian, Viking Age and later periods. The thick cultural layers derive mainly from the early Iron Age. However, two sunken-featured buildings, one with a complete oval brooch in Borre style, and remains of a longhouse, have been recorded.

In 1997 there was an opportunity to conduct a small excavation under the sanctuary in the present church, built in the 1860s. Foundations from the Romanesque medieval church under the present church were traced and beneath them, in a layer with occasional fragments of ceramic of Viking Age type, a skeleton in a stretched position with an east–west orientation was found. This could indicate an interment of Christian type before the medieval period. It is plausible to consider the possibility of a church older than the medieval one on the site. Not far from the present church a big encolpion, probably made in Germany around 1000, has been found (Staecker 1999). It could have belonged to a late Viking Age church.

Especially worth attention are the results from the excavations in 2001–4. South of the church an area has been investigated with manifold cultic or ritual manifestations. In its centre there is a house with an exceptionally long continuation, at least from the Roman Iron Age up to the beginning of the Viking Age. In the house a large number of depositions have been recorded, among them more than 110 gold-foil figures, a metal beaker with embossed figure foils in gold and a glass bowl from the Black Sea region. Around the house there are depositions of weapons, partly destroyed and dated from the Roman Iron Age to the Merovingian period, perhaps to the early Viking Age. Close to the house there is a stone paving with abundant animal bones. Here a Þórr's hammer ring of iron has been found. The house was pulled down around AD 800 and the depositions in the area ceased at the same time, probably indicating a fundamental religious change (Larsson 2001b; *Uppåkrastudier* vol. 10).

The main share of the Viking Age record comes from detector investigations. The distribution of the finds covers the entire cultural layer. The site appears as one of the richest Viking Age settlement sites, especially as regards ornament types. The number of finds of various types from Uppåkra surpasses several times what previously was known from the entire Skåne. For example, more than 100 fragments of oval brooches have been found. More than 40 three-foil brooches, complete and fragments, and 43 equal-armed brooches have been registered so far. A category worth attention is a group of about 40 round, cast and gilded bronze brooches and pendants with spiral or Terslev decoration and, in one case, animal decoration in Jelling style. This type of brooch and pendant is known mainly from places such as Birka, Hedeby and Tissø at Zealand.

Several of the ornaments are fragments and it is probable that they were intended to be remelted and thus are to be seen as raw material for metal handicraft. Some patrices show, together with moulds, the presence of metalwork in the Viking Age as in previous periods. The indications for metal handicraft suggest that it was at a large scale and of high quality (Kresten *et al.* 2001).

Over 380 weights have been found, among them several of the cubo-octahedric and of spherical types, characteristic of the Viking Age. Also some fragments of balances have been found. Coins dated to the Viking Age so far number 277. The dominant group (*c.* 250 coins) is Arabic issues. Their composition has an early emphasis with mainly Abbasid coins from the eighth and ninth centuries. From the tenth century there are 40 Samanid dirhams, dating up to *c.* AD 950, while from the second half of the tenth century and the eleventh century the number of coins is considerably smaller. There are some German, English and Danish coins but although the number of coins has decreased, the entire late part of the Viking Age is represented (Silvegren 2002).

Beside the coins there are several indications of long-distance contacts in the Viking Age as well as in previous periods: for example a collection of ornaments and mountings of west European, mainly Carolingian, origin, enamelled mountings from the British Isles, probably from Ireland, and an oriental mounting, perhaps from the Khazarian region.

There are many manifestations of the uniqueness of Uppåkra in the Viking Age. A small silver statue in the shape of a fantastic lion-like animal with two snakes was probably made in west Europe around 800 (Figure 8.9.1). The best parallels to the animal are to be found among the illustrations in the Book of Kells. A well-known little statue represents a one-eyed man with horns on his head. The figure is closely associated to horned figures with weapons, for example, on coins, stamped metal foils or patrices

Figure 8.9.1 Imaginative animal in solid silver with necklace of gold (44 mm in length) found at Uppåkra. Parallels to the animal can be found in the Book of Kells. It was probably manufactured in western Europe *c.* 800. (Photo: Bengt Almgren. Copyright © The Historical Museum, University of Lund.)

for these (cf. Arrhenius 1994: 211 ff.). There are also a couple of close parallels in Tissø. Apparently it is a representation of Óðinn.

A small gilded silver head has its best parallels on the famous caskets from Kammin and Bamberg, as well as on the belt mountings from the tomb under the church of Jelling. It is of course not possible to tell whether this highly prestigious object was made in Uppåkra, came there as scrap silver or shows the presence of some person connected to the Jelling court. It indicates, however, direct or indirect connections to the uppermost social levels in tenth-century Denmark.

As regards the variety, number and quality of finds, Uppåkra is fully comparable to the largest Viking Age central and trading places such as Birka, Hedeby and Tissø. A severe obstacle for the interpretation is, as mentioned, the damaged cultural layers, which means that traces of constructions are almost completely missing in Uppåkra. A central question is of course the character of settlement. The inland location, 7 km from the coast, indicates that the place was hardly a site with shipping trade as the main activity. In contrast to several of the Viking Age central and trading places, Uppåkra is not the result of a royal foundation in the early Viking Age. At the beginning of the Viking Age Uppåkra had already existed for at least 800 years and kept a position as an exceptional site, a mighty centre for centuries. Thus it is obvious that Uppåkra is not a parallel to Birka or Hedeby. Tissø on Zealand is characterised as an aristocratic residence, a manorial farm with abundant finds of prestigious objects, traces of qualitative handicraft and external contacts. The site has also continuity back into the migration period. The settlement of the central place Gudme on Fyn covered a vast area but was obviously not dense. Instead the record has been interpreted as a collection of about fifty farms with dwelling houses and outhouses. This is a model which is also possible for Uppåkra, especially as the site is located centrally in a most fertile agrarian region. It is also appropriate to consider that the earliest settlement of Lund, from the eleventh century, has been reconstructed as a collection of spacious plots with a settlement structure rather similar to concentrated rural farms (Carelli 2001: 107).

In the 990s Lund was established a few kilometres north of Uppåkra. In this case it is a foundation initiated by the king and with the Church as an active and powerful partner. It is also most probable that the localisation of Lund is connected to the presence of the mighty Iron Age centre. Here an infrastructure, roads and other communications and a large population were already present. Whether the king had influence in Uppåkra or whether he saw it as a competing power is hard to know. About 100 years later, as the above-mentioned donation charter shows, the king possessed substantial estates in Uppåkra. It is obvious that Uppåkra was part of the political power game in eastern Denmark in the decades around 1000. Two fortresses, Borgeby and Trelleborg, are dated to this period. Borgeby is situated at the estuary of the rivulet Lödde Å, the entrance to the province of Skåne from the Strait of Öresund, and Trelleborg is situated in the present town of Trelleborg on the south coast of Skåne. Both sites are also situated at a communication link that connects the south and west coasts of Skåne and which, in a north–south direction, runs through Uppåkra as well as Lund (Eriksson 2001; Jacobsson 2003). It is probable that the two fortresses also played an important part in politics, even if it is too early yet to state how.

The investigations in Uppåkra have shown the complexity of centre formations during the entire first millennium. They show a central place different from the well-known Viking Age trading places, and neither is it a manorial farm like Tissø. The size and continuity of the place are exceptional. Notwithstanding societal changes and political turbulence, Uppåkra kept its dominant position for 1,000 years. Only with the establishment of Lund did Uppåkra lose its position as a centre and become a mere agricultural settlement.

NOTE

Numbers of objects from Uppåkra given in this article refer to the standing of registered objects in 2003.

BIBLIOGRAPHY

Arrhenius, B. (1994) 'Järnåldern', in *Signums svenska konsthistoria*, vol. 1, Lund: Signum.

Carelli, P. (2001) *En kapitalistisk anda. Kulturella förändringar i 1100-talets Danmark*, Lund: Almqvist & Wiksell International.

Eriksson, M. (2001) 'En väg till Uppåkra', in L. Larsson (ed.) *Uppåkra. Centrum i analys och rapport* (Uppåkrastudier 4), Stockholm: Almqvist & Wiksell International.

Hårdh, B. (2000) 'Uppåkra – a centre in south Sweden in the 1st millennium AD', *Antiquity*, 74(285): 640–8.

Helgesson, B. (2002) *Järnålderns Skåne. Samhälle, centra och regioner* (Uppåkrastudier 5; Acta archaeologica Lundensia. Series in 8°, no. 38), Stockholm: Almqvist & Wiksell International.

Jacobsson, B. (2003) 'Trelleborg and the southern plain during the Iron Age a study of a coastal area in south-west Scania, Sweden', in L. Larsson and B. Hårdh (eds) *Centrality – Regionality. The Social Structure of Southern Sweden during the Iron Age* (Uppåkrastudier 7), Stockholm: Almqvist & Wiksell International.

Jørgensen, L. (2001) 'From tribute to estate system, 3rd–12th century', in B. Arrhenius (ed.) *Kingdoms and Regionality. Transactions from the 49th Sachsensymposium 1998 in Uppsala*, Stockholm: Archaeological Research Laboratory, University of Stockholm.

Kresten, P., Hjärthner-Holdar, E. and Harryson, H. (2001) *Metallurgin i Uppåkra. Icke-järnmetaller under tusen år; LUHM 31000, Uppåkra sn, Skåne* (Geoarkeologiskt Laboratorium. Analysrapport 10-2001), Uppsala: Raä.

Larsson, L. (2001a) 'Uppåkra, an Iron Age site with a long duration: internal and external perspectives', in B. Arrhenius (ed.) *Kingdoms and Regionality. Transactions from the 49th Sachsensymposium 1998 in Uppsala*, Stockholm: Archaeological Research Laboratory, University of Stockholm.

—— (2001b) 'A building for ritual use at Uppåkra, southernmost Sweden', *Antiquity*, 75(290): 679–80.

Silvegren, U. (2002) 'Mynten från Uppåkra', *Svensk numismatisk tidskrift*, 2002(3): 52–7, 2002(4): 76–80.

Staecker, J. (1999) *Rex regum et dominus dominorum. Die wikingerzeitlichen Kreuz- und Kruzifix-anhänger als Ausdruck der Mission in Altdänemark und Schweden* (Lund studies in medieval archaeology 23), Stockholm: Almqvist & Wiksell International.

Uppåkrastudier, 10 vols (Acta Archaeologia Lundensia), Lund 1998–2004: Almqvist & Wiksell International.

CHAPTER NINE

LOCAL AND
LONG-DISTANCE EXCHANGE

—— ·◆· ——

Søren Michael Sindbæk

Exchange was a delicate matter in the Viking period. Objects moved for many reasons: gifts were exchanged to maintain personal allegiances, goods were dispersed freely within families or organisations, treasures were robbed and trade was conducted on strictly economic terms. The greater and more important share of exchange was certainly conducted through the mesh of personal ties. Yet it is the impersonalised commercial relations that have attracted the attention of modern scholars.

Viking trade has inspired bright visions and exorbitant claims: it has been identified as a decisive vehicle for urbanisation, state formation and colonisation. Some even see a commercial revolution that introduced market-trade in northern Europe. The search for the origin of markets and a 'spirit of capitalism' has no doubt contributed unfairly to the fame of the Vikings. But though its scope and importance have often been over-emphasised, trade was a quintessential cultural phenomenon in Viking Age northern Europe, and a hub of important change and innovations.

CONFLICTS AND CONJUNCTURES: A BRIEF HISTORY

The Viking Age is renowned as an era when trade and war went happily together – raids being, so to speak, a continuation of trade by other means. When we examine the sources more thoroughly, though, the common theme in the history of Viking trade was that trading networks grew during relatively peaceful periods, and declined in periods of conflict.

The first distinctive phase of growth is associated with the network of *wics* or emporia – undefended port sites such as Hamwic, Dorestad, Ribe, Birka or Truso that developed almost simultaneously in the eighth century from Wessex in the west to the Wisła bay in the east. The geographical scope of the network is reflected in the distribution of many artefacts: the small silver coins or *sceattas*, and imports such as basalt quernstones from the Mayen region, Frankish glass beakers, textiles etc. (Gabriel 1988; Parkhouse 1997; Näsman 2000). They share a centre of gravity, and probably a locus of agency, in the Rhine mouth, from which contacts extend down the Rhine valley, over the Channel to southern England, and along the Frisian coast to southern Jutland. More limited finds occur in Scandinavia proper, in the Baltic region and in the northern parts of Britain.

The character of the sites, as well as the quantity and nature of the commodities, show that long-distance exchange had attained a level of intensity and regularity not found in other parts of northern Europe in this period. But, there were other spheres of interaction. One emerges from the end of the eighth century when Staraya Ladoga in north-west Russia and possibly Truso in Prussia became critical links in the near-eastern economy through fur and possibly slave trade. Towards the end of the eighth century Arabic silver coins, or dirhams, appear first in Russian then Scandinavian and other sites along with mass-produced glass beads and other items of near-eastern origin (Noonan 1980; Davidan 1995; Callmer 1995). The beads arrived in sufficient quantities to oust the local production of glass beads in such sites as Ribe and Åhus within a few years.

The first decades of the ninth century marked the apogee and a change of guard for the emporia network. Hedeby (Haithabu) was established at the southern Danish border and quickly took on the role as a bridge between the North Sea and the Baltic. As the Royal Frankish Annals inform, its foundation happened in direct consequence of political conflicts, and its protection was a matter for the Danish king. Kaupang in Norway was established at the same time, and very possibly on the same initiative (see Skre, ch. 8.3, above). It is worth noting that characteristic Norwegian products such as Eidsborg hones and steatite vessels first occur in southern Scandinavia at the same time (Figure 9.1) (Myrvoll 1985; Sindbæk 2005: 137 ff.).

While the first decades of the ninth century appear to be a culmination of developments through the past century, the following period bears every mark of crisis. Many of the sites that had previously transmitted long-distance exchange were either extinguished or substantially reduced during the mid-ninth century, when the Carolingian Empire disintegrated and Viking raids escalated.

Figure 9.1 Eidsborg hones and fragments of steatite vessels from Norway, found in Aggersbog, Denmark. Stone objects, whose provenance can often be established by petrological analyses, are some of the archaeologically most perceptible traces of interregional exchange in Viking Scandinavia. (Photo: Department of Medieval and Renaissance Archaeology, Aarhus University.)

Figure 9.2 Tenth-century hoard of brass bars from Myrvälde, Gotland. The seventeen complete bars are 41–3 cm long and were carefully adjusted to a weight between 390–410 g. The standardisation shows that the bars were prepared to function as 'economic' objects of exchange. (Photo: Søren M. Sindbæk.)

Around AD900 little was left of the network that had existed 100 years earlier, though key sites like Hedeby, Birka, Kaupang and Staraya Ladoga persisted. The most thriving sites of this period were clearly those engaged with the eastern connections (Ambrosiani 2002). These culminated in the period 930–70 when the influx of Arabic silver was at its peak (Noonan 1994). The most distinguished economic feature of this network was the 'weight-money' system, based on oriental types of scales and weights introduced in the late ninth century (Steuer 1987; Gustin 2004). Their use as economic instruments is reflected in the many hoards of hack-silver which are found over most of the Viking world, but particularly in the Baltic region (Hårdh 1996). The great fragmentation in many hoards shows that 'weight-money' was employed for even very trivial transactions (Figure 9.2).

But a new and very different phase of focused trading networks was under way. In England the first *burhs*, or fortified regional centres, were organised in the 880s. During the tenth century a new series of urban foundations in Scandinavia and the Baltic Sea, such as Århus, Lund and Wolin, became fortified in a similar way. Domestic coins increasingly replaced 'weight-money' from the late tenth century. At the same time the introduction of slow bulk-carrying vessels reveal a new level of security on the seas. These developments all point to a new level of political organisation where trade, towns and institutionalised royal protection proceeded together – a historical situation very unlike that 200 years earlier.

A crux in discussions of Viking Age trade and exchange is the idea of 'commercial revolution', variously identified with the beginning (Näsman 1991, 2000; McCormick 2001; Hodges 2006) or the end of the period (Hodges 1982; Christophersen 1989; Saunders 1995). Ambiguous results appear from analyses of many supposedly important commodities like textiles, ceramics, iron, furs and other hunting products (Jørgensen 1992; Roslund 2001; Magnusson 1995; Wigh 2001; Mikkelsen 1994). But the late tenth-century changes noted above do coincide with increasing trade in at least one low-value staple product – fish (Barrett *et al.* 2004). Market and non-market exchange certainly coexisted throughout the Viking Age in northern Europe, their relative

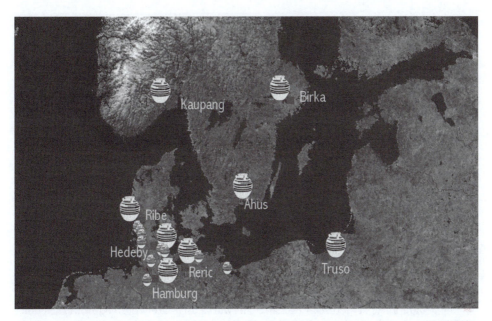

Figure 9.3   The distribution of the eighth–ninth-century Badorf-type ceramics from the middle Rhine area shows a characteristic pattern. In south-east Denmark and northern Germany the ceramics are found occasionally in rural sites (small symbols: less than five sherds). In the rest of Scandinavia and the Baltic Sea areas, they occur regularly in emporia, but were never received beyond them. Apparently this ware was not brought for trade, but for use by the traders, presumably Frisians. The map shows the ports that received foreigners from the Rhine area in early Viking Age Scandinavia. (Map: Søren M. Sindbæk, data according to Brather 2001 and Sindbæk 2005.)

importance changing by conjunctures rather than by revolution (Verhulst 2002: 135). But if an episode of more radical change must be identified, it occurred from the late tenth century.

ROUTES AND NETWORKS

The 'routes of the Viking' are celebrated in countless historical maps. These mostly reflect accounts of spectacular, individual journeys, and certainly not regular trade routes. In a preliterate society, 'routes' are journeys taken on a regular basis. They are defined by the knowledge of travellers, established through previous journeys or verbal exchange.

An early synthesis of Viking trade, still alive in many contemporary works, pictured a limited number of trading stations positioned along a few great trunk routes (e.g. Arbman 1937; Jankuhn 1953). This model, which reflects the diffusionist outlook of traditional historical archaeology, is related to the long-lived idea of Viking trade as a link that united the Carolingian Empire with the Abbasid Caliphate (Bolin 1953 (1939); Hodges and Whitehouse 1983; McCormick 2001).

Some recent reconstructions rather envisage a dense scatter of sites, suggesting that each would have acted as 'central place' to a region (Carlsson 1991; Näsman 1991; Callmer 1994; Ulriksen 1998). The implied view is that urban milieus evolved on a local basis by a process of 'urbanisation'. While this evolutionary perspective adds an important dimension, it tends to disregard a vital aspect of communication.

Viking trade operated as a network. Long-distance exchange took place in bulk along routes between specific localities, where large cargoes are loaded or unloaded. Archaeology shows that the distribution of imports, as well as crafts with imported raw materials, such as bronze casting, define a small group of sites as centres on quite another scale than other possible trading places (Figure 9.3). It is not trade as such that distinguishes these hubs from lesser sites. The latter were obviously important for local trade and communicated with the nodal points – but not with the long-distance traffic between them (Sindbæk 2006).

The nodal points were spatial and temporal buffers between different traffics. Hence, most were situated in locations where a topographical barrier caused a break in traffic and demanded a transshipment and perhaps a temporary storage of goods. In the Scandinavian climate, season was a critical factor, which may have affected more than the choice of location: the need for temporal buffers between inland transport, mostly carried out in the winter when grounds were firm and frozen, and sea-traffic, which took place in summer, may have been a decisive reason why permanently settled trading towns replaced the seasonal markets that seem to have prevailed earlier in the Iron Age.

The geographical structure of exchange networks ultimately derived from the choice of individuals: each participant in a long-distance exchange will have had a significant incentive to seek out what was considered the most favourable, safe and active places for trading. To a traveller spending weeks or months on the journey a few days extra were inessential compared to the ultimate objective of encountering suitable exchange partners. This would compel most travellers to seek the same few sites. The geographical outcome of these concerns would be exactly the situation that we seem to find: a ranked network with a few sites acting as hubs or nodal points for long-distance traffic within a widespread web of more local contacts.

COMMUNITIES, POLITICS AND PROTECTION

Commercial long-distance relations were rare connections in a network held together by personal and mostly local ties. Could we have asked a Viking Age person about his or her involvement in trade and exchange, we should very possibly have found long-distance connections to have been a marginal interest. Instead, our informant might have answered at length about the local exchange of essentials such as hay, cattle, food or textiles. Most of these, unfortunately, are perishable; even when found, there is usually little way of telling whence or in what way they were acquired.

Written sources are even less informative about local than about long-distance exchange. We are therefore left with little evidence to reflect on this obviously important subject. Interesting observations on scale and extent have emerged from studies on the hinterlands of towns and trading sites (Bäck 1997; Müller Wille 2002; Palmer 2003). A few other enlightening cases have been discussed (Resi 1987; Zachrisson 1997). But a comprehensive reconstruction of Viking Age rural exchange is still lacking.

Even commercial relations were preferably established within a frame of social ties. Where possible, trade was conducted in connection with assembly sites or magnates' residences, in which peace and protection were buttressed by political authority or sacrosanct protection (Skre 2006). This has provoked a long-standing debate on the relationship between economy and politics. Through recent decades, exchange was often subsumed as an aspect of political evolution. It has been argued that peaceful trade presupposes an institutionalised political (i.e. royal) authority in order to organise and protect trading sites (Hodges 1982: 184; Ambrosiani and Clarke 1991: 89), or to guarantee the safety and legal protection of individual foreigners (Sawyer 1978; Lund 1987), or both (Hedeager 1993).

Trading sites were certainly a concern of rulers and a target of political ambitions in early Viking Age Scandinavia. Written sources speak of kings in Ribe, Birka and Hedeby. But was edict and patronage enough to secure the trading network at this stage? The looting of Dorestad, Paris, London and many other sites demonstrates that no ruler in the early Viking Age could guarantee market peace without a large share of consensus; the lack of substantial fortifications in eighth–ninth-century emporia suggests that they knew this to be the case. According to ship finds, it was only in the tenth century that specialised cargo-vessels appeared in Scandinavian waters (Crumlin-Pedersen 1999). Before that, trading ships each brought an armed crew for protection.

It is becoming increasingly clear that the necessary protection for trade was often provided by the interdependence of groups and communities, rather than by coercive power. Individual safety and legal rights could be maintained by incorporating strangers in households and conducting transactions there (Roslund 1994, 2001). The essential relation of trust was facilitated, among other things, by symbolic communication through artefact style (Gustin 2004). Potential tensions in the exchange situation were accommodated for by establishing shared cultural norms and routine procedures for exchange (Sindbæk 2005). The basic conditions for trade and exchange were provided by township communities, by the *félag* or guilds of traders, and most importantly by accepting common law.

The constitution of trading communities was important in another sense too. The large trading sites are the only locations in the Viking world where great numbers of foreigners would live together on a regular basis, as we see from the distribution of items presumably brought as personal utensils (e.g. Brather 1996; Callmer 1998). Exchanges occurred not only in bulk cargoes between these sites, but on a personal level within them. As such, these motley communities must have been essential vehicles of cultural transmission and innovation.

BIBLIOGRAPHY

Ambrosiani, B. (2002) 'Osten und Westen im Ostseehandel zur Wikingerzeit', in K. Brandt, M. Müller-Wille and C. Radtke (eds) *Haithabu und die frühe Stadtentwicklung im nördlichen Europa*, Neumünster: K. Wachholtz.

Ambrosiani, B. and Clarke, H. (1991) *Towns in the Viking Age*, London and New York: Leicester University Press.

Arbman, H. (1937) *Schweden und das karolingische Reich*, Stockholm: KVHAA.

Bäck, M. (1997) 'No island is a society: regional and interregional interaction in central Sweden during the Viking Age', in H. Andersson, P. Carelli and L. Ersgård (eds) *Visions of the Past. Trends and Traditions in Swedish Medieval Archaeology* (Lund Studies in Medieval Archaeology 19), Stockholm: Raä.

Barrett, J.H., Locker, A.M. and Roberts, C.M. (2004) '"Dark Age economics" revisited: the English fish bone evidence AD 600–1600', *Antiquity*, 78(301): 618–36.

Bolin, S. (1953) 'Mohammed, Charlemagne and Ruric', *Scandinavian Economic History Review*, 1: 5–39. [Swedish version in *Scandia. Tidskrift för historisk forskning* 12 (1939): 181–222.]

Brather, S. (1996) 'Merowinger- und karolingerzeitliches "Fremdgut" bei den Nordwestslawen. Gebrauchsgut und Elitekultur im südwestlichen Ostseeraum', *Prähistorische Zeitschrift*, 71: 46–84.

—— (2001) *Archäologie der westlichen Slawen. Siedlung, Wirtschaft und Gesellschaft im früh- und hochmittelalterlichen Ostmitteleuropa* (Ergänzungsbände zum Reallexikon der Germanischen Altertumskunde 30), Berlin and New York: Walter de Gruyter.

Callmer, J. (1994) 'Urbanization in Scandinavia and the Baltic region *c.* AD 700–1100', in B. Ambrosiani and H. Clarke (eds) *Developments around the Baltic and the North Sea in the Viking Age. The Twelfth Viking Congress* (Birka Studies 3), Stockholm: The Birka Project, Raä.

—— (1995) 'The influx of oriental beads into Europe during the 8th century', in M. Rasmussen *et al.* (eds) *Glass Beads: Cultural History, Technology, Experiment and Analogy* (Studies in Technology and Culture 2), Lejre: Historical–Archaeological Experimental Centre.

—— (1998) 'Archaeological sources for the presence of Frisian agents of trade in northern Europe ca. AD 700–900', in A. Wesse (ed.) *Studien zur Archaeologie des Ostseeraumes. Von der Eisenzeit zum Mittelalter. Festschrift für Michael Müller-Wille*, Neumünster: Wachholtz Verlag.

Carlsson, D. (1991) 'Harbours and trading places on Gotland AD 600–1000', in O. Crumlin-Pedersen (ed.) *Aspects of Maritime Scandinavia AD 200–1200. Proceedings of the Nordic Seminar on Maritime Aspects of Archaeology*, Roskilde: The Viking Ship Museum.

Christophersen, A. (1989) 'Kjøpe, selge, bytte, gi. Vareutveksling og byoppkomst i Norge ca. 800–100: En modell', in A. Andren (ed.) *Medeltidens födelse* (Symposier på Krapperups borg 1), Lund: Gyllenstiernska Krapperupsstiftelsen.

Crumlin-Pedersen, O. (1999) 'Ships as indicators of trade in northern Europe 600–1200', in J. Bill (ed.) *Maritime Topography and the Medieval Town*, Copenhagen: Nationalmuseet.

Davidan, O.I. (1995) 'Material'naya kul'tura pervykh poselentsev drevnej Ladogij', *Peterburgskij arkheologicheskij vestnik*, 9: 156–66.

Gabriel, I. (1988) 'Hof- und Sakralkultur sowie Gebrauchs- und Handelsgut im Spiegel der Kleinfunde von Starigard/Oldenburg', *Bericht der Römisch-Germanischen Kommission*, 69: 103–291.

Gustin, I. (2004) *Mellan gåva och marknad. Handel, tillit och materiell kultur under vikingatid* (Lund Studies in Medieval Archaeology 34), Lund: Almqvist & Wiksell International.

Hårdh, B. (1996) *Silver in the Viking Age. A Regional-Economic Study* (Acta Archaeologica Lundensia series in 8°, 25), Stockholm: Almquist & Wiksell International.

Hedeager, L. (1993) 'Krigerøkonomi og handelsøkonomi i vikingetiden', in N. Lund (ed.) *Norden og Europa i vikingetid og tidlig middelalder*, Copenhagen: Museum Tusculanum.

Hodges, R. (1982) *Dark Age Economics. The Origins of Towns and Trade AD 600–1000*, London: Duckworth.

—— (2006) *Goodbye to the Vikings? Re-Reading Early Medieval Archaeology*, London: Duckworth.

Hodges, R. and Whitehouse, D. (1983) *Mohammed, Charlemagne and the Origins of Europe. Archaeology and the Pirenne Thesis*, London: Duckworth.

Jankuhn, H. (1953) 'Der fränkisch-friesische Handel zur Ostsee im frühen Mittelalter', *Vierteljahresschrift für Sozial- und Wirtschaftsgeschichte*, 40: 193–243.

Jørgensen, L.B. (1992) *North European Textiles until AD 1000*, Aarhus: Aarhus University Press.

Lund, N. (1987) 'Peace and non-peace in the Viking Age – Ottar in Biarmaland, the Rus in Byzantium and Danes and Norwegians in England', in J.E. Knirk (ed.) *Proceedings of the Tenth Viking Congress, Larkollen, Norway, 1985* (Universitetets Oldsaksamlings skrifter. Ny rekke 9), Oslo: Universitetets Oldsaksamling.

McCormick, M. (2001) *Origins of the European Economy. Communications and Commerce AD 300–900*, New York: Cambridge University Press.

Magnusson, G. (1995) 'Iron production, smithing and iron trade in the Baltic during the late Iron Age and early Middle Ages (*c.* 5th–13th centuries)', in I. Jansson (ed.) *Archaeology East and West of the Baltic. Papers from the Second Estonian–Swedish Archaeological Symposium. Sigtuna, May 1991*, Stockholm: Dept. of Archaeology, University of Stockholm.

Mikkelsen, E. (1994) *Fangstprodukter i vikingetidens og middelalderens økonomi. Organiseringen av massefangst av villrein i Dovre* (Universitetets Oldsaksamlings skrifter. Ny rekke 18), Oslo: Universitetets Oldsaksamling.

Müller-Wille, M. (2002) *Frühstädtische Zentren der Wikingerzeit und ihr Hinterland* (Abhandlungen der Geistes- und sozialwissenschaftlichen Klasse 2003:3), Stuttgart: Akademie der Wissenschaften und der Literatur.

Myrvoll, S. (1985) 'The trade in Eidsborg hones over Skien in the medieval period', *Iskos*, 5: 31–47.

Näsman, U. (1991) 'Seatrade during the Scandinavian Iron Age: its character, commodities, and routes', in O. Crumlin-Pedersen (ed.) *Aspects of Maritime Scandinavia AD 200–1200. Proceedings of the Nordic Seminar on Maritime Aspects of Archaeology*, Roskilde: The Viking Ship Museum.

—— (2000) 'Exchange and politics: the eighth–early ninth century in Denmark', in C. Wickham and I. Lyse Hansen (eds) *The Long Eighth Century. Production, Distribution and Demand* (The Transformation of the Roman World 11), Leiden: Brill.

Noonan, Th.S. (1980) 'When and how dirhams first reached Russia', *Cahiers du Monde Russe et Soviétique*, 21: 401–69.

—— (1994) 'The Vikings in the east: coins and commerce', in B. Ambrosiani and H. Clarke (eds) *The Twelfth Viking Congress* (Birka Studies 3), Stockholm: The Birka Project, Raä.

Palmer, B. (2003) 'The hinterlands of three southern English *emporia*: some common themes', in T. Pestell and K. Ulmschneider (eds) *Markets in Early Medieval Europe. Trading and 'Productive' Sites, 650–850*, Macclesfield: Windgather.

Parkhouse, J. (1997) 'The distribution and exchange of Mayen lava quernstones in early medieval northwest Europe', in G. de Boe and F. Verhaeghe (eds) *Exchange and Trade in Medieval Europe. Papers of the 'Medieval Europe Brugge 1997' Conference*, vol. 3, Zellik: Institut vor het Archeologisch Patrimonium.

Resi, H.G. (1987) 'Reflections on Viking Age local trade in stone products', *Proceedings of the Tenth Viking Congress* (Universitetets Oldsaksamling skrifter. Ny rekke 9), Oslo: Universitetets Oldsaksamling.

Roslund, M. (1994) 'Tools of trade: spatial interpretations of trade activities in early medieval Sigtuna', *Meddelanden från Lunds universitets historiska museum*, NS, 10: 145–57.

—— (2001) *Gäster i huset. Kulturell överföring mellan slaver och skandinaver 900 till 1300*, Lund: Vetenskapssocieteten i Lund.

Saunders, T. (1995) 'Trade, towns and state: a reconsideration of early medieval economics', *Norwegian Archaeological Review*, 28(1): 31–53.

Sawyer, P.H. (1978) 'Wics, kings and Vikings', in T. Andersson and K.I. Sandred (eds) *The Vikings. Proceedings of the Symposium of the Faculties of Arts of Uppsala University June 6–9 1977*, Uppsala: Almqvist & Wiksell International.

Sindbæk, S.M. (2005) *Ruter og Rutinisering. Vikingetidens fjernhandel i Nordeuropa*, Copenhagen: Multivers.

—— (2006) 'Networks and nodal points: the emergence of towns in early Viking Age Scandinavia', *Antiquity*, 80: 310.

Skre, D. (2006) 'Towns and markets, kings and central places in southwest Scandinavia ca 800–950 AD', in D. Skre (ed.) *Kaupang in Skiringssal. Excavation and Surveys at Kaupang and Huseby, 1998–2003 – Background and Results* (Kaupang Excavation Project 1), Aarhus: Aarhus University Press.

Steuer, H. (1987) 'Gewichtsgeldwirtschaften im frühgeschichtlichen Europa', in K. Düwel *et al.* (eds) *Untersuchungen zu Handel und Verkehr der vor- und frühgeschichtlichen Zeit in Mittel- und Nordeuropa. Teil IV. Der Handel der Karolinger- und Wikingerzeit* (Abhandlungen der Akademie der Wissenschaften in Göttingen), Göttingen: Vandenhoeck & Ruprecht.

Ulriksen, J. (1998) *Anløbspladser. Besejling og bebyggelse i Danmark mellem 200 og 1100 e.Kr.*, Roskilde: The Viking Ship Museum.

Verhulst, A. (2002) *The Carolingian Economy*, Cambridge: Cambridge University Press.

Wigh, B. (2001) *Animal Husbandry in the Viking Age Town of Birka and its Hinterland. Excavations in the Black Earth 1990–95* (Birka Studies 7), Stockholm: The Birka Project, Raä.

Zachrisson, I. (1997) *Möten i gränsland. Samer och Germaner i Mellanskandinavien* (Statens Historiska Museum. Monographs 4), Stockholm: Statens Historiska Museum.

CHAPTER TEN

COINAGE AND
MONETARY ECONOMIES

— • ◆ • —

Svein H. Gullbekk

When Scandinavians travelling outwards initiated the Viking Age in the eighth century, theirs was a society without coinage, towns or states. Three centuries later, in the mid-eleventh century, Viking society was familiar with coinage and towns, and possessed emerging states within a framework of Christianity. Without documentary evidence of any significance, the archaeological and numismatic evidence represents the building blocks for research on coinage and the monetary history of the Viking Age. Coins have been found in greater numbers, with a wider geographical distribution and continuity than any other objects in the Viking world. Viking coinage is first and foremost perceived as silver pennies issued in the names of such renowned Viking kings as Eirik Bloodaxe in York and Dublin (948 and 952–4), and Sven Forkbeard (*c.* 985–1014), Olof Skötkonung (*c.* 995–1022), Olaf Tryggvason (995–1000), Olaf Haraldsson (the Saint) (1015–28), Cnut the Great (1016–35, king of England 1018–35), Harthacnut (1035–42, king of England 1040–2), Magnus the Good (1042–7), Sven Estridsen (1047–74) and Harald Hardrade (1047–66) at different Scandinavian mints. All of these kings played key roles in the introduction and development of coinage within the Viking world, as was also the case for anonymous Nordic coinages of the ninth and tenth centuries in Haithabu and Ribe and the Scandinavian imitations of Anglo-Saxon pennies from *c.* 990 to the 1020s in Lund and Sigtuna (Figure 10.1–10.4).

Money and its use in the Viking world have been commented upon by anthropologists, archaeologists, ethnologists, historians and numismatists, and where there are many experts there are different opinions. Viking society has been described as one of gift-giving and as a status-oriented economy; in this view the coins found were brought to Scandinavia and immediately deposited in the ground. If coins were used it was rather in social contexts as part of a gift economy, or a redistributive economy, or that they were mainly melted down and used for the production of jewellery. Other scholars believe that the many coins found only represent a tiny fraction of what was once in use, and that money was widely distributed, and used for small-scale transactions, in some places on a daily basis. The use of coins in the Viking world has thus been connected with raiding and looting, tribute and taxation, ritual deposit, gift-giving and long-distance, regional and local trade.

Much research has been undertaken into the study of coinage in the Viking Age, less

Figure 10.1   Kufic dirhams found in a small hoard in Vestfold in south Norway.
(Courtesy of Museum of Cultural History, Oslo.)

Figure 10.2   The silver penny was the main coin in Europe from *c.* 800 to the thirteenth century. Small change was created by cutting pennies in halves or quarters. These cut pennies are all of Anglo-Saxon origin found in the Viking world. (Courtesy of Museum of Cultural History, Oslo.)

so with the use of coins and monetary economies. This is very much a topic of current development as a consequence of the many ongoing excavations and projects concerning marketplaces, productive sites and urban settlements in the Viking world. Also, the application of new technology has been very important and enriched Viking Age numismatics beyond measure during the past decades (Jensen 1994: 237–41). Metal-detectorists have discovered abundant numbers of single finds and archaeologists have improved their record in finding coins in excavations (Östergren 1989). Scholars who

Figure 10.3 Scandinavian royal coinages were imitations of contemporary Anglo-Saxon coin types. This Danish penny showing a snake as its main motif, issued for Cnut the Great (1018–35) in the 1020s or 1030s, is considered the first nationalised coin type in Scandinavia. (Courtesy of Museum of Cultural History, Oslo.)

Figure 10.4 Norwegian pennies from the 1050s and 1060s issued after Harald Hardrade (1047–66) had established a national coinage. (Courtesy of Museum of Cultural History, Oslo.)

have followed this development are less inclined to doubt that coins were used and used widely; however, the question has to be analysed in detail, and even though the concept of money being used does not meet the same resistance as before, the concept of monetary economies is still difficult to argue.

FROM ISLAMIC TO CHRISTIAN SILVER: A SHIFT FROM EAST TO WEST

There are three major shifts to be observed in the monetary scene in the Viking world from 750 to 1100. The first to occur is the flow of Islamic dirhams reaching Scandinavia

in the decades around 800. The second takes place in the last quarter of the tenth
century when Islamic dirhams disappear and are replaced with pennies of western
origin, first and foremost German and Anglo-Saxon. In the third shift, national state
coinages in Denmark and Norway replace foreign coins.

When the Viking Age commenced the greater part of all coins in the Viking world
were imported from the Abbasid and Samanid caliphates in the south-east, with smaller
numbers of dirhams from the Umayyad caliphate, and also dirham imitations struck
by the Volga Bulgars in Russia. The Islamic dirhams were introduced in the monetary
reforms carried out by the caliph Abd al-Malik in 696 and 698 (AH 77 and 79). As a
result of the Islamic iconoclasm dirhams were of uniform appearance with only
epigraphical design in Kufic writing, and for a long period also of stable weight and
good-quality silver. The weight started to vary significantly in the second half of the
ninth century, and the silver was debased in the second half of the tenth century when
the yield from mines in the Caliphate declined. When the caliphs in the Islamic world
went down the slippery slope of debasement, the Vikings turned their backs on their
coins. Instead an influx of silver from the west replaced the Islamic dirhams. While
coins from Francia, Germany and England had been neglible up to the second half of the
tenth century, discoveries of rich silver resources in the Harz mountains in Germany
fuelled minting in the Ottonian Empire and the Anglo-Saxon kingdom, especially from
c. 975 onwards. (For a recent discussion on Islamic, German and Anglo-Saxon coins in
the Viking world, see Metcalf 1997 and 1998.)

In the years around 995, uniform regal coinages were issued in the name of reigning
kings: Sven Forkbeard in Denmark, Olof Skötkonung in Sweden and Olaf Tryggvason
in Norway. In parallel with the vast imports of Anglo-Saxon pennies, Scandinavian
imitations of contemporary Anglo-Saxon coins were struck on a large scale within
Danish and Swedish territory. These coinages represent the first step in a process
whereby coinage gradually adopted national features, and which in the decades around
the mid-eleventh century culminated in substantial state coinages in Denmark and
Norway. Sweden did not produce any coinage in parallel with the Danish and Norwegian kingdoms in the second half of the eleventh century. Coinage in Sweden came
to a halt in the 1030s, and even though vast numbers of foreign coins have been found
in hoards in Sweden, minting was not resumed until the 1140s, when coinage was
produced on the island of Gotland.

The total number of coins found in Viking territory adds up to more than 800,000
coins, with an emphasis on the islands in the Baltic Sea, and the coastal areas of mainland Sweden, Denmark, then Norway and Finland. The finds from Iceland are few and
far between; it is only on Greenland that Viking Age coins have yet to be found, even
though it is likely that coins were there. The late eleventh-century penny struck in the
reign of the Norwegian king Olaf Kyrre (1067–93) found in Newfoundland reflects the
most western distribution of coins in the Viking world. Tracking the origin and final
destination of coins provides us with evidence for a beginning and an end; the question
to be answered is what happened to the monetary economy in between in the Viking world.

FROM SILVER TO COINS

In the Viking Age economy one can observe a transition from silver objects to coins in
the large hoard material. The shift from silver to coins took place gradually, with

jewellery, rings and hack-silver being predominant in the ninth and the first half of the tenth century. During the second half of the tenth century coins became more numerous, and by the eleventh century coins outnumbered and outweighed silver. Eventually, by the middle of the eleventh century, when state coinages were established, hoards were predominantly made up of coins, in total *c.* 90 per cent (Hårdh 1976: 140–2; Gullbekk 2003: 23–4). From this point silver was second to coins in the Danish and Norwegian economy and society until the collapse of state coinage after the mid-fourteenth century.

COINAGE IN THE VIKING WORLD

Wherever they settled the Vikings assimilated local customs and habits, adopting Christianity, statesmanship, law and coinage. The Vikings in England rapidly adopted the habit of striking their own coins, already from the 890s (Grierson and Blackburn 1986: 318–9). The Anglo-Saxon coinage became a major influence for Scandinavian coinage even in areas where contacts with German society were strong and German coins abundant. The explanation for this is the fact that the Anglo-Saxon coinage and monetary organisation were the most sophisticated at this time, and because Danish kings also reigned over England and Norway *c.* 1018 to 1047. Anglo-Saxon moneyers operating in Scandinavia had an important bearing on the early coinage of Denmark, Sweden and Norway, as in the case of the travelling moneyer Godwine who made the dies and inscribed his name on the reverses of the first royal coinages in Denmark, Sweden and Norway *c.* 995. Anglo-Saxon moneyers are reported to have worked in Denmark throughout the reigns of Cnut the Great, Harthacnut and Magnus the Good. English moneyers are especially prevalent in the reign of Cnut the Great when almost half of the moneyers were Anglo-Saxon. In some cases official English dies were brought to Denmark and used in combination with locally produced dies at Danish mints (Blackburn 1981: 425–47; 1985: 101–24).

Anglo-Saxon influence is clearly seen in monetary organisation and the use of coin design. The large series of Scandinavian imitations of contemporary Anglo-Saxon pennies in the first decades of the eleventh century are significant (Malmer 1997). Of the few coins issued by Olaf Haraldsson (the Saint) of Norway, one uses the extraordinary Agnus Dei-type issued in England *c.* 1009 as a prototype. Today only fifteen of Æthelred II's prototype Agnus Dei coins survive, most of which have been found within Scandinavia. It was struck for only a short period of time, and most probably the size of this coinage was only a fraction of the common series issued in England in the reign of Æthelred II (978–1016). This makes the adoption of the Agnus Dei-type in Norway remarkable, and it suggests that the people commissioning the dies had an awareness of coinage as an effective tool of communication. Otherwise the influence on Scandinavian coin design comes from Byzantine and not German coinage. This is especially the case for Danish and Norwegian coinage in the 1060s, 1070s and 1080s. (For Byzantine influence on Scandinavian coinage, see Skaare 1965: 99–111; Grierson 1966: 124–38; Hendy 1970: 187–97. For Finnish imitations, see Talvio 2002: 28–9).

The production of coinage was never developed in any of the island societies that in many ways played an important role in the history of the Viking world, especially for the history of wealth and money in this period: Gotland, Öland, Bornholm, Iceland, the Hebrides, the Faeroe Islands and Greenland. In fact, the production of coins can be attributed to a limited number of places within Viking Scandinavia: Haithabu, Ribe, Lund, Sigtuna and Nidarnes before the expansion of minting in earnest developed in Denmark in the 1030s and 1040s and in Norway in the 1050s and 1060s respectively. After minting became widespread in the Danish kingdom, coinage was produced at a number of mints: Lund, Roskilde, Slagelse, Ringsted, Viborg, Ribe, Ørbæk and Ålborg; and in Norway coins were minted at Nidarnes (Trondheim) throughout the eleventh century and in Hamar for a short period in the 1050s. In addition there are many coins struck in Norway in the reign of Olaf Kyrre (1067–93) with illegible legends, which have yet to be attributed to specific mints. These issues were either struck at minor mints of a temporary nature, or might have been struck by travelling mints, for example if travelling kings brought with them equipment for minting to be used on demand.

The monetary systems that developed within the Viking world must be regarded as the personal property of the king or issuing authority, which could be used for display purposes and personal enrichment. Sven Estridsen and Harald Hardrade were the first in Scandinavia deliberately to take advantage of manipulating the silver content of their coins to make additional income, beginning in the 1050s and 1060s (Skaare 1976; Gullbekk 1996).

THE USE OF MONEY AND MONETARY ECONOMIES

Arab historians writing in the ninth and tenth centuries describe northerners as tradesmen with a profound liking for silver and dirhams. In Frankish and English sources Norsemen are described as savage men raiding towns and sacred places with a lust for precious metal and exacting tribute in large figures with a beginning at Lindisfarne in 793.

Despite the emphasis on violence, the written sources also present Vikings as people trading and exchanging goods and services with the locals. Icelandic sagas describe a range of situations where culture, religion and economy came together within Viking society. In these tales we hear of coins and money used for display, gift-giving, taxation, bribery, fines, coins being buried in the ground to store wealth, the retrieval of hoards, the manipulation of coinage, testing of coins, and trade in different forms.

The many silver hoards are one of the characteristics of the Viking world. These hoards include more Viking Age coins from Germany and England than have ever been found in those respective countries. In consequence one label that is often used about the Viking Age is the Age of Silver. Coinage and economy in the Viking Age have been seen as evidence for the Viking's lust for silver, and often interpreted as a consequence of the 'Law of Óðinn', individuals securing wealth for their prosperity in the afterlife by hiding treasure in the ground. However, the question is whether they should be interpreted as evidence for a monetised society, or on the contrary if they are to be interpreted in the context of a society where coins were used only to a small extent.

On the basis of saga literature, the Viking Age economy and society are often perceived as having peasant characteristics, very much reliant on self-sufficiency. In this society a wide spectrum of goods and services were used as a means of exchange, with a multitude of different social and economic meanings, as was the case in medieval Scandinavia, and probably also before the Viking period. Even though the archaeological evidence at first sight seems overwhelming, one should not overemphasise the value of silver in this period. A hoard of a thousand silver coins is considered a large hoard, but the purchasing power would probably not be sufficient to pay a heavy fine or for a small farm. If we compare the silver hoards of the Viking Age with the 55 kg of gold from Merovingian Scandinavia, this represents, in total, almost the same value as the Viking Age silver. From this perspective most of the hoards deposited in Viking society must be considered small-value holdings, and only a few, as for instance the Spillings hoard with more than 14,300 coins and 50 k of silver, found on Gotland in 1999, are to be regarded as really large sums of money.

The large sums of money paid in tribute to Viking armies in Francia and England have traditionally been considered the main reason for the many large hoards in Viking Scandinavia. The evidence for tributes, however large, does not include any information about what was paid, whether silver, gold, coins, goods or property. Indeed, not only has the size of the sums been debated, but also whether the sums paid out to the Vikings were carried to Scandinavia (Lawson 1984: 721–38; 1989: 385–406; 1990: 951–61; Gillingham 1989: 373–84; 1990: 939–50. For a numismatic approach to this question, see Metcalf 1990: 165–76). The small number of Frankish coins from the ninth and tenth centuries found within the Viking world does not suggest a close connection between the recorded tribute payments and the import of coins to Scandinavia. The Anglo-Saxon Chronicle lists enormous sums paid in tribute to Viking armies in the years 991, 997, 1003, 1012 and 1018. If coins were used to pay Danegelds, and these were carried to Scandinavia, one should expect an increase in the hoards. This is also the case for the so-called Quadrofoil-type issued in the name of Cnut the Great *c*. 1017–25, which is most numerous in Scandinavian finds. These pennies were current when the enormous Danegeld of 82,500 pounds silver were paid to Scandinavian Vikings in 1018. However, the so-called Pointed Helmet-type, replacing the Quadrofoil issue in the years *c*. 1025–30/1, at a time where no records of tribute payments exist, is almost as numerous in Scandinavia (Jonsson 1994: 222–3). Instead, German coins are the most numerous in finds in the Viking world. The export of coins from Germany to Scandinavia reached a peak in 1025–40. More than three-quarters of the German coins in Swedish finds are made up of pennies from Lower Saxony, Cologne and the so-called Otto-Adelaide pennies. There are no records of tribute payments being made to Vikings from German territory. Instead the German coins have been labelled *Fernhandelsdenare*, reflecting that the main reason for them being issued was to be used in trade with the north and east. The evidence of tribute payments should not be disregarded, but the coin finds suggest that other sources were more influential, for instance trade with the Caliphate in the ninth and tenth centuries and Germany and England in the late tenth and eleventh centuries.

One key feature of Viking Age hoards is their composition of coins. Hoards usually contain a mixture of coins typical for the period when they were deposited, that is, before *c*. 975 a mixture of Abbasid, Samanid and Volga-Bulgar dirhams with intrusions of Merovingian, Carolingian, early Anglo-Saxon and Nordic coins. After *c*. 990 hoards contained German and Anglo-Saxon pennies with smaller numbers of Scandinavian imitations and eventually Danish and Norwegian coins, with intrusions of Hiberno-Norse, Bohemian, Italian, Russian, Frankish and Islamic coins. This mixed composition of coins from different regions is extraordinary, especially since neither German nor English hoards from the same period resemble anything as heterogeneous as the Scandinavian. The explanation for this is either that these coins arrived in Scandinavia ready mixed or that coins were used extensively after they arrived in Scandinavia. The fact that locally produced coins mixed with foreign coins only a short period of time after being struck, suggests that this was taking place within and not outside the Viking world. Only in exceptional cases do hoards contain coins from one region only, either Germany or England.

Regional variations exist not so much in the sense that some coins occur only in one region, and not others, but rather that German coins make up a relatively larger part than Anglo-Saxon coins in the hoards found in southern and eastern parts of Scandinavia, and vice versa in the Norwegian material. The regional differences in the composition of hoards, for instance the relatively large proportion of Anglo-Saxon coins in Norway, do include larger numbers of coins from the Danelaw, for example minted at York and Lincoln, while, on the other hand, hoards in Scania contain more coins from southern England, minted at London and Winchester (Jonsson 1993: 205–32; von Heijne 2004: 98–167). This reflects different points of contact and trade routes where the distance between the Danelaw in England was closer to Norway than other parts of Scandinavia.

The age structure of Scandinavian hoards is generally longer than what is usual for hoards from Germany and England. Many coins found in Scandinavia must have been in circulation for a considerable time after they were made obsolete in their respective home markets. That coins of different origins and different points of arrival in Scandinavia, at different times, ended up mixed in Scandinavian hoards suggests that they were used, and used intensively within Viking society. The degree of fragmentation of dirhams in tenth-century hoards suggests that they were used in Scandinavia, which is also supported by the fact that the metal-detectorists have unearthed more Islamic dirhams as stray finds than any coinage from the eleventh century. The many stray finds suggest that they were used in small-scale exchange and trade. This is also indicated by the testing of the silver quality which is described in documentary sources from Iceland. The many test marks on coins found within the Viking world proves that these coins were used outside the monetised areas in Germany and England, and tested by members of Viking society.

The size of coinages within the Viking world is difficult to establish, and without any documentary evidence estimates have to be made from the number of surviving dies used to strike coins, as recorded from the coins available for study. The numbers of dies in different coinages vary a great deal. It must be admitted that there are methodological concerns with this technique even though general conclusions may be drawn from this material. For instance, the survival rate of dies in the coinages struck in the name of Danish, Swedish and Norwegian kings around the millennium can only be seen as experimental in an economic sense. After state coinages were established in the mid-eleventh century, the number of dies in use for creating coinage in Denmark and Norway was much greater. Estimates consider Danish issues to have been in the range of millions, and Norwegian ones in the hundreds of thousands, presumably even millions (Suchodolski 1971: 20–37; Jensen 1983: 19–26; Gullbekk 2005: 551–72). These must be seen as evidence for the importance of state coinage and the use of coins within late Viking society.

The records of thousands of locally struck imitations of Anglo-Saxon pennies, mainly from Lund and Sigtuna, raise important questions about the use of coins in the decades around the millennium. The traditional view is that coins and coinage formed part of a universal weight economy (*geldwirtschaft*). Without natural resources of silver on any scale, the source for precious metal to issue these large series of coinages in Lund and

Sigtuna must have come from abroad of which foreign coins formed a substantial part. In a weight economy the silver being coined or scrap should, in principle, not make any difference. The extensive issues of Scandinavian imitations of Anglo-Saxon pennies *c.* 995–1020 cannot, however, be regarded as merely experimental coinages of crude nature. Involvement of skilled moneyers and the use of dies from official English coinage also suggest monetary operations on a grander scale. The evidence for either a weight or money economy is hard to interpret in the Viking Age, but the scale of locally made imitations of Anglo-Saxon coins suggests that coins were used with a premium, a concept that must have been familiar to Vikings in contact with foreign lands and merchants, a practice that became the rule rather than the exception with the introduction of state coinages.

MONETISATION OF THE MARKETPLACE

Recent excavations undertaken in early urban Viking societies such as Ribe, Birka, Hedeby, Tissø, Uppåkra and Kaupang make strong cases for the use of coins in a marketplace context. The number of single finds from these seasonal productive sites and urban settlements have increased manifold during the last decades. At Kaupang some twenty coins were found during excavations in the 1950s and 1960s, while the total has reached nearly 100 after using metal detectors for investigations in the 1990s and 2000s.

The transition phase from market towns to towns took place at the same time as the monetary import shifted from east to west in the second half of the tenth century. There is no reason to think these processes were sparked off in either way, but it is interesting to note that while the coins used in the market towns all over the Viking world were of Islamic origin, the coins used in the newly established towns in the eleventh century were of Christian origin.

Monetary influences in marketplaces became visible through local coin production in Haithabu and Ribe already from *c.* 825. Coin production is not conclusive evidence for the widespread use of coins in Viking Age society; however, it does provide an understanding of how important coinage and money were, more so with the emergence of state organisations in the eleventh century. Whatever perspective one takes on numismatics, coinage and monetary history, the Viking Age represents a bridge between Iron Age and medieval Scandinavia, and a decisive period in the history of coinage and monetary development.

BIBLIOGRAPHY

Blackburn, M. (1981) 'A Scandinavian crux/intermediate small cross die-chain reappraised', in M. Blackburn and D.M. Metcalf (eds) *Viking-Age Coinage in the Northern Lands* (The Sixth Oxford Symposium on Coinage and Monetary History; British Archaeological Reports International Series 122), Oxford: British Archaeological Reports.

—— (1985) 'English dies used in the Scandinavian imitative coinages', *Hikuin*, 11: 101–24.

Gillingham, J. (1989) 'The most precious jewel in the English Crown: levels of Danegeld and Heregeld in the early eleventh century', *English Historical Review*, 104: 373–84.

—— (1990) 'Chronicles and coins as evidence for levels of tribute and taxation in late tenth and early eleventh-century England', *English Historical Review*, 105: 939–50.

Grierson, P. (1966) 'Harold Hardrada and Byzantine coin types in Denmark', *Byzantinische Forschungen. Internationale Zeitschrift für Byzantinistik*, 1: 124–38.

Grierson, P. and Blackburn, M. (1986) *Medieval European Coinage*, vol. 1: *The Early Middle Ages (5th–10th centuries)*, Cambridge: Cambridge University Press.

Gullbekk, S.H. (1996) 'Myntforringelse i Danmark og innføring av monopolmynt under Sven Estridssen (1047–1074)', *Nordisk Numismatisk Årskrift* (1994–6): 111–29.

—— (2003) *Pengevesenets fremvekst og fall i Norge i middelalderen* (Acta Humaniora 157), Oslo: The Faculty of Arts, University of Oslo.

—— (2005) 'Lite eller mye mynt i Norge i middelalderen?', *Historisk Tidsskrift*: 2005(4): 551–72.

Hårdh, B. (1976) *Wikingerzeitliche depotfunde aus Südschweden. Probleme und Analysen* (Acta Archaeologica Lundensia, series in 8°, Minore no. 6), Lund: CWK Gleerup.

von Heijne, C. (2004) *Särpräglat. Vikingtida och tidigmedeltida myntfynd från Danmark, Skåne, Blekinge och Halland (ca. 800–1130)* (Stockholm Studies in Archaeology 31), Stockholm: Dept. of Archaeology, University of Stockholm.

Hendy, M. (1970) 'Michael IV and Harold Hardrada', *Numismatic Chronicle*: 187–97.

Jensen, J.S. (1983) 'Hvor stor var udmyntningen i Danmark i 1000- og 1100-tallet', *Fortid og Nutid*, 30: 19–26.

—— (1994) 'Do the coin finds of recent years change our ideas about the character of monetary circulation in Denmark in the Viking Age?', in B. Ambrosiani and H. Clarke (eds) *Developments Around the Baltic and the North Sea in the Viking Age* (The Twelfth Viking Congress; Birka studies 3), Stockholm: Birka Project, Raä & Statens historiska museer.

Jonsson, K. (1993) 'The routes for the importation of German and English coins to the Northern Lands in the Viking Age', in B. Kluge (ed.) *Fernhandel und Geldwirtscaft. Beiträge zum deutschen Münzwesen in Sächsischen und Salischer Zeit* (Römisch-germanisches Zentralmuseum. Forschungsinstitut für Vor- und Frühgeschichte. Monographien 31; Berliner numismatische Forschungen. N.F. 1), Sigmaringen: Thorbecke.

—— (1994) 'The coinage of Cnut', in A. Rumble (ed.) *The Reign of Cnut. King of England, Denmark and Norway*, London: Leicester University Press.

Lawson, M.K. (1984) 'The collection of Danegeld and Heregeld in the reigns of Aethelred II and Cnut', *English Historical Review*, 99: 721–38.

—— (1989) ' "Those stories look true": levels of taxation in the reigns of Aethelred II and Cnut', *English Historical Review*, 104: 385–406.

—— (1990) 'Danegeld and Heregeld once more', *English Historical Review*, 105: 951–61.

Malmer, B. (1997) *The Anglo-Scandinavian Coinage c. 995–1020* (Commentationes de nummis Saeculorum IX–XI, in Suecia repertis. Nova Series 9), Stockholm: KVHAA.

Metcalf, D.M. (1990) 'Can we believe the very large figure of £72,000 for the geld levied by Cnut in 1018?', in K. Jonsson (ed.) *Studies in Late Anglo-Saxon Coinage. In Memory of Bror Emil Hildebrand* (= *Numismatiska Meddelanden*, 35: 165–76), Stockholm: Swedish Numismatic Society.

—— (1997) 'Viking-Age numismatics 3: What happened to Islamic dirhams after their arrival in the northern lands?', *Numismatic Chronicle*: 296–335.

—— (1998) 'Viking-Age numismatics 4: The currency of German and Anglo-Saxon coins in the northern lands', *Numismatic Chronicle*: 347–71.

Östergren, M. (1989) *Mellan stengrund och stenhus. Gotlands vikingatida silverskatter som boplatsindikation* (Theses and papers in archaeology 2), Stockholm: Dept. of Archaeology, University of Stockholm.

Skaare, K. (1965) 'Heimkehr eines Warägers. Die Münzprägung Harald Hardrådes in Dänemark', in P. Berghaus and G. Hatz (eds) *Dona Numismatica. Festschrift for Walter Hävernick*, Hamburg: no publ.

—— (1976) *Coins and Coinage in Viking Age Norway*, Oslo: Universitetsförlaget.

Suchodolski, S. (1971) 'Die Anfänge der Munzprägung in Scandinavien und Polen', *Nordisk Numismatisk Årskrift*: 20–37.

Talvio, T. (2002) *Coins and Coin Finds in Finland c. 800–1200* (Iskos 12), Helsinki: The Finnish Antiquarian Society.

CHAPTER ELEVEN

VIKING SHIPS AND THE SEA

—•◆•—

Jan Bill

Geography has made shipbuilding and seafaring essential for the Scandinavians throughout history. In a landscape where the waterways offered much more ready communication lines than most of the inland, boats and ships were fundamental tools for survival and societal development. It was the presence of water – the many straits and fjords, and the ready access to the coast almost everywhere – that distinguished Denmark from the Continent and made it part of Scandinavia. State formation was dependent on ships, as only with ships some degree of control could be exercised over the populated, coastal stretches of Norway and Sweden, and over the archipelagic Denmark.

At the same time, ships were easy to build in Scandinavia as the primary resources – wood for hulls, iron for fasteners and wool for sails – were locally available or produced within the region. Ships could be, and were, built almost everywhere. Scandinavia was therefore well positioned to develop maritime power at an early point in history, because ships and seafaring played such a large role in the everyday life of much of the population. And southern Scandinavia, placed on the threshold between the Baltic and the North Sea, was also compelled by geography to play a role, as east–west trade started to emerge in the early Middle Ages.

Ships and seamanship are thus central issues to study if we want to learn about the Vikings, both at home and abroad; but they are reflections of what happened, not the reason for it. The changes that we see in shipbuilding during the Viking Age are not revolutionary, they represent improvements and adaptations to new uses rather than inventions. Still, or therefore, ships are valuable sources. They represent concrete material responses to needs that were important enough to be met with massive investments. Experimental archaeology has shown that building a 30 m longship may have taken as much as 40,000 working hours, including production of iron, ropes and sail, but excluding transport costs (Damgård-Sørensen *et al.* 2004: 44). Assuming a twelve-hour working day and a surplus production rate of 10 per cent, this means that to build such a ship one should command the surplus production of 100 persons for one year. Manning and sailing the ship was an even larger challenge. Taking it to sea for four months meant that 70 men were taken away from production and had to be fed. Calculated as above, this would require one year's surplus from 460 producers – which could, of course, be obtained by plundering. Smaller ships needed smaller investments, but the figures underline that shipbuilding and seafaring demanded organisation, and were a heavy burden on society. The *leidang* – the conscript naval organisation that was in effect in Scandinavia after and possibly already during parts of the Viking Age – exemplifies this, but the principle must have also been at work to a lesser extent in trade.

BEFORE THE VIKING AGE

The origin of lap-strake ships

The ships of the Vikings were built shell first on a backbone consisting of keel, stem and stern. The primary component was a shell of planks, fastened together with clench nails through their overlapping edges, hence the building technique is called 'lap-strake'. Finds of such vessels at the Nydam bog deposit in southern Jutland indicate that this way of building vessels was replacing sewn plank boats in Scandinavia and northern Germany in the first centuries AD. At the same time oars replaced paddles as means of propulsion. It might be that these changes reflect influences from the Roman navy, which was operating on the Rhine and in the southern North Sea then.

The lap-strake technique produces a hull which is strong and flexible. Caulking material inlaid between the overlapping planks during the construction made the hull watertight. Various materials were used, but the most common in Viking ships were loosely spun yarns of wool. To stiffen the hull, frames were inserted. In the Nydam vessels they consisted of a naturally curved timber – a compass timber – that was lashed to cleats carved out of the planks and of a thwart, also lashed. As the thwarts served as seats for the rowers, they – and thus the frames – sat roughly 1 m apart. This principle for spacing the framing remained in use until the end of the Viking Age. Rowlocks, mounted on the gunwale, served the oars, and the vessels could thus not be built higher than rowing allowed. Boats could be of a notable size; the best preserved of the Nydam boats, dated to *c.* AD 320, had twenty-eight oars and measured *c.* 23.5 m in length and 3.5 m in beam (Bill *et al.* 1997: 44).

During the fifth to eighth centuries, important improvements took place. Finds from the Anglo-Saxon ship grave Sutton Hoo in England and from Gredstedbro in south-western Denmark, show that in the seventh to eighth centuries lashing of frames was replaced with tree-nailed fastenings in the southern North Sea area. The Storhaug find from Avaldsnes in Norway shows a large rowing ship with a solid plank with oar holes instead of rowlocks. The grave, dated to between AD 680 and 750, is also the first find in Scandinavia of a ship where the compass timber in the frame does not reach from gunwale to gunwale (Christensen 1998).

The introduction of sail

Despite the widespread use of sail in Gaul and Britain in Roman times, there is little evidence that Scandinavians adopted this technology before the Viking Age. We find the earliest confirmation in the Baltic, where Gotlandic picture stones from the eighth century change from showing rowing vessels to showing ships with sails (Imer 2004). From around AD 800 depictions of sailing ships appear on Viking coins, runic stones and graffiti, but the Oseberg ship from AD 820 is the oldest find of a sailing vessel in

Scandinavia. Some written evidence points to the continuous use of sail in the southern North Sea and the Channel from Roman times on. That it seemingly was not adopted in Scandinavia is puzzling, but may reflect the unwillingness of shipowners rather than any technological restraint in shipbuilding.

THE CLASSIC VIKING SHIPS

The Oseberg ship

The ninth and tenth centuries may be considered the time of the classic Viking ship, as seen from today's perspective. The three famous Norwegian finds, Oseberg, Gokstad and Tune, dominate our impression of shipbuilding of this period (Brøgger and Shetelig 1951; Bonde 1994). All of them being ships that were reused in rich burials, they provide an insight into the vessels of the highest levels in society. They thus probably also represent state-of-the-art ships of their time. With the Gokstad and Tune ships having building dates close to AD 900, the three ships represent eighty years of ship-building in southern Norway, and, as it seems, eighty years of increasing knowledge of how to build ocean-going vessels.

The Oseberg ship, 21.5 m long and 5.1 m in beam, was propelled by thirty oars and by a single square sail on a mast, mounted in a keelson just ahead of amidships. This rigging remained characteristic of north European seafaring until the fifteenth century. The ship measured only 1.6 m from the bottom of the keel to the upper edge of the strake with the oar holes amidships, giving a modest draught of about 80 cm, but also providing a similar modest freeboard. As with all medieval north European vessels before *c.* 1150, a side rudder, mounted in starboard aft, provided steering. The hull has a solid keel and a marked transition between the V-shaped bottom and the two side planks. It is well suited for carrying sail but less so for rowing. The frames consist of compass or floor timbers that reach in one piece all over the bottom, and on the top of these beams that are secured with knees to the two side strakes. The floor timbers are lashed to clamps in the bottom planking, and the beams carry a deck. There are no thwarts for the rowers, who must have sat on chests or benches.

The arrangement around the mast – the oldest one preserved in Scandinavia – is of particular interest. The keelson, which is carrying the weight of the mast and rigging, and the tension of the shrouds and stays holding it, spans over two frames only. At deck level, a mast fish spanning over four beams supports the mast in lengthwise and transverse directions. The effect of the mast fish has been improved by giving it a domed design. The mast fish split during the life of the vessel and was repaired with a solid metal strap. Although clearly a refined design, the mast arrangement was thus seemingly inadequate, and it is notable that the Oseberg ship is the only find of a Scandinavian ship with a keelson spanning over only two frames. Apparently the ship-builder, when building this vessel, was at the limit of his knowledge about the powers of mast and rig in a vessel as large as the Oseberg ship (Bill 1997). (Figure 11.1.)

The Gokstad and Tune ships

Compared with the Oseberg ship, the Gokstad ship is a much more robust vessel. It is 23.2 m long, 5.2 m in beam, and measures 2.0 m from keel to gunwale, which makes it

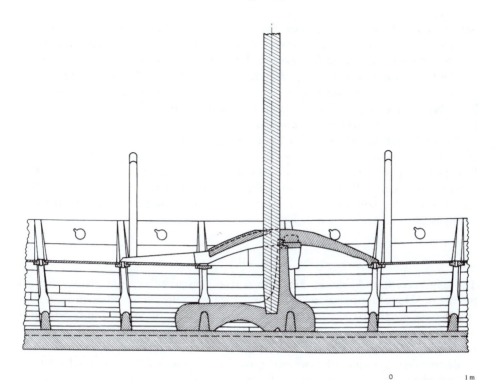

0   1 m

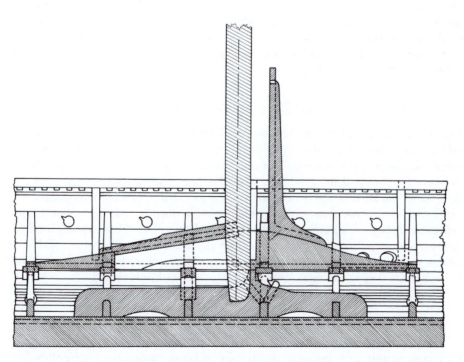

Figure 11.1   The central part of the Oseberg and Gokstad ships, showing the differences in keelson and mast fish construction. (Drawing: Werner Karrasch, Viking Ship Museum in Roskilde.)

not only about 8 per cent longer, but also 25 per cent higher than the Oseberg ship. This is achieved by adding two extra strakes above the one with the oar holes. Its interior structure is similar to that of the Oseberg ship, but it is equipped with thirty-two oars. The keelson spans over four frames, and the mast fish over six. The keel is significantly stronger, and the hull shape curved to provide good sailing. Full-scale reconstructions of both the Gokstad and the Oseberg ship have sailed in the Atlantic in modern times, proving the seaworthiness of the two vessels.

Recent analyses of the Tune ship, built *c.* AD 910, have shown that although smaller, even this 19 m long and 4.2 m wide vessel has been sea-going (Guhnfeldt 2005). In construction it is similar to the Gokstad and Oseberg ships, and it shares their proportions as well. Although being distinct and different vessels, the three ship finds give a remarkably homogeneous picture of how a ship sailing in the ninth- and early tenth-century Skagerak region looked.

Ladby

The ship grave from Ladby on Fynen in central Denmark, however, gives a different picture of Viking shipbuilding. The ship, which was only preserved as an impression and rows of metal fasteners in the soil, has recently been thoroughly analysed and its dimensions reconstructed (Sørensen 2001). The length was 21.5 m, the beam 2.9 m and the height amidships only 1.0 m. The vessel, which dates to around AD 900, was thus of a different design from the Norwegian grave ships. It was lower and more slender, like the rowed vessels from Nydam and Sutton Hoo. The reconstructed hull shape also appears less specialised for sailing than in the Norwegian ships, and the frames are tree-nailed, not lashed to the planking. While the latter may be a regional feature, it is likely that differences in hull shape reflect that the ships were built for use in different environments. Indeed the Ladby ship was suited for navigation in the Baltic and Kattegat, not in the North Sea.

THE TIME OF SPECIALISATION

From the late tenth century on, the frequency of shipfinds increases, and the ships turn up in other contexts. While the older finds are mainly vessels that have been selected for funeral use, the younger ones represent the everyday use of ships. These are vessels that have been lost by accident or warfare, that have been pulled ashore for scrapping, or which have been filled in with stones and sunk to form part of sea-route blockages. This may in part be why they show a much larger variation than the older finds, but it is also a reflection of the growing amount of transport needs in society. There was an increasing concentration of political power, and a growing trade channelled more and more through ports and towns. This conditioned a growing number of ships to be deposited at places where they would be preserved and later detected and studied.

The longships

The longship found in the harbour of Hedeby, known as Hedeby 1, is the first example of a Viking warship in a size range that until now has only appeared among ships from the end of the Viking Age (Crumlin-Pedersen 1997). It was severely damaged already by sinking, as it had served as a fireship in an attack on Hedeby at the most twenty-five years after its construction in *c.* AD 985. The ship, which was built with exquisite materials and craftsmanship, has a reconstructed length of *c.* 30.9 m, and had sixty oars. It is narrow, measuring only 2.6 m in beam, and has a height of 1.5 m amidships. Because of its dimensions it is believed that it was intended for use in the western Baltic and in coastal waters only. It was built from wood from the western Baltic region, perhaps even from the vicinity of Hedeby itself.

An example of a sea-going longship is Skuldelev 2 (Figure 11.2), excavated as part of a sea-route barrier protecting the access to Roskilde on Zealand (Crumlin-Pedersen *et al.* 2002). The ship, reconstructed to a minimum length of 29.2 m, was built in the Dublin area in 1042. Its sea-going capacity is reflected in its larger beam of *c.* 3.8 m and height of 1.8 m. It also had about sixty oars.

In 1997, ship remains excavated in Roskilde proved that ships were indeed built longer than this (Bill *et al.* 2000). The vessel, Roskilde 6, had been pulled ashore and partially scrapped, and the preserved remains include only the keel, the central bottom section and part of the port aft. The keel alone measured 32 m in length, and the overall length of the vessel has been preliminarily reconstructed to 36 m. It probably had as many as seventy-four oars. With a beam of about 3.5 m and a height of *c.* 1.7 m, its proportions place it between Skuldelev 2 and Hedeby 1. The keel had been joined from three pieces with two 2 m long, complicated scarfs. This solution is, until now, unique

Figure 11.2 The Viking Ship Museum's reconstruction of the 60-oared longship Skuldelev 2. Built in Dublin in 1042, the ship is constructed for use in the difficult waters of the Irish Sea. It probably came to Denmark in the late 1060s or early 1070s. (Photo: Werner Karrasch, Viking Ship Museum in Roskilde.)

in Viking Age shipbuilding and perhaps a testimony that longships of this size started to reach the borders of what the shipwright could achieve. Roskilde 6 dates dendro-chronologically to after 1025, and may be from the time of Canute the Great who, in the later – and exaggerating – saga literature, is said to have had a ship of 120 oars (Snorri's *Heimskringla*: 417)!

Longships were also smaller than this. Skuldelev 5, with a length of 18.3 m and only twenty-six oars, probably just deserved this title, as did vessels nos 3 and 5 of the five vessels from the mid-eleventh-century blockade at Foteviken on the east coast of Scania (Crumlin-Pedersen 1994; Crumlin-Pedersen *et al.* 2002). (Figure 11.3.)

The cargo ships

The most important development in shipbuilding in the late Viking Age was, however, the introduction of specialised cargo vessels. What marked out these was that they could be sailed by a small crew, that they had a large loading capacity per crewmember and that they were dependent on the sail for propulsion. They could have a few oars for manoeuvring purposes, but these would under normal circumstances not be used for moving the ship longer distances.

The oldest example of a Viking cargo ship in the archaeological record is the Klåstad ship. It was built in the closing years of the tenth century and wrecked near Kaupang, Norway, with a cargo partly consisting of hone stones. It had an estimated cargo capacity of *c.* 13 tons, and a length of *c.* 21 m (Crumlin-Pedersen 1999, also reports on the ship from Äskekärr).

Around AD 1000, the Äskekärr ship found in the Göta River, close to Gothenburg, shows a much more efficient hull shape, with a cargo capacity of *c.* 20 tons in an only 15.8 m long vessel. A few decades later, around 1025, shipbuilders around Hedeby produced much larger vessels, as the 25 m long Hedeby 3 ship shows. Calculations indicate that it could carry *c.* 60 tons.

The Skuldelev 1 find is a Norwegian-built, sea-going cargo ship from *c.* 1030. It is 16.3 m long and has a cargo capacity of 24 tons. Sailing experiments with several full-scale reconstructions of this vessel have shown that a crew size of five to seven is appropriate. Similar experiments with reconstructions of the much smaller Skuldelev 3, which carries only 4.6 tons, show that it needs a crew of four to five (Andersen *et al.* 1997: 267). Thus the general rule in seafaring that efficiency in tons cargo per crew-member increases with size also seems to fit on Viking cargo ships.

There were probably two factors that stimulated development of specialised cargo carriers in Viking Age Scandinavia. One was increasing volume of trade and exchange, and increasing stratification of society, which led to the need for more and more com-modities being transported at as low a cost as possible. Another one was the expansion into the Atlantic and keeping contacts with the North Atlantic settlements. This required seaworthy vessels with the capacity to transport people, horses and cattle, tools and supplies.

It is likely that specialised cargo ships started to be built earlier than reflected in the archaeological record. Cargo ships were clearly not used as grave ships, which is the only type of find that we have from before the late tenth century. Specialised cargo carriers are known from other parts of northern Europe, and Rimbert, in his *Vita Anskarii* (*c.* 870), several times mentions the presence of 'merchants' ships' in Hedeby in the

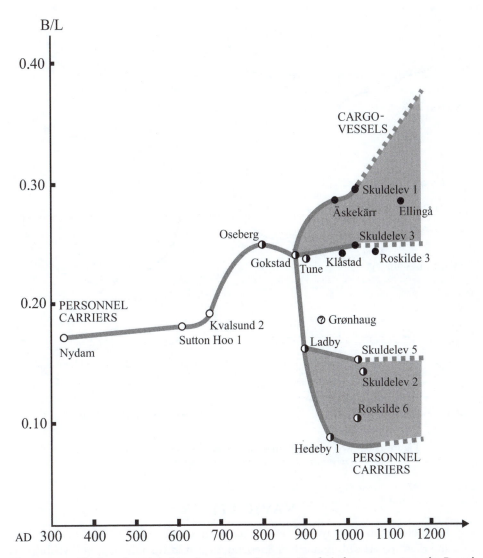

Figure 11.3   The beam/length index values for Scandinavian ship finds from AD 300 to 1060. Rowed boats are marked with open circles, combined rowing and sailing vessels with half open circles and sailing vessels with filled circles. The Grønhaug ship was rowed, but it is unknown if it also carried sail. (Revised after Crumlin-Pedersen 1999: 17.)

mid-ninth century (*Vita Anskarii* ch. 24; Fenwick 1978). The at that time pirate-infested Baltic may well also have made it necessary for trading expeditions to use well-manned, highly manoeuvrable vessels, and Rimbert's words cannot be taken to document the presence of specialised cargo carriers. Still it seems likely that the Hedeby 3 ship represents significantly more than thirty years of experience in using cargo ships. We may look for the oldest specialised cargo carriers from the establishment of extensive settlements in Iceland in the late ninth century onwards. (Figure 11.4.)

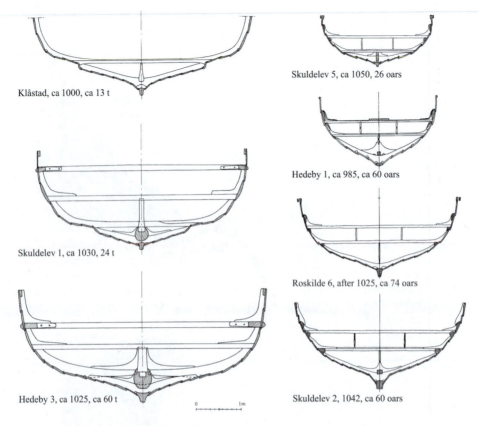

Klåstad, ca 1000, ca 13 t

Skuldelev 5, ca 1050, 26 oars

Skuldelev 1, ca 1030, 24 t

Hedeby 1, ca 985, ca 60 oars

Roskilde 6, after 1025, ca 74 oars

Hedeby 3, ca 1025, ca 60 t

Skuldelev 2, 1042, ca 60 oars

0   1m

Figure 11.4   Reconstructed amidships sections of ships mentioned in the text.
(Drawings: Werner Karrasch, Morten Gøthche del.)

NAVIGATION

From Hernar in Norway one should keep sailing west to reach Hvarf in Greenland
and then you are sailing north of Shetland, so that it can only be seen if visibility is
very good; but south of the Faeroes, so that the sea appears half-way up their
mountain slopes; but so far south of Iceland that one only becomes aware of birds
and whales from it.

(Trans. from Bill 1997: 198)

No navigation tools, apart from the lead, are known with certainty from the Viking
Age, and this description from *Hauksbók*, a fourteenth-century version of *Landnámabók*,
the Old Icelandic book on the colonisation of Iceland, is also likely to illustrate the
navigation method used 400 years earlier. It shows that crossing the Atlantic was an
'island-hopping' one where the course – with some luck – could be adjusted every few
days based on land observations. In between the seafarers travelled in a landscape where
any perceptible phenomenon was noticed and evaluated to provide clues about the
present position. Cloud formations, wind and smell would reveal the presence of land

beyond the horizon. Changes in the colour and taste of the water may tell when the currents changed. The sun, the moon, the stars, and the knowledge by heart of the common patterns of changing wind and wave directions would help one to stay on course. And sailors developed, as it happens for many today, an intuitive ability to estimate the speed and ground covered by their vessels.

Such a navigation based on experience is embedded in the mind of individuals, and this is also true for coastal navigation, which made up the larger part of Viking voyaging. Memorised characteristics of coasts and waters, helped along by descriptive toponyms, were essential navigation aids, and pilots with local knowledge were always valuable. This cognitive character of early medieval navigation must have benefited the Scandinavians compared with the people in other, less sea-oriented regions and been part of the background for their maritime success.

AFTER THE VIKING AGE

The most obvious change in the ship archaeological record by the end of the Viking Age is that longships disappear. Historically we know them to have played an important role well into the twelfth century, and their vanishing among the archaeological finds may be due to coincidence as well as real changes. What also happened, however, is that cargo vessels partly took over their role. Being higher and more strongly built, they were an adequate answer to more powerful missile weapons like the crossbow and heavier armour. As the much higher and more heavily built cog appeared in the twelfth century, it soon became the preferred warship, as often used against the now numerous coastal cities as against other ships (Bill 2002).

The clinker-built cargo ships continued to be used, and changed initially only slowly away from the design that they had achieved in the late Viking Age. The spacing between the frames shrank, and the lowermost beams almost became one with the floor timbers. From the late twelfth century change speeds up. The framing becomes simpler and more efficient for high-sided vessels, and the side rudder is replaced by the stern rudder. Decorations, which were everywhere in the Viking Age ships, gradually disappear, and handicraft becomes more economical. During the thirteenth century the changes become so extensive that shipbuilding in southern Scandinavia more or less loses its distinctive character and becomes part of a general, north European lap-strake tradition. Only in the northern parts of Scandinavia did traditional building style persist and led, in the nineteenth century, to the 'discovery' of Viking Age shipbuilding as a living tradition.

BIBLIOGRAPHY

Andersen, E. *et al.* (1997) *Roar Ege. Skuldelev 3 skibet som arkæologisk eksperiment*, Roskilde: Vikingeskibshallen.
Bill, J. (1997) 'Ships and seamanship', in P. Sawyer (ed.) *Oxford Illustrated History of the Vikings*, Oxford: Oxford University Press.
—— (2002) 'Scandinavian warships and naval power in the thirteenth and fourteenth centuries', in J.B. Hattendorf and R.W. Unger (eds) *War at Sea in the Middle Ages and the Renaissance* (Warfare in History), Woodbridge, Suffolk, UK and Rochester, NY: Boydell Press.
Bill, J. *et al.* (1997) *Dansk søfarts historie*, vol. 1: *Indtil 1588. Fra stammebåd til skib*, Copenhagen: Gyldendal.

—— (2000) 'Roskildeskibene', in T. Christensen and M. Andersen (eds) *Civitas Roscald – fra byens begyndelse*, Roskilde: Roskilde Museums Forlag.

Bonde, N. (1994) 'De norske vikingeskibsgraves alder. Et vellykket norsk-dansk forskningsprojekt', *Nationalmuseets Arbejdsmark*: 128–47.

Brøgger, A.W. and Shetelig, H. (1951) *The Viking Ships. Their Ancestry and Evolution*. Oslo: Dreyer.

Christensen, A.E. (1998) 'Skipsrestene fra Storhaug og Grønhaug', in A. Opedal (ed.) *De glemte skipsgravene. Makt og myter på Avaldsnes* (Ams Småtrykk 47), Stavanger: Arkeologisk museum i Stavanger.

Crumlin-Pedersen, O. (1994) 'Foteviken. En tidligmiddelalderlig naturhavn, slagmark og markedsplads i Skåne', *Sjöhistorisk årsbok* (1994–5): 89–110.

—— (1997) *Viking-Age Ships and Shipbuilding in Hedeby/Haithabu and Schleswig* (Ships and Boats of the North 2), Roskilde: Viking Ship Museum.

—— (1999) 'Ships as indicators of trade in northern Europe 600–1200', in J. Bill and B. Clausen (eds) *Maritime Topography and the Medieval Town* (Publications from the National Museum. Studies in Archaeology and History 4), Copenhagen: National Museum of Denmark.

Crumlin-Pedersen, O. *et al.* (2002) *The Skuldelev Ships*, vol. 1: *Topography, Archaeology, History, Conservation and Display* (Ships and Boats of the North 4:1), Roskilde: Viking Ship Museum.

Damgård-Sørensen, T. *et al.* (2004) 'Fuldblod på havet', in N. Lund (ed.) *Beretning fra toogtyvende tværfaglige vikingesymposium*, Højbjerg: Hikuin.

Fenwick, V. (1978) *The Graveney Boat. A Tenth-Century Find from Kent. Excavation and Recording; Interpretation of the Boat Remains and the Environment; Reconstruction and Other Research; Conservation and Display* (BAR British Series 53), Oxford: British Archaeological Reports.

Guhnfeldt, C. (2005) 'Glemt vikingeskip gjenskapt', *Aftenposten*, 8th of January.

Heimskringla eller Norges kongesagaer af Snorre Sturlassøn, C.R. Unger (ed.), Christiania: Brøgger & Christie 1868.

Imer, L. (2004) 'Gotlandske billedsten – dateringen af Lindqvists gruppe C og D', *Aarbøger for Nordisk Oldkyndighed og Historie* (2001): 47–111.

Landnámabók, 3 vols (*Hauksbók*, *Sturlubók*, *Mélabók* etc.), Copenhagen: Det Kongelige nordiske Oldskrift-Selskab 1900.

Sørensen, A.C. (2001) *Ladby. A Danish Ship-Grave from the Viking Age* (Ships and Boats of the North 3), Roskilde: Viking Ship Museum.

Vita Anskarii, accedit vita Rimberti, auctore Rimberto, G. Waitz (ed.) (Monumenta Germaniae historica. Scriptores rerum Germanicarum), Hannover: Hahn 1988 (1884).

CHAPTER TWELVE

VIKING AGE TEXTILES

—·◆·—

Annika Larsson

Textiles are perishable commodities and are not preserved over long periods unless special conditions are present. Animal fibres (wool and silk) nevertheless survive better than vegetable fibres (linen, nettle, hemp and cotton). An absence of air, constant moisture or direct contact with certain metals can all improve the survival chances of textile remains. These conditions are met in many high-status graves from the Viking period.

Rich textile finds of wool and silk have, for example, been preserved in the ship-burial from Oseberg in Norway, partly because the burial mound was constructed with an airtight turf layer and partly due to a deposit of damp and watertight blue clay that was pressed into the burial from below, due to the weight of the ship. A considerable quantity of textiles also survives from the graves at the Swedish site of Birka. Here, the presence of metal objects in the burials has been decisive in the preservation of the textiles, in that women's brooches and men's swords have both been in direct contact with the dress of the deceased. It is primarily cloth of wool and silk that has survived, but the metal salts exuded by bronze oval brooches have also conserved linen. In Viking dress it is not unusual to find work in silver thread, which in the same way has tended to preserve the cloth on which it was fastened.

If we look further east to the Russian, Mongolian and Chinese areas, we find rich textile preservation due to permafrost or permanent aridity in some areas. This makes it possible to analyse and compare finds from different regions, in order to understand how cultural traits have spread through trade and other contacts. Early literary sources and imagery can help us to confirm our hypotheses, and to explore the circumstances under which the raw materials of textile production, techniques and finished products were transmitted. We can also study equipment and even the design of textiles, as well as living craft traditions much later in time. The very terminology of textiles can also assist us in our interpretations.

The textiles of the Viking Age reflect long-distance trading networks. In the Birka graves are genuine Chinese silks from the Tang dynasty, but also rich finds of silk from Syria and Arabia. Exotic silks are also found at Oseberg. We often read of silk from Christian Byzantium as being typical of Viking Age graves, but we should exercise caution here as the trade with the empire first took off in the mid-tenth century. In the

Russian Primary Chronicle, there is a description of this textile trade and the peace treaties drawn up between the Greeks and the Rus'. Prior to this trade had flowed along the northern Silk Road, as part of which we should also include the culture area of the Vikings. In the Nordic region we see trade operating in fine woollens in the so-called diamond twill. It is still debated as to whether the origins of this trade should be sought in Syria or in the Frisian area. Already by the time of Charlemagne we find Frisian cloth mentioned as an important trade item. Old Norse sources also describe so-called Valland clothes, that is to say textiles from the Frankish Empire.

Even down to modern times we find Sassanid designs living on in Nordic folk arts. Close examination of the famous tenth-century wall hangings from Överhogdal in Swedish Jämtland reveals that many of the animals depicted there have direct parallels in Spanish medieval church textiles. Similarly we encounter the geometric forms of Nordic woven trim in Spanish ecclesiastical cloth as well as in the Viking Age dress of the Baltic region. Double-weaves and long-pile knots from the Nordic area can be found again in Turkey, the Viking Age handicrafts in silver thread can be seen even today in Sámi traditions, including the region of modern northern Russia, and so on. It is thus very difficult to speak of specifically *Nordic* textiles from the Viking Age.

By contrast, there are symbols within dress and clothing that are typical for the Viking Age cultures. One example is the oval brooch, worn in pairs by women. However, despite the fact that these brooches are represented in almost all the rich female graves of Viking Age Birka, the cloth to which they were fastened varies considerably – from crude domestic woollens to the finest oriental silk. It is interesting that this huge blend of qualities is often present in one and the same grave. The coarser textiles are sometimes found as lining in clothing of finer quality. Outerwear is also often sewn together from smaller pieces of cloth of different grades, then joined together by tablet-woven bands with geometric patterns in shining silver threads. The cloth has then been bordered with thin strips of silk – the same form in which we find the silk present in the Oseberg burial. Alongside these exotic materials we also see beaver furs, a typical Nordic phenomenon from the great forests of Scandinavia or Russia. It is clear that while the material changes, the cut of the clothing has been consistently made to fit a domestic tradition that includes the oval brooches.

Bearing in mind today's male costume of the grey suit and tie, it is easy to assume that women's clothing was the more spectacular even in the Viking Age. This was definitely not the case, as male burials contain in fact even more decorative textiles than the female graves. A large number of burials show that men wore headbands or thin diadems of gold and silver, from which small pendants (also in gold and silver) hung down at the neck, decorated with glittering mirror fragments. We also encounter embroidery in threads of precious metals, such as the extraordinary silver-on-silk finds from one of the Valsgärde boat graves from Swedish Uppland. It seems that the embroidery was once on a collar, and perhaps a pair of cuffs or similar, belonging to a fully armed male warrior buried with his horse. A number of silver-thread pendants also followed him into the grave. Similarly fantastic examples of embroidery can be found in the dress of the man buried at Mammen in Denmark.

This has something to say to us about male and female aesthetic ideals at this time. In examining, for example, the Eddic poem *Rígspula*, that may originally date from the tenth century, we should consider that what has often been interpreted as a description of female dress may in fact refer to that of a man – a warrior with bow and arrow, mail and helmet, with a cloak over his shoulders fastened with a beautiful brooch on his chest. We see similar figures on the Bayeux tapestry and on contemporary coinage from England and Scandinavia. Adult ideals are also reflected in children's clothing, in Birka just as in northern Germany, where we similarly find boys' burials with the same silver headbands, swords and so on.

It is entirely possible that differences in dress during the Viking Age were reflected far more by social status than through regional variation, unlike the folk costume of early modern times. Someone in England of a certain status probably looked very similar to a person of comparable standing in Kiev. In high-status burials all over the Viking world we find traces of a collective fashion. However, despite its standard cut, one emblem of this dress was its costly and exotic materials, reflecting a familiarity with innovation, mobility and perhaps a sense of adventure. The wearer was part of a culture that was used to travel.

We should also remember a different kind of production for daily use. Just as now, Viking Age people needed bedding, packing, sails and many other products for multiple purposes. In the Valsgärde boat graves, for example, there are remains of unspun wool, used for caulking the boats. However, it is worth emphasising that the finest textile-working implements – small, delicate spindle whorls, needles, scissors and tweezers, thin tablets for weaving – are found in rich contexts, the halls and graves of the wealthy.

The tiny spindle whorls were used to twine fine woollen threads from fleece, used for wool-comb weaving. Quality wool-comb textiles of this kind are hard to find today except in the houses of haute couture, but in the Viking Age were regularly woven on looms with a horizontal warp. Parts of such looms have been found in, for example, the trading town of Hedeby, and by no means all weaving at this time was done at upright looms with a hanging warp. While the market sites had a very high-quality output, finds from more everyday settlements indicate that domestic production continued much as it had for at least a thousand years. The real Viking Age innovation was the manufacture of the sail.

In Birka a different tool has been discovered that has implications for how we should view textile production – an instrument for drawing wires of the same kind used by the Sámi in their silver- and tin-thread work. Silver and tin were warmed and drawn successively through smaller and smaller holes to produce very thin but solid metal wires. The threads could be wound around a core of textile material, as the Sámi do today, and during the Viking Age we find this kind of work throughout Scandinavia, Poland and north-western Russia. In Christian Europe thin metal threads, often of gold, were worked in a quite different way. Even described in the Old Testament, gold was hammered into thin foil that was then cut into narrow strips, so-called *lan*. Such strips from the Viking Age have been found in tablet-woven bands, as displayed in Lund. They were found in a tenth-century urban context, and reflect contacts with the Continent.

Drawn metal threads, often of silver, have been used in tablet-weaving further north-east. The bands are only a centimetre or so in width (and sometimes even narrower), made of wires as thin as cotton threads. In fact, modern sewing threads must be used of necessity when making reconstructions of them.

In wool production, archaeological finds indicate that sheep were specially bred for white wool to be used for yarn, and clothes were dyed bright red, blue and yellow colours. These played a role in demonstrating status through clothing, and in achieving a certain effect through the use of woven bands. Grey and brown wool, less impressive, was used for more everyday purposes, for example homespun production.

The importance of wool quality is often forgotten now when sheep are reared primarily for meat and a degree of knowledge has been lost. Wool from the old country breeds consists of long, strong and very shiny outer hairs, and very soft inner hairs. There is also a major difference in quality between lambs' and sheep's wool. By separating the outer and inner hairs one could produce woollen fibres with radically different properties and uses. The shearing period is also crucial, the best time for fine-quality wool being in the autumn after the rich grazing, and when there are no lambs whose nourishment affects the wool proteins. This level of knowledge in textile production can be seen even in Bronze Age finds.

Two underestimated textile elements in the Viking Age are feathers and down, of which examples are preserved in graves – perhaps as stuffing in cushions and bolsters on which the dead have lain. Clothing may also have been stuffed with down, for winter warmth.

Otherwise typical for the Viking Age are the so-called twill weaves. These are woven in three- or four-shed twill and have names such as 'goose-eye', 'chevron-twill' and 'diamond-twill'. This means that the cloth was woven on the loom in a certain order with several so-called sheds. The simplest and eldest weaving technique is called tabby, consisting of only two sheds. In this technique, alternate warp threads are lifted with one shed while the second shed lifts the other threads so that a new one can be inlaid into the weave. In this way warp and weft threads are combined to make a fabric that cannot be torn. This process is continued until the desired length is reached. The resulting tabby cloth is rather stiff and in appearance resembles the surface of a woven basket.

With twill and the multiple sheds, the weaves became more flexible and thus more suited to a mobile horse and warrior culture. The cloth was also more durable and had a beautiful surface of shifting patterns, even though often simply coloured. When looms with horizontal warps were introduced, production capacity increased by 400 per cent. Greater efficiency in dyeing followed, when whole finished cloths were coloured rather than individual yarns that were then used in isolation. The latter method was long-lived on rural settlements, but the more effective production process assumed greater prominence in the towns as it was more suited for the production of surplus and thus for sale.

We see this in female textile equipment found in the Birka graves, especially when contrasted with its rural equivalent. In the country, women were buried with spindle whorls, but these are generally absent from Birka. There instead we find needles, scissors, tweezers, weights and coins, suggesting trade and fine sewing. The access that towns provided to costly materials such as silk probably meant that this too was incorporated in the work, though clearly these kinds of cloths were cut up into narrow strips for economy. Sewn on to make exotic borders on woollen clothes, these shining silks still played their part in indicating status, membership of the Viking Age culture area and a set of shared norms spanning the north from England to Scandinavia and Russia.

BIBLIOGRAPHY

Christensen, A.E., Ingstad, A.I. and Myhre, B. (1994) *Osebergdronningens grav. Vår arkeologiske nasjonalskatt i nytt lys*, Oslo: Schibsted.

Dronke, U. (ed. and trans.) (1997) *The Poetic Edda*, vol. 2: *Mythological Poems*, Oxford: Clarendon.

Elsner, H. (1989) *Wikinger Museum Haithabu. Schaufenster einer frühen Stadt*, Neumünster: Wacholtz.

Eriksson, M., Gustavsson, G. and Lovallius, K. (1999) *Varp och inslag. Bindningslära*, vol. 1, Stockholm: Natur och kultur.

Geijer, A. (1938) *Birka. Untersuchungen und Studien*, vol. 3: *Die Textilfunde aus den Gräbern*, Stockholm: KVHAA.

—— (1979) *A History of Textile Art*, London: Pasold research fund in ass. with Sotheby Parke Bernet.

—— (1983) 'The textile finds from Birka', in N.B. Harte and K.G. Ponting (eds) *Cloth and Clothing in Medieval Europe. Essays in Memory of Professor E.M. Carus-Wilson* (Studies in Textile History 2), London: Heinemann Educational Books.

Gräslund, A.-S. (2001) ' "Kvinnan satt där, snodde sin slända . . .". Några reflektioner om fynd av sländtrissor i Birka', in B. Magnus *et al.* (eds) *Vi får tacka Lamm*, Stockholm: Statens historiska museum.

Hägg, I. (1974) *Kvinnodräkten i Birka. Livplaggens rekonstruktion på grundval av det arkeologiska materialet* (Archaeological studies 2), Uppsala: Uppsala University, Institute of North European Archaeology.

Hoffmann, M. (1963) *The Warp-weighted Loom. Studies in the History and Technology of an Ancient Implement* (Studia Norvegica 14), Oslo: Universitetsforlaget.

Kjellberg, S.T. (1943) *Ull och Ylle. Bidrag till den svenska yllemanufakturens historia*, Lund: University of Lund.

Larsson, A. (2001a) 'Fåret och ryaullen', in A. Parholt, E. Anderson and L. Rothquist Ericsson (eds) *Nock, ragg, rya. Det glänser om ullen*, Örebro: Föreningen Sveriges hemslöjdskonsulenter.

—— (2001b) 'Oriental warriors in Viking Age Scandinavia – nothing but an illusion?', *Offa*, 58: 141–54.

—— (2007) *Klädd krigare. Skifte i skandinaviskt dräktskick kring år 1000* (Opia 39), Uppsala: Dept. of Archaeology and Ancient History, Uppsala University.

Strömberg, E. *et al.* (1974) *Nordisk textilteknisk terminologi. Förindustriell vävnadsproduktion*, new edn, Oslo: Tanum.

Wilson, D.M. (2004) *The Bayeux Tapestry. The Complete Tapestry in Colour*, London: Thames & Hudson.

CHAPTER THIRTEEN

HANDICRAFTS

—◆—

John Ljungkvist

Around the middle of the eighth century the Scandinavians became involved in increasing warfare, trade and cultural contacts with areas all around Scandinavia. These changes also had an impact on handicrafts. Factors such as the increasing use of raw materials, the rise of towns to become new places for craftspeople to dwell in, and intensified trade, made the craftspeople and their products more important for the society. Some parts of the handicrafts did however change slowly. These contrasts between 'sudden' changes and long-lived technology and tradition make handicraft a problematic term as it covers a wide range of different activities and specialities. Some of them altered quickly, depending on changes in fashion, trading routes and politics. Others remained the same for centuries, because of strong traditions and stagnant technology.

The Viking Age is different from previous periods because of the rise of towns and trading centres. But large production centres for different goods were uncommon. Most of the objects needed in people's daily life had to be manufactured by local specialists or ordinary people in rural farms and villages. Most people in Scandinavian society were craftspeople; basic carpeting and textiles were produced in their households.

From the evidence of the Old Norse sagas it is possible to recognise crafts that can be tied to men and women respectively. Carpeting and smithing were mainly male crafts, while working with textiles was primarily a female occupation. The strongest evidence does however come from the grave materials in different parts of Scandinavia. Objects related to work with textiles, such as needles and spindle whorls, are primarily found in female graves. Objects connected to woodworking or smithing, such as axes, chisels and files, are almost exclusively found in male graves. One must however remember that the sagas and the graves reflect primarily the social conventions in the society, and not necessarily all the real situations. It is not impossible that men, women and children could cross over the gender-related borders. This could for example happen when a craft became a true profession or necessary for the support of a family.

THE CRAFTSPEOPLE

In Viking Age society it is difficult to recognise when a craft became so complicated, economically important or exclusive that it required professional specialists. To identify these specialists is problematic as there is no real evidence for a guild system, or similar, that can help us. This society, with very few towns, looked completely different compared to the late medieval one, where numbers of craftspeople lived permanently in a number of towns.

One of the most prominent finds related to crafts is the Mästermyr chest found on the island of Gotland. This chest contained a complete set of tools for a craftsperson. One of the most interesting features in the find is the variety of the objects. They show that the person who owned the objects was not only a blacksmith, but also a carpenter, and someone who could melt bronze and deal with precious metals. This chest is evidence that at least some craftspeople had a wide range of skills. The true specialists were probably quite few.

Some people in the Viking Age can in some degree be identified with crafts since they were buried with tools. For example, a number of male graves with smithing tools have been interpreted as smiths' graves. A problem is that some of these graves contain not only a number of smiths' or carpenters' tools, but they are also high-status burials with much of everything: weapons, horse equipment, vessels and cooking utensils, a large number of sacrificed animals etc. These persons can be identified with many things: warfare, hunting, lordship etc. To say that these high-status persons were more craftspeople than others is difficult and not very likely. These graves have primarily been found in Norway and Sweden. There are no certain ways to identify the specialists among the craftspeople and determine their rank in society.

THE CRAFTS

Scandinavian craftspeople were capable of dealing with almost all materials available: wood, textiles, bone, antler and metals. Perhaps the most important limitation lay within the treatment of stone. In the Christian hemisphere, the Roman tradition of building stone constructions with mortar had been upheld, primarily for the building of churches. Building with mortar and the cutting of ashlar did not reach Scandinavia until some time after Christianisation. In Denmark the first stone church was erected in 1026, probably by a British master (Liebgott 1989: 119).

Stoneworking is not likely to have been a very prominent craft in most parts of Scandinavia. The exception is probably in those parts where quarrying was important. Most well known is the quarrying of soapstone in Norway and on the Swedish west coast. This soft type of rock could be shaped into vessels. Parts of these have been found in many places in Scandinavia. Another craft that seems to increase during the Viking Age is the production of whetstones and querns made primarily of slate and sandstone. Production areas of these materials have been found in Norway, central Sweden and the island of Öland, Sweden. By the end of the Viking Age the number of raised runestones increased dramatically. Many of the runestone carvers were amateurs, but from the evidence that comes from the carvers' signatures, it is apparent that some of them became specialists in the art of chiselling ornaments and runes. Curiously this was a group of specialists that hardly existed for more than 100 years as the runestones ceased to be raised around AD 1100.

Wood was the most important material in society for most parts of Scandinavia, used for buildings, tools, fences etc. Unfortunately very little wood is preserved that can tell us about how the wooden objects were decorated. Most of them we have preserved today come from wet culture layers in towns such as Hedeby, Staraya Ladoga and Lund, where parts of houses as well as objects have been well preserved. A few objects, such as the ship, sledge and wagon from the Oseberg grave, and the later stave churches, reveal some extraordinary high artistic levels as regards wooden objects.

Textiles are also quite rarely preserved. In most cases they are found either on metal objects in graves, where metal salts have preserved the fabric next to the object, or in the wet culture layer of the towns. Complete clothes from the Viking Age are very rare. Wool is the main textile represented, but textiles made of plants, such as linen or hemp and nettles, are even more rarely preserved, and little is known about the use and manufacture of these materials. The textile craft was very time consuming; almost all the women in society were involved in it. Traces of textile crafts are quite common in archaeological settlement excavations. The loom that was used was of a primitive standing type with weights in clay or sometimes stone, which held down the warp threads. These weights as well as spindle whorls – used for transforming the raw wool into threads – are often found on excavations. Brick weaving was popular in the Viking Age for producing decorative borders on clothes, sometimes with threads in silk, gold and silver. Probably the most prominent examples of Scandinavian textile crafts have been found in the Oseberg ship-burial, where both the tools and the textiles have been preserved.

Leather craft was almost as important as textile craft and was used for shoes, ropes, straps etc. Unfortunately leather does require a wet environment for preservation and this material is almost only ever found in excavations in towns with wet culture layers, such as Hedeby, York and Staraja Ladoga. The material from these places gives us a good idea of what kind of products were made. On the other hand it is hard to discuss how widely spread leather craft was and who in society performed the not-so-pleasant handling of tanning and what kind of speciality the leather cutters had.

Bone and antler were the raw material for a wide range of objects. Especially favoured was thick metatarsal bones from cattle, horses, sheep and goats for the manufacture of needles for different functions. Antler was the favoured material for making combs. The material was primarily taken from elk, red deer and reindeer, all depending on where the manufacture was taking place. In general the availability of the material dictated how the objects were produced. In Norway the working with bone and antler was slightly different because of the catch of walruses and whales in the North Atlantic. One speciality from this area are gaming pieces made of ivory, another one is the production of 'washing boards' made of whalebone. These often richly decorated boards are primarily found in rich female graves in Norway, but occasionally they have been found in other areas within and outside Scandinavia. A few objects have been found in Swedish graves and also on the Orkneys and in Ireland.

Smithing was by far the most common metal craft and also the most important one for making tools, nails, rivets and weapons etc. Traces of smithing can be found on many excavated settlements in Scandinavia as it was often easy to get the ore, whether from bog, stone or sand. The ore was then transformed to iron in relatively simple clay-built ovens.

The manufacture of iron and smithing took place in many areas, such as in the northern parts of Sweden and eastern Norway; it was not only a profession for true specialists. In these areas, the production of iron was probably an almost regular work and performed side by side with other activities. The production in these areas was certainly far bigger than for local needs and some of it was hence exported to within and outside Scandinavia.

In other areas, where the manufacture of iron has not been found, smithing was still a quite common feature on the excavated settlements, normally with finds of iron slag and forging pits. In many villages, at least one individual seems to have known how to produce simple tools or repair broken ones.

A debated question is to what extent iron objects were imported to Scandinavia and how skilled the Scandinavian smiths were. Most iron objects have a Scandinavian origin, but there are some exceptions, especially among the weapons, that often exemplify the most delicate skills. In the Roman period, large numbers of swords were imported to Scandinavia from the Roman provinces. This taste for Continental swords also existed in the Viking Age. Smiths' stamps and signatures such as the famous *Ulfberht* are evidence of imported Frankish swords. How many of the other swords in Scandinavia are imported we do not know. What can be assumed, however, is that even though iron was common and easily accessible in Scandinavia, people still preferred to import some iron objects connected to a certain value and status.

Bronze, silver and gold were metals used for the same type of objects, such as brooches, buckles, and inlays in weapons. In contrast to iron, these metals were not manufactured in Scandinavia, they all had to be imported. Much of this import was in the shape of scrap metal. One exceptional find has been discovered in Spilling, Gotland. Together with the largest silver hoard hitherto found, the excavators also found a chest containing scrapped imported bronze jewellery. Many of the Scandinavian objects in bronze and gold probably originated from such reused Continental objects.

Bronze was the most common material for the Viking Age jeweller. It was the material that the ordinary Scandinavians could afford. On a number of sites, such as Ribe, Birka and Kaupang, many fragments from moulds and crucibles have been revealed. The largest recent find is an excavated workshop on Birka, where thousands of mould fragments have been found. One skill that the Scandinavian bronze specialists (except for perhaps on Gotland) never seem to have achieved, is the production of bronze vessels.

During the late eighth century Arabic silver began to arrive in Scandinavia via Russia. This inflow, primarily in the shape of coins, is not only reflected in an increasing amount of treasure hoards containing coins and jewellery, but is also shown in the crafts. Some coins were transformed into pendants used in the female jewellery set, others were melted down and used in moulding, silver-plating or in objects and decorations made of silver wire. Brooches and bracelets of this material are however rarely found. Silver was still so precious that it was mainly used for making small objects.

Gold was, in comparison with bronze and silver, a very rare material. In combination with mercury, it was most often used for gilding bronze objects. True gold objects are also very rare compared to silver and bronze. Where they do occur, the craftsmanship is often of very high quality. Gold was especially used for filigree and granulation-decorated jewellery.

The manufacture of melted glass was probably not a skill that Scandinavian craftspeople were capable of, nor was the making of glass vessels. The handling of glass was primarily limited to the production of beads. The raw material was imported in the shape of cubic glass pieces that were melted and manufactured into beads for the Scandinavian taste. In the Viking period beads were also made of carnelian or rock crystal, highly valued by the Scandinavians. These beads, arriving via Russia, were previously thought to be imported as finished products. However, new evidence from Gotland has revealed that in some degree they were shaped in Scandinavia. The manufacture of beads has been found on most of the trading centres but traces can also occur on rural sites.

Pieces of amber often turn up on the trading centres and are evidence for the production of beads and other small objects. Amber is a raw material that is common in the southern Baltic and from here was exported to other parts of Europe.

THE PLACES FOR SPECIAL MANUFACTURE

Knowledge about Viking Age crafts has increased a great deal since the 1970s. A number of excavations have been made in both previously known and recently found towns and trading centres. Especially in Denmark and Sweden a dramatically increased number of rural excavations have revealed a lot of information, not least regarding crafts, that previously was almost only represented in the towns.

The largest number of traces of crafts come from towns where Scandinavians had big interests, such as York, Dublin, Hedeby, Birka, Kaupang and Staraya Ladoga. In these cities a number of craftspeople dwelt, such as bronze forgers, comb-makers and pottery-makers. These were probably the most prominent places for crafts. But it is far from certain that all craftspeople stayed here for the whole year, or that the production was on a large scale. It is not very common that traces of large-scale production reveal themselves. This indicates that many craftspeople stayed only temporarily in the cities. Perhaps they dwelt there only when the towns were busy.

In recent years new places with traces of specialised crafts have turned up on average every second year. The problem is that it is very difficult to define and categorise these sites.

What many of these places have in common is that they can be connected to people belonging to the upper strata of society. Some places have been connected to Danish and Swedish kings, such as Lejre and the Trelleborg forts in Denmark or Old Uppsala in Sweden. But not only kings gathered craftspeople around them. It almost seems to be a significant feature for a Viking Age chieftain to have specialised crafts such as moulding on his estate. This means that the chieftain was not completely dependent upon special crafts in towns such as Birka, where other chieftains, who were perhaps competitors in power, had control of the place and the production. We do not know whether the craftspeople stayed permanently on these estates. The traces of the production are however mostly quite small, which indicates that it was sporadic.

Some of the other sites can be interpreted as trading centres like the above-mentioned towns, though smaller and perhaps not permanently inhabited. Other sites, whether placed by the coast or inland, seem to be a magnate's estate or a village with an estate, where some production has taken place. The intention behind the specialised crafts seems to have varied a lot. Some craftspeople dwelt at the magnate's estate and produced objects probably for the magnate and the people around him. Other craftspeople produced larger amounts of objects at the trading and crafts centres, to which many people travelled.

It is interesting to wonder if it was the same craftspeople who upheld themselves in the magnate's estate as well as in the trading centre. Sporadic production in the towns and in the rural sites is evidence that craftspeople travelled between different places. An important question is whether the craftspeople were connected to a special lord, or if they in some degree were independent people. There is probably no definite answer to this question. The kings and queens probably had their personal goldsmith or jeweller, who travelled with them to different places. Some of the places connected to royalty reveal traces of high-quality crafts. People belonging to the low aristocracy could perhaps not afford to permanently support a specialised craftsperson. Instead they probably had to engage a travelling craftsperson to produce specialised products.

On rural farms, where fire-related crafts such as smithing, moulding or bead-making were taking place, craftspeople regularly worked on the outskirts of the farm, often in the same areas where one finds hearths and ovens for cooking. This is probably because of the fear of fire. A real smithy in the shape of a house is not always found. Occasionally a small post-built building or a pit-house is found, but in some cases there are no traces of a house construction over the forge or melt pits. Craftspeople seem in many cases to have conducted their work outdoors. This was perhaps not always pleasant, but was positive in some ways. There were difficulties in finding sufficient light when complicated details were required. Weaving on the other hand always seems to have been conducted indoors, whether in small pit-houses dug into the ground or inside the normal living quarters.

BIBLIOGRAPHY

Ambrosiani, K. (1981) *Viking Age Combs, Comb Making, and Comb Makers. In the Light of Finds from Birka and Ribe*, Stockholm: Dept. of Archaeology, University of Stockholm.

Andersson, E. (1999) *The Common Thread. Textile Production During the Late Iron Age–Viking Age*, trans. M. Gaimster, Lund: Institute of Archaeology, University of Lund.

Armbruster, B.R. (2002) 'Goldschmiede in Haithabu. Ein Beitrag zum frühmittelalterlichen Metallhandwerk', in *Das archäologische Fundmaterial der Ausgrabung Haithabu* (Berichte über die Ausgrabungen in Haithabu 34), Neumünster: Wachholtz.

Arwidsson, G. and Berg, G. (1983) *The Mästermyr Find. A Viking Age Tool Chest from Gotland*, Stockholm: Almqvist & Wiksell International.

Bayley, J. (1992) *Anglo-Scandinavian Non-ferrous Metalworking from 16–22 Coppergate* (Archaeology of York 17:7), London: Council for British Archaeology.

Bender Jørgensen, L. (1992) *North European Textiles. Until AD 1000*, Aarhus: Aarhus University Press.

Brinch Madsen, H. (1984) 'Metal-casting', in M. Bencard (ed.) *Ribe Excavations 1970–76* (Ribe Excavations 1970–76, vol. 2), Esbjerg: Sydjysk universitetsforlag.

Carlsson, A. (1983) *Djurhuvudformiga spännen och gotländsk vikingatid* (Stockholm studies in Archaeology 5), Stockholm: Dept. of Archaeology, University of Stockholm.

Christophersen, A. (1980) *The Transformation of Handicraft. Studies in the Development of Antler and Bone Working in Lund ca. 1000–1350*, Bonn: Habelt.

Duczko, W. (1985). *Birka Untersuchungen und Studien*, vol. 5: *The Filigree and Granulation Work of the Viking Period*, Stockholm: Almqvist & Wiksell International.

Groenman-van Waateringe, W. (1984) 'Die Lederfunde von Haithabu', in *Das archäologische Fundmaterial der Ausgrabung Haithabu* (Berichte über die Ausgrabungen in Haithabu 34), Neumünster: Wachholtz.

Liebgott, N.-K. (1989) *Dansk middelalderarkæologi*. Copenhagen: Gad.

Lønborg, B. (1998) *Vikingetidens metalbearbejdning*, Odense: Odense bys museer.

Macgregor, A., Mainman, A.J. and Rogers, N.S.H. (1999) *Craft, Industry and Everyday Life. Bone Antler, Ivory and Horn from Anglo-Scandinavian and Medieval York* (Archaeology of York 17:12), York: Council for British Archaeology.

Mould, Q., Carlisle, I. and Cameron, E. (2003) *Craft, Industry and Everyday Life. Leather and Leatherworking in Anglo-Scandinavian and Medieval York* (Archaeology of York 17:16), York: Council for British Archaeology.

Oldeberg, A. (1966) *Metallteknik under vikingatid och medeltid*, Stockholm: Seelig.

Ottaway, P.J. (1992) *Anglo-Scandinavian Ironwork from 16–22 Coppergate* (Archaeology of York 17:6), London: Council for British Archaeology.

Petersen, J. (1951) *Vikingetidens redskaper*, Oslo: Dybwad.

Rogers, P.W. (1997) *Textile Production at 16–22 Coppergate* (Archaeology of York 17:11), York: Council for British Archaeology.

Steppuhn, P. (1998) 'Die Glasfunde von Haithabu', in *Das archäologische Fundmaterial der Ausgrabung Haithabu* (Berichte über die Ausgrabungen in Haithabu 32), Neumünster: Wachholtz.

Thunmark-Nylén, L. (1983) *Vikingatida dosspännen. Teknisk stratigrafi och verkstadsgruppering*, Uppsala: Dept. of Archaeology, Uppsala University.

Trotzig, G. (1991) *Craftmanship and Function. A Study of Metal Vessels found in Viking Age Tombs on the Island of Gotland, Sweden*, Stockholm: Statens historiska museum.

Wallander, A. (1989) 'Smedsgravar eller gravar med smides- och snickarverktyg? Genomgång av definitioner och redskapskombinationer', *Tor*, 22: 105–59.

CHAPTER FOURTEEN

RAIDING AND WARFARE

———•◆•———

Gareth Williams

Raiding and warfare are central to our understanding of the Viking Age. For many years the only popular image of the Vikings was the Viking warrior, brutal and terrifying, raping and pillaging, burning monasteries, committing a variety of atrocities and demanding Danegeld. This image has been increasingly downplayed since the 1960s and 1970s, as scholars have rightly pointed out that there were many other important aspects to Scandinavian society in the Viking Age, and that only a small proportion of the population were warriors, while also noting that, since the surviving historical accounts were written by the Vikings' Christian victims, they may give an exaggerated picture of both the impact and the barbarity of raids by the pagan Vikings. Nevertheless, although the term *Viking* has come to be used for the whole society of the period, it is raiding and warfare that define 'Viking' activity – a Viking (OE *wicing*, ON *víkingr*) was a raider or pirate, and although trading, crafts, seafaring and settlement and many other aspects of Viking society may be equally important, it is the raiding which gives us the concept of a Viking Age. It is increasingly clear from archaeological evidence that there was contact between Scandinavia and the rest of northern Europe before the late eighth century, and historical sources show the Scandinavian kingdoms increasingly becoming part of the European mainstream from the eleventh century, if not earlier. It is only the visible military expansion from the late eighth century to the eleventh that makes the Viking Age a meaningful concept.

The motivation behind the earliest raids remains the subject of debate. According to one school of thought, the early raids on monasteries represented a pagan political/ religious response to the aggressive Frankish Christian mission against the Saxons and the Danes (Myhre 1998). However, this interpretation has not been widely accepted, not least because the earliest raids seem to have been launched from western Norway, not Denmark, and against the British Isles and Ireland, not against the Franks (Wamers 1998). It is clear that later raids were primarily motivated by the desire to gain wealth, and it seems likely that this was the main motivation for raiding and external warfare throughout the Viking Age. This leaves aside internal warfare within and between the emerging Scandinavian kingdoms, which was apparently motivated by the desire for political power, but the raids against western Europe are characterised by a desire to gain wealth abroad. This might then be translated into political power either abroad, as in the formation of new Viking kingdoms and earldoms in Britain, Ireland and Normandy, or at home, where successful Viking leaders such as Óláfr Tryggvason and Óláfr Haraldsson used their success in England to press their claims to kingship in Norway.

The results of raiding brought wealth in different forms. Conquest brought landed wealth abroad, and the fact that the military expansion of the Viking Age coincided with the more peaceful settlement of the North Atlantic serves as a reminder of the importance of landed wealth, however it could be acquired. However, raiding which fell short of conquest could also generate portable wealth, which might then be converted into land and status at home or elsewhere. This could be acquired directly through plunder, or through the ransoming of captured people or precious objects, such as the Codex Aureus (an ornate Gospel book from Canterbury) (Webster and Backhouse 1991: 199–201), or through the imposition of tribute. Although the payment of 'Danegeld' is particularly associated with the later Viking Age, and especially the reign of Æthelred II, large payments to the Vikings for peace are recorded in Frankish sources from the ninth century, and even Alfred the Great was forced to 'make peace' with the Vikings on occasion (Coupland 1999; Abels 1998: 79, 105–14, 140–2). Archaeological finds of Insular material in Scandinavia provide clear evidence of looting in the early Viking Age, while the vast number of late Anglo-Saxon coins found in Denmark and Sweden (more survive there than in England) must in part reflect the success of the later Vikings in taking gelds (Wamers 1998; Blackburn 1991: 156–69; Metcalf 1989: 178–89; 1990: 165–76; Gillingham 1989, 1990; Lawson 1984, 1989).

Clearly the Viking raids were significant enough to be recorded as major events by their victims, but how important were the raids, and how distinctive was Viking warfare? Scholarly interpretations on these points differ, especially on the scale and importance of the raids, not least because Viking raiding followed different patterns in different areas. In England, Ireland and the kingdom of the western Franks, there is an apparent progression from small-scale seasonal raiding at the end of the eighth century through larger seasonal raids, then over-wintering, then conquest and permanent settlement in the ninth century. However, it is clear from historical sources that the pattern in Frisia was different, with a series of Danish chieftains settling in Frisia in the early ninth century, under Frankish overlordship, as part of an ongoing dynamic of political relations between Danish and Frankish rulers (Coupland 1998). Similarly, archaeological evidence suggests that Norwegian settlement in the Northern Isles of Scotland may have begun as early as the first half of the ninth century (Crawford 1987; Graham-Campbell and Batey 1998; Hunter *et al.* 1993; Ballin Smith 2007). It would also appear that although there was relative peace from Viking raids in England in between 954 and the reign of Æthelred II (978–1016), this gap in England saw extensive Viking activity in northern Scotland and around the Irish Sea (Crawford 1987; Williams 2004). The idea of a First Viking Age and Second Viking Age, found in the works of some English historians, thus represents a narrowly English perspective on Viking raiding.

The earliest raids seem all to have been on a small scale. Where numbers are given, only very small numbers of ships or men are cited, such as the three ships that attacked Portland in what may have been the earliest recorded Viking raid, in the reign of Beorhtric of Wessex (786–802). Where numbers are not given, the choice of wealthy but exposed coastal monasteries such as Lindisfarne and Iona rather than larger targets also suggests relatively small forces. Such small raids were probably undertaken by local groups under their own leaders. The raiders at Portland apparently came from Hordaland in western Norway, while Frankish sources identify attacks by men from Vestfold in southern Norway (*ASC* E–F, *sub* 787 [789]; Nelson 1991: 55 n. 2). Raiding on a small scale continued throughout the Viking Age. A battle off the coast of Wessex in 896, described in unusual detail by the Anglo-Saxon Chronicle (*ASC* A, *sub* 897 [896]) involved only six shiploads of Vikings, and much of the raiding around Scotland and the Irish Sea apparently continued to involve small fleets as late as the eleventh and twelfth centuries.

However, the ninth century certainly saw an increase in the scale of Viking forces. The size of fleets mentioned in English, Irish and Frankish sources increased, often numbered in hundreds of ships by the mid-ninth century, and led by named kings or earls. These titles probably reflect personal status and lineage, and do not necessarily mean that such leaders ruled major territories in the Viking homelands. These were not yet fully unified into the modern Scandinavian kingdoms, which begin to emerge fully only towards the end of the Viking Age. Nevertheless, such titles indicate that the leaders of Viking raids now came from the highest levels of Scandinavian society, although lesser chieftains no doubt also continued to play a major part.

While there is no doubt that the scale of the raids increased in this period, historians have disagreed over the extent of the increase, and on the impact of these larger forces. Peter Sawyer, in his influential book *The Age of the Vikings*, argued that while the smaller numbers such as three and six ships seemed to be exact, the larger fleets were always in suspiciously round numbers, and were therefore unreliable. He questioned whether any Viking leader could realistically have mustered fleets of hundreds of ships, and suggested that the figures in the sources are much exaggerated, with even the largest Viking armies numbering only several hundred men (Sawyer 1962: 117–28). However, Nicholas Brooks (1979) noted that there is close agreement between independent Anglo-Saxon, Irish and Frankish sources on the size of fleets, and argued that the figures cited in the various chronicles were more reliable than Sawyer had suggested, and that the larger armies probably numbered in the low thousands. More recent thinking has tended to fall between these two positions. Interpretations of early medieval warfare generally since the mid-1980s have tended towards relatively small armies, but it does seem hard to reconcile contemporary accounts of the largest Viking forces with numbers below the low thousands.

This is not least because of the scale of the achievement of the Vikings in war. It may be true, as Janet Nelson (1997) has argued, that Frankish chronicles suggest that internal conflicts between the rival successors to the Carolingian Empire were seen as more important than the Viking raids in the late ninth century, and that the Vikings suffered a number of major defeats. Raids on Britain and Ireland also need to be seen in the context of the recurrent warfare between the petty kingdoms there – Viking raids did not take place in a peaceful vacuum. However, the Vikings in turn inflicted major defeats on the Franks and succeeded in extorting large amounts of silver as the price of peace. In England, three of the four great kingdoms of the late ninth century were conquered, while the fourth came close. In the second wave of large-scale attacks on England, vast quantities of coin were paid for short-lived peace, and eventually the whole kingdom was brought under Danish rule for more than a generation. In Scotland, Vikings successfully conquered the Northern and Western Isles, and large parts of the northern and western mainland, and probably contributed substantially to the collapse of both the Pictish kingdom and the kingdom of Dál Riata and to the emergence of a new kingdom of the Scots. Territorial conquest was more limited in Ireland, but the Vikings did succeed in establishing a number of defended trading centres on the coasts from which they were never permanently expelled. It is hard to see how any of this could have been achieved if the Vikings had been quite as insignificant in numbers and military prowess as some modern historians seem to suggest.

This does not mean, however, that historians have been wrong to question some elements of the Viking reputation as warriors. In particular, their reputation for atrocity seems to have been exaggerated. Certainly they showed little respect for churches and churchmen, and inevitably this provided material for religious polemic by monastic chroniclers. However, attacks on churches by Christian rulers were not unknown, while Charlemagne notably treated the pagan Saxons extremely harshly (Foot 1991; Halsall 1992). The one specifically 'Viking' atrocity, the so-called blood-eagle (in which a victim's ribs were split, and his lungs pulled out behind him like wings), does not appear in contemporary sources, and may well be a later literary invention (Frank 1984, 1988, 1990; Bjarni Einarsson 1988, 1990). Vikings were certainly capable of brutality by modern standards, but it is hard to argue that they were much more unpleasant than their Christian contemporaries.

Nor was the emphasis on raiding and plunder particularly unusual. Raiding in order to plunder portable wealth is typical of the warfare between the petty kingdoms of pre-Viking Britain and Ireland, and survived long after across medieval Europe, with the *chevauchée* continuing to play an important role even in the era of more obviously 'national' warfare in the later Middle Ages. Similarly, taking tribute seems to have been a central part of the relationship between greater and lesser kings in early medieval Britain (Charles-Edwards 1989; Dumville 1997), and although Anglo-Saxon sources tend not to equate payment of geld to the Vikings in return for temporary peace with the payment of 'legitimate' tribute to overkings, it is hard to see much difference in substance, and successful Viking leaders may well have regarded those who paid them gelds as tributaries. Frankish sources explicitly refer to such payments as tribute, and often imply that it was demeaning for the Franks to be in that situation (Coupland 1999).

Timothy Reuter (1985) argued persuasively that even the campaigns of a great European ruler like Charlemagne were largely carried out on the basis of a combination of raids against neighbouring kingdoms in pursuit of conquest where this was feasible, tribute where long-term dominance could be established that fell short of full conquest, and plunder when Charlemagne had the resources to raid but not to establish lasting domination. This provides a useful paradigm for much of early medieval warfare, and the Vikings are only unusual in that their expeditions were often led by 'private' warlords rather than by national leaders, and even this distinction becomes blurred in the eleventh century, when one looks at the campaigns of figures such as Sveinn Forkbeard and Cnut the Great of Denmark, and Harald Hardruler and Magnús Barelegs of Norway.

If the Vikings were not markedly more atrocious than others, and campaigns based around the combination of plunder and tribute were not unusual, it is probably also fair to say that their reputation on the battlefield has also been exaggerated. An important part of their campaign strategy often seems to have been to avoid battle unless they felt confident of victory. For example, although Viking raids continued in southern England following Alfred's victory at Edington in 878, the various Viking forces seem to have done their best to avoid being brought to battle, and although the Anglo-Saxon Chronicle for this period is dominated by the activities of the Vikings, it presents a picture of Alfred and Edward repeatedly pursuing the Vikings as they moved from one temporary base to another, rather than a series of glorious battles. Viking armies did have notable victories, but they also had notable defeats. The limited evidence available suggests that Viking battle techniques were broadly similar to those of their enemies, based around the shield wall, with some use of missile weapons (Williams forthcoming: ch. 5). Although the sources indicate that Viking forces often moved on horseback, and emphasise the acquisition or loss of horses on more than one occasion, they seem to have fought primarily as mounted infantry, dismounting for battle, and rarely fought on horseback, unlike the Franks, who regularly used horses on the battlefield (Davis 1989). As discussed elsewhere in this volume, their weapons and armour were also very similar to those of their enemies, and many of their finest weapons and armour were of Frankish manufacture (Pedersen, ch. 15, below; Williams forthcoming: ch. 2).

There are, however, some distinctive features of Viking warfare. Closely related to each other, these are the use of ships in war, the effective use of mobility in their campaigns and a strong awareness of the importance of supplying themselves when on campaign. The use of ships in warfare was not unique to the Vikings, and both Anglo-Saxons and Franks had a history of seafaring before the Viking Age (Haywood 1991), while the Scots of Dál Riata appear to have had a comparatively sophisticated levy system based on boats (Bannerman 1974; Williams 2002). However, technological developments in the early Viking Age meant that the Vikings had access to vessels which were suitable for use at sea, and which were also of sufficiently shallow draft to be used on at least the larger inland rivers, and large enough to carry significant numbers of men. They could also be used to carry both supplies and loot, and ships and boats were far more effective than any form of land transport for transporting bulk goods throughout the Middle Ages and beyond.

These ships are most commonly associated with the ability to arrive suddenly on a hostile coastline, attack a vulnerable target and leave again before local forces could be raised against them — the archetypal Viking park-and-raid approach. This was the strategy of all of their early raids, and a recurrent strategy throughout the period. However, ships also played a vital role in the large-scale campaigns of the mid- to late ninth century. The carrying capacity of the ships allowed Viking forces to transport both their accumulated wealth and stores, without the necessity for slow and cumbersome baggage trains, which would have made it much easier for their enemies to launch attacks on them. The shallow ships were able to penetrate far inland, and thus we hear of fleets, not just land forces, descending on completely landlocked targets such as Paris or Repton (Williams forthcoming: ch. 6). On occasion, the Vikings also divided their forces, sending one force overland and another by sea, to rendezvous at an agreed target, as with Exeter in 876 (*ASC* A and E, *sub* 877 [876]). This meant that the land force could travel unencumbered, moving quickly with the advantage of surprise, while the supplies moved in the ships, safe from counter-attack, although vulnerable to the weather, especially since they presumably sailed with reduced crews, since some crew-members would have served in the land force.

As mentioned above, the Vikings sought to equip themselves with horses on land whenever possible, which also provided additional carrying capacity as well as speed

(Clapham 1910; Davis 1989; Williams forthcoming: ch. 6). Horses provided a similar mobility on land to that provided by the ships along the rivers and the coast, and allowed the Vikings to extend the idea of the surprise attack in areas without access by water.

This emphasis on mobility was coupled with a shrewd sense of where to raid. Familiarity with western Europe prior to the outbreak of Viking raids enabled them to target wealthy and isolated monasteries for the early raids, as well as major coastal trading centres such as Dorestad in Frisia, which was raided repeatedly (Coupland 1988). However, the choice of targets became even more important with the shift towards larger-scale raiding, especially once the Vikings began to overwinter, rather than simply raiding seasonally. This overwintering is again one of the most distinctive aspects of Viking warfare, with a significance that has largely been underrated. The early Viking raids tended to be seasonal, of necessity, since their ships were not well suited to winter sailing. However, it is easy to ignore the fact that land-based warfare was normally seasonal in this period as well. Even Charlemagne, despite his impressive record for conquest and tribute-taking, rarely campaigned over winter, although he tended to campaign in most years (Reuter 1985). Although Alfred the Great eventually recognised the importance of maintaining a standing army to counter the Viking threat, this was not easy to maintain, and on one occasion a besieged Viking force was able to escape because the besiegers were forced to withdraw before their relief arrived (*ASC* A, *sub* 894 [893]). When even major kingdoms struggled to maintain permanent field armies, the fact that the Vikings managed to campaign for years on end, often in hostile territory, is perhaps a more impressive achievement than any success they may have enjoyed on the battlefield.

They managed to do this by careful selection of overwintering places, descending on monasteries, towns and royal estates early in the winter. That meant that they arrived in places where supplies had already been gathered, which they could take over for their own use, while the onset of winter made it difficult for anyone to raise and supply an army to remove them before the spring. The Vikings then probably spread out over the surrounding area, making it easier to supply the smaller groups, but retaining the centre as a rallying point and defence in case they were attacked, and there is growing evidence for secondary Viking activity close to Viking overwintering centres such as Repton, London and York (Brooks and Graham-Campbell 2000: 69–92; Richards 2001: 97–104; Blackburn 2002: 89–101; Williams forthcoming: ch. 6). Some sites already had defences, such as Roman forts and fortified towns, but where they did not, the Vikings simply created their own fortifications, as at Repton, and the many fortified centres in Ireland known as *longphorts* (Price 1991; Kelly and Maas 1995; Docherty 1998; Kelly and O'Donovan 1998; Ó Floinn 1998; Biddle and Kjølbye-Biddle 2001; Gibbons 2004, 2005; McKeown 2005; O'Brien *et al.* 2006; Williams forthcoming: ch. 4, 6).

While tribute payments provided short-term relief, battles were rarely decisive enough to provide a lasting solution to Viking raiding (Coupland 1999: 68–9), and it was only when the twin issues of mobility and supply were tackled that the Viking raids could successfully be contained. Charles the Bald introduced fortified bridges to deny the Vikings access to the Frankish river system, making it difficult for them to penetrate far inland, although this strategy failed when bridges were not built or maintained properly. Fortified bridges were also used by Alfred the Great, who also built ships to defend the coastline, and introduced a network of fortified towns across Wessex (Abels 1997; Peddie 1999; Williams forthcoming: ch. 4). These acted not only as refuges, but also as supply centres, denying the supplies to Viking raiders, and facilitating the resupply of his own army (Abels 1997: 257–65; Williams forthcoming). Despite initial difficulties, these *burh*s proved successful in Wessex, and the system was extended across England by his successors as they gradually conquered the Danelaw from its Viking rulers (Hill and Rumble 1996).

The social and organisational structures which underpinned Viking raiding and warfare have been hotly debated. Later laws from Denmark, Norway and Sweden all record the existence of a form of ship-levy system known as ON *leiðangr*, and although these laws date from the twelfth and thirteenth centuries, many historians have sought to project such systems back to the Viking Age. This view has been questioned since the 1980s, most notably by Niels Lund (1985, 1994, 1996, 1997; cf. Gelting 1999), who argued that no form of *leiðangr* existed before the late eleventh century at the earliest, and that the Viking raids were basically private ventures, carried out by war-leaders with whatever followers they were able to attract through their own reputations and the promise of wealth, rather than any sort of national army, even when the leaders were important Scandinavian kings. This view has received some support for the ninth century from Richard Abels (2003), who notes that Anglo-Saxon sources tend to describe Viking forces as *here* (warband) rather than *fyrd* (army), and argues that describing Viking forces as 'armies' implies much more structure than probably existed.

Lund's views have not been universally accepted, and there is evidence that some form of *leiðangr* existed in the tenth century, although since the *leiðangr* seems originally to have been linked to defensive warfare, it is not clear that this would have much impact on Viking incursions into western Europe (Malmros 1985, 2002; Crumlin-Pedersen 1988, 1997, 2002; Williams 2002, forthcoming: chs. 7–9). There is certainly a case for arguing that some of the conflicts between Danes and Franks in the ninth century reflect some form of national warfare (Wamers 2002; Williams 2002, forthcoming: ch. 7), and it is difficult to separate entirely the roles of 'king' and 'viking leader' for figures such as Svein Forkbeard and Harald Hardruler. Nevertheless, it is fair to say that the majority of Viking raiding and warfare was carried out by individual warbands. These might band together into larger groups, and their leaders might be kings or earls, or lesser chieftains. Occasionally, with the 'great' warbands of the late ninth century we see several kings or earls jointly leading their forces, again implying a merging of smaller independent forces. This apparent lack of formal structure makes their achievements in long-term campaigning and strategic and logistical planning even more impressive.

To conclude, raiding and warfare were typical features of the Viking Age, not just for the Vikings but for the whole of northern Europe. In many ways, Viking warfare is little different from their contemporaries', and the only really distinctive features are the emphasis on ships, and the strong emphasis on strategic mobility and logistics, which allowed Viking forces to campaign for years at a time. However, it is important not to underplay the significance of Viking raids, in terms of either their perceived impact by contemporaries, or the lasting effects of their conquests. Other 'Viking' achievements may be more impressive, and certainly more positive, but many of these rest in part on their military success, and without Viking raiding and warfare, we would have no 'Vikings'.

BIBLIOGRAPHY

Abels, R. (1997) 'English logistics and military administration 871–1066: the impact of the Viking wars', in A. Nørgård Jørgensen and B.L. Clausen (eds) (1997).
—— (1998) *Alfred the Great. War, Kingship and Culture in Anglo-Saxon England*, London: Longman.
—— (2003) 'Alfred the Great, the *micel hæðen here* and the Viking threat', in T. Reuter (ed.) *Alfred the Great. Papers from the Eleventh-Centenary Conferences*, Aldershot: Ashgate.
ASC = Swanton, M. (ed. and trans.) (1996), *The Anglo-Saxon Chronicle*, London: J.M. Dent.
Ballin Smith, B. (2007) 'Norwick: Shetland's first Viking settlement?', in B. Ballin Smith, S. Taylor and G. Williams (eds) *West over Sea. Studies in Scandinavian Sea-Borne Expansion and Settlement Before 1300* (The Northern World 31), Leiden: Brill.
Bannerman, J.W.M. (1974) *Studies in the History of Dalriada*, Edinburgh: Scottish Academic Press.
Biddle, M. and Kjølbye-Biddle, B. (2001) 'Repton and the "great heathen army" 973–4', in J.A. Graham-Campbell, R. Hall, J. Jesch and D.N. Parsons (eds) *Vikings and the Danelaw. Select Papers from the Proceedings of the Thirteenth Viking Congress*, Oxford: Oxbow.
Bjarni Einarsson (1988) 'De Normanorum Atrocitate, or on the execution by the Aquiline method', *Saga-Book of the Viking Society for Northern Research*, 22: 79–82.
—— (1990) 'The blood eagle once more: A. Blóðörn – an observation on the ornithological aspect', *Saga-Book of the Viking Society for Northern Research*, 23: 80–1.
Blackburn, M.A.S. (1991) 'Æthelred's coinage and the payment of tribute', in D. Scragg (ed.) *The Battle of Maldon, AD 991*, Oxford: Basil Blackwell.
—— (2002) 'Finds from the Anglo-Scandinavian site of Torksey, Lincolnshire', in B. Paskiewicz (ed.) *Moneta Mediævalis: studia numizmatyczne i historyczne ofiarowne Profesorowi Stanislawowi Suchodolsiemu w 65. rocznicę urodzin*, Warsaw: DiG.
Brooks, N.P. (1979) 'England in the crucible of defeat', *Transactions of the Royal Historical Society*, (5) 29: 1–20.
Brooks, N.P. and Graham-Campbell, J. (2000) 'Reflections on the Viking-Age silver hoard from Croydon, Surrey', in N. Brooks, *Communities and Warfare 700–1400*, London: Hambledon.
Charles-Edwards, T. (1989) 'Early medieval kingships in the British Isles', in S. Bassett (ed.) *The Origins of Anglo-Saxon Kingdoms*, London and New York: Leicester University Press.
Clapham, J.H. (1910) 'The horsing of the Danes', *EHR*, 25: 287–93.
Clarke, H.B., Ní Mhaonaigh, M. and Ó Floinn, R. (eds) (1998) *Ireland and Scandinavia in the Early Viking Age*, Dublin: Four Courts.
Coupland, S. (1988) 'Dorestad in the ninth century: the numismatic evidence', *Jaarboek voor Munt- en Penningkunde*, 75: 5–25.
—— (1998) 'From poachers to gamekeepers: Scandinavian warlords and Carolingian kings', *Early Medieval Europe*, 7(1): 85–114.
—— (1999) 'The Frankish tribute payments to the Vikings and their consequences', *Francia*, 26(1): 57–75.
Crawford, B.E. (1987) *Scotland in the Early Middle Ages*, vol. 2: *Scandinavian Scotland*, Leicester: Leicester University Press.
Crumlin-Pedersen, O. (1988) 'Gensyn med Skuldelev 5 – et ledingsskib?', in A. Andersen *et al.* (eds) *Festskrift til Olaf Olsen på 60-årsdagen, den 7. Juni 1988*, Copenhagen: Kongelige nordiske oldskriftselskab.
—— (1997) 'Large and small warships of the north', in A. Nørgård Jørgensen and B.L. Clausen (eds) (1997).
—— (2002) 'Splendour versus duty – 11th-century warships in the light of history and archaeology', in A. Nørgård Jørgensen *et al.* eds (2002).

Davis, R.H.C. (1989) *The Medieval Warhorse. Origin, Development and Redevelopment*, London: Thames and Hudson.

Docherty, C. (1998) 'The Vikings in Ireland: a review', in H.B. Clarke, M. Ní Mhaonaigh and R. Ó Floinn (eds) *Ireland and Scandinavia in the Early Viking Age*, Dublin: Four Courts.

Dumville, D.N. (1997) 'The terminology of overkingship in early Anglo-Saxon England', in J. Hines (ed.) *The Anglo-Saxons from the Migration Period to the Eighth Century. An Ethnographic Perspective*, Woodbridge: Boydell.

Foot, S. (1991) 'Violence against Christians? The Vikings and the Church in ninth-century England', *Medieval History*, 1(3): 3–16.

Frank, R. (1984) 'Viking atrocity and Skaldic verse: the rite of the blood-eagle', *EHR*, 332–43.

—— (1988) 'The blood-eagle again', *Saga-Book of the Viking Society for Northern Research*, 22: 287–89.

—— (1990) 'The blood-eagle once more: B. Ornithology and the interpretation of skaldic verse', *Saga-Book of the Viking Society for Northern Research*, 23: 81–3.

Gelting, M.H. (1999) 'Det komparative perspektiv i dansk højmiddelalderforskning. Om familia og familie, lið, leding og landeværn', *Dansk Historisk Tidsskrift*, 99(1): 146–88.

Gibbons, M. (2004) 'The longphort phenomenon in early Christian and Viking Ireland', *History Ireland*, 12(3): 19–23.

—— (2005) 'Athlunkard (Ath-an-longphort): a re-assessment of the proposed Viking fortress in Fairyhill, County Clare', *The Other Clare. Annual Journal of the Shannon Archaeological and Historical Society*, 29: 22–5.

Gillingham, J. (1989) ' "The most precious jewel in the English Crown": levels of Danegeld and Heregeld in the early eleventh century', *EHR*, 104: 373–84.

—— (1990) 'Chronicles and coins as evidence for levels of tribute and taxation in late tenth- and eleventh-century England', *EHR*, 105: 939–50.

Graham-Campbell, J.A. and Batey, C.E. (1998) *Vikings in Scotland. An Archaeological Survey*, Edinburgh: Edinburgh University Press.

Halsall, G. (1992) 'Playing by whose rules? A further look at Viking atrocity in the ninth century', *Medieval History*, 2(2): 2–12.

Haywood, J. (1991) *Dark Age Naval Power. A Re-assessment of Frankish and Anglo-Saxon Seafaring Activity*, London and New York: Routledge.

Hill, D. and Rumble, A.R. (eds) (1996) *The Defence of Wessex. The Burghal Hidage and Anglo-Saxon Fortifications*, Manchester: Manchester University Press.

Hunter, J.R., Bond, J.M. and Smith, A.M. (1993) 'Some aspects of early Viking settlement in Orkney', in C.E. Batey, J. Jesch and C.D. Morris (eds) *The Viking Age in Caithness, Orkney and the North Atlantic*, Edinburgh: Edinburgh University Press.

Kelly, E.P. and Maas, J. (1995) 'Vikings on the Barrow: Dunrally Fort, a possible Viking longphort in County Laois', *Archaeology Ireland*, 9(3): 30–2.

Kelly, E.P. and O'Donovan, E. (1998) 'A Viking longphort near Athlunkard, Co Clare', *Archaeology Ireland*, 12(4): 13–16.

Lawson, M.K. (1984) 'The collection of Danegeld and Heregeld in the reigns of Aethelred II and Cnut', *EHR*, 99: 721–38.

—— (1989) ' "Those stories look true": levels of taxation in the reigns of Aethelred II and Cnut', *EHR*, 104: 385–406.

Lund, N. (1985) 'The armies of Swein Forkbeard and Cnut: *leding* or *lið*?', *Anglo-Saxon England*, 15: 105–18.

—— (1994) 'If the Vikings knew a *Leding* – what was it like?', in B. Ambrosiani and H. Clarke (eds) *Developments Around the Baltic and the North Sea in the Viking Age* (Proceedings of the Twelfth Viking Congress; Birka Studies 3), Stockholm: Birka Project, Raä and Statens historiska museer.

—— (1996) *Lið, leding og landeværn. Hær og samfund i Danmark i ældre middelalder*, Roskilde: Vikingeskibshallen.

—— (1997) 'Is *leidang* a Nordic or a European phenomenon?', in A. Nørgård Jørgensen and B.L. Clausen (eds) (1997).

McKeown, M. (2005) 'Anagassan, a study of a Viking longphort', *County Louth Archaeological and Historical Journal*, 26: 67–79.

Malmros, R. (1985) 'Leding og skaldekvad. Det elvte århundredes nordiske krigsflåder, deres teknologi og organisation og deres placering i samfundet belyst gennem den samtidige fyrste- digtning', *Aarbøger for Nordisk Oldkyndighet og Historie*: 89–139.

—— (2002) 'Leiðangr in Old Norse court poetry', in A. Nørgård Jørgensen *et al.* (eds) (2002).

Metcalf, D.M. (1989) 'Large danegelds in relation to war and kingship: their implications for monetary history, and some numismatic evidence', in S.C. Hawkes (ed.) *Weapons and Warfare in Anglo-Saxon England* (Committee for Archaeology, Oxford University. Monograph 21), Oxford: Oxford University Committee for Archaeology.

—— (1990) 'Can we believe the very large figure of £72,000 for the geld levied by Cnut in 1018?', in K. Jonsson (ed.) *Studies in Late Anglo-Saxon Coinage. In Memory of Bror Emil Hildebrand*, Stockholm: Svenska numismatiska föreningen (= *Numismatiska Meddelanden*, 35: 165–76).

Myhre, B. (1998) 'The archaeology of the early Viking Age in Norway', in H.B. Clarke *et al.* (eds) (1998).

Nelson, J.L. (trans. and ed.) (1991) *The Annals of St-Bertin* (Ninth-century histories 1), Manches- ter: Manchester University Press.

—— (1997) 'The Frankish Empire', in P. Sawyer (ed.) *The Oxford Illustrated History of the Vikings*, London: Oxford University Press.

Nørgård Jørgensen, A. and Clausen, B.L. (eds) (1997) *Military Aspects of Scandinavian Society in a European Perspective, AD 1–1300* (Publications from the National Museum 2), Copenhagen: National Museum.

Nørgård Jørgensen, A., Lind, J., Jørgensen, L. and Clausen, B. (eds) (2002) *Maritime Warfare in Northern Europe. Technology, Organisation, Logistics and Administration 500 BC–1500 AD* (Publications from the National Museum. Studies in Archaeology and History 6), Copenhagen: National Museum.

O'Brien, R., Quinney, P. and Russell, I. (2006) 'Preliminary report on the archaeological excavation and finds retrieval strategy of the Hiberno-Scandinavian site of Woodstown 6, County Waterford', *Decies. Old Waterford Society*, 61: 13–107.

Ó Floinn, R. (1998) 'The archaeology of the early Viking Age in Ireland', in H.B. Clarke, M. Ní Mhaonaigh and R. Ó Floinn (eds) *Ireland and Scandinavia in the Early Viking Age*, Dublin: Four Courts.

Peddie, J. (1999) *Alfred, Warrior King*, Stroud: Sutton.

Price, N.S. (1991) 'Viking armies and fleets in Brittany: a case study for some general problems', in. H. Bekker-Nielson and H.F. Nielsen (eds) *Tiende tværfaglige Vikingesymposium*, Højbjerg: Hikuin.

Reuter, T. (1985) 'Plunder and tribute in the Carolingian Empire', *Transactions of the Royal Historical Society*, (5) 35: 75–94.

Richards, J.D. (2001) 'Boundaries and cult centres: Viking burial in Derbyshire', in J.A. Graham-Campbell, R. Hall, J. Jesch and D.N. Parsons (eds) *Vikings and the Danelaw. Select Papers from the Proceedings of the Thirteenth Viking Congress*, Oxford: Oxbow.

Sawyer, P.H. (1962) *The Age of the Vikings*, London: Edward Arnold.

Smyth, A. (1989) *Warlords and Holy Men. Scotland AD 80–1000*, Edinburgh: Edinburgh Uni- versity Press.

Wamers, E. (1998) 'Insular finds in Viking Age Scandinavia and the state formation of Norway', in H.B. Clarke *et al.* (eds) (1998).

—— (2002) 'The 9th century Danish–Norwegian conflict: maritime warfare and state formation', in A. Nørgård Jørgensen *et al.* (eds) (2002).

Webster, L. and Backhouse, J. (eds) (1991) *The Making of England. Anglo-Saxon Art and Culture AD 600–900*, London: British Museum Press.

Williams, D.G.E. (2002) 'Ship-levies in the Viking Age: the methodology of studying military institutions in a semi-historical society', in A. Nørgård Jørgensen *et al.* (eds) (2002).

—— (2004) 'Land assessment and the silver economy of Norse Scotland', in G. Williams and P. Bibire (eds), *Sagas, Saints and Settlements* (The Northern World 11), Leiden: Brill.

—— (forthcoming) *Viking Warfare and Military Organisation*, London.

CHAPTER FIFTEEN

VIKING WEAPONRY

—·◆·—

Anne Pedersen

Numerous sources offer information on Viking weaponry. The annals and chronicles of royal courts and monasteries in western Europe record the violent acts committed against Christian communities by armed warriors from Scandinavia. Old Norse sagas and poetry on the other hand praise the art of the warrior and not least his weapons, many of which are described and named in poetic terms (Falk 1914: 47–65; Drachmann 1967). Contemporary illuminated manuscripts, stone carvings and the famed Bayeux tapestry created in the late eleventh century provide further insight into the world of the warriors and the tools of their craft. However, precise technical descriptions or accurate depictions of individual weapons are rare. Modern knowledge of Viking Age weaponry is largely derived from the many weapons recovered over the past two centuries – swords, axes, spears and lances, bows and arrows as well as the much rarer wooden shields and defensive body armour. Descriptions of Viking activity indicate that Scandinavians also had experience in using large constructions for direct attack or siege warfare, although the physical remains have long since vanished.

OFFENSIVE WEAPONS

Iron swords designed for single-hand use were doubtless the most prestigious and expensive weapons of the time. Single-edged swords, some of them up to 1 m long, were still in use in the early Viking Age thus continuing the tradition of the Germanic sax (Nørgaard Jørgensen 1999). However, double-edged swords measuring about 90 cm in length were by far the most common. A characteristic feature intended to reduce the weight of these weapons is the broad shallow groove or 'fuller' running along the centre of the blade; special treatment of the edges and pattern-welding of the core provided extra strength and pliability.

The iron blades, both single- and double-edged, were fitted with lower and upper guards and usually also a pommel made of iron or cast copper alloy; less common are silver and organic materials such as bone or antler. Ornaments may be cast, but iron fittings are most often decorated with silver and copper inlay forming geometric patterns, animal motifs and in some cases even Christian symbols such as on the

Carolingian sword recovered from the boat-chamber grave excavated at Hedeby in northern Germany (Müller-Wille 1976; Wamers 1994: 9–14). The lower guard, typically about 10–11 cm long, is increased up to 16–17 cm in the late Viking Age, and the upper guard and pommel are reduced to a single pommel. The grip between the guards measured about the breadth of a hand. Its core, the iron tang of the blade, was covered by, for instance, wood, leather, horn or bone and on some swords also decorated with metal-plating or silver and gold wire as seen on a sword from Dybäck in southern Sweden (Rydbeck 1932).

Remains of scabbards are preserved in the corrosion layers on many sword blades. Scabbards were made of wood, probably a single board which could be split lengthwise, hollowed out and then joined again (Malmros 1987; Geibig 1991: 104–6). Beechwood, easy to split and yet difficult to bend, was suitable for the purpose but required a protective leather covering. Cast metal scabbard mounts could be added, mainly copper-alloy sword chapes depicting, for instance, animal figures in the Jelling style or bird motifs. Compared to the total number of swords, such chapes are few, and function not only as protection for the scabbard point but also as a badge of rank or group member-ship, possibly even a magical symbol has been suggested (Strömberg 1951; Paulsen 1953; see also Kulakow 1985).

In 1919 Jan Petersen published a typology based on Norwegian finds from the eighth to eleventh centuries, in which about 1,700 swords were grouped into twenty-six main types, A to Æ, and twenty distinctive types, the main criteria being the shape and decoration of the hilts. The typological sequence reflects changes through time, but also a distinction between simple and ornate weapons. Petersen's work includes most north-west and central European types and is still widely used, although adjustments have been made to certain types and type groups, such as the swords of the eighth and ninth centuries (Menghin 1980). The sword types leading up to the Viking Age are discussed in a detailed analysis of late Iron Age weapon graves in Scandinavia by A. Nørgaard Jørgensen (1999).

A. Geibig chose a different approach to that of Jan Petersen. Based on an extensive analysis of late eighth- to twelfth-century material, the hilts are grouped into nineteen combination types and three construction types, and fourteen types of blade are identi-fied by morphological and metric criteria (Geibig 1991). Although Geibig's focus lies outside Scandinavia, his system can be applied to Scandinavian finds, and in more recent publications either system – a classification based largely on a visual evaluation of the hilt and to a lesser extent sword blade or a classification focusing on constructional criteria – may be referred to.

Next to the swords, axes were widely used in battle, and numerous axes (or rather axe-heads) have been recovered. In well-equipped graves axes may be found alongside other weapons, but they appear to be more common as single weapons in less conspicuous burials, suggesting a difference in rank and economic means among the deceased and their families (see Näsman 1991). On the other hand, deposition of axes alone is not limited to poorly furnished graves. The Danish Bjerringhøj chamber burial contained a highly decorated axe-head (Iversen and Näsman 1991), and to judge from the quality of the silver inlay it must have represented considerable value. In the case of the Ladby ship grave, also from Denmark, the axe-head found in the front half of the ship most likely represents the tool used to slaughter the horses and dogs led into the ship to accompany the deceased (Thorvildsen 1957). Axe-heads found in female graves give equal cause for speculation. Are they true weapons or rather part of the assemblage of tools and kitchen utensils used by the mistress of a household?

Axe-heads were made of iron, and most are plain although the line between head and blade may be emphasised by narrow grooves. However, decoration in silver and copper does occur, and even gold, as seen on a rare eleventh-century axe-head from Botnhamn in Norway, decorated in the Ringerike style (*Viking to Crusader* no. 114). Other axe-heads are exceptional due to their small size (see Trotzig 1985) or unusual shape, a rare type having a blade reduced to a narrow frame surrounding a cross-shaped figure (Paulsen 1956: 66–8).

A typology based on Norwegian finds was published by J. Petersen in 1919 and includes twelve types, A to M, distinguished by way of the head, the shape of the blade and its cutting edge (Petersen 1919: 36–47). The axe-heads range from light, slender forms with more or less pronounced spurs on either side of the head to the well-known broad-bladed battle axes, also with projecting spurs. The latter type resembles the weapons featured in the Bayeux tapestry, and its basic shape continues in use well into the medieval period.

Axe-heads with a long 'helm' at the back of the head were most likely introduced from the eastern Baltic region (Hallinder 1986: 47), whereas others with elongated, often decorated blades and in some instances extremely long spurs at the head probably originated in the area south of the Baltic (Paulsen 1956: 156–67). These axes are very likely prestige weapons, possibly even exotica, brought home by their owner or received as gifts.

Similar to the swords and axes, spears were deposited in Viking Age burials, but have also come to light in settlements and a few weapon deposits. Most of the spearheads belong to heavy thrusting spears or lances. They were made of iron, some of them pattern-welded or showing elaborate geometric or vegetal/zoomorphic designs in silver and copper on the socket (Blindheim 1963; Horn Fuglesang 1980; Lehtosalo-Hilander 1985). The blades are usually leaf-shaped with rounded or angular shoulders towards the socket and have a more or less pronounced rib along the centre. They were fitted to the shafts by rivets; on one long and narrow type up to fifteen rivets formed an additional decorative element along the socket. Based on evidence from burial finds the shafts were up to 2 m long, and analysis of wood remains suggests that, for instance, ash was chosen for strength and flexibility.

In his work on Viking Age weapons J. Petersen also arranged a classification of the spearheads using the shape of the blade and the socket as basic diagnostic features. Twelve types, A to M, were identified, of which type L differs from the others in having short barbs and, instead of a socket, a long tang not unlike that of Viking Age arrow-heads (Petersen 1919: 22–36). A more accurate and detailed framework with a revision of Petersen's chronology, but also based on Norwegian material, has since been provided by B. Solberg, whereas the late type M is treated by K. Creutz (Solberg 1984; for a summary of recent typologies see Creutz 2003: 28–34).

Bows and arrows form the fourth weapon group of the Viking Age. The first complete longbow was recovered from Hedeby in northern Germany. No bowstring was preserved but the wooden bow made of yewwood and measuring 192 cm in length is intact (Graham-Campbell 1980: 74). Unlike the wooden bows, arrowheads of iron are common, occurring in burials and as single arrowheads in settlement contexts. Mineralised remains of organic material corroded together with tightly packed arrowheads in several graves suggest that whole bundles were deposited in a quiver made of leather or wood.

Scandinavian arrowheads usually have an iron tang, whereas socketed arrowheads appear to be more typical of the area south of Scandinavia (Kempke 1988). On the basis of Swedish finds several types have been identified (Wegraeus 1973, 1986). Most common is a lanceolate multipurpose type, but other forms are known, and during the Viking Age points with a triangular or square cross-section especially suited for military use were introduced.

Arrow-shafts and feathered flight-ends are rarely preserved. Evidence from the Hedeby boat-chamber grave indicates that the shafts, in this case made of birchwood, had been fitted not only with feathers but with cast copper-alloy nocks consisting of a sub-conical base with a deep notch and tang (Müller-Wille 1976: 80–6). It is often difficult to determine whether arrows deposited in graves represent offensive weaponry or rather were intended for hunting. The latter seems most likely for the bundle from Hedeby which, with copper-alloy fittings, may well have been a gift of some value (Wamers 1994: 29).

DEFENSIVE WEAPONRY

According to the older Gulathing and Frostathing laws every man on board a leding ship was required to have a shield. Very few complete shields have survived, but remains of originally sixty-four shields in the Gokstad ship-burial uncovered in Norway give an impression of their size and construction (Nicolaysen 1882: 62). The circular wooden disc, at Gokstad 94 cm in diameter, was joined by thin wooden boards, and many were probably fitted with an additional covering of leather (Arwidsson 1986: 39). The hole for the hand-grip at the centre of the shield was covered by an iron boss, usually one of three main types distinguished by the shape of the dome, the neck and the flange for attachment (see Rygh 1885: nos 562–5). Other metal fittings for the shields include rim-bindings, and occasionally also a metal grip instead of one of wood and sheet metal or cast copper-alloy grip-mounts (Arwidsson 1986: 40–3).

Shields could be distinguished by colour. An inscription on a Danish runestone from Rønninge on Fyn speaks of the son of 'Asgot of the red shield' (Moltke 1976: 313), and the shields from Gokstad were painted in alternate colours, black and yellow, similar to those depicted in the Bayeux tapestry (Nicolaysen 1882: 63). Sagas and law texts mention red and white, the latter possibly the natural colour of the wood but also signifying peaceful intentions (Falk 1914: 128), and according to the saga of Saint Olaf King, gilt, red and blue crosses marked the white shields of the king's men.

King Olaf's men were also equipped with body armour. Images of Viking warriors indicate that helmets were used, but archaeological finds, usually only metal fragments, are extremely rare. Leather, a probable alternative to metal, has left no trace. The most complete helmet, a simple iron cap fitted with eye-guards, was recovered from a richly furnished cremation at Gjermundbu in Norway (Grieg 1947: 3–4). Small rings at the edge of the cap suggest that the neck was protected by a cover of chain mail.

Apart from the helmet, the Gjermundbu grave contained fragments of a chain-mail shirt, and at Birka protective armour made of narrow metal plates has been identified (Arbman 1939: 63; Grieg 1947: 4). Shirts made of thousands of iron rings welded together or closed with a rivet were doubtless expensive and available only to the very

~~wealthy,~~ although scenes in the Bayeux tapestry indicate that mail shirts in later times were no longer so unattainable.

WEAPONS TRADE

Most complete swords and spearheads are recovered from burials. They appear far less common in settlement contexts where instead axes for different tasks, arrowheads and single sword fittings may be found. The arrowheads and sword fragments testify to the presence of weapons in individual households as well as the local manufacture and/or repair of weapons. Although it can be difficult to distinguish between indigenous and foreign production, some of the finest swords and spearheads were doubtless imported (Solberg 1991; Martens 2004).

Trade in weapons is recorded and forbidden in a number of Frankish capitularies, although apparently related to specific events rather than general export (Horn Fuglesang 2000), and plunder or gift exchange are equally valid explanations for some foreign swords in Scandinavia. The early Carolingian so-called 'King's sword' from the Hedeby boat-chamber grave was fully fitted when acquired; in other swords foreign blades are combined with Scandinavian-type guards. Inscribed blades, many with the name VLFBERHT or the word INGEL, are widely distributed from Ireland in the west to Russia in the east (see Geibig 1991: 113–33). The inscriptions are rarely identical, and obvious distortions or imitations suggest that they do not represent single workshops in western Europe but rather designations of quality that could be imitated, also in Scandinavia (Andresen 1993).

RITUAL CONTEXT

In spite of close interregional contacts leading to exchange and use of similar weapons, traditions of deposition differed within Scandinavia. Thus the percentage of weapon graves in relation to the corpus of known burials varies considerably, and not least the sheer number of weapons from Norway is impressive (Jakobsson 1992; Martens 2003). Based on the combination of artefacts selected for burial at a local or regional level, the role and meaning of weapons in the burial rite – and in the living society – were not uniform across Scandinavia (Jakobsson 1992; Pedersen 1997).

Visual quality as evident in the decorative use of contrasting metals was important, and weapons probably had considerable value not only in battle but also as symbols of power, rank and wealth. Swords are often singled out, and their importance is supported by numerous sources, among them the highly ritualised scenes depicted in illuminated manuscripts. However, axes and spears most likely held similar functions (Trotzig 1985; Näsman 1991). Although not Scandinavian, one of the most renowned spearheads of the time was the Carolingian *sancta lancea* belonging to the imperial insignia. Dated to *c.* 800, the spearhead was copied *c.* 1000 and presented by Otto III to Bolesław Chrobry of Poland in return for relics of St Adalbert, an act of great religious as well as political significance (*Bernward von Hildesheim* no. II-33).

Apart from burial, other ritual acts may have involved weapons. Surprisingly many stray finds from Denmark are recovered from wetland areas – bogs, lakes or rivers – and although conflict or extensive traffic near major crossing points and important settlements may explain certain finds, others appear to be sacrificial offerings (Lund 2003).

Occasional swords and not least spearheads have been recovered in similar circumstances suggestive of ritual deposition elsewhere in Scandinavia, for instance at Gudingsåkrarna in Valstena parish on Gotland (Müller-Wille 1984: 188–93). Here about 500 weapons and weapon parts have come to light since the nineteenth century, most of them spearheads or parts of spearheads and many of them damaged.

Ritualised and symbolic use of weapons in the late Iron Age and Viking Age is finally supported by finds of miniature weapons or amulets, among them swords and spearheads less than 5 cm long. Their exact purpose and meaning are uncertain, and it has been suggested that both groups are possible attributes of the pagan god Óðinn. However, they may equally well be magical amulets, intended to ward off evil forces against which real weapons despite their efficiency in battle were powerless (Koktvedgaard Zeitzen 1997: 18 with references).

BIBLIOGRAPHY

Andresen, K. (1993) 'Dekor og innskrift på vikingsverd – hvordan ble det utført?', *Spor – fortidsnytt fra midt-norge*: 8–39.

Arbman, H. (1939) *Birka. Sveriges äldsta handelsstad* (Från forntid och medeltid 1), Stockholm: Thule.

Arwidsson, G. (1986) 'Schilde', in G. Arwidsson (ed.) *Birka II:2. Systematische Analysen der Gräberfunde*, Stockholm: Almqvist & Wiksell.

Bernward von Hildesheim = M. Brandt and A. Eggebrecht (eds) *Bernward von Hildesheim und das Zeitalter der Ottonen. Katalog der Ausstellung Hildesheim 1993*, vol. 2, Hildesheim: Bernward Verlag and Mainz am Rhein: Verlag Philipp von Zabern.

Blindheim, C. (1963) 'Smedgraven fra Bygland i Morgedal', *Viking*, 26 (1962): 25–80.

Creutz, K. (2003) *Tension and Tradition. A Study of Late Iron Age Spearheads Around the Baltic Sea* (Theses and Papers in Archaeology N.S. A:8), Stockholm: Dept. of Archaeology, University of Stockholm.

Drachmann, A.G. (1967) *De navngivne Sværd i Saga, Sagn og Folkevise*, Copenhagen: G.E.C. Gads Forlag.

Falk, H. (1914) *Altnordische Waffenkunde* (Videnskapsselskapets Skrifter, II. Hist.-Filos. Klasse. 1914. No. 6), Kristiania: no publ.

Geibig, A. (1991) *Beiträge zur morphologischen Entwicklung des Schwertes im Mittelalter. Eine Analyse des Fundmaterials vom ausgehenden 8. bis zum 12. Jahrhundert aus Sammlungen der Bundesrepublik Deutschland* (Offa-Bücher 71), Neumünster: Karl Wachholtz.

Graham-Campbell, J. (1980) *Viking Artefacts. A Select Catalogue*, London: British Museum.

Grieg, S. (1947) *Gjermundbufunnet. En Høvdingegrav fra 900-årene fra Ringerike* (Norske Oldfunn 8), Oslo: Universitetets Oldsaksamling.

Hallinder, P. (1986) 'Streit- und Arbeitsäxte', in G. Arwidsson (ed.) *Birka II:2. Systematische Analysen der Gräberfunde*, Stockholm: Almqvist & Wiksell.

Horn Fuglesang, S. (1980) *Some Aspects of the Ringerike Style. A Phase of 11th Century Scandinavian Art* (Mediaeval Scandinavia. Supplements 1), Odense: Odense University Press.

—— (2000) 'Skriftlige kilder for karolingisk våpeneksport til Skandinavia', *Collegium Mediaevale*, 13: 177–84.

Iversen, M. and Näsman, U. (1991) 'Mammengravens indhold', in M. Iversen *et al.* (eds) *Mammen. Grav, kunst og samfund i vikingetid* (Jysk Arkæologisk Selskabs Skrifter 28), Højbjerg: Jysk Arkæologisk Selskab.

Jakobsson, M. (1992) *Krigarideologi och vikingatida svärdstypologi* (Stockholm Studies in Archaeology 11), Stockholm: Dept. of Archaeology, University of Stockholm.

Kempke, T. (1988) 'Zur überregionalen Verbreitung der Pfeilspitzentypen des 8.–12. Jahrhunders aus Starigard/Oldenburg', *Bericht der Römisch-Germanischen Kommission*, 69: 292–306.

Koktvedgaard Zeitzen, M. (1997) 'Amulets and amulet use in Viking Age Denmark', *Acta Archaeologica*, 68: 1–74.

Kulakow, W.I. (1985) 'Kultsymbole und Kriegerembleme aus dem Baltikum, aus Skandinavien und Osteuropa im 10. und 11. Jahrhundert', *Zeitschrift für Archäologie des Mittelalters*, 13: 53–64.

Lehtosalo-Hilander, P.-L. (1985) 'Viking Age spearheads in Finland', in S.O. Lindquist (ed.) *Society and Trade in the Baltic During the Viking Age*, Visby: Gotlands fornsal.

Lund, J. (2003) 'Hændelser ved Vand – an analyse af våbendeponeringer fra vikingetid på Sjælland og i Skåne', Copenhagen: Dept. of Archaeology, University of Copenhagen. (Unpubl. thesis.)

Malmros, C. (1987) 'Vikingernes brug af træ – Grimstrupgraven', *Nationalmuseets Arbejdsmark*: 107–13.

Martens, I. (2003) 'Tusenvis av sverd. Hvorfor har Norge mange flere vikingtidsvåpen enn noe annet europæisk land?', *Collegium Mediaevale*, 16: 51–65.

—— (2004) 'Indigenous and imported Viking Age weapons in Norway – a problem with European implications', *Journal of Nordic Archaeological Science*, 14: 125–37.

Menghin, W. (1980) 'Neue Inschriftenschwerter aus Süddeutschland und die Chronologie karolingischer Spathen auf dem Kontinent', in K. Spindler (ed.) *Vorzeit zwischen Main und Donau* (Erlanger Forschungen A:26), Erlangen and Nürnberg: no publ.

Moltke, E. (1976) *Runes and their Origin. Denmark and Elsewhere*, Copenhagen: The National Museum.

Müller-Wille, M. (1976) *Das Bootkammergrab von Haithabu* (Berichte über die Ausgrabungen in Haithabu 8), Neumünster: Karl Wachholtz Verlag.

—— (1984) 'Opferplätze der Wikingerzeit', *Frühmittelalterliche Studien*, 18: 187–221.

Näsman, U. (1991) 'Grav og økse. Mammen og den danske vikingetids våbengrave', in M. Iversen *et al.* (eds) *Mammen. Grav, kunst og samfund i vikingetid* (Jysk Arkæologisk Selskabs Skrifter 28), Højbjerg: Jysk Arkæologisk Selskab.

Nicolaysen, N. (1882) *Langskibet fra Gokstad ved Sandefjord / The Viking-Ship Discovered at Gokstad in Norway*, Christiania: Alb. Cammermeyer.

Nørgaard Jørgensen, A. (1999) *Waffen und Gräber. Typologische und chronologische Studien zu skandinavischen Waffengräbern 520/30 bis 900 n.Chr.* (Nordiske Fortidsminder B:17), Copenhagen: Det Kongelige Nordiske Oldskriftselskab.

Paulsen, P. (1953) *Schwertortbänder der Wikingerzeit. Ein Beitrag zur Frühgeschichte Osteuropas*, Stuttgart: W. Kohlhammer Verlag.

—— (1956), *Axt und Kreuz in Nord- und Osteuropa*, Bonn: Rudolf Habelt Verlag.

Pedersen, A. (1997) 'Similar finds – different meanings? Some preliminary thoughts on the Viking-age burials with riding equipment in Scandinavia', in C.K. Jensen and K.H. Nielsen (eds) *From Burial to Society. The Chronological and Social Analysis of Archaeological Burial Data*, Århus: Aarhus University Press.

Petersen J. (1919) *De norske vikingesverd. En typologisk-kronologisk studie over vikingetidens våben* (Videnskapsselskapets Skrifter II. Hist.-Filos. Klasse 1919 no. 1), Kristiania: no publ.

Rydbeck, M. (1932) 'Skånska praktsvärd från vikingatiden', *Meddelanden från Lunds Universitets Historiska Museum*: 38–47.

Rygh, O. (1885) *Norske Oldsager*, 2 vols, Christiania: Alb. Cammermeyer.

Solberg, B. (1984) 'Norwegian spear-heads from the Merovingian and Viking periods', Bergen: Dept. of Archaeology, University of Bergen. (Unpubl. thesis.)

—— (1991) 'Weapon export from the Continent to the Nordic countries in the Carolingian period', *Studien zur Sachsenforschung*, 7: 241–59.

Strömberg, M. (1951) 'Schwertortbänder mit Vogelmotiven aus der Wikingerzeit', *Meddelanden från Lunds Universitets Historiska Museum*: 99–121.

Thorvildsen, K. (1957) *Ladby-Skibet* (Nordiske Fortidsminder 6:1), Copenhagen: Det Kongelige Nordiske Oldskriftselskab.

Trotzig, G. (1985) 'An axe as sign of rank in a Viking community', in M. Backe *et al.* (eds) *In Honorem Evert Baudou* (Archaeology and Environment 4), Umeå: Dept. of Archaeology, University of Umeå.

Viking to Crusader = E. Roesdahl and D.M. Wilson (eds) (1992) *From Viking to Crusader. Scandinavia and Europe 800–1200*, New York: Rizzoli.

Wamers, E. (1994) 'König im Grenzland. Neue Analyse des Bootkammergrabes von Haithabu', *Acta Archaeologica*, 65: 1–56.

Wegraeus, E. (1973) 'Pilspetsar under vikingatid', *Tor*, 15 (1972–3): 191–208.

—— (1986) 'Die Pfeilspitzen von Birka', in G. Arwidsson (ed.) *Birka II:2. Systematische Analysen der Gräberfunde*, Stockholm: Almqvist & Wiksell.

CHAPTER SIXTEEN

THE RELIGION OF THE VIKINGS

——— •◆• ———

Anders Hultgård

What will be outlined here are the religious beliefs and rituals of the Scandinavians in the eighth to the eleventh centuries including those who went for trade, plunder or settlement abroad, that is, the 'vikings' properly speaking. Some among them were already Christians but the vast majority of the population still clung to their traditional religion. From a modern point of view their religion can be classified as a 'non-doctrinal community religion' in contrast with the 'doctrinal transnational religions' as represented by Christianity, Buddhism and Islam. Religion was strongly integrated with social life, warfare and subsistence activities, and this means that religious elements can be expected to occur within the total range of Viking Age culture and society.

Cultural and political contacts with Continental Europe and the British Isles slowly paved the way for Christianity, and towards the end of the Viking period many among the ruling elites of Scandinavia and Iceland had adopted the new religion. They also succeeded in imposing it on the rest of the population, and by the early thirteenth century Christianity was firmly established. In the transition period there was still room for the development of syncretistic phenomena, but with the full power of the Christian Church implemented, Scandinavian religion could survive only fragmentarily in popular beliefs and practices which were soon to disappear or to be mixed with medieval European folklore.

The attempt to grasp the main features of Scandinavian religion in the Viking period is beset with many difficulties. The written sources date roughly from the end of the tenth to the thirteenth century when a process of decisive religious and cultural change was already going on. Our knowledge of ancient Scandinavian religion is thus primarily based on sources that have passed through the intermediary of medieval Christian culture. In addition these written sources stem almost exclusively from Iceland and Norway. There is also an imbalance in the transmission of relevant texts. Only very scarce information on ritual is available whereas several myths and legends have survived the shift to Christianity. Archaeological evidence presents us with details of ritual and worship that do not appear in the written sources. On the other hand we are faced with greater problems when interpreting archaeological remains than with texts. The toponymic record is important in giving information about the deity or deities worshipped at a particular place and about the character of the cult place (grove, hill, hall, etc.). Iconographic evidence from runestones and various archaeological objects also provides knowledge on aspects of the religion.

THEOLOGY, MYTHOLOGY AND WORLD-VIEW

As in other religions of pre-Christian Europe the belief in divine and other supernatural beings permeated most aspects of human life. The Greeks used the term *theologia* to denote ideas and reflections on divine beings, and this use is retained here as a scholarly category. The main Scandinavian gods and goddesses were inherited from a distant past but their character may have changed over time. The deities were often referred to as a group: *goð* 'the gods', the original meaning of which is unknown, *regin* literally 'those who rule' (gen. pl. *ragna* cf. *Ragnarǫk* 'the destiny of the gods'), *bǫnd* (gen. pl. *banda*) and *hǫpt* (gen. pl. *hapta*), literally 'those who bind'. The connotations that the two last terms carried in the Viking period cannot be precisely recovered but the meaning is probably that the gods 'bind', that is, decide the destinies of the world and people whom they also tie to themselves in friendship and awe. Different classes of supernatural beings were distinguished. The *æsir* and the *vanir* represent mythologically the two main families of gods but in practice the term *æsir* could include all the prominent deities. Female deities were the *dísir* who seem to have played an important part in private worship especially in western Scandinavia. The *álfar* 'supernatural beings' were divine beings of lower rank who were related to the *vanir*. The *jǫtnar* 'giants' and the *dvergar* 'dwarfs' represent other classes. The mythology often reveals a complicated relationship between giants and gods. The former are not always regarded as hostile and male gods can have giant women as mothers and wives.

The deities were spoken of as 'most holy' (*ginnheilǫg goð* in Vǫluspá 6 etc.; Lokasenna 11), 'helpful' (*nýt regin* in Vafþrúðnismál 25) and 'gentle' (*in sváso goð* in Vafþrúðnismál 17–18). We do not know how the idea of a divine world with many and different supernatural beings worked in reality. It can be assumed that people believed in the existence of the deities that were worshipped by the community as a whole but that in practice only one god or a couple of gods were important for the individual. Different attitudes ranging from fear and awe to trust and friendship could be taken towards the gods depending on the prevailing situation and on the persons involved. The relationship between man and deity which the modern terms 'piety' or 'personal religion' intend to denote can be expressed in many ways, but only few traces of such individual relationships have survived the shift to Christianity. In addition what has been preserved is often discarded as due to Christian influence and as being alien to Scandinavian 'paganism'. Combining the scraps of evidence from the written sources with the archaeological record (mostly amulets and divine symbols of various kinds) we are, however, able to get glimpses of genuine personal devotion to a particular deity. Literary sources sometimes characterise this individual devotion by saying that the deity was considered a person's *fulltrúi* 'confidant' or *ástvinr* 'close friend'. Even if these terms were first applied to pre-Christian conditions by authors of the twelfth and thirteenth centuries – an assumption which is still open to discussion, however – it is likely that memories of personal devotion to the old deities were passed on by oral tradition into later centuries.

In non-doctrinal community religions *myths* are the foremost verbal expression of religion because they convey the world-view, ideas, emotions and values of a specific culture. Myths have several contexts, they may accompany rituals or be re-enacted in a dramatic form, but they may also be told in a variety of other situations. Myths have different functions, they explain the origins of the universe and humankind, they serve as models for ritual and social behaviour and they legitimise fundamental institutions of the society. After the shift to Christianity Scandinavian mythology was still handed down by many Icelandic and Norwegian families thanks to their interest in the traditions of the past. The anonymous collection of Eddic poems in the famous manuscript Codex Regius (latter half of the thirteenth century) is the best example. Skaldic poetry from the tenth century includes many allusions to living myth. Medieval written compilations such as the various versions of the Prose Edda of Snorri Sturluson from the early thirteenth century and the *Gesta Danorum* composed in Latin some decades earlier by the Dane Saxo helped to preserve parts of the mythological heritage for the future albeit in reworked or historicised forms.

The world-view of the ancient Scandinavians is incompletely known. Eddic poems such as the *Vǫluspá*, the *Vafþrúðnismál* and *Grímnismál* give selected but reliable information whereas Snorri's descriptions should be read more critically. The Scandinavians undoubtedly believed in a sort of universal history beginning with the creation of the world including that of humankind and ending with the destruction of the world in the Ragnarǫk. The end would, however, be followed by the emergence of a new world in which some of the ancient gods reappeared and human life became regenerated through a primordial couple (called Líf and Lífþrasir) who survived the catastrophe.

The cosmogony is described by Snorri as a process and has its origin in the polarity between a cold place, Niflheimr, and a hot place, Muspell, separated by an empty space called Ginnungagap, which eventually became filled with ice in the north and light and warmth in the south. When the soft sparks from the south met the frost from the north it thawed and dripped and from that two figures emerged, the giant Ymir and the cow Auðhumla. She licked the ice-blocks and a human figure called Buri appeared. He had a son Borr who married a woman, named Bestla. From them three sons were born, Óðinn and his two brothers. They killed Ymir and fashioned the world from the parts of his body. Finally, walking along the seashore the gods found two trees (or wooden pieces) which they endowed with human qualities. They named the man Askr and the woman Embla and gave them clothes. Snorri's narrative has clearly been compiled from different sources, mainly Eddic poems, and it is doubtful whether such a systematic account ever existed as a living myth. On the other hand some details unknown in the Eddic poems (e.g. the cow Auðhumla) seem to be rooted in genuine pre-Christian tradition. Judging from the evidence of the Eddic poems different creation myths were circulating. One represented by the *Vǫluspá* (stanzas 3–6) told how in distant times nothing existed:

> there was no sand nor sea, nor chill waves, there was no earth nor heaven above (*upphiminn*), a great void only (*gap var ginnunga*) and grass nowhere.
>
> (*Vǫluspá* 3)

Then the gods lifted the earth up from the sea and created the glorious Miðgarðr. The sun appeared and shone on the barren soil, which was grown with green plants. The ordering of the cosmos by the gods is then allusively told but the wording is partly obscure. Another myth – the one preferred by Snorri – imagined the world being created from the body of Ymir (*Vafþrúðnismál* 21; *Grímnismál* 40–1). The earth was

Story of creation

fashioned from his flesh, the sky from his skull, the sea from his blood. Other parts of the body were used to shape further elements of the world, which are differently described in the two poems, however. Both types of myth have parallels in other religions and the Scandinavian versions are certainly expressions of an inherited archaic tradition. An allusion to a third creation myth has probably been preserved in a skaldic poem from the tenth century, which mentions a struggle between Heimdallr and Loki appearing in the shape of two seals over a piece of earth (*rein*) that presumably came up from the sea (*Husdrápa* 2; *Skaldskaparmál* 8).

The creation of humankind is only mentioned in *Vǫluspá* stanzas 17–18, which are retold by Snorri with some additional details. The wording and context of these stanzas are far from clear and many diverging interpretations have been proposed. One point concerns the question of which shape Askr and Embla had when they were found by the gods. Carved human figures, wooden trunks drifted ashore or slender trees growing up from the soil have all been suggested. Comparative Indo-European evidence may speak in favour of the last alternative.

The world is mythically imagined as a cosmic tree, the Yggdrasill, which represents both time and space. The prophetess of *Vǫluspá* remembers it in the beginning growing beneath the earth (stanza 2), then it appears as a mighty tree (stanza 19) and when the end of the world draws near, the old tree quivers (stanza 47) and is finally consumed by the flames of the great fire in the Ragnarǫk (stanza 57). The closest correspondence to the idea of Yggdrasill is found in ancient Iranian religion where we find myths depicting the world as a tree and the branches as world ages. The trunk of the cosmic tree is also thought to contain nine mountains from which all waters of the earth flow forth. These similarities together with evidence from Greek, Phrygian and Indic traditions indicate that the Scandinavian idea of the world-tree is part of an Indo-European mythic heritage, which has analogies also among Finno-Ugric peoples of northern Eurasia.

RITUALS AND WORSHIP

Information on Scandinavian public ritual is scanty since this sort of religious expression was among the first things to be abolished when Christianity was introduced. Some aspects of the wide variety of ritual life in the Viking period can be gleaned from the sources, however. We may distinguish between several types of religious practices among the Scandinavians. Sacrificial feasts (*blótveizlur, blótdrykkjur*) seem to have occupied a prominent place and were also part of the great seasonal festivals which attracted a large number of people. Family rituals were usually performed in or around the farmhouses, for example the *álfablót* in western Sweden mentioned by Sigvatr Þorðarson in an early eleventh-century poem. An important group of religious practices are the rites of the life cycle ('rites de passage'), that is, birth, initiation, wedding and funerary rites. With the exception of the burials only a few hints at ritual detail performed at these occasions have survived. Funerary rituals can partly be reconstructed by the archaeological record, which indicates the diversity of ritual expressions. At rare occasions burials could include ritual killing as in the funerary ceremony of an eastern Scandinavian chieftain in Russia that was witnessed by Ibn Fadlan in the tenth century. His account survives only in later excerpts and reworkings, however.

Public rituals had certain basic forms in common but varied otherwise over time and geographical space. Animal sacrifices together with libations are clearly attested by skaldic verse and prohibitions in provincial laws, and by a few medieval literary sources. These types of sacrificial offerings seem to have been prominent in public and family rituals, whereas human sacrifices – if they were practised at all in the Viking Age – appear to have been occasional, perhaps performed only as crisis rituals. The references to human sacrifices in the medieval sources are rather to be interpreted as literary motifs. Descriptions of sacrificial feasts are found in secondary sources only and have varying claim on reliability. Snorri attempts to depict the usual procedure of a pre-Christian religious feast in *Hákonar saga ins góða* (ch. 14), but his account may not be true in all details. The report given by Adam of Bremen around 1075 of the temple and sacrificial rites in Old Uppsala (*Gesta Hammaburgensis Ecclesiae Pontificum* 4: 26–30) preserves several elements which bear the mark of authenticity, but is otherwise characterised by polemical stereotypes that cast doubt on his information. What cannot be questioned, however, is the importance of the Uppsala festival as a religious and political manifestation, the existence of a sacred grove and a building for ritual community meals, probably a hall (*triclinium*). Some further details reported by Adam seem likewise to derive from genuine tradition. It was customary to perform various songs during the ritual offerings and some of them were most probably addressed to the god Freyr who, according to Adam, was invoked for weddings and fertility. Snorri has an independent notice of the seasonal festival at Uppsala in the *Saga ins helga Ólofs konungs* (ch. 77) which confirms the main points of Adam's account and brings some additional details. The festival was held in the month called *gói* (late winter/early spring) and was connected with a law assembly (*þing*) and a market. The short remark of Thietmar of Merseburg (beginning of the eleventh century) on the religious festivals celebrated by the Danes at Lejre on Sjælland is not trustworthy in detail and explains the meaning of the ritual by using Christian polemic commonplaces.

More reliable glimpses of individual worship and smaller community rituals are given by a Gotlandic source, the Guta Law and its appendix the *Guta saga*, codified at the beginning of the thirteenth century, a date still rather close in time for people to be able to remember something of the ancient tradition. The evidence points to the fact that it was not until the end of the twelfth century that Christianity became implemented as the sole official form of religion on Gotland. The Guta Law states in the chapter entitled *af blótan* 'on pagan ritual' that when somebody is guilty of worship (*haizl*) with offerings of food or drink that does not conform to Christian tradition he shall pay a fine to the Church. The *Guta saga* reports that local communities used to have worship with animal sacrifices, food and beer which was known as the ritual of the 'cooking friends since they all cooked together' (*suðnautar þí æt þair suðu allir saman*).

Little has survived pertaining to prayers and ritual formulas. Two fragments of skaldic verse invoke Þórr as protector of the world of men against the giants, addressing him directly in the second person. An Eddic poem has preserved a praise and prayer formula, which addresses the divine beings in the second person plural:

> *Heilir æsir, heilar ásynior, heil siá in fjǫlnýta fold!*
> *Mál ok manvit gefið okr mærom tveim ok læknishendr meðan lifom!*

> Hail you, gods and goddesses, hail you, bounteous earth, give the two of us, glorious ones, word and wisdom and healing hands as long as we live.
>
> (*Sigrdrífumál* 4)

The concept of *ár* 'good harvest, good crops' occurs in various ritual formulas, the most well known being *ár ok friðr* 'good crops and peace'. The origin of this formula has been much discussed and some scholars claim a Christian background. The formula is not attested in the Poetic Edda nor in pre-Christian skaldic verses, but this may be explained by the fact that these sources are not ritual texts. Since a Christian model is lacking and since Indo-European parallels are found, the evidence suggests that the formulas with *ár* represent an ancient ritual legacy.

CULT PLACES

These were manifold and included natural sites such as mountains and hills (*fjall, berg*), groves (*lundr*), meadows and arable fields (*vangr, akr*), islands (*ey*), lakes (*sjór, sær*), rivers (*á*) and springs, but also funeral barrows (*haugr*) and grave-fields. The designations for such sites also form part of sacral place names. At these places different constructions could be added to enhance the religious character of the site: stone-settings in the form of ships (*skæið*) or circles, raised stones sometimes inscribed with runes (*kumbl, mærki*), hearths and other constructions for ritual purposes. Acts of worship were also performed indoors in farmhouses and chieftains' halls, the religious function of these buildings being one of many others. In several places specific cult houses were built; they were fairly small and served probably as a sort of shrine. The existence and importance of these houses have been brought out more clearly in recent decades through archaeological excavations (Tissø in Denmark; Uppåkra, Järrestad, Borg and Lunda in Sweden; Mære in Norway). The only undisputed Scandinavian word denoting a cult site is ON *vé* (ODa *væ* and OSw *vi*). A runic inscription at Oklunda in Östergötland shows that a cult site could also offer the right of asylum. It is said that Gunnar who carved the runes 'fled under penalty (*sakr*), he sought this holy place (*vī*)'.

RELIGIOUS PERSONNEL

There seem not to have been any professional priests similar to the druids among the Celts and the hereditary priestly classes of the Indo-Iranians. Religious ritual functions of different kinds were performed by various persons besides their ordinary occupations and roles in society. Kings and chieftains are known to have played an important part in public sacrificial feasts, as is witnessed by the kings' sagas for Norway and by Adam of Bremen for Sweden. In medieval Iceland we find the institution of the *goði*, a chieftain who in his person combined political, judicial and religious functions. It is probable that the *goði* institution also reflects the conditions prevailing in pre-Christian Iceland; the term *goði* is also known from three Danish runestones (DR 190, 192, 209) and possibly on a Swedish runestone from Småland (Sm 144). Another person who seems to have had some sort of religious function was the *þulr*, perhaps being the one who preserved and taught ritual and mythic traditions. The Snoldelev runestone in Sjælland mentions a man named Roald who was *þulr ā salhaugum*. In communicating with the world of supernatural beings both men and women played important roles, but women had a particular fame for foretelling the future. The *vǫlva* was not just a mythic figure as in the *Vǫluspá* ('the prophecy of the sibyl') but the help of the *vǫlva* seems to have been much asked for in real life when difficult and uncertain situations came up as is told in several

Old Norse texts. The *vǫlva* appears to have a long continuity in Scandinavia since Germanic prophetesses like Veleda were renowned already in the Roman Empire.

BIBLIOGRAPHY

The two classic treatments of ancient Scandinavian and Germanic religion, J. de Vries, *Altgermanische Religionsgeschichte*, 2 vols, Berlin: W. de Gruyter (1956–7; reprint 1970), and G. Turville-Petre, *Myth and Religion of the North. The Religion of Ancient Scandinavia*, New York: Holt, Rinehart and Winston (1964), are still valuable but need to be complemented with more modern textbooks and articles, such as: T.A. Dubois, *Nordic Religions in the Viking Age*, Philadelphia: University of Pennsylvania Press (1999); B. Maier, *Die Religion der Germanen*, Munich: C.H. Beck (2003) and R. Simek, *Religion und Mythologie der Germanen*, Darmstadt: Wissenschaftliche Buchgesellschaft (2003). In Scandinavian languages are F. Ström, *Nordisk hedendom. Tro och sed i förkristen tid*, Göteborg: Esselte (rev. edn 1985), B.-M. Näsström, *Fornskandinavisk religion*, Lund: Studentlitteratur (2001) and G. Steinsland, *Norrøn religion*, Oslo: Pax (2005). Articles on religious topics (in German and English) which are useful and include bibliographies, are to be found in *RGA* 1–35 (1973–2007).

Dillmann, F.-X. (2005) *Les magiciens dans l'Islande ancienne*, Uppsala: Kungl. Gustav Adolfs Akademien.

DR = *Danmarks runeindskrifter*, 3 vols, L. Jacobsen and E. Moltke (eds), Copenhagen (1941–2).

Dumézil, G. (1973) *Gods of the Ancient Northmen*, Berkeley and Los Angeles: University of California Press.

—— (2000) *Mythes et dieux de la Scandinavie ancienne*, édition établie et préfacée par F.-X. Dillmann, Paris: Gallimard.

Hultgård, A. (2001) 'Menschenopfer', *RGA* 19: 533–46.

—— (2003) 'Religion', *RGA* 24: 429–57.

—— (2006) 'The Askr and Embla myth in a comparative perspective', in A. Andrén, K. Jennbert and C. Raudvere (eds) *Old Norse Religion in Long-term Perspective*, Lund: Nordic Academic Press.

Marold, E. (2000) 'Kosmogonische Mythen in der Húsdrápa des Ulfr Uggason', in M. Dallapiazza (ed.) *International Scandinavian and Medieval Studies in Memory of Gerd Wolfgang Weber*, Trieste: Parnaso.

Platvoet, J.G. and Molendijk, A.L. (1999) *The Pragmatics of Defining Religion*, Leiden: Brill.

Sm = *Smålands runinskrifter*, 2 vols (SRI 4), Stockholm: Almqvist & Wiksell International (1935–61).

Vikstrand, P. (2001) *Gudarnas platser. Förkristna sakrala ortnamn i Mälarlandskapen*, Uppsala: Swedish Science Press.

CHAPTER SIXTEEN (1)

THE OLD NORSE GODS

———·◆·———

Jens Peter Schjødt

Our knowledge of the Old Norse gods stems mostly from medieval sources. The sources from pre-Christian times (skaldic poems, runic inscriptions etc.) only give us some names and hints of certain myths which would be almost impossible to reconstruct as narrative units if we could not take into consideration the *Poetic Edda* and Snorri's *Edda* and other medieval sources. This situation, of course, suggests that what we have is only 'the tips of the narrative icebergs' (Clunies Ross 1994: 25). For instance it is remarkable that only three gods have more than one known myth attached to them (*Óðinn, Þórr* and *Loki*), a situation which is not likely to be representative for the pre-Christian situation. Nevertheless, what we face in the extant source material gives us an idea of what the world-view was like among the pagan Norsemen.

It is not possible in the limited space available here to go into detailed discussions of the historical development of the individual gods. There is no doubt that many different influences can be traced in not only the source material of post-pagan times but also in the pagan religion of the Viking Age itself. There are no doubt traces of Indo-European mythical structures, of ideas originally belonging to the Sámis, and of Christian notions. The picture presented in the following is thus the basic characteristics which we may ascribe to the last period of the pagan religion, that is, the Viking Age, being well aware that we will never know exactly which information in the sources is a pagan view and what is due to Christian influence by the medieval authors.

The god we know most about is no doubt *Óðinn*. He is an old god, but many scholars believe that his outstanding position in the Viking pantheon is due to a late development, although this cannot be proved in any way. There is no doubt that he was especially worshipped by certain social groups: kings, chieftains and warriors. Mythologically he was himself the king among the gods, and as is reported by Adam of Bremen in his *Gesta* he was especially called upon when war was being prepared. It is remarkable, however, that he is never portrayed as a warrior himself. When he interacts with human beings we usually see him as an old, one-eyed man, giving advice concerning warfare or presenting special gifts, such as weapons, to his favourites. *Óðinn* is characterised as a great magician (the best description of *Óðinn* and his characteristics is seen in Snorri's *Ynglinga saga* chs 6 and 7), and almost all of the myths in which he is the main character tell us either how he seeks knowledge or how he passes it on to his special devotees. It is related how he hung on the world-tree for nine nights in order to obtain the runes, how he went into a mountain in order to have sex with the giant daughter *Gunnlǫð*, so that she would let him have the mead of wisdom and poetry, and we have a strange myth in which he gains the head of the wise *Mimir*, which can tell him things from other worlds. Besides this he knows all kinds of magical skills, and many of these remind us of the skills of the Sámi shamans, which have caused many modern scholars to see him as a shaman (Solli 2002; Price 2002). On the other hand it is obvious that he has no special connection to human magicians and those who perform the *seiðr*. His worshippers were, as stated, kings and warriors; he can often be seen in connection with groups of warriors (Kershaw 2000), the *Männerbünde*. This connection seems to indicate that *Óðinn*'s magical skills must be seen not primarily as those of a specialised magician, but as those being necessary for a king or a warrior in a society whose world-view was strongly based on the conviction that everything happening in our world was connected to things in the other world.

In the same way as the king was responsible for the wellbeing of society and thus for the communication with the other world, *Óðinn* was responsible for the wellbeing of the world as such. Therefore he gathered the best warriors in *Valhǫll*, the heavenly abode of the dead, in order that they could defend cosmos against the powers of chaos at *Ragnarǫk*. This final battle has no doubt existed as a collective notion in the consciousness of the old Scandinavians, and they no doubt also had an idea of how it was going to take place. In this connection in particular two gods in the sphere around *Óðinn* should be mentioned, namely *Baldr* and *Loki*. The first one is known from one myth only, namely the one in which he is killed. He is described as the most innocent of the gods, and eventually his killing is the worst thing that has happened among gods and men. It is noteworthy that in the religious present of the Viking Scandinavians *Baldr* is dead, and he will return only after *Ragnarǫk*. This probably means that his killing is the introduction to the end of the world, so that the religious or mythical present is characterised as the last time before the destruction. And the god responsible for the death of *Baldr* was *Loki*, who is one of the most ambiguous figures in the pantheon. It is related how he mingled his blood with *Óðinn*'s, at the beginning of time, and how he helped the gods in many situations, often by playing tricks on them or his opponents. He may thus be seen as a trickster god. But on the other hand we also know from several myths how he endangered the whole cosmos, culminating in the killing of *Baldr*, and about his part in *Ragnarǫk* where he leads one of the giant armies. The figure of *Loki* may thus be seen as the catalyst of the happenings that eventually bring about the end of the world, and even if it has been suggested that he represents the dark side of *Óðinn* (the two gods have many characteristics in common), it seems obvious that the two gods are true antagonists in relation to the cosmic development.

As a third side in a triangle we may look upon the very powerful god *Þórr* who is second only to *Óðinn*, and is depicted as his son. *Þórr* is a fighting god. In the myths in which he is the main character he is almost exclusively seen as an opponent of the giants. As opposed to *Óðinn* he is very physical in his way of fighting, but he is, as far as our sources let us see, never connected to human warriors. He is to be seen more as the god of the peasants, who worship him, because he is seen, as is especially accentuated by Adam of Bremen, as a god of fertility, since he is the master of thunder (his name means he who causes thunder) and rain. In that way it can be discussed whether he was primarily a god of fertility or of war. However, he, in the same way as *Óðinn*, is seen as an opponent of *Loki*, and it seems as if his main characteristic is that he is defending the cosmos against chaos, but, unlike *Óðinn*, with physical means. In the same way his role as a god of fertility may best be seen, not as a direct giver of fertility, but as the one who protects the right order (including fertility) against the interference of chaos. It should also be mentioned that when he creates rain it is due to his cosmic battles where he drives in his carriage, drawn by goats, through the sky, throwing his hammer, *Mjǫllnir*, against the giants and producing thunder and lightning as a by-product of his cosmic fights.

Fertility gods of the more traditional kind are the gods of the *vanir* family (as opposed to the *æsir* family, including *Óðinn*, *Þórr* and most of the other gods). There are three of them, namely *Njǫrðr* and his children *Freyr* and *Freyja*. They are connected with sexuality and wealth, and thus represent another aspect of the needs of the society. It is also related how the cult of the *vanir* had many sexual aspects. The myth of the war between the *æsir* and *vanir* reflects some kind of opposition between the activity of the peasants and the warriors, but the exchange of hostages which takes place as part of the peacemaking at the same time shows that the different social classes have to be united in order to make the society run. *Freyja* is one of the few individual goddesses who has had a major role in the more official religious cult (whereas many female deities seen as collectives played a part in both myth and ritual). She incorporates many traits that can be found in fertility goddesses all over the world (Nässtrom 1995), among whom is a clear connection also to death.

Apart from the major gods mentioned above, we meet many gods about whom we do not know very much, either because they were more or less forgotten by the time our sources were written down – which seems to be the case for instance with *Týr* and *Heimdallr* – or because they never played any significant part in the religion – which seems to be the case with *Bragi, Hermóðr* and others, at least in the official religion. There is no doubt that many of the collective groups just mentioned played an important role in private cult at the farmsteads, and were probably more important than many of the so-called great gods. It is thus characteristic that we do not know much about the beliefs of the lower classes, and we have only vague ideas about the differences from one place to another in the Nordic countries. On the other hand there seems to be no reason to doubt that there were some general structures that were known throughout the north, even if we must accept that a lot of details differed; myths were told in different ways, rituals were performed differently from one place to another and so forth. This also goes for the development in history. It is obvious that the religion of the Vikings differed from that of the Germanic peoples by the time of, let us say Tacitus, but on the other hand there is no doubt that certain gods as well as mythical and ritual structures must be seen as continuity.

BIBLIOGRAPHY

Bertell, M. (2003) *Tor och den nordiska åskan. Föreställningar kring världsaxeln*, Stockholm: Religionshistoriska inst., Stockholms universitet.

Clunies Ross, M. (1994) *Prolonged Echoes. Old Norse Myths in Medieval Northern Society*, vol. 1: *The Myths* (The Viking Collection 7), Odense: Odense University Press.

DuBois, Th.A. (1999) *Nordic Religions in the Viking Age* (The Middle Ages), Philadelphia: University of Pennsylvania Press.

Kershaw, K. (2000) *The One-Eyed God. Odin and the (Indo)-Germanic Männerbünde* (*Journal of Indo-European Studies*. Monograph 36), Washington, DC: Institute for the Study of Man.

Maier, B. (2003) *Die Religion der Germanen. Götter, Mythen, Weltbild*, Munich: Beck.

Näsström, B.-M. (1995) *Freyja – the Great Goddess of the North* (Lund Studies in History of Religion 5), Lund: Almqvist & Wiksell International.

Nordberg, A. (2004) *Krigarna i Odins sal. Dödsföreställningar och krigarkult i fornnordisk religion*, Stockholm: Religionshistoriska inst., Stockholms universitet.

Perkins, R. (2001) *Thor the Wind-raiser and the Eyrarland Image* (Viking Society for Northern Studies. Text series 15), London: Viking Society for Northern Research.

Price, N. (2002) *The Viking Way. Religion and War in Late Iron Age Scandinavia* (Aun 31), Uppsala: Dept. of Archaeology and Ancient History, Uppsala University.

Schjødt, J.P. (1999) *Det førkristne Norden. Religion og mytologi* (Verdensreligionernes hovedværker), Copenhagen: Spektrum.

Simek, R. (2003) *Religion und Mythologie der Germanen*, Darmstadt: Wissenschaftliche Buchgesellschaft.

Solli, B. (2002) *Seid. Myter, sjamanisme og kjønn i vikingenes tid*, Oslo: Pax.

Steinsland, G. (2005) *Norrøn religion. Myter, riter, samfunn*, Oslo: Pax.

CHAPTER SIXTEEN (2)

CULT LEADERS, RULERS AND RELIGION

————•◆•————

Olof Sundqvist

An important aspect of religious and social life was the public sacrifices, where some rituals were probably complicated and needed experts. There has been debate regarding whether Viking Scandinavians had some kind of priesthood (see Sundqvist 2003a). Some scholars state that they had (e.g. Andersson 1992): they have observed terms and names which seem to indicate such a specialised office (see below). Other scholars argue that there were no priests (e.g. Ström 1985). According to them the ruler, the king or earl, made contact with the deities on behalf of the people at the sacrificial feasts and in other rituals. Recently it has been argued that the term 'priest' is not appropriate as a cross-cultural concept since it is strongly influenced by Christian and western thinking. When examining traditional societies, such as ancient Scandinavia, more neutral analytical categories should be applied, such as 'cult leader' (Sundqvist 2003b). The problem still remains, however. Were there ever exclusive religious specialists who took care of the rituals at the public cult?

NAMES AND DESIGNATIONS INDICATING CULT LEADERS

It has been suggested that some composite personal names and designations including ON -vé(r), -vi(r), -væ(r) (< *wīha-) (cf. Goth weiha 'priest') indicate a 'differentiated hierarchical priesthood' (Kousgård Sørensen 1989). Sometimes these composites have *guð* 'god' as the first element, for example in *Guðir*. In other cases the first element is a name of a deity, as for instance in *Þóri(r)*. The first element may also refer to a denomination of a cult place, such as *Al-*, *Sal-*, *Vi-*, *Hargh- (Hǫrgr)*. The name *Qlvir* belongs to this group, which has been interpreted as **alu-wīhaz* 'Priester eines "*alu- (alh-)*" Heiligtums' (de Vries 1956–7). Hence, the composites with the element **wīha-* probably refer to an office including religious functions. When analysing historical and narrative sources, however, the interpretation 'priest' (or 'religious specialist') fits badly in this context. In most cases this designation refers to a kind of multi-functional leader (see e.g. Sundqvist 2003a, b).

Also the denomination ON *goði*, attested in medieval Icelandic prose (cf. Goth *gudja*, OHG **goto*), refers to a leader who performed with many roles (e.g. Sundqvist 2003a, b).

223

The word is derived from ON *goð* 'god', thus indicating a cultic function. The *goði* cared for the cult of specific gods, at the cult building called ON *hof*. Beside his religious assignments he also had other societal functions, such as a lawman and a leader in battle and trade etc. The religious aspect is sometimes emphasised in the sources. Widely known is the story in *Eyrbyggja saga* (3–4) about the *goði* Hrólfr Mostrarskegg who emigrated from Norway to Iceland. Since he was such a good friend of the god Þórr he changed his name and called himself *Þórólfr*. He built his new farm in Iceland on the peninsula *Þórsnes* and called it *Hofstaðir*, and there he had a *hof* erected.

Other sources indicate that the *goðar* functioned in similar roles also in Norway, Denmark and Sweden. OSw *gudhe*, *guþi* appears in Swedish place names. The farm name *Gudby*, in Fresta parish, Uppland, has been interpreted as 'the *goði*'s farm' (Hellberg 1986). Three Danish Viking Age runic inscriptions contain the word *goði* (Moltke 1985). The Glavendrup-inscription (DR 209) in Odense amt, Fyn, for instance, tells us about 'Alle, the *goði*'. He was not only the religious leader, but also an honourworthy *þegn*, that is, a 'warrior, champion'. There are slight evidences of designations referring to other types of cult leaders, for example the female equivalent of the *goði*, the *gyðja*, as well as the *þulr*, *véseti*, *vífill* and *lytir* (Proto-Scand. *hluti-wīha-*) (e.g. Brink 1996; Vikstrand 2001; Moberg 2002; Elmevik 2003).

THE KING AND THE EARL AS CULT LEADERS

It is certain that the cult leaders mentioned above never monopolised the public sacrifices as officials. According to Old Norse narrative sources the king (*konungr*) or the earl (*jarl*) could appear in religious roles or perform central rituals during the ceremonial feasts. They were also the custodians of the sanctuaries. Snorri Sturluson, for instance, depicts in his *Hákonar saga góða* (14–18) the ceremonial feasts in Lade and Mære, Trøndelag, where Sigurðr Hlaðajarl was involved. During the sacrifices the ruler carried the beaker around the fire and blessed it as well as the sacrificial food. When drinking the toasts to the gods ritual formulas were recited by him, such as *til árs ok friðar*. King Hákon was expected to perform similar roles. In Snorri's passage about these feasts no cult leaders are mentioned other than the earl and the king. This text has been criticised for reflecting Jewish–Christian notions. Klaus Düwel (1985) felt that Snorri either misunderstood concepts or mixed them up with Christian ideas with no basis in pre-Christian culture. Düwel's criticism is partly well founded.

There are some elements in Snorri's text, however, that are also present in the primary sources. The idea that Earl Sigurðr played important roles in the religious sphere may be supported by the contemporary skaldic poem *Sigurðardrápa* (6) (AD 960). In this poem Earl Sigurðr is praised for his generous banquets and he is addressed as *vés valdr* 'the protector of the sanctuary'. There is also archaeological support for cultic activities in Mære. Underneath the church of Mære, traces of a building from the Viking period were discovered. Nineteen gold-foil figures were found in relation to some post-holes. They are probably sacrificial objects and undoubtedly indicative of rituals performed in the context of rulers.

Earl Hákon Sigurðarson is praised in the skaldic poem *Vellekla* (15–16) (AD *c.* 990) as the one who restored Þórr's sanctuaries and the shrines of the gods, which had been plundered by the sons of Eiríkr. In this poem the ruler's cult is connected with the prosperity of the land. 'Now the soil flourishes as before – again the destroyer of the wealth of the spear-bridge allows the merry messengers of the gods to inhabit the sanctuaries.' This information has been associated with the idea of sacral kingship (see below).

Narratives from the conversion period mention rulers who refused to perform the sacrifices at the ceremonial feasts. Often such rulers were driven from the land and deposed from the rulership (see e.g. *Hervarar saga*). Some of these accounts may reflect historical facts. A passage in Adam of Bremen's *Gesta* (scholion 140) mentions that when the most Christian king of the Swedes, Anunder, would not offer to the demons the prescribed sacrifice of the people, he was deposed and driven away from the place. The people thus expected that the king would perform the great calendric sacrifices as other kings used to do.

A SACRAL KINGSHIP?

It has been argued that the early Scandinavians had a religiously legitimated kingship (e.g. Ström 1954). This discussion has been associated with a trans-cultural category and theory called 'the sacral kingship'. This implied that in ancient agrarian societies the king's authority was built on specific religious elements. In addition to the cultic aspects of the kingship the king was regarded as divine or as the offspring of the gods. He was also supposed to possess supernatural powers in order to gain legitimacy, that is, an intrinsic ability to give prosperity to his people. Scholars stated that these features were visible in the traditions about the Swedish–Norwegian royal family called the *Ynglingar* and there was a widespread consensus among them that the ancient Scandinavians had a sacral kingship (e.g. Ström 1954).

When Walther Baetke published his work *Yngvi und die Ynglinger* in 1964, this entire issue was reconsidered. Employing a radical source criticism, Baetke argued that the fundamental features of the sacral theory were not visible in the reliable primary sources. They could only be seen in the uncertain Icelandic saga literature. Today scholars accept that royal families legitimated their position by referring to their divine or mythic origin (e.g. Steinsland 1991; Sundqvist 2002). In the pre-Christian poem *Ynglingatal* (*c.* 890) the Ynglinga-kings' divine descent is proclaimed by epithets of kings, such as *Freys afspringr* 'Freyr's offspring' and *týs ǫttungr* 'the descendant of the god'. Also the cultic aspects are accepted in recent research, while the notions of *Königsheil* or 'divine kings' are still very controversial (*ibid.*).

There is thus weak evidence of exclusive religious specialists or 'priests' performing rituals in public cult. Certain terms and names indicate, however, that some individuals had religious assignments. In the narrative sources these persons seem to appear with several societal functions. According to these sources also the king or the earl played important roles at the ceremonial feasts. Whether Scandinavian kingship should be regarded as sacral is uncertain.

BIBLIOGRAPHY

Andersson, Th. (1992) 'Orts- und Personennamen als Aussagequelle für die altgermanische Religion', in H. Beck *et al.* (eds) *Germanische Religionsgeschichte. Quellen und Quellenprobleme*, Berlin and New York: de Gruyter.

Baetke, W. (1964) *Yngvi und die Ynglinger. Eine quellenkritische Untersuchung über das nordische*

'*Sakralkönigtum*' (Sitzungsberichte der sächsischen Akademie der Wissenschaften zu Leipzig. Philologisch-historische Klasse 109: 3), Berlin: Akademie Verlag.

Brink, S. (1996) 'Political and social structures in early Scandinavia: a settlement-historical pre-study of the central place', *Tor*, 28: 235–81.

Düwel, K. (1985) *Das Opferfest von Lade. Quellenkritische Untersuchungen zur germanischen Religionsgeschichte* (Wiener Arbeiten zur germanischen Altertumskunde und Philologie 27), Vienna: Verlag Karl M. Haloser.

Elmevik, L. (2003) 'En svensk ortnamnsgrupp och en hednisk prästtitel', *Ortnamnssällskapets i Uppsala årsskrift*: 68–78.

Hellberg, L. (1986) 'Hedendomens spår i uppländska ortnamn', *Ortnamnssällskapets i Uppsala årsskrift*: 40–71.

Kousgård Sørensen, J. (1989) 'Om personnavne på -vi/-væ og den før-kristne præstestand. Med nogle overvejelser over en omstridt passage i Glavendrup-stenens indskrift', *Danske studier*: 5–33.

Moberg, L. (2002) 'Gödåker som språkligt problem', *Namn och bygd*, 90: 45–52.

Moltke, E. (1985) *Runes and their Origin. Denmark and Elsewhere*, trans. P. Foote, Copenhagen: The National Museum.

Steinsland, G. (1991) *Det hellige bryllup og norrøn kongeideologi. En analyse av hirogami-myten i Skírnismál, Ynglingatal, Háleygjatal og Hyndluljóð*, Oslo: Solum.

Ström, F. (1954) *Diser, Nornor, Valkyrjor. Fruktbarhetskult och sakralt kungadöme i Norden* (KVHAA. Filol.–Filos. Serien 1), Stockholm: Almqvist & Wiksell.

—— (1985) *Nordisk hedendom. Tro och sed i förkristen tid*, Stockholm: Akademiförlaget.

Sundqvist, O. (2002) *Freyr's offspring. Rulers and Religion in Ancient Svea Society* (Historia Religionum 21), Uppsala: Acta Universitatis Upsaliensis.

—— (2003a) 'Priester und Priesterinnen', *RGA* 23: 424–35.

—— (2003b) 'The problem of religious specialists and cult performers in early Scandinavia', *Zeitschrift für Religionswissenschaft*, 2003(1): 107–31.

Vikstrand, P. (2001) *Gudarnas platser. Förkristna sakrala ortnamn i Mälarlandskapen* (Acta academiae regiae Gustavi Adolphi 77), Uppsala: Almqvist & Wiksell.

de Vries, J. (1956–7) *Altgermanische Religionsgeschichte*, 2 vols (Grundriss der germanischen Philologie 12:1–2), Berlin: de Gruyter.

CHAPTER SIXTEEN (3)

RULERS AS OFFSPRING OF GODS AND GIANTESSES: ON THE MYTHOLOGY OF PAGAN NORSE RULERSHIP

———•◆•———

Gro Steinsland

One of the main themes in the theory of the probable sacral rulership of pagan Scandinavia has been a genealogical one: the question of whether the king or the earl was looked upon as the offspring of a god. A new aspect was added to the debate in the 1990s, which in several ways may influence the theory. It was argued that the prototypic ruler was the offspring not only of a god, but of a giantess as well (Steinsland 1991). The further hypothesis is that the feminine element in the myth changes the deeper meaning of the mythical pattern connected to Norse ideology of rulership. This is a story about a myth of marriage, a so-called *hieros gamos*, a holy wedding, in different variations well known from several other cultures. The Norse myth about the holy marriage is, however, of a special structure and meaning.

THE HOLY WEDDING – *HIEROS GAMOS*

The source that most broadly unfolds the erotic myth or *hieros gamos* connected to rulership is the Eddic poem *Skírnismál*. The protagonists are the god Freyr and the giantess Gerðr. The poem tells that the vegetation god Freyr was enflamed by great passion when taking his place in the high seat of Óðinn, from where he was able to look all around the world and even into the *Jǫtunheimar*, 'the domain of the giants'. There he got a glimpse of the giant maiden Gerðr as she walked across the yard. Immediately Freyr was filled by desire for the beautiful maiden. Though an alliance across the borders of gods and giants would mean a cosmic threat, the servant of Freyr, Skírnir, was sent to the world of the giants to make an offer of marriage on behalf of his master.

As a messenger Skírnir brings three specific objects: apples, a ring and a staff. Gerðr is tempted by these highly valuable gifts: eleven golden apples shall be hers if she will promise to give Freyr all her love. The gift is identical with the apples of the goddess Iðunn, the fruits securing the youth and health of the gods. But Gerðr refuses to accept. Skírnir then offers her the ring of Óðinn, called *Draupnir*. But Gerðr still refuses, proud and independent as she is. To carry out his task, the messenger is forced to change his attitude. On the third object, the staff, he writes terrible magical runes, able to bring the maiden to madness and insanity. The threat alters the mind of Gerðr, and she promises to meet Freyr for love in the grove called *Barri* after nine nights.

In earlier research *Skírnismál* was primarily looked upon as a myth of vegetation. The classical analysis of Magnus Olsen (1909) interpreted Freyr as a god of heaven who in holy intercourse with the goddess of earth, Gerðr, regenerated the vegetation in the springtime.

It is however possible to argue that the myth of marriage between the god and the giantess has much deeper political and ideological connotations. When a giantess emerges on the mythical scene, it means as a rule that something new is coming forth. The wild women are shaking the gods in their rest, they force the gods to activity and deeds. Using an iconographic perspective, one may discover that the myth points to the rulership of the pagan north. Several literary sources disclose as well that the *hieros gamos* myth has been multi-functional, containing an aspect of enthronisation, a genealogical myth and a myth legitimising the ruling families of *ynglingar* and earls of Lade.

The story of *Skírnismál* is determined by a set of requisites: high seat, apples, ring and staff, on an iconographical level these elements point to the prime kingly regalia. The high seat is the king's throne, and the three groups of requisites, apple, ring and staff, represent the kingly regalia from antiquity in use in Europe. The apple was the symbol of the cosmos (the globe), the ring and staff are well-known signs of dignity and power. People in the north obviously did have knowledge of the symbols of European kingship quite early on.

By analysing the myth of *Skírnismál* in relation to other sources dealing with the ideology of kingship, primarily *Ynglingatal, Ynglinga saga, Háleygjatal* and *Hyndluljóð* (Steinsland 1991), one may see the outlines of a mythical pattern that concerns the ideology of kingship. Other sources tell that a son, the prototypical ruler, is the result of the erotic alliance between the mythical parents. Snorri Sturluson tells in *Ynglinga saga* (ch. 10) that the first of the kings of the *Ynglingar*, Fjǫlnir, is the son of Freyr and Gerðr. Thus Snorri seems to have knowledge of the function of the *hieros gamos* myth as a genealogical myth connected to the ruling family. His main source is *Ynglingatal* and traditions connected to the poem that most scholars link to the poet Þjódolfr or Hvini, dated approximately to 870.

The myth of the holy marriage between a god and a giantess has also been used as a genealogical base for of the greatest ruling family in Trøndelag in Norway, the family of the earls at Lade. The genealogy of the earls is presented in the praise poem *Háleygjatal*, which is approximately a hundred years younger than *Ynglingatal*, created by Eyvindr Finnsson skáldaspillir. In the tradition of the earls, the mythic proto-parents are Óðinn and the giantess Skaði. From this couple comes the first earl: *Sæmingr*.

What does the strange myth about a marriage across the borders of gods and giants mean when it comes to the actual ruler? In the mythology the giants are known as the gods' antagonists. The threats against the gods always come from the *Jǫtunheimar*. When the prototypic ruler is presented as the son of a god and a giantess, it means that the actual ruler in himself contains the whole spectrum of cosmic powers. The ruler is representing both the qualities of the gods, their will and ability to order, and the enormous creativity and primitive force of the giantesses. It is as an exceptional holder of godly abilities and primitive force as well that the actual ruler comes out as number one. It is from his dual origin that the ruler gets his outstanding destiny. The myth of the twofold origin of the rulers explains why the destiny of the ruler is rather tragic or even may be called apparently dishonourable.

The *hieros gamos* myth is thus multi-functional. The genealogical function has been in focus here so far, but the giantess has other symbolic meanings than as a proto-mother to ruling families. She may also be interpreted as a representative of the territory ruled by the king or earl. She is a personification of the land that is to be conquered and governed by the ruler. In Norse poetry the relationship between the territory and the ruler may be pronounced in erotic metaphors as a love relation between woman and man. In scaldic poems connected to the earls of Lade, the territory is called 'the bride of Óðinn' or 'the broad-cheeked bride of Óðinn', lying in the arms of the earl as his mistress (Ström 1983).

DEATH AND FATE

It is self-evident that a myth that deals with an erotic relationship between man and woman contains a fertility motif. But the myth of this extremely exogamous marriage includes further meaningful elements. The polar relationship involves a unification of opposites that contain within themselves the seed of *a fate-laden new creation*. In this way, the myth falls into a pattern that is characteristic of the pagan Norse view of life. New forms spring from the merger of opposite forces. An essential point is that the initial situation determines the consequences. In the powerful semantic field of the myth of *hieros gamos* – the abnormal relationship between the gods and the giant world – we can find the explanation of the fated life and death.

The poem *Ynglingatal* offers several variations of the theme 'the death of the king'. This material has led scholars to regard the poem as a major source of the tradition of Scandinavian royal sacrifice or cult of the dead king. A common feature in the portrayal of the deaths of the different kings by this poet is the fact that death appears as meaningless and dishonourable as that of the prototypic king, Fjǫlnir, who drowned in a butt of mead in far from honourable circumstances (*Ynglingatal saga* ch. 11). Things hardly went better for the remaining kings of *ynglingar*.

The motif of dramatic destiny of the rulers is probably expressed in the myth of the extreme exogamy between representatives of the gods and the giant world. Genealogical explanatory models are typical of the pagan Norse society. If one considers the saga literature, one will recognise that the saga narrator uses the same original model when he introduces a new pagan character (Meulengracht Sørensen 1977). It is typical of these heroes that their life is determined by fate to a special degree, and this destiny is in the end rooted in its own, inherited constitution. The pattern is based on the fact that the hero derives on his father's side from a recognised social milieu, but on the mother's side from *Útgarðsættir* – in other words from a socially unrecognised group. Just like the king, the hero is presented as an incarnation of opposition between order and chaos. He bears within himself the whole spectrum of possibilities for life. The powerful tension in his being is only released through his fated death, which is usually violent and dramatic. The Norse marriage myth with its extreme polarity reflects the Norse cosmology where both the polarity and the interaction between the two poles is the main theme.

An interesting question is from where this important pattern of mythology originates. Frands Herschend (1996) seems to have found some strange parallels in south Germanic poetry of the sixth century. Johan Wickström (2001) has examined the Norse heroic poems and concluded that traces of the wedding myth are working in heroic poetry as well. Else Mundal (1997) has followed the myth in the historical writing in the

Middle Ages and argued that the marriage myth is in use as an underlying pattern in the narratives about the alliance between the Sámi people and the Norsemen.

A SACRAL KINGSHIP?

As the son of a god and a giantess, the ruler is not himself a god, neither could he represent the god as a sacrifice in the cult. His supposed 'luck' is balanced by his dramatic destiny. What is left to the theory of a sacral kingship is the basic mythology concerning genealogy, destiny and *eros*, and maybe also some elements of enthronement rituals (Steinsland 2002). A sacral kingship? It finally becomes a question of how to define and employ the main concepts in use.

BIBLIOGRAPHY

Herschend, F. (1996) 'A note on late Iron Age kingship mythology', *Tor*, 28: 283–303.

Meulengracht Sørensen, P. (1977) 'Starkaðr, Loki og Egill Skallgrímsson', in Jónas Kristjánsson and Einar G. Pétursson (eds) *Sjötíu ritgerðir helgaðar Jakobi Benediktssyni 20. júlí 1977* (Stofnun Árna Magnússonar á Íslandi. Rit 12), Reykjavík: Stofnun Árna Magnússonar á Íslandi.

Mundal, E. (1997) 'Kong Harald hårfagre og samejenta Snøfrid. Samefolket sin plass i den norske rikssamlingsmyten', *Nordica Bergensiana*, 14: 39–53.

Olsen, M. (1909) 'Fra gammelnorsk myte og kultus', *Maal og Minne*: 17–36.

Steinsland, G. (1991) *Det hellige bryllup og norrøn kongeideologi. En analyse av hierogami myten i Skírnismál, Ynglingatal, Háleygjatal og Hyndluljóð*, Oslo: Solum.

—— (2002) 'Herskermaktens ritualer. Kan mytologien sette os spå spor av riter, gjenstander og kult knyttet til herskerens intronisasjon?', in K. Jennbert, A. Andrén and C. Raudvere (eds) *Plats och praxis. Studier av nordisk förkristen ritual* (Vägar till Midgård 2), Lund: Nordic Academic Press.

Ström, F. (1983) 'Hieros gamos-motivet i Hallfreðr Óttarsons Hákonardrápa och den nord-norska jarlavärdigheten', *Arkiv för nordisk filologi*, 98: 440–58.

Sundqvist, O. (2002) *Freyr's offspring. Rulers and religion in ancient Svea society* (Historia Religionum 21), Uppsala: Acta Universitatis Upsaliensis.

Wickström, J. (2004) 'Bröllopsmyten i Helgakvida Hjörvarzsonar. Ett exempel på fornskandinavisk härskarideologi i Codex Regius hjältediktning', *Arkiv för nordisk filologi*, 119: 105–23.

CHAPTER SIXTEEN (4)

THE CREATION OF OLD NORSE MYTHOLOGY

————— • ◆ • —————

Margaret Clunies Ross

The word 'mythology' refers to a body of myths that form part of the intellectual fabric of a particular human culture and is known in some form by the whole community. In times before the present, and still in some communities today, traditional mythic narratives about the creation of the world, supernatural beings and the origins of human society and the natural environment formed a coherent mythological system that served its owners as a point of reference in a variety of social, religious and conceptual situations. This is likely to have been the case in Viking Age Scandinavia.

There are major methodological and evidential questions concerning the study of Viking Age mythology that can never be fully resolved. For an oral society, as Scandinavia was for the most part at this time, its mythology poses a special problem, because access to mythological creation at that time exists for us now largely through material objects, datable to the Viking Age, that recorded visual images or written texts. In the Viking Age itself Old Norse myths were accessible to people through such material objects and through oral recitation and transmission of particular mythic narratives, which have mostly left no trace in the historical record. To the extent that orally transmitted Old Norse myths inspired the creation of written mythological literature in Scandinavia during the Middle Ages, we can speak meaningfully about the creation of Old Norse mythology, viewed retrospectively through medieval Christian eyes. What we call 'Old Norse mythology' existed in Viking Age Scandinavia. The problem is how to access it from sources available to us now, most of which date from the period after the Viking Age, when the new religion of Christianity caused people to qualify and sometimes reject the old traditional mythology (Clunies Ross 1994).

Evidence for Old Norse myths of the Viking Age is available from various contemporary sources: material objects, including standing stones, with or without runic inscriptions, the poetry of the Vikings which can reliably be ascribed to the Viking Age and, indirectly, the study of place and personal names of the Viking Age, as well as ethnographic accounts of the religion of the Scandinavians deriving from non-Scandinavian sources. All these kinds of sources, especially the last, must be used with great care. The evidence they provide is often slender and frequently cannot be understood except in the context of fuller narratives in much later written texts. In such cases, strictly speaking, the modern interpreter is recreating an Old Norse myth from the evidence provided by a Viking Age object, itself understood in the light of a medieval mythic narrative. Such a process is legitimate if the parallels between the two kinds of evidence can be securely established, but this has often not been the case.

An example of a legitimate identification with a particular myth is the well-known standing stone, dated *c.* 1000, from Altuna in Sweden, which depicts an anthropomorphic figure full-face, in a boat, a hammer raised in its right hand, and a foot shown in profile below the boat. The details of hammer-wielder, boat and serpentine object beneath the boat are specific enough to allow the figure to be identified as the god Þórr, wielding his hammer Mjǫllnir on his fishing expedition to catch the World Serpent, Miðgarðsormr. This myth was very popular during the Viking Age, when it existed in several versions (Meulengracht Sørensen 2002). However, there is one detail on the Altuna stone that sets its depiction of this myth apart from all others. This is the way the artist shows Þórr's foot sticking through the bottom of the boat. We find a parallel for this motif only in the medieval Icelander Snorri Sturluson's *Edda* (*c.* 1225): 'Then Thor got angry and summoned up his Ás-strength, pushed down so hard that he forced both feet through the boat and braced them against the sea-bed' (Faulkes 1987: 47; cf. Faulkes 2005: 44–5). If we did not know the Altuna stone, we might be tempted to consider Snorri's version his own embroidery of the myth; conversely, the Altuna stone's image gains greater mythic density when one is able to compare it with Snorri's narrative.

Runic inscriptions from the Viking Age and skaldic (or court) poetry which can reliably be dated to the period offer a fairly limited perspective on the creation of Old Norse mythology. Runic inscriptions tend to be short and formulaic, while skaldic poetry of this period is largely focused on 'war, sailing and remuneration' (Jesch 2001: 32), though its richly nominal style, which employs periphrases known as kennings (*kenningar*) and poetic synonyms for everyday nouns known as *heiti*, makes use of references to Old Norse mythological beings and sometimes to myths themselves, though these references tend to be stereotyped and allusive. For example, there is a myth told only by Snorri Sturluson in his *Edda* and, in a different version, in *Ynglinga saga*, the prefatory section of his *Heimskringla*, which represents poetry as taking the form of an inspiring mead, a gift from the god Óðinn. Poets often alluded to this myth when they drew attention to the divine origin of their own verse making, particularly at the beginning of formal poems. The tenth-century Icelander Glúmr Geirason begins a poem, possibly his *Gráfeldardrápa* in honour of the Norwegian king Haraldr gráfeldr ('grey cloak', d. 970), with an allusion to the mead of poetry myth: 'Listen! I begin the feast [the mead, a poem] of the gods' ruler [Odin] for princes. We crave silence, for we have heard of the loss of men' (Faulkes 1987: 70; cf. Faulkes 1998, vol. 1: 12, verse 32). There are many similar examples, but none of them actually narrates the mead myth. If we did not know Snorri's two versions, our understanding of this complex myth would be reduced to guesswork.

Viking Age skaldic poetry names many mythological figures, often within kennings, and alludes to a number of myths, but its audience was expected to supply the full mythological context from its general cultural knowledge. Thus skaldic verse of the Viking Age reveals the existence of Old Norse mythology as a system in its listeners' minds through its allusive referential habit, but it does not reveal Old Norse mythology itself. We are like Ariadne without her clue to the labyrinth; the only way we can understand mythological references in early skaldic verse is to follow the lead of the major medieval Scandinavian mythographers, of whom Snorri Sturluson is the pre-eminent authority.

Snorri composed his *Edda* ('Poetics') during the 1220s. It is a unique creation, not only in Old Icelandic literature, but within medieval European literature as a whole (Clunies Ross 1987). Although it exists in somewhat different versions in several medieval manuscripts, its general purpose seems clear: it is a treatise on both Old Norse mythology and poetics. The reason for linking the two subjects is precisely because traditional Old Norse poetry was predicated upon a knowledge of mythology. Young poets of Snorri's day needed a refresher course in mythology and the second part of the *Edda*, named *Gylfaginning* ('The Deception of Gylfi'), gave them an ordered overview of the major topics of Norse myth, beginning with the creation of the world and concluding with its ending at Ragnarǫk. Snorri quotes a number of important mythological poems in the common Germanic alliterative (or 'Eddic') verse form in *Gylfaginning*; it is difficult to determine the age of this poetry, but some at least is probably as old as the Viking Age, although it did not enter the written record until the thirteenth century or later.

Throughout Snorri's cohesive mythological exposition, something probably never before attempted in Scandinavia, there are echoes of Christian belief and eschatology, but, though his view of the old myths is qualified, it is never polemical. The fullest manuscripts of the *Edda* have a *Preface* to *Gylfaginning*, in which Scandinavian paganism is placed within the Christian intellectual tradition (Dronke and Dronke 1977; Faulkes 1983), as something to be explained both as a natural religion that grasped many of the fundamental tenets of Christianity and as euhemerised history, in which the gods of the Scandinavians were to be understood as clever and powerful humans, who colonised Scandinavia from Troy and taught the indigenous people of the area their language, religion and poetry.

A near contemporary of Snorri, the Danish historian Saxo Grammaticus, followed a different path by completely historicising, and possibly also allegorising (Johannesson 1978), Old Norse myths in the first part of his *Gesta Danorum*, a Latin work first published in 1514 but probably completed by the second decade of the thirteenth century. This history of Denmark in sixteen books is introduced by a lengthy section dealing with the Danes before the birth of Christ, while Books 5–8 cover the period down to the establishment of the Christian Church in Denmark. Books 9 and 10 enter the historical Viking Age. Saxo, by his own admission, was dependent on the men of Iceland for a good deal of his legendary and mythic material, and a number of his sources were almost certainly Old Norse poems that he had learnt from Icelanders and turned into Latin hexameters (Friis-Jensen 1987).

The Old Icelandic *fornaldarsögur* ('sagas of ancient time') are an indigenous kind of historicised Norse myth and legend (Ármann Jakobsson *et al.* 2003). Although none in their present form can be older than *c.* 1200, and many are probably much younger, they tell of the events and personages of prehistory, and thus of the Viking Age and earlier, in a pronouncedly mythological mode (Torfi H. Tulinius 2002) and they incorporate poetry, much in Eddic verse forms, and some of it probably at least as old as the Viking Age, into their prose.

BIBLIOGRAPHY

Ármann Jakobsson, Lassen, A. and Ney, A. (eds) (2003) *Fornaldarsagornas struktur och ideologi*, Uppsala: Swedish Science Press.

Clunies Ross, M. (1987) *Skáldskaparmál. Snorri Sturluson's Ars Poetica and Medieval Theories of Language* (The Viking Collection 4), Odense: Odense University Press.

—— (1994) *Prolonged Echoes. Old Norse Myths in Medieval Northern Society*, vol. 1: *The Myths* (The Viking Collection 7), Odense: Odense University Press.

Dronke, U. and Dronke, P. (1977) 'The Prologue of the Prose Edda: explorations of a Latin background', in Einar G. Pétursson and Jónas Kristjánsson (eds) *Sjötíu ritgerðir helgaðar Jakobi Benediktssyni 20. júlí 1977*, 2 vols, Reykjavík: Stofnun Árna Magnússonar. (Reprinted in U. Dronke, *Myth and Fiction in Early Norse Lands*, Aldershot and Brookfield, VT; Variorum 1997.)

Faulkes, A. (ed.) (1983) 'Pagan sympathy: attitudes to heathendom in the Prologue to Snorra Edda', in R.J. Glendinning and Haraldur Bessason (eds) *Edda. A Collection of Essays*, Winnipeg: University of Manitoba Press.

—— (trans.) (1987) *Snorri Sturluson Edda* (Everyman's Library), London and Rutland, VT: J.M. Dent & Sons Ltd and Charles E. Tuttle Co., Inc.

—— (ed.) (1998) *Snorri Sturluson Edda. Skáldskaparmál*, 2 vols, London: Viking Society for Northern Research.

—— (2005) *Snorri Sturluson Edda. Prologue and Gylfaginning*, London: Viking Society for Northern Research.

Friis-Jensen, K. (1987) *Saxo Grammaticus as Latin poet: studies in the verse passages of the Gesta Danorum* (Analecta Romana Instituti Danici. Supplementum 14), Rome: L'Erma di Bretschneider.

Jesch, J. (2001) *Ships and Men in the Late Viking Age. The Vocabulary of Runic Inscriptions and Skaldic Verse*, Woodbridge: The Boydell Press.

Johannesson, K. (1978) *Saxo Grammaticus. Komposition och världsbild i Gesta Danorum*, Stockholm: Almqvist & Wiksell.

Meulengracht Sørensen, P. (2002) 'Thor's fishing expedition', in P. Acker and C. Larrington (eds) *The Poetic Edda. Essays on Old Norse Mythology*, London and New York: Routledge. (Reprinted from G. Steinsland (ed.) (1986) *Words and Objects. Towards a Dialogue Between Archaeology and History of Religion*, Oslo, Oxford and New York: Norwegian University Press and Oxford University Press.)

Torfi H. Tulinius (2002) *The Matter of the North. The Rise of Literary Fiction in Thirteenth-century Iceland*, trans. R. Eldevik (The Viking Collection 13), Odense: Odense University Press.

CHAPTER SEVENTEEN

POPULAR RELIGION IN THE VIKING AGE

——·◆·——

Catharina Raudvere

The assignment of presenting the popular religion of the Viking world converges with complex issues such as the connection between mythology as cosmological narration and as literature, between mythology as belief system and as part of ritual practice, between mythology as cultural memory and as history-writing. The few and feeble sources of such an ancient world-view make the problem even more demanding especially when early Christian influences are taken into consideration.

We are aware from available legal documentation that the focus of the conflict between the old religion and the new was not primarily over dogma, but over public ritual behaviour instead. According to *Íslendingabók* baptism was required of everyone, although sacrifices could be accepted as long as there were no witnesses. The early medieval laws were products of a long process of interaction between a missionary church with universal claims and an ethnic religion that had formulated no dogmas, nor definitions regarding who was an insider and who was not, and appears to have been oriented more towards the performance of rituals. In Old Norse society there was scarcely any conceptual difference between religion and social community. The former was conspicuously entailed in the latter, and the idiom that comes closest to an equivalent of religion is the expression 'ancient custom' (*forn siðr*).

When the early medieval laws of Iceland, Norway and Sweden stated prohibitions against the old religion the primary emphasis was on unacceptable pagan behaviour and practices, and not on the question of belief. It was, for example, considered as punishable to execute rituals in order to awaken the trolls, employ formulas and charms (*galdr*), perform divination or ride like a night-hag (a practice which was condemned and rejected, while treated as a possibility for evil-minded persons).

Most Christian laws identify pagan (*heiðinn*) practice in terms similar to those found in the Icelandic collection of early legal texts *Grágás* which state that: 'A man worships heathen beings (*blotar hæiðnar vættir*) when he assigns his property to anyone but God and His saints. If a man worships heathen beings, the penalty is lesser outlawry' (Grágás 1: 38).

The narratives of Old Norse religion were recorded for purposes of preservation by Christians, its rituals appearing in the sources mostly as contrasts or examples of mis-behaviour. The members of the *populus* were to be converted, corrected and generally disciplined; if their beliefs were ignorant and foolish, their rituals were – even worse –

ingenuous and vulgar. There are good reasons to assume that these thirteenth- and fourteenth-century texts mirror the genres and expressions of an elite well in touch with the learned and courtly modes of the Continent, as opposed to the provincial religion more followed as rural everyday religion. This dichotomy lingers in most scholarly overviews of the Nordic religion: 'In folklore there is a belief in beings such as dwarfs, elves, trolls and giants which is on the whole independent from the higher forms of religion and actual mythological concepts' as Rudolf Simek states (1993: 67).

Some of the mythological characters appearing in Old Norse texts have resided in folk-narratives of various genres: dwarfs, giants and elves appear more frequently in texts written after the medieval period, but in these they almost exclusively take up jocular and/or obtuse roles. In the nineteenth century these beings were transposed into the angelic fairyland of children's literature, where they remain petrified for all time in roles they were never meant to occupy in the ancient myths.

Dwarfs for example appear only in mythological narratives and in metaphors based upon myths, and seem not to have been recipients of any cult. Whereas spirits like the *dísir*, a female collective associated with fertility and warfare, emerge as acting characters, elements in metaphors and symbolism; there are also hints indicating they were receivers of cult.

DWARFS

The dwarfs (sg. *dvergr*) in Old Norse mythology do not represent a clear-cut category of supernatural beings, and they are not considered to be any particularly active collective in the narratives. For the most part, dwarfs make their appearance in listings of names. Some of these names have meanings that are comprehensible; while others have meanings that are not, their etymological origins having been obscured by the passage of time.

Regardless of what their original roles might have been in Old Norse mythology, dwarfs lived on as creatures of wisdom in the later Christian folklore of northern Europe, and from there entered the realm of artistic fairy tales and children's literature.

The dwarfs have diffuse origins. According to Snorri's *Skáldskaparmál* (39) some dwarfs are understood to be a sub-group of the 'black elves' (*svartálfar*) with whom they are thought to share dwellings in the underworld.

In the Poetic Edda the lay *Vǫluspá* ('The Prophecy of the Seeress') relates in stanza 8 that the lord of the dwarfs is formed of the blood and bones of the primordial giant and in the following stanza dwarfs are described as 'manlike'. But in this particular lay of the creation and final destruction of the universe, the dwarfs play no further role. Stanzas 143 and 160 of the *Hávamál* ('The Sayings of the High One') speak of dwarfs as individual agents with unique insight and wisdom. In stanza 160, which is part of the catalogue wherein Óðinn ('the High One') imparts his extraordinary potentials in terms of acumen and might, we can read:

> I know a fifteenth, which the dwarf Tiodrerir
> chanted before Delling's doors:
> powerfully he sang for the Æsir and before the elves,
> wisdom to Sage
>
> (trans. Carolyne Larrington)

In the Eddic poem *Alvíssmál*, the dwarf *Alvíss* ('All Wise' or 'Omniscient') is himself an active narrator. The lay is essentially a knowledge contest structured as a dialogue that bears similarities to other poems of the Poetic Edda, generally classified as 'wisdom contests'. The frame story begins with Þórr's promise to Alvíss of his daughter's hand in marriage – a recurring theme in Old Norse mythology in which such mixed alliances almost always lead to a host of vexing tribulations. In this particular lay, when Alvíss arrives to claim his bride, the thunder-god demands that he first pass the test of wisdom by providing appropriate answers to a number of questions. The story provides one of only a handful of examples in which there is a lengthy verbal exchange between a representative of the Æsir and a dwarf.

Strongly linked to the notion of the dwarfs as bearers of unique wisdom is the notion of the dwarfs as artisans who have crafted some of the most precious paraphernalia possessed by the Æsir, including: *Draupnir*, Óðinn's arm-ring; *Mjǫllnir*, Þórr's hammer; and *Brísingamen*, Freyja's collar. Their handicraft is incomparable and is often allied with cunning insight.

ELVES

There was, according to Snorri's *Gylfaginning* (17), a mythological division between the black elves and the light elves: 'There is one place that is called Alfheim. There live the folk called light-elves (*ljósálfar*), but dark-elves (*dökkálfar*) live down in the ground, and they are unlike them in appearance, and even more unlike them in nature. Light-elves are fairer than the sun to look at, but dark elves are blacker than pitch.' Snorri is perhaps influenced by Christian dualism in his description, and thus translates the various groups of *álfar* into a kind of 'angels' and 'demons'.

There are many names for the spirits and deities of a certain place. The *landvættir* and the *álfar* both appear to dwell close to the farmhouse, with the latter also receiving a standardised form of worship known as *álfablót*, according to some texts. In *Kórmaks saga* (ch. 22) the *álfablót* is described as a healing ritual, while *Ynglinga saga* describes *álfablót* as an ancestral celebration. As is obvious from their name, the *landvættir* are closely connected to the land surrounding the farm and the cultivated soil. This is confirmed in *Egill Skalla-Grímssonar saga* (ch. 57): when Egill forcefully employs poetry (*níð*) against King Eirik Bloodaxe and his queen, the *landvættir* are offended and abandon the place, after which not even the royal inhabitants are able to remain.

FATE AND DESTINY

The saga literature tells of ceremonies and rituals that aim to reveal future events. The task of conducting such ceremonies was assigned to persons with special capabilities. Fate in these texts appears to function both as a convenient literary motif and as a conceptual belief.

Already Tacitus, the Roman historian, had noted in both his *Germania* and *Historiae* that prophetic women were held in high esteem among the Germanic peoples because of their capacity to foretell the future, with one of them even having been worshipped as a goddess. Moreover, both priests and heads of the families could, according to Tacitus, seek for premonitory signs and perform lottery oracles by means of twigs carved with signs.

A multitude of conceptions describing human interrelations were invariably linked to the ideas of fate and destiny, and the desire for power, control and domination, if not blatant, lurked very near to the surface when various fortunes were foretold.

The myths about creation, cosmogony and anthropogony were woven into a grand narrative about the end. The predicted destinies of individuals, families, gods and other mythological beings, and even of the universe itself, at *Ragnarǫk* are consistently mentioned in the various texts, and all in relation to the fate of final destruction – the culminating point of destiny itself. There appears to have been a strong correspondence between conceptions of personal destiny and the Old Norse narratives of creation and destruction, which also surface in details revealing more small-scale dimensions of how individuals could have related to destiny.

NORNS

The norns (pl. *nornir*) are perhaps the most renowned agents of fate. They are depicted as the carvers of the rune or the weavers of destiny and fortune. The portrait of the norns weaving represents a beautiful image of how individual destinies are invariably entwined. In mythological narratives they are said to dwell at the foot of *Yggdrasill*, close to the well associated with insight and clandestine knowledge. In *Vǫluspá* they seem to control the destiny of the whole universe, which is doomed to inevitable destruction. The 'wise maidens' (*meyjar, margs vitandi*) who appear in this text are given individual symbolic names, *Urðr*, *Verðandi* and *Skuld*, popularly understood as 'Past', 'Present' and 'Future'. Stanza 20 offers the following portrayal:

> From there come three girls, knowing a great deal,
> from the lake which stands under the tree;
> Fated one is called, Becoming another –
> they carved on wooden slips – Must-be the third;
> they set down laws, they chose lives,
> for the sons of men the fates of men.
>
> (trans. Carolyne Larrington)

To establish a possible connection between runes and providence, the act of carving with respect to fate has been linked to the divination ceremonies outlined by Tacitus, Egill Skallagrimson's use of runes, and descriptions of Óðinn's efforts to gain runelore.

Although mythical by definition, *nornir* make a brief appearance in the sagas as well – there in more or less imaginary circumstances. In the *fornaldarsaga Norna-Gests þáttr* it is difficult to distinguish between *nornir* establishing a destiny and the invited seeresses (*vǫlur*) reading the future. The text tells of a gathering at a wealthy farmhouse to celebrate the birth of a newborn son – a gathering to which three honoured women have been invited. In the course of the affair, however, Norna Gestr's mother inadvertently offends one of the special guests, who then decides to punish her by giving the child a short span of life. Fortunately, the other two women intervene to salvage the happy day. Snorri explains in *Gylfaginning* (15): 'Good norns, ones of noble parentage, shape good lives, but as for those people that become the victims of misfortune, it is evil norns that are responsible.'

FYLGJA, FYLGJUR

The *fylgjur* are guardian spirits or fetches connected to individual persons or families (Mundal 1993a; Lindow 1987, 1993). The word derives from the Old Norse verb *fylgja* 'to follow', and is also associated with the noun for 'caul' or 'afterbirth'. They appear in the distinctly visible forms of either animals or women. Else Mundal has shown that the guises are employed in two very distinct ways in the texts and concludes: 'These two types have little in common but the name' (Mundal 1993a: 624). The animal *fylgja* was a symbolic image pointing towards the inner qualities of its owner, a constant symbolic characterisation. As a metaphor the *fylgja* reveals much about the person it follows. Strength, evil-mindedness, or social status were visualised in the image of a bear, a wolf, or an eagle. The animal shape was thought not to vary over time and was thus considered easy to identify. In the texts *fylgjur* bring warnings or advice. The animal *fylgja* is said to appear in front of its owner, often in dreams, and offer portents of events to come. As such it is a representation of the future itself, not the character of a person. Like a person's fate the *fylgja* is not changeable, nor can it improve or act on its own. As noted by Else Mundal, the animal *fylgja* operates as a mirror image of its possessor; the identity of the two is inextricable and therefore the death of a *fylgja* is considered predictive of the imminent demise of its owner.

A *fylgja* in the shape of a woman is more of a guarding and helping spirit that protects not merely an individual but a whole family. This is a more abstract idea closely related to the conceptions of the *hamingja*. The two are hardly separable even for analysis. The *fylgja* in this latter aspect is not even always given a physical form, but spoken of more diffusely as standing behind the family. Sometimes the *fylgja* is called *spádís*, indicating that she functions as a diviner for the protection of the family. When she appears within dreams she may be called a dream-woman, *draumkona*. These aspects of fate are very concrete in their bodily appearance, and although they show themselves for only a short time no room remains for alternative interpretations.

The *hamingja* represents the shape of a person's fate and it is difficult to distinguish this notion from the notion of the female *fylgja*. It is acting as a protective spirit and can appear before its owner to give hints about the future. The *hamingja* is also closely connected to the notions of *gipta* 'luck', *gæfa* 'personal qualities' and future prosperity. In *Víga-Glúms saga* (ch. 9), Glúmr encounters an enormous woman in a dream and considers this to mean that his grandfather has died and that his *fylgja* has now come to be possessed by him.

FERTILITY, PROSPERITY

In accordance with the cross-currents of destiny, each individual and family were thought to have received their share of fortune, both materially and in terms more abstract. Fortune and the good things in life were conceived of as quantitatively fixed things and thus, as a law of necessity, when somebody gained a measure of prosperity, that very measure was lost to somebody else. Ideas of luck and fortune were used to explain not only the current situation, but also social stratifications in general, and the reason why there were more and less prosperous families in the world. Fortune was considered a settled fact of life – something that could be altered only through the sorcerer's charms and incantations. Not surprisingly, more attention was paid to bad

239

luck than to success, and the literature is rife with story after story about destructive evil forces, personal ill-will and greed.

DÍSIR

The *dísir* comprise yet another collective of female deities involved with fate and prosperity who are hard to distinguish from the *fylgjur*. Indeed in the sagas, a *vǫlva* is also referred to as *spádís*, or female diviner. Conceptual figures in these texts are often mentioned in conjunction with ritual activities, although of the three groups mentioned here – the *fylgjur*, *hamingja* and the *dísir* – only the *dísir* appear to have been the recipients of cult. The *dísablót* is mentioned in some texts as a form of sacrifice or feat in the wintertime, and shows similarities to fertility rituals of a more private character. In popular divisions of high and low mythology, the *dísir* are often consigned to a lower realm, despite the fact that they most certainly played a vital role in everyday ritual life, and were not without their connections to the major gods. Freyja, for instance, is known as *vanadís*, the *dís* of the Vanir.

The function of the *dísir* is understood to have been the protection of the prosperity and good fortune of a specific place. Thus they are more closely connected to the land and also have a more pronounced protective aspect as compared to the largely abstract *fylgjur*. The *fylgjur* are invariably attached to a particular individual or family, whereas the *dísir* are more attached to a particular location or space. There are some texts, however, that draw no meaningful distinctions between *dísir* and *fylgjur*, considering them both to be guardian spirits of a sort.

At the close of this section it should be mentioned that there are also evil-minded *dísir* whose wrath is spoken of with fear in the *Grímnismál* (53): if the *dísir* are against a person or family, only destruction can follow. When the valkyries are occasionally associated with revenge and struggle they are known as Óðinn's *dísir*.

VǪLSI

The story of an embalmed horse phallus (*vǫlsi*) that is worshipped as an idol in the most remote region of northern Norway is part of the saga of St Óláfr. The subject of the saga concerns the saint's encounter with pagans who had no previous contact with Christianity – a motif which, according to the text itself, is based upon an old lay (*kvæði*).

The prepared object is said to be kept in a casket from which it is brought each night so that the family may gather about it to perform a special ceremony that is led by the lady of the house. In the ceremony each member of the household sings over the phallus and the verses are concluded with a prayer requesting the *mǫrnir* to receive their offering. And while the *mǫrnir* are never explicitly defined in the text, they appear to be a collective of spirits similar to *dísir* or *vættir*.

The emphasis on the horse, fertility and the potency of the object is thought to be indicative of the cult of Freyr. Whether the text should be taken as a scurrilous Christian portrait of pagan ceremonies or a glimpse into rural worship remains a matter of some controversy.

THE HUMAN SOUL

There are many Old Norse stories about gods and humans with the capacity to transform themselves into temporal guises in order to fulfil a particular intention while their bodies lay in wait. The ability of the human soul to function outside the body is a fundamental conception in sagas as well as in myth where the direct influence of a particular character is in want of explanation – be it Óðinn, an evil-minded woman or a lovesick youth.

There are two fundamental terms for the conception of the human soul: *hugr* and *hamr*. *Hugr* is often translated plainly as 'soul', but is said to have had wider connotations entailing notions such as personhood, thought, wish and desire. Some people with a strong *hugr* had the ability to act over long distances without actually moving their bodies. In the tangible guise of an animal or object they could cause harm while their physical bodies lay as if dead. The shape adopted for the temporary appearance most often revealed the purpose or the moral status of the sender: a strong bear, an aggressive wolf, a noble eagle.

Hamr, literally 'skin', was the name of the temporary guise the *hugr* was able to adopt for its movements. The ability to change shape and act out of the ordinary body in a new guise was either inborn or acquired through learning.

To be *hugstolinn* or *hamstolinn*, to be deprived of the *hugr* or *hamr*, was a metaphor for illness, that is, the infirmity was caused by an ill-willed attack from the outside.

SHAPESHIFTERS

There were many names for persons with the capacity to change their shape and temporarily act outside the ordinary body. The term 'shapeshifters' is used here as an umbrella for a wide range of characters in Old Norse literature who were said to have the ability to propel their *hugr* into a temporary body or guise, *hamr*, that is, of being a *hamhleypa* or someone who *leaps* into a *hamr*. Individuals with such capacities appear in both the mythological narratives and the sagas.

Thus between reports of the factual existence of *hamhleypa* and the abundance of their appearances in Old Norse literature, it is quite impossible to distinguish the assumed ability of transformation from the metaphorical metamorphosis found in poetry and myth.

In *Ynglinga saga* (ch. 7) Óðinn is described as the foremost shapeshifter. Snorri depicts how Óðinn would lie as if dead or asleep while his *hugr*, in the guise of a bird, animal, fish or serpent, enacted various deeds for the benefit of himself and others. His regular body was said to have been left behind, while his soul alone assumed temporary forms, a scenario that is common to most Old Norse shapeshifting narratives. There is, in fact, no mention in any of the literature of a single instance in which a transformation occurred that involved the complete disappearance of the corporal body; some part of the body was always left behind. Thus the time of transformation was viewed as a time of grave danger for the shapeshifter since it provided his or her enemies with a golden opportunity to either steal or harm the temporary body – an action that would immediately cause a parallel stigma to appear on the inert regular body.

The expressive term *sendingar* is frequently employed in Old Norse literature as the name for certain figures that were dispatched by individuals who possessed a strong *hamr, hamrammr*. In eddic poetry there is mention of various night-riders, apparently women, who were seen flying through the air. These *riður* can best be understood as 'night hags' moving in a temporary body.

Another chapter of *Ynglinga saga* describes the prowess of Óðinn's personal warriors, who were said to be as strong as bears or bulls, and could fight without coats of mail while holding their shields between their teeth, appearing like a pack of maddened dogs. One particular group of shapeshifters appear in the fantastic sagas about ancient times (*fornaldarsǫgur*) where they are given appellations indicative of their character, appellations such as *berserkr* ('bear shirt') and *ulfheðnar* ('wolf coat').

CONCLUDING REMARKS

Antiquarian religions too often share the fate of being reduced to mythological systems, a structuralist legacy in the history of the discipline. Most information about Old Norse popular religion is to be found in mythological narratives and in prose and poetry – including skaldic poetry – that employ characters, symbols and stories from mythology in order to construct intricate metaphors. The paucity of information in these literatures regarding the performance of ritual, however, is strikingly apparent.

The medieval traces of the Viking Age, which serve as the primary resource whenever an attempt is made to analyse pre-Christian religion, most certainly do not come from strata that were popular at the time, that is, common in an ordinary sense. Comparative research indicates that each strata of Viking society maintained its own focus of interest: farmers were interested in prosperity, chieftains in warrior ideology. In balance, however, one must also mention the fact that most Viking settlements were close-knit communities comprised of individuals who were wholly dependent upon one another for the maintenance of social accord and the attainment of life's basic needs.

However one sees it, one thing is clear: the enterprise of separating high from popular religion is fraught with valuational assumptions that require the designation of one division as advanced and sophisticated, and the other as backward and primitive. This sort of approach almost always ends in giving preferential interpretation to the former, thus making it difficult to observe the beliefs that both high and popular segments of Viking society held in common.

BIBLIOGRAPHY

Acker, P. (2002) 'Dwarf-lore in Alvíssmál', in P. Acker and C. Larrington (eds) *The Poetic Edda. Essays on Old Norse Mythology*, London: Routledge.

Boberg, I.M. (1966) *Motif-Index of Early Icelandic Literature* (Bibliotheca Arnamagnaeana 27), Copenhagen: Munksgaard.

Clunies Ross, M. (1994) *Prolonged Echoes. Old Norse Myths in Northern Society*, vol. 1: *The Myths* (Viking Collection 7), Odense: Odense University Press.

DuBois, Th. (1999) *Nordic Religions in the Viking Age*, Philadelphia: University of Pennsylvania Press.

Egils saga Skalla-Grímssonar, ed. Sigurður Nordal (Íslenzk fornrit 2), Reykjavík: Hið íslenzka fornritafélag, 1933. (In trans. by B. Scudder in *The Complete Sagas of the Icelanders*, vol. 1, Reykjavík: Leifur Eiríksson Publishing, 1997.)

Grágás = *Laws of Early Iceland. Grágás. The Codex regions of Grágás with material from other manuscripts*, 2 vols, trans. by A. Dennis, P. Foote and R. Perkins (University of Manitoba Icelandic Studies 3 and 5), Winnipeg: University of Manitoba Press 1980 and 2000).

Íslendingabók, ed. Jakob Benediktsson (Íslenzk fornrit 1), Reykjavík: Hið íslenzka fornritafélag, 1968.

Kórmáks saga, ed. Einar Ól. Sveinsson (Íslenzk fornrit 8), Reykjavík: Hið íslenzka fornritafélag, 1939. (In trans. by Rory McTurk in *The Complete Sagas of the Icelanders*, vol. 1, Reykjavík: Leifur Eiríksson Publishing, 1997.)

Lindahl, C., McNamara, J. and Lindow, J. (2000) *Medieval Folklore. An Encyclopedia of Myths, Legends, Tales, Beliefs, and Customs*, 2 vols, Santa Barbara: ABC-CLIO.

Lindow, J. (1987) 'Fylgjur', in M. Eliade *et al.* (eds) *Encyclopedia of Religion*, vol. 5, New York: Macmillan.

—— (1993) 'Mythology', in Ph. Pulsiano *et al.* (eds) *Medieval Scandinavia*, New York: Garland.

—— (2001) *Norse Mythology. A Guide to the Gods, Heroes, Rituals, and Beliefs*, Oxford: Oxford University Press.

Mundal, E. (1993a) 'Supernatural beings: fylgja', in Ph. Pulsiano *et al.* (eds) *Medieval Scandinavia*, New York: Garland.

—— (1993b) 'Supernatural beings: norns', in Ph. Pulsiano *et al.* (eds) *Medieval Scandinavia*, New York: Garland.

Naumann, H.-P. (1993) 'Supernatural beings: dísir', in Ph. Pulsiano *et al.* (eds) *Medieval Scandinavia*, New York: Garland.

The Poetic Edda, vol. 2: *Mythological Poems*, ed. and trans. U. Dronke, Oxford: Clarendon, 1997.

Raudvere, C. (2002) 'Trolldómr in early medieval Scandinavia', in B. Ankarloo and S. Clark (eds) *Witchcraft and Magic in Europe*, vol. 3: *The Middle Ages*, London: Athlone.

Schmitt, J.-C. (1987) 'Magic and folklore: western Europe', *Dictionary of the Middle Ages*, 12: 25–31.

Simek, R. (1993) *Dictionary of Northern Mythology*, Cambridge: Brewer.

Snorri Sturluson, Edda, ed. and trans. A. Faulkes, Oxford: Clarendon, 1982–7.

Víga-Glúms saga, ed. Jónas Kristjánsson (Íslenzk fornrit 9), Reykjavík: Hið íslenzka fornritafélag, 1956. (In trans. by John McKinnell in *The Complete Sagas of the Icelanders*, vol. 2, Reykjavík: Leifur Eiríksson Publishing, 1997).

Ynglinga saga, in Snorri Sturluson, *Heimskringla*, ed. Bjarni Aðalbjarnarson (Íslenzk fornrit 26), Reykjavík: Hið íslenzka fornritafélag, 1941.

SORCERY AND CIRCUMPOLAR TRADITIONS IN OLD NORSE BELIEF

——— ·•· ———

Neil Price

Over the past decade or so of research into the pre-Christian religion of the Norse, new understanding has been gained of the early northern mind by scholars working in all disciplinary branches of Viking studies. For the people of late Iron Age Scandinavia, this special view of the world – 'religion' is far too simple a word for it – ultimately encompassed every aspect of life, though it particularly concerned beliefs relating to the supernatural.

One of the key elements of this mindset was a channel of communication, through which Viking Age men and women interacted with the invisible population of gods and other beings that shared their lives (Raudvere, ch. 17, above). It is hard to find an adequate word for this in modern languages, though something like 'sorcery' or 'magic' perhaps comes closest. In Old Norse we find several different terms for it, but it is clear from the sources that the most important of these was *seiðr*, to which a great deal of study has recently been devoted (Strömbäck 2000; Raudvere 2001, 2003; Price 2002, 2004; Solli 2002; Dillmann 2006; Heide 2006a, b).

THE EVIDENCE FOR SORCERY

Our sources for this phenomenon are overwhelmingly literary in character, drawn from the corpus of writings primarily composed in Iceland in the centuries immediately following the Viking Age. Among the key texts for the study of Nordic sorcery are the mythological and heroic poems of the *Poetic Edda*, the Icelandic sagas, and the passages of spiritual lore found in Snorri Sturluson's *Prose Edda*. To these we may add a handful of references in the skaldic praise poetry, and the occasional disapproving entry on magic in the early medieval Scandinavian law codes.

There is also a scattering of archaeological evidence, though this is very hard to interpret. While some of it may best be understood in the light of the written sources, it is vital to remember not only the contemporary nature of the material culture (unlike the literary record, which was formed centuries later), but also the fact that in the archaeology we see traces of ideas and practices that have left no documentary trace at all.

When we take these sources together, it seems that *seiðr* – and other named forms of magic such as *gandr, galdr, útiseta* and so on – formed a kind of collective, a package of techniques and principles for contacting the supernatural powers and either binding or persuading them to do one's bidding. It can be helpful to view them as tools in a toolkit of magic, to be selected and combined in different ways in order to suit the task at hand. They remain individual and distinctive, but nonetheless part of a recognisable whole, the portfolio of a Viking Age sorcerer. As we might expect, there was great variation not only in what could be achieved through sorcery, but also in the ways that this could be brought to completion and in the abilities of those who would attempt to do so.

GODS AND HUMANS

From the beginning *seiðr* was a prerogative of the gods, and it is clear that its origins predate the Viking Age by several centuries (Hedeager 1997). The sources relate how Óðinn became the supreme master of sorcery, having learnt of its powers from the goddess Freyja. In their combined connotations of violence, sex and the powers of the mind, these two deities embody many of the key attributes of Nordic magic, as we shall see below.

Sorcery was also learned by humans, however, and it is clear from the texts that it was primarily the province of women. Men were certainly known to perform *seiðr*, though its practice brought with it a strange kind of dishonour and social rejection, combining cowardice and general 'unmanliness' with suggestions of homosexuality (against which Viking society held extremely strong prejudices; Meulengracht Sørensen 1983). Begging the question as to why some men were nevertheless prepared to follow this life, the answer seems to have been that its very risks also brought male sorcerers a peculiarly vital power. This might also explain the contradiction of Óðinn achieving mastery of this female domain, in keeping with his willingness to make great sacrifices for knowledge that could be bought in no other way (Solli 2002).

We know of some forty-five terms for Viking sorcerers of both sexes, though women predominate, and the names emphasise that a range of specialists provided services of different kinds according to their skills. Chief among these seem to have been the *vǫlur* (*vǫlva* in the singular), powerful sorceresses who could see into the future and whom even Óðinn consulted. One of their main attributes was a staff of sorcery, and objects believed to be such tools have been excavated from almost forty burials in Scandinavia and beyond (Price 2002: ch.3). They have been convincingly interpreted as metaphorical distaffs (Heide 2006a and b), used to 'spin out' the souls of their users, though it is clear that they also have many other symbolic overtones.

From these graves, supplemented by literary descriptions, we can gain an idea of how these masters and mistresses of *seiðr* may have appeared. Dressed often in clothes of great richness, with gold and silver embroidery that would have shimmered as they moved, some of these people also wore exotic jewellery such as facial piercings and toe-rings (Figure 17.1.1). Along with staffs they carried amulets and charms of various kinds, including preserved body-parts of animals, and in a handful of graves evidence has also been found for mind-altering drugs such as cannabis and henbane (Price 2002: ch. 3).

Figure 17.1.1   A reconstruction of the *vǫlva* Þórbjǫrg's costume and equipment from the description in *Eiríks saga rouða*. (Drawing: Þórhallur Þráinsson, after Price 2002.)

THE USES OF SORCERY

Seiðr and the other magics were evidently used for a wide range of purposes, varying from the solution of domestic problems to major affairs of state.

Among the gods, Óðinn used *seiðr* primarily to seek out information about the future, especially by asking questions of the dead. He is described as falling into trances, as leaving his body behind and travelling abroad in the spirit-form of an animal, and several times as having visions of wisdom provoked by various kinds of ordeal. Freyja uses sorcery as disguise, changing her shape and using her physical charms to wreak havoc in the lives of her enemies.

If we turn to sorcery in the human world, from examples in the literature we find it employed for bringing good or bad luck to individuals or a community, for affecting the weather and the abundance of game and fish (all useful things in an agrarian or pastoral society), and for healing the sick. One of the most common circumstances in which we encounter *seiðr* is as a tool for divining the future, when *vǫlur* and other sorcerers are specially commissioned to come to a district and predict what the coming years will bring for its inhabitants. Again, it is no accident that this also frequently occurs in the context of famine, crop failure or other preoccupations of economic subsistence.

Another theme also runs through the descriptions of sorcery, namely its connections with sexuality, a link that is consistent both for gods and for humans. We not only find a variety of love charms intended to attract the opposite sex, cure impotence and so on, but also to do the opposite. Óðinn especially uses *seiðr* as a means of seduction. It is noticeable too how many of the rituals involve sexual elements in their performance, and indeed it has been suggested by several scholars that the very practice of magic itself was either a real or a simulated sexual act. Suggestive double meanings seem to have attached to the tools of sorcery such as the staff (in a manner that is probably obvious), as well as to what one did with them. Even the language used for describing the practice of magic mirrors that used to suggest the rhythms of lovemaking. If the completion of a *seiðr* ritual really did involve an actual sexual performance, with an emphasis on the woman's physically receptive role in intercourse, then this – together with the distaff imagery of female handicrafts – may explain why it held such negative connotations for men.

Finally there is also a form of *seiðr* that was very clearly aggressive in nature, building up from small-scale private disputes to a practical involvement on the battlefield. On the one hand we frequently find sorcerers accused of causing mild injury to people, animals or property (they often appear in the sources as medieval 'neighbours from Hell'). On the other hand, the same individuals are also found playing a role in warfare, using their sorcery in a proactive sense for both offence and defence. This kind of magic is described in many, many sources, including very specific catalogues of war-charms listed among the supernatural skills of Óðinn. In particular these charms affected the state of a warrior's mind, making him fearful or clumsy, confused and weak – or the opposite of these. Armour and weapons could be rendered unbreakable through sorcery, or alternatively as brittle as ice. At the final extreme, *seiðr* could be used to kill and maim outright, being employed against either individuals or even whole armies: one especially dramatic description relates how the shield-wall of a king's bodyguard breaks under the sheer weight of a barrage of spells, raining down on it like artillery fire.

SEIÐR, SHAMANISM AND CIRCUMPOLAR RELIGION

In thinking about Nordic sorcery, we should remember that all of this was far from static. It was in fact highly dynamic, with a pattern of regional variation and change over time. Above the level of these local differences, however, there is also an overarching pattern that can be perceived.

The Vikings are usually understood as part of the Germanic cultures of north-western Europe. However, there is also a sense in which Scandinavia at this time formed a border between the Germanic world and that of the circumpolar, arctic cultures – represented in Sweden and Norway by the Sámi people, but ultimately extending around the northern hemisphere through Siberia, northern North America and Greenland. It is in this vast region that scholars usually locate the origins of what is known as shamanism, a set of spiritual practices that bears a remarkable similarity to the Scandinavian *seiðr* and its related rituals.

The possible shamanic overtones of Óðinn's powers have been recognised for more than a century, embracing the complex beliefs in transformation and shapeshifting and the northern thought-world of spirits and supernatural communication. Though there is still fierce debate on the subject, it now seems increasingly likely that *seiðr* was firmly a part of this circumpolar shamanic sphere, evolving not under the influence of Sámi religion but alongside it, as part of the common spiritual heritage of the north.

BIBLIOGRAPHY

Dillmann, F.-X. (2006) *Les magiciens dans l'Islande ancienne*, Uppsala: Kungl. Gustav Adolfs Akademien.

Hedeager, L. (1997) *Skygger af en anden virkelighed. Oldnordiske myter*, Copenhagen: Samleren.

Heide, E. (2006a) *Gand, seid og åndevind*, Bergen: University of Bergen (Dr art. thesis).

—— (2006b) 'Spinning *seiðr*', in A. Andrén, K. Jennbert and C. Raudvere (eds) *Old Norse Religion in Long-term Perspectives* (Vägar till Midgård 8), Lund: Nordic Academic Press.

Meulengracht Sørensen, P. (1983) *The Unmanly Man. Concepts of Sexual Defamation in Early Northern Society* (The Viking Collection 1), trans. J. Turville-Petre, Odense: Odense University Press.

Price, N.S. (2002) *The Viking Way. Religion and War in Late Iron Age Scandinavia* (Aun 31), Uppsala: Dept. of Archaeology and Ancient History, Uppsala University.

—— (2004) 'The archaeology of seiðr: circumpolar traditions in Viking pre-Christian religion', in S. Lewis-Simpson (ed.) *Vínland Revisited. The Norse World at the Turn of the First Millennium*, St John's: Historic Sites Association of Newfoundland & Labrador.

Raudvere, C. (2001) 'Trolldómr in early medieval Scandinavia', in B. Ankarloo and S. Clark (eds) *Witchcraft and Magic in Europe. The Middle Ages*, Philadelphia: University of Pennsylvania Press.

—— (2003) *Kunskap och insikt i norrön tradition. Mytologi, ritualer och trolldomsanklagelser* (Vägar till Midgård 3), Lund: Nordic Academic Press.

Solli, B. (2002) *Seid. Myter, sjamanisme og kjønn i vikingenes tid*, Oslo: Pax.

Strömbäck, D. (2000) *Sejd och andra studier i nordisk själsuppfattning*, 2nd edn, Uppsala: Kungl. Gustav Adolfs Akademien.

CHAPTER EIGHTEEN

THE MATERIAL CULTURE OF OLD NORSE RELIGION

———— ·•· ————

Anne-Sofie Gräslund

Religion has always existed in the form of ideas about supernatural powers guiding people's lives. Religious practice allows people to communicate with these powers through rituals and cults. Bronze Age sites contain evidence of rituals documented in rock carvings as well as in a large number of sacrificial artefact deposits. These finds indicate that fertility cult was an important part of old Scandinavian religion.

A common theme in Scandinavian prehistory is the widespread use of sacrifices in water or wetlands. Many sacrificial finds from the Stone Age up to the middle of the first millennium AD have been discovered in springs and bogs, the most famous ones being the large bog finds containing booty, weapons and other military equipment, dated to AD 100–500. At the end of this period the religious cult seems to have changed: old wetland sacrificial sites were abandoned, and thereafter the rituals were mainly performed on dry land, in the halls of the chieftains or in the open air. Cults were organised on a regional basis in different levels within society: on a local level in the farm, on a regional level in the chieftain's farm and on a superregional level, as for example probably in Old Uppsala and in Uppåkra in Skåne.

In the Old Norse language there was no specific word for religion. The closest concept was *siðr*, meaning 'custom', showing how integrated religion was in daily life. Unlike today, when religion is often separated from secular life, it was then a natural part of all occupations. Old Norse religion should not be regarded as a static phenomenon, but as a dynamic religion that changed gradually over time and doubtless had many local variations. By the second half of the first millennium AD, the influence of Christianity is evident, for by that time there were frequent contacts with western Europe. In particular, the myths about the end of the world, Ragnarǫk, have many features in common with the Biblical treatment of the Day of Judgement.

Is it possible to trace Old Norse religion – or any religion – through the evidence of material culture? The answer is yes, to a certain degree. Religious practice includes ceremonies and rituals, normally very difficult to trace. But sometimes these actions have left some material remains. As always in Viking Age research an interdisciplinary approach is needed, we have to use all available evidence in order to get a better picture. Some fields of research are of special archaeological interest in this connection: sacrifices, meaning communication with the gods and the supernatural world, taking place at cult sites, and burial customs, indicating ideas of what happened after death, revealed in the graves. Artefacts should also be mentioned, as some of them may be loaded with religious meaning. There are also regular illustrations, as for example on the Gotlandic picture stones and on preserved textile wall hangings, so iconography is essential in this connection.

CULT SITES

The description by Adam of Bremen of the cult site in Old Uppsala is well known. He mentions a big temple, totally covered in gold, where three idols were placed, representations of Óðinn, Þórr and Freyr. Men, horses and dogs were sacrificed in a holy grove nearby, the bodies hanging in the trees. However, there are many source-critical aspects to be considered. Adam himself had never visited Uppsala – or even Scandinavia – he got his information from persons who had been there, for example the Danish king Sven Estridsen, who spent some time in the town of Sigtuna and then probably visited Uppsala or at least was told about what happened there. It may also be a question of glorifying Adam's own diocese by describing Uppsala as primitive and as pagan as possible – that made the successful Hamburg–Bremen mission among the *Svear* the more important. The question of the Uppsala temple is one of the most discussed through the years. After an excavation in 1926, under the medieval church, Sune Lindqvist published a reconstruction of the pagan temple, based on the evidence of post-holes found under the church (Nordahl 1996). However, he later denied that the temple could be reconstructed from his excavation. A new analysis in the 1990s of all evidence from the 1926 excavation has finally rejected the temple (Nordahl 1996). The post-holes belong to one or more buildings, probably a hall, and ^{14}C-analyses from various layers under the church give dates from the third and up to the tenth century. Therefore perhaps the cult performances that Adam had been told about took place in the hall of the royal manor at the site, which is what could be expected. There is evidence from Snorri's *Heimskringla* as well as from many sites of halls where the cult was practised. Important sites of this kind to be mentioned are Mære in Trøndelag, Borg in Lofoten, Järrestad in Skåne, Helgö in Lake Mälaren and so on. One indication of cultic performances in the hall is the presence of the so-called *guldgubbar*, tiny picture foils of gold depicting either a couple or a single man or woman. The couple motif has been interpreted as a representation of the 'holy marriage' between the god Freyr and the giantess Gerðr (Steinsland 1991).

It has long been argued that the pre-Christian Scandinavians had no cult houses and that the cult was performed in the open air. Descriptions of cult houses, such as Adam's, are late and probably influenced by Christianity or by knowledge of classical antiquity. However, in the beginning of the 1990s examples of possible cult houses were recovered at large settlement excavations of farmsteads, one at Borg in Östergötland (Nielsen 1997), the other at Sanda in Uppland (Åqvist 1996). At Borg (Figure 18.1) a small house, situated close to an elevated rock, was built on sills and probably made of corner-joint timber. It was erected on a paved yard with an area of about 1,000 m^2. Outside the building a large number of animal bones were found and iron slag together with depositions of many amulet rings of fire-steel shape with attached Þórr's hammers; inside there were few finds. Among the animal bones there were dog and horse bones, normally very rare at settlements but frequent in graves and in sacrifices, and, above all,

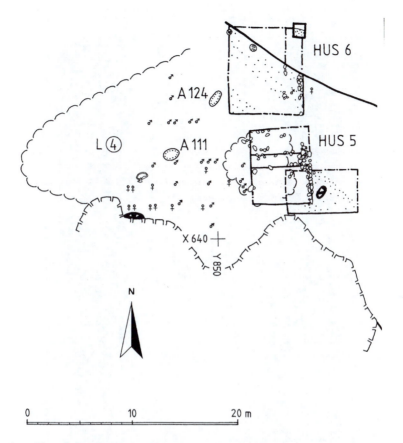

Figure 18.1 Plan of the cult house at Borg (no. 5), the yard, amulet rings and iron furnaces (A 111 and A 124). Also shown is the distribution of bones from pigs whose sex has been identified. (Drawing: Mari-Anne Grönwall, from Nielsen 1997.)

a lot of pig bones, mostly parts of the jaw. At the Viking Age site of Sanda a stone structure of about the same size as the cult house at Borg was found at the border between the settlement and the cemetery, with concentrations of hearths outside the structure and finds of many miniature sickles. It has been interpreted as a cult house (by the excavator tentatively called a *hǫrgr*).

In 2002 an excavation carried out at the Iron Age site of Lunda, Södermanland, revealed a large hall building and close to it on the north side a smaller building, where two small figurines were found, naked phallic men (3.5 and 2 cm respectively) (Andersson *et al.* 2004). To the south of the hall a third figurine was found, also a naked phallic man (3 cm high). Two of the figurines were made of bronze and partly gilded, the third of pure gold. Two of them had feet, one lacked feet due to damage. The smallest one, the one made of gold, has his feet in a position with the toes pointing downwards (Figure 18.2), which may be interpreted as if he is hanging (cf. Adam's account from Old Uppsala). The small building has been interpreted as a cult house (by the excavator tentatively called a *hof*). The cemetery occupied the sloping area behind the hall, and at a distance of *c.* 100 m to the west of the buildings, on a hilltop, a possible sacrificial site

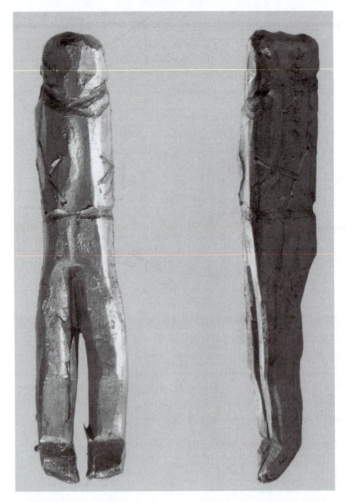

Figure 18.2   One of the figurines from Lunda, made of gold, 2 cm high. His toes point downwards, indicating that he was hanged. (Photo: Bengt A. Lundberg, from Andersson *et al.* 2004.)

has been identified with burnt bones and burnt clay spread all over the area. This phase of the settlement seems to be dated to the middle of the Iron Age, hence the migration period or the beginning of the Vendel period (*c.* AD 450–600). The place name *Lunda* means 'grove', and maybe the hilltop site was the holy grove, the sacrificial site of the whole region.

Recently a cult house has been excavated at the central place of Uppåkra in Skåne (Larsson and Lenntorp 2004). It seems to be older than the house at Borg and the structure at Sanda. The most spectacular finds are a beaker of bronze and silver, covered with ornamented gold bands, dated to *c.* AD 500, and a glass bowl, made of two layers of glass, one colourless and one blue, with the same dating. The Lunda and the Uppåkra finds indicate that cult houses were used already from the middle of the first millennium AD in Scandinavia.

Remains of an open-air cult site, probably a holy grove, similar to the one suggested at the hilltop of Lunda, have been found at Frösön in Jämtland. In 1984 excavations were carried out under the chancel of Frösö medieval church, and a dark, cultural layer with large amounts of animal bones was found around a partly mouldered birch stump (Iregren 1989). On stratigraphical grounds it can be concluded that the bones had been placed there when the tree was still growing. ^{14}C-analyses of samples from carbon in the cultural layer, from bones and from the stump, have all given a Viking Age dating, from AD 745 ±85 up to AD 1060 ±75. The species determined from the bones consist of both domesticated (40%) and wild (60%) animals. The most striking is the large proportion of bear, from at least five individuals. The site has been interpreted as a sacrificial site, probably a grove, and comparisons have been made between the tree and Adam's description of the bodies hanging in the trees of the holy grave of Uppsala, and with the tapestry from the Oseberg ship, where bodies hanging in a tree are depicted.

Another type of sacrifice, difficult to verify in the material culture but obviously also carried out in the open air, is described by the Arab writer Ibn Fadlan (in AD 922). In his account of the behaviour of the Rus' in the Volga region he gives us a lot of valuable information concerning the rituals of the Rus' merchants. When they arrive at a new place, they sacrifice food to a god, an idol in the form of a big wooden pole with a human face on top of it, standing together with smaller poles. This is a sacrifice to get success in their trade. And if the trade is good, they bring a thank-sacrifice to the pole god, consisting of the meat of slaughtered goats or cows. During the night the dogs come and eat the meat, and next day the merchant declares that his god has accepted the sacrifice.

As already mentioned, the place names can give significant information on pre-historic cult sites. There are specific place-name elements meaning 'cult site', such as *vi/væ/vé, lundr, akr* etc., and there are theophoric place names, where the name of a god makes up the first element, followed by such an element denoting a cult site, as for example the Swedish *Torsåker, Odensvi* and *Frölunda*. Judging from the frequency of such names, we have indications of cult sites spread all over Scandinavia.

ARTEFACTS

Examples of artefacts have already been mentioned, such as figurines and amulets. Starting with figurines there are some – in all probability – representing gods. The most well known was found in Rällinge, Södermanland, not far from the above-mentioned Lunda site (Andersson *et al.* 2004). It is a bronze statuette, *c.* 7 cm high, depicting a phallic man sitting cross-legged, naked but wearing a conical cap and an arm-ring. It is usually interpreted as a representation of the god Freyr, due to the big phallus, and references are made to Adam's description of the three god statues in the Uppsala temple, where Freyr is said to be the god of fertility who brings peace and enjoyment to the mortals and is depicted with an immense male organ. Ornaments on the back of the Rällinge figurine indicate a dating to the late Viking Age. He is grasping his beard with his left hand (the right hand is missing). This is a recurring element on some other statuettes, one from Eyraland in Iceland, where the male figure, naked but wearing a conical cap, is sitting in a chair, grasping his beard with both hands. The lower part of the beard is shaped like a hammer, and because of that the figurine is suggested to represent the god Þórr. In Adam's account Þórr is described as the god of thunder, all kinds of weather and crops, and as 'the mightiest of the gods, having his throne in the centre of the temple', so the chair/throne has been stressed as an argument for this interpretation of the figurine. Similar seated and beard-grasping figurines are known from Lund in Skåne, from Roholte in Sjælland, from Baldursheimur in Iceland and from Chernigov in Ukraine, all of them normally interpreted as representations of Þórr (Perkins 2001; Andersson *et al.* 2004).

Maybe images of Óðinn, the god of war, occur as well, or maybe he is represented only by his helpers and attributes? Warriors like those depicted on the Vendel-period helmets from the boat graves of Vendel and Valsgärde, and the so-called weapon-dancers from Viking Age graves in Birka and in Kungsängen in Uppland, and on belt buckles from Ribe, Tissø and Uppåkra can be interpreted as real images of the god or perhaps just symbols of his presence. A small standing bronze statuette from Lindby in Skåne has only one eye, the other one is closed, therefore it has been identified as the one-eyed god Óðinn.

People have always worn amulets as good-luck charms or as protection against danger (Gräslund 1992), but the symbolic meaning of the amulets, if we can grasp it, may give us some indication of which gods or powers were expected to help and protect. The worship of and belief in the help of the gods may be recognised by the occurrence of their specific attributes. The Þórr's hammer is a form of pendant of distinct amuletic character; this interpretation is supported by the Eddic poems as well as by contemporary iconographic evidence, such as the picture on the runestone in Altuna, Uppland, where Þórr is depicted holding his hammer while trying to catch the Miðgarðr serpent. Small Þórr's hammers of iron threaded onto neck-rings made of iron rods are found in ninth- and tenth-century graves, almost always cremations and nearly all from the east Mälar area. They are also found on Åland and in Russia. About fifty silver Þórr's hammers are known from hoards, graves and settlements. They have a wide distribution, mostly being found in south and central Scandinavia, but some also in Trøndelag and Iceland. They can be dated to the tenth and eleventh centuries. A few are known from England and Poland. It is impossible to say whether the Þórr's hammers were used in cult ceremonies, although the frequent deposition of Þórr's hammer rings in the top of an urn in a cremation layer suggests a role in burial rites. A similar custom may be represented by axe-shaped amber pendants from graves in Gotland, which have been shown, by examination under the microscope, to have been made specifically for burial, as they display no traces of wear. In Viking Age graves on Åland and in Russia bears' claws made of clay may have had a magical and ceremonial significance.

Óðinn's spear is one of his most important attributes. Miniature spearheads are known from Birka and from many other places in south and central Sweden. Other attributes connected to Óðinn are his two ravens, his eight-legged horse, Sleipnir, and probably also the eagle, the wolf and the snake. Óðinn as shaman means that the staff is significant. Small amulet rings with several pendants including staffs and spearheads are known from Birka and from Köping on Öland. In Óðinn's entourage we find the valkyries, taking care of the fallen warriors at the battlefield and bringing them to Valhǫll. In all probability the small, two-dimensional female figurines made of silver, in some cases holding a drinking horn, are valkyrie representations, and by that, symbols of worship of Óðinn. The identification of probable *vǫlva* graves in Birka, Köping on Öland, Fyrkat in Jutland, and other places (Price 2002) should also be seen in this connection.

References to the god Freyr, the third of the gods mentioned by Adam, as the god of fertility, may also be found in the artefact assemblages. Pendants in the form of strike-a-light have been interpreted as signifying the life-giving and purifying fire and by that connected to the fertility cult and Freyr. There are miniature fire-steels as both pendants and rings with an unmistakable fire-steel shape. On such rings, other pendants are sometimes attached, sickles, scythes and spades, all with an obvious association to agriculture. Another important attribute of Freyr is his ship, Skíðblaðnir, and whether the boat-grave custom could have its ideological root in this has also been discussed.

Many other kinds of supposed amulets are known from the Viking Age (Gräslund 2005), for example miniature chairs, interpreted as thrones and by some scholars attributed to Þórr, by others to Óðinn, shield-shaped pendants decorated with a whorl pattern, interpreted as a sun symbol and by that associated to the fertility cult. The shield as protective symbol should also be pointed out. There may be a connection to some brooches, found for example in Tissø in Sjælland, depicting a mounted woman with a spear and in front of the horse another woman with a shield. Maybe they could be interpreted as valkyries and, by that, that the woman wearing the brooch stood under the protection of the valkyries and – behind them – Óðinn. Pendants in the shape of a coiled snake are known from the Scandinavian countries and from England. No other species has played a more important role universally in religion, mythology and folklore than the snakes. Their way of living underground, their venomousness and their way of sloughing their skin have fascinated people in all periods and cultures. They have been regarded as symbols for rebirth and life.

Looking at the Birka graves, it is striking that some of the women buried there have got several amuletic pendants. In two cases the women in question have been identified as *vǫlur* (Price 2002), and it is possible that also some other women with more than one amulet pendant had a function in the cult.

Regarding the Viking burial customs, I would like to add a remark on possible remains of the rites de passage, from the living to the dead. Having studied the occurrence of dog bones in Scandinavian graves from the second half of the first millennium, I am convinced that the dogs in the graves should not be interpreted only as faithful and loyal companions, or as expressions of social status (Gräslund 2004). Dogs are very frequent in the graves, almost every grave where the bones have been analysed contains a dog, and combined with the evidence of the Eddic poems and with archaeological and literary evidence from other European cultures from the first millennium AD, I find it conclusive that the dogs had an important function as media in the transformation from living to dead, guarding the entrance of Hel, the realm of Death, and bringing the souls to the afterlife.

ICONOGRAPHY

Iconographical evidence has already been mentioned, such as the *guldgubbar*, probably depicting the holy marriage between Freyr and Gerðr, the picture foils of the Vendel-period helmets, in some cases maybe depicting Óðinn, and the bodies hanging in a tree on the Oseberg wall hanging. (For two other wall hangings from Överhogdal and from Skog, with both pagan and Christian motifs see Gräslund, ch. 46.1, below.)

Evidence of Old Norse cult practice can probably be found on the picture stones of Gotland (Lindqvist 1941–2), for example a possible human sacrifice and a body hanging in a tree. We also have clear examples of mythological narratives on the stones, such as a possible valkyrie with a drinking horn welcoming a man on an eight-legged horse, Sleipnir, Gunnar in the pit with the snakes and the legend of Vǫlundr the smith, and perhaps also Óðinn transformed into a bird. Turning to the artefacts, there are several human figures with animal masks, for example from Torslunda in Öland and from Kungsängen in Uppland (Price 2002). The latter grasps a snake reaching up to the man's head. On the Oseberg tapestry a woman with a boar mask and skin is depicted. A reference must also be made to the two felt masks found in the harbour of Hedeby. Those who wore animal masks have been seen as connected to shamanistic rituals.

BIBLIOGRAPHY

Andersson, G., Beronius Jörpeland, L., Dunér, J., Fritsch, S. and Skyllberg, E. (2004) *Att föra gudarnas talan – figurinerna från Lunda*, Stockholm: Raä.

Åqvist, C. (1996) 'Hall och harg – det rituella rummet', in K. Engdahl and A. Kaliff (eds) *Religion från stenålder till medeltid. Artiklar baserade på Religionsarkeologiska nätverksgruppens konferens på Lövstadbruk den 1–3 december 1995*, Stockholm: Riksantikvarieämbetet.

Gräslund, A.-S. (1992) 'Thor's hammers, pendant crosses and other amulets', in E. Roesdahl and D. Wilson (eds) *From Viking to Crusader. The Scandinavians and Europe 800–1200*, Copenhagen: Nordic Council of Ministers.

—— (2004) 'Dogs in graves – a question of symbolism?', in B. Santillo Fritzell (ed.) *Pecus. Man and Animal in Antiquity. Proceedings of the Conference at the Swedish Institute in Rome, September 9–12, 2002* (Swedish Institute in Rome. Projects and Seminars 1), Rome: Swedish Institute.

—— (2005) 'Symboler för lycka och skydd – vikingatida amuletthängen och deras rituella context', in K.A. Bergsvik and A. Engevik jr (eds) *Fra funn til samfunn. Jernalderstudier tilegnet Bergljot Solberg på 70-årsddagen* (UBAS 1), Bergen: Arkeologisk institutt, Universitetet i Bergen.

Iregren, E. (1989) 'Under Frösö kyrka – ben från en vikingatida offerlund?', in L. Larsson and B. Wyszomirska (eds) *Arkeologi och religion. Rapport från arkeologidagarna 16–18 januari 1989* (Institute of Archaeology. Report series 34), Lund: Arkeologiska inst., Lunds universitet.

Larsson, L. and Lenntorp, K.-M. (2004) 'The enigmatic house', in L. Larsson (ed.) *Continuity for Centuries. A Ceremonial Building and its Context at Uppåkra, Southern Sweden* (Uppåkrastudier 10), Stockholm: Almqvist & Wiksell International.

Lindqvist, S. (1941–2) *Gotlands Bildsteine*, 2 vols (KVHAAs Monografier 28), Stockholm: Wahlström & Widstrand.

Nielsen, A.-L. (1997) 'Pagan cultic and votive acts at Borg', in H. Andersson, P. Carelli and L. Ersgård (eds) *Visions of the Past. Trends and Traditions in Swedish Medieval Archaeology* (Lund Studies in Medieval Archaeology 19), Stockholm: Almqvist & Wiksell International.

Nordahl, E. (1996) *Templum quod Ubsola dicitur . . . i arkeologisk belysning* (Aun 22), Uppsala: Dept. of Archaeology, Uppsala University.

Perkins, R. (2001) *Thor the Wind-raiser and the Eyrarland Image*, London: Viking Society for Northern Research.

Price, N. (2002) *The Viking Way. Religion and War in Late Iron Age Scandinavia* (Aun 31), Uppsala: Dept. of Archaeology and Ancient History, Uppsala University.

Steinsland, G. (1991) *Det hellige bryllup og norrøn kongeideologi*, Oslo: Solum.

CHAPTER NINETEEN

DYING AND THE DEAD: VIKING AGE MORTUARY BEHAVIOUR

—·◆·—

Neil Price

> In his country Óðinn instituted such laws as had been in force among the Æsir before. Thus he ordered that all the dead were to be burned on a pyre together with their possessions, saying that everyone would arrive in Valhǫll with such wealth as he had with him on his pyre and that he would also enjoy the use of what he himself had hidden in the ground. His ashes were to be carried out to sea or buried in the ground. For notable men burial mounds were to be thrown up as memorials. But for all men who had shown great manly qualities memorial stones were to be erected; and this custom continued for a long time thereafter.
>
> (Snorri Sturluson, *Ynglingasaga* 8, trans. Hollander 1964: 11–12)

This brief passage from the first book of Snorri's *Heimskringla* is the only specific, as opposed to incidental, description of Viking Age burial ritual left to us by a Norse author. Written two centuries after pre-Christian mortuary behaviour was the norm, in isolation we have little way of evaluating the degree to which the ideological filters of his own time shaped Snorri's presentation of these rites. However, alongside the occasional descriptions of funerary settings in the Icelandic sagas and poems, and observations from outside the Scandinavian world (especially those of Arab travellers), we now have a vast amount of archaeological evidence that enables us to review in some detail Viking attitudes to dying and the dead. That the excavated material should not only corroborate but also to an extent sharply contradict the textual sources should not surprise us, but of key importance is the fact that the archaeology reveals mortuary practices that have left no documentary trace at all.

This chapter will confine its review to non-Christian burials, with some occasional exceptions, as these are otherwise discussed elsewhere in this volume.

DIVERSITY IN DEATH

Perhaps the central element of Viking Age Scandinavian funerary ritual was its individual character. After more than a century of excavations there can remain no doubt whatever that we cannot speak of a standard orthodoxy of burial practice common to the whole Norse world: Snorri's 'law of Óðinn' is an illusion, even for the rather vague 'country' to which it allegedly applied. This does not mean that every part of his description is inaccurate, but instead we should examine it in specific rather than generalised contexts.

In landmark studies of specific burial practices right across Scandinavia, Johan Callmer (1991, 1992; Figure 19.1) has demonstrated how local variation was present at the level of individual communities, villages and even extended farmsteads. From one settlement to another people handled the dead in broadly consistent ways – essentially through cremation or occasionally inhumation – but differed in the details of grave construction and elaboration, the placement of the body and the selection and deposition of objects that accompanied the deceased. It should be stressed that these 'grave goods' could include not only small artefacts but also vehicles, furniture, farm equipment, slaughtered livestock and even (in isolated instances) other humans who were apparently killed in connection with the funerals.

We find special rituals in island communities, and in general the funerary rites of places such as Gotland, Öland, Bornholm and Åland are unlike those of their respective mainlands, which differ in turn from the surrounding areas (Thunmark-Nylén 1998–2006; Beskow Sjöberg *et al.* 1987–2001). Recognisably Scandinavian burial traditions are also found across the Viking world, again with local traditions in evidence. In the North Atlantic colonies such as Iceland and Greenland, cremation is extremely rare

Figure 19.1   Settlement distribution in southern Scandinavia, *c.* AD 800, based on differentiation in the detail of funerary custom. Circled areas show affinities of burial ritual (after Callmer 1992).

(Eldjárn 2000), while in England there are few burials under mounds (Halsall 2000). In the eastern areas of Viking expansion, Norse funerary rituals are found amalgamated with Slavic, Khazar and other ethnic practices (see Androshchuk, ch. 38, below). Some areas, such as Continental Europe, have noticeably few graves that can be unequivocally interpreted as of Norse origin. No Scandinavian burials have so far been found in North America.

It has been suggested that this diversity is a signal not of varying treatment of the dead within a single society, but is instead evidence for the illusory nature of the 'Viking Age' itself: that the highly regional burial traditions are indicators of distinctive ethnic, social or political groupings that make a mockery of the notion of a pan-Scandinavian culture (Svanberg 2003). The problem with this interpretation is that it ignores the very real, general similarities of material culture within the region (not to mention language and settlement pattern) and focuses only on variations that are nonetheless practised within a broader, consistent framework. That villages or even larger communities promote their own identities does not mean that they have no part of larger ones. As will become clear (and, not least, is also demonstrated by the other contributions to this volume) the culture of the Viking Age Scandinavians is as evident in their burials as in other aspects of their society.

CREMATIONS

Before discussing specific rites for the burial of the dead, it is important to mention an aspect of Viking Age mortuary behaviour that is often overlooked: quite simply, it is clear from settlement–burial correlations that not everyone was accorded a grave at all. Estimates of the proportion of the populace not accorded a formal grave are unreliable, but more than half is not impossible.

It is perhaps reasonable to assume that these 'missing' dead were marked by low status, either the very poor or slaves, but we cannot be sure. We have no identifiable evidence for the burials of slaves in their own right, as opposed to their presumed presence as sacrificial offerings in a few cases treated below. Whether these people were cremated and their ashes then scattered or disposed of in water, or whether they were just discarded in an informal version of excarnation, is impossible to say. It is worth noting that these archaeologically invisible burial forms are mentioned not only in *Ynglingasaga* 8 as we have seen, but also in first-hand accounts left by Arab writers such as Ibn Fadlan who described in the tenth century how dead slaves were simply abandoned, at least while on the move (Montgomery 2000).

Children are also under-represented in the burial record, which may reflect a number of factors. We know little of how the child to adult transition was regarded at this time, and accordingly whether dead children were seen as 'worthy' of formal burial; the fact that we have child burials at all suggests, however, that the same criteria of familial and personal status may have been applied. The practice of child exposure and abandonment may also account for a large number of the children missing from the archaeological burial record.

For those that received a burial, the most common means of disposing of the dead was through cremation, followed by the interment of the ashes either in unmarked graves or under mounds. The corpses were most often burned *in situ* and the grave raised over them, sometimes with a burial pit dug down through the pyre to accommodate the ashes. In most cases the bones of the humans, and sometimes the animals, have been retrieved from the ashes, sorted and cleaned before being laid back on the charred remains of the pyre – either directly or in a container such as a ceramic vessel, a box or a bag. In most cremations objects were burned together with the dead and the resulting fragments interred with them, though sometimes the ashes are overlain by unburnt items placed there during the construction of the grave. In some cases objects were deliberately broken before being burned, perhaps to mark their 'death' alongside that of their owner.

It is among the objects deposited with the dead that the great variety noted above can be found. The most commonly encountered range of artefacts includes items of personal dress and ornament such as jewellery; weapons; implements for textile production and food preparation; smithying tools; agricultural implements; household utensils, containers and fixtures of various kinds; horse equipment; furniture including beds, chairs and stools; textiles of varying quality and quantity; food and drink, among many other kinds of objects. The selection, combination, particular type, quality, quantity and exact positioning of this material are all factors in the variation within Viking Age mortuary ritual, but there are also more indicative, local expressions. On Öland in Sweden, for example, fossils such as ammonites were sometimes deposited with the deceased (Beskow Sjöberg *et al.* 1987–2001). On the Åland islands between Sweden and Finland, the ashes of the dead were buried in pottery vessels on the top of which was placed a miniature animal paw made of clay (Figure 19.2). The paws, which were not present on the funeral pyre, have been identified as characteristic of either bears or beavers. This rite is found only on Åland, and in specific clusters of graves on the Volga and Kljaz'ma rivers in Russia; from the accompanying grave goods, these burials have been convincingly interpreted as those of travelling Ålanders (Callmer 1994).

Burial mounds could be of widely varying shapes and sizes, ranging from low humps in the ground to monumental barrows up to 10 m high or more. Circular forms predominate, but oval, rectangular and triangular mounds are also known. In some instances the mounds are augmented by what appear to have been posts set up in them, for unknown reasons, or by small pits dug into the sides, again of indeterminate

Figure 19.2   A clay animal paw from Hjortö, Saltvik, characteristic of those found in cremation burials on the Åland islands (after Roesdahl and Wilson 1992: 290).

purpose but presumably relating to the extended rituals of the burial, discussed further below.

In general burials seem to have been unmarked in the sense of personally recording their occupants, but Ibn Fadlan's account, mentioned above, describes how a mound was topped by a wooden pole, on which was cut (presumably in runes) the dead person's name and that of his lord. Leaving little archaeological trace this form of commemoration might have been more common than we suppose, and may also explain some of the post-holes found in barrows. In other ways the marking of graves was elaborate and widespread, and usually achieved with stones. These range from individual Sw *bautastenar*, standing stones erected on a single grave, to complex settings in an enormous variety of shapes (Bennett 1987). The latter include kerb rings, circles, rectangles, star patterns, triangles and curious three-sided forms with concave sides known in the absence of an English term as Sw *treuddar*, 'three-pointers'. The meaning, if any, of all these stone-settings is undetermined but several explanations have been proposed – by way of example, a recent idea has seen the *treuddar* as representing the roots of a tree, perhaps Yggdrasill, the World Tree (Andrén 2004).

A particularly striking form of stone setting is shaped like a ship, occurring in a range of sizes up to an enormous 170 m long at Jelling in Denmark (Roesdahl, ch. 48, below). The ship settings are sometimes empty but found among graves, often with the remains of fires and meals within – perhaps some form of commemorative place. Other ship settings contain one or more cremations spaced around their interior. In general most graves contain single cremations, but multiple burials in the same mound are known and are not uncommon within the larger stone settings. There is also a wider but related issue in the erection of memorials to the dead beyond the burial itself. These will not be treated in detail here, but include runestones, standing stones, bridges, and monumental acts of commemoration such as colossal mounds, fortresses and churches (see Roesdahl 2005 and ch. 48, below; also Gräslund, ch. 46.1, below).

Cremation burial in earthen mounds is frequently mentioned in the saga corpus, and it is clear that afterwards the named landmarks that resulted played a part in the cognitive landscape of the community. The degree to which the mounds' incumbents were still thought to 'reside' in their graves, and thus remain members of their communities, is arguable though their metaphorical presence seems assured. The Old Norse prose sources contain many stories of the living dead in the sense of the physically reanimated corpse, but while the majority of these tales concern evil beings there are also a significant number that merely relate how the dead live on in their graves. Two examples among many are Gunnar of Hliðarendi from *Njáls saga*, who is seen happily singing in his mound one night, and the dead warriors of the rather eerie poem known as *The Waking of Angantyr* who seem to sleep uneasily in their burials, 'down among the tree-roots' (Terry 1990: 248–53).

INHUMATION

Inhumation was rarer, but occurred across Scandinavia. In the later Viking Age it has been argued that some of these burials represent transitional Christian graves, but this is debated (see Gräslund, ch. 46.1, below). Bodies were generally laid in rectangular grave cuts, either directly on the ground, on textiles or on mats of bark (the latter especially in northern Norway), in shrouds or in coffins of various kinds including the detachable cargo bodies of wagons. Many different body postures are found, though the dead are most often laid out either supine or slightly curled over on their sides, as if sleeping. In some graves remains of blankets, pillows and other bedding have been found under and around the bodies, reinforcing this suggestion. In a few unusual instances the dead are buried prone or in a variety of unnatural postures that necessitate actual damage to the body, for example by the removal of limbs. Whether this relates to some kind of punishment or legal censure is hard to say, but the large stones placed on top of some of these bodies imply a fear that they might somehow leave the grave and presumably cause harm to the living.

Inhumation burials normally exhibit the same or even greater range of grave goods as the cremations, though the apparent profusion is perhaps a factor of preservation. Like the cremations, inhumations were also accompanied by animal and occasionally human offerings, along with considerable quantities of foodstuffs and, to judge by the containers, drink as well. Crampons on the shoes of the dead may suggest a winter burial, or that they were thought to be journeying somewhere cold; there are saga references to special 'hel-shoes' that the dead would need (Strömbäck 1961).

In the archaeological material, there are numerous examples of burials associated with what are undoubtedly means of transport – ships, wagons, sledges or simply horses – and which might suggest that the dead were on their way somewhere. However, the same graves sometimes also contain elements that imply the opposite: the Oseberg ship in southern Norway, for example, was 'moored' in the grave by a massive hawser tied around an immovable rock. The obvious question also remains as to whether these vehicles of various kinds were there for a functional purpose or merely as expensive possessions.

Both cremations and inhumations occur singly, in small groups and in cemeteries of varying sizes from a dozen or so burials to thousands. The great variety of constellations reflects the spatial and no doubt social patterning of the communities that they served, from individual farms with 'family plots' to larger villages and urban centres such as Birka and Hedeby. There also seem to be political factors at work, in that some areas tend to aggregate the dead in clusters whereas others maintain traditions of local burial. In general the dead were not buried far from settlements, but instead their graves can be seen as an extended component of the inhabited areas.

The best example of such a cemetery as it originally appeared is found at Lindholm Høje in northern Jutland, where a grave-field was buried by wind-blown sand and has survived intact. Almost every burial is marked by stones, often without apparent pattern, but clearly comprising an integral part of the funerary ritual. Elsewhere in Scandinavia the countryside is still dotted with small groups of Viking Age burial mounds in the tens of thousands, with massive cemeteries still visible at sites such as Birka. In the overseas colonies similarly sized cemeteries are found especially in the east at sites such as Gnezdovo near Smolensk (Androshchuk, ch. 38, below), but here Scandinavian burials are intermingled with those of other groups. In an English example, the mound cemetery at Heath Wood/Ingleby is one of the largest of its kind outside Scandinavia (though virtually alone in England), and is typically complex in including a number of empty 'graves' (Richards, ch. 27, below).

In addition to the kinds of inhumation grave usually found, there are a few isolated examples of mass graves, the main one being that excavated at Repton in Derbyshire, England (Richards, ch. 27, below). Like that deposit, similar though smaller mass graves have been ~~interpreted as the burials of battle casualties or deaths otherwise incurred on campaign.~~

CHAMBER BURIALS

A prominent form of high-status inhumation found in concentrations throughout Scandinavia sees the dead buried not in a coffin or other container but instead placed in an underground chamber. In the more modest examples, especially in Norway, this may resemble a kind of large box built *in situ* in the grave cut. The majority of the chambers, however, are the size of small rooms, constructed as square or rectangular pits with wooden walls and a raftered roof, over which a mound is usually raised. Chamber graves are known from the centuries before the Viking Age, especially in the Roman Iron Age and migration period, but it is in the ninth and especially tenth century that they reached their zenith.

They are most common in Sweden, where 111 examples have been found at Birka alone (Arbman 1940–3), while around 60 are known from Denmark and northern Germany (Eisenschmidt 1994). The latter examples cluster around Hedeby, and it ~~seems likely that the early towns were epicentres for the spread of what became an unusual but interregional burial rite~~ (Stylegar 2005). In Norway the custom was not as widespread and no such burials have yet been found at Kaupang (the nearest equivalent to Birka and Hedeby), and on present knowledge chamber graves appear as a primarily eastern and southern phenomenon. This burial form is also found in areas of Scandinavian settlement or influence abroad, especially in Russia and Ukraine where elaborate chamber graves have been excavated at Chernigov among other sites.

~~Some of the chamber graves are among the most spectacular burials known from the Viking Age. Every grave is different and many can be reconstructed as microcosms of local belief and funerary practice.~~ Only isolated examples of this rich variety can be given here, but at Hedeby the burials include a large chamber with a ship placed on top of it (Müller-Wille 1976) and the Mammen grave from Denmark represents what may be the resting place of a Viking man of princely rank. Dating to *c.* 970, the chamber was built to resemble a hall, with a pitched roof and sturdy wooden walls, all buried by a mound. Inside was a wooden coffin-box, on the lid of which lay a candle. The rich textile finds in particular have revolutionised our knowledge of high-status male dress, and the silver-inlaid axe is among the most famous finds from the whole period, giving its name to the Mammen art-style (Iversen 1991). The greatest chamber grave of Denmark, probably built for his father by King Harald Bluetooth as part of the Jelling monuments, is covered elsewhere (Roesdahl, ch. 48, below).

~~In some of the chamber graves, especially at Birka, the dead are found to have been buried seated, presumably on chairs or stools though the latter have decayed.~~ The deceased sometimes have objects placed in the hands or on the lap, with grave goods laid out around and particularly in front of them. In rare examples, as in the tenth-century grave IX at the Vendel cemetery, Uppland, Sweden, individuals are found seated in chairs on the decks of ships (Stolpe and Arne 1912: 37). Female seated burials are more common in the chambers, whereas on ships the rite is largely confined to men. Exceptionally in two chamber graves from Birka, men and women have been found buried sitting on top of each other in the same chair, the woman uppermost in both cases

(Price 2002: 132–9). Remains of slim iron chains around the bodies suggest that the corpses were tied to the back of a chair to hold them in place.

The meaning of seated burial is not known, though it is clear that in at least some instances the graves have been deliberately oriented so that the dead seem to 'look out' over a specific vista. At Birka, for example, the chamber graves with seated women are all positioned so that their occupants' faces would be turned inwards to the town, perhaps watching over it (Robbins 2004).

Seated burials are vividly described in some of the Icelandic sources, with especially detailed examples being found in *Njáls saga* and *Grettis saga* (discussed in Price 2002: 134–5). In the former, the burial mound of Gunnar of Hliðarendi inexplicably opens when two passers-by are near, and by moonlight they see him sitting in a chair, with 'lights' in his grave, singing happily. In *Grettis saga* an episode of attempted grave-robbing turns nasty when the undead occupant of the burial objects to the theft and starts to fight the intruder. The rather disturbing description of this battle inside the lightless mound makes it clear that it is a chamber grave, with even the rafters over the burial pit being mentioned. Jumping through a hole dug in the ceiling of the chamber, the robber lands on horse bones at one end of the grave, and blundering about in the dark he can feel the upright back of a chair with someone sitting in it. Even the stale air of the long-sealed tomb is described.

We should also note that seated burial is mentioned in a different kind of source, Ibn Fadlan's eyewitness account of the Volga ship cremation. Here, cushions are used to prop up the dead chieftain's body in a sitting position on top of a bench that has been made up as a bed.

SHIPS AND THE DEAD

Stone settings in the shape of ships have been mentioned above, but the most spectacular burial rite of the Viking Age involved the deposition of actual ships in the graves (Müller-Wille 1970). A second category of ship graves involves the burning of the vessel, as in the famous account of Ibn Fadlan discussed further below.

In Sweden ship burials cluster in the Mälar valley, especially at the site of Valsgärde in central Uppland, which has a continuity of boat graves at a rate of one per generation since several centuries prior to the Viking Age (Lamm and Nordström 1983). Danish ship burials are fewer in number but no less dramatic, including the remarkable grave from Ladby (Sørensen 2001) and the example from Hedeby (Müller-Wille 1976). Here the tradition of boat burial has its origins earlier in the Iron Age, and may offer clues as to the significance of the vessels in that parts of ships were buried with the dead in the absence of the complete craft (as at Slusegård: Andersen *et al*. 1991). The most dramatic examples of the ship-burial rite have been found in Norwegian Vestfold, with the famous burials at Oseberg, Gokstad and Tune (Nicolaysen 1882; Brøgger *et al*. 1917–28). Due to their unusual degree of preservation which has left not just the vessels themselves but also organic grave goods intact, these burials are among our richest sources for the detailed inventories of high-status graves anywhere in the Viking world.

Beyond Scandinavia, boat burials are found in the British Isles, especially in island communities on the Orkneys and Man. In the Northern Isles especially, these burials are sometimes lined with stones in the prow and stern (Graham-Campbell and Batey 1998: 135–40). Beyond Denmark, there is only one Scandinavian ship burial in Continental

Europe, located on the Île de Groix off the south coast of Brittany (Müller-Wille 1976; Price 1989).

The ships have usually been dragged into position within a trench dug to hold them, afterwards covered by a mound. In some cases the mast seems to have been left standing, protruding out of the top of the barrow. The burial monuments themselves can be augmented with other features, such as the circle of standing stones surrounding the Groix ship grave, and the line of stone uprights that appear to form a 'processional way' leading up to it (Müller-Wille 1976). There is also evidence that some of the burials, as at Valsgärde and Oseberg, may have been left open and accessible for some time (see below).

Typical features of ship burials include the deposition of at least one and sometimes up to three or four bodies, often interred in a small chamber built amidships, or simply laid out on the deck timbers. Many ship graves also contain very high numbers of animal sacrifices – up to twenty decapitated horses, for example, accompanied the Oseberg grave. As well as domesticates and household animals, exotic creatures such as peacocks and owls have also been found.

A massive range of grave goods can be found, including the full complement of items noted in other contexts above. At graves such as Oseberg in particular, we are able to see the variety of organic containers, baskets, boxes, chests and textiles that were present in very large quantities alongside much larger wooden items such as furniture. Sometimes subsidiary 'ship's boats' may be included, as well as a variety of land and ice vehicles (Brøgger *et al.* 1917–28).

Here too we find regional variation, sometimes startlingly so as in the case of the island of Gotland. No ship graves have been found on the island but instead Viking Age (and earlier) burials are sometimes marked by large 'picture stones' covered with engraved images and occasionally runic texts in the later examples (Lindqvist 1941–2). Common to many of these stones is a depiction of a ship under sail that occupies most of the lower section of the memorial, above which are a variety of scenes either laid out in horizontal fields or more informally arranged. The latter can sometimes be identified as motifs from Norse mythology, such as scenes from the life of the famous hero Sigurðr, but are equally often of unknown meaning. It has been suggested that these picture stones are in effect the Gotlandic equivalent of ship burials, but with their message content expressed through images rather than the physical objects that are customary on the mainland (Andrén 1993).

The exact nature of this meaning has been subject to long debate, focusing principally on the ship as means of transport for a symbolic journey or as a high-status possession either of the dead or of their wealthy relatives (Crumlin-Pedersen and Munch Tyhe 1995). While this question is not easy to resolve it is clear that the ships often contain deliberate markers of ethnicity, religion and power, and may also hold the clue to remarkable cultural interchange. One example comes from the Uppland graves as a whole, in which the presence of Sámi objects has been found in some profusion, including whole sheets of decorated birch-bark tent covers that seem to have been laid over the ships at both Vendel and Valsgärde (Price 2002: 237). DNA and dietary work at the Tuna in Alsike grave-field has also suggested that the dead interred there may have had Sámi ancestry (Price 2002: 237), raising the question of whether some of the ship-burial occupants may actually have actively maintained Sámi identities. Similarly startling results were recently obtained from new work on one of the two women from the Oseberg burial. Originally thought to have been aged about sixty–seventy and twenty-five–forty respectively when they died, analysis of tooth-root translucency in the 'younger' woman has shown that she was probably at least fifty and perhaps older still, thus closing the age gap between the two. Most interestingly, successful extraction of aDNA from one of her teeth has revealed that she belongs in mitochondrial sub-haplogroup U7, which strongly suggests that she came from the Middle East, particularly the area of modern Iran (Holck 2008: 205, 208). Very close matches in radiocarbon-dating sequences indicate that the two women most likely died at the same time, while ^{13}C analysis showed that both women had followed the same diet, perhaps implying that they were of similar status (Holck 2008: 204, 205).

Another striking aspect of the ship burials is their construction for both women and men – indeed the two women of Oseberg occupied the richest Viking Age grave ever found (though on the basis of the artefactual assemblage, one scholar has even argued that the primary burial at Oseberg was actually that of a man, whose body was completely removed when the chamber was disturbed, see Androshchuk 2005). This egalitarian ritual has considerable implications for the status of women in Viking society and accords well with other female-sponsored memorials such as the runic inscriptions mentioning bridge-building and similar activities.

HUMAN SACRIFICE

Human sacrifice in association with burial can be hard to identify with certainty, as graves with more than one occupant may represent family groupings or multiple burials due to disease, among other possibilities. However, a significant number of Viking Age graves contain individuals who were clearly killed to accompany the primary occupant of the burial in death – diagnostic injuries in these cases include decapitation, stabbing, broken necks and hanging, with the hands and/or feet sometimes being bound.

Famous examples include a man buried at Stengade with a decapitated, bound man placed beside him, both bodies covered by a heavy spear (Skaarup 1972), and a similar burial from the hill fort wall at Birka, in which the decapitated body of a young male was laid partly over that of an older man furnished with weapons and with elk antlers placed behind his head (Holmquist-Olausson 1990). Another tied, decapitated man accompanied the male buried at Lejre (Andersen 1960) while a woman's grave from Gerdrup near Roskilde contained the body of a man with a broken neck (Christensen 1981). At Ballateare on the Isle of Man, an armed male youth had been buried with grave goods and covered by a mound, on top of which a young woman was killed with a sword blow from behind, apparently while kneeling; the blow actually removed the back of her head, and the resulting detached skull fragment was oddly absent from the grave. A second layer of earth was then added to the mound, covering the woman's body (Bersu and Wilson 1966).

The human accompaniment of the dead seems to have been particularly common in connection with ship burials. The example of Oseberg has been noted above, but the most dramatic case comes from the account of Ibn Fadlan mentioned several times previously (Montgomery 2000). The ship cremation ceremony includes the murder of a young slave girl (the Arabic implies that she was about fourteen or fifteen years old), stabbed and strangled after at least six acts of rape and many more of semi-consensual sex. During the course of the rites she is seemingly drugged with some sort of beverage, and has (or says she has) a series of visions. Ibn Fadlan states specifically that the girl volunteers to accompany her owner in death, though how much coercion was involved is another matter. He mentions that slaves of both sexes might do this, and also dead men's wives. The latter are also mentioned by other Arab writers such as Ibn Rustah and Ibn Miskaweih, who describes how women might be buried alive in the chamber graves of their male partners, something perhaps confirmed by the Russian burials at Chernigov (Price 2002: 46). It is clear that more than one person might be sacrificed at Viking funerals, and there are Byzantine accounts of a Rus' army burying its war dead by full moonlight, accompanied by the mass killing of prisoners of both sexes (Price 2002: 369).

FUNERARY DRAMA AND THE RITES OF PASSING

In surveying the archaeological evidence for mortuary behaviour, we have considered the end result of burial practices but not the process by which these graves were created. An important strand of recent work on Viking death rituals has been a focus on a kind of funerary drama, in which the burial is preceded, accompanied and followed by extended periods of orchestrated action and activity. Pioneered by Terry Gunnell's research on the dramatic nature of Eddic poetry (1995 and ch. 22.1, below), and Martin Carver's work on similar 'theatres of death' at Anglo-Saxon sites (1992: 181) this approach has also been inspired by the vivid written records of Viking funerals left by several Arab travellers including Ibn Fadlan.

The latter's description of a ship cremation on the Volga in 922 is well known but not without complexity; the best English translation and commentary on its problems can be found in Montgomery (2006) and its archaeological implications are discussed in Price (2008). In brief, Ibn Fadlan relates as part of a longer journey how he witnessed the elaborate rituals surrounding the burial of a leading man among the Rus'. Involving ten days of carefully supervised activity prior to the final cremation, including the temporary burial of the dead man in a provisional grave that itself contains grave goods, the ceremonies of feasting, drinking and sex culminate in a funeral that involves dozens of people and the rape and murder of a slave girl noted above.

The central importance of this text for our understanding of Viking Age burials can hardly be overstated, especially in its implication that what we see in the archaeological remains is merely the 'stage set' at the close of a 'play', leaving only hints of the possible days of activity that precede and contextualise the actual interment or cremation. We should also consider the 'afterlife' of burials in terms of their continued active use within the community. The most striking evidence comes from the Oseberg ship burial, which has been shown to have been covered only part-way by the original mound, leaving the entire prow and forepart of the ship exposed, including the entrance to the burial chamber (Gansum 2004; Figure 19.3). Although the mound was later completed to cover the whole vessel, we do not know what kinds of activities took place around and even inside the burial in the intervening period.

More evidence for these drawn-out rituals of death comes from other ship burials, such as a boat grave from Kaupang, which exhibits a particularly prolonged sequence of activity. The scene begins with an unremarkable ninth-century male inhumation burial. Some years later in the early tenth century, and for unknown reasons, a boat was laid on top of this grave, exactly aligned with the keel covering the buried man from head to toe

Figure 19.3 A reconstruction of the Oseberg ship burial as originally built, with the ship left partially uncovered and accessible. (Drawing: Morten Myklebust, after Gansum 2004.)

– the location of the earlier grave must therefore have been carefully remembered. Within the boat lay a man and a woman laid out head-to-head along the keel line, furnished with high-status clothing and equipment; a baby lay by the woman's hip. The body of the boat was filled with objects and animals, the latter including a horse and a dismembered and butchered dog whose body parts had been carefully placed on a variety of items. Seated in the stern was a second woman, possibly with the tiller in her hands and with the severed head of the dog either in her lap or resting on an adjacent bronze cauldron. Buried with costly jewellery and dressed unusually in what appears to have been an outfit of leather, beside her on the deck lay the kind of iron object interpreted at other sites as a staff of sorcery. An axe and shield were deposited next to her and seem to be associated with this woman rather than the man on the boat floor (Stylegar 2007: 95–100). A similarly complex sequence at Klinta on Öland involved a double male–female cremation on board a boat, with the later separation of the ashes from the man, woman and animals and their deposition in separate graves nearby, all with secondary rituals over an extended period (see Price 2002: 142–9 for a detailed review of the process). These examples are far from unique.

The chamber graves in particular also exhibit a complexity that must reflect an intricate series of actions during their construction, such as the burials of possible sorceresses on Birka (Price 2002: 128–41; Figure 19.4). One of these, Bj.834, contains a double chair burial as described above, and a lance has been thrown across the seated figures in order to strike deep into the wood of the platform upon which rests a pair of draught-harnessed horses. Other burials also exhibit weapons being either stuck into chamber walls or else plunged vertically into cremation deposits (Nordberg 2002).

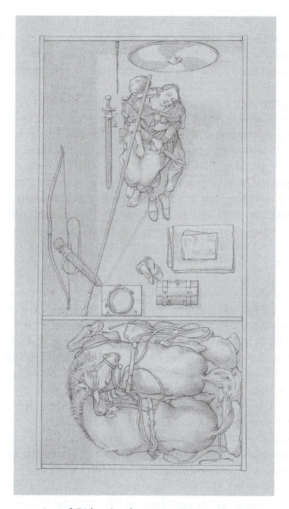

Figure 19.4 A reconstruction of Birka chamber grave Bj.834, showing a couple buried together seated on the same chair, with horses and a lance thrown over the bodies. (Drawing: Þórhallur Þráinsson, after Price 2002.)

One further element of this extended funerary behaviour may be the practice of so-called grave-robbing. While clearly some burials were merely plundered for their valuables, many of the break-ins to mounds and other graves are so extensive that they simply cannot have been done in secret or without wider social sanction – the disturbance of the Oseberg burial is a case in point. Often burials were opened (perhaps a better term than 'broken into') soon after the original interment, as seen in the still partial articulation of the corpses when they were disturbed. While some of these removals have a relatively clear motive, such as the translation of Gorm the Old's bones to the new church at Jelling, others are more obscure. Often the bodies are moved around or taken out altogether, some objects are taken while others are left alone, and sometimes it is possible to see how piles of items were shifted en masse and left where they were placed, presumably in order to access something else. Some of these interventions were very considerable in nature, such as the cutting into of the chambers in the Vestfold ship burials. Not enough work has been done on this phenomenon at present, but it seems likely to represent an integral part of the 'mortuary behaviour' that has hitherto been erroneously considered only in relation to the actual burial itself.

In considering the wider dramas of burial, Viking Age attitudes to dying and the dead should not be seen as restricted to the material culture of the graveside. One example of this is the phenomenon of hoard deposition. It has long been clear that buried hoards of silver and other metals are too numerous for them to represent nothing more than primitive banking, the Viking Age equivalent of hiding one's money under the mattress. Given the very large numbers of hoard finds within relatively small areas, especially Gotland, it is similarly evident that those doing the burying cannot *all* have died without telling anyone else where their wealth was concealed. There were probably many concurrent explanations for hoarding behaviour, but it is possible that it could relate to mortuary ritual either in the absence of a corpse or in addition to one disposed of elsewhere. There is also an alternative, relating to the actions of a person in advance of their own death. We know that some ambitious individuals were capable of erecting runic memorials to themselves in their own lifetimes, and we should therefore reconsider Snorri's suggestion that hoarded wealth could be buried by the person who had accumulated it *in order to enjoy it themselves in the afterlife*. Scholars have often been too ready to dismiss details of the *Ynglingasaga* account, and yet this is the kind of telling observation that is at least as likely to reflect Viking Age reality as it is Snorri's imagination.

Clearly, Viking funerals were complex affairs, and there is no reason to suppose that this did not apply right across the social spectrum beyond the spectacle of the ships and chambers. The vast diversity of ritual practice, and perhaps belief that underpinned it, has been mentioned above and it may be that we are looking in effect at a complex world of funerary narratives, linking the living with the dead through the storytelling medium that we know played such a central role in Viking culture (Price 2008).

THE VIKING WAYS OF DEATH

The above review of ancient burial practices is a conventional one in terms of its perhaps rather cold packaging of archaeological terminology and 'mortuary behaviour'. It is also worth remembering the individual component of emotion and loss. While we cannot know the exact feelings present in the onlookers at any funeral, grief must surely be a recurring theme. Confronting the material remains of death is not always a straightforward process for archaeologists (cf. Downes and Pollard 1999), but in an ethical context it is appropriate to respect the general dignity of the dead, and to spare a thought for the very human pain that was probably present at the construction of many of the Vikings' burial monuments.

To pursue this subject further, it may well be that the variability present in the graves is also to some degree a result of relatively spontaneous gesture, the deposition of favourite things and objects with an emotional resonance: a pebble from a habitual fishing spot, the shiny coin played with as a child, the last treasured fragment of the wine glass awarded years earlier to a warrior by his commander. The presence in graves of material culture with an enhanced personal value might also reflect a formal custom for its disposal in this way, individual but again part of a wider system. This too would fit with the idea of burials as components in a narrative, significant objects as the visual markers that identify a 'character' to an audience – the latter now being that of our own time.

The Viking ways of death were not those of the twenty-first century, but they nonetheless contained within them the human universals of loss, separation, memory and the (un)certain concern for a possible life beyond.

BIBLIOGRAPHY

Andersen, H. (1960) 'Hovedstaden i riget', *Nationalmuseets arbejdsmark*.

Andersen, S.H., Lind, B. and Crumlin-Pedersen, O. (1991) *Slusegårdgravpladsen*, vol. 3: *Gravformer og gravskikke – bådgravene*, Aarhus: Jysk Arkæologisk Selskab.

Andrén, A. (1993) 'Doors to other worlds: Scandinavian death rituals in Gotlandic perspective', *Journal of European Archaeology*, 1: 33–56.

—— (2004) 'I skuggan av Yggdrasil. Trädet mellan idé och realitet i nordisk tradition', in A. Andrén, K. Jennbert and C. Raudvere (eds) *Ordning mot kaos – studier av nordisk förkristen kosmologi*, Lund: Nordic Academic Press.

Androshchuk, F. (2005) 'En man i Osebergsgraven?', *Fornvännen*, 100: 115–28.

Arbman, H. (1940–3) *Birka I. Die Gräber*, 2 vols, Stockholm: KVHAA.

Bennett, A. (1987) *Graven – religiös och social symbol. Strukturer i folkvandringstidens gravskick i Mälarområdet* (Theses and papers in North-European archaeology 18), Stockholm: University of Stockholm.

Bersu, G. and Wilson, D.M. (1966) *Three Viking Graves in the Isle of Man* (The Society for Medieval Archaeology. Monograph 1), London: Society for Medieval Archaeology.

Beskow Sjöberg, M. *et al.* (eds) (1987–2001) *Ölands järnåldersgravfält*, 4 vols, Stockholm: Raä.

Brøgger, A.W., Falk, H. and Shetelig, H. (eds) (1917–28) *Osebergfundet*, 4 vols, Oslo: Universitetets Oldsaksamling.

Callmer, J. (1991) 'Territory and dominion in late Iron Age southern Scandinavia', in K. Jennbert, L. Larsson, R. Petré and B. Wyszomirska-Werbart (eds) *Regions and Reflections. In Honour of Märta Strömberg* (Acta archaeologica Lundensia. Series in 8°, vol. 20), Stockholm: Almqvist & Wiksell International.

—— (1992) 'Interaction between ethnical groups in the Baltic region in the late Iron Age', in B. Hårdh and B. Wyszomirska-Werbart (eds) *Contacts across the Baltic Sea* (University of Lund, Institute of Archaeology. Report 43), Lund: University of Lund.

—— (1994) 'The clay paw rite of the Åland islands and central Russia: a symbol in action', *Current Swedish Archaeology*, 2: 13–46.

Carver, M. (1992) 'Ideology and allegiance in East Anglia', in R. Farrell and C. Neuman de Vegvar (eds) *Sutton Hoo. Fifty Years After* (American early medieval studies 2), Oxford, Ohio: American Early Medieval Studies.

Christensen, T. (1981) 'Gerdrup-graven', *Romu. Årsskrift fra Roskilde Museum*, 2: 19–28.

Crumlin-Pedersen, O. and Munch Thye, B. (eds) (1995) *The Ship as Symbol in Prehistoric and Medieval Scandinavia*. (PNM – Publications from the National Museum 1), Copenhagen: National Museum of Denmark.

Downes, J. and Pollard, T. (eds) (1999) *The Loved Body's Corruption. Archaeological Contributions to the Study of Human Mortality*, Glasgow: Cruithne Press.

Eisenschmidt, S. (1994) *Kammergräber der Wikingerzeit in Altdänemark* (Universitätsforschungen zur prähistorischen Archäologie 25), Bonn: Habelt.

Eldjárn, K. (2000) *Kuml og haugfé. Úr heiðnum sið á Íslandi*. 2nd edn by Adolf Friðriksson, Reykjavík: Mál og menning.

Gansum, T. (2004) *Hauger som konstruksjoner – arkeologiske forventninger gjennom 200 år* (GOTARC. Gothenburg archaeological thesis. Serie B, vol. 33), Göteborg: Arkeologiska institutionen, Göteborgs universitet.

Graham-Campbell, J.A. and Batey, C. (1998) *Vikings in Scotland. An Archaeological Survey*, Edinburgh: Edinburgh University Press.

Gunnell, T. (1995) *The Origins of Drama in Scandinavia*, Woodbridge: Brewer.

Halsall, G. (2000) 'The Viking presence in England? The burial evidence reconsidered', in D.M. Hadley and J.D. Richards (eds) *Cultures in Contact. Scandinavian Settlement in England in the Ninth and Tenth Centuries*, Turnhout: Brepols.

Holck, P. (2008) 'The Oseberg ship burial, Norway: new thoughts on the skeletons from the grave mound', *European Journal of Archaeology*, 9(2/3): 185–210.

Hollander, L.M. (trans.) (1964) *Snorri Sturluson. Heimskringla. History of the Kings of Norway*, Austin: University of Texas Press.

Holmquist-Olausson, L. (1990) '"Älgmannen" från Birka. Presentation av en nyligen undersökt krigargrav med människooffer', *Fornvännen*, 85: 175–82.

Iversen, M. (ed.) (1991) *Mammen. Grav, kunst og samfund i vikingetid* (Jysk Arkæologisk Selskab. Skrifter 28), Højbjerg: Jysk Arkæologisk Selskab.

Lamm, J.-P. and Nordström, H.-Å. (eds) (1983) *Vendel Period Studies. Transactions of the Boat-grave Symposium in Stockholm, February 1981* (The Museum of National Antiquities. Studies 2), Stockholm: Statens Historiska Museum.

Lindqvist, S. (1941–2) *Gotlands Bildsteine*, 2 vols (KVHAA. Monografier 28), Stockholm: Wahlström & Widstrand.

Montgomery, J. (2000) 'Ibn Fadlān and the Rūsiyyah', *Journal of Arabic and Islamic Studies*, 3: 1–25.

—— (2006) *Ibn Fadlan and the Caliphal Mission through Inner Asia to the North. Voyaging the Volga.* Permanent internet resource, accessed 28 March 2008. http://wonka.hampshire.edu/abbasidstudies/html/abbasids/culture/works.html.

Müller-Wille, M. (1970) *Bestattung im Boot. Studier zu einer nordeuropäischen Grabsitte* (Offa 25/26), Neumünster: Wachholtz.

—— (1976) 'Das Bootkammergrab von Haithabu', *Berichte über die Ausgrabungen von Haithabu* 8, Neumünster: Wachholtz.

Nicolaysen, N. (1882) *Langskibet fra Gokstad ved Sandefjord*, Kristiania: Hammermeyer.

Nordberg, A. (2002) 'Vertikalt placerade vapen i vikingatida gravar', *Fornvännen*, 97: 15–24.

Price, N.S. (1989) *The Vikings in Brittany* (Saga-Book 22:6), London: Viking Society for Northern Research.

—— (2002) *The Viking Way. Religion and War in Late Iron Age Scandinavia* (Aun 31), Uppsala: Dept. of Archaeology and Ancient History, Uppsala University.

—— (2008) 'Bodylore and the archaeology of embedded religion: dramatic licence in the funerals of the Vikings', in D.M. Whitley and K. Hays-Gilpin (eds) *Faith in the Past. Theorizing Ancient Religion*, Walnut Creek, CA: Left Coast Press.

Robbins, H. (2004) 'Seated burials at Birka: a select study'. (Unpublished MA thesis, Dept. of Archaeology and Ancient History, Uppsala University.)

Roesdahl, E. (2005) 'Jordfaste mindesmærker i Danmarks yngre vikingetid', *Hikuin*, 32: 55–74.

Roesdahl, E. and Wilson, D.M. (eds) (1992) *From Viking to Crusader. Scandinavia and Europe 800–1200* (Council of Europe exhibition 22), Copenhagen: Nordisk Ministerråd.

Skaarup, J. (1972) 'Rejsekammeraten', *Skalk*, 1972(1): 4–9.

Sørensen, A.C. (2001) *Ladby. A Danish Ship-grave from the Viking Age* (Ships and boats of the North 3), Roskilde: The Viking Ship Museum.

Stolpe, H. and Arne, T.J. (1912) *Graffältet vid Vendel* (KVHAA. Monografier 3), Stockholm: KVHAA.

Strömbäck, D. (1961) 'Helskor', *KL* 6: 412.

Stylegar, F.-A. (2005) 'Kammergraver fra vikingtiden i Vestfold', *Fornvännen*, 100: 161–77.

—— (2007) 'The Kaupang cemeteries revisited', in D. Skre (ed.) *Kaupang in Skiringssal* (Kaupang Excavation Project. Publications 1), Aarhus: Aarhus University Press.

Svanberg, F. (2003) *Decolonizing the Viking Age*, 2 vols (Acta archaeologica Lundensia. Series in 8°, vol. 43 and Series in 4°, vol. 24), Stockholm: Almqvist & Wiksell International.

Terry, P. (trans.) (1990) *Poems of the Elder Edda*, Philadelphia: University of Pennsylvania Press.

Thunmark-Nylén, L. 1998–2006 *Die Wikingerzeit Gotlands*, 4 vols, Stockholm: KVHAA.

CHAPTER TWENTY

THE SCANDINAVIAN LANGUAGES IN THE VIKING AGE

———— •◆• ————

Michael P. Barnes

GERMANIC AND SCANDINAVIAN

The Scandinavian languages belong to the Germanic branch of the Indo-European language family. They are closely related to Dutch, Frisian, German, English and the extinct Gothic, and more distantly to most other European and some Asian tongues (for details, see Nielsen 1989). Precisely when Indo-European speech first arrived in what now constitutes Denmark, Norway, Sweden and north-west Germany is unclear, but recent estimates suggest a time around, or a little earlier, than 2000 BC. Germanic is thought to have begun evolving as a separate language branch soon after this, in part because of the gradual attenuation of contacts with speakers of other forms of Indo-European, but also due to influence from neighbouring tongues. A gradual expansion, dated by many between 1000 and 500 BC, saw the frontiers of Germanic pushed as far south as the present-day Netherlands and central Germany and as far east as the Wisła (Vistula). It is reckoned that at this period all Germanic speakers shared a common language, though probably with some dialectal differentiation. However, further migrations around the beginning of the Christian era led to a split into an East and North-West branch of Germanic. The latter, probably from the start a dialect continuum, was itself by the sixth century splitting into two recognisably different branches, North and West Germanic. It is from North Germanic that the Scandinavian languages are descended.

Language branches are classified on the basis of shared features. All forms of Germanic, for example, have a two-tense verb system, distinguishing present and past (there is no future, perfect or other tense form, as in many European tongues). In addition, Germanic languages form the past tense in two different ways, either by vowel change (English *sing–sang*, 'strong' inflexion) or by the addition of a dental suffix (English *walk–walked*, 'weak' inflexion). North Germanic or Scandinavian languages are also recognisable from the features they share, such as the suffixed definite article (ON *hestr* 'horse', *hestrinn* 'the horse'; Sw *häst*, *hästen*), or the *-s(k)/-st* form of the verb (ON *gerask* 'happen', from *gera* 'do'; Norw *gjøres* 'be done' from *gjøre* 'do').

VIKING AGE SCANDINAVIAN

North Germanic, just as North-West Germanic and 'Common Germanic' before it, is unlikely to have been a uniform language. The centralised authority that would seem to be a prerequisite for the development of a koiné or norm was absent. Such unity as may have existed must in any case have been disrupted by the radical linguistic changes of the syncope period (*c.* 550–700), which mark the emergence of an indubitably Scandinavian form of speech. It is inconceivable that the shortening of words, the restructuring of vowel and consonant systems and the creation of new grammatical categories associated with the syncope period can have been accomplished without massive dialectal variation. What is remarkable is the degree of linguistic uniformity that appears to have prevailed in Scandinavia after *c.* AD 700. So uniform has the language of the Vikings and stay-at-home Scandinavians appeared to some that it has been christened 'Common Scandinavian' (Haugen 1976: 150). This is clearly in part an illusion, arising from the extreme scarcity of linguistic sources. There is no doubt, however, that some unifying forces were at work, whatever they may have been. It is otherwise hard to explain why, for example, loss of initial /j-/ should have come to characterise all forms of Scandinavian, but no other kinds of Germanic (contrast mainland Scandinavian *år*, Faroese/Icelandic *ár* with English *year*, German *Jahr*; Scandinavian *ung(ur)* with English *young*, German *jung*); or why the reform of the runic alphabet that led to the jettisoning of eight of the original twenty-four characters and the simplification of many of the others should have been accepted Scandinavia-wide, apparently in the space of a few decades at the end of the seventh/beginning of the eighth century.

With the help of the meagre sources at our disposal – chiefly runic inscriptions – we can reconstruct in broad outline what Scandinavian was like in the Viking Age. Following the changes of the syncope period it had developed into a language not unlike classical Old Norse. It had twenty-seven vowel phonemes or thereabouts: nine qualitatively different sounds (/i, e, æ, a, ɔ, o, u, y, ø/) with length and nasality as additional distinctive features. Most consonants might also be long or short. There were four types of stressed syllable: short vowel + short consonant; short vowel + long consonant or consonant cluster; long vowel + short consonant or no consonant; long vowel + long consonant or consonant cluster. Length went hand-in-hand with stress; in unstressed syllables all sounds were short, and the vowel system was by and large reduced to a three-way contrast (/I, A, U/). As in all the early Germanic languages, three genders and four cases (nominative, accusative, genitive, dative) were distinguished in nouns, pronouns and adjectives; there was also a distinction between 'strong' and 'weak' adjective inflexion, strong marking indefinite and weak definite function. Viking Age Scandinavian verbs (as indicated above), had two tense forms, present and past, and the past tense might have 'strong' or 'weak' inflexion. The verb also had three moods (indicative, subjunctive, imperative), and all tensed forms had personal inflexion (different forms in most cases for 1st, 2nd and 3rd person singular and plural). There was a suffixed definite article, and an -*sk* form of the verb (cf. above). The vocabulary was inherited from earlier Germanic, with few loan words. No adequate description of Viking Age Scandinavian exists, but in its essential structure it can be taken not to have differed greatly from the more archaic forms of Old Norse.

Attempts to flesh out this skeletal structure with detail bring our ignorance about Scandinavian at the dawn of the Viking Age into sharper focus. With some forces pushing the language apart and others pulling it together, we can only speculate about how closely speech in the eighth or ninth century resembled the mixture of uniformity and diversity we find at the beginning of the manuscript age (Iceland and Norway *c.* 1100, Denmark and Sweden *c.* 1250). Possibly, as has sometimes been suggested (Liestøl 1971: 75; 1981: 262; Widmark 2001: 76–7, 82–5, 91–6), linguistic development in the early Viking Age was steered by a mercantile coastal culture based in a few influential trading centres. Imitation (or attempted imitation) of this allegedly prestigious form of speech might have promoted a rudimentary linguistic uniformity. Or there might have been rivalry between different centres of power, leading to different prestige varieties. The scenario envisaged here has to be set against the rise of royal power in Denmark and Norway in the tenth century, which must have offered alternative models of speech. Handbooks on Scandinavian linguistic history report as the earliest dialect split one between East and West, with (by and large) medieval Danish and Swedish representing East, Icelandic and Norwegian West Scandinavian. However, the age of this dichotomy is difficult to establish. It is based chiefly on phonological and morphological criteria found in medieval manuscripts, and to a lesser extent on runic inscriptions of the late Viking Age. The inscriptions do provide evidence of some differences between East and West. They indicate, for example, that monophthongisation of /ei/, /au/, /øy/ spread through Denmark in the tenth and Sweden in the eleventh century, while failing to make much headway in Norway. On the other hand, *u*-mutation (chiefly yielding /ɔ/, written ǫ in normalised Old Norse spelling) is well documented in Danish and Swedish inscriptions, and there are examples of the -*sk* verb suffix, notwithstanding two of the characteristics of (later) East Scandinavian are lack of *u*-mutation and the reduction of the -*sk* suffix to -*s*. In reality, a great many of the features presented in the handbooks as shibboleths dividing East and West (cf. e.g. Wessén 1957: 28–9) cannot be shown to have functioned as such in the Viking Age.

While it is impossible to offer anything like an adequate account of Viking Age Scandinavian, the flavour of the language can be gauged from examples. Below are given the Kälvesten (*Ög* 8, Östergötland, early 800s), Jelling II (*DR* 42, Jutland, mid-900s) and Dynna (*NIyR* 68, south-eastern Norway, early 1000s) runic inscriptions. Each is presented in transliteration (where ( ) denotes uncertain reading, [ ] editorial suppletion), followed by an edited text, an English translation and brief notes on the language.

Kälvesten

stikuʀ:karþi:kubl͡þau:
aftauintsunusin:safialaustr
miʀaiuisli:uikikʀfaþi
aukrimulfʀ

Stygguʀ gærði kumbl þau aft Øyvind sunu sinn. Sá fial austr meʀ Øyvísli. Víkingʀ fáði auk Grímulfʀ.

Stygguʀ made these memorials after Øyvindʀ his son. He fell east with Øyvísl. Víkingʀ wrote and Grímulfʀ.

R/*R* denotes the reflex of Germanic /z/, a voiced palatal fricative with sibilant quality. In Norway it seems to have coalesced with /r/ by the ninth century, but in Danish and Swedish runic tradition r and R were distinguished in some phonological environments until well into the twelfth century; in Gotland even longer. In the earliest Viking Age inscriptions, as in those from before the Viking Age, there seems to be no way of distinguishing between 'that' and 'this': *þau* defines *kumbl*, but not obviously as something close at hand or more distant. *Aft* is a short form of the preposition *eptir*, parallel to *fyr* for *fyrir* and *und* for *undir*. The short forms are on the whole earlier than their longer counterparts. *Sunu* is an old acc. sg. form with the original (pre-syncope) *-u* preserved (thus possibly also the *u* in *StygguR*, but the etymology of this name is uncertain). The demonstratives *sá, sú* are regularly used in Viking Age runic inscriptions to denote 'he', 'she'. *Fial* is an East Scandinavian variant of West Scandinavian *fell*. *Auk* is an older form of *ok* with the diphthong preserved (the conjunction is related to the verb *auka* 'increase').

Jelling II

haraltr:kunukʀ:baþ:kaurua
kubl:þausi:aft:kurmfaþursin
aukaft:þ̣aurui:muþur:sina:sa
haraltr[:]ias:sạʀ:uan:tanmaurk
ala:auk:nuruiak
:auk:t(ạ)ni[:](karþi)[:]kristnạ

Haraldr konungʀ bað gǫrva kumbl þausi aft Gorm faður sinn auk aft Þórví móður sína. Sá Haraldr es séʀ vann Danmǫrk alla auk Norveg auk dani gærði kristna.

King Haraldr ordered these memorials to be made after GormR, his father, and after Þórví, his mother. That Haraldr who won for himself all Denmark and Norway and made the Danes Christian.

There is disagreement about what the sequences **au** and **ia** denote in Danish inscriptions of the mid- and late Viking Age. Some argue that after the East Scandinavian monophthongisation /ei/ > /e:/, /au, øy/ > /ø:/, digraphic spellings were used to denote vowel sounds for which the runic alphabet of the time had no specific symbols, **au** denoting /ø/ or /ɔ/ and **ia** /æ/. Others believe that in the case of **ia**, at least, some kind of diphthongisation is reflected (cf. Swedish dialectal *jär* as a reflex of *hér* 'here', sometimes seen as a relic of the Viking Age 'trading-centre norm'). We may note that **au** became a common way of indicating /ɔ/ throughout the Scandinavian runic world – including the West where there was no monophthongisation. While acc. *faður* lacks labial mutation, as commonly in East Scandinavian, the second element of *Danmǫrk* would seem to have a mutated vowel. In the East Scandinavian of the Viking Age the demonstrative pronoun meaning 'this/these' usually consisted of the basic pronoun *sá, sú, þat* plus the deictic (pointing) particle *-sa* or *-si*. Hence *þennsi* (acc. m. sg.), *þassi* (< *þaʀ + si*, acc. f. pl.), *þausi* (acc. n. pl.).

Dynna

×**kunuur**×**kirþi**×**bru**×**þririkstutir**×**iftira̞sriþi**×**tutur**×**sina**×**suuasmarhanarst**×**a̞haþalanti**

Gunnvǫr gerði brú, Þrýðriks dóttir, eptir Ásríði, dóttur sína. Sú vas mær hǫnnurst á Haðalandi.

Gunnvǫr, Þrýðrikr's daughter, made a bridge after Ásríðr, her daughter. She was the handiest maid in Haðaland.

How far the carver of this inscription used mutated ǫ in his/her speech is uncertain. The third **u** in **kunuur** clearly indicates a vowel other than /a/, but there the rounding of the vowel is assisted by the immediately preceding [w]. In **hannarst**, on the other hand (normalised as *hǫnnurst* in keeping with standardised Old Norse orthography), a pronunciation /hanːarst/ seems most likely. This fits with what we know of later eastern Norwegian, where *u*-mutation is much less consistent than in the West. *Mær* is from older *māʀ*, with replacement of the palatal fricative (see Kälvesten above) by /r/, and front mutation /a/ > /æ/ presumed to have been caused by the palatal before its replacement.

SCANDINAVIAN IN THE COLONIES

As a result of Viking expansion and settlement Scandinavian-speaking communities were established in areas as diverse as Normandy, the British Isles, the Faroes, Iceland, Greenland, coastal Finland and Russia. If we assume that dialectal variation of one kind or another existed during the period of settlement, it follows that differing forms of Scandinavian will have been in use in the colonies. It is, however, impossible to know what first-generation immigrant speech in, say, England, Iceland, Ireland or Russia, was like. In those areas where Scandinavian subsequently died out, the most we can hope for are occasional glimpses of the language, mostly from well after the original period of settlement. It is no surprise to discover that a recent book on linguistic relations between speakers of Old Norse and Old English stresses how hard it is to identify dialectal features in the Scandinavian of England (Townend 2002: 28). The varieties of colonial Scandinavian that survived – Icelandic, Faroese and Finland-Swedish – by the time they are first attested, represent the products of several hundreds of years (at least) of linguistic levelling (Finland-Swedish, indeed, must be in part, if not wholly, the legacy of Swedish incursions into Finland in the twelfth century and later).

Certain things can nevertheless reasonably be concluded about the linguistic legacy of the Viking expansion. In Normandy and Russia the kind of Scandinavian spoken is likely to have reflected that in use in ninth- and tenth-century Denmark and Sweden respectively, since it is from those regions that the bulk of the settlers appear to have come. In both places Scandinavian is likely to have died out after two or three generations, and in neither did it leave more than a faint impression on the indigenous language(s).

In most parts of the British Isles Scandinavian will have lasted a while longer: in England because of new waves of immigration in the tenth and early eleventh centuries; in Ireland as a result of its concentration in urban centres; in the Isle of Man and the

Hebrides due to the relatively high density of Scandinavian speakers; in north-eastern Caithness, Orkney and Shetland because of the total subjugation, possibly even extermination, of the native population. Scandinavian influence on English was heavy: scores of everyday words were borrowed, including even the 3rd person pronouns *they, them, their*; in the areas of settlement in England place names of Norse origin abound. How long the language survived as a spoken idiom is uncertain, but there is runic evidence for the use of (a very aberrant form of) Scandinavian in north-west England as late as the twelfth century (Barnes 2003a: 7–8). Scandinavian influence on Irish is less profound; a number of loan words have been identified, but few place names. Runic inscriptions of both Danish/Swedish and Norwegian type were being carved in Dublin in the period *c.* 950–1100, but whether by residents of the town or visitors is impossible to say. The Isle of Man boasts over thirty runic inscriptions, mainly of Norwegian type, and a spread of Norse place names. With its apparently large and dominant immigrant population, one might expect Scandinavian speech to have survived longer here than in England or Ireland, and some have suggested a date in the fourteenth century for its final demise. However, there is already considerable evidence of Gaelic influence in the Norse of the earliest (tenth-century) inscriptions and two of the latest, perhaps from the end of the twelfth century, show signs of having been made by someone unacquainted with runic script, possibly even with the Norse language (Page 1992: 136). Scandinavian speech left its mark on Hebridean place nomenclature and on Hebridean Gaelic, especially in the island of Lewis. Estimates of how long the language survived there have varied from the thirteenth to the early fifteenth century (Barnes 1993: 77–8).

In Orkney, Shetland and north-eastern Caithness Scandinavian must have completely replaced the indigenous language or languages by the end of the tenth century, if not before. We nevertheless know very little about the form of Scandinavian in use in the Orkney earldom during the Viking Age since almost all our sources are from a later period. A few of the runic inscriptions preserved in the islands are probably from the tenth or eleventh century, but they are extremely laconic and confirm nothing more than that Orkney and Shetland were part of the West Scandinavian runic province (Barnes 1998: 9–11). The literary, onomastic and later linguistic records combine to suggest that the bulk of the settlers hailed from western Norway (roughly the area between present-day Nord-Trøndelag and Vest-Agder; Barnes 1998: 2–4), and that clearly coloured the type of language that developed there. Ultimately Northern-Isles and Caithness Scandinavian succumbed to Lowland Scots and English, in Caithness perhaps in the fourteenth or fifteenth century, in Orkney and Shetland between 1750 and 1800.

Greenland Scandinavian, according to medieval literary sources, was first and foremost an Icelandic emigrant language. That does not help us greatly in determining what form or forms it took during the Viking Age since we do not know how uniform or varied speech in Iceland was around AD 1000. The hundred or so runic inscriptions that have been found in Greenland indicate, unsurprisingly, that the Scandinavian in use there in the Middle Ages was of West Scandinavian type. Greenlandic Scandinavian died out with the demise of the Eastern settlement *c.* 1500.

Faroese and Icelandic are also West Scandinavian, quintessentially so, but whether that was the case from the beginning is unclear (Iceland has no runic inscriptions of Viking Age date, and the few from the Faroes are no more linguistically informative than those from Orkney and Shetland). Both countries seem to have been settled from a variety of places, and by speakers of other languages besides Scandinavian. It is thus something of a surprise to find that the so-called *First Grammatical Treatise*, compiled in Iceland probably in the first half of the twelfth century (Haugen 1972), treats Icelandic as though it were a variation-free tongue. Possibly 200–250 years was enough to even out all major differences of speech, but conceivably the author was describing a literary norm used by poets and scholars.

Viking Age Finland is all but bereft of Scandinavian documents (a runic fragment has recently been found, but it tells us nothing about the type of Scandinavian spoken there; Åhlén *et al.* 1998). The modern Swedish dialects of Finland do not exhibit all the East Scandinavian features associated with Swedish in Sweden. For example, they preserve the historical diphthongs /ei/, /au/, /øy/, but that can hardly reflect West Scandinavian input since they share this characteristic with Gotlandic and a number of dialects in the north of Sweden.

BIBLIOGRAPHY

Åhlén, M., Tuovinen, T. and Myhrman, H. (1998) 'Ett nyfunnet runstensfragment från Hitis i Åboland, Finland', *Nytt om runer*, 13: 14–15.

Barnes, M. (1993) 'Norse in the British Isles', in A. Faulkes and R. Perkins (eds) *Viking Revaluations*, London: Viking Society for Northern Research.

—— (1998) *The Norn Language of Orkney and Shetland*, Lerwick: Shetland Times.

—— (2003a) 'Norse, Celtic and English in the Scandinavian runic inscriptions of the British Isles', in L.-O. Delsing *et al.* (eds) *Grammatik i fokus/Grammar in Focus*, 2 vols, Lund: Institutionen för nordiska språk, Lunds universitet.

—— (2003b) 'Standardisation and variation in Migration- and Viking-Age Scandinavian', in Kristján Árnason (ed.) *Útnorðr. West Nordic Standardisation and Variation*, Reykjavík: University of Iceland Press.

—— (2005) 'Language', in R. McTurk (ed.) *A Companion to Old Norse-Icelandic Literature and Culture*, Oxford: Blackwell.

DR = Jacobsen, L. and Moltke, E. (1941–2) *Danmarks runeindskrifter*, 2 vols, Copenhagen: Munksgaard.

Haugen, E. (1972) *First Grammatical Treatise*, 2nd edn, London: Longman.

—— (1976) *The Scandinavian Languages*, London: Faber and Faber.

Liestøl, A. (1971) 'The literate Vikings', in P. Foote and D. Strömbäck (eds) *Proceedings of the Sixth Viking Congress*, London: Viking Society for Northern Research.

—— (1981) 'The Viking runes: the transition from the older to the younger *fuþark*', *Saga-Book*, 20: 247–66.

Nielsen, H.F. (1989) *The Germanic Languages*, Tuscaloosa: University of Alabama Press.

NIyR = Olsen, M. *et al.* (1941, in progress) *Norges innskrifter med de yngre runer*, 6 vols, Oslo: Kjeldeskriftfondet.

Ög = Brate, E. (1911–18) *Östergötlands runinskrifter*, Stockholm: KVHAA.

Page, R.I. (1992) 'Celtic and Norse on the Manx rune-stones', in H.L.C. Tristram (ed.) *Medialität und mittelalterliche insulare Literatur*, Tübingen: Gunter Narr Verlag.

Parsons, D.N. (2001) 'How long did the Scandinavian language survive in England? Again', in J. Graham-Campbell *et al.* (eds) *Vikings and the Danelaw*, Oxford: Oxbow Books.

Townend, M. (2002) *Language and History in Viking Age England*, Turnhout: Brepols.

Wessén, E. (1957) *De nordiska språken*, 5th impr., Stockholm: Filologiska föreningen vid Stockholms Högskola.

Widmark, G. (2001) *Det språk som blev vårt*, Uppsala: Kungl. Gustav Adolfs Akademien för svensk folkkultur.

CHAPTER TWENTY-ONE

RUNES

———— ·◆· ————

Henrik Williams

In the church of Forsa in the province of Hälsingland in north-eastern Sweden there has hung from ancient times a ring of iron, a foot in diameter and covered with some 200 runic characters that have been impressed into the metal by means of a chisel. The inscription has been interpreted as dealing with fines to the bishop when divine services had been illicitly cancelled. The word *staff* was taken to imply the bishop and the sequence **lirþiR** to be *lærðir* 'learned men', hence the Christian context and a dating of the ring to the twelfth century.

In 1979 the great Norwegian runologist Aslak Liestøl published a new reading of a single rune in the text, the **r** in **lirþiR**. By comparing it to all other **r**:s and **u**:s, he could prove that in fact we are dealing with a **u**-rune and the word **liuþiR** *ljóðir* 'people'. All Christian connections disappear and, instead, we have the first Scandinavian legal act in writing, dated (now in consistency with the language used) to the early Viking Age (Brink 1996, 2002).

Herein lie the value and importance of the scholarship devoted to the runes. The correct reading of a single character can change the entire meaning of a runic text and make it older by several hundred years. The runic evidence in itself is of unsurpassed value to our knowledge of life in the Viking Age. Runestone texts and other runic inscriptions constitute the only original sources to this period. Through the first stages of Old Danish, Old Norwegian and Old Swedish we hear a faint echo of the voices of the Vikings, and their documents give us unique insight into intellectual culture, mentalities and society. Runic writing provides evidence of legal practices, naming patterns including the aspect of social history, religious faiths and influence, burial customs, rules for inheritance, and literary tastes. Also as sources to settlement history, gender studies and the early Scandinavian languages the runic data is irreplaceable.

RUNES AND RUNIC ORTHOGRAPHY

Yet, all of this knowledge is derived from one of the least sophisticated writing systems in the world. The sixteen runes of the Viking Age are insufficient to represent all of the phonemes (speech sounds) used. Thus many runes had to serve more that one purpose. These sixteen runes were arranged in three groups (called *ættir* 'families') and in a deviant, yet unexplained order. This writing system is called the *Futhark* after the initial six runes and it exists in two main variants, the long-branch runes (also called normal or Danish runes) and the short-twig runes (also called Swedo-Norwegian runes), plus one unusual variant, the staveless runes (also called the Swedish or Hälsinge runes). The latter lack the main staff (except for the i-rune) and always had to be written within a text band, since height placement was crucial (Peterson 1994a). This variant has been derived from short-twig runes, but recently a case has been made for the long-branch runes being the origin (Fridell 2000).

The runes are commonly 'transliterated', that is, printed with bold type Latin letters, which tells you little about the actual pronunciation (cf. Thompson 1981). Runes, transliterations, Old Icelandic designation ('rune name') and *ætt*, and the most important pronunciation variants of each rune are listed in Table 21.1.

Some comments are needed. Most runes had minor or major variants, such as ↑ **s** and ↑ **m**. They could also be reversed (Sw *vändrunor*) or inverted (Sw *stuprunor*): ↑ ~ ↑ and ↑ ~ ↑, respectively, and they could be ligatured (Sw *bindrunor*): ↑ + ↑ = ↑, sometimes many on a common staff (see comprehensive treatment by MacLeod 2002).

The runic designations are nouns which start, or in one case ends, with the sound that the rune was primarily used for (cf. Bauer 2003: 7). The *ætt* division is ancient and of unexplained origin, but constituted a handy way of creating ciphers based on placement in respective *ætt* (the order of which also could be reversed). Thus the s-rune would be designated 2:5 in some manner (for example by 2 long and 5 short strokes, the so-called *ísrúna*-system). A few of the phonetic symbols perhaps need an explanation (Table 21.2).

Table 21.1   The three Viking Age variants of the runic script

Number	Long-branch	Short-twig	Staveless	Designation	Transliteration	Common sound values	Ætt
1	ᚠ	ᚠ	ᛁ	*fé*	**f**	*f ff w*	Freyr's
2	ᚢ	h	|	*úrr*	**u**	*u y o ø au øy w*	
3	þ	ᛑ	!	*þurs*	**þ**	*θ ð*	
4	ᚦ	ᚴ	≤ ?	*óss, áss*	**o ą**	*o ã*	
5	R	R	l	*reið*	**r**	*r ř R RR*	
6	ᚲ	ᚲ	ᛁ	*kaun*	**k**	*k kk g gg nk ng*	
7	ᚼ	ᛏ	l	*hagall*	**h**	*h γ*	Hagall's
8	ᛏ	ᚽ	᛬	*nauð*	**n**	*n nn*	
9	|	|	ᛁ	*íss*	**i**	*i æ e æi*	
10	ᛏ	ᚽ	᛬	*ár*	**a**	*a æ e æi*	
11	ᛍ	ᛁ	ᛁ	*sól*	**s**	*s ss*	
12	ᛏ	ᛁ	ᛨ	*týr*	**t**	*t tt d dd nt nd*	Tyr's
13	ᛒ	ᚽ	᛬	*bjarkan*	**b**	*b bb p pp mb mp*	
14	ᚤ	ᛏ	ᛓ	*maðr*	**m**	*m mm*	
15	ᚱ	ᚱ	᛬	*lǫgr*	**l**	*l ll*	
16	ᛘ	ᛁ	᛬	*ýr from ýʀ*	**ʀ**	*ʀ ʀʀ y æ*	

Table 21.2 Phonetic symbols

Symbol	Pronounced as
y	Germ. *Tür*, Fre. *lune*
ø	Eng. *bird*, Fre. *peu*
θ	Eng. *thin*
ð	Eng. *other*
ǫ	Eng. *tall*
ã	Fre. *blanc* (cf. Williams 1990: 28–34)
r	Scott. *red*
R	Eng. *red*? (Larsson 2002b: 28–33)
γ	Dan. *bog* (a fricative *g*)
æ	Eng. *man*

Spacing of words was not mandatory. Runes were not always doubled if the same character happened to occur at the end of one word and initially in the following, nor were they doubled when representing long phonemes. If /n/ or /m/ preceded a similar consonant no representation was necessary (Williams 1994). This parsimonious system sometimes leads to texts that are difficult to interpret. A modern parallel would be if we wrote the sequence **buliftusitunilusuks** to express the (admittedly somewhat unexpected) sentence 'Pull left to send down Nelly's socks!' If we add the complications of a thousand-year-old language and an imperfect knowledge of the contents to be expected in a Viking Age runic text, it stands to reason that interpretation of an inscription can be quite a formidable exercise.

The rune carvers were, however, conscious of this difficulty and had ways to make it easier on the reader. First of all, most inscriptions do separate at least some individual words by using word dividers in the form of (double) points, (double) crosses, or other punctuation marks. Secondly, already in the tenth century there appeared dots on three of the most common runes to mark that these were not used in their usual manner. The **u-**, **k-** and **i-**runes were dotted to create ø (**y**), g (**g**), and e (**e**), respectively.

READING RUNESTONE INSCRIPTIONS

But the best help to the reader then as well as now when deciphering a runic text was that almost all of the ones occurring on stone memorials followed an established pattern. Since runestones constitute the great majority of extant runic markers, most inscriptions are therefore not that difficult to understand.

The runestone formula may be summarised in the following way: 'X (and Y) raised this stone in memory of Z, their relative.' Each part of the formula may vary, but the pattern is very regular. In addition to this memorial formula up to three additional elements may occur: obituaries, prayers, and signatures (Hübler 1996: 38–41), usually in that order but seldom all three present simultaneously. On the runestone from Söderby in the province of Gästrikland (Gs 13), however, the three additional elements are found:

Brúsi lét rétta stein þenna eptir Egil, bróður sinn. En hann varð dauðr á Tafeistalandi, þá Brúsi fœrði langlenz(?) eptir bróður sinn. Hann fór meðr Freygeiri. Guð hjalpi hans sálu ok Guðs móðir. Sveinn ok Ásmundr þeir mǫrkuðu.

Brúsi had this stone erected in memory of Egill, his brother. And he died in Tafeistaland, when Brúsi carried long-lance after his brother. He travelled with Freygeirr. May God and God's mother help his soul. Sveinn and Ásmundr, they marked (=carved).

Tafeistaland is part of present-day Finland and this is where Egill met his fate. His brother, who also commissioned the runestone, presumably took over the job as *merkis-maðr* ('carrier of the battle banner') after Egill died (Williams MS).

By knowing and expecting this formulaic content, the reader of an inscription was well equipped to decode inscriptions with even the most challenging orthography. For example, an inscription such as the one on the runestone at Eckersholm in the province of Småland (Sm 55) reads:

hakR:kulkR:aukR·kuþkurR:riþ:itRn:þan:isunR:auti:Rtinf

By applying strictly logical arguments based on the expected formula, Evert Salberger (2001: 101–2) finally managed to 'crack the code' of this apparent gibberish and propose an interpretation which may be summarised:

Haki, Kolki, Auki, mœðgur rei(s)t(u) (s)tein þenn(a), syni(r), epti(r) Stein f(ǫður).

Haki, Kolki, Auki (and) mother and daughter(s) erected this stone, the sons after Steinn, (their) father.

Except for the word *mœðgur* this is a very convincing suggestion. The 'formulaic words' of this inscription are frequently abbreviated or written in a deviant fashion, whereas the personal names are less aberrant, as indeed they had to be. Through the established formula, the reader knew which words were names and which were not. For the latter, only a suggestion has to be made through orthographic means in order for the reader to understand which word is implied. For the former, however, stricter spelling is necessary if the reader is to know exactly which personal name is intended (Salberger 2001: 67, 83).

But the formula alone serves the purpose in the vast majority of cases, without the need for intricate analysis. What is of interest is the distribution and contents of the runic texts when decoded.

NUMBER AND DISTRIBUTION OF RUNIC INSCRIPTIONS

We know of almost 3,000 Scandinavian runic inscriptions from the Viking Age. In the most recent inventory of the Scandinavian runic-text database (accessed 26 August 2004), these inscriptions are distributed in the following manner within the borders of present-day countries: Sweden 2,270, Denmark 400, Norway 138, the Faroes 2,

Great Britain and Eire 76. But more are being added continuously due to new finds and updated sources.[1]

It must be stressed, however, that both the period and the material itself are problematic (cf. Palm 1992). The 'Viking Age' to runologists ends as late as 1130, and indeed a third of this type of runestones are now dated to the period after 1050. Also, hundreds of inscriptions are found on, for example, grave slabs and coins, artefacts usually associated with the Middle Ages. It is evident, therefore, that the runic material should rather be divided into two parts, the split occurring around the year 1000. Before this date the Danish runestones command the scene although there are also small amounts of monuments in Norway and Sweden, as well as some runic inscription on other artefacts. After the shift of the millennium, the runestone tradition of Sweden really gains ground and inscriptions with a Christian content and/or ornamentation begin to dominate. From this point on the runic medium is used for other purposes, as well, but the fashion of 'proper runestones' does not lose its popularity for more than a century, at least not in the central part of Sweden where the Christian Church is slowest to establish itself in more formal respects. Once the building of (public) church buildings is widespread in an area, runic memorials take the form of standing or lying grave markers in or outside the temple.

The method of dating runestones based on their ornamentation is a recent discovery, developed by Anne-Sofie Gräslund (2003 with references). (For a deeper discussion of this problem, see Gräslund and Lager, ch. 46, below.) Earlier, linguistic methods have proved unreliable (Williams 1990: 183; Lagman 1990: 157), although linguistic variation with a typological chronology may in the future become important as a supplementary means of dating.

Just as the runestones are unevenly spread in time, they are unsymmetrically distributed within the Scandinavian countries. In Norway there are no concentrations to talk of, runestones occurring throughout inhabited areas. In Denmark there are centres in north-eastern Jutland and southern Skåne, as well as on Bornholm. On Swedish soil the majority of memorials are erected in the provinces around Lake Mälaren in central Sweden, although Östergötland, Västergötland, Småland, Öland and Gotland also evidence about a hundred or more stones. For the most recent distribution maps, see Sawyer (2000: 12–13). Runic practices did vary regionally to some extent, usually depending on variation in the dialect spoken (Williams 1996 with references).

CONTENTS OF RUNIC TEXTS

Contents, finally, vary as much as do other factors, although the memorial formula is always present. The reason for this could be purely commemorative. But it has been suggested that 'almost *all* inscriptions reflect inheritance and property rights' (Sawyer 2000: 47). This implies that literacy had become more formalised in Scandinavian eleventh-century society than previously thought, an intriguing possibility, but fraught with problems. It has also been proposed that almost all missionary-period inscriptions had a Christian purpose, even the 'neutral' ones without cross or prayer (Williams 1999). Since I am responsible for the latter idea, it behoves me to admit that I now consider all absolute positions too extreme. Runestone production obviously has its roots in the memorial tradition. In the later part of the Viking Age, the medium was expanded to include other aspects of commemoration such as obituaries, but also for adding other types of material. Hereditary information was deemed interesting, whether it was 'useful' in a legal sense or not. (Obituaries certainly are not.) The Church could not fail to see the worth of the runestone medium, used as it was to written documents. The concluding prayer *Einn er Guð* 'God is one' on the Galteland stone (N 184) reached a wide audience. The combination of a traditional memorial inscription and ornamentation with a Christian prayer and incorporated cross was a powerful means of demonstrating your adherence to a presumably fashionable faith, as well as a method of spreading the religion. Runestone raising was, we must remember, almost exclusively restricted to the landed class of society. If this group accepted the new creed, others could be influenced or coerced to embrace it.

But runic texts do not only deal with the mundane and the religious exclusively. There are also literary aspects: commemoratory poetry occurs regularly, especially in the Swedish province of Södermanland (Hübler 1996: 167–8). The earliest attested *dróttkvætt* stanza occurs on the Karlevi stone (Öl 1), as well as the first stanza of *fornyrðislag* on the Rök stone (Ög 136). Runic poetry fits in well with the rest of the Old Norse corpus, and should not be forgotten when discussing it. The material is presented fully in Larsson (2005).

The memorial formula varies little, but it nevertheless provides crucial information about Viking Age society. The sex of the commemorator(s) and the deceased and the family structure are data that have been used for important studies (Sawyer 2000), although not all are equally convincing (see Jesch 1994).

As important are the personal names prolific in the inscriptions, some 1,400 separate names in all, 75 per cent of which denote men (Peterson 2002: 3). Only approximately half a per cent of all names are of non-Scandinavian origin, the exceptions stemming from names 'borrowed' from Christian saints or royal families (Larsson 2002a: 50, 53–4 with references). Most of the names are made up of two parts, for example *Guðlaug* and *Þorsteinn* to choose the most common ones of either sex. In the Viking Age this type of name no longer had any 'meaning' but was simply handed down through the generations or made up from randomly combined elements, resulting in unique combinations.

More interesting, perhaps, are appellations which are only secondary as names, that is, the bynames (nicknames) so commonly found in medieval sources, for example *Haraldr hinn hárfagri* 'fair-haired'. In the runic inscriptions names of this type usually stand alone, as the only name of a person. These 'absolute bynames' constitute a unique source to the social history and mentality of Viking Age Scandinavians. Many common names were probably bynames originally, such as *Dóttir* 'daughter' and *Gás* 'goose'. Others are of a more obvious byname character: *Spjúti* 'he with a spear', *Kárr* 'curly hair' and *Fundinn* 'foundling'. Many phenomena could inspire a byname, for example characteristics of the human body such as the colour of hair (*Hvíthǫfði* 'white head = hair') and beard (*Kanpr* 'moustache'), or shape of parts of the body like the forehead (*Ennibrattr* 'steep forehead'), nose (*Eikinefr* 'oaken nose'), lips (*Varrfeitr* 'fat lips') and feet (*Fótr*). Distinctive speech (*Dragmáll* 'drawling speech'), abilities (*Spár* 'prophetic') or behaviour (*Styrr* 'tumult') could also lead to the coining of a nickname.

Names which certainly stimulate our imagination are the ones that start with the negative prefix *Ó-* 'un-', such as *Ófeigr* 'undying', *Órœkja* 'uncaring' and *Óþveginn* 'unwashed' (Williams 1993). The type is old, but seems especially popular in the Old Scandinavian society, perhaps because these superficially negative names had become favourites among the Viking warriors, where hurtful actions and bad behaviour were not always frowned upon. Successful Vikings bearing names of this type probably passed them on to later generations.

RUNIC RESEARCH: ISSUES AND FUTURE CHALLENGES

Most of the runic inscriptions are now published in scholarly editions, and almost all are available in some form (see note 1). But the work for runologists is far from over. It is now time to utilise the material, which has so far mostly been inventoried, at least from the linguistic point of view. Historians of all creeds have already, as I have shown, begun to mine the runic texts, but there is so much more to be learned. Runology as a discipline, however, is primarily philological (Peterson 1995). Until an inscription is properly published and its meaning firmly established, the text cannot be utilised by other scholars. And there is much to be done in this field. Many passages are still unclear, due to damages or misunderstandings. Since the material is not that large, even a few inscriptions can make a lot of difference. Many names are misinterpreted or yet remain wholly uninterpreted. Behind these are often found the more uncommon types of bynames, the very material that tells us the most about naming patterns. Personal names have been erroneously analysed regarding the sex of their bearers, which can lead historians to the wrong conclusions.

We also have a poor understanding of the communicative situation of the runic texts: who and how many could read and write runes? What were the mental tools used to decode an inscription and what were the orthographical rules more precisely? Since the runes are ambiguous, we have to spend extra care in determining which interpretations are at all possible and which one is obviously the correct one, or at least the most likely. What role did the 'nonsense' inscriptions play in the corpus (cf. Meijer 1997)? Why would anyone carve a runic text or a part of one that does not make sense, and are these inscriptions and passages really meaningless? The first steps towards the understanding of these complex issues have been taken (Lagman 1989), but much remains to be done.

As for the linguistic issues, there is a word index to the Rune-Swedish inscriptions (Peterson 1994b), which is currently being translated into English (http://runic dictionary.nottingham.ac.uk/). There are also book-length studies of some runic orthographic/phonological phenomena (Williams 1990; Lagman 1990; Larsson 2002b) and much material on Old Scandinavian languages to be found in Bandle *et al.* (2003). But there is no proper dictionary of Viking Age language, no grammar dealing with its phonology, morphology and syntax (Peterson 1996: 23), nor is there any handbook of runology (stepping-stones are laid in Thompson 1975 and Barnes 1994). All of these works need to be written, not least because many reinterpretations are likely to result from such work.

Another major runological research effort must be directed towards the runographers, the artists carving the runestone inscriptions and sometimes signing with their names. Many runographers have received some attention and a couple, Asmundr Kárason and Øpir, full-length treatments (Thompson 1975 and Åhlén 1997, respectively). One monograph has been published on all the carvers in a region (Stille 1999) and one on the technical aspects of rune carving (Kitzler 2002). But we are still far from understanding all the important circumstances relating to the runographers (cf. Williams 2000): did several usually cooperate and, if so, is there a pattern to who was responsible for (what parts of) the runic inscription and who for the ornamentive parts? Why are only certain inscriptions signed, and does the signature always indicate who actually carried out the work? Were there carvers' schools with masters and pupils? Is the orthography of the runographer influenced by her or his dialect, region, colleagues or customers?

CONCLUSION

The study of runology is old, but still in its beginnings. Viking Age runestones have received much attention but have much more to contribute to our knowledge of contemporary society and language. Other inscriptions, for example on so-called runic amulets, are only beginning to be studied as a group. The runic material may not be large, but it is of extraordinary richness, variety and value.

NOTE

1   The runic inscriptions of the various countries are published as follows. Britain: Barnes and Page (2006), Holman (1996), Page (1995); Denmark (including Skåne, Halland and Blekinge): DR and Moltke (1985); Gotland: SRI 11–12, Snædal (2002); Ireland: Barnes *et al.* (1997); Norway (including Bohuslän and Jämtand): Niyr and Spurkland (2001); Sweden: SRI and Jansson (1987). New finds are published in *Nytt om runer*, now also available on the Internet. The entire corpus, including unpublished texts, is available through *Scandinavian runic-text data base*, now also available in English, along with updated readings and interpretations in addition to translations of (virtually) all texts.

BIBLIOGRAPHY

Åhlén, M. (1997) *Runristaren Öpir. En monografi* (Runrön 12), Uppsala: Swedish Science Press.

Bandle, O. *et al.* (eds) (2003) *The Nordic Languages. An International Handbook of the History of the North Germanic Language*, vol. 1, Berlin and New York: Walter de Gruyter.

Barnes, M.P. (1994) 'On types of argumentation in runic studies', in J. Knirk (ed.) *Proceedings of the Third International Symposium on Runes and Runic Inscriptions, Grindaheim, Norway, 8–12 August 1990* (Runrön 9), Uppsala: Swedish Science Press.

Barnes, M.P., Hagland, J.R. and Page, R.I. (1997) *The Runic Inscriptions of Viking Age Dublin* (Medieval Dublin excavations 1962–81, B:5), Dublin: Royal Irish Academy.

Barnes, M.P. and Page, R.I. (2006) *The Scandinavian Runic Inscriptions of Britain* (Runrön 19), Uppsala: Institutionen för nordiska språk, Uppsala universitet.

Bauer, A. (2003) *Runengedichte. Texte, Undersuchungen und Kommentare zur gesamten Überlieferung* (Studia Medievalia Septentrionalia 9), Vienna: Fassbinder.

Brink, S. (1996) 'Forsaringen. Nordens äldsta lagbud', in E. Roesdahl and P. Meulengracht Sørensen (eds) *Beretning fra femtende tvaerfaglige vikingesymposium* (Beretning fra Det Tvaerfaglige Vikingesymposium 15), Højbjerg: Hikuin.

—— (2002) 'Law and legal customs in Viking Age Scandinavia', in J. Jesch (ed.) *Scandinavians from the Vendel Period to the Tenth Century* (Studies in historical archaeoethnology 5), Woodbridge: Boydell and Brewer.

DR = *Danmarks runeindskrifter*, 2 vols, L. Jacobsen and E. Moltke (eds) together with A. Bæksted and K.M. Nielsen (1941–2), Copenhagen: Ejnar Munkgaards Forlag.

Fridell, S. (2000) 'De stavlösa runornas ursprung', *Saga och sed*: 85–100.

Gräslund, A.-S. (2003) 'Runensteine', *RGA* 25: 585–91.

Gs = *Gästriklands runinskrifter* (SRI 15).

Holman, K. (1996) *Scandinavian Runic Inscriptions in the British Isles. Their Historical Context* (Senter for middelalderstudier. Skrifter 4), Trondheim: Tapir.

Hübler, F. (1996) *Schwedische Runendichtung der Wikingerzeit* (Runrön 10), Uppsala: Swedish Science Press.

Jansson, S.B.F. (1987) *Runes in Sweden*, Stockholm: Gidlunds.

Jesch, J. (1994) 'Runic inscriptions and social history: some problems of method', in J. Knirk (ed.) *Proceedings of the Third International Symposium on Runes and Runic Inscriptions, Grindaheim, Norway, 8–12 August 1990* (Runrön 9), Uppsala: Swedish Science Press.

Kitzler Åhfeldt, L. (2002) *Work and Worship. Laser Scanner Analysis of Viking Age Rune Stones*, Stockholm: Archaeological Research Laboratory.

Lagman, S. (1989) 'Till försvar för runristarnas ortografi', in *Projektet De vikingatida runinskrifternas kronologi. En presentation och några forskningsresultat* (Runrön 1), Uppsala: Swedish Science Press.

—— (1990) *De stungna runorna. Användning och ljudvärde i nordiska runinskrifter* (Runrön 4), Uppsala: Swedish Science Press.

Larsson, P. (2002a) 'Recent research on personal names and place-names in runic inscriptions', *Onoma*, 37: 47–68.

—— (2002b) *Yrrunan. Användning och ljudvärde i nordiska runinskrifter* (Runrön 17), Uppsala: Swedish Science Press.

—— (2005) 'Runes', in R. Turk (ed.) *A Companion to Old Norse-Icelandic Literature and Culture* (Blackwell companions to literature and culture 31), Malden, MA, Oxford and Carlton, Victoria: Blackwell Publishing.

Liestøl, A. (1979) 'Runeringen i Forsa. Kva er han, og når vart han smidd?', *Saga och sed*: 12–27.

MacLeod, M. (2002) *Bind-runes. An Investigation of Ligatures in Runic Epigraphy* (Runrön 15), Uppsala: Swedish Science Press.

Meijer, J. (1997) 'Literacy in the Viking Age', in *Blandade runstudier*, vol. 2 (Runrön 11), Uppsala: Swedish Science Press.

Moltke, E. (1985) *Runes and Their Origin. Denmark and Elsewhere*, Copenhagen: The National Museum of Denmark.

N = Runic inscription in Niyr.

Niyr = *Norges innskrifter med de yngre runer*, M. Olsen (ed.) (Norsk historisk kjeldeskrift-institutt: Norges indskrifter indtil reformationen 2), Oslo 1941 ff.: Jacob Dybwad/A.S. Bokcentralen.

Nytt om runer, Meldingsblad om runeforskning, 1–, Oslo 1986 ff. Online: http://ariadne.uio.no/runenews/issues.htm.

Ög = Östergötlands runinskrifter (SRI 2).

Öl = Ölands runinskrifter (SRI 1).

Page, R.I. (1995) 'The Manx rune-stones', in *Runes and Runic Inscriptions. Collected Essays on Anglo-Saxon and Viking Runes*, Woodbridge: Boydell and Brewer.

Palm, R. (1992) *Runor och regionalitet. Studier av variation i de nordiska minnesinskrifterna* (Runrön 7), Uppsala: Swedish Science Press.

Peterson, L. (1994a) 'The graphemic system of the staveless runes', in J. Knirk (ed.) *Proceedings of the Third International Symposium on Runes and Runic Inscriptions, Grindaheim, Norway, 8–12 August 1990* (Runrön 9), Uppsala: Swedish Science Press.

—— (1994b) *Svenskt runordsregister*, 2nd edn (Runrön 2), Uppsala: Swedish Science Press.

—— (1995) 'Runologi. Försök till ett aktuellt signalement', *Saga och Sed*: 39–54.

—— (1996) 'På vägen mot en runsvensk grammatik', *Kungl. Humanistiska Vetenskaps-Samfundet i Uppsala årsbok* (Annales Societatis Litterarum Humaniorum Regiae Upsaliensis): 23–38.

—— (2002) *Nordiskt runnamnlexikon*, 4th rev. edn, Uppsala. Online: www.sofi.se/SOFIU/runlex/.

Salberger, E. (2001) 'Eckersholm-stenen. Ett tydningsförsök', *Sydsvenska ortnamnssällskaps årsskrift*: 61–102.

Sawyer, B. (2000) *The Viking-Age Rune-Stones. Custom and Commemoration in Early Medieval Scandinavia*, Oxford and New York: Oxford University Press.

Scandinavian runic-text data base/Samnordisk runtextdatabas. Online: www.nordiska.uu.se/forskn/samnord.htm.

Sm = Smålands runinskrifter (SRI 4).

Snædal, Th. (2002) *Medan världen vakar. Studier i de gotländska runinskrifternas språk och kronologi/ While the World Wakes. Studies in the Language and Chronology of the Runic Inscriptions of Gotland* (Runrön 16), Uppsala: Swedish Science Press.

Spurkland, T. (2001) *I begynnelsen var fuþaRk. Norske runer og runeinnskrifter*, Oslo: Cappelen Akademisk Forlag/Landslaget for norskundervisning.

SRI = *Sveriges runinskrifter*, 1–, Stockholm 1900 ff.: KVHAA.

Stille, P. (1999) *Runstenar och runristare i det vikingatida Fjädrundaland. En studie i attribuering* (Runrön 13), Uppsala: Swedish Science Press.

Thompson, C.W. (1975) *Studies in Upplandic Runography*, Austin and London: University of Texas Press.

—— (1981) 'On transcribing runic inscriptions', *Michigan Germanic Studies*, 7(1): 89–95.

Williams, H. (1990) *Åsrunan. Användning och ljudvärde i runsvenska steninskrifter* (Runrön 3), Uppsala: Swedish Science Press.

—— (1993) 'Ó-namn. Nordiska personnamn med det privativa prefixet Ó-', *Personnamn i nordiska och andra germanska fornspråk. Handlingar från NORNA:s artonde symposium i Uppsala 16–19 augusti 1991* (NORNA-rapporter 51), Uppsala: NORNA-förlaget.

—— (1994) 'The non-representation of nasals before obstruents: spelling convention or phonetic analysis?', in J. Knirk (ed.) *Proceedings of the Third International Symposium on Runes and Runic Inscriptions, Grindaheim, Norway, 8–12 August 1990* (Runrön 9), Uppsala: Swedish Science Press.

—— (1996) 'Till frågan om runsvenska dialekter', *Svenska landsmål och svenskt folkliv*, 119: 433–40.

—— (1999) 'Runestones and the conversion of Sweden', in C.M. Cusack and P. Oldmeadow (eds) *This Immense Panorama. Studies in Honour of Eric J. Sharpe* (Sydney Studies in Religion 2), Sydney: School of Studies in Religion.

—— (2000) 'Om attribuering av runstenar i Fjädrundaland', *Arkiv för nordisk filologi*, 115: 83–118.

—— (2005) 'Vittnar runstenen från Söderby (Gs 13) om Sveriges första ledungståg?' Does the runestone from Söderby (GS 13) bear witness to the first Swedish levy? Runic Philology and the art of reading what is there, *Kungl. Humanistiska Vetenskaps-Samfundet i Uppsala* Årsbok 2004 (Annales Societatis Litterarum Humaniorum Regiae Upsaliensis).

CHAPTER TWENTY-TWO

POETRY IN THE VIKING AGE

——·◆·——

Judith Jesch

Long before the Viking Age, Scandinavians liked to remember their dead by erecting large stones in their honour, sometimes with an inscription carved in runes, sometimes decorated, sometimes both. These could be further embellished by formulating the inscription, or part of it, in verse. One such stone, from Tune in Østfold, Norway, dated to around 400, is for a man called *Wōdurīdaʀ*. Despite the difficulties of interpreting this early inscription, it is clearly in verse, and records that a man called *Wiwaʀ* made the monument, and that three daughters held a funeral feast for the deceased (Naumann 1998: 697–8; Spurkland 2005: 35–42). Other kinds of important messages could also be embellished by the use of verse forms. One of the gold drinking horns found at Gallehus, in Denmark, from the fifth century, had a runic inscription recording who made it. On this fine piece of craftwork in the most precious metal, the maker's simple inscription is appropriately couched in verse form (Naumann 1998: 702–3; Spurkland 2005: 21–5):

> *ek Hlewagastiʀ Holtijaʀ horna tawidō*
> I, Hlewagastiʀ son of Holtiʀ, made the horn.
> (Spurkland 2005: 22)

This poetic line is in *fornyrðislag* ('the metre of old sayings'), the standard alliterative long line used throughout the Germanic-speaking world, and also found in the mythological and legendary poetry collected in the late thirteenth-century Icelandic manuscript of the Poetic Edda, while the Tune inscription is recognisably in *ljóðaháttr*, another metre also found in the Edda, both suggesting a remarkably long-lived continuity of poetic form. The Viking Age falls in the middle of the eight centuries that separate the Tune and Gallehus inscriptions from the medieval Icelandic manuscript. In formal, metrical and linguistic terms, the poetry of the Vikings is thus just a slice of a much longer history of Scandinavian poetry that can be traced from at least AD 400 to around AD 1500 (Fidjestøl 1997; Gade 2000; Clunies Ross 2005).

Studying Viking Age poetry involves making a number of assumptions about it from indirect evidence. Despite the Scandinavians' familiarity with runes, their poetry in the Viking Age was predominantly oral: it was composed, performed and transmitted without the benefit of writing. In the long run, such poetry could only survive if it was recorded in writing, and we have to rely heavily on later written evidence for our knowledge of Viking Age poetry (Roesdahl and Meulengracht Sørensen 2003: 134–40). It is true that runes were used to record snatches of verse on memorial stones from the Viking Age, like the earlier Tune memorial, but these texts are short, highly restricted in genre and style, and not especially interesting as poetry. Such inscriptions show poetry in action, verse forms put to work in the more serious business of commemorating the dead, and of establishing and reinforcing the kin group and local hierarchies. Two stones still standing on the assembly site at Bällsta in Uppland, Sweden, contain this verse in *fornyrðislag*, framed by the names of three men who commissioned the monument and a fourth who carved the runes:

> *Munu æigi mærki*
> *mæiRi verða,*
> *þan Ulfs syniR*
> *æftiR gærðu,*
> *snialliR sveinaR,*
> *at sinn faður.*
> *Ræistu stæina*
> *ok staf unnu*
> *auk inn mikla*
> *at iartæiknum.*
> *Auk Gyriði*
> *gats at veri.*
> *Þy man i grati*
> *getit lata.*

> There shall no mightier
> memorials be found
> than those Ulv's sons
> set up after him,
> active lads
> after their father.
> They raised the stones
> and worked the staff
> also, the mighty one,
> as marks of honour.
> Likewise Gyrid
> loved her husband.
> So in mourning
> she will have it mentioned.
> (Jansson 1987: 121)

Such occasional uses of verse reflect a culture whose habit of thinking was poetical, one in which it came naturally to embellish important messages with well-worn verse forms (Wulf 2003). That such inscriptions are poetic embellishment, rather than 'poetry', is clear both from their brevity, and the difficulty of deciding whether individual inscriptions are in verse or not (Hübler 1996).

This easy familiarity with poetry continued after the Viking Age, as can be seen from the verse fragments carved for instant consumption on throwaway sticks of wood preserved in the waterlogged Bryggen area of medieval Bergen, in Norway (Liestøl 1974). These, too, are very like the poetry found in medieval Icelandic manuscripts, both Eddic and the kind that is usually called skaldic (see below). Like the Icelandic manuscripts, the runic poetry from medieval Bergen is mainly from the thirteenth and fourteenth centuries, and shows affinities with contemporary manuscript culture. While there are strong indications of the continuity of poetic forms from before the Viking Age until well after it, the actual contemporary evidence for the poetry of the Vikings is thus limited to a small number of runic inscriptions, mainly on memorial stones.

For a fuller appreciation of the range and variety of this poetry we have to turn to the later written evidence from medieval Iceland. The flowering of literary culture there began a century or so after its conversion to Christianity and the subsequent introduction of writing, using the roman alphabet and the technology of pen, ink and parchment. An important part of the Icelanders' literary activity involved the recording and preservation of ancient oral traditions: historical, mythological and poetical (Quinn 2000; Whaley 2000). While works like *Íslendingabók* and the sagas of Icelanders stressed the novelty and distinctiveness of Iceland and its literary culture, the poetry often stressed its own antiquity, and historical and cultural ties with the Scandinavian homeland, especially Norway. A vast quantity of poetry of many different kinds is preserved in Icelandic manuscripts from the thirteenth century onwards (Clunies Ross 2005). Much of this poetry was composed at the time of writing, or at least in the literate period from the twelfth century onwards. Yet it is also clear that a substantial proportion of the poetry preserved in medieval Icelandic manuscripts has its roots in the Viking Age, and that some of it may even be an accurate and faithful reproduction of the oral poetry of the Vikings. The main problem is to identify which medieval Icelandic verse originates in the Viking Age, and to determine how faithfully it reproduces its oral antecedents.

It is usual to divide medieval Icelandic poetry into two main categories, labelled 'Eddic' and 'skaldic' (Gunnell 2004; Whaley 2004). Like most binary divisions, this categorisation is an oversimplification of a large, diverse and chronologically extensive corpus. Nevertheless, these categories are useful for thinking about the possible Viking Age origins and contexts of poetry, and its transmission into the literate period.

Eddic poetry takes its name from a manuscript now generally referred to as the Codex Regius of the Poetic Edda (though it has borrowed this name from Snorri's *Edda*, also an important medieval source for ancient poetry). The Codex Regius was produced in Iceland in the 1270s and is a collection, or even an anthology, of twenty-nine poems of the kind we now call Eddic (Neckel and Kuhn 1983; Larrington 1996; Hallberg 1993). These poems have subjects from myth and heroic legend, and are in a variety of metres including *fornyrðislag* and *ljóðaháttr*, as noted above. They differ from other early Germanic poetry in being stanzaic, but there is some similarity, even overlap, of subject matter. They employ a wide variety of narrative, discursive and even dramatic stylistic techniques, and the tone ranges from the scurrilous to the high serious and visionary. The interest and variety of this collection suggest that it is just a sampling of a much richer literary tradition. The Codex Regius is not the first collection of this particular group of poems, but a copy of earlier versions, which can be traced back to around 1200 (Pétursson 1993). The early thirteenth century was also the time Snorri Sturluson was compiling his *Edda*, a handbook of mythology and poetry which both paraphrases and quotes from poems like those in the Poetic Edda (Faulkes 1982–98, 1987). Snorri clearly knew some poems not in the Poetic Edda, and others he seems to have known in different versions. A further manuscript, from around 1300, contains seven of the mythological poems from the Codex Regius, and an additional one (*Baldrs draumar*) not found there (Pétursson 1993), and Eddic-style poems are found in other manuscripts (Hallberg 1993). It is clear that scribes and authors of the thirteenth century knew a lot of Eddic-type poetry and took pains to collect, record and study it.

But how old is this poetry and did it originate in the Viking Age? By this time Iceland was thoroughly Christian, and yet much of the poetry deals with the pre-Christian mythology of Scandinavia, or with semi-historical heroes from the Migration period. Again, a runic inscription comes to our aid to demonstrate that both the form and the subject matter of Eddic verse were known in the Viking Age. The Rök stone from Östergötland in Sweden cites a *fornyrðislag* stanza that would not be out of place in the Codex Regius, and which alludes to heroic legends:

> *Reð ÞioðrikR*
> *hinn þurmoði,*
> *stilliR flutna,*
> *strandu HraiðmaraR.*
> *SitiR nu garuR*
> *a guta sinum,*
> *skialdi umb fatlaðR,*
> *skati Mæringa.*

> Theodric the bold,
> king of sea-warriors,
> ruled over
> Reid-sea shores.
> Now he sits armed
> on his Gothic horse,
> shield strapped,
> prince of Mærings.
> (Jansson 1987: 32)

This stone is dated to the beginning of the Viking Age, around AD 800. Theodric is the famed ruler of the Ostrogoths in the fifth/sixth century – quite what he is doing on a Swedish runestone nearly three centuries later is hard to determine, but he fits the pattern of Migration-period heroes celebrated in Eddic verse, like Attila the Hun and Gunnar the Burgundian who appear in several of the legendary poems in the second half of the Codex Regius.

The Rök stone shows that the type of poetry found in the Codex Regius was known in Viking Age Scandinavia, but not that the Eddic poems themselves are from that period. There have been many attempts to date the Eddic poems on the grounds of their language, metre, style, literary connections or contents (Hallberg 1993; Fidjestøl 1999), but there is no consensus on their age, though scholars agree that some of the poems are older than others, and, in particular, that some of them were composed as late as the twelfth century. The mythological poems, for instance, have been judged on whether they seem to be thoroughly pagan (like *Vafþrúðnismál*), touched by Christianity (like *Völuspá*), or a Christian pastiche of pagan beliefs (as some scholars believe *Þrymskviða* is), but such judgements are inevitably subjective. Instead, we need to ask what it means to say that an Eddic poem is 'old' (Meulengracht Sørensen 1991). The manuscript transmission cannot with certainty be traced further back than 1200. To reach the Viking Age, we have to assume either an untraceable early manuscript tradition, or a period of oral transmission, or probably both. Yet it is clear that much of the material in the Eddic poems – the stories of gods and heroes, the conceptual vocabulary, the ideologies and beliefs – is of great antiquity. A common pool of stories and cultural knowledge can be traced in art, iconography and other sources from before, during and after the Viking Age, and it is from this pool that the Eddic poems drew their material. But to argue that the poems themselves, as they are preserved, are old, would depend on an assumption of extensive oral transmission in fixed form of poems that are actually rather loose in their structures, which accords ill with what we know about oral poetry from other cultures (Finnegan 1988: 139–74). It is more likely that the Eddic poems are reworkings, at various times, of material from the pool of ancient cultural knowledge (Meulengracht Sørensen 1991). In this way, the surviving Eddic poems represent a Viking Age cultural practice, without necessarily being Viking Age texts in their current form.

Skaldic poetry can more easily be traced to its Viking Age origins. The term is often used rather broadly to cover most kinds of medieval Scandinavian and Icelandic poetry other than the Eddic poems (Fidjestøl 1993). Unlike Eddic poems, named after a manuscript, the (modern) name of the skaldic genre focuses on the figure of the poet, the *skald*. Whereas the anonymous Eddic poems come from an ancient, timeless and common cultural pool, skaldic verse is ascribed to a named poet and situated in a particular historical or literary context, either the patron for whom he composed, or the occasion for which he made his verses (although we know of some female skalds, they are very rare, see Jesch 1987). The preservation of such ancillary information about skaldic verse is related to its transmission. Unlike the Poetic Edda, an anthology, or Snorri's Edda, a handbook with illustrative quotations, the manuscripts which preserve skaldic poems generally cite them in a narrative context, and in such a way as to indicate their chronological, geographical and social context, which is often in the Viking Age. However, there is still a problem of dating.

Although skaldic verse is now accessible mostly in Icelandic manuscripts of the thirteenth century or later, much of it purports to be a product of the Viking Age, composed and performed in an oral context (Jesch 2001: 9–12, 15–33). We do not know for sure how such oral texts were transmitted, and how they survived the transition to literacy to be preserved for posterity, though one answer was provided by Snorri Sturluson. In the prologue to *Heimskringla*, he explains that he has taken his examples from those 'poems which where recited before the chieftains themselves or their sons' because *kvæðin þykkja mér sízt ór staði færð, ef þau eru rétt kveðin ok skynsamliga upp tekin* 'the poems seem to me least likely to be corrupted, as long as they are correctly composed and carefully interpreted' (Aðalbjarnarson 1979 I: 7, my trans.). This is the origin of the idea widespread among modern scholars that the form of skaldic verse is a guarantee of its more-or-less accurate preservation in an oral tradition, until the advent of literacy enabled the text to be fixed in a different, and more permanent, way. The extent to which the form of skaldic verse is fixed is much greater than in other early Germanic genres, so that, while all verse is designed to be memorable, skaldic verse seems particularly designed to be memorable in exactly the form in which it was originally composed. It is characterised by complex metrical rules applied within a small poetic space: almost any changes to the text may violate one or more of these metrical rules (Gade 1995: 1–7). As Snorri said, as long as the poem is 'correctly composed' in the first instance, and then 'carefully interpreted', it will not be 'corrupted'.

Skaldic verse that can in this way be relatively confidently attributed to the Viking Age needs to be defined somewhat more narrowly. In the Viking Age, kings and chieftains employed poets who composed formal poems in their praise, recording and celebrating their warlike and other accomplishments (Frank 1978: 120–5). This genre (known from its form as *dróttkvætt* 'composed in court metre') flourished particularly in the late tenth and eleventh centuries. The poets were mainly Icelanders and the kings were mainly Norwegian, though Swedish, Danish and English kings, and other rulers, could also be celebrated. The poems were composed in the poet's head and recited before an audience of the king and his retainers, or of his heirs if it was posthumous. The skaldic poet often appears as an authorial presence in his text, drawing attention to his sources. His authorial personality is also of importance outside the text, guaranteeing its authenticity and authority. For historians like Snorri, the poet is the authority for the information they take from his poems. But it is also clear to us that the poet is in some sense the creator of that information. Handsomely rewarded for his poem, he presents a flattering and definitive version of the life and works of the king or chieftain being praised, securely enmeshed in the strict and complex forms of *dróttkvætt* which ensure its enduring testimony. The poem then becomes part of the treasure-chest of other poets, who ensure it is remembered and passed on.

Arnórr Þórðarson's *Þorfinnsdrápa* records the earl of Orkney's raids on mainland Scotland in the late 1020s, including a battle against a Scottish leader called Karl Hundason, at Tarbat Ness, south of the River Oykell:

Ulfs tuggu rauð eggjar,
eitt þar's Torfnes heitir,
– ungr olli því þengill –
(þat vas mánadag) fránar.
Sungu þar, til þinga,
þunn fyr Ekkjal sunnan,
sverð, es siklingr barðisk
snarr við Skotlands harra.

Bright blades grew red on the wolf's mouthful [carrion] at a place
called Torfnes. Young, the ruler caused that. It was a Monday.
Slender swords sang there south of the Ekkjall, as the princeling,
swift into conflict, fought with Scotland's lord. (Whaley 1998: 236–7)

This is a typical *dróttkvætt* stanza, with eight half-lines of six syllables each, alliteration binding the half-lines into pairs, and internal rhyme (full rhyme in the even-numbered lines and half-rhyme in the odd-numbered). It makes use of poetic tropes such as 'the wolf's mouthful', and descriptive adjectives ('bright', 'slender'). But it also demonstrates a concern for naming significant places, and has a precise concern with chronology, specifying the day of the week on which the battle took place. In this way it is both poetry and chronicle, both entertainment and praise. The combination of significant historical details, interesting literary embellishment and strict metre all helped to ensure the survival of this stanza, like many others in *dróttkvætt*, for an unknown length of time in the oral tradition, and for subsequent recording in Icelandic historical texts. Like the runic memorials, these poems are verse in action, used for a variety of social purposes. The art of the Viking Age, including its poetry, is rarely just decorative (though it is highly decorative), but usually also functional. The surviving Eddic poems, however, hint at an alternative, less functional, aesthetic, which might also be located in the Viking Age.

BIBLIOGRAPHY

Aðalbjarnarson, B. (1979) *Snorri Sturluson. Heimskringla*, 3 vols, Reykjavík: Hið íslenzka fornritafélag.

Clunies Ross, M. (2005) *A History of Old Norse Poetry and Poetics*, Woodbridge: D.S. Brewer.

Faulkes, A. (1982–98) *Snorri Sturluson. Edda*, 4 vols, London: Viking Society for Northern Research.

—— (1987) *Snorri Sturluson. Edda*, London: Dent.

Fidjestøl, B. (1993) 'Skaldic verse', in P. Pulsiano *et al.* (eds) *Medieval Scandinavia. An Encylopedia*, New York: Garland.

—— (1997) 'Norse-Icelandic composition in the oral period', in O.E. Haugen and E. Mundal (eds) *Bjarne Fidjestøl. Selected Papers*, Odense: Odense University Press.

—— (1999) *The Dating of Eddic Poetry*, Copenhagen: Reitzel.

Finnegan, R. (1988) *Literacy and Orality*, Oxford: Blackwell.

Frank, R. (1978) *Old Norse Court Poetry. The* Dróttkvætt *Stanza*, Ithaca, NY: Cornell University Press.

Gade, K.E. (1995) *The Structure of Old Norse* Dróttkvætt *Poetry*, Ithaca, NY: Cornell University Press.

—— (2000) 'Poetry and its changing importance in medieval Icelandic culture', in M. Clunies Ross (ed.) *Old Icelandic Literature and Society*, Cambridge: Cambridge University Press.

Gunnell, T. (2004) 'Eddic poetry', in R. McTurk (ed.) *A Companion to Old Norse-Icelandic Literature and Culture*, Oxford: Blackwell.

Hallberg, P. (1993) 'Eddic poetry', in P. Pulsiano *et al.* (eds) *Medieval Scandinavia. An Encylopedia*, New York: Garland.

Hübler, F. (1996) *Schwedische Runendichtung der Wikingerzeit*, Uppsala: Institutionen för nordiska språk, Uppsala Universitet.

Jansson, S.B.F. (1987) *Runes in Sweden*, Stockholm: Gidlunds.

Jesch, J. (1987) 'Women poets in the Viking Age: an exploration', *New Comparison*, 4: 2–15.

—— (2001) *Ships and Men in the Late Viking Age. The Vocabulary of Runic Inscriptions and Skaldic Verse*, Woodbridge: Boydell.

Larrington, C. (trans.) (1996) *The Poetic Edda*, Oxford: Oxford University Press.

Liestøl, A. (1974) 'Runic voices from towns of ancient Norway', *Scandinavica*, 13: 19–33.

Meulengracht Sørensen, P. (1991) 'Om eddadigtenes alder', in G. Steinsland *et al.* (eds) *Nordisk hedendom. Et symposium*, Odense: Odense Universitetsforlag.

Naumann, H.-P. (1998) 'Runeninschriften als Quelle der Versgeschichte', in K. Düwel and S. Nowak (eds) *Runeninschriften als Quellen interdisziplinärer Forschung*, Berlin: De Gruyter.

Neckel, G. and Kuhn, H. (eds) (1983) *Edda. Die Lieder des Codex Regius nebst verwandten Denkm-älern*, Heidelberg: Carl Winter.

Pétursson, E.G. (1993) 'Codex Regius', in P. Pulsiano *et al.* (eds) *Medieval Scandinavia. An Encylopedia*, New York: Garland.

Quinn, J. (2000) 'From orality to literacy in medieval Iceland', in M. Clunies Ross (ed.) *Old Icelandic Literature and Society*, Cambridge: Cambridge University Press.

Roesdahl, E. and Meulengracht Sørensen, P. (2003) 'Viking culture', in K. Helle (ed.) *The Cambridge History of Scandinavia*, vol. 1, Cambridge: Cambridge University Press.

Spurkland, T. (2005) *Norwegian Runes and Runic Inscriptions*, Woodbridge: Boydell.

Whaley, D. (1998) *The Poetry of Arnórr Jarlaskáld. An Edition and Study*, Turnhout: Brepols.

—— (2000) 'A useful past: historical writing in medieval Iceland', in M. Clunies Ross (ed.) *Old Icelandic Literature and Society*, Cambridge: Cambridge University Press.

—— (2004) 'Skaldic poetry', in R. McTurk (ed.) *A Companion to Old Norse-Icelandic Literature and Culture*, Oxford: Blackwell.

Wulf, F. (2003) 'Runenverse und Runenritzer', in W. Heizmann and A. van Nahl (eds) *Runica – Germanica – Mediaevalia*, Berlin: De Gruyter.

THE PERFORMANCE OF
THE POETIC EDDA

——•◆•——

Terry Gunnell

There are a number of central facts that should be borne in mind by anyone who intends to study the Eddic poems in the context of the early Middle Ages:

First of all, the two main manuscripts containing the earliest complete versions of these works, the so-called Codex Regius and the AM 748 4°, both come from the late thirteenth century (see Vésteinn Ólason 2001; and Wessén 1945). Prior to this, Snorri Sturluson quotes directly from some of the poems contained in these manuscripts in his Prose Edda, which was written in about 1220.

Secondly, most scholars agree that the majority of the works contained in the Eddic manuscripts must have lived in the oral tradition prior to the time at which they were recorded, although opinions vary about how long this might apply to different works (see e.g. Gísli Sigurðsson 1998; Harris 1979, 1983, 1985, 2000a, b, 2003, 2004, forthcoming; Lönnroth 1971, 1978, 1979). Some argue, logically, that a number of the works contained in the Poetic Edda might have roots in pagan times 200 years earlier, although considering the arguments that have been made about the workings of the oral tradition by scholars such as Milton Parry and Albert Lord (1960), Ruth Finnegan (1977), Jeff Opland (1980), Walter Ong (1982) and John Miles Foley (2002), it must be regarded as questionable exactly how much the texts of these works would have remained unchanged during all of this time.

The above statement underlines a third fact, that these works were 'collected' rather than composed by those who recorded them, although it seems clear that different editorial approaches were used by those who recorded different sections of the manuscript, the Codex Regius manuscript being a compilation of other earlier compilations (see Lindblad 1954, 1980). The mere fact that they were collected, however, does not mean that these works were known all over Scandinavia, nor, if they were well known, that all the 'versions' known at the time around Scandinavia would have taken the same form. As Gísli Sigurðsson (1998: xlv–xlvi) has argued, it is likely that the performer would have adapted the work to suit the occasion, as happens in many other oral cultures.

In short, the Eddic poems were essentially works that were presented 'live' by performers, and received by audiences not only aurally, but also visually as *one-off* living performances, not least because, as with a play, every performance of these works would have been different in one way or another, at least in terms of audience and accompanying atmosphere. Indeed, this fact would also have applied to the period after these works came to be recorded, because it is probable that the recorded and copied Eddic poems, like the sagas, would have tended to have been received by most people read aloud rather than through private reading. This means, in essence, that for most people, as with a play (or at the very least, a poetry-reading or a stand-up comedy performance), the actual *text* of these works was only one relatively limited part of the overall received 'work'. In short, these works were not composed solely of words: they were also received as a form of music with varying tones, rhythms and inflections, although it is hard to say whether they were sung, spoken or chanted.[1] In short, as John Miles Foley (2002: 60) has noted recently about oral poetry:

> Oral poetry is endemically plural, naturally diverse … Any oral poem, like any utterance, is profoundly contingent on its context. To assume that it is detachable – that we can comfortably speak of 'an oral poem' as a freestanding item – is necessarily to take it out of context. And what is that lost context? It is the performance, the audience, the poet, the music, the specialised way of speaking, the gestures, the costuming, the visual aids, the occasion, the ritual, and myriad other aspects of the given poem's reality … And when we pry an oral poem out of one language and insert it into another, things will inevitably change. We'll pay a price.

In other words, scholars who ignore the aural and visual aspects of the performance of Old Norse poetry and limit themselves to the 'safe' fixed text are doing little more than examining the equivalent of a dead butterfly pinned to a board in a museum. The object they are viewing has little to do with the work as it was conceived by the original performer.

A natural reaction to the above statement is to argue that we know nothing about the context of the Eddic poems, since there are no objective accounts of the presentation of the Eddic poems outside the fictional, and slightly questionable account given in *Norna-Gests þáttr* in the *Flateyjarbók* manuscript from the fourteenth century, where Norna-Gestr recites *Helreið Brynhildar* and parts of *Reginsmál* apparently to the accompaniment of a harp (see *Norna-Gests þáttr*). Certainly, nothing at all exists from the prehistoric pagan times about the performance of such works. All the same, as has been implied above, the extant versions of the Eddic poems were collected from the oral tradition, and these can be assumed, for the main part, to be relatively trustworthy records of the form and content of these works as they existed in the thirteenth century (see further Tangherlini 2003). Furthermore, it can also be safely assumed that the extant form of these works was shaped by the performance conditions they were intended for at that time, if not also in earlier centuries, just as the form of Shakespeare's plays was governed by the theatrical conditions of Elizabethan England, and the shape of oral ballads and folk tales is governed by the fact that their audience had to be able to follow what was going on at any given time: they could not flick back through the pages of the book (see also Lönnroth 1978: 12).

This brings us to the additional information about performance provided by the form of the Eddic poems themselves and the manuscripts in which they are contained. First of all, it is clear that the use of the expression 'Eddic poem' as a genre description is highly misleading, not least because the main Eddic manuscript, the Codex Regius, actually contains two very different types of poetic work, written in two quite different metres. The former metre, *fornyrðislag*, is used essentially for epic narrative works, most of them dealing with ancient Germanic heroes. In these works, which for the main part are composed in the third person, the audience is informed of earlier events by a narrator who refers back to the past, thereby acting as a middle-man between the past and the present (the audience). They recount actions and dialogues, but never personally leave the present world of the performance situation. The latter metre, *ljóðaháttr*, is totally different: all of the works in this metre, which deal with the world of the gods and those archetypal heroes like Sigurðr Fáfnisbani who had business with the gods, take the form of monologues and dialogues in the first person. Although the works have prose introductions in the Codex Regius, these have been shown to be of questionable origin. A number of them are taken directly from Snorri Sturluson's *Prose Edda* (see Gunnell 1995: 218–35). In short, in these works, there is no middle-man: the form forces the performer to take on the role(s) of the characters in question, in other words, the gods and their followers, who are simultaneously 'brought to life' in front of the audience. This is even more likely if the performer in question adds tone, emotion or gesture to the words they are presenting, thereby encouraging a degree of identification between themselves and the characters. At the same time, the audience is brought actually to 'witness' the events of the past. Two times are thus present simultaneously. All of the implications are that the *ljóðaháttr* works in question have strong dramatic qualities in performance, quite different from those works in *fornyrðislag* (see Phillpotts 1920; Gunnell 1995).

The dramatic aspects of the dialogic *ljóðaháttr* works are emphasised still further by the fact that in *both* main manuscripts of the Poetic Edda, when recording five dialogic works (*Skírnismál*, *Hárbarðsljóð*, *Vafþrúðnismál*, *Lokasenna* and *Fáfnismál*) the scribes felt a need to adapt a form of marginal speaker notation that was never used anywhere else in medieval Scandinavian manuscripts before or after that time. In other Icelandic and mainland Scandinavian manuscripts containing dialogue (e.g. the Dialogues of Gregory the Great), names of speakers are always given in abbreviated form in the main text (sometimes rubricated). This is attempted and then rejected in the Eddic manuscripts before being replaced by the marginal notation (see Gunnell 1995: 282–329). The marginal notation form is only encountered elsewhere during this period in manuscripts from northern France and England containing dramas in the vernacular (such as *Le Mystère d'Adam*, or *La Seinte Resureccion*) or works meant to be performed in dramatic fashion (such as *Babio* and *Dame Sirith*) (see further Gunnell 1995: 206–18, 282–329). Furthermore, careful analysis of the texts of these Eddic poems underlines the fact that a single performer would have immense difficulty in presenting them and conveying the various changes of character *without* making use of some form of acted character presentation in voice or action (especially in *Skírnismál*, *Fáfnismál* and *Lokasenna*). Indeed, as I have noted elsewhere, the humour of *Hárbarðsljóð* and *Lokasenna* seems to depend on this (see Gunnell 1995: 182–281). The likelihood must then be that two or more performers would have been involved in presenting these dialogues. It might be noted that *Skírnismál*, *Lokasenna* and *Hárbarðsljóð* have all been presented effectively as dramas in Iceland in recent years.

In short, it appears that the two main types of poetic works within the Eddic corpus had different forms of performance. Those in *fornyrðislag* might have been performed as Norna-Gestr presents his poems (although it must remain somewhat questionable whether harps were commonly used in Scandinavia in the early Middle Ages), while those in *ljóðaháttr* (including the monologues) involved dramatic presentation. Indeed, several of them seem to imply movement and living gesture (especially *Skírnismál*, which not only involves movement but the carving of magical runes, something that one cannot expect a good Christian scribe to have dreamed up for actual performance).

This leads to the natural questions of the possible setting and background of these works. Of course, the *fornyrðislag* poems could have been performed anywhere, although one can expect an indoor setting. As for the dialogic poems and monologic poems mainly in *ljóðaháttr*, it is interesting to note the fact that several of them (*Fáfnismál*, *Sigrdrífumál*, *Skírnismál* and *Hárbarðsljóð*) largely take place outside in a liminal setting, while others (*Vafþrúðnismál*, *Grímnismál*, *Lokasenna* and probably *Hávamál*) are all deliberately set inside a hall, something that provides an additional religious context if, as I have argued elsewhere, the hall building itself had a potentially microcosmic symbolism in pagan times (the roof being the sky, held up by 'dwarfs', while the chieftain sitting in the high seat between the tree-like high-seat pillars has the role of the *goði/goð*: see further Gunnell 2004). Indeed, it is hard to ignore the strong 'initiatory' ritual elements of *Grímnismál*, *Vafþrúðnismál*, *Fáfnismál* and *Sigrdrífumál*.

In short, it would appear that in the *ljóðaháttr* poems of the Poetic Edda we have the earliest extant 'dramatic' works in northern Europe. There is good reason to consider whether the form of works such as these might originally have some connection to those archaeological finds and foreign historical accounts implying ritual dramatic activities, such as the Torslunda matrices, the Oseberg tapestry, the horned and sometimes dancing figures found in Birka, Ekhammar, Finglesham and Sutton Hoo, the felt animal masks found in Hedeby harbour, Adam of Bremen's talk of a 'theatrum' at Uppsala, and the accounts of masked Varangians in skins dancing a Christmas *gothikon* for the emperor in Constantinople (see Gunnell 1995: 36–80).

NOTE

1   The words most commonly used with poetic performance are *þylja* ('to recite or list') and *kveða*, which might mean chanting, or some heightened form of speech. Readers are recommended to listen to the recent experiments into the 'music' and performance of the Edda undertaken by the medieval music ensemble Sequentia, who have attempted to present the works as they might have sounded in the thirteenth century: Sequentia *Edda* (1995): Deutsche Harmonia Mundi 05472 77381 2; and *The Rhinegold Curse* (2001): Deutschland Radio and Westdeutscher Rundfunk; Marc Aurel edition MA 20016. On the question of music and song, see also Harris (2000a, 2003, 2004, forthcoming).

BIBLIOGRAPHY

Finnegan, R. (1977) *Oral Poetry. Its Nature, Significance and Social Context*, Cambridge: Cambridge University Press.

Foley, J.M. (2002) *How to Read an Oral Poem*, Urbana and Chicago: University of Illinois Press.

Gísli Sigurðsson (1998) 'Inngangur', in Gísli Sigurðsson (ed.) *Eddukvæði*, Reykjavík: Mál og menning.

Gunnell, T. (1995) *The Origins of Drama in Scandinavia*, Cambridge: D.S. Brewer.

—— (2004) '*Hof*, halls, *goð(ar)* and dwarves: an examination of the ritual space in the pagan Icelandic hall', *Cosmos*, 17(1): 3–36.

Harris, J. (1979), 'The Senna: from description to literary theory', *Michigan Germanic Studies*, 5(1): 65–74.

—— (1983) 'Eddic poetry as oral poetry: the evidence of parallel passages in the Helgi poems for questions of composition and performance', in R.J. Glendinning and Haraldur Bessason (eds) *Edda. A Collection of Essays*, Manitoba: University of Manitoba.

—— (1985) 'Eddic poetry', in C.J. Clover and J. Lindow (eds) *Old Norse-Icelandic Literature. A Critical Guide* (Islandica, 45), Ithaca, NY: Cornell University Press.

—— (2000a) 'The performance of Old Norse Eddic poetry: a retrospective', in K. Reichl (ed.) *The Oral Epic. Performance and Music* (Intercultural Music Studies 12), Berlin: VWB, Vlg für Wissenschaft und Bildung.

—— (2000b) 'Performance, textualization, and textuality of "Elegy" in Old Norse', in L. Honko (ed.) *The Textualization of Oral Epic* (Trends in Linguistics: Studies and Monographs 128), Berlin and New York: Mouton de Gruyter: 89–99.

—— (2003) 'Ethnopaleography and recovered performance: the problematic witnesses to "Eddic music"', in J.F. Nagy (ed.) *Models of Performance in Oral Epic, Ballad, and Song* (= *Western Folklore*, 62(1/2): 97–117.

—— (2004) 'Sänger', *RGA* 2: 79–86.

—— (forthcoming) 'Eddic poetry and the ballad: voice, vocality, and performance. With special reference to DgF 1', forthcoming in a volume based on the conference 'Ballade und Stimme. Vokalität als theoretisches und historisches Phänomen in der skandinavischen Balladentradition', ed. Jürg Glauser, Zurich.

Lindblad, G. (1954) *Studier i Codex Regius af Äldre Eddan*, Lund: Gleerup.

—— (1980) 'Poetiska Eddans förhistoria och skrivskicket i Codex regius', *Arkiv för nordisk filologi*, 95: 142–67.

Lönnroth, Lars (1971) 'Hjálmar's death song and the delivery of Eddic poetry', *Speculum*, 46: 1–20.

—— (1978) *Den dubbla scenen. Muntlig diktning från Eddan till ABBA*, Stockholm: Prisma.

—— (1979) 'The double scene of Arrow-Odd's drinking contest', in H. Bekker-Nielsen, P. Foote, A. Haarder and P. Meulengracht Sørensen (eds) *Medieval Narrative. A Symposium*, Odense: Odense University Press.

Lord, A.B. (1960) *The Singer of Tales*, Cambridge, MA: Harvard University Press.

Norna-Gests þáttr, in Guðbrandur Vígfússon and Unger, C.R. (eds) (1860–8) *Flateyjarbók*, 3 vols (Det norske historiske kildeskriftfonds skrifter 4), Christiania: Malling (vol. 1: 346–59).

Ong, W.J. (1982) *Orality and Literacy. The Technologizing of the Word*, London: Methuen.

Opland, J. (1980) *Anglo-Saxon Oral Poetry. A Study of the Traditions*, New Haven: Yale University Press.

Phillpotts, B.S. (1920) *The Elder Edda and Ancient Scandinavian Drama*, Cambridge: Cambridge University Press.

Tangherlini, T. (2003) 'Performing through the past: ethnophilology and oral tradition', *Western Folklore*, 62(1/2): 143–9.

Vésteinn Ólason (ed.) (2001) *Konungsbók Eddukvæða. Codex Regius, Stofnun Árna Magnússonar á Íslandi Gl. Kgl. Sml. 2365 4to* (Íslensk miðaldahandrit: Manuscripta Islandica Medii Aevi 3), Reykjavík: Lögberg Edda.

Wessén, E. (ed.) (1945), *Fragments of the Elder and the Younger Edda AM 748 I and II 4:o* (Corpus Codicum Islandicorum Medii Ævi 17), Copenhagen and Reykjavík: Munksgaard.

CHAPTER TWENTY-THREE

THE ICELANDIC SAGAS

——— •◆• ———

Lars Lönnroth

Saga in the Old Norse language simply meant a story – any story. The word is related to *segja*, 'say', and could be used about anything told or related, regardless of form, origin or subject matter. In modern English usage, however, an 'Icelandic saga' is a specific type of long epic prose narrative written in Old Norse in medieval Iceland at some time after 1150, at least partly based on indigenous oral tradition and primarily dealing with the legendary past of the Scandinavian people. The three most ancient and famous indigenous saga types – or genres – are called *fornaldarsögur* ('mythical-heroic sagas'), *konungasögur* ('sagas of kings', normally about the kings of Norway) and *Íslendingasögur* ('family sagas' or 'sagas of Icelanders', about prominent Icelandic families and individuals living in the period 850–1050).

There are also other saga genres: *samtíðarsögur*, 'contemporary sagas', which are chronicles about events in twelfth- and thirteenth-century Iceland; *heilagra manna sögur*, saints' lives; *biskupa sögur*, hagiographic biographies of bishops; *riddarasögur*, chivalric romances (particularly about the knights of King Arthur and Charlemagne), plus various translations of Latin works about Roman history, the Trojan war and other matters which indicate that the Icelanders were by no means ignorant of classical culture. Although most of these sagas, including the translations, are important for the understanding of Icelandic medieval literature and its relation to the literary history of Europe, we must confine ourselves here to *fornaldarsögur*, *konungasögur* and *Íslendingasögur*, which are the only genres that can be assumed to preserve some narrative traditions from the Viking period.

The earliest saga texts have been preserved in manuscripts from the latter half of the twelfth century, a few of them Norwegian but generally Icelandic; most of these texts were clearly written by priests or monks and their content is mostly of a clerical or hagiographic nature. Most of the famous and classical sagas, however, are decidedly secular in their orientation and were written in Iceland during the thirteenth century. This period is often referred to as the 'Sturlung Age', so named after the Sturlung family, which played a dominant role in both politics and saga-writing under the leadership of powerful chieftains such as Snorri Sturluson and Sturla Thorðarson, who were not only themselves prominent saga-writers but were also in a position to sponsor literary production by other people.

A precondition for the amazing literary output of the Icelanders was the unique cooperation that existed in their country between the servants of the Church and the secular chieftains. While pagan and secular stories from oral traditions were rarely at this time recorded in other countries of Europe, since writing was more or less monopolised by the Church, the situation was very much different in Iceland. Here the chieftain families controlled the Church and the clerical schools and hence also literary production. In spite of their role as church leaders, the chieftains also saw themselves as the guardians and preservers of traditional lore from the pre-Christian era in the form of skaldic poetry, heroic tales, genealogies and legends about their ancestors, particularly insofar as these ancestors were reputed to have played an important role in the history of Norway and Iceland. Hence the chieftains took an interest in saga-writing and in promoting various kinds of literary activities. The first manifestations of this interest was the writing of the Book of Settlement (*Landnámabók*) about the first settlers of Iceland, and brief historical surveys of Icelandic and Norwegian history by the priests Ari the wise and Sæmundr the Wise in the twelfth century. But it was not until the thirteenth century that indigenous and secular saga production started on a large scale. It seems to have started with *konungasögur*, while *Íslendingasögur* came some decades later, and *fornaldarsögur* towards the end of the century, but the dating of early saga texts is so notoriously uncertain and has in later years been challenged so often, that it may be wisest to avoid the dating problems altogether.

While the *fornaldarsögur* contain traditional legends and Eddic poems about mythical heroes who are supposed to have lived in the *forn öld* or 'ancient era' before the vikings, both the *konungasögur* and the *Íslendingasögur* present extensive narratives about historical events and characters of the Viking Age, and they do so in a manner that appears more realistic and trustworthy than that of the *fornaldarsögur*. For this reason, *konungasögur* and *Íslendingasögur* have often been classified as 'historiography', while *fornaldarsögur* have been classified as 'fiction' or 'entertainment'.

Such a classification, however, can hardly be defended from either a literary or a historical point of view, since all three of these saga genres are obviously meant to be both entertaining and, in some sense, loyal to what actually happened in the past. No clear distinction was originally made by the saga-writers between 'historiography' and 'fiction', although it became gradually accepted that a story did not necessarily have to be perfectly true in order to be entertaining. From a modern historian's point of view there is enough fiction in all sagas to make them unreliable as sources, but this does not mean that any saga should be read as pure fiction like a modern novel, since they all claim to present some kind of truth, even though it would hardly be recognised as such by modern scholars. And although events in a *fornaldarsaga* often seem more fantastic than events in a *konungasaga* or an *Íslendingasaga*, this is not so much a result of generic difference as a result of the fact that *fornaldarsögur* deal with prehistorical and hence mythical times about which people loved to talk and speculate but actually knew almost nothing. The saga-writers knew a great deal more about the Viking Age but their knowledge was embedded in legendary tales and supplemented with the help of their own creative imagination.

To what extent were the sagas then based on oral tradition and to what extent on literary authorship? This is one of the main problems of saga scholarship, discussed primarily with regard to *Íslendingasögur* but equally relevant with regard to *fornaldarsögur* and *konungasögur*. Scholars used to adhere either to the 'Freeprose theory' or the

'Bookprose theory'. According to the first theory, the sagas were essentially oral texts transmitted from generation to generation before they were finally recorded in writing. According to the second theory, the saga texts were essentially created by writers in the Middle Ages, although partly on the basis of oral sources. Today most scholars agree that neither the first nor the second theory is completely valid, because the relationship between oral tradition and literary authorship varies considerably, not only between different saga genres but also between individual sagas or even chapters within the same saga text.

In the case of *fornaldarsögur*, the main source of the earliest written texts obviously consists of very ancient poetry in Eddic metre, often about famous Germanic heroes from the migration period such as Sigurd the Volsung, Attila the Hun or Theoderic the Great. Some of the oldest poems of the Edda, transmitted in oral tradition since the early Viking Age, are in fact extensively quoted and often provide the core of the narrative in such *fornaldarsögur* as *Völsunga saga*, *Hervarar saga* and *Hrólfs saga kraka*. The prose of these sagas, however, especially in the later texts, is often influenced by written prose literature, especially courtly romances translated from French into Old Norse.

Konungasögur, on the other hand, are partly based on skaldic poetry composed in honour of the king about whom the saga is told. These poems, which have also in some cases been preserved in the oral tradition since the Viking Age, are often quoted in the text. In addition to skaldic poetry, the writers of *konungasögur* must have had access to numerous anecdotes and prose tales circulating within the court or *hirð* about the king's battles, his relationship to various famous people in his environment. Finally, the composition and style of some sagas of kings – for example *Ólafs saga helga* and *Sverris saga* – are to some extent based on foreign (primarily Latin) literary models such as saints' lives or secular biographies of princes.

Íslendingasögur, finally, are sometimes also based on skaldic poetry, especially sagas about the lives of prominent viking skalds such as Egill Skallagrímsson or Hallfreðr Vandræðaskáld. In addition, they often seem to be based on genealogical lore about the early settlers of Iceland plus oral traditions about famous legal cases involving feuds between local chieftains or other prominent members of the community. Some of these sagas give the impression of being very faithful to the oral traditions of a particular region or family, while others, such as *Njáls saga*, are highly literary compositions by sophisticated authors who are at least partly influenced by the style, narrative technique and vocabulary of foreign literature.

A few Icelandic texts contain information about *sagnaskemtan*, 'saga entertainment', where sagas were told and later read aloud, for example at feasts or public meetings. From these sources we may possibly draw some conclusions about the oral performance of sagas before they were committed to vellum or parchment by literate authors in the twelfth and thirteenth centuries. One of the most interesting accounts, included in an early collection of kings' sagas (*Morkinskinna*), concerns a young Icelander who is said to have visited the court of King Harald Harðráði in Norway around 1050. The king asks him if he has some kind of learning or talent, and he answers that he knows sagas. He is then asked to entertain the court with these sagas, and he does so regularly for some time during the winter months. When Christmas comes around, the Icelander has only one saga left but that is the one he does not dare to tell, since it describes King Harald's youthful adventures as a Varangian guard in Constantinople. Encouraged by the king, the Icelander finally tells this saga during the Christmas holidays while men are drinking.

On the thirteenth day, when the story had been finished earlier in the day, the king said:

> 'Aren't you curious to know, Icelander,' he asked, 'what I think of the story?'
>
> 'I am afraid to ask, sire,' he said.
>
> The king said: 'I am very pleased with it. It is perfectly faithful to the actual events. Who taught you the story?'
>
> He replied: 'It was my custom out in Iceland to go to the thingmeeting every summer, and every summer I learned something of the story from Halldórr Snorrason.'
>
> 'Then it is not surprising,' said the king, 'that you know the story well, and it will turn out to your benefit. You are welcome to stay with me whenever you wish.'

Although this account may not be historically accurate, it may still be used as a valuable source of information about the custom of *sagnaskemtan*. The telling of stories was evidently a well-known pastime at festive occasions, and it was known to have taken place both at the Norwegian court and at Icelandic thingmeetings. Furthermore, it appears to have been of some importance that the saga was not only entertaining but also historically accurate, at least if it concerned a still living king such as Harald. This is obviously why the Icelander refers to Halldórr Snorrason as his source, because Halldórr was known to have been the king's closest and most trusted companion during his stay in Constantinople. Finally, we can learn from this source that an Icelander visiting the Norwegian court could improve his situation and his social status by being a good storyteller. This could well have been a major incentive for the production of sagas, oral as well as written. Quite a few Icelandic saga manuscripts have in fact been preserved in Norway, where they were probably read aloud, particularly at court and in aristocratic surroundings.

Another interesting description of saga entertainment is found in a description of a prominent wedding that is known to have taken place at the Icelandic farm of Reykjahólar in 1119:

> And now there was much merriment and happiness, good entertainment and many kinds of games, dancing as well as wrestling and saga entertainment (*sagnaskemtan*) . . . People have told, although this is hardly a matter of importance, who provided the entertainment and how it was done. Such tales were told which now many people object to and pretend not to have known, for many are ignorant about truth and believe in lies while they cast doubt upon facts. Hrólfr from Skálmarnes told the saga about Hröngviðr the Viking and Oláfr Liðsmanna King and how Thráinn the Berserk broke into the burial mound and about Hrómundr Gripsson – and several verses were included. This saga was used for King Sverre's entertainment, and he said that such lying sagas were the most enjoyable. And yet people know how to trace their ancestry back to Hrómundr Gripsson! Hrólf himself had composed this saga. Ingimundr, the priest, told the saga of Ormr Barreyjasrskáld including many verses and at the end of the saga a good poem that Ingimundr had made – and yet many wise men hold this saga to be true.

It would appear from this account that mythical-heroic sagas could also be used as entertainment at large weddings on Icelandic farms, and although certain of these sagas were evidently regarded by some as untrustworthy or even 'lying', they were believed by many people to be true. We also learn from this source that farmers as well as priests would at least occasionally be expected to compose oral poems or prose sagas for the entertainment of their friends and neighbours. We may conclude that not only *konunga-sögur* but also *fornaldarsögur* – such as the saga of Thráinn the Berserk and Hrómundr Gripsson – were sometimes brought to the Norwegian court and used for the king's entertainment. The quotation from King Sverre, furthermore, indicates that at least this king – who was a highly literate and sophisticated sole ruler of Norway between 1184 and 1202 – understood the value of fiction, even though many other people at this time clearly did not.

Unfortunately, there is no account of *sagnaskemtan* where *Íslendingasögur* were told or read aloud. Although there is no reason to suppose that these sagas ever reached Norway, as *fornaldarsögur* and *konungasögur* evidently did, we may assume that stories about Icelandic families and their feuds were told both at thingmeetings, where the legal aspects of the feuding would be appreciated, and at festive occasions in Icelandic farms, where the inhabitants traced their ancestry back to prominent saga heroes.

The oral character of early saga prose is apparent in many different ways, particularly in the *Íslendingasögur* but also in many *konungasögur* and *fornaldarsögur*. The language is colloquial, straightforward, full of dialogue and containing a large number of epic formulas, type-scenes and stereotyped narrative patterns, for example when a new character is introduced ('A man was called X, the son of Y'), when a visit is described ('He was received well') or when the story moves to a new scene ('Now it is time to tell of X'). There are frequent references to what people in the district have said or told: 'It is said that . . .', 'Some people have said . . .', 'Some say this . . . but others say that . . .' The whole story is normally told in an apparently 'objective' manner suggesting that it has come down from reliable witnesses and trustworthy community spokesmen through several generations. The narrator sometimes refers to characters or events as if they were already well known to the audience, even though they have in fact not been mentioned earlier: 'At this time X lived in the Eastfjords,' 'This happened the winter after X was killed.' Such features may sometimes be explained as literary devices or as references to previously written texts, but in most cases they indicate that the text has its roots in a living oral tradition.

As in most oral narratives, the development of the plot is to a large extent predictable. When a man from family A kills a man from family B we know that revenge will soon follow and that the women on both sides will goad their brothers and husbands on to battle by suggesting that they are cowards if they do not fight. Legal battles at the Thing follow ritualistic patterns as do killings, weddings, travels abroad, viking adventures, flytings, encounters with giants and troll women, not to speak of formal presentations at a foreign court. When a hero has a horrible dream involving wolves or other predatory beasts, we know for certain that he is doomed to be attacked and killed. And we can expect him to make some salty and memorable remark in his moment of death.

In spite of all these recurrent patterns, some of the sagas are highly artistic in their overall structure, style and characterisation. It is also obvious that some of the longest sagas are written compositions, combining many episodes or *þættir*, a word originally meaning 'strands in a rope'. While each individual episode or strand may have originated in oral tradition, plaiting them together was a task that required a literate author. For a long and well-integrated saga form was hardly possible to achieve for an oral storyteller who had to divide his saga into several episodic instalments, as the Icelander entertaining King Harald's court evidently did. It is thus not very surprising that the earliest saga texts are either short or very loosely structured, consisting of several semi-independent episodes. At a later stage, however, writers like Snorri Sturluson or the author of *Njáls saga* managed to integrate material from many different sources into large and complicated literary structures.

The world picture of the sagas usually appears to modern readers as 'pagan' or at least as distinctly different from that of Christianity. Events seem to be governed by Fate (*auðna*) or Luck (*gæfa, gipta, hamingja*) and anticipated in prophetic dreams or visions. The ethic of retribution prevails, prompting men to take revenge whenever their honour has suffered a serious blow. Heathen rituals are sometimes described, sorcerers cast their magic spells, and mythical figures such as fetches (*fylgjur*), trolls or giants may occasionally appear. Yet the pagan gods are almost never present in the narrative, except in a few *fornaldarsögur*, and the attitude to the heathen religion is decidedly critical. It is characteristic of the noblest pagan heroes that they refuse to worship Odin, Thor and the other *æsir* but instead believe in their own power or in some unknown and invisible Creator, who will eventually turn out to be identical with the Christian God. Heroes living in the period after the conversion of Scandinavia are pictured as good Christians, even though their religious faith is rarely emphasised in the text. It would therefore be mistaken to characterise the world picture of the sagas as pagan, even though it is only rarely piously Christian either. Perhaps one can say that the sagas are told from a Christian perspective but nevertheless reveal a great deal of genuine admiration for the lost world of pagan ancestors.

To what extent, then, can the sagas be said to mirror this lost world? This is a question which has been much debated by historians. Generally speaking, scholars nowadays agree that you cannot trust the sagas as sources about major events and developments in the Viking Age, for example the settlement of Iceland, the conversion of Scandinavia, the battle of Svolder, or the Danish invasion of England. The testimony presented by the sagas about such matters has often been proved wrong when compared to archaeological evidence or earlier written documents. It is also obvious that the sagas give a rather distorted picture of the pagan religion and a much too idealised presentation of certain legendary heroes such as Olaf the Saint or Olaf Tryggvason, even though the ideological bias of the narrators is usually cleverly concealed under a protective layer of formal objectivity.

Nevertheless, the sagas are often good sources concerning mentality, ideas, social structure, farmlife and everyday customs in Old Norse society, because that society evidently had not changed very much in Iceland – except in the religious sphere – between the Viking Age and the Sturlung Age. As we can see from contemporary sagas about the Sturlung Age, people at this time still lived the same kind of lives in similar houses and with similar customs as their legendary ancestors. They also still followed the ethics of revenge, even though they considered themselves Christian, and they evidently believed in Fate, Luck, fetches, giants, troll women, skaldic poetry and prophetic dreams, even though they rejected Odin and Thor. Although political historians no longer read the saga texts with the same veneration as their nineteenth-century colleagues, these texts have therefore remained important sources for ethnologists, folklorists and historical anthropologists studying *histoire de mentalité*.

Yet it is as literary works, foreshadowing the modern novel, that the sagas are today primarily read and admired, not just in Scandinavian or Germanic countries, but all over the world. To the general reader their value as art has turned out to be more important than their value as sources.

BIBLIOGRAPHY

Clover, C.J. and Lindow, J. (eds) (1985) *Old Norse-Icelandic Literature. A Critical Guide* (Islandica XLV), Ithaca, NY and London: Cornell University Press.

Jónas Kristjánsson (1988) *Eddas and Sagas. Iceland's Medieval Literature*, trans. P. Foote, Reykjavík: Hið íslenzka bókmenntafélag.

Lönnroth, L. (1991) 'Sponsors, writers and readers of early Norse Literature', in R. Sampson (ed.) *Social Approaches to Viking Studies*, Glasgow: Cruithne.

Meulengracht Sørensen, P. (1993) *Saga and Society. An Introduction to Old Norse Literature*, trans. J. Tucker (Studia Borealia 1), Odense: Odense University Press.

Steblin-Kamenskij, M.I. (1973) *The Saga Mind*, trans. K. H. Ober, Odense: Odense University Press.

SNORRI STURLUSON: HIS LIFE AND WORK

—◆—

Anthony Faulkes

Snorri Sturluson is the first major writer of Old Icelandic prose from whom we have a large body of extant writing, including some poetry, and whose life is, in outline, well documented. Unlike most earlier writers of prose, he was not a cleric, but an aristocratic layman, and nearly all he wrote is on secular topics. The main sources for his life besides annals are the nearly contemporary *Íslendinga saga* and the saga of Hákon Hákonarson (king of Norway 1217–63), both by Snorri's nephew Sturla Þórðarson; and the sagas of Guðmundr Arason (bishop at Hólar in northern Iceland 1203–37).

Snorri was born in western Iceland in 1178 or 1179, son of the powerful chieftain Hvamms-Sturla whose family gave their name to the turbulent period of Icelandic history leading up to the loss of political independence in 1262–4, the Age of the Sturlungs, which was also the great age of Icelandic saga-writing. When he was three (his father died in 1183) Snorri was sent to be fostered (i.e. educated) at Oddi in southern Iceland, with the chieftain Jón Loptsson (d. 1197), grandson of the historian (writing in Latin) and priest Sæmundr fróði (the Learned). Jón himself was a deacon, but was prominent in the resistance of secular leaders to the extension of church power in the later twelfth century.

Many have thought that there must have been some sort of school at Oddi, but at that period in Iceland as elsewhere in Europe, most formal education took place in monasteries and cathedrals, and was based on training in Latin and preparation of pupils for ordination as priests. There is no trace in Snorri's writings of any knowledge of Latin; he almost never uses Latin words and never quotes Latin works. Where he shows knowledge of Latin concepts or theological ideas that were not already available in Icelandic translations, it is mostly of a fairly general nature and could easily have been derived from listening to vernacular preaching in churches or from conversation with clerical friends such as the priest and historian Styrmir Kárason (d. 1245). But there would undoubtedly have been books at Oddi, and they may have included secular writings in the vernacular such as Eddic poems and historical records about Icelandic and Norwegian history. Snorri was a learned writer, but his learning was mostly in native lore rather than Continental European writings in Latin.

At the age of twenty, Snorri married Herdís, daughter of Bersi Vermundarson 'the Wealthy' of Borg in western Iceland, formerly the home of the Viking poet Egill

Skallagrímsson, and Snorri went to live at Borg in 1202 on the death of his father-in-law. He went on to acquire, by inheritance, bargaining, purchase, or just plain intimidation, many chieftaincies (*goðorð*), or a share in them, in the Borgarfjörður area and even in part of one in northern Iceland. After about four years at Borg, he moved to Reykholt, about 50 km further inland, and took over the church property there, and probably the Reykholt chieftaincy at the same time, and thereafter also gained possession of several other churches. There is a document listing the property of and gifts to the church at Reykholt which has a short entry thought by some to be in Snorri's own hand – if so, it is the only autograph by him extant. Herdís, who seems to have remained on what had been her family property at Borg (their two children were both born before 1206), died in 1233. Snorri also had several children by other women.

Thus, Snorri became a very wealthy and powerful man. This accumulation of chieftaincies and properties in the hands of one man is characteristic of the social and economic changes in thirteenth-century Iceland, and led to most of the chieftancies and much of the property coming into the possession of a small number of very powerful families, who then fought it out among themselves, hoping to make one individual or family predominant – or even king. In the end it did no one in Iceland much good, and the king of Norway eventually gained control of the whole country, though he did not live to enjoy it.

Snorri began soon to make use of his powerful position, and already in 1202 had a violent dispute with some merchants from Orkney, whom he seems to have treated very badly. In the following years he was involved in several disputes, sometimes legal ones, some more warlike, but seems often to have worked for reconciliation. He served two periods as president (lawspeaker) of the General Assembly (*Alþingi*), 1215–18 and 1222–31. One attractive feature of his character is that he gave his booth at the General Assembly the mythological name Valhǫll; the association of the name with warfare was occasionally justified in practice.

At the same time, Snorri was making himself a name as a poet. He sent a poem to Earl Hákon galinn (d. 1216) and received gifts in return, and also composed about the earl's wife Kristín, King Sverrir (d. 1202) and King Ingi Bárðarson (d. 1217). These poems are all lost. He composed two poems about Earl Skúli Bárðarson, probably during his first visit to Norway (1218–20); only three lines of a refrain of one of them survives. *Háttatal*, the only substantial poem of his that survives, was composed in honour of Earl Skúli and King Hákon, probably soon after his return to Iceland. Two lines survive of a poem addressed to a bishop, perhaps Guðmundr Arason, and six and a half stanzas of occasional poetry.

While he was in Norway, Snorri became known to the young King Hákon (still only fourteen), and first received the honorary title of 'cupbearer' (*skutilsveinn*), then 'landed man' (*lendr maðr*). It was understood that he was to work to make Iceland subject to the king of Norway, and was to send his son Jón to Norway as a guarantee. But he came to be on much closer terms with Earl Skúli, the king's father-in-law and regent for the time being; Snorri managed to persuade Skúli to abandon a projected invasion of Iceland and stayed with him for his two winters in Norway.

On his return, Snorri met considerable hostility from other Icelandic chieftains, and was even lampooned in verse, but this seems gradually to have subsided, and moreover he did nothing towards fulfilling his promise to King Hákon and Earl Skúli. In 1224 he entered into partnership with Hallveig Ormsdóttir (it is not said that they ever married). Hallveig was said to be the richest woman in Iceland, and Snorri himself now became the richest, and probably the most powerful, man. In 1224 he married his daughter Ingibjǫrg to Gizurr Þorvaldsson.

During his second period of presidency of the Alþingi and on until his second visit to Norway in 1237, Snorri was involved in various violent disputes with other Icelandic chieftains, including his brother Sighvatr and Sighvatr's son Sturla, not always getting the best of it.

In Norway this time, Snorri had even less to do with King Hákon, but spent much time with Earl Skúli or the latter's son Pétr in Trondheim. Snorri returned to Iceland in 1239, in defiance of the king's express ban, but was rumoured to have been made a 'secret earl' (*fólgsnarjarl*) by Earl Skúli. In 1240 Skúli, hoping himself to become king of Norway, rebelled against the king and was killed, while in Iceland Gizurr Þorvaldsson was becoming dominant over all other chieftains and became King Hákon's chief agent in Iceland. Gizurr received a commission from the king to force Snorri to return to Norway or else to kill him, on the grounds that he had become a traitor to the king. Gizurr, with a great following, surprised Snorri at Reykholt on the night of 23 September 1241. Snorri took refuge in his cellar, but Gizurr's men found him there and killed him.

Scholars have come to very different conclusions about Snorri's character and attitudes from a study of his works. There are four main sections of his *Edda*, a treatise on poetry. The final section, *Háttatal*, offering patterns of nearly a hundred verse forms and metres for Icelandic poets, is remarkable for its technical ingenuity, in which the author shows some pride, but few readers are very impressed by the content or the style. But it has an impressive commentary, and *Skáldskaparmál*, an analysis of poetic language with examples from the work of more than seventy earlier poets, was expressly designed as an aid to young poets. *Gylfaginning* may have been added later, as a collection of mythological narratives to show the background and origin of skaldic kennings. The Prologue gives a narrative account of the origin of the heathen religion of the author's ancestors. It is clear that Snorri was fully Christian; but he shows no polemic tendency towards heathendom, and many of his stories are told with irony and humour.

His separate *Óláfs saga helga* is based on earlier lives of the saint, but is remarkable for its secular attitudes and the enhanced realism of his portrayal of the king. Although the miracles are not all suppressed, Snorri often gives a rationalistic explanation of them, and does not emphasise the king's saintliness. *Heimskringla*, a more mature work than his *Edda*, and thought to be an expansion of his *Óláfs saga*, begins the history of Norway in legendary times and continues down to 1177. The earliest attribution of the work to Snorri is from the seventeenth century, but it is now accepted. Though much is said in *Heimskringla* about relations between Norway and Iceland, the author's political views do not come out clearly. It is obvious that Snorri had nothing against kingship, admired some Norwegian kings immensely and enjoyed being a courtier; on the other hand, the oft-quoted speech of Einarr Þveræingr in defence of Iceland's independence (*Íslenzk fornrit* 27: 216) suggests that Snorri realised the dangers of Iceland coming under the power of Norway. Recent writers have stressed that Snorri and others who entered a feudal relationship with the king of Norway were not at the time seen as traitors to Iceland.

There is little real doubt that he was the author, or at any rate compiler, of these three works. They must have been compiled between his two visits to Norway (according to

Sturlunga saga, in the summer of 1230, Snorri's nephew Sturla Sighvatsson spent much time in Reykholt having Snorri's histories copied). Many have thought it possible that he also wrote *Egils saga*, one of the earliest of the sagas of Icelanders, which gives an archetypal picture of the heathen Viking that perhaps in some respects reflects Snorri's own character – or perhaps the character he would have liked to have been.

The best books about Snorri are Nordal (1920) and *Snorri. Átta alda minning* (1979).

BIBLIOGRAPHY

Egils saga (Íslenzk fornrit 2), Reykjavík: Hið íslenzka fornritafélag 1933.

Íslenzk fornrit, vols 1–, Reykjavík: Hið íslenzka fornritafélag 1933 ff.

Nordal, S. (1920) *Snorri Sturluson*, Reykjavík: Þór. B. Þorláksson.

Snorri. Átta alda minning, Reykjavík: Sögufélag 1979.

Snorri Sturluson, Heimskringla, 3 vols (Íslenzk fornrit 26–28), Reykjavík: Hið íslenzka fornritafélag 1941–51.

Snorri Sturluson, Edda, 4 vols, ed. A. Faulkes, London: Viking Society for Northern Research, 1998–2005.

Snorri Sturluson, Edda, trans. A. Faulkes (Everyman's Library), London: Dent 1987.

Sturla Þórðarson, Hákonar saga Hákonarsonar, ed. Guðbrandur Vigfússon, trans. G.W. Dasent (Icelandic Sagas 2 and 4), London: Rolls Series 1887–94.

Sturla Þórðarson, Íslendinga saga, in *Sturlunga saga*, 2 vols, ed. Jón Jóhannesson *et al.*, Reykjavík: Sturlunguútgáfan 1946.

CHAPTER TWENTY-THREE (2)

THE SAGAS OF ICELANDERS

——·◆·——

Guðrún Nordal

The sagas of Icelanders (*Íslendingasögur*) are often mentioned in the same breath as the Vikings. It is true that the sagas dramatise events and vividly portray the lives of people that hypothetically lived in the ninth, tenth and eleventh centuries in the Viking diaspora, and by noting the Norwegian king who is in power at the time of events the saga's narration seems to be anchored in time. The listing of genealogies of many of the saga characters, some stretching back to their Scandinavian, Irish or British ancestors, and the evocation of well-known locations in the northern region, Iceland, Scandinavia and the British Isles, renders a further air of historical truthfulness to the narrative. But can we evaluate the factual evidence of the sagas of Icelanders as regards their depiction of the settlement period, the migration from Norway and the British Isles to Iceland, and their representation of the period in which the pagan religion was practised? The sagas of Icelanders have caught the imagination of the modern reader not least their portrayals of the pagan period, but these portrayals are borne out of, and modified by, a culture which is certainly closely rooted in the scholastic and Christian learned traditions of the thirteenth and fourteenth centuries in Europe. The complex relationship between the orally transmitted memories of the past and the literary culture of the Christian Middle Ages draws attention to the challenge of using the sagas as reliable sources for the Viking period.

The generic characteristics of the sagas of Icelanders (in contrast to other saga genres, e.g. *fornaldarsögur* and the kings' sagas) are determined by three features in particular: the time of events, the scene and place of events, and the time of writing. However, these three criteria are by no means consistent in all forty sagas. The sagas' sense of time of events is not the same from one saga to the next, even though they seem to inhabit the same timeframe, *c.* 870–1070. Some sagas begin in the ninth century and do not cross over the significant line of the conversion to Christianity *c.* 1000, while other sagas focus on events in the Christian period of the eleventh century. The time of writing is equally widely spread: spanning the period from the early thirteenth century to the beginning or the middle of the fifteenth century. The earliest manuscripts of some of the sagas are even dated to the seventeenth century, even though it is clear that they are copies of older, now lost, manuscripts. It is therefore important to distinguish on the one hand between sagas portraying the earlier pagan period in contrast with the later period, and

315

on the other hand between the earliest manuscript versions of each of the sagas, and the later ones, and thus take into account the variability in the transmission of the texts (see e.g. the transmission of *Njáls saga*, Guðrún Nordal 2005). The sagas' sense of geography is furthermore decisive for the narrative mode. Most of the sagas focus on events in Iceland, while the narration is also played out to a smaller or greater degree in Greenland (and even America if the Vinland sagas, *Eiríks saga rauða* and *Grænlendinga saga* are grouped with the sagas of Icelanders), in the British Isles and Scandinavia, and some characters even travel as east as Constantinople. It has been argued that the narrative mode changes according to the change of location; that the 'realistic' mode is relaxed when events depart the familiar space in Iceland and Norway (Torfi Tulinius 1990). But it is equally evident that among the sagas there is varied interest in other countries outside Iceland and in the 'other', as will become evident in this chapter.

Modern scholars have approached the categorisation of the *c.* forty sagas of Icelanders from different angles. These attempts are always linked to the scholars' ideas about the growth and evolution of the genre in the thirteenth and fourteenth centuries. I will mention three such endeavours. Sigurður Nordal attempted a grouping based on the balance between the historical and the fantastic in each saga and suggested a timeline for the writing of the sagas from the beginning of the thirteenth century to *c.* 1400. His division of the sagas into five groups is based on the chronology in the writing of the sagas (Sigurður Nordal 1953: 235). Vésteinn Ólason (2005: 101–18, cf. 1993: 23–163), in the most recent Icelandic literary history, categorised the sagas into three groups according to their content matter and time of writing: (1) early sagas *c.* 1200–80, (2) classical sagas *c.* 1240–1300 and (3) late sagas *c.* 1300–1450. Theodore Andersson in his recent study of the early sagas, written in the period 1180–1280, attempted to define more clearly the sagas' relationship with other narrative genres, such as the kings' sagas, for their artistic development. Andersson (2006: 17) suggests three types of sagas which are particularly frequent: (1) the biographical mode, (2) the regional or chronicle saga and (3) the feud or the conflict saga.

Memories about the pagan past in Iceland and the settlement period were most likely preserved in oral memory from the ninth and tenth centuries to the period in which the sagas of Icelanders were written (see Gísli Sigurðsson 2004). The early writing of the Book of Settlement (*Landnámabók*) reveals a social, cultural or economic need in the early twelfth century to establish an official account of the settlement. The motivation behind the construction of the Book of Settlement is contested, but the early settlements of Iceland may have been set in writing in order to secure land claims by ruling families at the time of writing. The different versions of the work from the thirteenth century to the beginning of the fifteenth century reflect a continuing interest in and demand for passing on the stories of the migration from Norway and the British Isles and an account of the settlement.

The inclusion of the stories of the migration to Iceland and the settlement in a saga clearly affects its beginning and determines through which door the reader or listener enters the house of the narrative, to use a metaphor from Geoffrey from Vinsauf's *Poetria nova*. Unusually for a fictitious medieval genre, the sagas of Icelanders do not contain literary prologues that place the narrative in a context with other medieval genres at the very outset, nor is there any discussion of the writers' attitudes to the factual or fictive quality of the narrative. For this reason, the beginning of each saga may serve as a prologue, in many cases foreshadowing the main narrative, in some cases comparing or contrasting the forefather or foremother to the main character. In the context of the Viking period it is illuminating to focus on the sagas which open at the time of settlement of Iceland *c.* 870–950, and thus reflect the author's or the audience's interest in the migration period and their interest in the neighbouring countries in the Viking period. These sagas are, in alphabetical order: *Bárðar saga Snæfellsáss, Egils saga, Eyrbyggja saga, Flóamanna saga, Gísla saga Súrssonar, Grettis saga, Hallfreðar saga, Harðar saga, Hrafnkels saga, Kjalnesinga saga, Kormaks saga, Laxdæla saga, Reykdæla saga, Svarfdæla saga, Vatnsdæla saga, Víga-Glúms saga, and Þórðar saga hreðu Víglundar saga, Þorskfirðinga saga.*

Iceland had become part of the Norwegian kingdom (*c.* 1262–4) when most of the sagas of Icelanders are written, with perhaps the exception of *Egils saga,* the skalds' sagas and possibly *Laxdæla* and *Eyrbyggja.* Some of these sagas may reflect an interest by members of the Icelandic aristocratic elite to argue for the close ties between Iceland and Norway, the old homeland for many of the settlers, now the seat of the king. But each saga treats the topic of the settlement differently, and the sagas that begin their story in Iceland and omit the migration story place less importance on these ties. Moreover, the sagas that begin their narration after the settlement treat the topic with lack of interest. Four patterns in the sagas' depiction of the settlement emerge:

1   Sagas containing a complex migration story and detailed elucidation of the migrating family's relationship with the king. This theme is rehearsed in sagas such as *Laxdæla saga, Vatnsdæla saga, Eyrbyggja saga,* and the sagas of the court poets, such as *Egils saga, Hallfreðar saga* and *Kormaks saga.* Some of these sagas are preserved in old manuscript fragments from the thirteenth century, and are probably among the oldest written sagas of Icelanders.

2   The emphasis on the history of a fighter-poet's family, where the family's life in Norway is played out in detail in sagas such as *Grettis saga* and *Gísla saga Súrssonar* (particularly the longer version). Other sagas of this kind are *Harðar saga og Hólmverja* (no migration story), *Víga-Glúms saga, Víglundar saga* and *Þórðar saga hreðu* (see Guðrún Nordal 2007). The portrayals of the hero seem to be modelled on the sagas of the court poets, but in fact these sagas focus on different themes from the skalds' sagas. All of them deal with personal loss, the loss of land, the loss of freedom, as in the outlaw sagas, and some end on a very tragic note. There is a strong tendency in all of these sagas to deepen the portrayal of the hero by linking him to the family's past in Norway. *Víga-Glúms saga* is not a typical settlement saga, but the family's 'fylgja' in Norway settles in Iceland.

3   Learned interest in the settlement and the mythic past of Iceland is attested in sagas such as *Bárðar saga Snæfellsáss, Flóamanna saga, Kjalnesinga saga* (not a migration story, the saga begins at the time of the settlement), *Þorskfirðinga saga.* Some of the settlement stories are even drawn from external written sources such as in *Flóamanna saga.* In this group there is an apparent interest in travels to Greenland.

4   In some sagas we find a very short reference to the settlement, where there is no migration story and little importance placed on the settlement process. Among those are sagas such as *Hrafnkels saga* and *Reykdæla saga.*

The shifting emphasis on the migration to Iceland and the settlement in the sagas of Icelanders reveals the ambiguity in the sagas' deliberation and reconfiguration of the Viking past. The many Christian writers of the sagas regarded the pagan past in a markedly different way, and some went as far as to disregard the settlers' ties to their old homelands. The sagas of the Eastfjords reveal a noteworthy indifference to the memories of the settlement. Only two sagas out of ten begin at the time of settlement (*Reykdæla saga* and *Hrafnkels saga*), but with no accompanying genealogy connecting the families with the 'old' Viking world. The stories of the settlement seem to be predominantly associated with events and characters in west and north-west Iceland: the area where the interest in skaldic poetry and the writing about pagan myth was also most clearly attested. This geographic distinction within the genre of the sagas of Icelanders can be no coincidence, and throws into relief the importance of constantly keeping in mind the subtle differences between the sagas of Icelanders in their depiction of the Viking past.

BIBLIOGRAPHY

Andersson, Th.M. (2006) *The Growth of the Medieval Icelandic Sagas (1180–1280)*, Ithaca, NY and London: Cornell University Press.

Gísli Sigurðsson (2004) *The Medieval Icelandic Saga and Oral Tradition. A Discourse on Method*, trans N. Jones (Publications of the Milman Parry Collection of Oral Literature 2), Cambridge, MA: Cambridge University Press.

Guðrún Nordal (2005) 'Attraction of opposites: skaldic verse in *Njáls saga*', in P. Hermann (ed.) *Literacy in Scandinavia from Middle Ages to Early Modern Time* (The Viking Collection in Northern Civilization 16), Odense: Odense University Press.

—— (2007) 'The art of skaldic poetry and the sagas of Icelanders', in J. Quinn, K. Heslop and T. Wills (eds) *Learning and Understanding in the Old Norse World. Essays in Honour of Margaret Clunies Ross* (Medieval Texts and Cultures of Northern Europe 18), Turnhout: Brepols.

Sigurður Nordal (1953) 'Sagalitteraturen', in Sigurður Nordal (ed.) *Litteraturhistorie*, vol. B (Nordisk kultur 8B), Stockholm, Oslo and Copenhagen: Bonnier *et al.*

Torfi H. Tulinius (1990) 'Landafræði og flokkun Íslendingasagna', *Skáldskaparmál*, 1: 142–56.

Vésteinn Ólason (1993) 'Íslendingasögur', in Vésteinn Ólason (ed.) *Íslensk bókmenntasaga*, vol. 2, Reykjavík: Mál og menning.

—— (2005) 'Family sagas', in R. McTurk (ed.) *A Companion to Old-Norse Icelandic Literature and Culture*, Oxford: Blackwell.

THE HEROIC AND
LEGENDARY SAGAS

——·•·——

Stephen Mitchell

The heroic and legendary sagas, also known by such varied terms as Mythical-Heroic Sagas and *fornaldarsögur norðrlanda* ('Nordic sagas of antiquity'), constitute a group of some thirty late medieval Icelandic texts. Although the genre was given its canonical shape by modern editors, especially P.E. Müller (1818) and Carl C. Rafn (1829), few readers fail to sense the unity of these narratives. Characteristic features include the valorisation of Nordic heroes, wide-ranging exploits across the map of Europe, frequent pagan theophanies, and a remarkable array of supernatural creatures and villains. These features, and a frequent suspension of normal temporal and spatial frames of reference, contrast sharply with the more realistic saga genres (e.g. *íslendingasögur, Sturlunga saga*). Many of these same formal features are also true of a group of texts closely resembling the *fornaldarsögur* but which, due to their foreign origins and non-Nordic heroes, are usually assigned to a separate genre of translated and original chivalric romances (e.g. *Karlamagnús saga, Kirjalax saga*).

The *fornaldarsögur* are generally subdivided into several broad, and occasionally overlapping, sub-categories, Adventure Tales and Heroic Legends, corresponding to comic and tragic modes within the genre. Typically, the Adventure Tales (e.g. *Bósa saga*) sport a so-called 'Ashlad' hero and end with a felicitous conclusion to the hero's quest. By contrast, the Heroic Legends (e.g. *Ragnars saga loðbrókar*) generally close with the deaths of their champions. To the extent the protagonist is presented as a Viking, a further subgroup is sometimes drawn from the previous sub-categories, namely the Viking Sagas. The taxonomic imprecision evident in such a statement underscores the difficulty in making overly narrow genre assignments, yet the themes associated with these sub-categories are helpful in understanding the genre as a whole. Alternatively, some critics have looked to categorise – and evaluate – the *fornaldarsögur* in terms of the individual saga's relation to such external categories as myth, folktale, history and heroic poetry. In addition to the extant texts, a number of lost *fornaldarsögur* (e.g. **Ásmundar saga flagðagæfu*) can be perceived in the literary record.

That something like our modern perception of the genre was also recognised in medieval Iceland is strongly suggested by the fact that several manuscripts consist almost entirely of *fornaldarsögur* and other 'romantic' sagas (e.g. AM 343a, 4to). The popularity of these sagas in Iceland is attested to by the large number of manuscripts in which they are preserved, and that these texts are even found in the inventories of medieval Icelandic churches indicates the audiences for them were large and diverse. On the other hand, some sagas (e.g. *Hálfs saga ok Hálfsrekka*) are preserved in unique medieval manuscripts, while still others (e.g. *Hrólfs saga kraka*) have come down to us only in post-Reformation codices. Significant too in understanding the character and complexity of these sagas is the fact that a number of them have survived in highly varied multiforms. The variations often include lengthy interpolations, and the overall effect of the codicological testimony indicates the ready acceptance, and practice, of textual massaging according to the tastes of subsequent scribes, audiences and patrons. And as with other saga genres, although perhaps to a greater degree in this instance, the *fornaldarsögur* are ornamented with details drawn from a diverse and eclectic set of sources, including the learned clerical culture that informs encyclopaedic works like *Alfræði íslenzk* (AM 194, 8vo). Yet the hallmark of the legendary sagas remains, as the various names given to the genre suggest, their fascination with the old heroic traditions of northern Europe. Typically, the exploits of their champions take place before the settlement of Iceland, and the few exceptions (e.g. *Yngvars saga víðförla*) explicitly set the adventures outside the historical worlds of their audiences. Characteristically, these sagas play out either on the undefined landscape of Germanic heroic literature or in the exotic, far-off venues of adventure tales; in any event, the locales (and resulting atmospheres) are far from the realistic, workaday world of medieval Iceland so characteristic of the *íslendingasögur* and other more realistic saga genres.

Testimony to the popularity of the heroic traditions these sagas celebrate – throughout the Nordic world, not just in Iceland – is provided by a wide variety of adjacent cultural monuments. The most impressive work in this regard is surely *Völsunga saga*. Although this *fornaldarsaga* is preserved only in a single fifteenth-century manuscript, the fame of the traditions at its heart is evident in a wide array of media throughout northern Europe. Scenes from the story are found in sculpted and carved representations, most notably in the many Norwegian stave-church carvings, but also on such impressive works as the Ramsund petroglyph in Sweden (see Figure 23.3.1) and the Andreas carving on the Isle of Man. Literary works in related Germanic traditions (e.g. *Beowulf*, *Nibelungenlied*) refer to, and are informed by, this material, as is the case in other genres of Old Norse literature (i.e. in an encapsulated form in *Snorra Edda* and in the heroic cycle constituted by more than a dozen poems in the *Poetic Edda*). Within Scandinavian narrative tradition, the popularity of many of the *fornaldarsögur* materials is also readily apparent, nowhere more so than in the twelfth-century *Gesta Danorum* of Saxo Grammaticus. This text is rich with characters and episodes also known from the *fornaldarsögur* (e.g. *Örvar-Odds saga*, *Hervarar saga ok Heiðreks*), a knowledge of which Saxo attributes to the Icelanders' love of legendary materials. Given the popularity of the *fornaldarsögur* traditions, it is hardly surprising that they are well represented in the ballad traditions of the Faroes, Norway, Sweden and Denmark and in the Icelandic metrical romances (*rímur*). Many of the motifs and characters of the *fornaldarsögur* corpus are also found in the folklore materials collected in the nineteenth century, although questions of authenticity and direction of influence, or even of reticulated influences, naturally abound in such contexts.

How the *fornaldarsögur* were used by medieval audiences, and to what purpose, has attracted much attention in recent years. Were they written through the patronage of individuals whose ambitions and concerns influenced the shape of the text? Were they of some larger extra-literary value to the Icelanders? Were they written under the moderate, or even deep, influence of the oral tradition which informs them? To what degree can we reconstruct the performance contexts of these materials? The possibility of orally composed and recited *fornaldarsögur* has been eagerly pursued, although until recently arguments in this area have principally been based on such passages as those in *Þorgils saga ok Hafliða* and *Sturlu saga*, both of which portray orally performed *fornaldarsögur*. As to their function, it has been noted that prominent Icelandic families and individuals may have found advantageous the genealogical connections reported in the *fornaldarsögur* between the heroes of these texts and themselves (e.g. *Hálfs saga ok Hálfsrekka*). Along similar lines, there is reason to believe that Icelanders may have found such ancestral ties to the champions of the legendary sagas important and useful, providing as they do an intimate and prestigious connection between the world of medieval Iceland and the Scandinavian heroic age. Precisely this logic is offered by a writer looking to explain the Icelanders' renowned interest in history, legends and genealogies: 'But we can better answer the criticism of foreigners when they accuse us of coming from slaves or rogues, if we know for certain the truth about our ancestry' (*Melabók*, ch. 335).

Scholarly assessments of the *fornaldarsögur* vary widely: some (e.g. *Völsunga saga*) attract much attention in literary criticism, whereas most others have been dismissed in contemptible terms. As scholarship increasingly prizes the genre's potential to augment our knowledge of the Nordic Middle Ages in cultural and social, not merely literary, terms, the worth of the *fornaldarsögur* rises steadily, and modern readers perhaps begin to understand the texts in terms closer to those valued by their medieval audiences.

Figure 23.3.1   Sigurðr impaling the dragon Fafnir from below, from the Ramsund petroglyph in Sweden. Copyright S. Mitchell

BIBLIOGRAPHY

Boberg, I. (1966) *Motif-Index of Early Icelandic Literature* (Bibliotheca Arnamagnaeana 27), Copenhagen: Ejnar Munksgaard.

- *Stephen Mitchell* -

— *Stephen Mitchell* —

Buchholz, P. (1980) *Vorzeitkunde. Mündliches Erzählen und Überliefern im mittelalterlichen Skandinavien nach dem Zeugnis von Fornaldarsaga und eddischer Dichtung* (Skandinavistische Studien 13), Neumünster: Wachholtz.

Einar Ól. Sveinsson (1929) *Verzeichnis isländischer Märchenvarianten, mit einer einleitenden Untersuchung* (Folklore Fellows Communications 83), Helsinki: Suomalainen Tiedeakatemia.

Genzmer, F. (1948) 'Vorzeitsaga und Heldenlied', in *Festschrift Paul Klukhohn und Hermann Schneider gewidmet zu ihren 60. Geburtstag*, Tübingen: J.C.B. Mohr.

Gísli Sigurðsson (2002) *Túlkun íslendingasagna í ljósi munnlegrar hefðar. Tilgáta um aðferð* (Rit Stofnun Árna Magnússonar á Íslandi 56), Reykjavík: Stofnun Árna Magnússonar á Íslandi. [In trans. as: *The Medieval Icelandic Saga and Oral Tradition. A Discourse on Method* (Publications of the Milman Parry Collection of Oral Literature 2), Cambridge, MA: Harvard University Press 2004].

Guðni Jónsson (ed.) (1954) *Fornaldar Sögur Norðurlanda*, 4 vols, Reykjavík: Íslendingasagnaútgáfan.

Hallberg, P. (1982) 'Some aspects of the *Fornaldarsögur* as a corpus', *Arkiv för nordisk filologi*, 97: 1–35.

Hermannsson, H. (ed.) (1912) *Bibliography of the Mythical-Heroic Sagas (Fornaldarsögur)* (Islandica 5), Ithaca, NY: Cornell University Library.

—— (1937) *The Sagas of the Kings (Konunga sögur) and the Mythical-Heroic Sagas (Fornaldar sögur). Two Bibliographic Supplements* (Islandica 26), Ithaca, NY: Cornell University Press.

Holtsmark, A. (1965) 'Heroic poetry and legendary sagas', *Bibliography of Old Norse-Icelandic Studies*: 9–21.

Jakobsson, Ármann, Lassen, A. and Ney, A. (eds) (2003) *Fornaldarsagornas struktur och ideology* (Nordiska texter och undersökningar 28), Uppsala: Institutionen för nordiska språk, Uppsala universitet.

Liestøl, K. (1915) *Norske trollvisor og norrøne sogor*, Oslo: Olaf Norlis forlag.

—— (1970) *Den norrøne arven* (with an English summary 'The Norse Heritage'), Oslo: Universitetsforlaget.

Mitchell, S.A. (1991) *Heroic Sagas and Ballads*, Ithaca, NY: Cornell University Press.

—— (2002) 'Performance and Norse poetry: the hydromel of praise and the effluvia of scorn', *Oral Tradition*, 16(1): 168–202.

Müller, P.E. (1818) *Saga-Bibliothek med Anmærkninger og indledende Afhandlinger*, vol. 2, Copenhagen: no publ.

Mundt, M. (1993) *Zur Adaption orientalischer Bilder in den* Fornaldarsögur Norðrlanda. *Materialien zu einer neuen Dimension altnordischer Belletristik*, Frankfurt am Main: Lang.

Pálsson, H. (1979) 'Early Icelandic imaginative literature', in H. Bekker-Nielsen *et al.* (eds) *Medieval Narrative. A Symposium*, Odense: Odense University Press.

Pálsson, H. and Edwards, P.G. (1970) *Legendary Fiction in Medieval Iceland* (Studia Islandica/Íslenzk fræði 30), Reykjavík: University of Iceland and the Icelandic Cultural Fund.

Rafn, Carl C. (ed.) (1829–30) *Fornaldar Sögur Nordrlanda, eptir gömlum handritum*, 3 vols, Copenhagen: no publ.

Reuschel, H.I. (1933) *Untersuchungen über Stoff und Stil der Fornaldarsaga* (Bausteine zur Volkskunde und Religionswissenschaft 7), Bühl-Baden: Konkordia.

Righter-Gould, R. (1980) 'The *Fornaldar Sögur Norðurlanda*: a structural analysis', *Scandinavian Studies*, 52: 423–41.

Schlauch, M. (1934) *Romance in Iceland*, Princeton: Princeton University Press for the American–Scandinavian Foundation.

Schneider, H. (1928–34) *Germanische Heldensage*, 3 vols (Grundriss der germanischen Philologie 10), Berlin: de Gruyter.

Torfi H. Tulinius (1995) *La 'Matière du Nord'. Sagas légendaires et fiction dans la littérature islandaise en prose du XIIIe siècle*, Paris: Presses de l'Université de Paris-Sorbonne. [In trans. as: *The Matter of the North. The Rise of Literary Fiction in Thirteenth-Century Iceland* (The Viking Collection 13), Odense: Odense University Press 2002].

CHAPTER TWENTY-FOUR

THE DEVELOPMENT OF VIKING ART

——·◆·——

David M. Wilson

Viking-Age ornament was chiefly rooted in a continuous tradition common to much of north-western Europe which emerged in the fourth century AD. From that period until the end of the Viking Age and beyond Scandinavian artists were obsessed by a convoluted animal ornament which had its roots in Roman art and embellished objects of everyday use, particularly jewellery and weapons. But from the end of the seventh century onwards such foreign influences and many others were quickly – and often almost unrecognisably – subsumed into a self-confident native art.

Salin (1904) first systematised the European Germanic animal ornament, dividing it into three styles (I, II and III). The two latter were subdivided by Arwidsson (1942a and b) into three further styles: style C, which flourished in the seventh century but continued into the eighth century, when it was largely replaced – particularly in southern Scandinavia – by style D. These two styles provided inspiration for the chief animal ornament (style E) of the early Viking Age. Styles D and E, although well in tune with northern and western Europe animal ornament, were developed within Scandinavia with little influence from abroad.

Style E, which appeared at the end of the eighth century and survived until nearly the end of the ninth century, is best represented by twenty-two gilt-bronze bridle-mounts from a grave at Broa, parish of Halla, Gotland, which were the property of a man wealthy enough to ride a well-caparisoned horse (Figure 24.1). The glittering surface of the bridle would have made a brave show, but (as with so much of Viking art) has to be examined in detail in order first to discern and then to understand the ornament. Thus the circle a little to the left of centre is the animal's eye, (Figure 24.1a), exaggerated to fill almost the whole of the head. The ear is produced as a frond to the left, while the snout forms two small tendrils and an irregular extension above the knot to the right of the eye. The head having been identified, the rest of the animal is easily traced.

Three distinct animal motifs appear in style E. The first consists of a double-contoured creature with a subtriangular body, stylised, beak-like head and fork-like feet. Limbs and lappets form boldly curved open loops. Second, a more coherent animal with rounded head, a long lappet and small claws. One of the hips or the neck is often treated as a heart-shaped opening interlaced with a limb or a lappet. Third, in rather more chunky technique, are 'gripping-beasts', (Figure 24.1d), which apparently lack symmetry and coherence. The hips are emphasised (the body often disappears); the feet grip, or reach towards, the border of the field in which they are placed, or actually grip part of their own body. The heads appear as masks. The bodies of all these animals frequently pass from one field to another.

The most important style III find comes from the early ninth-century Norwegian ship burial from Oseberg (Shetelig 1920; Christensen *et al.* 1992). The wooden prow and stem of the ship and many other wooden associated finds – tent-posts, bed-posts, four sledges and a cart are decorated in this style, in a manner well adapted to the objects which they embellish. While the objects differ widely in form and appearance, their ornament is stylistically coherent (although a cart, with its narrative scenes, stands slightly outside the series).

Not all style E artefacts are of the quality of Oseberg and Broa. Humbler objects were decorated in this style: oval brooches (an adjunct of smart dress – equivalent of later folk costume jewellery), for example, were widely dispersed and demonstrate a pan-Scandinavian taste. The brooches were copied, often by being moulded from each other (Jansson 1985), the shrinkage in the clay moulds at each stage of the process resulting in the ornamental detail becoming smaller and more degenerate over time. Other simple objects were clearly produced in a similar fashion.

Early scholars were much exercised by the possibility of a British – and particularly an Irish – origin for much of Viking art. While there are tenuous links with both Britain and the Continent, there is no evidence that style E, while related to a common

Figure 24.1 Style E ornament on gilt-bronze harness-mounts from Broa, Halla, Gotland, Sweden. Scale 1 : 1. © D.M. Wilson.

European tradition, was anything but native. If any foreign element was introduced, it was immediately absorbed – almost unrecognisably – into the native repertoire.

The dendrochronological date for the Oseberg ship, built *c.* 820 and buried in 834, provides a firm chronological point in the development of style E (Bonde and Christensen 1993) – a style which faded towards the end of the century (although the gripping-beast motif survived into the succeeding Borre style).

Not all Viking art was zoomorphic; narrative art also occurs, particularly in Gotland, where a series of 'picture stones' (Sw *bildstenar*) – unique to the island – date from the fifth to well into the eleventh century (Lindqvist 1941; Nylén 1978). Slabs of limestone, engraved with images representing a cult of death, were erected in pagan grave-fields. In the Viking Age, however, they were often set up as memorials away from the burial grounds. Within a frame, on a grand stone from Ardre (Figure 24.2), are two panels – in the upper frame is a rider on an eight-legged horse; to his left a semicircular design is usually interpreted as a building. Below is a complicated scene of armed warriors and at least one woman. The lower field is dominated by a ship in full sail with rising prow- and stern-posts. Below the ship – to the left – are two figures in a boat, fishing. In the middle is a forge with various smiths' tools. To the right are two recumbent bodies, apparently headless, and a man within a rectangle apparently caught up in interlaced snakes. Two men (bottom left) spear a fish from a boat. Other figures, structures and implements are scattered seemingly at random throughout the field.

It is assumed that the scenes on the stones are drawn from Old Norse mythology. Apart from what are clearly representations of the hero Sigurðr, and of the god Þórr, fishing, few clear and understandable representations of Old Norse myth and religion in Viking art can be related to literary sources which recount pagan tales. A common motif of the Gotland stones is the ship, which in the Viking Age is shown in full sail crewed by armed men, and is clearly in continuous tradition from oared vessels depicted on stones as early as the fourth century. The idea of a funerary ship is familiar in Germanic mythology and both ship burials and ship settings in Scandinavia witness – as do these images of ships – to the belief in a journey to an afterlife by ship.

Lindqvist (1941–2) erected a chronology for the stones which spanned the period from *c.* AD 400 to *c.* 1100, but with a gap in the sequence, between say 850 and 1000. This gap is unlikely (Wilson 1998), particularly as the ornament of some eleventh-century stones are closely related to that of Ardre, which is conventionally dated to the eighth or ninth century. It is more likely that the Viking series extended from the late eighth or early ninth century – a date strengthened by stylistic and figural parallels in narrative textiles from Oseberg – until the mid-eleventh century.

Outside Gotland, narrative stones largely date from the tenth and eleventh centuries and are only marginally related to those on the island. There are significant parallels to the scenes on the Gotland stones, however, on a wooden wagon and on tapestries from Oseberg (Krafft 1956), and on a fragment of tapestry from Över-hogdal, Härjedalen, Sweden, although here chronological opinions differ (Franzén and Nockert 1992: 49–50; Wilson 1995: 81–5). Further, representational art reminiscent of that on the stones occurs on metalwork of the early Viking Age (Arwidsson 1989: 58 ff.).

The sequence of zoomorphic ornament continues with the Borre style which, succeeding style E, is found throughout Scandinavia and the Viking colonies. Named after a group of gilt-bronze harness-mounts found in a ship burial at Borre, Vestfold, Norway

Figure 24.2   Picture stone from Ardre, Gotland. (Bildsten; Ardre k:a; Go; Inv. nr. 11118: VIII.
Copyright © Bengt A Lundberg/Museum of National Antiquities, Stockholm, Sweden.)

(Brøgger 1916; Myhre 1992), its most important diagnostic element is the ribbon plait
– the 'ring-chain' (Figure 24.3b) – a symmetrical interlaced pattern, each intersection of
which is bound by interlacing circles overlaid by lozenges or by hollow-sided squares or
triangles. Often constructed as a double ribbon, it is often given added glitter by means
of transverse nicks. The second major motif of the style is a single gripping-beast, its
body normally forming a curved ribbon between two hips (Figure 24.3a). The head
consists of a mask (basically a triangle with prominent eyes and a snout), usually with
one or two lappets or pigtails. The ribbon-like neck passes to a hip in one corner of the

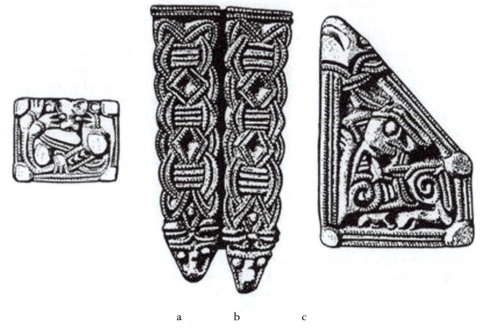

a   b   c

Figure 24.3   Bronze harness-mounts from Vestfold, Norway. Scale 1 : 1.
© 3a Eva Wilson; b and c after Brøgger (1916).

field and the body curves up below (exceptionally above) the mask to a hip at the opposite side of the field. The legs are produced from the hip and some of the feet grip either the border of the field or another part of the animal's body. The Borre animal differs from the gripping beast of the preceding style in that it forms a single articulated creature and tends to be symmetrical within the field. The third Borre-style motif is an animal (normally standing alone in a field) seen from the side (Figure 24.3c). Although formalised, it is of more-or-less naturalistic proportions, its head frequently bent backwards; the hips are spiraliform, and the feet sometimes grip the border of the field. This motif is occasionally treated three-dimensionally. The style probably originated in metalwork: the metalworkers' interpretation of the style being developed in precious metal, the transverse nicks on base metal objects imitate gold or silver filigree. The style is widely diffused in the British Isles, where it was adapted enthusiastically in stone sculpture and to a lesser extent in metalwork (Bailey 1980: 54–5; Wilson 1976, 1983), and in the metalwork in the Swedish settlements and graves of Russia (e.g. Roesdahl and Wilson 1992: 307, nos 301, 304, 305, 307, 310).

Dates for the Borre style depend almost entirely on coin hoards. A mid-ninth-century date for the beginning of the style might be suggested on the basis of the hoard from Hoen, Norway (Horn Fuglesang and Wilson 2006), and it is reasonable to allow for the production of the Borre style for more than a century after 850, as objects decorated in the style are found in the late tenth-century circular fortresses in Denmark. Danish coin hoards provide an acceptable chronological series for the first three-quarters of the tenth century (Wilson and Klindt-Jensen 1966: 92–3).

The fact that Borre-style objects are so common in Scandinavia may in part be explained by the fact that this was the last period of full paganism. By the last quarter of the tenth century Denmark was officially Christian and the practice of accompanied burial was dying out. Norway and Sweden had not yet achieved that state, but Christianity was beginning to seep in, and burial customs were beginning to change. Another reason for the style's popularity was that this was the period of maximum Viking expansion, when the kingdom of York and other parts of the Danelaw flourished. Ireland, the Isle of Man, the north and west of Scotland and even parts of Wales were settled by Scandinavians. In the east the Swedes largely influenced the river routes of eastern Europe, founding trading stations and even a proto-Russian state; they traded southwards with Byzantium and the Arab world. The Scandinavian Borre style appeared commonly in more or less pure form in all these colonies. No other style was so widespread.

The succeeding Jellinge style has its roots in style III and is closely related to, and largely contemporary with, the Borre style. The two styles, however, rarely merge. The name is taken from the ornament on a small (4.3 cm high) silver cup, with traces of gilding and niello, found in the burial chamber of the North Mound at the royal burial place of Jelling (Figure 24.4), Jutland, which is dated dendrochronologically to 958/9. The mound was presumably raised to take the body of King Gorm, whose remains were later removed to a grave in the church built at the foot of the mound by his son Harald Bluetooth when Denmark became officially Christian, a few years after Gorm's death. (An accident of dialect introduced the term 'Jellinge' – with a final -e – to describe the style, a label which is by general consent retained to distinguish the style from the site.)

The style's chief motif is a beast with a ribbon-like (approximately S-shaped) body; the head – unlike most Borre-style animal heads – is normally seen in profile and has a round eye, a pigtail and a lip lappet. The body is often beaded, usually double contoured and usually has an insubstantial hook-like hip. Its most diagnostic feature is a ribbon-like body, which distinguishes it from the more substantial and slightly more natural-istic body of animals of the succeeding Mammen style (Figure 24.5).

The style can be considered only with reference either to the Borre style or to the Mammen style, with both of which it is often associated. Links with the Borre style are clearly seen on the composite rectangular silver brooch from Ödeshög, Östergötland (Wilson 1995: fig. 79). One of a pair, the midrib and its ends are decorated with a design

Figure 24.4 Ornament on cup from Jelling, Jutland. © Eva Wilson

Figure 24.5   Inlaid iron axe-head from Bjerringhøj, Mammen, Jutland , Denmark. Length: 19 cm.
© Holger Arbman.

derived from the Borre ring-chain. On either side of the midrib is an animal with ribbon-like body, spiral hips, legs which interlace with the body, and a pigtail.

Many features of the Jellinge style may be derived from style III, as, for example, from the ribbon-formed animals on the runners of Shetelig's sledge at Oseberg (Shetelig 1920 fig. 159a and c). It must be stressed, however, that, by the time the Jellinge style had reached its full maturity – on the Mammen horse-collar, for example (Näsman 1991: figs 11–17) – all distinct traces of style E had been subsumed into the new style.

The earliest datable Jellinge-style object is a strap-end from the Gokstad mound (Wilson and Klindt-Jensen 1966: pl. 30d), which is dated dendrochonologically *c.* 900–5, suggesting that the style developed towards the end of the ninth century. The Jelling beaker was deposited 958/9. Other dates are provided by coin hoards – Vårby (deposited *c.* 940), Eketorp (deposited after 954), Sejrø (deposited *c.* 953) and the mid-ninth-century Gnezdovo hoard. Emerging just before 900, the Jellinge style gradually developed into the Mammen style, dying out towards the end of the tenth century.

The Mammen style (Fuglesang 1991) is named after an axe from a richly equipped man's grave in the mound at Bjerringhøj, Mammen, Jutland. Decorated on both faces with inlaid silver wire, it bears on one face (Figure 24.5) an asymmetrical bird-like creature with back-turned head, lip-lappet and various foliate offshoots. There is a large spiral hip, and the offshoots interlace elaborately with the body to form double loops (sometimes described as pretzel loops) to fill the whole field. There are curved nicks in the contour and the body is embellished with a regular pattern of inlaid dots. The other face of the axe is decorated in the same technique and has similar billeting. As befits an object which is itself asymmetrical, the face encloses an asymmetrical plant ornament, the tendrils of which rise to cover the whole field (best seen if viewed with the axe-edge at the bottom). The Mammen style occurs importantly on the Jelling stone (Figure 48.4) and on a number of stone, ivory and bone objects. The motifs are generally set in an unaxial and asymmetrical fashion, often forming irregular closed loops; the ribbons (which sometimes have zoomorphic elements) and plants often bifurcate and the contours are often angled at a major curve and frequently have a curved indented nick. The body is almost always billeted in regular rows. As it gradually merges with the succeeding Ringerike style, traits such as asymmetry and unaxiality tend to disappear and, as they were not universal traits of the Mammen style, it is sometimes difficult to distinguish between the two.

Objects decorated in the Mammen style are found widely (if sparsely) throughout Europe – in the Ukraine, at Leon in Spain, Bamberg in Germany, the River Thames at London, the Isle of Man, and Møre og Romsdal in Norway. In Sweden the style mostly occurs on runic-inscribed stones. Its most important appearance, however, is on the Danish royal memorial at Jelling, which almost certainly influenced a new style of stone-carving in southern Scandinavia.

The origin of the 'lion', first seen on the Jelling stone, seems to be in native Scandinavian art. In stance and treatment its precursors are found in more or less recognisable form on a brooch from Birka (grave 854; Wilson 1995: fig. 19), on the runner of the fourth sledge from the Oseberg grave (Wilson 1995: fig. 111), on the Borre mounts (Figure 24.3c) and, in three-dimensional form, on some of the baroque Borre-style brooches (Wilson 1995: fig. 58). Persistent attempts have, however, been made to find its origins in Anglo-Saxon or Ottonian art (Fuglesang 1991: 101), for the lion – a universal Christian motif – is clearly ultimately of foreign origin. No immediate prototypes have, however, been identified, and definite conclusions concerning archetypes have not been established. It may have been derived from any of a number of countries – France, Byzantium, Italy, Germany, or England – and from any of a number of media: manuscript art or figured textiles, for example. A telling argument for foreign influence must be that there were few or no carved stone reliefs in Denmark before the production of the Jelling stone. It is also clear that the nearest source for such a technique was the Scandinavian areas of Britain, where the long tradition of Hiberno-Saxon stone sculpture had been adapted to the incomers' taste (for a general discussion, see Wilson 1984). It is conceivable that the Danish carver of the Jelling stone had learnt his trade in the English Danelaw (although sculpture of granite is a rarity in an area of ubiquitous freestone). Even if this is the case, the zoomorphic element of the stone need not be derived from Britain; stylistic similarities may be explained by a common origin of the ornament in the two areas, which, by the time it reached Denmark, had been subsumed into the local taste. It is, however, inherently likely that the animal's general design originated in the stone sculpture of England, whence surely came the style's vegetal elements. The acanthus-like fleshy scrolls are closely related to, and must be derived from, those of the Anglo-Saxon Winchester style, which flourished in the period of greatest Danish influence in England – in the first half of the tenth century. The Jelling stone is the most important representative of the Mammen style surviving in Scandinavia. It is also remarkable in bearing the earliest datable representation of Christ in Scandinavia (Wilson 1995: fig. 129). Finally, it is unique in being a decorated royal monument and as such would have been an object of wonder and prestige throughout the kingdom.

It was almost certainly the direct inspiration for a group of stones from Skåne, from Tullstorp (Wilson 1995: fig. 115) and Hunnestad, the latter group, of which only three stones survive (seven were illustrated by Ole Worm in 1643, see Wilson 1995: fig. 114), really belongs to the Mammen/Ringerike overlap. There are a number of central dates for the Mammen style. First, the Jelling stone, which is to be dated about 965 (i.e. the conversion of Denmark, an event referred to in the inscription on the stone), a date which might well, as the stone is so innovative in both form and ornament, be near the period of the birth of the style. Second, there is the axe from the Mammen grave itself, buried in the winter of 970/1. Then there is the small wooden figure of a man from the North Mound at Jelling, which was constructed in 958/9 (Wilson 1995: figs 118–19). The only hoard which contains objects ornamented in the Mammen style comes from Skaill, Orkney, which is bracketed within the period 950–70 (Graham-Campbell 1995: 34–48). It has been suggested that the brooches were ornamented somewhere in the Irish Sea region, perhaps in the Isle of Man where sculptured cross-shafts from the parish church of Kirk Braddan (Figure 27.3.3) bear classic Mammen-style decoration (Graham-Campbell 1995: 70–1). This suggested provenance is of interest as a single piece of wood decorated in the Mammen style has been found in Dublin in an archaeo-logical context with coins dating between the 920s and 950s (Lang 1988: 45 and fig. 20). Thus a date in the 950s is likely for the production of the Skaill brooches (which in some instances show traces of the Jellinge/Mammen overlap), a date which would chime with that of the Jelling stone. By the end of the century the Mammen style was merging with the Ringerike style. On the basis of all this rather precise evidence a date of 950–1000 would seem an acceptable bracket for the Mammen style.

The Ringerike style takes its name from the Ringerike district to the north of Oslo in Norway, where the reddish sandstone common in the region is widely used for stones carved with designs in this style, although only one stone, from Tanberg (Fuglesang 1980: pl. 38), has been found in Ringerike itself. The object usually used to define the Ringerike style is the stone from Vang, Oppland, Norway (Figure 24.6). 215 cm high; it bears on the right-hand edge a runic memorial inscription. The main field of the stone is filled with a balanced tendril ornament, which springs from two shell spirals at the base. The main stems cross twice and terminate in lobed tendrils. Further tendrils spring from loops at the crossing, while pear-shaped elements appear from the centre of the tendrils on the upper loop. Although the design is axial, there is a basic asymmetry in the deposition of the tendrils. Above the tendril pattern is a striding animal, double contoured, with spiral hips and a lip lappet. If the design on the Vang stone is compared with the clearly related design on the Mammen axe-head (Figure 24.5), it will be seen that the latter lacks the axiality of the pattern on the Vang stone and its tendrils are much less disciplined. The Mammen scroll is wavy and the Vang scroll is taut and evenly curved. These features in general distinguish the Mammen and Ringerike scrolls. In general the latter are more taut and disciplined; but the close relationship between the two styles is more than adequately demonstrated by the animal at the top of the stone, which is in almost every respect interchangeable with that on the Jelling stone (Figure 48.4).

In metalwork the style is best seen on two copper-gilt weather-vanes – one from Källunge, Gotland, and the other from Söderala, Hälsingland. On one face of the former (Wilson 1995: fig. 138) are two axially constructed loops which take the form of snakes, which produce symmetrically placed tendrils. The heads of the snakes, and the animal and snake on the reverse, are more floridly treated than that on the Vang stone; all have a lip lappet and the snakes have pigtails. Each has a pear-shaped eye with the point towards the snout (a diagnostic feature of the Ringerike style). In two corners are acanthus-bud motifs of a type often encountered in this style (Wilson 1995: fig. 137). The borders are filled with various plant-scroll motifs. The scrolls have shell spirals and elongated tendrils of a form which was to develop as the scrolls became more attenuated. The lion and snake motif on one face of the vane clearly has a common origin with the similar motif on the Jelling stone (Figure 48.4). The pattern of the Söderala vane (Wilson 1995: fig. 139), which is executed in openwork, has the more restless, filament-like characteristics of the succeeding Urnes style, but the substantial body of the main animal and its axial form place it firmly in the Ringerike style. Another animal (a biped) bites the main animal and foreshadows the combat motif of the succeeding Urnes style.

Although stones with runic inscriptions first appear in Sweden in the early Viking Age, it is the Ringerike style which gave full rein to their ornamental embellishment from the late tenth century onwards. They are most plentiful in south and middle Sweden and on Gotland, but occur in some numbers in present-day Denmark and occasionally, although in a rather different form, in Norway. Proclaiming public or private works, the creation of a bridge or causeway, a place of assembly, or the record of the ownership of property, or recording a good deed, the stones are often set up in prominent places to stress a message conveyed in the inscription. Some record a death – often far from home of warriors or merchants in the settlements abroad, or in the lands where Scandinavian merchants traded or soldiers fought. Few stones are specifically pagan (Sawyer 1991: 111) and, where they express religious sentiments or portray symbolism, it is usually Christian (even using apparently pagan scenes in a Christian context). They form the first consistent evidence for the conversion.

The carving on the great rock of Ramsundsberget in Jäder, near Eskilstuna, Södermanland (Wilson 1995: figs. 151 and 152), is one of the most remarkable monuments of the Viking Age in Sweden. Skilfully carved, it tells a coherent and recognisable story, part of the Eddic legend of *Sigurðr*, slayer of *Fafnir* – one of the most popular stories of the period from the tenth to the thirteenth century, and one which occurs throughout Scandinavia, which is represented as far away as in Scandinavian Russia and the Isle of Man. The main scene at Ramsundsberget is framed by three snakes, the heads and tails of which produce typical Ringerike tendrils; the lowermost snake containing a runic inscription which was carved by the order of a woman. Outside the frame (which is some 4.7 m long) is the figure of *Sigurðr* with his sword stuck through the soft underbelly of the lowermost snake. Within the field defined by the snakes lies, to the left, the body of a decapitated *Regin* (the treacherous forger of *Sigurðr*'s sword), together with the tools of his smithy – bellows, hammer, anvil tongues, and so on. *Sigurðr* again appears in the centre of the picture with his finger in his mouth. (This refers to the story that, having slain the dragon, *Sigurðr* cut out its heart and roasted it over a fire; burning himself on the heart, he put his finger in his mouth to cool it down and thus tasted some of the dragon's blood – an accident which enabled him to understand the language of the birds, who warn him of the treachery of *Regin*, whom he then kills.) The birds are seen in the tree to which is tethered *Sigurðr*'s horse *Grani* with the treasure which *Sigurðr* had taken from *Fafnir* on his back. The figures are cleanly cut, with firm outline, and *Sigurðr* is portrayed putting obvious effort into his task of killing the dragon. A clumsier and smaller (250 cm long) version of the same composition is to be found not far away on a boulder at Näsbyholm, Åker, the Gök stone (Wilson 1995: fig. 153). *Sigurðr* appears elsewhere on a number of other – more conventional – stones in Scandinavia.

A comparison between the tendril ornament on the Mammen axe and that on the Norwegian Vang stone demonstrates the roots of the Ringerike style in the Mammen style. Its deeper roots are more obscure. It has been shown that prototypes for such elements of the style as the 'lion' cannot easily be recognised outside Scandinavia – either in Anglo-Saxon England or in Ottonian Europe. Its origins cannot, however, be truly determined. It is reasonable to suggest that the vegetal motifs in both Mammen and Ringerike styles were derived from England, where the acanthus scrolls of the Anglo-Saxon Winchester style provide convincing parallels. The presence of the Danes in England during the whole of the period during which the Ringerike style flourished strengthens the argument. Although Ottonian motifs, which might serve as prototypes particularly for asymmetrical tendril scrolls, have been identified; the arguments for an English origin seem stronger.

The Ringerike style in both Denmark and Norway (and to a lesser extent in Sweden) provides early examples of Christian iconography. Christianity – a religion that was ultimately to introduce new styles and new motifs into the north – was seeping in from both the south and the west; but the Viking styles, conceived in pagandom, were to survive for some time. A syncretism with the art of the pagan period appears in the late tenth century; as, for example, on a stone carving from Kirk Andreas in the Isle of Man (Margeson 1981: fig. 1). It is a syncretism which was to survive. It occurs, for example, as late as *c.* 1200, when the pagan *Sigurðr* legend appears in a totally Christian context on the portal from the stave-church at Hylestad, Setesdal, Norway (Hohler 1999: pl. 220).

The best dating evidence for the style comes from the British Isles, where it appears in various media – manuscripts, stone sculpture, metalwork and woodcarving. The style was presumably introduced into England with Knut (Canute the Great), in the period after his assumption of the throne in 1016; it chimed well with the Winchester style and indeed gave it added liveliness. Classically it appears on a rune-inscribed stone from St Paul's Cathedral in London (Wilson 1974). Its presence in manuscript art helps in dating, as in the so-called Winchcombe Psalter (Cambridge University Library Ff.I.23) (Wilson 1984: fig. 276), dated to the 1020s or 1030s. In Ireland early eleventh-century dates are provided archaeologically by a number of motif-pieces and other decorated objects found during excavation in Dublin (Lang 1988: 18 f.; O'Meadhra 1979: figs 8 ff.), but it must be stressed that elements of the Ringerike style may be traced in Ireland long after this (Wilson and Klindt-Jensen 1966: 143 ff.).

The Ringerike style was incidentally highly influential in Insular art, but most notably in Ireland, where it was adopted enthusiastically, appearing, for example, on a number of pieces of religious metalwork and in illuminated service books. Most interestingly it is seen among the bone motif-pieces from Dublin referred to above – the detritus of metalworkers' workshops, on which the Irish craftsmen had worked out their patterns (e.g. O'Meadhra 1979: figs 114–29).

In Scandinavia the best evidence for the date of the style is provided by coin hoards (Fuglesang 1980: 56 f. and 159 f.), which generally reflect the more reliable English chronology. To fit the style in sequence after the Mammen style (with which it clearly overlaps) we may date the Ringerike style between, say, 990 and 1050 – in historical terms during the period of the growth, maximum expansion and fall of the so-called Danish North Sea Empire.

The ultimate phase of Viking Age art is named after the stave-church at Urnes, Sogn, in western Norway (Figure 24.6). The church was rebuilt in the twelfth century, but a number of earlier timbers were used in its reconstruction, and it is these which give the name to the style. Some of these timbers were decorated, namely the portal and door, two planks now in the north wall of the church, the north-west corner post and the gables at the east and west. The sculptor at Urnes used three basic motifs. First, a standing quadruped; second, a snake-like animal with a single foreleg and a hindleg which appears as a terminal foot, with a hip hinted at by an angular break in the curve of the body; and, third, a thin interlacing or interpenetrating ribbon which terminates either in an animal head or in a trefoil. The creatures are sinuous and curve gently, with few breaks in the curves. The designs are rarely symmetrical. The animals tend to bite each other and this 'combat' element, while not universal, is fairly general.

Some Urnes elements survive from earlier styles: the spiral hip, the lip lappet and the pointed eye (which latter now nearly fills the whole head of the animal), for example. The interlace is filament-like, and forms large, even, almost circular loops. The feet are hardly emphasised, but the lip lappet is sometimes extended to form a tendril. The heads are generally in profile; although some – particularly the secondary (often biting)

Figure 24.6 Stone from Vang, Oppland, Norway. Height: 2.15 m. After Wilson (1995)

snake heads and, on some Swedish runestones, the heads of some of the coarser snakes – are seen from above.

The decoration of the earliest elements of the Urnes stave-church provides a rare example of what must have been a considerable body of high-quality woodcarving which would have been seen throughout Scandinavia in the second half of the eleventh century and in the early twelfth century. Other Urnes-style wooden sculpture survives – though rarely – from church sites throughout Scandinavia. The fact that so much of this art is found in Christian contexts re-emphasises that there is nothing specifically pagan in Viking Age art styles.

The Urnes style dominates the ornament of the runestones of central Sweden; as a result the style itself has sometimes been labelled as the 'rune-stone style'. The sweeping deeply curved relief seen for example in wood on the Urnes portal (Figure 24.7) is not attempted in the harder medium of Swedish stone. Much of the decoration is highly competent; but unfortunately the ornament on these stones is not easily related to the classic Urnes style, being simple and often more coarsely executed. More than a hundred Swedish rune carvers are named, and it is assumed that the writer of the runes also provided the design of the snake in which the inscription was enclosed. Many 'unsigned' stones have been attributed to named carvers on grounds of orthography, language and style; but there is only general agreement concerning the relative chronology of the different craftsmen.

On the basis of the historical content of the inscriptions of some of the runestones, some sort of chronology has been erected. Twenty-five stones, for example, commemorate

Figure 24.7   Portal of the wooden stave-church from Urnes, Norway. Copyright Leif Anker, Oslo.

men who died on an expedition in the east *c.* 1041 (Larsson 1986: 99 discusses these stones in the context of the written sources). Although there are a number of problems in relation to this date, it is at least plausible to place all the stones which mention this expedition to within a decade of that date (Gräslund 1990–1). Attempts to date stones which record expeditions to England (Jansson 1966), which took place between *c.* 1000 and 1020, are of little use, as the people who are commemorated returned alive to Sweden and may have died a generation or more later.

The true variety of the Urnes style is best seen in metalwork. Some is of high competence, as is the silver bowl from Lilla Valla, Rute, Gotland, deposited in a coin hoard *c.* 1050 (Wilson 1995, figs. 185–6). A large number of filigree-ornamented silver disc-brooches of this period, many found in Gotland hoards, are loosely dated by coins to the eleventh century (e.g. Stenberger 1947: figs 190:1, 205:1, 223:4). Some are of gold – from Johannishus, Hjortsberga, Blekinge in Sweden, and Frederiksborg (Stenberger 1947: fig. 73) and Hornelund, in Denmark (Roesdahl and Wilson 1992: 201). Danish wealth at this period is emphasised by the fact that while nearly all the objects found in Sweden are of silver, many found in Denmark are of gold. The gold Orø cross and its chain, with Urnes-style animal-head terminals, from Issefjord, Sjælland (Jensen *et al.* 1992: 261), which weighs 309.6 g, emphasises this fact, while similar crosses and chains with their delicately moulded terminals from Sweden are all made of silver.

At a humbler level the bronze-smith was producing masterworks in the Urnes style. Bronze buckles and strap-distributors, brooches and mounts for boxes and other objects were manufactured in increasing numbers. In Lund metalworking remains (chiefly moulds) excavated on the site of PK-banken (Bergman and Billberg 1976: 206 ff.) represent an early twelfth-century workshop which produced a type of openwork brooch (in the form of a sinuous Urnes animal) of a type more popular in Denmark and Norway than in Sweden. Finds in Denmark suggest the presence of a similar workshop for related brooches in the Ålborg region (Bertelsen 1991). It is probable that similar workshops existed in England. Particularly noticeable is the increasing tally of cast bronze stirrup-mounts decorated in the Urnes style (Williams 1997: figs 177–93), which reflect the higher-quality material typified by the Pitney brooch (Wilson and Klindt-Jensen, pl.73e).

There is little difficulty in dating the Urnes style. Its central period of production must span the period from *c.* 1040 to *c.* 1110: a dating most firmly based on coin hoards, particularly that from Lilla Valla (deposited *c.* 1050). In general terms it can be related to the historically based dating of the runestones. These cannot – with the exception of the artistically rather dreary Ingvar stones – be dated with any great degree of certainty, although there is a likelihood that the stones with inscriptions that refer to the English expeditions of Sven and Knut the Great may be dated to the second quarter of the eleventh century. In considering the dating of this style it should be emphasised that the runestones display only a limited proportion of the ornamental elements of the wider style. The end date of 1110 is only an indicator; the style clearly extends into the twelfth century – but how far is unclear.

Dendrochronology at the moment provides only a single date – from a short plank found at Hørning church, Jylland (Krogh and Voss 1961: pl. 1). A probable dendrochronological date for this fragment places it between *c.* 1060 and *c.* 1070 (Bonde *et al.* 1990: 234), which fits well with dates arrived at by traditional methods expressed here and elsewhere. The evidence for the fact that the Urnes style goes on into the twelfth century is overwhelming. It occurs in Denmark on a major piece of church furniture, the twelfth-century Lisbjerg altar, while in the Scandinavian settlements abroad it survives in a modified form in Ireland, at least until the 1130s and probably later (Wilson and Klindt-Jensen 1966: 160). In Scandinavia however it survives in a less vital manner and in a less pure form, largely due to the introduction from abroad of the first major international style – the Romanesque – to be received in its entirety into the north.

BIBLIOGRAPHY

Arwidsson, G. (1942a) *Valsgärdestudien 1. Vendelstile: Email und Glas im 7.–8. Jahrhundert* (Acta Musei antiquitatum septentrionalium Regiae Universitatis Upsaliensis 2), Uppsala: Almqvist.

—— (1942b) *Die Gräberfunde von Valsgärde 1, Valsgärde 6* (Acta Musei antiquitatum septentrion-alium Regiae Universitatis Upsaliensis 1), Uppsala: Almqvist & Wiksell.

—— (ed.) (1989) *Birka II:3. Systematische Analysen der Gräberfunde*. Stockholm: KVHAA.

Bailey, R.N. (1980) *Viking Age Sculpture in Northern England*, London: Collins.

Bergman, K. and Billberg, I. (1976) 'Metallhantverk', in A.W. Mårtenson (ed.) *Uppgrävt förflutet för PKbanken i Lund. En investering i arkeologi* (Archaeologica Lundensia 7), Lund: Kulturhistor-iska Museet.

Bertelsen, L.G. (1991) 'Præsentation af Ålborg-gruppen – en gruppe dyrefibler uden dyreslyng', *Aarbøger for nordisk oldkyndighed og historie*: 237–64.

Bonde, N. and Christensen, A.-E. (1993) 'Dendrochronological dating of the Viking Age ship burials at Oseberg, Gokstad and Tune', *Antiquity*, 67: 575–83.

Bonde, N. *et al.* (1990) 'Dendrokronologiske undersøgelser på Nationalmuseet', *Arkæologiske udgravninger i Danmark 1990*: 226–42.

Brøgger, A.W. (1916) *Borrefundet og Vestfoldkungernes graver* (Videnskapsselskapets Skrifter 2. Hist.-Filos. Klasse 1916:1), Kristiania: no publ.

Christensen, A.-E. *et al.* (1992) *Osebergs-dronningens grav. Vår arkeologiske nasjonalskatt i nyt lys*, Oslo: Schibsted.

Franzén, A.M. and Nockert, M. (1992) *Bonaderna från Skog och Överhogdal och andra medeltida väggbeklädnader*, Stockholm: KVHAA.

Graham-Campbell, J. (1995), *The Viking-Age Gold and Silver of Scotland*, Edinburgh: National Museums of Scotland.

Gräslund, A.-S. (1990–1) 'Runstenar – om ornamentik och datering', *Tor*, 23: 113–40.

Hohler, E.B. (1999) *Norwegian Stave Church Sculpture*, vol. 2, Oslo: Scandinavian University Press.

Horn Fuglesang, S. (1980) *Some Aspects of the Ringerike Style. A Phase of 11th Century Scandinavian Art* (Mediaevel Scandinavia. Supplements 1), Odense: Odense University Press.

—— (1991) 'The axehead from Mammen and the Mammen style', in M. Iversen (ed.) *Mammen. Grav, kunst og samfund i vikingetid* (Jysk Arkæologisk Selskabs skrifter 28), Højbjerg: Jysk Arkæologisk Selskab.

Horn Fuglesang, S. and Wilson, D.M. (eds) (2006), *The Hoen Hoard, a Viking Gold Treasure of the Ninth Century* (Acta ad archaeologiam et artium historiam pertinentia 14), Rome: Bardi Editore.

Jansson, I. (1985) *Ovala spännbucklor. En studie av vikingatida standardsmycken med utgångspunkt från Björkö-fynden* (Archaeological Studies 7), Uppsala: Inst. för arkeologi, Uppsala universitet.

Jansson, S.B.F. (1966) *Swedish Vikings in England. The Evidence of the Rune Stones* (The Dorothea Coke Memorial Lecture in Northern Studies 1965), London: Viking Society, University College London.

Jensen J.S. *et al.* (1992) *Danmarks middelalderlige skattefund c.1050–c.1550* (Nordiske Fortids-minder. Serie B 12), Copenhagen: Det konglige nordiske oldskriftselskab.

Krafft, S. (1956) *Pictorial Weavings from the Viking Age*, Oslo: Dreyer.

Krogh, K.J. and Voss, O. (1961) 'Fra hedenskap til kristendom i Hørning', *Nationalmuseets Arbejdsmark*: 1–34.

Lang, J.T. (1988) *Viking Age Decorated Wood. A Study of its Ornament and Design*, Dublin: National Museum of Ireland.

Larsson, M.G. (1986) 'Ingvarstågets arkeologiska bakgrund', *Fornvännen*, 81: 98–113.

Lindqvist, S. (1941–2) *Gotlands Bildsteine*, 2 vols (KVHAA. Monografier 28), Stockholm: Wahlström & Widstrand.

Margeson, S. (1981) 'Saga-Geschichten auf Stabkirchenportalen', in C. Ahrens (ed.) *Frühe Holzkircher im nordlichen Europa*, Hamburg: Helms Museum.

Myhre, B. (1992) 'The royal cemetery at Borre, Vestfold: a Norwegian centre in a European periphery', in M. Carter (ed.) *The Age of Sutton Hoo. The Seventh Century in North-west Europe*, Woodbridge: Boydell.

Näsman, U. (1991) 'Mammen 1871. Ett vikingatida depåfund med beslag till selbågskrön och annat', in M. Iversen (ed.) *Mammen. Grav, kunst og samfund i vikingetid* (Jysk Arkæologisk Selskabs skrifter 28), Højbjerg: Jysk Arkæologisk Selskab.

Nylén, E. (1978) *Bildstenar i Gotlands fornsal*, Visby: Barry Press.

O'Meadhra, U. (1979) *Early Christian, Viking and Romanesque Art. Motif-pieces from Ireland*, Stockholm: Almqvist & Wiksell.

Roesdahl, E. and Wilson, D.M. (1992) *From Viking to Crusader. The Scandinavians and Europe 800–1200*, New York: Rizzoli.

Salin, B. (1904) *Die altgermanische Thierornamentik*, Stockholm: Wahlström & Widstrand.

Sawyer, B. (1991) 'Viking-Age rune-stones as a crisis symptom', *Norwegian Archaeological Review*, 24: 97–112.

Shetelig, H. (1920) *Osebergfunnet*, vol. 3, Kristiania: Universitetets Oldsaksamling.

Stenberger, M. (1947) *Die Schatzfunde Gotlands der Vikingerzeit*, vol. 2 (KVHAA. Monografier 34), Stockholm: Almqvist & Wiksell.

Williams, D. (1997) *Late Saxon Stirrup-strap-mounts*, York: Council for British Archaeology.

Wilson, D.M. (1974) 'Men de ligger i London', *Skalk*, 1974(5): 3–8.

—— (1976) 'The Borre style in the British Isles', in B. Vilhjálmsson *et al.* (eds) *Minjar og Menti. Afmælisirit helga Kristjáni Eldjárn*, Reykjavík: Menningarsjóðs.

—— (1984) *Anglo-Saxon Art from the Seventh Century to the Norman Conquest*, London: Thames & Hudson.

—— (1995) *Vikingatidens konst*, Lund: Signum.

—— (1998) 'The Gotland picture-stones: a chronological re-assessment', in A. Wesse (ed.) *Studien zur Archäologie des Ostseeraumes. Von der Eisenzeit zum Mittelalter*, Neumünster: Wacholtz.

Wilson, D.M. and Klindt-Jensen, O. (1966) *Viking Art*, London: Allen & Unwin.

PART II

THE VIKING EXPANSION

———•◆•———

CHAPTER TWENTY-FIVE

VIKINGS IN ENGLAND

———•◆•———

Clare Downham

Vikings had a profound impact on the history of the English-speaking people. In the period from the first recorded raids in the late eighth century, until the conquest of England by Knútr (Cnut) in 1016, the political geography, culture and identities of the Anglo-Saxons were transformed. As a result of their impact, the image of vikings has loomed large in English historical literature from the Middle Ages to the present. Their historiography can be seen to reflect developments in attitudes across the centuries to various issues including regional identity, conquest, migration and cultural assimilation.

Modern scholarly debates have tended to focus on the scale and impact of viking settlement in England (see Richards, ch. 27, and Hadley, ch. 27.1, below). However, there have been calls for more research on the leaders of vikings and their contacts abroad (Wormald 1982: 44; Hadley 2000a: 107). Nevertheless the political history of vikings has proved controversial due to a lack of consensus as to what constitutes reliable evidence. The paradigms of viking history have been much coloured by texts which post-date the Viking Age. These include writings which emanated from the church of Durham from the eleventh century onwards and Icelandic sagas from the thirteenth century and later (Schlauch 1949; Rollason *et al.* 1998: 22–7, 33). The value of these late accounts has been increasingly called into question (McTurk 1977; Page 1982; Dumville 1987). The use of skaldic verse has also been problematised due to uncertainties over the date of its composition and its original context (Downham 2004; but see Jesch 2004).

An awareness of the partial nature of contemporary evidence has also been highlighted by in-depth analysis of major texts. For example, 'The Anglo-Saxon Chronicle', Asser's Life of King Alfred, royal diplomas and the chronicle of Æthelweard were each connected with the household of English kings. They are, for the most part, Wessex-based accounts with less information on other parts of England and they can be seen, at times, to promote the cause of royal government. Recent re-evaluations of the written evidence pose interesting questions which can challenge received accounts of Anglo-Saxon history (e.g. Keynes 1978) and reveal how the terminology used by historians has been influenced by selectivity and biases in the written evidence (see Dumville, ch. 26, below).

The first recorded viking attacks on the Anglo-Saxons took place during the reign of Beorhtric, king of the West Saxons (786–802). The Anglo-Saxon Chronicle reports that three ships of Northmen arrived at Portland (Dorset) where they killed the local reeve and his followers. Another attack was led against the church of Lindisfarne in 793 and a further attack on Northumbria is reported in 794. The Anglo-Saxon Chronicle mentions no further raids until 835. However, it is clear that the Chronicle does not give the whole story. A series of diplomas issued by kings of the Mercians from 792 to 822 refer to intensive viking activity in Kent, including the existence of viking camps (Sawyer 1968: nos 134, 160, 168, 177, 186, 1264).

From the 830s to the 850s raids appear to be more frequent. An alliance between vikings and Cornishmen against Wessex is recorded in 838, but they were defeated (Whitelock *et al.* 1965: *s.a.* 838). A major English defeat is recorded in the Frankish Annals of St-Bertin under the year 844, after which the vikings 'terra pro libitu potiuntur' (seized or wielded power over land at will; Nelson 1991). This was soon followed by a great defeat of viking forces at *Aclea* in Greater Wessex in 851, recorded in the Anglo-Saxon Chronicle, the Annals of St-Bertin and in the so-called 'Fragmentary Annals of Ireland' (Whitelock *et al.* 1965: *s.a.* 851; Nelson 1991: *s.a.* 850; Radner 1978: §250). These records of battles between vikings and Anglo-Saxons in foreign chronicles demonstrate wider concern about vikings' activity in western Christendom. Contact between vikings in different areas is indicated in the composition of silver hoards deposited during this period (Blackburn and Pagan 1986), and it can sometimes be deduced by a comparison of written sources from different areas.

In 865/6 'a great army' arrived in East Anglia. Over the next thirteen years, detachments of this army and its allies enjoyed a remarkable series of victories. York was seized in 867, and the kingdom of Northumbria was subjugated. Then in 869, the East Anglian kingdom was conquered after the defeat and martyrdom of its king Edmund. More vikings ('a summer army') arrived at Fulham in 871 and allied with vikings already active in Britain. In 873 Mercia was subjugated. Wessex fell under viking control in the early months of 878, but a victory by King Alfred that year stemmed the tide of viking conquest. The background of the warriors active in England during these years has been debated. The original force seems to have been a coalition of different fleets. It may have included vikings active in England in the early 860s and contingents from West Francia as opportunities there were in decline (Wormald 1982: 137; Sawyer 1998: 90) as well as a contingent from Ireland (Keynes 1997: 54). Ívarr, one of the viking leaders in England, can be identified with Ívarr, king of the vikings of Ireland (Haliday 1884: 24–56; Smyth 1977; Wormald 1982: 143). His followers had been campaigning in North Britain in the early 860s and their ambitions soon extended to control of Northumbria. According to the Anglo-Saxon Chronicle, Ívarr's brother and successor Hálfdan shared out lands in Northumbria to viking settlers. His exploits in North Britain are also recorded in Irish chronicles (Mac Airt and Mac Niocaill 1983: *s.aa.* 874 [=875].3, 874[=875].4, 876[=877].5).

Three viking leaders who may have arrived in England in 871, namely 'Guthrum', 'Anwend' and 'Oscetyl', took control of East Anglia in 874. Over the next four years their followers seized control of parts of Mercia and campaigned against the West Saxons. King Alfred was temporarily driven into hiding in the Somerset marshes, but his great victory at Edington secured the independence of Wessex. As a result of this setback a fleet of vikings left England late in 878 to campaign in Francia (which they did to devastating effect: Maclean 1998). Land in East Anglia was distributed among Guthrum's followers. A boundary between areas of English and viking control (stretching from the River Thames, via Bedford, to Watling Street) was recognised in a treaty drawn up between Alfred and Guthrum some time before 890 (Whitelock 1979: no. 34).

Another major viking threat to Alfred's reign was posed in 892. In this year two large fleets arrived in Kent. They made little headway despite receiving support from vikings based in Northumbria and East Anglia. In 896 the viking army, which represented the greatest menace to Alfred, dispersed. Some of these troops settled in areas under viking control in England, while others travelled to the Continent. The failure of this viking campaign may be attributed to Alfred's policies, which included the construction of a network of fortresses, the reorganisation of his army, the cultivation of propaganda aimed at unifying his subjects, as well as treaties aimed at dividing his enemies (Keynes and Lapidge 1983).

Alfred's successors developed his policies and worked to bring areas of viking settlement under their control. However, the character of viking settlement during the ninth century and beyond is obscure and has been much debated. Peter Sawyer invigorated this question over forty years ago (Sawyer 1962) by arguing that the number of immigrants was much lower than had been supposed. This provoked a series of studies either supporting or attacking his thesis from a range of viewpoints. Debates have raged about the size of viking armies, the use of place-name evidence, and the nature of cultural and linguistic change. From this a new consensus has emerged largely as a result of Sawyer's theory, namely that numbers of immigrants cannot be simply deduced from their impact on the host society. Rather, the impact of vikings in the areas of England which they settled owes more to the duration of viking rule and to the nature of interaction between vikings and English (Hadley and Richards 2000b).

The viking conquests of the 860s and 870s brought large swathes of territory in eastern and northern England into Scandinavian hands. Successive kings of Wessex campaigned to seize this land for themselves. London was one of the first gains, taken by Alfred. York, which was the last bastion of viking power in England, fell finally to the West Saxon royal dynasty in 954. Some areas of England therefore remained in Scandinavian control for the better part of a century. However, contemporary accounts give an incomplete picture of political organisation in areas under viking control.

Initially the Anglo Saxon Chronicle linked viking settlers to pre-existing population-groups, so in the 890s different viking armies are referred to as 'Northumbrians' or 'East Angles', each under the control of individual kings and numerous jarls. Mercia at this date was divided between English and Scandinavian control. The part which was in Scandinavian hands was seemingly divided between the northern and southern viking kings. The Alfred–Guthrum treaty indicates that East Anglian vikings ruled as far north as Stoney Stratford (Bucks.), and Northumbrian viking rule is attested as far south as Stamford (Lincs.) in 894 (Campbell 1962: 50–1; cf. 40–1). Northern Northumbria remained independent throughout this period, under the control of native kings based at Bamburgh. It is not clear that Northumbrian vikings ruled as far as the west coast in the 890s, although Manchester was in Northumbrian viking control in 919, immediately prior to being taken by the English. The use of pre-existing labels by English chroniclers is not always helpful if we wish to determine the boundaries of different viking kingdoms.

Shifts in borders are frequently attested in the Anglo-Saxon Chronicle in the early tenth century as rulers of Wessex advanced their power northwards. Alfred's son Edward acted in alliance with his sister Æthelflæd and brother-in-law, Æthelred, who ruled English Mercia, to bring East Anglia and viking Mercia into English control. Initially Edward had battled against his cousin Æthelwold who had a claim to the Wessex throne. Æthelwold enlisted the support of the East Angles and Northumbrians but he was killed in battle alongside a viking king called Eiríkr. The battle was followed by a short-lived truce. In 910 Edward defeated a viking army at Tettenhall (Staffs.) in which three kings 'Eowils', Hálfdan and Ívarr were killed. This succession of events seriously weakened viking power in England. This decline may have been exacerbated by a contemporary influx of vikings from the Gaelic world to north-western England. Political fragmentation may be hinted at, as no king of vikings in England is clearly identified from 910 until 918, but there is reference to jarls ruling individual fortified centres. It was during this period that King Edward and his Mercian allies made significant gains.

Viking Northumbria could have fallen into English hands in 918 had it not been for a viking invasion led from Ireland by Rǫgnvaldr, grandson of Ívarr. His campaign which culminated at the battle of Corbridge is recorded in Irish, Scottish and English accounts. Some historians have argued that there were two battles fought at Corbridge, but this is an error based on a reading of the eleventh-century text *Historia de Sancto Cuthberto* (Johnson-South 1990: 159). Chronicle records clearly indicate that only one battle was fought (Mac Airt and Mac Niocaill 1983: *s.a.* 917 [=918].4; Radner 1978: §459; Hudson 1998: 150, 157). After the battle Rǫgnvaldr became king of York.

It has long been argued that Northumbrian politics in the early tenth century can be interpreted in terms of rivalries between an Anglo-Danish and Hiberno-Norse faction. According to 'The Mercian Register' the people of York promised obedience to Æthelflaed of Mercia shortly before her death in 918, which has been deemed a sign of disaffection with Rǫgnvaldr's rule by the Anglo-Danes (Wainwright 1975: 178). However, this promise may have predated the Corbridge campaign, and need not suggest that English rule was preferred to that of Rǫgnvaldr, grandson of Ívarr. Indeed, Rǫgnvaldr himself found it necessary to recognise Edward's superiority at a meeting in 920. The theory of ethnic competition between Danes and Norwegians in England seems based on over-rigid translation of *Norðmann* as 'Norwegian' in English sources (Mawer 1923). A comparison of Insular chronicles suggests that familial connections between viking leaders of Dublin and York continued from the 860s until the 950s, and there was not an interchange of power between Danish and Norwegian factions (Dumville 2004).

Edward may have lost some land south of the Humber to the vikings of Northumbria towards the end of his reign. Nevertheless his son Æthelstan ousted the viking king of York in 927 and ruled Northumbria until his death in 939. Therefore Æthelstan is the first king who united England (Dumville 1992: 141–71). The most famous event of his career is the battle of Brunanburh, where the English defeated an alliance between the king of *Alba* (North Britain) and vikings of the dynasty of Ívarr in 937. The site of this battle is still a matter of debate (e.g. Halloran 2005). Scottish involvement can be explained by Æthelstan's attempts to extend his authority across Britain which had provoked a war with Constantine, king of Alba in 934. There were also some Welsh sympathies for the Northumbrians in the 930s or 940s, illustrated in the prophetic poem *Armes Prydein Vawr* (Williams and Bromwich 1972).

After Æthelstan's death, the kingdom of York, and lands south of the Humber called 'the five boroughs' (see Hadley, ch. 27.1, below), was once more taken into viking hands. The political situation in the north continued to be unstable, and the viking territories were won and lost once more before they were finally annexed by Eadred of Wessex in 954. The main historical sources for the decline of viking power are largely written from an English perspective. It is perhaps testament to the power of their rhetoric that historians often refer to the seizure of viking lands by Wessex as 'redemption' or 'reconquest' (e.g. Mawer 1923), and Alba's war against Æthelstan (which gave rise to an alliance with vikings) as 'rebellion' (e.g. Sawyer 1998: 121–2). As Wessex had no legitimate claim to rule across Britain, the appropriateness of such language is questionable. It is doubtful that the majority of contemporaries regarded this as the natural order of things, and such interpretations may also be unduly coloured by subsequent political events.

One striking feature of events during the last decade of viking rule in Northumbria is the support given to kings Óláfr and Eiríkr by Wulfstan I, archbishop of York (Keynes 1999). This is despite Wulfstan's promotion to power by the English king, Æthelstan. The question of vikings' relationship with the Church is closely related to debates about viking impact and integration. This relationship clearly changed from the arrival of the first viking fleets in the late eighth century to the mid-tenth century. Initial contacts were characterised by destruction as ecclesiastical sites were attacked. This destruction was followed in areas of viking settlement by the seizure of some, if not all, ecclesiastical lands. This removal of resources apparently dealt a fatal blow to monastic life in areas under viking control (Sawyer 1998: 98). Pastoral care may have continued with the support of priests by the Christian population who remained after viking settlement. Dawn Hadley has demonstrated that some pre-Viking Age church sites were used following (and perhaps during) conversion and integration of the viking population (Hadley 2000b: 216–97). As conversion seems to have begun fairly rapidly, churches which had been destroyed may have been quickly revived.

Only one see is known to have persisted without relocation in areas under viking control and that was at York. This won patronage from the Scandinavian kings of York from the 890s (Campbell 1962: 51; Abrams 2001). Coins bearing the name of St Peter were produced in York in the first decade of the tenth century (Grierson and Blackburn 1986: 322–3). Although the adult baptism of a viking king of York, Óláfr, is recorded as late as 943, this need not indicate the moment of conversion as has often been thought (Whitelock *et al.* 1965: *s.a.* 943). Adult baptism was not uncommon in Christian communities in the Middle Ages. The many stone crosses erected across northern England in the tenth century indicate some enthusiasm for Christianity among an Anglo-Scandinavian elite (albeit sometimes with representations of Scandinavian deities included in their designs). The distribution of these crosses and the evidence of urban churches indicates that a decentralised ecclesiastical structure prevailed (Hadley 2000b: 287–9). This may have resulted from the fragmentation of pre-viking landed estates and the growth of a merchant class of patrons (which was a corollary of urban growth in viking settled areas). It is not known what structures for pagan worship may have been in place.

From 954, kings of England sought to secure power in erstwhile viking territories. King Edgar (959–75) allowed areas of Scandinavian settlement to have a degree of legal autonomy as a reward for their loyalty, while imposing national legislation in cases of theft (Whitelock 1979: no. 41). The written sources from Edgar's reign demonstrate that inhabitants of 'Danelaw' perceived themselves as being different from those of the rest of England. The intermingling of Scandinavian and English peoples gave rise to a distinct regional identity. Edgar also met other Insular kings, including Maccus Haraldsson, king of the Isles, in 973, to ensure peaceful relations, perhaps in order to prevent disaffected elements in the Danelaw from seeking their support (Thornton 1997, 2001).

The efforts made by Edgar were somewhat undone during the reign of his son Æthelred (978/9–1016). Æthelred had come to power following the murder of his brother at the age of twelve. The consequent political instability seems to have encouraged vikings from the Gaelic world and Scandinavia to raid England. Initially attacks were focused on the west of Britain and this can be linked with the activities of Guðrøðr, king of Man and the Isles (Downham 2003: 59–60). In the early 990s a new wave attacks was led against eastern England under the leadership of Óláfr Tryggvason, future king of Norway, and Sveinn Haraldsson, future king of Denmark. Æthelred appeared unable to unite his subjects effectively against this threat. A series of peace agreements and payments of tribute to viking armies also failed to curb attacks. In 1002 Æthelred ordered his subjects to kill all the Danes in England. This was perhaps intended as a way of directing popular anger over the successive viking invasions away from the king. Æthelred's subjects were also urged to seek divine assistance against enemies through prayer (Keynes 1997: 74–81).

Nevertheless, in 1013 England was conquered by Sveinn Haraldsson. He arrived with an invasion fleet at Gainsborough (Lincs.) and quickly won local support. Niels Lund has suggested that Æthelred's efforts to curb the legal freedoms of the Danelaw encouraged the inhabitants to support this rival king (Lund 1976: 189, 193–4). London held out longest against this invasion but in Christmas 1013 Æthelred went into exile. The main Anglo-Saxon Chronicle entries for the reign of Æthelred (found in versions C, D, E and F) were written shortly after his reign ended, probably by a single author. These retrospective reports focus on the failures of Æthelred, and the Danish conquest is presented with a gloomy air of inevitability (Keynes 1978). This provides a salutary reminder that descriptions even of the recent past in written sources can be heavily influenced by partiality and hindsight.

Sveinn only ruled for a brief time before his death in 1014. His son Knútr succeeded to rule England in 1016 following the death of Æthelred's son Edmund, and he reigned until 1035 (see Lund, ch. 48.1, below). From the end of the eighth century to the early eleventh century the nature of viking activity in England changed radically. What began with hit-and-run raids by small warbands led to a reconfiguration of regional identities in England and to conquest by the armies of a powerful Scandinavian Christian king.

The fifty years from Knútr's accession until the Norman conquest was characterised by rivalry for control of the English throne. Following the death of Knútr and his two sons Haraldr and Harðaknútr, Edward son of Æthelred became king in 1042. Edward was assisted to power with the support of Godwine, earl of Wessex. Edward's subsequent promotion of Godwine's sons, and his childless marriage with Edith daughter of Godwine, led Harold Godwinesson to claim the English throne on Edward's death in 1066. A rival claim to the English throne was maintained by Knútr's successors in

Scandinavia. This may have been the cause of piratical attack on south-east England by twenty-five ships in 1048. Haraldr inn Harðráði, king of Norway, pursued a claim to the English throne by leading an invasion in 1066, but he was defeated and killed at Stamford Bridge. In addition, William, duke of Normandy claimed that he was Edward's appointed heir. (Edward had maintained close relations with Normandy as a consequence of his exile there during the reign of Knútr.) William invaded England and was crowned after his victory at the battle of Hastings.

It took some years before William had a firm grip over England. Two invasions of south-west England were attempted by sons of Harold Godwinesson in 1068 and 1069 with Irish support. A Danish army also landed in northern England in 1069. This was joined by Edgar Ætheling (a great grandson of Æthelred) and a large number of English troops. Despite initial gains the campaign failed and King William ordered the 'harrying of the north' to crush remaining opposition. As a result of the Norman invasion the political history of England during the later Middle Ages was to be linked more strongly with northern France than with Scandinavia.

BIBLIOGRAPHY

Abrams, L. (2001) 'The conversion of the Danelaw', in J. Graham-Campbell *et al.* (eds) *Vikings and the Danelaw. Select Papers from the Proceedings of the Thirteenth Viking Congress*, Oxford: Oxbow.

Blackburn, M. and Pagan, H. (1986) 'A revised checklist of coin hoards from the British Isles, *c.* 500–1100', in M.A.S. Blackburn (ed.) *Anglo-Saxon Monetary History. Essays in Memory of Michael Dolley*, Leicester: Leicester University Press.

Campbell, A. (ed. and trans.) (1962) *The Chronicle of Æthelweard*, Edinburgh: Thomas Nelson.

Downham, C. (2003) 'England and the Irish Sea zone in the eleventh century', *Anglo-Norman Studies*, 26: 55–73.

—— (2004) 'Eric Bloodaxe – axed? The mystery of the last Scandinavian king of York', *Mediaeval Scandinavia*, 14: 51–77.

Dumville, D.N. (1987) 'Textual archaeology and Northumbrian history subsequent to Bede', in D.M. Metcalf (ed.) *Coinage in Ninth-Century Northumbria*, Oxford: British Archaeological Reports.

—— (1992) *Wessex and England from Alfred to Edgar. Six Essays on Political, Cultural, and Ecclesiastical Revival*, Woodbridge: Boydell.

—— (2004) 'Old Dubliners and new Dubliners in Ireland and Britain: a Viking-Age story', *Medieval Dublin*, 6: 78–93.

Grierson, P. and Blackburn, M. (1986) *Medieval European Coinage, with a Catalogue of the Coins in the Fitzwilliam Museum, Cambridge*, vol. 1: *The Early Middle Ages (Fifth to Tenth Centuries)*, Cambridge: Cambridge University Press.

Hadley, D.M. (2000a) '"Hamlet and the princes of Denmark": lordship in the Danelaw, *c.* 860–954', in D.M. Hadley and J.D. Richards (eds) (2000a).

—— (2000b) *The Northern Danelaw, its Social Structure, c. 800–1100*, London: Leicester University Press.

Hadley, D.M. and Richards, J.D. (eds) (2000a) *Cultures in Contact. Scandinavian Settlement in England in the Ninth and Tenth Centuries*, Turnhout: Brepols.

—— (2000b) 'Introduction: interdisciplinary approaches to the Scandinavian settlement', in D.M. Hadley and J.D. Richards (eds) (2000a).

Haliday, C. (1884) *The Scandinavian Kingdom of Dublin*, 2nd edn, Dublin: Gill.

Halloran, K. (2005) 'The Brunanburh campaign: a reappraisal', *Scottish Historical Review*, 84: 133–48.

Hudson, B.T. (ed. and trans.) (1998) 'The Scottish Chronicle', *Scottish Historical Review*, 77: 129–61.

Jesch, J. (2004) 'Skaldic verse and the roots of history', *Quaestio Insularis*, 5: 1–22.

Johnson-South, T. (1990) 'The "Historia de Sancto Cuthberto": a new edition and translation, with discussions of the surviving manuscripts, the text, and Northumbrian estate structure'. (Unpubl. PhD thesis, Cornell University.).

—— (ed. and trans.) (2002) *Historia de Sancto Cuthberto. A History of Saint Cuthbert and a Record of his Patrimony*, Cambridge: Boydell.

Keynes, S. (1978) 'The declining reputation of King Æthelred the Unready', in D. Hill (ed.) *Ethelred the Unready. Papers from the Millenary Conference*, Oxford: British Archaeological Reports.

—— (1997) 'The Vikings in England, *c.* 790–1016', in P. Sawyer (ed.) *The Oxford Illustrated History of the Vikings*, Oxford: Oxford University Press.

—— (1999) 'Wulfstan I', in M. Lapidge *et al.* (eds) *The Blackwell Encyclopaedia of Anglo-Saxon England*, Oxford: Blackwell.

Keynes, S. and Lapidge, M. (trans. with an intro. and notes) (1983) *Alfred the Great. Asser's Life of King Alfred and Other Contemporary Sources*, Harmondsworth: Penguin.

Lund, N. (1976) 'King Edgar and the Danelaw', *Mediaeval Scandinavia*, 9: 181–95.

Mac Airt, S. and Mac Niocaill, G. (eds and trans.) (1983) *The Annals of Ulster (to* A.D. 1131), Dublin: Dublin Institute for Advanced Studies.

Maclean, S. (1998) 'Charles the Fat and the viking great army: the military explanation for the end of the Carolingian empire (876–88)', *War Studies Journal*, 3(2): 74–95.

McTurk, R.W. (1977) 'Review: Alfred P. Smyth, *Scandinavian York and Dublin*', *Saga-book of the Viking Society*, 19 (1974–7): 471–4.

Mawer, A. (1923) 'The redemption of the Five Boroughs', *English Historical Review*, 38: 551–7.

Nelson, J.L. (annot. and trans.) (1991) *Annales Bertinieni. Ninth-century Histories*, vol. 1: *The Annals of St-Bertin*, Manchester: Manchester University Press.

Page, R.I. (1982) 'A tale of two cities', *Peritia*, 1: 335–51.

Radner, J.N. (ed. and trans.) (1978) *Fragmentary Annals of Ireland*, Dublin: Dublin Institute for Advanced Studies.

Rollason, D.W. *et al.* (1998) *Sources for York History to* AD 1100, York: York Archaeological Trust.

Sawyer, P.H. (1962) *The Age of the Vikings*, London: Edward Arnold.

—— (1968) *Anglo-Saxon Charters. An Annotated List and Bibliography* (Royal Historical Society. Guides and handbooks 8), London: Royal Historical Society.

—— (1998) *Anglo-Saxon Lincolnshire*. Lincoln: History of Lincolnshire Committee.

Schlauch, M. (trans.) (1949) *The Saga of the Volsungs, the Saga of Ragnar Lothbrok, together with the Lay of Kraka*, 2nd edn, New York: American Scandinavian Foundation.

Smyth, A.P. (1977) *Scandinavian Kings in the British Isles 850–880*, Oxford: Oxford University Press.

Thornton, D.E. (1997) 'Hey Macc! The name *Maccus*, tenth to fifteenth centuries', *Nomina*, 20: 67–94.

—— (2001) 'Edgar and the eight kings, A.D. 973: *Textus et dramatis personae*', *Early Medieval Europe*, 10: 49–79.

Wainwright, F.T. (1975) *Scandinavian England. Collected Papers*, Chichester: Phillimore.

Whitelock, D. (trans.) (1979) *English Historical Documents*, vol. 1: *c. 500–1042*, 2nd edn, London: Eyre and Spottiswoode.

Whitelock, D. *et al.* (trans.) (1965) *The Anglo-Saxon Chronicle*, rev. imp., London: Eyre and Spottiswoode.

Williams, I. and Bromwich, R. (eds and trans.) (1972) *Armes Prydein. The Prophecy of Britain from the Book of Taliesin*, Dublin: Dublin Institute for Advanced Studies.

Wormald, C.P. (1982) 'Viking studies: whence and whither?', in R.T. Farrell (ed.) *The Vikings*, Chichester: Phillimore, 128–53.

CHAPTER TWENTY-SIX

VIKINGS IN INSULAR
CHRONICLING

——·◆·——

David N. Dumville

Each of the different cultural zones of what used to be called 'The British Isles' (namely Britain and Ireland, with their associated smaller islands; Davies 2000) had its own tradition or traditions of chronicling in the Viking Age. Nor should we forget Brittany, a complex Continental polity of Insular Celtic heritage situated alongside a predatory Frankish empire (Dumville 2007c). It is certain that these zones interacted variously. Because of shared ecclesiastical history there were significant, especially generic, points of similarity. But different interactions and differing local cultures generated chronicles whose character and tone differed between the cultural zones. When the Viking Age began, with apparent suddenness in the chronicle-records, shared experiences nonetheless seem to have provoked a range of generically different responses (see Dumville 2002c).

Some individual chroniclers are less difficult to isolate stylistically than others (on 'The Anglo-Saxon Chronicle' see Clark 1971, Keynes 1978; on 'The Annals of Ulster' see Dumville 1982), but in no certain Insular instance can we put a name or specific identity to any Viking Age chronicler, in spite of various attempts to recognise the work of Asser of St Davids (Hughes 1980: 68, 86–7) or King Alfred (see Shippey 1982) or Alcuin of York (Stubbs 1868–71, vol. 1: xi; Lapidge 1982: 121 and n. 74). We certainly do have literary work from the hand of each of these, in which vikings are mentioned: but only Asser's biography of King Alfred (datable, as it survives, to 893), with its translations from 'The Anglo-Saxon Chronicle', approaches the chronicling genre (Stevenson 1904; Cook 1906; Keynes and Lapidge 1983). What all Insular chronicling of this era does share is annalistic structure.

The annal, however it may be distinguished from its immediate neighbours, is, as the record of one year, these chronicles' essential structural unit (Dumville 2002a: 6; 1999: 104). Constituting it there may be nothing more than the annal-marker, whether *an.* (for *annus*, 'year') or *kl.* (for *kalendae Ianuarii*, 'the first day of January'), sometimes accompanied by a sequence-number or an AD date or a complex series of chronological notations; or there may be a single entry of information, or any number of such entries (of immensely various length and complexity, from a single word to some pages of modern print) though rarely many more than a dozen. The hierarchy of content is therefore constructed from individual entries (or items) which are joined to form the annal, and the annals (some left blank for lack of suitable information) together constitute the chronicle. While an individual chronicle-author might think his work to have beginning and end, the annalistic chronicle is widely recognised as history without an end; while time continues, we cannot expect or require closure of a chronicle constituted of successive annals (Van Houts 1980; Dumville 2002a: 18).

Before the Viking Age, Insular chronicles had limited terms of relevance of information for inclusion (Dumville 1982, 1999). Typically, succession to important office (whether described by the death of the former or the accession of the latter office-holder, or both) was a major concern, as were battles; disturbance of nature – plague, famine, great severity of weather, heavenly signs, miraculous events – also merited attention (MacNeill 1913/14: 81–5; Hughes 1957; cf. Cooke 1980; Hughes 1980: 99; Thornton 1996). While annalistic chronicles tended towards greater inclusiveness of information as the early Middle Ages progressed, nevertheless that development had not undergone radical change before the Viking Age.

In general, the events and processes of the Viking Age did greatly stimulate chroniclers, challenging them to record events of a character previously unknown. In effect, vikings, by their very disorderliness in the Insular societies which they encountered from the closing years of the eighth century, forced their way into the writing of contemporary chroniclers; the chroniclers were challenged to adapt their criteria of relevance and the vocabulary, style and even the very language which they used (Dumville 1982). By the eleventh century, the English and Irish chronicles were being written in more expansive styles, more information was being recorded and the local vernacular language had a larger role (Clark 1971; Dumville 1999). 'The Anglo-Saxon Chronicle' now included poetry (Dobbie 1942; cf. Abegg 1894).

In other words, we see changes over time in Insular chronicling, partly continuing the early medieval developments, partly reacting to the new circumstances of the Viking Age. Likewise, the Viking Age had its own internal dynamics, and we see these reflected above all in chroniclers' reactions to rulers of large Scandinavian polities, whose involvement in Insular politics evoked from eleventh-century chroniclers a response rather different from that which those writers' ninth-century predecessors had accorded the leaders of viking armies of their day (Lund 1986; Keynes 1978, 1986). All the Insular chronicles of this period, and particularly those which had begun earlier (and, indeed, continued later) than the Viking Age, can be seen in a process of continual (but by no means continuous) change.

However, the differing cultural traditions within which Insular chroniclers worked ensured varying presentations of information. Generic inheritance should not be underestimated as a factor determining what was recorded or excluded. Likewise, differing types of authorship, generic function and institutional (or authorial) outlook and purpose should all be recognised as contributors to the character of the texts which we possess.

Surviving Insular chronicles of the Viking Age show us a chronological order of recording of vikings: English and Gaelic (principally, but not exclusively, Irish) from the 790s, Welsh from 850, Breton, Scottish. We have no Cornish chronicle of the period, nor any certain chronicle-record native to Viking Age Strathclyde or Mann (on Strathclyde, see Hughes 1980: 95–100; Grabowski and Dumville 1984: 216–17). What is now northernmost Scotland (north of a line drawn due west from the Beauly Firth) is without any chronicle-record throughout the entire era, in spite of the momentous events and processes which the Viking Age brought to that complex region (on Skye, see Downham 2000). Within England and Ireland, some regions are much better covered than others (indeed, some areas generally lack coverage, although the distribution of record changes over time: on Ireland, cf. Etchingham 1996). Throughout the Viking Age, the extant Welsh chronicling is generally rather thin (Downham 2007; Maund 1991). And survival from Brittany is exceedingly poor: there are fragments and hints of Breton Viking Age chronicling record (and some external survival); but our knowledge of events in Brittany, insofar as it depends on chronicles, is largely drawn from foreign texts (Dumville 2007c; cf. Werner 1959 and Price 1986–9).

There is no doubt that in the Gaelic record we see contemporary chronicling from the first notices of vikings' activities – which begin once those impinge on Gaelic-speaking territory, particularly Ireland (from 795) and the Inner Hebrides (from 802), apart from generalising notices about Britain under 794 and 798 (Charles-Edwards 2006). No extant Gaelic chronicle is earlier in date than the late eleventh century (Dumville 1999), but we can be sure that contemporary record constitutes the mass of the entries for the Viking Age (cf. Ó Máille 1910; Hughes 1972: 129–35, 148–59). That corruptions of entries and insertions occurred during transmission is equally certain, however, as we shall see. Gaelic chronicling, while essentially bilingual in Gaelic and Latin, tends increasingly towards the vernacular in this period (Dumville 1982) – and this process was (as I have remarked above) greatly encouraged by the need to break away from generically conventional diction to record vikings' activities. For all that, Gaelic chronicles very much remain constituted of discrete entries and annals, however large these might become: the generic inheritance remained powerful. Both secular and ecclesiastical dimensions of vikings' presence in the Gaelic world are covered in the chronicles. For the most part, it is not possible to deduce large agenda on the part of Gaelic chroniclers – the record is generally local and specific, very much evenemental. One fragmentary eleventh-century text surviving in a seventeenth-century manuscript offers a very different perspective, however (Radner 1978; Downham 2004b).

Viking Age interaction between the Insular chronicling traditions must be recognised as possible. Welsh chronicles carry a notice of vikings' first activity in Ireland, in 795, derived from a tenth-century Irish chronicle (Grabowski and Dumville 1984; Downham 2000 and Griscom 1925–6: 95–7; Dumville 2002b: 8–9; 2005: 14–15). Native Welsh record of vikings begins only with an annal for 850 (Dumville 2002b: 10–11; 2005: 22–3).

The several chronicles in their different traditions display varying types of interest and angles of approach. All are local, whether in their sources or their production or their politics. In the Insular political circumstances of 800, it would have been difficult for a chronicler to articulate a national position in the absence of a political nation. After the formation of the kingdom of England in 927, an English chronicler might adopt a new stance (Dumville 1992: 141–71); but we should also remember that the creation of a single English polity may have been a West-Saxon project for at least a half-century before 927, and the chronicling of those decades must be scrutinised for such an outlook (for the texts see Thorpe 1861; Plummer 1892/9; Whitelock *et al.* 1961). The hypothetical Gaelic chronicle which Kathleen Hughes (1972: 99–115) named 'The Chronicle of Ireland' (substantially reconstructable as it stood in 911; Grabowski and Dumville 1984; Charles-Edwards 2006) may have been created and maintained by chroniclers who aspired to a national coverage (and it was not closed to foreign information), but it is hard to see in it a political project (despite Kelleher 1963).

'The Anglo-Saxon Chronicle' as it was originally created in 892 (Plummer 1892/9, vol. 2: lxiv, xciv, ci, cii, cxiii, cxiv–cxxii; Sawyer 1962: 13–25; Dumville 1992: 89–90), no doubt in the context of the Alfredian revival of learning, caught a moment of grave crisis for Alfred's '(over)kingdom of the Anglo-Saxons' (Keynes 1998) as a major army of vikings returned to southern England after thirteen years' campaigning on the Continent (Shippey 1982; cf. Vogel 1906: 260–372). Its narration of approximately a century of vikings' activity in England – and notably of previous grave peril for the West Saxons and the Mercians, first from the mid-830s to the mid-850s, and again from 865 to 879 when Scandinavian forces brought all the kingdoms of the English tetrarchy to their knees (Dumville 1993: IX; cf. Hill 1981: figs 49–64) – dominated the record; to read this was to be offered apocalyptic prospects. Alfred and his politico-literary circle compared the Viking Age with the Age of Migrations which brought down the Roman empire of the west (Godden 2004; Harris 2001: 505–10; cf. Bury 1928 and Musset 1971).

The approach of the author(s) of the original text of 'The Anglo-Saxon Chronicle' remained partial, however: not only were there political agenda (though by no means as straightforward as some interpretations of this work as 'propaganda' might imply: Wallace-Hadrill 1950; Davis 1971; Shippey 1982: 42), but in its ninth-century coverage much activity by vikings in England was unknown or forgotten or downplayed or deemed irrelevant (for an example concerning 855, see Sawyer 1968: no. 206; Whitelock 1979: no. 90). Continuators of the work for the next century had varied concerns, but we see no effort at a comprehensive treatment of events in England as they occurred and as news was received.

When we encounter the 'Chronicle of Æthelred and Cnut' – which begins with an annal for 983 and seems to have been written as a whole in the aftermath of the deaths of King Æthelred 'the Unready' and King Edmund II 'Ironside' in 1016 with succession passing to Cnut (it could not have been composed later than the early months of 1023) – we find a text with a strong political (and historical) message, giving detailed consideration to events in the struggle for Scandinavian, and especially Danish, domination of the kingdom of England (Keynes 1978). It is not clear whether this narrative of some thirty to forty years was intended as a continuation of 'The Anglo-Saxon Chronicle' of 892 (with its subsequent, varied continuations already attached), or as a continuation of a derivative revision, or as a freestanding text (Dumville 1983: 26–38, 52). What is certain is that its author had not only a very clear and hostile view of the Scandinavian invaders but also (secure in the knowledge of Danish success in 1013 and 1016) a strongly negative perception of the governance of the kingdom of England, and the failings of those who bore rule, throughout the period. His writing has coloured all historiography until the present generation (Keynes 1978; more generally on Anglo-Saxon attitudes to vikings, see Ashdown 1919–27).

Approximately coincident with Danish success in England was the famous battle of Clontarf, just north of Dublin, in 1014, which saw heavy and varied Scandinavian participation (Downham 2007). It attracted the lengthiest annals in Irish chronicling up to that date (Mac Airt and Mac Niocaill 1983: 446–9, annal 1014.2; cf. Goedheer 1938). Although the character and significance of the battle have long been under scrutiny, what chroniclers report of the kings of Scandinavian Dublin after 1014 has been taken to mark a sea-change in those kings' outlook in the context of Anglo-Scandinavian England under Cnut and his sons (1016–42) (Gwynn 1992).

'The Chronicle of Æthelred and Cnut' offers a more varied diet than its ninth-century predecessor, while remaining largely concerned with military activity and high politics (Clark 1971). Those who wrote the original text of 'The Anglo-Saxon Chronicle' drew on various sources for the years since the beginning of the Viking Age. The resulting annals give little sense of consistency of vikings' purposes, with a very fragmentary record of what they did, and no sense of who led the vikings in their actions, until 865. Then, suddenly, a marked consistency and named leaders become apparent: while the narrative from 865 to 892 is by no means without problems attracting questions, it does convey some sense of purpose on either side (but especially the Scandinavian). It is quite possible that all the annals 865–92 were written by one chronicler in a single authorial campaign (Dumville 1982: 333–4). The author(s) focused relentlessly on the most dangerous armies and their political effects: the ecclesiastical results of their activities seem to have been of no compelling interest. This gives the record of the First Viking Age in England a uniquely secular character among the west European chronicling of that era (Dumville 2002c).

In Insular chronicles, vikings are very variously referred to, and this has led to problematic interpretations of their ethnicity, geographical origins and religion. In general, in Latin chronicling of Viking Age date, vikings are *Nordmanni*, sometimes *Nortmanni* and (later) *Normanni*: 'Northmen' is a credible and sensible translation (while 'Norsemen' is variously problematic and best avoided: see Dumville 2002c: 209). When not 'Northmen' or *piratae*, 'pirates', they are usually *Dani*. To translate as 'Danes' may seem obvious but is in fact unwise, as has long been recognised. It seems clear that, in the usage of latinate writers of the era, both *Dani* and *Nordmanni* (and its variants) have the same semantic force and were used in free variation.

In Old English, when an ethnonym was used, *Dene* was usual; and (unlike Latin *Dani*) it has typically been translated 'Danes'. In the absence of Anglo-Latin chronicling of this era, until the work of Æthelweard in the last quarter of the tenth century (Campbell 1962; Van Houts 1992; on his latinity see Riley 1857, Winterbottom 1967, Howlett 2000), *Nordmanni* have not been an issue. The appearance of Old English *Norðmenn* has therefore caused excitement and sometimes been translated 'Norwegians' (Mawer 1923 seems to have been important), but whether this is an anachronism needs to be considered. *Norðmann* (not an Old Norse form) and *Norðmenn* appear in English place-names, another complicating factor. What is more, *Norðmann* is attested as a personal name, alongside *Wiking* and *Sumarlidi* (and Old and Middle Gaelic *Dubgall*, it might be added); this suggests that it might have meant 'viking' rather than bearing any geographical or ethnic significance (cf. Hermann Pálsson 1981). 'Danes' were late and brief entrants to Gaelic chronicles (Middle Gaelic *Danair* in the 980s) and the reasons are not yet clear (cf. Downham 2007). When we turn to Old Norse (viz Old Scandinavian) usage, it is highly significant that *dönsk tungu* is not 'the Danish language' but that of all ethnic Scandinavians (cf. Amory 1980).

It has often been observed that in Old English an army of vikings would be called *here* while that of the natives would be *fyrd* (Plummer 1892/9, vol. 1: 338, 360). (We should also note that *folc* could be used to mean an army: cf. John 1966: 121–2, 142, 292–3.) H.G. Richardson and G.O. Sayles (1963: 55; cf. John 1966: 132–50) protested against this, arguing that the two words were semantically equivalent. Their concerns were

[margin, handwritten: Problem of accurate translation/meaning of "vikings" @ insular chronicles]

proper, given the unfortunate common translations of *fyrd* in particular. But it has to be said that in the original text of 'The Anglo-Saxon Chronicle' (to 892) the distribution of usage does seem to be as has often been indicated. Nevertheless, it is clear – as Peter Sawyer observed more than forty years ago (Sawyer 1962: 120) – that there is more to these distinctions than an opposition of 'them' and 'us'; and, after the First Viking Age, the terminology found in 'The Anglo-Saxon Chronicle' for military forces becomes more complex in its usage. The rare employment of *wicing(as)*, 'pirates' (Plummer 1892/9, vol. 1: 415), in annals 879, 885 and 917A is a further aspect of this, but that word finds reflexes (as *pirata[e]*) in Continental Latin writing, which we also see in England after the Norman conquest (Richardson and Sayles 1963: 77, 102).

Another aspect of otherness of vikings was their difference in religion. Old English *hæðene*, 'heathens', is found – less in chronicles than in texts with overtly religious messages –, and in Latin writing (one thinks first of the 'Life of King Alfred' by Asser, with his Welsh, Frankish and English educational experiences; Stevenson 1904: xciii–xciv; Keynes and Lapidge 1983: 51–5) *pagani*, with the same meaning, is common currency. Æthelweard's Latin usage in relation to vikings is often quite vigorously racist (Page 1987; for various translations see Giles 1848: 1–40; Stevenson 1853–8, vol. 2, part 2: 407–40; Albrectsen 1986). Gaelic and Welsh chroniclers felt the difference of religion too, calling vikings Old Gaelic *gen(n)ti*, 'foreigners of different religion', borrowed from the Biblical usage of Latin *gentes*, *gentiles* ('Gentiles' in the traditional language of the English Bible), Old Welsh *gint*, *gynt* (we also find Welsh *pobloedd*, in effect a loan-translation from Christian Latin *gentes* or *nationes*). Abandonment of such terminology by Gaelic chroniclers has been taken as recognition of conversion to Christianity (Abrams 1997; Dumville 1997: 37–8).

Simple recognition of vikings as foreigners – even archetypal foreigners – is a manifest element of Gaelic usage. Old and Middle Gaelic *Gaill*, 'Foreigners' (Modern Gaelic *Goill*), is the word which from the first appearance of vikings in the Gaelic world until the third quarter of the twelfth century conveyed the idea of Scandinavians or colonists of Scandinavian speech or descent or mores (Mac Cana 1962; Ní Mhaonaigh 1998). Persons of hybrid Gaelic and Scandinavian culture could be called *Gall-Gaedil*, 'Foreigner-Gaels' (Dumville 1997: 26–9). The word *Gaill* etymologically means 'Gauls', who therefore until the beginning of the Viking Age were the archetypal foreigners: what they had done in Gaelic prehistory to gain that status is unknown and was probably unpleasant. The appellation passed in the later twelfth century to those foreigners of French speech who (after 1166) invaded and settled Ireland, the immediately successive Angevin king of England and his government who claimed lordship of Ireland, and by natural extension to the English at large (for colonial identity in Ireland in that period, see the important and controversial work of Gillingham 2000).

The other aspect of nomenclature which is characteristic of Gaelic and (probably derivatively) Welsh usage is the recognition of a pair of groups of vikings characterised by the prefixed adjectives Old Gaelic *find* (Middle Gaelic *finn*, Modern Gaelic *fionn*) and Old Gaelic and Old Welsh *dub*: literally, these mean 'light' and 'dark', 'white' and 'black', and there has long been speculation as to their usage in relation to vikings, when compounded with Gaelic *gen(n)ti* (Welsh *gint, gynt*) and *Gaill*. Racial or ethnic interpretations have long been favoured in modern scholarship, a characteristic reflex of contemporary culture (Downham 2004b). Seventeenth-century Gaelic writers took this opposition to mean 'the former' / 'the latter', and some recent scholars have accepted this usage (Smyth 1974–7; Dumville 2004): it allows us to see a distinction between two politically and genealogically defined groups of vikings operating in the Insular world (particularly in the ninth century) and especially associated with Dublin (Downham 2007).

The last terminological issue arising relates to the lands from which vikings arrived in the territories of Insular chroniclers. On the whole, what is striking is that chroniclers writing in the First Viking Age largely ignored this issue: either the origin or the immediate provenance of groups of vikings was unknown or it was obvious. If they were *Dani* / *Nordmanni*, their Scandinavian ethnicity and Northern origin could be taken for granted. Those familiar with the Latin Bible knew that it was prophesied, and a given, that evil would come from the north: but this sentiment is not, I think, openly expressed in Insular chronicling, although it is visible elsewhere (cf. Coupland 1991).

An instructive case is the famous notice in annal 787 (for 789) of 'The Anglo-Saxon Chronicle', in which we read that in the days of Beorhtric, king of the West Saxons (786–802), three ships of vikings landed in his kingdom. The chronicler concluded – no doubt with an eye to a similar sentiment expressed in annal 449 about the arrival of the English in Britain – that *Þæt wæron þa ærestan scipu deniscra monna þe Angelcynnes lond gesohton*, 'They were the first ships of "Danish" men who attacked England'. For Æthelweard, a century later, they were *Dani* (Campbell 1962: 26–7). 'The Northern Recension' of 'The Anglo-Saxon Chronicle', approximately contemporary with Æthelweard but written at York, tells us (on what authority we know not) that these were *.iii. scipu Norðmanna of Hereða lande*, 'three ships of Northmen from *Hereða lande*' (Dumville 2007a), where the last might be identified with Hǫrðaland in Norway (Plummer 1892/9, vol. 2: 59). In a fairly close Latin translation ('The Annals of St Neots') of a lost version of 'The Anglo-Saxon Chronicle' to 912 made in the earlier twelfth century, we read of *.iii. naues Normannorum `id est Danorum´* (Dumville and Lapidge 1985: 39)! We may conclude that in the late ninth century the precise date of the event was unknown, that the source of the Scandinavians in question was unknown, but that for the Alfredian chronicler(s) the Viking Age in England began in Wessex about a century earlier and had uncomfortable parallels with fifth-century British history (cf. Godden 2004). After a further century the story had begun to be elaborated and glossed with further ethnic, geographical and local statements (these have not all been discussed here).

A northern territory which loomed large in medieval Gaelic writing has been the subject of much modern scholarly discussion, often with little resulting profit. In some ninth-century Gaelic texts we read of *Lothlind* or *Laithlind* as a source of vikings (Mac Airt and Mac Niocaill 1983: 306 and 312, annals 848 and 853; Ahlqvist 2005). In eleventh-century and later Gaelic writing we find *Lochlann* used in the same way. These two words are not etymologically related but seem to occupy the same semantic space. Attempts at specific equations with Scandinavian locations (for example, Rogaland) have failed (Marstrander 1911, 1915; Greene 1975). And periodic attempts to locate this source of Scandinavians in a Scottish provenance have found little favour with other scholars (cf. Ó Corráin 1998 for the latest attempt). In Gaelic usage *Lochlann* came to mean 'Scandinavia' and may have done so from the time of its first attestation (cf. Greene 1975). It was used for Norway in relation to Magnús, its king, in 'The Annals of Ulster' for 1102 and 1103 (Mac Airt and Mac Niocaill 1983: 538–43).

Denmark and Norway, and Norwegians certainly identifiable thus, only enter English chronicling in the Second Viking Age. Denmark (Old English *Denemearce*) is found from 1005 in 'The Anglo-Saxon Chronicle'. Norway (*Norwege*) makes its first appearance in 1028, *Normen* means Norwegians in 1049D and 1066CD, and in 1066DE Haraldr is *se Norrena cyng* (E) and Óláfr Haraldsson is *þæs Norna cynges suna* (D). We may suspect, on the back of all this, that the use of *denisc* (from the 990s) and of *Dene* (from 1018DE) became more geographically and politically (and perhaps ethnically) precise in the context of the creation of the historical Scandinavian kingdoms. The Swedes have a single walk-on part in 'The Anglo-Saxon Chronicle' for their resistance to Knútr (Cnut; 1025E). To that era and its historiography in Insular chronicling we shall return.

I have written at length elsewhere about the historiographical problems created by national compartmentalisation of the history of the Viking Age (Dumville 2002c). In spite of various scholars' determined efforts, this remains a problem in the Insular world, in continental Europe and in Scandinavia. It cannot be said too often that vikings were not respecters of boundaries, whether mental or geographical or political, and certainly not of modern categories. Vikings must be followed and studied wherever they went. The historian's principal difficulty in dealing with vikings has been that the sources from one genre or area or language may give a very different impression of their activities from those derived from another. In spite of the unceasing flow of generalising (and usually undocumented) books about vikings as a whole, scholars have emerged who have cautioned against any kind of generalising approach. And yet it is arguable that to avoid generalising hypothesis on principle is unnecessarily to become the prisoner of the patchy distribution of partial sources. To take a simple contrast, we learn from English chronicles about vikings' roles in high politics; but from more abundant, if more laconic, Gaelic chronicling we learn (above all) of numerous attacks on Irish churches. Yet if we were to deduce that vikings in England were interested only in conquest and settlement and left the Church alone, while vikings in Ireland were more interested in plunder, we should undoubtedly have gained a severely distorted view of Insular history in the Viking Age. In other words, where historians, in a mood of cheerful positivism, have deduced themes from their national chronicle-record they have often seen only a fragment of the picture even of their own territory. It is arguable therefore that an infusion of themes by the historian into the chronicle-record will provide valuable tests of that evidence.

We can, of course, see common themes in different categories or groupings of sources. If we ask the extant chronicles what it was like to have vikings as visitors or neighbours, some shared experiences emerge across the boundaries between the several ethnic groups of the Insular world. But there are restraints: we learn nothing about northernmost Britain or the extreme west and south of Ireland, for example. That vikings had nothing to do with these areas is a manifestly nonsensical hypothesis (on Ireland, see Sheehan *et al.* 2001). For approximately a half-century after the first-recorded raids vikings remain anonymous: in effect, the encounters took place at the point of a weapon, with exchanges of name unlikely; the pre-existing conventions in all divisions of Insular chronicling were to name the leaders and groups participating in recorded armed activities, and long-standing opponents would be aware of each other's identities. Nameable leaders of vikings emerge in Irish, English and Welsh chronicles over a period of half a century from the middle of the ninth: at 837 in 'The Annals of Ulster' (Mac Airt and Mac Niocaill 1983: 294–5; cf. Downham 2006: 54); at 871 in 'The

Anglo-Saxon Chronicle'; at 902 in *Annales Cambriae* and *Brenhinoedd y Saeson* (900) (Dumville 2002b: 14; 2005: 32–3).

In Irish chronicling, groups of vikings then began to be distinguished by (Gaelic) names, *Findgenti* and *Dubgenti* (Dumville 2004) from 851 (cf. 849), for example (853, followed by 866 and 890 in the Welsh chronicles: Dumville 2002b: 12–13, and 2005: 24–5, 30–1), and then *Gall-Gaedil* from 856 (Dumville 1997: 26–9). Norse words begin to appear in the Gaelic chronicles (cf. Stokes 1892: 115–23): *erell* (848), and as a Gaelic dual *na da iarla* (918), both from Old Norse *jarl*, are the first examples (Mac Airt and Mac Niocaill 1983: 306, 368).

The use of names of vikings' leaders is effectively coincident with settlement: there was now no option but to recognise that Scandinavians were no longer hostile transients but instead hostile neighbours with whom it might be necessary or profitable sometimes to ally. These were in principle new permanent local competitors for status and resources, and ones about whose habits, language and patterns of thought it was necessary to learn fast. Just as vikings sought to – and did – exploit political differences between the natives of territories in which they operated, so the natives would have to find ways to profit from, and indeed encourage, dissension between or within viking-groups (on Ireland see Downham 2006; for the Scandinavian situation see Maund 1994).

How much settlement took place is very difficult to assess from the records offered by Insular chronicles – and impossible to quantify. However different from one another the various chronicling traditions may be, what they share is a level of selectivity – determined in great part by criteria of relevance – which largely excludes longer-term trends and events or processes lacking a strictly military or ecclesiastical character. In 1969 Peter Sawyer published a discussion-paper, with critical responses from a variety of colleagues, entitled 'The two Viking Ages of Britain' (Sawyer *et al.* 1969). In fact, this dealt almost exclusively with England, but it is a concept which can be expanded within Britain and to Ireland. Much of the criticism turned, however, on the extent and depth of Scandinavian settlement and in particular on the bearing of toponymic evidence on these issues. The problem was (and is) that 'The Anglo-Saxon Chronicle' has very little to say on the subject, beyond noting that armies – whether after success (876 and probably 877) or after their ambitions had reached a high-water mark (880) – divided land and settled among the Northumbrians, Mercians and East Angles. But was that all? Did subsequent settlement of Scandinavians take place in these areas of England controlled by Scandinavian rulers and armies? – in the southern and eastern 'Danelaw' until the 910s, and in the northern 'Danelaw' until (first) the creation of the kingdom of England in 927 and (even then) during the period of contested rule from 939/40 to 954.

After the defeat and death of Eiríkr, king of Scandinavian York, in 954 (Downham 2004a), and the permanent end (as it turned out) of the rule of the vikings of Dublin in England (cf. Dumville 2006: 51), there was a marked pause, lasting for a generation, in chroniclers' reporting of vikings' activities in England. This has long been noted and probably represents a historical reality. Historians' perception has been that, when raiding by (external rather than settled) Scandinavians resumed in England, it was of a distinctly different character. From this perception was developed the concept of the two Viking Ages. Although this concept has never been popular among Scandinavian academics, for it has not been identified as a phenomenon in Scandinavia itself (where the weight of evidence would have to be physical rather than literary), in Britain and Ireland, at least, it has served as a useful historical tool. It was quite explicitly adopted for Ireland by Donnchadh Ó Corráin (Ó Corráin 1994).

In relation to Ireland, a period of 'forty years' rest' from severe depredations by vikings (in the late ninth century and ending in 915) was commented on by an author of the beginning of the twelfth century in *Cocad Gaedel re Gallaib*, 'The War of the Irish with the Foreigners' (Todd 1867: 26–9, 232–3 [§26]; on the date of this text, see Ní Mhaonaigh 1995). Whether this has any historical credibility has been debated in the past generation. What is certainly the case is an almost total absence of chronicle-record for vikings' activities in Ireland from 902 (expulsion of the Scandinavian ruling dynasty from Dublin) until 914×917 when Uí Ímair re-established themselves there (Downham 2007). Ó Corráin has explicitly defined these latter years as marking the beginning of Ireland's Second Viking Age (Ó Corráin 1994). Certainly it can be argued that the character of vikings' activities in Ireland in the tenth century is in various ways different from that of the ninth. And the archaeology of Ireland's Scandinavian towns has a markedly different character from the tenth century, not least in the levels of fortification. These urban kingdoms came to be dominated by major Irish overkings of the late tenth century and later, but they retained their distinctive character and (especially in the case of Dublin) remained centres of viking activity until Angevin conquest from 1171/2 subjected them to an altogether more vigorous domination (for some of the complexities of 1166–75, see Duffy 1999).

The English position was rather different and developed in part from that observed in Wales. There too, the native chronicles show an apparent cessation of vikings' predatory activities – from the end of the 910s (Dumville 2002b: 14–15; 2005: 34–5) to the beginning of the 960s. (Perhaps in the middle of that period the Isle of Man was settled by bicultural vikings from the Hebrides; cf. Downham 2007.) The new attacks were due to vikings from Ireland (as before) and from the Hebrides: in the former case they were no doubt aimed at weakening English *imperium* in Wales as a prelude to another attempt on York, but the latter was never achieved. Resumption of vikings' attacks on England, as reported by chroniclers, began in 980 (Thorpe 1861, vol. 1: 234–5; Whitelock *et al.* 1961: 80; Dumville 2007a), in the immediate aftermath of the assassination of King Edward I 'the Martyr' (975–9) and his replacement by King Æthelred 'the Unready' (979–1013, 1014–16) (Dumville 2007b; Williams 2003). For the rest of the 980s, the source of such attacks in southern England (as also in Wales) seems to have lain in the Irish Sea. There is reason to think that, as Sveinn tjúguskegg Haraldsson, king of the Danes (and king of the English in 1013/14), came to be recorded as participating from 994 in campaigns in England, he continued for some while to draw on support from vikings based in Ireland (and perhaps the Hebrides) – where he himself may previously have been active – in addition to forces recruited in Scandinavia itself (Downham 2007). Sveinn's conquest of England, achieved in 1013, and the eventual succession there of his son Knútr (1016–35) created an Anglo-Scandinavian empire which lasted for a generation and inspired kings of Denmark and kings of Norway for the next century and more to dream of recreating it (for a couple of these possible manifestations see Bolton 2005; Dumville 2006: 18). In that sense, England's Viking Age continued until the mid-twelfth century.

From the time of Sveinn's campaigns in England (994–1014), it may be (and has been) argued, national monarchs in Denmark and Norway were a danger to the polities of Ireland and especially Britain. In respect of western Britain and the Irish Sea, it was indeed the case that two Norwegian royals, Magnús Haraldsson in 1058 (Stokes 1993, vol. 2: 291, annal 1058.4; cf. Welsh chronicles – Williams 1860: 25; Jones 1952: 14) and Magnús berfœttr Óláfsson in 1098–1103, presented problems for all the major parts of the region. In 1066 Haraldr harðráði Sigurðarson famously sought conquest in England, as his son Magnús had attempted in 1058. (We should note also the activities of Magnús góði Óláfsson, recorded in 'The Anglo-Saxon Chronicle' 1046–9D.) After the Norman conquest Sveinn Úlfsson or Ástríðarson, king of Danes, presented problems for the Anglo-Norman realm (Bolton 2005). Even in the 1150s, Eysteinn Haraldsson gilla plundered eastern Scotland and England with a Norwegian fleet (Dumville 2006: 18 and n. 63). And as late as the 1260s a Norwegian royal fleet might arrive in Scotland with hostile intent. All these events were recorded by writers of history, now Insular, now Scandinavian. But where are the various lines of definition to be drawn? On the evidence of the First Viking Age, earlier Scandinavian adventurers of unknown but royal and aristocratic origin had dreamt of and sought widespread conquest in Britain and Ireland: what power and resources any of them may have enjoyed in Scandinavia itself is wholly unknown. When the spread of Christianity and Latin-letter literacy in Scandinavia had changed the character of the source material available to us, we inevitably have a rather different perception of the resources and outlook of Northern rulership. This, together with the effects of modern history, has encouraged historians (and, more recently, archaeologists) to view the history of the Second, or Later, Viking Age according to a national paradigm. Scandinavian archaeologists have also tended to be prey to another paradigm, in which the word 'state' is used prematurely and inappropriately to describe socio-political structure in the Viking Age. It must be said that the contemporary chronicle-evidence does not straightforwardly encourage outlooks of this sort. For example, we can still gain the impression of significant Insular ignorance of the basic political structures of Scandinavia (this is suggested, for example, by the description of eleventh-century Norway as *Germania* in Welsh chronicles, and confusion of Denmark and Norway: Williams 1860: 31; Jones 1952: 11, 13, 15, 21, 24, 25).

The Viking Age in Insular chronicles inevitably ends *au courant*, with a lack of hindsight. The annalistic chronicle, as by definition 'a history without an end', deals in general with origin and development rather than closure. Across Britain and Ireland, what removed Scandinavians and locally based vikings from chroniclers' interests and writing was the advent of a new and more dangerous breed of invader, the French-speaker. In the chronicling traditions of England, Wales and Ireland, these newcomers were identified first in terms of their speech ('The Anglo-Saxon Chronicle' 1050D [Whitelock *et al.* 1961: 115]; *Annales Cambriae* 1071 [Williams 1860: 26; Jones 1952: 16]). In Irish chronicles we find evidence for a rapid semantic shift mimicking that which took place at the beginning of the Viking Age: as I have already noted, the word *Ga(i)ll*, 'Foreigner(s)', which around 800 came conclusively to mean vikings, now around 1200 shifted to mean 'French-speakers from Britain' (and eventually simply 'English'). These were the new vikings – and Normans of course had been trained by their own historians to think of themselves as reformed, civilised, ex-vikings, still endowed with the strength and adventurousness of vikings but fully absorbed within a French, Christian cultural paradigm (Davis 1976; Shopkow 1997).

It is only in subsequent historical writing that we find the work of authors who have begun to contemplate the Viking Age from a safe distance. Much research remains to be done on perceptions of vikings in later medieval (and especially Latin) historiography. It is my provisional impression that it is in thirteenth-century writing in particular that the image of vikings' impact on England became comprehensively bloodcurdling and transmitted the received image into modern perceptions. If one studies a standard older handbook of English ecclesiastical life – I think of *Medieval Religious Houses: England and Wales* by David Knowles and R.N. Hadcock (1953; 2nd edn 1971), for example – one finds that the sources which underpin notions of the complete destruction of monastic life by vikings' actions can be traced to that period (cf. Dumville 1992: 29–54). It is not that Anglo-Norman historians failed to reflect on the Viking Age; rather, it was in the thirteenth century that larger conclusions were vividly applied to local circumstances. I think in particular of the historical introduction to the cartulary of Chertsey Abbey (Surrey), which has almost everything one might expect and seek to find (*ibid.*, 34, n. 17). The carefully cultivated Norman self-image, which admitted but rejected heathen savagery, was blunted among the neighbours (one thinks of Brittany in particular) and was historically modified in post-Norman England; both recalled such evil (Dumville 2002d).

In Ireland, however, a thoroughgoing interpretation of Irish experience of vikings was achieved by the opening years of the twelfth century (in the text *Cocad Gaedel re Gallaib*, already mentioned, which was built on annalistic data but written racily as narrative: Todd 1867; cf. Dumville 1999: 104–5). Vikings were the heathen Other who sought to conquer Ireland and more or less succeeded. The island and nation were rescued by the heroic scions of an outstanding royal dynasty full of *uirtus*, and in particular by Brian *Bóruma* ('of the tribute') who repeatedly defeated vikings, even on his Good Friday death-day when, Christ-like, he sacrificed himself for his people at the battle of Clontarf.

All such interpretations coalesced to give the picture of the Viking Age which was a staple of historical writing until twentieth-century reconsideration, timid at first but eventually becoming perversely revisionist, brought us – in Danish cartoons (Ramskou and Bojesen 1967) and in English sloganeering ('traders not raiders') – to the brief era of the cuddly viking. The problem of the modern apologists' syllogism is focused squarely on the chronicle-evidence (Dumville 1997: 9; cf. Dumville 2002c: 249): 'We learn of vikings' aggression from ecclesiastical writers. Because vikings attacked churches and churchpeople, ecclesiastical writers were biased against them. Therefore we must discount their prejudiced testimony. Having rejected it, we possess no evidence that vikings attacked churches (or, indeed, did anything much else which a chronicler might report). . . . Narrow-minded clergy are responsible for the bad press which they have received.' Much of this syllogism (belonging to the category which gives logic a bad name) bears on larger issues. But, in so far as it makes the chronicler central, we are returned to questions of opportunity, relevance and style. No chronicle tells the whole story of vikings within its chosen territory: chroniclers did not receive total information; chroniclers had generic criteria of relevance, although these might develop over time, and this would cause non-recording of some available information. But style is a matter which has confounded readers of chronicles, especially chronicles of Gaelic origin. Take the following sequence from 'The Annals of Ulster' in its record for 812 (Mac Airt and Mac Niocaill 1983: 268–9):

Ár gennte la fíru Humhaill.
Ár Conmaicne la gennti.
Ár Calraighi Luirgg la Hu Briúin.
Ár Corco Roídhe Míde la Hua Mac Uais.
Ár gennte la Mumain, id est la Cobthach
        mac Maele Dúin, rí Locha Léin.

A slaughter of heathens by the men of Umall.
The slaughter of the Conmaicne by heathens.
The slaughter of the Calraige of Lurg by Uí Briúin.
The slaughter of Corcu Roídi of Míde by Uí Moccu Uais.
A slaughter of heathens in Mumu, viz. by Cobthach
        son of Mael Dúin, the king of Loch Léin.

It would be hard to argue from these five successive entries that vikings were being singled out and made to play stereotype. In this record their only difference from the native population-groups is that they are at once known but not known: they are heathens but they cannot be (or, at any rate, are not) described more precisely. We also need to ask whether these are blazing tabloid-newspaper headlines or tediously sober statements: if they are the former, then five successive instances of the same formula must have severely blunted their impact. In sum, chroniclers cannot carry the weight of accusations of cripplingly hostile bias. History-writing in highly coloured, imaginative prose is a much later phenomenon in respect of vikings – late tenth-century at the earliest and thirteenth-century in its more spectacular development. It is hard to fault the rather dry writing of Gaelic annalistic chronicles – which deliver copious quantities of information – except on aesthetic or frustratedly historiographical grounds. 'The Anglo-Saxon Chronicle' is an easier target, but detractors have often lacked the skills which could land damaging blows on it.

Even the blandest text can be innocently corrupted, however. I close with some instructive – but not necessarily generalisable – examples arising in later medieval manuscripts.

(a) 'The Annals of Ulster', 701:

> *Conall mac Donennaigh, rex nepotum Finngenti, moritur.*
> 'Conall, the son of Doinennach, the king of the descendants of the *Finngenti* [Old Heathens], dies.'

A copyist, dreaming of vikings or having recently copied a text about them, substituted *Finngenti* for *Fidgenti*, the name of an early mediaeval Irish dynasty (Mac Airt and Mac Niocaill 1983: 160–1, annal 701.10).

(b) 'The Annals of Tigernach', 752:

> *Taudar mac Bile, rex a Lochlandaid . . .*

If this has meaning, it is that Tewdwr ab Beli (who died in 752) was 'king from *Lochlann*', a name referring to a viking-homeland and not known to have been used before the eleventh century. The scribe should have written *rex Alo Chluaide*, 'the king of the Rock of the Clyde [Dumbarton]' (Stokes 1993, vol. 1: 253 and n. 1).

(c)   *Annales Cambriae* and *Brenhinoedd y Saeson*, 850:

AC (B)   *Cengen a Gentilibus occisus est.*
          'Cyngen was killed by Heathens.'

ByS (P)   . . . *laðawð y paganyeid Gyngen.*
          '. . . the pagans killed Cyngen.'

ByS (R)   *Ac y tagwyt Kyngen y gan y <K>enedloed.*
          'And Cyngen was strangled by the Heathens.'

ByS (S)   . . . *y llas Kyngen y gan y wyr ehun.*
          '. . . Cyngen was killed by his own men.'

The Latin source-text makes the meaning plain (Dumville 2002b: 10–11). It was translated into Welsh (Dumville 2005: 22–3) with stylistic freedom in P. The redactor of R preferred a different verb (a literal translation of *iugulauit*) and a closer rendering of *Gentilibus*. The redactor of S misunderstood *kenedloed* as 'kinsmen' (an analogous example is in 903/901: Dumville 2002b: 14–15; 2005: 32–3) and altered the wording to make the abandonment of heathen vikings explicit (as he also tried, but then failed, to do in 950.2; Dumville 2005: 40–1). By this last version, the vikings in question had escaped blame by a few strokes of the pen.

(d)   'The Chronicle of the Kings of Alba' (extending from the 840s to the 970s) contains examples of annal-entries where vikings remain but where kings of Alba whom they probably killed have disappeared from the text (Dumville 2000: 81).

In sum, textual corruption over centuries of copying the chronicle-record could lead to various distortions of vikings' activities, with no certain indication that this led to a better or a worse press for them. Slogans and twisted syllogisms cannot usefully be extracted from the overall evidence of Insular chronicles.

BIBLIOGRAPHY

Abegg, D. (1894) *Zur Entwicklung der historischen Dichtung bei den Angelsachsen*, Strassburg: Karl J. Truebner.
Abrams, L. (1997) 'The conversion of the Scandinavians of Dublin', *Anglo-Norman Studies*, 20: 1–29.
Ahlqvist, A. (2005) '*Is acher in gaíth . . . úa Lothlind*', *CSANA Yearbook*, 3–4: 19–27.
Albrectsen, E. (trans.) (1986) *To tidlige engelske Krøniker*, Odense: Odense Universitetsforlag.
Amory, F. (1980) 'The *dönsk tunga* in early medieval Normandy: a note', in K. Klar *et al.* (eds) *American Indian and Indoeuropean Studies. Papers in Honor of Madison S. Beeler*, The Hague: Mouton.
Ashdown, M. (1919–27) 'The attitude of the Anglo-Saxons to their Scandinavian invaders', *Saga-book of the Viking Society for Northern Research*, 10: 75–99.
Bolton, T. (2005) 'English political refugees at the court of Sveinn Ástríðarson, king of Denmark (1042–76)', *Mediaeval Scandinavia*, 15: 17–36.

Bredehoft, T.A. (2001) *Textual Histories. Readings in The Anglo-Saxon Chronicle*, Toronto: University of Toronto Press.

Bury, J.B. (1928) *The Invasion of Europe by the Barbarians*, London: Macmillan.

Campbell, A. (ed. and trans.) (1962) *The Chronicle of Æthelweard*, Edinburgh: Thomas Nelson.

Charles-Edwards, T.M. (trans.) (2006) *The Chronicle of Ireland*, 2 vols, Liverpool: Liverpool University Press.

Clark, C. (1971) 'The narrative mode of the *Anglo-Saxon Chronicle* before the Conquest', in P. Clemoes and K. Hughes (eds) *England before the Conquest. Studies in Primary Sources presented to Dorothy Whitelock*, Cambridge: Cambridge University Press.

Cook, A.S. (trans.) (1906) *Asser's Life of King Alfred*, Boston, MA: Ginn.

Cooke, W.G. (1980) '"Firy drakes and blazing-bearded light"', *English Studies*, 61: 97–103.

Coupland, S. (1991) 'The rod of God's wrath or the people of God's wrath? The Carolingian theology of the viking invasions', *Journal of Ecclesiastical History*, 42: 535–54.

Davies, R.R. (2000) *The First English Empire. Power and Identities in the British Isles, 1093–1343*, Oxford: Oxford University Press.

Davis, R.H.C. (1971) 'Alfred the Great: propaganda and truth', *History*, new series, 56: 169–82.

—— (1976) *The Normans and their Myth*, London: Thames and Hudson.

Dobbie, E. van K. (ed.) (1942) *The Anglo-Saxon Minor Poems*, New York: Columbia University Press.

Downham, C. (2000) 'An imaginary viking-raid on Skye in 795?', *Scottish Gaelic Studies*, 20: 192–6.

—— (2004a) 'Eric Bloodaxe – axed? The mystery of the last Scandinavian king of York', *Mediaeval Scandinavia*, 14: 51–77.

—— (2004b) 'The good, the bad, and the ugly: portrayals of vikings in "The Fragmentary Annals of Ireland"', *The Medieval Chronicle*, 4: 27–39.

—— (2006) 'Irish chronicles as a source for rivalry between vikings, 795–1014', *Northern Scotland*, 26: 51–63.

—— (2007) *Viking Kings of Britain and Ireland. The Dynasty of Ívarr to A.D. 1014*, Edinburgh: Dunedin Academic Press.

Duffy, S. (1999) 'The 1169 invasion as a turning point in Irish–Welsh relations', in B. Smith (ed.) *Britain and Ireland, 900–1300. Insular Responses to Medieval European Change*, Cambridge: Cambridge University Press.

Dumville, D.N. (1982) 'Latin and Irish in The Annals of Ulster, A.D. 431–1050', in D. Whitelock *et al.* (ed.) *Ireland in Early Mediaeval Europe. Studies in Memory of Kathleen Hughes*, Cambridge: Cambridge University Press.

—— (1983) 'Some aspects of annalistic writing at Canterbury in the eleventh and early twelfth centuries', *Peritia*, 2: 23–57.

—— (1992) *Wessex and England from Alfred to Edgar*, Woodbridge: Boydell Press.

—— (1993) *Britons and Anglo-Saxons in the Early Middle Ages*, Aldershot: Variorum.

—— (1997) *The Churches of North Britain in the First Viking-Age*, Whithorn: The Friends of the Whithorn Trust.

—— (1999) 'A millennium of Gaelic chronicling', *The Medieval Chronicle*, 1: 103–15.

—— (2000) 'The Chronicle of the Kings of Alba', in S. Taylor (ed.) *Kings, Clerics and Chronicles in Scotland, 500–1297. Essays in Honour of Marjorie Ogilvie Anderson on the Occasion of her Ninetieth Birthday*, Dublin: Four Courts Press.

—— (2002a) 'What is a chronicle?', *The Medieval Chronicle*, 2: 1–27.

—— (ed. and trans.) (2002b) *Annales Cambriae, A.D. 682–954: Texts A–C in Parallel*, Cambridge: Department of Anglo-Saxon, Norse, and Celtic, University of Cambridge.

—— (2002c) 'Vikings in the British Isles: a question of sources', in J. Jesch (ed.) *The*

Scandinavians from the Vendel Period to the Tenth Century. An Ethnographic Perspective, San Marino: Center for Interdisciplinary Research on Social Stress.

—— (2002d) 'Images of the viking in eleventh-century Latin literature', in M.W. Herren *et al.* (eds) *Latin Culture in the Eleventh Century*, Turnhout: Brepols.

—— (2004) 'Old Dubliners and New Dubliners in Ireland and Britain: a Viking-Age story', *Medieval Dublin*, 6: 78–93.

—— (ed. and trans.) (2005) *Brenhinoedd y Saeson, 'The Kings of the English', A.D. 682–954. Texts P, R, S in Parallel*, Aberdeen: School of Divinity, History, and Philosophy, University of Aberdeen.

—— (2006) *The Mediaeval Foundations of England?*, Aberdeen: School of Divinity, History & Philosophy, University of Aberdeen.

—— (ed. and trans.) (2007a) *The Anglo-Saxon Chronicle. A Collaborative Edition*, XI, 'The Northern Recension', 60 B.C.–A.D. 984, Cambridge: D.S. Brewer.

—— (2007b) 'The death of King Edward the Martyr – 18 March, 979?', *Anglo-Saxon*, 1: 269–83.

—— (2007c) 'Breton Latin chronicling in the central Middle Ages', *Journal of Celtic Studies*, 7 (forthcoming).

Dumville, D.N. and Lapidge, M. (eds) (1985) *The Anglo-Saxon Chronicle. A Collaborative Edition*, vol. 17: *The Annals of St Neots with Vita Prima Sancti Neoti*, Cambridge: D.S. Brewer.

Etchingham, C. (1996) *Viking Raids on Irish Church Settlements in the Ninth Century. A Reconsideration of the Annals*, Maynooth: St Patrick's College.

Giles, J.A. (trans.) (1848) *Six Old English Chronicles*, London: Henry G. Bohn.

Gillingham, J. (2000) *The English in the Twelfth Century. Imperialism, National Identity and Political Values*, Woodbridge: Boydell Press.

Godden, M. (2004) *The Translations of Alfred and His Circle, and the Misappropriation of the Past*, Cambridge: Department of Anglo-Saxon, Norse, and Celtic, University of Cambridge.

Goedheer, A.J. (1938) *Irish and Norse Traditions about the Battle of Clontarf*, Haarlem: Tjeenk Willink.

Grabowski, K. and Dumville, D. (1984) *Chronicles and Annals of Mediaeval Ireland and Wales. The Clonmacnoise-group Texts*, Woodbridge: Boydell Press.

Greene, D. (1975) 'The influence of Scandinavian on Irish', in B. Almqvist and D. Greene (eds) *Proceedings of the Seventh Viking Congress, Dublin, 15–21 August, 1973*, Dublin: Royal Irish Academy.

Griscom, A. (1925-6) 'The "Book of Basingwerk" and MS. Cotton Cleopatra B.v', *Y Cymmrodor*, 35: 49–116 and 36: 1–33.

Gwynn, A. (1992) *The Irish Church in the Eleventh and Twelfth Centuries*, Blackrock: Four Courts Press.

Harris, S.J. (2001) 'The Alfredian *World History* and Anglo-Saxon identity', *Journal of English and Germanic Philology*, 100: 482–510.

Hermann Pálsson (1981) 'The name *Somhairle* and its clan', in M. Benskin and M.L. Samuels (eds) *So meny people longages and tonges. Philological Essays in Scots and Mediaeval English Presented to Angus McIntosh*, Edinburgh: The Editors.

Hill, D. (1981) *An Atlas of Anglo-Saxon England*, Oxford: Basil Blackwell.

Howlett, D.R. (2000) 'The verse of Æthelweard's Chronicle', *Bulletin Du Cange: Archivum Latinitatis Medii Aevi*, 58: 219–24.

Hughes, K. (1957) 'Review', *Medium Aevum*, 26: 122–8.

—— (1972) *Early Christian Ireland. Introduction to the Sources*, London: The Sources of History.

—— (1980) *Celtic Britain in the Early Middle Ages. Studies in Scottish and Welsh Sources*, Woodbridge: Boydell Press.

John, E. (1966) *Orbis Britanniae and Other Studies*, Leicester: Leicester University Press.

Jones, T. (trans.) (1952) *Brut y Tywysogyon or The Chronicle of the Princes – Peniarth MS 20 Version*, Cardiff: University of Wales Press.

Kelleher, J.V. (1963) 'Early Irish history and pseudo-history', *Studia Hibernica*, 3: 113–27.

Keynes, S. (1978) 'The declining reputation of King Æthelred the Unready', in D. Hill (ed.) *Ethelred the Unready. Papers from the Millenary Conference*, Oxford: British Archaeological Reports.

—— (1986) 'A tale of two kings: Alfred the Great and Æthelred the Unready', *Transactions of the Royal Historical Society*, 5th series, 36: 195–217.

—— (1998) 'King Alfred and the Mercians', in M.A.S. Blackburn and D.N. Dumville (eds) *Kings, Currency, and Alliances. History and Coinage of Southern England in the Ninth Century*, Woodbridge: Boydell Press.

Keynes, S. and Lapidge, M. (trans.) (1983) *Alfred the Great. Asser's* Life of King Alfred *and Other Contemporary Sources*, Harmondsworth: Penguin.

Knowles, D. and Hadcock, R.N. (1953; 2nd edn, 1971) *Medieval Religious Houses. England and Wales*, London: Longman.

Lapidge, M. (1982) 'Byrhtferth of Ramsey and the early sections of the *Historia regum* attributed to Symeon of Durham', *Anglo-Saxon England*, 10: 97–122.

Lund, N. (1986) 'The armies of Swein Forkbeard and Cnut: *leding* or *lið*?', *Anglo-Saxon England*, 15: 105–19.

Mac Airt, S. and Mac Niocaill, G. (ed. and trans.) (1983) *The Annals of Ulster (to A.D. 1131)*, vol. 1, Dublin: Dublin Institute for Advanced Studies.

Mac Cana, P. (1962) 'The influence of the vikings on Celtic literature', in B. Ó Cuív (ed.) *Proceedings of the International Congress of Celtic Studies held in Dublin, 6–10 July, 1959*, Dublin: Dublin Institute for Advanced Studies.

MacNeill, E. (1913/14) 'The authorship and structure of the "Annals of Tigernach"', *Ériu*, 7: 30–113.

Marstrander, C.J.S. (1911) 'Lochlainn', *Ériu*, 5: 250–2.

—— (1915) *Bidrag til det norske sprogs historie i Irland*, Oslo: Videnskapsselskapet.

Maund, K.L. (1991) *Ireland, Wales, and England in the Eleventh Century*, Woodbridge: Boydell Press.

—— (1994) '"A turmoil of warring princes": political leadership in ninth-century Denmark', *The Haskins Society Journal*, 6: 29–47.

Mawer, A (1923) 'The redemption of the Five Boroughs', *English Historical Review*, 38: 551–7.

Musset, L. (1971) *Les Invasions: le second assaut contre l'Europe chrétienne (VIIe–XIe siècles)*, Paris: Presses universitaires de France.

Ní Mhaonaigh, M. (1995) '*Cogad Gáedel re Gallaib*: some dating considerations', *Peritia*, 9: 354–77.

—— (1998) 'Friend and foe: vikings in ninth- and tenth-century Irish literature', in H.B. Clarke *et al.* (eds) *Ireland and Scandinavia in the Early Viking Age*, Dublin: Four Courts Press.

Ó Corráin, D. (1994) 'The Second Viking Age in Ireland', in M. Rindal (ed.) *Three Studies on Vikings and Christianisation*, Oslo: Research Council of Norway.

—— (1998) 'The vikings in Scotland and Ireland in the ninth century', *Peritia*, 12: 296–339.

Ó Máille, T. (1910) *The Language of The Annals of Ulster*, Manchester: Manchester University Press.

Page, R.I. (1987) '*A Most Vile People'?* Early English Historians on the Vikings*, London: University College/Viking Society for Northern Research.

Plummer, C. (ed.) (1892/9) (revised impression, by D. Whitelock, 1952) *Two of the Saxon Chronicles Parallel with Supplementary Extracts from the Others*, 2 vols, Oxford: Clarendon Press.

Price, N.S. (1986–9) 'The vikings in Brittany', *Saga-book*, 22: 323–440.

Radner, J.N. (ed. and trans.) (1978) *Fragmentary Annals of Ireland*, Dublin: Dublin Institute for Advanced Studies.

Ramskou, T. and Bojesen, B. (1967) *Vikingernes hverdag – Everyday Viking-life*, Copenhagen: Rhodos.

Reuter, T. (1985) 'Plunder and tribute in the Carolingian empire', *Transactions of the Royal Historical Society*, 5th series, 35: 75–94.

Richardson, H.G. and Sayles, G.O. (1963) *The Governance of Mediaeval England from the Conquest to Magna Carta*, Edinburgh: Edinburgh University Press.

Riley, H.T. (1857) 'The chronicle of Fabius Ethelwerd', *The Gentleman's Magazine*, 203 (3rd series, 3): 120–31.

Sawyer, P.H. (1962) *The Age of the Vikings*, 1st edn, London: Edward Arnold.

—— (1968) *Anglo-Saxon Charters. An Annotated List and Bibliography*, London: Royal Historical Society.

Sawyer, P.H., *et al.* (1969) 'The two Viking Ages of Britain: a discussion', *Mediaeval Scandinavia*, 2: 163–207.

Sheehan, J., *et al.* (2001) 'A Viking Age maritime haven: a reassessment of the island settlement at Beginish, Co. Kerry', *Journal of Irish Archaeology*, 10: 93–120.

Shippey, T.A. (1982) 'A missing army: some doubts about the Alfredian *Chronicle*', *In Geardagum*, 4: 41–55; revised version in *Anglo-Saxon*, 1 (2007) 319–38.

Shopkow, Leah (1997) *History and Community. Norman Historical Writing in the Eleventh and Twelfth Centuries*, Washington, DC: Catholic University of America Press.

Smyth, A.P. (1974–7) 'The *Black* Foreigners of York and the *White* Foreigners of Dublin', *Saga-book*, 19: 101–17.

Stevenson, J. (trans.) (1853–8) *The Church Historians of England*, 5 vols in 8, London: Seeleys.

Stevenson, W.H. (ed.) (1904) (rev. impr. by D. Whitelock, 1959) *Asser's Life of King Alfred, together with The Annals of Saint Neots erroneously ascribed to Asser*, Oxford: Clarendon Press.

Stokes, W. (1892) 'On the linguistic value of the Irish annals', *Beiträge zur Kunde der indogermanischen Sprachen*, 18: 56–132.

—— (ed. and trans.) (1993) *The Annals of Tigernach*, 2 vols, 2nd edn, Felinfach: Llanerch.

Stubbs, W. (ed.) (1868–71) *Chronica Magistri Rogeri de Houedene*, 4 vols, London: Longmans.

Thornton, D.E. (1996) 'Locusts in Ireland? A problem in the Welsh and Frankish annals', *Cambrian Medieval Celtic Studies*, 31: 37–53.

Thorpe, B. (ed. and trans.) (1861) *The Anglo-Saxon Chronicle, according to the Several Original Authorities*, 2 vols, London: Longman.

Todd, J.H. (ed. and trans.) (1867) *Cogadh Gaedhel re Gallaibh. The War of the Gaedhil with the Gaill, or, The Invasions of Ireland by the Danes and Other Norsemen*, London: Longmans.

Van Houts, E. (1980) 'The *Gesta Normannorum Ducum*: a history without an end', *Proceedings of the Battle Conference on Anglo-Norman Studies*, 3: 106–18, 215–20.

—— (1992) 'Women and the writing of history in the early Middle Ages: the case of Abbess Matilda of Essen and Æthelweard', *Early Medieval Europe*, 1: 53–68.

Vogel, W. (1906) *Die Normannen und das fränkische Reich bis zur Gründung der Normandie (799–911)*, Heidelberg: Carl Winter.

Wallace-Hadrill, J.M. (1950) 'The Franks and the English in the ninth century: some common historical interests', *History*, new series, 35: 202–18.

Werner, K.F. (1959) 'Zur Arbeitsweise des Regino von Prüm', *Die Welt als Geschichte*, 19: 96–116.

Whitelock, D. (trans.) (1979) *English Historical Documents*, c. 500–1042, 2nd edn, London: Eyre Methuen.

Whitelock, D., *et al.* (trans.) (1961; rev. impr. 1965) *The Anglo-Saxon Chronicle. A Revised Translation*, London: Eyre and Spottiswoode.

Williams, A. (2003) *Æthelred the Unready, the Ill-counselled King*, London: Hambledon and London.

Williams, J. [Ab Ithel] (ed.) (1860) *Annales Cambriæ*, London: Longman.

Winterbottom, M. (1967) 'The style of Æthelweard', *Medium Aevum*, 36: 109–18.

CHAPTER TWENTY-SEVEN

VIKING SETTLEMENT IN ENGLAND

——·◆·——

Julian D. Richards

Accounts of Scandinavian activity in England have been dominated by debates surrounding the scale of settlement (e.g. Sawyer 1971) and the extent of assimilation of the colonists (e.g. Hadley 1997). Opinions concerning the scale of immigration have ranged from the view that movement was confined to a small group of elite land-takers to ideas of secondary mass migration in the wake of the raiding parties. Although interdisciplinary collaboration might appear to offer great potential for resolving these divergent perspectives, the problem has been that the different categories of evidence do not describe a coherent story (Trafford 2000). Partial documentary sources (see Dumville, ch. 26, above) inevitably focus on raiding activity and wars, while the proliferation of Scandinavian place names has been taken as evidence for large-scale rural colonisation (see Fellows-Jensen, ch. 28, below). Much has hung upon the level of interaction and integration within the area, which became known as the Danelaw (see Hadley, ch. 27.1, below). It has been difficult to observe Viking activity in material evidence and, as part of a general post-war reaction to migration theory, archaeologists have tended to subscribe to minimalist interpretations. In line with new approaches to other periods the debate has now shifted onto questions of ethnicity and has focused on the circumstances of the creation of a hybrid Anglo-Scandinavian cultural identity.

It is possible to identify some archaeological evidence corresponding with the intensity of ninth-century raiding activity described in the Anglo-Saxon Chronicle. The number of Anglo-Saxon coin hoards indicates a period of general insecurity, and there are also Scandinavian hoards of coins and hack-silver. One buried near Croydon, *c.* 872, may represent the plunder gained by an individual Viking warrior which was never retrieved (Brooks and Graham-Campbell 1986). A massive silver hoard was hidden in a lead chest at Cuerdale, on the banks of the River Ribble, *c.* 905, shortly after the expulsion of the Hiberno-Norse from Dublin. It comprised *c.* 7,500 coins, and *c.* 1,000 pieces of bullion silver, and was probably accumulated over several years as the cumulative wealth of a large Viking force (Graham-Campbell 1992b). Finds of weaponry and horse fittings, particularly from rivers, have traditionally been seen as losses during battle, but may also be offerings made after battle, in a revival of the long tradition of Scandinavian water-borne offerings (Wilson 1965; Seaby and Woodfield 1980; Graham-Campbell 1992a).

In addition, there are possible traces of the fortified camps which the Viking armies constructed when they overwintered, most notably at Repton, near Derby, in 873–4. Here a massive D-shaped encampment was built, using the River Trent as its long side, and incorporating the tower of the Mercian royal shrine of St Wigstan as a gatehouse. Adjacent to the shrine, a number of accompanied burials have been excavated. The most dramatic was the grave of a warrior who had been killed by a slashing cut to his inner thigh, but may also have had a sharp object thrust through the socket of an eye. He was buried with a knife, a key and a sword which had been deliberately broken and replaced in its fleece-lined scabbard. He wore a silver Þórr's hammer amulet at his neck, and a jackdaw leg bone and a boar's tusk had been placed between his legs, possibly symbols of Oðinn and Freyr respectively. Outside the encampment the Viking army had also desecrated a second mausoleum, levelling a two-roomed structure, and burying an important warrior in the centre of one of the rooms, arranged the reinterred remains of at least 250 individuals around him. A group of four young males, buried adjacent to this mound, may have been sacrificial victims. It has been argued that the charnel deposit, comprising 80 per cent males, may have consisted of warriors of the Viking army, although it has also been suggested that they may have been the Anglo-Saxon monks, either killed in the attack on Repton, or disturbed from their graves when the fortification was constructed (Biddle and Kjølbye-Biddle 1992, 2001; Halsall 2000; Richards 2004b).

On a hill overlooking Repton, 4 km to the south-east, there are the remains of the only Scandinavian cremation cemetery in the British Isles, at Heath Wood (Richards 2004b). Some fifty-nine burial mounds have been identified, in four clusters. Some mounds, where the dead had been cremated *in situ*, covered cremation hearths of charcoal, ash and cremated bone. These included human bone, sometimes representing more than one individual, as well as a wide range of offerings, including joints of mutton and beef, as well as the complete bodies of horses and dogs. Although the hearths had been raked over and larger pieces of iron removed, there is evidence that the bodies had been laid out with weaponry, including swords and shields, as well as more everyday objects. Other mounds had been thought to be empty, but complete excavation of one has led to the discovery of a small token offering of a few fragments of burnt bone and a ringed pin. Heath Wood may have functioned as a war cemetery of some of the Viking Great Army; perhaps the token offerings represent warriors who died in battle and were cremated elsewhere, with just small parcels of bone and personal items which had been brought back to Heath Wood. Use of the cemetery at Heath Wood appears to have been short-lived, whereas the cemetery at Repton continued in use into the tenth century. The finds at Repton and Heath Wood are remarkable and reflect the range of Scandinavian-style burial practices developed by the Viking force in the frontier zone of the valley of the River Trent.

In general, the relative scarcity of burials of identifiable Scandinavian character suggests that elsewhere the settlers soon gave up the practice of burial with traditional costume and grave offerings (Graham-Campbell 2001; Hadley 2002; Halsall 2000; Richards 2004a: 189–212). The exceptions are mostly clustered in north-west England and Cumbria, where burial practices are similar to those observed on the Isle of Man (see Wilson, ch. 27.3, below). In these areas most settlers lived in scattered farmsteads and were buried on their farms. A number of individual mound burials, frequently containing weaponry, have been excavated – generally in the nineteenth century – at sites such as Aspatria, Hesket in the Forest and Claughton Hall (Edwards 1998). The only cemetery has been discovered by a metal-detectorist, on a low hill overlooking the village of Cumwhitton, near Carlisle. It comprised just six burials – four males and two females – buried with weaponry and jewellery. A mound had been raised over one of the males (Pitts 2004).

In lowland and eastern England such burials are extremely scarce and it is probable that colonists may have been accommodated within existing Anglo-Saxon graveyards. A female burial at Adwick-le-Street, near Doncaster, provides an isolated exception (Speed and Walton-Rogers 2004). This woman had been buried with a non-matching pair of oval brooches, of late ninth-century date, and fragments of an iron knife and key or latch-lifter. A small copper-alloy bowl, probably manufactured in the Celtic west, had been placed at her feet. Strontium isotope analysis of her teeth shows she originated from the Trondheim area of Norway, or possibly north-east Scotland. There is no evidence for settlement or other burials in the locality and she must represent an individual first-generation immigrant. At Middle Harling (Norfolk), a single furnished burial recovered from the edge of a Christian graveyard may represent another first-generation settler (Rogerson 1995).

Although identifiable ninth-century graves are rare, in the tenth century subsequent generations of Scandinavian settlers invented new forms of distinctive grave marker. In northern and eastern England in particular they adapted the Christian tradition of erecting stone crosses at monastic sites, and turned them into individual memorials for the founder burials of rural graveyards (Bailey 1980; Everson and Stocker 1999; Sidebottom 2000; Stocker 2000). At Middleton in North Yorkshire, for example, there is a small group of warrior crosses, including one depicting an armed warrior on the front, with a dragon-like beast on the reverse (Lang 1991).

The so-called hogback tombstones reflect another newly invented monument type (Lang 1984; Stocker 2000). These recumbent stone memorials have arched sides and tops, like bow-sided halls; some are grasped at each end by animals, sometimes identified as muzzled bears. Although examples have been found as far afield as Orkney and Cornwall, the distribution is focused in North Yorkshire, in the Viking kingdom of York, with a particularly fine group at Brompton. The prototype may have been the grave slabs of the early Scandinavian rulers of England, such as those found under York Minster, combined with the form of Irish house shrines. Both the crosses and the hogback stones date from the first half of the tenth century and may reflect the arrival of Hiberno-Norse settlers from Ireland.

The patrons of these monuments were at least partially Christianised, and some of the sculpture incorporates Christian as well as pre-Christian themes. A massive cross at Gosforth in Cumbria depicts a Crucifixion scene populated with figures in Scandinavian costume on one face, and a scene from Ragnarǫk, the end of the world, on the others (Bailey 1980). They were also partially responsible for the great boom in church building in the tenth and eleventh centuries. Private chapels were constructed on the estates of the new landowners; many later developed into parish churches serving their local communities. At Wharram Percy, fragments of eighth- and ninth-century sculpture may represent an earlier minster church, and a timber church may have been established on a new site in the tenth century. This was enlarged in the eleventh century into a stone church with a separate nave and chancel, which became the focus for the burials of the early lords of the manor and their retainers (Bell and Beresford *et al.* 1987). An Old English inscription on the sundial at the site of the Anglo-Saxon minster church at

Kirkdale provides a graphic illustration of the process of Anglo-Scandinavian privatisation of minster estates. It relates how *Ormr*, son of *Gamal* – both Old Norse names – bought the minster when it was tumbled and ruined, and erected a new church on the site in 1055–65 (Watts *et al.* 1997).

Identifiable Scandinavian settlements have been elusive. In the upland areas of northern England isolated farmsteads such as those excavated at Simy Folds and Ribblehead have often been assumed to be the homes of colonists on the basis of their morphology (Batey 1995; Coggins 2004; King 2004). Farther south the appearance of bow-sided halls at sites such as Goltho (Beresford 1987) and Waltham Abbey (Huggins 1976) might indicate the residences of new Scandinavian lords, although there is nothing ethnically Scandinavian about the shape or form of a building. The date of the creation of the fortified aristocratic manor at Goltho has been debated, but the consensus is now that it took place in the later ninth or early tenth century, after the Viking takeover of Lincolnshire. At Wharram Percy, Borre-style belt fittings have been found on what became the site of one of the medieval manor houses, and it seems likely that the village was first laid out with regular plots in the tenth century (Stamper and Croft 2000). This process of village nucleation is repeated throughout lowland England during the tenth century, and represents part of an ongoing process of land privatisation. Former great estates, previously owned by the king or the Church, were divided up into smaller units held by individual lords. This process was happening both in the Danelaw and in Wessex and was not a direct result of Viking raids, although the disruption of the monasteries and the subsequent dislocation of landholdings clearly accelerated the process (Richards 2004a: 49–77).

The recording of finds recovered by metal-detecting has also transformed our knowledge of settlement density (Margeson 1997; Leahy 2004). In eastern England there is a growing number of finds of Scandinavian brooches and other personal ornaments which suggests more direct and continuing contact with Scandinavia in the tenth century than previously thought, and the presence of a peasant class. The indigenous population also acquired a taste for mass-produced copper-alloy costume jewellery. Although craftsmen often retained Anglo-Saxon forms, such as the disc-brooch, they frequently decorated them with Scandinavian motifs. There are also completely new types, such as tiny hexagonal bells, which may have been amulets or costume fittings. Such finds indicate widespread acceptance of an Anglo-Scandinavian cultural identity in tenth-century England.

The settlement at Cottam, East Yorkshire, was first discovered by metal-detectorists (Richards 1999). In the eighth and ninth centuries there had been an Anglian farmstead at Cottam, possibly an outlying dependency of a royal estate at Driffield. The residents had been part of a trading network and there were large numbers of low-denomination Northumbrian copper-alloy coins, or *stycas*. In the late ninth or early tenth century the Anglo-Saxon farm was abandoned and replaced by a new planned settlement set within rectangular paddocks and with a rather grand gated entrance. Judging by the Anglo-Scandinavian artefact types introduced, the new occupants may well have been Scandinavian colonists. They were no longer able to buy and sell with coins as the Northumbrian mints had ceased production, but this did not prevent them trading west with York and south of the Humber to Lincolnshire, weighing out bullion to conduct their transactions. They lived in their new farm for only a couple of generations before relocating to the site of what became the medieval village.

There is a growing body of evidence to suggest that the process of settlement drift, common throughout lowland England in the Anglo-Saxon period, came to an end in the tenth century. Excavations have rarely been large enough to prove this point, but the large-scale landscape project at West Heslerton provides another example where this seems to be the case (Powlesland 2000).

The Scandinavian settlement also brought major changes to towns in and provided a stimulus for the largest urban regeneration since Britain under the Romans (Richards 2004a: 78–108). In the Anglo-Saxon kingdoms of Mercia and Wessex systems of fortified towns, or *burhs*, were established in response to the Viking threat. They also functioned as civil and ecclesiastical administrative centres, and, in some, mints were established. In some cases, such as at Chester, Gloucester, Exeter and Winchester, Roman sites were refortified; in other cases, such as Langport, Wilton and Lydford, natural defences were used. Elsewhere, such as at Cricklade, Wallingford and Oxford, new defences were constructed based upon Roman models. Many *burhs* were established on rivers, often at bridging points. Many became important markets; at Chester a community of Hiberno-Norse traders settled between the Roman fort and the River Dee, where they constructed cellared buildings (Mason 1985).

Although Viking raids initially disrupted trade which had been organised through the urban markets or *wics*, at places such as *Hamwic* (Southampton), *Lundenwic* (London) and *Eoforwic* (York), these towns flourished in the tenth century. In most cases the trading sites were brought within, or adjacent to, the walls of the old Roman forts, and were then subject to rapid development. York is the best-known example (see Hall, ch. 27.2, below), although these towns were not necessarily always run by Scandinavian rulers and traders.

In the East Midlands the Danes established a series of urban strongholds, described as the Five Boroughs, comprising Derby, Leicester, Lincoln, Nottingham and Stamford (Hall 1989). Excavations have failed to reveal anything specifically Scandinavian about these towns and they may have been based upon Anglo-Saxon models. The best evidence comes from Lincoln, which lacks the regularity of the Wessex *burhs*, but still represents a planned development of streets and tenements. Several new industries developed, such as the production of glazed Stamford ware pottery, which may have resulted from skilled immigrant potters moving in with the Scandinavian traders. But industrialisation was not a direct result of Viking settlement. Throughout England specialised crafts which had hitherto been under the control of rural estates, were replaced by town-based industrialised mass production, and a little-known class of rural markets, the so-called 'productive' sites, went into decline (Pestell and Ulmschneider 2003).

In England, therefore, there was a complex process of interaction between incoming Scandinavians, or those of mixed Hiberno-Norse descent, and indigenous Anglo-Saxon inhabitants. This continued for some 300 years. As fresh archaeological finds provide greater resolution it is becoming possible to observe a variety of colonisation strategies and a range of responses, including both regional and chronological variation.

BIBLIOGRAPHY

Bailey, R. (1980) *Viking Age Sculpture in Northern England*, London: Collins.
Batey, C.E. (1995) 'Aspects of rural settlement in northern Britain', in D. Hooke and S. Burnell (eds) *Landscape and Settlement in Britain AD 400–1066*, Exeter: Exeter University Press.

Bell, R.D., Beresford, M.W. *et al.* (1987) *Wharram Percy: The Church of St Martin. Wharram: A Study of Settlement on the Yorkshire Wolds*, vol. 3 (Society for Medieval Archaeology. Monograph Series 11), London: Society for Medieval Archaeology.

Beresford, G. (1987) *Goltho. The Development of an Early Medieval Manor c.850–1150* (English Heritage. Archaeological Report 4), London: Historic Buildings and Monuments Commission for England.

Biddle, M. and Kjølbye-Biddle, B. (1992) 'Repton and the Vikings', *Antiquity*, 66: 36–51.

—— (2001) 'Repton and the "great heathen army", 873–4', in J. Graham-Campbell *et al.* (2001).

Brooks, N.P. and Graham-Campbell, J. (1986) 'Reflections on the Viking-Age silver hoard from Croydon, Surrey', in M.A.S. Blackburn (ed.) *Anglo-Saxon Monetary History. Essays in Memory of Michael Dolley*, Leicester: Leicester University Press.

Coggins, D. (2004) 'Simy Folds: twenty years on', in J. Hines, A. Lane and M. Redknap (eds) *Land, Sea and Home* (Society for Medieval Archaeology. Monograph Series 20), Leeds: Maney.

Edwards, B.J.N. (1998) *Vikings in North West England. The Artifacts*. Lancaster: Centre for North-West Regional Studies, University of Lancaster.

Everson, P. and Stocker, D. (1999) *Corpus of Anglo-Saxon Stone Sculpture*, vol. 5: *Lincolnshire*, Oxford: Oxford University Press for the British Academy.

Graham-Campbell, J. (1992a) 'Anglo-Scandinavian equestrian equipment in eleventh-century England', *Anglo-Norman Studies*, 14: 77–89.

—— (ed.) (1992b) *Viking Treasure from the North West. The Cuerdale Hoard in its Context* (National Museums and Galleries on Merseyside. Liverpool Museum Occasional Papers 5), Liverpool: National Museums and Galleries on Merseyside.

—— (2001) 'Pagan Scandinavian burial in the central and southern Danelaw', in J. Graham-Campbell *et al.* (eds) (2001).

Graham-Campbell, J., Hall, R., Jesch, J. and Parsons, D. (eds) (2001) *Vikings and the Danelaw. Select Papers from the Proceedings of the Thirteenth Viking Congress, Nottingham and York, 21–30 August 1997*, Oxford: Oxbow Books.

Hadley, D.M. (1997) '"And they proceeded to plough and support themselves": the Scandinavian settlement of England', *Anglo-Norman Studies*, 19: 69–96.

—— (2002) 'Burial practices in northern England in the later Anglo-Saxon period', in S. Lucy and A. Reynolds (eds) *Burial in Early Medieval England and Wales* (Society for Medieval Archaeology. Monograph Series 17), London: Society for Medieval Archaeology.

Hadley, D.M. and Richards, J.D. (eds) (2000) *Cultures in Contact. Scandinavian Settlement in England in the Ninth and Tenth Centuries*, Turnhout: Brepols.

Hall, R.A. (1989) 'The Five Boroughs of the Danelaw: a review of present knowledge', *Anglo-Saxon England*, 18: 149–206.

Halsall, G. (2000) 'The Viking presence in England? The burial evidence reconsidered', in D.M. Hadley and J.D. Richards (eds) (2000).

Huggins, P.J. (1976) 'The excavation of an eleventh-century Viking hall and fourteenth-century rooms at Waltham Abbey, Essex, 1969–71', *Medieval Archaeology*, 20: 75–133.

King, A. (2004) 'Post-Roman upland architecture in the Craven dales and the dating evidence', in J. Hines, A. Lane and M. Redknap (eds) *Land, Sea and Home* (Society for Medieval Archaeology. Monograph Series 20), London: Society for Medieval Archaeology.

Lang, J.T. (1984) 'The hogback: a Viking colonial monument', *Anglo-Saxon Studies in Archaeology and History*, 3: 85–176.

—— (1991) *Corpus of Anglo-Saxon Stone Sculpture*, vol. 3: *York and Eastern Yorkshire*, Oxford: Oxford University Press.

Leahy, K. (2004) 'Detecting the Vikings in Lincolnshire', *Current Archaeology*, 190: 462–8.

Margeson, S. (1997) *The Vikings in Norfolk*, Norwich: Norfolk Museums Service.

Mason, D.J.P. (1985) *Excavations at Chester: 26–42 Lower Bridge Street 1974–6. The Dark Age and*

Saxon Periods (Grosvenor Museum. Archaeological Excavation and Survey Reports), Chester: Grosvenor Museum.

Pestell, T. and Ulmschneider, K. (eds) (2003) *Markets in Early Medieval Europe. Trading and 'Productive Sites' 650–850*, Macclesfield: Windgather Press.

Pitts, M. (2004) 'Cumbrian heritage', *British Archaeology*, 79 (Nov.): 28–31.

Powlesland, D. (2000) 'West Heslerton settlement mobility: a case of static development', in H. Geake and J. Kenny (eds) *Early Deira. Archaeological Studies of the East Riding in the Fourth to Ninth centuries AD*, Oxford: Oxbow Books.

Richards, J.D. (1999) 'Cottam: An Anglian and Anglo-Scandinavian settlement on the Yorkshire Wolds', *Archaeological Journal*, 156: 1–110.

—— (2004a) *Viking Age England*, rev. edn, Stroud: Tempus.

—— (2004b) 'Excavations at the Viking barrow cemetery at Heath Wood, Ingleby, Derbyshire', *Antiquaries Journal*, 84: 23–116.

Rogerson, A. (1995) *A Late Neolithic, Saxon and Medieval Site at Middle Harling, Norfolk* (East Anglian Archaeology 74), Norwich: Field Archaeology Division, Norfolk Museums Service.

Sawyer, P.H. (1971) *The Age of the Vikings*, 2nd edn, London: Arnold.

Seaby, W.A. and Woodfield, P. (1980) 'Viking stirrups from England and their background', *Medieval Archaeology*, 24: 87–122.

Sidebottom, P. (2000) 'Viking Age stone monuments and social identity', in D.M. Hadley and J.D. Richards (eds) (2000).

Speed, G. and Walton Rogers, P. (2004) 'A burial of a Viking woman at Adwick-le-Street, South Yorkshire', *Medieval Archaeology*, 48: 51–90.

Stamper, P. and Croft, R. (2000) *Wharram. A Study of Settlement in the Yorkshire Wolds*, vol. 8: *The South Manor* (York University Archaeological Publications 10), York: Dept. of Archaeology, York University.

Stocker, D. (2000) 'Monuments and merchants: irregularities in the distribution of stone sculpture in Lincolnshire and Yorkshire in the 10th century', in D.M. Hadley and J.D. Richards (eds) (2000).

Trafford, S. (2000) 'Ethnicity, migration theory, and the historiography of the Scandinavian settlement of England', in D.M. Hadley and J.D. Richards (eds) (2000).

Watts, L., Rahtz, P., Osaka, E., Bradley, S.A.J. and Higgitt, J. (1997) 'Kirkdale – the inscriptions', *Medieval Archaeology*, 41: 51–99.

Wilson, D.M. (1965) 'Some neglected late Anglo-Saxon swords', *Medieval Archaeology*, 9: 32–54.

THE CREATION OF THE DANELAW

———•✦•———

Dawn M. Hadley

The term *Danelaw* is widely used to refer to those regions of northern and eastern England conquered and settled by Scandinavians in the ninth and tenth centuries. The term first occurs in legal compilations produced by Archbishop Wulfstan of York, the so-called 'Laws of Edward and Guthrum', dated to between 1002 and 1008, and a law code issued on behalf of King Æthelred II at Wantage (Berks.) in 1008, both of which draw a small number of distinctions between legal process in districts under English law and those under Danish law (*on Deone lage*) (Whitelock 1941, 1979: 439–46). Later legal compilations occasionally distinguish between laws among the English and those among the Danes (*mid Denum*), and shires are periodically, if inconsistently, grouped into those that follow the laws of the West Saxons, Mercians and Danes (*Danelaga* [*scire*]) (Stenton 1971: 505–6; Holman 2001: 2–3).

The legal provisions of the Danelaw were distinguishable from those of other parts of England in several respects, including the imposition of heavier payments for transgressions (Stenton 1971: 507–10). The legal terminology of the Danelaw incorporates many Scandinavian terms, including *landcop* (referring to the purchase of land), *lahslit* (a penalty for infringement of the law) and *witword* (possibly meaning 'the right to prove one's case'), and even the word *law* is borrowed from Old Norse (Stenton 1971: 507, 512; Neff 1989: 278–88). Yet direct Scandinavian influence on legal practice is difficult to demonstrate (Fenger 1972; Neff 1989; Holman 2001: 3–4). For example, the local administrative and law-enforcement districts known as wapentakes (ON *vápnatak* 'a taking of weapons'), which are found in the territory of the Five Boroughs and parts of Yorkshire (Loyn 1974), do not occur in Scandinavia as a legal district (Geipel 1971: 62; Holman 2001: 4), but rather served similar functions to the hundreds found elsewhere in England (Loyn 1974; Stenton 1971: 504–5).

Nevertheless, there was an enduring perception that the regions known as the Danelaw were distinctive. A peace treaty of *c.* 880–90 contracted between King Alfred of Wessex and Guthrum, the leader of a Viking army that had occupied East Anglia, regulated relations between the English and the Danes, and also defined 'the boundaries between us' as running along the rivers Thames and Lea, then in a straight line to Bedford, and up the River Ouse to Watling Street (Whitelock 1979: 416–17). This has provided the basis for many modern maps of the Danelaw, which typically depict its boundary as running along Watling Street to Chester, although the treaty does not specify this. While the treaty has often been regarded as a foundation charter for the Danelaw, it was contracted only on behalf of the Scandinavian settlers in East Anglia. Furthermore, the boundary established by the treaty did not endure and the West Saxons were obliged to capture *burh*s on the 'English' side in the early tenth century, while Scandinavian place names to the west of the boundary indicate Scandinavian settlement there (Davis 1982; Dumville 1992). Finally, the fortuitous survival of this treaty in later manuscripts obscures the fact that it was only one of a number of broadly contemporary peace treaties with the regions of Scandinavian settlement. The Anglo-Saxon Chronicle records the breaking of a peace between King Alfred and the Northumbrians and East Anglians in 893 (Whitelock 1979: 201), and in 905 notes that King Edward the Elder confirmed a peace (*frið*) at Tiddingford (Bucks.) with the East Anglians and Northumbrians (Whitelock 1979: 209), while the laws of this king (II Edward, 5.2) stipulate that certain legal provisions in eastern and northern England should be 'in accordance with the provisions of the treaties (*friðgewritu*)' (Attenborough 1922: 120–1).

The Danish qualities of parts of northern and eastern England were subsequently recognised in a law code issued by King Edgar (in the 960s or early 970s) where it is stipulated that 'there should be in force among the Danes (*mid Denum*) such good laws as they best decide on' (Whitelock 1979: 435–6). It is not, however, clear who would have been identifiable as Danes, and by what means, around a century after settlement had begun (Reynolds 1985: 406–8). Moreover, many of the most recent settlers in northern England had come not from the Danish provinces but from northern Scandinavia or Dublin, where there had been Scandinavian settlers since the mid-ninth century (Smyth 1999: 32–5).

The regions known as the Danelaw were accorded special provisions, but were, nonetheless, regarded as legal provinces within the English kingdom. Indeed, Edgar also demanded that other aspects of the law should 'be common to all the nation, whether, Englishmen, Danes or Britons' (Whitelock 1979: 435), and it has been argued that Æthelred's law code issued at Wantage, and addressed to the territory of the Five Boroughs, while laden with Scandinavian terminology was unquestionably English royal law, and may even have been an attempt to extend English customs to the Danelaw (Wormald 1978: 61–2; Neff 1989: 287). It has also been argued that ethnic terminology was employed from the mid-tenth century as part of the cultivation of the regional identities of parts of England. Edgar's separate legal provision for 'the Danes' may have been a reward for support received from the elite of northern England early in his reign (Lund 1976). The political language of the early eleventh century frequently invoked the friendship between English and Danes, and the forged document known as 'The Laws of Edward and Guthrum' sought to project such relations back to a much earlier date, 'when the English and the Danes unreservedly entered into relationships of peace and friendship' (Whitelock 1941; Innes 2000: 77). Yet expressions of ethnic difference coincided with the binding of the elites of northern and eastern England to the English kingdom (Innes 2000: 85), and the loyalty of secular and ecclesiastical leaders in northern England from the mid-tenth century was enhanced by the appointment of men who also held substantial possessions further south (Whitelock 1959). In spite of the ethnic terminology employed, the distinctive legal provisions for the Danelaw attest to the integration of the settlers and their descendants into English society (Innes

2000: 72–7; Holman 2001: 3). Indeed, the Danishness of northern and eastern England was but rarely documented, typically during times of political and military strife, and regional terminology continued to be employed to describe those regions (Reynolds 1985: 408–9). There is, finally, little evidence to support modern assumptions that the descendants of earlier Scandinavian settlers were predisposed to support Danish raiders of the late tenth and early eleventh centuries (Reynolds 1985: 406–12). Assaults launched at this time on southern England via the Danelaw are as likely to have been determined by its remoteness from the heartlands of the English king as by an expectation of ethnic loyalty, and regional grievances, rather than ethnic sympathies, provided the grounds for supporting the Danish raiders, who also received support elsewhere in England (Innes 2000: 74).

The regions of the Danelaw can be distinguished from 'English' England by a range of characteristics, but not consistently so. Scandinavian place names occur most frequently in Nottinghamshire, Leicestershire, Lincolnshire and Yorkshire, although there are smaller concentrations in the Wirral, Cumbria and Norfolk (Fellows-Jensen 1975). Stone sculpture influenced by Scandinavian art styles of the ninth and tenth centuries is most common in Yorkshire and the north-west, although the latter region was generally omitted from medieval lists of Danelaw shires (Bailey 1980; Abrams 2001: 130–1). Free peasants (*liberi homines* and sokemen) are often deemed to be characteristic of the Danelaw, but while numerous in the entries in the Domesday Book for East Anglia and Lincolnshire, they are found in much smaller numbers elsewhere (Stenton 1971: 515–17). The tenth century witnessed the emergence in eastern England of many new centres of trade and manufacture and the expansion of others, including Lincoln, Torksey, Thetford and Norwich. Pottery production became an urban phenomenon, and the industry was revolutionised by the adoption of new manufacturing techniques common on the Continent (Hinton 1990: 112). Coins minted in eastern England and York from the late ninth century display a mixture of influences, reflected in the use of Continental moneyers, the copying of West Saxon prototypes, the adoption of regional weight standards and the incorporation of Scandinavian personal names and insignia (Blackburn 2001). Recently large amounts of metalwork displaying Scandinavian characteristics have been recovered from eastern England, but although it has been suggested that this supports arguments for a mass migration of Scandinavians, relatively few items are typically Scandinavian and many more display a fusion of Scandinavian and English styles, along with Continental and Irish influences. Notably, eleventh-century Scandinavian art styles were more widely adopted in southern England than in the Danelaw (Leahy and Paterson 2001).

BIBLIOGRAPHY

Abrams, L. (2001) 'Edward the Elder's Danelaw', in N. Higham and D. Hill (eds), *Edward the Elder 899–924*, Manchester: Manchester University Press.

Attenborough, F. (1922) *The Laws of the Earliest English Kings*, Cambridge: Cambridge University Press.

Bailey, R. (1980) *Viking Age Sculpture in Northern England*, London: Collins.

Blackburn, M. (2001) 'Expansion and control: Anglo-Scandinavian minting south of the Humber', in J. Graham-Campbell, R. Hall, J. Jesch and D. Parsons (eds) *Vikings and the Danelaw*, Oxford: Oxbow.

Davis, R.H.C. (1982) 'Alfred and Guthrum's frontier', *English Historical Review*, 97: 803–10.

Dumville, D.H. (1992) *Wessex and England from Alfred to Edgar*, Woodbridge: Boydell.

Fellows-Jensen, G. (1975) 'The Vikings in England: a review', *Anglo-Saxon England*, 4: 181–206.

Fenger, O. (1972) 'The Danelaw and the Danish law: Anglo-Scandinavian legal relations during the Viking period', *Scandinavian Studies in Law*, 16: 85–96.

Geipel, J. (1971) *The Viking Legacy*, Newton Abbot: David and Charles.

Hinton, D. (1990) *Archaeology, Economy and Society*, London: Seaby.

Holman, K. (2001) 'Defining the Danelaw', in J. Graham-Campbell, R. Hall, J. Jesch and D. Parsons (eds) *Vikings and the Danelaw*, Oxford: Oxbow.

Innes, M. (2000) 'Danelaw identities: ethnicity, regionalism and political allegiance', in D. Hadley and J. Richards (eds) *Cultures in Contact*, Turnhout: Brepols.

Kershaw, P. (2000) 'The Alfred–Guthrum treaty: scripting accommodation and interaction in Viking Age England', in D. Hadley and J. Richards (eds) *Cultures in Contact*, Turnhout: Brepols.

Leahy, K. and Paterson, C. (2001) 'New light on the Viking presence in Lincolnshire: the artefactual evidence', in J. Graham-Campbell, R. Hall, J. Jesch and D. Parsons, *Vikings and the Danelaw*, Oxford: Oxbow.

Loyn, H. (1974) 'The hundred in England in the tenth and eleventh centuries', in H. Hearder and H. Loyn (eds) *British Government and Administration*, Cardiff: University of Wales Press.

Lund, N. (1976) 'King Edgar and the Danelaw', *Mediaeval Scandinavia*, 9: 181–95.

Neff, C. (1989) 'Scandinavian elements in the Wantage code of Æthelred II', *Journal of Legal History*, 10: 285–316.

Reynolds, S. (1985) 'What do we mean by "Anglo-Saxon" and "Anglo-Saxons"?', *Journal of British Studies*, 24: 395–414.

Smyth, A. (1999) 'The effect of Scandinavian raiders on the English and Irish churches: a preliminary reassessment', in B. Smith (ed.) *Britain and Ireland 900–1300. Insular Responses to Medieval European Change*, Cambridge: Cambridge University Press.

Stenton, F.M. (1971) *Anglo-Saxon England*, 3rd edn, Oxford: Oxford University Press.

Whitelock, D. (1941) 'Wulfstan and the so-called Laws of Edward and Guthrum', *English Historical Review*, 56: 1–21.

—— (1959) 'The dealings of the kings of England with Northumbria in the tenth and eleventh centuries', in P. Clemoes (ed.) *The Anglo-Saxons*, London: Bowes and Bowes.

—— (ed. and trans.) (1979) *English Historical Documents*, vol. 1: *c. 500–1042*, 2nd edn, London: Eyre and Spottiswoode.

Wormald, P. (1978) 'Æthelred the lawmaker', in D. Hill (ed.) *Ethelred the Unready*, Oxford: British Archaeological Reports.

CHAPTER TWENTY-SEVEN (2)

YORK

———— ·◆· ————

Richard Hall

A series of documentary references, written in the mid-ninth to mid-eleventh centuries, indicates that York was the most important and enduring focus of Scandinavian interests in England in the early medieval period. Documents and archaeology combine to indicate that, outside London, York was then the largest city in England, with an area of some 100 hectares and an estimated population of 10–15,000. Its Viking Age prominence reflects its geographical significance and earlier history.

York is 330 km north of London; although 60 km from the nearest coast, it is an inland port that could be reached from the North Sea by a journey of 120 km up the Humber Estuary and the River Ouse. Urban settlement at York was initiated by the Romans, who built a fortress (*Eboracum*) in AD 71 on the land between the Rivers Ouse and Foss; later there was a walled civilian town (*colonia*) on the opposite bank of the Ouse. After the Roman army evacuated Britain *c.* 410 there was a period of historical and archaeological obscurity in the fifth and sixth centuries, when it seems the fortress and *colonia* were largely abandoned. York again became regionally prominent in the early seventh century as *Eoforwic*, the religious epicentre of the Anglo-Saxon kingdom of Northumbria. It had royal associations, a bishop (627) and then an archbishop (735), a famous school and international trading connections. The cathedral stood near the centre of the former fortress, and mercantile and manufacturing activities took place along the banks of the River Ouse. Yet the population of *Eoforwic* may have numbered only 1,000–2,000 and, apart from the Roman defensive walls, much of the Roman townscape – buildings and streets – had already disappeared.

In 866 *Eoforwic* was captured by the Viking 'great heathen army'; it has been suggested that this force was commanded by members of a dynasty that, since 851, had ruled in Dublin. The Anglo-Saxon Chronicle reports that in 876 this army 'shared out the land of the Northumbrians and began to plough and to support themselves'. For much of the next century the modern county of Yorkshire, and areas beyond, were ruled by Viking kings of York who were members of the same Hiberno-Viking family; under Old Norse linguistic influence the city's name was transformed to *Jorvik* (ON *Jórvík*). Archbishops of York recognised a co-dependency with the Viking kings in their shared ambitions to maintain authority and independence, and this political détente was mirrored in the fusion of the Viking invaders and Northumbrian Anglo-Saxons into a new, Anglo-Scandinavian, culture. Military force and diplomacy were employed to fend off the expansionist ambitions of successive Anglo-Saxon kings of Wessex, who in the early tenth century had taken over other formerly independent Anglo-Saxon kingdoms previously conquered by Vikings. York's Viking king was expelled by Alfred's grandson, King Athelstan, in 927, but Irish-Viking rule was renewed on his death in 939. In the 940s–50s Eric Bloodaxe, an exiled Norwegian prince, also contended for control of York, an episode echoed in the *Saga of Egill Skallagrimsson*, but with his departure and death in 954 York became irrevocably absorbed into England. Yet Anglo-Saxon kings rarely ventured north to York; they appointed Anglo-Scandinavian churchmen and aristocrats to positions of authority in York to oversee the territory on their behalf. Untouched during the later tenth- and early eleventh-century invasions of Sven Fork-beard and his son Cnut, York played a pivotal role in the events of 1066. The Norwegian king Haraldr Harðráði won a battle at Fulford, just south of York, on 20 September 1066; the city submitted, but he was defeated and killed at the battle of Stamford Bridge, nearby, on 25 September. Even after William the Conqueror took over the city in 1068 York was a bastion of resistance to the Normans. Scandinavians attempted invasions in 1069, 1070 and 1075, but thereafter the city's political and social connection with Scandinavia faded, leaving as its only obvious legacy the majority of York's street names that incorporate elements derived from Old Norse such as -*gate*.

In 1972 York Archaeological Trust undertook the first archaeological excavations aimed specifically at elucidating Viking Age York. This showed that in part of York there is up to 9 m of archaeological strata, mostly dating to the Viking Age, and comprising peat-like anoxic deposits in which organic remains, including timber buildings and artefacts of leather, textile and wood, are well preserved. There is also a wealth of biological data within these layers; studies of plant and beetle remains have shown that York probably had slightly colder winters and slightly warmer summers than today.

Excavation of 1,000 m^2 at 16–22 Coppergate, in 1976–81 (Figure 27.2.1), investigated large parts of four long narrow tenement plots that had been laid out by *c.* 900; post and wattle buildings erected near the street frontage of Coppergate had housed specialist craftsmen. The remainder of each plot was used for ancillary purposes, with rubbish and cesspits dug there. In the 970s a new style of building was adopted, incorporating a plank-lined cellar below a ground-level room. On some plots there were two ranks of buildings at the frontage, an index that York was thriving. It was, however, a smelly place, with cesspits, rubbish pits, animal waste, and both domestic and industrial debris contributing to the malodour. In the damper parts of the city, where decomposition was inhibited, the ground level rose at an average rate of 1–2 cm per year in the tenth century.

City-wide, the evidence suggests that it was in the late ninth and tenth centuries that new streets and property plots were laid out in and around what had previously been a largely open, sparsely occupied townscape. Almost the only Roman street lines that remained in use were parts of those linking the four main gateways of the fortress. The sole Roman bridge across the River Ouse having disappeared, the crossing was re-established downstream on a site beyond the corner of the fortress. This encouraged, or perhaps necessitated, sweeping changes to the city's overall plan. As the ground surface was steadily heightened by the dumping of rubbish and the build-up of occupation debris, two sides of the Roman fortress defences, those facing the Rivers Ouse and Foss,

Figure 27.2.1   Excavations in 1967–81 by York Archaeological Trust in Coppergate, York, provide much of the currently available information about Viking Age York. In the tenth and eleventh centuries the Coppergate street frontage was occupied by timber buildings, with long and heavily pitted backyards behind them.

became less of a barrier, and may have been actively dismantled. They were perhaps replaced by an extension of the other two sides of the fortress walls down to the rivers, thereby defining the line taken by the city's medieval stone walls in this area. To the south of the River Ouse, within the former Roman *colonia*, the rectilinear street grid was totally disregarded by a new main road, Micklegate (ON *Miklugata* 'Main Street'), leading to the new river crossing. Meanwhile, to the east of the River Foss, there is evidence for a 500 m long ribbon development of properties in the tenth/eleventh century on the line of the street Walmgate. It is not certain that this part of Jorvik was defended, although a hypothetical bridge-head barrier on this east side of the River Foss has been suggested. Although the city's Viking Age defences have not been recorded often or in great detail, it seems that they consisted of an earth rampart, in places oversailing the surviving Roman walls, with a timber palisade along its top and a ditch outside it.

Many of the city's parish churches were founded in these centuries, as the survival of characteristic funerary monuments indicates. A handful of churches have also been investigated archaeologically, and shown to be Anglo-Scandinavian in origin; the contemporary cathedral, where some Viking kings were buried, has not been found. A few burials in some of the churchyards were accompanied by a small number of rather mundane items, but no elaborately ostentatious pagan Vikings' graves are known; local Christian custom, as regards both place and mode of burial, seems to have been quickly adopted by the incomers. The skeletons of only a few of the hundreds of thousands of people who lived in York during these centuries have been recovered. Demographically this was a population with a high infant mortality; 50 per cent of women died before the age of thirty-five; average life expectancy for men was about fifty years. Average height was 2–3 cm lower than today. Abundant eggs of human gut worms reveal that the population was heavily infested.

York was an important manufacturing centre, with specialist craftspeople mass-producing a variety of items on a scale and intensity not seen since the Roman era (Figure 27.2.2). There were high-temperature industries including the working of iron, copper-alloys, lead, silver and gold, and the making of high-lead glass; bone- and antlerworking, particularly the production of combs; lathe-turning wooden items; leatherworking to make shoes, horse-riding equipment, knife and sword scabbards; the making of amber and jet jewellery. Most textileworking was carried out in a domestic rather than an industrial milieu. Raw materials for these crafts came into the city from the farms and estates in its hinterland, and the finished goods were supplied to that same hinterland. To facilitate trade the debased, small-flan coinage issued by the Anglo-Saxon kings of York was replaced from *c.* 895 onwards by a high-quality silver penny coinage, with designs based initially on Continental as well as Anglo-Saxon models. Food for the citizens came from the same hinterland sources; fish and shellfish came from the rivers and from estuarine and coastal waters, and animals such as deer and birds were hunted. Goods also flowed into the city from further afield. Items from England included pottery made in Lincolnshire; a Pictish brooch and, perhaps, soapstone vessels originated in Scotland. Dress pins of Irish type have been found and, although they may have been manufactured locally, the name *Divelinestaynes* ('Dublin stones') at a riverside location, albeit first recorded in the thirteenth century, suggests a berth for ships trading between York and Dublin. Whetstones made of Norwegian schist were common. Goods imported from the Rhineland included wine (the pottery containers have been found) and lava quernstones. A series of silk fragments indicates contact with the east end of the Mediterranean, probably Byzantium (although Baghdad might also have been a supplier); a cowrie shell from the Red Sea reinforces these near-eastern contacts, as does an early tenth-century coin struck in Samarkand. York was part of a great international trading network that, for the most part, supplied high-value luxury goods; but the majority of its commerce and economic growth was focused on the provision of more mundane items to its extensive hinterland.

Figure 27.2.2 The epitomy of acculturation in early tenth-century York; this iron coin-die for a St Peter's penny, struck in York, combines a Christian inscription with a Viking sword and Thor's hammer motif.

BIBLIOGRAPHY

The Archaeology of York series includes many volumes on York's topography, buildings, artefacts, coins, environment, animal bones and human osteology, published by the Council for British Archaeology for the York Archaeological Trust.

Dumville, D.N. (2005) 'Old Dubliners and new Dubliners in Ireland and Britain: a Viking-Age story', in S. Duffy (ed.) *Medieval Dublin*, vol. 6: *Proceedings of the Friends of Medieval Dublin Symposium 2004*, Dublin: Four Courts.

Hall, R.A. (1994) *English Heritage Book of Viking Age York*, London: Batsford/English Heritage.

—— (2000) 'Anglo-Scandinavian attitudes: archaeological ambiguities in late ninth–mid eleventh century York', in D.M. Hadley and J.D. Richards (eds) *Cultures in Contact. Scandinavian Settlement in England in the Ninth and Tenth Centuries* (Studies in the Early Middle Ages 2), Turnhout: Brepols.

—— (2001) 'Anglo-Saxon and Viking-Age York', in P. Nuttgens (ed.) *The History of York from Earliest Times to the Year 2000*, Pickering: Blackthorn.

Lang, J.T. (1991) *Corpus of Anglo-Saxon Stone Sculpture*, vol. 3: *York and Eastern Yorkshire*, Oxford: Oxford University Press for the British Academy.

Phillips, D. and Heywood, B. (1995) *Excavations at York Minster*, vol. 1: *From Roman Fortress to Norman Cathedral*, ed. M.O.H. Carver, London: HMSO.

Rollason, D.W. (1998) *Sources for York History to AD 1100* (The Archaeology of York 1), York: York Archaeological Trust.

www.yorkarchaeology.co.uk (contains reports, bibliographies and publication lists relating to this topic).

CHAPTER TWENTY-SEVEN (3)

THE ISLE OF MAN

—◆·◆·◆—

David M. Wilson

In the early tenth century the name of the Island is inscribed in Old Norse (*maun*) on a cross at Kirk Michael; but written sources for the history of the Viking Age in the Isle of Man are mostly brief, tenuous, sometimes corrupt and difficult to use. English, Welsh, Irish and Scandinavian sources mention the Island, but no coherent story can be built up from them. Only snippets of history survive, such as the record of Edgar, King of England, being rowed in 974 on the Dee by eight sub-kings, including, 'Maccus [Magnús], king of many islands'. Magnús is assumed to have been king of Man (the 'many islands' referring to Man and the southern Hebrides). But there is no other record of him, although the suggestion that he was paying homage to an English king is highly relevant to the turbulent politics of the Irish Sea at this period.

The most important evidence for this period is provided by archaeology – particularly fortifications, graves, stone sculpture (with its associated epigraphy) and hoards. The Scandinavians appeared in the Irish Sea towards the end of the eighth century, and it is inconceivable that the raiders would have overlooked Man on their way from Norway. Of this, however, there is no evidence, and it is doubtful whether there was sufficient wealth to interest them on Man; but (initially at least) slaves could have been taken and ships provisioned. Further, it is possible that, after the establishment of the first Norse bases in Ireland in the mid-ninth century, Man became a place of interest for the Irish Vikings.

This earliest evidence for a Viking presence (and presumably settlement) in the Island is provided by twenty-four pagan, or semi-pagan, Norse burial sites, which start to appear at the beginning of the last quarter of the ninth century. All are inhumation burials, either in mounds or flat burials, sometimes in pre-existing Christian cemeteries. Two burials may be alluded to: a male grave from Balladoole and a female grave from Peel. At Balladoole an oak boat (11 m in length) set within a stone mound overlay a number of cist burials from a pre-existing Christian cemetery (Figure 27.3.1). The burial was of a male, but remains of an associated female skeleton may merely represent the disturbed remains of an earlier burial, although conceivably it was a double burial (in another grave on Man, at Ballateare, a sacrificed woman possibly provides a significant parallel). The grave goods are either of Irish-Sea type (shield-mounts, a ring-headed pin and bridle-mounts), of Carolingian or Anglo-Saxon origin (stirrups and

Figure 27.3.1   The Balladoole burial. The kerb of the Viking mound overlies earlier burials.
(© Bersu and Wilson.)

spur-mounts), or are of indeterminate origin (three knives, a hone, a flint strike-a-light, belt buckle and strap-end, and the iron handle of a bucket). Boat graves are rare in Scandinavian Britain – two are recorded from the Island, two from the Hebrides and three from Orkney: all contained the remains of four-oared clinker-built boats (*fer-æringr*). That few, if any, of the grave goods from Balladoole were made in Scandinavia is of little significance: the burial rite is Scandinavian.

On St Patrick's Isle, Peel, a middle-aged woman of high status was buried in a cist grave (Figure 27.3.2) in a pre-existing Christian graveyard which continued in use into the Middle Ages. Buried in a woollen dress with a tablet-woven sash, she may also have worn a head-covering. With her were an iron roasting-spit, the remains of three silver-mounted knives, shears, an antler comb, two needles, a miniature limestone 'pestle and mortar', a pierced ammonite and a necklace of seventy-three beads of coloured glass, amber and jet. Traces of textiles, cord and cooking herbs were also recovered. While of normal Viking type, the grave contained no specifically Scandinavian objects (save possibly the spit), and particularly no brooches of the type normal in female burials.

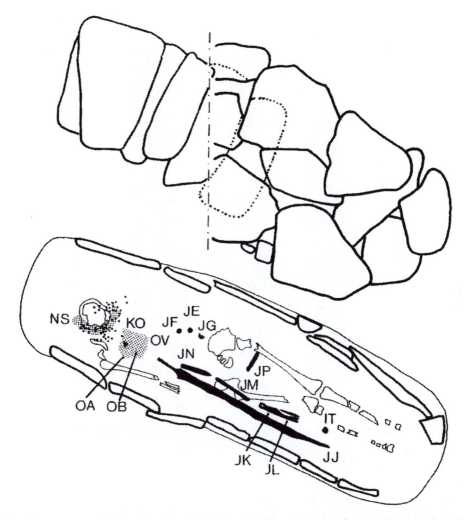

Figure 27.3.2 Plan of woman's grave, St Patrick's Isle. Above, capstones of the lintel-grave. Below, the skeleton and grave-goods: JM, JN knives; JL bone comb; JK iron shears; JJ iron cooking-spit; NS down pillow; the beads are below the skull.

The grave-goods suggest that the first Viking settlers arrived in the last quarter of the ninth century, possibly from north-west England and Scotland. Nothing is known of the mechanics of the settlement. The native inhabitants may initially have been overwhelmed, but inscriptional evidence shows them soon living alongside each other. Many single finds of weapons may well represent pagan graves (probably those of first-generation settlers) – this is particularly true of objects (chiefly swords) found in ancient graveyards, which continued in use into the Viking Age and beyond.

Interment in Christian flat-grave cemeteries is common and is best paralleled in north-west England and Ireland. Mounds of the size which cover some Manx burials, while rare in Scotland or Ireland, have been found in England, particularly in Cumbria – almost in sight of the Isle of Man.

Figure 27.3.3   Ornament on memorial cross from Kirk Braddan, Isle of Man.
(Copyright © Eva Wilson.)

The comparatively rich Manx burial material suggests that the strategic potential of the Island had early been recognised: Danish settlers from the Scandinavian kingdom of York and Mercia, who began to settle north-west England towards the end of the ninth century, would have recognised the potential of the Island, while the turmoil caused by the exodus of Scandinavians from Dublin in 902 may also have encouraged Manx settlements.

The incomers soon became Christian, a fact demonstrated by the monuments raised over the dead, on which the cross is usually the chief feature. Ranging in height from nearly 4 m to less than 1 m, many survive only as fragments. Of about 100 sculptured stones of Viking Age date about a third bear runic inscriptions in Old West Norse characters. Embellished with ornament basically of Scandinavian origin, they also show traits of contemporary north English, and even Scottish and Irish, taste (Figure 27.3.3). The ornament (of the Borre, Jellinge, Mammen and Ringerike styles) dates them between *c.* 925 and 1000. Much ornament – representing individual animal and human figures – presumably had iconographic significance. The figure of Christ occurs only once, but other Christian symbols are more frequent. Pagan iconography also occurs – for example, scenes from the *Sigurðr* cycle.

Figure 27.3.4 The remains of a pre-Norse round house and two other buildings at Braaid. (Copyright © Manx National Heritage.)

Other than the graves, physical evidence of Norse settlement is exiguous. Geomorphological and palynological studies of the landscape and vegetation of the Island have revealed little, although wetlands were clearly much more extensive and the marginal lands of the uplands were utilised. No traces of field systems have been recognised.

Only one Norse dwelling-house has been excavated in the lowlands; from St Patrick's Isle it dates from around 1100. However, perhaps as many as twenty promontory forts around the coast were occupied in the Viking Age. Created by cutting off a small headland overlooking the sea, by means of a bank and external ditch, the outworks enclosed an often continuous series of houses. The forts are multi-period; some pre-dating the Viking Age, some continuing in use afterwards. The sites are exposed and were probably used primarily as look-out stations.

One site – the Braaid – uniquely seems to show continuity between the pre-Norse inhabitants and the incomers. Here (Figure 27.3.4) are the remains of a pre-Norse round house and two other buildings, all built of stone and presumably turf. One (a byre) is rectangular (16.5 m × 6 m); the other (20 m × 8 m at its widest point) has curved long walls. The latter was probably entered through the gables. Few internal features remain, although there are hints of lateral benches. The floor surface is lost and no fireplace was found. After it became derelict the ruins enclosed a number of simple shelters.

The propinquity of the round house to the other buildings suggests a continuous history from the pre-Norse period into the Viking Age – the incomers introduced into Man a new architectural fashion, the rectangular building. The byre, while unremarkable in Viking contexts, suggests that the farmstead was at the centre of a sizeable

389

economic unit. The Braaid, while not strictly an upland site, is situated on the edge of what must have been marginal land, close to the point where arable infield downslope gave way to grazing outfield nearer the hill lands.

Another farm complex, at Doarlish Cashen, Patrick, was certainly on marginal land. Its buildings, while smaller than those at the Braaid, are more substantial than those found at Manx shieling sites of later (twelfth-century) date. Its main building, a rectangular house (7 m × 3 m internally), has a typical Norse layout; opposing doors at one end define a screen which cuts off the end of the building. The main room had lateral benches and a central hearth.

The many Scandinavian place names do not generally help in the study of the Viking Age settlement pattern. Although a substratum of Celtic language remained throughout the Viking period, Norse was dominant and much used in constructing place names, as is demonstrated by the fact that only three certain pre-Norse place names survive.

Interpretation of landholding is difficult. The suggestion that the quarterland system of tenure (a medieval term) existed in the Viking period is fragile. There is no documentary evidence of settlement structure in the Viking Age, and no evidence to suggest (by parallel with Scotland and Ireland) that it is earlier.

Twenty-two Viking Age coin hoards and three hoards without coins have been found in Man. The earliest coin hoards date between *c.* 955 and *c.* 995. Although not a sophisticated statistical sample, it suggests that hoarding in Man started soon after the beginning of the expansion of the Dublin trade. After 990 no hoard is dated earlier than 1030, but eleven hoards may be dated between 1030 and the 1070s. Some contain coins, based on the Dublin style and standard, minted in the Island. Clearly Dublin was deeply influential in Man at this period. Hoarding ceases after a new king, who may have looked more to Scandinavia, arrived in 1079.

From time to time a ruler of Man was sufficiently independent to play politics in the region, but his tenure was probably periodic and often nominal. The presence of a possible king of Man contemporary with Edgar in 974 supports this, although there is no evidence of an English political presence in the Island at this period. When Man developed a coinage (a royal prerogative), it was based on Dublin and not on an English mint, which probably indicates the direction of the Island's economic and political interests. The emergence of Man in the late eleventh century as a kingdom would suggest that the kingdom of Man and the Isles had been established in the late tenth century, and that the 974 reference may be the first indication of a later political entity. A national assembly, Tynwald, presumably has its roots in the Scandinavian period.

Nothing is known of the organisation of the Church in the Viking Age. The first bishop, Roolwer (ON *Hrólfr*), was appointed in the late eleventh century and presumably his diocese was some sort of predecessor to the present diocese of Sodor and Man.

BIBLIOGRAPHY

Wilson, D.M. (2008) *The Viking Age in the Isle of Man*, Aarhus, Aarhus University Press.

CHAPTER TWENTY-EIGHT

SCANDINAVIAN PLACE NAMES
IN THE BRITISH ISLES

———·◆·———

Gillian Fellows-Jensen

Scandinavian place names are found in varying densities over much of the British Isles. They occur in the Northern and Western Isles and along the northern, western and north-eastern seaboard of Scotland, in the Isle of Man, in eastern, northern and north-western England, as well as in the northern and southern seaboard of Wales and along the eastern seaboard of Ireland. It is impossible to date the coining of the place names concerned but it seems reasonable to assume that the first settlements arose some time after the first Viking raids in the British Isles.

Since documentation for Scandinavian settlement is earliest evidenced in England, the study will begin with the part of the region now known as the Danelaw. Three recorded partitions of land were made by the Danes in 876, 877 and 880, and it was earlier thought that these partitions marked the first settlements in England by the rank and file of the Danish army. It now seems more likely that most of the Scandinavian place names in the Danelaw were not coined until the tenth century, when the Danes began to split up between themselves the great English estates and large numbers of Scandinavian names were coined for individually owned units of settlement. It should not be forgotten, of course, that over half of the old names of Celtic and English origin in the Danelaw survived and that even where Scandinavian names were most numerous, namely in parts of Yorkshire and the East Midlands, less than a third of the Domesday place names were of Scandinavian origin.

The largest group of Scandinavian names in England is that consisting of the over 700 settlements with names ending in *-bý*, a word meaning 'settlement' and ranging in size from a flourishing town to a single farm (Figures 28.1 and 28.2). To begin with, these names would seem to have had as their first elements common nouns, for example topographical words such as *dalr* 'valley' in *Dalby* and *saurr* 'sour ground' in *Sowerby*, terms for trees and plants such as *askr* 'ash-tree' in *Ashby* and English *æppel* 'apple' in *Eppleby*, or animal terms such as *gríss* 'pig' in *Girsby* and *veðr* 'wether' in *Wetherby*. Such names occur not only in Yorkshire and the East Midlands but also, although less frequently, in East Anglia and north-west England. No fewer than forty-seven of the names ending in *-bý* take the form *Kirby* or *Kirkby*, meaning 'church settlement', and most of these were originally borne by English settlements later renamed by the Danes. It was probably at a slightly later date that the names ending in *-bý* in England began to

Figure 28.1   Skewsby, Yorkshire: Danish genitive *skógs* 'wood' and *bý* 'settlement'.

Figure 28.2   Stokesby, Norfolk: OE *stoc* 'outlying cattle-farm' and Danish *bý* 'settlement'. Thrigby, Norfolk: probably an OE place name *thric* 'narrow passage' and Danish *bý*. Mautby, Norfolk: Danish *malt* 'malt' and *bý*. Runham, Norfolk: probably OE *hruna* 'tree-trunk', used of a footbridge, and *hām* 'homestead'.

acquire personal names as their first element, most frequently names of Danish origin (here in ON spelling) such as *Eymundr* in *Amotherby*, *Ásketill* in *Asselby*, *Þorketill* in *Thirkleby* and *Ormr* in *Ormesby*.

The next most frequently occurring Scandinavian habitative place-name type in the Danelaw is that containing *thorp*, a word denoting a 'secondary dependent settlement', of which there are over 500 instances, some of which may reflect confusion with the related English element *throp*. More than half of the compound names in *thorp* contain Scandinavian first elements and it seems certain that the Danes must have been responsible for most of these, as well as of the majority of the simplex names in *Thorp* and *Thorpe*. Among the compound *thorp*s whose first element is of Scandinavian origin, many contain personal names such as *Ásgautr* in *Osgathorpe*, *Grímketill* in *Grimblethorpe*, *Ragnhildr* in *Raventhorpe*, *Þóraldr* in *Tharlesthorpe* and *Þórulfr* in *Tholthorpe*, while others contain the same type of common nouns as those occurring in the names ending in *-bý*, for example *brunnr* 'spring' in *Bonthorpe* and *bogi* 'bow, bend' in *Bowthorpe*, *birki* 'birch copse' in *Birthorpe* and *lundr* 'grove' in *Londonthorpe*, *gríss* 'young pig' in *Gristhorpe* and *lamb* 'lamb' in *Langthorpe*.

A third group of characteristic Danish names, although containing the common English element *tūn* meaning 'settlement', is those which are preceded by a Scandinavian personal name. These names would seem to represent pre-existing English place names that were taken over by Scandinavians with Scandinavian personal names, for example *Flík* in *Flixton*, *Friði* in *Fryton*, *Náttfari* in *Nafferton*, *Gunnulfr* in *Gonalston*, *Þorketill* in *Thurcaston* and *Þorgeirr* in *Thurgarton*. Some of these names date from the tenth century, while others may be over a century younger.

There are also various purely Scandinavian habitative names such as *Airy Holme* (*Ergum*) 'at the sheilings', *Thrintoft* (*Tirnetoste*) 'the toft with a thorn-tree', *Scraptoft* (*Scraptofte*) 'at the toft with a thin covering of grass', as well as even more frequently occurring Scandinavian topographical names, most of which would already seem to have come to denote settlement names in Domesday Book, such as *Aiskew* (*Aikescogh*) 'oak wood', *Askwith* (*Ascvid*) 'ash wood', *Ellerbeck* (*Elrebec*) 'alder stream', *Langwith* (*Languath*) 'long ford', *Micklethwaite* (*Muceltuoit*) 'great clearing', *Scargill* (*Scacreghil*) 'merganser cleft', *Skirpenbeck* (*Scarpenbec*) 'dried-up stream', *Wath* (*Wad*) 'ford', *Griff* (*Grif*) 'pit', *Lound* (*lund*) 'grove', *Skegness* (*Sceggenesse*) 'projecting headland', *Deepdale* (*Dupedale*) 'deep valley', *Thingoe* (*Thingehov*) 'assembly mound', *Thwaite* (*Thweit*) 'clearing', *Whinburgh* (*Wineberga*) 'gorse hill' (Figures 28.3 and 28.4).

The Scandinavian place names found in East Anglia, the East Midlands and Yorkshire are mostly recorded in Domesday Book, which can be dated to approximately 1086. Although comparatively few of the Scandinavian names in Cumberland survive in Domesday Book, many of them may well be older than this. A name such as *Carlatton*, for example, identical in origin with several *Carletons* (*karlatūn* 'home of the free peasants') but in which the name is stressed on the second syllable, shows that the Strathclyde Britons had reoccupied northern Cumberland in the tenth century.

Figure 28.3 Kettleshulme, Cheshire: Scandinavian personal name *Ketil* and Danish *holm* 'land almost surrounded by water' with the form *hulm* reflecting a dialect development with its core area in south-east Lancashire and north-east Cheshire.

Figure 28.4   Skirpenbeck, Yorkshire: Danish *skerpin(g)* 'dried up' and *bekk* 'stream'.

Men whose personal names in the north-west are of later date are those whose personal names were of Norman or Flemish origin but whose farm names end in *-bý*, for example *Richard* in *Rickerby* and *Robert* in *Robberby*. They were associated with the plantation of peasant settlers by William Rufus after the capture of Carlisle from Strathclyde in 1092. It is unlikely that such a large number of place names containing Norman personal names compounded with the element *-bý* would have been coined from scratch unless place names consisting of Scandinavian personal names and *-bý* had earlier become well established in the Viking period. The distribution pattern of the *bý*s in north-western England containing Scandinavian personal names and Norman ones respectively shows a negative correlation that can best be explained as the result of an outward movement from Carlisle of settlers with Norman names.

Some of the Scandinavian personal names in Cumberland were even borne by men still alive in the twelfth century, for example *Astin* (from a short form of *Ásketill*) in *Alstonby*, and *Gamall* in *Gamblesby* (Fellows-Jensen 1985: 22), while across the border from the North Riding in Durham there are two names in *-bý* containing personal names of French origin, namely *Folet* in *Follingsby* and *Race* in *Raisby*, while the same type of formation is found in the same century in the Annan valley in Dumfriesshire, where names such as *Lochard* and *William* occur in a string of names in *-bý* which are likely to have originally contained Scandinavian forenames.

There are other Scandinavian names in *-bý* in Scotland which reflect Danelaw influence (Fellows-Jensen 1989–90: 42). Ten of the names in Dumfriesshire and seven of those in Galloway have first elements other than personal names and most of these have exact parallels in England, for example *Sorbie* containing the appellative *saurr* 'sour land', *Applebie* and *Esbie* containing the plant terms *epli* 'apple' and *eski* 'place where ash-trees grow'. There are also similar names in *-bý* further north in the Central Lowlands of Scotland, for example those containing 'sour land' in *Sorbie, hundi* 'hound' in several *Humbies* and *veðr* 'wether-sheep' in *Weddersbie*. Several of these names have exact parallels in the Danelaw and must reflect Danelaw influence.

Unlike the *bý*s in Cumberland and south-western Scotland, where some of the names contain Norman personal names, most of the *bý*s in the Central Lowlands have first

394

elements that are not personal names. There are, for example, two *Busby*s and two *Busbie*s, which would all seem to be of the same origin as *Busby* in the North Riding of Yorkshire, namely *buski* 'shrub, bush', while two *Sorbie*s have several parallels in England, including four *Sowerby*s in Yorkshire and two in Lancashire. It seems likely that the names in both Dumfriesshire and central Scotland were formed on analogy with names in the Danelaw, probably as the result of the arrival of new settlers from areas of Scandinavian settlement in England. They would seem to have followed a similar route into Scotland in the second quarter of the tenth century as the type of monument known as hogbacks, whose development originated in northern Yorkshire around Brompton, which is not far from Busby. The popularity of the hogbacks spread from there along the Tees valley via the Stainmoor pass to the Eden valley and the Carlisle plain, from where the hogbacks continued on north to central Scotland. A stylistic analysis of the hogbacks in Scotland shows them to be later than, and derivative from, the English ones, and the same can probably be said of the Scottish place names ending in *-bý*. In a recent paper Simon Taylor has argued that *bý*-names in central Scotland tend to be situated on royal land or in baronies held directly by the Crown and that the Scottish kings may well have been encouraging limited Anglo-Scandinavian settlement within their kingdom in the tenth century (Taylor 2004: 130–8).

In addition to the names ending in *-bý* in Dumfriesshire there are also a number of names there in *-thveit*, a word denoting 'clearing', and to judge from the distribution pattern of these names, they would also seem to reflect Danelaw influence. Like many related names in Yorkshire the *thveit*s seem to be younger than most of the names recorded in Domesday Book. Many of the names in Dumfriesshire have forms with early spellings resembling those in Yorkshire, for example the Dumfriesshire names *Brakanepheit, Thorniethwaite, Langesweit, Litelsweit, Blindethuayt* and *Holthwayt* from *Howthat*, which probably reflect Danish influence (Nicolaisen 1982: 113). Some of the forms in Dumfriesshire, for example *Cowthat* and *Howthat*, however, reflect the usual Scottish spelling of the name-element, as do the few examples of names in *-thveit* in Orkney and Shetland, where these names in *Twatt* reflect Norse influence.

Other place names ending in *-bý* which can be assumed ultimately to reflect Danelaw influence are four place names in southern Wales, where three of the four: *Colby, Homri* and *Womanby*, have exact parallels in the Danelaw: several *Colby*s and *Hornby*s and *Hunmanby*. It seems likely that the four names were all imported from the Danelaw in the post-Viking period as analogical formations.

In the Isle of Man there are some names which belong to the period when Norse settlers arrived directly from Norway or indirectly via the Norse colonies in Scotland and the Isles, probably in the tenth or eleventh century, to which names I shall return later. The Manx names ending in *-bý*, however, would all seem to have been coined by settlers of Danish or Danelaw origin and there are several possible explanations for their presence (Fellows-Jensen 2004: 139–52). Some settlers came from the Danelaw in the course of the tenth century, while others, who may have been recruited there by Godred Crovan, were granted large farms in the fertile south of the island after his victory in 1079. Finally, there was a documented immigration to Man from northern England in the early fifteenth century.

A few of the names in Man, for example *Jurby* (from **djúrabý* 'deer farm') and *Sulby* (from **súlabý* 'farm in or by a cleft or fork'), show from their early recordings and their linguistic development that they must have been subject to Gaelic influence in the

Figure 28.5   Ramnageo, Shetland: Norn *hrafn* 'raven' and *gjá* 'cleft, ravine'.

tenth or eleventh century. Other Manx *býs*, however, are today identical in form and pronunciation with their parallels in England, for example *Dalby* in the parish of Kirk Patrick and *Dalby* in Yorkshire. Some of these analogical formations might perhaps have been introduced to Man after the crown had been granted by the English king to Sir John Stanley in 1405 but it is more likely that they simply reflect English influence.

Leaving the Scandinavian names of Danelaw origin behind us, both those coined in the Viking period in England and those coined in England, Scotland and Man on analogy with English names, the most impressive Scandinavian presence in the British Isles is that of the names in Shetland and Orkney, where Norse settlement would seem to have begun in the ninth century and gradually to have ousted all the older names there of Pictish or Celtic origin. No trace survives today of these earlier names. The Norse language in Shetland and Orkney is generally referred to as Norn and would seem to have come from western Norway and to have become totally dominant by the middle of the eleventh century. Norn survived here until the islands were pledged to the Scottish Crown by King Christian I of Denmark in 1468–9 but Lowland Scots became dominant in the late sixteenth century and subsequently English. Although most of the old Norn names survive in Shetland and Orkney, as a living language Norn must have died out by the end of the eighteenth century (Barnes 1998: 2–4, 26).

Many of the Norn settlement names originally denoted topographical features, for example *Bressay* 'broad island' and *Rousay* 'Hrólf's island', *Whiteness* 'white headland' and *Stenness* 'stone headland', *Leiraback* 'clay bank', *Stackhoull* 'stack rock', *Gillsbreck* 'ravine by a slope' and *Howth* 'head', *Gru* 'a pit' and *Dale* 'a valley', *Bretto* 'steep river' and *Laxo* 'salmon river', *Roerwater* 'reed lake' and *Groundwater* 'shallow lake', *Haroldswick* 'Harald's bay', *Sandwick* 'sandy bay', *Lerwick* 'clay bay' and *Snarravoe* 'snare bay', *Hamnavoe* 'harbour bay' and *Laxvoe* 'salmon bay', as well as *Ramnageo* 'raven cleft' and *Trolle Geo* 'trold cleft' (Crawford 1995: 26–41) (Figure 28.5).

There are also originally habitative Norwegian place names in the Northern Isles. Some of these names are of comparatively rare occurrence, for example those containing the element -*heimr*, for example *Sullom*, an original **sólheimr* 'sunny farm' and names reflecting older **leikvin* 'playground, sports field'. These are stereotype names that were brought over from Norway as names (Fellows-Jensen 1984: 154).

More frequently occurring habitative names are those discussed by Nicolaisen (2001: 112–22) ending in *-staðir*, *-setr* and *-sætr* and *-bólstaðr*. *Staðir*-names probably denoted small settlement units and often contained personal names, for example *Grimista* (*Grímr*), *Oddsta* (*Oddr*) and *Girlsta* (*Geirhildr*) in Shetland and *Germiston* (*Geirmundr*), *Cairston* (*Kjarrekr*) and *Grimeston* (*Grímr*) in Orkney. Settlement names in *-setr* and *-sætr* occur rather more commonly, particularly in Shetland. The elements they contain here are sometimes personal names, as in *Grimsetter* (*Grímr*), *Frakkaster* (*Frakki*) and *Kettlester* (*Ketill*), but it is more frequent for them to contain topographical terms such as *Crooksetter* (*krókr* 'curve'), *Gilsetter* (*gil* 'narrow valley') and *Vatsetter* (*vatn* 'lake'), or terms for animals or birds, for example *Oxensetter* (*yxn*), *Swinister* (*svín*), *Russeter* (*hross* 'horse') and *Goster* (*gás* 'goose'). In Orkney the same kinds of formations appear, although personal names there are of rare occurrence, for example *Grímr* in *Grymesetter*, and *Snjallr* in *Snelsetter*. There are many topographical terms such as *Melsetter* (*melr* 'sand') and *Inksetter* (*eng* 'meadow'). The most commonly occurring element is *bólstaðr* but its representation varies greatly. In Shetland it occurs as *Bousta* as a simplex name and as *-bister* in compounds, for example *Wadbister* (*vað* 'ford'), *Nesbister* (*nes* 'headland'), *Fladdabister* (*flati* 'flat'). In Orkney it occurs as *Busta* and *Bousta* as a simplex name and as *-bster* and *-bist* and *-bust* in compound names, for example *Ellibister* (perhaps *elf* 'elf'), *Skelbister* (perhaps *skáli* 'shieling') (Crawford 1995: 57–8). It is extremely rare for personal names to be compounded with the element *bólstaðr* anywhere in Scotland (Gammeltoft 2001: 275).

Whereas the Norse place names in the Northern Isles finally became embedded in English, the Norse names elsewhere in Scotland passed through a Gaelic stage before reaching English (Nicolaisen 1982: 98; 2001: 156). In the ninth and tenth centuries Gaelic and Norse must have confronted each other in Caithness and the Hebrides, as also in the Isle of Man. Norse place names are in fact found all round the coastal areas of north-western and western Scotland and in the Outer and Inner Hebrides and in Man, dating probably from the tenth century to the twelfth to thirteenth centuries.

In contrast to the names ending in *-bý* in the Danelaw, related names in northern Scotland are fairly rare. Possible examples in Orkney are *Trenaby* (containing **Thránd* or the related tribal name), *Cattaby* (containing *Káti* or *Kǫtt*) and *Yesnaby* (of doubtful origin) (Fellows-Jensen 1984: 156). Two personal names are compounded with *bær* in Caithness: Celtic *Dungal* in Duncansby and *Cano* in Canisbay (Figure 28.6). Other names of this type include *Europie*, probably containing a feminine name *Jórun* in Lewis, and *Golspie* (*Goldespy* 1330) in Sutherland, whose first element is of uncertain origin. In the Isle of Man, however, Norse personal names compounded with *bý* are more likely to reflect Danelaw influence.

In the eastern part of Caithness, Norse place names are very similar to those in Shetland and Orkney. Elsewhere, however, Gaelic-speaking settlers began to spread over Scotland from the west and while Norse names occur fairly commonly on the northern and western seaboard, the Outer Hebrides, the fertile islands of Coll and Tiree and the Isle of Man, they are much less easily identifiable in the heavily Gaelicised areas in the Inner Hebrides and mainland Scotland.

There is a fairly general distribution of topographical names, for example *Reay* (**vrá* 'corner, nook'), *Staxigoe* (*stakk-gjá* 'stack cleft'), *Sanwick* (**sand-vík* 'sand bay') and *Murkle* (**myrk-hól* 'dark hill') in Caithness, *Torrisdale* (**Þór(ir)s-dalr* 'Thór(ir)s valley') and *Melness* (**mel-nes* 'sandy headland') in Strathnaver, *Migdale* (**mjuk-dalr* 'glen with soft

Figure 28.6   Duncansby, Caithness: Celtic personal name *Dungal* and Norse *bæ* 'settlement'.

soil') and *Cyderhall* (**Sigvarth-haugr* 'Sigurd's howe') in Sutherland, *Durness* (**dýr-nes* 'deer headland') and *Sangomore* (**sand-gjá* 'sand cleft') on the north-west seaboard, *Gruinard* (**grunna-fjǫrðr* 'shallow firth') and Sand (**sand-á* 'sandy river') in Wester Ross, *Aignish* (**egg-nes* 'ridge headland') and *Galson* (**galt-sund* 'hog sound') in Lewis, *Hough* (**haugr* 'mound') and *Uig* (**víg* 'bay') in Coll, and *Skipnes* (**skip-nes* 'ship headland') and *Sandaig* (**sand-vík* 'sandy bay') in Tiree (Crawford 1995: 112–15), and further afield but still within the Norse zone, *Scarlett* (**skarf-klett* 'cormorants' cleft'), *Ramsey* (**hrams-á*) 'wild-garlic river') and *Swarthawe* (**svart-hǫfuð* 'black mound') in the Isle of Man, and *Strangford* (**strang-fjǫrð* 'strong-current firth') and *Leixlip* (**lax-hleypa* 'salmon leap') along the east coast of Ireland.

Habitative names include *staðir* in *Borrostoun* (*Borgarr*), *setr* in *Helsetter* (*hella*), and *bólstaðr* in *Lybster* (*hlíð*) and *Scrabster* (*skári* 'young seagull') in Caithness (Crawford 1995: 42–3), *staðir* in *Skegirsta* (*Skeggi*), *setr* in *Linshader*, and *bólstaðr* in *Garrabost* (*garða* gen. pl.) in Lewis, *staðir* in *Torastan* (*Þórr*) in Coll, and *Bhiosta* (with an obscure first element) in Tiree, and *bólstaðr* in the simplex name *Bousd* and in *Arnabost* (*Árni* or 'eagle') in Coll (Crawford 1995: 116–21), *staðir* in *Leodest* (*Ljótulfr*) and possibly *bólstaðr* in *Bravost* (*brú*) in Man (Gammeltoft 2001: 98, 100, 105, 136).

The picture of Scandinavian place names in the British Isles ranges from the almost wholly Norn names of Shetland and Orkney and the marked Danish influence in eastern England to areas of Scotland and the Isles where Gaelic influence has partly obscured the Norse names of the Viking period and areas where later Danish influence from the Danelaw has spread over north-western England, southern and central Scotland and even southern Wales, to the spread of seafaring influence around the coasts of Ireland and Wales, and, finally, to the Isle of Man, where Gaelic names have been overlaid by both Norse and Danish names before finally being subjected to a layer of English varnish (Figure 28.7).

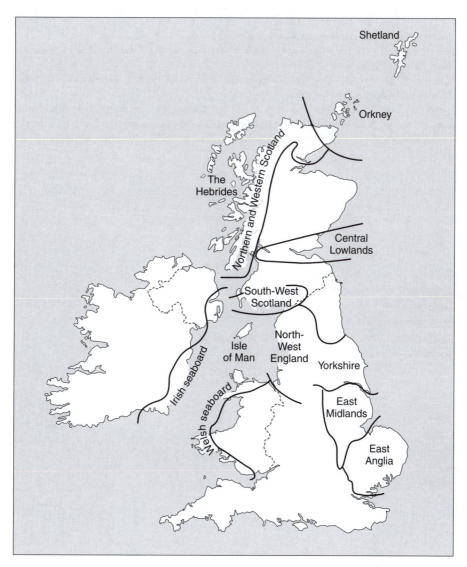

Figure 28.7   Map showing areas where Scandinavian place names occur.

BIBLIOGRAPHY

Barnes, M.P. (1998) *The Norn Language of Orkney and Shetland*, Lerwick: The Shetland Times.

Crawford, B.E. (ed.) (1995) *Scandinavian Settlement in Northern Britain. Thirteen Studies of Place-Names in their Historical Context*, London and New York: Leicester University Press.

Fellows-Jensen, G. (1984) 'Viking settlement in the Northern and Western Isles: the place-name evidence as seen from Denmark and the Danelaw', in A. Fenton and H. Pálsson (eds), *The Northern and Western Isles in the Viking World*, Edinburgh: John Donald Publishers.

—— (1985) *Scandinavian Settlement Names in the North-West*, Copenhagen: C.A. Reitzels Forlag.

—— (1989–90) 'Scandinavians in southern Scotland?', *Nomina*, 13: 41–60.

—— (2004) 'How old are the Scandinavian place-names in Man?', *Proceedings of the Isle of Man Natural History and Antiquarian Society*, 11(3): 421–36.

Gammeltoft, P. (2001) *The Place-name Element* bólstaðr *in the North Atlantic Area*, Copenhagen: C.A. Reitzels Forlag.

Nicolaisen, W.F.H. (1982) 'The Viking settlement of Scotland', in R.T. Farrell (ed.) *The Vikings*, London and Chichester: Phillimore.

—— (2001) *Scottish Place-Names. Their Study and Significance*, new edn, Edinburgh: John Donald.

Taylor, S. (2004) 'Scandinavians in central Scotland – *bý*-place-names and their context', in G. Williams and P. Bibire (eds) *Sagas, Saints and Settlements* (The Northern World 2), Leiden: Brill.

CHAPTER TWENTY-NINE

THE VIKINGS IN WALES

—·◆·—

Mark Redknap

The geographical position of north Wales and its close sea-borne connections to the Isle of Man, Dublin, the Wirral and Strathclyde, naturally led to some engagement between its coastal population and the Scandinavian world. The extent of this engagement has long been debated, but the term 'Cambro-Norse' has been usefully adopted for the period *c.* 850–*c.* 1100 (Knight 1984).

The annals of early Wales (*Annales Cambriae*), written in Latin, record raids by 'gentiles' (MW *Cenhedloedd*), 'Black Gentiles', 'pagans' (MW *Paganiaid*), 'foreigners' and 'Black Norsemen'. The medieval 'Chronicle of the Princes' (*Brut y Tywysogyon*) and 'The Kings of the Saxons' (*Brenhinedd y Saesson*; Jones trans. 1971), Welsh versions of a Latin text based on the annals, sometimes contain additional information. Apart from the annals, no Welsh chronicler produced a coherent story for the events of the ninth and tenth centuries.

Whether the semi-legendary Icelandic *Jómsvíkinga saga* refers to Wales is less clear. Written down around 1200, it tells of a warrior community of Vikings in the Baltic. In the saga, which is set in the tenth century, the founder of 'Jómsborg' on the south coast of the Baltic, Viking leader Pálna-Tóki (foster-father of King Svein), raided *Bretland* ('Land of British') where he married Earl Stefni's daughter Álöf and settled. Here Pálna-Tóki met Björn *hinn brezki* in Old Norse, who was put in charge of their interests. There is little to suggest that the person who wrote this saga down was alluding to Wales, and *Bretland* here may rather represent 'a distant land about which little is known' (Blake 1962; Moffatt 1903: 163–73).

THE EARLY VIKING RAIDS

The first definite recorded raid on Wales was in 852 (the killing of Cyngen by Pagans recorded in *Brut y Tywysogyon*: Jones 1952), and Anglesey (*Môn*) became a particular target from 855. Sporadic probing raids in the north and south, which occurred until about 919, have been described as a 'backwash' of Viking activity, their efforts being focused elsewhere (Loyn 1976: 21; 1994; Davies 1990; Maund 1996). Rhodri Mawr, ruler of Gwynedd, led initial Welsh resistance and was successful in slaying Orm (ON *Gormr*), leader of the 'New Dubliners' (*Dubh-gheinte*), in 855 (recorded in the

Annals of Ulster, s.a. 855; *Chron. Scot. s.a.* 856). In the light of the Dubliners' interest in north Wales and the assertion by the Welsh writer Asser that Rhodri Mawr's sons were dependent on the Scandinavians of York, a case has been made for Viking hegemony over north Wales by the 870s (Dumville 2001). External interest in Anglesey is further illustrated by the exploits of the Viking leader Ingimund (*Igmunt, Hingamund*). Having been expelled from Dublin *c.* 902/3, Ingimund attempted to establish a base on Anglesey (recorded in the eleventh-century Irish account presented in *Annals of Ireland, Three Fragments*, § 429; Jones trans. 1952: 6; Griffiths 2004). The *Annales Cambriae* also record that one of Rhodri Mawr's sons, Merfyn ap Rhodri (*Mervyn vab Rodri*), was slain by 'gentiles' (*s.a.* 904 in *Brenhinedd y Saesson*). Expelled by the Welsh king, Ingimund and his followers sailed east and were allowed to land near Chester, an event which was followed by the development of a Viking enclave in north-west England (O'Donovan 1860; Wainwright 1948; Jesch 2000).

During the reign of Rhodri Mawr's grandson, Hywel ap Cadell (*Hywel Dda* 'The Good', 920–50), the focus of native royal power shifted southwards with the expansion of Dyfed. Hywel Dda's pragmatic policy of active cooperation with the House of Wessex may have contributed to a period of relative security and unity against the Viking threat. This contrasts with the passionate sentiments expressed in a famous dissident poem in Welsh composed possibly by a monk from south Wales about 930, known as *Armes Prydein* ('The Prophecy of Britain'), which called upon the Scandinavians to help the Welsh and other Britons in a coalition to expel the English from the Island of Britain (Clancy 1970) – possibly a reaction to the size of Welsh tribute exacted by Æthelstan (924–39) at Hereford.

THE 'SECOND PHASE' OF VIKING RAIDS

If the lull in the annalistic references to raids in Wales reflects what really happened, there appears to be a 'Second Viking Phase' starting about 950, with renewed attacks on the coastal lowlands, and on monasteries at Penmon and Caer Gybi near Holyhead (Anglesey), Tywyn (Gwynedd), St David's (eleven times between 967 and 1091), Clynnog Fawr (978) and St Dogmaels (Pembrokeshire), Llanbadarn Fawr (Ceredigion), Llantwit Major and Llancarfan (Vale of Glamorgan). In 989 Maredudd ab Owain, great-great-grandson of Rhodri Mawr and king of Dyfed, was compelled to redeem captive Welshmen from slavery at a penny a head paid to *black gentiles*, and in 998 the Bishop of St David's, Morgeneu, was killed by Vikings.

By the mid-tenth century, some members of the Dublin community were as much engaged in commerce as Irish politics, and it has been suggested that Scandinavians were controlling Gwynedd (or large parts of it) between about 960 and 1025. According to the twelfth-century *Historia Gruffud vab Kenan*, Óláfr Sigtryggsson ruled Anglesey and mainland Gwynedd (as well as Dublin, a large part of Ireland, the Isle of Man, Galloway and the Rhinns) in the early eleventh century (Loyn 1977: 104–5; Davies 1990: 59; see also *Historia Gruffudd vab Kenan*: Evans 1990: 55; see also Russell 2005).

THE FINAL PHASE OF VIKING RAIDS

A third phase of raiding appears (according to the annals) to have commenced during the second half of the eleventh century, linked to events leading up to the Norman invasion of Wales. From the late tenth century, Scandinavian presence appears to have grown in the Severn Estuary, with Bristol replacing Chester as the main focus for Hiberno-Norse trading contact with Anglo-Saxon England. In one, famous account, following the plundering of Glamorgan by Count Eilaf (a Dane in the service of King Cnut 1018–24), the clergy fled from Llancarfan with relics and the shrine of St Cadog, only to be attacked at Mamhilad near Usk in Monmouthshire, one attacker damaging the shrine with his axe (*Vita Cadoci*, ch. 40; Wade Evans 1944: 110).

Gruffudd ap Llywelyn, king of Gwynedd (1039–63) extended his rule to the eastern reaches of the Bristol Channel (the kingdoms of Morgannwg and Gwent). Making use of both rivalries in England during the reign of Edward the Confessor and the actions of Vikings, Gruffudd eventually ruled the whole of what is now known as Wales and owned his own fleet.

To some during the eleventh century, the Scandinavians were allies and a source of mercenaries, and it was a period of alliance between Gwynedd and the Norse rulers of Dublin and Man. Gruffudd ap Llywelyn sacked Hereford in 1055 with the help of the banished Earl Ælfgar, and eighteen Norse ships from Ireland (Garmonsway 1986: 104–6, *s.a.* 1055; Davies 2002: 223–5). Gruffudd was murdered in 1063 after a series of defeats at the hands of Harold Godwinson and his brother Tostig. Harold married Gruffudd ap Llywelyn's widow Ealdgyth, only to meet his death a few years later at the hands of William of Normandy at Hastings in 1066.

Relations between Wales and Ireland during the eleventh century were complex, with both Scandinavian settlers in Ireland and the Irish having close political links with Wales (Duffy 1995: 378–96; Davies 1990: 50–1). Insight into the close political involvement between Wales and Ireland in the late eleventh and early twelfth centuries is provided by the *Life* of the ruler of Gwynedd, Gruffudd ap Cynan (1055–1137), grandson of Iago and a descendant of Rhodri Mawr, who had grown up among the Danish community in Dublin. After several failed attempts to re-establish the old line of Rhodri as ruler of Gwynedd, during which Gruffudd stayed with the king of Dublin (Diarmit Uí Briain), he eventually succeeded in returning to Anglesey in 1098, and consolidated his hold on Gwynedd by 1115 (Maund 1996). Gruffudd's death in 1137 was lamented by Irishmen and Danes, which suggests that he may never have divorced himself from his Scandinavian connections (*Historia Gruffudd vab Kenan*; see Evans 1990: 153, 157).

SETTLEMENT

The question of Viking settlement in Wales has been a matter of debate for some time. Early proposals for Scandinavian settlement using place-name evidence at a number of locations around the Welsh coast (Paterson 1921: 11–71) have been more cautiously refined, while some coastal names have been attributed to Scandinavian maritime activity (Charles 1934). The historian J.E. Lloyd, writing at the beginning of the twentieth century, did not believe in permanent Scandinavian colonisation anywhere in Wales (Lloyd 1912: 322), while Melville Richards in the 1960s argued for Norse trading stations but a smaller number of Scandinavian place names (Richards 1962).

Norse place names in Wales comprise two main groups. The first are those names which have been preserved for prominent coastal features which were used as navigational points (in the manner of a visual itinerary). These are particularly common along the sea route to Bristol, and reflect Norse domination of the seaways and their movements around the coast. This first group includes the common elements -*holmr* 'islet', 'island' as in *Priestholm, Grassholm, Skokholm, Gateholm, Burry Holms* and in the Bristol Channel, *Flat Holm* and *Steep Holm*; -*wick* 'bay' and -*ford* 'fjord' as in *Milford Haven*. Flat Holm, known to the Saxons as *Bradan Relice* 'broad burial-place', became a place of refuge in 1068 for Countess Gytha, mother of Harold; in 914 a Viking fleet under earls Hróald and Óttar eventually fled to neighbouring Steep Holm (*Steapan Relice* 'steep burial-place' to the Saxons), where many perished of hunger. Other Scandinavian names include *Fishguard, the Skerries* (*sker* 'isolated rock'), *Emsger, Tusker, the Stacks* (*stakkr* 'pillar-shaped rock'), *Stackpole, Midland* (*meðal* 'middle' and -*holmr*) and *Ormes Head* (*ormr* 'snake'). Islands were viewed as targets (if endowed with churches or monasteries) or places of refuge, and the element -*ey* 'island' appears a number of times, as in *Anglesey* (< *Onguls-ey*), *Bardsey, Caldy, Skomer* (*skálm* 'side of a cleft' and -*ey*), *Ramsey, Lundy* and possibly *Swansea* (Fellows-Jensen 1992: 34). In the case of Anglesey, it has been suggested that either the repeated attacks resulted in some limited period of Viking domination, or that the sustained contacts of Gruffudd ap Cynan and others somehow influenced the description of the island by outsiders.

Warning against attributing too much weight to the lack of explicit references to Scandinavian settlement in the annals and other literary sources, Wendy Davies has argued for significant Viking success in two areas of north Wales – Anglesey and Arfon in the north-west (on either side of the Menai Straits), and Tegeingl (north-east Wales west of the River Dee) in north-east Wales (in the Scandinavian settlement zone of the Wirral and Chester) (Davies 1990: 52). Such assessments have relied largely on documentary sources, the annals and Anglo-Norman histories, coupled with place-name studies and rare archaeological finds. For example, a probable Viking burial at Talacre and Viking-inspired ornament on crosses in the same area suggest the existence of an offshoot of settlement in the Wirral and west Cheshire.

The second group of place names comprises Scandinavian-style settlement names combined with personal names. Typical examples in England are -*bý*, but *Tenby* comes from the Welsh *din-bych*, not the Scandinavian, while *Womanby* (*hundamannabý* 'settlement of the dogkeepers') in Cardiff, *Homri* (*Horn(e)by*, possibly personal name *Horni*) and *Lamby* (*lang* 'long') in Monmouthshire are all late in date, and, as with such names in the central lowlands of Scotland, may represent settlement from the Danelaw *after* Norman conquests in Wales (Fellows-Jensen 1992: 34; Pierce 1984). In Pembrokeshire, a few names consist of a Scandinavian personal name, followed by the English/Anglo-Saxon element -*tun* such as *Furzton, Haroldston, Yerbeston*, but these probably reflect settlement *after* the Norman conquest by settlers from the areas of England where Danish names were common. In Flintshire, there is a small cluster of names such as *Kelston, Axton* and possibly *Linacre*, which may represent an infiltration from north-west England. Scandinavian elements are also evident in the Pembrokeshire names *Goultrop, Hasguard, Wolf's Castle* and *Scollock*. It is significant that Welsh vocabulary was scarcely affected, and Scandinavian place names only occur in coastal regions. While these place names entered the English language, some have little linguistic relationship with the corresponding Welsh names: *Bardsey* remains *Ynys Enlli*, *Anglesey* remains *Môn*, *Orme's Head* remains *Penygogarth*, which suggests limited contact with the native population.

ARCHAEOLOGICAL EVIDENCE

Archaeological evidence of Scandinavian activity has been limited: Viking graves, occasional finds, some Scandinavian place names, coin hoards and a handful of sculptured stones which display Scandinavian influences (e.g. Nash-Williams 1950: nos 37, 38, 190; Edwards 1999) – but the various elements were seen to be 'consistent with and reinforce each other'.

Until recently, there was little archaeological material from Wales to support the historical or place-name evidence. Recent reviews by Wilson and Graham-Campbell have placed this evidence (largely hoards and coins with a littoral distribution) in context (Wilson 1995; Graham-Campbell 1998). Davies (1990: 52–5, 57) considered that the early tenth-century five Red Wharf Bay silver arm-rings (Boon 1986) reflect a distinctively Scandinavian practice, and that it is exceptionally unlikely they were not deposited by Scandinavians. Sheehan (2004) has viewed such hoards of complete ornaments in social rather than economic terms alone: that they conferred status on patrons, donors or recipients. The Red Wharf Bay arm-rings are probably contemporary with the Cuerdale hoard (buried *c.* 905), and it has been suggested that Ingimund's activities on Anglesey in 903 might have led to the deposition and their non-recovery (Boon 1986: 30; Graham-Campbell 1998: 108) (Figure 29.1). Eleven silver hoards are known from Wales, which are thought to have been deposited between 850 and 1030. One of two hoards from Bangor, found on the High Street (within the precinct of the monastery established by St Deiniol in the sixth century), was probably deposited after *c.* 925. It is characteristically Scandinavian in coin composition, and includes hack-silver (Blackburn and Pagan 1986: no. 106). The mixed hoard may represent east–west or west–east movement of bullion rather than resulting from a raid from the Isle of Man. Discoveries of silver hoards on ecclesiastical sites in Ireland, particularly of ingot and

Figure 29.1   Early tenth-century silver arm-rings from Red Wharf Bay, Anglesey.
(Copyright © National Museum of Wales.)

coin hoards, appear to demonstrate the developing role of monasteries as market centres during the tenth century (Sheehan 1998: 175).

The discovery of a decorated sword guard by a diver off the Smalls Reef, some 25 km off the coast of Pembrokeshire, has provided an indication of stylistic transmission between Ireland and south Wales in the early twelfth century (Redknap 2000: 55, 85–7). The lower guard is made of brass with silver and niello decoration in the form of beasts in profile and snake-like animals, in Insular Urnes style, and was probably made in Ireland (*c.* 1100–25).

Four possible pagan Scandinavian burials of the Viking period have been discovered, all located close to the coast. Two contained skeletons associated with grave goods: Talacre, Flintshire (Smith 1931–2), and Benllech on Anglesey (Williams 1945; Edwards 1985). A third possible late ninth- or early tenth-century pagan grave has been proposed as a likely context for a pair of stirrups found at St Mary Hill in the Vale of Glamorgan (Seaby and Woodfield 1980), while a late tenth-/eleventh-century spear and axe found at Caerwent, Monmouthshire, may have come from a fourth grave (Knight 1996).

Excavations by Amgueddfa Cymru–National Museum Wales between 1994 and 2001 at Llanbedrgoch on Anglesey have revealed a strategically sited, fortified settlement near the coast. This supports Davies' suggestion of Scandinavian enclaves of small communities centred on Anglesey in the early tenth century, though the extent of their authority remains unclear. During the first half of the tenth century this settlement was economically and socially integrated with regional and long-distance exchange networks which operated around the Irish Sea (Redknap 2000, 2004). Many of the artefacts from the site are characteristic of Scandinavian or Irish Sea taste, among other objects of native or Irish type: hack-silver is indicative of an active bullion economy (Figure 29.2); lead weights and items of personal adornment have close parallels at Dublin, Meols, York and Whithorn, while Chester ware points to trade links with Chester and Viking Dublin. The site would have been a contained staging post of mutual benefit to both its Welsh lord and the Vikings, immediately before and during an upsurge in the importance of Chester as a port in the reign of Æthelstan (924–39), and in particular in trade with Ireland and the Dublin–Man–Chester sea routes. There is no evidence that Llanbedrgoch represents the setting up *de novo* of a temporary or permanent staging post on fortified or fortifiable ground, within Loyn's concept of 'first-stage' settlement (Loyn 1992: 218), and it probably has its origins in informal overseas contact prior to the land-taking attempts of Ingimund and his successors. Llanbedrgoch may be an early example in an area to the west of Red Wharf Bay of an aristocratic estate centre, or *caput*, for the land of a secular lord and a key element in royal regional administration (Longley 2001), perhaps with a fiscal and administrative role. The status of the site may even be considered to be equivalent to that of a royal *llys* – but without proof of royal ownership – at the upper end of the settlement hierarchy as a major non-regal lordship within an expanding Gwynedd.

The discovery of five casually buried skeletons in the enclosure ditch suggests that the consequences of raiding in the second half of the tenth century may have contributed to its eventual abandonment. Regular raiding and tribute-taking during the second half of the tenth century implies that the Scandinavians were the dominant political power in the region. In the 970s and 980s, the Man-based sons of Harald appear to have effectively controlled Gwynedd, and may have had bases on Anglesey in the 980s. Magnus Haraldsson and his brother Guðröð made efforts to gain political control of

Figure 29.2 These tenth-century silver ingots and fragments of arm-ring from Llanbedrgoch, Anglesey bear shear marks which indicate that they have been used as hack-silver bullion for trading. (Copyright © National Museum of Wales.)

Anglesey, which they raided in 971 (ravaging Penmon), 980 and 987 when, according to the annals, Guðröð seized as many as 2,000 men from Anglesey (Jones 1952; Davies 1990: 57).

LEGACY

Viking impact on Wales has to be seen as part of a broader pattern of activity in north-west Europe and is comparable with that on Brittany. The displacement of Viking leaders from Dublin in the early tenth century had repercussions around the Irish Sea, so that by the middle of the century its seaboard supported in some respects what has been termed a single 'Scandinavian' community of fashion or culture. No doubt the strength of such Scandinavian contributions to seaboard culture will have varied regionally, with pockets of intensity. By the middle of the tenth century the southern seaboard of the Irish Sea (the coast of north Wales) also shared the 'Norse-influenced' community of fashion or culture which should more appropriately be called 'Cambro-Norse', reflecting the contact between the two cultures in the territory.

There is broad agreement that the extent and impact of Scandinavian settlement in Wales were limited – there is no evidence for an equivalent to the Scandinavian kingdom of Dublin. However, a degree of Scandinavian rule in north Wales by the early eleventh century is likely; some leaders had strong Welsh connections and ruled in

Anglesey and mainland Gwynedd for a period (such as Óláfr in the early eleventh century).

The Red Wharf Bay armlets (Figure 29.1) may point to gift-giving to a local elite, and the formation of alliances at this period, while the evidence from Llanbedrgoch suggests a Scandinavian trading presence, a foothold which helped them maintain the Dublin–York axis within the Irish Sea cultural zone. The quantity of artefacts bearing the stylistic hallmarks of Scandinavian or Hiberno-Norse taste raises the possibility of a significant immigrant element among the occupants of the site, and the coexistence and integration of the native population with traders in terms of material culture, but not of language or significant self-conscious ethnicity. Llanbedrgoch is a manifestation of settlement in north-west Wales which learnt to operate within the Hiberno-Scandinavian political and commercial activity around the Irish Sea (perhaps ultimately being targeted by raids), and is providing a new perspective on Hiberno-Scandinavian influence and cultural hegemony in north Wales.

The available evidence indicates that there was little impact on the Welsh language and political structures. The Vikings initiated no urban developments, and the Welsh were effective in limiting Viking settlement to certain areas. The Vikings have been credited with indirect influence on the development of a sense among the Welsh of solidarity against an external threat. Some of their episodic impact is now invisible – the loss of treasures and the cultural damage caused by this plundering – although largely documented through the annals, place names and occasional finds.

BIBLIOGRAPHY

Annales Cambriae, A.D. 682–954, ed. and trans. David N. Dumville (Basic texts for Brittonic history 1), Cambridge: Department of Anglo-Saxon, Norse and Celtic, University of Cambridge (2002).

Annals of Ireland, Three Fragments, copied from ancient sources by D. Mac Firbisigh, ed. with trans. and notes . . . by J. O'Donovan, Dublin (1860).

Annals of Ulster, to A.D. 1131, vol. 1: Text and translation, ed. Seán Mac Airt and Gearóid Mac Niocaill, Dublin: Dublin Institute for Advanced Studies (1983).

Blackburn, M. and Pagan, H. (1986) 'A revised check-list of coin-hoards from the British Isles, *c.* 500–1100', in M.A.S. Blackburn (ed.) *Anglo-Saxon Monetary History. Essays in Memory of M. Dolley*, Leicester: Leicester University Press.

Blake, N.F. (ed.) (1962) *The Saga of the Jomsvikings* (Icelandic texts 3), London: T. Nelson.

Boon, G.C. (1986) 'The armlet hoard', in *Welsh Coin Hoards*, Cardiff: National Museum of Wales.

Charles, B.G. (1934) *Old Norse Relations with Wales*, Cardiff: University of Wales Press.

Chron. Scot. = *Chronicle of the Scottish Nation by John of Fordun*, trans. F.J.H. Skene, ed. W.F. Skene (Historians of Scotland 4), Edinburgh: Paterson (1872).

Clancy, J.P. (trans.) (1970) *Armes Prydein*, in *The Earliest Welsh Poetry*, London: Macmillan.

Davies, M. (2002) 'Gruffudd ap Llywelyn. King of Wales', *The Welsh History Review*, 21: 207–48.

Davies, W. (1990) *Patterns of Power in Early Wales*, Oxford: Clarendon Press.

Duffy, S. (1995) 'Ostmen, Irish and Welsh in the eleventh century', *Peritia*, 9: 378–96.

Dumville, D.N. (2001) 'Ethnicity, politics, and settlement in Viking-Age Britain and Ireland'. (Paper read at the Viking-period Settlement in Britain and Ireland Conference, Cardiff, July 2001.)

Edwards, N. (1985) 'A possible Viking grave from Benllech, Anglesey', *Anglesey Antiquarian Society and Field Club Transactions*: 19–24.

—— (1999) 'Viking-influenced sculpture in north Wales: its ornament and context', *Church Archaeology*, 3: 5–16.

Evans, D.S. (1990) *A Medieval Prince of Wales. The Life of Gruffudd ap Cynan*, Llanerch: Llanerch Enterprises.

Fellows-Jensen, G. (1992) 'Scandinavian place-names of the Irish Sea province', in J. Graham-Campbell (ed.) *Viking Treasure from the North West. The Cuerdale Hoard and its Context* (National Museums and Galleries of Merseyside Occasional Papers 5), Liverpool Museum.

Garmonsway, G.N. (trans.) (1986) *The Anglo-Saxon Chronicle* (Everyman's Library), London: no publ.

Graham-Campbell, J. (1998) 'The early Viking age in the Irish Sea area', in H.B. Clarke, M. Ní Mhaonaigh and R. Ó Floinn (eds) *Ireland and Scandinavia in the Early Viking Age*, Dublin: Four Courts Press.

Griffiths, D. (2004) 'Settlement and acculturation in the Irish Sea region', in J. Hines, A. Lane and M. Redknap (eds) *Land, Sea and Home* (Society for Medieval Archaeology Monograph 20), Leeds: Maney.

Jesch, J. (1996) 'Norse historical traditions and the *Historia Gruffudd vab Kenan*: Magnús berfœttr and Haraldr Hárfagri', in K. Maund (ed.) *Gruffudd ap Cynan. A Collaborative Biography* (Studies in Celtic History 16), Woodbridge: Boydell Press.

—— (2000) 'From Scandinavia to the Wirral', in P. Cavill, S.E. Harding and J. Jesch, *Wirral and its Viking Heritage* (English Place-Name Society Popular Series 2), Nottingham: English Place-Name Society.

Jones, T. (trans.) (1952) *Brut y Tywysogyon or The Chronicle of the Princes. Peniarth MS. 20 Version* (Board of Celtic Studies. History and Law Series 11), Cardiff: University of Wales Press.

—— (trans.) (1971) *Brenhinedd y Saesson or The Kings of the Saxons, BM Cotton MS. Cleopatra Bv and the Black Book of Basingwerk NLW MS. 7006* (Board of Celtic Studies. History and Law Series 25), Cardiff: University of Wales Press.

Knight, J.K. (1984) 'Glamorgan A.D. 400–1100: archaeology and history', in H.N. Savory (ed.) *Glamorgan County History*, vol. 2: *Early Glamorgan*, Cardiff: W. Lewis.

—— (1996) 'Late Roman and post-Roman Caerwent: some evidence from metalwork', *Archaeologia Cambrensis*, 145: 35–66.

Lloyd, J.E. (1912) *A History of Wales from the Earliest Times to the Edwardian Conquest*, London: Longmans, Green *et co.*

Longley, D. (2001) 'Medieval settlement and landscape change on Anglesey', *Landscape History*, 23: 39–59.

Loyn, H.R. (1976) *The Vikings in Wales* (Dorothea Coke Memorial Lecture), London: Viking Society for Northern Research.

—— (1977) *The Vikings in Britain*, London: Batsford.

—— (1992) *Society and Peoples. Studies in the History of England and Wales c. 600–1200* (Westfield Publications in Medieval Studies 6), London: Queen Mary and Westfield College, Centre for Medieval Studies.

—— (1994) *The Vikings in Britain* (Historical Association Studies), Oxford: Blackwell.

Maund, K.L. (ed.) (1996) *Gruffudd ap Cynan. A Collaborative Biography* (Studies in Celtic History 16), Woodbridge: Boydell Press.

Moffatt, A.G. (1903) 'Palnatoki in Wales', *Saga Book*, 3(2): 163–73.

Nash-Williams, V.E. (1950) *The Early Christian Monuments of Wales*, Cardiff: University of Wales Press.

O'Donovan, J. (ed.) (1860) *Annals of Ireland. Three Fragments by Dubhaltach mac Firbisigh*, Dublin: no publ.

Paterson, D.R. (1921) 'Early Cardiff: with a short account of its street-names and surrounding place-names', *Report and Transactions from the Cardiff Naturalists' Society*, 54: 11–71.

Pierce, G.O. (1984) 'The evidence of place-names', Appendix II in G. Williams (ed.) *Glamorgan County History*, vol. 2, Cardiff: University of Wales Press.

Redknap, M. (2000) *Vikings in Wales. An Archaeological Quest*, Cardiff: National Museum of Wales.

—— (2004) 'Viking-age settlement in Wales and the evidence from Llanbedrgoch', in J. Hines, A. Lane and M. Redknap (eds) *Land, Sea and Home* (Society for Medieval Archaeology Monograph 20), Leeds: Maney.

Richards, M. (1962) 'Norse place-names in Wales', in B. Ó Cuív (ed.) *Proceedings of the First International Congress in Celtic Studies, Dublin, 6–10 July, 1959*, Dublin: Dublin Institute for Advanced Studies.

Russell, P. (ed. and trans.) (2005) *Vita Griffini filii Conani. The Medieval Latin Life of Gruffudd ap Cynan*, Cardiff: University of Wales Press.

Seaby, W.A. and Woodfield, P. (1980) 'Viking stirrups from England and their background', *Medieval Archaeology*, 24: 87–122.

Sheehan, J. (1998) 'Early Viking Age silver hoards from Ireland and their Scandinavian elements', in H.B. Clarke, M. Ní Mhaonaigh and R. Ó Floinn (eds) *Ireland and Scandinavia in the Early Viking Age*, Dublin: Four Courts Press.

—— (2004) 'Social and economic integration in Viking-age Ireland: the evidence of the hoards', in J. Hines, A. Lane and M. Redknap (eds) *Land, Sea and Home* (Society for Medieval Archaeology Monograph 20), Leeds: Maney.

Smith, F.G. (1931–2) 'Talacre and the Viking grave', *Proceedings of the Llandudno, Colwyn Bay and District Field Club* 17: 42–50.

Wade-Evans, A.W. (trans.) (1944) *Vitae Sanctorum Britanniae et Genealogiae*, Cardiff: University of Wales Press.

Wainwright, F.T. (1948) 'Ingimund's invasion', *English Historical Review*, 63: 145–69.

Williams, I. (1945) 'Recent finds in Anglesey: Benllech', *Anglesey Antiquarian Society and Field Club Transactions*: 21–3.

Wilson, D.M. (1995) 'Scandinavian ornamental influence in the Irish Sea region in the Viking Age', in T. Scott and P. Starkey (eds) *The Middle Ages in the North West*, Oxford: Leopard's Head Press.

CHAPTER THIRTY

THE NORSE IN SCOTLAND

—·◆·—

James H. Barrett

The long-term Scandinavian influence on what is now Scotland was considerable. Scandinavian place names blanket the Northern Isles of Shetland and Orkney and are part of the onomasticon across the northern and western mainland, the Hebrides and as far south as the islands of the Firth of Clyde (Nicolaisen 1982; Jennings 1996; Gammeltoft 2005). A Scandinavian dialect, *Norn*, continued to be spoken in the Northern Isles into the eighteenth century (Barnes 1998). In the political sphere, much of western Scotland remained under at least nominal Scandinavian rule until the Treaty of Perth in 1266 (Cowan 1990) and Orkney and Shetland were only transferred to Scottish authority in 1468 and 1469 respectively (Crawford 1969). Genetically, this long period of interaction has led to a modern population in northern and western Scotland with Scandinavian ancestry in both the female and male lines (Goodacre *et al.* 2005). In the Northern Isles, the proportion of Scandinavian female ancestry may approximate that of the modern Icelanders.

Moving back in time, the greatest challenges to the expansion of the Scottish kingdom in the twelfth century were posed by independent petty kings and warlords of Norse ancestry such as Harald Maddadarson, earl of Orkney, and Somerled of Argyll (McDonald 2003). Earlier still, it has been argued that Scandinavian raiding and settlement in the ninth century played an important – if ambiguous – role in the emergence of a united kingdom of Alba (later Scotland) from the harassed remnants of the kingdoms of Dál Riata (in Argyll), Pictland (in eastern and northern Scotland) and Strathclyde (in the south-west) (Broun 1994; Driscoll 1998; Crawford 2000; Woolf 2004).

The need to understand this Scandinavian impact has been felt by the historically inclined in both the past and the present. In twelfth- and thirteenth-century Norway and Iceland, for example, it formed a significant theme in texts such as the Latin *Historia Norwegie* (written in Norway in the second half of the twelfth century) and the Old Norse *Orkneyinga saga* (written in Iceland *c.* 1200 and updated in the thirteenth century) (Finnbogi Guðmundsson ed. 1965; Ekrem and Boje Mortensen 2003). Their authors had broadly historical intent, but worked with source material of highly variable historicity (e.g. Jesch 1996). With minor caveats, these texts describe a largely Scandinavian world in the Northern and Western Isles – in terms of language, culture and politics. *Historia Norwegie* provides the classic and much cited example (Ekrem and Boje Mortensen 2003: 65–7):

> the Pents, only a little taller than pygmies, accomplished miraculous achievements by building towns, morning and evening, but at midday every ounce of strength deserted them and they hid for fear in underground chambers ... In the days of Harald Fairhair, king of Norway, certain vikings, descended from the stock of that sturdiest of men, Ragnvaldr jarl, crossing the Solund Sea with a large fleet, totally destroyed these people after stripping them of their long-established dwellings and made the islands subject to themselves.

Thus by the late twelfth century the Picts – the pre-Scandinavian cultural, linguistic and political group of northern Scotland (including at least the north mainland, Orkney and Shetland, and possibly the Outer Hebrides) – had faded into folklore, having been replaced by (real or fictional) migrants of Norwegian ancestry. *Orkneyinga saga* and other sources provide a slightly different rendition of the story, attributing the colonisation of the Northern Isles to Harald Fairhair himself, who then gifted them to members of the dynasty of the earls of Møre (Finnbogi Guðmundsson ed. 1965: 7–8). Otherwise, however, the two traditions are much the same.

These twelfth- and thirteenth-century sources thus provide a destination that an informed discussion of earlier, Viking Age, developments in Scotland must reach (Owen 2004: 6). By this date a self-consciously Scandinavian elite existed in northern and western (hereafter Atlantic) Scotland who were recognisable as part of a wider North Atlantic culture by their peers in Norway and Iceland.

The difficult questions, however, are the degree to which these sources can be extrapolated back in time and to which they relate to society beyond the elite. The danger of extrapolation is well recognised within the scholarly literature. Nevertheless, it is common in discussions of Viking Age Scotland for elements of these high medieval sources to be accepted as factual – despite heavy qualifications regarding their historicity (e.g. Hunter 1997; Crawford 2004; Forte *et al.* 2005). Two assumptions inherent in the twelfth–thirteenth-century sources are particularly resilient: that an earldom of Orkney was founded in the years around AD 900 (be it by Harald Fairhair or another) and that it was then ruled by a single dynasty (albeit not without internecine strife) into the lifetime of the medieval author in question.

Without corroboration these assumptions are potentially dangerous, leading to the need to tell history forwards as well as backwards. Fortunately this can be attempted by combining archaeological evidence (from settlements, graves and hoards) with the very limited contemporary historical evidence from annalistic sources – preferring the latter's laconic precision over the evocative anachronisms of later narrative sources. One can also make cautious use of skaldic poetry of probable early date incorporated into the twelfth- and thirteenth-century texts – using it as independent source material in much the same way as the medieval historiographers themselves.

This optimism must be tempered, however, with the observation that such attempts have led to widely divergent reconstructions of Viking Age Scotland (see Barrett 2004 and below). To oversimplify for brevity, these can be said to vary largely in the degree to which they assume continuity or discontinuity from pre-Viking to Viking times and thus in their interpretations of the nature of culture contact. Specific models will be discussed below, but to introduce the problem it is worth reviewing why it is that such different interpretations can be founded on the same evidence. Beyond the inevitable influence of a scholar's point of view, this problem emerges from a combination of semantics, superficially conflicting source material and poor chronological resolution. Each needs to be treated briefly in turn.

The semantic issue is a simple but critical matter of definition. It is often unclear whether the terms *Viking* and *Scandinavian* are used to refer to people or things (Barrett 2004). Within each category, the intended meaning also differs and is seldom made explicit. If people, is one discussing biological ancestry, speech community, ethnicity or simply those who lived in the Viking Age (variously defined)? If things, is one considering objects of Scandinavian manufacture, of Scandinavian style or of Viking Age date? These distinctions are non-trivial. For example, biological ancestry and ethnicity are of course not the same thing – despite dangerous assumptions to the contrary in various times and places in human history (Wolf 1994).

By 'superficially conflicting evidence' I refer to sources that seem to imply divergent interpretations when of course they must ultimately be reconcilable – either by accepting that they represent different voices from the past (groups of differing status for example) or by clarifying their divergent chronologies or degrees of historicity. The examples are too extensive to review in full, but a few will serve to illustrate the problem. Broadly speaking, they will be considered in reverse chronological order and from north to south.

One can begin with DNA evidence regarding the genetic ancestry of *modern* populations in different regions of Scotland. It implies considerable continuity of the indigenous female and male populations of these regions (albeit greater in northern and western mainland Scotland and the Hebrides than in the Northern Isles) (Helgason *et al.* 2001; Wilson *et al.* 2001; Goodacre *et al.* 2005). Superficially interpreted, this pattern could be mapped onto the Viking Age and read as evidence for considerable continuity of the indigenous population, greater in the west than in the north. Although possible, this result also reflects long-term processes such as the migration of Gaelic-speakers into the Hebrides later in the Middle Ages and the long duration of Scandinavian influence and rule in the Northern Isles (Goodacre *et al.* 2005). (Stable isotope analysis of teeth from Viking Age burials may ultimately illuminate the issue of migration with greater chronological precision, e.g. Montgomery *et al.* 2003.)

Turning to the evidence for Scandinavian place names, it is so extensive that in contrast with the genetic results it has led to the suggestion that the pre-Norse inhabitants of Atlantic Scotland were completely replaced by Norse migrants (see below). The place-name record of the Northern Isles and Outer Hebrides lacks any (or virtually any) evidence of pre-Norse onomastic survivals (Gammeltoft 2005; Jennings and Kruse 2005). The situation in the southern Hebrides is more complex, but Norse topographic names are nevertheless common as far south as the islands of the Firth of Clyde (Jennings 1996). Like the modern genetic evidence, however, the source material for the onomastic record is much later than the Viking Age – Scotland has no equivalent to the eleventh-century Domesday survey of England (see Gammeltoft 2000). The place names may thus reflect the duration of Scandinavian influence rather than its character in the ninth and tenth centuries.

Moving to archaeological evidence for Norse settlements (Figure 30.1), a number of excavated sites from the Northern Isles have produced late Viking Age and medieval

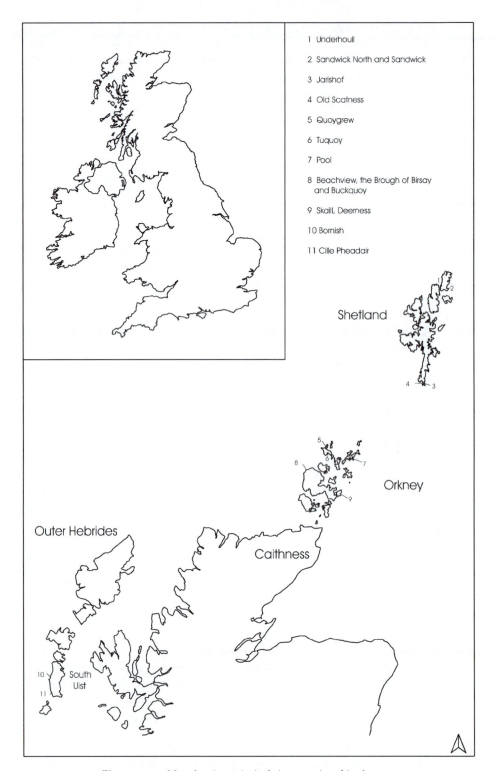

1 Underhoull

2 Sandwick North and Sandwick

3 Jarlshof

4 Old Scatness

5 Quoygrew

6 Tuquoy

7 Pool

8 Beachview, the Brough of Birsay
   and Buckquoy

9 Skaill, Deerness

10 Bornish

11 Cille Pheadair

Shetland

Orkney

Outer Hebrides

Caithness

South
Uist

Figure 30.1 Map showing principal sites mentioned in the text.

(i.e. post-Viking Age) longhouse architecture of North Atlantic type associated with portable material culture imported from Norway or influenced by Scandinavian styles. These settlements show little or no affinity with local pre-Viking Age precursors. In Shetland they include Underhoull (Small 1966; Stummann Hansen 2000: 89), Sandwick North (Stummann Hansen 2000), Sandwick (Bigelow 1987) and the later phases of Jarlshof (Hamilton 1956). In Orkney, they are Tuquoy (Owen 1993, 2005), Quoygrew (Barrett 2005; Barrett *et al.* 2005; see below), Beachview (Morris 1996a), and the later phases of Pool (Hunter *et al.* 1993), Skaill Deerness (Buteux 1997) and the Brough of Birsay (Curle 1982; Hunter 1986; Morris 1996a).

To elaborate on one example, Phase 2 at Quoygrew included a modest 'fisherman's house' of eleventh–twelfth-century date with unambiguous Scandinavian associations (Figure 30.2). It was between 7 m and 10 m long (its western end remains under the wall of a consolidated later building) and 4 m wide internally with low side aisles or 'benches' flanking each wall. The long walls and eastern gable, all slightly bowed, were composed of a dry-stone inner face and an informal outer face suggestive of mixed stone and turf construction. The portable material culture in this house was remarkable given its 'Scottish' location. It included hones of Eidsborg schist from Norway (G. Gaunt pers. comm.), shards of hemispherical soapstone vessels probably from Norway (C. Batey pers. comm.), a broken whalebone weaving batten of Norwegian type and several antler combs of types made in Norwegian towns at this date (e.g. Flodin 1989; S. Ashby pers. comm.). The house contained only a single shard of coarse pottery, the most ubiquitous find in pre-Viking Age indigenous settlements (e.g. Ross 1994) and in eleventh–twelfth-century sites in mainland Scotland (e.g. Hall 2001). The fishing associations of the building are made clear by an extensive fish midden that surrounds it (Barrett 2005; Simpson *et al.* 2005) and finds of a fishhook and probable boat anchor.

The story of medieval settlement in western Scotland is slightly more complex. Tenth- and eleventh-century longhouses with bowed walls and Scandinavian material culture have recently been excavated at Bornish on South Uist (Sharples 2004). However, other buildings of slightly later date at Bornish and Cille Pheadair (also on South Uist) seem to have developed as a distinctive regional tradition (Sharples and Parker Pearson 1999; Parker Pearson *et al.* 2004b). Moreover, ceramics continued to be used in the Outer Hebrides throughout the Viking Age and Middle Ages, albeit in different styles from their pre-Viking predecessors (Lane 1990; Campbell 2002). Yet further south, settlement of demonstrably Scandinavian style of any date in Argyll has not yet been found (e.g. Brown 1997). It must be noted, however, that there may have been some Scandinavian influence on the royal dynasty of Strathclyde in the tenth and eleventh centuries based on the hogback monuments known from the kingdom's ecclesiastical centre at Govan (Driscoll 1998).

Late Viking Age and medieval settlements from the Northern Isles may thus imply that Shetlandic and Orcadian society was explicitly 'Norse' in the tenth to twelfth centuries – insofar as material culture is related to identity (Jones 1997; Barrett 2003). Quoygrew and other sites like it are particularly noteworthy because they demonstrate that this observation holds true for individuals of modest or even low status in addition to the elite for whom manuscript sources were probably produced. In the Western Isles and mainland Argyll the situation may have been more complex. Here, however, one is assisted by a better record in the contemporary Irish historical sources which imply much involvement in the increasingly Hiberno-Norse world of the Irish Sea province to

Figure 30.2 Structure 5 at Quoygrew, Orkney, looking west. Most of the artefacts from this stone and turf longhouse of eleventh- to twelfth-century date were probably Norwegian imports. The edge-set stones along the north wall demarcate a partially dismantled side aisle or bench, a completely removed example of which also lined the south wall. The house underlies a later thirteenth-century building retained *in situ* for public display.

the west – and in the expansion of Alba (united Dál Riata and Pictland) to the east (Etchingham 2001; Woolf 2004).

Moving backwards in time, Scotland's *c.* 34 Viking Age silver hoards and *c.* 130 'pagan' graves (defined as Viking Age burials with grave goods) are also characteristically Scandinavian (Graham-Campbell 1995; Graham-Campbell and Batey 1998: 113–54; Owen and Dalland 1999; Paterson 2001; see Figure 30.3). The hoards were deposited between the 930s and 1060s, superseding the graves which are all datable to a window between *c.* 850 and *c.* 950. The hoards contain possible 'colonial' elements such as ring money – plain penannular rings which probably have their origin in the migrant Scandinavian communities of Scotland (Warner 1976; Graham-Campbell 1995) – but

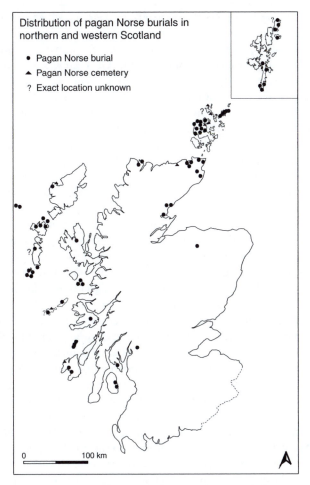

Figure 30.3 Distribution of Scottish Viking Age burials including grave goods.
(T. Simpson after Graham-Campbell and Batey 1998: fig. 7.1).

are otherwise characteristic of the wider Viking world (cf. Graham-Campbell 1995; Hårdh 1996). The burial rite has its closest parallels in Norway (and Scandinavian burials in Ireland) and many of the grave goods were probably manufactured in Scandinavia. Some of the men buried in these graves also had a highly marine diet, a characteristic of Norway rather than Scotland prior to the Viking Age (Barrett and Richards 2004 and references therein). Unlike the settlement evidence, these graves and hoards differ less between the Northern Isles, the Western Isles and Argyll. Nevertheless, they do continue to show some regional diversity (e.g. Bornholdt-Collins 2003).

Thus far, the evidence of the late place-names, the tenth–twelfth-century settlements, the tenth–eleventh-century hoards and the ninth–tenth-century pagan graves could all be read as indicative of a society that was predominately or entirely based on the use of Norse language and material culture – despite regional variability and considerable indigenous ancestry as implied by genetic research. However, interpretation becomes more complex when one considers the early Viking Age settlements. Several sites have been interpreted as producing a mixture of indigenous cellular and Scandinavian longhouse architecture and/or both indigenous and Scandinavian portable artefacts. The 'type site' for this argument is Buckquoy in Orkney, where combs and pins of indigenous style (i.e. with local pre-Viking Age parallels) were recovered from rectangular houses under a mid-tenth-century pagan grave (Ritchie 1974, 1977; Brundle *et al.* 2003; Thäte forthcoming). However, the co-occurrence of indigenous and Scandinavian material culture (in the form of objects and/or architecture) early in the Viking Age has also been argued at three other sites in Orkney (the Brough of Birsay, Pool and Skaill Deerness) and at Old Scatness in Shetland (Curle 1982; Hunter *et al.* 1993; Buteux 1997; Forster *et al.* 2004; Turner *et al.* 2005). Moving to the Outer Hebrides, one must note the added complication of continued pottery production (rather than a switch to soapstone vessels) in the Viking Age (Lane 1990; Campbell 2002) and some continuity in architectural methods (the building of semi-subterranean houses revetted into sand) (Sharples and Parker Pearson 1999; Owen 2002). Further south in Argyll, one can note the present lack of characteristically Scandinavian settlement of any date and the likelihood of continued occupation of indigenous sites such as Iona (as a monastery and perhaps royal burial ground) and Dunadd (as an elite centre) (Jennings 1998; Lane and Campbell 2000).

The discrepancies evident in most of the categories of evidence surveyed above are largely matters of chronology and regional diversity. The geographical issue is one of unsurprising divergence between the Northern Isles, the Western Isles and Argyll. In terms of chronology, the place-name, tenth- to thirteenth-century settlement and hoard evidence (and in other ways the genetic data) all post-date the early Viking Age settlement evidence. The same may not apply, however, to the burial evidence, which raises the last main reason for the existence of widely divergent interpretations of Viking Age Scotland – poor chronological resolution. Although the pagan graves have now been carefully studied and relatively tightly dated (Graham-Campbell and Batey 1998: 152–4), Viking Age settlements in Scotland can only be assigned the broadest of date ranges (see Barrett 2003: 82–8). We therefore cannot tell whether or not settlements with 'mixed' indigenous and Scandinavian assemblages predate or are contemporary with Scotland's pagan graves – or even if the different elements of the 'mixed' assemblages were really used at the same time. Moreover, we do not know whether 'unmixed' late Pictish settlements preceded sites with Scandinavian material culture or were contemporary with them. Similar problems exist regarding the question of whether Christian and pagan practice were contemporary or sequential in the ninth and tenth centuries – a complex topic which is also clearly important to the question of Scandinavian impact in Scotland (Morris 1996b; Dumville 1997; Barrett 2002; Crawford 2002).

These issues arise for a variety of reasons. Early Viking Age settlements at the Brough of Birsay and Skaill both lack convincing stratigraphy – due to antiquarian methods in the former case and the unfortunate premature death of the excavator in the latter case (Curle 1982; Buteux 1997). Another important site, Buckquoy, lacks radiocarbon dates and there is some debate regarding whether the (only partially preserved) rectangular buildings in its latest phase are actually of Scandinavian style (cf. Graham-Campbell and Batey 1998: 160–4; Brundle *et al.* 2003). These three settlements – plus Pool and Old Scatness also noted above – are also multi-period, sometimes making it difficult to ascertain which finds are contemporary and which are mixed from earlier or later layers. Finally, radiocarbon and other scientific dating methods usable in Atlantic Scotland – for settlements, ecclesiastical sites and burials without grave goods – typically produce error ranges of between one and three centuries (unlike the dendrochronological dates available elsewhere in the Viking world). Ongoing work regarding Old Scatness is attempting to resolve this last problem by using multiple stratified dates and Bayesian statistics (Dockrill and Batt 2004), but this approach cannot be applied retrospectively to sites such as the Brough of Birsay.

A related problem is establishing when one might *expect* to find the first Scandinavian settlement in Scotland. It was once assumed to have begun *c.* 800 (e.g. Hamilton 1956) based on the date of the earliest raids in the North and Irish Seas – and the assumption that these raids were launched from bases in Atlantic Scotland (cf. Morris 1998: 74; Ó Corráin 1998a; Sawyer 2003). However, early ninth-century settlement has been questioned by those who would argue for both earlier (Myhre 1993) and later (Graham-Campbell 1998: 106; Barrett 2003; Parker Pearson *et al.* 2004a: 129) alternatives. An early, pre-ninth-century, option is conceivable if envisioned as a period of trade and contact rather than migration and settlement (see below). A late, mid-ninth-century, option is favoured by the present author. It is only at this time that the historical and archaeological records provide explicit evidence for settlement rather than raiding in Scotland and it is also the period when Scandinavian warbands first began to overwinter elsewhere in the west – such as Ireland and England (see Barrett 2003 and references within). (An even later, mid-tenth-century, option has been proposed by Parker Pearson *et al.* 2004a: 129, but is inconsistent with the historical, burial and settlement evidence.) Clearly the contemporaneity of indigenous and Scandinavian material culture in Atlantic Scotland will depend on which of these interpretations is correct.

In sum, it is evident that one's interpretation of Viking Age Scotland will be dependent on which of the above bodies of evidence are favoured and what assumptions are made regarding chronology. The potential combinations are legion, but most published discussions can be categorised into one or more of four broad theories:

- The genocide hypothesis
- The *Laithlind* hypothesis
- The Myhre (or pagan reaction) hypothesis
- The earldom hypothesis

Not all of these alternatives are equally plausible, but insofar as each has been given credence in the published scholarly literature they will be discussed in turn.

The least credible (if nevertheless tenacious) option is the genocide hypothesis – which suggests that the indigenous populations of the Northern and Western Isles were eradicated by Scandinavian migrants (e.g. Crawford 1981; Smith 2001, 2003; Jennings and Kruse 2005). It is typically espoused by those who place most weight on the onomastic evidence, given the (virtual) absence of recognisable Pictish place names in the Northern Isles and of demonstrably pre-Norse Pictish or Gaelic place names in the Western Isles (Jennings and Kruse 2005: 284). This observation – sometimes in combination with ethnographic analogy citing tragedies such as the European extermination of the Tasmanians (e.g. Smith 2001, 2003) – is explicitly or implicitly interpreted as an indication of both language death *and* biological death in the early Viking Age. The problem with this hypothesis is straightforward. As noted above, the onomastic evidence is mostly very late and thus illuminates the end result of a lengthy process rather than events in (for the sake of argument) the ninth century. Languages can die over time, typically due to the adoption of a higher-prestige alternative by their former speakers (Dorian 1981).

The *Laithlind* hypothesis is almost equally improbable. It argues that *Laithlind* (variously spelled) of the Irish annals – from which the early royal dynasty of Dublin came – was a Viking kingdom in Atlantic Scotland which was fully established by the 840s and probably had its centre in Orkney (Ó Corráin 1998a; Sawyer 2003: 31). This is a departure from the traditional interpretation that *Laithlind* and related terms referred to Norway – which they clearly did by 1058 (Etchingham 2001: 153).

There are three problems with this hypothesis. The first is that its historical basis is controversial (e.g. Etchingham 2001: 153). More definitive, however, is the observation noted above that there is no independent historical or archaeological evidence that Scandinavian settlement occurred in Atlantic Scotland any earlier than in Ireland (Barrett 2003). Lastly, archaeology has provided a clear picture of the material correlates of royal and chiefly power in Viking Age Scandinavia. These include ship (rather than boat) burials, very large feasting halls and landscapes of power incorporating major earthworks (see elsewhere in this volume). None of these exist in Atlantic Scotland, even in nascent form.

An alternative hypothesis, speculatively raised by Bjørn Myhre (1993, 1998), has been both influential and controversial (cf. Solli 1996; Morris 1998: 91; Ambrosiani 1998: 411–14; Owen 2004: 22). It assumes a long tradition of Scandinavian, Gaelic (i.e. Irish or Gaelic Scottish) and Pictish mobility in the North Atlantic followed by crystallisation of ethnic tension and expression in the early Viking Age (variously defined) due to 'Christian' expansionism around the North Sea (Myhre 1993). In other words, some Scandinavian migrants were present in Scotland before the Viking Age, but were not making a point of signalling their identity with material culture. Following Barth's (1969, 1994) widely adopted interpretations of ethnicity, Myhre suggested that this only became necessary at a time of political and ethnic tension.

The four main arguments behind this hypothesis included: possible early pagan graves in Atlantic Scotland, early insular objects in Norwegian graves, possible evidence for pre-Viking Age settlement in the Faroe Islands and/or Iceland and combs from Orkney made in indigenous styles that were arguably of reindeer antler (and thus imported from Scandinavia). The first of these arguments has since been shown to be incorrect (Graham-Campbell and Batey 1998: 152–4) and the second is better interpreted as evidence of Viking Age raids on monastic treasuries containing centuries of accumulated wealth (Ó Corráin 1998b: 433; Wamers 1998: 42–51; Gaut 2002). The third argument, that there is evidence for pre-Viking Age settlement elsewhere in the North Atlantic, may now be corroborated in the Faeroe Islands based on new palynological evidence (Hannon *et al.* 2005; Prof. K. Edwards, Univ. of Aberdeen, pers. comm.).

Myhre's fourth argument – the 'Pictish' combs made of reindeer antler – has not been widely accepted due to scepticism regarding whether (native) red deer and (imported) reindeer antler can be distinguished when worked (e.g. Graham-Campbell and Batey 1998: 23; Smith 1998: 131; Owen 2004: 26). This problem was exacerbated by the fact that although the identifications were made by a very experienced Norwegian zooarchaeologist, Rolf Lie, an explicit methodology was not published along with the identifications (Weber 1992, 1993, 1994; Ballin Smith 1995) and that they had thus not been replicated. (The methodology for identifying worked reindeer antler has been replicated in the Bergen laboratory by Anne Karin Hufthammer, but this research was on Norwegian combs of Scandinavian style rather than Scottish combs of indigenous style; A.K. Hufthammer pers. comm.).

Recently, however, Ashby (2006) – building on Lie's work and analogous research in Novgorod by Smirnova (2005) – has studied worked antler identification in detail. His research corroborates many of the original attributions. Some combs of indigenous style found in Orkney have a high probability of being made from reindeer antler imported from Scandinavia (Figure 30.4). What Ashby has also observed, however, is that none of these combs demonstrably precedes the Viking Age. The earliest combs previously alleged to be of reindeer antler (including middle and late Iron Age examples from Howe, see Ballin Smith 1994: 177–8; 1995) he considers to be too poorly preserved for definitive identification and one is almost certainly made of red deer. Thus his research both supports and undermines the Myhre hypothesis, which probably cannot be accepted in its original form.

The earldom hypothesis is the most traditional of the four considered. It can be summarised as follows: a period of early ninth-century trade, migration and acculturation was followed by the creation of an earldom of Orkney in the late ninth

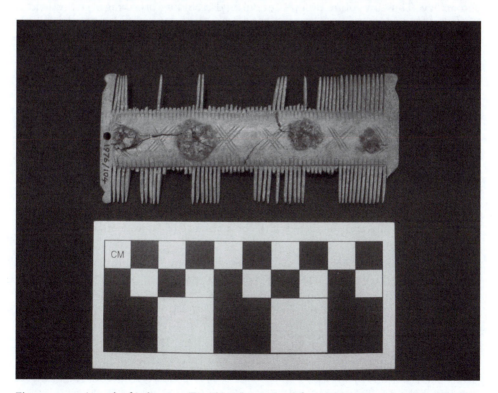

Figure 30.4 A comb of indigenous 'Pictish' style recovered from settlement predating a mid-tenth-century pagan grave at Buckquoy, Orkney. It is probably made of reindeer antler imported from Norway despite past scepticism regarding this suggestion (Ashby 2006).

~~or early tenth century~~ – which some assume dominated western Scotland and the Isle of Man as well as northern Scotland into the eleventh century (see Etchingham 2001 for a refutation of the evidence for lengthy Orcadian dominance of Man and the Hebrides in the tenth and eleventh centuries). The earldom then continued under the rule of a single dynasty until well into the Middle Ages (e.g. Morris 1985, 1998; Buteux 1997; Hunter 1997; Owen 2004; Crawford 2004; Helle 2005). In this vision of the past, the perspectives of *Historia Norwegie* and *Orkneyinga saga* survive largely intact. However, they are augmented by the possible evidence for mixed material culture at early Viking Age settlements such as Buckquoy, Pool, the Brough of Birsay and Old Scatness.

The potential weaknesses of this model are that it extrapolates from late sources, it *assumes* the existence of an earldom of Orkney before the eleventh century (the earliest unambiguous reference being to the death of Earl Sigurd of Orkney at the battle of Clontarf in Ireland in 1014; MacAirt and MacNiocaill 1983) and it derives its chronology largely from its theory. In other words, it assumes rather than demonstrates a gradual sequence from mixed (indigenous and Norse) to exclusively Scandinavian material culture (see Barrett 2003, 2004). This progression has not been demonstrated because of the issues clouding chronological resolution discussed above.

In sum, all of these hypotheses remain unproven. Nevertheless, the genocide and *Laithlind* hypotheses are arguably the least probable, leaving the Myhre and earldom models for further consideration. Both are problematic due to uncertainties over chronology. Thus any future progress in our understanding of Viking Age Scotland is likely to hinge on a better understanding of time – be it by stratigraphic excavation of early Viking Age settlements, further typological study of poorly stratified collections, improved archaeometric dating or a combination of all these approaches. While the quality of the available evidence can be improved in these ways, the issues must also be clearly theorised – with due attention to what one means by the Norse in Scotland.

ACKNOWLEDGEMENTS

I thank Stefan Brink and Neil Price for the invitation to contribute to this volume and for their patience as editors. The paper benefited from discussions and correspondence with Steve Ashby, Kristin Bornholdt-Collins, Anne Brundle, Colman Etchingham, Peder Gammeltoft and Eva Thäte – some of whom have kindly allowed me to cite their forthcoming work. Excavations at Quoygrew in Orkney were principally funded by Historic Scotland and conducted with the assistance of James Gerrard and Jennifer Harland.

BIBLIOGRAPHY

Ambrosiani, B. (1998) 'Ireland and Scandinavia in the early Viking Age: an archaeological response', in H. Clarke, M. Ní Mhaonaigh and R. Ó Floinn (eds) *Ireland and Scandinavia in the Early Viking Age*, Dublin: Four Courts Press.

Ashby, S. (2006) 'Time, trade and identity: bone and antler combs in early medieval northern Britain'. (Unpubl. PhD thesis, University of York.)

Ballin Smith, B. (ed.) (1994) *Howe: Four millennia of Orkney prehistory* (Society of Antiquaries of Scotland Monograph Series 9), Edinburgh: Society of Antiquaries of Scotland.

—— (1995) 'Reindeer antler combs at Howe: contact between late Iron Age Orkney and Norway', *Universitetets Oldsaksamling. Årbok*, (1993–4): 207–11.

Barnes, M.P. (1998) *The Norn Language of Orkney and Shetland*, Lerwick: Shetland Times.

Barrett, J.H. (2002) 'Christian and pagan practice during the conversion of Viking Age Orkney and Shetland', in M. Carver (ed.) *The Cross Goes North*, Woodbridge: Boydell Press.

—— (2003) 'Culture contact in Viking Age Scotland', in J.H. Barrett (ed.) *Contact, Continuity and Collapse. The Norse Colonization of the North Atlantic* (Studies in the Early Middle Ages 5), Turnhout: Brepols.

—— (2004) 'Beyond war or peace: the study of culture contact in Viking-age Scotland', in J. Hines *et al.* (eds) 2004.

—— (2005) 'Economic intensification in Viking Age and medieval Orkney, Scotland: excavations at Quoygrew', in A. Mortensen and S.V. Arge (eds) 2005.

Barrett, J., Gerrard, J. and Harland, J. (2005) 'Farming and fishing on medieval Westray', *Current Archaeology*, 199: 336–41.

Barrett, J.H. and Richards, M.P. (2004) 'Identity, gender, religion and economy: new isotope and radiocarbon evidence for marine resource intensification in early historic Orkney, Scotland', *European Journal of Archaeology*, 7: 249–71.

Barth, F. (ed.) (1969) *Ethnic Groups and Boundaries. The Social Organization of Culture Difference*, Boston: Little, Brown and Company.

—— (1994) 'Enduring and emerging issues in the analysis of ethnicity', in H. Vermeulen and C. Govers (eds) *The Anthropology of Ethnicity. Beyond 'Ethnic Groups and Boundaries'*, Amsterdam: Het Spinhuis.

Bigelow, G.F. (1987) 'Domestic architecture in medieval Shetland', *Review of Scottish Culture*, 3: 23–38.

Bornholdt-Collins, K.A. (2003) 'Viking-Age coin finds from the Isle of Man: a study of coin circulation, production and concepts of wealth'. (Unpubl. PhD thesis, University of Cambridge.)

Broun, D. (1994) 'The origin of Scottish identity in its European context', in B.E. Crawford (ed.) *Scotland in Dark Age Europe*, St Andrews: The Committee for Dark Age Studies, University of St Andrews.

Brown, M.M. (1997) 'The Norse in Argyll', in G. Ritchie (ed.) *The Archaeology of Argyll*, Edinburgh: Edinburgh University Press.

Brundle, A., Lorimer, D.H. and Ritchie, A. (2003) 'Buckquoy revisited', in J. Downes and A. Ritchie (eds) *Sea Change. Orkney and Northern Europe in the Later Iron Age AD 300–800*, Balgavies, Angus: The Pinkfoot Press.

Buteux, S. (ed.) (1997) *Settlements at Skaill, Deerness, Orkney* (British Archaeological Reports. British Series 260), Oxford: BAR.

Campbell, E. (2002) 'The Western Isles pottery sequence', in B. Ballin Smith and I. Banks (eds) *In the Shadow of the Brochs*, Stroud: Tempus.

Cowan, I. (1990) 'Norwegian sunset – Scottish dawn, Hakon IV and Alexander III', in N. Reid (ed.) *Scotland in the Reign of Alexander III*, Edinburgh: John Donald.

Crawford, B.E. (1969) 'The pawning of Orkney and Shetland: a reconsideration of events of 1460–9', *The Scottish Historical Review*, 48: 35–53.

—— (2000) 'The Scandinavian contribution to the development of the kingdom of Scotland', *Acta Archaeologica*, 71: 123–34.

—— (ed.) (2002) *The Papar in the North Atlantic: Environment and History* (St John's House Papers No. 10), St. Andrews: University of St Andrews.

—— (2004) 'Earldom strategies in north Scotland', in G. Williams and P. Bibire (eds) *Sagas, Saints and Settlements*, Leiden: Brill.

Crawford, I.A. (1981) 'War or peace: Viking colonization in the Northern and Western Isles of Scotland reviewed', in H. Bekker-Nielsen, P. Foote and O. Olsen (eds) *Proceedings of the Eighth Viking Congress*, Odense: Odense University Press.

Curle, C.L. (1982) *Pictish and Norse Finds from the Brough of Birsay 1934–74* (Society of Antiquaries of Scotland Monograph Series Number 1), Edinburgh: Society of Antiquaries of Scotland.

Dockrill, S.J. and Batt, C.M. (2004) 'Power over time: an overview of the Old Scatness Broch excavations', in R.A. Housley and G. Coles (eds) *Atlantic Connections and Adaptations. Economies, Environments and Subsistence in Lands Bordering the North Atlantic*, Oxford: Oxbow Books.

Dorian, N.C. (1981) *Language Death*, Philadelphia: University of Pennsylvania Press.

Driscoll, S.T. (1998) 'Church archaeology in Glasgow and the kingdom of Strathclyde', *The Innes Review*, 49: 95–114.

Dumville, D.N. (1997) *The Churches of North Britain in the First Viking Age* (5th Whithorn Lecture), Whithorn: Whithorn Trust.

Ekrem, I. and Boje Mortensen, L. (eds) (2003) *Historia Norwegie*, Copenhagen: Museum Tusculanum Press, University of Copenhagen.

Etchingham, C. (2001) 'North Wales, Ireland and the Isles: the Insular Viking zone', *Peritia*, 15: 145–87.

Finnbogi Guðmundsson (ed.) (1965) *Orkneyinga Saga* (Íslenzk fornrit 34), Reykjavík: Hið íslenzka fornritafélag.

Flodin, L. (1989) *Kammakeriet i Trondheim*, Trondheim: Riksantikvaren, Utgravningskontoret for Trondheim.

Forster, A.K., Thomas, J. and Dockrill, S.J. (2004) 'Spatial analysis and cultural indicators: Viking settlers at Old Scatness Broch, Shetland?', in J. Hines *et al.* (eds) 2004.

Forte, A., Oram, R. and Pedersen, F. (2005) *Viking Empires*, Cambridge: Cambridge University Press.

Gammeltoft, P. (2000) 'Why the difference? An attempt to account for the variations in the phonetic development of place-names in Old Norse *bólstaðr* in the Hebrides', *Nomina*, 23: 107–19.

—— (2005) ' "Look now stranger at this island". A brief survey of the island-names of Shetland and Orkney', in A. Mortensen and S.V. Arge (eds) 2005.

Gaut, B. (2002) 'Britain and Western Scandinavia in the Vendel period, *c.*570–*c.*800: the evidence of artefacts'. (Unpubl. thesis, University of York.)

Goodacre, S., Helgason, A., Nicholson, J., Southam, L., Ferguson, L., Hickey, E., Vega, E., Stefánsson, K., Ward, R. and Sykes, B. (2005) 'Genetic evidence for a family-based Scandinavian settlement of Shetland and Orkney during the Viking periods', *Heredity*, 95: 129–35.

Graham-Campbell, J. (1995) *The Viking-Age gold and silver of Scotland*, Edinburgh: National Museums of Scotland.

—— (1998) 'The early Viking Age in the Irish Sea area', in H. Clarke, M. Ní Mhaonaigh and R. Ó Floinn (eds) *Ireland and Scandinavia in the Early Viking Age*, Dublin: Four Courts Press.

Graham-Campbell, J. and Batey, C.E. (1998) *Vikings in Scotland: an archaeological survey*, Edinburgh: Edinburgh University Press.

Hall, D.W. (2001) 'Pottery from excavations at Robert's Haven, Caithness.' (Unpubl. report, SUAT Ltd.)

Hamilton, J.R.C. (1956) *Excavations at Jarlshof*, Edinburgh: HMSO.

Hannon, G.E., Bradshaw, R.H.W., Bradshaw, E.G., Snowball, I. and Wastegård, S. (2005) 'Climate change and human settlement as drivers of late-Holocene vegetational change in the Faroe Islands', *The Holocene*, 15: 639–47.

Hårdh, B. (1996) *Silver in the Viking Age: a regional-economic study*, Stockholm: Almquist & Wiksell International.

Helgason, A., Hickey, E., Goodacre, S., Bosnes, V., Stefánsson, K., Ward, R. and Sykes, B. (2001)

'mtDNA and the islands of the North Atlantic: estimating the proportions of Norse and Gaelic ancestry', *American Journal of Human Genetics*, 68: 723–37.

Helle, K. (2005) 'The position of the Faeroes and other "tributary lands" in the medieval Norwegian dominion', in A. Mortensen and S.V. Arge (eds) 2005.

Hines, J., Lane, A. and Redknap, M. (eds) (2004) *Land, Sea and Home. Proceedings of a Conference on Viking-period Settlement* (Society for Medieval Archaeology. Monograph 20), Leeds: Maney.

Hunter, J.R. (1986) *Rescue Excavations on the Brough of Birsay 1974–82* (Society of Antiquaries of Scotland. Monograph Series 4), Edinburgh: Society of Antiquaries of Scotland.

—— (1997) 'The early Norse period', in K.J. Edwards and I.B. Ralston (eds) *Scotland. Environment and Archaeology, 8000 BC–AD 1000*, New York: John Wiley & Sons.

Hunter, J.R., Bond, J.M. and Smith, A.M. (1993) 'Some aspects of Viking settlement in Orkney', in C.E. Batey, J. Jesch and C.D. Morris (eds) *The Viking Age in Caithness, Orkney and the North Atlantic*, Edinburgh: Edinburgh University Press.

Jennings, A. (1996) 'Historical and linguistic evidence for Gall-Gaidheil and Norse in western Scotland', in P.S. Ureland and I. Clarkson (eds) *Language Contact Across the North Atlantic* (Linguistische Arbeiten 359), Tübingen: Niemeyer.

—— (1998) 'Iona and the Vikings: survival and continuity', *Northern Studies*, 33: 37–54.

Jennings, A. and Kruse, A. (2005) 'An ethnic enigma – Norse, Pict and Gael in the Western Isles', in A. Mortensen and S.V. Arge (eds) 2005.

Jesch, J. (1996) 'Presenting traditions in Orkneyinga saga', *Leeds Studies in English*, 27: 69–86.

Jones, S. (1997) *The Archaeology of Ethnicity*, London: Routledge.

Lane, A. (1990) 'Hebridean pottery: problems of definition, chronology, presence and absence', in I. Armit (ed.) *Beyond the Brochs*, Edinburgh: Edinburgh University Press.

Lane, A. and Campbell, E. (2000) *Dunadd. An Early Dalriadic Capital*, Oxford: Oxbow Books.

MacAirt, S. and MacNiocaill, G. (eds) (1983) *The Annals of Ulster (to A.D. 1131)*, Dublin: Dublin Institute for Advanced Studies.

McDonald, R.A. (2003) *Outlaws of Medieval Scotland. Challenges to the Canmore Kings, 1058–1266*, Phantassie, East Linton: Tuckwell Press.

Montgomery, J., Evans, J.A. and Neighbour, T. (2003) 'Sr isotope evidence for population movement within the Hebridean Norse community of NW Scotland', *Journal of the Geological Society, London*, 160: 649–53.

Morris, C.D. (1985) 'Viking Orkney: a survey', in C. Renfrew (ed.) *The Prehistory of Orkney*, Edinburgh: Edinburgh University Press.

—— (ed.) (1996a) *The Birsay Bay Project*, vol. 2: *Sites in Birsay Village and on the Brough of Birsay, Orkney* (Department of Archaeology. Monograph series 2), Durham: University of Durham, Department of Archaeology.

—— (1996b) 'Church and monastery in Orkney and Shetland: an archaeological perspective', in J.F. Krøger and H. Naley (eds) *Nordsjøen. Handel, religion og politikk*, Karmøy: Karmøy Kommune.

—— (1998) 'Raiders, traders and settlers: the early Viking Age in Scotland', in H. Clarke, M. Ní Mhaonaigh and R. Ó Floinn (eds) *Ireland and Scandinavia in the Early Viking Age*, Dublin: Four Courts Press.

Mortensen, A. and Arge, S.V. (2005) (eds) *Viking and Norse in the North Atlantic. Select Papers from the Proceedings of the Fourteenth Viking Congress, Tórshavn, 19–30 July 2001* (Annales Societatis Scientiarum Færoensis Supplementum 44), Tórshavn: Føroya Fróðskaparfelag.

Myhre, B. (1993) 'The beginning of the Viking Age: some current archaeological problems', in A. Faulkes and R. Perkins (eds) *Viking Revaluations*, London: Viking Society for Northern Research.

—— (1998) 'The archaeology of the early Viking Age in Norway', in H. Clarke, M. Ní Mhaonaigh and R. Ó Floinn (eds) *Ireland and Scandinavia in the Early Viking Age*, Dublin: Four Courts Press.

Nicolaisen, W.F.H. (1982) 'The Viking settlement of Scotland: evidence of the place-names', in R.T. Farrell (ed.) *The Vikings*, London: Phillimore & Co.

Ó Corráin, D. (1998a) 'The Vikings in Scotland and Ireland in the ninth century', *Peritia*, 12: 296–339.

—— (1998b) 'Viking Ireland: afterthoughts', in H. Clarke, M. Ní Mhaonaigh and R. Ó Floinn (eds) *Ireland and Scandinavia in the Early Viking Age*, Dublin: Four Courts Press.

Owen, O.A. (1993) 'Tuquoy, Westray, Orkney: a challenge for the future?', in C.E. Batey, J. Jesch and C.D. Morris (eds) *Caithness, Orkney and the North Atlantic in the Viking Age*, Edinburgh: Edinburgh University Press.

—— (2002) 'Les Vikings en Écosse: quel type de maison les colons vikings construisaient-ils?', in E. Ridel and P. Bouet (eds) *L'Héritage maritime des Vikings en Europe de L'Ouest*, Caen: Presses Universitaires de Caen.

—— (2004) 'The Scar boat burial – and the missing decades of the early Viking Age in Orkney and Shetland', in J. Adams and K. Holman (eds) *Scandinavia and Europe 800–1350. Contact, Conflict and Co-existence* (Medieval texts and cultures of Northern Europe 4), Turnhout: Brepols.

—— (2005) 'History, archaeology and *Orkneyinga Saga*: the case of Tuquoy, Westray', in O. Owen (ed.) *The World of Orkneyinga Saga. 'The Broad-cloth Viking Trip'*, Kirkwall: The Orcadian Limited.

Owen, O. and Dalland, M. (1999) *Scar: a Viking boat burial on Sanday, Orkney*, Phantassie: Tuckwell Press.

Parker Pearson, M., Sharples, N. and Symonds, J. (2004a) *South Uist. Archaeology and History of a Hebridean Island*, Stroud: Tempus.

Parker Pearson, M., Smith, H., Mulville, J. and Brennand, M. (2004b) 'Cille Pheadair: the life and times of a Norse-period farmstead c. 1000–1300', in J. Hines *et al.* (eds) 2004.

Paterson, C. (2001) 'Insular belt-fittings from the pagan Norse graves of Scotland: a reappraisal in the light of scientific and stylistic analysis', in M. Redknap, N. Edwards, S. Youngs, A. Lane and J. Knight (eds) *Pattern and Purpose in Insular Art*, Oxford: Oxbow Books.

Ritchie, A. (1974) 'Pict and Norseman in northern Scotland', *Scottish Archaeological Forum*, 6: 23–36.

—— (1977) 'Excavation of Pictish and Viking-Age farmsteads at Buckquoy, Orkney', *Proceedings of the Society of Antiquaries of Scotland*, 108: 174–227.

Ross, A. (1994) 'Pottery', in B. Ballin Smith (ed.) *Howe. Four Millenia of Orkney Prehistory* (Society of Antiquaries of Scotland. Monograph Series 9), Edinburgh: Society of Antiquaries of Scotland.

Sawyer, P. (2003) 'Scotland, Ireland and Iceland: Norwegian settlers in the ninth century', in S. Lewis-Simpson (ed.) *Vínland Revisited. The Norse World at the Turn of the First Millennium*, St John's: Historic Sites Association of Newfoundland and Labrador, Inc.

Sharples, N. (2004) 'A find of Ringerike art from Bornais in the Outer Hebrides', in J. Hines *et al.* (eds) 2004.

Sharples, N. and Parker Pearson, M. (1999) 'Norse settlement in the Outer Hebrides', *Norwegian Archaeological Review*, 32: 41–62.

Simpson, I.A., Barrett, J.H. and Milek, K.B. (2005) 'Interpreting the Viking Age to medieval period transition in Norse Orkney through cultural soil and sediment analyses', *Geoarchaeology*, 20: 355–77.

Small, A. (1966) 'Excavations at Underhoull, Unst, Shetland', *Proceedings of the Society of Antiquaries of Scotland*, 98: 225–48.

Smirnova, L. (2005) *Comb-making in Medieval Novgorod (950–1450). An Industry in Transition* (British Archaeological Reports. International Series S1369), Oxford: Hadrian Books.

Smith, A.N. (1998) 'The worked bone and antler', in N. Sharples (ed.) *Scalloway: A Broch, Late*

Iron Age Settlement and Medieval Cemetery in Shetland (Oxbow Monograph 82), Oxford: Oxbow Books.

Smith, B. (2001) 'The Picts and the martyrs or did Vikings kill the native population of Orkney and Shetland?', *Northern Studies*, 36: 7–32.

—— (2003) 'Not welcome at all: Vikings and the native population in Orkney and Shetland', in J. Downes and A. Ritchie (eds) *Sea Change. Orkney and Northern Europe in the Later Iron Age AD 300–800*, Balgavies, Angus: The Pinkfoot Press.

Solli, B. (1996) 'Narratives of encountering religions: on the Christianization of the Norse around AD 900–1000', *Norwegian Archaeological Review*, 29: 91–114.

Stummann Hansen, S. (2000) 'Viking settlement in Shetland: chronological and regional contexts', *Acta Archaeologica*, 71: 87–103.

Thäte, E. (forthcoming) 'A question of priority: the re-use of houses and barrows for burials in Scandinavia in the late iron age (AD 600–1000)', *Anglo-Saxon Studies in Archaeology and History*, 14.

Turner, V., Dockrill, S. and Bond, J. (2005) 'Viking settlement in an Iron Age village: Old Scatness, Shetland', in A. Mortensen and S.V. Arge (eds) 2005.

Wamers, E. (1998) 'Insular finds in Viking Age Scandinavia and the state formation of Norway', in H. Clarke, M. Ní Mhaonaigh and R. Ó Floinn (eds) *Ireland and Scandinavia in the Early Viking Age*, Dublin: Four Courts Press.

Warner, R. (1976) 'Scottish silver arm-rings: an analysis of weights', *Proceedings of the Society of Antiquaries of Scotland*, 107: 136–43.

Weber, B. (1992) 'Norwegian exports in Orkney and Shetland during the Viking and Middle Ages', in R.A. Hall, R. Hodges and H. Clarke (eds) *Medieval Europe 1992. Exchange and Trade Pre-printed Papers*, York: Medieval York.

—— (1993) 'Norwegian reindeer antler export to Orkney', *Universitetets Oldsaksamling. Årbok* (1991–2): 161–74.

—— (1994) 'Iron Age combs: analyses of raw material', in B. Ambrosiani and H. Clarke (eds) *The Twelfth Viking Congress. Developments around the Baltic and the North Sea in the Viking Age*, Stockholm: The Birka Project.

Wilson, J.F., Weiss, D.A., Richards, M., Thomas, M.G., Bradman, N. and Goldstein, D.B. (2001) 'Genetic evidence for different male and female roles during cultural transitions in the British Isles', *Proceedings of the National Academy of Sciences*, 98: 5, 078–83.

Wolf, E.R. (1994) 'Perilous ideas: race, culture, people', *Current Anthropology*, 35: 1–12.

Woolf, A. (2004) 'The age of the sea-kings: 900–1300', in D. Omand (ed.) *The Argyll Book*, Edinburgh: Birlinn.

CHAPTER THIRTY-ONE

THE VIKINGS AND IRELAND

——·◆·——

Donnchadh Ó Corráin

There were contacts between Scandinavia and the British Isles long before the end of the eighth century. The best witness to Irish contact with Scandinavians is *Liber de mensura orbis terrae* (825) by Dícuill the Geographer, an Irish scholar at the Frankish court (Tierney 1967). He first describes a scientific expedition by Irish clerics to Iceland in 795 or so. They met no Vikings there or elsewhere during their voyage. He gives a detailed account of the Faroes, occupied by Irish hermits since at least 725. Some archaeologists have been reluctant to accept Dícuill's testimony. Faroese field evidence is as poor as one would expect from hermits – there are inscribed gravestones showing Irish features and recent palynological work shows that oats were cultivated and sheep reared *c.* AD 600–50. This fits well enough with Dícuill's record (Debes 1993: 454–64; Arge 1993: 465–72; Stummann Hansen, 1993: 473–86). Thus, the Irish monks who compiled the Irish annals, our richest source for the history of the Vikings in Ireland, knew more about them than one might suspect.

The raids began abruptly and unexpectedly. The *Annals of Ulster* report for 794: 'The devastation of all the islands of Britain by pagans' (Mac Airt and Mac Niocaill 1983). This pattern of sudden raids on islands and coasts was to continue for a generation. The first recorded Viking raids on Ireland took place in 795: 'The burning of Rechru by the pagans'. The Vikings soon swept south into the Irish Sea: in 798 the annalist reports 'the burning of Inis Pátraic by the pagans and they took the cattle-tribute of the territories and they smashed the shrine of Do Chonna and they made great incursions both in Ireland and in Scotland'. Inis Pátraic is St Patrick's Island near Skerries, Co. Dublin; St Do Chonna is its patron.

So far the raids were exploratory, by a few ships rather than larger fleets. The rich church of Iona was found and attacked in 802 and 806. By 807 they had rounded Donegal and had reached the west-coast bays and harbours. They burned the monastery of Inishmurray off the coast of Sligo and attacked Roscam, near Oranmore, on Galway Bay. They concentrated on the north and west coasts, but sometimes they met with determined opposition from local Irish lords. In 812 Viking raiders reached the Kerry coastline, in the far south-west, but they were slaughtered by local kings. By now, the Vikings knew all they needed about the coastline and its possibilities for plunder or colonisation, but suddenly there is silence. There are no reports of activities anywhere in

Ireland for eight years. This may be the time when a powerful Viking settlement was made in Scotland.

Attacks began again in 821 in the Irish Sea and on the south coast. In 821 Vikings raided Howth and 'took a great prey of women' – as slaves, very likely. By 822 they had reached Cork on the south coast and in 824 they raided the remote island monastery of Skellig, 13 km off the Kerry coast.

In the 830s, the raids became more threatening and from 836 large-scale attacks began with 'the first prey of the pagans from Southern Brega [south Co. Meath] . . . and they carried off many prisoners and killed many and took very many captives'. That autumn the annalist reports 'a most cruel devastation of all the lands of Connacht by the pagans'. The great monastery of Clonmore, Co. Carlow, was burned on Christmas Eve, and many captives were taken. Mid-winter raiding for slaves proves that the Vikings were already overwintering, possibly on islands that could hold many prisoners.

In 837, a fleet of sixty ships appeared on the Boyne and another on the Liffey, very likely from the Scottish settlements, each bringing about 1,500 men. They ravaged the east-coast kingdoms and defeated the Uí Néill kings 'in a countless slaughter'. These appear to be royal expeditions with large resources. The Vikings now appear on the inland waterways – the Shannon, the Erne, the Boyne, Lough Neagh and the Bann. They overwintered on Lough Neagh for the first time in 840–1. They now began to build *longphoirt*, fortresses that protected them and their ships, some of which became permanent (Kelly and Maas 1999: 123–59). They first overwintered in Dublin in 841–2.

These large-scale raids marked the beginning of the occupation of the Irish east midlands and were mounted from Scandinavian Scotland, where a powerful royal dynasty had established itself in the north and west. Leaders of that dynasty, the brothers Amlaíb (Óláfr) and Ímar (Ívarr), exercised authority over the Irish Vikings through a series of royal expeditions – the annals report ones in 848, 849 and 853 but there may have been more. For nearly two centuries this dynasty played a major role in the history of Ireland and Britain (Ó Corráin 1998a: 296–339).

The Irish church leaders, who had borne the brunt of attacks, were aristocrats with close ties to the dominant dynasties, and well used to war and violence. This conditioned their reaction: they trusted in God and in their own arms. The Vikings fell on no unworldly clerics but on a confident church organisation determined to defend itself. That determination meant aggression. Armagh was on the attack when it first encountered the Vikings in 831: 'the heathens defeated the community of Armagh in the Carlingford Lough area and great numbers of them were taken captive' – evidently Armagh troops were defending its dependent coastal churches, now under attack. In 845, the abbot of Terryglass and Clonenagh and the deputy abbot of Kildare were killed by Vikings at the fortress of Dunamase leading their monastic levies. Dunamase is about 13 km from Clonenagh, 24 km from Kildare – near enough to show they were engaged in local defence. A contemporary ironic comment on prayers for defence occurs in the notice of a raid on Armagh in 895:

Alas, holy Patrick!
unavailing your orisons –
the Vikings with axes
are hacking your oratories.

It seemed to some that Ireland was about to be overrun and made subject to the Vikings – the view of the Irish *émigré* sources that lie behind the *Annales Bertiniani* for 847: 'After they had been for many years under attack from the Vikings, the Irish were made tributaries to them; the Vikings have possessed themselves without opposition of all the islands round about and have settled them.'

The Irish provincial kings, who spent their energies on their own power struggles, slowly turned on the Vikings (Ó Corráin 1979: 283–323). In 845 Niall Caille, king of Tara and king of the northern Uí Néill, defeated them in battle in Donegal. In 848, Mael Sechnaill, king of Tara since 846, defeated the Vikings near Skreen (Co. Meath), and killed 700 of them. In the same year, Ólchobar mac Cináeda, king of Munster, and Lorccán mac Cellaig, king of Leinster, joined forces and defeated the Vikings in a major battle near Castledermot, Co. Kildare.

These victories lie behind an important embassy sent to Charles the Bald, the Frankish emperor, in 848 and an exaggerated report in the *Annales Bertiniani*: 'The Irish attacked the Vikings and with the help of our Lord Jesus Christ they were victorious and drove them out of their territory.'

By the second half of the ninth century the Vikings were a familiar element in Irish life and militarily impressive (Ó Corráin 1987: 287–93). They had small permanent settlements and had become part of the country's politics. The Irish aristocracy found them useful as allies and mercenaries. From this point Viking–Irish alliances become commonplace, and no matter for reproach. The annalists report frequent Irish–Viking alliances in the ninth century and there was intermarriage at the very highest levels of Irish society.

Relatively unsuccessful as conquerors in Ireland, the Vikings turned to Scotland, with dramatic results. The Irish annals report:

> Amlaíb and Auisle [the kings of Dublin] went to Fortriu with the Vikings of Ireland and Scotland and they ravaged the whole of Pictland and took their hostages.

The Dublin dynasty, commanding the Viking forces of Ireland and of their original settlement in Scotland, invaded southern Pictland, then plundered the whole of Pictland, and took hostages, as overkings, to enforce their authority. This leaves no room for independent kings: Constantine I (r. 862–76), called 'rex Pictorum', will have given hostages with the rest. And they placed Pictland (southern and eastern Scotland) under tribute. They returned to Dublin, and for the next four years there is a detailed account of their activities – enough to show that Dublin was their base of operations and that the Irish did not make things easy for them. There was a successful attack on Dublin itself in 867 and a major defeat in battle in 868, in which Carlus, son of Amlaíb, fell.

It is not surprising, then, that in 870–1 the Dublin leadership turned again to Scotland, now to the south-west British kingdom of Strathclyde:

> [870] The siege of Dumbarton by the Nordmanni i.e. Amlaíb and Ímar the two kings of the Nordmanni besieged that fortress and at the end of four months they destroyed the fortress and plundered it. [871] Amlaíb and Ímar came back to Dublin from Scotland with 200 ships and they brought with them in captivity to Ireland a great prey of Angles, Britons and Picts.

This was a major event. The plunder taken from Scotland was vast. The Dublin kings smashed the power of the Strathclyde Britons and established their authority over them. Given the captives they took, they also reasserted their authority over Pictland as a whole and, if the Anglian captives were taken in their homeland, they may have been raiding Lothian as well. They had now brought the whole of Scotland under their suzerainty.

Ímar continued to rule in Dublin and died in 873. His death notice in the *Annals of Ulster* reads:

> Ímar king of the Norwegian Vikings of the whole of Ireland and Britain ended his life.

This record means that Ímar was overking of all the Norwegian Vikings in Ireland and Britain. One may infer, too, that Dublin had become the dynastic caput. The evidence suggests that Dublin was the capital of a sea-kingdom: Man and all Scotland and it is probable that Galloway and Cumbria from the Solway Firth to the Mersey formed part of the same overkingship.

Dublin was soon being fought over by rival groups within the dynasty. There were intense dynastic feuds and killings in 883 and 888. In 893 there was a major conflict between the Vikings of Dublin and they divided into two main groups, one led by the son of Ímar and the other by Earl Sigfrith. In 896 his fellow Vikings killed Sitric, son of Ímar, and the rulers of a small kingdom in Louth, to the north of Dublin, killed his brother Amlaíb. The Dubliners were still able to raid the monastic centres in the Irish hinterland. In 890–1 they plundered Ardbraccan, Donaghpatrick, Dulane, Glendalough, Kildare and Clonard – all within easy striking distance. In 895 they attacked Armagh and took 710 prisoners. But the power of Dublin was ebbing fast. The decisive defeat came in 902 when the kingdoms of Brega to the north and Leinster to the south joined forces against them. As the annalist records: 'The pagans were driven from Ireland, i.e. from the fortress of Dublin . . . and they abandoned a good number of their ships, and escaped half-dead after they had been wounded and broken.' The first Viking settlement of Dublin had ended.

When Dublin fell its rulers went to Scotland and to territories that had long been their dependencies. In 903 we next find them engaged in fierce warfare in southern Pictland. They attacked Dunkeld, an attack on the king of south Pictland, Constantine II (r. 900–43), now the most important ruler in Scotland. Very likely, he had been considered a dependent king by the dynasty of Dublin, and the fall of Dublin was the signal for his revolt. In 904 Ímar grandson of Ímar, the former king of Dublin, was killed with great slaughter. And then there is silence. However, some time between 904 and about 914 (when historical sources again become available), the exiled Dublin dynasty rose to power again and embarked on another career of conquest that led to the re-establishment of the Viking kingdom of Dublin, the taking of York by the same dynasty, and the establishment of close relationships between Dublin, York and northern England generally (Smyth 1975–9).

The second Viking Age began suddenly in 914 with 'the arrival of a great sea-fleet of pagans in Waterford Harbour'. In 917 the Dublin dynasty joined in the renewed attack: Ragnall, who is called *rí Dubgall* 'king of the Danes' because he ruled Danish Northumbria, and his kinsman, Sitric Caech. Their arrival sparked off a major conflict with the Irish kings, but the newcomers were victorious. Sitric repossessed Dublin, and Ragnall led his troops back to northern England to campaigns that made him king of York and ruler of Northumbria. Henceforth, Dublin and York were ruled by a single dynasty and this brought about dramatic change in Ireland, in trade, urbanisation and in the resources of its kings. Dublin became a sea-kingdom, the centre of far-flung economic and political interests. It had real power and influence in the Irish Sea, Scotland and northern England – resources that made it much more formidable than the limited assets in land and manpower it held in Ireland.

Dublin aimed to make strategic conquests. There was an intense campaign in eastern Ulster, 921–7 and again later, led by Dublin and using large fleets, to create a Scandinavian kingdom like that on the other side of the Irish Sea, and to control north–south transit and trade (Smyth 1975–9 vol. 2: 23). This was foiled by Muirchertach mac Néill, king of the northern Uí Néill, who was later defeated and slain by the Dubliners.

Amlaíb, king of Dublin, led the opponents of King Athelstan at the great battle of Brunanburh: at stake was the kingship of England. Athelstan won a decisive victory, but Amlaíb escaped to Dublin in 938. On Athelstan's death in October 939 Amlaíb sailed for England, reached York before the year's end and was made king by the Northumbrians. He followed this with a campaign south of the Humber. The result was a negotiated settlement with Edmund, Athelstan's successor, by which Amlaíb was recognised as king of York and ruler of Danish Mercia – almost half the kingdom of England. He died in 941.

York was soon lost by his successor, Amlaíb Cuarán, who returned to Ireland in 945 to fierce Irish–Viking warfare. In 944 Congalach, king of Brega, and the king of Leinster had united against Dublin in a pincer movement and sacked the city with a new ferocity: 'The destruction brought upon it was this: its houses, house-enclosures, its ships and its other structures were burned; its women, boys and common folk were enslaved; its men and its warriors were killed; it was altogether destroyed, from four persons to one, by killing and drowning, burning and capture, apart from a small number that fled in a few ships and reached Dalkey.' Congalach attacked Dublin again in 948, killed its ruler and 1,600 of its troops were either killed or taken prisoner. Amlaíb Cuarán tried his luck in England again and he held the kingship of York from about 948 until he was driven out in 953. He returned to Dublin.

Though a powerful king of Dublin, Amlaíb Cuarán fatally overreached himself. He battled with the major Irish kings: he defeated and killed the king of Leinster in battle near Athy and attacked Meath. In 980 he invaded Meath but Mael Sechnaill mac Domnaill, its king, inflicted a crushing defeat (the annalist calls it 'a red slaughter') on him at the battle of Tara. His long-planned attempt at conquest failed disastrously, and his signal defeat decisively broke the power of Dublin. Mael Sechnaill besieged the city and it met his terms: the release of all Irish hostages, the handing over of treasure and the freeing of all Uí Néill lands from tribute. Mael Sechnaill further proclaimed the liberty of all Irish slaves in Viking territory – that, says the annalist, was 'the Babylonian captivity of Ireland, second only to the captivity of hell'. Amlaíb Cuarán went to Iona as a penitent, and died there in religious retirement.

This marked the end of Viking military power in Ireland. All the Viking cities – Dublin, Limerick, Waterford, Cork and Wexford – were henceforth ruled directly or indirectly by Irish kings. Dublin and Waterford were often autonomous, though they were sometimes ruled directly. Limerick was under the Uí Briain kings of Munster: they had a governor in the city. ~~Generally, the Irish kings milked the cities for men, fleets and taxes, and it is likely that they encouraged their wealth-creating trade~~. Irish writers appreciated the skills of the merchants and this may reflect the attitudes of the political class they served: *seolad crann dar muir co beacht / cráes Gall is cennaigecht* 'sailing ships skilfully over the sea / the gluttony and commerce of the Vikings'. Their influence, which was significant, was henceforth commercial and cultural – in art, language and literature (Bugge 1900, 1904). The Viking past, which now looked more like a remote heroic age, a time when dynastic ancestors fought a fearsome foe, was drawn upon for the historical propaganda that gave status to twelfth-century kings and expressed their ambitions. The Christian and relatively peaceful Vikings were the whipping boys of this new royal patriotism (Goedheer 1938). Ironically, their world of urbanisation, trade and communications provided the means by which these very kings grew great (Ó Corráin 1987: 287–93; 1998b: 420–52).

BIBLIOGRAPHY

Arge, S.V. (1993) 'On the landnam of the Faroe Islands', in C. Batey, J. Jesch and Ch.D. Morris (eds) *The Viking Age in Caithness, Orkney and the North Atlantic*, Edinburgh: Edinburgh University Press.

Bugge, A. (1900) 'Nordisk sprog og nordisk nationalitet i Irland', *Aarbøger for Nordisk Oldkyndighed og Historie*, 279–332.

—— (1904) 'Bidrag til det sidste afsnit af nordboernes historie i Irland', *Aarbøger for Nordisk Oldkyndighed og Historie*, 248–315.

Debes, H.J. (1993) 'Problems concerning the earliest settlement in the Faroe Islands', in C. Batey, J. Jesch and Ch.D. Morris (eds) *The Viking Age in Caithness, Orkney and the North Atlantic*, Edinburgh: Edinburgh University Press.

Goedheer, A.J. (1938) *Irish and Norse Traditions about the Battle of Clontarf*, Haarlem: Willinck & Zoon.

Kelly, E.P. and Maas, J. (1999) 'The Vikings and the kingdom of Laois', in P.G. Lane and W. Nolan (eds) *Laois. History and Society*, Dublin: Geography Publications.

Mac Airt, S. and Mac Niocaill, G. (1983) *The Annals of Ulster*, vol. 1, Dublin: Institute for Advanced Studies.

Ó Corráin, D. (1979) 'High-kings, Vikings and other kings', *Irish Historical Studies*, 21: 283–323.

—— (1987) 'The semantic development of Old Norse jarl in Old and Middle Irish', in J. Knirk (ed.) *Proceedings of the Tenth Viking Congress, Larkollen, Norway, 1985* (Universitets Oldsaksamlings Skrifter. Ny rekke 9), Oslo: Universitets Oldsaksamling.

—— (1994) 'The second Viking age in Ireland', in M. Rindal (ed.) *Three Studies on Vikings and Christianization* (KULT skriftserie 28), Oslo: Research Council of Norway.

—— (1997) 'Ireland, Wales, Man and the Hebrides', in P. Sawyer (ed.) *The Oxford Illustrated History of the Vikings*, Oxford: Oxford University Press.

—— (1998a) 'The Vikings in Scotland and Ireland in the ninth century', *Peritia*, 12: 296–339.

—— (1998b) 'Viking Ireland: afterthoughts', in H.B. Clarke, M. Ní Mhaonaigh and R. Ó Floinn (eds) *Ireland and Scandinavia in the Early Viking Age*, Dublin: Four Courts Press.

—— (2001) 'The Vikings in Ireland', in A.-Ch. Larsen (ed.), *The Vikings in Ireland* , Roskilde: Roskilde Ship Museum.

Smyth, A.P. (1975–9) *Scandinavian York and Dublin*, 2 vols, Dublin: Templekieran.

Stummann Hansen, S. (1993) 'Viking-Age Faroe Islands and their Southern Links in the Light of Recent Finds at Toftantes, Leirvik', in C. Batey, J. Jesch and Ch.D. Morris (eds) *The Viking Age in Caithness, Orkney and the North Atlantic*, Edinburgh: Edinburgh University Press.

Tierney, J.J. (1967) *Dicuili Liber de mensura orbis terrae*, Dublin: Institute for Advanced Studies.

CHAPTER THIRTY-TWO

ARCHAEOLOGICAL EVIDENCE FOR THE DIFFERENT EXPRESSIONS OF SCANDINAVIAN SETTLEMENT IN IRELAND, 840–1100

———•◆•———

Patrick F. Wallace

Instead of speculating on what exactly the Irish chroniclers who described the mid-ninth-century Scandinavian fortresses in Ireland as *longphuirt* (literally 'ship fortresses') meant by the term, it is intended here merely to provide an overview of the archaeological evidence as it presently exists for the different types of Scandinavian-inspired settlements which existed in Viking Age Ireland.

Best understood and most enduring are the *towns* of Dublin, Waterford, Limerick and Wexford. In their developed form in the tenth-, eleventh- and early twelfth-century Hiberno-Norse phase, these consisted of large defended settlements at the tidal confluences of main rivers and their tributaries. They were located on high ground traversed by ascending streets which, together with laneways and intramural accesses, formed irregular rather than gridded networks. Boundary fences radiated from the streets forming rows of contiguous rectangular or trapezoid plots into which settlements were divided. The archaeological record preserves rich evidence for the buildings and layout of plots particularly at Dublin, Waterford and Wexford as well as at Cork where recent excavations have unearthed what had hitherto been regarded as urban houses of Hiberno-Norse type in an indigenous urban settlement of the later eleventh- and early twelfth-century period.

It appears that access through individual plots was controlled. Main buildings had their narrow ends to streets or laneways, had pathways leading to the entrances and from back entrances to lesser outbuildings and sheds in the yards at the back of the plots. Front and back entrances in the main buildings meant that access was through them although obviously this would have had to be at the behest of house/plot owners or their agents. It is likely that there would be widenings and crossings in the street network as well as outside town gates to facilitate markets and public gatherings, though evidence for these are inferential rather than evidential.

The only town gateway of the period excavated to date comes from Waterford where piers for such were identified. There is good evidence for defences and port facilities particularly at Dublin where a succession of two main palisaded earthen banks from the tenth and eleventh centuries respectively have been identified in succession to one another, each completely encircling the settlement. At Dublin and Waterford and probably also at Wexford and Limerick these were replaced by stone walls –

both freestanding and partly revetted fronts for earthen banks – in the later eleventh century.

A number of different house types have been identified in Ireland's Viking Age urban settlements and an overall national pattern has been suggested. By far the most numerous among these is the *type 1*, an Irish urban variant (built in local materials and in indigenous building methods to the dictates of local climate) of the more widespread north-west European rectangular three-sided building characteristic of the Norse in their western expansion.

The large-scale excavation campaigns at Dublin and Waterford have provided us with the most complete picture anywhere of the cramped urban atmosphere of the Viking town in the tenth, eleventh and early twelfth centuries. Commensurate volumes of animal bone and organic samples have provided detail on economy and everyday life and thousands of artefacts in different media form the subject of ongoing reports on trade and commerce and craft studies.

Over the past decade or so, however, new discoveries have led to the recognition of several other forms of Scandinavian settlement in Ireland, particularly from the early phase of contact around the mid-ninth century. Apart from the recognition by John Ó Néill of the first (of what must have been very many) farmsteads at Loughlinstown, south of Dublin, excavations in Dublin city's Parliament Street, Essex Street West, South Great Georges Street and Great Ship Street – mainly by Linzi Simpson – and a review of discoveries of burials and artefacts, particularly at Islandbridge and Kilmainham by Raghnall Ó Floinn, Elizabeth O'Brien and Stephen Harrison, contribute to our having to entertain possibly several different settlement forms of Scandinavian origin in the ninth century.

The coincidence of the 841 annalistic reference to the Scandinavian establishment of *longphuirt* has led historians such as Edel Bhreathnach and archaeologists such as Michael Gibbons to speculate on how this term can be applied to known ninth-century archaeological sites. Principal among such candidates is the seemingly remarkable site at Woodstown near Waterford, identified in April 2004. Much speculation has also centred on the nature of the Dunrally, Co. Laois and Athlunkard, Limerick sites by Eamonn Kelly, while John Sheehan's work on probable Scandinavian settlements in the Atlantic south-west also come into the reckoning.

The Essex Street West excavation showed that Dublin's main house type went back to the ninth century and the division of the settlement into plots also dated from well before the apparent 902 expulsion of some of the Scandinavians from Dublin. Georgina Scally's work at Parliament Street was the first to show that the focus of the earliest Scandinavian settlement may have been on the Poddle rather than on the Liffey along which the town may only have developed later. Ó Floinn suggested that burials and associated farmstead-type settlements were 'strung out' along both sides of the Liffey. It may have been such an early farmhouse that Simpson found at the south of her later urban Essex Street West site.

In the recent past, Simpson's sites on either side of the Pool – the 'Black Pool' or *Dubh Linn* from which Dublin gets its name and which was near a pre-Viking indigenous monastic settlement – on the Poddle watercourse at South Great Georges Street and Ship Street Great (west bank) both revealed early Viking burial remains mainly of warriors and the former 'an inlet of the Pool and a good stretch of the southern bank'. The burials were found on the south-east shore of the Black Pool on the east side of an islet. Ships' rivets were recovered from the gravel of the Pool along with a bearded axe. What Simpson took to be evidence for a palisade, possibly to control flooding along the eastern edge of her islet, she suggests may have been a landing stage to link the Pool with the eastern part of the later Viking town which, thanks to the Parliament Street and Essex Street excavations and their early layers, now looks like the earliest part of the town. Simpson goes beyond this to suggest that the Pool may have been where boats laid up during the winter, in what in effect was the *longphort*. The apparently early and relatively pure content of the Scandinavian warrior burials found here seem to enhance the possibility that this was the *longphort*. It seems right to link the Poddle channel and the Pool as central to understanding the earliest Scandinavian settlement in Dublin, though to prove that the *longphort* (whatever it was!) 'must be on the western side . . . in an area later subsumed by the tenth-century settlement' is probably impossible to be fully confident about. Simpson suggests that it was at least 300 m north–south, protected on three sides by water and 'including the naturally defensive ground at the extreme southern end' where Dublin Castle 'always a contender for the site of the *longphort*' was later built. Simpson poses an alternate possibility that the Poddle is the western protection of a *longphort* that existed east of the Pool with burials close to or within the fortress, as has been speculated for Woodstown. There is little doubt that with the advantage of dating evidence Simpson is right about a settlement and probable landing activity around the Pool, followed somewhat later by more concerted habitation nearer the mouth of the Poddle to the north. After this, in the tenth century, there was an expansion northwards and westwards with the building of earthen defensive banks and the development of the Dublin we know so well from our forty-year excavation campaign.

Considerable speculation has centred on the nature of Viking settlement in the mid-830s and 840s when it appears bases were first established in Ireland as a result of the intensification of Scandinavian interest. We cannot be sure about what exactly the 840 Lough Neagh or the 841 Dublin and Annagassan bases looked like, upon what Scandinavian prototypes they were based, or that they even resembled one another. It is not without relevance that the word *Linn* ('Pool') also occurs in the Annagassen place name Linn Duchail; the *longphort* in question also occurs at the confluence of two rivers with the possible (as yet unexcavated) settlement incorporating a D-shaped island and a separate high citadel (?) feature.

The 840s saw the proliferation of bases on Carlingford Lough, the Boyne Estuary, Narrow Water, Lough Swilly, the Shannon and Lough Ree. In the 850s and early 860s a Norse Viking leader, Rodulf or Rothlaibh, became active in the Nore and Barrow river systems 'attacking Laois from a base probably located in the Waterford harbour area', a prophetic remark now that an apparently major site of the era has been identified at Woodstown near Waterford. Rodulf may have been the son of a former king of Denmark and was later active in Friesia until his death in 873.

Rodulf's '*longphort*' may have been deep inland at Dunrally, Co. Laois, which is west of the junction of the Barrow and its tributary, the Glasha. This appears to have been destroyed in 862 along with the fleet it protected by the combined armies of the kings of Ossory and Laois. It is possible that originally this foundation had been established by the Dublin Vikings for their own political purposes being in line with the kind of bases then being established by the Vikings on some of the main rivers of mainland Europe and England.

Dunrally fort survives as a 360 m × 150 m area enclosed by a large D-shaped rampart with an outer ditch, 5.3 m wide and 1.8 m deep. According to Kelly and Maas (1995) 'the enclosure was sufficiently large to ensure that the biggest of Viking fleets could have been protected on-shore and . . . there was a pool on the river Barrow, immediately adjacent where ships could have anchored'. Dunrally has a smaller 52 m × 41 m (citadel?) enclosure within the larger *enceinte*. Kelly and Maas believe construction of a *longphort* at Dunrally would have been consistent with known Viking practice elsewhere including within the Carolingian Empire. They suggest Dunrally belongs 'to a class of Viking inland forts chosen for their defendable terrain of marsh and river', but suggest that the choice of location of the fort is similar to that of the Irish Viking towns. Only excavation will really tell.

It is possible that the mid-ninth-century Viking *longphuirt* in Ireland were all long D-shaped enclosures like Dunrally. Linn Duchail (Annagassan), Co. Louth and Athlunkard (Limerick), Co. Clare – the latter 75 m × 30 m and also with an enclosed feature internally – and maybe the original *longphort* on the Poddle fit a pattern which is discernible at sites (like Repton) in England and in the north-west of the Continent.

Easter 2004 witnessed acknowledgement of the discovery of the rich and apparently ninth-century Viking riverine site at Woodstown. Although still only trenched in advance of road construction and awaiting full archaeological excavation, it seems to predate the Hiberno-Norse town of Waterford a couple of miles downriver which, unlike Woodstown, was to endure. Metal finds including lead weights, a sword pommel and several pieces of hack-silver indicate a seemingly strong Scandinavian presence which seems to fulfil Eamonn Kelly's prophecy about Rodulph having such a place near the mouth of the River Barrow in Waterford harbour. Woodstown is located on the sister river Suir but is otherwise in the right place. Geophysical indications are that this is a large elongated D-shaped enclosure in line with what we have been thinking may constitute a *longphort*, or at least a mid- to later ninth-century fortified base in Ireland. The only problem is that trial excavation of the suggested ditch gives a much earlier (sixth–seventh-century) date for the lowest ditch infill which cautions against acceptance of the site as a Scandinavian foundation and suggests more a reuse and a possible expansion in an undoubted Viking Age heyday. Again, large-scale excavation is necessary.

The discovery at Woodstown raises questions of the extent to which the ninth-century settlement relates to the later town of Waterford. Was it a short-lived earlier precursor, did it overlap with its neighbour and how was it managed in relation to the town that endured? When, why and by whom was Woodstown established? Was it related to the possible inland sister fortress at Dunrally and like the latter was it abandoned after being destroyed by native forces? Only excavation will tell. And are Waterford and maybe Dublin's two names related to each having pairs of Scandinavian settlements in which case it can be asked if Port Láirge is Woodstown and not Waterford?

The excitement of the recent work in Ireland means that physical evidence for the forms which Scandinavian settlement took is more varied and inevitably of more military character than the impressions of more developed urban character which forty years' excavation of the great urban sites at Dublin, Waterford and to a lesser extent Limerick, Wexford and in its way Cork have hitherto provided us with. When recent discoveries at Dumore Cave, Co. Kilkenny, Cloghermore, Co. Kerry and the exotic burial at Finglas near Dublin are added, the growing rush of evidence for the complicated and seemingly varied physical nature of Scandinavian presence in Ireland becomes stronger. And this is before even admitting to the possibility of as many as nine or ten Hiberno-Scandinavian maritime havens or way-stations as a recent reassessment of the Viking presence at Beginish island off the south-west coast 'on the sea route between Cork and Limerick' has it. Similar way-stations for coasts between Ireland's other main Viking town settlements are postulated along with the idea of a stubborn adherence to their cultural identity on the part of the Scandinavians! Not bad for a people of whom it used to be thought came to Ireland in small numbers effecting a legacy disproportionate to those numbers. A rush to see Scandinavian settlements in more places than they may have been may not be unrelated to modern Irish society's desire to be seen as welcoming of the new waves of strangers currently arriving on its shores.

BIBLIOGRAPHY

Archaeology Ireland, 9(3) (1995) [An issue devoted to Viking archaeology.]

Clarke, H. (ed.) (1990) *Medieval Dublin. The Making of a Metropolis*, Dublin: Irish Academic Press.

Clarke, H.B., Ní Mhaonaigh, M. and Ó Floinn, R. (eds) (1998) *Ireland and Scandinavia in the Early Viking Age*, Dublin: Four Courts Press.

Holm, P. (1986) 'The slavetrade in Dublin: ninth to twelfth centuries', *Peritia*, 6: 317–45.

Hurley, M.F. (1998) 'Viking Age towns: archaeological evidence from Waterford and Cork', in M. Monk and J. Sheehan (eds) *Early Medieval Munster*, Cork: Cork University Press.

Kelly, E.P. and Maas, J. (1995) 'Vikings on the Barrow', *Archaeology Ireland*, 9(3): 30–2.

Kelly, E.P. and O'Donavan, E. (1998) 'A Viking *longphort* near Athlunkard, Co. Clare', *Archaeology Ireland*, 12(4): 13–16.

Larsen, A.-Ch. (ed.) (2001) *The Vikings in Ireland*, Roskilde: The Viking Ship Museum.

Mytum, H. (2003) 'The Vikings and Ireland: ethnicity, identity, and culture change', in J. Barrett (ed.) *Contact, Continuity, and Collapse. The Norse Colonization of the North Atlantic*, Turnhout: Brepols.

Ó Néill, J. (1999) 'A Norse settlement in rural County Dublin', *Archaeology Ireland*, 13(4): 8–10.

Sheehan, J. (2000) 'Ireland's early Viking-Age silver hoards: components, structure, and classification', *Acta Archaeologica*, 71: 49–63.

Simpson, L. (1994) *Excavations at Isolde's Tower, Dublin* (Temple Bar archaeological report 1), Dublin: Temple Bar Properties Ltd.

—— (1995) *Excavations at Essex Street West, Dublin* (Temple Bar archaeological report 2), Dublin: Temple Bar Properties Ltd.

Wallace, P. (1985) 'The archaeology of Viking Dublin', in H.B. Clarke and A. Simms (eds) *The Comparative History of Urban Origins in Non-Roman Europe* (British Archaeological Reports. International Series 255), Oxford: British Archaeological Reports.

—— (1992) *The Viking Age Buildings of Dublin*, 2 vols, Dublin: Royal Irish Academy.

CHAPTER THIRTY-THREE

SCANDINAVIA AND THE CONTINENT IN THE VIKING AGE

————·◆·————

Johan Callmer

During the entire Viking Age Scandinavia was profoundly influenced by the spiritual and material culture of Continental Europe. As we might expect, this cultural Continental impact was most influential in the southern and south-western parts of Scandinavia. From there it often reached other parts of Scandinavia as a secondary phenomenon but there are several exceptions to this rule. The influence was very significant and the culture in Scandinavia at the end of the Viking Age had adopted numerous important cultural patterns of Continental origin. At that date Scandinavian culture in many respects had already become a variant of a west and central European culture. This *rapprochement* with Continental culture then continued in the high and late Middle Ages. For once rather legitimate political reasons this Continental influence has been generally undervalued by much Scandinavian twentieth-century research. As a consequence the study of this cultural process has been neglected in comparison with the broad study of Insular influence. Although highly relevant and indeed in many ways central, the Christianisation of Scandinavia will not be treated here but separately (see Brink, ch. 45, below).

Continental cultural influence in Scandinavia is of course an obvious consequence of the geopolitical position of Scandinavia. However, we must also consider the fact that Scandinavian cultural exchange with other parts of Europe from the Stone Age onwards mainly followed a north–south pattern. The east–west perspective so important in the high medieval period and later in the modern period begins only on a modest level in the centuries preceding the Viking Age (Callmer 1990). The Continental cultural influence is not homogeneous and the process is dynamic, including both phases when change is radical and rapid and others when culture influence is slow and steady. Also the geography of the homeland of this Continental influence is different and changing over time. Continental cultural influence in Scandinavia emanates from four different geographical zones: (1) the North Sea coastal lands from southern Jutland down to the Channel, a region often named Frisia; (2) the central part of the Merovingian and Carolingian state including the major part of Neustria and north-western Austrasia; (3) Saxony (the heartland of the East Frankish and later German kingdom); (4) the lands of the Slavs on the southern coast of the Baltic from the southern end of the Jutish peninsula in the west to the mouth of the Vistula in the east. The first three zones were in mutual connection with each other but their chronological phases and their factual content are different. Saxony only becomes important in the tenth century. Frisia is important at the beginning of the Viking Age and possibly also towards the end of the period. The Carolingian heartland is most important in the late eighth and ninth centuries. The lands of the Baltic Slavs are important throughout the Viking period but seemingly this cultural link also has an early and a late main focus. Certainly the cultural interaction was no one-way process. Scandinavia also influenced the Continent of Europe. Mainly, we must sadly contend that this influence was negative and destructive (Zettel 1977). The picture of the Vikings in the west also as carriers of economic initiative and culture is a grave misconception initiated as a positive model from the past some fifty years ago in the name of contemporary west European cooperation. Connections between the western Slavs and the Scandinavians had a more mutual character.

FRISIA

In the early medieval period, as for the Barbarian parts of the coast much earlier, the populations along the southern North Sea coast had developed a number of similar variations of a coastal culture with strong internal links. These links of cultural exchange and political connections not only bound this zone together but also brought ideas and cultural patterns along the coast, mostly from the south-west to the north-east. This communication system was bound together effectively by links of coastal shipping routes. These coastal populations were known under the label of Frisians and they spoke a language of their own, although not so unlike those of their inland neighbours and the insular population on the other side of the Channel. Politically the entire Frisian territory was never united under one single polity. However, considerable power had been wielded by Frisian kings in the central part of the Frisian area in the late seventh and early eighth centuries (Heidinga 1997). Later the Carolingian state expanded stepwise into the entire Frisian coastal zone. Frisia was Christianised during the eighth and ninth centuries. The process was however slow and only in the later part of the ninth century did the population of the coastal lands north of the Elbe estuary convert.

Groups in Frisia had for a considerable time kept up regular shipping both across the sea to England and along the Continental coast northwards into Scandinavian waters at least to south-western Jutland and possibly even further. The most important entrepot for this shipping was Dorestad in the Rhine estuary but there were some additional ports of great importance. In the pre-Viking Age centuries traditional links with Scandinavia had increased and Frisians certainly played an important role in connection with the foundation of the earliest major trading place in Scandinavia (later emporium) at Ribe in south-western Jutland in the early eighth century. In fact the idea behind the artificial tongue of sand on which the market at Ribe was located may be more Frisian than Scandinavian. In fact the whole idea of the emporium as a socio-economic focal point was taken over from north-western Europe to northern Europe and the Baltic region. There are of course some differences but the general pattern is very similar. It has often been assumed that Scandinavians took over the further transport of goods as soon as the Continentals reached Danish territory in southern Jutland. This remains very unclear and it is indeed not unlikely that some individuals and some ships crossed into

Scandinavian waters. That Frisians were exclusively acquainted with ships intended for the shallow waters inside the chain of offshore islands on the North Sea coast is unlikely. The traffic across to the Thames estuary and further north along the east coast of England called for a type of ship that could also be used for travel into Scandinavian waters. The number of Frisians at trading sites like Hedeby and Birka was probably limited, but their presence is well confirmed by literary sources. Archaeologically Frisian connections are certified by numerous finds of Frisian coins, combs and decorative bronze keys (sometimes with Christian symbols). Also the occurrence in the southern part of the Baltic region of Frisian *Muschelgrus*-pottery is a weighty indication. The numerous finds of Frisian combs which distinctively but only subtly differ from Scandinavian combs at south Scandinavian coastal sites are also indicative of the presence of Frisians in the north in the late eighth and early ninth centuries. Specific grave customs have also been discussed in connection with the question of Frisians in Scandinavia. West–east orientated inhumation graves in early contexts (Hedeby and Birka) may be the graves of Christian Continental guests, and then preferably Frisians. Also at Hedeby some pagan cremations with pottery of North Sea type have been discussed under a similar viewpoint (Callmer 1998). South-western Jutland intensively interacted with the northernmost Frisian groups (La Baume 1953). Here in the eighth and ninth centuries a culture evolved which was largely similar on both sides. It seems likely that this culture was common for both the Scandinavian-speaking and Frisian-speaking populations.

The Frisian agents of exchange could have brought parts of the important Continental imports to the north. We are here dealing with imports that were essential for the reproduction of Scandinavian culture. Among these products were casting metal (for the production of brooches and ornaments), metal vessels (non iron), raw glass (for the production of beads), glass vessels, quernstones of basalt lava, high-quality textiles and high-quality offensive weapons. The social system and the political structures in Scandinavia were, long before the Viking Age, partly dependent on these imports for the maintenance of gift-giving and exchange. They were also directly or indirectly important for the expression of social roles and ranks. These commodities from the south-west were certainly exchanged or traded for Scandinavian products. The Frisians were involved in the transportation of the major products of the north such as fine furs, amber and slaves towards the south. There is also evidence of Scandinavians visiting (not only plundering) important Frisian entrepots like Dorestad.

Indirect influence from the female sector of Frisian culture is the introduction of equal-armed brooches in the second half of the eighth century (see Callmer 1998: 473). Equal-armed brooches interestingly enough were not a characteristic of the closest variants of Frisian culture. They are mostly found in contemporary Holland, Belgium and northern France (Normandy and Département du Nord). Carolingian coins from the mint at Dorestad and Frisian *sceattas* were the prototypes for early experiments with minting undertaken within Scandinavia.

This evidence of interaction between Scandinavia and Frisia can be followed from the eighth century well into the ninth. The finds indicating interaction in Scandinavia from the late ninth and tenth centuries are relatively few; they are mainly pottery finds. Most frequent is Frisian *Kugeltopf*-pottery in western Jutland but it also occasionally turns up on the Baltic side of the peninsula and further afield in the Baltic region (Madsen 2004). It is only natural that this close connection between the southern North

Sea coast and south-western Denmark remains significant through the centuries. It seems reasonable that earlier activities continued into later periods. The numismatic material from the late tenth century indicates that persons and groups in the central parts of the Frisian area are again very active in trade directed towards the Baltic and beyond, to north-eastern Europe. An interesting confirmation of these indications is provided by two inscriptions on runestones at Sigtuna, dating to the mid-eleventh century, providing evidence of the existence of a guild of people trading with Frisia or with Frisians.

The spiritual influence of the Frisians on Scandinavian culture is very difficult to ascertain. However, the seemingly sudden occurrence of some mythological themes in the eighth century could find its explanation in this way. We are here especially concerned with the Wayland myth and the Vǫlsunga/Niebelungen motif. The iconography of the pictorial stones of Gotland shows the familiarity with these motifs on the island in the second half of the eighth century, and we may suppose that they were disseminated also along the mainland coasts.

THE CENTRAL PART OF THE MEROVINGIAN AND CAROLINGIAN KINGDOM AND EMPIRE

The cultural influence of the central part of the Merovingian and Carolingian realm (major parts of Neustria and north-western Austrasia) on large parts of Europe was huge. Already in the early days of this political formation the ruling dynasties, the high aristocracy and their entourage developed an exclusive elite culture mainly from elements of Late Antiquity but also from contemporary Byzantine culture. Some Barbaric traditions were also included but did not prevail in all parts of this area. From the beginning of the sixth century the Christian Church, its major institutions and its high officials were integrated into this culture. From the very beginning the influence of this elite culture was strong on the other side of the Channel in Anglo-Saxon England (Hawkes 1982). Along the North Sea coast it was important in Frisia and in Lower Saxony and Westphalia. The latter parts were also reached from the south. Coming up from the south-west it also had quite early an impact on Scandinavia. How much of this influence was secondary and how much was direct (some direct connection cannot be ignored), is a complicated question. Beginning in the eighth century but remarkably powerfully in the ninth century these influences reached the central European Slavs and other Slav communities in the Carpathian Basin and in the northern Balkans. Although this process must mainly be studied with the help of material traces we should, of course, from the beginning, consider the immaterial side of it much more important. Ideas of kingship, empire and dominion also on a lower level as well as socio-economic principles for the organisation of landed wealth through an elaborate estate economy were significant. These ideas gradually transformed the political and economic structures of the Carolingian periphery. This is not to say that the process of transmission was simple. The disseminated elements of political organisation and an aristocratic lifestyle were sometimes indeed partly rejected, but always locally modified and integrated in local cultural tradition. In Scandinavia, especially in the south-west, we can note an increase in this influence in the eighth century (Arbman 1937; Arwidsson 1942). However, the real breakthrough comes only in the tenth century and is connected with the Saxon kingdom (see below). The study of this very complex cultural influence from the Merovingian and Carolingian state has been rather neglected, as already hinted at above. It has been understood as German influence. This is a misconception since Germany indeed did not exist at that time either as a political entity or as a cultural province.

The study of this development of an aristocratic lifestyle under Continental influence in Scandinavia can be followed only with great difficulty in the archaeological record. The main reason is the almost complete discontinuation of articulate aristocratic graves in southern Scandinavia beginning already in the Migration period. In other parts of Scandinavia some graves from the top level of society are known, but being cremations they have few and in some cases not very representative fragments. Thus we have little or no possibility of studying significant complexes of personal artefacts of various types. During the past fifteen years our knowledge of aristocratic milieus in Scandinavia has expanded immensely. The main traits of aristocratic residences both in the pre-Viking period and in the Viking period have become increasingly clear. These complexes with their halls, cult houses, cult enclosures, houses and workshops have been brought into connection with supposed influence from Carolingian palaces. So far this seems to be a misconception. The tradition of the layout of aristocratic compounds and their buildings must rather be seen as a northern, Barbarian cultural phenomenon developed already in the Roman Iron Age or even earlier. This northern tradition consequently has little to do with the southern developments. The concept of the Carolingian palace is firmly rooted in the tradition of Late Antiquity and Byzantine tradition and it reaches Scandinavia only at the very end of the Viking Age.

Accepting this negative situation for a closer study of the Merovingian and Carolingian influence on Scandinavian aristocratic culture we can pick out some secondary cultural traits, which can give us some idea of the connection. It is very notable that it is primarily in the masculine sector of Scandinavian society that we can best record this influence. Although ceremonial drinking of alcoholic drinks in the northern cultures also had a long history, the cultural requisites employed at the highest social level, from the late migration period onwards, were largely copied from Continental cultural patterns. Ceremonial drinking at this level of society was connected with drinking from glass beakers imported from the Continent. Although glass vessels had already been brought to the north in the Roman Iron Age the volume of this importation expanded in the Merovingian and especially the early Carolingian period. Huge numbers of shards of glass vessels have been recovered on the trading sites of the pre-Viking and Viking Age around Scandinavia (Näsman 1986, 1990; Jensen 1991: 15). It is very likely that the local drinking ceremonies were also influenced by those of the Merovingian aristocracy. Exclusive foreign drinking practices were integrated into the aristocratic culture of the halls. Whether wines were imported throughout the period must remain uncertain, but it is most likely that at least in Jutland aristocrats could occasionally drink wine (mulled?). Especially in south-western Scandinavia this influence has been strong, but it also reached out further towards the north and north-east.

Hunting was another socially significant pastime among the Merovingian and Carolingian aristocracy. Hunting of course also had a long history in Scandinavia with its large woodlands. It is however a tendency especially in south-western Scandinavia that venison disappears completely from the menu of ordinary people already in the Roman Iron Age if not even earlier. The right to hunt for the big game available seemingly becomes a prerogative of the uppermost stratum of society. The Continental aristocratic hunting culture with mounted hunters, beaters and packs of dogs spread to the Merovingian and Carolingian periphery and probably also to the north. Hunting parks may also be an innovation in Scandinavia brought over from the Continental hunting culture in the pre-Viking Age. The existence of hunting parks for deer hunting is indicated by the availability of red deer antler in masses from the seventh century on. Since a high percentage of antlers found at comb-making sites is shed antler it is most likely that these numbers of antlers could be collected only in delimited parks (Callmer 2001). The importance of hunting with trained birds of prey also increased as a result of Continental impulses in the same period (Åkerström-Hougen 1981; Sten and Vretemark 1988). The Scandinavian uppermost stratum in the Viking Age was familiar with both these pastimes.

To what extent masculine dress in Viking Age Scandinavia was influenced by Frankish prototypes is little known. It is less likely that feminine dress was profoundly influenced before the tenth century. It is however most likely that the intensive inter-action of south-western Scandinavia with the central parts of the Carolingian Empire in the middle and second half of the ninth century resulted in a number of imitated elements of dress on the masculine side. Also the possibility of earlier Merovingian and Carolingian influences on dress on the highest social level should not be excluded. Here again our archaeological sources are unfortunately insufficient. There is a better basis for such considerations when we turn to weapons and sword belts, bandoliers and horse equipment. Already before the eighth century Scandinavians followed the main trends in the Continental development of arms and armature although somewhat tardily (see Arbman 1937). Still in the middle of the eighth century sword hilts with parts made of cast bronze and with animal ornamentation were produced in eastern Scandinavia. In western Scandinavia a sharp break can be noted in the middle of the century with a massive import of Carolingian high-quality weapons (as mentioned above in connection with the Frisian trade), mainly swords and lance-heads. A similar pattern of change could be noted in the (mainly) Slav lands beyond the eastern border of Carolingia. Modern Continental, highly efficient arms soon became a standard for warriors all over Scandinavia. Soon they were also traded or exchanged on the eastern side of the Baltic. As far as the archaeological sources can inform us this influence is mainly confined to offensive arms whereas protective weapons remained more traditional. Finds of real armour are however too few to give us the possibility of judging the question. The mounted warrior already appears in the Merovingian period if not earlier but only slowly becomes important. There is much to suggest that mounted troops copying Carolingian standards were organised in southern Jutland already in the late eighth century. Occa-sional finds show us that these impulses also reached other parts of Scandinavia such as Norway. These changes in armaments most probably equalled changes in fight-ing technique and military culture in general. The cavalry of the Jutish kings may however have become disorganised as the royal power disintegrated in the second half of the ninth century.

So far little discussed but very significant is the question of the influences of Carolingian manorial organisation on the north. For a long time the evaluation of the level of Carolingian agriculture by historians was very negative and the breakthrough of west European agriculture with numerous important innovations was dated to the eleventh century (Devroey 1993; cf. Duby 1976). During the past twenty years it has become increasingly clear that, mainly as a result of archaeological studies, the majority of these innovations must be dated to the Carolingian period. ~~The fact that Scandinavians came into direct contact with the Carolingian agrarian economy and estate organisation as territorial lords in Carolingia in the ninth century makes it very likely that the Scandinavians did pick up some of their ideas and became aware of their superiority.~~ Estate organisation in Scandinavia certainly antedates the ninth century and the Viking period change is rather a qualitative one (Callmer 2001). One very important innovation is the water mill, which in Europe rapidly spread from the south-west to the east, beginning in the eighth or ninth century. The earliest water mill so far known was excavated at Omgård in west Jutland and dates to the tenth century but that does not mean that the mills had not already reached south-western Scandinavia in the ninth century (Nielsen 1986). ~~Elaborate forms of field rotation and enclosures may also have been innovations from the Continent as well as the equalisation of dependent farms.~~

For a long time it has been recognised that Carolingian ornamental art influenced Scandinavia profoundly. One of the major problems is to make out what is Continental influence and what is Insular. This is to a certain extent a pseudo-question since artists and artisans circulated between the Continent and the British Isles. The Continental connection of style D (*sensu* Arwidsson 1942), the dominating style of the first half of the eighth century, remains unclear. The development of style E in the second half of that century is however closely connected with the development of the Tassilo chalice style. The regional, south-west Scandinavian style F is even more closely connected with this Continental ornamentation and may be understood as a close but qualitatively often questionable rendering of the Tassilo chalice style. The so-called gripping-beast style has often been discussed in connection with Continental influences. Recently some scholars have argued for a purely Scandinavian innovation (e.g. Neiss 2004). This seems less convincing and the problem seems to be partly of chronological character. Gripping animals, with the exception of ornamentation on some oval brooches produced in south-western Scandinavia from *c.* AD 790, are hardly datable before AD 800. The vast majority are later. Further, the best parallels to the Scandinavian gripping beasts are still the small animals on the Lindau book cover (late eighth century). When considering these questions we must realise the possible ways of influence from artisan to artisan including a process of recurrent confirmation by the customer or employer.

In the late ninth century Carolingian plant ornamentation is used on trefoil brooches produced in Scandinavia for women. This clear influence is obviously of a secondary character. ~~As a result of intensive raiding of the central part of the Carolingian realm in the 860s, complete Carolingian sword belts set with mounts with plant ornamentation were brought as loot to southern Scandinavia~~ (see Schilling 2003), where they sometimes ended up on production sites as raw metal. Trefoil mounts from these sword belts were sometimes converted into brooches and soon copied by south Scandinavian producers. Initially only plant ornamentation was used on these brooches, but very soon various animal ornaments appeared on the flaps (Skibsted-Klæsøe 1998). The same story is told by some less numerous but generally similar strap-end-shaped brooches.

Unfortunately we have very little primary archaeological evidence for the earliest initiatives for the Christianisation of the north. Secondary material, especially Christian symbols used in ornamental art, are numerous from the late eighth century on. When primary evidence turns up it will certainly be closely connected with the Christian culture of the central Carolingian area.

SAXONY

When the central Carolingian territory treated above began to disintegrate politically after the Treaty of Verdun in 843, this only gradually led to a division of the earlier cultural unity of Carolingia. The political and economic consolidation of the German kingdom during the first half of the tenth century, however, brought about a new situation of great significance for Scandinavia. During the tenth and eleventh centuries the connections with Continental Europe were mainly with this successor state of the Carolingian Empire. With its centres more closely situated to Scandinavia and with great territorial ambitions towards the east, the German kingdom was bound to play a significant role in the connections between Scandinavia and the Continent. The political connections between the Danish kingdom(s?) and the German kingdom were complicated and Jutland was invaded probably twice in the tenth century. For some short periods the German king controlled parts of southern Jutland. When Christianisation of the entire population in Scandinavia begins in the tenth century, Christian mission and ecclesiastical organisation are dominantly connected with the Church in the German kingdom.

The development of kingship with pretensions to controlling state territories in Scandinavia in the tenth and eleventh centuries is connected with models taken from the German kingdom although inspiration also from post-Alfred England should not be completely ruled out. The cultural expression of this new idea of kingship was to a considerable degree taken over from the Continent. Only during the end of the tenth century and at the beginning of the eleventh was Anglo-Saxon influence strong. The architectural expression of the ambitions, both secular and ecclesiastical, of central power in the eleventh century is stone architecture. In these manifestations we find influences from the German kingdom and from Anglo-Saxon England as well. Unfortunately we have no basis for an evaluation of external influence on the development of aristocratic architecture of the late Viking Age. The Scandinavian aristocratic residences mentioned above were in existence until the beginning of the eleventh century or until *c.* AD 1000. What their replacements looked like we do not know.

It is likely that the foreign influence on the culture of the topmost social stratum in Scandinavia continued to be strong in the tenth and eleventh centuries. The culture of the German royal household and the high aristocracy, both spiritual and material, was a very influential model for the upper social strata in Scandinavia. As before this was probably primarily the situation in south-western Scandinavia but it was from there as a secondary phenomenon also felt in other, more remote parts of Scandinavia. The very restricted availability of investigated graves and the low standard of knowledge of the material culture of aristocratic residences of the eleventh century, as pointed out above, make detailed evaluation difficult. Difficulties for example with the recovery of unstable potassium glass make it uncertain to what extent ceremonial drinking from glass vessels was still important. Metal beakers may have been increasingly favoured. Hunting as a pastime was still popular but we do not know to what extent new innovations were taken over from the Continent (signal horns?). The dress of the aristocratic stratum in Scandinavia was certainly strongly influenced by the Continental pattern (see below).

The economy of the German kingdom was strong as it could fall back on considerable deposits of silver in the Harz highlands. Coined silver from the German kingdom begins to play an important role in treasure finds and stray-finds collections already at the end of the tenth century. This German silver stimulated trade and exchange relationships especially in the Baltic region. As has been shown for the contemporary connections with Frisia, it is not unlikely that traders from the German kingdom did travel in Scandinavia and carry out transactions there. There is however no basis for an interpretation of this state of affairs as evidence of the existence of a Hansa organisation before the foundation of the Hanseatic League in the twelfth century. On the contrary it is more likely that it is evidence of a continuation of a tenth-century pattern of trade between the German kingdom and Scandinavia and regions beyond towards the north-east.

As before in the ninth century and earlier, arms and armour as well as horse-riding equipment are some of the most significant sources for our understanding of the Continental connections of Scandinavia. The general Continental trends in weaponry are well reflected in the Scandinavian material and there are large numbers of imported weapons from Continental workshops. The relatively great importance of the axe as an offensive weapon in Scandinavia, however, shows the relative independence and originality of Scandinavian combat techniques. During the eleventh century arms and armour in the north as well are internationalised and become almost universally European. In comparison with ninth-century standards much more efficient cavalry develops in the tenth century in the German kingdom, partly as a response to the disastrous large-scale raids of the Magyars, who were established in the Carpathian Basin at the very end of the ninth century. This is the beginning of the formation of the heavy cavalry of the European type so characteristic of the Middle Ages. Unfortunately our knowledge of armour in this period in Scandinavia is nil with the exception of the probably rather outdated equipment in the Gjermundbu grave in Norway. Lances become lighter but more efficient and the increase in mail-penetrating arrowheads tells of a much wider use of mail coats and other types of armour. The new bridles, saddles, stirrups and spurs that were developed (and partly taken over from the Magyars) gave the equestrian warrior a new efficiency and control (Pedersen 1997). To what extent taller horses for mounted combat were introduced in Scandinavia from the Continent is yet uncertain. Importation is however most likely especially in the second half of the tenth century, when King Harald (certainly with cavalry) fights back against German troops in southern Jutland. An earlier importation of taller horses already in the ninth century cannot be ruled out completely.

The new wave of urbanisation in Scandinavia beginning in the second half of the tenth century (after the first which was connected with the rise of the emporia) is closely connected with similar patterns in Saxony. Initiatives of the Church for a firm ecclesiastical administration and of the secular royal power for the establishment of dominion, separately or in union, play a key role notwithstanding the often very obvious connection with the trade network.

The basic innovative ideas of the agricultural regime and the organisation of estates were connected with the central parts of Carolingia, as pointed out above. These innovations were also important in the German kingdom and the influence on later Scandinavian development rather came from there. This is especially important in the very active period of new formations of estates in the wake of the general power-political restructure of the Danish kingdom in the late tenth and early eleventh centuries (see below). In addition to the innovations mentioned in connection with the central

Carolingian region, we can note an important innovation in house-building technique comprising large parts of southern Scandinavia in the late tenth and eleventh centuries (Meier 1994). House building with the weight of the roof resting on the posts in the wall had been developed much earlier in Continental western Europe. This way of building the house gave better access to the entire indoor surface of the house. Probably there was also a social and cultural aspect to this change. The posts in the earlier post-built, mostly three-aisled main buildings had religious and mythical significance. This means that the idea of the house as a micro cosmos changed. It is significant that this change comes simultaneously with the consolidation of Christianity in south-western Scandinavia. The house-building technique is introduced from German territory and from Jutland expands east to contemporary south-western Sweden.

When the Scandinavian production of traditional dress ornaments collapsed *c.* AD 970–80, dress at all levels of Scandinavian society was strongly influenced from the south (Kaland 1992). This influence from the south however begins already in the first half of the tenth century when round brooches are introduced as an innovation inspired by the *fibula* fashion of the Continent. In Scandinavia at first the small round brooches were incorporated in the traditional Scandinavian feminine status dress. Whereas most other brooches were almost only produced in bronze (sometimes gilded), small round brooches are more often produced in silver. The ornamentation on the round brooches may feature traditional animal figures but it is more common that the bronze specimens show interlace patterns and patterns connected with the filigree decoration on silver specimens. At the end of the tenth century the round fibula is the only one to survive the demise of the old canon of dress ornament.

In the final century of the Viking Age the main stream of innovations from the south and from the west passed through the territory of the German kingdom. Major cultural concepts and models with this origin were adopted. This does however not mean that the Frisian regions were completely eclipsed but rather that Frisian influence gradually became restricted to south-western Jutland. Insular influence is not altogether non-existent but mainly becomes restricted to certain centres like Lund in eastern Denmark, where people from the west also played a role in the royal administration.

THE WESTERN SLAVS ON THE SOUTHERN COASTS OF THE BALTIC

When we now turn to the Slavic cultural milieu to the east of the Continental Saxons we meet a culture and socio-economic patterns that in many respects are basically similar to those of the Scandinavians. The culture of the Continental west was stronger and, in general, when Scandinavians were confronted with elements of that culture the Continental patterns were ultimately accepted. The northern part of the Continent to the east of the Elbe had a cultural history quite different from that of the west. Parts of the most probably once Germanic population in the area had migrated towards the south-west in the fifth century, but still minor groups remained in the area in the sixth century. Slavic colonisation from the south-east reached the Baltic coast in the seventh century. The important question of how these populations with different traditions interacted is unfortunately still insufficiently elucidated. In contrast to the former inhabitants on the southern coast of the Baltic the new ones were, notwithstanding certain parallels, in many details culturally rather different from the Scandinavians and they spoke a language with little resemblance to that of the Scandinavians. It is however not to be excluded that mixing with the remaining small population groups resulted in a certain cultural and linguistic competence among the Slavs which could make communication with the Scandinavians on the opposite coasts more easy and desirable. The shipbuilding traditions on the southern Slav coast of the Baltic may have something to tell of continuation of earlier cultural patterns. The ships and boats of the Slavs and the Scandinavians were built according to similar principles, although a few characteristic differences can be noted (Slaski 1978). We have no reason to assume that shipbuilding was part of the Slavic culture before the Slavs reached the Baltic coast.

Intensive interaction between Scandinavians and Slavs starts already in *c.* AD 700. The interaction is concentrated in special places and regions. The main interaction is channelled through trading places, which were organised on both the Scandinavian and the Slavic sides of the Baltic. On the Scandinavian side these contacts, which are already well documented from the first half of the eighth century, could be demonstrated for example through the regular import of distinct Slavic pottery to trading places and to a certain degree also further afield (Callmer 1988). Scandinavian products to some extent also penetrated into the Slavic hinterland. We are here mainly concerned with jewellery, combs, quality cutting tools and weapons. The rather low population density in large parts of the Slav hinterland could have contributed to a considerable volume of fur hunting and trading, especially beaver. The slave trade was certainly also important because of the high economic value of this commodity. These connections continue in the ninth century and the trading sites played an important role on both sides for socio-economic development. Scandinavian patterns of political dominion may have stimulated the development of increasingly complex political structures among the Slavs although the Carolingian influence was stronger in large parts of the lands of the western Slavs. Early forms of Scandinavian estate building and management could also have been introduced among the Slavs at this date. The special character of Slav material culture before the tenth century with few distinct characteristics other than pottery makes an assessment of the breadth and weight of Slav and Scandinavian interaction difficult. It may however have been very considerable. Possibly Scandinavian religious patterns influenced west Slavic temples. The Slavic cult sites with rectangular houses and fenced yards are intriguingly similar to south Scandinavian cult complexes. If this is so, interaction must have had a very deep dimension.

Interaction with the Slav lands was, as we may expect, best developed in eastern Denmark, Skåne and on Bornholm. For lack of targeted research we can follow the process only to a certain extent in Skåne. West Slav culture is well represented at Hedeby in the tenth century, whereas more distant trading sites like Birka have much less evidence. West Slav culture developed strongly in the tenth century when influences from the Danubian lands and from Bohemia reached the Baltic. Slav silverwork taking up this southern impulse, mainly jewellery, is increasingly common in Scandinavian hoards of the late tenth century.

A more intensive and important period of interaction according to our sources begins in the late tenth century. This interaction is complex and has for both Scandinavians and Slavs far-reaching cultural consequences. We have good reason to connect this phase with the radical political and social transformation of the Danish kingdom and surrounding territories. In parts of this south Scandinavian zone a new and loyal aristocracy was established by the kings, and corresponding landholdings for their maintenance were carved out. The kings also needed loyal warriors. A considerable part of this personnel (and we are here talking of whole families) was recruited, kidnapped or bought as slaves from the Slav lands on the southern side of the Baltic. The most convincing evidence for this cultural and demographic process is the broad introduction of a standard pottery in Insular Denmark, Skåne, Bornholm and adjoining parts, which strikingly imitates west Slavic pottery (Roslund 2001). Very significant is the occurrence of genuine west Slavic pottery on the Danish side in the last two decades of the tenth century and the beginning of the secondary, local pottery production in the eleventh century. The beginnings are connected with certain important places and from there the innovation is diffused throughout society. Sunken-featured buildings have been discussed in connection with Slav cultural influence. There is probably no reason to presuppose a Slavic connection for this house form, not even for variants with corner stone ovens. The type is well known from Lower Saxony and surrounding areas. In the cultural development of the eleventh century a notable convergence between west Slavic and Scandinavian material culture can be noted. Unfortunately a broad analysis of this cultural phenomenon for southern Scandinavia as a whole has not yet been carried out (see Andersen 1982). We can, however, maintain that the close dynastic ties at the top level of society between southern Scandinavia and the west Slav lands corresponded to considerable interaction and cultural transfer also at lower levels of society.

CONCLUSION

The cultural development of Scandinavia is not conceivable without a thorough and positive evaluation of the importance of Continental influence. Although Viking warbands and armies for certain short periods could wield considerable political power in Continental Europe, their cultural impact, that is, the transfer of Scandinavian cultural elements to Continental milieus, was virtually nil. Much more significant is the rather steady development of Continental cultural influence on Scandinavia throughout the Viking Age. From the present viewpoint of archaeological research, the trend seems to be strong in the eighth and early ninth centuries, followed by a certain decrease. A century later the cultural impact of the Continent is again very strong. We can here only repeat what has been stated above: in the eleventh century Scandinavian culture is well on the way to the common west and central European culture of the twelfth and later centuries of the Middle Ages. Continental influence often first reached the upper levels of Scandinavian society and only later was generally adopted. In some cases the process of change is so rapid that this difference is difficult to document. So perhaps it was not there at all.

BIBLIOGRAPHY

Åkerström-Hougen, G. (1981) 'Falconry as a motif in early Swedish art: its historical and art historical significance', in R. Zeitler (ed.) *Les Pays du Nord et Byzance. Actes du colloque nordique et internationale de byzantinologie tenu à Upsal 20–22 avril 1979*, Uppsala: Almqvist & Wiksell International.

Andersen, M. (1982) 'De dansk-vendiske forbindelser ca. 950–1225. En karakteristik af arten og omfanget især med henblick på disse forbindelsers betydning for Danmark'. (Unpubl. MA diss., University of Aarhus.)

Arbman, H. (1937) *Schweden und das karolingische Reich. Studien zu den Handelsverbindungen des 9. Jahrhunderts* (KVHAAs Handlingar 43), Stockholm: Wahlström & Widstrand.

Arwidsson, G. (1942) *Vendelstile, Email und Glas im 7.–8. Jahrhundert* (Acta Musei antiquitatum septentrionalium Regiae Universitatis Upsaliensis 2), Uppsala: Almqvist.

Callmer, J. (1988) 'Slawisch-skandinavische Kontakte am Beispiel der slawischen Keramik in Skandinavien im achten und neunten Jahrhundert', *Bericht der Römisch-Germanischen Kommission*, 69: 654–74.

—— (1990) 'The beginning of the Easteuropean trade connections of Scandinavia and the Baltic Region in the eighth and ninth centuries A.D.', *A Wosinsky Mór Múzeum Evkönye*, 15: 19–51.

—— (1998) 'Archaeological sources for the presence of Frisian agents of trade in northern Europe ca. AD 700–900', in A. Wesse (ed.) *Studien zur Archäologie des Ostseeraumes. Festschrift für M. Müller-Wille*, Neumünster: Wachholtz.

—— (2001) 'Extinguished solar systems and black holes: traces of late prehistoric and early medieval domains in Scandinavia', in B. Hårdh (ed.) *Uppåkra. Centrum och sammanhang* (Acta archaeologica Lundensia. Series in 8° no. 34; Uppåkrastudier 4), Lund: Almqvist & Wiksell International.

Devroey, J.-P. (1993) *Etudes sur le grand domaine carolingien* (Variorum reprints 391), Aldershot: Variorum.

Duby, G. (1976) *Rural Economy and Country Life in the Medieval West*, Columbia: University of South Carolina Press.

Hawkes, S.Ch. (1982) 'Anglo-Saxon Kent *c.* 425–725', in P. Leach (ed.) *Archaeology in Kent to AD 1500* (The Council for British Archaeology. Research report 48), London: Council for British Archaeology.

Heidinga, H.A. (1997) *Frisia in the First Millennium. An Outline*, Utrecht: Matrijs.

Jensen, S. (1991) *Ribes vikinger*, Ribe: Den antikvariske samling.

Kaland, S. (1992) 'Dress', in E. Roesdahl and D.M. Wilson (eds) *From Viking to Crusader. The Scandinavians and Europe 800–1200* (Council of Europe exhibition 22), Copenhagen: Nordisk ministerråd.

La Baume, P. (1953) 'Die Wikingerzeit auf den nordfriesischen Inseln', *Jahrbuch des Nordfriesischen Vereins für Heimatkunde und Heimatliebe*, 29 (1952–3): 5–184.

Madsen, H. (2004) 'Pottery from the 8th–9th centuries', in M. Bencard *et al.* (eds) *Ribe Excavations 1970–76*, vol. 5, Højbjerg: Jutland Archaeological Society.

Meier, D. (1994) *Die wikingerzeitliche Siedlung von Kosel (Kosel-West), Kreis Rendsburg-Eckernförde.* (Siedlungsarchäologische Untersuchungen in Angeln und Schwansen, vol. 3; Offa Bücher 76), Neumünster: Wachholtz.

Näsman, U. (1986) 'Vendel period glass from Eketorp II, Öland, Sweden', *Acta Archaeologica*, 55 (1984): 55–116.

—— (1990) 'Om fjärrhandel i Sydskandinaviens yngre järnålder. Handel med glas under germansk järnålder och vikingatid', *Hikuin*, 16: 89–118.

Neiss, M. (2004) 'Midgårdsormen och fenrisulven. Två grundmotiv i vendeltidens djurornamentik. Kontinuitetsfrågor i germansk djurornamentik', *Fornvännen*, 99: 9–25.

Nielsen, L.-Chr. (1986) 'Omgård: the Viking Age water mill complex. A provisional report on the 1986 excavations', *Acta Archaeologica*, 57: 177–204.

Pedersen, A. (1997) 'Weapons and riding gear in burials – evidence of military and social rank in 10th century Denmark', in A. Jørgensen and B. Clausen (eds) *Military Aspects of Scandinavian Society in a European Perspective AD 1–1300*, Copenhagen: National Museum of Denmark.

Roslund, M. (2001) *Gäster i huset. Kulturell överföring mellan slaver och skandinaver 900 till 1300*, Lund: Vetenskapssocieteten i Lund.

Schilling, H. (2003) 'Duesmindeskatten', *Skalk*, 2003(6): 5–12.

Skibsted-Klæsøe, L. (1998) 'Plant ornament: a key to a new chronology of the Viking Age', *Lund Archaeological Review*, 3: 73–87.

Slaski, K. (1978) 'Slawische Schiffe des westlichen Ostseeraumes', *Offa*, 35: 116–27.

Sten, S. and Vretemark, M. (1988) 'Storgravsprojektet – osteologiska analyser av yngre järnålderns benrika gravar', *Fornvännen*, 83: 145–56.

Zettel, H. (1977) *Das Bild der Normannen und der Normanneneinfälle*, Munich: Beck.

THE DUCHY OF NORMANDY

———•◆•———

Jean Renaud

THE TREATY OF SAINT-CLAIR

By the turn of the tenth century, the Vikings had sailed up and down the River Seine many times and plundered the area far and wide since their first attack in 820. Some of them had even settled along the estuary and lower part of the river, taking over several abandoned harbours (Le Maho 2003: 153–67). It is under these circumstances that the Frankish king, Charles the Simple, agreed to negotiate with their chief, Rollo (ON *Hrólfr*). (Figures 33.1.1 and 33.1.2.)

We have no written record of the so-called 'treaty of Saint-Clair-sur-Epte', and even the date is unknown: probably autumn 911. Dudo of Saint-Quentin has left us the only known account of that event, written a hundred years later and much criticised, perhaps too much, by historians (Neveux 1998: 19–27). The king apparently granted Rollo a

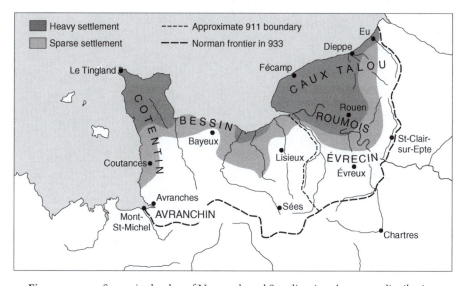

Figure 33.1.1   Successive borders of Normandy and Scandinavian place-name distribution.

453

Figure 33.1.2   Rollo's statue in Rouen.

territory already more or less under Danish control, demanding that the Vikings should defend it, thus protecting the realm from further attacks, and become Christians. On accepting these terms, Rollo – no one can say for sure whether he came from Denmark or Norway (Douglas 1942: 417–24; Renaud 1989: 47–55) – acquired mainly the *pagi* (circumscriptions) of Talou, Caux, Roumois and Evrecin, the area now called Upper Normandy. But it turned out only to be the first step. In 924 King Raoul extended that 'county of Rouen' westward to the River Vire, including Bessin, where more Danes, coming over from England, had recently settled. Then in 933, Raoul gave Rollo's son and successor, William Longsword, Cotentin and Avranchin, which the Bretons had ruled before. North-Cotentin had long been settled by Norwegians coming from the Irish Sea area, who now showed much hostility to the new Danish elite of Rouen.

The Vikings must have insisted that their new land could not be taken back. A diploma dated to 918 is the only contemporary testimony which indirectly confirms the agreement; the verb *annuere* is used. It expresses a genuine donation and that is probably why we never hear of Rollo's duties as a vassal. He accepted baptism and the new name of Robert, and encouraged the return of priests and monks in order to gain the people's favour, thus asserting personal political strength.

The three grants of 911, 924 and 933 enlarged the Scandinavian annexation to an area roughly reproducing the former ecclesiastical province of Rouen. Normandy was born, first as a county, but Rollo's great-grandson (Richard II) already called himself a duke, so one often refers to Normandy as a duchy from the very start (Helmerichs 1997: 57–77).

THE SCANDINAVIAN SETTLEMENT

The Vikings did not settle all over Normandy, nor did they sever the country from its roots. But each of the two mainly settled areas reflects a different attitude and different structures.

In Caux and Roumois, it was a coherent process of both settling and integrating. As the successor to Frankish counts, Rollo found it advisable to keep the current Carolingian system in place: he became the *Rúðujarl* (count of Rouen), as the Norse sagas later referred to him, but did not recreate a *þing*, an assembly, where all free men would meet and take decisions. He seems to have shared the larger estates fairly equally among his close companions and offered agricultural land to the remaining majority of his men without segregating the local population from the incomers, who cleared the land, built new farms and worked the fields.

In the less inhabited North-Cotentin, on the other hand, the settlement was purely Scandinavian. There is even evidence for the existence of a *þing*, situated at today's Le Tingland (Renaud and Ridel 2000: 304). The names given in their own language to lots of coastal features also indicate intense navigation. And when the area eventually became part of Normandy too, three of the ancient *pagi* happened to bear Norse names (still attested in a document of 1027): *Haga, Sarnes* and *Helganes*.

We do not know how much Scandinavian legislation Rollo originally enforced on his new territory: we only find traces of it in Norman customary law once it is written down in the thirteenth century, and in some older documents written by clerics who had no particular knowledge in matters of the north.

The right to exile is of undeniable Scandinavian origin. In a charter of 1050 listing the so-called 'ducal cases' which aroused the duke's anger (a Frankish tradition!), *ullac* (< ON *útlagr* 'banishment') is mentioned. The word is also found in Robert Wace's *Roman de Rou* in the twelfth century, and today's family names *Dodeman* and *Floteman* (< *dauðamaðr* 'man condemned to death' and *flóttamaðr* 'fugitive') also bear witness of it. Free union, *more danico* ('the Danish way'), was long admitted together with legal marriage before the Church. It was common practice in Scandinavia and the first rulers all had a concubine: Rollo's was Poppa, William's Sprota, Richard's Gunnor, who ensured their lineage.

Scandinavian influence has obviously been most significant in maritime organisation. The dukes had a monopoly on shipwrecks, the so-called 'droit du varech' (< ODa *vrek*), in the eleventh century. Besides, they had a right on whales and sturgeon – which reminds us of the law of Jutland (1241) stating that treasures, jetsam and fish larger than sturgeon were the king's property. All fishing must originally have depended on Scandinavian law. In a charter of 1030 we hear for example of *fisigardum* 'fisheries' (< ON *fiskigarðr*). The law of Scania also mentions *fiskigardha*. And in several documents from the eleventh century, whalers are known as *valmanni* (< *hvalmenn*) and the word *valseta* (< *hval*[*manna*]*setr*) describes a whaling station. But this activity existed before the arrival of the Vikings, and that also applies to the making of salt, in which they obviously took a great part as well.

Yet we have no details about the military structures under the first dukes. Did Rollo have his own *hirð* 'bodyguard'? Possibly, but reference to this appears nowhere: the only hint is the surname *Huscaille*, attested in 1263, derived from Norse *húskarl* 'housecarl'. Likewise, some sort of *leiðangr* must have existed, allowing the duke to levy an army (such as William the Conqueror did in 1066): but no document ever states it (Musset 1997 [1976]: 245–61).

A SUCCESSFUL INTEGRATION

One of the main features of the Viking settlement in Normandy is the rapid and successful mixing of Franks and Scandinavians, which created the Norman people in only a few generations' time. The eleventh-century author of the *Miracles of Saint Vulfran* understood it perfectly when he wrote: 'Rollo was not long in bringing together men of various extractions and crafts, shaping all races into one single people.'

While the Vikings integrated into the local community, their language declined fairly quickly. But many Norse words remained, some about everyday life, others for which there existed no precise equivalent. The Norman dialect has kept a few hundred of them, out of which modern French has borrowed a good number (de Gorog 1958). Among these are *homard* (< *humarr* 'lobster'), *vague* (< *vágr* 'wave'), *crique* (< *kriki* 'nook'), *duvet* (< *dúnn* 'down'), *girouette* (< *veðrviti* 'vane'), *débiter* (< *bita* 'to cut into bits'). And still today a French sailor currently uses some fifty Norse loan words without thinking of it, such as *quille* (*kjölr* 'keel'), *tolet* (*þollr* 'thole pin'), *hauban* (*höfuðbenda* 'stays'), *cingler* (*sigla* 'to sail'), *haler* (*hala* 'to haul') or *gréer* (*greiða* 'to rig').

Such words were actually used very early in Normandy in order to name places, such as *La Dalle* (< *dalr* 'valley'), *La Londe* (< *lundr* 'wood, grove'), *Le Torp* (< *þorp* 'isolated farm'), *Le Thuit* (< *þveit* 'clearing').

Indeed, although the country was already inhabited, the Scandinavian settlers named many topographical features and their new dwellings. All these place names allow us to mark the boundaries of the settled areas; they show a substantial and lasting influence, but by no means a deep upheaval (Fellows-Jensen 1988: 113–37; Renaud 1989: 153–98). Over a hundred names end in *bec*, like *Bricquebec* (< *brekka* 'slope' + *bekkr* 'brook'), and just as many in *tot*, like *Appetot* (< *epli* 'apple' + *toft* 'piece of land, often with a farm on it') or *Tourmetot* (< the man's name *Þormóðr* + *toft*). One finds many other different kinds, such as *Carquebut* (< *kirkja* 'church' + *býr* 'village'), *Lindebeuf* (< *lind* 'lime-tree' + *búð* 'shanty'), *Houlgate* (< *holr* 'hollow' + *gata* 'path'), *Sanvic* (< *sandr* 'sand' + *vík* 'inlet'), *Touffrécale* (< the man's name *Þorfrøðr* + *skáli* 'shed'), *Quettehou* (< the man's name *Ketill* + *hólmr* 'islet'). It is also possible that the Vikings who first received extensive landed estates kept the local element *villa* 'farm' and associated their own personal name to it: a very distinctive way which was imitated many times afterwards, like *Gonneville* (< *Gunni*), *Éculleville* (< *Skúli*), *Trouville* (< *Þorólfr*), *Barneville* (< *Barni*), *Hatainville* (< *Hásteinn*), *Colleville* (< *Koli*).

Integration has also meant the use of many Scandinavian personal names in Normandy, attested not only in place-names but also in many ancient documents. They became surnames when those were forged in the fifteenth century, and are still very common Norman family names: *Toutain* (< *Þorsteinn*), *Turgis* (< *Þorgils*), *Auzouf* (< *Ásúlfr*), *Osmond* (< *Ásmundr*) etc.

The new Norman aristocracy gradually departed from the Norse (Bates 1982: 15–38). William Longsword's murder in 942 was a threat to the fragile existence of Normandy. But his young son Richard I, who succeeded him, eventually regained control of the situation and ruled firmly until 996, and so did his own son, Richard II, after him. From the beginning of the eleventh century onwards, the Scandinavian flavour of the duchy faded more and more. Yet the Normans remained a people apart in the eyes of their contemporaries, and still today, Normandy's originality mainly derives from its Viking past.

BIBLIOGRAPHY

Bates, D. (1982) *Normandy before 1066*, London and New York: Longman.

Douglas, D.C. (1942) 'Rollo of Normandy', *English Historical Review*, 57: 417–36.

Dudo of Saint-Quentin's *History of the Normans*, trans. E. Christiansen, Woodbridge: Boydell (1998).

Fellows-Jensen, G. (1988) 'Scandinavian place-names and Viking settlement in Normandy: a review', *Namn och Bygd*, 76: 113–37.

Helmerichs, R. (1997) '*Princeps, Comes, Dux Normannorum*: early Rollonid designators and their significance', *Haskins Society Journal*, 9: 57–77.

de Gorog, R. (1958) *The Scandinavian Element in French and Norman*, New York: Bookman.

Le Maho, J. (2003) 'Les premières installations normandes dans la basse vallée de la Seine', in A.-M. Flambard-Héricher (ed.) *La progression des Vikings, des raids à la colonisation, Cahiers du GRHIS*, 14: 153–69.

Musset, L. (1997) *Nordica et Normannica. Recueil d'études sur la Scandinavie ancienne et médiévale, les expéditions des Vikings et la fondation de la Normandie*, Paris: Société des Etudes nordiques.

Neveux, F. (1998) *La Normandie des ducs aux rois, X^e–XIIe siècle*, Rennes: Ouest-France.

Renaud, J. (1989) *Les Vikings et la Normandie*, Rennes: Ouest-France.

Renaud, J. and Ridel, E (2000) 'Le Tingland: l'emplacement d'un *þing* en Normandie', *Nouvelle Revue d'Onomastique*, 35–6: 303–6.

CHAPTER THIRTY-THREE (2)

THE VIKING CONQUEST
OF BRITTANY

——•◆•——

Neil Price

Throughout the Viking Age, the small province of Brittany – the westernmost Atlantic peninsula of what is now France – stands out as an anachronism. The Celtic-speaking Bretons continually maintained a determined independence from the Frankish Empire, across a defensible border on the imperial 'mainland' of Continental Europe. The Breton March, in only slightly varying form, would survive temporary occupation by Carolingians, Vikings and eventually Normans to continue even today as the boundary of a polity that many of its inhabitants would still prefer to see as a nation in its own right.

When Scandinavian raiding parties began appearing around the shores of Francia in the ninth century, Brittany was nominally a client state of the empire, ruled by a Breton regent – Nominoë – in the name of Louis the Pious. Faithful during the emperor's lifetime, Nominoë's regime saw off repeated Viking raids on monastic sites around the Breton coasts that from a Scandinavian perspective simply formed part of the overall seaborne assault on Francia. However, on the emperor's death in 840, Nominoë declared independence in a move which set the pattern for the following century. Interspersed with brief periods of peace, over the next eighty years his successors would fight increasingly vicious and internecine wars on two fronts, against both the Carolingians and the Scandinavians (all primary and secondary sources for the Viking contacts with Brittany are discussed in detail in Price 1989, to which the reader is referred for deeper references; subsequent material is taken up and reviewed in Price 1991, 2000 and 2008).

THE HISTORICAL PICTURE

The fulcrum of Viking operations in Brittany, initially in the form of aggravated raids but later expanding in scope, was the base established at the former monastery on the island of Noirmoutier. Controlling the mouth of the Loire and thus access to one of the great arterial rivers of Francia, it was natural for Scandinavian fleets to occupy this strongpoint as they did from 843 onwards. For the rest of the century several different Viking forces campaigned in Francia and Brittany, fighting a range of Carolingian and Breton factions who were in turn engaged in civil wars with colonial ambitions. Scandinavians fought as mercenaries for all sides, and occasionally even against each other.

This was to change in the tenth century, when after decades of peace Brittany was subjected to a repeated pattern of intense raiding, culminating in a four-year occupation that was itself followed by a complete takeover of the province in 919. Two Viking fleets of different origins, almost certainly composed of individuals who had fought in the whole north-west European theatre in previous years, together managed to overcome all Breton resistance. This is of course the period following the establishment of Normandy, and it seems clear that the Vikings in Brittany had in mind a similar kind of colony – but the outcome was very different: not only was the settlement short-lived, but it left behind hardly any trace of its existence.

What we know seems entirely military in character. The Breton Vikings used their new home as a base for further raiding, often in tandem with the fledgling Normans on the Seine. In 921 the Franks even confirmed the Scandinavians in their territory, happy perhaps to contain a potential problem in the lands of their Breton enemies. But there is no external sign of the trappings of Viking colonial ambition that are familiar from other areas of settlement: there is no trade, no coinage, no thriving market centres – there appears to be only war. The peculiar nature of this colony perhaps explains why it was evidently so heavily resisted, though alongside a failed Breton revolt in 930–1 we also find men with probable Breton names among the leaders of the occupiers. In 936 the exiled Breton royalty returned with a fleet from England, driving the Vikings away after a costly three-year war. Although sporadic raiding continued around the province's coasts into the early eleventh century, there was no other attempt at settlement or conquest. The Viking colony in Brittany had lasted only twenty years, and was never to be refounded.

ARCHAEOLOGICAL REMAINS

Archaeological traces of the raiding and occupation are relatively slight, but tend towards the spectacular where they occur. The site of what may have been an earlier raid has been excavated at the abbey of Landévennec on the western coast, where destruction levels bear witness to extensive burning of this monastery which we know was attacked in the ninth century (Bardel and Perennec 1996, 2002, 2004). Other relics of this early phase of military contact may be the weapons dredged from the Loire at Nantes and found on the Île de Bièce (Arbman and Nilsson 1968: 166–71), though these may also be the result of deliberate deposition.

One of the most dramatic monuments is the circular fortified enclosure at Camp de Péran on the north coast near St-Brieuc (Nicolardot 1991, 2002, 2004). Although we know little about the interior of the fortress, it is clear from excavations that it was attacked and burned early in the tenth century. A Scandinavian presence and signs of fighting are clearly evident, though whether the Vikings were inside or outside the walls is not known. Along with many other artefacts, swords, spears and other weapons of Scandinavian type have been found in the ashes of the rampart, together with a coin minted at York *c.* 905–25. The datings make a close match with the Breton invasion of the 930s, and the site lies close to their landfall, suggesting that Péran was the site of an early battle in the reconquest. Other enclosures possibly relating to the Viking presence have been found at Trans and a number of sites known to have been occupied by Carolingian forces (Price 1989: 56–63).

The burial data are very different, and perhaps surprisingly Brittany can boast the most elaborate pre-Christian Scandinavian burial in Continental Europe, as well as the region's only ship burial. On the Île de Groix, a rocky island off the south coast, in the mid-tenth century a longship was set on fire, having been dragged into a stone-setting on a headland overlooking the sea. Two individuals – an armed man and a youth – were burned within, accompanied by dogs, birds and a very large array of grave goods including high-status gaming-pieces and many weapons. Up to twenty-four shields were present of a type unknown elsewhere, and were perhaps manufactured by the isolated Scandinavian occupation army itself (Müller-Wille 1976; Price 1989). New work has demonstrated that the Groix warrior's connections stretched to England, northern Germany along the Rhine and the Elbe, southern Norway and even Birka (Tarrou 2002, 2004). At l'Île Lavret off the Breton coast, raided several times by Vikings, two more warrior burials have been found cut into a rocky slope, badly eroded, with only the most fragmentary grave goods and generally poor preservation (Renaud 2000: 96). What has survived, however, are pieces of shield-bosses that resemble those found in the Groix burial.

The singular nature of the ship burial on the Île de Groix and its dating that coincides with the height of the occupation raise inevitable questions of attribution. Assigning named individuals to archaeological graves is usually a foolhardy business, but it is not impossible that Groix marks the resting place of one of the Viking commanders whose ambitions for this tiny province briefly raised it to the level of its Norman neighbour. If this is the case, this unique burial would be a fitting memorial for a unique endeavour.

BIBLIOGRAPHY

Arbman, H. and Nilsson, N.-O. (1968) 'Armes Scandinaves de l'époque viking en France', *Meddelanden från Lunds Universitets Historiska Museum* (1966–8): 163–202.

Bardel, A. and Perennec, R. (1996) 'Les Vikings à Landévennec: les traces du "passage" des Normands en 913', *Chronique de Landévennec*, 85: 32–40.

—— (2002) 'Les Vikings à Landévennec', in É. Ridel (ed.) *Les Vikings en France* (Dossiers d'Archéologie 277), Dijon: Éditions Faton.

—— (2004) 'En 913 à Landévennec', in C. Glot and M. le Bris (eds) *L'Europe des Vikings*, Daolas: Éditions Hoëbeke.

Müller-Wille, M. (1976) *Das Bootkammergrab von Haithabu* (Berichte über die Ausgrabungen in Haithabu 8), Neumünster: Wachholz.

Nicolardot, J.-P. (1991) *Le Camp de Péran de la bêche à l'épée*, Rennes: CAP.

—— (2002) 'Le Camp de Péran et les Vikings en Bretagne', in É. Ridel (ed.) *Les Vikings en France* (Dossiers d'Archéologie 277), Dijon: Éditions Faton.

—— (2004) 'Le Camp de Péran', in C. Glot and M. le Bris (eds) *L'Europe des Vikings*, Daolas: Éditions Hoëbeke.

Price, N.S. (1989). *The Vikings in Brittany*, London, Viking Society for Northern Research.

—— (1991) 'Viking armies and fleets in Brittany: a case study for some general problems', in H. Bekker-Nielsen and H. Frede Nielsen (eds) *Beretning fra tiende tværfaglige Vikingesymposium*, Odense: Odense University Press.

—— (2000) '"Laid waste, plundered and burned": Vikings in Frankia', in W.W. Fitzhugh and E. Ward (eds) *Vikings. The North Atlantic Saga*, Washington, DC: Smithsonian Institution.

—— (2008) 'Viking Brittany: revisiting the colony that failed', in A. Reynolds and L. Webster (eds) *Early Medieval Art and Archaeology in the Northern World*, Leiden: Brill.

Renaud, J. (2000) *Les Vikings en France*, Rennes: Éditions Ouest-France.

Tarrou, L. (2002) 'La sépulture à bateau viking de l'Île de Groix (Morbihan)', in É. Ridel (ed.) *Les Vikings en France* (Dossiers d'Archéologie 277), Dijon: Éditions Faton.

—— (2004) 'Le bateau funéraire de Groix', in C. Glot and M. le Bris (eds) *L'Europe des Vikings*, Daolas: Éditions Hoëbeke.

CHAPTER THIRTY-FOUR

THE VIKINGS IN SPAIN, NORTH AFRICA AND THE MEDITERRANEAN

——•◆•——

Neil Price

L ike the Carolingian kingdoms, the Iberian peninsula was also a divided land in the Viking Age. No borders can really be considered fixed at this time, but the southern limits of the Frankish Empire of Charles the Bald most often ran approximately along the natural barrier of the Pyrenees, and extended a short way into modern Spain. This 'Spanish March' was of variable size and subject to continual dispute, but the sphere of Frankish influence sometimes stretched as far south as Barcelona and the River Ebro. The rest of northern Iberia, especially in the north-west, was occupied by a number of smaller Christian kingdoms and principalities. Some of these, such as the tiny kingdom of Pamplona, had come into being in the context of border conflicts with the Franks. Others, including the largest and most powerful such as the kingdom of Galicia and the Asturias, had been formed in the aftermath of the event which more than any other shaped the political map of Spain in the Viking Age: the Arab invasion of the early eighth century. Over and above their individual rivalries, the northern states joined with the Franks in manning what they saw as the front line against the potential advance of Islam, which was perceived as an even greater threat to Christian Europe than the Vikings themselves (see Hodges and Whitehouse 1983 for some still controversial observations on the complications, even benefits, of these tensions, with a more current view in McCormick 2001).

In 661 a new Arab dynasty, the Umayyads, had fought their way to power in Damascus and at once begun a massive campaign of conquest. North Africa had been overrun in the 670s (Brett 1978a), and in 711 the first Muslim troops landed in Spain, their ranks primarily filled with newly converted Berbers from Morocco and Algeria. They rapidly advanced north and in a few years most of Iberia was under Islamic control (Collins 1994). The remnants of the earlier Visigothic kingdom managed to survive in the north-east of the peninsula, and the Christian realm of the Asturias had been established after the battle of Covadonga in 718 or 722. By the time of the Vikings, the Umayyad caliphate had in turn been swept away by a revolt that had spread from Persia in the mid-eighth century, an event which had a great impact on Spain and by extension on Christian Europe. The leaders of the rebellion were descendants of Abbas, one of the prophet Muhammad's uncles, and were known as the Abbasids. Their rule, from a new capital at the recently founded city of Baghdad, was to continue for much of the

Viking period and would see a gradual shift in the focus of Islamic interests from the Mediterranean and the west to the more lucrative trade with India, China and the east.

The great exception was Spain, whose Islamic governor Yusuf al-Fihri was facing grave civil disturbances at the time of the Abbasid revolt. This situation was exploited by the sole surviving member of the Umayyad family, one 'Abd al-Rahman, who in the aftermath of the Abbasid takeover had first fled to North Africa and then in 756 had quickly crossed into Spain. There he assumed command of the Muslim forces opposed to the governor, defeated Yusuf, and established his own independent realm. At the very beginning of the Viking Age, forty years before the first longships beached at Lindisfarne, a new Umayyad emirate called al-Andalus was thus proclaimed in Spain, with its capital at Córdoba (Collins 1995: 181–221). This city quickly became a centre for learning, science and culture as the royal court was swelled by refugees who flocked there from Mesopotamia and Syria, and in later centuries it was from Córdoba that many of the most important intellectual developments would spread to the medieval courts of France and Italy. During the Viking period, however, an uneasy peace was established with the Iberian Christians and the Franks to the north, and much of modern Castilla y León and the Duero valley in northern Portugal was only sparsely populated, forming a sort of demilitarised zone between the warring states (see Hill 1981: 38). The entire Viking Age saw constant skirmishing across the border, often developing into full-scale campaigns in which the Muslims sometimes struck deep into Frankia.

This was the complex situation in Iberia at the time of the first Scandinavian incursions, with the political intricacies of the region fortunately reflected in the richness of the historical source material that has survived (Dozy 1881; Jón Stefánsson 1910; Birkeland 1954; Melvinger 1955; Wikander 1978; Almazán 1986; Morales Romero 2004a: 55–7; see González Campo 2002a for a comprehensive bibliography).

The earliest confirmed Viking attack on the region occurred in 844, but prior to this there are occasional hints in Arab and European sources at Scandinavian encounters in the Basque Country in the early ninth century (Pons-Sanz 2001; Erkoreka 2004). The first substantial contact seems, however, to have been a violent one, when the great raid of 844 saw a fleet of fifty-four ships sailing southwards from Brittany and their base on the Loire at Noirmoutier (see Price, ch. 33.2, above). This first expedition to Iberia is worth recounting in detail, as it was to set a pattern for much of the Vikings' subsequent contacts with the region including the other major raids.

Navigating along the coast, the Scandinavians first raided on the Garonne in southern France before continuing west to the kingdom of Galicia and the Asturias (Morales 1997; Almazán 2004). Sources such as the *Chronicon Rotensis* from *c.* 883 refer to the 'naval army' of the Northmen (Ruiz de la Peña 1985: 38–41) that launched two attacks on the ports of Giljón and La Coruña. According to the *Annals of St-Bertin*, the Vikings were driven off partly by a storm and partly by the defenders' use of missile-throwing war machines; other sources refer to an even greater defeat. The coordinated resistance that King Ramiro I of the Asturias presented to the raids was perhaps made more effective by the Christians' more-or-less constant state of mobilisation, in readiness to counter the Arab threat from the south. Having met with only poor returns for their efforts in Galicia, the Vikings rounded Cape Finisterre and headed for Muslim territory.

Here their luck seemed to turn, and for several weeks the Scandinavians were extraordinarily successful in the emirate – it must have seemed that the rich pickings in Frankia were expanding limitlessly to the south. Lisbon was taken and sacked on

20 August with little or no defence being mounted, and for a short time the fleet harried the area immediately west of the Straits of Gibraltar. The towns of Cádiz, Medina Sidonia and Algeciras were burned on the Spanish side, and possibly Asilah on the Moroccan coast, a settlement under the distant control of the Abbasid Caliphate. The Vikings then turned briefly northwards again, and entered the Guadalquivir River to take Seville on 3 October, where they halted and plundered the surrounding countryside for over a month. During this period Castillo de Azaguac, Coria and Beja were sacked, while the invaders harried at will in the lower Guadalquivir valley, basing themselves on a defendable island, Isla Menor (Collins 1995: 193; Morales Romero 2004a: 58–62).

It was at this point that the emir ʿAbd al-Rahman II mobilised his forces, perhaps due to Seville's proximity to the capital at Córdoba which may even have come under attack (Pons-Sanz 2004: 5). A large Andalusian army was then sent out against the Vikings, who held their ground at Tablada but suffered heavy losses: according to Muslim sources, more than 1,000 Scandinavians were slain and thirty ships lost. Many of the vessels were set ablaze by a highly volatile and lethal substance known as Greek Fire, which was thrown from catapults and resembled a primitive form of napalm. The same chronicles record that more than 400 raiders were captured, almost all of whom were later hanged from palm-trees at Seville.

It was not a complete victory for the emirate, but the surviving Vikings had little choice but to negotiate their way out of the area in return for surrendering the prisoners that they had taken to sell as slaves, together with all the plunder they had seized. A thirteenth-century Arab poet, Ibn Dihya, describes these presumably somewhat tense discussions in his collation of earlier sources, noting also that the Scandinavian commander had been killed in the fighting (Allen 1960: 19). The remnants of the Viking fleet managed to evade the ships sent after them by the emir, and limped home to the Loire after brief raiding in the Algarve (Lévi-Provençal 1944: 152 f.). Back in Frankia they presumably recounted the disaster that had befallen them in Iberia, and it would seem to have been as a direct result of this that no further Scandinavian raids were mounted in the peninsula for thirteen years.

The Andalusians sometimes referred to the Vikings as *majus*, 'fire-worshippers', presumably referring to their religious customs, though the term could also be applied to other non-Muslim foreigners (Pritsak 1990; al-Azmeh 1992). Although relations between the Umayyads and the Scandinavians were often violent, the possibility of Muslim trading contacts with the Vikings cannot be ruled out (El-Hajji 1967). Indeed, one of the leading scholars of early medieval Spain has suggested that the Vikings were among the main sources for the constant supply of slaves that the emirate required (Collins 1995: 192).

The negotiation of some aspects of this trade may have been on the agenda of a diplomatic delegation that ʿAbd al-Rahman II sent to the Scandinavians, a mission led by the poet Yahya b. Hakam al-Jayyani, whose looks earned him the name al-Ghazal ('the Gazelle') by which he is more commonly known to scholarship. The exact date of the embassy is uncertain but has been assumed to shortly post-date the 844 raid, nor is its objective or even destination clear (Hiberno-Norse Ireland, the Scandinavian territories in Frankia and Denmark have all been proposed). Its very existence has also been called into question, and it may be a conflation with an earlier mission to Byzantium led by the same man (Lévi-Provençal 1937; González Campo 2002b, 2004; Pons-Sanz 2004). If it even occurred, deeper study of the mission is made difficult by the fanciful nature of the sources, which describe a complex attempt made by the king of the *majus* to humiliate the Arab ambassador, perhaps not unconnected with the effect that his handsome appearance was said to have had on the queen. Interesting detail nevertheless emerges, such as the note that on his return journey to al-Andalus, al-Ghazal was asked by the Scandinavians to act as their intermediary in diplomatic discussions with the Asturians. This may be spurious, or to be taken at face value, or may alternatively represent an attempt by the Arabs to divide their enemies.

There is little archaeological evidence to support the idea of Muslim–Viking trade, and only a few objects of Scandinavian manufacture have been found in Spain, such as the small, late tenth-century box of deer antler now in the museum of the Colegiata of St Isidoro in León (Morales Romero 2004b). However, there are three place names – *Lormanos* in Portugal, *Lordemanos* in León and *Lodimanos* in Galicia – that all contain variations on an element meaning 'men of the north' (Almazán 2004). These names may indicate sites where Scandinavians came regularly to barter, but their exact interpretation is unclear. The only other indication of Viking contact at this time with the Muslims of Córdoba comes in 854, when there is a brief note of two Scandinavian ships being captured off the coast near Lisbon.

In 859, however, a second fleet set out for Spain from the Scandinavian base on the Loire, this time under the command of two of the most famous Vikings from the entire European theatre, Hásteinn and Bjǫrn Ironside, who had both fought with the Great Army against the Anglo-Saxons and would later do so against the Franks. We read of their departure first in the Frankish *Annals of St-Bertin* and in Galician sources (Morales Romero 2004a: 65), but the subsequent story of the voyage is also taken up in tenth-century Muslim documents such as the accounts written by al-Maqqari (de Gayangos 1840–3) and Ibn al-Athir (Fagnan 1901; Almazán 2004; see Melvinger 1955 for a comprehensive corpus of Arab sources).

The fleet seems to have been large at 62 ships (one source says 100), but not exceptionally so for a major campaign. Their objective, however, was anything but usual: they intended to sack the city of Rome. Such an undertaking, in ambition, scale and content, was unique among Viking operations of this period. Even in later centuries, the only voyage that comes close is the great journey into southern Russia and Asia made by Ingvar the Far-Travelled around 1036. Hásteinn and Bjǫrn would appear to have formulated their plan partly in terms of the fabulous wealth that was surely to be gained, but partly too as a conscious quest for fame and glory, both central qualities in the Nordic heroic ideal.

The voyage began badly, and the Vikings had as little success in Galicia and Asturias as their predecessors. After taking the bishopric at Iria Flavia, the Vikings were driven back from the walls of Santiago, after which they left the Galician coast (Almazán 2004: 42–4). They continued south to Seville and burned the mosque there, though an attempt on the city itself was repulsed after the Scandinavians retired in the face of a large Muslim force that the new emir Muhammad I had assembled to block their path. At this point the Viking commanders must have made a crucial decision, and decided to proceed east despite the disappointments in Spain. Sometime in the late autumn of 859 the fleet passed the Straits of Gibraltar unopposed and, as far as we know, thus became the first Vikings to enter the Mediterranean from the west.

In the course of their passage Cádiz and Algeciras were attacked again, but once through the Straits the fleet made for the North African coast and their first real success.

Mazimma in the small Moroccan state of Nekor was sacked, and occupied for eight days according to al-Bakri. Two of the royal women – Amaar-rahaman and Kanula – were captured, and a large ransom was paid by the emir of Córdoba for their return (Morales Romero 2004a: 66–7). The Vikings then crossed back to Spain and ravaged Andalucia and Murcia, before harrying northwards along the Mediterranean coast. Many settlements were attacked in Valencia, including Orihuela, and the Balearic islands of Formentera, Ibiza, Majorca and Minorca were all raided. The fleet then continued north-eastwards into southern Frankish territory, assaulting monasteries and towns in Roussillon and burning Norbonne, before wintering in the marshy fastnesses of the Camargue.

In the spring of 860, Hásteinn and Bjǫrn entered the Rhône, sacking Nîmes and Arles before continuing upriver to Valence. Here the Vikings met with the most organised resistance they had encountered since the defence of Seville, and therefore turned back to the sea and eastwards towards Italy. With ships so fully laden with plunder that they sat low in the water, at last the Scandinavians reached Rome and achieved their prize – or so they thought, and one must imagine their consternation in finding that they had sacked Luna (modern Lucca) by mistake. For a time the fleet sailed inland up the River Arno to attack Pisa and Fiesole, but they soon returned to the open water.

After this, the movements of the Vikings are uncertain. There are some indications that they sailed beyond Italy into the eastern Mediterranean (they do not seem to have attempted an assault on Rome after all), but the next confirmed report of them is a year later in 861, when the Vikings tried to pass the Straits of Gibraltar a second time. In contrast to the previous occasion, they found a Muslim fleet waiting for them. The battle went against the Scandinavians and a great many Viking ships were destroyed before they managed to break through the blockade to the Atlantic. With two-thirds of their vessels gone, Hásteinn and Bjǫrn turned north for the Loire and home, pausing only in Pamplona for one last raid. Here they captured the local regent, King García, and then ransomed him for the vast sum of 70,000 gold pieces. When it emerged that not all the money was forthcoming, they released him but kept his children as hostages (Morales Romero 2004a: 68, with references to the numerous Arab sources that mention this episode). In the spring of 862, after nearly three years on campaign, the Viking fleet returned to its base in France.

The voyage seems to have taken on a truly epic quality in the minds of succeeding generations of Scandinavians, a process that no doubt began very early as the survivors' tales grew in the telling; a later Hiberno-Norse saga eloquently built on the facts to create a myth of heroic endeavour. However, there must also have been much more tangible evidence of the raid, not least in the fabulous wealth gained by the admittedly relatively few survivors. At least some of the Vikings who participated in the campaign moved on from the Loire and took their spoils with them, and even the final sea battle near Gibraltar may not have been a complete loss, because the Irish chronicler Duald Mac-Fuirbis records that 'after that the Norsemen brought a great host of Moors in captivity with them to Ireland . . . long were these blue men in Ireland'.

After the great raid of 859–62, Scandinavian contacts with Spain again seem to have tailed off to almost nothing, and this time it would be nearly a century before the attacks were renewed. Even though the above-mentioned possibility of trade cannot be discounted, the degree of disorder that the Vikings brought to the already troubled affairs of ninth-century al-Andalus should not be underestimated. Potentially at least, from the 850s onwards the Umayyads could well have borne the brunt of continuous Scandinavian depredations similar to those endured by the Franks to the north – indeed, given the initial success of the 844 expedition this prospect had almost certainly occurred to the Vikings themselves. In contrast to the actions of the Carolingians, the rapid and crushing response of the Muslims, together with the considered strength of their defences, were decisive in averting such an eventuality. The military arm of the emirate was well organised both on sea and on land, and most towns and major settlements were encircled by walls and towers. A new chain of forts had also been constructed in response to the Viking raids of the ninth century, distinguished by their *rapita* place names. Above all, successive emirs focused their attentions on the navy as the first line of defence against the Scandinavians, something which the Franks had failed to do. ʿAbd al-Rahman II built new shipyards at Seville and established a naval base at Almería, while Muhammad I ordered the construction of a completely new fleet – an example that was followed by ʿAbd al-Rahman III who did the same in the 950s (Collins 1995: 193).

It was thus not until the second half of the tenth century that Viking raiders attacked Spain again, by which time there had been many changes in Islamic politics. In the early years of the century a new power had arisen in North Africa, where a Shiʾite rebellion in 909 had proclaimed an *al Mahdi* descended from the prophet's daughter, Fatima (Brett 1978b). Over the next sixty years, the Fatimids expanded and conquered as far east as Egypt, where they founded Cairo as the capital of a new caliphate. This was established in opposition to the Abbasids, who still ruled from Baghdad as before. In response to this and the perceived threat from North Africa, the Umayyad emir of Córdoba then proclaimed himself caliph too, thus making three simultaneous caliphates in the Islamic world (relations between al-Andalus and the other Muslim states are ably summarised in Scales 1994).

Against the background of these complex events, which naturally involved a high degree of military preparedness among the Muslim states, it is perhaps not surprising that the bulk of the renewed Viking raids on Iberia were confined to the Christian kingdoms in the north. Galicia was attacked in 951, 965 and 966, with a naval battle being fought on the latter occasion in the mouth of the Silves River. During this period forays were also made to the south as far as Lisbon. Two years later in 968, a Viking army under a commander called Gunnrauðr defeated the Galician forces, and killed Sisnando, the bishop of Santiago de Compostela. From their base on the Ulla River this group of Scandinavians then seem to have raided inland for some three years afterwards, causing devastation that is still related in Galician folklore today (Almazán 2004: 44–7). The Spanish coasts were attacked again in 970 and 971, with a raid the following year on the Algarve in what is now southern Portugal. In general, the Muslim fleets were successful in resisting these attacks (Morales Romero 2004a: 69–75).

Sporadic Viking assaults continued in the north of Spain even into the eleventh century. In 1008 Galicia and the Douro region were attacked, and in 1014 or 1015 a major raid was launched against the city of Tui at the mouth of the Miño River. The Vikings seem to have been led on this occasion by Óláfr Haraldsson, and managed to successfully capture the bishop and many of the town's inhabitants. It is uncertain if these prisoners were ransomed, or even sold as slaves in the emirate. Galicia was again attacked in 1028, by a fleet perhaps under the command of a Viking called

Ulfr. The last recorded raids occurred during the period 1047–66 when Cresconio, the bishop of Santiago de Compostela, fought several battles against the Scandinavians. The intensity of these attacks against the Spanish Christians may imply some kind of attempt at settlement or even conquest: the assaults of 968–71 and 1047–66 seem to have been virtually military campaigns. The documentary sources are unfortunately too meagre to draw any firm conclusions, and in the absence of new archaeological evidence the motivations behind the later Viking raids on northern Spain remain obscure.

If we take the long view of Scandinavian activity in Iberia, despite the spectacular nature of the 859–62 expedition and the undoubted violence of the tenth- and eleventh-century raids, Viking contacts with the Muslim and Christian polities of Spain were minimal (see also Price 1994: 146–7). This is in stark contrast to the experiences of the Frankish kingdoms, and there is little doubt that Spain and the western Mediterranean formed the south-western periphery of the Viking world. However, the memory of the Gibraltar passage and what lay beyond was not lost in Scandinavia (Musset 1992: 92), and was revived as early as the twelfth century by Norwegians attempting a new kind of assault on Islam: the Crusades.

BIBLIOGRAPHY

Allen, W.E.D. (1960) *The Poet and the Spae-wife. An Attempt to Reconstruct al-Gazal's Embassy to the Vikings*, Dublin: Figgis.

Almazán, V. (1986) *Gallaecia Scandinavica. Introducción ó estudio das relacións galaico/escandinavas durante a Idade Media*, Vigo: Galaxia.

—— (2004) 'Vikingerne i Galicien', in [no editor] *Vikingerne på Den Iberiske Halvø*, Madrid: Dronning Isabella Fonden.

al-Azmeh, A. (1992) 'Barbarians in Arab eyes', *Past and Present*, 134: 3–18.

Birkeland, H. (1954) *Nordens historie i middelalderen etter arabiske kilder* (Norske Videnskaps-Akademi Skrifter 2:2), Oslo: Dybwad.

Brett, M. (1978a) 'The Arab conquest and the rise of Islam in North Africa', in J.D. Fage (ed.) *The Cambridge History of Africa*, vol. 2, Cambridge: Cambridge University Press.

—— (1978b) 'The Fatimid revolution (861–973) and its aftermath in North Africa', in J.D. Fage (ed.) *The Cambridge History of Africa*, vol. 2, Cambridge: Cambridge University Press.

Collins, R. (1994) *The Arab Conquest of Spain, 710–797*, 2nd edn, Oxford: Blackwell.

—— (1995) *Early Medieval Spain. Unity in Diversity, 400–1000*, 2nd edn, New York: St Martin's Press.

Dozy, R. (1881) *Recherches sur l'histoire et la litterature de l'Espagne pendant le Moyen Âge*, 2 vols, 3rd edn, Leiden: Brill.

El-Hajji, A.A. (1967) 'The Andalusian diplomatic relations with the Vikings during the Umayyad period', *Hespéris Tamuda*, 8: 67–110.

Erkoreka, A. (2004) 'Vikingerne i Vasconia', in [no editor] *Vikingerne på Den Iberiske Halvø*, Madrid: Dronning Isabella Fonden.

Fagnan, E. (1901) *Ibn al-Athir. Annales du Maghreb et de l'Espagne*, Algiers: no publ.

de Gayangos, P. (trans.) (1840–3) *The History of the Mohammedan Dynasties in Spain*, 2 vols, London: no publ.

González Campo, M. (2002a) 'Bibliographia Normanno-Hispanica', *Saga-Book*, 26: 104–13.

—— (2002b) *Al-Ghazal y la embajada hispano-musulmana a los vikingos en el siglo IX*, Madrid: Miraguano Ediciones.

—— (2004) 'En stor ø i oceanet', in [no editor] *Vikingerne på Den Iberiske Halvø*, Madrid: Dronning Isabella Fonden.

Hill, D. (1981) *An Atlas of Anglo-Saxon England*, Oxford: Blackwell.

Hodges, R. and Whitehouse, D. (1983) *Mohammed, Charlemagne and the Origins of Europe. Archaeology and the Pirenne Thesis*, London: Duckworth.

Jón Stefánsson (1910) 'The Vikings in Spain: from Arab (Moorish) and Spanish sources', *Saga-Book*, 6: 31–46.

Lévi-Provençal, E. (1937) 'Un échange d'ambassades entre Cordove et Byzance au IXᵉ siècle', *Byzantion*, 12: 1–24.

—— (1944) *Histoire de l'Espagne musulmane*, vol. 1: *De la conquête à la chute du Califat de Cordove (710–1031 J.C.)*, Cairo: L'institut français d'archéologie orientale de Caire.

McCormick, M. (2001) *The Origins of the European Economy. Communications and Commerce AD 300–900*, Cambridge: Cambridge University Press.

Melvinger, A. (1955) *Les premières incursions des Vikings en Occident d'après les sources arabes*, Uppsala: Almqvist & Wiksell.

Morales, E. (1997) *Os vikingos en Galicia*, Santiago de Compostela: Universidad de Santiago de Compostela.

Morales Romero, E. (2004a) 'Vikingerne i al-Andalus', in [no editor] *Vikingerne på Den Iberiske Halvø*, Madrid: Dronning Isabella Fonden.

—— (2004b) '"San Isidoro-æsken" i León', in [no editor] *Vikingerne på Den Iberiske Halvø*, Madrid: Dronning Isabella Fonden.

Musset, L. (1992) 'The Scandinavians and the western European continent', in E. Roesdahl and D.M. Wilson (eds) *From Viking to Crusader. Scandinavia and Europe 800–1200*, New York: Rizzoli.

Pons-Sanz, S.M. (2001) 'The Basque Country and the Vikings during the ninth century', *Journal of the Society of Basque Studies in America*, 21: 48–58.

—— (2004) 'Whom did al-Ghazal meet? An exchange of embassies between the Arabs from al-Andalus and the Vikings', *Saga-Book*, 28: 5–28.

Price, N.S. (1994) 'The Vikings overseas: western Europe', in J.A. Graham-Campbell (ed.) *Cultural Atlas of the Viking World*, Oxford: Andromeda.

Pritsak, O. (1990) 'Did the Arabs call the Vikings "Magians"?', in T. Pàroli (ed.) *Poetry in the Scandinavian Middle Ages. The Seventh International Saga Conference* (Atti del Congresso Internazionale di Studi sull'Alto Medioevo 12), Spolet: Centro Italiano di Studi sull'Alto Medioevo.

Ruiz de la Peña, J.I. (1985) 'Estudio preliminar: la cultura en la corte ovetense del siglo IX', in J.G. Fernández and J.L. Moralejo (eds) *Crónicas asturianas*, Oviedo: Universidad de Oviedo.

Scales, P.C. (1994) *The Fall of the Caliphate of Córdoba. Berbers and Andalusis in Conflict*, Leiden: Brill.

Wikander, S. (1978) *Araber, Vikingar, Väringar*, Lund: Svenska Humanistiska Förbundet.

CHAPTER THIRTY-FIVE

THE VIKING AGE IN FINLAND

———•◆•———

Torsten Edgren

THE SETTLEMENT

During the Viking Age (AD 800–1050) the settlement of present-day Finland underwent a number of changes. While the number of western Finnish cemeteries and consequently also of farms and villages increased in the old core settlement areas of Finland Proper, Satakunta, and Häme, the settled population was also expanding into areas that had formerly been sparsely inhabited. A number of new cemeteries appeared in the inner coastal zone while former population centres shrank. In the province of Finland Proper, the expansion can nevertheless only be termed moderate, since the borders of the settled area did not change radically. Individual settlements, which were primarily concentrated in the river valleys and heads of inlets with their farmable land, were isolated pockets surrounded by uninhabited forests. The distances between the river valleys were not great and contacts occurred naturally, but both trade and subsistence considerations would have directed the inhabitants' interests towards the sea while the river valleys were first-class conduits to the inland with its boundless hunting grounds. A parish church was raised in each of these settlements during the early Middle Ages, and they developed into local administrative centres. The medieval churches were often built on or next to the pre-Christian cemeteries. The foundations for the medieval parishes may thus have been laid already in the Viking Age.

In the province of Häme (Tavastia), on the other hand, settlement expanded beyond the borders of the old core area and the first cemeteries appear in several districts outside the actual core cluster located around the lake region of southern Häme. Archaeological remains are also found in the province's eastern part and they also include female burials with a full range of western Finnish jewellery. As a rule, however, finds that originate from outside the core settlements come from male graves, apparently those of trappers.

During previous periods, signs of habitation were almost totally absent from the archipelago off the coast of Finland Proper. Now, however, these appear as well. The most important site is a harbour and trading centre located on the northern side of the narrow sound of Kyrksundet on the island of Hiittinen in the south-western Finnish archipelago, which lies right on the Eastern Route of the Vikings. Up to now no remnants of houses have been found, only some remains of a workshop with many finds, such as bronze bars and scrap metal for casting, raw-glass, glass and mosaic beads, small whetstones, amber and small pieces of German and Anglo-Saxon silver coins for the production of jewellery. The workshop seems to have been in operation at the end of the eleventh century.

On the other hand, the northern coast of the Gulf of Finland and the province of Uusimaa appear almost deserted during the Viking Age. It has been suggested that the great trade route to the east that followed the southern coast of Finland was actually detrimental to settlement near the coast, and that the lively traffic along the route made the coast a dangerous place to live. This could explain the abandoning of the previously rich Iron Age villages in Karjaa, western Uusimaa, around AD 800. On the other hand, the new finds from Hiittinen show that the coastal farmers could also form productive relationships with the voyagers on the Eastern Route. Both parties were astute enough to take advantage of the Viking Age economic boom.

In this connection one should recall that in the Old Norse sagas of both Njáll and St Óláfr the coastline of southern Finland is called 'Balagårdssidan'. The name refers to the custom of lighting fires on high rocks to warn the population against enemy attacks. In the saga of St Óláfr it is described how he sailed to Finland after returning from a plundering expedition to Saaremaa in Estonia, the Nordic *Eysyssla*.

In the south-western part of the province of Ostrobothnia, so rich in archaeological remains during the earlier periods, all signs of permanent occupation disappear at the beginning of the Viking Age, *c.* AD 800. So far, archaeologists have not come up with a satisfactory explanation for this phenomenon. Some have seen it as the result of the struggle between the realms of Kaleva and Pohjola described in Finnish folk epics, others have discussed the possible role of the Justinian plague in emptying the province of inhabitants. In fact, however, the settlements were not struck by a sudden catastrophe but rather were gradually abandoned as a result of the rapid land rise in the region – some 100 cm every 100 years – which, in combination with the province's flat topography, turned the formerly lush coastal meadows into useless bog. Consequently, the economic boom that is evident elsewhere as a result of the intensified trade activity in the Baltic Sea region did not reach Ostrobothnia, but then again the region was a rather remote corner far from the main trade highways of the day.

A new settlement area arose in Savo around the present-day city of Mikkeli, which became a provincial population centre over the following centuries. Both the grave types and the artefact forms of the early period were clearly western Finnish in origin, and it is obvious that the region was colonised by settlers from Tavasthia. A new silver coin hoard with some 140 Anglo-Saxon and German coins was found in the area at the end of the 1990s. Contacts with Ladoga Karelia intensified during the eleventh century and became predominant during the following centuries. The development of permanent settlement in Savo and Karelia seems to have been primarily related to a notable increase in the market for frontier products, especially furs.

Western Finnish influence can also be discerned in the Iron Age culture of Ladoga Karelia. Whether this was due to an actual influx of westerners or to the original population adopting a western-style material culture is not clear. The settlements on the western and northern shores of Lake Ladoga might perhaps best be seen as a counterpart to the villages on the lake's southern and south-eastern sides, where the Scandinavian influence on the local Iron Age culture is notable. This Scandinavian expansion can be seen as a bid to establish a bridgehead on the Eastern Route.

The Åland archipelago, Finland's westernmost province, received a strong influx of immigrants from central Sweden in the sixth century AD and formed a part of the Scandinavian culture area throughout the Viking Age. Both the material culture and the graves – cremation burials in earth mounds – are totally Scandinavian in character, but objects imported from Finland are also present. The latter consist primarily of women's jewellery, possibly indicating that at least some of the local men obtained wives from Finland, if voluntarily or not remains an open question.

A notable rise in the numbers of archaeological finds during the Viking Age can also be observed in northern Finland, in northern Ostrobothnia and Lapland. Most of the artefacts are pieces of jewellery manufactured in western Finland, but a number of Scandinavian artefacts have been found as well. The finds also include weapons. Most of the archaeological finds come from the region between the Gulf of Bothnia and the White Sea, from Kainuu, Kuusamo and Salla, which were important centres in the Lapland trade. The White Sea and the Gulf of Bothnia were connected by several major water routes. The archaeological finds include both single graves and a few silver hoards, all of which have connections with the White Sea region, particularly the mouth of the Dvina, where the land of Biarmia, mentioned in historical sources, is supposed to have been located. It appears that traders from northern Norway originally travelled to the White Sea coast via the Lapland river routes, but in the ninth century the trade traffic shifted to the sea route around the North Cape, discovered and described *c.* 875 by Ottar (Othere) of Halogaland. Finds from the eleventh century show that the Karelian population also maintained trade relations with the White Sea region.

Finally, only a small portion of present-day Finland was permanently settled during the Viking Age. The rest of the country was a vast uninhabited wilderness that offered excellent hunting, fishing and trapping, the latter being economically the most important of the three. It has been estimated that the population of Finland at the end of the Viking Age amounted to around 50,000 people.

HOUSES, FARMS AND BURIAL CUSTOMS

The archaeological material available for the study of Viking Age society is fairly limited in scope, and the majority of analyses focus exclusively on the grave forms and grave goods typical of the period. The reason for this lies in the fact that archaeological fieldwork has concentrated on graves while house remains and other settlement-related structures have received less attention.

Another contributing factor is the fact that the remains of late Iron Age settlements are almost invisible above ground, which makes them difficult to locate and consequently rare. Our knowledge of late Iron Age house forms is scant and was limited for many years to the results of excavations in Åland house foundations. Later research has shown, however, that the houses were usually constructed of wall panels woven from branches and fastened between upright posts that formed the actual load-bearing frame. The space between the posts could also be filled in with a tight row of thin, split saplings. Log houses came into use later, but were presumably much smaller than the large Scandinavian halls. In all cases the walls were caulked with clay daub and the floor was of hard-packed earth.

In both Finland Proper and Häme the dominant form of burial was in level-ground cremation cemeteries. These had been introduced late in the seventh century and remained in use until *c.* AD 1000. Mixed stone/earth cairns also appear in Häme until the end of the pagan period. Level-ground cremation cemeteries are a pronouncedly Finnish phenomenon. They have extensive pavings of stone consisting of one to three layers but rarely visible on the present surface. In between, under and on top of the stones lay strewn the remnants of the pyres of the dead: burnt bones, ashes and grave goods. It has been presumed that the large cremation cemeteries were used by whole villages. Many villages, however, had several cemeteries; therefore these apparently belonged to individual farms. Cremation cemeteries sometimes contain boat graves, burials in which the deceased were burned in their boats – as can be seen from large amounts of rivets. This parallels the Scandinavian boat graves, although the latter were not cremations.

CLOTHING AND JEWELLERY

The parishes of Eura and Köyliö in the province of Satakunta were exceptions as far as burial customs were concerned. In Eura and Köyliö the dead were buried in inhumation graves, a custom that did not spread to other parts of the country before the early eleventh century. The Luistari cemetery in Eura is the largest Viking Age cemetery in Finland with more than 1,300 excavated graves. The dead were interred dressed in their best clothes and finest jewellery (Figures 35.1 and 35.2). Organic materials such as cloth are rarely preserved in graves, but thanks to the custom of decorating women's garments with spiral tubes of bronze wire that eventually oxidised and preserved the surrounding cloth, it has been possible through painstaking studies in the field and laboratory to reconstruct a number of women's costumes. The most reliable reconstructions are based on grave finds from the Luistari cemetery mentioned above. The Eura costume dates from the early eleventh century and thus represents dress fashions around the end of the Viking Age.

The pieces of jewellery that appear in grave finds from the ninth and tenth centuries are predominantly heavy and massive bronze objects, while silver jewellery remains relatively rare until the eleventh century. Bronze seems to have been the period's precious metal of choice and was imported from central Europe in the form of ingots. In addition to imported raw bronze, recycled jewellery also provided an important source of metal. Certain mass finds of scrap-bronze jewellery show fire patina. This probably indicates that they came from a cremation cemetery, where the grave goods might lay completely in the open. These finds, in other words, constitute evidence of grave robbery from the prehistoric period.

The population increase that took place during the Viking Age led to a notable boom in jewellery production, which had a detrimental effect on quality. Viking Age jewellery was typically made by backyard businesses. The pieces were mostly cast by village blacksmiths; large Viking Age caches of jewellery-making equipment such as found in the other Nordic countries are missing from Finland. The jewellery was cast in clay moulds using the *á cire perdue* or 'lost wax' technique, which may explain why finds that illustrate the actual casting process are so rare. Another method suited for mass production and used by village blacksmiths up to modern times was sand casting, which also made it possible to copy existing designs.

As noted above, silver was rare during the ninth and tenth centuries with the exception of Åland, which has produced a few early silver hoards. The situation changed over the following centuries when silver, as a result of the flood of silver coins that

Figure 35.1   Convex round shoulder brooches and other ornaments characteristic of women's dress in western Finland during the Viking Age. Grave no. 56, Luistari cemetery in Eura, Satakunta. (Photo: National Board of Antiquities/Ritva Backman 1990. Copyright © National Museum of Finland.)

washed over the Nordic countries, became common in south-western Finland. The coins, like chopped silver and silver scraps, were used as currency in trading since an actual monetary system did not yet exist. The coins were often cut into pieces, which indicates that their value was based on weight. The scales and weights that start to appear in archaeological finds from the beginning of the Viking Age onwards clearly relate to commerce and the influx of silver.

Figure 35.2 Ornaments from grave no. 16, Tuukkala cemetery in Mikkeli, Savo. Characteristic of women's dress in eastern Finland at the end of the Viking Age are the oval tortoise brooches decorated with plant ornament, round thin silver brooches, big thin penannular brooches of silver decorated with acanthus ornament, and women's knives, the sheet and handle decorated with plant ornament.

(National Board of Antiquities/Ritva Backman 1990. Copyright © National Museum of Finland.)

Coins also furnished the most important raw material for silver jewellery. Silver coins were frequently used as coins, and were either perforated or furnished with a loop for hanging on a necklace or chain assembly, for example. Arabian dirhams were especially popular in Finland, which is evident from the fact that 'counterfeit' dirhams were manufactured specifically for use as jewellery hangings. A large number of coins mimicking the Byzantine silver *miliaresion* have also been discovered in Finland. Among these, numismatists have identified five different types, four of which have not been found elsewhere. Many of the copies have identical stampings and are therefore probably of Finnish manufacture. The *miliaresion* copies have been dated to AD 1025–50. They are all perforated and have been used as hanging jewellery. For some reason, the fact that the Byzantine coins were larger than other coins of the period appears to have attracted the western Finns, as have the Byzantine designs.

IRON PRODUCTION

Our present information concerning the presumably large-scale iron foundry of the Viking Age is extremely limited. The large amounts of slag discovered in settlements and mixed earth/stone cairns naturally indicate that iron was produced in notable quantities. Merely the replacing of the iron tools, weapons and other objects that were taken out of circulation through being deposited in graves would have required a sizeable output of iron. The raw material was bog and lake ore, which was available in quantity and has been used up to the present day, but we do not know what form the iron was distributed in. Since commerce and distribution technology required that the iron be refined into products of a standard form and weight, it may be assumed that some form of ingots were used also in Finland.

WEAPONS

The most important weapons of the Viking Age were the two-edged sword, the long-handled axe and the spear.

The swords were made in western European smithies in the Frankish kingdom and were exported to the Nordic countries as half-finished goods, the blades being provided with grips by Nordic craftsmen. While damascened blades are typical of the early Viking Age, the tenth century introduced the practice of furnishing the blades with signs, symbols and texts, the latter being the trade marks of certain workshops and smiths. Of the texts, the most noteworthy is + ULFBERHT +, a master's name that appears over a period of around 150 years. Other masters' names on Finnish swords include Beno, + BENO ME FECIT +, INGELRII, and Gicelin, who furnished the products of his workshop with the text + GICELIN ME FECIT +. During the eleventh century the blades were made slightly longer, which also led to longer texts. Typical inscriptions are + IN NOMINE DOMINI + and + AMEN +. One sword blade bears the inscription CONSTANTINUS REX, which probably refers to the Byzantine emperor Constantine VIII (976–1028); the sword may have belonged to a member of his varangian or varjag (east Viking) bodyguard. During the late eleventh century the finest blades might be decorated by Christian symbols or text in silver or gold wire that was hammered into grooves on the blade. These swords were luxury swords, but the majority were plain swords intended for use. Finnish finds have produced a large number of swords, close to 330 examples, all identified as to type.

Perhaps the most common weapon of the Viking Age was the spear, mostly of Scandinavian types. The socket tube of later spear types may be handsomely decorated with silver inlay and gilded looped animals in the style of the late runestones. Most of these spear points, like the most artistically silver-inlaid sword grips, may have been manufactured on Gotland.

SILVER HOARDS

Finnish coin hoards from the Viking Age number some forty separate finds and consist of *c.* 1,600 Islamic, *c.* 1,000 Anglo-Saxon and *c.* 4,000 German coins together with a few Scandinavian, Irish, Bohemian, Hungarian, Spanish and Byzantine pieces. The oldest Finnish hoards, which contain only oriental coins, come from Åland and date to the ninth and tenth centuries. The others, which also include various other kinds of silver objects, are from Finland Proper and Häme and date to the latter part of the eleventh century. Viking Age silver apparently came to Finland from two different directions. During the early part of the period silver was obtained on voyages to the east, later on it came from western Europe.

The silver hoards of the Viking Age have generally been interpreted as evidence of war and troubled times: when danger threatened, people hid their silver in the ground. The actual reasons for burying treasures are really much more complicated. Objects of value have always been hidden away, while troubled times and outside threats have increased the number of hoards only temporarily. We can only speculate on the reasons why the hoards were left in the ground rather than being retrieved once the threat was past. It often appears as if the owner had died suddenly or in a foreign land without being able to tell his or her heirs where the silver was hidden. Other possibilities, however, have also been suggested based on, for example, the fact that the Icelandic chronicler Snorri Sturluson wrote in the thirteenth century that Óðinn had laid down laws whereby anything one buried away during one's lifetime could be enjoyed in the afterlife. We must therefore take into account that there are also other possible explanations for stowing away treasures besides purely practical considerations.

The number of hoard finds is naturally dependent on the influx and availability of coins. The fact that no eleventh-century coin hoards are known from Åland does not mean that the archipelago was depopulated, as has been suggested. The answer lies in the fact that the eastern influx of coins dried up, a phenomenon that has also been considered one of the contributing factors to the decline and fall of the central Swedish trading centre, Birka.

TRADING CENTRES AND TRADE ROUTES

The trading town of Birka, located on the island of Björkö in Lake Mälaren, is an important archaeological monument. At least during the trading season, Birka must have been a meeting place for many nations, making up a polyethnic trading centre. The finds include Finnish objects such as pottery and round brooches, indicating that women from south-western Finland visited Birka.

Due to its favourable location both from a regional and a trans-Baltic viewpoint, Birka came to play a central role in the Baltic trade up to the time when it was abandoned. At the same time, Birka was one of the most important points of departure for trade voyages via the Eastern Route, which commenced somewhat later than the Viking raids in western Europe. One of the two most important routes to Russia and Byzantium led across the Baltic to the Duna River in present-day Latvia, while the other, mentioned in medieval sources, led via Åland and the sheltered archipelago of south-western Finland to Hanko Peninsula and Porkkala on the southern Finnish coast. One could either sail south from Porkkala to *Lindanes* (today's Tallinn) and then eastward along the Estonian coast, or one could follow Finland's south coast from Hanko onwards. In either case, the objective was the Neva River at the head of the Gulf of Finland, which led to the open waters of Lake Ladoga. From Lake Ladoga one could either follow the River Svir to Lake Onega or take the Volkhov towards the south and the heartland of present-day Russia.

Evidence of the Scandinavians appears in many places along the water routes to the Black Sea, and it is often difficult to assess their meaning. Grave mounds of Scandinavian type and containing Scandinavian grave goods are found, for instance, at Gnezdovo near Smolensk, an imposing cemetery containing more than 4,500 grave monuments. On the other hand, the Scandinavian-type grave finds from the south-eastern shore of Lake Ladoga come from kurgan burials of local type.

The archaeological material has been said to contain no evidence to support the idea that the Finns took part in the Viking voyages, not even on the Eastern Route, but Åland may be an exception. It has been pointed out that the Viking Age hoards from Åland consist exclusively of Islamic coins, which were presumably obtained by the local people themselves on voyages to the east. The Islamic coins found in western Finnish graves and hoards were probably brought to Finland by Viking voyagers, who were not necessarily Finns. It has been noted that the coin finds from the northern coast of the Gulf of Finland are best characterised as traces left by the transiting Vikings, and that aside from a few Finnish round brooches, no finds of Finnish character are known from the Russian water routes. That is the classical interpretation of the route, in Scandinavian as well as in Russian archaeology.

New observations based on travelling with reconstructed Viking ships, however, seem to indicate that sailing on the rivers in north-west Russia was more complicated than previously thought. Since the water level in the rivers Volkhov and Lovat must have been much lower during the Viking Age than nowadays, some Russian scholars believe that some of the most important rivers were in fact not navigable at all during the Viking Age, at least not with heavy oak-built ships. Instead it has been stressed that travel in north-west Russia by horse and sledge on the frozen plains and on the ice of the rivers enables longer distances to be covered in relatively short periods, at least when travelling upstream. Several written accounts of Viking Age winter travel, for instance by Snorri, support the importance of this version of travelling in the east.

Viking Age trading voyages were usually arranged by a group of men who outfitted a ship together, or by traders who obtained part of their trade goods from others who stayed home but received a share of the profits afterwards. Trading voyages were undertaken primarily by men. It has been noted that Viking Age male costumes were almost identical all over the Baltic area and that Finnish men also followed this fashion, while the women were more conservative as far as dress was concerned. Since the weapons found in graves also represent common types, it is difficult to say with certainty whether a Viking buried somewhere along the Eastern Route was a Finn or not.

The finds also include certain groups of finds that are considered evidence of direct contacts with the east. These include a number of so-called Permian belt mountings and the so-called Permian strike-a-light with bronze handle, which was widespread in the Nordic countries and known, for instance, from Hedeby and Birka. The wide distribution indicates, however, that the strike-a-lights were valued trade goods, not that they were brought to Finland by Finnish voyagers.

One special find category that points to the east is the so-called clay paws, which are common in late Iron Age graves on Åland. Most of these objects represent beaver paws, some have been thought to represent bear paws or perhaps human hands. The Åland paws have no parallels on the Finnish mainland, but similar objects are common in central Russia. The Russian paws derive from graves that have been characterised as Finnish. They are thought by Russian archaeologists to represent specifically beaver paws and have been connected with a particular beaver cult that appeared among Finnic tribes in eastern Russia. It is evident that there is a connection between the clay paws from Åland and central Russia, and according to chronological evidence the implement originated on Åland. The question is nevertheless complicated by the fact that the beaver is not found on Åland, nor is there any other archaeological evidence of close contacts between the two areas. One possible explanation is that the beaver cult, like the bear cult, had a wider distribution than the finds indicate, and that the original custom was to place real beaver and bear paws in the graves. When real paws were not available, clay substitutes were used. In the same way, bear teeth were represented by bronze 'copies'.

One prerequisite for the Viking Age Nordic expansion and trade was the double-ended, clinker-built ship known from Nordic ship finds and including graceful sea-going long (war)ships for coastal voyages and wider freight-carrying types with a greater draught and dimensions. Viking Age boat graves show that large ships with oars and sails were also built – or at least used – in Finland. A different boat-building technique was used in the inland area, and the vessels were smaller. Instead of being fastened together with iron rivets, the planks were sewn together with spruce roots. Sewn boats are known from a number of bog finds. These vessels, which were especially flexible and well adapted for running rapids, represent an old tradition and technique.

TRAVEL AND TRANSPORTATION

Due to its geography Finland, like the other Nordic countries, is a region where various methods of travel and transportation have always played an extremely important role. Hunting required both sleds and skis. The most simple type of sled was the ski sled, a low hand-drawn sled on thin and narrow runners that had up-curved ends in order to clear snow obstacles. Heavier loads, of course, required larger-capacity sleds. Many runners for sleds like these have been found in bogs. Sleds were also used for travelling in the Viking Age; evidence for this includes drawings on Gotland picture stones. Communications, both commercial and social, undoubtedly improved once the winter ice set in, and the freeze-over also made special winter resources available. At the same time, however, ice travel also required special knowledge about the ice and its

479

properties. Archaeological finds contain, among other things, bone skates made from the long bones of moose, horses or oxen.

Skis were particularly important for winter hunting and travel. More than 100 skis have been discovered in bogs, where the preservation of wood is exceptionally good; one-third of these have been dated by pollen analysis and radiocarbon to before the year AD 1200. The skis were all carved of pine, an elastic and hard material that had good sliding properties due to the natural resin content. The most widespread ski type is known as the Bothnic ski, which already appeared in its oldest form towards the end of the Bronze Age. The Bothnic ski is typically short (less than 165 cm) and lanceolate; it has a flat bottom, an elevated foot platform and a horizontal transverse hole for the binding. The Bothnic ski was used primarily north of the 62nd parallel, and many of the known examples are beautifully decorated.

Quite early in the Stone Age, Finnish skis were already furnished with a bottom channel. Thanks to this channel, which during the early Iron Age was almost as wide as the ski itself, but shrank later to less than half of the ski's breadth, the ski slid better and was consequently faster and easier to steer. These slender skis could be up to 3 m long and were often decorated with grooved lines or artistically executed band patterns.

A special type is the asymmetrical-paired skis, which consist of a long left ski with bottom channel and a notably shorter right ski. The bottom of the latter was covered with stiff-haired hide, the hairs pointing backward for traction. This type of ski required a different technique than even-paired skis: the skier slid along on the long left ski while kicking with the shorter right ski and maintaining balance with a ski pole. At least during the historical period, asymmetrical-paired skis were used primarily for moose hunting. We do not know for sure exactly when they came into use, but judging from the fact that they are mentioned in ancient Finnish folk poems, they were probably known already in the prehistoric period.

The contacts between the Iron Age villages that are reflected in the archaeological finds naturally required seasonal or year-round travel routes. The shallow and narrow rivers of south-western Finland were not exceptionally well suited for boat traffic; for instance the Kokemäenjoki River, which was an important connecting route between the settlement area of Häme and the coast during the early Iron Age; became unnavigable during the Viking Age. Rivers could nevertheless be used for local traffic and winter travel. However, the most important route between the two settlement areas was the Häme Ox Road, which became the primary connection between Finland Proper and Häme as early as the ninth century.

The winter season with its severe weather of ice, snow and freezing temperatures naturally entailed a form of isolation as far as trade traffic and foreign contacts were concerned, but it was in no way a season of passiveness and isolation. As the sagas relate, winter was a time for social contacts, when people hosted each other and traded experiences and news while planning for the coming spring and summer.

SOCIETY AND ECONOMY

Seen as a whole, the Viking Age can be characterised as a period when the country's population had access to a higher standard of living than ever before. The international-isation of trade and the economic boom stimulated the community and created resources for domestic fine handicrafts, for example. The boom also brought with it a population increase and an expansion of settlement, which in turn produced an increase in the number of cemeteries, but it did not result in any marked expansion of the core area in Finland Proper, which had been inhabited already from the end of the preceding Merovingian period (AD 600–800). On the other hand, an expansion and colonisation of new areas did take place in Häme, Savo and Karelia. The population increase does not appear to have caused the same problems in Finland as it did in Scandinavia. Ostrobothnia is the exception; the factors behind the crisis that struck the settlements in this province can only be guessed at.

The flourishing economy cannot be explained solely through foreign contacts and trade relationships. On the contrary, the changes appear to emanate from a domestic economic evolution, which included, for example, a definitive shift to permanent fields (as opposed to shifting swiddens in a slash-and-burn culture) and the birth of village communities. At the same time, it is apparent that the rise in the standard of living affected an ever-larger portion of the population. As opposed to the stratified society of the Merovingian period, Viking Age grave finds point to an egalitarian society of the type that usually characterises affluent farming communities. None of the graves differs from the others – whether in construction, location or grave goods – to the extent that they could be thought of as belonging to leaders with exclusive political power. This does not mean, of course, that there were no affluent landowners or merchants who could afford to buy expensive swords, nor indeed paupers and slaves. But the archaeological material is incapable of explaining the nature of the differences in wealth and social status that the grave finds nevertheless do reflect.

The social structure was probably based primarily on the kinship group, the family headman taking care of the community's economic interests and its religious needs as well. The point has been raised, however, that the building of the numerous hill forts that dot the inhabited regions demanded a collective work effort of a magnitude that could have been maintained only through the cooperation of several villages, as well as a degree of defence coordination that required some form of political leadership.

Although the culture carries a stamp of uniformity, certain geographical areas nevertheless differ from the rest in their exceptional affluence. One such area is the region known as Vakka-Suomi south of the present town of Uusikaupunki, which had closer ties with central Sweden than with the other settlements in south-western Finland. One reason for this might be the area's geographical location, another the fact that the rich farming villages in Kokemäki, Eura and Köyliö maintained their ties with the Baltic world via Vakka-Suomi. Since the area is not known for having exceptionally productive fields, one explanation for the affluence may be that the region already in the Viking Age became famous for its manufacture of wooden containers, particularly the bushels (Finn. *vakka*) that gave the region its name. During the Viking Age with its growing village clusters, there was a thriving market for storage vessels of all kinds. Containers were also required on trading voyages, both for storing the merchandise and for packing provisions.

Although the decisive importance of agriculture to the Iron Age community and its economy cannot be overemphasised, the role played by fur trapping and hunting must also be pointed out. Furs, seal products and skins – not to mention beeswax, which was an old household commodity among the Baltic Finns – were unquestionably among the most important trade goods of the Viking Age. Especially the fur trade required intensive hunting, which took place primarily in the deep forests that spread around the inhabited Iron Age villages. Besides the bow and arrow, hunters used various kinds of traps, pitfalls and snares as well as other passive devices. The most important game animals were the beaver, the moose, the wolf, the lynx and the brown bear. The arrows often had a transverse cutting edge, the points being shaped like chisels or two-pronged forks. Both types are of eastern origin and appear mainly in central and northern Finland.

As the market for furs grew and the hunting grounds near the villages were depleted, hunting trips became longer and longer. The hunting grounds were now frontier wilderness areas hundreds of miles from the core villages. Hunting trips were made at certain times of the year and to particular areas that came to be considered the common property of individual farms or villages. The foundation of the Finnish 'frontier usufruct institution', whereby villages owned land-use rights and even taxation rights in large tracts of outback country primarily in the east and north, was laid during the closing phase of the Iron Age. Hunting voyages to these distant hunting grounds were undertaken by the village's whole male population, and winter – especially late winter – was the main season for these trips. The frontier usufruct economy that had originally developed to supply domestic needs became increasingly commercial and large-scale.

In addition to hunting, fishing also played an important role in the economy. In the inland zone, fishing was mainly carried out by individual households for their own needs. On the coast, on the other hand, it was a cooperative enterprise involving several people. To what degree the Iron Age communities practised true deep-water fishing is beyond our knowledge. The settlements obviously lay in the coastal zone, but there is no archaeological evidence of large-scale fishing on the open sea. These activities belong in the Middle Ages, when the consumption of fish rose steeply in western Europe.

BIBLIOGRAPHY

Appelgren-Kivalo, H. (1907) *Suomalaisia pukuja myöhemmältä rautakaudelta – Finnische Trachten aus der jüngeren Eisenzeit*, Helsinki: no publ.

Cleve, N. (1929) 'Jüngereisenzeitliche Funde von der Insel Berezan', *Eurasia Septentrionalis Antiqua*, 4: 250–62.

—— (1978) *Skelettgravfälten på Kjuloholm i Kjulo*, vol. 2: *Vikingatid och korstågstid* (SMYA–FFT 44:2), Helsingfors: Finska fornminnesföreningen.

Edgren, T. (1968) 'Zu einem Fund von Gussformen aus der jüngeren Eisenzeit in Finnland', *Suomen Museo* (1968): 37–51.

—— (1992) 'Den förhistoriska tiden', in T. Edgren and L. Törnblom, *Finlands historia*, vol. 1, Esbo: Schildt.

—— (1995a) '". . . De Aspø usque Ørsund.vi.Inde usque Hangethe.iij . . ." An archaeological research project concerning one of the harbours in Finland's south-western archipelago referred to in "the Danish itinerary"', in O. Olsen, J. Skamby and F. Rieck (eds) *Shipshape. Essays for Ole Crumlin-Pedersen. On the occasion of his 60th anniversary February 24 1995*, Roskilde: Viking Ship Museum.

—— (2000) 'The Eastern Route: Finland in the Viking Age', in W.W. Fitzhugh and E.I. Ward (eds) *Vikings. The North Atlantic Saga*, Washington, DC: Smithsonian Inst. Press.

—— (2005) 'Kyrksundet in Hitis, SW Finland: a Viking Age resting place and trading post on the sailing route to the east', in A. Mortensen and S.V. Arge (eds) *Viking and Norse in the North Atlantic. Selected Papers from the Proceedings of the Fourteenth Viking Congress, Tórshavn, 19–30 July 2001*, Tórshavn: Føroya Fróðskaparfelag.

Granberg, B. (1966) *Förteckning över kufiska myntfynd i Finland* (Studia Orientalia 34), Helsinki: Societas Orientalis Fennica.

Kivikoski, E. (1937) 'Studien zur Birkas Handel im östlichen Ostseegebiet', *Acta Archaeologica*, 8: 229–50.

—— (1964) *Finlands förhistoria*, Helsingfors: Schildt.

—— (1965) 'Magisches Fundgut aus finnischer Eisenzeit', *Suomen Museo* (1965): 22–35.

—— (1967) *Finland* (Ancient People and Places 53), London: Thames & Hudson.

—— (1973) *Die Eisenzeit Finnlands. Bildwerk und Text*, new edn, Helsingfors: Finska fornminnesföreningen.

Lehtosalo-Hilander, P.-L. (1980) 'Common characteristic features of dress-expressions of kinship or cultural contacts', in *Fenno-ugri et slavi 1978. Papers Presented by the Participants in the Soviet–Finnish Symposium 'The Cultural Relations between the Peoples and Countries of the Baltic Area during the Iron Age and the Early Middle Ages' in Helsinki May 20–23, 1978* (Department of Archaeology. The University of Helsinki. Stencil 22), Helsinki: Department of Archaeology. The University of Helsinki.

—— (1982a) *Luistari*, vol. 1: *The Graves* (SMYA–FFT 82:1), Helsingfors: Finska fornminnesföreningen.

—— (1982b) *Luistari*, vol. 2: *The Artefacts* (SMYA–FFT 82:2), Helsingfors: Finska fornminnesföreningen.

—— (1982c) *Luistari*, vol. 3: *A Burial-ground Reflecting the Finnish Viking Age Society* (SMYA–FFT 82:3), Helsingfors: Finska fornminnesföreningen.

—— (1984) *Ancient Finnish Costumes*, Helsinki. The Finnish Archaeological Society. See also Lehtosalo-Hilander, P.-L. (2001).

—— (1985) 'Viking Age spearheads in Finland', in S.-O. Lindquist (ed.) *Society and Trade in the Baltic during the Viking Age* (Acta Visbyensia 7), Visby: Gotlands fornsal.

—— (1991) 'Le Viking finnois', *Finskt Museum* (1990): 55–72.

—— (1992) 'Finland', in E. Roesdahl and D.M. Wilson (eds) *From Viking to Crusader. Scandinavia and Europe 800–1200* (Council of Europe exhibition 22), Copenhagen: Nordisk Ministerråd.

—— (1994) 'Bijoux et modes vestimentaires en Finlande à l'époque Viking', *Proxima Thule. Revue d'études nordiques*, 1: 111–21.

—— (2000) *Luistari*, vol. 4: *A History of Weapons and Ornaments* (SMYA–FFT 107), Helsingfors: Finska fornminnesföreningen.

—— (2001) *Euran puku ja muut muinaisvaatteet*, Eura: Euran Muinaispukutoimikunta. (Revised and enlarged edition of Lehtosalo-Hilander 1984.)

Leppäaho, J. (1964) *Späteisenzeitliche Waffen aus Finnland. Schwertinschriften und Waffenverzierungen des 9.–12. Jahrhunderts. Ein Tafelwerk* (SMYA–FFT 61), Helsingfors: Finska fornminnesföreningen.

Meinander, C.F. (1980) 'The Finnish society during the 8th–12th centuries', in *Fenno-ugri et slavi 1978. Papers Presented by the Participants in the Soviet–Finnish Symposium 'The Cultural Relations between the Peoples and Countries of the Baltic Area during the Iron Age and the Early Middle Ages' in Helsinki May 20–23, 1978* (Department of Archaeology. The University of Helsinki. Stencil 22), Helsinki: Department of Archaeology. The University of Helsinki.

Mikkola, E. and Talvio, T. (2000) 'A silver coin hoard from Orijärvi, Kihlinpelto in Mikkeli rural commune, province of Savo, eastern Finland', *Fennoscandia archaeologica* (2000): 129–38.

Nordman, C.A. (1921) *Anglo-Saxon Coins Found in Finland*, Helsingfors: The Finnish Antiquarian Society.

—— (1942) 'Schazfunde und Handelsverbindungen in Finnlands Wikingerzeit', *Acta Archaeologica*, 8: 272–93.

Salmo, H. (1948) *Deutsche Münzen in vorgeschichtlichen Funden Finnlands* (SMY–FFT 47), Helsingfors: Finska fornminnesföreningen.

Sarvas, P. (1966) 'Kaiser und Jungfrau Maria. Barbarische Darstellungen auf einigen in Finnland gefundenen Nachahmungen byzantinischer Münzen', *Suomen Museo* (1966): 5–13.

—— (1973) 'Bysanttilaiset rahat sekä niiden jäljitelmät Suomen 900- ja 1000-lukujen löydöissä', in *Honos Ella Kivikoski* (SMYA–FFT 75): Helsingfors: Finska fornminnesföreningen.

SMYA–FFT = Suomen Muinaismuistoyhdistyksen Aikakauskirja – Finska Fornminnesföreningens Tidskrift – *Journal of the Finnish Antiquarian Society*, 1–, Helsingfors – Helsingfors 1870 ff.

Taavitsainen, J.-P. (1990) *Ancient Hillforts of Finland. Problems of Analysis, Chronology and Interpretation with Special Reference to the Hillfort of Kuhmoinen* (SMYA–FFT 94), Helsingfors: Finska fornminnesföreningen.

—— (1991) 'Cemeteries or refuse heaps? Archaeological formation process and the interpretation of sites and antiquities', *Suomen Museo* (1991): 5–14.

Talvio, T. (1980a) 'Coin imitations as jewellery in eleventh century Finland', *Finskt Museum* (1978): 26–38.

—— (1980b) 'The Finnish coin hoards of the Viking Age', in *Fenno-ugri et slavi 1978. Papers Presented by the Participants in the Soviet–Finnish symposium 'The Cultural Relations between the Peoples and Countries of the Baltic Area during the Iron Age and the Early Middle Ages' in Helsinki May 20–23, 1978* (Department of Archaeology. The University of Helsinki. Stencil 22), Helsinki: Department of Archaeology. The University of Helsinki.

—— (1980c) 'Finland's place in Viking-Age relations between Sweden and the eastern Baltic/ northern Russia: the numismatic evidence', *Journal of Baltic Studies*, 13: 245–55.

—— (2002) *Coins and Coin Finds in Finland AD 800–1200* (Iskos 12), Helsingfors: Finska fornminnesföreningen.

Uino, P. (1997) *Ancient Karelia. Archaeological Studies* (SMYA–FFT 104), Helsingfors: Finska fornminnesföreningen.

CHAPTER THIRTY-SIX

THE VIKINGS AND THE EASTERN BALTIC

——•◆•——

Heiki Valk

VIKING TRADE AND VIKING SILVER

The waterways

In the Viking Age, the eastern Baltic was involved in the large waterways leading to the east, as well as in the local Baltic Sea trade networks (Figure 36.1). The two main routes to Old Rus were the Gulf of Finland and the Daugava River in present-day Latvia. The Viking way crossed the gulf between Finland and Estonia near present-day Tallinn, passing on along the north Estonian coastline. The importance of the Daugava, the main continental waterway, has changed in the course of time (Berga 1988: 31). In Latvia the earliest, ninth-century, finds of Viking silver are from the western part of the country and have come, evidently, via Gotland. In the early tenth century the Daugava road emerged and became the main route of Viking trade, but already in less than a century silver coins arrived in Latvia mainly from the north-east, from the basin of the Velikaya River. The Gauja River area, especially the lands at its lower course, was also influenced by Scandinavian culture (Tõnisson 1974; Apala and Apals 1992).

An important water route from the Gulf of Finland to Old Rus, especially Pskov, consisted of the Narva River and Lake Peipsi between present-day Estonia and Russia. Another, smaller waterway in inland Estonia was formed by the Emajõgi River, Lake Võrtsjärv and the Pärnu River with its tributaries. This communication channel joined Lake Peipsi with the Baltic Sea and contributed to the formation of late Iron Age centres in Tartu and Viljandi. In Tartu, which belonged in 1030–61 to Old Rus, a large settlement existed in that period.

Viking silver

In the eastern Baltic, Viking trade is most clearly expressed in silver hoards (Figure 36.2), which consist until the mid-tenth century mainly of Arabic coins. Probably, the main goods exchanged for silver were furs, especially beaver, which were demanded at the large markets (Leimus and Kiudsoo 2004). Hoards with Kufic coins appear in Latvia

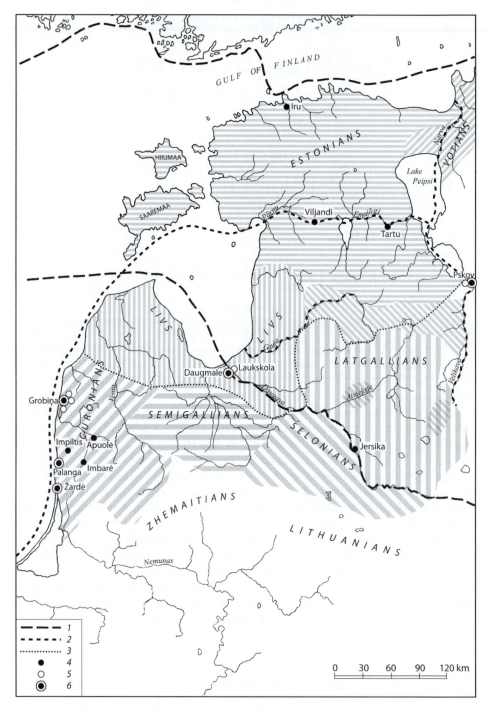

Figure 36.1 Map of the eastern Baltic in the Viking Age: (1) main branch of the 'Austrvegr', (2) major local waterways, (3) presumed Finnic–Baltic ethnic border, (4) hill forts and power centres, (5) cemeteries with Scandinavian graves mentioned in the text, (6) trading places at hill forts.

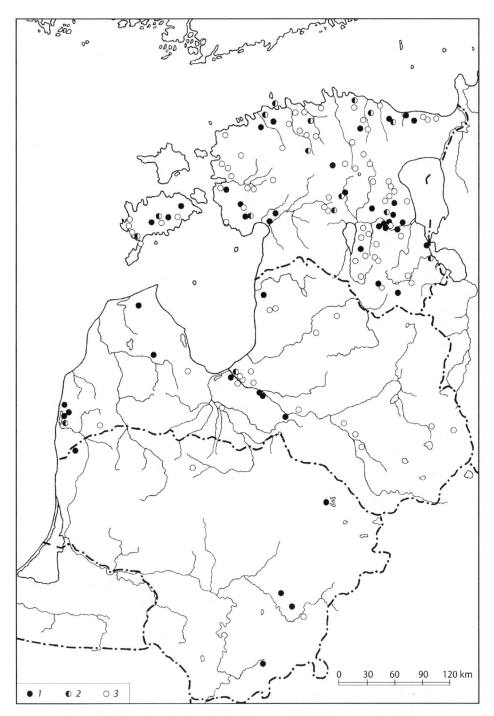

Figure 36.2 Viking Age coin hoards from the eastern Baltic: (1) hoards with Arabic coins,
(2) hoards with Arabic and west European coins, (3) hoards with west European coins.

in the 850s–60s and in Estonia in the first quarter of the tenth century (Berga 1988: 27–9; Leimus 2004). From Estonia there are data for over *c.* 3,700 dirhams (Leimus 2007a). Thirty-five hoards consist of exclusively Arabic coins and there are also 1,521 oriental coins from thirty-three Estonian hoards with west European denars (Molvõgin 1994: table 7). From the *c.* 2,400 dirhams from Latvia, *c.* 1,200 are from thirteen hoards of only Arabic coins, *c.* 750 from hoards with west European coins and 140 from other sites (Berga 1988, 2005). In Latvia the main inflow of Arabic coins was in the first half of the twelfth century, although they circulated up to the 1020s and the latest occur in the hoards buried in the 1070s. The inflow of Kufic coins to Estonia continued up to the turn of the millennium or a little longer (Molvõgin 1994: 566–7; Leimus 2007b). Judging by the frequency of scratch-marks on Kufic coins, the silver seems to have come to Estonia in the ninth century via Sweden (Gotland), but in the tenth century from Russia, mediated mainly by merchants trading with the Swedes (Leimus 2003, 2004).

Continuous inflow of west European coins started in Estonia in the 980s–90s and in Latvia at the very end of the tenth century (Molvõgin 1994; Leimus and Molvõgin 2001; Berga 1988: 32–9). In Estonia the deniers replaced the formerly predominating oriental silver in 1015–18 but their inflow decreased greatly about 1020 and coin hoards are almost missing up to the 1060s. In Latvia, however, the European deniers arrived most intensively in the 1030s–60s. From between *c.* 965 and 1050 the thirty-three Estonian hoards include more than 1,500 coins of west European origin (Molvõgin 1994: 565–74). Respective numbers from Latvia are smaller: ten and *c.* 550 only (Berga 1988: 29–34).

The Viking Age coin hoards of Estonia and Latvia, but also of Finland, are rather small: more than half of them consist of fewer than 100 coins and about one-third have 101–500 coins. Larger hoards are not numerous and there are no finds with more than 2,000 coins (Molvõgin 1994: 580). In Russia the number of hoards is less but on average they are much bigger.

Lithuania remained outside the 'Austrvegr' and there the number of Viking Age silver hoards is small (Duksa 1981; Aleksiejúnas 1992). There are data for about 300 Arabic dirhams from fourteen places (including six hoards) and only for two hoards with west European coins. In Lithuania silver ingots were used instead of coins.

Proto-urban centres

In the Viking Age proto-urban centres emerged also in the eastern Baltic. In Grobiņa, western Latvia, a Scandinavian colony was founded in about 650 and it developed into an important centre (called *urbs* by Rimbert in 857). The large archaeological complex of Grobiņa from the seventh–ninth/tenth centuries consists of cemeteries, a settlement and a hill fort (Petrenko and Urtans 1995). The cemeteries (once with more than 2,000 grave mounds) give evidence of migrants from eastern Sweden or Gotland. In the emergence of the colony parallels can be drawn with the *Guta saga*, the ancient saga of the people of Gotland: the legend says that, due to overpopulation, one-third of the island's inhabitants left first for Dagö (Hiiumaa) island, then moved along the Daugava River to Russia and further on to Greece/Byzantium.

The main proto-urban trade and handicraft centre at the Daugava waterway was Daugmale hill fort of a polyethnic background in the contact zone of the Livs and the

Semgals (Radiņš and Zemītis 1992; Radiņš, 2001; Zemītis 2007). The hill fort, which controlled the waterway, emerged in early tenth century, probably as a reaction to the Viking raids, and was in use up to the mid- or late twelfth century. Its rise correlates well with Daugava's becoming the main east–west Viking trade route. Finds from Daugmale include several imports of the tenth and eleventh centuries and over 190 silver coins from the eighth to twelfth centuries. The other numerous hill forts at Daugava, such as Jersika, are of different character: local power and administrative centres with only the most limited traces of Viking contacts (Radiņš 2001).

From coastal Lithuania there are data for two multicultural proto-urban trade and handicraft centres, oriented on the Baltic Sea, namely Palanga and Žardė, which both arose in the ninth–tenth centuries (Žulkus 1997, 2004: 90, 107–18; Genys 1995, 1997: 149–51). Likewise at Daugava, the major Viking Age centres in southern Curonia (e.g. Apuolė, Impiltis, Eketė, Imbarė) were not oriented on foreign contacts but served as internal power, handicraft and trade centres.

From Estonia there are no data for proto-urban centres. Evidently, communication with the passing Vikings was based on several local harbours.

General involvement in Viking trade

For the long-distance trade between Scandinavia and Old Rus the eastern Baltic offered no special interest. Nor was it reflected on runestones as the destination: only the large water routes to the east were important. The east Baltic region or its toponyms occur on runestones only if someone perished there and thus Viking finds of ritual character are missing from the area (Mickevičus 1997: 192–4). The interests of the Scandinavians were limited to a safe passage and some trading on the way.

Local involvement and the importance of inland rivers in Viking Age trade contacts were especially remarkable in Estonia, being reflected in the equal distribution of Viking silver. In Latvia traces of Viking trade are mainly limited to the areas near the main waterways. Lithuania remained outside the network of long-distance trade but its western coast was part of the trade system of the Baltic Sea. The northern part of the country formed a remote hinterland of the Daugava water route.

THE VIKINGS AND THE NATIVES

On their way to Rus, as well as in their Baltic Sea activities, the Vikings encountered people with a different linguistic and ethnocultural background (Figure 36.1). Among the natives of the eastern Baltic, the Finnic ethnicities were represented by the Estonians and the Livs. The latter inhabited northern and north-western Latvia, including the lower course of the Daugava and Gauja rivers, and up to the eleventh century, probably, most of the Curonian peninsula (Vasks 2004: 13). The Curonians lived near the Baltic Sea, closest to Scandinavia, in the western part of present-day Lithuania and south-western Curonia. This ethnonym was probably used by people living in the west also for the peninsula's Livic population. The Daugava waterway met the lands of the Semgals and Sels to its south and the Latgalian territories at its middle course. Lithuania was involved in the Viking world mainly via the coastal, south Curonian areas, although the big rivers were sometimes also touched by Viking activities. As a whole, Scandinavia and the eastern Baltic represented worlds with different cultures and societies. Their dissimilarities are expressed for example in language, religion, art, fashion and building traditions.

The relations of the Scandinavians with the natives of the eastern Baltic had both mercantile and military aspects. In communication, evidently private initiatives at the local level and the activities of the emerging Scandinavian state formations must be distinguished.

Trading contacts

In the eastern Baltic, the impact of Viking activities on native culture is the strongest in Latvia, in the densely populated Livic areas at the lower course of the Daugava River, up to *c.* 30 km from its mouth (Caune 1992). Probably a strong impetus for the emerging Livic culture was provided by its location at important trading routes. At the large Salaspils Laukskola cemetery (Zariņa 2006), Scandinavian imports occurred in 6 per cent of the tenth- and eleventh-century graves (Zariņa 1992: 184), mainly in rich burials of native character. The Scandinavian contacts are represented, in addition to silver coins, by oval brooches which were imported between 950–1000 (Jansson 1992; Spirgis 2004, 2007), silver penannular brooches, pendants, belt details, bone combs etc. The importance of Scandinavian contacts is most clearly expressed in the local imitations of Scandinavian artefact forms: oval brooches from the eleventh to thirteenth centuries (Tõnisson 1974: 120–1; Jansson 1992: 72–4), weapons (Creutz 2003) and belt buckles.

In Estonia Scandinavian influences on the local culture are much weaker. Their presence is not expressed in fashion and costume – for example, oval brooches are rare (Luik 1998) – but mainly in imported silver coins. Finds of Scandinavian Viking Age ornaments (Figure 36.3) are rare in Estonian cemeteries and hoards (Tamla 1995).

In spite of the Viking routes, traces of Scandinavian permanent settlement are virtually absent in the eastern Baltic. In the well-investigated cemeteries of the Daugava Livs just some single graves can be interpreted as 'Scandinavian'. Thus, from the 610 graves excavated at Laukskola cemetery merely four (incl. a warrior) can be regarded as

Figure 36.3   Scandinavian silver pendants from Estonian hoards: (1) Kose (AM 25159: 1),
(2) Olustvere (AI 5005: 1).

Scandinavian burials) (Zariņa, 2006; 318, 425). Only in and around Grobiņa numerous grave mounds speak of a large colony of Scandinavian migrants who preserved their cultural identity and kept contacts with their homeland. Archaeology speaks of their peaceful coexistence with the native Curonian population.

At the main waterways, especially the Daugava, relations between the Scandinavians and the natives seem to have been predominantly peaceful and based on mutual interests. Gifts to the local elite granted the Vikings the right to trade and passage. The role of the numerous hill forts at Daugava was evidently not to block the waterways, but to control the situation. Contacts with the Livic areas were presumably based on relationships, including marriage (indirectly reflected also in Livs' personal names). The inland areas were probably involved in trade through local mediators – either independent or representatives of the native elite – who exchanged local goods for silver at harbours and trading places. The presence of trading Scandinavians themselves on smaller waterways seems likely only where they had good contacts with the native elite.

A special role in Scandinavian–eastern Baltic relations belonged to Gotland, which differed greatly from Continental Sweden both in culture and in society. The large and numerous silver hoards indicate the Gotlanders' special role in Viking raids and also the non-centralised character of Viking trade (Thunmark-Nylén 1992: 156–7). Archaeology indicates close, peaceful and intensive contacts between Gotland and the eastern Baltic. Close similarity in men's costume and weapons (silver-plated spearheads, scabbards, belt mounts with animal ornamentation) manifest the common identity and solidarity of traders from the Gotland, Curonia, Saaremaa and Livic areas in the tenth–eleventh centuries. The contacts were especially intensive with Curonia, geographically the closest area (Thunmark-Nylén 2000). Eastern Baltic women's ornaments from Gotland have been interpreted not as ordinary imports, but as signs of marriage relations (Thunmark-Nylén 1992: 157–60), and breast pins, alien to Scandinavia, were even produced on Gotland (Jansson 1995). In the light of new research, the old model of Gotlandic expansion to the east (Nerman 1929) is no longer valid. The recent analysis of E-type spearheads around the Baltic shows that, although 'Scandinavian' in form and ornament, they were produced in different workshops and areas (Creutz 2003) and in this light the same may be the situation concerning also other 'Scandinavian' artefacts (Figure 36.4). The relations between Gotland and the eastern Baltic, especially its closest eastern neighbours – Saaremaa and Curonia – were probably mainly of mercantile, not of military, character. The Gotlanders had peace with Saaremaa even during the crusades of the early thirteenth century when Visby had become a centre of German activities.

Thus, in the local networks of Baltic Sea trade an active role belonged also to the eastern Baltic, especially the inhabitants of western coastal areas. It has even been suggested that from the eleventh century Saaremaa was involved in transit trade between the estuary of Daugava and Gotland (Ligi 1995a: 237). But, on the whole, trade on the Baltic Sea was not equal: finds of Scandinavian origin are numerous in the eastern Baltic but eastern Baltic artefacts are quite rare in Scandinavia.

Military relations

The military aspects of relations are also considerable. The written sources show that Scandinavian early state formation had different zones of interest in the eastern Baltic

Figure 36.4 Local imitations of Scandinavian oval brooches from the Gauja Livonians' Krimulda cemetery (AI 1222: XXV. 1).

(Mickevičius 1997: 196–8). Denmark was more oriented to Prussia and south Curonia, mainly in coastal areas. The interests of Sweden were directed towards the extensive eastern routes, while the eastern Baltic was just a place *en route*. The concentration of power increased the attempts of Scandinavian rulers to control the strategically important waterways. The sagas repeatedly tell of the activities of kings against both the Curonians and the Estonians (Nerman 1929: 55–6; Mugurēvičs 1997: 88–9; Mickevičius 1997: 196–8; Apals and Mugurēvičs 2001: 371–2). Rimbert in his *Vita Ansgarii* mentions already in 857 the besieging of the Curionian centres of Seeburg (probably Grobiņa) and Apuole (in present-day Lithuania). Raids not only against the Curonians but also deep inland are evinced by Scandinavian arrowheads from Lithuania (Zabiela 1997). The hill fort of Iru near Tallinn, in the place where the Vikings crossed the Gulf of Finland, was burnt down four times during the Viking Age and the finds include arrowheads of Nordic origin (Lang 1995). Viking arrowheads were found also in other centres of north Estonia and Saaremaa. Probably, it was not only internal concentration of power but also an external danger which made the people of Saaremaa construct in the eighth and ninth centuries round-wall forts, similar to those on Gotland and Öland. The fact that the Viking Age and post-Viking Age settlements in north Estonia are not located on the coast but some kilometres inland is, evidently, also conditioned by danger from the sea. Arrowheads from east Estonian centres (e.g. Tartu) indicate the participation of Scandinavians in the Russian princes' attacks on eastern Estonia.

The military raids caused, however, no permanent Scandinavian supremacy.

Although the sagas repeatedly mention the Scandinavian kings subordinating different areas and peoples in the eastern Baltic, the stated conquests remained only temporary and are not reflected in archaeology. In spite of the Scandinavian activity on the 'Austrvegr', its shores were still controlled by the native, Finnic and Baltic population.

Evidently, Baltic tribes had different relations with Scandinavia. Scandinavian sources tell about piracy and plundering attacks from the east, mentioning especially the Curonians. As archaeology in northern Curonia speaks of trade contacts with Scandinavia, and as finds referring to long-distance trade are not numerous from the south Curonian coast (Genys 1997: fig. 1), the data on piracy seem to concern rather the latter area (Mickevičius 1997: 196). In Estonia, Saaremaa was most actively involved in piracy, and its relations with Scandinavia (except for Gotland) were probably of a mostly military character. From the early tenth century the island was overpopulated and the lack of arable land forced part of its population to live by means of plunder (Ligi 1995b). At the lower course of the Daugava River, but also in the Gauja Basin, mainly trade contacts are reflected in the archaeology. North Estonian coastal areas were not touched much by the passing Vikings but the silver hoards speak of involvement in a broad trade system.

Although the initiative on the Baltic Sea and the main waterways to the east belonged to the Scandinavians in the Viking Age, the situation seems to have changed in the eleventh century. The transition to the Middle Ages and the genesis of new political, social and religious structures in Scandinavia not only caused a decline in Viking activities, but also increased the social and cultural distance of the eastern Baltic where Iron Age societies continued. Economic and population growth and the lasting practices of a plundering economy even increased the 'eastern' military pressure on Scandinavia. In the mid-twelfth century a new power – the German merchant – appeared on the Baltic Sea. This change shifted the balance of force, in which semi-professional traders began to be expelled, both from Scandinavia and the eastern Baltic, and prepared the ground for the east Baltic crusades.

BIBLIOGRAPHY

Aleksiejuńas, V. (1992) 'Monetary circulation in the territory of Lithuania before the introduction of its own coinage', in B. Hårdh and B. Wyszomirska-Werbart (eds) *Contacts across the Baltic Sea during the Late Iron Age (5th–12th Centuries)* (Inst. of Archaeology, University of Lund. Report series 43), Lund: Inst. of Archaeology, University of Lund.

Apala, Z. and Apals, J. (1992) 'Die Kontakte der Lettgallen des Gauja-Raumes mit Skandinavien', in A. Loit, E. Mugurevics and A. Caune (eds) *Die Kontakte zwischen Ostseeeraum und Skandinavien im frühen Mittelalter* (Studia Baltica Stockholmiensia 9), Stockholm: Almqvist & Wiksell International.

Apals, J. and Mugurēvičs, E. (2001) 'Vēlais dzelzs laikmets (agrie viduslaiki)', in E. Mugurēvičs and A. Vasks (eds) *Latvijas senākā vēsture. 9. g.t. pr. Kr – 1200 g*, Riga: Latvijas vēstures institūts.

Berga 1988 = Берга, Т.М. (1988) *Монемы в археологических памятниках Латвии IX–XII вв*, Рига (Riga): Зинатне.

Berga, T. (2005) 'Austrumu monēti atdarināumi Latvijā', *Arheoloģija un etnogrāfija*, 22: 127–34.

Caune, A. (1992) 'Die Siedlungszentren des 10.–12. Jh, im Gebiet des Daugava-Unterlaufs und ihre Beziehungen zu skandinavischen Ländern', in A. Loit, E. Mugurevics and A. Caune (eds) *Die Kontakte zwischen Ostseeraum und Skandinavien im frühen Mittelalter* (Studia Baltica Stockholmiensia 9), Stockholm: Almqvist & Wiksell International.

Creutz, K. (2003) *Tension and Tradition. A Study of Late Iron Age Spearheads around the Baltic Sea* (Theses and Papers in Archaeology. New Series A:8), Stockholm: Dept. of Archaeology, University of Stockholm.

Duksa, Z. (1981) 'Pinigai ir jų apyvarta', in R. Volkaitė-Kulikauskienė (ed.) *Lieutuvių materialinė kultūra IX–XIII amžiuje*, vol. 2, Vilnius: Mokslas.

Genys, J. (1995) 'Žardė-Pilsoto žemės prekybos ir amatų centras', in N. Vélius *et al.* (eds) *Lietuvininkų kraštas*, Kaunas: Litterae Universitatis.

—— (1997) 'Trade routes and trade centres in western Lithuania during the early Middle Ages', *Archaeologia Baltica*, 2: 141–54.

Jansson, I. (1992) 'Scandinavian oval Brooches found in Latvia', in A. Loit, E. Mugurēvičs and A. Caune (eds) *Die Kontakte zwischen Ostseeraum und Skandinavien im frühen Mittelalter* (Studia Baltica Stockholmiensia 9), Stockholm: Almqvist & Wiksell International.

—— (1995) 'Dress pins of east Baltic type made on Gotland', in I. Jansson (ed.) *Archaeology East and West of the Baltic. Papers from the Second Estonian–Swedish Archaeological Symposium. Sigtuna, May 1991* (Theses and Papers in Archaeology. New Series A:7), Stockholm: Dept. of Archaeology, University of Stockholm.

Lang, V. (1995) 'The hill-fort of Iru', in I. Jansson (ed.) *Archaeology East and West of the Baltic. Papers from the Second Estonian–Swedish Archaeological Symposium. Sigtuna, May 1991* (Theses and Papers in Archaeology. New Series A:7), Stockholm: Dept. of Archaeology, University of Stockholm.

Leimus, I. and Molvõgin, A. (2001) *Estonian Collections: Anglo-Saxon, Anglo-Norman and later British Coins* (Sylloge of the coins of the British Isles 51) Oxford.

Leimus, I. (2003) 'Graffitid Eestis leitud araabia müntidel', *Arheoloogia Läänemeremaades. Muinasajà Teadus*, 13: 143–52.

—— (2004) 'Finds of Cufic coins in Estonia: preliminary observations', *Wiadamości Numizmatyczne*, 178(2): 153–66.

Leimus, I. (2007a) *Sylloge of Islamic coins 710/1–1013/4 AD. Estonian public collections* (Thesaurus historiae 2), Tallinn: Eesti Ajaloomuuseum.

Leimus, I. (2007b) 'Die letzte Welle des orientalischen Münzsilbers im Norden', in *Magister Monetae. Studies in Honour of Jøgen Steen Jensen. Publications of the National Museum* (Studies in Archaeology and History 13), Copenhagen: National Museum of Denmark.

Leimus, I. and Kiudsoo, M. (2004) 'Koprad ja hõbe', *Tuna*, 4: 31–47.

Ligi, P. (1995a) 'Ühiskondlikest oludest Eestis hilispronksi- ja rauaajal', in V. Lang (ed.) *Eesti arheoloogia historiograafilisi ja teoreetilisi probleeme* (Muinasaja Teadus 3), Tallinn: Teaduste Akadeemia Kirjastus.

—— (1995b) 'Saaremaa during the Viking Age', in I. Jansson (ed.) *Archaeology East and West of the Baltic. Papers from the Second Estonian–Swedish Archaeological Symposium. Sigtuna, May 1991* (Theses and Papers in Archaeology. New Series A:7), Stockholm: Dept. of Archaeology, University of Stockholm.

Luik, H. (1998) 'Ovaalsõled Eestis – importesemed mitmest piirkonnast', *Eesti Arheoloogia Ajakiri*, 2: 3–20.

Mickevičus, A. (1997) 'Curonia in the "Eastern Policy" of Viking Age Scandinavia', *Archaeologia Baltica*, 2: 191–9.

Molvõgin, A. (1994) *Die Funde Westeuropäischer Münzen des 10. bis 12. Jahrhunderts in Estland* (Numismatische Studien 10), Hamburg: Museum für Hamburgische Geschichte.

Mugurēvičs, E. (1997) 'Kurlands Siedlungsplätze in frühgeschichtlicher Zeit', *Archaeologia Baltica*, 2: 85–93.

Nerman, B. (1929) *Die Verbindungen zwischen Skandinavien und dem Ostbaltikum in der jüngere Eisenzeit* (KVHAAs Handlingar 40: 1), Stockholm: KVHAA.

Petrenko, V. and Urtans, J. (1995) *The Archaeological Monuments of Grobiņa*, Stockholm: Museum of National Antiquities.

Radiņš, A. (1992) 'The Daugmale antiquities complex', in B. Hårdh and B. Wyszomirska-Werbart (eds) *Contacts across the Baltic Sea during the Late Iron Age (5th–12th Centuries)* (Inst. of Archaeology, University of Lund. Report series 43), Lund: Inst. of Archaeology, University of Lund.

—— (2001) 'Daugmale, Jersika, Riga: the development of economic and political centres along the lower reaches of the Daugava', in M. Auns (ed.) *Lübeck Style? Novgorod Style? Baltic Rim Central Places as Arenas for Cultural Encounters and Urbanisation 1100–1400 AD* (CCC Papers 5), Riga: Nordik.

Radiņš, A. and Zemītis, G. (1992) 'Die Verbindungen zwishen Daugmale und Skandinavien', in A. Loit, E. Mugurevics and A. Caune (eds) *Die Kontakte zwischen Ostseeraum und Skandinavien im frühen Mittelalter* (Studia Baltica Stockholmiensia 9), Stockholm: Almqvist & Wiksell International.

Spirgis, R. (2004) 'Lībiešu 3.–5. tipa bruņrupuču saktas Daugavas Lejtecē 12.–13. gadsimtā', *Latvijas Vēstures Institūts Zurnāls*, 2: 27–48.

Spirģis, R. (2007) 'Liv Tortoise Brooches in the Lower Daugava Area in the 10th–13th Centuries', in U. Fransson, M. Svedin, S. Bergerbrant and F. Androshchuk (eds) *Cultural interaction between east and west. Archaeology, artefacts and human contacts in northern Europe* (Stockholm Studies in Archaeology 44), Stockholm: Stockholm University.

Tamla, Ü. (1995). 'Scandinavian influences on the Estonian silver ornaments of the 9th–13th centuries', in I. Jansson (ed.) *Archaeology East and West of the Baltic. Papers from the Second Estonian–Swedish Archaeological Symposium. Sigtuna, May 1991* (Theses and Papers in Archaeology. New Series A:7), Stockholm: Dept. of Archaeology, University of Stockholm.

Thunmark-Nylén, L. (1992) 'Gotland: neighbour between the west and the east', in A. Loit, E. Mugurēvičs and A. Caune (eds) *Die Kontakte zwischen Ostseeraum und Skandinavien im frühen Mittelalter* (Studia Baltica Stockholmiensia 9), Stockholm: Almqvist & Wiksell International.

—— (2000) 'Some notes on the contacts between Gotland and the east Baltic area', *Archaeologia Baltica*, 4: 173–80.

Tõnisson, E. (1974) *Die Gauja-Liven und ihre materielle Kultur im 11. Jh. – Anfang 13. Jhs*, Tallinn: Eesti Raamat.

Vasks, A. (2004) 'Kurši un baltijas somi Kurzemē 1. gadu tūkstotī', *Latvijas Vēstures Institūta Žurnāls*, 3(52): 5–17.

Zabiela, G. (1997) 'Scandinavian arrowheads in Lithuania', *Archaeologia Baltica*, 2: 133–40.

Zariņa, A. (1992) 'Die Kontakte der Liven mit Skandinavischen Ländern nach den Schmucksachen des Gräberfeldes aus dem 10.–13. Jh. zu Salaspils Laukskola', in A. Loit, E. Mugurēvičs and A. Caune (eds) *Die Kontakte zwischen Ostseeeraum und Skandinavien im frühen Mittelalter* (Studia Baltica Stockholmiensia 9), Stockholm: Almqvist & Wiksell International.

Zariņa, A. (2006) *Salaspils Laukskola kapulauks. 10.–13. gadsimts*, Rīga: Latvijas Vēstures Institūta Apgāds.

Zemītis, G. (2007) '10th–12th Century Daugmale. The earliest Urban Settlement along the Lower Daugava and Forerunner of Riga', in U. Fransson, M. Svedin, S. Bergerbrant and F. Androshchuk (eds) *Cultural interaction between east and west. Archaeology, artefacts and human contacts in northern Europe* (Stockholm Studies in Archaeology 44), Stockholm: Stockholm University.

Žulkus, V. (1997) *Palangos viduramžių gyvenvietės* (Acta Historica Universitatis Klaipedensis 6), Klaipeda: Klaipedos univ. 1-kla.

—— (2004) *Kuršiai Baltijos jūros erdvėje*, Vilnius: Versus aureus.

CHAPTER THIRTY-SEVEN

THE VIKING RUS AND BYZANTIUM

——.•.——

Jonathan Shepard

Byzantium was far from being the main attraction for persons drawn from the Nordic world to lands east of the Baltic in the early Middle Ages. Mostly their priorities lay closer to hand, trapping animals for their furs in the vicinity of Lake Ladoga and dealing in furs at trading posts such as Staraia Ladoga from the mid-eighth century onwards. At that time the Abbasid caliphate stimulated or revived multifarious nexus of exchange through issuing silver coins on a massive scale and general promotion of commerce (Noonan 1986).

Silver was prized by virtually all the peoples living in the forest zones to the north of the Eurasian steppes and in the opening stages of the trafficking in Islamic silver most routes led through territories under the Khazars' control. The Khazars' power could hardly have failed to make an impression on those from the Nordic world who joined with indigenous populations of the eastern lands in a common quest for silver, and in fact the head of their first recorded polity to the east of the Baltic sported the same title as that of the Khazar ruler, *chaganus* or kagan. The Khazars probably supplied the inspiration for authority-symbols and customs, including that of setting a more or less sacral figurehead at the polity's head. As with the Khazars, this totem-like overlord (reportedly residing on an immense bed-cum-throne) acted in tandem with a military commander who handled earthly affairs in the later ninth and early tenth centuries (Lewicki 1985: 75–6; Montgomery 2000: 21–2; Golden 1982: 45–50, 52–3; Golden 2006).

Such adaptations are understandable, in that the Khazars could make their presence felt well to the north of the Black Sea steppes: they were still exacting tribute in the mixed-forest zone from Slavic tribes such as the Viatichi in the mid-960s (*PVL*: 31; *RPC*: 84). In contrast, no continuous land route led from the eastern lands to Constantinople, nor was there any question of the Byzantines seeking tangible hegemony to the north of the steppes.

But while the Greco-Byzantine world played second fiddle to the semi-nomadic Khazars and to Islamic markets in the opening stages of the exchanges of Abbasid silver for produce from the northern forests, northern traders did encounter Greek-speakers. One of the earliest hoards of Islamic silver found in the north, near modern St Petersburg, contains several pieces on which Scandinavian and Turkic runes have been scratched but one dirham has the name 'Zacharias' scratched in Greek-style letters, perhaps with reference to a temporary owner (Mel'nikova 2001: 107, 115–19). The coins in the hoard, probably deposited early in the ninth century, will mostly have passed through the Khazars' dominions, which housed enough Christians of the eastern orthodox rite for a metropolitanate to be devised for them by the Constantinopolitan authorities, probably in the second quarter of the ninth century (Darrouzès 1981: 31–2, 241–2, 245). Later in the century, the well-informed Abbasid director of posts and intelligence Ibn Khurradadhbeh noted that northern traders brought furs and swords down to the Black Sea coast and paid customs duties to the Byzantines, probably at Cherson in the Crimea (Lewicki 1956: 76–7). He terms them 'Rūs', and in fact persons 'stating that they, that is their people (*gens*), were called *Rhōs*' were already at the Byzantine emperor's court by 838. Reportedly, their 'king called *chaganus*' had sent them 'for the sake of friendship'. These envoys are best known for what befell them later, at the court of the western emperor, Louis the Pious. After making enquiries Louis identified them as 'of the people of the Swedes (*Sueoni*)' and detained them on suspicion of espionage. The episode provides a central plank in the case for regarding the Rūs/*Rhōs* who appear in the eastern lands as incomers, a 'people' of Nordic stock (Grat *et al.* 1964: 30–1; Shepard 1995a). But it also suggests that exchanges of embassies and other marks of recognition with the Byzantine emperor mattered to the Rus from the moment that an elite group tried to establish hegemony over populations between the Gulf of Finland and the fringes of the steppes. The likeliest location for the Rus *chaganus*' base is Riurikovo Gorodishche, at the hub of several long-distance waterways radiating out from Lake Il'men. A Byzantine official's seal of the first half of the ninth century has been found there as well as a copper coin of Theophilos, the Byzantine emperor visited by the forementioned embassy. These form part of a trail of copper coins and of seals belonging to another official found at Hedeby, Ribe, Tissø and Birka, hints of Byzantine as well as Rus emissaries moving between Nordic courts and kingly halls around this time (Shepard 1995a: 48–55; Bulgakova 2004: 53–4; Duczko 2004: 50–9, 101–4). Byzantine emperors' gifts and greetings could bolster the status of would-be dynasts near and east of the Baltic, while the emperor was ever alert for allies and potential 'barbarian' recruits for his armies, the further-flung and fiercer the better.

One unintended by-product of the Byzantine emissaries' probings may have been to whet Nordic arms-bearing groups' appetite for fame and wealth from long-range ventures to the inland seas. Viking expeditions harried Spanish and Italian coastlines in the 840s and 850s, and in June 860 a sizeable fleet bore down on Constantinople from the north — like 'a thunderbolt' according to Patriarch Photios. They reportedly amassed 'immense wealth' from looting the suburbs and other coastal settlements, and in activities that lasted no more than a few weeks, they made a point of terrifying Constantinople's citizens. Photios describes them as sailing past the walls and raising their swords, 'as if threatening the city with death by the sword' (Laourdas 1959: 44; Mango 1958: 101). Such displays and the desecration of altars showed up the shortcomings of the God whom the Christians claimed was their protector, while the terrified Greeks' failure to respond militarily gained further kudos for the expedition's leaders. Photios' rhetorical claim that what had been a rabble had now gained fame may hit upon one of the reasons for the undertaking: a couple of hundred or so boatloads of even the bravest warriors stood little chance of storming Constantinople's walls, while the amount of loot they could ship back north was finite. But a notably bloody, destructive raid served notice on the Greeks that marks of respect were expected, while plausible claims to have humbled the 'God-protected city' could overawe the indigenous populations of the eastern lands. The Rus *chaganus* had not necessarily initiated the expedition, and (as with later Rus attacks on Byzantium), many participants were probably fresh arrivals from the Baltic region. However, retainers and associates of the *chaganus* probably played a key part in equipping and guiding what Photios called 'the unbelievable course of the barbarians'.

Whatever the Rus expedition's rationale and exact organisation may have been, the fleet reportedly succumbed to a storm on its way back north. Perhaps this intervention from Above, belated but deadly, prompted the Rus leadership's next known move, the despatch to Constantinople of envoys requesting baptism. By 867 Photios was boasting that the famed *Rhōs* had received a 'bishop and pastor' and it is likely enough that a mission was sent: a later Byzantine text depicts him as astounding the Rus prince and his assembled 'elders' with his flameproof Gospel book (Laourdas and Westerink 1985: 50; Bekker 1838: 343–4). However, neither missionaries nor miracles could guarantee political order and the archaeological hints of conflagration at Staraia Ladoga and Gorodishche datable to the 860s and early 870s (Zuckerman 2000b: 110–14) suggest upheavals and strife; the Byzantine mission seems to have folded at that time without lasting gains to its name.

Twenty or so years later groups of eastern-based Rus made the move to the Middle Dnieper area, some taking up residence on the hills overlooking the river at Kiev. Neither their provenance nor the exact circumstances of their arrival are known, although the *Rus Primary Chronicle*'s tale of successive would-be warlords is not implausible (*PVL*: 13–14; *RPC*: 60–1). What is reasonably clear is that they were few in number, newcomers to a region inhabited mainly by Slavs and overshadowed by the steppe-nomads: the Khazars and their proxies had exacted tribute there and it is likely that a Khazar official resided in Kiev at the time when the northerners installed themselves. Others made for the town of Chernigov and settlements nearby such as Shestovitsa. That this occurred in the last decade or so of the ninth century is suggested by archaeological finds at Shestovitsa and at Kiev, whose docklands beside the Dnieper only began to be built over with log cabins from around that time onwards (Sahaidak 1991: 82–4, 88; Franklin and Shepard 1996: 98–103; Androščuk 2000; Kovalenko *et al.* 2003: 60–4). The region was attractive less for its own fertility or land routes running from east to west than for the megalopolis that was a few weeks' sailing-distance away in springtime. Hopes of gaining access to the markets of Constantinople probably induced the Rus to try and establish themselves there: the tribute customarily paid by local Slavs to the Khazars might now be shipped overseas rather than borne overland to the Khazar core-lands. The scheme was almost as audacious as the expedition of 860, although now it was a matter of trading with the Greeks, not raiding. There had never been a regular waterway between the Middle Dnieper region and ports lying to the south of the Black Sea before. The exchanges in primary produce of the forest regions, furs, wax, honey and slaves, had mostly been conducted by nomads, associates of the Khazars and, in the ninth century, the Hungarians. The Chersonites were themselves important shippers of goods and passengers across the Black Sea, while also standing to gain from the customs dues payable on all goods brought to their hometown (Shepard 2008). But their trafficking did not involve river journeys across the steppe and they most probably looked askance at newcomers ferrying goods down the Dnieper and then plying the same craft across the unpredictable waters of the Black Sea.

Yet that is what the Rus embarked upon soon after installing themselves at Kiev and a few other points along riverways converging on that town. We catch a glimpse of how they proceeded from the agreements with Byzantium that gave them the advantage of direct access to the many markets and broader choice of goods on offer in the empire's capital. This brought them opportunities for more lucrative deals than were available in Crimean towns, cutting out the Chersonite middleman. For the Byzantines the benefits were less commercial than political: by engaging their potentially troublesome new neighbours in trade they could dampen enthusiasm for alternative methods of self-enrichment, such as raiding: Leo VI had noted their capacity for trouble in his tactical treatise, but their river-going boats did not seem a threat at the time of writing, the 890s (Dain 1943: 32).

The earliest accord was issued not long afterwards, in 907. Although the text is known only from the fragments incorporated in the *Rus Primary Chronicle*, enough survives to suggest that it was laying down house-rules for regular visits to Constantinople; a fuller treaty followed soon afterwards, providing for various contingencies likely to arise in the course of trading. This agreement, dated 2 September 911, included among its attesters all five of the men named as Rus negotiators in the text datable to 907, Karl, Farulf, Vermund, Hrollaf and Steinvith. The total number of northerners personally vouching for the bilateral treaty 'of peace and friendship' between Leo VI and the Rus ruling elite came to fifteen; they probably represented power-nodes across the land of Rus, with the locus of authority still lying far to the north, embodied in the palace-bound kagan.

The 907 accord amounts to a set of privileges vouchsafed by the emperor, compensating the Rus for the costs and dangers which trading visits incurred and encouraging them to persist. They were exempted from all customs dues, and monthly allowances supplemented the free board and lodging provided for periods up to six months. Unlimited baths were part of the treatment and, for the return journey, sailcloth and anchors were supplied. But such 'perks' were only available to prospective traders: 'Rus coming here without goods shall receive no monthly allowances' (*PVL*: 17; *RPC*: 65). And the Byzantines remained on their guard. The Rus were to reside north of the Golden Horn and were only to enter the city through one gate, fifty at a time, unarmed and escorted by an imperial agent. Politico-military considerations likewise underlie the terms for dispute-settlement and determination of rightful ownership of chattels in the 911 treaty. Opportunities for strife between individual Rus and Byzantines are expected to be numerous, with detailed regulations as to what was to be done with the crews and cargoes of any stricken 'Christian' vessels the Rus might encounter. These apply Romano-Byzantine law to conditions in the tenth-century Black Sea. (*PVL*: 19; *RPC*: 67; Malingoudi 1998: 59–64). But the notion of compensatory fines based on a duo-decimal system to resolve issues of murder and property was alien to Byzantine law. So was the right of the victim of theft to slay a thief caught red-handed and to undertake a house-search of a suspect. Robbery, in contrast, was treated more leniently: a foiled robber must repay three times the value of what he had seized, but vengeance is not countenanced. These procedures, with thieves deemed utterly contemptible, are in the spirit, if not the letter, of laws codified two or three centuries later in Nordic societies and they show the lengths the Byzantines went to accommodate their Rus guests in the megalopolis (*PVL*: 18–19; *RPC*: 66–8; Stein-Wilkeshuis 1991: 43–5). These are the nuts and bolts of a working document which both sides thought met their needs, judging by the fact that the terms feature in comparable form in the Russo-Byzantine treaty ratified a generation later. The 944 treaty to some extent fills in the gaps left by the earlier texts and is slightly more forthcoming about the commodities in play: besides ships' cargoes and slaves, silk is mentioned and Rus are forbidden from buying silks worth more than 50 *solidi* (*PVL*: 24; *RPC*: 75).

These treaties give an impression of joint-concern on the part of the Rus and imperial leaderships with orderly commerce, involving constant exchanges over such matters as restitution of the property of a Rus who has died intestate to kinsfolk in the north. That correspondence went on between Rus and Byzantine officials is confirmed by finds of earlier and mid-tenth-century seals at Kiev and Shestovitsa (Bulgakova 2004: 49–51, 55–7). A picture of a militarised elite geared to trading with the south also emerges from a text drafted for Constantine VII around 950. Chapter Nine of Constantine's *De administrando imperio* depicts the Rus as based on the Middle Dnieper, while also occupying Smolensk and points north, and 'all the Rus' constitute an elite preoccupied with tribute-collection and trade. The cycle of their 'hard way of life' revolves around winter spent among Slav tribute-payers and then, 'as the Dnieper ice melts', they reassemble in Kiev while simple craft made from newly felled trees are floated downstream to Kiev by Slavs who are paid for their labours. The boats are fitted out and laden, and the Rus set forth in convoy as far as the Dnieper Rapids. Constantine's account of the journey derives from an eyewitness. The Rapids' names are given 'in Rus' and 'in Slavic', certain of the former being clearly identifiable as Old Norse, for example *Oulvorsi*, a compound deriving from words for 'island' (*hólmr*) and 'waterfall, rapid' (*fors*) (*DAI*: 58–9; Jenkins 1962: 45). The Rus have to disembark with their goods at the deadliest Rapid of all, helped by the fact that their foremost commodities, slaves, are self-propelling. But the Pecheneg nomads try to attack them there and follow them downstream, stalking them as far as the Danube delta: 'and if it happens that the sea casts a *monoxylon* to shore, they all put in to land, to present a united front against the Pechenegs' (*DAI*: 62–3).

The Rus' journey appeared noteworthy to Byzantine observers, and their feats of organisation, boatmanship and endurance can hardly be overstated. As Emperor Constantine's informant perceived, stragglers from the encumbered flotillas had few prospects of survival and this might serve as a paradigm for the Rus presence on the Middle Dnieper as a whole. Compared with the diverse nexuses that still brought Muslim silver to the north in the first half of the tenth century and involved caravans of camels, boatmen on the Upper Volga and countless small-scale fur-traders and trappers (including part-time agriculturalists), the Byzantine connection was largely a matter for those already disposing of resources, coercive and material. There may have been more than one trading flotilla of container-craft each year and some Rus boats of the more seaworthy kind could have made the journey solo or in small groups. But boats and armaments were prerequisite for transporting valuables, and the essence of profitable dealing lay in exaction of goods by means of tribute for minimal outlay and in the collective security provided by a trading convoy. For these purposes, a fairly tight form of politico-military organisation was indispensable, capable of intimidating tribute-payers, guarding the convoys and enforcing the terms agreed with the Byzantines.

Enlightened self-interest weighed in favour of mutual cooperation among the tribute-raisers, especially since both Constantine's account and archaeological evidence imply that Rus numbers on the Middle Dnieper were limited. Some Slav tribes, such as the Derevlians, had effective hierarchies of their own, headed by a 'prince' (*PVL*: 27; *RPC*: 78–9). The Rus had a corresponding need for 'princes' of their own, forming some sort of hierarchy but jointly concerned with policing the exchanges with Byzantium. This is, roughly speaking, the picture that Constantine VII's writings and the *Rus Primary Chronicle* disclose. Constantine's address-formula provided for letters to 'the prince of *Rhōsia*' (*DC*: 691) but other texts produced under his aegis mention 'princes' of the Rus (*DC*: 595, 597; *DAI*: 62–3) in the plural and twenty-five persons were substantial enough to send their own representatives to negotiate the 944 treaty with Byzantium. The lengthy line-up, which includes a few Slavic names, suggests keen interest in the Byzantine connection on the part of the elite and by around 940, at latest, the locus of political authority had shifted south: Igor (ON *Ingi*), the earliest indisputably historical paramount prince of the Rus, was based at Kiev while his infant son, Sviatoslav, 'sat' in 'Novgorod', by the site of Gorodishche (*DAI*: 56–7). Igor was probably styled kagan, and his relationship with his chief commander, Sveneld, has overtones of Khazar-style dual rulership. But unlike the kagan described by Arabic writers of earlier generations, Igor was himself a war-leader, conducting tribute-rounds and commanding a major expedition in 941. Such personal activity is what might be expected by way of response to all the challenges facing the Rus on the Dnieper.

What one would not expect, from the scenario pictured, is that Byzantium would be the target of Igor's expedition. The Byzantines themselves were taken by surprise and the emperor is said by Liudprand of Cremona to have spent 'sleepless nights' (Chiesa 1998: 131) pondering what to do when a large war fleet appeared in June 941. The Rus ravaged along the Bosporos, paying special attention to churches, which they burnt, and also to priests, through whose heads iron nails were driven (Bekker 1838: 425). But they could not penetrate well-fortified Byzantine towns and their low-slung boats were no match for the elderly vessels that were brought out of mothballs and rigged out with Greek Fire (Chiesa 1998: 132). The expedition was, for the Rus, a disaster, for all their courage and ingenuity. In fact the episode probably reflects the Dnieper Rus' vulnerability to pressures from external powers. According to a Khazar text, the Rus leadership had been induced by the Byzantine emperor 'with great presents' to seize the main Khazar fortress on the Straits of Kerch. The paramount prince complied, gained control of the fortress but was subsequently driven out; the defeated Rus then had reluctantly to accept the Khazars' demand that they mount an expedition against Constantinople and this Khazar text, like Liudprand's account, makes Greek Fire the chief instrument of the Rus' destruction (Golb and Pritsak 1982: 118–19). The episode suggests that the Rus were amenable to Byzantine wishes because of their need for access to the markets of Constantinople, while still ultimately inferior to the Khazars in the steppes. In fact they were soon seeking renewal of their trading privileges, which were confirmed with some elaborations and restrictions in the 944 treaty. Byzantine apprehensions are registered in new clauses such as the ban on Rus from wintering in the Dnieper estuary. Constantine VII's account of the Rus trading organisation, compiled soon after the war, presupposes that their leadership had a strong stake in maintaining the sea-link, even while it emphasises the need to woo the Pechenegs as allies, to forestall any further attack on 'this imperial city of the Romans' (*DAI*: 50–1).

There were other constraints on Rus aggressiveness besides Pechenegs, Khazars and the Byzantines' mix of trading-privileges and Greek Fire. Christianity was known to the Rus from several quarters, including communities in the Baltic world. But the Byzantines vaunted their special relationship with heavenly powers and, like their precursors in the early 860s, many Rus after 941 probably inclined to link the superior firepower discharged at their fleet with the Christians' God. The Byzantines fostered such tendencies, singling out Christian Rus representatives for special treatment during the ratification of the post-war treaty and by 946 'the baptised Rus' had a prominent position in ceremonial receptions (*PVL*: 26; *RPC*: 76–7; *DC*: 579). Finds of Christian cross-pendants in the mid-tenth-century graves of some women and children at Kiev suggest that families among the elite were adopting Christian rites. The most spectacular devotee of all was Prince Igor's widow, who acted as regent for more than a decade. She is known in Byzantine sources by the Nordic name of 'Helga' and in Rus sources by the Slavic form, 'Olga'. The exact date of Olga's baptism is highly contentious. A case can be made for 946, mainly on the strength of what seems to be a dossier of materials for that year contained in Constantine VII's *De cerimoniis* (Kresten 2000: 6–19, 33–41; Zuckerman 2000a: 647–60). But on balance, and giving weight to general historical considerations, a somewhat later dating – probably to 957 – seems preferable (Nazarenko 2001: 219–310; Featherstone 2003; see overview in Tinnefeld 2005: 551–63). Perhaps most telling is the location of Olga's baptism – not Kiev but Constantinople, probably in the Great Palace itself. She was, together with her entourage of 'princesses of her kin', 'nobler ladies-in-waiting', 'envoys of the princes of Rus' and 'merchants', treated to two formal receptions. At one of these Olga ate dessert at table with Constantine VII and his family (*DC*: 597–8), and she took the name of his wife, Helena, in baptism. She was known by this Christian name to the chronicler Adalbert of Trier, who himself led a religious mission to Rus on behalf of Otto of Saxony in 961 (Bauer and Rau 2002: 214). Olga-Helena's bid for this mission in itself shows that she was not committed to eastern orthodoxy to the exclusion of all other variants of Christianity: she was then probably reacting to the Byzantines' failure to provide her with a bishop and priests. But by having Helena and Constantine for godparents, adopting Helena's name and receiving hundreds of Constantine's silver coins as gifts, Olga associated herself with this imperial order in ritual fashion, before eminent Rus traders and the representatives of other princes. Her pre-eminence was recognised by the fact that she merely 'nodded her head slightly' whereas her fellow princesses duly prostrated themselves before the emperor (*DC*: 597). Yet her gesture also signalled deference of a sort and, in its way, expressed the relationship of the Rus leadership towards Byzantium. Their capacity for 'first strikes' might give emperors 'sleepless nights', but for sustainable prosperity they needed regular commerce with the Byzantines, on generous yet ultimately imperial terms.

Personal devotion seems to have compounded with *Realpolitik* in Olga's reverence for the God of the Greeks. She maintained a priest, apparently keeping to Christian observances for the rest of her life; on her deathbed in 969 she forbade any funeral-feast or the raising of a barrow over her grave (*PVL*: 32; *RPC*: 86; Musin 2002: 81–2). But religious affiliation remained a matter of individual or familial choice and prominent counter-forces were in play against a religion whose close associations with Greek superpower could repel as well as attract. The German mission on behalf of another, western, overlord, was, according to its leader, futile and dangerous, with Adalbert only narrowly escaping death at Rus hands on his way back. Adalbert's claim chimes in with the *Rus Primary Chronicle*'s tale of the response of Olga's son, Sviatoslav, to her efforts to convert him: allegedly he exclaimed, 'My retainers will laugh at this!' (*PVL*: 30; *RPC*: 83–4). Around this time a prince or notable was buried in a huge barrow at Chernigov and among his grave goods was a figurine of a god, seemingly Thor. Thor had devotees among the wealthier echelons of the Rus, judging by the finds of his pendant hammerlets on iron neck-rings in graves and settlements. The use of these amulets seems to have peaked around the mid- and second half of the tenth century, and pendants in the form of valkyries were being worn at commercial centres such as Gnezdovo in the second half of that century (Pushkina 2001: 313–16; 2004: 51; Novikova 1992: 79–87; Duczko 2004: 132–3, 239–40). The profusion of amulets may well register the mutual awareness of cross-bearers and the devotees of hammerlets and other pagan pendants, some individuals opting for multiple affiliations. It also reflects the diverse directions which the Rus faced in their desire for trading and self-enrichment. Dessert at the emperor's high table was one manner whereby a Rus ruler could express her politico-cultural affiliation, but others, no less politic, were available.

Sviatoslav's policy, upon taking over effective power from his mother, was to remain on amicable terms with the Byzantines, still letting warriors serve with their forces in hundreds if not thousands, but he also sought conspicuously to align himself with the peoples of the steppes. A Byzantine eyewitness account and the *Rus Primary Chronicle* agree that Sviatoslav took on the hair- and lifestyle of a Eurasian steppe chieftain: his scalp was shaven save for one long strand of hair, denoting nobility of birth, and a ring was in one ear; life in the saddle was his delight, 'making many wars' and sleeping beneath the open sky. Sviatoslav's prime target was the Khazars who, as his own father had found, could threaten the Rus from across the steppes and still raised tribute from some Slav populations. Allying, probably, with the Uzes, Sviatoslav led an attack on their core-lands, laying waste the main towns and dealing a deathblow to Khazaria as a steppe-power.

Soon afterwards the Byzantines approached him to carry out a similar job on their truculent neighbours, the Bulgarians, in return for 1,500 pounds of gold, paid in advance. The Rus overwhelmed the Bulgarians at a stroke in, probably, late summer and autumn 968, but Sviatoslav proceeded to seize on the opportunities that a river-mouth offered, in the manner of Vikings on the other side of Europe. Reportedly, he proclaimed that he would make Pereiaslavets on the Lower Danube 'the centre of my land, for there all good things flow' (*PVL*: 32; *RPC*: 86). Sviatoslav's desire to base himself at the intersection of several trade routes near the sea, without reliance on any single market, made strategic sense: no attempt was made to repeat past expeditions against the 'God-protected city', but the Rus could hope to trade with the Greeks from a more favourable vantage-point than the Middle Dnieper. Sviatoslav hastened back to Kiev when the Pechenegs – perhaps at Byzantine instigation – threatened to seize it in his absence. A deal was struck, Pechenegs joined forces with Rus to return to the Balkans and soon the Bulgarian tsar Boris was reigning over his people from his palace in Preslav, in effect a puppet of the Rus occupation-force. Sviatoslav's project of maintaining hegemony over steppe-peoples and Rus was not inherently absurd: his governors assigned to Danubian towns might soon have begun raising revenues sufficient to remunerate retinues and nomads to police the steppes. Sviatoslav's miscalculation was to take apparent Byzantine inertia for acceptance of the status quo. In the spring of 971

Emperor John I Tzimiskes launched a surprise attack, a pincer-movement: his cavalry made for Preslav while a fleet equipped with Greek Fire sailed up the Danube. The Rus garrison-troops under their commander Svenkel fought bravely, 7,000 of them making a last stand in the palace even after it was set ablaze (Hase 1828: 137; Talbot *et al.* 2005: 183). And even when beleaguered in Silistra on the banks of the Danube, Sviatoslav and his warriors took on the Byzantine heavy cavalry, the footsoldiers vainly attempting mounted combat, and their womenfolk enlisted for combat, as the Byzantines observed when they came to strip the dead. Our main Byzantine source, Leo the Deacon, depicts a series of Homeric contests and doubts may be cast on the historicity of some of his details about 'Scythian' pagan sacrifices and beliefs. In any case, the Rus resisted furiously and after months of heavy fighting they did not so much surrender as agree to withdraw together with their ample stocks of loot and captives. These trophies were probably Sviatoslav's ultimate undoing: they encumbered his withdrawal from the Danube and the winter of 971–2 was spent on the Dnieper estuary. The Rus, weakened by hunger, were set upon by Pechenegs in the spring and annihilated. Sviatoslav's own skull found new uses as a plated Pecheneg drinking-cup.

The disappearance of Sviatoslav and much of the Rus warrior elite left a power vacuum which his youthful sons were ill-equipped to fill. One of them, Prince Iaropolk, managed to defeat and kill his brother, whom Sviatoslav had set over the Derevlians, but another son, Vladimir, fled 'overseas' from his seat in Novgorod to a court or courts in the Nordic world. Iaropolk's regime was less than robust, seeing that some Slav tribes ceased to render tribute while opportunists from the Scandinavian world tried to set themselves up among the Rus, a 'prince' named Ragnvaldr at Polotsk and a certain Tury at the place which took its name from him, Turov (*PVL*: 36; *RPC*: 91). These moves bespeak political volatility, but they also imply that trading with the Byzantines persisted. Polotsk controlled one branch of what became known as 'the way from the Varangians to the Greeks' (Figure 37.1), skirting Novgorod; and Turov lay on the River Pripet, leading from the Middle Dnieper towards the Western Bug, or overland to Cracow and other markets where German-struck silver might be had. By the 970s a major reorientation in Rus trading was underway, as supplies of high-quality dirhams from central Asia dwindled, and exchanges of furs for western goods and silver grew in value and volume. But access to Byzantine silks and other de luxe goods carried a special cachet. Ragnvaldr's and Tury's choice of seats implies as much, and one of Sviatoslav's conditions for vacating the Danube had been that the Rus should be allowed to travel 'to Byzantium to trade, as has been the custom from of old' (Hase 1828: 156; Talbot *et al.* 2005: 198–9). Smolensk owed much of its prosperity to its role as a service-station for boats hauled over portages on 'the way to the Greeks', and its ostentatious barrows, some raised over boat-burnings, suggest that business was booming through the second half of the tenth century. In that sense, the trading connection with Byzantium was now too widely prized to be subject to the vagaries of particular regimes. Sviatoslav's Danubian venture, after all, amounted to a variant on the earlier move made by the Rus to the Middle Dnieper the better to trade with the Greeks.

Nonetheless, the question of the future course of political relations between the Dnieper Rus and the Byzantines remained open. Byzantine observers were struck by the organisational skills as well as the fighting prowess shown by the Rus during their Balkan campaigning, and in the late tenth century the popular interpretation placed on a relief sculpture in Constantinople was that it portended the city's fall to the Rus

(Preger 1907: 176; Mango 1953: 460). The institution of a military command-post on the Straits of Kerch marks one Byzantine measure to contain the Rus in the aftermath of Sviatoslav, but from 976 the emperor Basil II was too preoccupied with his rebel generals and Bulgarian insurgents to pay much attention to the Rus, who were anyway themselves in disarray.

More to the point was the question of what stand any powerful Rus ruler should take towards Christianity and its burgeoning practitioners. Olga had personally associated herself with the sacred palace of the Greeks and their ruling family's God, whereas Sviatoslav took a flamboyantly contrary line. His regime was to rest on personal command over the steppes and on the material patronage that plundering wealthy targets and supervision of trade routes could yield. The gods by which he swore to uphold terms with the Greeks in 971 were the Slav god of lightning and power, Perun, and Volos, god of herds. Sviatoslav had envisaged long-term hegemony over the Bulgarians, a wholly Christian people, and the core-lands of Rus could have continued to harbour a medley of practising Christians and non-Christians. Coexistence of populations with different faiths, Judaist, Christian, Muslim and pagan, had, after all, been a characteristic of Khazaria, and the elite burial ground on the Starokievskaia Hill at Kiev in the later tenth century seems to have accommodated pagan shrines and Christian coffins (Borovs'ky and Kaliuk 1993: 8–12). However, when a masterful prince wrested control of all the Rus branches of the 'way from the Varangians to the Greeks' and set about reimposing tribute on dissident outlying populations, he resolved to institute public worship closely associated with his personal authority and victories. Prince Vladimir Sviatoslavich was tainted with the blood of Iaropolk, murdered after coming out from Kiev to negotiate with Vladimir, and also by his mother's questionable status, as Slavic key-holder of Sviatoslav's hall who had succumbed to her master's will.

A legitimacy-deficit could in itself account for Vladimir's desire to raise his status through unprecedentedly elaborate associations with heavenly powers. But he would have been well aware that prominent leaders to his north-west and west now associated their rule with the Christian God, notably Mieszko of the Poles and Harald Blue-Tooth of the Danes. There are hints that Christian Danes frequented Rus in the later tenth century, perhaps serving as princely retainers; Vladimir himself may have spent his exile at a Danish kingly court or at least had Christians among the Varangian warriors who helped him seize control of Novgorod, Polotsk and, eventually, Kiev (Shinakov 2004: 247–9). Against this background it is hardly surprising that Vladimir, declining to commit his regime to the Christian God, sought to institute a kind of counter-cult, by way of monuments and sacrifices, some of them human. A wooden idol of Perun was raised outside Vladimir's main hall in Kiev and another idol stood near the governor's hall in Novgorod; Vladimir's partially silver and gilded Perun was accompanied by several other gods, some quite local, others known throughout the Slavic-speaking world. This organised cult, which had strong connotations of princely victory, served as a riposte to the Christian cult of Vladimir's northerly neighbours as well as a counter-force to goings-on in the Great Palace in Constantinople.

Vladimir's early years after seizing Kiev around 978 were followed up by successful campaigning to secure regular tribute-payments, and his ruthlessness and resources were such as to enforce compliance with his cult's demands. Victories were celebrated with communal sacrifices to his idols, candidates being chosen by lot from among the free. The objections of a 'Varangian' Christian returnee from the Greeks, who had settled

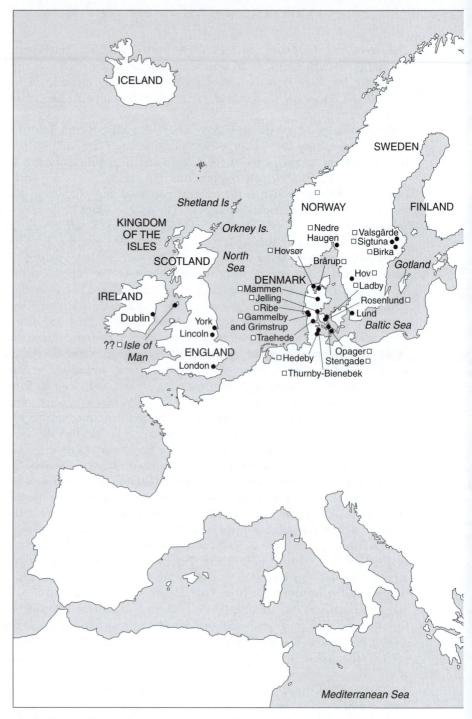

Figure 37.1 Map of 'the way from the Varangians to the Greeks'. The 'way' is described in the *Rus Primary Chronicle c.* 1100 and is also attested by the many eleventh-century Swedish runestones commemorating individual travellers to 'the Greeks'. The routes – which could enter Rus via the western Dvina or the VolkLov and Lovat rivers – were in use much earlier, but the sea-link from the Middle Dnieper to Constantinople was regularised only in the early tenth century. Very few goods went all the way from the North Atlantic to Byzantium, but the slave trade spanned the British Isles, the Baltic and Rus, and Byzantine silks have been unearthed in York, Lincoln and Dublin. Scandinavians, including Icelanders, attended the emperor at court and served with his forces. Many eventually returned home, probably bringing Byzantine luxury goods with them. Exchanges of embassies and courtesies between Nordic,

L. Ladoga

Volkhov
Luga
Msta
L. Ilmen
Volga

● Staraia Ladoga □

● Novgorod (Gorodishche)
□ Pskov
Velikaia
Lovat
W. Dvina
● Timerevo □

RUS

● Toropets

● Vitebsk
● Polotsk ● Smolensk (Gnezdovo)□

Desna

BYZANTINE EMPIRE

● Turov
Pripet
● Liubech
● Chernigov □
● Vyshgorod
□ Kiev ● Shestovitsa □
● Kitaevo
● Voyn
Sula
Dnieper
Don
Donets

Dniester

RAPIDS

● Oleshe

Caspian Sea

● Cherson
STRAITS OF KERCH

Black Sea

● Silistra
● Preslav
Danube

BULGARIA

● Constantinople

Mediterranean Sea

0   300 miles

0   300 km

Key
□ = Chamber graves

Rus and Byzantine courts were the background to all this trafficking. Tenth-century chamber graves denoted exceptional wealth, social and/or political status and aspirations to retain these in the next world. Their precise significance varied across the huge area in which they occur, and in Denmark they are found at rural settlements as well as emporia. But the goods and types of funeral ritual found in them attest to people for whom travel and ample equipment for the afterlife were status symbols, a kind of self-consciously international elite. To that extent, the chamber graves offer a tracer of 'the way from the Varangians to the Greeks'.

in Kiev and upon whose boy the lot fell, were overridden: father and son were slain in their hall (*PVL*: 38–9; *RPC*: 95–6). It was not so much Vladimir's patronage of this cult cutting an odd figure with other Christian rulers as the cessation of victories that made him think again. A campaign against the Bulgars on the Middle Volga in the mid-980s failed to yield tribute, the first such setback recorded among Vladimir's campaigns (*PVL*: 39; *RPC*: 96). Soon afterwards, according to the *Rus Primary Chronicle*, Vladimir embarked on what is sometimes termed his 'investigation of the faiths', Islam, the faith of his formidable Bulgar foes, the Christianity of the Germans and the Greeks, and Judaism.

Stylised as they are, the *Chronicle*'s tales of high-status investigative emissaries and of discourses conducted before the prince probably register actual, high-profile, signals in favour of a monotheistic cult on Vladimir's part (Shepard 1992: 76–81). But a series of accidents seems to have determined which particular cult was adopted. Basil II was, by *c.* 988, virtually besieged in his capital, his army mostly in rebellion and the Bulgarians at large to his west. In circumstances which have yet to be fully elucidated, a deal was struck between Vladimir and the beleaguered emperor. At some stage in the proceedings, perhaps by way of pressurising Basil to honour an agreement already made, Vladimir showed the Rus' striking-power and nuisance-value, capturing Cherson and sacking much of it. At all events, he sent an army, reportedly 6,000-strong, and the new arrivals surprised the rebels encamped across the Bosporos, enabling Basil eventually to regain control of Asia Minor. Vladimir's reward was marriage in Cherson to Anna, Basil's sister, and the match in itself implied Vladimir's comparable standing with members of the imperial family born in the palace's purple chamber (Franklin and Shepard 1996: 162–4). As Vladimir would have foreseen, he could only wed such a princess after being baptised, and Anna's entourage was accompanied or followed by a religious mission comprising prelates, priests and church-builders. Vladimir, withdrawing from Cherson to Kiev, summoned the citizens to the riverbank and oversaw their mass-baptism to the sound of clergymen's prayers. Monumental halls decorated with mosaics and wall-paintings were erected on the Starokievskaia Hill, flanking a sizeable church built of brick and stone and dedicated to the Mother of God. The builders were Byzantines, and the church's layout and function seem to have echoed those of the Mother of God of the Pharos, a prominent church in Constantinople's Great Palace. Vladimir thus set in stone his claims to comparability in status with the Greek emperor, treating his retainers and 'nobles' to feasts and Sunday worship in his own palace-complex. The foundations of Vladimir's regime were very different from those of the *basileus*. But the long-established monotheistic cult serviced mainly by the Greeks brought a degree of coherence to the nexus under Vladimir's care, and a German missionary, visiting his court in 1008, took it for granted that Rus was a Christian realm. Only upon passing through gates of a 'massive rampart' did Bruno of Querfurt enter the land of the pagans (Karwasińska 1973: 99). The rampart was the outermost of a series of earthworks and fortified settlements built under Vladimir's direction in what had been nomads' pasturing grounds. Reclaiming them for intensive agricultural cultivation, he created a robust defensive shield for his city, transplanting 'the best men' from Slav and Finnish populations in the north to live in his settlements (*PVL*: 54; *RPC*: 119). The Rus were embedded on the Middle Dnieper more securely than ever before, and there would be no further attempts at large-scale migration to the south.

Vladimir's adoption of Christianity as mandatory cult for his subjects accelerated the Slavicisation of the ruling elite already underway. Slavic was in use among the Rus leadership on the Middle Dnieper by the mid-tenth century: their tribute-rounds were termed *poliude*, from the Slavic for 'among the people' (*DAI*: 62–3) and Igor and Olga gave their son a Slavic name by which he was known to the Byzantines, Sviatoslav. But, as noted above, the Dnieper Rapids still bore distinct Rus and Slavic names at that time. And the Rus' reliance on axes, broadswords and shield-walls during Sviatoslav's Balkan campaigns, the names of certain commanders (including the *beserkr* 'Ikmor' [= *Ingimarr?*]) and, back in Rus, the occurrence of boat-burnings and chamber graves in burial grounds in urban centres, attest close affinities of the militaro-commercial elite with tactics and religious rites practised elsewhere in the Nordic world. But Sviatoslav's wars followed by the succession-struggle took a heavy toll on the Rus elite, and Vladimir (whose name was Slavic) drew on the counsel of his maternal uncle, the Slav Dobrynia, for victory. Moreover the gods whose idols Vladimir made such a show of venerating outside his hall had mostly Slav rather than overtly Nordic characteristics; and after his baptism Slavic probably became the language of liturgical worship quite swiftly, aided by the assortment of texts readily available from Bulgarian and other Slavophone Christians. Vladimir himself upheld Slavic as the language of authority, judging by the legends on the gold and silver coins he struck. One reads: 'Vladimir on the throne!' (Sotnikova and Spasski 1982: 80). The retainers and notables remunerated with these pieces were presumed to be able to make out the Cyrillic lettering, indecipherable as the later issues became. And waxed wooden tablets excavated at Novgorod suggest that by the early eleventh century the repeated writing out of psalms in Slavic was one means of teaching functional literacy (Ianin 2001: 38–42; Franklin 2002: 46–7). Yet Greek remained the mother tongue of most of the senior clergy in Rus, who corresponded with colleagues in the empire. The seal of an earlier eleventh-century metropolitan of Laodicaea found at Staraia Ladoga may register such correspondence: the town was, in the second quarter of the century, guarded for Prince Iaroslav Vladimirovich by a relative of his Swedish wife (Bulgakova 2004: 85–8).

Vladimir's adoption of Byzantine-style Christianity as the religion to be imposed on diverse subject-populations launched a new written culture for a polity structured differently from its counterparts elsewhere in the Scandinavian world. Exactly when newcomers from Scandinavia began to be denoted by the Rus elite with a generic term is uncertain but 'Varangian' was most probably being used partly for this purpose by the beginning of the eleventh century. In that sense, Rus and the rest of the Scandinavian world were going their separate ways. But many persons of high status and fortune-seeking Nordic warbands took advantage of the more or less continuous waterways to reach Rus, often travelling on to Byzantium. A Saxon visitor to the Middle Dnieper in 1018 gained the impression that Kiev 'like all this region' was teeming with 'speedy Danes' and runaway slaves (Holtzmann and Trillmich 2002: 474; Warner 2001: 384), and river journeys across the steppes became somewhat less hazardous once Rus cavalry squadrons based as far south as the confluence of the Dnieper and the Sula could escort vessels to the Rapids. Besides, the Byzantines now let a Christian Rus trading settlement develop in the Dnieper estuary. Such improved communications strengthen the likelihood that Norse sagas' depictions of warriors in the service of the Byzantine emperor denote historical figures from the late tenth century onwards (Blöndal and Benedikz 1978: 193–209; Carroll 2005: 40–3). And in the case of Haraldr Harðráða sagas' boasting of his exploits gains some corroboration from a Byzantine contemporary who was probably acquainted with him, Kekaumenos (Litavrin 2003: 298–300).

Byzantium, rather than Rus, seems to have been proverbial for its wealth in the eleventh-century Scandinavian world, and sagas' claims for the riches brought back by Haraldr from 'Micklegarth' echo those of Adam of Bremen (Trillmich 2000: 394). The greed and unruliness of Varangian mercenaries is, conversely, a motif of the *Rus Primary Chronicle* alongside sagas for the late tenth and earlier eleventh centuries (Pálsson and Edwards 1989: 73, 79–80). But their appetites were more or less manipulable by Rus rulers and employers, as by Byzantine emperors. Only internal dynastic strife opened the door to interlopers such as Ragnvaldr and Tury in the 970s or Sveinn Hákonarson, who sacked Staraia Ladoga shortly before Vladimir's death in 1015. A personal bond with forceful Nordic dynasts appeared politic to the capable yet hard-pressed Iaroslav Vladimirovich. In 1018, after being routed by his half-brother Sviatopolk and the Polish ruler Bolesław, he contemplated flight 'across the sea' to Scandinavia (*PVL*: 63; *RPC*: 132), and his marriage the following year to Olof Skottkonung's daughter Ingigerðr was probably intended to bring security to Staraia Ladoga and a supply of cooperative warriors from Swedish courts. Many years later, Iaroslav wedded his daughter Elizabeth to an ambitious *konungr* now heading back north after nearly ten years at Byzantium – Haraldr Harðráði. Shortly before the marriage, in 1043, Iaroslav had drawn on his Nordic contacts to raise fresh warriors for the last great Rus expedition against Constantinople. This attack seems to have been prompted by Iaroslav's need to save face after a supposed slight, a matter of honour that would have been familiar enough to those involved with the famous embassy of the *Rhōs* some 200 years earlier.

Besides contacts at the ruling elite's level, commercial exchanges went on between persons based in the Baltic region and those who called themselves Rus and resided in the land of Rus. Trade was most conveniently and profitably conducted across fairly short distances, from emporia such as Sigtuna or Gotland's markets to Staraia Ladoga or Novgorod. Traders from Scandinavia had, together with warriors, their own compound in Novgorod by 1016 at the latest, and within a few years of Olaf Haraldsson's death he was believed to be working miracles for fellow Northmen there: a church in Novgorod was subsequently dedicated to him (Mel'nikova 1999: 542–4, 553–4; Antonsson 2003: 148–53). But 'Varangians' were still a common enough feature of the Middle Dnieper region for the mid-eleventh-century law code promulgated by Iaroslav's sons to provide specifically for escaped or stolen slaves whom they harboured: the slaves were to be handed back to their rightful owners, and a fine of 3 *grivnas* paid 'for the offence' (*Kratkaia Pravda* in Kaiser 1992: 16). Brawls involving 'a Varangian or a Kolbiag' (another term designating northerners from across the sea) were also specially catered for (*Kratkaia Pravda* in Kaiser 1992: 16). The association of Varangians with runaway slaves calls to mind the forementioned Saxon's impression of Kiev in 1018: it also suggests that Scandinavian armsbearers still had some involvement with slave-trading.

At any rate, commercial as well as court-level exchanges between Rus and the rest of the Nordic world were still intensive in the mid-eleventh century. In fact goods and produce of Byzantine origin were reaching Baltic emporia such as Lund and Sigtuna in increasing quantities, not only silks but also bulkier commodities such as glazed wares and amphorae that probably brought oil and wine (Roslund 1998: 359–68, 380–5). The land of Rus may now have been forming into a distinctive politico-cultural order whose language of Christian worship and literary culture was Slavic. But this order engendered conditions facilitating exchanges of goods, albeit through multiple transactions in Rus, between the Nordic and Mediterranean worlds on a scale not seen before.

ABBREVIATIONS

DAI   Moravcsik, G. (ed.) (1967) *Constantine VII Porphyrogenitus, De administrando imperio*, trans. R.J.H. Jenkins, second edn, Washington, DC: Dumbarton Oaks Center for Byzantine Studies.

DC   Reiske, J.J. (ed.) (1829–30) *Constantine VII Porphyrogenitus, De cerimoniis aulae byzantinae*, 2 vols, Bonn: Weber.

PVL   Adrianova-Peretts, V.P. and Likhachev, D.S. (eds) (1996) *Povest' Vremennykh Let*, with revisions by M.B. Sverdlov, second edn, St Petersburg: Nauka.

RPC   Cross, S.H. and Sherbowitz-Wetzor, O.P. (trans.) (1953) *The Russian Primary Chronicle*, Cambridge, MA: Mediaeval Academy of America.

BIBLIOGRAPHY

Androščuk, F. (2000) 'Černigov et Šestovica, Birka et Hovgården: le modèle urbain scandinave vu de l'est', in M. Kazanski *et al.* (eds) *Les centres proto-urbains russes entre Scandinavie, Byzance et Orient* (Réalités byzantines 7), Paris: P. Lethielleux.

Antonsson, H. (2003) 'The cult of St Olaf in the eleventh century and Kievan Rus', *Forum Medievale*, 3: 143–60.

Avdusin, D.A. (ed.) (1991) *Smolensk i Gnezdovo (k istorii drevnerusskogo goroda)*, Moscow: Moskovskii Universitet.

Avdusin, D.A. and Pushkina, T.A. (1988) 'Three chamber-graves at Gnezdovo', *Fornvännen*, 83: 20–33.

Bauer, A. and Rau, R. (eds) (2002) *Quellen zur Geschichte der Sächsischen Kaiserzeit. Widukinds Sachsensgeschichte, Adalberts Fortsetzung der Chronik Reginos, Liudprands Werke . . .* (= *Fontes ad historiam aevi Saxonici illustrandam*), Darmstadt: Wissenschaftliche Buchgesellschaft.

Bekker, I. (ed.) (1838) *Theophanes Continuatus . . .* (Corpus Scriptorum Historiae Byzantinae 33), Bonn: Weber.

Blöndal, S. and Benedikz, B.S. (1978) *The Varangians of Byzantium. An Aspect of Byzantine Military History*, Cambridge: Cambridge University Press.

Borovs'ky, I.E. and Kaliuk, O.P. (1993) 'Doslidzhennia kyivs'kogo dytyntsia', in P.P. Tolochko *et al.* (eds) *Starodavniy Kyiv. Arkheolohichni doslidzhennia 1984–1989*, Kiev: Naukova dumka.

Brisbane, M. and Gaimster, D.R.M. (eds) (2001) *Novgorod. The Archaeology of a Russian Medieval City and its Hinterland*, London: British Museum.

Bulgakova, V. (2004) *Byzantinischen Bleisiegel in Osteuropa. Die Funde auf dem Territorium Altrusslands*, Wiesbaden: Harrassowitz.

Carroll, A. (2005) 'The role of the Varangian guard in Byzantine rebellions'. (Unpubl. PhD thesis, Queen's University Belfast.)

Chiesa, P. (ed.) (1998) *Liudprandi Cremonensis opera omnia* (Corpus Christianorum Continuatio Mediaevalis 156), Turnhout: Brepols.

Dain, A. (ed.) (1943) *Leo VI, Naumachica* (Nouvelle collection de texts et documents), Paris: Belles Lettres.

Darrouzès, J. (1981) *Notitiae Episcopatuum Ecclesiae Constantinopolitanae*, Paris: Institut français d'études Byzantines.

Djakson, T.N. (2001a) *Austr í Görðum. Drevnerusskie toponimy v drevneskandinavskikh istochnikakh*, Moscow: Iazyki slavianskoi kul'tury.

—— (ed.) (2001b) *Norna u istochnika Sud'by. Sbornik statei v chest' Eleny Aleksandrovny Mel'nikovoi*, Moscow: Indrik.

Duczko, W. (2004) *Viking Rus. Studies on the Presence of Scandinavians in Eastern Europe*, Leiden: Brill.

Egan, G. (2007) 'Byzantium in London? New archaeological evidence for 11th-century links between England and the Byzantine world', in M. Grünbart *et al.* (eds) *Material Culture and Well-being in Byzantium (400–1453)* (Österreichischen Akademie der Wissenschaften. Philos.–Hist. Klasse. Denkschriften 356; Veröffentlichungen zur Byzanzforschung 11), Vienna: Verlag der Österreichischen Akademie der Wissenschaften.

Featherstone, J.M. (1990) 'Olga's visit to Constantinople', *Harvard Ukrainian Studies*, 14: 293–312.

—— (2003) 'Olga's visit to Constantinople in *De ceremoniis*', *Revue des études Byzantines*, 61: 241–51.

Franklin, S. (2002) *Writing, Society and Culture in Early Rus, c. 950–1300*, Cambridge: Cambridge University Press.

Franklin, S. and Shepard, J. (1996) *The Emergence of Rus 750–1200*, London: Longman.

Glazyrina, G.V. (2002) *Saga ob Ingvare puteshchestvennike. Tekst, perevod, kommentarii*, Moscow: Vostochnaia Literatura.

—— (2004) 'O genealogii islandtsa Torval'da, stranstvovavshego na Rus' v X veke', *Drevneishie gosudarstva vostochnoi Evropy 2002 g.*, Moscow: Vostochnaia Literatura.

Golb, N. and Pritsak, O. (1982) *Khazarian Hebrew Documents of the Tenth Century*, Ithaca, NY: Cornell University Press.

Golden, P.B. (1982) 'Imperial ideology and the sources of political unity amongst the pre-Činggisid nomads of western Eurasia', *Archivum Eurasiae Medii Aevi* 2: 37–76. (Reprinted in P.B. Golden (2003) *Nomads and their Neighbours in the Russian Steppe. Turks, Khazars and Qipchaks*, Aldershot: Ashgate.)

—— (1994) 'Rūs', in *The Encyclopaedia of Islam*, vol. 8, Leiden: Brill

—— (2006) 'Sacral kingship among the Khazars', in K.L. Reyerson *et al.* (eds) *Pre-modern Russia and its World. Essays in Honor of Thomas S. Noonan*, Wiesbaden: Harrassowitz.

Grat, F. *et al.* (eds) (1964) *Annales de Saint-Bertin* (Société de l'histoire de France 470), Paris: C. Klincksieck.

Hannick, C. (1993) 'Les nouvelles chrétientés du monde byzantin: Russes, Bulgares et Serbes', in G. Dagron, P. Riché and A. Vauchez (eds) *Histoire du christianisme des origines à nos jours, IV. Évêques, moines et empereurs (610–1054)*, Paris: Desclée.

Hase, C.B. (ed.) (1828) *Leo the Deacon, Historiarum libri decem* (Corpus Scriptorum Historiae Byzantinae 11), Bonn: Weber.

Holtzmann, R. and Trillmich, W. (ed. and German trans.) (2002) *Thietmar von Merseburg, Chronik*, Darmstadt: Wissenschaftliche Buchgesellschaft.

Ianin, V.L. (2001) 'Tri sezona otkrytii v Novgorode', *Istoricheskie Zapiski*, 4(122): 5–45.

Jenkins, R.J.H. (1962) *Constantine VII Porphyrogenitus, De administrando imperio*, 2: *Commentary*, London: Athlone Press.

Kaiser, D.H. (ed. and trans.) (1992) *The Laws of Rus' – Tenth to Fifteenth Centuries* (The Laws of Russia. Series 1, Medieval Russia 1), Salt Lake City, UT: C. Schlacks Jr.

Karwasińska, J. (ed.) (1973) 'Bruno of Querfurt, *Epistola ad Henricum regem*', in *Monumenta Poloniae Historica, series nova* 4:3, Warsaw: Państw. Wydaw. Naukowe.

Kazanski, M. *et al.* (eds) (2000) *Les centres proto-urbains russes entre Scandinavie, Byzance et Orient* (Réalités byzantines 7), Paris: P. Lethielleux.

Kisterev, S.N. (2004) 'Cheliadin v russko-grecheskikh dogovorakh X v.', *Drevneishie gosudarstva vostochnoi Evropy 2002 g.*, Moscow: Vostochnaia Literatura.

Kovalenko, V. *et al.* (2003) 'Arkheologicheskie issledovaniia Shestovitskogo kompleksa v 1998–2002 gg.', in P.P. Tolochko, *et al.* (eds) *Druzhynni starozhytnosti tsentral'no-skhidnoi Evropy VIII–XI st.*, Chernigov: Institut arkheologii NAN Ukrainy.

Kovalev, R.K. (2000–1) 'The infrastructure of the northern part of the "fur road" between the Middle Volga and the east during the Middle Ages', *Archivum Eurasiae Medii Aevi*, 11: 25–64.

Kresten, O. (2000) *'Staatsempfänge' im Kaiserpalast von Konstantinopel um die Mitte des 10. Jahrhunderts. Beobachtungen zu Kapitel II, 15 des sogenannten 'Zeremonienbuches'* (Sitzungsberichte der philosophisch-historischen Klasse, Österreichische Akademie der Wissenschaften 670), Vienna: Verlag der Österreichischen Akademie der Wissenschaften.

Kuzenkov, P.V. (2003) 'Pokhod 860 g. na Konstantinopol' i pervoe kreshchenie Rusi v srednevekovykh pis'mennykh istochnikakh', *Drevneishie gosudarstva vostochnoi Evropy 2000 g.*, Moscow: Vostochnaia Literatura.

Kuz'min, S.L. (2003) 'Pozhary i katastrofy v Ladoge: 250 let nepreryvnoi zhizni?', in D.A. Machinksy (ed.) *Ladoga pervaia stolitsa Rusi. 1250 let nepreryvnoi zhizni, Sed'mye chteniia pamiati Anny Machinskoi*, St Petersburg: Nestor-Istoriia.

Laourdas, B. (ed.) (1959) *Photios, Patriarch of Constantinople, Homiliai*, Thessalonica: Hetaireia Makedonikōn Spoudōn.

Laourdas, B. and Westerink, L.G. (eds) (1983) *Photios I, Patriarch of Constantinople, Epistulae et Amphilochia*, vol. 1, Leipzig: B.G. Teubner.

Leont'ev, A.E. (1996) *Arkheologiia Meri. K predystorii severo-vostochnoi Rusi*, Moscow: Institut Arkheologii RAN.

Lewicki, T. (ed.) (1956) 'Ibn Khurradadbeh, *Kitab al-Masalik wa'l Mamalik*' in *Źródła arabskie do dziejów słowiańszczyzny*, vol. 1, Wrocław-Cracow: Zakład Narodowy im. Ossolinskich.

—— (ed.) (1985) 'Ibn Fadlan, *Risāla*', in *Źródła arabskie do dziejów słowiańszczyzny*, vol. 3, Wrocław, Warsaw, Cracow, Gdansk and Łodz: Polska Akademia Nauk.

Likhachev, D.S. *et al.* (eds) (1997) 'Ilarion, *Slovo o zakone i blagodati*', in D.S. Likhachev *et al.* (eds) *Biblioteka literatury drevnei Rusi*, vol. 1, St Petersburg: Nauka.

Litavrin, G.G. (ed. and Russian trans.) (2003) *Sovety i rasskazy Kekavmena*, 2nd edn, St Petersburg: Aleteiia.

Machinsky, D.A. (2004) 'Krest i molot', in D.A. Machinsky (ed.) *Ladoga i Gleb Lebedev, Vos'mye chteniia pamiati Anny Machinskoi*, St Petersburg: Nestor-Istoriia.

McCormick, M. (2001) *Origins of the European Economy. Communications and Commerce AD 300–900*, Cambridge: Cambridge University Press.

Makarov, N. (2004) 'Rural settlement and landscape transformations in northern Russia, AD 900–1300', in J. Hines *et al.* (eds) *Land, Sea and Home. Proceedings of a Conference on Viking-period Settlement, at Cardiff, July 2001*, Leeds: Maney.

Makarov, N.A. *et al.* (eds) (2001) *Srednevekovoe rasselenie na Belom Ozere*, Moscow: Iazyki russkoi kul'tury.

Malingoudi, J. (1994) *Die russisch-byzantinischen Verträge des 10. Jhds. aus diplomatischer Sicht* (Bibliothēkē Slabikōn Meletōn 5), Thessaloniki: Vanias.

—— (1998) 'Der rechtshistorische Hintergrund einiger Verordnungen aus den russisch-byzantinischen Verträgen des 10. Jhds.', *Byzantinoslavica*, 59: 52–64.

Mango, C. (1953) 'A note on the Ros-Dromitai', *Prosphora eis Stilpōna P. Kyriakiden: epi tē eikosipentaetēridi tēs kathēgesias autou (1926–1951)* (Hellēnika 4), Thessalonica: Hetaireia Makedonikōn Spoudōn.

—— (trans.) (1958) *The Homilies of Photius, Patriarch of Constantinople*, Cambridge, MA: Harvard University Press.

Martin, J. (1986) *Treasure of the Land of Darkness. The Fur Trade and its Significance for Medieval Russia*, Cambridge: Cambridge University Press.

Mel'nikova, E.A. (ed.) (1999) *Drevniaia Rus' v svete zarubezhnykh istochnikov*, Moscow: 'Logos'.

—— (2000) 'The death in the horse's skull: the interaction of Old Russian and Old Norse literary traditions', in S. Hansson and M. Malm (eds) *Gudar på jorden. Festskrift till Lars Lönnroth*, Stockholm and Stehag: Symposion.

—— (2001) *Skandinavskie runicheskie nadpisi. Novye nakhodki i interpretatsii*, Moscow: Vostochnaia Literatura.

—— (2005) 'Vizantiia v svete skandinavskikh runicheskikh nadpisei', *Vizantiiskii Vremennik*, 64(89): 160–80.

Mikhailov, K. (2001) 'Drevnerusskie kamernye pogrebeniia i Gnezdovo', *Trudy Gosudarstvennogo Istoricheskogo Muzeia*, 124: 159–74.

Minorsky, V. (1942) *Sharaf al-Zamān Tāhir Marvazī on China, the Turks and India* (James G. Forlong Fund 22), London: Royal Asiatic Society.

Montgomery, J.E. (2000) 'Ibn Fadlān and the Rūsiyyah', *Journal of Arabic and Islamic Studies*, 3: 1–25.

Morgunov, I.I. (1999) 'O pogranichnom stroitel'stve Vladimira Sviatoslavicha na pereiaslavskom levoberezh'e', *Rossiiskaia Arkheologiia*, 3: 69–78.

Mühle, E. (1991) *Die städtischen Handelszentren der nordwestlichen Ruś. Anfänge und frühe Entwicklung altrussischer Städte (bis gegen Ende des 12. Jahrhunderts)*, Stuttgart: Franz Steiner.

Musin, A. (2002) *Khristianizatsiia Novgorodskoi zemli v IX–XIV vekakh. Pogrebal'nyi obriad i khristianskie drevnosti*, St Petersburg: PV.

Nazarenko, A.V. (1995) 'Eshche raz o date poezdki kniagini Ol'gi v Konstantinopol': istochniko-vedcheskie zemetki', *Drevneishie gosudarstva vostochnoi Evropy 1992–1993gg.*, Moscow: Vostochnaia Literatura.

—— (2001) *Drevniaia Rus' na mezhdunarodnykh putiakh*, Moscow: Iazyki slavianskoi kul'tury.

Nelson, J. (trans.) (1991) *The Annals of St-Bertin*, Manchester: Manchester University Press.

Noonan, T.S. (1986) 'Why the Vikings first came to Russia', *Jahrbücher für Geschichte Osteuropas*, 34: 321–48. (Reprinted in T.S. Noonan (1998) *The Islamic World, Russia and the Vikings, 750–900*, Aldershot: Variorum.)

—— (forthcoming) *Catalogue of Finds of Islamic Coins in Northern and Eastern Europe*, ed. R.K. Kovalev, Stockholm.

Nosov, E.N. (1990) *Novgorodskoe (Riurikovoe) Gorodishche*, Leningrad: Nauka.

—— (2000) 'Rjurikovo Gorodišče et Novgorod', in M. Kazanski *et al.* (eds) *Les centres proto-urbains russes entre Scandinavie, Byzance et Orient* (Réalités byzantines 7), Paris: P. Lethielleux.

Novikova, G.L. (1992) 'Iron neck-rings with Thor's hammers found in eastern Europe', *Fornvännen*, 87: 73–89.

Obolensky, D. (1971) *The Byzantine Commonwealth. Eastern Europe 500–1453*, London: Weiden-feld and Nicolson.

—— (1989) 'Cherson and the conversion of Rus': an anti-revisionist view', *Byzantine and Modern Greek Studies*, 13: 244–56.

—— (1994) *Byzantium and the Slavs*, New York: St Vladimir's Seminary.

Pálsson, H. and Edwards, P. (trans.) (1989) *Vikings in Russia. Yngvar's saga and Eymund's saga*, Edinburgh: Edinburgh University Press.

Peskova, A.A. (2004) 'O drevneishei na Rusi khristianskoi relikvii', in D.A. Machinsky (ed.) *Ladoga i Gleb Lebedev, Vos'mye chteniia pamiati Anny Machinskoi*, St Petersburg: Nestor-Istoriia.

Petrov, N.I. (2005) 'Ladoga, Ryurik's stronghold, and Novgorod: fortifications and power in early medieval Russia', in F. Curta (ed.) *East Central and Eastern Europe in the Early Middle Ages*, Ann Arbor, MI: The University of Michigan Press.

Petrukhin, V.I. (1995a) 'The early history of Old Russian art: the rhyton from Chernigov and Khazarian tradition', *Tor*, 27: 475–86.

—— (1995b) *Nachalo etnokul'turnoi istorii Rusi IX–XI vekov*, Smolensk-Moscow: Rusich-Gnozis.

—— (2000) 'Drevniaia Rus': Narod. Kniaz'ia. Religiia', in *Iz istorii russkoi kul'tury*, vol. 1 (Drevniaia Rus'), Moscow: Shkola 'Iazyki russkoi kul'tury'.

Poppe, A. (1976) 'The political background to the baptism of Rus'', *Dumbarton Oaks Papers*, 30: 197–244. (Reprinted in A. Poppe (1982) *The Rise of Christian Russia*, London: Variorum.)

Preger, T. (ed.) (1907) *Scriptores originum Constantinopolitanarum*, vol. 2, Leipzig: B.G. Teubner.

Pushkina, T.A. (2001) 'Podveska-amulet iz Gnezdova', in T.N. Jackson *et al.* (eds) *Norna u istochnika Sud'by. Sbornik statei v chest' Eleny Aleksandrovny Mel'nikovoi*, Moscow: Indrik.

—— (2004) 'Viking-period pre-urban settlements in Russia and finds of artifacts of Scandinavian character', in J. Hines *et al.* (eds) *Land, Sea and Home. Proceedings of a Conference on Viking-period Settlement, at Cardiff, July 2001*, Leeds: Maney.

Roslund, M. (1998) 'Brosamen vom Tisch der Reichen. Byzantinische Funde aus Lund und Sigtuna (ca. 980–1250)', in M. Müller-Wille (ed.) *Rom und Byzanz im Norden. Mission und Glaubenswechsel im Ostseeraum während des 8.–14. Jahrhunderts*, vol. 2 (Akademie der Wissenschaften und der Literatur Abhandlungen der Geistes- und Sozialwissenschaftlichen Klasse, Jahrgang 1997 no. 3:2), Stuttgart: Franz Steiner Verlag.

Sahaidak, M.A. (1991) *Davn'okyïvs'kyi Podil. Problemy topohrafiï, stratyhrafiï, khronolohiï*, Kiev: Naukova dumka.

Schramm, G. (2002) *Altrusslands Anfang. Historische Schlüsse aus Namen, Wörtern und Texten zum 9. und 10. Jahrhundert*, Freiburg im Breisgau: Rombach Verlag.

Shepard, J. (1978–9) 'Why did the Russians attack Byzantium in 1043?', *Byzantinisch-Neugriechischen Jahrbücher*, 22: 147–212.

—— (1984–5) 'Yngvarr's expedition to the east and a Russian inscribed stone cross', *Saga-Book of the Viking Society*, 21: 221–93.

—— (1986) 'A cone-seal from Shestovitsy', *Byzantion*, 56: 252–74.

—— (1992) 'Some remarks on the sources for the Conversion of Rus', in S.W. Swierkosz-Lenart (ed.) *Le origini e lo sviluppo della cristianità slavo-bizantina* (Nuovi Studi Storici 17), Rome: Istituto storico italiano per il Medio Evo.

—— (1995a) 'The Rhos guests of Louis the Pious: whence and wherefore?', *Early Medieval Europe*, 4: 41–60.

—— (1995b) 'Constantinople – gateway to the north', in C. Mango and G. Dagron (eds) *Constantinople and its Hinterland*, Aldershot: Ashgate.

—— (forthcoming) 'Mists and portals: the Black Sea's north coast', in M. Mundell Mango (ed.) *Byzantine Trade (4th to 12th centuries): recent archaeological work*, Aldershot: Ashgate.

Shinakov, E.A. (2004) 'Datskii sled v sobytiiakh 977–980 gg. na Rusi', in A.M. Volkov *et al.* (eds) *XV Konferentsiia po izucheniiu istorii, ekonomiki, iazyka i literatury skandinavskikh stran i finlandii. Tezisy dokladov*, vol. 1, Moscow: Institut Vseobshchei Istorii RAN.

Sotnikova, M.P. and Spasski, I.G. (1982) *Russian Coins of the X–XI Centuries AD. Recent Research and a Corpus in Commemoration of the Millenary of the Earliest Russian Coinage* (BAR International Series 136), Oxford: British Archaeological Reports.

Staecker, J. (1999) *Rex regum et dominus dominorum. Die wikingerzeitlichen Kreuz- und Kruzifix-anhänger als Ausdruck der Mission in Altdänemark und Schweden* (Lund Studies in Medieval Archaeology 23), Stockholm: Almqvist & Wiksell International.

—— (2003) 'The cross goes north: Christian symbols and Scandinavian women', in M. Carver (ed.) *The Cross goes North. Processes of Conversion in Northern Europe, AD 300–1300*, York and Woodbridge: York Medieval Press.

Stalsberg, A. (2001) 'Scandinavian Viking-age boat graves in Old Rus'', in R.K. Kovalev and H.M. Sherman (eds) *Festschrift for Thomas S. Noonan* (= *Russian History* 28: 359–401).

Stein-Wilkeshuis, M. (1991) 'A Viking-age treaty between Constantinople and northern merchants, with its provisions on theft and robbery', *Scando-slavica*, 37: 35–47.

Talbot, A.-M. *et al.* (2005) *The History of Leo the Deacon. Byzantine Military Expansion in the Tenth Century*, Washington, DC: Dumbarton Oaks Research Library and Collection.

Tinnefeld, F. (2005) 'Zum Stand der Olga-Diskussion', in L. Hoffmann (ed.) *Zwischen Polis,*

Provinz und Peripherie. Beiträge zur byzantinischen Geschichte und Kultur, Wiesbaden: Harrassowitz.

Trillmich, W. (ed.) (2000) 'Adam of Bremen, *Gesta Hammaburgensis ecclesiae pontificum*', in W. Trillmich and R. Buchner (eds) *Quellen des 9. und 11. Jahrhunderts zur Geschichte der Hamburgischen Kirche und des Reiches* (Ausgewählte Quellen zur Deutschen Geschichte des Mittelalters 11), Darmstadt: Wissenschaftliche Buchgesellschaft.

Vasil'evskii, V.G. (1908–30) *Trudy*, 4 vols, St Petersburg: Imperatorskaia akademiia nauk/ Akademiia nauk SSSR.

Warner, D.A. (trans.) (2001) *Ottonian Germany. The Chronicon of Thietmar of Merseburg*, Manchester: Manchester University Press.

Zalizniak, A.A. and Ianin, V.L. (2001) 'Novgorodskii kodeks pervoi chetverti XI v. – drevneishaia kniga Rusi', *Voplaz*, 5: 3–25.

Zuckerman, C. (2000a) 'Le voyage d'Olga et la première ambassade espagnole à Constantinople en 946', *Travaux et Mémoires*, 13: 647–72.

—— (2000b) 'Deux étapes de la formation de l'ancien État russe', in M. Kazanski *et al.* (eds) *Les centres proto-urbains russes entre Scandinavie, Byzance et Orient* (Réalités byzantines 7), Paris: P. Lethielleux.

CHAPTER THIRTY-EIGHT

THE VIKINGS IN THE EAST

——•◆•——

Fjodor Androshchuk

The number of Scandinavian artefacts from the Viking Age found in eastern Europe is much larger than that in western Europe and even in Denmark (Figure 38.1). This material is known in different regions of the modern independent states of Russia, Ukraine and Belarus and also in the south-eastern Baltic area. These finds came from fortified and unfortified urban and rural settlements, from graves and hoards; there were also stray finds.

VIKINGS IN THE SOUTH-EASTERN BALTIC AREA: GROBIŅA AND WISKIAUTEN

Latvia and the Kaliningrad region are two areas that have yielded a large quantity of Scandinavian jewellery (Apala and Apals 1992; Atgāzis 1992; Jansson 1992; Kulakow 1992). Single finds of jewellery, swords and scabbard chapes have also come from Lithuania, where they were found in a local cultural context (Kazakevičius 1992).

A large number of Scandinavian artefacts were found in two barrows (Priediens II, Porāni) and a flat (Rudzukalns I) cemetery of the Iron Age at Grobiņa (Nerman 1958; Petrenko 1991; Jansson 1994; Lamm and Urtāns 1995). Scandinavian male and female artefacts, typical for sites and cemeteries in central Sweden and Gotland in the Vendel and Viking periods were found here. Recently researchers have pointed out some south Scandinavian parallels in the Vendel material of Grobiņa (Jansson 1994: 14–15). In one of the barrows a fragment of a shield and a stone stele of the Gotlandic type from the Vendel period came to light (Petrenko 1991; Lamm and Urtāns 1995). It had been suggested that some of the population from central Sweden left barrow cemeteries, while people from Gotland were buried in flat graves (Nerman 1958). However, new excavations have yielded a number of cremation graves of local character, which were connected to the Curonian population. On the basis of the polyethnic character of the revealed remains, Grobiņa was considered as a trade centre (Petrenko and Virse 1993: 102). However, a settlement investigated south-west of the Priediens cemetery (Lamm and Urtāns 1995: 14) has a local character without any indication of trade. The Scandinavian cultural elements of Grobiņa are usually discussed in association with another centre, Wiskiauten or Kaup (the modern village of Mokhovoe in the Kaliningrad

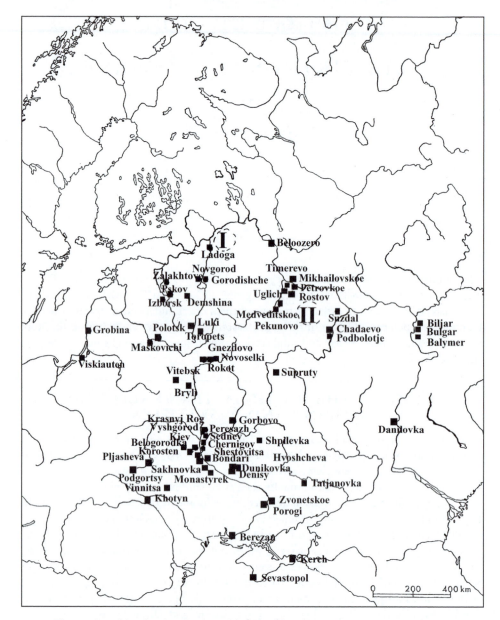

Figure 38.1 Map showing the sites with finds of Scandinavian origin in eastern Europe.

region, former eastern Prussia) (Figure 38.2). It was supposed that in the Vendel period, Scandinavians of Grobiņa moved to the Sambian peninsula and founded a new settlement there (Martens 1996: 54). This conclusion is not supported by Scandinavian jewellery from the ninth–tenth centuries found in the vicinity of Grobiņa (Šturms 1949: 207 fig. 2, 213 fig. 4).

The Scandinavian elements at Wiskiauten were mainly found in the cemetery (*c.* 215 mounds) with cremation and inhumation graves (Nerman 1936; Mühlen 1975; Martens

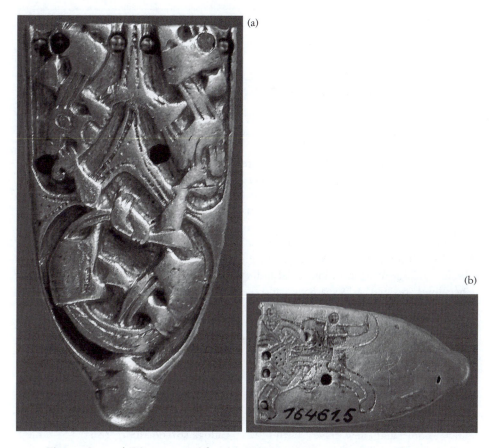

(a)

(b)

Figure 38.2   a, b Silver strap-end found in Kaliningrad. (Photo: Constantine Skvortsov.)

1996). In some of the graves typical Scandinavian ritual traits like folded weapons and stone-settings were recorded (Androshchuk 2004a: 112–13 fig. 4). The place of the Wiskiauten settlement is uncertain. But it seems that it was situated in the wet meadow terrain. For example, such a topography is characteristic of another site in the Baltic area, Janow Pomorski, which yielded a large number of Scandinavian objects (Jagodziński and Kasprzycka 1991: 706). Jewellery and weapons characteristic of Gotland, central Sweden and Denmark were found in different graves at Wiskiauten (Mühlen 1975; Androshchuk 2004a with parallels). A unique find is a hoard which contained silver bracelets of the so-called Hiberno-Norse type from the ninth–tenth centuries discovered at Kivitten (Mühlen 1975: Taf. 50: 1–6). From the territory of the modern Kaliningrad area there are forty-two swords from the Viking Age, which conform to eleven main sword types common in Scandinavia. There are three interpretations of the character of the settlement at Wiskiauten. According to one of them it was a Swedish colony/garrison that also had trade functions (Nerman 1936: 79). According to another interpretation the settlement was originally Gotlandic and then a Danish colony (Mühlen 1975). A third point of view considers Wiskiauten as a 'polyethnic trade centre' (Kulakow 2000, 2003). None of the interpretations seems to be convincing since they only treat the Scandinavian finds from the burials. Objects of local origin were not taken into consideration and the place of the settlement and its character are still uncertain.

GEOGRAPHICAL DISTRIBUTION OF SCANDINAVIAN ARTEFACTS IN EASTERN EUROPE

Within the territory of modern Russia several areas are characterised by a considerable number of Scandinavian artefacts: Staraya Ladoga with the area to the south and east of Lake Ladoga; Rjurikovo Gorodishche near Novgorod on the Upper Volkhov River; the Jaroslavl'–Vladimir area with the river system of the Volga; Gorodok on the Lovat' in the Upper Lovat' River area, and the Upper Dnepr (Dnieper) area, in the vicinity of the modern town of Smolensk (Gnëzdovo and Novosëlki). Single objects of Scandinavian origin have been found in the cemeteries of rural character in the country between the Dnepr and the Dvina.

In Belarus there are only single finds known from excavations of old towns (Vitebsk, Polotsk), hill forts (Menka, Maskovichi), graves (Menka, Uklja) and hoards (Bryli). In Ukraine a large concentration of Scandinavian artefacts came from the Chernigov (Chernihiv) area on the Desna River, and the middle and lower part of the Dnepr River (Kyiv [Kiev], Chortica island area and Berezan'). Single finds are known in the area of Siverskyj Dinets and Buh Rivers and Crimea (Kerch, Sevastopol'). One grave with weaponry of Scandinavian character has been found in the cemetery of Chersoneses (Sevastopol').

The Volkhov River and Lake Ladoga area

Most of the earliest Scandinavian finds have been found in the oldest cultural layers of Staraya Ladoga and a few graves south of Lake Ladoga (Brandenburg 1895: 122 table I: 2). The presence of Scandinavians in Staraya Ladoga can be dated to the second part of the eighth century. At this time Ladoga, situated on the western bank of the Volkhov River at the mouth of a small brook, Ladozhka, in a place now called Zemljanoe gorodishche, was a small settlement occupied by people from northern Europe (Kuz'min 2000: 129–30). There are signs of possible blacksmiths' activity, which was later supplemented by jewellery production (Rjabinin 1994: 26). The types of tools have close parallels in Scandinavia. In the course of the 780s and beginning of the 800s the Ladoga settlement takes on more of the appearance of a trade centre. Two different house-building traditions could be seen in Ladoga at this time. One of them is represented by large houses with a central fireplace and is usually interpreted as Scandinavian. Another Slavic tradition is represented by small rectangular wooden houses with a fireplace in one of the corners.

In the earliest horizons of the Staraya Ladoga settlement some objects characteristic of Scandinavian culture of the Vendel period around AD 600 have been found. A small oval brooch and a bronze handle with a small head with a horned head-dress and a collection of smiths' tools indicate that there were both Scandinavian men and women settled in Ladoga at that time (Davidan 1993: 27 Abb. 8: 8).

In the 830–40s the site was expanding considerably. New houses were built on the northern side of the Ladozhka brook. Metal-, antler-, amberworking and glass bead-making as well as weaving are characteristic traits in the settlement activity (Davidan

1993). During the second part of the ninth century the population of Zemljanoe gorodishche were still living in the same two types of house, as mentioned above. Some artefacts interpreted by Russian scholars as Slavic have close parallels in the area of the Upper Dnepr, populated by *Krivichi* tribes, according to the *Russian Primary Chronicle*. One large house with a fireplace in the centre is known from this period. A rune stick with a disputed inscription was found in this house (Melnikova 2001: 202). A mould for producing lunula-shaped pendants popular in many Slavic cultures has been found in the earth hill fort and could be dated to the same period (Davidan 1993: 32 nr 39 Abb. 11: 39). Several gaming-pieces of Scandinavian type could be dated to this and later periods (Davidan 1993: 50 Abb. 22, 146–8, 151–4).

Scandinavian objects have also been found in the later horizons of Staraya Ladoga dated to the tenth century. These artefacts consist of fragmentary bronze oval brooches, equal-armed brooches, a small circular brooch, one animal-head brooch, pendants, oval strike-a-light-shaped pendants, iron rings with Þórr's hammer pendants, bronze decorated mounts of bridles and a decorated ringed pin (Davidan 1993: 28 Abb. 8: 4–6, 8–12, 9: 13–14, 21–2; Golubeva 2003: 75 figs 128–34, 79 figs 150–2, 154, 83 fig. 176; Kirpichnikov 2004: 189 figs 10–11). Around AD 894 a large house was constructed at Zemljanoe gorodishche. Among the finds in the house were ceramic, spindle whorls, beads, pieces of amber, weights, a gold finger-ring, fragments of glass cups, combs, a gaming-piece, an axe-shaped pendant and a wooden cylinder with a bird motif (Rjabinin 2002: 15). This house was used until the 930s and has been interpreted as a building belonging to a group, most probably well-to-do Scandinavian traders (Duczko 2004: 87). Recently a suggestion has been made that the house was the residence of a deputy of the prince or a prince's palace (Rjabinin 2002: 23). In the ninth–eleventh centuries the settlement covered an area of no less than 10–12 ha (Jansson 1997: 27).

To the south-east of the earth hill fort and to the west of the part of the settlement on the northern side of the Ladozhka brook three cemeteries from the Viking Age were situated. One of them, in a place now called Pobedishche, consisted of barrows with cremation and inhumation graves. The cemetery was destroyed in the twentieth century but a stray find of an oval brooch from the tenth century is known from there (Mikhailov 2003: 154 fig. 312). Other grave finds discovered here have close parallels in Finnish barrows south of Lake Ladoga and one of them contained a pendant with a Rurikids' symbol – a trident symbol used today as a coat of arms of Ukraine, which is believed to emanate from the first ruler of Rus', Rurik (Golubeva 2003: 104 fig. 315).

On the eastern side of the Volkhov River, near Chernavino village, in a place called Plakun, a small cemetery consisting of eighteen barrows has been excavated (Nazarenko 1985; Mikhailov 2003; Duczko 2004: 91). The barrows contained male and female cremation graves, probably burnt in boats or with the use of parts of boats. In one of the female graves a fragmentary so-called Tating-ware jug was found. It has been stated by some scholars that they were made in the Rhineland for liturgical use. In one of the barrows a coffin with the skeleton of a man in a chamber grave was discovered. The chamber grave is dated to *c.* 895 and has close parallels in southern Scandinavia (Mikhailov 1996, 2003: 155). Another chamber grave from the tenth century also with southern Scandinavian burial traits was discovered on the top of a large barrow situated about 250 m to the south of the small barrows (Nosov 1985; Mikhailov 1996). A male individual with two horses, riding gear, a knife, arrowheads, a bucket, an animal-headed bone point and Byzantine bronze buckle were found in the chamber.

Most Russian archaeologists have considered Plakun to be the cemetery for the Scandinavian fraction of the Ladoga population (Bulkin *et al.* 1978: 88; Nazarenko 1985: 165; Mikhailov 2002: 66; 2003: 158). This conclusion doesn't seem convincing. A stray find of the above-mentioned oval brooch in the area of the cemetery at Pobedishche doesn't exclude the possibility of finding graves with more Scandinavian artefacts in the same area. The very special topography of the Plakun cemetery, its location on the opposite side of the Volkhov River, the large number of women's graves, such high-status traits as the Tating-ware jug, two chamber graves and a large barrow underline a very special position for the buried people, who were in close connection with southern Scandinavia during the eighth–tenth centuries.

From the barrows of twenty-three sites in the area south-east of Lake Ladoga came about eighty Scandinavian objects (Pushkina 1997: 88). Most of them were found in barrows with cremation and inhumation graves together with elements of local Finnish culture (Pushkina 1997: 88). Types of female brooches belonging to the middle Viking Age and some peculiarities in their manufacture and use show that they were made by local craftsmen (Jansson 1992: 62 fig. 2, 71 fig. 5). The context of the weapon finds suggests that we are dealing with representatives of powerful rural families. Two different interpretations have been proposed concerning the character of the Scandinavians' activity in this area. One of them – by Ture J. Arne and Holger Arbman – claims that the Ladoga area was subjected to Swedish agrarian colonisation (Jansson 1997: 775 with references; Duczko 2004: 99). Another point of view considers the activity in this area to be connected with the fur trade and the Volga trade route (Raudonikas 1930: 134; Boguslavskij 1993: 135; 2003: 162).

Rjurikovo Gorodishche

The remains of an early urban centre have been revealed on a hillock now called Rjurikovo Gorodishche about 2 km south of Novgorod (Nosov 1990, 1992, 2000; Jansson 1997: 31–5). The settlement covers an area between 4 and 7 ha and is interpreted as the original Novgorod mentioned in the *Russian Primary Chronicle*. In contrast to Ladoga, Rjurikovo Gorodishche was already fortified from the very beginning, which gives the place a clear eastern European character (Jansson 1997: 35). Here we don't find any large houses of Scandinavian type as in Ladoga. However, Scandinavian material from the ninth–tenth centuries from the cultural layer of Rjurikovo Gorodishche is very abundant (Nosov 1990, 2000; Jansson 1997: 35; 1999; Duczko 2004: 103). These finds consist of male and female dress accessories and ornaments, tools, weaponry and objects related to cult and magic, which originated from central Sweden (Jansson 1999: 48; Mikhailov and Nosov 2002; Duczko 2004: 103). One oval brooch from the early Viking Age probably comes from a destroyed burial on the northern slope of the hill (Jansson 1999: 55). Careful analysis of these finds has shown that most probably the population of this site included both local inhabitants and Scandinavian immigrants, who however quite quickly melted into one society (Jansson 1999: 56).

Other towns in north-western Russia

Scandinavian male and female objects are also known in the Old Russian towns of Pskov, Novgorod and Beloozero. Old Pskov emerged at the confluence of the rivers Pskovka and Velikaya. During the tenth century the settlement area expanded and consisted of a fort, a trading centre and a cult site. In Pskov the Scandinavian finds come from the cultural layer and graves (Sedov 1992; Duczko 2004: 112). Five of eighty excavated graves have Scandinavian traits. A rich chamber grave with the remains of a woman was recently found in the town (Jakovleva 2004).

The Volga–Oka region

Along the Volga waterway, Scandinavian artefacts have been found in different cultural contexts and different types of sites (Figure 38.3). The earliest objects have been found at Sarskoe Gorodishche near Lake Nero in the Upper Volga area (Leont'ev 1996, 2000). This hill fort was a local centre inhabited from the late seventh to the early eleventh century. Islamic coins and also Scandinavian male and female artefacts give evidence of long-distance connections in the ninth–tenth centuries (Leont'ev 1996: 18–21; Pushkina 1997: 89).

A large concentration of such finds came to light in an area between the towns Jaroslavl' on the Volga and Vladimir on the River Kljaz'ma. About 12 km from Jaroslavl' city is the Timerëvo archaeological complex, which consists of a settlement of about 5–6 ha and cemeteries (Murasheva 1997; Sedyh 2000). About 500 mounds with cremations and inhumations including chamber graves have been excavated here, as well as about fifty dwellings with roof-bearing posts, pits and other structures clustered together and sometimes fenced. A large hoard of Islamic coins dated to 864/5 found in the settlement and also oriental and Scandinavian objects from the graves indicate the importance of international contacts in the activity of the Timerëvo population. It has been suggested that three different ethnic groups lived here during the Viking Age but now it seems that 'the material culture does not indicate separate population groups, but rather a community with people of different genetic origins but viewing themselves as one community and most probably as one ethnic group' (Jansson 1997: 42). There are two different interpretations of the character of the Timerëvo settlement. According to one it was an urban site (Dubov 1982). The other view is that Timerëvo was a rural settlement (Fekhner 1963: 17; Jansson 1997: 44). A large number of barrows with Scandinavian artefacts were also found at Mikhailovskoe and Petrovskoe in the Vladimir area. These finds are interpreted either as evidence for centres of the Old Russian population (Pushkina 1997: 89) or as evidence of Scandinavian immigration (Jansson 1997: 47). Scandinavian weapons and jewellery have also been found at sites on the Upper Volga, which suggests that these were centres to control the traffic along the Volga way (Tomsinski 1999: 171; Islanova *et al.* 2005: 72–7).

Scandinavian penetration into the areas of the Volga Bulghars is reflected by a single find of an equal-armed brooch and a sword found in the town of Bulgar. One bronze scabbard chape decorated in the Jellinge style has been found in Biljar. Five more swords and one shield-boss come from different places in an area between the rivers Kama and Volga (Izmailov 1997: 34, 44, 125 fig. 81). So far only one grave with clear Scandinavian traits is known from this area. In a mound with a cremation grave containing a folded sword, remains of a bag and bronze decorative mounts of local production and a strike-a-light have been revealed at Balymer (Izmailov 1997: 49 fig. 23). In the Lower Volga area there is a single Scandinavian find, a bronze scabbard chape in Jellinge style from Danilovka (Paulsen 1953: 41 Abb. 39). Contacts of Scandinavians with the Slavic

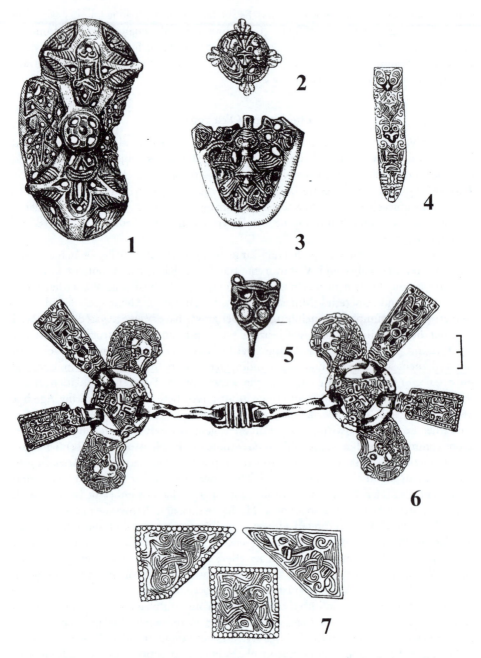

Figure 38.3   Scandinavian finds from the area of the Upper Volga: 1, 3 Medveditskoe; 5 Pekunovo; 2, 4, 7 Bezhitsy; 6 Supruty (from articles by Islanova *et al.* 2005).

population in the Oka River area can be seen in the Supruty hoard that contained a richly decorated snaffle-bit, made on Gotland (Duczko 2004: fig. 58). During the Viking Age Oka was an important waterway leading to the rivers Don and Desna. Only one find marks the movement of Scandinavians along the Don River, a richly decorated silver equal-armed brooch in Borre style from Elets in the Voronezh region (Arbman 1960: 120 Abb. 2–6).

The region of the Desna River (Shestovitsa and Chernigov)

A considerable amount of Scandinavian objects were revealed in the area of the Desna River, especially in such sites as Shestovitsa and Chernigov. The Shestovitsa archaeological complex is situated about 14 km south-east of Chernigov, on the right bank of the Desna River (Blifeld 1977; Androshchuk 1999, 2000; Kovalenko 2000). Two hill forts, a large settlement and six groups of barrows are known in this area. The dating of the hill fort in the centre of the modern village is uncertain; however, some barrows excavated on village land definitely dated to the Viking Age (Blifeld 1977: 187–8). The current level of knowledge about Shestovitsa allows us to construct the following for the development of the site. Before *c.* 900 a small fortified settlement existed at the south end of the Korovel' headland. Then in the course of the tenth century, westwards from the headland, on the wet meadows and on the headland itself a large settlement was established. Westwards and north-eastwards from the settlement numerous barrows were raised. Because of intensive fortification works at the south end of the headland in the twelfth century it is still unclear if any hill fort existed here in the tenth century (Androshchuk 1999: 29, 75; Kovalenko *et al.* 2003: 56, 60). During excavations of the headland area, several dozen buildings were revealed. Along the western edge of the headland beside the wet meadows, a rectangular building with evidence for the production of iron and pitch was discovered (Kovalenko *et al.* 2003: 57). Evidence of pitch production was also revealed on the wet meadow part of the settlement. Among the finds were a fragmentary Scandinavian oval brooch, numerous rivets, beads and a bronze button from the tenth century. A large number of Scandinavian artefacts came from mounds with cremations and inhumations. Around thirty chamber graves with clear Scandinavian identities (jewellery, weapons and ritual traits) could be distinguished among the Shestovitsa graves (Androshchuk 1999: 42 table 7). Most of the Scandinavian objects from Shestovitsa dated to the tenth century; however, one south Scandinavian beaked brooch from the seventh century was found recently on the settlement. The Scandinavian cultural traditions of Shestovitsa point towards central Sweden (especially Birka, but also Denmark and Åland).

North-eastward from Shestovitsa, on the right bank of the Desna River, was situated Chernigov, the capital of the medieval principality (Rybakov 1949; Kovalenko 2000). The topography and character of the site in the tenth century are still disputed (Androshchuk 1999, 2000; Kovalenko 2000). All we know about Chernigov at this time are the remains of numerous barrow groups, which occupy a wide area. Scandinavian objects were found in large and smaller barrows with cremation and chamber graves. Two large barrows were situated on the high right bank of the Desna River. One of them, called Gulbishche, contained a sword with a scabbard chape decorated in Jellinge style (Duczko 2004: 241). The third large barrow, called Chornaja Mogila, was situated far from the bank of river close to the hill where the medieval Eletskij monastery was built. Here a large number of various objects were found including two swords, boat rivets and a little bronze figure of the Old Norse god Þórr (Duczko 2004: fig. 70 b–d). Close to the barrow a chamber grave with riding gear and weaponry was discovered (Androshchuk 2000: fig. 1). It seems that the topography of Chernigov was very similar to Gnëzdovo. The centre consisted of one hill fort, a settlement on marshy land and surrounding satellite settlements with cemeteries. One of these cemeteries, which had barrows with cremations and chamber graves, has been excavated in the city, on the bank of the brook Strizhen', in a place called Berizki. In two barrows Scandinavian horse crampons and a pendant were found (Androshchuk 1999: 107). Single Scandinavian finds are also known from rural cemeteries in the Chernigov area, such as Sednev, Persazh and Liskove. Chernigov and Shestovitsa emerged at a meeting-point of the routes along the Desna, Seim and the Northern Dinets. Movements and contacts along the Seim and Desna rivers are reflected by a sword and other single finds (Androshchuk 1999: 107–8 fig. 60).

The Dnepr River (Gnëzdovo and Kiev)

The Gnëzdovo archaeological complex is situated on the right bank of the Dnepr (Dnieper), about 13 km from the city of Smolensk, between two tributaries of the Dnepr, Svinets and Olsha (Mühle 1989; Jansson 1997: 49; Duczko 2004: 157). The complex consists of the central settlement with the hill fort Tsentalnoe on the brook Svinets and surrounded by large cemeteries. The dating of the second hill fort and the remains of the settlement at the mouth of the River Olsha is uncertain. The total number of barrows in several groups in the cemetery, according different scholars, is between 3,000–5,000 (Avdusin 1969; Mühle 1989). There are two explanations for the relationship between such a huge number of mounds and the cemetery. One suggestion is that all these barrows belonged to one settlement, while another is that they were made by the population of small satellite settlements that lay on the lower land outside the large settlements (Jansson 1997: 49). Recent archaeological excavations in the area of the lower land revealed a cultural layer with remains of wooden structures and finds from the tenth century. Most of the early cultural remains were found in the Tsentralnoe hill fort, the south-western part of the settlement and the southern part of the Lesnaya group of barrows and included more than 250 artefacts of Scandinavian origin (Pushkina 1997: 89; Duczko 2004: 159) (Figure 38.4). Scandinavian jewellery and weaponry were found in barrows with cremations, inhumations and chamber graves, and especially from the hill fort and settlement of Gnëzdovo. Fragmentary moulds were also found in the Tsentralnoe hill fort (Eniosova 2001: figs 7–10), as well as the majority of the coins, a hoard of jewellery and sword fragments (Androshchuk 1999 with references) that testify to the dominating and controlling role of the hill fort during the history of Gnëzdovo. In the cemeteries of Gnëzdovo the large barrows were either concentrated in separate groups or stood alone among smaller mounds. They contained graves cremated in boats and some Scandinavian artefacts (Bulkin *et al.* 1978: 33; Duczko 2004: 161). Scandinavian artefacts from Gnëzdovo have close parallels in graves in central Sweden and in Denmark, and with single objects in Gotland (Thunmark-Nylén 2001; Duczko 2004: 181). There are different interpretations of Gnëzdovo. Some Russian scholars have interpreted Gnëzdovo as an important industrial centre belonging to the prince's retinue (Petrukhin and Pushkina 1979: 101; Pushkina 1997: 89; see critique in Jansson 1997: 51). Scandinavian scholars have considered this site to be a central proto-urban settlement surrounded by a number of farming settlements belonging to the same society that also included people of Scandinavian origin (Jansson 1997: 51), or 'a

Figure 38.4 Some finds from a hoard found in 1868 in Gnëzdovo (from Gushchin 1936: tables I–IV).

mixture of Birka and Rjurikovo Gorodishche, with a culture that is exposing its origin in Svealand' (Duczko 2004: 188). A number of Scandinavian objects have been also found in hill forts, rural settlements and cemeteries in an area between the Western Dvina and the Upper Dnepr.

Kiev (Kyiv) is situated on the high right bank of the Dnepr River. During the Viking Age, this centre of Rus' consisted of the upper part or the town hill, in medieval written sources called Gora and now known as Starokievska gora, and the lower part called Podol'e/Podil. Northward from Gora, a row of hills stretch towards another centre of the tenth century, Vyshgorod. Two of the hills rising over the lower town still preserve their medieval names, Zamkova and Shchekovitsa.

Archaeological excavations on Starokievska gora revealed a small hill fort from the seventh century, which could be connected to the hill fort of the Slavic prince Kiy, mentioned in the *Russian Primary Chronicle*. According to the *Chronicle* this town still existed when the Northmen Askold and Dir arrived in Kiev in 862. The *Chronicle* relates how they gathered other Varangians and remained as princes in the town built by Kiy. Excavations in the 1970s discovered on the lower part of the town several well-preserved wooden buildings and even complete merchant properties from the late ninth to tenth centuries. The finds testify that merchants and craftsmen were the main inhabitants there. No artefacts of Scandinavian origin were found in Podil during these excavations (see discussion in Androshchuk 2004b; Zotsenko 2003). However, a large number of such objects came from the tenth-century cremation and chamber graves in the upper town. A hoard of six gold bracelets of Scandinavian type was also found here. These and other finds indicate that no regular townscape existed there prior to the eleventh century. What most likely existed were individual homesteads, around which barrows arose. A chain of satellite-settlements situated below the hills stretched northwards from the town. One of them existed in the area of the modern Jurkivska street, where remains of several destroyed barrows with cremation and inhumation graves were revealed. The graves yielded jewellery and swords of Scandinavian character (Androshchuk 2004b: 36). In the same area was also found a hoard of Islamic coins with jewellery dated to 935/6.

Single Scandinavian objects including brooches, bronze pendants and scabbard chapes decorated in Borre and Jellinge style and also swords have come to light in towns, hill forts and settlements to the north and west of Kiev (a total of about ten finds from Vyshgorod, Bilgorod, Korosten', Lystvyn, Pljasheva and Bycheva) (some of them discussed in Zotsenko 2004).

South of Kiev, downriver on the Dnepr, single finds of Scandinavian character have been made as far as the Old Rus' town of Pereyaslav (Androshchuk 1999: 108; Duczko 2004). Objects of Scandinavian origin have also come to light in the Lower Dnepr area. Here, close to Khortitsa island, five swords from the late Viking Age and other objects were found in the river. Taking into account the character of the finds and also evidence of Rus' sacrificing on St. Gregory island (Moravchik 1985) this could be interpreted as weapon sacrifice well known from this period in Sweden and Denmark.

Crimea (Krym)

There is only one Scandinavian grave known on the territory of the Krym peninsula. It was revealed in the cemetery of Byzantine Chersoneses and contained one scramasax and lancet-shaped arrowheads (Kolesnikova 1975). A scabbard chape decorated in Borre style was also found in the town. Another chape with a bird motif came to light at Kerch (Frenkel 2002: 134–7). There are no finds of Scandinavian female character known from this area. Such exceptional military character of the finds is also characteristic of objects found in Bulgaria, where six bronze scabbard chapes decorated in Borre and Jellinge style and also some swords of Scandinavian origin have been found. It has been suggested that all these elements of weaponry came to Bulgaria probably via the Dnepr way (Yotov 2002).

CURRENT DISCUSSIONS ON SCANDINAVIAN ACTIVITIES IN THE EAST

Since Hans Hildebrand's article was published as an archaeological contribution to the Swedish version of Vilhelm Thomsen's book about the origin of the Russian state (Hildebrand 1882: 131–41), the archaeological sources have become an important argument for both Normanists and Antinormanists in discussions on the role, of the Scandinavians in the creation of the Russian state (Schmidt 1970; Šaskol'skij 1970). Yet, in his article, Hildebrand raised the question of the criteria in searching for Scandinavians in Russia. According to him the percentage relationship between foreign and local items is important in such studies (Hildebrand 1882: 135). Firstly he came to the conclusion that especially the finds of oval brooches, which are characteristic of the costume of Scandinavian women, represent serious evidence for Scandinavian settlement in Russia (Hildebrand 1882: 139). However, he never wrote on the role of such finds in his discussion of the foundation of the Russian state and underlined only their importance for Swedish cultural history (Hildebrand 1882: 141). The discussion was continued by Ture J. Arne, who, on the basis of his personal studies of museum collections and excavations of graves and grave goods in both countries, suggested a wider list of indicators for Scandinavians in the east, including even spikes, rivets, weapons, fire-steels, combs and scissors. Graves with such finds he regarded as evidence of the existence of Swedish colonies (Arne 1914, 1940). Arne's approach was developed by Holger Arbman (1955, 1960), who, while stating the existence of Scandinavian colonies in the east, nevertheless came to the conclusion that there is no archaeological evidence supporting the idea of the 'foundation' of a state by Scandinavians (Arbman 1955: 78–9, 94). Many of Arne's indicators were called into question by some researchers, who suggested trade and exchange as possible ways for Scandinavian artefacts coming to Russia. Moreover, neither Arne nor Arbman explained in detail their own concepts of colonies and colonisation. That is why their conclusions very soon came to be challenged by Soviet scholars.

One reason was that all conclusions about Scandinavian migration, expansion and colonisation that mixed with the foundation of the Russian state became an extremely touchy subject during and after the Second World War. Adolf Hitler's statement: 'Unless other people, beginning with the Vikings, had imported some rudiments of organisation into Russian humanity, the Russians would still be living like rabbits' (Duczko 2004: 4; Härke 1998: 22) puts a shadow over the questions related to Scandinavian activities in the east. The purpose of the 1930s' and post-war Soviet research was to look for social processes and state formation in the archaeological data. The theoretical foundation of the Soviet scholars was that the Marxist belief about the socio-economic processes and class differentiation formed the background of state formation (Klejn 1975: 3; Latvakangas 1995: 23). According to this point of view, finds in most ancient towns 'demonstrate the unity of Russian culture' (Avdusin 1970: 97). It did not leave any space for discussions about the cultures of other populations apart from those that had been colonised (Balodis 1943: 609). At the beginning of the 1930s, one of the prominent founders of Soviet archaeology, Artemij V. Artsykhovskij, was very nervous about investigating the earliest cultural layers of Novgorod, because of probable Scandinavian finds. Even simple interlacing decoration on some ancient items made him irritated. Only in private conversation was he able to say: 'Nevertheless, there is something Scandinavian in this interlacing' (Avdusin 1994: 30).

During the 1950s to 1980s a concept of so-called retainer culture was developed. It was concluded that various grave types reflected the social differentiation in the society of Old Rus'. All graves containing a rich inventory were determined as retainers' graves (Melnikova 1996: 71–2). It was possible to speak only of other cultural elements which were first incorporated and assimilated by Old Russian culture. Singling out strange elements in material culture became a method of discussion for both Normanist and Antinormanist. On the basis of this approach different calculations of the number of Scandinavian graves were suggested (Avdusin 1969: 58; Stalsberg 1989: 464; Zharnov 1991: 203). Ornaments decorated in Scandinavian style, ritual traits such as the bending of weapons and boat graves were regarded as typical Scandinavian traits, but not simply shaped tools such as knives, iron crampons for horses and strike-a-lights, which could be produced by the local population (Kirpičnikov 1970: 55–6; Stalsberg 1989: 450–1). At the same time burials with a cremation under a circular mound were not recognised as Scandinavian (Stalsberg 1989: 451), although these graves form the normal type of burial in Sweden (Šaskol'skij 1970: 26; Gräslund 1980: 72; Jansson 1987: 775). Chamber graves known in both Rus' and Scandinavia were not regarded by Scandinavian scholars as typical Scandinavian graves. They were interpreted as showing Continental influence on the burial practice of such Scandinavian urban centres as Hedeby and Birka (Gräslund 1980: 46). Even outside these centres in some rural areas of Sweden (Arbman 1936), Denmark and Norway (Eisenschmidt 1994; Stylegar 2005) they were interpreted as an interregional burial rite.

It is a paradox that both the Normanists, who believe in the Scandinavian origin of the Old Russian state, and the Antinormanists, who oppose this, in looking for the traces of Vikings have been dealing with the study of female items in order to explain male actions. It has became a common view to refer most of the Viking Age swords to the so-called Carolingian type. Many swords have blades with pattern-welding or inscriptions with Latin letters that are usually interpreted as the marks of Carolingian manufacture. Interpreting some damaged signs as the name of a Slavic blacksmith on the blade of a unique sword decorated with Scandinavian ornamentation made it possible to argue that some swords could be produced in Rus' (Avdusin 1970: 55; Kirpičnikov 1970: 67; Androshchuk 2003). It is also claimed that it is impossible to establish a sword's provenance because the same types were in use all over Europe (Avdusin 1969: 55). Swords could also be captured in battle, bought, stolen or lost (Blindheim 1970: 114). Nevertheless, it is remarkable that finds of swords are restricted to the same areas where Scandinavian women's brooches were found (Callmer 1971: 68 figs 1–2). Some scholars have suggested that some of the swords found in Rus' might have been imported there by Scandinavians (Kivikoski 1970: 117).

From a modern point of view, it seems that the frequency of various types of sword hilts shows clear regional peculiarities. It is possible to suggest that some types were much more popular in Denmark, others in Sweden and some in Norway (Androshchuk 2003: 43; 2004c; Martens 2003: 56–7). At last there are some technological peculiarities testifying that swords were produced in Scandinavia (Stalsberg 1989: 451; Kirpichnikov *et al.* 2001: 231; Martens 2003, 2004). A find of a deposition of five blades with inscriptions without hilts on the island of Öland (Thålin Bergman and Arrhenius 2005: 51) on the one hand, and also unfinished pieces of sword hilts on Gotland and Birka make it possible to conclude that some imported blades could be assembled in Sweden with the hilts made according to local tastes.

During the 1970s the approach to the 'Varangian problem' moved from a focus on Scandinavian artefacts to their contextual analysis. For a long time, it was discussions concerning the problem of the adjacent location of such centres as Gnëzdovo and Smolensk, Rjurikovo Gorodishche and Novgorod, Sarskoe and Rostov. Such cases were interpreted from a theoretical point of view that towns were 'moved', hence someone (a king) decided to move a town to a new site. In 1974 an important Soviet article on the relationship between Scandinavia and Rus' was published (Bulkin and Lebedev 1974). Entitled 'Gnëzdovo and Birka', its purpose was to subdivide among the eastern European sites from the Viking Age a distinctive type of trade settlement similar to the northern trade centres of Ribe, Hedeby, Kaupang and Birka. Although most of the 'characteristic peculiarities' of these centres that were subdivided in the article (especially the absence of fortification and chaotic planning) did not get support during further excavations, it was a first attempt to put eastern European material into a wider geographical context. As it seems now, the topography and functions of these centres are different. Some of them have the same topography but completely different functions and 'fates' (e.g. Gnëzdovo compared with Kiev and Chernihiv). Others have both different topography and functions (e.g. Ladoga, Rjurikovo, Sarskoe, Timërevo). The only thing that unites all these centres is the presence of Scandinavian artefacts.

It has also been argued that centres like Rjurikovo, Gnëzdovo and Shestovitsa were the centres of great princely power, -*pogosts*, for the collecting of tribute and were in areas where powerful centres of local tribes existed (Novgorod, Smolensk, Chernihiv respectively) (Petrukhin and Pushkina 1979; Melnikova 1996: 71). However, as dating of the 'tribal centres' shows, they were established later than *pogosts*. On the other hand, their interpretation as military centres contradicts the large number of female Scandinavian artefacts.

During the 1930s–60s some Scandinavian scholars believed that it was possible to see a process of state formation in archaeological data (Nerman 1958: 174). It was pointed out that a large amount of Scandinavian artefacts were concentrated mainly along the eastern coast of the Baltic Sea, especially at Elbląg in Poland, Wiskiauten in Prussia and Grobiņa in Curonia and an opinion was expressed that they represented colonies of natives from Denmark, central Sweden and Gotland. Even Viking activity in the Rus' realm has been considered as deliberate political actions of the Swedish state (Nerman 1936: 88). One feature that characterises these works is the belief that the activities of Sweden on the Baltic Sea coast were large-scale political actions by the Swedish kingdom (Nerman 1936: 81). However, modern historians believe that it is not possible to talk about a Swedish state earlier than the second half of the twelfth and the beginning of the thirteenth century (Sawyer 1982: 9, 52; 1991: 62; Lindkvist 1988: 8, 59). Furthermore, nowadays the existence of colonies of natives from Gotland on the east coast of the Baltic Sea has been called into question by modern Scandinavian archaeologists (Carlsson 1983; Thunmark-Nylén 1983; Jansson 1994). Many items from Grobiņa in Latvia, identified as Rimbert's Seeburg, are indeed of Scandinavian origin and date from the Vendel period to the beginning of the Viking Age, but their connection to some sort of colonies with a population from Gotland is without foundation.

CULTURAL ASSIMILATION AND SHAPING IDENTITIES

The common concept of what was called Rus', also termed by historians and archaeologist as Kievan Rus' or Ancient Rus', as a well-defined area with fixed borders is due to our familiarity with modern geographical and political maps. However, this vision would have been alien to people living in the Viking Age. There is no word with the meaning of the modern word 'state' in the *Primary Chronicle* and even the concept of a capital did not exist until the twelfth century, when a borrowed Greek word *metropolis* was put into Prince Oleg's mouth when he proclaimed Kiev as 'the mother of the Russian towns' (Tolochko 1991: 15–16). Absence of a clear concept of a capital is supported by the story that Prince Sviatoslav had serious plans to abandon Kiev and move to the Balkans where 'all the riches are concentrated: gold, silks, wine and various fruits from Greece' (Cross 1930: 173).

The concept of Rus' itself has changed during the course of time and denoted completely different kinds of identity. The group of foreigners among the envoys from the Greeks sent by Emperor Theophilus to Ingelheim in 839 claimed that they belonged to the people (*gens*) called *Rhos'* and it was only the emperor Louis the Pious who gave them another identity, discovering that they belonged to the people of the Swedes (Nelson 1991: 44; Garipzanov 2006: 7). The Rus' had a distinctive identity among Islamic writers, who made a clear difference between the Rus' and neighbouring Slavs in almost all respects, from clothing to lifestyle and activities (Birkeland 1954). They described the Slavs as people dressing in linen shirts and leather boots, using spears and shields in battle, whereas the Rus' wore short caftan-like coats or jackets with buttons and wide trousers. Their women wore bracelets, beads and rings, with 'boxes' on the chest. Contrary to the settled Slavs, the Rus' had no fixed property and lived on what they could acquire with their swords. Sources from the eastern part of the Muslim world described that the Rus' were headed by a leader, which some records called *Malik*, while others say *Haqan*. Priests are also mentioned. These were involved in human and animal sacrifices. Certain of them had considerably more power than the kings. They were not only warriors. According to Ibn Rustah and Ibn Hauqal (tenth century), Rus' are traders of sable, ermine, squirrel, honey and wax and they deal with 'Chazars' and 'Byzans' (Birkeland 1954: 15–16, 49–51). Al-Ma-s'ūdī (tenth century) writes that some Rus' lived in the land of Chazars and were warriors of kings of Chazars; others lived on the shore of the *Buntus sea* (Caspian Sea) and had trade relations with the capital of the Bulgars, while others had trade relations with Rome, Byzantium and Chazars (Birkeland 1954: 33–4). The only source that gives a picture of a kind of permanent settlement of Rus' ruled by a king called *Rūs-ḫāqān* is a geographical work *Hudūd al-'Ālam* (*c.* 982). Among the Rus' there is also mention of a distinctive group of warriors, the *morrovat*. Rus' paid taxes, one-tenth of their profits, to the authority. Three main centres are distinguished by the source: *Kūyāba*, which is the king's seat and produces distinctive fur and valuable swords, *S.lābā*, where in peaceful times they travel to the Bulgar area, and *Urtāb*, an extremely protected site that produces valuable blades and swords (Birkeland 1951: 52).

A peace treaty between Rus' and Byzantium dated to 912 demonstrates a new kind of identity. Here among the envoys presenting themselves as 'from the kin of Rus'', thirteen emissaries bear Scandinavian names while two are more probably Finnish ones. More changes can be seen in the text of the treaty of 944 where we can still see Scandinavian and Finnish names while Slavic names appear for the first time (Melnikova 2003: 459). The Rus' in these treaties denotes representatives of the princely family, their emissaries, other agents and merchants, and does not take into account their ethnic origin. As it was defined recently, Rus' of this period 'was a family owned company, equipped with its own administration, military forces, laws and its own aborigines to exploit. The parallel that immediately comes to mind is that of European colonial companies of modern times' (Tolochko 2001: 131). Until the eleventh century the word *Rus'* still referred to Scandinavians and was then replaced by the word *Varangians*. It was first mentioned by the Byzantine historian John Skylitzes *c.* 1034. Then we find it in a number of official Byzantine charters from the eleventh century, where the names *Varangians* and *Rus'* are used as synonyms (Obolensky 1970: 161–2). From around the same time came the Arabic name *Bahr Warank* (Varangian Sea) (Birkeland 1954: 60) and *Varjagi* of *The Primary Chronicle*. The origin of the word is still not clear but it stood for different things in different languages. In Slavic and Greek it meant Scandinavians and/or Franks; in English or Old Norse it referred to Scandinavian mercenaries in the service of Byzantine emperors (Pritsak 1993: 688). *Hetaireia*, the imperial guard, had many foreign mercenaries. Whereas the Rus' mostly acted from their ships, the Byzantine *Varang*-guard chiefly consisted of heavy cavalry. Many of the Varangians also became part of the bodyguard of Kievan princes. The mercenary Varangians who came to Rus' and the Byzantine Empire were all males. The lack of women among them marks an essential difference compared to the Rus'. The Rus' came with their families and settled in Rus'. During the second part of the eleventh century the term increasingly signified west Christians/Catholics in Rus'.

How long did Scandinavians in other cultural settings remember their origin? How did they see their identity? It has been suggested by some archaeologists that Scandinavians were rapidly assimilated (Lebedev and Nazarenko 1975: 7). One of the arguments for this idea was the production in some centres of Rus' of so-called hybrid objects reflecting both Scandinavian and local cultural peculiarities (Arbman 1960; Avdusin 1969: 56; Lebedev and Nazarenko 1975: 7–8). This point of view found supporters among Russian archaeologists while Scandinavian ones do not regard these objects as being anything other than Scandinavian (Callmer 1971: 68; Jansson 1987: 780). It was concluded recently that already in the first quarter of the tenth century some Scandinavians could use Old Russian. The only basis for this conclusion is the famous cremated boat grave from Gnëzdovo, which together with such typical Scandinavian traits as a broken sword, oval brooch and Þórr's hammer ring contained also a Byzantine amphora with a Cyrillic inscription *gorouhsha* or *goroushcha* (Melnikova 2003: 456). Despite the disputed reading of the inscription, it is still treated as the oldest dated Russian inscription. Nevertheless, apart from the amphora, other objects of Byzantine origin were also found, which make it possible to conclude that inscribed amphora came to Gnëzdovo from the area of Bulgaria on the Danube (Arne 1952: 342; Nefedov 2001: 66). Thus this is not adequate proof for the existence of a bilingual population among the Northmen in the east at this time.

Some scholars have argued that the most important evidence that shows the cultural assimilation of Scandinavians is the time when they stopped speaking their native language and writing with runes (Melnikova 2003: 455). Runic inscriptions written on different artefacts from the ninth to twelfth centuries found in Old Ladoga, Riurikovo Gorodishche and Zvenigorod are evidence that some Scandinavians still kept their native language (Melnikova 2001, 2003: 456).

Another piece of evidence that could be taken into consideration in the problem of whether they kept their Scandinavian identity are the Old Norse personal names that appear in some inscriptions on the wall of the St Sofia Cathedral in Novgorod and birch-bark letters from Novgorod (Melnikova 2003: 462). According to these records, the bearers of these names lived in the north-eastern rural areas of the Novgorod land and until the fourteenth century kept their Scandinavian identity. On the basis of these data it was summarised that in these rural areas, the process of assimilation developed much more slowly than in the towns (Melnikova 2003: 464).

The comparative analysis of both archaeological and written sources shows that processes of cultural assimilation and shaping identities among the descendants of Scandinavians were more complicated in the urban communities. It could be seen on the basis of the social topography of Kiev and Chernihiv. In both centres, a strong continuity between family graves from the Viking Age, churches and graveyards from the tenth–twelfth centuries could be suggested. The founders of chapels, churches and monasteries often had Scandinavian origins. For example, Prince Yaroslav had the church of St Irina built close to where Prince Dir lay in his grave. A certain 'Olma' (*Holmi*), who had a property close to the grave of Prince Askold (*Haskuld*), had the church of St Nikolai built there. There was also a building in the upper town called *Turova bozjnica* (Þórr's chapel), indicating its Scandinavian connection (Androshchuk 2004b). The location of the Scandinavian graves in the upper part of the town, the exceptional character of the finds, and their continuation into and contact with the house plots of the aristocracy in the eleventh–twelfth centuries, of which we know from archaeological and written sources, are evidence that people of Scandinavian origin became a prominent part of the elite in the town. The biographies of two Scandinavian families could be traced on the basis of written sources. From *The Primary Chronicle* we learn that in Kiev on the domain of one royal estate two boyar properties existed in the latter part of the eleventh century, where the Boyars Mikyfor Kyanin and Mikula Chiudin lived. These two were involved in the compiling of the first code of law for Rus' territory entitled *Pravda Yaroslavichej* from 1072. Mikula Chiudin was later to receive the town of Vyshgorod on loan from Prince Izjaslav. Despite his Slavic name, there is reason to believe that Chiudin was a descendant of eminent members of the Scandinavian royal bodyguards in tenth-century Kiev. This is suggested by the name of his brother Tuki (*Tóki*), which was most frequent as a name in Scandinavia. The collection of tales of the monastery's history and inhabitants (*Pateric*) at the Cave Monastery in Kiev tells about Varangian Simon (*Sigmundr*), who was one of the sons of Varangian prince Afrikan (*Alfrékr*). He was a brother of Jakun (*Hákon*) who served with Prince Yaroslav and took part in the battle of Listven against Mstislav, brother of Yaroslav, in 1024. He lived the remainder of his life among the Rus', where he served first with Prince Yaroslav and then with his son. We also know the name of Simon's son Georgy who lived with his descendants in Suzdal' and made a generous donation for the Cave Monastery in Kiev.

There is written evidence from the early eleventh century, which testifies that there were many 'fast-moving Danes in Kiev' (Warner 2001: 384). Among the inscriptions of the Old Rus' elite in the St Sofia Cathedral in Kiev, there is one with the Old Norse name Yakun (*Hákon*) written with unsure Cyrillic letters (Vysotskij 1966: nr 29). The only find of a runestone in the east came to light on the island of Berezan' near the mouth of the Dnepr (Melnikova 2001: 200–2). A slab dated to the eleventh century was raised by *Grani* in memory of his companion *Karl*. The stone was found in a later grave and the original place is unknown. However, it is found on the island, which is mentioned in *De administrando imperio* as the island of *St Aitherios*, where Rus' usually had a rest on the way between Kiev and Byzantium (Moravchik 1985: 61). It is evident that *Grani* chose a place where his monument could be read and understood. Swedish runestones give evidence that many people were visiting eastern Europe at that time. On the other hand, it should be noted that the runestone from Berezan' belongs to the type of burial monument made of limestone or sandstone that had strong connections to churches and were raised on many graveyards in Sweden (Palm 2004: 196). Because archaeological excavations on Berezan' revealed remains of a settlement and graves from the tenth to twelfth centuries (Rolle 1989: 494) it would be possible to suggest the existence there of a church and Scandinavian visitors.

CONCLUSIONS

Contemporary Islamic and Byzantine and also later Russian and Scandinavian sources testify mainly about Scandinavian war and trade activities in the east. Archaeological sources show that the real picture was more complicated. From the archaeological point of view, the importance of trade between Rus' and Scandinavia seems to be exaggerated. The penetration of the Northmen into eastern Europe was not only from the north to the south and south-east. The context of the Scandinavian finds in Kiev, Chernihiv and Gnëzdovo testifies that many people settled after having visited Byzantium, the Bulgars and the Hungarians. Their presence in these lands is reflected in the introduction of a new type of dress, a short coat with bronze buttons originating from the Byzantine *skaramangion*, belts with decorated bronze fittings and even weapons, axes and new types of bows, arrowheads and helms. From a modern point of view it is possible to trace Scandinavians in both urban and rural settlements. The functional female jewellery such as oval brooches, finds of some unfinished ornaments in Staraya Ladoga, Gorodishche and Pskov as well as runic inscriptions and objects of cult testify that many Scandinavians were living there permanently with families. The name of their identity has been changed over time, shifting from Rus' to Varangians. The Nordic identity has been manifested by the use of traditional Old Norse personal names, runic inscriptions and burial customs. The places where some Scandinavian family graveyards were situated affected the reshaping of the cultural landscapes of some Old Rus' towns. Christian churches and monasteries were founded on some of the graveyards or in their vicinity. The chamber graves, which were common in the most prominent centres of north Europe, here obtained a new symbolic and ritual value. Their constructions reveal features characteristic of the local house-building tradition. Double graves and graves with the bodies in sitting position make it possible to see them as graves of famous ancestors with the help of whom the new 'homeland' should be 'settled'. The large barrows in Chernihiv reveal some rituals connected to the cult of Þórr, the Old Norse god of thunder and lightning. This cult found a transformed continuation in the foundation of a monastery dedicated to St Elias. In the south Rus' area some Scandinavian descendants became part of powerful elite families but still kept their identity through collecting biographical objects in their hoards.

BIBLIOGRAPHY

Androshchuk, F. (1999) *Normany i slovjany u Podesenni. Modeli kulturnoi vzaemodii doby rannjogo serednjovicha* (Biblioteka Vita Antiqua 1), Kiev: Kyiv's T. Shevchenko University and Society of Archaeology and Anthropology.

—— (2000) 'Cernigov et Sestovica, Birka et Hovgården: le modèle urban scandinave vu de l'est', in M. Kazanski, A. Narcessian and C. Zuckerman (eds) *Les centres proto-urbains russes entre Scandinavie, Byzance et Orient* (Actes du Colloque International tenu au Collège de France en octobre 1997; Réalités byzantines 7), Paris: P. Lethielleux.

—— (2001) 'Gnëzdovo, Dneprovskij put' i final Birki', in V.V. Murashova (ed.) *Gnezdovo 125 let issledovanija pamjatnika. Archeologicheskij sbornik*, Moscow: Gosudarstvennij istoricheskij muzej.

—— (2003) 'The Hvoshcheva sword: an example of contacts between Britain and Scandinavia in the late Viking period', *Fornvännen*, 98: 35–43.

—— (2004a) 'Ot Ragnara Lodbroka do Vidgautra. O datskikh i shvedkikh kontaktakh sembov i kurshej v epokhu vikingov i rannem srednevekovje', in D.A. Machinskij (ed.) *Ladoga i Gleb Lebedev. Vos'mye chtenia pamjati Anny Machinskoj*. St Petersburg: Izdatelstvo SPb II RAN 'Nestor-Istoria'.

—— (2004b) 'Skandinavskie drevnosti v sotsialnoj topografii drevnego Kieva', *Ruthenica*, 3: 7–47.

—— (2004c) 'Vikingar och bönder. Några anmärkningar om den sociala tolkningen av svärden och de långväga kontakterna under vikingatiden', in Garðar Guðmundsson (ed.) *Current Issues in Nordic Archaeology. Proceedings of the 21st Conference of Nordic Archaeologists, 6–9 September 2001, Akureyri, Iceland*, Reykjavík: Society of Icelandic Archaeologists.

Apala, Z. and Apals, J. (1992) 'Die Kontakte der Lettgalen des Gauja-Raumes mit Skandinavien', in A. Loit, Ē. Mugurēvičs and A. Caune (eds) *Die Kontakte zwischen Ostbaltikum und Skandinavien im frühen Mittelalter* (Studia Baltica Stockholmiensia 9), Uppsala: Almqvist & Wiksell International.

Arbman, H. (1936) 'En Kammargarv från vikingatiden vid Långtora, Uppland', *Fornvännen*, 31: 89–98.

—— (1955) *Svear i österviking*. Stockholm: Natur och Kultur.

—— (1960) 'Skandinavische handwerk in Russland in der Wikingerzeit', *Meddelanden från Lunds universitets historiska museum* (1959): 110–35.

Arne, T.J. (1912) 'Ett svensk gravfält i guvernementet Jaroslavl, Ryssland', *Fornvännen*, 13: 31–47.

—— (1914) *La Suéde et l'Orient*, Uppsala: K.W. Appelberg.

—— (1940) 'De svenska fynden i guvernementet Vladimir, Ryssland', *Fornvännen*, 35: 155–66.

—— (1952) 'Die Varägerfrage und die sowjetrussische Forschung', *Acta Archaeologica*, 23: 138–47.

Atgāzis, M. (1992) 'First finds of three-armed (trefoil) brooches in Latvia', in A. Loit, Ē. Mugurēvičs and A. Caune (eds) *Die Kontakte zwischen Ostbaltikum und Skandinavien im frühen Mittelalter* (Studia Baltica Stockholmiensia 9), Uppsala: Almqvist & Wiksell International.

Avdusin, D.A. (1969) 'Smolensk and the Varangians according to the archaeological data', *Norwegian Archaeological Review*, 2: 52–62.

—— (1970) 'Material culture in the towns of ancient Rus' (in the light of the excavations at Novgorod)', in K. Hannestad (ed.) *Varangian Problems* (Scando Slavica. Supplementum 1), Copenhagen: Munksgaard.

—— (1994) 'Artemij Vladimirovich Artsikhovky and Novgorod', in V.L. Yanin and P.G. Gaidukov (eds) *Novgorod Archaeological Conference. Materials of Scientific Conference Dedicated to the 60th Anniversary of Novgorod's Archaeological Study and the 90th Anniversary of A.V. Artsikhovsky, the Founder of the Novgorod Archaeological Expedition*, Novgorod: Tipografija 'Novgorod'.

Balodis, F. (1943) 'Varifrån härstammar det ryska folket?', *Svensk tidskrift*, 30: 604–14.

Birkeland, H. (1954) *Nordens historie i middelalderen etter arabiske kilder* (Skrifter utgitt av Det Norske Videnskaps-Akademi i Oslo II. Hist.-Filos. Klasse 1954:2), Oslo: Jacob Dybwad.

Blifeld, D.I. (1977) *Davnjorus'ki pamjatki Shestovytsi*. Kiev: Naukova dumka.

Blindheim, Ch. (1970) 'Comments on D. Avdusin: Smolensk and the Varangians according to the archaeological data', *Norwegian Archaeological Review*, 3: 113–15.

Boguslavskij, O.I. (1993) 'Juzhnoe Priladozhje v sisteme transevrazijskikh sviazei', in V.S. Masson, E.N. Nosov and E.A. Rjabinin (eds) *Drevnosti Severo-Zapada Rossii (slavjano-finno-ugordkoe vzaimodejstvie i russjie goroda Baltiki)*, St Petersburg: Centr 'Peterburgskoe vostokovedenie'.

—— (2003) 'Istorija Jugo-Vostochnogo Priladozgja i pogrebalnye pamjatniki', in G.V. Golubeva (ed.) *Staraya Ladoga – drevnjaja stolitsa Rusi. Katalog vystavki*, St Petersburg: Izdatelstvo Gosudarstvennogo Ermitaga.

Brandenburg, N.E. (1895) *Kurgany Juzhnogo Priladozhja* (Materialy po archeologii Rossii 18), St Petersburg: Tipografia Glavnogo Upravlenia Udelov.

Bulkin, V.A. (1973) 'On the Classification and Interpretation of Archaeological Material from the Gnezdovo Cemetery', *Norwegian Archaeological Review*, 6: 10–13.

Bulkin, V.A. and Lebedev, G.S. (1974) 'Gnezdovo i Birka (k probleme stanovlenija gorodov)', in A.N. Kirpichnikov and P.A. Rappoport (eds) *Kultura srednevekovoj Rusi*, Leningrad: Nauka.

Bulkin, V.A., Dubov, I.I. and Lebedev, G.S. (1978) *Arkheologicheskie pamjatniki Drevnei Rusi*, Leningrad: Izdatelstvo Leningradskogo universiteta.

Callmer, J. (1971) 'Comments on D. Avdusin: Smolensk and the Varangians according to the archaeological data', *Norwegian Archaeological Review*, 4: 65–8.

Carlsson A. (1983) *Djurhuvudformiga spännen och gotländsk vikingatid. Text och katalog* (Stockholm Studies in Archaeology 5). Stockholm: Inst. för arkeologi, Stockholms universitet.

Cross, S.H. (1930) 'The Russian Primary Chronicle', *Harvard Studies and Notes in Philology and Literature*, 12: [77]–320.

Davidan, O. (1993) 'Kunsthandwerkliche Gegenstände des 8. bis 10. Jahrhunderts aus Alt-Ladoga (Die Sammlung der Staatlichen Ermitage in St. Petersburg)', *Zeitschrift für Archäologie des Mittelalters*, 20 (1992): 5–61.

Dubov, I.I. (1982) *Severo-vostochnaia Rus v epokhu srednevekovia* (Istoriko-arkheologicheskie ocherki), Leningrad: Izdatelstvo LGU.

Duczko, W. (2004) *Viking Rus. Studies on the Presence of Scandinavians in Eastern Europe* (The Northern World 12), Leiden and Boston: Brill.

Eisenschmidt, S. (1994) *Kammergräber der Wikingerzeit in Altdänmark* (Universitätsforschungen zur prähistorischen Archäologie 25), Bonn: Habelt.

Eniosova, N. (2001) 'Skandinavskie rel'efnye fibuly iz Gnëzdova', in V.V. Murashova (ed.) *Gnëzdovo 125 let issledovanija pamjatnika. Archeologicheskij sbornik*, Moscow: Gosudarstvennij istoricheskij muzej.

Fekhner, M.V. (1963) 'Timerevskij mogi'lnik', in A.P. Smirnov (ed.) *Jaroslavskoe Povolzhe X–XI vv*, Moscow: Gosudarstvennyj Istoricheskij muzei.

Frenkel, Ya. (2002) 'O nakchodke azhurnoi buteroli severoevropejskogo kruga', in D.A. Machinskij (ed.) *Ladoga i Severnaya Evrazia ot Baikala do La-Mansha. Svyazujushchie puti i organizujush-
chie tsentry. Shestye chtenija pamjati Anny Machinskoi*, St Petersburg: Izdatelstvo SPb II RAN
'Nestor-Istoria'.

Garipzanov, I. (2006) 'The Annals of St Bertin (839) and *Chacanus* of the *Rhos*', *Ruthenica*,
5: 7–11.

Golubeva, G.V. (ed.) (2003) *Staraya Ladoga – drevnjaja stolitsa Rusi. Katalog vystavki*, St Petersburg: Izdatelstvo Gosudarstvennogo Ermitazga.

Gräslund, A.-S. (1980) *Birka*, vol. 4: *The Burial Customs. A Study of the Graves on Björkö*,
Stockholm: Almqvist & Wiksell International.

Gushchin, A.C. (1936) *Pamjatniki Khudozhestvennogo remesla Rusi*, Moscow and Leningrad: no
publ.

Härke, H. (1998) 'Archaeologists and migrations: a problem of attitude?', *Current Anthropology*,
39: 19–45.

Hildebrand, H. (1882) 'Om fynd af nordiska fornsaker i Ryssland', in V. Thomsen (1882):
131–41.

Islanova, I.V., Krymov, E.Yu. and Romanov, V.V. (2005) 'Varjagi na Verkhnej Volge', in
N.A. Makarov and A.V. Chernetsov (eds) *Rus' v IX–XIV vekakh. Vzaimodejstvie Severa i Juga*,
Moscow: Nauka.

Izmailov, I.L. (1997) *Vooruzhenie i voennoe delo naseleniya Volzhskoj Bulgarii X-nachala XIII vv*,
Kazan': Magadan.

Jagodziński, M. and Kasprzycka, M. (1991) 'The early medieval craft and commercial centre at
Janyw Pomorski near Elbląg on the south Baltic coast', *Antiquity*, 65: 696–715.

Jakovleva Je.A. (2004) 'New burial finds in central Pskov from the time of Princess Olga', in *Olga
and Ingegerd – Viking Princesses* (Historiska Nyheter), Stockholm: Statens historiska museum.

Jansson, I. (1987) 'Communications between Scandinavia and eastern Europe in the Viking
Age: the archaeological evidence', in K. Düwel, H. Jankuhn, H. Siems and D. Timpe (eds)
*Untersuchungen zu Handel und Verkehr der vor- und frühgeschichtlichen Zeit in Mittel- und
Nordeuropa*, vol. 4: *Der Handel der Karolinger- und Wikingerzeit* (Bericht über die Kolloquien der
Kommision für die Altertumskunde Mittel- und Nordeuropas in den Jahren 1980 bis 1983),
Göttingen: Vandenhoeck & Ruprecht.

—— (1992) 'Scandinavian oval brooches found in Latvia', in A. Loit, Ē. Mugurēvičs and
A. Caune (eds) *Die Kontakte zwischen Ostbaltikum und Skandinavien im frühen Mittelalter* (Studia
Baltica Stockholmiensia 9), Uppsala: Almqvist & Wiksell International.

—— (1994) 'Skandinavien, Baltikum och Rus under vikingatiden', in A. Loit (ed.) *Det 22.
Nordiske historikermøte Oslo 13.–18. August 1994*, vol. 1: *Norden og Baltikum*, Oslo: IKS, Avd.
for historie, Universitetet i Oslo.

—— (1997) 'Warfare, trade or colonisation? Some general remarks on the eastern expansion of
the Scandinavians in the Viking Age', in P. Hansson (ed.) *The Rural Viking in Russia and
Sweden*, Örebro: Örebro kommuns bildningsförvaltning.

—— (1999) 'Scandinavian finds from the 9th–10th centuries on Ryurikovo gorodishche', in
P. Purhonen (ed.) *Fenno-ugri et Slavi 1997. Cultural Contacts in the Area of the Gulf of Finland in
the 9th–13th centuries. Papers Presented by the Participants in the Archaeological Symposium 'Cultural
Contacts in the Area of the Gulf of Finland in the 9th–13th centuries', 13–14 May 1997 in the
National Museum of Finland*. Helsinki: Museovirasto.

Kazakevičius, V. (1992) 'Sword chapes from Lithuania', in A. Loit, Ē. Mugurēvičs and A. Caune
(eds) *Die Kontakte zwischen Ostbaltikum und Skandinavien im frühen Mittelalter* (Studia Baltica
Stockholmiensia 9), Uppsala: Almqvist & Wiksell International.

Kirpičnikov, A.N. (1970) 'Connections between Russia and Scandinavia in the 9th and 10th
centuries, as illustrated by weapon finds', in K. Hannestad (ed.) *Varangian Problems* (Scando
Slavica supplementum 1), Copenhagen: Munksgaard.

—— (2004) 'A Viking period workshop in Staraya Ladoga, excavated in 1997', *Fornvännen*, 99: 183–96.

Kirpichnikov, A.N., Thålin-Bergman, L. and Jansson, I. (2001) 'A new analysis of Viking-Age swords from the collection of the Statens Historiska museer, Stockholm, Sweden', *Russian History/Historie Russe*, 28(1–4): 221–44.

Kivikoski, E. (1970) 'Comments on D. Avdusin: Smolensk and the Varangians according to the archaeological data', *Norwegian Archaeological Rewiev*, 3: 115–17.

Klejn, L.S. (1975) 'Soviet archaeology and the role of the Vikings in the early history of the Slavs', *Norwegian Archaeological Review*, 5: 1–4.

Kolesnikova L.G. (1975) 'Pogrebenie voina na nekropole Khersonesa', *Sovetskaya arkheologia*, 4: 264–7.

Kovalenko, V. (2000) 'La période ancienne de l'histoire de Černigov', in M. Kazanski, A. Narcessian and C. Zuckerman (eds) *Les centres proto-urbains russes entre Scandinavie, Byzance et Orient* (Actes du Colloque International tenu au Collège de France en octobre 1997; Réalités byzantines 7), Paris: P. Lethielleux.

Kovalenko, V., Motsja, A. and Sytyj, J. (2003) 'Archeologicheskie issledovanija Shestotskogo kompleksa v 1998–2002 gg.', in P.P. Tolochko (ed.) *Druzhynni starozhytnosti Tsentralno-Skhidnoi Evropy VIII–X st.*, Chernigiv: Siverjanska dumka.

Kulakow, V.I. (1992) 'Preussische Gefolgschaft im 9. Jahrhundert', in A. Loit, Ē. Mugurēvičs and A. Caune (ed.) *Die Kontakte zwischen Ostbaltikum und Skandinavien im frühen Mittelalter* (Studia Baltica Stockholmiensia 9), Uppsala: Almqvist & Wiksell International.

—— (2000) 'La terre Prusse entre Scandinavie et Orient', in M. Kazanski, A. Narcessian and C. Zuckerman (eds) *Les centres proto-urbains russes entre Scandinavie, Byzance et Orient* (Actes du Colloque International tenu au Collège de France en octobre 1997; Réalités byzantines 7), Paris: P. Lethielleux.

—— (2003) *Istoria prussov do 1283 goda* (Prussia Antiqua 1), Moscow: Izdatelstvo 'Indrik'.

Kuz'min, S. (2000) 'Ladoga, le premier centre proto-urban Russe', in M. Kazanski, A. Narcessian and C. Zuckerman (eds) *Les centres proto-urbains russes entre Scandinavie, Byzance et Orient* (Actes du Colloque International tenu au Collège de France en octobre 1997; Réalités byzantines 7), Paris: P. Lethielleux.

Lamm, J.P. and Urtāns, J. (1995) *The Archaeological Monuments of Grobina*, Stockholm: Museum of National Antiquities and Riga: Latvian Cultural Foundation.

Latvakangas, A. (1995) *Riksgrundarna. Varjagproblemet i Sverige från runinskrifter till enhetlig historisk tolkning* (Annales Universitatis Turkuensis, Ser. B: 211), Turku: Turun Yliopisto.

Lebedev, G.S. and Nazarenko, V.A. (1975) 'The connections between Russians and Scandinavians in the 9th–11th centuries', *Norwegian Archaeological Review*, 5: 5–9.

Leont'ev, A.A. (1996) *Arkheologia Meri*, Moscow: Nauka.

—— (2000) 'Sarskoe et Rostov: deux centres de la Rus' du Nord-Est aux IXe–XIe siècles', in M. Kazanski, A. Narcessian and C. Zuckerman (eds) *Les centres proto-urbains russes entre Scandinavie, Byzance et Orient* (Actes du Colloque International tenu au Collège de France en octobre 1997; Réalités byzantines 7), Paris: P. Lethielleux.

Lindkvist, Th. (1988) *Plundring, skatter och den feodala statens framväxt. Organisatoriska tendenser i Sverige under övergången från vikingatid till tidig medeltid* (Opuscula Historica Upsaliensia 1), Uppsala: Historiska inst., Uppsala universitet.

Martens, I. (2003) 'Tusenvis av sverd. Hvorfor har Norge mange flere vikingtidsvåpen enn noe annet europeisk land?', *Collegium Mediaevale*, 16: 51–66.

—— (2004) 'Indigenous and imported Viking Age weapons in Norway – a problem with European implications', *Journal of Nordic Archaeological Science*, 14: 125–37.

Martens, J. (1996) 'Das Wikingergräberfeld von Wiskiauten, Samland', in O. Pelc and G. Pickhan (eds) *Zwischen Lübeck und Novgorod. Wirtschaft, politik und Kultur im Ostseeraum von frühen Mittelalter bis 20. Jahrhundert. Norbert Angermann zum 60. Geburtstag*, Lüneburg: Institut Nordostdeutsches Kulturwerk.

Melnikova, E.A. (1996) *The Eastern World of the Vikings. Eight Essays about Scandinavia and Eastern Europe in the Early Middle Ages* (Gothenburg Old Norse Studies 1), Göteborg: Litteraturvetenskapliga institutionen, Göteborgs universitet.

—— (2001) *Skandinavskie runicheskie nadpisi* (Vostochnaya literatura), Moscow: 'Vostochnaja literatura' RAN.

—— (2003) 'The cultural assimilation of the Varangians in eastern Europe from the point of view of language and literacy', in W. Heizmann and A. van Nahl (eds) *Runica – Germanica – Mediaevalia* (Ergänzungsbände zum Reallexikon der Germanischen Altertumskunde 37), Berlin and New York: Walter de Gruyter.

Mikhailov, K.A. (1996) 'Juzhnoskandinavskie cherty v pogrebalnom obrjade Plakunskogo mogilnika', in V.L. Yanin (ed.) *Novgorod i Novgorodskaya zemlya. Istoria i arkheologia* (Vypusk 10), Novgorod: Tipografia Novgorod.

—— (1997) 'Pogrebenie voina s konjami na vershine Plakunskoj sopkovidnoi nasypi v svete pogrebalnykh traditsij epokhi vikingov', in A.N. Kirpichnikov and E.A. Nosov (eds) *Drevnosti Povolkhovja*, St Petersburg: ABEVEGA.

—— (2002) 'Skandinavskij mogilnik v urochishche Plakun (zametki o khronologii i topografii)', in A.N. Kirpichnikov (ed.) *Ladoga i ejo sosedi v epokhu srednevekovja*, St Petersburg: 'Biznes-Elita'.

—— (2003) 'Kurgannye mogilniki Staroy Ladogi', in G.V. Golubeva (ed.) *Staraya Ladoga – drevnjaja stolitsa Rusi. Katalog vystavki*, St Petersburg: Izdatelstvo Gosudarstvennogo Ermitaga.

Mikhailov, K.A. and Nosov, E.N. (2002) 'Novye nakhodki nakonechnikov nozhen mechej na Rjurikovom gorodishche', *Arkheologicheskie Vesti*, 9: 136–40.

Moravchik, G. (ed.) (1985) *Constantine Porphyrogenitus. De administrando imperio* (Corpus fontium historiae Byzantinae), Greek text with English trans. by R.J.H. Jenkins, Washington, DC: Dumbarton Oaks Research Library and Collection.

Mühle, E. (1989) 'Gnezdovo – das alte Smolensk? Zur Deutung eines Siedlungskomplexes des ausgehenden 9. Bis beginnenden 11. Jahrhunderts', *Oldenburg-Wolin-Staraja Ladoga-Novgorod-Kiev. Handel und Handelsverbindungen im südlichen und östlichen Ostseeraum während des frühen Mittelalters* (Bericht der Römisch-Germanischen Kommission 69), Mainz am Rhein: Philipp von Zabern.

von zur Mühlen, B. (1975) *Die Kultur der Wikinger in Ospreussen* (Bonner Hefte zur Vorgeschihte 9), Bonn: Friedrich-Wilhelms-Universität.

Murasheva, V.V. (1997) 'The Viking Age monuments in the Jaroslavl region on the Upper Volga', in P. Hansson (ed.) *The Rural Viking in Russia and Sweden*, Örebro: Örebro kommuns bildningsförvaltning.

Nazarenko, V.A. (1985) 'Mogilnik v urochishche Plakun', in V.V. Sedov (ed.) *Srednevekovaya Ladoga*, Leningrad: Izdatelstvo 'Nauka'.

Nefedov, V.S. (2001) 'Arkheologicheskij kontekst "drevnejshej russkoj nadpisi" iz Gnezdova', in V.V. Murashova (ed.) *Gnezdovo 125 let issledovanija pamjatnika. Archeologicheskij sbornik*, Moscow: Gosudarstvennij istoricheskij muzej.

Nelson J.L. (ed.) (1991) *The Annals of St-Bertin*, Manchester: Manchester University Press.

Nerman, B. (1936) 'Svenskarna i Ösbaltiska länder och i Ryssland', in H. Shetelig (ed.) *Nordisk kultur*, vol. 1: *Befolkning i oldtiden*, Stockholm: Bonnier.

—— (1958) *Grobin-Seeburg* (KVHAA. Monografier 41), Stockholm: Almqvist & Wiksell.

Nosov, E.N. (1985) 'Sopkovidnaya nasyp bliz urochishcha Plakun v Staroy Ladoge', in V.V. Sedov (ed.) *Srednevekovaya Ladoga*, Leningrad: Izdatelstvo 'Nauka'.

—— (1990) *Novgorodskoe (Rjurikovo) Gorodishche*, Leningrad: 'Nauka'.

—— (1992) 'Ryurik gorodishche and the settlements to the north of Lake Ilmen', in M.A.

Brisbane (ed.) *The Archaeology of Novgorod, Russia* (The Society for Medieval Archaeology. Monograph series 13), Lincoln: Society for Medieval Archaeology.

—— (2000) 'Rjurikovo Gorodisce et Novgorod', in M. Kazanski, A. Narcessian and C. Zuckerman (eds) *Les centres proto-urbains russes entre Scandinavie, Byzance et Orient* (Actes du Colloque International tenu au Collège de France en octobre 1997; Réalités byzantines 7), Paris: P. Lethielleux.

Obolensky, D. (1970) 'The Byzantine sources on the Scandinavians in eastern Europe', in K. Hannestad (ed.) *Varangian Problems* (Scando Slavica supplementum 1), Copenhagen: Munksgaard.

Palm, R. (2004) *Vikingarnas språk. 750–1100*, Stockholm: Norstedts.

Paulsen, P. (1953) *Schwertorbänder der Wikingerzei. Ein Beitrag zur Frühgeschichte Osteuropa*, Stuttgart: Kohlhammer.

Petrenko, V. (1991) 'A picture stone from Grobin (Latvia)', *Fornvännen*, 86: 1–10.

Petrenko, V. and Virse, I.A. (1993) 'Issledovania mogilnika Pridiens v zapadnoj Latvii', *Kratkie soobshchenia Instituta arkheologii*, 208: 102–7.

Petrukhin, V.Y. and Pushkina, T.A. (1979) 'K predystorii drevnerusskogo goroda', *Istoria SSSR*, 18: 100–12.

Pritsak, O. (1993) 'Varangians', in P. Pulsiano (ed.) *Medieval Scandinavia. An Encyclopedia*, New York and London: Garland.

Pushkina, T.A. (1997) 'Scandinavian finds from Old Russia: a survey of their topography and chronology', in P. Hansson (ed.) *The Rural Viking in Russia and Sweden*, Örebro: Örebro kommuns bildningsförvaltning.

Raudonikas, V.I. (1930) *Die Normannen der Wikingerzeit und das Ladogagebiet* (KVHAAs handlingar 40:3), Stockholm: KVHAA.

Rjabinin, E.A. (1994) 'U istokov remeslennogo proizvodstva v Ladoge (k istorii obshchebaltijskikh svjazej v predvikingskuju epokhu)', in V.M. Masson and E.N. Nosov (eds) *Novye istochniki po arkheologii Severo-Zapada*, St Petersburg: Institut istorii materialnoj kultury.

—— (2002) 'Novye dannie o "bolshikh domakh" Staroy Ladogi (po materialam raskopok Zemljanogo gorodishcha v 1973–1985 gg.)', in E.N. Nosov and G.I. Smirnova (eds) *Staraya Ladoga i problemy archeologii Severnoj Rusi*, St Petersburg: Izdatelstvo Gosudarstvennogo Ermitaga.

Rolle, R. (1989) 'Archäologische Bemerkungen zum Warägerhandel', *Oldenburg-Wolin-Staraja Ladoga-Novgorod-Kiev. Handel und Handelsverbindungen im südlichen und östlichen Ostseeraum während des frühen Mittelalters* (Bericht der Römisch-Germanischen Kommission 69), Mainz am Rhein: Philipp von Zabern.

Rybakov, B.A. (1949) 'Drevnosti Chernigova', in N.N. Voronin (ed.) *Materialy i issledovania po arkheologii SSSR* (Vypusk 11), Moscow and Leningrad: Izdatelstvo akademii Nauk SSSR.

Šaskol'skij, I.P. (1970) 'Recent development in the Normanist controversy', in K. Hannestad (ed.) *Varangian Problems* (Scando Slavica supplementum 1), Copenhagen: Munksgaard.

Sawyer, P. (1982) *Kings and Vikings. Scandinavia and Europe AD 700–1100*, London: Methuen.

—— (1991) *När Sverige blev Sverige* (Occasional papers on medieval topics 5), Alingsås: Viktoria.

Schmidt, K.R. (1970) 'The Varangian problem: a brief history of the controversy', in K. Hannestad (ed.) *Varangian Problems* (Scando Slavica supplementum 1), Copenhagen: Munksgaard.

Sedov, V.V. (1992) 'Skandinavische Elemente im frühmittelalterlichen Pskov', in A Loit, Ē. Mugurēvičs and A. Caune (eds) *Die Kontakte zwischen Ostbaltikum und Skandinavien im frühen Mittelalter* (Studia Baltica Stockholmiensia 9), Uppsala: Almqvist & Wiksell International.

Sedyh, V. (2000) 'Timerevo – un centre proto-urbain sur la grande voie de la Volga', in M. Kazanski, A. Narcessian and C. Zuckerman (eds) *Les centres proto-urbains russes entre Scandinavie, Byzance et Orient* (Actes du Colloque International tenu au Collège de France en octobre 1997; Réalités byzantines 7), Paris: P. Lethielleux.

Stalsberg, A. (1989) 'Scandinavian Viking Age finds in Rus', *Oldenburg-Wolin-Staraja Ladoga-Novgorod-Kiev. Handel und Handelsverbindungen im südlichen und östlichen Ostseeraum während des frühen Mittelalters* (Bericht der Römisch-Germanischen Kommission 69), Mainz am Rhein: Philipp von Zabern.

Šturms, E. (1949) 'Schwedische Kolonien in Lettland', *Fornvännen*, 44: 205–17.

Stylegar, F.-A. (2005) 'Kammergraver fra vikingtiden i Vestfold', *Fornvännen*, 100: 162–77.

Thålin Bergman, L. and Arrhenius, B. (2005) *Weapon Investigations. Helgö and the Swedish Hinterland* (Excavations at Helgö 15), Stockholm: Almqvist & Wiksell International.

Thomsen, V. (1882) *Ryska rikets grundläggning genom Skandinaverna*, Stockholm: Samson & Wallin.

Thunmark-Nylén, L. (1983) 'Gotland och Ostbaltikum', in I. Jansson (ed.) *Gutar och vikingar*, Stockholm: Statens Historiska Museum.

—— (2001) 'Gnezdovskij mech – izdelie gotlandskogo mastera?' in V.V. Murashova (ed.) *Gnezdovo 125 let issledovanija pamjatnika. Archeologicheskij sbornik*, Moscow: Gosudarstvennij istoricheskij muzej.

Tolochko, O. (1991) 'Polshcha i Rus. Sproba stvorennja modeli evoljuciji potestarnykh struktur', in V.M. Smolij (ed.) *Ukraina i Polshcha v period feodalismu*, Kiev: 'Naukova dumka'.

—— (2001) 'Kievan Rus around the year 1000', in P. Urbanczyk (ed.) *Europe around the Year 1000*, Warsaw: Institute of Archaeology and Ethnology Polish Academy of Science.

Tomsinskij, C.V. (1999) 'Skandinavskie nakhodki iz uglichskogo kremlja i legenda ob osnovanii Uglicha', *Stratum plus*, 5: 169–78.

Vysotskij S.A. (1966) *Drevnerusskie nadpisi Sofii Kievskoj XI–XIV vv* (Vypusk 1), Kiev: Naukova dumka.

Warner, D.A. (2001) *Ottonian Germany. The Chronicon of Thietmar of Merseburg*, trans. and annotated by D.A. Warner, Manchester and New York: Manchester University Press.

Yotov, V. (2002) *Vorzhenieto i snarjazhenieto ot blgarskoto srednovekovie (VII–XI vek)*, Varna: Knigoizdatelstvo ZOGRAF.

Zharnov Y. (1991) 'Zhenskie skandinavskie pogrebenia v Gnëzdove', in D.A. Avdusin (ed.) *Smolensk i Gnëzdovo*, Moscow: Izdatelstvo Moskovskogo Universiteta.

Zotsenko, V. (2003) 'Skandinavskie drevnosti i topogrfija Kieva "druzhinnogo perioda"', *Ruthenica*, 2: 26–52.

—— (2004) 'Skandynavski artefakty Pivdenno-Zakhidnoi Rusi', in A.P. Mocja (ed.) *Starodavnij Iskorosten' i slovjanski grady VIII–X st.*, Kiev: Korvin Press.

CHAPTER THIRTY-NINE

THE VIKINGS AND ISLAM

———•◆•———

Egil Mikkelsen

The main sources at hand studying the contacts between the Vikings and Islam are documentary sources, Arabic coins and archaeological objects.

THE DOCUMENTARY SOURCES

Old Norse sources, including runic inscriptions that tell about Viking relations to the east during the Viking Age, never mention direct contacts with the Islamic world. Far more information is found in the Arabic written sources. The authors were geographers, diplomats, missionaries or merchants.

The two — and only — Arabs that we know by name who reached Scandinavia both came from Spain. The Arab diplomat al-Ghazal, in the year 845, gives a description of what must be Scandinavia. He says that people here once were *majûs* (Vikings), but were now Christians. People on some islands further north were still worshipping their old religion. The first land was probably Denmark that for a period had converted to Christianity, 'the islands' are interpreted as present-day Norway (Wikander 1978). Around 970 the Spanish Arab, al-Tartuschi, visited Hedeby. He described the town and its people: it was a big town, poor and dirty. The people lived on fish, were singing like howling dogs and worshipped Sirius (Piltz 1998: 29).

Ibn Horradadbeh was the first Arab writer, between 844 and 848, to mention the people ar-Rus and Scandinavia (Birkeland 1954: 10 f.). He speaks of ar-Rus and their roads to the east, the commodities they brought with them and that they were taxed. He also tells that ar-Rus often took their commodities by camel the last part of the way to Baghdad. And he says: 'They pass them off as Christians.' This story tells us that the Vikings went as far as the capital of the Caliphate and that it was probably easier to do so when they claimed to be Christians. Islam, Christianity and Judaism are all 'book religions' with one god and their people lived in peaceful neighbourliness. The polytheistic Norse religion was reckoned as infidelity, and Vikings belonging to that religion would have had far greater problems trading with the Caliphate.

The most famous Arabic source concerning the descriptions of the Vikings is Ibn Fadlan who wrote an account of a journey from Baghdad to the Volga Bulgars in 921–2. His main task was to spread the Muslim faith to this people (Wikander 1978). He tells

543

that he saw among these people 5,000 men and women, who had all converted to Islam. They were called *al-baringâr*, which is interpreted as an Arabic rendering of the Old Norse name *væringar*, another name for Vikings (Lewicki 1972: 12; Wikander 1978: 21). Ibn Fadlan built a mosque of wood for them to perform Islamic service and he taught them to pray. There are some difficulties in interpreting this part of the Arabic source (*ibid.*). It is, however, interesting if Vikings really were converted to Islam in Volga Bulgar, although the number of converted is probably highly overstated. It is tempting to speculate if any of these Vikings ever went back to Scandinavia and brought their Islamic faith with them. The Vikings obviously settled along the River Volga, built their houses and traded with the Volga Bulgars (Wikander 1978: 63).

Several Arabic writers tell about the Khazar society (Wikander 1978: 71 f.; Birkeland 1954: 33–4, 49 f.). The best information is given by al-Mas'udi (written 947). In their capital Itil lived Muslims, Christians, Jews and pagans. Their king converted to Judaism. Among the pagans al-Mas'udi mentions as-Saqaliba (Slavs) and ar-Rus (Vikings) who lived in this city. The different religious groups had their own judges, using their own laws. The Muslims had their mosque. They were mainly occupied by trade and handicraft (Birkeland 1954: 33–4). The land of the Khazars has thus also been an important meeting place between Vikings, Muslims and people of other religions. The fact that Vikings lived here more permanently must have given them a clear impression of what Islam meant.

Many of the Arabic descriptions of the Vikings must be understood on the bases of different religions and customs related to religious practice. One such aspect is the way the Arabs looked upon the lack of cleanliness among the Vikings: they did not wash after having relieved themselves, after having intercourse or after a meal. Ibn Fadlan obviously believed that a stranger who did not perform the daily five ritual ablutions as Muslims are obliged to do, was terribly filthy (Wikander 1978).

Amin Râzi, describing Rûs among the Volga Bulgars, says that they highly valued pork. Even those who had converted to Islam aspired to it and were very fond of pork (Wikander 1978: 73). We know that Muslims are not allowed to eat pork. The Spanish Arab Abu Hamid who visited Bulgar in the twelfth century complained that it was very cold and there were only four-hour days during winter and twenty-hour days in summer. When he visited Bulgar, Ramadan – the Muslim's month of fasting – came in summer. As the fasting is set to last all day when the sun is shining, Abu Hamid admitted he had to abstain from fasting (Wikander 1978: 78–9).

Women had a free position in Viking society. They were allowed to marry and divorce on their own will. According to Amin Râzi, referred to by Ibn Fadlan, Rûs did not look upon having intercourse in public as a shame (Wikander 1978: 73). This was most common between men and their bondswomen. Muslims were allowed to have several wives and concubines, but their sex life was a highly private matter.

When Ibn Fadlan described the Vikings in Volga Bulgar he also mentioned that Rûs had idols: long poles with human-like faces dug into the ground. This is in contrast to Muslims who are not allowed to depict human faces. Many Arab writers tell of ar-Rûs who burn their dead, again in contrast to their own custom of burying them in the ground. A discussion between a Viking and a Muslim on their different burial customs, told by Ibn Fadlan, is interesting: 'You Arabs are really stupid. You take the man who you love and honour most of all and dig him into the ground where insects and worms are eating him. We [the Rûs] burn him on a fire in a moment and he goes immediately to Paradise.' Another contrast between Old Norse religion and Islam is that the Vikings buried their dead with a lot of their equipment, whereas the Muslims left nothing with the dead. Well known is Ibn Fadlan's description of the rich boat burial. Ibn Miskawaih wrote about the Rûs raid on the trading town of Barda'a in Azerbaijan in 943 including the burial custom of al-Rûs. Then he says: 'The Muslims, after the Rûs had left, were looking into their graves and picked out their swords that were in great demand up to this day because they are so bright and of such an exquisite quality' (Birkeland 1954). This is difficult to see as other than regular grave robbery by the Muslims.

Many of the Arab writers tell about trade relations between Vikings and Arabs, directly or with Russians, Volga Bulgars or Khazars as middlemen (Birkeland 1954: 16, 29, 50). The Vikings brought slaves (male and female), fur of sable, black fox, grey squirrel, beaver and ermine, the tusk of walrus, honey and beeswax, amber and weapons of good quality (Duczko 1998: 107). What the Vikings got in return, according to the Arab written sources, were Arabic silver coins, dirhams, which were the main object of exchange, beads, luxury clothing and silk (Jansson and Nosov 1992: 80).

It was not only through trade that Arab objects reached other people. Gift exchange was also of great importance. When the Spanish Arab al-Ghazal visited the Danish king in 845 he brought gifts: chests containing clothes and vessels. On his journey from Baghdad to the Volga Bulgars Ibn Fadlan gave gifts to the different people he stayed with. Islamic costumes, jackets and caftans are mentioned, obviously gifts for men. Women were given a veil or a signet ring. Other gifts mentioned are pieces of textile, shoes, beads, perfume, etc. Ibn Fadlan tells that Muslim tradesmen had to start a friendly relationship with someone who would accommodate him when doing business in foreign countries. The host and his wife are given gifts of the kind mentioned (Wikander 1978). This is one way that Vikings also may have got goods of Arabic origin.

Another way of obtaining goods was by raiding and plundering. The Arab sources speak of Viking expeditions to Arab territory, mainly around the Caspian Sea, attacking several towns (Kromann and Roesdahl 1996: 10). Well known is also the Viking raid against Seville in Spain in 843/4, where they took prisoners, plundered and killed. New attacks were carried out in different parts of Spain early in the tenth century (Birkeland 1954: 13, 38).

ARCHAEOLOGICAL OBJECTS AND COINS OF ARAB ORIGIN FOUND IN SCANDINAVIA

A considerable number of Viking Age archaeological finds testify to contacts with the Arabic world: they are known as 'oriental imports'. These artefacts have been interpreted as expressions of trade (Arne 1914; Jansson 1985, 1987, 1988). Is it possible that ideas and religious concepts associated with these objects also reached Scandinavia?

The largest and possibly also the most important group of artefacts demonstrating the connections between the Arab world and Viking Age Scandinavia are the Arabic or Cufic coins, mostly silver dirhams. About 85,000 coins have been found in Sweden, most of them in silver hoards on the islands of Gotland and Öland (Hovén 1981). Nearly 700 come from Norway (Khazaei 2004), 5,000 from Denmark (Kromann 1990). About 100,000 have been found in Russia (Noonan 1998). A few of the coins come from the

Arabic colonies in Spain and the western Mediterranean. The stream of coins started at the end of the eighth century and reached a climax during the tenth; it came to an almost total stop around AD 1015 (Hovén 1985).

The Cufic coins provide information, written in Arabic, of the name of the person who had ordered the coin to be struck, the caliph, the mint master, the place and year of minting. In addition the coins bear quotations from the Quran (Hovén 1985: 74 f.). These quotations were reminders of central parts of the Islamic doctrines for their own fellow believers. The Muslim traders and officials were the most active missionaries during the Viking Age. Bearing this in mind, it seems natural that the exchange medium, the coins, should act as small, yet important 'missionary tracts'.

We know of several cases of graffiti and inscriptions on the Arabic coins which reached northern Europe. Although the significance of these has in some cases been overstated, especially as concerns the runes, there is no doubt about this being an important source. Some studies on the Swedish and Russian material have been carried out (Hammarberg and Rispling 1985; Dobrovolskij *et al.* 1991). The most common types of graffiti and inscriptions on Arabic coins are oriental and runic inscriptions, objects such as weapons and boats, and religious and magic symbols. Most graffiti were probably made in Scandinavia, some possibly also in Scandinavian Russia.

I have investigated graffiti among about 15,000 Arabic coins found in Sweden, concentrating on religious signs and symbols. I found 12 instances of Þórr's hammers and 28 coins with graffiti which were interpreted as Christian crosses of various types (Mikkelsen 1998: figs 7–8). The year of minting of these coins lay between AD 814 and 970.

Why were Þórr's hammers and Christian crosses scratched across the quotations from the Quran? Islam must have been a well-known religion among Vikings travelling in the east. It is likely that they knew some of the main aspects of the Islamic doctrine, and must surely also have been aware of the fact that the Arabic texts found on the coins conveyed messages from this religion. When our ancestors scratched Þórr's hammers and crosses on the surface of the Arabic coins, they must presumably have wanted to show that they dissociated themselves from the other faith, Islam. During the Viking Age, people of northern Europe tried, for some reason or other, to render the quotations from the Quran harmless, or to confront Allah with their own Norse or Christian god, by scratching their symbols over the Islamic messages.

Arabic inscriptions or imitations of that writing have also been observed on artefacts found in Scandinavia other than coins, as follows.

Five bottle-shaped bronze vessels have been found, four in Sweden and one on Åland (Jansson 1988: 646; Mikkelsen 1998: 41 f.). Two were used as containers for coin hoards, mostly Cufic coins, three come from richly equipped graves. These bronze vessels were probably made in the late ninth or the tenth century. T.J. Arne (1932: 104 f.) has suggested west Turkestan, Samarqand or Bukhara as their place of origin. One of the bronze vessels, from Aska, Hagebyhöga, Östergötland bears a conventionalised Arabic inscription. It has been transcribed and reads as follows: *el-fadl el-akmal wa- (l-a) san qabisa, lillah*: 'The most perfect beneficent and most beautiful gift [is] for God.' It is thought that the inscription was added to the bronze bottle at a later date, probably by someone not familiar with Arabic letters (Arne 1932: 107). The bronze vessel from Bertby, Saltvik, Åland is very similar to the vessel from Aska, and the two are thought to have been made at the same place. Even the inscriptions are almost identical. They were probably made by the same person: a man in Bulgar (Arne 1932: 108).

Vessels of this kind were normally used as water jugs in Islam, for purifying water used for ritual ablution before praying. The Scandinavia find contexts do not support the hypothesis that the function came north together with the object. Both context and function changed.

A cast bronze object with openwork plant ornamentation, interpreted as a censer, was found together with a fragment of an oil lamp and three glow tongs at Åbyn, Hamrånge, Gästrikland, Sweden. The censer probably comes from the province of Khorasan in Iran, and should be dated to the late ninth century (Ådahl 1990). It may have come from a prosperous home, but we cannot rule out the possibility that it was connected with religious activities. The censer bears two inscriptions in Arabic: *bi'ism Allah* 'in the name of God', and: *rahim* 'merciful'. These inscriptions relate the objects to the Islamic faith in some way or other.

In the rich female Birka grave 515 a finger-ring with an amethyst was found. The stone bore the legend 'Allah' engraved in Arabic. Finger-rings with semi-precious stones of this kind are common in Russia, among the Volga Bulgars and the Khazars and also in the Caliphate (Duczko 1998: figs 7–9). From the Arab written sources we know that rings like this were common gifts from Muslim traders to people in the east, especially women.

Among objects from the Arab world reaching Scandinavia during the Viking Age were balances and weights. This shows the importance of trade between the two, and many archaeologists have suggested that the Viking Age weight system in parts of Scandinavia originated from the Arabic system (Sperber 1996). Most common in Viking Age graves are the weights made of lead or bronze/brass. Some of them display pseudo-Arabic symbols or letters on the poles (Mikkelsen 1998: fig. 4). On one of them, from Nysätra, Gotland, we may read: *rasûl Allah* 'Allah's prophet', and: *bakh* 'choice'. The latter text occurs also on two other weights, and may be seen as a kind of warranty quality. Many of the Birka graves in Sweden from the period AD 890–930 contained weights belonging to the Islamic weight system. Sperber (1996: 104–7) believes that Muslim people most probably stayed at Birka during that period.

Costumes and costume accessories of different kinds are one of the biggest group of artefacts of Islamic origin in Scandinavia. Many graves, especially in Birka, have yielded textiles deriving from so-called 'oriental' costumes; this applies to women's as well as to men's burials. Silk and other textiles and ornaments of gold and silver, as well as fur trimmings, are interpreted as part of such 'oriental' costumes (Jansson 1988).

Agnes Geijer (1938) saw these as foreign luxury goods which the individual Viking trader had acquired during his travels in the east. Anne-Sofie Gräslund (1980: 80 f.) interpreted the rich chamber graves of Birka, often containing luxury costumes, as probably representing the burials of Scandinavians as well as foreign traders and their wives. Inga Hägg (1983) is more inclined to regard these garments as symbols of rank, belonging to people who were in close contact with the Byzantine court, with the court in Kiev probably acting as an important intermediator.

If we return to the written Arabic sources, we have seen that gift exchange between Arabs and other people included Islamic costumes, sometimes with embroidered gold or made of silk, jackets, caftans and veils. Using these sources as models, it is obvious that all the above interpretations may be possible.

One group of artefacts which has been found in a great many Viking Age graves in Scandinavia consists of rock-crystal and carnelian beads (Jansson 1988: 584 f., 633 f.). Certain types may have been produced in Gujarat, India, but other places of origin have also been suggested. Beads like these were used as votive gifts in Buddhist cultures, and as rosary beads in Islam. When the beads came to Scandinavia during the Viking Age, Gujarat had been conquered by the Muslims. It thus seems likely that they came to Scandinavia as part of the Arabic trade. However, we have at present no indications of any religious ideas or functions linked to the beads in their original context having come to Scandinavia. Here they are usually found in women's graves, as parts of necklaces.

BIBLIOGRAPHY

Ådahl, K. (1990) 'An early Islamic incense burner of bronze in a Swedish collection', in Gh. Gnoli and A. Panaino (eds) *Proceedings of the First European Conference of Iranian Studies*, vol. 2, Rome: Instituto Italiano per il Medio ed Estremo Oriente.

Arne, T.J. (1914) *La Suède et L'Orient. Etudes archéologiques sur les relations de la Suède et de L'Orient pendant l'Age des Vikings* (Archives d'Etudes orientales 8), Uppsala: K.W. Appelberg.

—— (1932) 'Ein bemerkenswerter Fund in Östergötland', *Acta Archaeologica*, 3: 67–112.

Birkeland, H. (1954) *Nordens historie i middelalderen etter arabiske kilder* (Skrifter utgitt av Det Norske Videnskaps-Akademi i Oslo II. Hist.-Filos. Klasse No 2), Oslo: Universitetsforlaget.

Dobrovolskij, I.G., Dubov, I.V. and Kuzmenko, J.K. (1991) *Graffiti na vostotsjnikh monetakh. Drevnjaja Rus i sopredelnye strany*, Leningrad: University of Leningrad.

Duczko, W. (1998) 'Viking Age Scandinavia and Islam: an archaeologist's view', in E. Piltz (ed.) *Byzantium and Islam in Scandinavia. Acts of a Symposium at Uppsala University June 15–16 1996*, Göteborg: Åström.

Geijer, A. (1938) *Birka. Untersuchungen und Studien*, vol. 3: *Die Textilfunde aus den Gräbern*, Stockholm: KVHAA.

Gräslund, A.-S. (1980) *Birka. Untersuchungen und Studien*, vol. 4: *The Burial Customs. A Study of the Graves on Björkö*, Stockholm: Almqvist & Wiksell International.

Hägg, I. (1983) 'Birkas orientaliska praktplagg', *Fornvännen*, 78: 204–23.

Hammarberg, I. and Rispling, G. (1985) 'Graffiter på vikingatida mynt', *Hikuin*, 11: 63–78.

Hovén, B.E. (1981) 'On oriental coins in Scandinavia', in M.A.S. Blackburn and D.M. Metcalf (eds) *Viking Age Coinage in the Northern lands* (British Archaeological Reports. International series 122), Oxford: British Archaeological Reports.

—— (1985) 'Islamic coins', in M. Fahlander *et al.* (eds) *Islam – konst och kultur* (Sagt, hänt, meddelat 2), Stockholm: Statens historiska museum.

Jansson, I. (1985) 'The Caliphate and the northern barbarians', in M. Fahlander *et al.* (eds) *Islam – konst och kultur* (Sagt, hänt, meddelat 2), Stockholm: Statens historiska museum.

—— (1987) 'Communication between Scandinavia and eastern Europe in the Viking Age: the archaeological evidence', in K. Düwel, H. Jankuhn, H. Siems and D. Trimpe (eds) *Unter-suchungen zu Handel und Verkehr der vor- und frühgeschichtlichen Zeit in Mittel- und Nordeuropa*, vol. 4 (Abhandlungen der Akademie der Wissenschaften in Göttingen. Philol.-Hist. Klasse 3:156), Göttingen: Vandenhoeck & Ruprecht.

—— (1988) 'Wikingerzeitlicher orientalischer Import in Skandinavien. Oldenburg – Wolin – Starja Ladoga – Novgorod – Kiev. Handel und Handelsverbindungen im südlichen und östlichen Ostseeraum während des frühen Mittelalters', *Bericht der Römisch-Germanischen Kommision*, 69: 564–647.

Jansson, I. and Nosov, E.N. (1992) 'The way to the east', in E. Roesdahl and D.M. Wilson (eds) *From Viking to Crusader. The Scandinavians and Europe 800–1200*, Copenhagen: Nordisk Ministerråd.

Khazaei, H. (2004) 'Et samanidisk myntfunn fra Porsgrunn', *Norsk numismatisk tidsskrift*, 2: 5–14.

Kromann, A. (1990) 'The latest Cufic coin finds from Denmark', in K. Jonsson and B. Malmer (eds) *Sigtuna Papers. Proceedings of the Sigtuna Symposium on Viking Age Coinage 1–4 June 1989* (Commentationes de nummis saeculorum IX–XI in Suecia repertis. Nova series 6), Stockholm: KVHAA; London: Spink & Son.

Kromann, A. and Roesdahl, E. (1996) 'The Vikings and the Islamic lands', in K. von Folsach, T. Lundbaek and P. Mortensen (eds) *The Arabian Journey. Danish Connections with the Islamic World over a Thousand Years*, Århus: Prehistoric Museum Moesgård.

Lewicki, T. (1972) 'Handel Samanidow ze wschodnia I srodkowa Europa. Res. Le commerce des Samanides avec l'Europe Orientale et Central', *Slavia Antiqua* 19: 1–18.

Mikkelsen, E. (1998) 'Islam and Scandinavia during the Viking Age', in E. Piltz (ed.) *Byzantium and Islam in Scandinavia. Acts of a Symposium at Uppsala University June 15–16 1996*. Göteborg: Åström.

Noonan, T.S. (1998) *The Islamic World, Russia and the Vikings, 750–900. The Numismatic Evidence* (Variorum reprints. Collected studies series 595), Aldershot: Variorum.

Piltz, E. (1998) 'Byzantium and Islam in Scandinavia', in E. Piltz (ed.) *Byzantium and Islam in Scandinavia. Acts of a Symposium at Uppsala University June 15–16 1996*. Göteborg: Åström.

Sperber, E. (1996) *Balances, Weights and Weighting in Ancient and Early Medieval Sweden* (Thesis and Papers in Scientific Archaeology 2), Stockholm: Archaeological Research Laboratory, University of Stockholm.

Wikander, S. (1978) *Araber – Vikingar – Väringar* (Svenska Humanistiska Förbundet. Skrifter 90), Lund: H. Hansson.

CHAPTER FORTY

ARABIC SOURCES ON THE VIKINGS

—•◆•—

J.E. Montgomery

The Vikings appear sporadically across some six centuries in Arabic texts. These texts provide information, of varying degrees of accuracy and reliability, on two (broadly conceived) groups of Vikings (I make no distinction between Vikings, Varangians, Norsemen and Scandinavians): those Vikings who, with Ireland as a base, operated in and around the Atlantic seaboard of western Europe and who occasionally made their presence felt in parts of Islamic Spain (in this entry, such texts are marked {a}); and those who made inroads into northern mainland Europe via the Baltic Sea and the Volga portage routes, coming into contact with Muslims in and around the Caspian Sea (marked {b}). Issues of nomenclature will be raised where appropriate: the Vikings in {a} texts tend to be called 'Magians', that is, Zoroastrians (Ar. *al-Majus*), while those in {b} texts are known as 'Rus' (Ar. *al-Rus*, written as *al-rws*), and variously connected with either the Slavs (Ar. *Saqaliba*) or the Turks (Ar. *Atrak*). A third group, the Rus who entered the military service of the Byzantines (as distinct from the Varangian Guard) are occasionally mentioned {c}. Works from the early periods of contact (approximately two centuries) will be discussed 'chronologically', in terms of either the putative date of composition of the work, or, failing that, the floruit of the author: thus, the issue of whether these texts are chronologically stratified with material from earlier periods will be only tangentially addressed. The earliest occurrence of the word *Warank* (Varangians) [d] in an astronomical work by al-Biruni (d. after 1050) determines the chronological limits of this chapter. One source and one individual who have benefited from exaggerated assessments of their relevance will be touched briefly upon in the conclusion, in an attempt to highlight those works which warrant greater exposure.

The most comprehensive treatment of the Arabic source material remains Harris Birkeland, *Nordens historie i middelalderen etter arabiske kilder* (*Det Norske Videnskaps-Akademi i Oslo. Skrifter II: Historisk-filosofiske klasse* 2 [1954]), Oslo: Dybwad, 1955, a Norwegian trans., with notes, of A. Seippel's pioneering work in two volumes, *Rerum Normannicarum Fontes Arabici*, Oslo: Brøgger, 1896–1928. André Miquel's four volume *La géographie humaine du monde musulman jusqu'au milieu du 11e siècle*, Paris: Mouton, 1967–87, is absolutely indispensable. See also P.B. Golden, 'Rus', in *Encyclopaedia of Islam, New Edition* (hereafter *EI2*), vol. 8: 618–29 and

J.E. Montgomery, 'Vikings and Rus in Arabic Sources', in Y. Suleiman (ed.) *Living Islamic History: Studies in Honour of Carole Hillenbrand*, Edinburgh: Edinburgh University Press (forthcoming). A convenient overview of the principal features of geographical writings in Arabic and their study is P. Heck, *The Construction of Knowledge in Islamic Civilization*, Leiden: Brill, 2002: 94–145.

[?] The earliest reference to the Rus in an Arabic text is the phrase 'the mountain of the Rus from which the river *Drws* flows', which Novosel'tsev (according to Golden, 'Rus', 620) finds in the *Treatise on the Shape of the Earth*, a revision by the geodesist al-Khwarazmi (fl. 800–47) of the coordinates given in Ptolemy's *Geography*, designed to accompany the map which the Caliph al-Ma'mun (r. 813–33) commissioned. In the section of this work on 'the Islands in the Exterior Sea of the West', the coordinates for the islands of *Bwbarnya* (Ireland), *Thwly* (Thule), *Sqydya* (Scandia) and the all-male and all-female islands of *Amratws* (Amazones) are listed, among others. In the corresponding account of 'the Rivers and Water-sources beyond the Seventh Clime', Bwbarnya and Thwly are again mentioned. The enigmatic Suhrab, writing his *Treatise on the Marvels of the Seven Climes* about one century later, revised al-Khwarazmi's text and his coordinates, though he retains these mysterious islands and their rivers in his sections on 'the Islands in the Exterior Western and Northern Sea' and 'Knowledge of the Rivers and Water-sources beyond the Seventh Clime'. Neither author reveals any indication that these islands may be the home of the Majus or the Rus.

> *Bibliography:* Al-Khwarazmi, *Kitab Surat al-Ard*, H. von Mžik (ed.), Leipzig: Harrassowitz, 1927; Suhrab, *Kitab 'Aja'ib al-Aqalim al-Sab'a*, H. von Mžik (ed.), Wiesbaden: Harrassowitz, 1930; J. Vernet, 'Al-Khwarazmi', *EI2*, vol. 4: 1070–1.

[a] and [b] The earliest reference to the Rus in an Arabic text which is as good as fully extant is that contained in Ibn Khurradadhbih's *Treatise on the Highways and the Kingdoms*. Ibn Khurradadhbih, of Persian descent, was the head of intelligence and postal communications in an eastern province of the Islamic Empire (the Jibal) and was a prominent member of the Baghdad court famous for his expertise in music. His work (which is an account of the territories of the Caliphate dedicated to the ruler presented according to the Iranian tradition as the Just King) was written before AD 850 and then rewritten some thirty years later. It is available in two different recensions. The passage on the Rus is found in the recension which ante-dates AD 850, and provides two itineraries through which these 'Slav' traders with their furs and swords came to Muslim lands: via Spain or Francia and North Africa (their terrestrial route); and from the north (their maritime and riverine route). The former itinerary has been incorrectly assimilated by some scholars with the fabled and oft-disputed Jewish trading federation, the Radhanites (Ar. *Radhaniyya*). In the first case, the Rus are said to travel as far as al-Sin (Turko-China), while the destination of the second group is Baghdad. The author notes that this group claims to be Christians.

[b] In AD 903 a quarter of a century or so after the second recension of this work, Ibn al-Faqih of Hamadhan completed his *Treatise of the Regions*, a work which is extant today in two different abridgements of varying degrees of completeness. In a municipal eulogy, the author rings the praises of al-Rayy as the 'bride of the earth', the destination

of mercantile goods from all around the world: Armenia, Azerbaijan, Khurasan, Khazaria and Burjan, brought there by the 'merchants of the sea', that is, presumably the Jewish trading confederation of the Radhanites. To their merchandise is to be added that of the 'merchants of the Saqaliba', presumably the Rus of Ibn Khurradadhbih, who bring fox and beaver pelts from the furthermost reaches of Saqlaba to the Mediterranean or who sail down the 'river of the Khazar', the Volga, to the Caspian (here: the Khurasanian Sea). Their wares, having been sold in Jurjan, are then taken to al-Rayy. On account of their similarities, this report is thought to be one of Ibn al-Faqih's many borrowings (both avowed and unavowed) from his predecessor or at least to share a common source, though it is not clear whether the route used by these Saqaliba to reach the Mediterranean is identical with the Rus merchants of the earlier text. Their identification as Saqaliba may imply that Dnieper and Volga Rus, and not North Sea Majus, are meant.

Bibliography: Ibn Khurradadhbih: Arabic text (with a French trans.): *Kitab al-Masalik wa-l-Mamalik* (*Bibliotheca Geographorum Arabicorum*, vol. 6), M.J. de Goeje (ed.), Leiden: Brill, 1967 [1889]; C.E. Bosworth, 'Ebn Hordadbeh', *Encyclopaedia Iranica* (= *EIr*), vol. 8: 37–8; J.E. Montgomery, 'Serendipity, Resistance, and Multivalency: Ibn Khurradadhbih and his *Kitab al-Masalik wa-l-Mamalik*', in P. Kennedy (ed.), *On Fiction and Adab in Medieval Arabic Literature*, Wiesbaden: Harrassowitz, 2005: 177–230.

Ibn al-Faqih, *Mukhtasar Kitab al-Buldan* (*Bibliotheca Geographorum Arabicorum*, vol. 5), M.J. de Goeje (ed.), Leiden: Brill, 1967 [1885]; (Mashhad recension) *Kitab al-Buldan*, Y. al-Hadi (ed.), Beirut: 'Alam al-Kutub, 1996; French trans. by H. Massé, *Abrégé du livre des pays*, Damascus: Institut Français de Damas, 1973; A.B. Khalidov, 'Ebn al-Faqih Hamadani', *EIr*, vol. 8: 23–5.

[a = b] Al-Ya'qubi was a state bureaucrat who composed his *Treatise on the Regions* in Egypt in AD 891, a chorography in the Islamic administrative tradition. In his discussion of al-Andalus (Islamic Spain), he notes that Seville, which is situated 'on a mighty river, the river of Cordoba', was penetrated in the year 844 by 'al-Majus who are called al-Rus, who took captives, slaughtered, burnt and plundered'. This corroborates the identification of Ibn Khurradadhbih's first group of Rus as North-Sea Vikings.

Bibliography: Arabic text: *Kitab al-Buldan* (*Bibliotheca Geographorum Arabicorum*, vol. 7), M.J. de Goeje (ed.), Leiden: Brill, 1967 [1892]; French trans. by Gaston Wiet, *Les pays*, Cairo: Institut Français d'Archéologie Orientale, 1937; M.Q. Zaman, 'Al-Ya'kubi', *EI2*, vol. 11: 257–8; A. Melvinger, *Les premières incursions des Vikings en Occident d'après les sources arabes*, Uppsala: Almqvist & Wiksell, 1955.

[b] Ibn Rusta was a native of Isfahan who performed the Pilgrimage to Mecca in 903, the *terminus post quem* for his work *The Treatise of Precious Objects*. This work was thought by its first editor M.J. de Goeje to represent the seventh volume of a multi-volume work, variously identified as an encyclopedia in the tradition of the polythematic compositional style known in Arabic as *Adab* (i.e. edifying and diverting instruction). De Goeje based his conclusion on the phrase 'the seventh part' which is prominently scored out on the first folio of the earliest extant manuscript (British Library Add 23,378). There is no internal evidence to support the restoration of the phrase and it

is absent in the late copy kept in Cambridge University Library (Suppl. 1006). The question is important for understanding the nature of the information about the Rus provided by Ibn Rusta: if his work is an encyclopedia, it is most likely to be a (partial) compilation of earlier works, whence derives the notion that his report on the Rus is a quotation of an anterior, anonymous account (as his account of the Khazar seems to be). He was certainly aware of Ibn Khurradadhbih's composition, whom he criticises for his fanciful exaggerations, but the passage on the Rus should be connected with the Samanid geographical (and ultimately cosmographical) enterprise coordinated from the capital Bukhara. The account of the northern peoples in which it is set was certainly in part garnered from personal observation; and his description of Rus funerary practices are a better fit for the Middle Dnieper than the Volga Rus, i.e. the Rus' who were destined to transform Kiev from a trading outpost into an imperial capital.

Bibliography: Arabic text: *Kitab al-A'laq al-Nafisa VII* (*Bibliotheca Geographorum Arabicorum,* vol. 7), M.J. de Goeje (ed.), Leiden: Brill, 1967 [1892]; French trans. by Gaston Wiet, *Les Atours Précieux*, Cairo: La Société de Géographie d'Égypte, 1955: C.E. Bosworth, 'Ebn Rosta', *EIr*, vol. 8: 49–50; J.E. Montgomery, 'Ibn Rusta's Lack of "Eloquence", the Rus and Samanid Cosmography', *Edebiyât* 12 (2001): 73–93.

[b] Ibn Fadlan was a member of the Caliphal embassy dispatched from Baghdad on 21 June 921 by the Caliph al-Muqtadir (r. 908–32) in response to an epistolary petition requesting assistance from Almish ibn Yiltawar (Elteber), the king of the Volga Bulghar and the self-styled king of the Slavs (*Saqaliba*), who had converted to Islam. Note that, as with the phrase Khaqan of the Rus, the king of the Slavs need not himself be ethnically consanguineous with his subjects. The embassy reached Bulghar on the Volga–Kama confluence on 11 May 922. Little is known but much has been speculated about Ahmad ibn Fadlan ibn al-'Abbas ibn Rashid ibn Hammad. The Mashhad manuscript discovered by Zeki Validi Togan in 1923 tells us (though the passage is *not* by Ibn Fadlan himself) that he was the client of the commander and functionary Muhammad ibn Sulayman, presumably the successful officer who died in the siege of the city of al-Rayy in 919. In all probability Ibn Fadlan was himself a soldier of some sort, albeit a reasonably educated one. His function in the embassy (the exact composition of which is far from clear) was to read out the letters to the king of the Slavs in Volga Bulgharia and to ensure that appropriate gifts were rendered to him and to supervise the religious instructors, whose duties he was constrained to assume after they had abandoned the embassy en route. This led the geographer and lexicographer Yaqut (d. 1229), prior to 1923 our only source for Ibn Fadlan's work, to refer to him as a jurisconsult (*faqih*). I do not know what the authority is for identifying him as a Greek convert to Islam. The manuscript itself is lacunose: it ends with the description of the king of the Rus and a garbled section on the Khazar and there is no narrative of the return to Baghdad (though it is by no means certain that the return would have featured as part of the work). In the Arabic tradition, the work disappears without a trace, for about three centuries until the Mashhad manuscript was compiled in the thirteenth century, where it is juxtaposed with two epistolary travel accounts by Abu Dulaf al-Khazraji (fl. mid-tenth century), and a version of the *Kitab al-Masalik wa-al-Mamalik* of Ibn al-Faqih. Indeed, Yaqut, when travelling in the erstwhile Samanid domains, mentions a number of copies in circulation. The two late Persian 'translations'-cum-quotations

of Ibn Fadlan require further study. Too much has been made of the text's status as an 'official' chancellery report of the embassy, which is just wishful thinking. Among the several astonishing accounts of the various peoples through whom the embassy travelled, the passage on the Rus, and especially its weird account of a horrific cultic marriage and magnificently pyrotechnical ship burial, has been especially prized but it has not, despite repeated attempts, been satisfactorily explained. It may represent a 'snapshot' of the Viking Rus at a stage of the ethnogenesis which would lead to their emergence as the Rus' who created Russia, though most recently several resolutely Vikingist readings of these Rus have been offered. Curious texts often lead curious lives: the fictional 'completion' of Ibn Fadlan imagined by Michael Crichton as *Eaters of the Dead: The Manuscript of Ibn Fadlan, Relating his Experiences with the Northmen in AD 922* (New York: Alfred A. Knopf 1976), has been translated back into Arabic as a fortuitous discovery of the rest of the account, though Crichton's whimsy went undetected by the translator.

Bibliography: Facsimile of the Meshed MS: F. Sezgin, A. Jukhush, F. Neubauer and M. Amawi, *Majmū fi al-Jughrafīya*, Frankfurt: Publications of the Institute for the History of Arabic-Islamic Science, 1987; Arabic text: *Risalat Ibn Fadlan*, S. al-Dahhan (ed.), Damascus: Matbuʿat al-Majmaʿ al-ʿIlmi al-ʿArabi bi-Dimashq, 1959; English translations: J.E. McKeithen, 'The Risalah of Ibn Fadlan: an annotated trans. with introduction' (unpublished PhD diss.), Indiana University 1979; Richard Frye, *Ibn Fadlan's Journey to Russia. A Tenth Century Traveller from Baghdad to the Volga River*, Princeton: Markus Wiener, 2005; J.E. Montgomery, *Ibn Fadlan and the Caliphal Mission through Inner Asia to the North. Voyaging the Volga* (http://wonka-.hampshire.edu/abbasid studies/html/abbasids/culture/works.html); J.E. Montgomery, 'Ibn Fadlan', in J. Speake (ed.), *Literature of Travel and Exploration. An Encyclopedia*, London: Fitzroy Dearborn, 2003, vol. 2: 578–80; 'Ibn Fadlan and the Rusiyyah', *Journal of Arabic and Islamic Studies* 3 (2000): 1–25 (www.uib.no/jais); 'Pyrrhic scepticism and the conquest of disorder: prolegomenon to the study of Ibn Fadlan', in M. Maroth (ed.), *Problems in Arabic Literature*, Piliscsaba: The Avicenna Institute of Middle East Studies, 2004: 43–89; 'Travelling autopsies: Ibn Fadlan and the Bulghar', in *Middle Eastern Literatures*, 7.1 (January 2004): 4–32; T. Taylor, *The Buried Soul. How Humans Invented Death*, London and New York: The Fourth Estate, 2002; W. Duczko, *Viking Rus. Studies on the Presence of Scandinavians in Eastern Europe*, Leiden: Brill, 2004.

[b] According to the *Primary Chronicle* (or the *Chronicle of Nestor*), the Rus are said to live in that part of the world where the descendants of Japheth, son of Noah, are to be found. An earlier version of this genealogy is also found in the *Chronology Compiled on the Basis of Verification and Assent*, a world history completed in 937–8 by the Melkite patriarch of Alexandria Saʿid ibn al-Bitriq (Eutychius) (d. 940), who notes, in his account of the construction of the tower of Babel, that among the sons of Yafith (Japheth) are the inhabitants of the north: they include the Turk, the Pechenegs, Gog and Magog, the Khazar, the Alan, the Rum, the Rus, Daylam, the Bulghar, the Saqaliba and the Ifranja (Franks).

Bibliography: Arabic text: *Annales* (*Corpus Scriptorum Christianorum Orientalium: Scriptores Arabici*, series 3, vol. 6), L. Cheikho (ed.), Beirut: Matbaʿat al-Abaʾ al-Yasuʿiyyin, 1905; F. Micheau, ʿSaʿid b. al-Bitrik, *EI2*, vol. 8: 853–6.

{b} During the course of the tenth century an approach to the presentation of geographical knowledge (known today as 'the Atlas of Islam') emerged in the eastern province of Khurasan. It was initiated by the philosopher Abu Zayd al-Balkhi (d. 934) in his *Representations of the Climes* (no longer extant in its own right), was continued by al-Istakhri (fl. mid-tenth century) whose *Treatise of the Highways and the Kingdoms* is thought principally to be an extensive quotation of al-Balkhi's work, and found fullest expression in the maps and text of *The Representation of the Earth* by Ibn Hawqal (d. *c.* 988), which is itself frequently a verbatim quotation of al-Istakhri's work. From al-Istakhri's work (and Ibn Hawqal's version of it: IH), we learn that the Rus inhabit a territory between the Bulghar and the Saqaliba on the river Volga (IH); that the Khazar import from the Rus, the Bulghar and Kwyaba (Kiev) honey, wax and pelts (IH); that Kwyaba is not situated in any formal administrative province (*iqlim*) (not in IH); that al-Rus, like al-Khazar and al-Sarir, is the name of a kingdom, and not a town or a people (not in IH); that the Rus language differs from the language of the Khazar and the Burtas (IH); that there are three distinct groupings of the Rus: those of Kwyaba, closest to Bulghar (which it surpasses in size) (IH), where the king resides (not in IH); al-Slawiyya, with their capital in al-Sla, to the north; and al-Arthaniyya, with their capital in al-Artha, whence merchandise is brought to Kwyaba: an impenetrable region, its people xenophobic and secretive, whence lead, marten and black fox furs come (IH); that the Rus burn their dead (IH adds several other ethnic groups who have the same practice, among them the Indians); and that slave-girls willingly accompany their rich masters in cremation; that some shave their faces while others plait their beards like curried horse tails (IH adds or women's hair-braids); that they wear short qurtaqs, unlike the Khazar, Bulghar and Petchenegs who wear the full qurtaq; that they are very numerous and powerful, imposing land-taxes on the neighbouring territories of the Byzantines and 'Inner' (i.e. Volga) Bulghar. Ibn Hawqal updates this last item of information by describing the sorry plight of the Bulghar, Burtas and Khazar whose lands have been ravaged by the Rus. Al-Istakhri also refers to the 'Island of the Rusiyya' in the Caspian Sea (?).

Bibliography: Arabic text: Al-Istakhri, *Kitab al-Masalik wa-l-Mamalik*, M.J. ʿAbd al-Hini (ed.), Cairo: Dar al-Qalam, 1961; (*Bibliotheca Geographorum Arabicorum*, vol. 1), M.J. de Goeje (ed.), Leiden: Brill, 1967 [1870]; Ibn Hawqal, *Kitab Surat al-Ard* (*Bibliotheca Geographorum Arabicorum*, vol. 2), J.H. Kramers (ed.), Leiden: Brill, 1967 [1938]; French trans. by J.H. Kramers and G. Wiet, *Configuration de la terre*, Beirut and Paris: UNESCO, 1964; W.M. Watt, ʿAbu Zayd Balki, *EIr*, vol. 1: 399–400; O.G. Bolshakov, ʿEstakri, *EIr*, vol. 8: 646–7.

{a} {b} and {c} The geographical scientist al-Masʿudi (d. 956) took an especial interest in the riverine topography of the Caspian Sea, which he himself visited and about which he quizzed the merchants and travellers whom he met. This desire to revise the theories of his predecessors concerning whether the Caspian was land-locked or not led him to investigate the peoples of the Caspian. The results of this in large part empirically conducted research are an invaluable account of the Rus, second only to Ibn Fadlan's more famous (and more dramatic) description. Of al-Mas'udi's works, only two have survived: *The Meadows of Gold and Mines of Jewels*, written originally in 943 (only the author's revision of 947 has survived: it was revised by him once more in 956) (*MG*); *The Treatise of Reference and Supervision*, his last work written in 955–6, a reformulation of many of his earlier works (*RS*). A third work which has survived (and from which Seippel quotes two excerpts: *The Treatise of the Accounts of the Age*) attributed to al-Mas'udi is in fact a work of popular geography written in the eleventh century.

[b] According to al-Mas'udi, on the authority of Ptolemy and Marinus, the island of Thwly is the most northerly inhabited region of the earth (*RS*), and it forms part of Brytanya (*MG*), situated in a lake, the Mayts (the Sea of Azov). Lake Mayts is connected with the Bnts (i.e. the Pontus, the Black Sea), the sea of the Bulghar, the Rus (*RS*), the Petchenegs and the Bashjirt (*RS* and *MG*). The Bnts Sea stretches from the lands of al-Ladhqah (for which a plethora of suggestions exist: see Shboul, p. 174: it is orthographically cognate with Wdh'ana, and may be a scribal corruption of Kwyaba, Kiev), and is fed by the Don (Tnys), the river along which many of the descendants of Yafith b. Nuh (Japheth the son of Noah) live: they include the Franks, the pre-Islamic Andalusians and the Rus (*MG*). The Saqaliba in particular are the descendants of Madhay b. Yafith (*MG*) (see Sa'id ibn al-Bitriq above and Ibrahim ibn Ya'qub below). Al-Mas'udi suggests that some of his predecessors may have confused the Rus with the Khazar, because the Rus vessels use the River Atil as their sole means of access to the Caspian (*MG*). The Rus, along with the Bulghar, the Ifranja and the Saqaliba, inhabit the vicinities of al-Qabq Mountains (*RS*); the Rum (Byzantines) call them Rwsya, meaning 'red' (*RS*), and have built a settlement on the Black Sea and forts along the Hellespont to repulse the vessels of al-Kwdhkanah (another scribal corruption of al-Kwyabah, Kiev?) and other types of al-Rus (*RS* and *MG*); [c] in the 950s the Byzantines used the Rus who had settled in their lands to garrison the fortresses along their northern marches (*RS*).

According to the *MG*, the Rus have a sea which only they use (presumably the Bnts and its contiguous lake the Mayts); they are a mighty, pre-scriptural people with no revealed law, and do not recognise the sovereignty of any king; their merchants frequent the king of the (Volga) Bulghar; and they have a silver-mine in their territory; they are made up of many kinds, the most numerous among whom are al-Lwdh'ana who frequently sail to al-Andalus, Rome, Constantinople and Khazaria; around the year 912–13, the Rus raided the Caspian Sea with dramatic consequences for the geopolitical organisation of the region: al-Mas'udi notes that after the wholesale slaughter of these raiders on their return journey up the Volga, the Rus have not dared to return.

Al-Mas'udi also describes another group of Rus: the Saqaliba and the Rus who serve the Khazar king as slave-soldiers, living in the capital Atil on one bank of the Volga; they are a pre-scriptural people who cremate their dead, along with their horses, equipment and jewelery; a man's wife is burned along with his body, but he is not burned when she dies; if one of them dies a bachelor, he is married after his death; the women believe that by sacrificing themselves thus they will enter the Garden (i.e. Paradise); they have a judge in the Khazar imperial administration who judges in accordance with reason (and not revealed law); the king of the Khazar is not to be confused with the Khaqan (*MG*). This passage covers all of the principal features of the Rus as described by

~~Ibn Fadlan, though it is not even remotely indebted to Ibn Fadlan's account:~~ Ibn Fadlan does not make the observation concerning conjugal disparity in the matter of cremation. It explains the nature of the cultic marriage which Ibn Fadlan describes (the detail concerning Paradise is very telling), confirms his identification of the Rus with the Saqaliba in a very precise manner and explains why the Rus should have a Khaqan-like king. It strongly suggests, therefore, that Ibn Fadlan's Rus in Volga Bulgharia were slave-soldiers or mercenaries who originated from Khazaria and not from Gorodische or Ladoga or anywhere further to the north.

[a = b] Finally, al-Masʿudi conjectures that the people who raided al-Andalus before 912–13 and whom the inhabitants identified as the Majus, because of a chiliastic prophecy which claimed that the Majus would raid them from the Atlantic every 200 years, were in fact the Rus because they are the only people to sail the seas which are connected with the ʾQyans (i.e. the Greek Okeanos, also known as the Encircling Sea) (*MG*).

> *Bibliography*: Arabic text (*MG*): *Muruj al-Dhahab wa-Maʿadin al-Jawhar*, Ch. Pellat (ed.), Beirut: Manshurat al-Jamiʿa al-Lubnaniyya, 1966; French trans. by B. de Maynard, P. de Courteille and Ch. Pellat, *Les prairies d'or*, Paris: Société Asiatique, 1965; Arabic text (*RS*): *Kitab al-Tanbih wa-l-Ishraf* (*Bibliotheca Geographorum Arabi-corum*, vol. 8), M.J. de Goeje (ed.), Leiden: Brill, 1967 [1894]; French trans. by C. de Vaux, *Le livre de l'avertissement et de la révision*, Paris: Société Asiatique, 1897; A. Shboul, *Al-Masʿudi and his World*, London: Ithaca Press, 1979.

[a] Ibn al-Qutiyya (whose name indicates that his mother was a Goth), philologist and historian, died in Cordoba in 977. ~~His *Chronology of the Conquest of al-Andalus*, a celebration of the Muslim presence in Islamic Spain, gives an account of the raids of al-Majus in 844 during the Umayyad emirate of ʿAbd al-Rahman II (r. 822–52) and the measures taken to repulse them. After their retreat from Seville, the Majus are said by this source to betake themselves to Byzantium and to settle in Alexandria for four-teen years, when in 858 they launched an unsuccessful raid on Seville, on their way back from Alexandria~~ (as the chronicle seems to suggest).

> *Bibliography*: Arabic text with Spanish trans.: *Colección de obras arábigas de historia y geografía que publica la Real Academia de la Historia. Historia de la Conquista de España*, vol. 2, Madrid: Revista de Archvos, 1926; J. Bosch-Vila, ʿIbn al-Kutiyyaʾ, *EI2*, vol. 3: 844.

[c] In one of a series of panegyrics in honour of his patron the Hamdanid Sayf al-Dawla, emir of Aleppo, al-Mutanabbi (d. 965) ('the Shakespeare of the Arabs') celebrated his patron's victories over the Byzantine Domesticus Bardas Phocas at al-Hadath (in 953 and 954), taunting the Rum and the Rus with their despair at ever destroying the fortress.

> *Bibliography*: R. Blachère and Ch. Pellat, ʿal-Mutannabiʾ, *EI2*, vol. 7: 769–72; Th. Bianquis, ʿSayf al-Dawlaʾ, *EI2*, vol. 9: 103–110.

[a] and [b] The Spanish Jew Ibrahim ibn Yáqub al-Turtushi travelled across northern Europe *c.* 965–6. From the quotations of his work in later authors we learn that Ireland was the main residence of the Majus (incontrovertibly the North Sea Scandinavians and not a generic term for Normans and the maritime peoples of north-west Europe, as some have argued); that the Saqaliba were descended from Madhay ibn Yafith (see Saʿid ibn al-Bitriq and al-Masʿudi above); that the Rus and the Saqaliba travelled to Prague (Fraghah) from Krakow (Krakawa) with their wares; that the territory of Mshqh (?), king of the North, bordered on the Rus in the east and the Brws (Prussians) on the coast of the Encircling Sea (i.e. the Okeanos), whom the Rus reach by ships from the west; that west of the Rus (read al-Rus and not al-Brws) lies the 'Isle of Women' (see al-Khwarazmi, above: this rare connection between the Islands of the North and the Rus is reminiscent of al-Masʿudi's location of Thwliya in Lake Myts, next to the Sea of the Rus); that the Saqaliba trade by land and sea with the Rus and Constantinople; and that the Saqaliba had intermarried with various tribes of the north, including the Petchenegs, the Khazar and the Rus, to the point that Saqlab had become their common language.

> *Bibliography*: (partial) Arabic text: *Relatio Ibrahim ibn Yákub de Itinere Slavico quae traditur apud al-Bekri* (Monumenta Poloniae Historica, New Series, 1), Krakow, 1946; (partial) English trans. by D. Mishin, 'Ibrahim Ibn-Yáqub At-Turtushi's Account of the Slavs from the Middle of the Tenth Century', in M.B.L. Davis and M. Sebok (eds), *Annual of Medieval Studies at the CEU 1994–1995*, Budapest: CEU, 1996: 184–99; P. Charvát and J. Prosecky (eds), *Ibrahim ibn Yáqub at-Turtushi. Christianity, Islam and Judaism meet in East-Central Europe, c. 800–1300 A.D.: Proceedings of the International Colloquy, 25–29 April 1994*, Prague: Academy of Sciences of the Czech Republic, 1996.

[b] The *Hudud al-ʿAlam*, an anonymous geography written in Persian in 982 and dedicated to an emir of the Farighunid dynasty in northern Afghanistan, is clearly indebted to the tradition of the 'Atlas of Islam' for much of its arrangement and information, especially al-Istakhri. As far as the Rus are concerned, it does not (contrary to conventional wisdom) share a common source with Ibn Rusta (i.e. al-Jayhani). Its author describes the Rus, after the account of the Saqlab and before that of the 'Inner' (Volga) Bulghar, as bordered to the east by the Petchenegs, to the west by the Saqaliba and to the south by the river Rwtha (?). To the north lie the frozen wastes. The Rus are bellicose and ungovernable; their king is the Khaqan of the Rus; their lands are fertile and prosperous; they pay tithes annually to the Sultan; they revere their doctors (i.e. shamans); they are served by Saqlab slaves; they wear distinctive dress (pantaloons and a woollen cap); they have distinctive burial customs; and there are three principal settlements: Kuyaba, Slaba and Urtab.

> *Bibliography*: V. Minorsky, *Hudud al-ʿAlam*, C.E. Bosworth (ed.), Cambridge: Gibb Memorial Trust, 1982.

[a] and [b] The information on the Rus which Ibn Hawqal provides and which has no equivalent in al-Istakhri is significant. He notes that Volga Bulgharia had been sacked by the Rus in 969 and adds cryptically that 'they immediately advanced on Byzantium

and al-Andalus and then divided into two groups'; that they are a 'rabble without leadership' who inhabit the Atil between the Bulghar and the Saqaliba, and had formed an alliance with the Petchenegs who had migrated to the lands between the Khazar and Byzantium; that the Petchenegs were the military might of the Rus; and that (together) they were those who, of old, raided al-Andalus and Bardha'a (on the Caspian). In his discussion of al-Andalus, Ibn Hawqal continues in the same vein and notes that 'often vessels of the Rus, the Turk, and the Petchenegs, including, in their host, a force of Saqaliba and Bulghar' raided Islamic Spain (unsuccessfully) during the Umayyad caliphate of ʿAbd al-Rahman III (r. 912–61). His ultimate source here may be al-Masʿudi's *The Treatise of Reference and Supervision*, according to which furs are transported via the river of the Khazar (the Volga) to the northern lands of the Saqaliba, and from there to al-Ifranja (Francia) and al-Andalus, as these three territories are contiguous. This may be an attempt by Ibn Hawqal to account for the identification of the pre-Islamic inhabitants of al-Andalus as Saqaliba and for the two principal spheres of Rus activity (as *al-Majus* and *al-Rus*), and may involve a confusion of the Petcheneg Turks with the Oghuz Turks, Svyatoslav's allies in the destruction of Khazaria in 965, though the text is very specific in its identification of the Turkic tribes. The Rus alliance with the Petchenegs is elsewhere unattested (Minorsky's emendations [see Golden, 'Rus', 623] are untenable, the term *shawka* for 'military might', and not 'thorn', being attested of the Majus by Ibn al-Qutiyya, and of a tribe of the Saqaliba by Ibrahim b. Yaʿqub), while the raids on Bardha'a are mentioned in several places. Rus raids on their trading partners in Bulghar and Khazaran in the year 969 and on Samandar in Khazaria are also mentioned.

Bibliography: A.B. Khalidov, ʿEbn Hawqal', *EIr*, vol. 8: 27–8.

{b} and/or {c} It is a paradox, from our present perspective, that al-Muqaddasi (d. *c.* 990), the author of what is generally considered to be the definitive and most accomplished work of classical Arabic geography, *The Best Divisions for Knowledge of the Climes* (the summation and revision of the 'Atlas of Islam' project initiated by al-Balkhi) reveals but a perfunctory interest in the Rus. This is completely in keeping with the insouciance he displays towards non-Islamic lands. In his discussion of the town of Atil, subsumed within the region of Daylam, according to his general schematisation of the kingdom of Islam, he notes that the inhabitants of Atil had been raided by the caliph al-Maʾmun from Gurganj and, without specifying a date, he adds that he had heard that 'a military force from al-Rum (Byzantium) known as al-Rus had raided and conquered their territories', presumably referring to the Rus destruction of Khazaria by Svyatoslav in 965 (though this is said to have been achieved by the Rus and their allies, the Oghuz Turks).

Bibliography: Arabic text: *Ahsan al-Taqasim fi Maʿrifat al-Aqalim* (*Bibliotheca Geographorum Arabicorum*, vol. 3), M.J. de Goeje (ed.), Leiden: Brill, 1967 [1877]; English trans. by B.A. Collins, *The Best Divisions for Knowledge of the Regions*, Reading: Garnet, 2001; A. Miquel, ʿAl-Mukaddasi', *EI2*, vol. 7: 492–3.

{b} An example of writing on (birch-)bark is recorded in his *Catalogue* by the Baghdad bibliophile Ibn al-Nadim (d. 990) where it is reproduced along with specimens of

Chinese, Soghdian and northern Indian (Sindi) scripts. The author mentions that a trustworthy informant had been sent by one of the kings of Mount al-Qabq (the Caucasus) to the king of al-Rusiyya and had brought back to Ibn al-Nadim a sample of 'writing through incision on wood'.

Bibliography: Arabic text: *Al-Fihrist*, R. Tajaddud (ed.), Teheran: Maktabat Danishkah, 1971; English trans. by B. Dodge, *The Fihrist of al-Nadim*, New York: Columbia University Press, 1970; R. Sellheim and M. Zakeri, 'Al-Fehrest', *EIr*, vol. 9: 475–7.

[b] In his history, the *Experiences of the Communities*, the philosopher, bureaucrat and librarian Miskawayh (d. 1030) describes the Rus assault on Bardha'a in the year 943–4. His description is vivid and is accompanied by intriguing observations on the appearance of the Rus; their ethnic traits (ferocity, courage, willingness to die rather than be taken prisoner); their weaponry; their insatiable hunger for spoils; and their burial customs. Miskawayh notes that after the Rus had been driven from the town, the Muslims disturbed the Rus graves and retrieved the valuable swords which had been buried with the warriors. Miskawayh also describes how the Rus tried to coerce the inhabitants of Bardha'a into cooperation and how they were defeated because of a disease which spread when the Rus ate too much of the local fruit (diarrhoea?).

Bibliography: Arabic text with English trans.: *The Eclipse of the 'Abbasid Caliphate*, by A.H.F. Amedroz and D.S. Margoliouth, Oxford: Blackwell, 1921; M. Arkoun, 'Miskawayh', *EI2*, vol. 8: 143–4.

[d] In *The Book of Instruction in the Elements of the Art of Astrology*, the great scientist al-Biruni is the first author in Arabic to mention the Warank, a people who live in the northernmost reaches beyond the seventh clime. They have a sea, which is connected with the Encircling Sea (i.e. the Okeanos of the Greeks) and passes the lands of the Saqaliba and approaches the lands of the Bulghar (presumably Volga Bulgharia), and a capital, Balyd (which has been identified as Poland); it is not to be confused with the Bnts (the Black Sea) which flows past the lands of the Saqaliba and the Rus; that those who live in the seventh clime as far north as Thwly are more like wild beasts than men: this is where some Turkish tribes live, along with the Volga Bulghar, the Rus and the Saqaliba. Beyond the seventh clime, live the likes of the Warank, the Ysw (the people Ibn Fadlan refers to as Wysw: the Ves), and the Bardah (or possibly the Ywrah, the Ugrians?). The Warank and the Rus are also located on a map in the principal manuscript of the work.

Bibliography: Arabic text with English trans.: *The Book of Instruction in the Elements of the Art of Astrology*, R. Ramsay Wright (ed.), London: Luzac, 1934; C.E. Bosworth et al., 'Biruni', *EIr*, vol. 4: 274–87.

And so to our 'false' sources: the Andalusi Yahya ibn al-Hakam al-Ghazal (?) and al-Jayhani. The bibliographers credit three generations of al-Jayhanis with the composition of a work entitled the *Treatise on the Highways and the Kingdoms*, a work which al-Mas'udi and al-Muqaddasi say they consulted. The work was a family composition of a type not infrequent in the classical Arabo-Islamic tradition, one not designed originally for general use but for exposure to a strictly circumscribed group of readers. The al-Jayhani who began the book was vizier of the Samanid emirate in Bukhara and is presumably the individual visited by Ibn Fadlan on the embassy to Volga Bulgharia. Like the treatise of Ibn Rusta and the *Hudud al-'Alam*, the Jayhani treatise was probably an information-gathering exercise which included the tribes to the north and west of the Samanid realm. Only a few snippets of this work have been recovered, though scholars have been tempted to discern the Svengali-like influence of al-Jayhani in many geographical writings. The passage on the Rus contained in the work of al-Bakri is a conflation of the accounts of Ibn Rusta and al-Istakhri.

Bibliography: J.-C. Ducène, 'Al-Gayhani: fragments (Extraits du *K. al-masalik wa l-mamalik* d'al-Bakri)', *Der Islam* 75 (1998): 259–82; H. Göckenjan and I. Zimonyi, *Orientalische Berichte über die Völker Osteuropas und Zentralasiens im Mittelalter. Die Gayhani-Tradition*, Wiesbaden: Harrassowitz, 2001.

[a] Yahya ibn al-Hakam al-Ghazal is said to have been the envoy of the Andalusian caliph 'Abd al-Rahman the Second (r. 822–52) at the court of Theophilus of Byzantium and the Norsemen of Jutland or Ireland. Al-Ghazal (the Gazelle) of Jaen was a renowned poet. The story of his participation in the embassy to the emperor of Byzantium as told by Ibn Hayyan (d. 1076) is inspired by a descriptive passage in one of his love poems which describes the charms of a youth and his mother said to descend from Caesar. The account of his diplomatic mission to the north recounted by Ibn Dihya (d. 1235) is but a rehash of the embassy to Byzantium, fuelled by the fame of the Majus raids of the ninth century and has nothing to commend it beyond the charms of its fancy.

Bibliography: S.M. Pons-Sanz, 'Whom did al-Ghazal meet? An exchange of embassies between the Arabs from al-Andalus and the Vikings', *Saga-Book* 28 (2004): 5–28.

CHAPTER FORTY-ONE

THE NORTH ATLANTIC EXPANSION

——•◆•——

Gísli Sigurðsson

Our main source of information about the settlement of the North Atlantic (Figure 41.1) is Icelandic writings, supplemented by both archaeological evidence and writings of foreign historians. Strong doubts have sometimes been raised about the credibility of these texts which were first written in the twelfth and thirteenth centuries given that they describe events supposed to have taken place two to four centuries before: the Book of the Icelanders, the Book of Settlement and the sagas of Icelanders

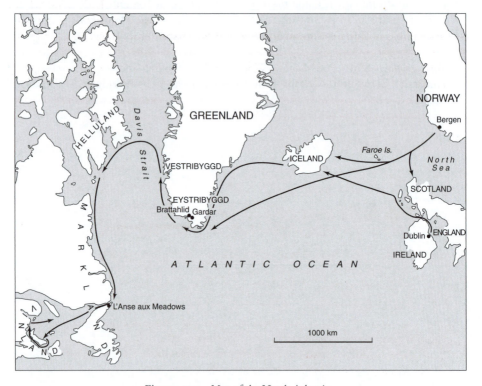

Figure 41.1   Map of the North Atlantic.

that deal specifically with the Icelanders and their adventures from the settlement of their country in the late ninth century until shortly after they had all been converted to Christianity in 999/1000. Greenland plays a vital role in these sagas as well as the voyages to Vinland, all in all filling five thick volumes (400–500 pages each) of printed text in the recent first complete English translation. The sagas about the people in the Faroe Islands and the Orkney earls fall outside this literary genre.

THE SETTLEMENT OF ICELAND IN BOOKS AND ARCHAEOLOGY

Christianity brought literacy to Iceland, and medieval historians who applied their knowledge of book-making to write about the past in Iceland sought all their informa- tion in oral stories and lore. Living oral traditions studied in many parts of the world have shown a tendency to adapt to contemporary reality, whereby facts change according to the context in which they are repeated even though people consider themselves to be preserving memories from the past. Despite this mutability, however, it is still possible to talk about a continuous tradition lasting several centuries and embodying essential truths which are archaeologically verifiable. For example, the written accounts are correct insofar as Iceland was rapidly settled after 870 by people from Norway and Britain, with several hundred large estates owned by chieftains and some 3,000 farms. Their dating can be ascertained from the 'Settlement Layer' of volcanic ash which covered a large part of the country following an eruption in 871 (± 1 year), as may be corroborated by ice-core samples from the Greenland glacier. Immediately above this layer of ash are relics of the oldest settlements in Iceland. The saga-writers and chron- iclers also knew that people left Iceland to settle in Greenland near the end of the tenth century. Likewise they knew stories about sailings to the continent of North America around 1000 – as was confirmed when relics left by people from Greenland and Iceland were found in the 1960s at L'Anse aux Meadows on the northern point of Newfound- land. The saga-writers knew that heathendom was the prevailing faith during the settlement of Iceland, and that Christianity was adopted by law around 1000. All this was known because people preserved the memories of these events, told stories about them and linked the names and lineage of certain individuals to specific incidents. It is an inherent feature of narrative art and the oral tradition that various details inevitably stray from the straight and narrow path of truth on their long journey through the centuries. Inconsistencies in detail, however, do not alter the overall picture that is presented and is well compatible with archaeological findings.

Ancient writings mention the island of Thule, far to the north. Although their reliability is questionable, the fact that the English cleric Bede (d. 735) mentions this island in his *History of the English Church and People* could show that he had already heard real accounts of voyages to Iceland by that time. Writing around 825, the Irish monk Dicuil mentions that thirty years previously priests had told him about the island Thule in the far north, where they stayed in summer when the nights were so bright they could look for lice on their shirts. And Ari the Learned mentions Irish hermits (*papar*) who were already in Iceland when the Viking settlement began.

There is no reason to doubt that Irish monks visited Iceland; Irish hermits commonly sought out islands where they would be left in peace. But these visitors would have been few in number and sporadic, and would not have had any significant impact on the development of the settlement of Iceland after 870. No confirmed relics left by the *papar* have been found in Iceland.

The first settlers of Iceland came from a variety of backgrounds. Different cultural elements from Norway and Britain met and merged in Iceland to create a society with no direct prototype in the old world. The majority of settlers could trace their roots to Norway and many came directly from there, especially the south and western regions, but it was also common among men and women of Scandinavian descent, who had been brought up in the Viking colonies in Britain, to leave there for Iceland once news of the settlement began to spread. With them were Gaelic people, from Ireland, Scotland and the Scottish isles, as either independent settlers, or the wives of Scandinavian men, or as slaves. Recent genetic studies suggest that among the first settlers in Iceland about 60% of the women were Gaelic and about 20% of the males.

Many settlers from Britain and Ireland are said to have made their homes in the Kjalarnes and Akranes districts of south-west Iceland. Some place names there are of Gaelic origin, while several correspond to names found in a small area on the eastern shore of the Isle of Lewis in the Hebrides. Thus place-name evidence supports the written accounts of the settlers' origins.

It is also noteworthy that many of the settlers coming from the British Isles seem to have had an eye for salmon fishing as many of the best salmon rivers in the country are associated with the settlement of either Gaelic people or Norsemen coming from that part of the world. Stories about the Irish hermit Ásólfr alskik also confirm that Irishmen were believed to be able to catch salmon in rivers, which were empty when Norsemen arrived – showing a difference between the two peoples.

Many of the settlers were Christian, even though Scandinavian culture and heathendom prevailed at first after the settlement. People of Scandinavian descent were in charge of administration as well as farming and other work, and provided the crafts and skills, household articles and domestic animals by which society was sustained. Slaves were given Scandinavian names and had to learn the language of their masters, so their culture was never dominant. Although it is impossible to assess the distribution of different religions in the ninth and tenth centuries, archaeological finds tell us that the Scandinavians in Shetland and Orkney had adopted Christianity long before the end of the tenth century when, according to written sources, Óláfr Tryggvason is supposed to have converted them. The people who left Breidafjord in Iceland with Eiríkr the Red in 985 or 986 and settled in Greenland have not left behind any signs of heathen burial customs in Greenland. The oldest graves in the cemetery of Þjóðhild's church are Christian and date from the end of the tenth century. This shows that Christianity was the living religion of these people, even though Óláfr Tryggvason is supposed to have sent Leifr Eiríksson the Lucky to convert them in 1000. Many of the settlers around Breiðafjörður originated from Britain and are likely to have brought the Christian faith to Iceland when they arrived.

More than 300 Viking Age graves have been found in Iceland at a total of 150 sites, none of them containing cremated remains. Few heathen graves have been discovered in west Iceland, where Christian settlers are mentioned most frequently in early sources. Considerable amounts of grave goods, weapons and even horses have been buried with the dead.

Egils saga describes Skallagrímr's burial mound as follows: 'Egil had a mound made on the edge of the promontory, where Skallagrim was laid to rest with his horse and weapons and tools. It is not mentioned whether any money was put into his tomb.' The saga of Gísli Súrsson also mentions a ship burial at the tomb of Þorgrímr, Gísli's brother-in-law, which shows that the saga-writers were familiar with ancient burial customs.

Details of Viking rites of worship are not known for certain. Sacrifices are frequently mentioned in written sources, and place names in Iceland testify to the presence of temples at large farm estates, where churches were later built. Special words are used in the texts for the site of blood sacrifices (*hǫrgr*), the sacrificial altar (*stallr* or *stalli*) and cups (*hlautbollar*) and sticks (*hlautteinar*) used in rites.

Scholars have strong doubts about the veracity of ancient descriptions of heathen temples and consider it more likely that rites were conducted in the open air, in groves, at sacred springs and near burial mounds, as was the case elsewhere in the Germanic cultural area. The oldest Christian laws in Scandinavia banned heathen rites in such places.

During the first phase of the Viking Age the Scandinavians started to develop a form of poetry which was unique in Germanic culture, but reflects some peculiarities of Old Irish poetry. The art of scaldic poetry flourished in Iceland and Icelandic poets soon monopolised all posts for professional court poets on the mainland.

At home the poets studied both mythology and poetic diction, and trained their skills in the complex prosody before they went abroad to try their luck at noble courts. The art of poetry is therefore one of the oldest export items from Iceland.

Lore and knowledge about the different kings accumulated at royal courts through poems composed about them. The names of the poets were associated with these poems, thus preserving their memory in connection with the kings and earls whose praise they had sung – such as in a list of poets from the Uppsala manuscript of Snorra Edda.

Early on in the settlement period, Iceland was divided into geographically delimited parishes (*hreppar*) and chieftaincies (*goðorð*), which did not depend on where people lived. The incumbents, the *goðar*, had both a religious and a secular administrative function. District assemblies were held regularly and when the General Assembly or Althing was established at Þingvellir in 930, chieftains started convening once a year to consult, make laws and pass judgements about disputes. Implementation of sentences was generally on the initiative of the *goðar* and/or parties to the disputes, not a central executive. Around that time Iceland's population would have been 10–20,000. A Lawspeaker, responsible for preserving the law, was chosen at the Althing for a term of three years. His function was to recite the law, which was preserved orally until the introduction of writing, and also to rule on disputes about interpretations of it.

Many of the sagas hinge on the way personal disputes overlapped with the legal authority of the *goðar* and Althing. Tension often develops between the ancient duty of revenge and the sentences imposed under the rule of law, leading to escalating feuds and bloody conflict which could only be appeased by the new attitudes ushered in by the Christian philosophy of peace and forgiveness.

At first, the chieftains and major farmers in Iceland sailed abroad and traded for themselves; the main imports would have been weapons, clothes, honey, wheat, timber, wax, tar and canvas. Gradually trading sites and harbours developed on main travel routes around the country. One of the largest trading posts in the Middle Ages was at Gasar on Eyjafjörður, which archaeological finds show had already begun to develop in the tenth century.

Gísli Sigurðsson

Studies of farm waste show that relatively more beef, pork and goat were eaten when Iceland was first settled, before mutton became progressively more dominant. Fish from the sea played an important part in the diet, at the coast and inland alike, and salmon and trout were commonly eaten in many parts of the country.

EIRÍKR THE RED AND THE ICELANDIC SETTLEMENT OF GREENLAND

Greenland was settled from Iceland towards the end of the tenth century. The settlement was led by Eiríkr the Red whose background is explained in two different ways in the sources. In the oldest source, Ari the Learned's Book of the Icelanders, he is said to be 'a man from Breiðafjǫrðr', which is Ari's customary way of describing people who are born in Iceland. He identifies people from Norway differently. In later sources, the Book of Settlement and sagas in which he appears, Eiríkr the Red is said to have hailed from Jæren in Norway and gone to Iceland with his father. The two men were said to have lived first at Drangar on Hornstrandir, after which Eiríkr moved to Dalir when he married Þjóðhildr, daughter of Jǫrund and Þorbjǫrg *knarrarbringa*, who was by then living with her second husband at Vatnshorn in Haukadalr according to the Book of Settlement. Þjóðhildr's paternal grandmother Bjǫrg was the sister of Helgi the Lean and the daughter of Eyvindr, whose wife was Rafarta, daughter of King Kjarval of Ireland. Thus Eiríkr and Þjóðhildr's son, Leifr the Lucky, the first explorer of the Vinland area west and south of Greenland, had Irish blood like so many other people in Dalir.

Archaeologist Guðmundur Ólafsson has excavated a 50 m^2 hall at Eiriksstaðir in Haukadalr which was lived in for a short while at the end of the tenth century. Two stages have been identified in its construction; the hall was abandoned shortly after it was completed. It was fitted in at the eastern boundary of Vatnshorn between two existing farms, and archaeological evidence about the history and location of the hall corroborates what the sagas say about Eiríkr the Red.

Many people of Gaelic descent lived around Breiðafjörður and undoubtedly knew the tales from Ireland about fantastic countries to the west, lands of plenty where the Irish envisaged beautiful women, endless wine, rivers full of huge salmon, and eternal bliss. These highly fanciful stories resemble Viking notions of Ódáinsvellir (the Plains of the Undead) insofar as those who go to this paradise have no way of returning to their earthly lives. Accounts in the Book of Settlement and later sources about Ari Másson and other people from Breiðafjörður reaching the 'Land of the White Men' could be an offshoot of these legends, and it is not improbable that such stories may have encouraged people to sail and search for land to the west. When Eiríkr the Red went to settle in Greenland, for example, a Christian from the Hebrides is mentioned as accompanying him. After people from Iceland and Greenland had travelled all the way to the North American mainland where the flora and climate resembled the descriptions in these legends, it is not unlikely that fact and fiction merged, leading people to believe they had actually reached the countries they were already familiar with from these accounts.

The oldest relics left in Greenland by people of Icelandic origin are at the site thought to be Brattahlíð, Eiríkr the Red and Þjóðhildr's farm in the Eastern Settlement. These are ruins of a little church in Viking Age style. Radiocarbon dating of skeletons from the cemetery there indicates that they are from near the end of the tenth century

566

(AD 976 ±50 years). Radiocarbon dating of the oldest relics in the Western Settlement, most recently from the 'Farm under the Sand', shows that people settled there during the first decades of the eleventh century.

All the graves found in Greenland are Christian ones and there is no evidence of heathen burial customs. In Brattahlíð, however, a whetstone has been found with a Þórr's hammer carved on it, which is the only evidence of the Viking paganism in Greenland.

Studies of core samples drilled from the Greenland icecap have provided important information about the climate on Earth and climatic fluctuations in the past. The successive strata of the Greenland icecap can be read year by year for indications about temperature, precipitation, volcanic eruptions in Iceland, etc., like a kind of natural chronicle.

Before the settlement of Iceland in 874 the climate was cold. When Raven-Flóki visited Iceland and supposedly coined its chilly name, he probably encountered a harsh winter with heavy sea ice off the West Fjords. It would have been about as cold then as at the end of the seventeenth century when Iceland was completely surrounded by sea ice, which stretched as far south as the Faroe Islands. From 860 onwards the temperature began to rise and in the tenth century it was somewhat warmer than today.

When Eiríkr the Red settled in Greenland in 985, a continuous period of favourable weather had prevailed for a whole century and vegetation there was at a historical peak. By the middle of the thirteenth century the climate had turned much colder, and there is a clear correspondence with the abandonment of the Western Settlement around 1350.

Archaeological evidence in Greenland clearly shows that people were able to live well there and did not lack food or suffer from any particular ailments. Clothes from Herjólfsnes cemetery testify to direct trading with Europe at a time when contact with Iceland had begun to dwindle sharply, and there are several indications of contact with the English in the fifteenth century.

Hypotheses have been put forward that the last Icelandic Greenlanders simply moved out of the country, perhaps returning to Iceland where there was plenty of land after the plague, or heading west to the North American mainland and Newfoundland where the English were fishing by then, or even that they were captured by the Portuguese and sold into slavery to work on sugar plantations in the Canary Islands – possible evidence of which is a Portuguese map from 1502, named after Alberto Cantino, with a Portuguese flag in Greenland's Eastern Settlement. The only written account of the end of the Scandinavian settlement in Greenland was recorded around 1750 by the son of missionary Hans Egede. A sorcerer from Siglufjǫrðr in the Eastern Settlement told him how the Scandinavians had been taken away by pirates while some had sailed southwards themselves and several women and children fled to join the Inuit. The time that elapsed between these events and their being written down was similar to that from the settlement of Iceland to Ari the Learned's Book of the Icelanders.

THE SAGAS AND THE VINLAND VOYAGES

The Vinland sagas contain the oldest written descriptions of the North American continent and tell the story of several voyages undertaken by people from Iceland and Greenland to North America around the year 1000: the first authentically documented voyages across the Atlantic Ocean in which the peoples of America and Europe met for the first time. Earlier references also exist which show that the Vinland voyages were well known in Iceland and on the European continent before these two sagas were actually written down. The sagas about Vinland have been the subject of many learned studies. Numerous contradictory theories about the voyages described in them have been put forward, with these sagas as their major source. These contradictions, however, can largely be explained by the different methodologies used by different generations of scholars. If we understand the basic problems behind the different answers and take into account the progress made in Vinland studies in the past decades, on the archaeological front and in the minute philological analysis of the texts and the major achievements in studies of oral storytelling traditions around the world, we can once again revisit the old problem of the whereabouts of Vinland.

As literary products the Vinland sagas fit well into the genre of forty sagas of Icelanders. It is important to be aware of the nature of the sagas as source material. They are not written accounts by eyewitnesses, but written accounts derived from oral tradition, containing stories and information (in the case of Vinland) about highly exceptional voyages which were undertaken more than 200 years earlier. Thus the stories about these voyages changed and were reshaped in oral tradition, which can have been kept alive not only by descendants of the people who took part in the voyages themselves but also others, in particular seafarers who were continually telling each other stories and exchanging information about faraway places, how to reach them and recognise the landscape.

When Anne and Helge Ingstad found L'Anse aux Meadows in Newfoundland in the early 1960s and identified it somewhat speculatively as Leifr's Vinland of the sagas, Helge Ingstad operated on the theory that the saga of Eiríkr the Red was a rewriting of the saga of the Greenlanders – which is no longer believed to have been the case. Of course it is difficult to argue against someone who has actually found something which proves that the Vikings were there, but it is clear from the L'Anse aux Meadows findings that this location was used as a staging post for exploring the lands further south. There the explorers would have repaired their ships and gathered strength before and after the crossing from Greenland. The northern tip of Newfoundland in L'Anse aux Meadows is hardly the sort of place which would create memories like the ones preserved about Vinland, the land of wine and grapes, in the sagas.

Among the artefacts found at L'Anse aux Meadows was a ringed pin with decorated head, of the type associated with Viking Dublin. Such pins have not been found in Norway, but they are common in Ireland, Britain and Denmark, and many have been found in Iceland as well. The ringed pin discovery supports the impression given by the Vinland sagas that the voyages to the New World were undertaken by people from Iceland who had strong family connections with Britain and Ireland. Not only was Leifr's maternal family of Irish background but the leaders of the major subsequent voyage, Þorfinnr Karlsefni and Guðríðr Þorbjarnardóttir, both had Gaelic blood in their veins.

Other objects from the site confirm the story as it is told in the sagas: a butternut and a butternut burl which has been cut with a metal tool prove that the Norse inhabitants went further south, at least to where the wild grapes and butternut trees grow, namely in the southern Gulf of St Lawrence, ship rivets show that ship repairs took place and a spindle whorl indicates the presence of women among the explorers of Vinland – all reflecting similar activities as are mentioned in the texts.

The overall picture of the voyages which emerges from the texts is reasonably clear: around the year 1000 people from Greenland and Iceland made several voyages along the eastern coast of North America, into the Gulf of St Lawrence, to Prince Edward Island and New Brunswick, and farther south. They built camps in more than one location in this area and spent from one winter to a few years in them. They came into contact with natives, partly on friendly trading terms, but also fought battles with them. Internal conflicts as well as attacks from the natives eventually led them to leave. After that it is unlikely that the Greenlanders ever ventured again as far south as the places mentioned in the sagas, but it is highly probable that they went to Labrador on a regular basis to gather wood, all through the Middle Ages – since in an Icelandic annal for 1347 we have a casual reference to such a trip, which seems to be regarded as commonplace.

On the Vinland voyages people are bound to have sought out the fruits and plants which Greenland lacks and they may even have tried to settle in some places, only to find the land already crowded with native people. So they ended up going back home and spent the rest of their lives boasting of the great time they had when they sailed all summer long across the seven seas, finding new and previously unheard-of lands . . . just as the Icelandic sagas tell us.

BIBLIOGRAPHY

Barrett, J.H. (ed.) (2003) *Contact, Continuity, and Collapse. The Norse Colonization of the North Atlantic* (Studies in the Early Middle Ages 5), Turnhout: Brepols.

Batey, C.E., Jesch, J. and Morris, Ch.D. (eds) (1993) *The Viking Age in Caithness, Orkney and the North Atlantic. Select Papers from the Proceedings of the Eleventh Viking Congress, Thurso and Kirkwall, 22 August–1 September 1989*, Edinburgh: Edinburgh University Press.

Fitzhugh, W.W. and Ward, E.I. (eds) (2000) *Vikings. The North Atlantic Saga*, Washington, DC: Smithsonian Institution Press.

Gísli Sigurðsson (1988) *Gaelic Influence in Iceland. Historical and Literary Contacts. A Survey of Research* (Studia Islandica 46), Reykjavík: Bókaútgáfa Menningarsjóðs.

—— (2004) *The Medieval Icelandic Saga and Oral Tradition. A Discourse on Method*, trans. N. Jones (Publications of the Milman Parry Collection of Oral Literature 2), Cambridge, MA: Harvard University Press.

Goodacre, S., Helgason, A., Nicholson, J., Southam, L., Ferguson, L., Hickey, E., Vega, E., Stefánsson, K., Ward, R. and Sykes, B. (2005) 'Genetic evidence for a family-based Scandinavian settlement of Shetland and Orkney during the Viking periods', *Heredity*, 95: 129–35.

Guðmundur Ólafsson (1998) *Eiríksstaðir í Haukadal. Fornleifarannsókn á skálarúst*, Reykjavík: Þjóðminjasafn Íslands.

Helgason, A., Nicholson, G., Stefánsson, K. and Donnelly, P. (2003) 'A reassessment of genetic diversity in Icelanders: strong evidence from multiple loci for relative homogeneity caused by genetic drift', *Annals of Human Genetics*, 67: 281–97.

Jónas Kristjánsson (2005) *The First Settler of the New World. The Vinland Expedition of Thorfinn Karlsefni*, Reykjavík: University of Iceland Press.

Jones, G. (1986) *The Norse Atlantic Saga. Being the Norse Voyages of Discovery and Settlement to Iceland, Greenland, and North America*, 2nd edn, Oxford: Oxford University Press.

Lewis-Simpson, Sh. (ed.) (2003) *Vínland Revisited. The Norse World at the Turn of the First Millennium. Selected Papers from the Viking Millennium International Symposium, 15–24 September 2000, Newfoundland and Labrador*, St John's: Historic Sites Association of Newfoundland and Labrador.

McEvoy, B. and Edwards, C.J. (2005) 'Human migration: reappraising the Viking image', *Heredity*, 95: 111–12.

Mortensen, A. and Arge, S.V. (eds) (2005) *Viking and Norse in the North Atlantic. Select Papers from the Proceedings of the Fourteenth Viking Congress, Tórshavn, 19–30 July 2001* (Annales Societatis scientiarum Faeroensis. Supplementum 44), Tórshavn: Føroya Fróðskaparfelag.

Wawn, A. and Thórunn Sigurðardóttir (eds) (2001) *Approaches to Vínland. A Conference on the Written and Archaeological Sources for the Norse Settlements in the North-Atlantic Region and Exploration of America. The Nordic House, Reykjavik 9–11 August 1999* (Sigurður Nordal Institute Studies 4), Reykjavík: Sigurður Nordal Institute.

CHAPTER FORTY-TWO

ICELAND

———— ◆•◆ ————

Jón Viðar Sigurðsson

Scholarly discussion about the Icelandic Free State (*c.* 930–1262/4) was up to 1970 focused on the political development (which also includes the debate about the relationship between the Church and chieftains), the introduction of Christianity, the source value of the Icelandic family sagas and finally the constitution of the Free State. Around 1970, under the influence of social history, cultural history and social anthropology, new topics were introduced in the discussion and there was renewed interest in some old ones, such as the settlement of disputes, women's and gender history, political culture and the role of honour. The discussion about the source value of the Icelandic family sagas continued, but now from a social anthropological perspective (Jón Viðar Sigurðsson 2000).

SETTLEMENT PERIOD

Until recently little attention has been paid to the settlement period (*c.* 870–930), but recent archaeological excavations will undeniably throw a new light on this period. There is general agreement among scholars that Ari fróði's ('the learned') dating of the first settlement to *c.* 874 is reliable. Just before the first settlers arrived there was a volcanic eruption in Iceland and the ash from this eruption has been dated in Greenland's glacier to 872 ±2, and according to the results from the archaeological excavations in Iceland there are no traces of a settlement below the ash layer from this volcanic eruption (Árný E. Sveinbjörnsdóttir *et al.* 2004).

According to the sagas most of the settlers came from Norway and the British Isles, and many of them brought slaves from the Irish Sea area with them. Recent DNA studies have confirmed this mixture of people (Agnar Helgason *et al.* 2001). *Landnámabók* (the Book of Settlement) lists *c.* 415 settlers: 404 men and 13 women (Haraldur Matthíasson 1982); it was this group that was in charge of the settlement process. The majority of the settlers were either wealthy farmers or chieftains; what most of them had in common was that they owned ships which were large enough to transport people and livestock to Iceland. The period between *c.* 870–930 is usually labelled *landnámsöld*, 'the settlement period'. It is Ari's statement in *Íslendingabók*, that all land was claimed (*albyggt*) within sixty winters 'so that there was no further settlement made

571

afterwards', together with the foundation of a general assembly for the whole country *c.* 930 that marks the end of the settlement period.

The settlers brought with them domestic animals, cattle, sheep, horses, goats and pigs, but it took some time to build up a stock of domestic animals that was large enough to sustain the population. In the earliest phase of the settlement, therefore, fish was the staple food. Consequently we find the highest number of settlers in the Western Quarter and along the coast. Inner regions became more important than the costal areas only after the stock of domestic animals became large enough.

The single farm was the main feature of the settlement; there were no villages or towns developed in medieval Iceland. In the earliest phase of the settlement, settlers experimented with the location of their farms, so many farms were moved or were abandoned completely. It was not until the twelfth century that a settlement pattern which has dominated the Icelandic landscape to modern times was established. The number of farms in the fourteenth century did not exceed 6,000 (Björn Teitsson and Magnús Stefánsson 1972).

The main emphasis after the initial settlement period was on animal husbandry and some agriculture, with fishing in rivers, lakes and the sea as an additional food source. The cultivation of crops, especially barley, took place at some major farms all across the island in the early and high Middle Ages. Most of the production was consumed domestically. Self-sufficiency was the goal for most households. Not all farms could produce all the resources they needed, such as iron. We can therefore assume that some farms specialised in the production of certain products (Jón Jóhannesson 1956; Kristján Eldjárn 1959; Sturla Friðriksson 1982; Árný E. Sveinbjörnsdóttir and Sigfús J. Johnsen 1996).

Population growth was an important underlying factor for the development of this new society. Nothing accurate is known about the number of emigrants in the settlement period, but a qualified guess is 10,000 (Björn Þorsteinsson 1966). If we accept this number and argue that the growth of the population in Iceland was the same as elsewhere in western Europe in the period *c.* 900–1300 – that is, a duplication every *c.* 200 years – the number of inhabitants was 20,000 *c.* 1100 and 40,000 *c.* 1300 (Björn Teitsson and Magnús Stefánsson 1972).

THE CONSTITUTION

The settlers were familiar with assembly organisations and according to tradition assemblies were established in Þórsnes and Kjalarnes before the national assembly at Þingvellir was founded *c.* 930. There is agreement among most scholars that the main elements of the constitution of the Free State, which only the *Konungsbók* version of *Grágás* (*c.* 1250) describes, were introduced at the first assembly meeting (i.e. Maurer 1874; Sigurður Nordal 1942; Jón Jóhannesson 1956). At the time the General Assembly (*alþing*) was established there were thirty-six chieftaincies (*goðorð*); later, in *c.* 965, when the country was divided into quarters and the quarter courts were introduced, three new chieftaincies were established in the Northern Quarter. In order to maintain the balance between the quarters, the Eastern, Southern and Western Quarters each got three 'additional' chieftains (sg. *goði*), who were nominated by the nine chieftains in each of these three quarters. The total number of chieftaincies represented at the General Assembly was thus forty-eight, or twelve from each quarter.

Within each quarter, three chieftains would hold a spring assembly (*várþing*) together, so that the Western, Southern and Eastern Quarters had three such assemblies each, while the Northern Quarter had four.

The court system consisted of the spring assembly courts (*várþingsdómar*), the quarter courts and the Fifth Court (*fimtardómr*), which was the highest court of the Commonwealth, established around 1005.

All the 48 chieftains (*goðar*) sat in the Law Council (*lǫgrétta*), with two assembly men each to advise them. The chieftains and their chosen men thus made up 144 of the members of the Law Council. In addition, the Lawspeaker (*lǫgsǫgumaðr*) and, later, the country's two bishops brought the total to 147, but only the 48 chieftains had the right to vote. The Law Council had three particular tasks: to make new laws, to interpret the laws when there was disagreement about them and to decide on various kinds of exemption from the laws.

POLITICAL DEVELOPMENT

There are two main opinions in the discussion about the political development in Iceland in the period *c.* 930–1120. The first one, which has dominated the discussion for more than a century, is based on the view that it is the constitutional paragraphs in *Grágás*, and not the family sagas, which give the most coherent picture of the political system in the period *c.* 930–1120, that is that the number of chieftaincies were thirty-six to thirty-nine. As a result, the history of the Free State in this period has for the most part been a constitutional history (i.e. Jón Jóhannesson 1956). The second opinion rejects *Grágás* as a source for the political system, and relies on the 'picture' given by the family sagas. According to this view there was at no time a fixed number of chieftains, and moreover that their numbers reduced from about fifty to sixty to about twenty in the period *c.* 930–1120 (Jón Viðar Sigurðsson 1999).

There is however no disagreement among scholars over the main features of political development *c.* 1120–1262/4. This period is characterised by the concentration of power: in *c.* 1200 seven families controlled most of the country. By 1220 it is possible to divide the country into *ríki*, small domains with fairly fixed boundaries (Jón Jóhannesson 1956; Jón Viðar Sigurðsson 1999).

After 1220 the Norwegian monarchy started to interfere in the political development of Iceland, and the king's involvement resulted in the fall of the Free State. After 1238, both of Iceland's bishops were appointed from Norway, and served partly as agents of the king's policies. In the power struggle, Icelandic chieftains considered it advantageous to become a member of the king's *hirð* ('body of retainers'). The chieftains' positions in Iceland were strengthened by this, but they had to pay for this support by giving their *goðorð*, or their permission to administrate the *goðorð*, to the king. Thus, by *c.* 1250 the king had managed to acquire control over all of the *goðorð* in the country except in the Eastern Quarter, which were acquired in 1264. Having taken control over the *goðorð* the king started to appoint his own governors and arguably became the country's leading 'chieftain' (Berlin 1909; Jón Viðar Sigurðsson 1999). Once this process had started, it was only a matter of time before Iceland became part of the Norwegian kingdom, and in 1262/4 the leading persons in the country swore fealty to the king.

If we return now to the constitution it is worth mentioning that most scholars disregard how the political development eventually influenced it and the fact that most of the information in the sagas does not support the type of constitution described in *Grágás*. The spring assemblies were never held regularly, and the number of chieftaincies in the family sagas is significantly higher than is assumed in *Grágás*, and in the contemporary sagas it is significantly lower (Jón Viðar Sigurðsson 1999).

SOCIAL HISTORY

Around 1970 new topics under the influence of cultural history, social history and social anthropology, and inspiration from the works of Michael Ivanovich Steblin Kamenskij (1973), Aaron Ja. Gurevich (1968) and Victor Turner (1971), for example, were introduced into the discussion of Iceland in the Free State period. The most important consequences of these changes were that women were introduced into the history of the Free State. Especially important were the works of Anna Sigurðardóttir (1985, 1988) and Jenny Jochens (1995, 1996), dealing with almost all aspects of women's lives in this period.

Feuds and settlement of disputes now became important topics. The majority of disputes were settled through arbitration or direct negotiation. The decision was usually acceptable to all parties involved and the likelihood of the case ending there was good. Arbitration and negotiation were the most effective methods of resolving conflicts because the Icelandic Free State had no central authority that could implement sentences. The arbitrators had to find a long-term solution that would satisfy all the parties involved so that they could withdraw from the case with their honour intact. If the conflicting parties did not accept the arbitration decision, they would offend the arbitrators and would not be able to rely on their support in future cases. The same applied to the judges. They had to find a suitable solution or they would insult one of the parties involved and risk a similar decision if their roles were ever reversed (Heusler 1911, 1912; Lúðvík Ingvarsson 1970; Miller 1990; Jón Viðar Sigurðsson 1999).

An important consequence of the shift around 1970 was that the source value of the Icelandic family sagas was emphasised. Scholars now started to use the sagas as sources for the period from the middle of the twelfth to the end of the thirteenth century (e.g. Miller 1990). But one major oversight was that the contemporary sagas, which deal with the Icelandic society in the twelfth and thirteenth centuries, were forgotten in the heat of the debate. There is a big difference in how these two different types of sources depict the society; for example, in the Icelandic family sagas there are about fifty to sixty named chieftains, but only about six to seven *c.* 1220 in the contemporary sagas. This approach meant that the picture of the social development was more static than it was in reality.

There is little doubt that the most important social institution in Iceland in the Middle Ages was the commune (*hreppr*), but scholarly discussion has neglected it. The communes were independent geographical units led by five commune leaders, elected for one year at a time (Jón Jóhannesson 1956; Lýður Björnsson 1972; Stein-Wilkeshuis 1987). Little is known about when the system of communes was introduced, but its organisation had reached an advanced stage by 1096/7, when tithes were introduced; the communes then received the right to distribute the tithe revenue intended for the poor. In other European countries the Church itself distributed this part of the tithes.

In the Free State, each family was primarily responsible for looking after its own members. If it was unable to do so, or if there were no relatives, this duty fell on the communes, the spring assembly parish, the Quarters or the country as a whole. It was one of the main duties of the communes to fulfil this task. The leaders of the communes had to distribute the tithes and food to the poor, and organise their movements round the commune.

The communes' other main task was to arrange mutual insurance between the farmers. They had to jointly pay half the compensation needed for two types of losses: if a farmer lost more than a quarter of his cattle and horses or if parts of his farm, dwelling, outhouse for washing and baking, or food store burned down. This compensation was not to be paid out more than three times to the same farmer and should never constitute more than 1 per cent of the wealth of each farmer, even if it did not cover half the damage.

The chieftains had a strong influence over the communes in the Free State period, but when Iceland became part of the Norwegian kingdom, and especially after the introduction of the legal codes *Járnsíða* in 1271 and *Jónsbók* in 1281, the relationship between the chieftains and the farmers changed significantly. The chieftains had been obliged to defend and assist their supporters, but as the king's servants they had to prosecute and punish those who had formerly been their friends. The chieftains' power over the communes was reduced, and it can be argued that it was after *c.* 1271 that the communes took on the function they retained for the rest of the Middle Ages (Jón Viðar Sigurðsson 1995).

RELIGION

One of the major themes in Icelandic history is the introduction of Christianity in the year 999 or 1000, and especially the peaceful nature of the process, but also how this change affected the power of the chieftains. The Lawspeaker Þorgeirr Ljósvetningagoði has been the focal point for much discussion, and his contribution towards the peaceful outcome of the conflict between the heathens and Christians has been underlined (Maurer 1855–6; Jón Hnefill Aðalsteinsson 1999; Hjalti Hugason 2000).

Around the middle of the nineteenth century the German legal historian Konrad Maurer presented his theory about the sacred origins of the chieftaincy system. He maintained that these chieftains, like other Germanic chieftains, were guardians of religion, but that this function was of secondary importance to their secular duties (Maurer 1874). The strongest argument against Maurer's thesis is the assertion that it would have been impossible for the chieftaincy system to survive the introduction of Christianity at the General Assembly of 999/1000 if it had been based on sacred–heathen foundations (Ólafur Lárusson 1960: 363–4). However, it has been argued that it was because of the chieftains' control of the old religion that it was possible to introduce the new one via a resolution at the General Assembly. Discussion about the introduction of Christianity has also failed to take into consideration the chieftains' leading role in society, or the bonds that tied them and their supporters (*vinir*) together. In this kind of relationship, the chieftains were dominant and the farmers had to accept their decisions (Jón Viðar Sigurðsson 1999).

In 1056 the bishopric of Skálholt was founded, and in 1106 the see of Hólar, which included the Northern Quarter, was established. Until 1104, Iceland and the rest of Scandinavia belonged to the archdiocese of Hamburg–Bremen, and from 1104 to 1152–3 that of Lund. In 1152–3 the archbishopric in Niðarós, which included Norway and the Norse settlement on the islands in the west, was founded. An important factor behind the foundation of the archbishopric in Niðarós was the church reform movement. The aim of the reform was to free the Church from secular influence and place it under the leadership of the pope.

As soon as Iceland became part of the archbishopric in Niðarós, the archbishop introduced the universal church demands in Iceland. But to do that successfully he needed support from the Icelandic bishops. He got support from Þorlákur Þórhallsson who became bishop in Skálholt in 1178. But after a dispute with Jón Loftsson, the country's leading chieftain, Þorlákr relinquished his claims, and did not raise them again. The main reason for this shift in Þorlákr's policy was a change in the political situation in Norway. Archbishop Eysteinn was, due to conflicts with the king, forced to leave Norway in 1180. Without the archbishop's support there was little Þorlákur could do on his own and he was therefore forced to concede (Jón Jóhannesson 1956; Gunnar Karlsson 2000; Magnús Stefánsson 2000).

After the death of Bishop Þorlákur in 1193, the chieftains in the Skálholt bishopric elected Páll Jónsson as his successor. He was a chieftain from the powerful Oddaverja family, and by choosing Páll as a bishop the chieftains in the Skálholt see could prevent the archbishop from intervening in ecclesiastical matters in the bishopric.

The chieftains in the Hólar see thought that they had done this when they elected Guðmundr Arason as a bishop in Hólar in 1201. But this was not the case. Guðmundr instead became a strong advocate for the church reform programme. Two issues were at the heart of the disputes between Bishop Guðmundr and the chieftains. The first one was on the administration of the bishopric at Hólar, where Guðmundr wanted to be more generous to poor people than the chieftain liked. The second and main conflict between Guðmundr and the chieftains concerned the judicial status of clergymen, whether they should obey church law or the secular law of the country. These conflicts lasted for decades. It was not until 1234 that Guðmundr was left in peace at Hólar. The outcome of this dispute was a kind of status quo; the Church gained no new rights.

Both bishops in Iceland died in 1237. As usual, the chieftains in Iceland elected candidates and sent them to Niðarós. This time the archbishop rejected the Icelandic candidates, and appointed two Norwegians as bishops in Iceland. After the archbishop had gained control of the election of bishops in Iceland, it became easier for him to influence the ecclesiastical and political developments in the country. Consequently over the course of the next fifty years he managed to transform the Icelandic Church to a bishop's Church which better suited the general ecclesiastical structure that was created in Europe in the eleventh, twelfth and thirteenth centuries (Magnús Stefánsson 1978; Gunnar F. Guðmundsson 2000).

BIBLIOGRAPHY

Agnar Helgason *et al.* (2001) 'mtDNA and the islands of the North Atlantic: estimating the proportions of Norse and Gaelic ancestry', *American Journal of Human Genetics*, 68: 723–37.

Anna Sigurðardóttir (1985) *Vinna kvenna á Íslandi í 1100 ár* (Úr veröld kvenna 2), Reykjavík: Kvennasögusafn Íslands.

—— (1988) *Allt hafði annan róm áður í páfadóm. Nunnuklaustrin tvö á Íslandi á miðöldum og brot úr kristnisögu* (Úr veröld kvenna 3), Reykjavík: Kvennasögusafn Íslands.

Árný E. Sveinbjörnsdóttir *et al.* (2004) '14C dating of the settlement of Iceland', *Radiocarbon*, 46(1): 387–94.

Árný E. Sveinbjörnsdóttir and Sigfús J. Johnsen (1996) 'Ískjarnar. Skuggsjá liðinna alda', in Guðrún Ása Grímsdóttir (ed.) *Um landnám á Íslandi. Fjórtán erindi* (Ráðstefnurit 5), Reykjavík: Vísindafélag íslendinga.

Berlin, K. (1909) *Islands statsretlige stilling efter fristatstidens ophør*, Copenhagen: Salomonsens Boghandel.

Björn Teitsson and Magnús Stefánsson (1972) 'Um rannsóknir á íslenzkri byggðarsögu tímabil-sins fyrir 1700', *Saga*, 10: 134–78.

Björn Þorsteinsson (1966) *Ný Íslandssaga. Þjóðveldisöld*, Reykjavík: Heimskringla.

Gunnar F. Guðmundsson (2000) *Íslenskt samfélag og Rómakirkja* (Kristni á Íslandi 2), Reykjavík: Alþingi.

Gunnar Karlsson (2000) *Iceland's 1100 Years. History of a Marginal Society*, London: Hurst.

Gurevich, A.Ja. (1968) 'Wealth and gift-bestowal among the ancient Scandinavians', *Scandinavica*, 7: 126–38.

Haraldur Matthíasson (1982) *Landið og landnáma*, 2 vols, Reykjavík: Örn og Örlygur.

Heusler, A. (1911) *Das Strafrecht der Isländersagas*, Leipzig: Dunker & Humblot.

—— (1912) *Zum isländischen Fehdewesen in der Sturlungenzeit* (Abhandlungen der Königlich Preussischen Akademie der Wissenschaften. Philosophisch-historische Classe 4), Berlin: Königliche Akademie der Wissenschaften.

Hjalti Hugason (2000) *Frumkristni og upphaf kirkju* (Kristni á Íslandi 1), Reykjavík: Alþingi

Jochens, J. (1995) *Women in Old Norse Society*, Ithaca, NY: Cornell University Press.

—— (1996) *Old Norse Images of Women* (The Middle Ages), Philadelphia: University of Pennsylvania Press.

Jón Hnefill Aðalsteinsson (1999) *Under the Cloak. A Pagan Ritual Turning Point in the Conversion of Iceland*, 2nd edn, Reykjavík: Háskólaútgáfan.

Jón Jóhannesson (1956) *Íslendinga saga*, vol. 1: *Þjóðveldisöld*, Reykjavík: Almenna bókafélagið.

Jón Viðar Sigurðsson (1995) 'The Icelandic aristocracy after the fall of the Free State', *Scandinavian Journal of History*, 20: 153–66.

—— (1999) *Chieftains and Power in the Icelandic Commonwealth*, trans. J. Lundskær-Nielsen (The Viking Collection 12), Odense: Odense University Press.

—— (2000) 'Allir sem sjá líta þó ekki jafn á: sagnaritun um íslenskar miðaldir fram um 1300', *Saga*, 38: 33–57.

Kristján Eldjárn (1959) *Stakir steinar. Tólf minjaþættir*, Akureyri: Bókutgáfan Norður.

Lúðvík Ingvarsson (1970) *Refsingar á Íslandi á þjóðveldistímanum*, Reykjavík: Menningarsjóður.

Lýður Björnsson (1972) *Saga sveitarstjórnar á Íslandi*, vol. 1, Reykjavík: Almenna bókafélagið.

Magnús Stefánsson (1978) 'Frá goðakirkju til biskupskirkju', in Sigurður Líndal (ed.) *Saga Íslands*, vol. 3, Reykjavík: Hið íslenzka bókmenntafélag.

—— (2000) *Staðir og staðamál. Studier i islandske egenkirkelige og beneficialrettslige forhold i middelalderen*, vol. 1 (Skrifter fra Historisk institutt, Universitetet i Bergen 4), Bergen: Historisk institutt, Universitetet i Bergen.

Maurer, K. (1855–6) *Die Bekehrung des norwegischen Stammes zum Christenthume in ihrem geschichtlichen Verlaufe quellemäßig geschildert*, 2 vols, Munich: Christian Kaiser.

—— (1874) *Island von seiner ersten Entdeckung bis zum Untergange des Freistaats*, Munich: no publ.

Miller, W.I. (1990) *Bloodtaking and Peacemaking. Feud, Law, and Society in Saga Iceland*, Chicago: University of Chicago Press

Ólafur Lárusson (1960) 'Goði og Goðorð', in *KL* 5: 363–6

Sigurður Nordal (1942) *Íslenzk menning*, Reykjavík: Mál og menning.

Steblin Kamenskij, M.I. (1973) *The Saga Mind*, trans. K.H. Ober, Odense: Odense University Press.

Stein-Wilkeshuis, M.W. (1987) 'Common land tenure in medieval Iceland', *Recueils de la société Jean Bodin*, 44: 575–85.

Sturla Friðriksson (1982) 'Línakrar á Bergþórshvoli', in Helga Þórarinsdóttir *et al.* (eds) *Eldur er í Norðri. Afmælisrit helgað Sigurði Þórarinssyni sjötugum 8. janúar 1982*, Reykjavík: Sögufélag.

Turner, V.W. (1971) 'An anthropological approach to the Icelandic Saga', in T.O. Beidelman (ed.) *The Translation of Culture. Essays to E.E. Evans-Pitchard*, London: Tavistock.

THE FAROE ISLANDS

———•◆•———

Símun V. Arge

The Faroe Islands are located in the North Atlantic at the latitudes of 62°N and 7°W almost midway between Norway, Iceland and Scotland; the closest neighbour is Shetland, 300 km to the south-east. The Faroes consist of eighteen islands, separated by narrow fjords and sounds, seventeen of which are inhabited. The islands are approximately 14,000 km². The longest distance from north to south is 118 km, and east to west 79 km. The climate can be described as wet, windy and relatively mild, which is caused by the island's position within the Gulf Stream.

When the first settlers arrived at the islands in the ninth century they were met with a natural vegetation characterised by grasses, sedges and ericaceous shrubs. Woodland – small populations of juniper and tree birch – seem to have been of minor importance. In other words, the landscape has been rather similar to what we see today (Lawson *et al.* 2005). The topography of the islands has limited the settlements mainly to the coastal strip along the sounds and by the fjords.

SETTLEMENT

The first professional archaeological excavation in the Faroes took place as late as 1941. Through this excavation, remains from the islands' early history were brought to light for the very first time. Ever since, this site, located in the village of Kvívík on Streymoy, has been regarded as the classic example of a Faroese Viking farm: a longhouse (the dwelling), *c.* 20 m long with a central hearth and earthen benches along the long curved side walls made of stone and earth; the roof was carried on two rows of posts. Beside the dwelling there was a shorter house, which in a modified version was built as a byre, capable of holding about a dozen cattle in the winter. Stalls were allocated along each side wall and a drain ran down the centre of the structure. A recent reanalysis of the excavation has altered this interpretation (Dahl 1951; Matras 2005). Furthermore, the abundance of artefacts found told about the daily life at the farm and about links to the outside world.

Characteristic for the investigation at Kvívík was that most attention was paid to the oldest phases on the site – the Viking Age. That's why layers from younger periods were not really taken into account. In Kvívík it was obvious that the Viking layers were capped by layers from a medieval settlement on the same site. Because of the excavation method, medieval artefacts were found mixed with those from the Viking Age.

The picture we see here is of interest and a good example of the settlement-historical development in the Faroes. Investigations regarding the settlement history during recent years have shown that the localisation of settlements in the Faroes has been fairly stationary: if special circumstances did not cause your removal you stayed where you had settled in the *landnám* ('colonisation') period. The settlement sites where the actual core of the farm was found was a specially defined area called *heimrúst*. Usually this settlement core was separated from the outlying infield by a stone fence and a *geil*, a stone-walled cattle path, that connected the settlement core with the outfield (Arge 2005). Since the excavations in Kvívík, Viking settlement remains have been mapped and investigated around the islands both within the infields and in the outfields as well (Arge *et al.* 2005).

RECENT INVESTIGATIONS AND RESEARCH

Á Toftanesi, Leirvík

It was not until the excavation of the site of Toftanes (Figure 42.1.1), during 1982–7, that a Viking Age farm was unearthed, which presented a clearer picture of the layout of a Viking farm as well as Viking everyday life, compared to the site in Kvívík. The farm consisted of four buildings. The dwelling structure, a longhouse, was preserved in its *c.* 20 m length and had an internal width of 5 m. The curved walls were 1 m thick, and were made of an outer and an inner wall of dry-stones, interspersed with turf to give a more windproof structure. In the middle of the western half of the building, a fireplace

Figure 42.1.1   The Viking farm at Toftanes, Leirvík. (Photo: S.S. Hansen.)

almost 5 m long was recorded. The eastern part of the longhouse may have contained a byre. Added to the southern wall of the longhouse was a small structure with a floor space of *c.* 12 m². Its western gable end was probably a wooden wall. On the northern side of the long dwelling house, there was a building, 13 m long and 4 m wide. Its walls were constructed from only a single built dry-stone wall and no turf. Its function has preliminarily been interpreted as an outhouse.

A small building, 5 m long and 3 m wide, was located close to the northern side of the longhouse. The side walls were constructed similarly to the walls of the dwelling house, while the gable wall to the west was probably a wooden wall; the eastern end was eroded by a stream. The floor was paved with flat stones, and covered with thick layers of ashes and charcoal, and with a small stone-built ember pit in the eastern end. The building was interpreted as a firehouse (Stummann Hansen 1991).

As in other farmsteads known from this period, the buildings were basically constructed of wood, but had thick insulating outer walls of stone and earth. Even though building timber was scarce, the wooden stave-building tradition based on Norwegian/ Scandinavian architecture was employed with modifications to suit local conditions (Stoklund 1984; Stummann Hansen 1999).

The artefact record is of great interest. This consists of a large number of objects of steatite, for example fragments of bowls and saucepans, but also spindle whorls and line- or netsinkers for fishing, as well as hones and querns of schist. As steatite is not a local material these objects must have been imported, apparently from Norway. Only a few artefacts of local material, such as basalt and tufa, were found. There were huge numbers of well-preserved wooden objects such as bowls, spoons and staves from barrels. A large group of the wooden objects consists of cords of twined juniper branches which no doubt were used as handles for the barrels and as ropes for the roof stones. While the afore-mentioned stone artefacts may have been imported from the east, the artefact record also includes imported goods and jewellery originating from and indicating links to the south, the Irish Sea, for example two ringed pins of Hiberno-Norse type and a jet bracelet (Larsen 1991; Stummann Hansen 1993). The settlement at Toftanes has been dated to the ninth–tenth centuries (Vickers *et al.* 2005).

Argisbrekka

Among the place names to whose existence philologists paid special attention from early on were names containing the Celtic name-element *ærgi*. It had possibly become inte-grated into the Norse language during the ninth century, and it was assumed that the place names meant something like summer grazing pastures or shielings for cattle (Matras 1956). Archaeological surveys of the eighteen localities retaining such place names – all but one situated in the outfield – ascertained that at several of these localities were the remains of small ruins. From the archaeological excavation of one of these localities, Ergidalur on the island of Suðuroy, it was concluded that this was a Viking Age summer or seasonal settlement (Dahl 1970: 362).

Due to the damming of Lake Eiðisvatn, located in the northernmost part of the island of Eysturoy, extensive archaeological excavations were initiated at the site of Argisbrekka during 1983–7 (Mahler 1991, 1998, 2007). The locality is in the outfield of the village of Eiði, at an altitude of 130 m above sea level. It was possible to divide the archaeological remains on the plain west of Argisbrekka into roughly two settlement areas. Twenty-two buildings were unearthed, with eight and thirteen in the afore-mentioned areas respectively. Within these two areas, there were two to three lesser construction areas, which consisted of a residential house and one or two outhouses and storage houses. All were constructed with walls of turf, sand, clay and pebbles. These are all smaller buildings, 7–8 m long and 3–4 m wide, and even smaller. Stratigraphical observations indicate that two shielings were in operation simultaneously during the area's last active period in the Viking Age. Functionally the Faroe *ærgir* resemble full-time Norwegian shielings.

The dating indicates that all activity ceased sometime during the middle of the eleventh century. Stratigraphical observations and ^{14}C dating indicate a commencement of activities in the eastern area sometime during the ninth century. Regarding the artefact assemblage, it's interesting to note that except for local ceramics the assemblage did not differ much from the one found at the stationary farm. The local ceramics are a distinct category for Faroese archaeology, documented from the late tenth century and into the nineteenth century (Arge 1991, 1997).

We must conclude that in the Viking Age the *ærgi* and farm were closely intertwined elements, which together characterise the special operational method, also that the traces of these operations are widely dispersed throughout the Faroes. The operational method does however become adjusted to existing local conditions. As the shieling operational method is not mentioned in a special enactment for the Faroes, *Seyðabrævið* 'the Sheep Letter', issued in 1298, which relates to the dominant extensive sheep farm-ing, it is concluded that a combination of a greater emphasis upon fishing and extensive sheep farming led to the disappearance of the Faroe *ærgir* as part of an outdated operational method (Mahler 2007).

Sandur

Sandur is one of the largest and wealthiest agricultural societies on the islands (Figure 42.1.2). There can be no doubt that ever since the first settlers, who had a farming background, arrived at the islands in the Viking Age, that is, the *landnám* period, this village must have been among the most prominent in the rural societies of that time (Arge 2001). The local church lies rather isolated from the rest of the habitation, which is not common in the Faroes. But ever since a coin hoard containing ninety-eight eleventh-century silver coins, deriving from what we now know as European and Scandinavian countries, was found in the churchyard by a grave digger in 1863 (Steen Jensen 2004), there have been expectations that something more would turn up.

When the first archaeological excavation in Sandur took place in 1969–70, efforts were focused within the actual church. The results were outstanding and rather unexpected, in that what was found were the remains of five successive churches under the present one, built in 1839. The oldest was a small single-aisled stave-church, as we know them from Norway, and dated to the eleventh century. Thus, all in all six churches have been built one on top of another on this very spot (Krogh 1975).

In 1972 a small-scale excavation in the churchyard revealed the eastern gable of a building with a beautifully stone-paved floor. This structure has been interpreted as part of a boat-shaped longhouse, which may have been the living house at the local farm. It is very likely that the coin hoard was placed below the floor paving in this building by the end of the eleventh century, thus indicating that the building has been in use during the

Figure 42.1.2   Sandur, Sandoy. The site of Junkarinsfløttur is central in the photo – in the fields north of the church. (Photo: S.V. Arge.)

eleventh century at least (Krogh 1975, 1983). When the churchyard in the 1970s was extended towards the south remains of Viking Age activities were revealed throughout this large *c.* 3,000 m² area. In 1989 eleven graves were uncovered in this area, of which seven were excavated (Arge and Hartmann 1992). Prior to this the only Viking burial site had been the one in Tjørnuvík unearthed in 1956 (Dahl and Rasmussen 1956). It can be dated to the tenth century both archaeologically as well as by ¹⁴C (Arge 2001). The burial site in Sandur gives the impression of having been well regulated: it consists of a series of burials placed end to end in a number of more or less parallel rows. All of the graves are aligned east–west and all of the uncovered skeletons lay with their skulls pointing west.

The state of preservation of the skeletal material was fairly poor. However, teeth or rather dental enamel was found preserved in all seven of the excavated graves. The objects recovered from the graves can be classified as personal belongings, for example finger-rings of silver and bronze, pearls of bone, glass and amber and iron knives. Two of those interred had been buried with an iron knife which had thin silver threads entwined around the handle; one of these, a young man, also had a pouch or a purse – possibly a woven pouch containing a leather purse. In this pouch were seven plain lead weights – three pairs, and each pair contained a circular and a rectangular weight. Also a strap-end was found in the grave, ornamented with an animal head; further a bronze fragment was found, which was decorated with an interlaced motif of Irish origin, and some small silver fragments.

In one of the graves was found a clipped Cufic coin, the first and only coin of this type found in the islands so far. This has been identified as a late ninth-century imitation of an Abbasid-style dirham, which may be suggestive for dating the burial to the mid-tenth century (Blackburn 2005; Graham-Campbell 2005).

We must suppose that around AD 1000, at the time when it is commonly supposed that the Faroes were converting to Christianity, there existed a settlement here, important enough to warrant the erection of a church. The activity on the site continued for a period, perhaps until the early thirteenth century, after which the site was abandoned. Only the church and the churchyard remained.

JUNKARINSFLØTTUR, SANDUR AND THE VIKING ECONOMY

A phosphate survey in 1989 in Junkarinsfløttur, Sandur, to the north of the church site, which has been cultivated for centuries, indicated a large settlement area. Erosion of the cliff just below these fields in 2000 made 2 m deep cultural layers visible, and subsequent archaeological investigations have now revealed an extensive settlement in that area of which we hitherto had no knowledge (Arge 2001) (Figure 42.1.3). The preliminary zooarchaeological analysis of the remains from Junkarinsfløttur – the first of its kind in the Faroes – presents a diverse range of economic practices employed by the Norse settlers at a key time and geographical position in their expansion across the North Atlantic. Their economic strategy appears to have relied heavily upon the exploitation of a broad spectrum of the local wild resources to supplement a mixed agricultural base of animal husbandry and cereal cultivation.

Domestic mammals recovered included sheep, cows and pigs with single bones of goat and dog. Significant numbers of pig bones were recovered throughout the site sequence, indicating sustained pig keeping up to and beyond the thirteenth century, a situation unique compared to Iceland and Greenland. Birds comprised a relatively large proportion of the archaeofauna. The Faroese at Junkarinsfløttur remained dependent upon bird resources, especially puffins, far longer and to a greater degree than any of the other Viking Age settlers of the North Atlantic islands. A wide range of marine resources were also recovered, suggesting the Norse settlers of the Faroes were heavily reliant on natural resources to sustain their economy.

The procurement of wood would have been a major consideration for the Norse in the Faroes. The islands never sustained extensive woodland, and heather and juniper were the only wood resource available on Sandoy at the *landnám*, though fragments of various coniferous timber species would have arrived as driftwood picked up from the shore. In the archaeological assemblage in Sandur wood charcoal was very rare and consisted of locally derived roundwood, coniferous driftwood and imported oak. Peat and turf were the main fuel sources in the treeless landscape. A hulled six-row barley monoculture was

Figure 42.1.3 Junkarinsfløttur, Sandur. Excavation of a ruin in 2004. (Photo: S.V. Arge.)

in place, with small-scale yet intensive cultivation undertaken. Cereal cultivation seems to have played a lesser role in the economy than in other areas of the eastern North Atlantic and some of the barley may have been imported (Church *et al.* 2005).

The recent excavations at Junkarinsfløttur, Sandoy, represent a key site for investigating early Faroese palaeoeconomy. We must assume that this site is part of an extensive settlement area comprising the church site. The archaeological record from the area leaves us with the impression of a high-status Faroese society, which had strong links with the outside world.

BIBLIOGRAPHY

Arge, S.V. (1991) 'The *landnám* in the Faroes', *Arctic Anthropology*, 28(2): 101–20.
—— (1997) 'Í Uppistovubeitinum: site and settlement', *Fróðskaparrit*, 45: 27–44.
—— (2001) 'Forn búseting heima á Sandi', *Frøði*, 2001(2): 4–13.
—— (2005) 'Cultural landscapes and cultural environmental issues in the Faroes', in A. Mortensen and S.V. Arge (eds) *Viking and Norse in the North Atlantic. Select Papers from the Proceedings of the Fourteenth Viking Congress, Tórshavn, 19–30 July 2001* (Annales Societatis scientiarum Færoensis. Supplementum 44), Tórshavn: Føroya Fróðskaparfélag.
Arge, S.V., Guðrún Sveinbjarnardóttir, Edwards, K.J. and Buckland, P.C. (2005) 'Viking and medieval settlement in the Faroes: people, place and environment', *Human Ecology*, 33(5): 597–620.
Arge, S.V. and Hartmann, N. (1992) 'The bural site of við Kirkjugarð in the village of Sandur, Sandoy', *Fróðskaparrit*, 38/39 (1989–90): 5–21.

Blackburn, M. (2005) 'Coinage and contacts in the North Atlantic during the seventh to mid-tenth centuries', in A. Mortensen and S.V. Arge (eds) *Viking and Norse in the North Atlantic. Select Papers from the Proceedings of the Fourteenth Viking Congress, Tórshavn, 19–30 July 2001* (Annales Societatis scientiarum Færoensis. Supplementum 44), Tórshavn: Føroya Fróðskaparfélag.

Church, M.J., Arge, S.V., Brewington, S., McGovern, T.H., Woollett, J.M., Perdikaris, S., Lawson, I.T., Cook, G.T., Amundsen, C., Harrison, R., Krivogorskaya, Y. and Dunbar, E. (2005) 'Puffins, pigs, cod, and barley: palaeoeconomy at Undir Junkarinsfløtti, Sandoy, Faroe Islands', *Environmental Archaeology*, 10: 179–97.

Dahl, S. (1951) 'Fornar toftir í Kvívík', *Varðin*, 29: 65–96.

—— (1970) 'Um ærgistaðir og ærgitoftir', *Fróðskaparrit*, 18: 361–8.

Dahl, S. and Rasmussen, J. (1956) 'Víkingaaldargrøv í Tjørnuvík', *Fróðskaparrit*, 5: 153–67.

Graham-Campbell, J. (2005) 'The Viking-Age gold and silver of the North Atlantic region', in A. Mortensen and S.V. Arge (eds) *Viking and Norse in the North Atlantic. Select Papers from the Proceedings of the Fourteenth Viking Congress, Tórshavn, 19–30 July 2001* (Annales Societatis scientiarum Færoensis. Supplementum 44), Tórshavn: Føroya Fróðskaparfélag.

Krogh, K.J. (1975) 'Seks kirkjur heima á Sandi', *Mondul*, 2: 21–54.

—— (1983) 'Gård og Kirke. Samhørighed mellem gård og kirke belyst gennem arkæologiske undersøgelser på Færøerne og i Grønland', *hikuin*, 9: 231–44.

Larsen, A.-Ch. (1991) 'Norsemen's use of juniper in Viking Age Faroe Islands', *Acta Archaeologica*, 61 (1990): 54–9.

Lawson, I.T., Church, M.J., McGovern, T.H., Arge, S.V., Woollett, J., Edwards, K.J., Gathorne-Hardy, F.J., Dugmore, A.J., Cook, G., Mairs, K.-A., Thompson A.M. and Guðrún Sveinbjarnardóttir (2005) 'Historical ecology on Sandoy, Faroe Islands: palaeoenvironmental and archaeological perspectives', *Human Ecology*, 33(5): 651–84.

Mahler, D.L. (1991) 'Argisbrekka: new evidence of shielings in the Faroe Islands', *Acta Archaeologica*, 61 (1990): 60–72.

—— (1998) 'The stratigraphical cultural landscape', in H. Andersson, L. Ersgård and E. Svensson (eds) *Outland Use in Preindustrial Europe* (Lund Studies in Medieval Archaeology 20), Lund: Institute of Archaeology, University of Lund.

—— (2007) *Sæteren ved Argisbrekka. Økonomiske forandringer på Færøerne i Vikingetid og Tidlig Middelalder* (Annales Societatis Scientiarum Færoensis. Supplementum 47), Tórshavn: Faroe University Press.

Matras, A.K. (2005) 'The Viking settlement "Niðri á Toft", Kvívík, Faroe Islands – a reanalysis', in A. Mortensen and S.V. Arge (eds) *Viking and Norse in the North Atlantic. Select Papers from the Proceedings of the Fourteenth Viking Congress, Tórshavn, 19–30 July 2001* (Annales Societatis scientiarum Færoensis. Supplementum 44), Tórshavn: Føroya Fróðskaparfélag.

Matras, Ch. (1933) *Stednavne paa de færøske Norðuroyar*, Copenhagen: Thieles.

—— (1956) 'Gammelfærøsk ærgi, n., og dermed beslægtede ord, *Namn och bygd* 44: 51–67.

Steen Jensen, J. (2004) 'Møntskatten fra Sand, Færøerne', *Nordisk numismatisk årsskrift* (1997–9): 65–93.

Stoklund, B. (1984) 'Building traditions in the northern world', in A. Fenton and H. Pálsson (eds) *The Northern and Western Isles in the Viking World. Survival, Continuity and Change. For the Bicentenary of the National Museum of Antiquities of Scotland 1781–1981*, Edinburgh: John Donald.

Stummann Hansen, S. (1991) 'Toftanes: a Faroese Viking farmstead from the 9th–10th centuries AD', *Acta Archaeologica*, 61 (1990): 44–53.

—— (1993) 'Viking-Age Faroe Islands and their southern links in the light of recent finds at Toftanes, Leirvík', in C.E. Batey, J. Jesch and C.D. Morris (eds) *The Viking Age in Caithness, Orkney and the North Atlantic. Selected Papers from the Proceedings of the Eleventh Viking*

Congress, Thurso and Kirkwall, 22 August–1 September 1989, Edinburgh: Edinburgh University Press.

—— (1999) 'I Jan Pedersens fodspor på Oma. Nyt om Vikingetidens Gårdsanlæg', in I. Fuglestvedt, T. Gansum and A. Opedal (eds) *Et hus med mange rom. Vennebok til Bjørn Myhre på 60-årsdagen*, vol. A (AmS-rapport 11A), Stavanger: Arkeologisk museum i Stavanger.

Vickers, K., Bending, J., Buckland, P.C., Edwards, K.J., Stummann Hansen, S. and Cook, G. (2005) 'Toftanes: the Paleoecology of a Faroese *landnám* farm', *Human Ecology*, 33(5): 685–710.

CHAPTER FORTY-THREE

THE NORSE SETTLEMENTS
IN GREENLAND

——•❖•——

Jette Arneborg

In the late tenth century Viking settlers moved further west into the North Atlantic. According to early Icelandic history-writing, settlers from Iceland colonised the southern part of the Greenland west coast in the late 980s:

> The land which is called Greenland was discovered and settled from Iceland. Eirik the Red was the name of a Breidafjord man who went out there from here and took land in settlement . . . When he began to settle the land, that was fourteen or fifteen years before Christianity came to Iceland.
>
> (*The Book of the Icelanders* by *Arí Fróði Þorgilsson* (1067–1148), trans. Jones 1986: 148)

Greenland is the world's largest island. However, more than 75 per cent is covered by ice and only the narrow rim between the massive Inland Ice and the sea is inhabitable. The south-west Greenland landscape is mountainous with deep fjords, valleys and rivers draining the water from the Inland Ice into the sea. In general the climate of Greenland is Arctic (the mean temperature of the warmest month of the year is below +10° C): in the protected inner parts of the south-west Greenland fjords (around 60° to 61° N) and the Nuuk hinterland (around 64°N) temperatures in the warmest month crawl up above +10° C. It was here – in subarctic Greenland – that the Icelandic Norse immigrants settled. In the Middle Ages the southernmost settlement area was called the Eastern Settlement and the settlement area around Nuuk the Western Settlement (Figure 43.1).

Contacts with the Norse Greenland settlements broke off during the fifteenth century and almost ever since the fate of the Norse has been discussed in Iceland and in Scandinavia. At the beginning of the eighteenth century contacts with Greenland were re-established and the deserted and collapsed farms spoke for themselves. The last evidence of life in the settlements is the letter written by a Greenland priest testifying a wedding in the Hvalsey fjord church in the Eastern Settlement in 1408.

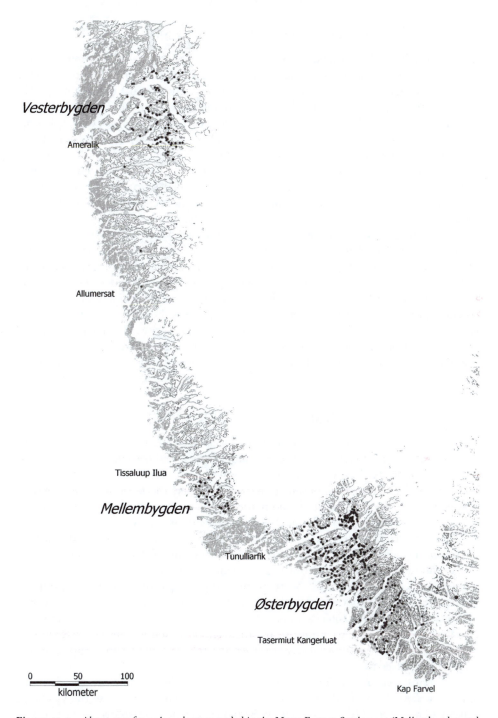

Figure 43.1 About 500 farms have been recorded in the Norse Eastern Settlement (Mellembygden and Østerbygden on the map). About 100 farms have been recorded in the Western Settlement (Vesterbygden). (Map: Niels Algreen Møller 2004. Copyright © National Museum of Denmark.)

589

CONDITIONS FOR SETTLEMENT

Geographically the Greenland settlements were several days' sailing from Iceland, and a well-developed ship technology was a prerequisite for navigation in the at times very dangerous North Sea. Several theories have been put forward to explain why the sedentary Norse population settled in an environment that was basically marginal for the pasture economy they brought with them. Among the push factors, overpopulation in Iceland has been put forward (Ólafsson 2000). As pull factors, the uninhabited land and a relative abundance of fish and seal in the sea and caribou on land have been pointed out (Krogh 1982: 66 f.) as has access to the sought-after Arctic commodities such as walrus ivory, narwhal tusks and polar bear skins (Arneborg 2000, 2002). For the Norse way of life to survive in Greenland, contacts with the homelands were prerequisite. The settlements especially needed supplies of iron from Scandinavia, and the Greenlandic ivory and furs were the main means of trade (Arneborg 2000, 2002; Roesdahl 1995). Already in the Iron Age trade networks were established in Norway that – among other things – included iron, walrus tusk, hides and furs (e.g. Christophersen 1989: 126 ff.), and in the late ninth century the north Norwegian chieftain Ottar went from Hålogaland to Hedeby to sell his Arctic commodities (see Lund 1983: 23 f.). Although sedentary, the resource utilisation of the Norse settlers was therefore not restricted to the settlement areas. The Norse settlements depended on resources that included most of the west coast of Greenland from Thule in the north to Kap Farvel in the south and also the most southern part of the east coast was their exploitation territory (Arneborg 2004).

FARMS AND SUBSISTENCE

The many well-preserved ruins dating from the Norse settlers that are visible in the south-west Greenland landscape today are from the medieval period, but archaeological excavations indicate that the settlement pattern did not alter from the Viking to the medieval period. From the *landnám* (landtaking) period the farms were scattered on the moraine plains along the fjords and in the fertile and protected valleys reflecting the pastoral economy of the settlements. A few farms occur on sites with very little pasture-land available. Here especially the seal hunt was decisive for the choice of settlement.

Zooarchaeological analysis of the animal bone collections (McGovern 1985; Enghoff 2003) and isotope analysis (^{13}C) of human bones (Arneborg *et al.* 1999) show that subsistence economy was based on the combination of pastoral farming, fishing and hunting. Seal and caribou were the main meat supplies. Cattle, sheep and goats were primarily kept for the secondary products such as milk, cheese and butter. Sheep were also kept for the wool. According to the distribution of animal bones the individual farms were self-sufficient at subsistence level and the exchange of foodstuffs does not seem to have taken place.

The farms were run in an infield–outfield system. In the summer the domestic animals grazed the outfields, while in the growing season to maximise the yields the infields were manured (e.g. Schweger 1998) and at some farms also irrigated (Arneborg 2005). Unlike the cattle that had to be stalled for many months of the year, sheep and goats can survive the winter outside in Greenland. But they may have needed supplementary fodder, and the production of grass was fundamental for the farmers.

Until now about 500 Norse sites have been recorded in the Eastern Settlement and about 100 in the Western Settlement. The average number of inhabitants in Greenland has been estimated as about 1,400 with a peak around the year 1200 of over 2,000 individuals (Lynnerup 1998: 118), and even though not all sites can be regarded as self-sufficient farms it is evident that the recorded farms cannot have been in use simultaneously. Some farms may have been abandoned after years of settlement, and some farms may have been populated periodically, depending on the state of vegetation resources (Figure 43.2).

In spring and autumn either in groups or separately the farmers organised hunting trips to the outer coast of the settlements to hunt the passing migratory seals, and in early summer they went further to the north along the Greenland west coast to hunt walrus, narwhal and polar bear. Some went south and rounded Kap Farvel (Arneborg 2004). On the west coast the southernmost area to hunt walrus today is the Disko Bay about 600 km north of the Western Settlement. Items of Norse origin found at Thule Culture Inuit sites as far north as in Thule and on the Canadian Ellesmere Island show that Norse hunters travelled even that far north (Sutherland 2000; Schledermann 2000).

BUILDING A NEW SOCIETY

Even though the environment differed and the newcomers had to adjust economic strategies to the new realities the adaptation to the new land took place within the social system of the homelands of the settlers, and settlement pattern, farm layout, architecture and economy of the farms reflected the stratified society that the settlers transferred from their homelands.

The quality of the land and the number of buildings at the farms was the visible sign of social and economic status and – in the later periods – so was the layout of the farm buildings. The living house underwent most changes during the settlement period. In the *landnám* period the setting of domestic life was the longhouse of the Scandinavian

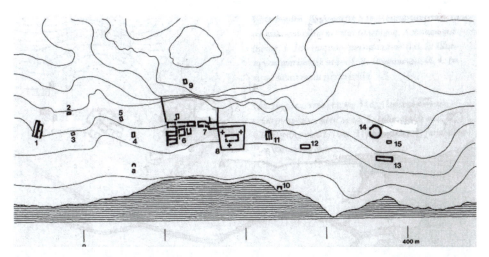

Figure 43.2 The Hvalsey fjord farm was a typical medieval Norse high-status farm. Among the buildings were (1) byre and barn, (6) living houses with a large stone-built celebration hall, (8) church, (9) storehouse and (10) warehouse (after Krogh 1982. Copyright © National Museum of Denmark).

type with a main room furnished with a central long hearth and benches along the long walls (e.g. Vebæk 1993; Albrethsen and Ólafsson 1998). Later the large multi-functional room was divided up into smaller rooms with specific functions (Roussell 1941). At the high-status farms the houses remained dispersed whereas at the lower-status farms, especially in the Western Settlement, living houses, stables, cowsheds, barns and outhouses were moved so close together that from the outside they appeared as one single building, and the inhabitants could move from the living quarters to the other buildings without having to go outside. The two types of layout have been named the longhouse (or the dispersed farm) and the centralised farm (Roussell 1941). The development from the dispersed to the centralised farm has been regarded as a response to climate change whereas the development of the living quarters reflects the changes in social relations between humans that took place in the Middle Ages and which is not specific to Greenland (Poulsen 2003: 39).

Despite their dependence on marine resources, wealth in Greenland was based on the ownership of land. The elite farmers lived on large coastal farms where the yields were best. Even though they were not profitable, the elite farmers owned prestigious cattle, unlike at the ordinary and smaller farms where sheep and goats dominated. As additional signs of status the high-status farms had stone-built warehouses where export commodities were kept until they were shipped to Norway, and they had large celebration halls attached to the churches (Figures 43.2 and 43.3).

Figure 43.3   The celebration hall at the Hvalsey fjord farm. (Photo: J. Arneborg 2004.
Copyright © National Museum of Denmark.)

THE CHURCH

No pagan graves have been found in Greenland, and from the initial settlement the leading *landnám* families may have had Christian churches and burial grounds attached to their farms. In time some churches were demolished while others were enlarged. No doubt as in Iceland the churches were privately owned and formed an important part of the economic and social organisation of the society (Arneborg 1991). Directly contrary to the interests of the Roman Church the system of privately owned churches gave the secular church owners opportunities to gain economic advantages, and the payments to the church may have been a sizeable source of income for the church owners. Thus, the development from many small churches to fewer and larger churches may reflect the concentration of power in Norse Greenland society.

However, despite this development, power in the society never seems to have been monopolised by the few, and the group of elite families seems to have maintained some kind of mutual equilibrium that did not permit one family to gain superiority. In Iceland the family at Skálholt was powerful enough to seize the crosier in the middle of the eleventh century and turn their family farm into the first Icelandic Episcopal residence; contrary to that the bishop's see in Greenland was established by Norwegian initiative at the beginning of the twelfth century. The bishop of Norse Greenland was never a Greenlander. The effect was twofold. No Greenland family gained power and position on the basis of the office, and the influence of the Roman Church in Greenland seems to have been restricted during the entire settlement period (Arneborg 1991). The last bishop residing in Greenland died in 1378, which was thirty years before the wedding (mentioned above) took place in the Hvalsey fjord church.

THE GREENLANDERS AND EUROPE

Greenland never adopted a monetary economy. Both external trade and internal exchange were dominated by the exchange of what were considered valuables in Europe and in Greenland. The Greenlanders exported first and foremost walrus ivory, which was considered valuable on the European market in the Viking and early medieval period, and they imported the requisite iron, which they could not produce in Greenland (Buchwald 2001). They also imported other items that were considered luxuries or valuables in Greenland. Trade and internal exchange were organised in a redistributive system with the high-status or elite farmers in the role as distributors. The control of exchange and trade formed part of the position of power of the elite farmers and not only did they organise and profit by the system they also took an active part in acquiring the trade commodities. According to the written accounts of Haukur Erlendsson (d. 1334) the elite farmers owned the ships that went to the hunting grounds, and they also owned the hunting equipment (see Halldórsson 1978: 55).

In the first period of settlement the Greenlandic farmers had their own ships to take them and their commodities to the markets in Europe. In the late twelfth century they were among the merchants that traded in Bergen (Magerøy 1993: 34). Less than a century later the Greenlanders depended on Norwegian merchants sailing to Greenland and in 1261 they – as the Icelanders – subjected to the Norwegian king in order to ensure the traffic between Greenland and Norway (Magerøy 1993: 62). The reasons for this development are obscure. One explanation is the lack of sea-going ships; this however is hardly consistent with the fact that in the same period they had ships to cross the Melville Bay in North Greenland (see below). Another explanation could be the wish of the Norwegian kings – especially King Håkon Håkonsson (1204–63) was successful – to subject the North Atlantic colonies, and an effective means to succeed was to refuse their traders admittance to Norwegian harbours.

Despite the agreement of 1261, the numbers of Norwegians sailing to Greenland declined during the late fourteenth century. The famous late medieval garments from the churchyard at Ikigaat (in Old Norse *Herjólfsnes*) clearly show that communication between Greenland and Europe lasted at least to the beginning of the fifteenth century (Arneborg 1996; Østergaard 2004); the number of ships that arrived in Greenland is however unknown, and in the later part of the century the official Norwegian sailings to Greenland had stopped completely (Magerøy 1993: 228).

THE HUNTERS OF THE NORTH

On their hunting trips to the north the Norse Greenlanders may have met both the late Dorset people and the Thule culture people. The late Dorset Palaeo Eskimos appeared in the Nares Strait/Smith Sound region in the eighth century and the Thule Inuit arrived around 1200. Both people seem to have been in the region in the period 1200–1300: the late Dorset declining; the Thule culture on the rise (Gulløv 2000). The Norse Greenlanders regarded the late Dorset and the Thule people as the same as the Vinland *skrælings* (weaklings), and most probably the name expresses their opinion of the hunters of the north. Archaeological finds and written sources indicate some interaction between the Dorset, Thule and Norse people; the nature of the contacts is however hardly known, but written sources indicate Norse interest in the *skrælings* (see Halldórsson 1978: 53 f.) and one explanation could be the exchange of commodities (Arneborg 1997). The Norse may have acquired walrus ivory from the Palaeo Eskimo and Inuit hunters in return for metals. The majority of Norse finds found in Thule culture context are metals (Gulløv 2000: 326).

During the fourteenth century the Thule culture people moved southwards to Greenland's west coast. They arrived in the Western Settlement region around the middle of the fourteenth century about the same time as the Norse deserted the settlement and they may have lived for a generation or two on the outer coast of the Eastern Settlement region while the Norse were still living on their farms in the inner parts of the fjords. How the relations between the two people developed, as they physically got closer to each other, are unknown but we may guess that the two very different ways of understanding the world may have caused problems.

DESERTED SETTLEMENTS

The written and the archaeological record agree that the northernmost Western Settlement was depopulated in the second half of the fourteenth century, and according to the archaeological finds in the Eastern Settlement it is most likely that this settlement was abandoned about 100 years later. For many years the predominant theory pointed to the advancing Thule culture people who were thought to have wiped out the Norse population. The theory was, however, based on one interpretation of the written sources

(Arneborg 2003: 117 ff.), and today hostilities between the Thule culture people and the Norse do not play a dominant role in the discussions.

The basis for settlement in the first place was the natural resources of Greenland and the maintenance of contact with the homelands – and both conditions were vital for the survival of the colonies. Contacts with the homeland declined and the official sailings from Norway terminated at the beginning of the fifteenth century threatening the position of the elite farmers. But the archaeological record does not seem to reflect any changes in the social relations of the society. Simultaneously climate changes most certainly influenced the Norse subsistence economy. *Landnám* took place at the end of the Medieval Warm Period (*c.* 885–1235), with the beginning of the Little Ice Age around 1200 the climate got colder and drier. In the period up to the beginning of the Little Ice Age the wind increased (Jensen *et al.* 2004: 161; Lassen *et al.* 2004), and either because of the wind, overexploitation of the vegetation resources, or a combination of both, erosion became a serious threat to the Norse farmers (Jakobsen 1991; Mainland 2000). At the same time the sea level rose with the loss of valuable grassland as the result (Kuijpers *et al.* 1999). Isotope ^{13}C of the human bones and the animal bones indicates a growing dependence on marine resources (Arneborg *et al.* 1999), but the isotope studies also show that the farmers maintained the pasture economy they introduced at *landnám*. For instance, 'hunger feeding' of the domesticates with fish refuse did not take place.

Certainly conditions for the Greenlanders deteriorated and with an eye to the supposed number of inhabitants the yearly emigration of a few discontented individuals – as argued by Lynnerup (1998: 115 ff.) – unavoidably would result in the depopulation of the Norse Greenland settlements.

BIBLIOGRAPHY

Albrethsen, S.E. and Ólafsson, G. (1998) 'A Viking Age hall', in J. Arneborg and H.C. Gulløv (eds) *Man, Culture and Environment in Ancient Greenland* (Danish Polar Center 4), Copenhagen: Danish Polar Centre, Danish National Museum.

Arneborg, J. (1991) 'The Roman Church in Norse Greenland', *Acta Archaeologica*, 61: 142–50.

—— (1996) 'Burgunderhuer, baskere og døde nordboer i Herjolfsnæs, Grønland', *Nationalmuseets Arbejdsmark* (1996): 75–83.

—— (1997) 'Cultural borders: reflections on Norse–Eskimo interaction', in R. Gilberg and H.C. Gulløv (eds) *Fifty Years of Arctic Research. Anthropological Studies from Greenland to Siberia* (Publications of The National Museum of Denmark. Ethnographical Series 18), Copenhagen: Department of Ethnography and the National Museum of Denmark.

—— (2000) 'Greenland and Europe', in W.W. Fitzhugh and E.I. Ward (eds) *Vikings. The North Atlantic Saga*, Washington, DC: Smithsonian Institution Press.

—— (2002) 'Inhospitable regions and marginality: settlement at the end of the world', in G. Helmig, B. Scholkmann and M. Untermann (eds) *Centre – Region – Periphery*, vol. 3, Hertigen: Wesselkamp.

—— (2003) 'Norse Greenland archaeology: the dialogue between the written and the archaeological record', in S.M. Lewis-Simpson (ed.) *Vinland Revisited. The Norse World at the Turn of the First Millennium. Selected Papers from the Viking Millennium International Symposium 15–24 September, Newfoundland and Labrador*, St John's: Newfoundland Historic Sites Association of Newfoundland and Labrador.

—— (2004) 'Nordboernes rejser i Grønland og på det nordamerikanske kontinent', *Grønland*, 2004(1–2): 1–10.

—— (2005) 'Greenland irrigation systems on a west Nordic background', in J. Klápště (ed.) *Water management in medieval rural economy* (Ruralia 5) (Památky archeologické. Suppl. 17), Prague: Inst. of Archaeology.

Arneborg, J., Heinemeier, J., Lynnerup, N., Nielsen, H.L., Rud, N. and Á.E. Sveinbjarnardóttir (1999) 'Change of diet of the Greenland Vikings determined from stable carbon isotope analysis and ^{14}C dating of their bones', *Radiocarbon*, 41(2): 157–68.

Buchwald, V.F. (2001) *Ancient Iron and Slags in Greenland* (Meddelelser om Grønland; Man and society 26), Copenhagen: Danish Polar Centre, Danish National Museum.

Christophersen, A. (1989) 'Kjøpe, selge, bytte, gi. Vareutveksling og byoppkomst i Norge ca 800–1100: En model', in A. Andrén (ed.) *Medeltidens födelse* (Symposier på Krapperups borg 1), Lund: Wallin & Dalholm.

Enghoff, I. (2003) *Hunting, Fishing and Animal Husbandry at the Farm beneath the Sand, Western Settlement* (Meddelelser om Grønland; Man and society 28), Copenhagen: Danish Polar Centre, Danish National Museum.

Gulløv, H.C. (2000) 'Natives and Norse in Greenland', in W.W. Fitzhugh and E.I. Ward (eds) *Vikings. The North Atlantic Saga*, Washington, DC: Smithsonian Institution Press.

Halldórsson, Ó. (1978) *Grænland í Miðaldaritum*. Reykjavík: Sögufélag.

Jakobsen, B. (1991) 'Soil resources and soil erosion in the Norse settlement area of Østerbygden in southern Greenland', *Acta Borealia* (1991): 56–68.

Jensen, K.G., Kuijpers, A., Koc, N. and Heinemeier, J. (2004) 'Diatom evidence of hydrographic changes and ice conditions in Igaliku fjord, south Greenland, during the past 1500 years', *The Holocene*, 14(2): 152–64.

Jones, G. (1986) *The Norse Atlantic Saga*, Oxford and New York: Oxford University Press.

Krogh, K.J. (1982) *Erik den Rødes Grønland*, Copenhagen: Nationalmuseet.

Kuijpers, A., Abrahamsen, N., Hoffmann, G., Hühnerbach, V., Konradi, P., Kunzendorf, H., Mikkelsen, N., Thiede, J. and Weinrich, W. (1999) 'Climate change and the Viking-age fjord environment of the Eastern Settlement, south Greenland', in A.K. Higgins and W. Stuart Watt (eds) *Review of Greenland Activities 1998* (Geology of Greenland Survey Bulletin 183), Copenhagen: Danmarks og Grønlands Geologiske undersøgelse (GEUS).

Lassen, S., Kuijpers, A., Kunzendorf, H., Hoffmann-Wieck, G., Mikkelsen, N. and Konradi, P. (2004) 'Late-Holocene Atlantic bottom-water variability in Igaliku fjord, south Greenland, reconstructed from foraminifera faunas', *The Holocene*, 14(2): 165–71.

Lund, N. (1983) 'Af den oldengelske Orosius', in J.S. Madsen (ed.) *Ottar og Wulfstan. To rejsebeskrivelser fra vikingetiden*, Roskilde: Vikingeskibshallen i Roskilde.

Lynnerup, N. (1998) *The Greenland Norse. A Biological-anthropological Study* (Meddelelser om Grønland; Man and society 24), Copenhagen: The Commission for Scientific Research in Greenland.

McGovern, T.H. (1985) 'Contributions to the paleoeconomy of Norse Greenland', *Acta Archaeologica*, 54: 73–122.

Magerøy. H. (1993) *Soga om austmenn. Nordmenn som siglde til Island og Grønland i mellomalderen* (Norske Videnskaps-Akademi. II, Hist.-Filos. Klasse. N.S. 19), Oslo: Det norske samlaget.

Mainland, I. (2000) 'The potential of dental microwear for exploring seasonal aspects of sheep husbandry and management in Norse Greenland', *Archaeozoologia*, 11: 79–100.

Ólafsson, H. (2000) 'Sagas of western expansion', in W.W. Fitzhugh and E.I. Ward (eds) *Vikings. The North Atlantic Saga*, Washington, DC: Smithsonian Institution Press.

Østergård, E. (2004) *Woven into the Earth*, Århus: Aarhus University Press.

Poulsen, B. (2003) 'Privatliv i middelalderens huse', in E. Roesdahl (ed.) *Bolig og familie i Danmarks middelalder*, Aarhus: Jysk Arkæologisk Selskab.

Roesdahl, E. (1995) *Hvalrostand, elfenben og nordboerne i Grønland*, Odense: Odense Universitetsforlag.

Roussell, Aa. (1941) *Farms and Churches in the Mediaeval Norse Settlements of Greenland* (Meddelelser om Grønland 89), Copenhagen: Kommissionen for videnskabelige Undersøgelser i Grønland.

Schledermann, P. (2000) 'Ellesmere', in W.W. Fitzhugh and E.I. Ward (eds) *Vikings. The North Atlantic Saga*, Washington, DC: Smithsonian Institution Press.

Schweger, C. (1998) 'Geoarchaeology of the GUS site: a preliminary framework', in J. Arneborg, and H.C. Gulløv (eds) *Man, Culture and Environment in Ancient Greenland*, Copenhagen: The Danish National Museum and Danish Polar Centre.

Sutherland, P.D. (2000) 'The Norse and native North Americans', in W.W. Fitzhugh and E.I. Ward (eds) *Vikings. The North Atlantic Saga*, Washington, DC: Smithsonian Institution Press.

Vebæk, C.L. (1993) *Narsaq. A Norse Landnáma Farm* (Meddelelser om Grønland; Man and society 18), Copenhagen: Kommissionen for videnskabelige Undersøgelser i Grønland.

CHAPTER FORTY-THREE (1)

THE NORTH ATLANTIC FARM
AN ENVIRONMENTAL VIEW

—— ·❖· ——

Paul Buckland

Viking expansion across the North Atlantic, to the Faroes, Iceland, Greenland and briefly to Newfoundland between the ninth and early eleventh centuries, took a north European farming system to islands which were either previously unoccupied or intermittently utilised by hunter–fisher communities. According to the one near-contemporary source, Dicuil, writing at the court of Charlemagne's successors in France *c.* 825, Irish hermits may have been present in the Faroes and possibly Iceland, although they have been singularly difficult to trace in the archaeological and palaeoecological record (Buckland 1992; Buckland *et al.* 1995; but see Hannon and Bradshaw 2000). The *Landnámsmenn* therefore may have found feral sheep on the Faroes (ON *Færeyjar*, maybe meaning 'sheep islands'), but they also introduced a regular European set of farm animals – cattle, pig, horse, goat and sheep – and crops – principally barley (ON *bygg*), to landscapes previously showing little or no human impact (Amorosi *et al.* 1997; Dugmore *et al.* 2005). In the late twelfth century Ari Froði wrote of Icelandic *landnám* – *Í þann tíð var Ísland viði vaxið á milli fjalls og fjöru* (*Íslendingabók*) – and the destruction of the predominantly birch woodland cover is well documented in the pollen record (Einarsson 1961; Hallsdóttir 1987). Subsequent soil loss, largely as a result of over-grazing, has been extensively researched (e.g. Þórarinsson 1961; Dugmore and Buckland 1991; Simpson *et al.* 2001). A similar pattern is evident in south-west Greenland (Fredskild 1988, 1992), but the absence of woodland in the Faroes leads to difficulties in the pinpointing of *landnám* (lit. 'the taking of land') by palynological means, and the macrofossil record is more precise, if still debatable (cf. Jóhansen 1985; Buckland and Dinnin 1998).

Onto this backdrop, Norse farmers placed a farming system which relied heavily upon secondary products: milk and cheese from sheep, goats and cattle, supplemented by some meat and cereals in the Faroes and Iceland, where cultivation and sporadic imports of grain were possible; as the author of the thirteenth-century *Konungs Skuggsjá* remarks, the Greenlanders did not know of bread. McGovern and others (2001) have noted how the domestic herbivore package was tailored to each environment – more goats in Greenland, and a higher frequency of pigs in early deposits, until they effectively destroyed their wooded and scrubland landscapes. In the absence of land-based mammals in Iceland, with the exception of the arctic fox, marine resources were early exploited, with seal, seabird and fish forming a significant component of the diet, and a similar pattern has recently emerged from the Faroese data (Church *et al.* 2005). In Greenland, fish are remarkably rare in the middens, but reindeer (caribou), particularly in the more northerly Western Settlement, provided an important dietary component, supplemented by seal, seabirds and the occasional stranded whale. The distribution of animal bones on sites shows that all farms contributed to the communal hunt, although dispersal of the results was not always equitable (McGovern *et al.* 1996).

Iceland plugs early into mainland Europe's need for stockfish to sustain standing armies and urban growth, supplementing and partly replacing sources in the Lofoten islands of Arctic Norway (Perdikaris 1999), but Greenland's trade in prestige goods, walrus ivory, its hide for making ropes and the intermittent polar bear (exchanged for a bishop in Einar Sokkasson's saga) and unicorn horn (narwhal) was always subject to the fluctuating supply from other sources to the east and south, and it was never effectively integrated into the European world system. Survival at a level close to subsistence, however, did not need contact for anything beyond the spiritual, but it did require an ability to provide sufficient fodder to overwinter core domestic stock. Its importance is indicated in the tale of Iceland's failed first settler, Nadodd, who found the hunting of marine resources so good that he neglected to collect fodder for his animals. Come the winter, natural resources disappeared and a disappointed Nadodd returned to Norway, with a poor report of the new land, which he consequently christened Iceland; Eirik the Red's sales pitch on Greenland shows a similar concern. The didactic nature of these foundation myths is evident – the neurosis of any northern farmer is whether he has sufficient fodder for his animals for the winter (cf. Jónsson 1877). Archaeological and palaeoecological data provide evidence for the storage of fodder (Amorosi *et al.* 1998), represented not only by the preservation of seeds in anaerobic conditions on archaeological sites but also by the extensive synanthropic insect faunas, largely species which feed on slime moulds on the decaying hay and their predators, introduced with the first settlers, including many species which are only able to survive in the artificially warmed habitats created by humans in the turf houses of farms and byres and the decaying plant debris in middens (Sadler and Skidmore 1995). Despite extensive burning in both Iceland and Greenland to convert birch and willow woodland and scrub to grassland, twig and leaf hay remained an important element in the diet of much stock, and the larger numbers of goats in Greenland may as much reflect their greater ability to metabolise woody tissue as the fact that woollen cloth (ON *vaðmál*) formed a lesser element in its taxation. At the *Gården under Sandet* (GUS) site in the Western Settlement in Greenland, the pollen spectra of faecal pellets of sheep or goat contain up to 98 per cent birch, perhaps reflecting spring collection of additional fodder (personal information from Robert Craigie, Dept. of Archaeology, University of Sheffield).

The use of seaweed as animal fodder, and as a source of salt, is evident on sites from Orkney to Greenland, and in organic deposits where the alga itself does not survive, its presence is often indicated by the remains of the marine colonial epizoote *Dynamena pumila*, which lives attached to it (Buckland *et al.* 1993). The presence of littoral elements in beetle faunas and puparia of flies which live in the debris thrown up on the tide line in middens and house floors further stresses the supplementation of terrestrial with marine resources, and the marine component of human and animal diet is also evident in the isotope composition of human and animal bone (Arneborg *et al.* 1999). Charred fragments of wrack are not uncommon even on inland sites (Buckland *et al.*

1998), and seaweed must have provided a source of essential salts for balancing the Norse diet. That other scourge of humans in Arctic systems, which largely close down for up to six months of the year, scurvy, vitamin C deficiency (e.g. Troup 1987), could be countered by the consumption of sheep and goat milk; the contrast with Inuit diet, where all essential elements were provided by the consumption of raw meat and fish, with a different consequent set of health risks (Hart Hansen *et al.* 1991), is striking.

Throughout the North Atlantic region, the basic building material for both farm and outbuilding was turf, sometimes on a stone foundation. Without grazing, however, natural turf is poorly matted, and it is probable that the earliest phase of at least Faroese and Icelandic *landnám* utilised other materials. In Iceland, pit-houses are often the earliest structures on sites (Einarsson 1992; Simpson *et al.* 1999). The more typical longhouse structure with outshots is illustrated by the farm at Stöng in Þjórsárdalur in Iceland, abandoned after the eruption of Hekla in 1104/58. Since its excavation by the Scandinavian Archaeological Expedition of 1939 (Stenberger 1943), it has become perhaps the most widely reproduced plan in the history of Norse archaeology (e.g. Foote and Wilson 1970; Fitzhugh and Ward 2000). Construction is of turf sods on dry-stone footings with a central fire trench in the main hall, loom and small hearth in the end room. At Stöng, the two outshots have traditionally been interpreted as a larder and communal latrine (Ólafsson and Ágústsson 2003), although Buckland and Perry (1989) have argued that at least one of the barrels set in the floor may have been for the collection and storage of human urine to provide an alkali for cleaning wool rather than for food storage, and that the lined trenches either side of the other room reflect the washing and dyeing of the finished cloth. There is relatively little animal bone from the Þjórsárdalur sites, but the Stöng evidence, which also includes a small cow byre with standing stall slabs, could be interpreted as the remains of a mixed livestock farm with an emphasis on sheep. At Stóraborg on the south coast of Iceland, large numbers of ectoparasites of sheep, both the ked, *Melophagus ovinus*, and the fleece louse, *Damalinia ovis*, in a drain beneath a room in the farm reflect residues from the cleaning of wool (Buckland and Perry 1989), and the presence of sheep, or fleeces, in several rooms on many sites is evident in the widespread distribution of the remains of keds; at GUS in Greenland these are supplemented by goat lice, both *D. capreae* and *Linognathus stenopsis* (Panagiotakopulu *et al.* forthcoming).

In both Iceland and Greenland, fly faunas from within the farm buildings and in deposits dumped out onto the middens are dominated by the puparia of *Heleomyza borealis* and *Telomarina flavipes*, both breeding in protein-rich material in either faeces or food debris within the rooms. The thermal requirements of the latter would have restricted its life cycle entirely to within buildings (Panagiotakopulu 2004), and Panagiotakopulu and others (2007) have suggested that its high frequency in the terminal stage of the farm at Nipaitsoq in the Western Settlement of Greenland reflects a community under stress. In general, however, the carefully constructed floors of farms on the permafrost in Greenland provide suitable habitats for a wide range of introduced species of insect, from flies to fleas (Buckland and Sadler 1989). Human lice are also present in large numbers, probably both head and body lice (Sveinbjarnardóttir and Buckland 1983), where preservation permits their identification. The large numbers of the human flea, *Pulex irritans*, from sites in Greenland (Panagiotakopulu 2001) are not matched elsewhere, although it should be stressed that living conditions do not seem to have differed significantly from contemporary urban Oslo (Kenward 1980), York (Kenward and Hall 1995) or Dublin (Coope 1981).

In Iceland, local crop production was clearly early supplemented by imported cereals, evident in the insect pest faunas of grain weevil, *Sitophilus granarius*, and saw-toothed grain beetle *Oryzaephilus surinamensis*. The former is not recorded in the modern fauna of the country, but both appear in the midden at Bessastaðir in the twelfth century (Amorosi *et al.* 1992), probably having been deposited in human faeces. The relative frequency of this fauna on this site, compared with material from the more extensively sampled lesser farm at Stóraborg on the south coast, is probably an indication of site status. Large numbers of false puparia, probably of the Hessian fly, *Mayetiola* sp., in a medieval pit within the Stóraborg farm might reflect the difficulty of sieving this important field pest out of imported grain (Buckland *et al.* 2005). The connection between exported fish and imported grain is particularly evident at the medieval fishing station at Langenes in the Norwegian Arctic, where insect pest faunas are supplemented by accidental import of more southerly beetles (Buckland *et al.* 2006).

BIBLIOGRAPHY

Amorosi, T., Buckland, P.C., Dugmore, A.J., Ingimundarson, J.H. and McGovern, T.H. (1997) 'Raiding the landscape: human impact in the Scandinavian North Atlantic', *Human Ecology*, 25: 491–518.

Amorosi, T., Buckland, P.C., Edwards, K.J., Mainland, I., McGovern, T.H., Sadler, J.P. and Skidmore, P. (1998) 'They did not live by grass alone: the politics and palaeoecology of fodder on the North Atlantic islands', *Environmental Archaeology*, 1: 41–54.

Amorosi, T., Buckland, P.C., Ólafsson, G., Sadler, J.P. and Skidmore, P. (1992) 'Site status and the palaeoecological record: a discussion of results from Bessastaðir, Iceland', in Ch. Morris and J. Rackham (eds) *Norse and Later Settlement and Subsistence in the North Atlantic*, Glasgow: Dept. of Archaeology, University of Glasgow.

Arneborg, J., Heinemeier, J., Lynnerup, N., Nielsen, H.L., Rud, N. and Sveinbjarnardóttir, A.E. (1999) 'Change of diet of the Greenland Vikings determined from stable isotope analysis and 14C dating of their bones', *Radiocarbon*, 41(2): 157–68.

Buckland, P.C. (1992) 'Insects and the pre-Norse settlement of Faeroe: a case not proven', *Fróðskaparrit*, 38/39: 107–14.

Buckland, P.C., Buckland, P.I. and Skidmore, P. (1998) 'Insect remains from GUS: an interim report', in J. Arneborg and H.C. Gulløv (eds) *Man, Culture and Environment in Ancient Greenland*, Copenhagen: Danish National Museum and Danish Polar Centre.

Buckland, P.C. and Dinnin, M.H. (1998) 'Insect faunas at *landnám*: a palaeoentomological study at Tjørnuvík, Streymoy, Faroe Islands', *Fróðskaparrit*, 46: 277–86.

Buckland, P.C., Edwards, K.J., Blackford, J., Dugmore, A.J., Sadler, J.P. and Sveinbjarnardóttir, G. (1995) 'A question of Landnám: pollen, charcoal and insect studies on Papey, eastern Iceland', in R. Butlin and N. Roberts (eds) *Ecological Relations in Historical Times*, Oxford: Blackwell.

Buckland, P.C., Panagiotakopulu, E., Buckland, P.I., Perdikaris, S. and Skidmore, P. (2006) 'Insect faunas from medieval Langenes, Arctic Norway', in R. Engelmark and J. Linderholm (eds) *Proceedings of the 8th Nordic Conference on the Application of Scientific Methods in Archaeology, Umeå, Sweden 2001* (Archaeology and Environment 21), Umeå: Dept. of Archaeology, University of Umeå.

Buckland, P.C., Panagiotakopulu, E., Skidmore, P. and Buckland, P.I. (2005) 'Insect remains from Stóraborg, Iceland'. (Unpubl. File Report, National Museum of Iceland.)

Buckland, P.C. and Perry, D. (1989) 'Ectoparasites of sheep from Stóraborg, Iceland and their interpretation: piss, parasites and people, a palaeoecological perspective', *hikuin*, 15: 37–46.

Buckland, P.C. and Sadler, J.P. (1989) 'A biogeography of the human flea, *Pulex irritans* L. (Siphonaptera: Pulicidae)', *Journal of Biogeography*, 16: 115–20.

Buckland, P.C., Sadler, J.P. and Smith, D. (1993) 'An insect's eye-view of the Norse farm', in C.E. Batey, J. Jesch and Ch.D. Morris (eds) *The Viking Age in Caithness, Orkney and the North Atlantic*, Edinburgh: Edinburgh University Press.

Church, M., Arge, S.V., Brewington, S., McGovern, T.H., Woollett, J.W., Perdikaris, S., Lawson, I.T., Amundsen, C., Harrison, R. and Krivogorskaya, K. (2005) 'Puffins, pigs, cod and barley: palaeoeconomy at Undir Junkarinsfløtti, Sandoy, Faroe Islands', *Environmental Archaeology*, 10: 179–97.

Coope, G.R. (1981) 'Report on the Coleoptera from an eleventh-century house at Christ Church Place, Dublin', in H. Bekker-Nielson, P. Foote and O. Olsen (eds) *Proceedings of the Eighth Viking Congress (1977)*, Odense: Odense University Press.

Dugmore, A.J. and Buckland, P.C. (1991) 'Tephrochronology and Late Holocene soil erosion in south Iceland', in J.K. Maizels and C. Caseldine (eds) *Environmental Change in Iceland. Past and Present*, Dordrecht: Kluwer Academic Press.

Dugmore, A.J., Church, M.J., Buckland, P.C., Edwards, K.J., Lawson, I., McGovern, T.H., Panagiotakopulu, E., Simpson, I.A., Skidmore, P. and Sveinbjarnardóttir, G. (2005) 'The Norse *landnám* on the North Atlantic islands: an environmental impact assessment', *Polar Record*, 41: 21–37.

Einarsson, B. (1992) 'Granastaðir-grophuset och andra isländska grophus i ett nordiskt sammanhang. Deras funktion och betydelse i kolonisationforloppet i Island', *Viking. Tidskrift for norrøn arkeologi*, 55: 95–119.

Einarsson, T. (1961) 'Pollenanalytische Untersuchunngen zur spät- und postglacialen Klimageschichte Islands', *Sonderveröffliche der geologische Institut der Universitat Köln*, 6: 1–52.

Fitzhugh, W.W. and Ward, E.I. (2000) *Vikings. The North Atlantic Saga*, Washington, DC: Smithsonian Institute.

Foote, P.G. and Wilson, D.M. (1970) *The Viking Achievement. The Society and Culture of Early Medieval Scandinavia*, London: Sidgwick & Jackson.

Fredskild, B. (1988) 'Agriculture in a marginal area: south Greenland from the Norse Landnam (985 A.D.) to the present (1985 A.D.)', in H.H. Birks, H.J.B. Birks, P.E. Kaland and D. Moe, *The Cultural Landscape. Past, Present and Future*, Cambridge: Cambridge University Press.

—— (1992) 'Erosion and vegetation change in south Greenland caused by agriculture', *Geografisk Tidsskrift*, 92: 14–21.

Hallsdóttir, M. (1987) *Pollen Analytical Studies of Human Influence on Vegetation in Relation to the Landnam Tephra Layer in Southwest Iceland* (Lundqua Thesis 18), Lund: Acupress.

Hannon, G.E. and Bradshaw, R.H.W. (2000) 'Impacts and timing of the first human settlement on vegetation of the Faroe Islands', *Quaternary Research*, 54: 404–13.

Hart Hansen, J.P., Melgaard, J. and Nordqvist, J. (eds) (1991) *The Greenland Mummies*, London: British Museum.

Jóhansen, J. (1985) *Studies in the Vegetational History of the Faroe and Shetland Islands* (Annales Societatis Scientiarum Faeroensis. Supplementum 11), Tórshavn: Føroya Fróðskaparfélag.

Jónsson, J. (1877) 'Jón Jónsson's saga: the genuine autobiography of a modern Icelander (G.R. Fitz-Roy Cole ed.)', *Frazer's Magazine*, New Series 15: no. 85.

Kenward, H.K. (1980) 'Insect remains', in E. Schia (ed.) *De Arkeologiske Utgravninger i Gamlebyen, Oslo*, vol. 2: *Feltene 'Oslogate 3 og 7'*, Oslo: Universitetsforlaget.

Kenward, H.K. and Hall, A.R. (1995) *Biological Evidence from 16–22 Coppergate*, York: Council for British Archaeology.

McGovern, T.H., Amorosi, T., Perdikaris, S. and Woollett, J. (1996) 'Zooarchaeology of Sandnes

V51: economic change at a chieftain's farm in west Greenland', *Arctic Anthropology*, 33: 94–122.

McGovern, T.H., Perdikaris, S.P. and Tinsley, C. (2001) 'Economy of *landnam*: the evidence of zooarchaeology', in A. Wawn and T. Sigurðardóttir (eds) *Westward to Vinland*, Reykjavík: The Nordahl Institute.

Ólafsson, G. and Ágústsson, H. (2003) *The Reconstructed Medieval Farm in Þjórsárdalur and the Development of the Icelandic Turf House*, Reykjavík: National Museum of Iceland.

Panagiotakopulu, E. (2001) 'Fossil records of ectoparasites', *Antenna*, 25: 41–2.

——— (2004) 'Dipterous remains and archaeological interpretation', *Journal of Archaeological Science*, 31: 1675–84.

Panagiotakopulu, E., Skidmore, P. and Buckland, P.C. (2007) 'Fossil insect evidence for the end of the Western Settlement in Norse Greenland', *Naturwissenschaften*, 94: 300–6.

Panagiotakopulu, E. *et al.* (forthcoming b) *Insect Faunas from GUS in the Western Settlement of Norse Greenland*.

Perdikaris, S. (1999) 'From chiefly provisioning to commercial fishery: long-term economic change in Arctic Norway', *World Archaeology*, 30: 388–402.

Sadler, J.P. and Skidmore, P. (1995) 'Introductions, extinctions or continuity: faunal change in the North Atlantic', in R. Butlin and N. Roberts (eds) *Human Impact and Adaptation. Ecological Relations in Historical Time*, Oxford: Blackwell.

Simpson, I.A., Dugmore, A.J., Thomson, A. and Vésteinsson, O. (2001) 'Crossing the thresholds: human ecology and historical patterns of landscape degradation', *Catena*, 42: 175–92.

Simpson, I.A., Milek, K.B. and Guðmundsson, G. (1999) 'A reinterpretation of the great pit at Hofstaðir, Iceland, using sediment thin section micromorphology', *Geoarchaeology*, 14: 511–30.

Stenberger, M. (ed.) (1943) *Fornitida gårdar i Island. Meddelanden från den nordiska arkeologiska undersökingen i Island sommaren 1939*, Copenhagen: Ejnar Munksgaard.

Sveinbjarnardóttir, G. and Buckland, P.C. (1983) 'An uninvited guest', *Antiquity*, 48: 32–3.

Þórarinsson, S. (1961) 'Uppblastur á Islandi í ljósi öskulagarannsokna', *Arsrit Skogræktarfélags Íslands* (1961): 17–54.

Troup, J.A. (1987) *The Ice-bound Whalers. The Story of the Dee and the Grenville Bay, 1836–37*, Kirkwall: The Orkney Press.

CHAPTER FORTY-FOUR

THE DISCOVERY OF VINLAND

———•◆•———

Birgitta Wallace

In 1837 Carl Christian Rafn published the Vinland sagas in his *Antiquitates Americanae* (Rafn 1837), followed in 1838 by *Discovery of North America* (Rafn 1838), the English translation. Ever since, there has been speculation, on both sides of the Atlantic, as to the location of Vinland and the two other areas of Norse landfalls, Markland and Helluland. Archaeological work at L'Anse aux Meadows, in Newfoundland, in the 1960s and 70s provides compelling evidence that Vinland was, in fact, the Gulf of St Lawrence in eastern Canada. While situations and events described in the sagas have been ritualised, conflated and adjusted for the political biases of their day, the L'Anse aux Meadows site proves that Vinland was indeed a physical reality. The site is *Leifsbúðir-Straumfjǫrðr*, and Vinland itself the coastal region encircling the Gulf of St Lawrence, extending from the Strait of Belle Isle in the north to New Brunswick in the south.

THE NAME VÍNLAND

The name *Vínland*, written and pronounced with a long /ī/, means 'Land of Wine'. Suggestions that the name should be *Vinland* with a short /ĭ/, translated as 'Grasslands' or 'Land of Pastures', have never been accepted by philologists. Where intended, there are instances of the long /ī/ in the actual saga manuscripts (Crozier 1998: 39). Theories that the sagas' *vínber* does not refer to grapes but to other berries, such as cranberries or currants, are untenable since the Norse had specific terms for these berries. Furthermore, none of these theories explains the sagas' equal emphasis on *vínviðr* 'grape trees'. Another notion, that the reference to wine was simply an invention to lend Vinland a paradisiacal quality (Nansen 1911; Keller 2001), is contradicted by archaeological evidence that proves the Norse had indeed visited regions where grapes grew wild.

THE LITERARY EVIDENCE – THE VINLAND MANUSCRIPTS

Although Vinland is mentioned in passing in several sources, the real descriptions of Vinland are to be found in *Grænlendinga saga* ('The Greenlanders' Saga') (hereafter GS) preserved in the larger *Flateyjarbók* ('Flat Island Book'), dated to the first half of the fourteenth century (Helgi Þorláksson in Wawn and Þórunn Sigurðardóttir 2001: 69), and in *Erik's Saga* (AM 544 and 557). *Erik's Saga* (hereafter ES) exists in two versions, the *Skalholt Book* (hereafter SB), dated to the mid- to late thirteenth century, and the *Hauk's Book* (hereafter HB), dated to the beginning of the thirteenth century (cf. Gísli Sigurðsson 2004: 265–302).

The Greenlanders' Saga and Eric's Saga describe the same events, but with discrepancies. The GS describes four expeditions and a fifth which never reached its goal. The new lands were accidentally discovered around 985 by the Icelander Bjarni Herjólfsson *en route* to his father in Greenland. They were explored a few years later by Leifr Eiríksson, who established a base there, *Leifsbúðir* ('Leif's Booths'). Here he discovered grapes and good lumber, which he brought back to Greenland. The explorations were continued by Leif's siblings Þórvaldr, Þorsteinn and Freydís, and sister-in-law Guðríðr, with her husband, the Icelandic trader Þorfinnr Karlsefni.

In ES all four expeditions have been combined into one single expedition as large as all the others together. The leader of the expedition is Þorfinnr Karlsefni with his wife Guðríðr. This saga has two major bases, *Straumfjǫrðr* ('Fjord of Currents') and *Hóp* ('Estuary Lagoon'). *Straumfjǫrðr* is a base in northern Vinland from which expeditions leave in the summer to explore in all directions, returning to spend the winter. *Hóp* is a summer camp in the south where grapes are collected and lumber harvested. *Straumfjǫrðr* is described as an attractive place, with tall grass, plenty of game, and offshore islands so covered with seabirds and eggs that there was hardly room to set foot. Although the winter proved difficult because no provisions were laid up and the hunting and fishing failed, it was sufficiently mild for the livestock to go out all winter.

Hóp was a summer camp at a considerable distance south of *Straumfjǫrðr*. It derived its name from the many tidal estuary lagoons protected by offshore sandbars. The lagoons were so shallow that ships could be brought in only during high tide. It was a more hospitable area than *Straumfjǫrðr*. On the shores there were fields of self-sown wheat, and forests with *mausir* wood, wood burls and grapevines climbing trees. However, the area was inhabited by large groups of native people, and the Norse feared them.

Frequently, *Leifsbúðir*, *Straumfjǫrðr* and *Hóp* have been regarded as three separate spots. *Leifsbúðir* is, however, likely a combination of *Straumfjǫrðr* and *Hóp*. Like *Straumfjǫrðr* it is a base for explorations in several directions, but many of its physical characteristics are close to those of *Hóp*, and both grapes and lumber are harvested there.

The Icelandic saga scholar Ólafur Halldórsson has suggested that the purpose of ES was to magnify Guðríðr's role to establish antecedents for the canonisation sought *c.* 1200 for Bishop Björn Gilsson, a direct descendant of Karlsefni and Guðríðr (Wawn and Þórunn Sigurðardóttir 2001: 47, 50). To magnify the importance of Þorfinnr Karlsefni and Guðríðr, ES reduces Leifr Eiríksson to the accidental discoverer of Vinland. Karlsefni usurps Leif's position as leading explorer, combining all the expeditions of the GS into one mega-expedition led by himself. The name *Leifsbúðir* is accordingly erased and replaced with *Straumfjǫrðr*.

PURPOSE OF THE VINLAND SETTLEMENTS

It is often assumed that the purpose of the Vinland settlements was colonisation. In fact, the chief goal of the Vinland voyages was exploration for resources and exploitation of these resources so that they could be brought back to Greenland: 'They did nothing but explore the land' (ES and HB); 'for the profitable resources' (ES and HB); 'Thorvald . . . thought that the land had been explored in too small a portion' (ES and HB); 'good for both property and fame' (GS). The GS does state that Karlsefni's expedition 'took with them all sorts of livestock because they intended to settle *if they could*' (emphasis added). On the other hand, ES asserts that Thorstein took 'little livestock . . . no more than what they took of weapons and provisions' (ES and SB). The participants in the Vinland expeditions were not families but male work crews, hired for a particular voyage for a share in the profits. Only a few women were present to handle domestic chores. Þorsteinn Eiríksson's voyage was launched specifically to retrieve the body of his brother Þórvaldr. This would not have been necessary had the site been intended for permanent occupation.

The initial buildings were 'booths', sod walls roofed over with tent cloth, giving rise to the name *Leifsbúðir*. It was only when the expedition decided to spend the winter that they built 'big houses'. No buildings were constructed for livestock, but the animals grazed out of doors all winter.

The size of the expeditions varied between 30 and 70 people. Karlsefni's crew of 160 is a fictional combination of three separate crews into one. The crews reflected the west Norse social stratification. At the top was the leader, in all cases a member of Leifr Eiríksson's family. The leader might be accompanied by his or her spouse. The leader could have a business partner, one or more traders with their own ship and crew. The crews consisted mostly of hired workers but included some of the leader's personal staff. Slaves such as Tyrkir the German were also included for special chores.

The activities consisted first of exploration. As useful resources were encountered, they were collected and brought to the base in order to be carried back to Greenland. The resources in question were grapes, lumber, especially 'grape trees', and furs. In GS, the same settlement was occupied by all the expeditions. There were no aboriginal people at *Straumfjǫrðr*, but the Norse encountered large groups of native people in both *Hóp* and *Markland*.

The expeditions took place shortly after the year 1000. Each expedition stayed one to three years. In the end, they were given up altogether. The presence of aboriginal people was given as the major reason.

THE ARCHAEOLOGICAL EVIDENCE – THE L'ANSE AUX MEADOWS SITE

L'Anse aux Meadows is located on the western side of the northernmost tip of Newfoundland's Northern Peninsula, on the Strait of Belle Isle, facing Labrador (Figure 44.1). It is an easily recognisable landmark for any navigator *en route* from the north: at the entrance to a large strait, with distinctive landmarks such as Belle Isle, Cape Bauld and Cape Onion, Great and Little Sacred Islands (Figure 44.2). The site comprises eight buildings located on a former beach terrace surrounding a sedge peat bog. A small brook cuts through the terrace. There are three dwelling complexes, each consisting of a large hall and a small hut. One complex also includes a small house. A fourth complex, consisting of a charcoal kiln and a hut with furnace for direct-reduction iron manufacture is located on the seaside portion of the terrace, at some distance from the dwellings (Figure 44.3).

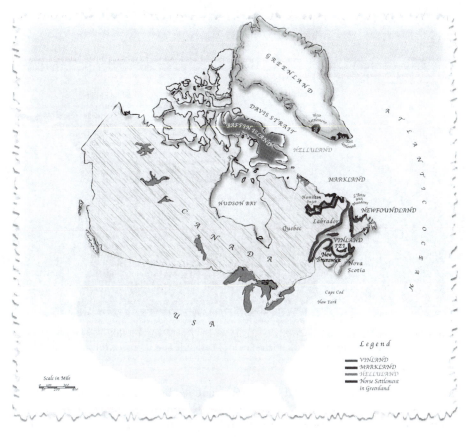

Figure 44.1   Map of Vinland. (Drawing: Vis-à-Vis Graphics, St. John's.)

Although L'Anse aux Meadows is unquestionably Norse and of an early eleventh-century date (the date is based on architectural evidence, artefacts and fifty-eight radio-carbon dates), the only site in the Norse world to which it corresponds in structure, function, social organisation and size is *Straumfjǫrðr* of ES and, in part, *Leifsbúðir* of GS. What sets L'Anse aux Meadows apart from all other Norse sites is its location, the lack of structures for livestock and its size. The site is much more exposed than usual for an Icelandic or Greenland site. This is in spite of the fact that more sheltered coves and protected harbours could be found short distances to the east and south. Access to the Strait of Belle Isle was definitely the deciding factor for the location of the site. The buildings are almost exclusively dwellings. They are solid, roofed-over dwellings, built for year-round use, not seasonal *búðir*. There are no barns and byres, or any structures associated with domestic animals otherwise so prominent on all west Norse living sites. If domestic animals were present, they would have been left outside in the winter or consumed before then. The dwellings exhibit the same range in size and type as those found on large estates in Iceland and Greenland, mirroring the full spectrum of social classes in Norse society. Present are two large chieftain's halls (A and F), of which F is larger and more complex than the other, a more modest hall (D), a smaller one-roomed

Figure 44.2 The L'Anse aux Meadows site, facing north. The Norse buildings were on the terrace to the right. The low cape points towards the Strait of Belle Isle and Labrador. (Photo: B. Wallace.)

house (B), two sunken huts (E and G) and one rounded hut of even simpler construction (C). All huts are equipped with fireplaces indicating human, not animal, use. The size of the buildings and their relationship to each other indicate an organisation with a leader-in-command, a near-equal associate, work crews numbering between about twenty and thirty per dwelling complex, a few women but not regular families, and domestic labour of low status. Some specialisation is discernible within the work crews: carpentry, iron manufacture, smithing and boat repair. Storage spaces within the dwellings are conspicuously large. The total size of the settlement was substantial, anywhere between seventy and ninety people. This is an unusual concentration of people, even for a large estate.

From L'Anse aux Meadows, the Norse made voyages to areas further south. They reached areas of wild grapevines as demonstrated by the presence in the Norse deposits of butternuts, *Juglans cinerea*, a North American species of walnut, and a burl of butternut wood. The northern limit of this species, in the St Lawrence river valley and north-eastern New Brunswick, corresponds to the limit of wild grapes.

Although there was abundant evidence of aboriginal groups on the site, ranging in date from 5000 BC to *c.* AD 850, and *c.* AD 1200–1500, no aboriginal people were on the site at the time of the Norse.

The occupation of the settlement was short, only a few years, as indicated by the minute scale of the middens and sparseness of the cultural deposits. Another indication of short occupation is the absence of graves, Christian or pagan.

L'Anse aux Meadows was not a colonising venture. The site resembles winter camps set up in Europe by marauding Vikings as 'safe havens' during the winter months when

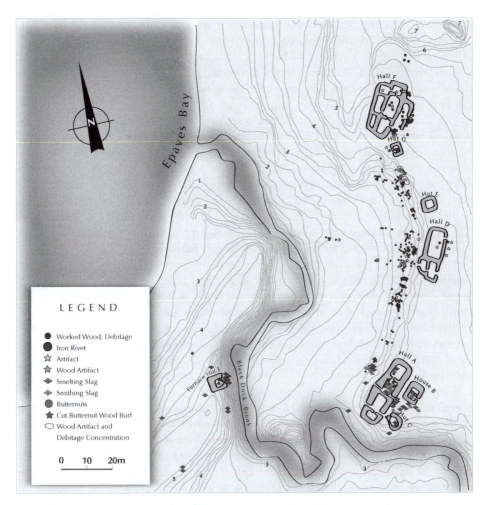

Figure 44.3 Plan of the L'Anse aux Meadows site. (Plan by Vis-à-Vis Graphics, St. John's.)

no pillaging took place. However, unlike the conditions in those winter camps, the L'Anse aux Meadows site served as a port-of-trade, or gateway. It was a safe haven, where goods from remote areas were collected and prepared for shipment back home. It was controlled by a chieftain or king via a deputy. In this case it was controlled by Eiríkr rauði (Erik the Red), and after his death by Leifr. The presence of large storage rooms at L'Anse aux Meadows is consistent with a port-of-trade function.

CORRELATION OF THE ARCHAEOLOGICAL AND LITERARY EVIDENCE

The function, the structures, the size, the social organisation and the time and length of occupation of L'Anse aux Meadows clearly parallel those of *Straumfjǫrðr*. The climate historian Astrid Ogilvie has shown that in the eleventh century temperatures were warmer, with a special warming peak around the year 1000 (Wawn and Þórunn

Sigurðardóttir 2001: 173–88). Under these circumstances winters would have been snow free, and the livestock could have grazed out of doors all winter.

The very size of the L'Anse aux Meadows settlement makes it certain that it is *the* site of the Vinland sagas. Calculations of the Greenland population have shown that during the time of the Vinland voyages, the entire Greenland colony had no more than 400 to 500 individuals (Lynnerup 1998: 113, 116–18). Given that it took anywhere between seventy and ninety people to run L'Anse aux Meadows, it is clear that there was not sufficient labour available to build and maintain another settlement of this size. Even if as much as two-thirds of the crew were Icelandic, at least 5 per cent of the Greenland population would have been required to operate L'Anse aux Meadows. Considerable effort had gone into its construction. For the three halls alone, eighty-six trees had been felled and dressed, and this does not include wood required for the large roofs and the smaller structures. A minimum of 1,500 m^3 of sod had been cut for the walls and roofs. The construction would have taken sixty men about two months. The small Greenland colony could not have supported another site of this magnitude.

Butternut trees grow in the same areas as wild grapes. Thus we can state with certainty that the Norse encounter with wild grapes is based on fact. In their wild state, grapes grow in stands of deciduous trees, the vines winding themselves up the tree trunks. These are the *vínviðr*, the grape trees of the sagas. Grapes and butternuts occur in the hardwood forests of New Brunswick, as do large maples and oaks typical of New Brunswick. Such hardwood was more valuable than the small birch and softwood lumber of northern Newfoundland. It would have been a significant cargo to bring back to Greenland.

Wine, and walnuts, were the type of luxury items served during large banquets by chieftains to impress their followers and to gain influence and power. For Leifr and his family, a potential supply of wine would have been a welcome prospect for maintaining their new position as the first family of Greenland.

ES is clear that the grapes and lumber were obtained at *Hóp*, not at *Straumfjǫrðr. Hóp* means inlet or lagoon, generally at the mouth of a river, a tidal saltwater lake protected from the open sea by sand barriers at the entrance. North-eastern New Brunswick is famous for its warm, shallow, tidal lagoons behind sandbars guarding the estuaries of several large rivers, of which Miramichi is the largest (Figure 44.4). Here, also, are butternuts and grapes. This area was also home to the largest concentration of aboriginal people in Atlantic Canada, the ancestors of the Mi'kmaq. This region is *Hóp*.

While butternut trees and wild grapes can also be found in New England, skin canoes, a prominent feature associated with the native people of *Hóp*, were never used there. The Mi'kmaq, on the other hand, did use hide canoes (Wallis and Wallis 1955: 50–1).

Vinland must have been the entire area from the Strait of Belle Isle to the southern shores of the Gulf. L'Anse aux Meadows was the gateway to its riches. Its location on the Strait of Belle Isle and the western shore of Newfoundland's Northern Peninsula shows that the main traffic south was through the Strait. The Strait is a natural funnel into the Gulf of St Lawrence. The Gulf forms an inland sea, which can be circumnavigated by beginning and ending the voyage in L'Anse aux Meadows. The southern part of the Gulf is marked by large leafy forests, warm waters and great diversity in fauna and flora, including wild grapes and walnuts. It is a rich landscape like that of legendary Vinland but totally unlike that of Iceland, Greenland and Newfoundland.

Figure 44.4   The Miramichi River at Metepenagiaq Mi'kmaq First Nation, New Brunswick.
(Photo: R. Ferguson.)

Given that L'Anse aux Meadows is Leifsbúðir–Straumfjǫrðr, it follows that Markland is the central forest belt of Labrador, chiefly the area around Hamilton Inlet. It was here that Þórvaldr met his death from an arrow shot fired by aboriginal people.

North of Markland was Helluland, 'Land of Flat Rocks'. The sagas' descriptions of this area as one with big glaciers and mountains, and 'as a slab of rock was everything between the mountains and the sea' (GS) is an apt description of the area north of 58° latitude north, including Baffin Island.

Vinland was a short-lived venture. This is understandable, considering the size of the Greenland population and the distance to L'Anse aux Meadows and Vinland. By coastal ship, it is 3,000 km to L'Anse aux Meadows, and 4,000 km to north-eastern New Brunswick. This is nearly 2,000 km longer than from south-western Greenland to Bergen in Norway. Given the short sailing season in the western Atlantic, it would have been impossible for the small population in Greenland to maintain regular traffic to two such distant locations, in opposite directions. The traffic with Europe was essential, the one to Vinland was not. Lumber and wine could be obtained in Europe, but so could goods such as metals, spices, exotic textiles and other luxury items. Europe also held personal and political connections. For the small Greenland colony, Vinland remained an impractical paradise.

BIBLIOGRAPHY

Bergersen, R. (1997) *Vinland Bibliography. Writings Relating to the Norse in Greenland and America* (Ravnetrykk 10), Tromsø: University of Tromsø.

Crozier, A. (1998) 'The Vinland hypothesis: a reply to the historians', *Gardar. Årsbok för samfundet Sverige–Island i Lund–Malmö*, 29: 37–66.

Fitzhugh, W.W. and Ward, E.I. (eds) (2000) *Vikings. The North Atlantic Saga*, Washington, DC: The Smithsonian Institution.

Gísli Sigurðsson (2004) *The Medieval Icelandic Saga and Oral Tradition. A Discourse on Method* (Milman Parry Collection of Oral Literature. Publications 2) Cambridge, MA and London: Harvard University Press.

Ingstad, A.S. and Ingstad, H. (1986) *The Norse Discovery of America*, 2 vols. Vol. 1: *Excavations at L'Anse aux Meadows, Newfoundland 1961–1968*. Vol. 2: *The Historical Background and the Evidence of the Norse Settlement Discovered in Newfoundland*, Oslo: Norwegian University Press.

Jones, G. (1986) *The Norse Atlantic Saga. Being the Norse Voyages of Discovery and Settlement to Iceland, Greenland, and North America*, 2nd edn, Oxford and New York: Oxford University Press.

Keller, Ch. (2001) *Leiv Eriksson, Helge Ingstad og Vinland. Kjelder og tradisioner*, Trondheim: Tapir Akademisk Forlag.

Lewis-Simpson, S. (ed.) (2004) *Vínland Revisited. The Norse World at the Turn of the First Millennium. Selected Papers from the Viking Millennium International Symposium 15–24 September 2000, Newfoundland and Labrador*. St John's NL: Historic Sites Association of Newfoundland and Labrador, Inc.

Lynnerup, N. (1998) *The Greenland Norse. A Biological-Anthropological Study* (Meddelelser om Grønland. Man and Society 24), Copenhagen: Kommissionen for videnskabelige Undersøgelser i Grønland.

Nansen, F. (1911) *In Northern Mists. Arctic Exploration in Early Times*, 2 vols, trans. A.G. Chater, New York: F.A. Stokes Co.

Rafn, C.Ch. (1837) *Antiquitates Americanae sive scriptores septentrionalies rerum ante-columbianarum America. Samling af de i Nordens Oldskrifter indeholdte Efterretninger om de gamle Nordboers Opdagelsereiser til Amerika fra de 10e til det 14de Aarhundrede*, Copenhagen: Det Kongelige Nordiske Oldskriftselskab.

—— (1838) *Discovery of North America*, New York: Jackson.

Wallace, B. Linderoth (1991) 'L'Anse aux Meadows: gateway to Vinland', *Acta Archaeologica*, 61 (1990): 166–97.

—— (2003) 'L'Anse aux Meadows and Vinland, an abandoned experiment', in J. Barrett (ed.) *Contact, Continuity and Collapse. The Norse Colonisation of the North Atlantic* (Studies in the Early Middle Ages 5), Turnhout: Brepols.

—— (2006) *Westward Vikings. The Saga of L'Anse aux Meadows*, St John's, NL: Historic Sites Association, Newfoundland and Labrador, Inc.

Wallis, D. Wilson and Wallis, R. Sawtell (1955) *The Micmac Indians of Eastern Canada*, Minneapolis: University of Minnesota Press.

Wawn, A. and Þórunn Sigurðardóttir (eds) (2001) *Approaches to Vinland. Proceedings of a Conference on the Written and Archaeological Sources for the Norse Settlements in the North-Atlantic Region and Exploration of America. Held at The Nordic House, Reykjavik 9–11 August 1999* (Sigurður Nordal Institute Studies 4), Reykjavík: Sigurdur Nordal Institute.

NORSE AND NATIVES IN THE EASTERN ARCTIC

———•◆•———

Patricia Sutherland

When the Norse lived in Greenland between the tenth and fifteenth centuries AD, two distinct aboriginal populations were present in the eastern Arctic: the Dorset Palaeo-Eskimos, descendants of the first inhabitants of Arctic North America, occupied Arctic Canada and far north-western Greenland when the Norse arrived. The Thule Inuit, who were the ancestors of the present-day inhabitants of the area, immigrated to the eastern Arctic from Alaska at some time between the eleventh and thirteenth centuries AD.

Historical accounts of meetings between native groups and the Norse are rare and vague. The earliest mention of Arctic natives appears in the *Historia Norwegiae*, an Icelandic manuscript which may have been copied from an original dating to the mid-twelfth century. This brief description tells of apparently hostile meetings with natives living beyond Greenland, whom the Norse called *Skrælings*, and who used tools and weapons made from stone and walrus ivory rather than iron (Jones 1986: 18). This account may refer to either Dorset or Thule people.

The archaeological evidence bearing on the question of Norse–Dorset contact derives from a number of different localities (Figures 44.1.1 and 44.1.2). A fragment of a bronze vessel, of a type made no earlier than the end of the thirteenth century, was found in a Dorset dwelling in the Thule District of north-western Greenland and is interpreted as an indication of direct contact (Appelt *et al.* 1998). Small pieces of smelted copper have been recovered from two Dorset villages, one on the east coast of Hudson Bay (Harp 1975) and the other on the south coast of Hudson Strait (Plumet 1982). These objects are assumed to be of Norse origin, but probably reached their final locations through native trade routes, and therefore tell us little about the nature of meetings between the two groups or where they occurred. Objects which appear to be consistent with a knowledge of medieval European technologies – whetstones, artefacts of soapstone, fibre and wood – have been recovered from several Dorset sites on Baffin Island and in northern Labrador (Sutherland 2000a). The findings from these sites suggest direct contact and more complex interactions than previously thought.

A few later historical records refer to Arctic natives who were encountered in Greenland. These people were first met in the *Norðrsetr*, the northern hunting grounds to which the Norse travelled in summer in order to obtain walrus ivory and other

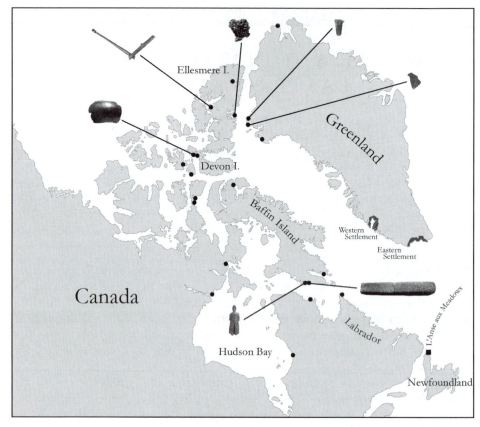

Figure 44.1.1 Map showing the distribution of objects relating to Norse contact recovered from aboriginal archaeological sites (see p. 615).

commodities for use in their trade with Europe. The *Norðrsetr* is usually considered to be the western coast of Greenland to the north of the Norse farming settlements in the area around Disko Bay, but it may have extended as far north as the Upernavik region at almost 73° latitude. A Norse presence in this region is confirmed by the discovery of a small runestone apparently dating to the latter half of the thirteenth century. A letter written by a Greenlandic priest states that in 1266 a hunting party returned from travelling further north in the *Norðrsetr* than ever before, but they had seen native dwellings only at one location, probably on the Nuussuaq Peninsula at the northern boundary of Disko Bay. The church then sent an expedition still further north, perhaps to the Upernavik region or possibly beyond the heavily glaciated coast of Melville Bay and as far as the Thule District of north-western Greenland. The explorers reported an abundance of seals, whales and bears, as well as native dwellings (Jones 1986: 80). Jette Arneborg (1997: 44) argues that this account seems to indicate that the Norse were looking for natives with whom to trade, probably for walrus ivory and hides.

Archaeological evidence suggests that both Dorset Palaeo-Eskimos and Thule Inuit were living in the Thule District at the time of this Norse voyage (Appelt *et al.* 1998), but the dominant occupation of the area, as well as of the adjacent regions of Ellesmere

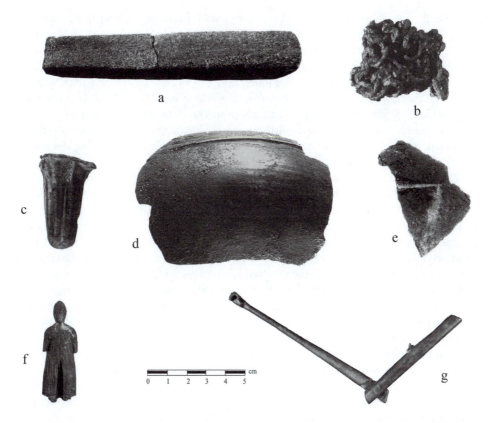

Figure 44.1.2   Selected artefacts relating to Norse contact recovered from aboriginal archaeological sites in Arctic Canada and adjacent regions of north-western Greenland: (a) squared and tapered whetstone (quartzite) (KdDq-9:618, 5183); (b) fragment of chain mail (SfFk-4:2); (c) leg of bronze vessel (L3.1466); (d) bowl portion of bronze vessel (RbJu-1:269); (e) bowl portion of bronze vessel (KNK 2280 × 613); (f) wooden figurine apparently representing a person in European dress (KeDq-7:325); (g) arm portion of bronze folding balance (SlHq-3:4). (a, b, d, f, g: Canadian Museum of Civilization; c, e: Danish National Museum.)

Island in Arctic Canada, was that of the Inuit. The dwellings and middens of the Thule people on both sides of Smith Sound have produced a wide variety of objects of Norse origin. In addition to small pieces of metal that have been reworked into blades for Inuit tools and weapons, these finds include ship rivets, fragments of chain mail, the leg of a bronze cooking vessel, woollen cloth, a double comb, chess pieces, a wooden spoon case, wooden box and tub parts, and a carpenter's plane (Holtved 1944; McCullough 1989; Gulløv 1997; Schledermann 2000). Peter Schledermann (1993) has suggested that the concentration of materials and the nature of the finds indicate a Norse visit to the area, which perhaps ended in shipwreck. Part of a bronze balance of the type used by medieval Norse traders, which was found in a Thule Inuit site on the west coast of Ellesmere Island, likely relates to this event and is suggestive of an intention to engage in trade (Sutherland 2000b).

Objects of European origin, which reached the Inuit through contact with the Norse, are found in association with a number of other sites in Arctic Canada and northern

Greenland. The majority of these objects are small pieces of smelted iron, copper or bronze which were valuable commodities to the Thule Inuit, and would have been widely distributed through native trade routes. Other items include a piece of oak wood incorporated in the frame of an umiak found on the north coast of Greenland (Knuth 1980), and a portion of a bronze vessel found on Devon Island (McGhee 1984), which is similar to that recovered from a Dorset site in north-western Greenland. It is currently impossible to determine whether this scatter of materials may have originated from one contact episode, such as the thirteenth-century event in the Thule District described by Schledermann (1993), or whether it resulted from multiple contacts along the eastern coasts of the Canadian Arctic and Greenland

The latter interpretation is supported by an archaeological find from the southern coast of Baffin Island: a small wooden carving that appears to represent an individual in European dress (Sabo and Sabo 1978). The figure is typical of Thule Inuit carving of humans, with a blank featureless face and stumpy arms, but the clothing style is European. It would seem unlikely that such an object would have been traded from Inuit who had met Norsemen in north-western Greenland, and more probable that the artist depicted a European encountered in the area which the Norse referred to as Helluland and which they coasted on their way to Markland and Vinland. It is interesting to note that the Thule village from which this carving was recovered is located only a few kilometres from Dorset sites, mentioned earlier, that have produced evidence suggestive of direct contact.

Historical records contain no further mention of Inuit in the regions to the north or west of the Norse colonies. A few confusing and suspect accounts refer to Inuit attacks on the Norse settlements (Gad 1971: 141–57), but no archaeological confirmation of such attacks has been found, and archaeological evidence that Inuit had actually appeared in the area of the settlements prior to Norse abandonment (Gulløv 1997) is inconclusive. Early Inuit sites in western Greenland contain many objects of Norse origin, but it is impossible to assess whether these were obtained by trade or were scavenged from abandoned farms after the Norse settlements disappeared. The oral traditions of the Greenlandic Inuit refer to trade between Norse and Inuit, and of a more complex relationship between the two peoples occupying western Greenland than is suggested by Norse historical accounts (Gad 1971: 158).

A divergence also exists between the historical records and the archaeological evidence from north-western Greenland and the eastern Canadian Arctic. The archaeological finds suggest considerably more interaction than do the historical accounts. Direct contact between the Norse and aboriginal groups appears to have occurred in at least two regions: the High Arctic coasts of Smith Sound, and the area of southern Baffin Island/Hudson Strait. Relationships between these groups probably included cautious trade as well as the hostile encounters mentioned in historical reports, and while most evidence relates to the twelfth to fourteenth centuries, meetings may have taken place throughout the period that the Norse occupied Greenland.

BIBLIOGRAPHY

Appelt, M., Gulløv, H.Ch. and Kapel, H. (1998) 'The gateway to Greenland: report of the field season 1996', in J. Arneborg and H.Ch. Gulløv (eds) *Man, Culture, and Environment in Ancient Greenland. Report on a Research Programme*, Copenhagen: Dansk Polar Center.

Arneborg, J. (1997) 'Cultural borders: reflections on Norse–Eskimo interaction', in R. Gilberg and H.Ch. Gulløv (eds) *Fifty Years of Arctic Research. Anthropological Studies from Greenland to Siberia* (National Museum of Denmark. Ethnographical Series 18), Copenhagen: Department of Ethnography.

Gad, F. (1971) *The History of Greenland*, vol. 1: *Earliest Times to 1700*, Montréal: McGill-Queen's University Press.

Gulløv, H.Ch. (1997) *From Middle Ages to Colonial Times. Archaeological and Ethnohistorical Studies of the Thule Culture in South West Greenland 1300–1800 AD* (Meddelelser om Grønland; Man and Society 23), Copenhagen: Commission for Scientific Research in Greenland.

Harp Jr, E. (1975) 'A late Dorset copper amulet from southeastern Hudson Bay', *Folk*, 16/17: 33–44.

Holtved, E. (1944) *Archaeological Investigations in the Thule District*, 2 vols (Meddelelser om Grønland 141/1–2), Copenhagen: Reitzel.

Jones, G. (1986) *The Norse Atlantic Saga*, 2nd edn, Oxford: Oxford University Press.

Knuth, E. (1980) *Umiaq'en fra Peary Land*, Roskilde: Vikingeskibshallen.

McCullough, K.M. (1989) *The Ruin Islanders. Early Thule Culture Pioneers in the Eastern High Arctic* (Canadian Museum of Civilization. Mercury Paper 141), Hull: Archaeological Survey of Canada.

McGhee, R. (1984) 'Contact between Native Americans and the medieval Norse: a review of the evidence', *American Antiquity* 49(1): 4–26.

Plumet, P. (1982) 'Les maisons longues dorsétiennes de l'ungava', *Géographie Physique et Quaternaire*, 36(3): 253–89.

Sabo, D. and Sabo III, G. (1978) 'A possible Thule carving of a Viking from Baffin Island, N.W.T.', *Canadian Journal of Archaeology*, 2: 33–42.

Schledermann, P. (1993) 'Norsemen in the High Arctic?', in B.L. Clausen (ed.) *Viking Voyages to North America*, Roskilde: The Viking Ship Museum.

—— (2000) 'Ellesmere: Vikings in the far north', in W.W. Fitzhugh and E. Ward (eds) *Vikings. The North Atlantic Saga*, Washington, DC: Smithsonian Institution Press.

Sutherland, P. (2000a) 'Strands of culture contact: Dorset–European interactions in the Canadian eastern Arctic', in M. Appelt, J. Berglund and H.Ch. Gulløv (eds) *Identities and Cultural Contacts in the Arctic*, Copenhagen: National Museum of Denmark and Danish Polar Centre.

—— (2000b) 'The Norse and Native North Americans', in W.W. Fitzhugh and E. Ward (eds) *Vikings. The North Atlantic Saga*, Washington, DC: Smithsonian Institution Press.

PART III

SCANDINAVIA ENTERS
THE EUROPEAN STAGE

———•◆•———

CHAPTER FORTY-FIVE

CHRISTIANISATION AND THE EMERGENCE OF THE EARLY CHURCH IN SCANDINAVIA

———•◆•———

Stefan Brink

Scandinavia was Christianised at more or less the same time as other polities on the European fringe, that is, roughly in the tenth and eleventh centuries. The traditional and political-historical dates for this religious change are: Bohemia *c.* 970, Hungary *c.* 1000, Poland *c.* 1000 etc. There are interesting anomalies, for example Prussia, with a conversion around 1300, and even more so Lithuania, which continued to be a 'pagan state' in nearly all of the Middle Ages, with an official conversion as late as *c.* 1400. Another polity on the European fringe, Ireland, was on the other hand one of the earliest to convert to the new religion: it was Christianised already in the fifth century. In between the Anglo-Saxons (seventh century), the Frisians (eighth century) and, by military force, the Saxons (*c.* 800) had become part of the quickly expanding Christian world.

Already at the beginning of this chapter it has to be emphasised that all these dates for 'Christianisation' and 'conversion' relate to certain mainly political events, which in later historical writings were considered as important dates or decisive moments for the religious change. Of course, Christianisation is more of a process, a slow cultural change and an adoption of new ideas.

The new religion probably did not bring any immediate changes to people: the old chieftains and aristocratic families continued to be the social elite, people continued, as a collective, to participate in a communal 'cult', if not at the district's old cult site, so in a church, which was sometimes erected on the old cult site; life continued on the whole as before, with cultivating the land, raising the stock, and probably still being aware of and appeasing the invisible 'small people' living on the farm, the *landvættir* residing on the farm's land, the elves and *vittror* in the forest and other supernatural powers living among the people. However, in the longer perspective the change to a new religion was very profound, probably the biggest mental and social change Scandinavia has seen in history, that is, concerning policy, society, economy, art, gender relations etc. Gradually the Scandinavians exchanged an entire pre-Christian world system, including constitutional beliefs on life and aftermath, to a new, Christian world-system.

Scandinavians went from an oral society in principle, which used runes on erected stones in order to honour the deceased, to a literacy society, with books and written documents. They transcended into a society based on documents and the written word, where the scribal technology was in the hands of a new social elite, the clergy. With the establishment of the Church a new hierarchy in society emerged. The Church became the prime mover and the dominant force in Europe in the Middle Ages.

We have a big problem when it comes to the study of the Christianisation of Scandinavia due to the deficiency of reliable – or in fact any – written sources. We have from the critical period – the ninth, tenth and eleventh centuries – only a handful of written sources: *Vita Ansgarii*, the history of Archbishop Ansgar and his life in the ninth century, written by the disciple Rimbert, who became the second archbishop in Hamburg–Bremen at Ansgar's death in 865. It is believed that Rimbert completed this hagiography sometime before 876. Adam of Bremen's history of the archdiocese Hamburg–Bremen (*Gesta Hammaburgensis ecclesiae pontificum*), written *c.* 1070, and then some scattered notices in Frankish and English annals and chronicles. In addition, we of course have the Old Norse sagas and their tales of what happened a couple of centuries earlier. Every one of these sources is marred by source-critical problems of various kinds; none has of course been written as a historical account on the basis of modern source-critical methods. Hence, the written sources we have to build our reconstruction on are biased in several respects. However, archaeology can provide us with more material to take into account; and comparisons with neighbouring people with more written sources describing their Christianisation process, as with the Anglo-Saxons, also offer interesting parallels.

THE CHRISTIANISATION PROCESS

For many centuries, ever since the early Middle Ages, the historical writings on the conversion have intimately been connected to the activities of certain missionaries in Scandinavia. In principle every province has a tradition of 'their' missionary, who is said to have converted people and made them able to see the new light. Iceland had Þangbrandr, Vestlandet in western Norway had St Sunniva, Västmanland in Sweden had St David, Södermanland had St Eskil and St Botvid, Småland had St Sigfrid, Hälsingland had Stenfi or St Staffan. There were more local saints, such as St Elin in the town of Skövde and St Elav in Borgholm. The history of the introduction of the Christian religion in Scandinavia became the history of these holy men and women, who in principle had to give their lives in the religious struggle, but which eventually resulted in a local cult and a canonisation of the one killed. A legend was produced and became part of the history of the early Church.

This traditional view of the Christianisation of Scandinavia can be described as a process which starts at the bottom of society and eventually climbs up on the societal ladder. The missionaries were assumed to have been wandering around among people, just like Jesus did in Palestine, preaching, converting and baptising them, and not least stressed was the importance of Christian slaves, taken abroad. The Christian religion was supposed to successively have permeated society.

Modern research has in a way turned this picture upside-down. Today we stress the importance of kings and chieftains in the Christianisation process, toning down the importance of Christian slaves, furthermore stressing that it was very much a process, stretching over several centuries in time. The Christianisation is looked upon as part of a much larger cultural shift, which has sometimes been termed a 'Europeanisation', where Scandinavia adapted to a Continental situation. This culture revolution took place in the

Viking Age, with a consolidation in the early Middle Ages, and is probably the most dynamic period in our history. We are dealing with a 'top–down' process, where first kings and chieftains adopted the new religion and Continental culture, which, eventually, trickled down in society over time.

To exemplify we can study the Norwegian kings Óláfr Tryggvason and Óláfr Haraldsson. The former was a youth of royal lineage (of which there were several in Norway at that time). He had been on the Continent and in England and made himself quite a reputation and wealth as a mercenary. He also had been baptised in England. That was the smart way for a pretender to get access to a throne, so that he could come back home and claim power and the kingship. These youngsters had on their journeys of course watched and understood how to be and act as a king by the grace of God, also that the Church was an important ally for a kingdom, and that the document-based church administration was unsurpassed and utterly useful to rule and administer a kingdom. Óláfr Tryggvason returned home to Norway at the end of the 990s and managed to be accepted as king, first in Trøndelag, then in the rest of Norway. In the early historical tradition King Óláfr is considered the one who Christianised Norway. The Icelandic medieval historian Ári fróði wrote in his *Íslendingabók* that Óláfr Christianised Norway as well as Iceland, and in *Ágrip* one can read that 'the five years he carried the king's name in Norway, he Christianised five countries: Norway and Iceland and Hjáltland [Shetland], Orkney and fifth the Faroes'.

Óláfr Haraldsson had a similar background and journey to the crown. Thus, he had been down to the Continent and offered his services as a warrior to different kings in their battles, and thereby accrued reputation and wealth. Also he was baptised, according to tradition in Rouen in France. After a famous battle at Nesjar, where he defeated Svein jarl and an army from Trøndelag, he could proclaim himself king of Norway. Mirroring the Continental kings, Óláfr had by his side an (probably) English clergyman, Grímkell, who functioned as his court bishop and personal counsellor. In Sweden the situation was probably similar to that in Norway at this period. One example is King Emund the Old, who in the mid-eleventh century had a bishop, Osmund, by his side.

A central figure in the traditional historiography of the Christianisation of Scandinavia is Ansgar, the first archbishop in Hamburg–Bremen's archdiocese. He has been given the epithet 'the apostle of Scandinavia'. This monk of the Benedictine order followed in 827 the Danish king Harald Klak to Denmark, an occasion which traditionally is seen as the beginning of the Christianisation of Denmark. However, in *Vita Ansgarii* we read that Harald, Ansgar and his follower Autbert reached the 'confina' of the Danes, hence approximately 'border zone' and not 'country' or 'kingdom', and furthermore that Harald did not dare to be in Denmark due to struggle and fighting there, and therefore he had received the peninsula Rüstringen as a county and 'asylum' from Emperor Louis the Pious. Ansgar's journey seems hence not to have resulted in any deeper religious impact on Danish society. Ansgar was perhaps more successful with the Danish king Horik I, when a church was erected and a priest placed at Hedeby(Haithabu)/Schleswig. Under the reign of King Horik II another church was established in the town of Ribe. It is however to be noted that neither of these kings was willing to be baptised.

Ansgar played a special role in the Swedish Christianisation tradition. According to this, some envoys, sent out by the Swedes, came to Louis the Pious in Germany and said that many people (*gentes*) among them wished to become Christian (the story has already become improbable here!), and that their king would be glad if priests could be sent to the Swedes and convert them. The aforementioned monk, Ansgar, was some time in the 820s chosen to go and check if the Swedes really were ready to be converted to Christendom. And after a dramatic journey he arrived in the town of Birka, where he met the Swedish king Björn.

In Birka Ansgar's most important contact was a man, Hergeirr, who in the *Vita* is called a *praefectus*, hence some kind of chieftain or royal steward. He was the first to convert and to be baptised by Ansgar, and within a short time they built a church on his plot of land (presumably in the town). Rimbert relates several stories of pious people in Birka and of miracles conducted in the town. After Ansgar left Birka, the people are said to have returned to paganism and the Swedes became hostile towards Christians. One story tells about the missionary bishop Gautbert, who was forced to leave Birka, and his follower, Nithard, who became the first Christian to be killed, and hence the first martyr. This sad situation led Ansgar to go on a second journey to Birka in 852. He then met King Olof, and urged him to secure the rights of the Christians in his kingdom.

Of course, this is not a true story, but bears all the signs of having a core of truth that has been amended and 'improved', a *vita* of a holy man, the first archbishop of a struggling Hamburg–Bremen archdiocese which laid claim on this northerly province. We don't know if Ansgar's journeys on the whole resulted in a Christian community, and traces of the church mentioned by Rimbert have not yet been found in Birka. There are actually reasons to believe that Christians were residing in Birka already before the visits of Ansgar. The early emporia, such as Birka, Hedeby, Ribe etc., were probably cultural melting pots, where people from a wide range of countries and cultures lived. It is more than probable that in Birka people belonging to the eastern Church lived alongside, for example, Frisians belonging to the Catholic Church and so on.

As regards Iceland, we have the paradox that this island was already 'Christianised' when the first Norwegian colonisers settled here in the ninth century. According to the written sources these settlers met Irish monks, hermits ('papar'), who – so typically for the Irish Church – had left Ireland in search of remote islands to live in solitude.

The Christianisation of the Norwegians on Iceland is often mentioned in the Icelandic sagas, perhaps to be understood as a topos, such as Ari fróði's *Íslendingabók*, Njál's saga, the large saga of Óláfr Tryggvason, Saint Óláfr's saga, Kristni saga etc. The story is that a first mission took place at the end of the tenth century, when the archbishop Adaldag of Bremen sent out two missionaries, the Icelander Þorvaldr Kóðransson and a Saxon bishop Frederik, who made themselves unwelcome in Iceland after killing two men. A decade later the Norwegian king, Óláfr Tryggvason, is said to have sent two more missionaries to Iceland, who, however, were similarly violent, destroyed several pagan cult sites, and had to leave.

According to the sagas the conversion of the Icelanders was a significant event. Two expelled Christian Icelanders, Gizzur hvíti and Hjalti Skeggjason, returned to Iceland in the summer of 999 or 1000 and went to the Alþing, and were able to talk at the Lǫgberg. That year a Christian party stood against a pagan party, and there was a risk that Iceland could be divided as a result of this clash. The Christian goði, Hallr frá Síðu, therefore asked the pagan Lawspeaker, Þorgeirr, to work out a compromise, which both parties could agree upon. And according to the sagas the Lawspeaker sat in his thing hut under a cloak and thought all night and in the morning addressed the people saying that if Iceland should continue to be undivided, they had to agree on one law and one faith. And this faith must be the Christian religion, the pagan Þorgeirr concluded. However, there should be three exemptions: you should still be allowed to eat horsemeat, you could continue to leave unwelcome newborn children in the outback, and you could continue to sacrifice to the old, pagan gods as long as you did it in secrecy. This has been taken as an example of the pragmatic stance regarding the transfer from the old to the new religion.

How 'true' this tradition and story are is a question of debate. Today we know that it cannot be the whole truth. We know that many settlers who came to Iceland came from Orkney, Shetland, England, Scotland and Ireland, and several of them were probably already Christians. Furthermore we know today that not only Norwegians settled on Iceland, but also many Irish and Scottish, especially Celtic women (recent DNA analyses suggest). In other words both religions probably already lived side by side from the beginning in Iceland. The tradition we can read in the Icelandic sagas is – again – a biased and embellished story, produced by later, Christian authors.

THE EVIDENCE ON THE RUNESTONES

During the eleventh century more than 1,000 runestones were carved and erected in eastern Sweden. This has been seen in conjunction with strife between Christians and pagans, where the runestones should be seen as Christian propaganda. This may be the case. But it is remarkable that there is nothing in the actual runic inscriptions that supports such a 'religious war'. Perhaps the transformation was peaceful, and therefore the erection of runestones has quite another background. Maybe they are to be looked upon as a kind of regional fashion in eastern Sweden, on which people have manifested their new Christian faith.

Apart from Christian crosses of various kinds, many runestones have pious Christian prayers for deceased relatives: 'He died in Denmark in white baptismal clothes,' 'God help his soul,' 'God and God's mother help his soul and spirit, give him light and paradise.'

Three runestones are of special interest. On a runestone at Jelling on Jutland in Denmark, dated to *c.* 970, one reads: 'King Harald made these memorials after Gorm, his father, and after Tyra, his mother, the Harald who won Denmark and the whole of Norway, and made the Danes Christians.' This remarkable inscription has been discussed intensively: is it a lie, bragging, a political 'statement' or has it some historical bearing? One thing is for sure, Harald cannot have converted the Danes. Perhaps his words are to be seen in a socio-political context, alluding to some political event, when Denmark 'officially' changed religion, in the same way as on Iceland.

On the Frösö runestone, the northernmost in Sweden, one can read: 'Austman Gudfast's son had this stone erected and this bridge built, and he Christianised Jämtland. Åsbjörn made the bridge. Tryn [Trjónn] and Sten carved these runes.' Also in this case this statement may be looked upon as a political one, saying that the *Jämtar*, perhaps on their thing site, *Jamtamot*, 'officially' had accepted the Christian religion.

The Kuli runestone stood beside an ancient road in Edøy, Nordmøre in Norway. The stone has the text: '. . . twelve winters had Christendom been in Norway'. The runestone has obviously been a so-called 'bridge stone', and the 'bridge' can be dated to 1034. Therefore it seems plausible to connect the statement to the event when King Óláfr Haraldsson together with his bishop, Grímkell, declared the first Christian law

(*Kristinn réttr*) on the island of Moster in 1024, hence again a testimony of a political event.

FROM WHERE DID THE NEW RELIGION COME?

The traditional view has been that Norway was Christianised from England, whereas Denmark and Sweden were mainly from Germany. The reason for focusing on the German Church is of course Rimbert's *Vita Ansgarii* and Adam of Bremen's *Gesta*. Both are biased in favour of the Hamburg–Bremen diocese, and both writers obviously have a mission – claim ecclesiastical authority over the northern provinces. Today research instead stresses the importance of the Anglo-Saxon Church especially during the early phase of Christianisation. There is today also a great interest in possible links to the eastern Church. The contacts between Scandinavia and eastern Europe have been extensive, but obvious evidence for a religious impact from the Byzantine Church is more or less lacking.

Traditionally – and for good reasons – a focus in the discussion on the Christianisation of Scandinavia has been on the tenth and eleventh centuries. Today we are more inclined to accept that Christian culture had infiltrated and influenced Scandinavian society for a long time, probably for all of the late Roman and early medieval periods (the Iron Age in Scandinavia). This influence may be seen in a change of cult practice, the emergence of a new kind of nobility, perhaps the emergence of new gods, new burial customs etc., changes not necessarily of a religious kind.

We therefore look upon the Christianisation as a prolonged process, which partly has been a successive influence of a socio-cultural kind over a long period of time, which eventually resulted in a conversion and a change in religion of a more official kind. The real impact and decisive change, however, come when the Church has gained such power that it is possible to organise the Scandinavian provinces and implement the new religion in society with the parish church and parish priest. By then we have reached the twelfth and thirteenth centuries.

THE FIRST BISHOPS AND THE ORGANISATION OF THE CHURCH

The first bishops we know of are those who were ordained to some emerging town, a *civitas*, and then those who functioned as the itinerant king's counsellor, attached to his personal court. In the 960s the archbishop of Hamburg–Bremen appointed three suffragan bishops to be placed in Hedeby, Ribe and Aarhus, probably as a way of announcing the interest and superiority over the northern province. At least two of these bishops, however, never set foot in Denmark. It seems obvious that there was competition between the German and English Churches in this period, leading to the paradox that up to the mid-eleventh century, Scandinavia from a judicial and administrative point of view belonged to the German Church, but more or less all the bishops came from England. Today there is a tendency to tone down the impact of the Hamburg–Bremen's diocese even more, changing focus to the archbishopric in Cologne, especially for the tenth century. It seems obvious that the English Church must have had an important role especially during the first part of the eleventh century, when Canute the Great was king over England, Denmark, Norway and 'parts of Sweden'.

In Norway we have a well-known example of a bishop attached to a king's court, acting as the king's counsellor, namely the aforementioned Bishop Grímkell. He is the one who was decisive for the translation of the dead king Óláfr to Nidaros and the creation of the legend which introduced the first and by far the most important of the Scandinavian saints, St Óláfr, *Perpetuus Rex Norvegiae*. The early cult of St Óláfr was decisive in the Christianisation process and many churches were dedicated to the Norwegian saint.

In the middle of the eleventh century a consolidation and an expansion of the ecclesiastical organisation took place. With the initiative of the dynamic archbishop Adalberth in Hamburg–Bremen (1043–72) some twenty new bishops were ordained to Scandinavian dioceses, to Hedeby/Schleswig, Ribe, Aarhus, 'the island of Vendel', 'the islands of Fyn and the Faroes', Roskilde, Dalby and Lund for Denmark, Skara, Sigtuna, 'Hälsingland' and Birka for Sweden, the bishops Tholf and Sigvardr for Norway, a bishop to Orkney and Bishop Ísleifr to Iceland. The letter describing this achievement is problematic in many ways, but it shows that there was a definite interest in the ecclesiastical organising of Scandinavia from Hamburg–Bremen.

A more fundamental organisation of Scandinavia by the Church came later on with the parish formation, but then we have left the Viking Age and entered into the Middle Ages of Scandinavia. This process took place in the twelfth and thirteenth centuries.

BIBLIOGRAPHY

Adam of Bremen's *Gesta = Hamburgisch Kirchengeschichte. Magistri Adam Bremensis gesta Hammaburgensis ecclesiae pontificum*, B. Schmeidler (ed.), 3rd edn (Monumenta Germaniae Historica. Scriptores 7), Hannover and Leipzig: Hahn 1917 (reprint 1977).

Brink, S. (1990) *Sockenbildning och sockennamn. Studier i äldre territoriell indelning i Norden* (Acta Academiae Regiae Gustavi Adolphi 57), Stockholm: Almqvist & Wiksell International.

—— (2004) 'New perspectives on the Christianization of Scandinavia and the organization of the early Church', in J. Adams and K. Holman (eds) *Scandinavia and Europe 800–1350. Contact, Conflict and Coexistence* (Medieval Texts and Cultures of Northern Europe 4), Turnhout: Brepols.

Brunius, J. (2005) 'Medieval manuscript fragments in the National Archives: a survey', in J. Brunius (ed.) *Medieval Book Fragments in Sweden. An International Seminar in Stockholm, 13–16 November 2003* (KVHAA. Konferenser 58), Stockholm: Almqvist & Wiksell International.

Carver, M. (ed.) (2003) *The Cross Goes North. Processes of Conversion in Northern Europe, AD 300–1300*, Woodbridge: Boydell & Brewer.

Gräslund, A.-S. (2001) *Ideologi och mentalitet. Om religionsskiftet i Skandinavien från en arkeologisk horisont* (Opia 29), Uppsala: Uppsala universitet. Institutionen för arkeologi och antik historia.

Helgi Þorláksson (ed.) (2005) *Church Centres. Church Centres in Iceland from the 11th to the 13th Century and their Parallels in other Countries* (Snorrastofa. Rit 2), Reykholt: Snorrastofa.

Hjalti Hugason (2000) *Kristni á Íslandi*, vol. 1: *Frumkristni og upphaf kirkju*, Reykjavík: Alþingi.

Lund, N. (ed.) (2004) *Kristendommen i Danmark før 1050. Et symposium i Roskilde den 5.–7-februar 2003*, Roskilde: Roskilde Museums Forlag.

Nilsson, B. (ed.) (1996) *Kristnandet i Sverige. Gamla källor och nya perspektiv* (Projektet Sveriges kristnande. Publikationer 5), Uppsala: Lunne.

—— (1998) *Sveriges kyrkohistoria*, vol. 1: *Missionstid och tidig medeltid*, Stockholm: Verbum.

Nyberg, T. (2000) *Monasticism in North-Western Europe 800–1200*, Aldershot: Ashgate.

Orri Vésteinsson (2000) *The Christianization of Iceland. Priests, Power, and Social Change 1000–1300*, Oxford: Oxford University Press.

Rimbert's *Vita Anskarii = Vita Anskarii. Accedit vita Rimberti*, recensuit G. Waitz (Monumenta Germaniae historica. Scriptores rerum Germanicarum in usum scholarum separatim editi 55), Hannover: Hahn 1884 (reprint 1988).

Sanmark, A. (2004) *Power and Conversion. A Comparative Study of Christianization in Scandinavia* (Opia 34), Uppsala: Dept. of Archaeology and Ancient History, Uppsala University.

Sawyer, B. and Sawyer, P. (1993) *Medieval Scandinavia. From Conversion to Reformation, circa 800–1500* (The Nordic Series 17), Minneapolis: University of Minnesota Press.

Sigurdhsson, J.V., Myking, M. and Rindal, M. (eds) (2004) *Religionsskiftet i Norden. Brytinger mellom nordisk og europeisk kultur 800–1200 e.Kr.* (Senter for studier i vikingtid og nordisk middelalder. Skriftserie 6), Oslo: Senter for studier i vikingtid og nordisk middelalder.

Skre, D. (1995) 'Kirken før sognet. Den tidligste kirkeordningen i Norge', in H.-E. Lidén (ed.) *Møtet mellom hedendom og kristendom i Norge*, Oslo: Universitetsforlaget.

—— (1998) 'Missionary activity in early medieval Norway: strategy, organization and the course of events', *Scandinavian Journal of History*, 23: 1–19.

CHAPTER FORTY-SIX

RUNESTONES AND THE CHRISTIAN MISSIONS

——·◆·——

Anne-Sofie Gräslund and Linn Lager

During the last decades of the tenth century the Scandinavian runestone tradition went through a major transformation. The erection of the Jelling stone in Denmark by King Harald Bluetooth in the 960s is usually considered the starting point of this transformation, even though the majority of the late Viking Age runestones were produced during the eleventh century. The Jelling stone is unique in many ways, but it contains all of the elements that came to characterise the late Viking Age runestone tradition.

The runic inscription begins with stating who had the stone erected in memory of whom, also clarifying in which way these individuals were related to each other. In this case, King Harald had 'these monuments' made in memory of his father Gorm and his mother Tyra. This introductory memorial phrase constitutes the least denominator on virtually every runestone erected during the eleventh century, and it soon became very formulaic. Many inscriptions then proceed to mention admirable qualities or achievements that characterise the deceased and/or the commemorator, in Harald's case that he had come to reign over both Norway and Denmark and that he converted the Danes. The northernmost stone in Sweden, at Frösön in the province of Jämtland, is in some respects compatible to the Jelling stone (although considerably later), as the inscription goes: 'Östman, Gudfast's son, had this stone raised and this bridge made, and he had Jämtland made Christian . . .'. There is also a Norwegian stone, explicitly mentioning the conversion, the Kuli stone from the province of Møre. The normal memorial sentence is followed by the text 'Twelve winters Christianity has been in Norway.' References to the conversion, and to Christianity in general, were a new addition to the Scandinavian runestone tradition. These references generally occur in the shape of a prayer and/or a centrally placed cross. Nearly 60 per cent of the Swedish runestones have references to Christianity; in Denmark and Norway the percentage is considerably lower. While the ornamentation on the Jelling stone is unique, it signifies the introduction of a regular and more standardised element of ornamentation on the eleventh-century runestones, usually in the shape of zoomorphic rune bands in Scandinavian styles. From a chronological perspective, the standardisation of the memorial phrase and the introduction of references to Christianity preceded the introduction of zoomorphic rune bands by a few decades. Last, but not least, a major difference between the runestone tradition prior to the Jelling stone and after, is the number of runestones produced. From the end of the tenth century until the beginning of the twelfth about 3,000 runestones were produced in Scandinavia (*c.* 2,400 in Sweden, *c.* 400 in Denmark and *c.* 140 in Norway), gradually transforming a unique event reserved for the absolute elite of society, into a relatively common affair practised by the upper middle classes.

STYLISTIC GROUNDS FOR A CHRONOLOGY

Since there are few remaining written sources from this period, the runestones are an invaluable historical source material, and also for the history of mission. A more precise dating for the runestones than just to the eleventh century is therefore most desirable. Over the years, several scholars have presented suggestions for a systematisation of the ornamentation and layout of the runestones as a means of obtaining a more detailed chronology. The grouping of the ornamentation on the Upplandic runestones by Otto von Friesen (1913), based on his linguistic knowledge and the information obtained from the so-called historical inscriptions, was generally accepted until the 1980s. New research then implied that the runological and linguistic variations in the material were caused more by regional variation than chronology (Lagman 1990: 157; Williams 1990: 183), and this caused a sense of pessimism concerning the possibilities of a closer dating of the material.

By this time a Southern and a Central Scandinavian style in the Swedish runestones had already been defined through analyses of the curves and rhythm of the rune bands (Christiansson 1959), largely corresponding to the Mammen–Ringerike style and the Urnes style respectively. The former is characterised by close, hard lines and additive elements, the latter by softly sweeping, continuous lines. The differences between the styles were then seen as caused by regional variation, but have later been proved to originate in the chronological development of the Mammen–Ringerike and Urnes styles respectively. Comparisons between the runestone ornamentation and archaeologically well-dated material have in recent years proved to be a very fruitful way of obtaining a more detailed chronological sequence for the runestone material (Gräslund 1994, 2003). The artists/carvers of the runestones were subjected to the same stylistic ideals as those influencing the rest of society, and consequently well-dated ornamented artefacts can help pinpoint their time of production.

NON-ZOOMORPHIC CARVINGS

For the non-zoomorphic (or 'unornamented') carvings, a classification into three groups has been suggested which does not necessarily form a chronological sequence: row system, central loop and edge loop (Kinander 1935: 10–11). Most of the unornamented carvings seem to belong to the oldest phase, *c.* 970–1020, but attention must be paid to the fact that also later stones may be decorated in this style. Elements forming typical parts of the Ringerike style occur rather often on the non-zoomorphic stones, giving a means for dating such carvings to the very end of the tenth, or the first half of the eleventh, century (Gräslund 2002: 149). This is also indicated by the linear rhythm of the carvings.

ZOOMORPHIC CARVINGS

The Upplandic runestones hold an exceptional position in the Swedish material, above all in number (*c.* 1,400 out of *c.* 2,400), but also in ornamentation, with the runes often carved in a band-shaped animal body. A stylistically based system of classification has been suggested for the zoomorphic carvings based on the following criteria: the overall impression, the design of the rune animal's head, feet and tail, the loops of the snake(s) and the layout of the pattern. A rough sorting of all zoomorphic carvings of Uppland resulted in six distinct groups with different characteristics. The chronological order of these groups was established by comparisons with archaeologically well-dated material and occurrences of genealogically connected runestones (Gräslund 1994, 2003). One of the stylistic groups is characterised by the rune animal's head seen from above, therefore called 'Bird's-eye's-view' (B-e-v). The other five groups (called Pr 1–5) show the rune animal's head seen in profile. These five groups can, very compressedly, only regarding their overall impression, be characterised in the following way:

- Pr 1: a compact, close and blunted overall impression. The curves of the rune animal are often angular and the bow line pressed together.
- Pr 2: a compact and unresilient impression with angular curves of the rune animal.
- Pr 3: a firmly rounded overall impression with moderately sweeping lines.
- Pr 4: an elegant overall impression with elongated sweeping bow lines.
- Pr 5: a characteristic overall impression of chequer pattern, formed by parallel lines crossing each other at right angles, made up of parts of the loops of the rune animal and a serpent.

The most common variants of the criteria 'head, tail, feet and union knot' (common in B-e-v, Pr 1, 2 and 3) of each group are presented in Figure 46.1. Examples of the layout of both non-zoomorphic and zoomorphic carvings are presented in Figure 46.2.

The following approximate dates may be suggested: non-zoomorphic/unornamented stones: *c.* 970?–1020, Bird's-eye's-view: *c.* 1010–50, Pr 1: *c.* 1010–40, Pr 2: *c.* 1020–50, Pr 3: *c.* 1045–75, Pr 4: *c.* 1070–1100, Pr 5: *c.* 1100–30. The group 'B-e-v' seems to be contemporary with Pr 1 and Pr 2, as there are carvings where rune animal heads typical for these stylistic groups occur together. If this chronology is accepted, it enables us to see a chronological pattern in the production of the runestones, and it also implies that the time of production of some known rune carvers has to be redefined. Of course, the stylistic groups should not be seen as a strictly chronological sequence, instead, large overlaps should be expected. Conscious imitations of earlier stones are also possible. However, the general tendency is clear, and the order of the groups is distinct on the basis of both the stylistic analysis and the examination of the genealogically related stones.

This system of classification seems to be applicable not only for Uppland and the Mälar area, but also for other Swedish provinces (Gräslund 2002: 146–7). Zoomorphic carvings constitute 10 per cent of the late Viking Age carvings of the provinces of Skåne and Småland, 25 per cent of the carvings of Västergötland and Östergötland and as much as 65 per cent of the carvings of Öland. They are also represented to a high degree in Norrland (Gästrikland, Hälsingland, Medelpad and Jämtland) and on Gotland. On the other hand, they occur seldom in Denmark and practically never in Norway. It can

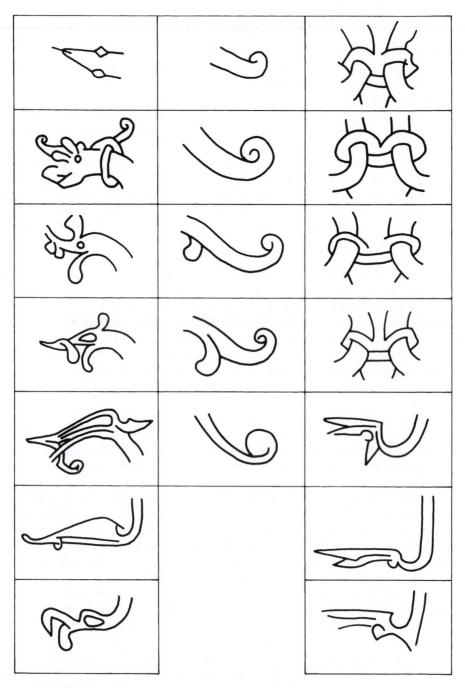

Figure 46.1   Typical details of zoomorphic carving, stylistic groups B-e-v and Pr 1–Pr 5. (Drawing: Alicja Grenberger.)

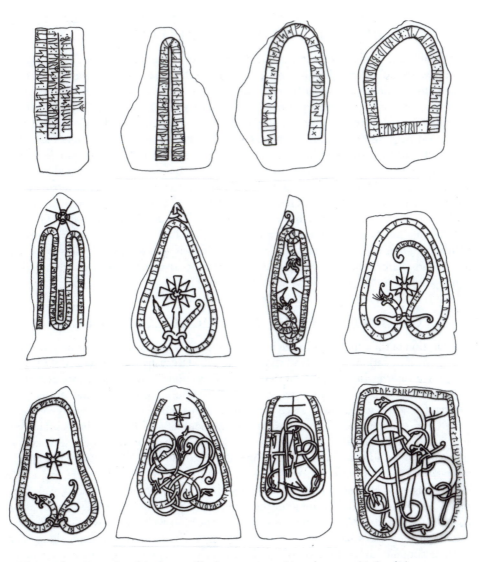

Figure 46.2 Examples of the layout of both non-zoomorphic and zoomorphic Swedish runestones.
(Drawing: Alicja Grenberger.)

be argued that this system of classification puts too much weight on the shapes of specific details. However, they are not arbitrarily formed but instead modelled in a certain style, and it is the combination of specifically formed details that is making up the totality of each style. The importance given to detail also has practical significance, as many runestones are fragmented and have to be dated on the basis of a few remaining details.

RUNESTONES AND CHRISTIANITY

The connection between runestones and Christianity is clearly witnessed by the large amount of stones decorated with a cross; in Uppland there are crosses on over 50 per cent of the stones. Crosses seem to be more frequent in the earlier style groups, perhaps indicating that it was more important to show one's Christian faith in the early part of the conversion than towards the end. Many inscriptions are finished by a simple prayer: 'May God help his/her soul.' In some cases there are more elaborate prayers like 'May God and God's mother help his spirit and soul and grant him light and paradise' on a stone decorated in Pr 1 or 'May Christ let Tumme's soul come into light and paradise and into the world best for Christians,' on a stone decorated in Pr 4. Pilgrimage is mentioned twice, once on a stone decorated in Pr 2 erected in memory of Östen, grandfather of the famous Jarlabanke: 'he went out to Jerusalem and died in Greece'. The second pilgrimage inscription, with decoration in Pr 3, tells us that 'Ingerun, Hård's daughter, had the runes cut in memory of herself. She wanted to go eastward and out to Jerusalem.' There are also some inscriptions that mention persons who died in 'white clothes', in all probability baptismal gowns.

CHRISTIANITY IN THE LOCAL COMMUNITY

The location of the runestones in the landscape may also give us some information of the Christian connotation. In Uppland there are about seventy-five stones with inscriptions that mention the building of bridges for the soul(s) of the commemorated dead (Gräslund 1989: 228–33). In order to promote the building of roads and bridges the Church had already at an early stage incorporated this in the system of indulgence – in return the Church offered intercession for the soul of the dead and/or absolution. Judging from the location near water or wetlands another approximately seventy-five stones could be added. The female component in these inscriptions (52%) is clearly higher than in the total number of runestones. Women are generally more frequently seen as raisers or commemorated, alone or together with men, in Uppland (39%), than in the rest of Sweden (for example in the province of Småland they make up only 8%). As runestones and bridges should be seen in connection with the conversion, women's actions in these cases have special significance, an interesting combination along with other testimonies to their active role in the conversion. However, both men and women had runestones raised and bridges built, certainly acts of prestige and therefore worth mentioning. Judging from their ornamentation, bridge stones occur throughout the eleventh century, represented by stylistic groups from 'unornamented' to Pr 4. Bridge inscriptions also occur in Denmark and Norway. A famous Norwegian example is the Dynna stone with the inscription 'Gunvor, Thrydrik's daughter, made a bridge in memory of Astrid, her daughter. She was the handiest maiden in Hadeland.' The stone is decorated with scenes from the Christmas gospel and it is a good example of classic Ringerike style. Obviously, the Christmas gospel was reasonably well known in Norway in the first half of the eleventh century.

A study of records left by Swedish researchers of runes from the seventeenth, eighteenth and nineteenth centuries reveals that many runestones were placed in cemeteries, sometimes directly on a mound or in a stone-setting with a shape that allows a dating to the Viking Age (Gräslund 1987: 256–7; 2000: 89). In many cases the graves have completely disappeared due to extensive cultivation, and only the runestone is left in place. Runestones affiliated with cemeteries are decorated with crosses at an unusually high degree (75 per cent), and these runestones might cast an interesting light on the relationship between pagan cemeteries and Christianity (see e.g. U 661; Figure 46.3). It is possible that these stones served as a consecration of the cemetery or a part of it. Christians could then be buried there until a real churchyard was available. That runestones actually could serve as gravestones is shown by two Pr 5 stones in eastern Uppland with the inscription 'Here lies . . .'. They are both found at church sites, a location that is more frequent for the later stones than for the early. In the province of Öland a unique inscription on a bridge runestone in style Pr 3, raised by a wife to the memory of her husband, ends with '. . . he is buried in the church'.

Many runestones have been built into the walls of medieval churches, dating from the twelfth to the fourteenth century. There is an ongoing discussion if this should be interpreted as an ideological act – to move the ancestors to the church – or if the runestones were regarded as nice flat stones, ideal to use in the building. The fact that several of the pillars in the chancel of Uppsala Cathedral rest on runestones

Figure 46.3 Runestone U 661, Håtuna parish, Uppland. Drawing (from U) from the beginning of the eighteenth century by Peringskiöld. The inscription read: 'Gervi and Gulla raised this stone in memory of Anund, their father. He died in the east with Ingvar. May God help Anund's spirit.' This is one of the so-called Ingvar stones, raised by two daughters in memory of their father. The stone, placed at a grave-field, is carved in 'Bird's-eye's-view' style and decorated with a cross.

(Gustavson 1986: 14), indicates a conscious use and speaks in favour of the ideological interpretation.

RUNESTONES AND THE CHRISTIANISATION

The conversion of Scandinavia is a very complicated process with major geographical and chronological differences and fluctuations. To facilitate the analyses of this process it is usually considered as comprised by different periods or phases with different characteristics; a phase of infiltration, a phase of mission and a phase of organisation (Birkeli 1973: 14 ff.). During the phase of infiltration Christian influences reached a region passively through the interaction with Christians in a nearby region or country, or through trade communication with more remote areas. During the phase of mission Christian influences were actively directed towards a region through the efforts of missionaries, and Christian ideas and beliefs were beginning to settle in among a growing part of the population. During the phase of organisation the majority of the population was already converted, and an organised ecclesiastical structure was developing. Even though the conversion as a whole gradually moved from a phase of infiltration towards a phase of organisation, it was not a linear process, and there were setbacks. We have to assume that the conversion advanced at different rates in different regions, and that all of these phases could occur simultaneously in different areas of the same country or region. Using this terminology, the production of runestones can mostly be said to occur during the phase of mission. The tradition seems to have been discouraged in regions where a more organised ecclesiastical structure had developed. There the social, political and economic resourses were instead channelled towards the Church and more traditional expressions of Christian faith.

THE PROCESS OF CONVERSION

Christianity came to Scandinavia from Europe, and so did the concept of the Christian cross and its use on Christian monuments. While the majority of the Swedish runestone crosses are uniquely Scandinavian in their overall design, some of their details quite naturally have similarities with cross-shapes found on contemporary European monuments and artefacts. To most parts these similarities can be traced to the British Isles, either as details found on carved stone crosses or on details on imported objects from this area, such as cross-pendants or coins (Lager 2002: 156). These similarities indicate interaction between these areas during the production of the runestones, and hence also during the phase of mission. The impact of British influences in Sweden during this period is further supported by philological analyses of runic inscriptions and early Scandinavian liturgical manuscripts (Thors 1957: 360–1). While words with an English origin seem to have been dominant in the formation of a basic Scandinavian Christian vocabulary, words with German origins can mostly be associated with a more advanced and organised ecclesiastical structure. Based on both art-historical and philological analyses it seems reasonable to assume that contacts with Christians in, and from, the British Isles were very influential in Scandinavia during the initial phases of infiltration and mission. When contacts with this area ceased after the battle of Hastings in 1066, the continued involvement from the German Church led to an increased dependence on a German vocabulary during the phase of organisation. Since most of the remaining historical sources were written within the realms of the German Church, they generally downplay the impact of British Christianity during the Scandinavian conversion. Although the German mission undisputedly played an important role, the information supplied by the runestones adds to a more nuanced picture.

SCANDINAVIAN CHRISTIANITY AND EUROPE

The phase of mission was a phase of transformation, and the runestones produced during this phase can be considered a transitory phenomenon with a mix of old and new influences, indigenous as well as foreign. The late Viking Age runestones have their origins within the Scandinavian culture and the runestone tradition of previous centuries, but with significant additions through new influences from European Christianity. The combination of visual and ideological elements from both of these cultures makes these runestones into Christian monuments with a very distinct, and uniquely Scandinavian, character. Those who produced and ordered cross-pendants, runestones and other Christian objects in Scandinavia during the later part of the Viking Age, were well acquainted with the European material through travels and imports. Since most of these foreign ornamental influences seem to have been discarded in the indigenous production of artefacts, the Scandinavian characteristics found on these objects were most likely developed and maintained intentionally (Staecker 1999; Lager 2002).

Converting to Christianity implied a change of religious identity. However, by this time Christianity was far more than just a system of religious belief. It was a cultural, political and social institution that defined most of the kingdoms and empires in Europe. From a Scandinavian perspective Christianity was synonymous with 'the others', with areas and people that they had spent centuries trading with, but also ravaging and conquering (Lager 2004: 147 ff.). Scandinavia was a powerful region, and it was probably imperative for many Scandinavians that their conversion was not perceived as a sign of cultural or political defeat. Converting to Christianity consequently raised questions about cultural, political and ethnic identity. While many Scandinavians were willing to convert, and change their religious identity, they might not have been equally willing to convert their Scandinavian identity. The conversion had to be done without losing face and with a maintained sense of integrity. Christianity itself had to be, at least seemingly, converted from something that used to define 'the others' into something that could also define themselves: as Christian Scandinavians.

The design and concepts behind the late Viking Age runestones, as well as other indigenously produced Christian artefacts, were familiar, yet innovative, ensuring a sense of cultural continuity despite profound changes (Lager 2004: 147 ff.). By carefully combining an eclectic selection of foreign designs with indigenously developed traditional elements and motifs, Christianity was made Scandinavian. This also enabled the Scandinavian culture to function as a mediator or catalyst in understanding and explaining the Christian faith. Metaphorical allusions and comparisons with the traditional worldview, its legends and values, were facilitated by the use of Scandinavian ornamentation. Through this solution, Christianity enriched the Scandinavian culture and identity, instead of depriving it of its fundaments. It was only when these new influences were fully absorbed into the Scandinavian culture that steps towards more orthodox expressions of Christian faith were possible, and the production of runestones ceased.

BIBLIOGRAPHY

Birkeli, F. (1973) *Norske steinkors i tidlig middelalder. Et bidrag til belysning av overgangen fra norrøn religion til kristendom* (Skrifter utg. av det Norske Videnskaps-Akademi i Oslo. II. Hist–Filos. Klasse, NS 10), Oslo: Universitetsforlaget.

Christiansson, H. (1959) *Sydskandinavisk stil. Studier i ornamentiken på de senvikingatida runstenarna*, Uppsala: no publ.

von Friesen, O. (1913) *Upplands runstenar. En allmänfattlig öfversikt*, Uppsala: Akademiska bokhandeln.

Gräslund, A.-S. (1987) 'Runstenar, bygd och gravar', *Tor*, 21: 241–62.

—— (1989) ' "Gud hjälpe nu väl hennes själ" – om runstenskvinnorna, deras roll vid kristnandet och deras plats i familj och samhälle', *Tor*, 22: 223–44.

—— (1994) 'Runestones – on ornamentation and chronology', in B. Ambrosiani and H. Clarke (eds) *Developments around the Baltic and the North Sea in the Viking Age* (Birka studies 3), Stockholm: Birka Project, Raä & Statens historiska museer.

—— (2000) 'The conversion of Scandinavia – a sudden event or a gradual process?', *Archaeological Review from Cambridge*, 17(2): 83–98.

—— (2002) 'De senvikingatida runstenarna i Jönköpings län – deras ornamentik och datering', *Småländska kulturbilder*: 139–54.

—— (2003) 'Runensteine – late Viking Age runestones: ornamentation and chronology', *RGA* 25: 585–91.

Gustavson, H. (1986) 'Runstenarnas Uppsala', in *Från Östra Aros till Uppsala. En samling uppsatser kring det medeltida Uppsala* (Uppsala stads historia 7), Uppsala: Uppsala historiekommitté.

Kinander, R. (1935) 'Inledning', in *Smålands runinskrifter* 1 (Sveriges runinskrifter 4), Stockholm: Almqvist & Wiksell International.

Lager, L. (2002) *Den synliga tron. Runstenskors som en spegling av kristnandet av Sverige* (Opia: Occasional Papers in Archaeology 31), Uppsala: Dept. of Archaeology and Ancient History, Uppsala University.

—— (2004) 'Art as a medium in defining "us" and "them": the ornamentation on runestones in relation to the question of "Europeanisation" ', in J. Staecker (ed.) *The European Frontier. Clashes and Compromises in the Middle Ages* (Lund Studies in Medieval Archaeology 33; CCC papers 7), Lund: Almqvist & Wiksell International.

Lagman, S. (1990) *De stungna runorna. Användning och ljudvärde i nordiska runinskrifter/Die Punktierte Runen. Gebrauch und Lautwerte in runenschwedischen Steininschriften* (Runrön 4), Uppsala: Swedish Science Press.

Staecker, J. (1999) *Rex regum et dominus dominorum. Die wikingerzeitlichen Kreuz- und kruzifixanhänger als Ausdruck der Mission in Altdänemark und Schweden* (Lund Studies in medieval Archaeology 23), Stockholm: Almqvist & Wiksell International.

Thors, C.-E. (1957) *Den kristna terminologien i fornsvenskan* (Studier i nordisk filologi 45), Helsingfors: Svenska litteratursällskapet.

U = *Upplands runinskrifter*, 4 vols (Sveriges runinskrifter 6–9), Stockholm: Almqvist & Wiksell International (1940–58).

Williams, H. (1990) *Åsrunan. Användning och ljudvärde i runsvenska steninskrifter/The Os-rune. Use and Phonetic Value in Rune-Swedish Inscriptions on Stone* (Runrön 3), Uppsala: Swedish Science Press.

THE MATERIAL CULTURE
OF THE CHRISTIANISATION

——·◆·——

Anne-Sofie Gräslund

Referring to the chapter 'The material culture of Old Norse religion' (Gräslund, ch. 18, above), our question must be: is there any evidence of the Christianisation to be seen in the material culture as well? Yes, there is, in at least four different fields: the burial customs, the cult places, the artefacts and the iconography. To this should be added the evidence of the runestones (see Williams, ch. 21, above). If we accept the opinion that the Christianisation was not an event but a process, going on for centuries, there were of course many possibilities for Christian impact on the material culture, especially in the phase of mission, starting at the end of the eighth century. The influences accepted could then be seen as an expression of syncretism, a wish to adapt the new ideas at the same time as a wish to keep the old ones.

BURIAL CUSTOMS

Starting with the burial customs, this is maybe where it is easiest to discern a gradual transition, from pagan cremation graves furnished with rich grave goods, artefacts of various kinds as well as animals, via inhumation graves still with rich grave goods, through oriented inhumation graves without grave goods, culminating with oriented graves in churchyards (Gräslund 2000, 2001). It must be noted, however, that it is very difficult, not to say impossible, to decide whether a specific grave is Christian or not; instead we have to look at the general tendency of a larger number of graves at a certain cemetery. It is necessary to qualify the vague term 'grave goods'. Objects which the deceased wore or suspended from his/her clothing, including jewellery, often of impressive quality and variety, knives, combs etc. just imply that he or she was buried in his/her dress, a custom that continued for a long time in both high and low social circles. Objects signifying the rank of the deceased could follow him/her into the grave even in Christian contexts. On the other hand, true grave gifts like boxes, vessels of glass, metal, wood or pottery, weapons and tools, intended to be used in the afterlife, must be regarded as conflicting with Christian ideas, as they express a belief in a bodily life with needs for functional objects from our world. In Gotland this is clearly demonstrated by the differences between the so-called churchyard graves from the eleventh century and the contemporary graves in pagan cemeteries: both categories contain the same type of jewellery, but the pagan graves also contain metal vessels with food.

However, when discussing Christian elements in the burial customs in order to understand the progression of the conversion, we should not forget the remaining pagan traits. The Danish historian of religions Jens Peter Schjødt has expressed it in this way: depending on which aspect we choose to focus on – for example the view of the missionaries or the view of the convert, the official attitude (the king) or the individual (the people), our evaluation of the extent to which something or someone was Christian will vary (Schjødt 1989: 193).

The external structure of Viking Age graves is normally mounds or stone-settings; even flat-graves occur, probably an influence from western Europe. At Viking Age cemeteries in east Sweden there is sometimes a special kind of rectangular stone frame over east–west oriented inhumation graves, datable to the eleventh century. Such rectangular stone frames are often placed close to each other, sharing one side. In all probability, these are the graves of the first Christian generation in the area, those who died before there was access to a consecrated churchyard (Gräslund 2001).

Some of our preserved runic monuments may be the remains of the earliest church-yards. Runestones with the inscription 'Here lies X . . .' found in churchyards may be regarded as real tombstones, with the inscription pointing towards the medieval tombstones. Another indication of an early churchyard is the so-called Eskilstuna sarcophagus, made of limestone or sandstone and consisting of five big slabs, two long walls, a roof or lid and two tall gable ends (Figure 46.1.1). They are richly ornamented with carving in animal art and have runic inscriptions. They were raised on top of graves from the middle of the eleventh century, to judge from the ornamentation, but have normally been disturbed by later burials. They got their name from the first find, at an old churchyard in Eskilstuna, Södermanland, but the largest amount of such monuments – today mainly preserved as fragments – are found in the province of Östergötland. Gotland has its own type of similar monument, a stone coffin, made of four upright slabs with runic inscriptions and pictorial illustrations in relief, standing on top of the grave. Concerning Gotland and the so-called churchyard finds already men-tioned: women's graves from the eleventh century, found to the north of the medieval churches in many parishes (Thunmark-Nylén 1995). The reason why these graves are always female is that sex segregation (women were buried to the north and men to the south of the church) was often practised in the eleventh, twelfth and beginning of the thirteenth centuries, and they are undisturbed because, from the high Middle Ages, the north side of the church was not used for burials, due to superstition.

CULT PLACES AND CHURCHES

The topic of cult-site continuity has been vividly discussed for a long time. New archaeological material supports the hypothesis of continuity; the most striking examples are the offering site excavated under the church of Frösö (see Brink 1996 *passim*), and the Danish excavations of Viking Age manors in direct contact with early medieval churches (e.g. at Lisbjerg, see Jeppesen and Madsen 1990). If the pre-Christian cult was performed in the hall of the manor, the chieftain may, after the conversion, have given place for a small private church at the farm. A good example of this seems to be the aforementioned Lisbjerg in Jutland, where the excavation immediately outside the

Figure 46.1.1   The Eskilstuna sarcophagus (Sö 356), with ornamentation and runic inscriptions on the slabs. (From Sö.)

churchyard wall in 1988 revealed a Viking Age estate with many and unusually large buildings. This farm was encircled by a robust fence, making up an almost square plot. In the centre of this plot the medieval stone church is situated, that probably had a wooden predecessor. This was not just an ordinary manor but rather a royal estate (Jeppesen and Madsen 1990). Similar sites have been excavated at other places in south Scandinavia.

Remains or foundations of older wooden churches have sometimes been found at investigations of medieval stone churches. For Sweden, several examples of this are known from, for example, Gotland, Öland and Östergötland. In Karleby, Västergötland, the remains of two rectangular wooden churches were found in 1986, the younger datable to the first half of the twelfth century, indicating a date for the older church at the end of eleventh century or 1100 at the latest (Vretemark 1998). In Klåstad, Östergötland, the foundations of a stave-church from the second half of the eleventh century were excavated in 2000 (Hedvall 2003). At the churchyard thirty fragments of so-called 'Eskilstuna sarcophagi' were found, with ornaments datable to the middle of the eleventh century. One of the monuments was found *in situ*, placed 60–70 cm on top of the grave of a young woman.

The first certainly documented stone church in Scandinavia was built in Roskilde *c.* 1027. Its patron was Estrid, the sister of Knútr (Cnut the Great) (Olsen 1992). There are several stone churches from the second half of the eleventh century preserved in Denmark, but in Sweden and Norway they are somewhat later: the earliest ones date to the last decades of the century or even to *c.* 1100. In Norway the wooden stave-churches were an original contribution to ecclesiastical architecture. There were once hundreds of them, but only about thirty have survived. In Urnes at Sognefjord in Vestlandet a portal with rich carved animal ornament from the last quarter of the eleventh century, belonging to the oldest stave-church on the site, has been reused in the succeeding stave-church built in the 1130s.

ARTEFACTS

Artefacts reflecting the conversion are above all the silver pendant-crosses from graves, settlements and hoards (Staecker 1999). Normally, they do not occur until the tenth century. Pendant-crosses in graves are primarily found in Sweden and Finland, whereas those from hoards occur in all Scandinavian countries. The crosses from the Birka graves are all found in tenth-century female graves; the crosses are simple, cast or cut, with stamped or punched decoration or with filigree. The earliest Scandinavian crucifix is the filigree example from a tenth-century grave at Birka, where the crucifix is one of several amulets, worn by a woman, identified as a *vǫlva* by the presence of an iron staff in the grave (Price 2002). This casts light on the problem of syncretism, a concept with a wide meaning denoting a mixture of religions. A requirement is that the two religions in question have some similarities. Probably there was a long period of influence or even interaction between Old Norse religion and Christianity, and in the literary evidence we can see similarities: the end of the world and Ragnarǫk, Christ and the good *áss* Balder, the crucifixion of Christ and Balder's death etc. This also facilitates the phenomenon *interpretatio Christiana*, signifying that a pagan object or feature gets a Christian meaning. An example may be the shield-shaped amulets seen as pagan (see Gräslund, ch. 18, above) Recently a new interpretation was suggested, that they should be seen as symbols of the defenders of the Christian faith (Trotzig 2004). In my view such a transition is exactly what can be expected.

Other Christian amulets are reliquary pendants and pendants with images of saints. There are also *encolpia*, reliquary crosses, originally a Byzantine type. A Scandinavian version was found in Gåtebo in Öland, where the artist has elegantly translated the eastern form into a Scandinavian one, using native Urnes style.

Imported originally probably liturgical vessels should also be mentioned. The so-called Tating-ware jugs, produced in Westphalia, are found on the early trading centres in north-west Europe, including Birka, Hedeby and Kaupang. They have applied tin-foil decoration with equal-armed crosses at the base. The large hanging bowls of insular origin, made of copper alloys, have sometimes fish-shaped escutcheons. Both these categories are found in chamber grave Bj 854 at Birka, together with rich jewellery, a lot of other artefacts and a bronze key, which is another artefact with a possible Christian connotation. The keys are distributed over north-west Germany and southern England and Scandinavia, and chronologically they fit in well with the progression of the mission. They have been interpreted as the keys of St Peter or the Keys to Heaven. The strange thing is that in Bj 854 a Þórr's hammer ring was also found, lying by the skull of the deceased. This mix may be regarded as an example of syncretism. Further artefacts are coins with Christian symbols, both foreign and native, and pendants of rock crystal with connotations to baptismal symbolism.

ICONOGRAPHY

Finally a few words on iconographical evidence of the Christianisation: the Jelling stone in Denmark, the Dynna stone in Norway and the crucifixes display pictures of Christ. Churches are depicted on two wall hangings, from Överhogdal, Härjedalen and from Skog, Hälsingland (Franzén and Nockert 1992). They have been interpreted as showing both pagan and Christian motifs. The weavings from Överhogdal (tenth century) have recently even been regarded as a complete illustration of Ragnarǫk (Wikman 1996), but doubtless there are pictures of churches too. A common interpretation of the Skog tapestry (thirteenth century), with the church and the bell-tower in the centre, is that it is illustrating the conflict between Old Norse religion and Christianity. Three giant beings at the left end of the tapestry have been interpreted as Óðinn, Þórr and Freyr, threatening the church. However, today an interpretation of them as the three Scandinavian royal saints, St Óláfr, St Knútr and St Erik is more accepted.

BIBLIOGRAPHY

Brink, S. (ed.) (1996) *Jämtlands kristnande* (Sveriges kristnande. Publikationer 4), Uppsala: Lunne.

Franzén, A.-M. and Nockert, M. (1992) *Bonderna från Skog och Överhogdal och andra medeltida väggbeklädnader*, Stockholm: KVHAA.

Gräslund, A.-S. (2000) 'The conversion of Scandinavia – a sudden event or a gradual process?', *Archaeological Review from Cambridge*, 17(2): 83–98.

—— (2001) *Ideologi och mentalitet – om religionsskiftet i Skandinavien från en arkeologisk horisont* (Opia: Occasional Papers in Archaeology 29), Uppsala: Dept. of Archaeology and Ancient History, Uppsala University.

Hedvall, R. (2003) 'Kyrkorna i Klåstad. En presentation av ett pågående projekt', *Hikuin*, 30: 103–14.

Jeppesen, J. and Madsen, H.J. (1990) 'Stormansgård og kirke i Lisbjerg', *Kuml* (1988–9): 289–310.

Olsen, O. (1992) 'Christianity and churches', in E. Roesdahl and D. Wilson (eds) *From Viking to Crusader. The Scandinavians and Europe 800–1200*, Copenhagen: Nordic Council of Ministers.

Price, N. (2002) *The Viking Way. Religion and War in Late Iron Age Scandinavia* (Aun 31), Uppsala: Dept. of Archaeology and Ancient History, Uppsala University.

Schjødt, J.P. (1989) 'Nogle overvejelser over begrebet religionsskifte med henblik på en problematisering av termens brug i forbindelse med overgangen til kristendommen i Norden', in A. Andrén (ed.) *Medeltidens födelse* (Symposier på Krapperups borg 1), Nyhamnsläge: Gyllenstiernska Krapperupstiftelsen.

Sö = *Södermanlands runinskrifter*, 3 vols (Sveriges runinskrifter 3), Stockholm: Almqvist & Wiksell International.

Staecker, J. (1999) *Rex regum et dominus dominorum. Die wikingerzeitliche Kreuz- und Krucifixanhänger als Ausdruck der Mission in Altdänemark und Schweden* (Lund Studies in Medieval Archaeology 23), Stockholm: Almqvist & Wiksell International.

Thunmark-Nylén, L. (1995) 'Churchyard finds from Gotland (11th–12th centuries)', in I. Jansson (ed.) *Archaeology East and West of the Baltic. Papers from the Second Estonian–Swedish Archaeological Symposium Sigtuna, May 1991* (Theses and Papers in Archaeology. New Series A7), Stockholm: Dept. of Archaeology, University of Stockholm.

Trotzig, G. (2004) 'Trons försvarare i Birka', *Fornvännen*, 99: 197–207.

Vretemark, M. (1998) *Karleby kyrka – traditionen som blev sann*, Skara: Skaraborgs länsmuseum.

Wikman, S. (1996) *Fenrisulven ränner. En bok om vävarna från Överhogdal*, Östersund: Jamtli/ Jämtlands läns museum.

CHAPTER FORTY-SEVEN

THE CREATION OF NORWAY

——·◆·——

Claus Krag

'Norway' was originally a geographical concept. This is particularly conveyed in the English and German name for the country, more clearly than in the modern Scandinavian form (*Norge*). 'The way to the north' was the long sailing route along the Norwegian coast. It began in the Skagerrak–Kattegat area, went round Lindesnes – the country's southernmost point – and continued northwards to the extent of permanent settlement. In the Viking Age this was represented by the islands around Tromsø.

In 890 or thereabouts a man called Ottar travelled from the very northernmost part of this area, all the way to England. He told King Alfred of the journey he had made, and his account was written down (Lund 1984: 18–22). Ottar said that all the way south he had had 'the land of the northmen' (*norðmanna land*) on his port side. This country was long and narrow. Ottar called it *Norðweg*. Ottar's tale is not the only mention of 'northmen' (Norwegians) at this time. In a contemporary skaldic poem (*Haraldskvæði*, see below) we find Harald Finehair called 'king of the northmen' (*dróttinn norðmanna*; Finnur Jónsson 1912: 22). From this we can deduce that names such as 'Norway' and 'northmen' were in common use in the second half of the ninth century. The terms themselves almost certainly derive from southern Scandinavia, because it is from that perspective that the Norwegian coast and its people lay to the north.

Nothing indicates that 'Norway' formed a political unit in the early Viking period, and there are no surviving sources that suggest this even as a possibility. There were also several Norwegian territories (*landskaper*), probably with roots stretching back into prehistory, that possessed names of their own – for example, Hålogaland, Trøndelag, Møre, Hordaland, Rogaland, Agder, and so on, together with equivalent ethnic or tribal names for their populations (*háleygir, þrændir, mærir, hǫrðar, rygir, egðir*). Similarly when we consider these 'tribes' (an area of this kind is called a *folkland*, 'people's land', in Old Norse), it is likely that this was an identity shaped by geographical proximity and not, for example, a matter of political organisation. A possible exception is Trøndelag, which originally consisted of a tightly populated area around the inner part of the Trondheim fjord. The Trønderne's collective assembly organisation, with Frosta as a central meeting place, may have its origins in the early Viking Age or even farther back (Sandnes 1967).

In modern times 'the creation of Norway' (or *rikssamlingen* as it is known, literally 'the unification of the realm') has taken up a much greater space in Norwegian historiography than the equivalent processes have done in neighbouring countries. In a frequently cited pan-Scandinavian historical encyclopaedia, the Norwegian article on the subject takes up seven entire columns, while the comparative Swedish text spans two and the Danish one (Simensen *et al.* 1969). This difference depends on several factors. When modern historical science developed around the middle of the nineteenth century, Norwegians – as citizens of a resurgent nation after several centuries in union with Denmark – were active in seeking their historical specificity (Dahl 1990: 43–85). This they claimed to have found, in a Herderian spirit, especially manifest in the creation of the nation and in its earliest history. In addition, we should remember that Norwegians could build such a history on remarkably rich and comprehensive sources: the Old Norse saga literature and above all the kings' sagas, which treat the Norwegian monarchs in particular.

The thirteenth-century kings' sagas (building on learned historical enquiry that began on Iceland with Sæmundr fróði 100 years earlier) contained much that could sustain the independence of nineteenth-century Norwegians. Especially important was the saga-writers' construction of a close connectedness in Norwegian history, right from the first half of the ninth century to the saga-authors' own time. This connection took the form of a long dynastic line. This began with Halfdan the Black and Harald Finehair around 850, and ended with the kings of the Sverre family in the thirteenth century. In some of the sagas this long lineage was extended further back in time, as far as the legendary Ynglinga kings of Gamla Uppsala (Krag 1991).

Harald Finehair's significance as a national king and dynastic founder was summarised in the saga called *Fagrskinna* (*c.* 1220–30; author unknown):

> Harald, son of Halfdan the Black, took the kingdom after his father. He was then a young man reckoned in winters, but had in full measure the manliness that a courtly king should possess. His hair was of a remarkable colour and in this respect could be likened most to silk. He was the most handsome of all men and unusually strong, and as tall as can be seen from the stone on his grave that lies at Haugesund. He was a very wise man, forward-looking and courageous, and he also brought luck with him. He set himself the objective of becoming king over the realm of the Norwegians, and with increasing honour the country has been in the hands of his line even to our own time, and so shall it always be.
>
> (Old Norse text in Bjarni Einarsson 1985: 58–9; trans. Neil Price)

With the exception of a few skaldic verses there is no contemporary source that sheds any light on Harald's conquest. The most important source, *Haraldskvæði* (Finnur Jónsson 1912: 22–5), contains information that does not entirely match the picture painted by the sagas. Snorri Sturluson constructed a systematic description of the whole conquest from one region to another, encompassing all of what would become the later kingdom. To him the battle at Hafrsfjǫrðr (a little south of Stavanger) that is the focus of the verses, marked the completion of Harald's conquest. According to Snorri, in this battle Harald's last opponents, who were kings of the Vestlands in the region south of Bergen (Bjarni Aðalbjarnarson 1979: 114–17), were defeated. But if we work from the verses that are a contemporary source, the situation (not the outcome of the battle) appears to have been different: here it is Harald in *his* south-west Norwegian kingdom who was attacked by rivals that came from the east, probably with Danish support (von See 1961: 105–11).

This, together with the fact that the royal manors mentioned in connection with Harald and his immediate successors lay in the Vestlands, suggests that the kingdom Harald first took over included the central and southern parts of the Vestland region. From what we know it seems that the starting point for Harald's conquest was Sogn, where his maternal grandfather was king, and not Vestfold as Snorri writes (Ólafía Einarsdóttir 1971).

In the Nordvestland and further north it appears that Harald had no more than a purely formal overlordship, while jarls who were subordinate only in name in fact possessed the real power. The best known of these jarls are Håkon Grjotgardsson and his successors. Their seat lay at Lade in Trøndelag, but the family came originally from Hålogaland, where they also continued to enjoy considerable influence. Håkon was an expansionist ruler in his own right and in many senses Harald's equal.

It can hardly be coincidence that the regions that were unified around 900 also formed the 'north way'. This was a rich trade route that could certainly tempt a would-be conqueror, whether beginning from the south like Harald or from the north like Håkon. Alongside the process of unification, and partly preceding it, we also see a significant inner network being created, sometimes over great distances, by family ties within the highest social strata of chieftains, even though the political structures in the new kingdom were weak.

Viken, that is the coastal region of south-east Norway, was not part of Harald's kingdom. Here Danish kings had been influential from the beginning of the Viking Age. At the start of the ninth century the Frankish annals mention a certain King Godfred, who was a formidable opponent even for Charlemagne. Concerning his descendants it is written there that for a time they were resident in 'Vestfold' – the northernmost part of their kingdom – to quell an uprising (Rau 1968: 102). Throughout the entire tenth century there were petty kings in Viken, who at least in the second half of the century were sub-regents to the Danish kings.

The dynasty of Finehair was a reality insofar as Harald (d. *c*. 932) was succeeded as king by two of his sons, first Eirik Bloodaxe (r. *c*. 930–4) and subsequently Håkon the Good (r. *c*. 934–61). Around the middle of the tenth century the Danish kingdom again became strong, and King Harald Bluetooth (r. *c*. 958–87) was able to become overking of Norway, including both Viken and the kingdom that Harald Finehair had unified. At first the sons of Eirik Bloodaxe were sub-kings, and afterwards Håkon Sigurdsson Ladejarl (grandson of Håkon Grjotgardsson) ruled the greater part of Norway as the Danish king's jarl. In the last years of his reign, Håkon (who died in 995) managed to establish more independent control over the coastal area from Lindesnes and northwards.

During the period from *c*. 950 to 1035 we find that the dominance of the Danish kings was extending over the whole south Scandinavian region. The Danish monarchs were attractive collaborative partners for chieftains elsewhere in the north, because they could offer their allies lucrative participation in the Danish Viking enterprises overseas, especially in England. Jarl Håkon's son, Eirik jarl (d. *c*. 1024), revived cooperation with the Danish kings, and ended his career as Knut the Great's jarl in Northumberland.

Olaf Tryggvason (r. 995–1000) and Olaf Haraldsson (St Olav, r. 1015–28/30) eventually succeeded in breaking the Danish hegemony in Norway. But before their assumption of the national throne, both of these men had gained power and wealth in England, in connection with the Danish conquest there (Krag 2003: 191–6). Without these resources that they brought home with them, they would hardly have been able to lay the foundations on which to build a kingdom at home. Later saga tradition depicted the two Olafs, both sons of Danish sub-kings of the Viken region, as inheritors of Harald Finehair. For this we find no support in contemporary sources, that is to say the skaldic verses, and it appears to be a later construction (Nielsen 1908; Krag 1989, 2002).

Events that took place later in the eleventh century, from 1035 onwards, meant that the reigns of Olaf Tryggvason and Olaf Haraldsson were not just isolated episodes in Norwegian history. When the Danish Empire of the North Sea disintegrated on the death of Knut the Great in 1035, a genuine Norwegian dynasty could establish itself in their homelands. The first of these kings was the son of Olaf Haraldsson, Magnus the Good (r. 1035–47), and the next was Olaf's half-brother, Harald Sigurdsson Hardrada (the 'Hard-Ruler' or the 'Ruthless', r. 1046–66). A few years after his death Olaf Haraldsson was also canonised, and this contributed to the legitimation of his successors' thrones. The later Norwegian kings of the Middle Ages were all descendants of Harald Hardrada. Under Olaf Haraldsson and Harald Hardrada we also find the Østlands – not merely Viken but also the inner territories – for the first time incorporated in the national kingdom. The skald Ottar the Black tells how Olaf Haraldsson broke down resistance in the interior: all the kings of Hedmark fled, 'apart from he who sat furthest north, and whose tongue you ordered to be cut out . . . Now you rule over wide-ranging lands, that five kings possessed before, as far east as Eidskog. No king previously had such a kingdom' (Finnur Jónsson 1912: 271–2).

The shift in religion was equally important. Christianity had already penetrated most parts of the coastal regions by the tenth century (Rolfsen 1981; Solberg 2000: 311–20). Håkon the Good had taken pains to bring English missionaries to the country (Birkeli 1960). It was under Olaf Tryggvason and Olaf Haraldsson that the whole country was converted, and a Norwegian church established (Krag 2003: 196–201). The process of Christianisation met with little resistance. It was not this, but instead his conflicts with Knut the Great, the Lade jarls and the Norwegian coastal aristocracy that led to Olaf Haraldsson's downfall in 1028–30.

It was after 1035 that the unification of Norway became a continuing process moving in a single direction. A decisive element was the disappearance of the Danish kings as a power in Norway. The same is true for the Lade jarls, whose line died out on the male side in 1029, thereby ending the last princely family that could match itself with the kings. This meant that it was the new Norwegian dynasty, the descendants of Olaf Haraldsson and Harald Hardrada, with whom the local chieftains would have to cooperate if they wished to retain their power and influence.

Collaboration between the kingdom and the chieftains found its organisational expression in the king's *hird* and the institution of the *lendmann* (Krag 2001). The *hird* was originally the king's bodyguard and continued to be so. But under a peaceful king such as Olaf Kyrre (r. 1066–93) we see that it to some degree altered in character and began to take on civil functions as a royal court (Andersen 1977: 289–94; Hamre 1961).

While the members of the *hird* stayed with the king, his *lendir menn* were set up around the country as his representatives. The actual word *lendr maðr* refers to the fact that a *lendmann* had received 'land' (i.e. landholdings) in the name of the king. The land symbolised the bond between the two, and meant that the *lendmann* had the king's authority behind him. This connection, and loyalty, stretched equally in the opposite direction. The *lendmann* was as a rule a chieftain in his home district, and possessed an estate of his own that far exceeded in value that which he received from the king. The support that the kings gained from such men, with their considerable local influence, was fundamental for the cohesion of the kingdom.

This network also made it possible for the king to assert himself abroad. When military-minded kings took to the warpath, they brought with them not only their own *hird*, but also the *lendmenn* and their *'huskarls'*. This was the situation during Magnus the Good's and Harald Hardrada's campaigns in Denmark in the 1040s and 1050s (the latter fell at Stamford Bridge in 1066), and under the last 'Viking' king Magnus Barelegs (r. 1093–1103) on his invasion of Scotland and Ireland. We see something similar in connection with Sigurd Jerusalem-farer's (r. 1103–30) crusade to the Holy Land in 1108–11. Sigurd was incidentally the first European king to take up a crusade.

The parallel development of ecclesiastical organisation was a prerequisite for the consolidation of the kingdom, and meant simultaneously that Norway took its place among the European Christian monarchies. The religion itself and its accompanying ideals supported the notion of a Christian king, as a necessary institution in this world, ordained by God. Through its preaching and its administration of the sacrament, the Church prepared ordinary people for life in the next world. Christianity in this way also came to shape popular mentalities and ideas in Norway, as it had elsewhere. With time the Church became a social institution that in many ways was more powerful than the throne. The clearest expression of this can be seen around 1300, when 40 per cent of landownership in Norway, measured by value, was in the hands of the Church, a remarkably high proportion (Andersen 1977: 301–39; Helle 1974: 236–42).

As an institution the Church eventually achieved independence of the king. This development began with the establishment of permanent bishoprics around 1100 (Trondheim, Bergen, Oslo, later also Stavanger and Hamar), prior to which the bishops had been part of the royal *hird* and had accompanied the king on his travels around the country. An important step was taken in 1152–3, when the archbishopric of Nidaros was established. In addition, numerous monastic houses had been founded from around 1100 and onwards. Apart from the five Norwegian bishoprics, the Nidaros church province also included Greenland, Iceland (with two bishoprics), the Faroes, the Orkneys, and the kingdom of Man and the Isles.

The link between the Church and the monarchy had great practical significance. It was quite simply decisive for the development of a royal administration that made use of script, which gradually came into being from the second half of the eleventh century. At this time the first laws were written down, having previously been passed on through oral tradition (Helle 2002).

In the eleventh century and the beginning of the twelfth, the kingdom was largely undeveloped in institutional terms. There were no fixed rules for royal succession. All the king's sons – of whom few were born in wedlock – had the right of inheritance. It was therefore common to find joint kingdoms, in which two or more pretenders shared the throne, without splitting up the territory, between them. If the kings got on well, this arrangement could promote peace and stability (Bjørgo 1970). However, in the period 1134–1217 there arose by phases a struggle between various pretenders to the throne and their adherents. An especially intense conflict developed between King Magnus Erlingsson (r. 1161–84) and his successors on one side, and on the other Sverre Sigurdsson (r. 1177–1202) and his followers within the party known as the *birkibeinar* ('Birchlegs'; Helle 2003: 369–76; Gathorne-Hardy 1956). The strife ended when Sverre's grandson, Håkon Håkonsson (r. 1217–63), managed to consolidate a reunited kingdom, with a strongly personal control of power, and left it to his successors as an uncontested and formalised inherited monarchy.

Throughout the period of civil war the organisational expansion of the Norwegian kingdom continued (Helle 1974). For the state as a whole, it was of especial importance that the local administration became more solid than before. Earlier the *lendmenn* had shared the king's interests at a local level together with another group of 'civil servants', the so-called *ármenn* ('service-men'), without any formal system. Now the whole country was divided into administrative districts called *sýslur*, and in each *sýsla* sat a royal bailiff called *sýslumaðr* (Andersen 1972). In the second half of the thirteenth century there were forty to fifty such districts.

At this time the *hird* also changed in nature. It came to embrace not only those *hirdmenn* who always accompanied the king, but also ex-*hirdmenn* who at the conclusion of their service formed a royal network over the whole country. As time passed this was transformed into an ever more formalised aristocratic corporation, in effect a nobility, though with less comprehensive privileges than in neighbouring countries. The *lendmenn* formed the most senior section of the *hird* (Hamre 1961).

For most Norwegians the thirteenth century represents their country's time of grandeur. Several elements have come to characterise this period: political stability, a cultural flowering and a 'Pax Norvegica' that drew to itself vast areas – from the Göta River to Greenland, from the Irish Sea to Finnmark – and laid them under the Norwegian Crown (Helle 2003: 385–91). Three generations of kings, all of them Sverre's descendants, reigned in this period. Håkon Håkonsson was the dominant figure of the century because of the length of his reign. On his death he was succeeded by his son Magnus Lagabøte (r. 1263–80), who was in turn followed by his sons – first Eirík Magnusson (r. 1280–99) and thereafter Håkon Magnusson (r. 1299–1319).

While Håkon Håkonsson completed the territorial expansion which brought both Greenland and Iceland under Norwegian dominion (in respectively 1261 and 1262), Magnus Lagabøte devoted most of his energies to the inner consolidation of the realm. In 1274 the National Legal Code (*Landsloven*) replaced the earlier provincial laws, and Norway was thereby among the first European countries to have a single law. This occurred seventy years earlier than in Sweden, whose national law followed the Norwegian model, and all of 400 years before the same happened in Denmark. The king's personal power was also far greater in Norway than in its neighbours.

Magnus Lagabøte pursued a peaceful foreign policy. He recognised that it was impossible for the Norwegian king to maintain long-term possession of the Hebrides and Man, and relinquished these territories at the Peace of Perth in 1266, ceding them to the Scottish king Alexander III. At the same time there occurred a reorientation of foreign policy, away from those regions that were colonised by Norwegians in the Viking Age and towards a greater concentration on Scandinavian affairs. Parallel with this, however, the Norwegian kingdom was let down by generally poor military and economic development during this period (Bjørgo 1995: 95). In the fourteenth and fifteenth centuries this made Norway the underdog of the Scandinavian collective that grew into being at this time. ~~From 1450, Norway was part of a durable union with Denmark that lasted until 1814.~~

BIBLIOGRAPHY

Andersen, P.S. (1972) 'Syssel: Norge', *KL* 17: 646–8, Oslo: Gyldendal.

—— (1977) *Samlingen av Norge og kristningen av landet 800–1130*, Oslo: Universitetsforlaget.

Birkeli, F. (1960) 'Hadde Håkon Adalsteinsfostre likevel en biskop Sigrid hos seg?, [*Norsk*] *Historisk tidsskrift*, 40: 113–36.

Bjarni Aðalbjarnarson (ed.) (1979) *Heimskringla*, vol. 1 (Íslenzk fornrit 26), Reykjavík: Hið íslenzka fornritafélag.

Bjarni Einarsson (ed.) (1985) *Ágrip. Fagrskinna* (Íslenzk fornrit 29), Reykjavík: Hið íslenzka fornritafélag.

Bjørgo, N. (1970) 'Samkongedøme kontra einekongdøme', [*Norsk*] *Historisk tidsskrift*, 49: 1–33.

—— (1995) '800–1536. Makt og avmakt', in *Norsk utenrikspolitisk historie*, vol. 1, Oslo: Universitetsforlaget.

Dahl, O. (1990) *Norsk historieforskning i 19. og 20. århundre*, 4th edn, Oslo: Universitetsforlaget.

Finnur Jónsson (ed.) (1912; 2nd edn 1967) *Den norsk-islandske skjaldedigtning*, vol. 1B: *Rettet tekst*, Copenhagen: Rosenkilde og Bagger.

Gathorne-Hardy, G.M. (1956) *A Royal Impostor. King Sverre of Norway*, Oslo: Aschehoug.

Hamre, L. (1961) 'Hird', *KL* 6: 567–77, Oslo: Gyldendal.

Helle, K. (1974) *Norge blir en stat 1130–1319*, Oslo: Universitetsforlaget.

—— (2002) 'Fra muntlig rett til skreven lov', *Forum Mediaevale*, 5: 5–31.

—— (2003) 'The Norwegian kingdom: succession disputes and consolidation', in K. Helle (ed.) *The Cambridge History of Scandinavia*, vol. 1, Cambridge: Cambridge University Press.

Krag, C. (1989) 'Norge som odel i Harald Hårfagres ætt', [*Norsk*] *Historisk tidsskrift*, 68: 288–301.

—— (1991) *Ynglingatal og ynglingesaga. En studie i historiske kilder*, Oslo: Universitetsforlaget.

—— (2001) 'Lendir menn', *RGA* 18: 259–62.

—— (2002) 'Myten om Hårfagreættens "odel" ', [*Norsk*] *Historisk tidsskrift*, 81: 381–94.

—— (2003) 'The early unification of Norway', in K. Helle (ed.) *The Cambridge History of Scandinavia*, vol. 1, Cambridge: Cambridge University Press.

Lund, N. (ed.) (1984) *Two Voyagers at the Court of King Alfred. The Venture of Othere and Wulfstan*, York: William Sessions.

Nielsen, Y. (1908) 'Den gamle hadeland-ringerikske Kongeæt og Snefridsagnet', in *Sproglige og historiske Afhandlinger tilegnede Sophus Bugges Minde*, Kristiania/Oslo: Aschehoug.

Ólafia Einarsdóttir (1971) 'Harald Dovrefostre af Sogn', [*Norsk*] *Historisk tidsskrift*, 50: 131–66.

Rau, R. (ed.) (1968) *Quellen zur karolingischen Reichsgeschichte. Annales regni Francorum*, Darmstadt: Wissenschaftliche Buchgesellschaft.

Rolfsen, P. (1981) 'Den siste hedning på Agder', *Viking*, 44: 112–28.

Sandnes, J. (1967) 'Trøndelags eldste politiske historie', [*Norsk*] *Historisk tidsskrift*, 46: 1–19.

von See, K. (1961) 'Studien zum Haraldskvæði', *Arkiv för nordisk filologi*, 76: 96–111.

Simensen, J. *et al.* (1969) 'Rikssamling', *KL* 14: 260–71, Oslo: Gyldendal.

Solberg, B. (2000), *Jernalderen i Norge*, Oslo: Cappelen.

CHAPTER FORTY-EIGHT

THE EMERGENCE OF DENMARK AND THE REIGN OF HARALD BLUETOOTH

———— •◆• ————

Else Roesdahl

On the great runestone at Jelling, King Harald Bluetooth (r. *c.* 958–87) mentions among his deeds that he had 'won the whole of Denmark for himself' (*sar uan tanmaurk ala*; Moltke 1985: 207). This is sometimes understood today as meaning that he unified the kingdom. However, in concrete terms the inscription tells us that he took power in all of Denmark, which implies that 'Denmark' signified a polity that was already recognised. It is not known exactly when Denmark became unified. For the early Danish chroniclers of the 1100s, this had already happened in the remote age of stories, when their tales began. No historically known king was famed for having unified the country that from the second half of the tenth century clearly appears as one realm under a single monarch.

It comprised the southernmost part of Scandinavia (Figure 48.1): the Jutland peninsula as far as the Ejder River (in what is now northern Germany), the islands of Fyn and Sjælland with nearby islets, together with Skåne and Halland (in modern south Sweden). Apart from areas of Blekinge (now also in southern Sweden) and the island of Bornholm, which both became part of the kingdom after the Viking period, and Viken (the area around the Oslo fjord) which at times was also included, this region marked the limits of Denmark throughout the Middle Ages. The kingdom was bound together by the sea, and good ships were a prerequisite for its unity. The sea also opened up the potential for contact – both hostile and friendly – with many neighbouring countries and peoples to the north, east and west. The marine link between western Europe and the Baltic region also passed through the Danish belts and sounds: Denmark was the gateway, and could control access.

To the east the great forests and bogs of Småland formed a natural border between Skåne and the Swedish lands. To the south, at the foot of Jutland, was a narrow connection to the European mainland. Around the year 700 an impressive boundary wall was erected here, the Danevirke (Figure 48.2), that was later rebuilt many times (Andersen 1998) and also marked a cultural and linguistic border. South of it lived the Saxons and Frisians, who during the eighth century found themselves incorporated into the Carolingian Empire, along with the Slavic Obodrites whose lands lay in the western Baltic. Over time there were many confrontations, but also shifting alliances between Denmark and the Slavic territories, as Denmark was pressured by the powerful

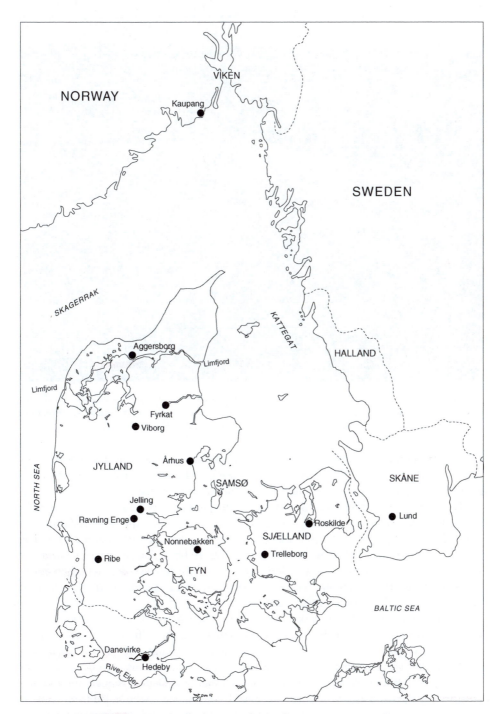

Figure 48.1   Map of Viking Age Denmark. (Drawing: Louise Hilmar.)

Figure 48.2   Aerial photo of the 'Main Wall' of the Danevirke, which marked the Danish border with Germany. Seen from the west where it meets the 'Crooked Wall'. In the foreground is a fortification from 1864. In the far background Schleswig town. (Photo: Thorkild Balslev.)

Carolingian Empire and later the German realm. Denmark's location in southern Scandinavia meant that many European influences reached the region first, seen for example in the unification of the country and the introduction of Christianity.

But when did Denmark come into being? (The question is discussed in, among other works, Christensen 1969: 25–32; Skovgaard-Petersen 1977: 23–44, 88–96; Albrectsen 1994; Näsman 1999; Olsen 1999: 23–37; cf. Sawyer 1988: 11–48; Lund 1991). The matter can be illuminated from written sources, but today archaeology also provides us with considerable information, not least because of the precise dendrochronological dating of the great military and politically loaded engineering projects that can help us understand these developments (Roesdahl 1994).

The oldest mention of Denmark (*Denameark*) as the name of a geographic area comes from around 890 and can be found in two accounts given to Alfred the Great, king of the southern English realm of Wessex. Among other things, the north Norwegian chieftain Ohthere provided him with a short description of his sailing route from Kaupang in southern Norway to Hedeby at the southern Danish border. Jutland and possibly also Sjælland are mentioned. The merchant Wulfstan, who sailed from Hedeby to the eastern Baltic region, mentions the southern Danish islands of Langeland, Lolland and Falster, together with Skåne, as part of Denmark.

The terms 'Danes' and 'king of the Danes' (*rex danorum*) are in fact known from as far back as the sixth century, and at that time the Danes must have been a leading tribe in what later became the kingdom. From the end of the eighth century, when the Carolingians' northern expansion and the Danish Viking raids on the empire resulted in mutual political and military confrontation, the 'king of the Danes' is often mentioned – and named – in Frankish sources. Among them was Charlemagne's opponent Godfred, about whom is written among other things that in 808 he ordered a wall to be raised across the border at the base of Jutland. This must have been an expansion of the Danevirke, but this phase has not yet been archaeologically identified. Even though no other king than that of the 'Danes' is mentioned in the Frankish sources, it has been debated whether he and many of his successors reigned over the area that we now know as Denmark, or perhaps only Jutland.

However, archaeological analyses of developments in the eighth century strongly suggest that Denmark was a single kingdom at this time, under the 'king of the Danes' (especially Olsen 1999: 23–37; Näsman 1999, 2000). Among these developments were increased production and major new trading networks, making possible greater exchange and surplus. Impressive building projects around the year 700 and in the decades following enabled the control of large areas of land (the oldest phases of the Danevirke) and of the inner Danish waterways (the Kanhave canal built on Samsø in 726), in addition to the seventh–eighth-century development of sailing vessels that made possible the efficient control of the sea and a kingdom with many islands.

The unification of the kingdom was undoubtedly a long process (Näsman 1999, 2000), which probably followed a pattern from originally independent tribes through to growing tribal federations with an overking from the leading tribe, and finally to a single kingdom with a single ruler. This took place under pressure from the south in connection with decisive socio-economic changes, and also through war. The process was almost certainly uneven and dramatic, accelerating in the later Roman Iron Age and resulting – prior to the Viking Age, perhaps around 700 – in the unification of a number of 'lands' (*lande*) within the Denmark that we now recognise. During and after the Viking period the nature of royal power, its duties and prerogatives, and the governance of the kingdom changed many times. There are instances of several kings reigning simultaneously, and also cases when the kingdom was periodically divided between a number of kings and then subsequently reunited again.

There were still many very considerable regional differences that were politically centred on the 'lands'. In the twelfth century, when we have written sources, the larger 'lands' of Jutland, Sjælland and Skåne each had their assembly at which kings would be elected and important decisions and laws made. The interaction between kings and magnates was of decisive importance. Through the earliest surviving literature and historical writings we glimpse the powerbrokers' construction of traditions around the kingdom as a legitimate unit of great antiquity and with an identity linked to a royal line that led back far into the past. These traditions are probably very old. Great pains and expense were taken to visually mark the power and success of kings – prestige banquets, halls and decoration together with large public monuments and memorials. The latter reached their zenith under Harald Bluetooth.

Over the course of the ninth and the beginning of the tenth century the Danish kings and conditions in Denmark can be followed sporadically through written sources, especially in their relation to the Frankish and German empires (e.g. Christensen 1969: 115–222; Skovgaard-Petersen 1977: 148–64; Sawyer 1988: 103–30, 213–19). By their nature these frequently discuss confrontations, but also several missions, normally at the behest of the Carolingian and German emperors and kings. The Frankish missionary Ansgar thus visited the country around 830 and 850, and on the latter occasion was given permission from King Horik to build churches and ring bells in Hedeby and Ribe. These were international market towns with a great many foreign visitors, places that were particularly suitable for mission work. Ansgar's mission was hardly significant at the time, but laid a modest foundation for the conversion a century later. This took place after Danes had become gradually acquainted with Christianity abroad over a 150-year period, about 30 years after the Danish king Gnupa had been forcibly converted following defeat at the hands of the German king, and about 20 years after we hear of German bishops installed in the towns of Schleswig (Hedeby), Ribe and Århus.

THE REIGN OF HARALD BLUETOOTH

The mid- to late tenth century formed in many ways an end of one era and the beginning of another, especially after the official shift of religion around 965. But it was also a time of upheaval in economic, cultural, social and political terms, as Denmark was increasingly affected by Christian Europe. Among the examples of this is the introduction of special cargo ships in contrast to warships and personal transport vessels, undoubtedly as a result of increased trade; towns grew and others were established; comparatively cheap wares were paid for in silver by weight, in the form of coins or parts of them – most often foreign issues, but Danish mints became more frequent and increased production; the traditional Nordic female dress with its particular jewellery was abandoned; a new decorative form, the Mammen style, developed; large royal monuments were built as never before, with a focus on the king himself; the erection of runestones underwent a boom, and so on (summarised with references in Roesdahl 2002). All this took place or began in the time of Harald Bluetooth, and the change of religion is a part of this.

The image of Harald and his policies can today be illuminated through a combination of different sources. His reign was a shifting one, and questions of continuity and schism, traditions and innovation are central (Christensen 1969: 223–40; Skovgaard-Petersen 1977: 164–78; Sawyer 1988: 221–45; Albrectsen 1994; Roesdahl 2002). He succeeded his father Gorm, who probably died in 958/9 and who was one of the first kings in a new dynasty. For about twenty years Harald was the greatest king in the north, who apart from ruling over Denmark also held power over part of Norway. From there he gained both troops and tribute, undoubtedly in the form of typical Norwegian products such as furs, falcons, iron, soapstone vessels and whetstones, all of which were sought after and could be redistributed. Through successful politics he secured the country against the German Empire, with the help of an expanded Danevirke and alliances with Slavic princes. He also married Tove, the daughter of the Obodrite ruler Mistivoj. The raising or enlargement of the defensive walls around the three Jutland towns is also part of this picture.

The conversion was one of Harald's great achievements. He 'made the Danes Christian', as it says on the great Jelling stone, though as in Iceland in the year 1000 this undoubtedly occurred with the assent of the kingdom's magnates, the acceptance of the regional assemblies and with a few exceptions made to Christian rules. The new religion was no stranger to the country. Its teachings would have appealed to many, its hierarchical structure could support a central power and the real transition took place gradually. According to the Saxon Widukind, who also described Harald as 'eager to listen but late to speak', the cleric Poppo played a decisive role by proving the truth of the Christian faith through an ordeal of iron. However, the conversion was probably also a countermeasure against the emperor Otto I's expansionist mission policy (cf. Wamers 2000: 156 ff.). There seem to have been earlier pagan reactions against Christianity's inroads, and a focus on the reinforcement of Nordic cultural traditions (Roesdahl 2005), expressed in various ways. These included aristocratic burial ritual and a revived monumentalisation of memorials and other sites of a religious character from earlier times, such as mounds and ship settings, together with the practical reuse of ancient monuments. Many of these traditions, including those relating to mortuary behaviour, continued for a time after the conversion, though probably in a moderated form. These soon died out, however, and around the year 1000 we find for example that Christian crosses have completely replaced pagan Þórr's hammers as personal religious symbols.

In 974 Harald was defeated at the Danevirke by the German emperor Otto II, and Schleswig/Hedeby was taken. At the same time dominion in Norway was lost together with its concomitant soldiery and income. At around this period economic conditions also shifted in that the traditional flow of silver from the Orient to the north, via Russia, suddenly ceased due to a changing situation out east. Silver and honour were pre-requisites for a king's success, and this loss of military and political prestige (and not least income, including the profits from Hedeby) must have altered the configuration of power in Denmark. In 983 a combined Slavic–Danish force made a successful attack on northern Germany, laying waste Hamburg among other places, but only a few years later in 987 King Harald was driven out and killed in a rebellion led by his son and heir, Svein Forkbeard.

JELLING

Harald Bluetooth also raised a remarkable series of large, innovative buildings and memorials, and he is the first Nordic king whose name can with certainty be associated with surviving monuments. The most spectacular and important are situated at Jelling (Figures 48.3 and 48.4). They mark the zenith of his power and at the same time give us an insight into his political and cultural programme, as well as the period's architecture and art of power. These are large, dynastic monuments with a focus on power, identity, tradition and continuity spanning the change of religion, as well as on Harald himself, his deeds and his parents. At the same time they are the central monuments of the conversion itself, in that a major pagan site was developed into an even bigger and more complex Christian memorial. It is notable that all of these things had Nordic roots, apart from the Church, and that everything was done on a royal scale. Together with an undoubtedly impressive royal manor, whose location and appearance are unknown, the monuments provided the physical framework for the exercising of power, religion and (probably) law.

The monuments are connected to Harald and his parents by the inscriptions on two runestones. The text on the older and smaller stone, whose original position is unknown, reads: 'King Gorm made this monument in memory of Thorvi [Thyre], his wife, Denmark's adornment.' The inscription on the larger runestone (Figure 48.4), which stands on its original spot exactly between two great mounds, reads: 'King Harald commanded this monument to be made in memory of Gorm, his father, and in memory

Figure 48.3 Jelling in the late nineteenth century, seen from the south-west. The stone church, which was built around 1100 and is the successor of earlier stave-churches, is seen between the two huge mounds. King Harald Bluetooth's large runestone (Figure 48.4), which forms the centre of his composite monument, is seen to the left of the church porch. The North Mound (right) was the burial place of his pagan father, King Gorm, who was presumably moved to a grave in the first church at Jelling after Harald's introduction of Christianity in *c.* 965. The South Mound (left) had no grave; it was built a few years after the conversion and was probably a memorial and a thing mound (after Kornerup 1875).

of Thorvi [Thyre], his mother – that Harald who won the whole of Denmark for himself, and Norway and made the Danes Christian.' Apart from the inscription the stone is decorated with large pictures of an animal interlaced with a snake, and an image of Christ. On both stones we find the word *kubl*, in the plural form. This has been interpreted as meaning a monument, of a kind that could have multiple component parts (Moltke 1985: 206–16).

The Jelling monuments were probably constructed over three decades and in three phases, from the 940s to the 970s. They are situated prominently in the landscape and in each phase form a coherent, planned whole built along the same axis. This is monumental architecture of turf, stone and wood and must have demanded an extraordinary investment of labour, probably carried out by men seconded to do so. All the most important monument types of the Viking Age are found here writ large. Today the site is bounded by the two great mounds around the church and the runestones (Kornerup 1875; Krogh 1982, 1993; Krogh and Olsen 1993; Roesdahl 2005).

The first phase originally took the form of a stone alignment *c.* 170 m long, probably a ship setting (the largest in the north), which at its northern end adjoined a small Bronze Age mound. It was a pagan monument, whose real function is unknown – perhaps the ship setting formed the stage for cultic performances. It was probably built

Figure 48.4   King Harald's great runestone in Jelling, *c.* 970. Height: *c.* 245 cm above ground level. It has text and ornament on one side. The two other sides each have a text line and a large picture of, respectively, a prancing animal and Christ. The idea of the large pictures was probably inspired by Christian book illustrations, while the organisation of the rune-lines in horizontal bands must have been inspired by lines in a book. But the style used is unmistakably the Viking Mammen style. In the foreground King Gorm's runestone raised for his queen; its original position is unknown. (Photo: Else Roesdahl 1996.)

by King Gorm, perhaps as a memorial to Queen Thyre. We do not know where she was buried.

In the second phase the site was enlarged by the construction of the North Mound, Denmark's largest barrow. It covered the Bronze Age mound and the northern point of the ship setting. The runic inscriptions, the dating of the burial chamber (958/9), the remains of the funerary objects found inside and the scale of the work in itself all combine to suggest that the mound was the grave and memorial for King Gorm, raised in a pagan country for a pagan king, by his son and heir, King Harald. It was a royal version of the magnate graves of the time and a dramatic pagan manifestation.

The third and last phase was the major expansion in association with the change of religion, which took place five to seven years after Gorm's death, around 965. There was clearly a coordinated plan for the whole site, but the construction of the South Mound was begun *c.* 970 at the earliest. The work thus probably continued in stages over ten years or so, most likely with the larger runestone and the great wooden church (under the present stone one) as its first elements. The church was probably a baptismal foundation dedicated to John the Baptist. At the same time King Gorm was probably 'Christianised' by the translation of his remains from the North Mound to a chamber grave in the church, for here lay the reburied bones of a man, packed in gold-threaded textiles with costly mounts in the same style as objects found in the North Mound. The South Mound, which is even bigger than its northern counterpart, covered the southern end of the ship setting and thereby destroyed this pagan monument. The South Mound did not contain a grave, and its real function has been debated. Perhaps it was a memorial for King Harald himself, or maybe for his mother. It may also have been built as an assembly mound – on its flat summit legal proceedings could be publicly conducted in a prominent space connected to religion, as we find in many other places.

The Jelling memorials were in every phase a national monument focusing on royal power, legitimacy, religion and the kings themselves, Gorm and Harald. In the final, Christian phase we might also see a message that, despite the new religion, Harald wished to follow custom and respect tradition. At the same time his success as a politician and warrior was underlined, an important demarcation in relation to the German Empire that generated the main political, cultural and religious movements of the age.

The location of the monuments in Jelling may partly be explained by its proximity to the *Hærvej* (literally 'army-road'), the great communication route through Jutland, not far from the southern border of the kingdom that was then the political focus. It may also be understood through the presence of a large royal manor, where the leading people of the realm could be gathered for important meetings and councils, conflict resolutions or great banquets – a context which undoubtedly suits the monuments. But Jelling's golden age was short-lived and no noteworthy memorials were raised here after Harald's time. The centre of power shifted, which is why so much has survived intact. The monuments have, however, always been known and admired. The larger runestone also provided inspiration to the images on several of the following generations' runestones, and the great beast of the stone, whose exact symbolism is unknown, became the prototype for half a century of similar images (Wilson and Klindt-Jensen 1966: 119–22 and *passim*).

THE RAVNING ENGE BRIDGE AND THE TRELLEBORGS

The Ravning Enge bridge and the four Trelleborgs (Figures 48.1 and 48.5) date to a few years after the Jelling monuments but share many of their characteristics: they are large, resource-intensive, prestige-oriented, innovative and very short-lived. The Trelleborgs were constructed *c.* 980 and the bridge is either contemporary with them or perhaps a few years later. They must have been built by Harald Bluetooth in the last years of his monarchy, both for a specific purpose and also as national monuments and memorials. Their use-life does not extend much, if at all, beyond the end of his reign.

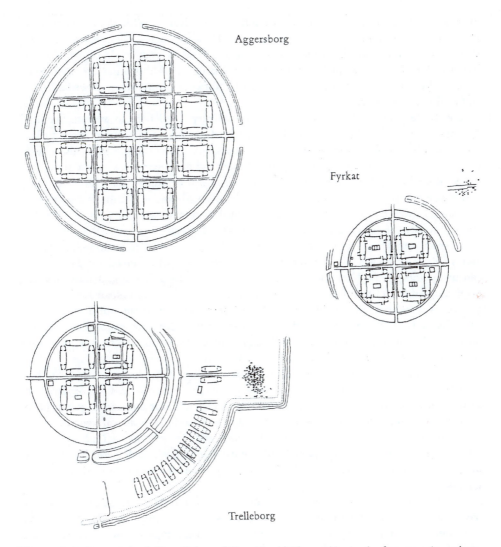

Aggersborg

Fyrkat

Trelleborg

Figure 48.5 Reconstructed plans of three of King Harald Bluetooth's circular fortresses: Aggersborg, Fyrkat and Trelleborg. Their inner diameter was 240 m, 136 m and 120 m respectively. The building materials were timber, turf and earth. All had a circular rampart with gates at the four points of the compass linked by roads. The inner space was divided into four quarters, each with four buildings, *c.* 30 m long (at Aggersborg there were twelve buildings in each quarter). Trelleborg had an outer ward with fifteen buildings and a cemetery. A cemetery was also excavated at Fyrkat, while none has been identified at Aggersborg and Nonnebacken. All fortresses were built *c.* 980, undoubtedly as a response to a specific political situation. They lasted only a few years. (Drawing: Holger Schmidt.)

The bridge lay not far to the south of Jelling. It was made of wood, *c.* 760 m long and over 5 m wide (Schou Jørgensen 1997; for exact dating see Christensen 2003). It is the oldest known bridge in Denmark and by far the largest from the Nordic Viking Age. There is no doubt of its practical function in providing a comfortable passage across the wide Vejle river valley and therewith a good approach to Jelling from the south. If this impressive bridge is seen in relation to Jelling as a slightly later follow-up to those *kumler* that, according to the runestone, King Harald had made for his mother and father, then it may have been viewed as a 'bridge of souls' that could ease the way to Paradise for the pagan spirits of his parents. Bridges of this kind are mentioned on several slightly later Swedish and a couple of Norwegian runestones (Roesdahl 1990; cf. Gräslund 1989; Peterson 1991).

The Trelleborgs are distributed around the country: Trelleborg in western Sjælland, Nonnebakken on Fyn, Fyrkat in north-east Jutland and Aggersborg in northern Jutland by the Limfjord (Olsen and Schmidt 1977; Roesdahl 1977, 1987, 1996; Olsen 1999: ch. 6). They have the same unique ground plan and are Denmark's oldest royal fortresses. Borgeby in Skåne, north of Malmö, might also belong to the group (Svanberg and Söderberg 1999). The Trelleborgs undoubtedly had practical military functions as permanent strongpoints for the king and as royal manors in stressful times. With their special, consistent layout and the large numbers of major structures (that must have been rather impractical to live and work in), they were clearly also prestige foundations and symbols of power. The design with a circular rampart pierced by gates at the cardinal points was probably inspired by earlier Flemish fortresses, and details may have been adopted from Ottonian imperial residences. But the location of the houses within the fortified space is unique, and both the structural types and the building materials (principally timber and turf) are of a domestic nature. This type of fortress is known only from Denmark and must have originated there. It combines both innovation and tradition, but was ultimately a failure.

For comparison (Roesdahl 2002) we can consider Sigtuna in central Sweden, founded at the same time as the Trelleborgs by the Svear king Erik Segersal but along quite different lines – it developed into a bishop's seat and into a town. Other royal manors from the late 900s also became towns and ecclesiastical centres around 1000, such as Roskilde and Lund in Denmark and Trondheim in Norway. At the same time important former pagan cult centres and royal manors declined in significance, as was the case with Tissø in western Sjælland, Lejre near Roskilde and Uppåkra near Lund.

Harald Bluetooth's religious conversion, politics and great engineering projects have a firm place among the major achievements of the Viking Age. The former was successful but the building works had only a short lifespan – they were created under special conditions and as expressions of his new concepts of royal power, but did not succeed, perhaps not least due to the burdens that they placed on his people. With Svein Forkbeard came different times. There appears to have been a militarisation of society, and after the consolidation of his power the king's energies were directed outward, concentrating on Viking expeditions against England which was conquered in 1013. Svein died the following year, and two years after that the country was retaken by his young son Knut, who both in England and Denmark was known as 'the Great'. He too focused his powers on England. Probably deterred by precedent, neither Svein nor Knut challenged the traditional division of power in Denmark or raised major royal memorials there.

BIBLIOGRAPHY

Albrectsen, E. (1994) 'Harald Blåtand og Danmark', in C. Due-Nielsen *et al.* (eds) *Struktur og Funktion. Festskrift til Erling Ladewig Petersen* (Odense University studies in history and social sciences 174), Odense: Odense Universitetsforlag.

Andersen, H.H. (1998) *Danevirke og Kovirke. Arkæologiske undersøgelser 1861–1993*, Højbjerg: Jysk Arkæologisk Selskab.

Christensen, A.E. (1969) *Vikingetidens Danmark*, Copenhagen: Gyldendal.

Christensen, K. (2003) 'Ravning-broens alder', *Kuml*: 213–26.

Gräslund, A.-S. (1989) 'Gud hjälpe nu väl hennes själ', *Tor*, 22: 223–44.

Kornerup, J. (1875) *Kongehøiene i Jellinge*, Copenhagen: Det Kgl. Nordiske Oldskriftselskab.

Krogh, K.J. (1982) 'The royal Viking Viking-Age monuments in Jelling in the light of recent archaeological excavations', *Acta Archaeologica*, 53: 183–216.

—— (1993) *Gåden om Kong Gorms Grav. Vikingekongernes Monumenter i Jelling*, vol. 1, Herning: Poul Kristensens Forlag.

Krogh, K.J. and Olsen, O. (1993) 'From paganism to Christianity', in S. Hvass and B. Storgaard (eds) *Digging into the Past. 25 Years of Archaeology in Denmark*, Copenhagen: Det Kgl. Nordiske Oldskriftselskab & Jysk Arkæologisk Selskab.

Lund, N. (1991) ' "Denemearc", "Tanmarkar But" and "Tanmaurk ala" ', in I. Wood and N. Lund (eds) *People and Places in Northern Europe 500–1600. Essays in Honour of Peter Hayes Sawyer*, Woodbridge: The Boydell Press.

Moltke, E. (1985) *Runes and their Origin. Denmark and Elsewhere*, Copenhagen: Nationalmuseet.

Näsman, U. (1999) 'The ethnogenesis of the Danes and the making of a Danish kingdom', in T. Dickinson and D. Griffiths (eds) *The Making of Kingdoms* (Anglo-Saxon Studies in Archaeology and History 19), Oxford: Oxbow Books.

—— (2000) 'Exchange and politics: the eighth–early ninth century in Denmark', in I.L. Hansen and C. Wickham (eds) *The Long Eighth Century*, Leiden, Boston and Cologne: Brill.

Olsen, O. (1999) *Da Danmark blev til*, Copenhagen: Fremad.

Olsen, O. and Schmidt, H. (1977) *Fyrkat. En jysk* vikingeborg, vol. 1: *Borgen og bebyggelsen*, Copenhagen: Det Kgl. Nordiske Oldskriftselskab.

Peterson, L. (1991) 'Gæra bro fyrir sial', in G. Alhaug *et al.* (eds) *Heidersskrift til Nils Hallan på 65-årsdagen 13. desember 1991*, Oslo: Novus Forlag.

Roesdahl, E. (1977) *Fyrkat. En jysk* vikingeborg, vol. 2: *Oldsagerne og gravpladsen*, Copenhagen: Det Kgl. Nordiske Oldskriftselskab.

—— (1987) 'The Danish geometrical Viking fortresses and their context', *Anglo-Norman Studies*, 9: 208–26.

—— (1990) 'At bygge bro – om det ældste brobyggeri i Norden', in A. Bistrup *et al.* (eds) *Gulnares hus. En gave til Hendes Majestæt Dronning Margrethe den Anden . . .*, Copenhagen: Samleren.

—— (1994) 'Dendrochronology and Viking studies in Denmark, with a note on the beginning of the Viking Age', in B. Ambrosiani and H. Clarke (eds) *Developments Around the Baltic and the North Sea in the Viking Age. The Twelfth Viking Congress* (Birka Studies 3), Stockholm: Raä and Statens historiska museer.

—— (1996) 'Fyrkat', *RGA* 10.

—— (2002) 'Harald Blauzahn. Ein dänischer Wikingerkönig aus archäologischer Sicht', in J. Henning (ed.) *Europa im 10. Jahrhundert. Archäologie einer Aufbruchzeit*, Mainz am Rhein: Philipp von Zabern.

—— (2005) 'Jordfaste mindesmærker i Danmarks yngre vikingetid', *hikuin*, 32: 55–74.

Sawyer, P. (1988) *Da Danmark blev Danmark. Fra ca. år 700–ca. 1050* (Gyldendal og Politikens Danmarkshistorie 3), Copenhagen: Gyldendal og Politiken.

Schou Jørgensen, M. (1997) 'Vikingetidsbroen i Ravning Enge – nye undersøgelser', *Nationalmuseets Arbejdsmark*: 74–87.

Skovgaard-Petersen, I. (1977) 'Oldtid og vikingetid', in I. Skovgaard-Petersen, A.E. Christensen and H. Paludan, *Danmarks historie*, vol. 1, Copenhagen: Gyldendal.

Svanberg, F. and Söderberg, B. (1999) *Den vikingatida borgen i Borgeby* (Arkeologiska studier kring Borgeby och Löddeköpinge 1), Lund: Avd. för arkeologiska undersökningar, Raä.

Wamers, E. (2000) 'Der grosse Jellingstein im Spiegel ottonischer Kunst', *Frühmittelalterliche Studien*, 34: 132–58.

Wilson, D.M. and Klindt-Jensen, O. (1966) *Viking Art*, London: George Allen and Unwin.

CNUT THE GREAT AND HIS EMPIRE

——— •✦• ———

Niels Lund

In a letter of 1027 *Cnut* (Eng. *Canute*, ON *Knútr*) styles himself 'king of all England, and Denmark, and the Norwegians, and part of the Swedes'. He appears, by then, to have restored the power his father had at his death. When he died in February 1014 Sven Forkbeard was king of England and Denmark and overlord of Norway and Sweden. Cnut, however, could not take over his father's position immediately. He was outlawed from England when the *witan* (the king's council) chose to recall Æthelred from Normandy to resume power, in Denmark his elder brother Harald succeeded their father; in Norway the earls of Lade, Erik and Sven Hakonsson, who had acknowledged Sven's overlordship, were driven out by Olav Haraldsson, returning from England, and in Sweden Sven's stepson Olof Skötkonung took the opportunity to assert his independence.

Cnut was therefore reduced to a landless viking leader and had to start all over again. He recruited a fresh army in Scandinavia, including Swedes and Norwegians as well as Danes, and attacked England again in 1015. His first battles were not particularly successful but his campaign took a lucky turn at Assandun in Essex on 18 October 1016. After this Edmund Ironside, who had succeeded Æthelred in April of that year, and Cnut agreed to share England. After Edmund's death on 30 November Cnut succeeded to all England. He divided it into four large earldoms, giving Northumbria to Erik Hakonsson, Mercia to Eadric Streona – who was, however, killed soon after – and East Anglia to Thorkel the Tall, while taking over Wessex for himself. His position as king of England was agreed with the English magnates in Oxford in 1018. This involved royal promises and legislation resembling a coronation charter.

Cnut's elder brother Harald is probably the Danish king about whom least is known. His reign has left practically no record. Even his death was not recorded and we can only guess that Cnut paid his visit to Denmark in 1019 in order to succeed his brother. Very little is known also about how Denmark was ruled in the rest of Cnut's reign. According to the Anglo-Saxon Chronicle Cnut outlawed Thorkel the Tall in 1021; they were reconciled in 1023 and Thorkel immediately given custody of Denmark and Cnut's son Harthacnut. This is, however, the very last thing heard of Thorkel, he disappears from history and Harthacnut remained in England for the time. A few years later Cnut's brother-in-law Earl Ulf appears to have been viceroy in Denmark. He was killed in

Roskilde for conspiring with King Anund Jakob of Sweden and St Olav of Norway to overthrow Cnut in Denmark and replace him by Harthacnut. They failed in the battle of the Holy River (probably not the *Helgeå* in Skåne), after which Cnut was able to go to Rome to attend the imperial coronation of Konrad II in the Easter of 1027, but had to return to Denmark to negotiate a settlement with his adversaries. After these events Harthacnut, still a young boy, may have taken over; coins were apparently struck in his name before 1030 and certainly before Cnut's death in 1035.

Cnut tried to introduce a Danish coinage modelled on the English system by which types were centrally controlled and exchanged at regular intervals. The main mint appears to have been in Lund but, as in England, a number of mints were in operation, evenly distributed across the country.

Cnut made little effort to unite his kingdoms politically or administratively. He did, however, draw on the English Church for clergymen to work in Denmark, and very likely he was planning to raise the see of Roskilde to archiepiscopal status, subordinated to Canterbury in the same way as York was. This brought him on a collision course with the archsee of Hamburg–Bremen, keen to protect its position in Scandinavia. Almost 200 years after its foundation the archsee still did not have the suffragans in Scandinavia needed to justify its existence. Archbishop Unwan of Hamburg went to the length of capturing newly appointed Gerbrand of Roskilde and holding him prisoner till he promised to acknowledge him as his proper head. This problem was probably settled when Cnut and Konrad met in 1027.

Cnut's grandfather Harald Bluetooth claimed on his runic monument in Jelling (*c.* 970) (Figure 48.4) that he had conquered Norway, and Sven Forkbeard maintained Danish overlordship over Norway for most of his reign; his position was challenged, with English support, by Olav Tryggvason, who was killed in the battle of Svold in 999 (or 1000). There was a long tradition, certainly going back to the beginning of the ninth century, of Danish rule in south-eastern Norway and for attempts to control the rest through native earls. After Sven's death, however, Olav Haraldsson, who had been campaigning in England with Thorkel the Tall and been in the service of Æthelred with Thorkel, returned from England with Æthelred's support and possessed himself of Norway at the expense of the earls of Lade. Erik joined Cnut in England and Sven was beaten in the battle of Nesjar.

Cnut probably never meant to give up traditional Danish claims to overlordship over Norway and before 1023 styled himself king of Norway. Only in 1028, however, did he send a force to Norway, before which Olav Haraldsson yielded without a battle and went to Russia. Cnut now appointed Hakon Eriksson, whose father was earl of Northumbria, to rule Norway. When he was drowned on his way to take up this position, Olav Haraldsson returned from Russia and made a new bid for power but was beaten and killed by the Norwegian magnates at Stiklestad on 29 July 1030. Perhaps short of suitable Norwegian candidates Cnut then sent his concubine Ælfgifu of Northampton and their son Sven to rule Norway. They quickly became very unpopular, apparently because they tried to introduce English habits of administration and taxation. Christmas presents became particularly unpopular, being a tax to be paid at Christmas. 'Alfiva's time' is remembered in Norway as a period of harsh rule. In 1034 Ælfgifu and Sven had to leave England, and before Cnut's death Magnus, the young son of Olav Haraldsson, was brought back from Novgorod and proclaimed king of Norway.

Cnut's claim to be king of part of the Swedes is less straightforward. After the death of his stepfather Sven Forkbeard, whom he had acknowledged as his overlord, Olof Skötkonung began to pursue a more independent policy towards the Danes. He married a daughter to Olav Haraldsson and he requested a bishop for the see of Skara in Västergötland from the archsee of Hamburg–Bremen; Thorgut, who had himself attended the consecration of Unwan as archbishop in 1013, was consecrated to this see by Unwan. According to John of Worcester, Cnut sent the sons of Edmund Ironside, Edward and Edmund, to the king of Sweden to have them killed by him, clearly expecting the Swedish king to obey his orders, but Olof refused to do so and sent the boys to Hungary. He also included Jaroslav, prince of Novgorod, who married a daughter of Olof in 1019, in his anti-Danish alliance with Olav of Norway.

Olof's successor Anund Jacob continued his hostility to Cnut and joined Olav Haraldsson and Ulf Jarl in an attack on Denmark in 1026. The outcome of this battle is uncertain but it certainly was not any subjugation of the Swedes by Cnut. A series of coins struck in Sigtuna in the name of Cnut has been regarded as evidence of his rule in Sweden, but these coins are more likely to be imitations of Cnut's English coins than coins struck in Sweden for Cnut. The reality of Cnut's claim to be king of part of the Swedes probably is that in an extremely decentralised land a number of Swedes had recognised Cnut as their lord, and had probably helped him conquer England in 1015–16. They appear in a number of runic inscriptions commemorating 'thegns' and 'drengs'.

Cnut, thus, had a hard job trying to recreate the sort of control that his father had in Scandinavia and England. He was immediate lord of only England and Denmark, and his only attempts to unite his possessions in any sense was his plan to subordinate the Danish Church to Canterbury. He never held joint meetings of the magnates of his realms, neither does he seem to have appointed English officials to serve in Denmark, or Danes to serve in England on any noticeable scale. His plan seems rather to have been to leave a kingdom for each of his three sons. At his death Norway was already lost, and seven years later, after the death of Harthacnut, the old West Saxon dynasty was reinstated in England, and a Norwegian king was accepted in Denmark.

BIBLIOGRAPHY

Gräslund, B. (1986) 'Knut den store och sveariket. Slaget vid Helgea i ny belysning', *Scandia*, 52: 211–38.

Lawson, M.K. (2004) *Cnut. England's Viking King*, London: Tempus.

Lund, N. (1993) *De hærger og de brænder. Danmark og England i vikingetiden*, Copenhagen: Gyldendal.

—— (1997) 'The Danish Empire and the end of the Viking Age', in P. Sawyer (ed.) *The Oxford Illustrated History of the Vikings*, Oxford: Oxford University Press.

Rumble, A.R. (ed.) (1994) *The Reign of Cnut. The King of England, Denmark and Norway*, London: Leicester University Press.

Sawyer, P. (1989) 'Knut, Sweden and Sigtuna', in S. Tesch (ed.) *Avstamp för en ny Sigtunaforskning. 18 forskare om Sigtuna. Heldagsseminarium kring Sigtunaforskning den 26 november 1987 Gröna Ladan, Sigtuna. 1989*, Sigtuna: Sigtuna museer.

CHAPTER FORTY-NINE

THE EMERGENCE OF SWEDEN

——·◆·——

Thomas Lindkvist

In 1442 the second version of the law code of the realm of Sweden was officially promulgated by King Christopher (Sw *Kristoffers landslag*). It was initially stated that the kingdom of Sweden had once originated from a heathen world, from a *Svea* and a *Göta rike* (realm). The view that Sweden emerged through a union of two realms or 'kingdoms' is actually a statement about a great and profound transformation. From a 'heathen world' Sweden had been Christianised and Sweden had been united of two different parts: *Svealand* 'the *land* of the *Svear*' and *Götaland* 'the *land* of the *Götar*'. It the late Middle Ages this idea of a national origin of Sweden as a kingdom was invented and articulated.

The conversion and the making of a Christian monarchy were the great transformations in the breaking up from a Viking to a medieval world; but how and when all this took place in Sweden has been much debated.

In modern research it is now stressed that the emergence of Sweden was a very long and gradual process. Earlier scholarly reconstructions of a political and military conquest of a *Svea rike* over a *Göta rike* in the sixth century, based upon archaeological evidence and imaginative readings of the Icelandic *Ynglingatal* and the Anglo-Saxon *Beowulf* are now more or less rejected (Stjerna 1905; Behre 1968; Gahrn 1988). It has also been suggested that it was about the year 1000 that Sweden existed as a kingdom; then there was a Christian king who can be connected to both Svealand and Götaland (Weibull 1921). But Sweden was far from a coherent political unit with a more or less undisputed kingship on the eve of the second millennium.

The making of a Christian monarchy is a later and more unclear and incomprehensible process in Sweden than in Denmark and Norway. In Sweden there never developed the great high medieval history-writing like Saxo for Denmark and Snorri for Norway that has served as the great narratives for later interpretations of the making of kingdoms. The source material is sparse and open to many interpretations. (Concerning the discussion of the origins of Sweden and the early medieval political history, see Sawyer 1989, Hyenstrand 1996 and Lindkvist 2003.)

The emergence of Sweden was the establishment of Christian and royal institutions and organisations, as well as the emergence of a new economic and social structure. These transformations meant a form of Europeanisation. Sweden, as well as the other

Scandinavian kingdoms, became integrated into the wider cultural and political community of western Christianity. New forms of lordship, new economic and social structures, new cultural concepts emerged and were introduced, but also adapted to existing structures. The political transformation differed, however, regionally in Sweden.

The main element of this Europeanisation was of course Christianisation. The first missionary to visit present Sweden was Ansgar in 829 or 830 at Birka, also with the intent to establish relations between Emperor Louis the Pious and a king of the *Svear*. But Ansgar and the foundation of an ephemeral congregation were but an incident in the Christianisation. For a long period Christianity was brought to Sweden by Swedes through contacts. Missionaries, mostly from the British Isles and in the eleventh and twelfth centuries, are known through later saints' legends. From an organisational point of view the emerging ecclesiastical organisation was under the supervision and hegemony of the archbishopric of Hamburg and Bremen, until the archbishopric of Lund was founded in 1103 and exercised a Danish hegemony for more than half a century.

The assumption is often that Sweden became Sweden when the two main provinces, Svealand and Götaland, were under the same political rule and order. But that emerged gradually during the Middle Ages and without any direct military conquest. Medieval Sweden remained a very confederate kingdom, consisting of different provinces (Sw *land* sg., *länder* pl.). There were great regional variances concerning the monetary system, land measurements, tax systems etc. The structures of new overlordships of Church and kingdom were the results of different regional developments. There were diverse ways in the emerging of Sweden.

The *Svear* and the *Götar* are elusive terms and not to be understood exclusively as ethnic terms, or as tribes, but are also functional and political. The *Svear* were often mentioned as seafarers and as warriors. As such they were probably more known and notorious than the *Götar*. The *Götar* are in some sources from the ninth century onwards a separate 'people', but also a subdivision or branch of the *Svear*. From the Middle Ages the two terms distinctly denoted the inhabitants in the two main regions of Sweden.

Rulers of petty kingdoms are known long before Christianisation and the political organisation can be discussed using archaeological evidence, although we have but rudimentary glimpses of lords' and kings' position and functions. The kings at Birka, recorded through the mission of Ansgar, were for example dependent on an assembly. The pre-Christian kingdom or kingdoms in central Sweden (ON *Svíþjóð*) seems to have had a rather highly structured political organisation. Gamla (Old) Uppsala is especially in the Old Norse literary tradition, not least in the *Ynglingasaga* of Snorri Sturluson, associated with kings and kingship; Uppsala was known as the political, royal and religious, cultic centre. There is hardly any evidence of a similar kingship in the Götaland provinces (cf. Larsson 2002).

The kingdom of the *Svear* was a loose and partly seaborne empire (Lönnroth 1977: 7–16). According to Wulfstan in his description of a sea voyage in the ninth century from Hedeby to Truso, the *land*s Blekinge, Möre, Öland and Gotland belonged to the *Svear* (*to Sweon*). Evidently the *Svear* exercised a form of seaborne hegemony in the Baltic Sea, with some territorial control. In the ninth century we know, for example, that the *Svear* demanded and took tributes from the inhabitants of Curonia. The kings were often war leaders. The power structure was based on warfare, pillage and demanding tribute.

Such activities are also connected with Erik *Segersäll* ('the Victorious') at the end of the tenth century. About him we have more records than any previous king in Sweden. He was partly a typical seafaring Viking king, with plundering and predatory activities in foreign areas. Erik is also connected with Uppland. He was probably the king that founded Sigtuna as a royal residence around 975. Erik was baptised while in Denmark. He also allowed missionaries in his realm, but was also blamed by the Christian chronicler Adam of Bremen for having relapsed into paganism at home. He was, however, married to a Christian woman, the daughter of the Polish prince Mieszko.

Erik's son was Olof, often later called OSw *Skot-/Skøtkonunger* (Sw *Skötkonung*). He is known as the first Christian king in Sweden. According to a late tradition he was baptised at Husaby in Västergötland. During his reign we find the first coinage with a mint house at Sigtuna. The minting was extensive and the coinage has to be interpreted as a demonstration of royal power. Inscriptions and symbols testified to the intent to promote Christianity (Malmer 1996). Olof is also connected with the promotion of the bishopric at Skara in Västergötland. Although there is but a small number of sources, Olof was a king who strove for a new form of kingship, legitimised through Christianity.

After Olof his sons Anund Jakob and Emund followed as kings. In the middle of the 1020s Anund Jakob was defeated by King Canute the Great of Denmark, who for a period was in control over Sigtuna. After Emund a new dynasty emerged. A Stenkil was *c.* 1060 recognised as king. In the sources he is mostly associated with Västergötland. His origin is unknown, but evidently he legitimised his title through marriage to a daughter of Emund. Four of Stenkil's sons are known to have followed him as kings. The kingdom was fragile and contested and co-regency between brothers evidently occurred. In the 1070s a certain King Håkon is, however, known to have exercised power in at least the province of Västergötland.

Even if there were kings with ambition to be rulers of Sweden, they seldom held power over the two main parts of Sweden. A dynastic principle prevailed, although the kingship was elective. Sweden was throughout the Middle Ages an electoral monarchy.

The election was often more or less formal, but it also implied a weak monarchy. In the electoral procedures, at least as they were formalised in the late thirteenth and early fourteenth centuries, the influence of a political elite, the bishops and the law speakers (Sw *lagmän*), was great and the authority of the king was restricted. An election of a king was not just formal, but implied the possibility of the aristocracy restricting royal authority.

The 1120s in particular seem to have been a period when internal struggles culminated. No king was recognised for the whole realm of the *Svear*, but possibly local kings were to be found in some regions. A consolidation of royal power started from *c.* 1130. Sverker I was evidently an aristocrat who became recognised as king. His position was partly legitimised through marriage with the widowed queen of King Inge II. With the active support of Sverker and Queen Ulfhild the Cistercians were established in Sweden. This was the great introduction of monasticism in Sweden. One of the great spiritual and cultural organisations thus gained a foothold in Sweden. The connections between the royal power and the Cistercian houses were close. The collaboration between the kingship and the Church, especially the bishopric of Linköping, and hereby the papacy as well, was good in Sverker's days.

King Sverker was murdered in 1156 and after him an Erik became king. His ancestry is unknown, but he represented another dynasty. From the middle of the twelfth century there were dynastic competitions mainly between the descendants of King Sverker I and King Erik until the beginning of the thirteenth century. King Erik was shortly after his death in 1160 during dynastic struggles promoted as a saint. The cult was mainly supported by his dynasty and by Uppsala Cathedral, and St Erik never gained the unquestioned role as a national patron that his Norwegian counterpart, St Olav, had.

After Erik's death, Karl Sverkersson was recognised as king, but was murdered in 1167 by Knut, son of Erik. Knut Eriksson reigned for a long period. After his natural death in 1195 or 1196 a son of Sverker, Karl Sverkersson, became king, but was defeated in a battle at Lena in 1208 and fell two years later. After him the Eriks, represented by Knut's son, Erik Knutsson, ruled until his death in 1216. He was followed by Johan Sverkersson, who, when he died in 1222, was the last of his dynasty. He was followed by the last of the descendants of Erik, Erik Eriksson. During a short period (1229–34), Knut Länge of the *Folkung* fraction was in power, while King Erik Eriksson was in exile in Denmark.

In spite of the inter-dynastic struggles kingship and kingdom became more stabilised. In 1164, when the archbishopric of Uppsala was founded, the king of Sweden was addressed by the pope as king of the *Svear* and the *Götar*. It was the first time that title was used. The making of a Swedish ecclesiastical province; and the breaking up of the Danish archdiocese of Lund, also contributed to making Sweden definitely recognised as one of the independent, European and Christian monarchies and as such was recognised by the papacy. In the reign of Knut Eriksson we have the first traces of a written royal administration. The earliest preserved royal charters are from his reign. King Knut was the first known king who had more substantial control over both Svealand and Götaland and thus created a further step in the emergence of a Sweden.

In the process of the emergence of Sweden there were great regional differences. The tendencies towards Europeanisation of the institutions and organisations took place earlier in Östergötland and Västergötland. Christianisation developed earlier in the Götaland provinces, especially in Västergötland. An ecclesiastical organisation developed earlier and stone churches were built earlier there. Skara in Västergötland was the first bishop's see in the eleventh century. Linköping in Östergötland was a see at least at the beginning of the twelfth century. Sigtuna, the royal town on the shore of Lake Mälaren, was the see of a bishop between the 1070s and 1130s, but evidently vacant for certain periods. In his chronicle Adam of Bremen juxtaposes a pagan – or supposed pagan Uppsala – to a Christian Sigtuna.

The early Christian monarchy was mostly based in the Götaland provinces. The Sverker dynasty had its origins in Östergötland; the Erik dynasty seems to have had its ancestral estates in Västergötland, while the often fractioning *Folkungar* had their base in Uppland (Lönnroth 1959: 13–29). The first monasteries were founded in Götaland. Alvastra monastery was the sepulchral church of the Sverker kings, Varnhem monastery of most of the Erik dynasty.

When taxes were introduced, mainly in the thirteenth century, they originated in Götaland in the burdens of the peasantry to support the king during his itineraries. It was there kingship was exercised through physical presence. A small castle on Visingsö, the small island in Lake Vättern between Västergötland and Östergötland, was a frequent royal residence in the twelfth century.

In the Svealand the permanent taxes were mainly replacements of the military obligation of the peasantry to provide ships, victuals and men to the royal naval organisation, called the *ledung*. The *ledung* was described in a legal sense in the late thirteenth century as the fleet under royal command and had its origins in the old ability of local aristocrats to muster a maritime retinue. In the thirteenth century the king got control over the *ledung*, which was transformed into a fiscal duty (Lönnroth 1940: 57–136).

In Svealand there were tendencies of opposition or reluctance towards the making of a Christian monarchy. 'Pagan' uprisings are recorded as having taken place around 1080 and 1120. In the 1080s, according to the Icelandic *Hervararsaga*, the Christian king Inge was overthrown, when he refused to perform pagan rites in *Svíaríki* (probably at Uppsala), by the supposed pagan king Blot-Sven for three years.

Adam of Bremen portrays Uppsala as a pagan centre, especially in locating and describing a 'pagan' temple there. A later saint legend and other sources describe a revitalising of pagan rituals in Svealand in the first and second decades of the twelfth century. These trends of opposition are in the sources described as pagan, as the opposite of Christianity, but could also, and more precisely, be understood as opposition to the monarchy and the ecclesiastical ideals and organisation supporting it (see discussion in Hultgård 1997).

The area around Lake Mälaren and the plain areas in Östergötland and Västergötland were the central political areas and the most prosperous agrarian regions. They were the homelands of the old aristocracy, the social elite. Peripheries outside these areas became gradually integrated into the political community of the kingdom; initially through the expansion of an ecclesiastical organisation and administration. Present Finland became an integrated part of Sweden during the high Middle Ages. A colonisation from Sweden in the coastal areas from around the beginning of the twelfth century and onwards took place. This colonisation was carried out by peasant communities. According to the legend of St Erik, the king and the missionary, Bishop Henry, carried out a conversion crusade to Finland, probably in the middle of the 1150s. But there is no contemporary historical evidence of a Swedish military conquest. Through the establishment of an ecclesiastical organisation, including the making of Turku (Åbo) as a bishopric under the archbishop of Uppsala, and a later royal administration, Finland became part of the Swedish realm (Sjöstrand 1994; Ivars and Huldén 2002).

Gotland had an autonomous position in relation to the king of Sweden and the Swedish bishop of Linköping. According to the *Gutasaga*, written in the late thirteenth century, a tributary relationship to the Swedish king had once been established. An overlordship was recognised, but the community of the island was less integrated into the kingdom than many other parts.

Jarl or earl was a title that at least from the late twelfth century appears for politically powerful men alongside the king. There was no evident splitting up of functions, but *jarls* were often engaged in warfare. Jarl Birger brosa had a powerful position in the late twelfth century. Birger Magnusson, *jarl* from *c*. 1246 until his death in 1266, was for a long period the most powerful person; when King Erik Eriksson died in 1250, Birger's son, Valdemar, was elected king. But Birger ruled all but in name as a king until his death. During his reign the first legislative activity concerning the whole realm took place. Revolts of the opposing aristocratic fraction of the *Folkungar* were crushed. In Birger's time, the kingdom obtained more significant and substantial control in the Lake Mälaren region. During the middle and second half of the thirteenth century Svealand became more of the political centre. Eastern Sweden also became a more dynamic economic region with, for example, growing urbanisation.

In Birger's and his son's reigns, especially Magnus Birgersson's (1275–90), the political structure became more stabilised and institutionalised. Permanent taxes were introduced, an incipient administration began, castles were built, not least for control of land and people, and the royal council emerged gradually as more or less a permanent political institution. Offices or permanent more or less specialised functions beside the king emerged. Birger Magnusson upheld good relations with the papacy and the Swedish bishops (Harrison 2002; Schück 2003).

The emergence of Sweden also meant the gradual transformation of the economy. Slavery faded away. A variant of a manorial economy emerged, partly initiated by the Church and monasteries. The peasantry became burdened with innovative demands: taxes, fines, different kinds of leases and fees were introduced. A European social order based mainly on control and appropriation of agrarian produce gained ground, although acclimatised to existing social and economic structures.

In the second half of the thirteenth century many of the formal and legal frameworks of the general social and political order of the Europeanised Christian monarchy became settled. With the synod of Skänninge in 1248 vital parts of the canonical law were introduced. The chapters of the cathedrals were introduced and established. An autonomous position of the Church was hereby strengthened.

The privileges of the aristocracy and the Church became settled in around 1280. According to the statutes of Alsnö in 1280 all men serving the king with a knight and mounted horse were exempted from the permanent royal taxes and duties. And the collaboration between the king and the Church resulted in a general privilege with comprehensive exemption of royal duties and levies. The clergy and the aristocracy became separate and privileged groups (Rosén 1952; Andræ 1960: 146–71).

The first great achievement in literacy in the vernacular – and with Latin script – was the provincial law codes. The oldest is the first version of *Västgötalagen* (the provincial law of Västergötland) from probably the 1220s. It reflected very much the interests of the provincial aristocracy. The great volume of laws comes, however, from the late thirteenth and early fourteenth centuries. *Upplandslagen* from 1296 was promulgated in the name of the minor king Birger Magnusson. The influence of Church and of canonical law in this legislation is nowadays considered to be great. It was probably not, as has been suggested, entirely a result of a reception of foreign law, but they were all mainly in the interests of the secular and spiritual aristocracy. But in many respects, a new, Europeanised social order is found there, not least concerning the rights of land, property and marriage (Sjöholm 1990; Lindkvist 1997).

With the election of Valdemar Birgersson the royal title was confined within one family, but it was far from uncontested within the royal family. The late thirteenth and early fourteenth centuries were characterised by internal and intensive struggles between royal brothers. During the late thirteenth century there was a mighty aristocracy, secular and spiritual, that in many respects formulated the new political culture in Sweden. The internal inter- and intra-dynastic struggles paved a way for a very aristocratic monarchy. The charter issued in 1319 when the infant Magnus Eriksson was elected king after inter-dynastic disastrous conflicts circumscribed the rights of the king. And it was the identical group of leading aristocrats, the law speakers, who swore the oath on behalf of the king; and then swore the loyalty of the different provincial communities (*land*) to the king. The position of the political elite, the council with the bishops and the law speakers, was confirmed, the possibilities for the king of taxation and using the material resources were formalised and restricted (Rosén 1939: 331–43; Schück 2003). Sweden was then in many respects a European monarchy. It was, however, the clergy and the Europeanised aristocracy who essentially set the rules of the political game.

BIBLIOGRAPHY

Andræ, C.G. (1960) *Kyrka och frälse i Sverige under äldre medeltid* (Studia historica Upsaliensia 4), Uppsala: Almqvist & Wiksell.

Behre, G. (1968) *Svenska rikets uppkomst*, Göteborg: Läromedelsförlaget.

Gahrn, L. (1988) *Sveariket i källor och historieforskning* (Meddelanden från historiska institutionen i Göteborg 36), Göteborg: no publ.

Harrison, D. (2002) *Jarlens sekel. En berättelse om 1200-talets Sverige*, Stockholm: Ordfront.

Hultgård, A. (ed.) (1997) *Uppsalakulten och Adam av Bremen*, Nora: Symposion.

Hyenstrand, Å. (1996) *Lejonet, draken och korset. Sverige 500–1000*, Lund: Studentlitteratur.

Ivars, A.-M. and Huldén, L. (eds) (2002) *När kom svenskarna till Finland?* (Skrifter utgivna av Svenska litteratursällskapet i Finland 646), Helsingfors: SLS.

Larsson, M.G. (2002) *Götarnas riken. Upptäcktsfärder till Sveriges enande*, Stockholm: Atlantis.

Lindkvist, Th. (1997) 'Law and the making of the state in medieval Sweden: kingship and communities', in A. Padoa-Schioppa (ed.) *Legislation and Justice*, Oxford: Clarendon Press.

—— (2003) 'Kings and provinces in Sweden', in K. Helle (ed.) *The Cambridge History of Scandinavia*, vol. 1, Cambridge: Cambridge University Press.

Lönnroth, E. (1940) *Statsmakt och statsfinans i det medeltida Sverige. Studier över skatteväsen och länsförvaltning* (Göteborgs högskolas årsskrift 46), Göteborg: no publ.

—— (1959) *Från svensk medeltid* (Aldus-böckerna 19), Stockholm: Bonnier.

—— (1977) *Scandinavians. Selected Historical Essays*, Göteborg: Eckersteins bokhandel.

Malmer, B. (1996) 'Sigtunamyntningen som källa till Sveriges kristnande', in B. Nilsson (ed.) *Kristnandet i Sverige. Gamla källor och nya perspektiv*, Uppsala: Lunne.

Rosén, J. (1939) *Striden mellan Birger Magnusson och hans bröder. Studier i nordisk politisk historia 1302–1319*, Lund: no publ.

—— (1952) 'Kring Alsnö stadga', in *Festskrift Gottfrid Carlsson 18.12.1952*, Lund: no publ.

Sawyer, P. (1989) *The Making of Sweden*, Alingsås: Victoria.

Schück, H. (2003) 'Sweden under the dynasty of the Folkungs', in K. Helle (ed.) *The Cambridge History of Scandinavia*, vol. 1, Cambridge: Cambridge University Press.

Sjöholm, E. (1990) 'Sweden's medieval laws: European legal tradition – political change', *Scandinavian Journal of History*, 15: 65–87.

Sjöstrand, P.O. (1994) 'Den svenska tidigmedeltida statsbildningsprocessen och den östra rikshalvan', *Historisk tidskrift för Finland*: 520–73.

Stjerna, K. (1905) 'Svear och götar under folkvandringstiden', *Svenska fornminnesföreningens tidskrift*, 12: 339–60.

Weibull, C. (1921) 'Om det svenska och danska rikets tillkomst', *Historisk tidskrift för Skåneland*, 7: 307–60.

INDEX

——•◆•——

Related titles from Routledge

The Vikings in History
F. Donald Logan

Completely updated to include important primary research, archaeological findings and debates from the last decade, this third edition of F. Donald Logan's successful book examines the Vikings and their critical role in history.

The author uses archaeological, literary and historical evidence to analyze the Vikings' overseas expeditions and their transformation from raiders to settlers. Focusing on the period from 800–1050, it studies the Vikings across the world, from Denmark and Sweden right across to the British Isles, the North Atlantic and the New World.

This edition includes:

- a new epilogue explaining the aims of the book
- updated further reading sections
- maps and photographs.

By taking this new archaeological and primary research into account, the author provides a vital text for history students and researchers of this fascinating people.

Hb: 978–0–415–32755–8
Pb: 978–0–415–32756–5

Available at all good bookshops
For ordering and further information please visit:
www.routledge.com

Related titles from Routledge

An Archaeology of the Early Anglo-Saxon Kingdoms
C. J. Arnold

An Archaeology of the Early Anglo-Saxon Kingdoms is a volume which offers an unparalleled view of the archaeological remains of the period. Using the development of the kingdoms as a framework, this study closely examines the wealth of material evidence and analyzes its significance to our understanding of the society that created it. From our understanding of the migrations of the Germanic peoples into the British Isles, the subsequent patterns of settlement, land-use, trade, through to social hierarchy and cultural identity within the kingdoms, this fully revised edition illuminates one of the most obscure and misunderstood periods in European history.

Hb: 978–0–415–15635–6
Pb: 978–0–415–15636–3

Available at all good bookshops
For ordering and further information please visit:
www.routledge.com